THE JOHN LOCKE COLLECTION

By
John Locke

The Fundamental Constitutions of Carolina

March 1, 1669 [1] [2]

Our sovereign lord the King having, out of his royal grace and bounty, granted unto us the province of Carolina, with all the royalties, properties, jurisdictions, and privileges of a county palatine, as large and ample as the county palatine of Durham, with other great privileges; for the better settlement of the government of the said place, and establishing the interest of the lords proprietors with equality and without confusion; and that the government of this province may be made most agreeable to the monarchy under which we live and of which this province is a part; and that we may avoid erecting a numerous democracy, we, the lords and proprietors of the province aforesaid, have agreed to this following form of government, to be perpetually established amongst us, unto which we do oblige ourselves, our heirs and successors, In the most binding ways that can be devised.

One. The eldest of the lords proprietors shall be palatine; and, upon the decease of the palatine, the eldest of the seven surviving proprietors shall always succeed him.

Two. There shall be seven other chief offices erected, viz: the admirals, chamberlains, chancellors, constables, chief justices, high stewards, and treasurers; which places shall be enjoyed by none but the lords proprietors, to be assigned at first by lot, and, upon the vacancy of any one of the seven great offices, by death or otherwise, the eldest proprietor shall have his choice of the said place.

Three. The whole province shall be divided into counties; each county shall consist of eight signiories, eight baronies, and four precincts; each precinct shall consist of six colonies.

Four. Each signiory, barony, and colony shall consist of twelve thousand acres; the eight signiories being the share of the eight proprietors, and the eight baronies of the nobility; both which shares, being each of them one-fifth of the whole, are to be perpetually annexed, the one to the proprietors, the other to the hereditary nobility, leaving the colonies, being three-fifths, amongst the people; so that in setting out and planting the lands, the balance of the government may be preserved.

Five. At any time before the year one thousand seven hundred and one, any of the lords proprietors shall have power to relinquish, alienate, and dispose to any other person his proprietorship, and all the signiories, powers, and interest thereunto belonging, wholly anti entirely together, and not otherwise. But after the year one thousand seven hundred, those who are then lords proprietors shall not have power to alienate or make over their proprietorship, with the signiories and privileges thereunto belonging, or any part thereof, to any person whatsoever, otherwise than in section eighteen; but it shall all descend unto their heirs male, and for want of heirs male, it shall all descend on that landgrave or cazique of Carolina who is descended of the next heirs female of the proprietor; and, for want of such heirs, it shall descend on the next heir general; and, for want of such heirs, the remaining seven proprietors shall, upon the vacancy, choose a landgrave to succeed the deceased proprietors, who, being chosen by the majority of the seven surviving proprietors, he and his heirs. successively shall be proprietors, as fully to all intents and purposes as any of the rest.

Six. That the number of eight proprietors may be constantly kept, if, upon the vacancy of any proprietorship, the seven surviving proprietors shall not choose a landgrave to be a proprietor before the second biennial parliament after the vacancy, then the next biennial parliament but one, after such vacancy, shall have power to choose any landgrave to be a proprietor.

Seven. Whosoever, after the year one thousand seven hundred, either by inheritance or choice, shall succeed any proprietor in his proprietorship, and signories thereunto belonging; shall be obliged to take the name and arms of that proprietor whom he succeeds; which from thenceforth shall be the name and arms of his family and their posterity.

Eight. Whatsoever landgrave or cazique shall any way come to be a proprietor, shall take the signiories annexed to the said proprietorship; but his former dignity, with the baronies annexed, shall devolve into the hands of the lords proprietors.

Nine. There shall be just as many landgraves as there are counties, and twice as many caziques, and no more. These shall be the hereditary nobility of the province, and by right of their dignity be members of parliament. Each landscape shall have four baronies, and each cazique two baronies, hereditarily and unalterably annexed to and settled upon the said dignity.

Ten. The first landgrave and caziques of the twelve first counties to be planted shall be nominated thus, that is to say: of the twelve landgraves, the lords proprietors shall each of them, separately for himself, nominate and choose one; and the remaining four landgraves of the first twelve shall be nominated and chosen by the palatine's court. In like manner, of the twenty-four first caziques, each proprietor for himself shall nominate and choose two, and the remaining eight shall be nominated and chosen by the palatine's court; and when the twelve first counties shall be planted, the lords proprietors shall again in the same manner nominate and choose twelve more landgraves and twenty-four more caziques, for the next twelve counties to be planted; that is to say, two-thirds of each number by the single nomination of each proprietor for himself, and the remaining third by the joint election of the palatine's court, and so proceed in the same manner till the whole province of Carolina be set out and planted, according to the proportions in these fundamental constitntions.

Eleven. Any landgrave or cazique, at any time before the year one thousand seven hundred and one, shall have power to alienate, sell, or make over, to any other person, his dignity, with the baronies thereunto belonging, all entirely together. But after the year one thousand seven hundred, no landgrave or cazique shall have power to alienate, sell, make over, or let the hereditary baronies of his dignity, or any part thereof, otherwise than as in section eighteen; but they shall all entirely, with the dignity thereunto belonging, descend unto his heirs male; and for want of heirs male, all entirely and undivided to the next heir general; and for want of such heirs, shall devolve into the hands of the lords proprietors.

Twelve. That the due number of landgraves and caziques may be always kept up, if, upon the devolution of any landgraveship or caziqueship, the palatine's court shall not settle the devolved dignity with the baronies thereunto annexed, before the second biennial parliament after such devolution, the next biennial parliament but one after such devolution shall have power to make any one landgrave or cazique in the room of him who dying without heirs, his dignity and baronies devolved.

Thirteen. No one person shall have more than one dignity, with the signiories or baronies thereunto belonging. But whensoever it shall happen that any one who is already proprietor, landgrave, or cazique shall have any of these dignities descend to him by inheritance, it shall be at his choice to keep which of the dignities, with the lands annexed, he shall like best; but shall leave the other, with the lands annexed, to be enjoyed by him who, not being his heir apparent and certain successor to his present dignity, is next of blood.

Fourteen. Whosoever, by right of inheritance, shall come to be landgrave or cazique, shall take the name and arms of his predecessor in that dignity, to be from thenceforth the name and arms of his family and their posterity.

Fifteen. Since the dignity of proprietor, landgrave, or cazique cannot be divided, and the signiories or baronies thereunto annexed must forever all entirely descend with and accompany that dignity, whensoever, for want of heirs male, it shall descend on the issue female, the eldest daughter and her heirs shall be preferred, and in the inheritance of those dignities, and in the signiories or baronies annexed, there shall be no coheirs.

Sixteen. In every signiory, barony, and manor, the respective lord shall have power, in his own name, to hold court-leet there, for trying of all causes, both civil and criminal; but where it shall concern any person being no inhabitant, vassal, or leet-man of the said signiory, barony, or manor, he, upon paying down of forty shillings to the lords proprietors' use, shall have an appeal from the signiory or barony court to the county court, and from the manor court to the precinct court.

Seventeen. Every manor shall consist of not less than three thousand acres, and not above twelve thousand acres, in one entire piece and colony, but any three thousand acres or more in one piece, and the possession of one man shall not be a manor, unles it be constituted a manor by the grant of the palatine's court.

Eighteen. The lords of signiories and baronies shall have power only of granting estates not exceeding three lives, or twenty-one years, in two-thirds of said signiories or baronies, and the remaining third shall be always demesne.

Nineteen. Any lord of a manor may alienate, sell, or dispose to any other person and his heirs forever, his manor, all entirely together with all the privileges and leet-men thereunto belonging, so far forth as any colony lands; but no grant of any part thereof, either in fee, or for any longer term than three lives, or one-and-twenty years, shall stand good against the next heir.

Twenty. No manor, for want of issue male, shall be divided amongst coheirs; but the manor, if there be but one, shall all entirely descend the eldest daughter and her heirs. If there be more minors than one, the eldest daughter first shall have her choice, the second next, and so on, beginning again at the eldest, until all the manors be taken up; that so the privileges which belong to manors being indivisible, the lands of the manors, to which they are annexed, may be kept entire and the manor not lose those privileges which, upon parcelling out to several owners, must necessarily cease.

Twenty-one. Every lord of a manor, within his own manor, shall have all the rights, powers, jurisdictions, and privileges which a landgrave or cazique hath in his baronies.

Twenty-two. In every signiory, barony, and manor, all the leet-men shall be under the jurisdiction of the respective lords of the said signiory, barony, or manor, without appeal from him. Nor shall any leet-man or leet-woman have liberty to go off from the land of their particular lord and live anywhere else, without license obtained from their said lord, under hand and seal.

Twenty-three. All the children of leet-men shall be leet-men, and so to all generations.

Twenty-four. No man shall be capable of having a court-leet or leet-men but a proprietor, landgrave, cazique, or lord of a manor.

Twenty-five. Whoever shall voluntarily enter himself a leet-man in the registry of the county court, shall be a leet-man.

Twenty-six. Whoever is lord of leet-men, shall, upon the marriage of a leet-man or leet-woman of his, give them ten acres of land for their lives; they paying to him therefor not more than one-eighth part of all the yearly produce and growth of the said ten acres.

P>Twenty-seven. No landgrave or cazique shall be tried for any criminal cause in any but the chief justice's court, and that by a jury of his peers.
Twenty-eight. There shall be eight supreme courts. The first called the palatine's court, consisting of the palatine and the other seven proprietors. The other seven courts of the other seven great officers, shall consist each of them of a proprietor, and six councillors added to him. Under each of these latter seven courts shall be a college of twelve assistants. The twelve assistants of the several colleges shall be chosen, two out of the landgraves, caziques, or eldest sons of the proprietors, by the palatine's court; two out of the landgraves by the landgraves' chamber; two out of the caziques by the caziques' chamber; four more of the twelve shall be chosen by the commons' chamber, out of such as have been or are members of parliament, sheriffs, or justices of the county court, or the younger sons of proprietors, or the eldest sons of landgraves or caziques; the two others shall be chosen by the palatine's court, out of the same sort of persons out of which the commons' chamber is to choose.

Twenty-nine. Out of these colleges shall be chosen at first, by the palatine's court, six councillors, to be joined with each proprietor in his court; of which six one shall be of those who were chosen into any of the colleges by the palatine's court, out of the landgraves, caziques, or eldest sons of proprietors; one out of those who were chosen by the landgraves' chamber; one out of those who were chosen by the caziques' chamber; two out of those who were chosen by the commons' chamber; and one out of those who were chosen by the palatine's court, out of the proprietors' younger sons, or eldest sorts of landgraves, caziques, or commons, qualified as aforesaid.

Thirty. When it shall happen that any councillor dies, and thereby there is a vacancy, the grand council shall have power to remove any councillor that is willing to be removed out of any of the proprietors' courts, to fill up the vacancy; provided they take a man of the same degree and choice the other was of, whose place is to be filled up. But if no councillor consent to be removed, or upon such remove, the last remaining vacant place, in any of the proprietors' courts, shall be filled up by the choice of the grand council, who shall have power to remove out of any of the colleges any assistant, who is of the same degree and choice tliat that councillor was of into whose vacant place he is to succeed. The grand council also have power to remove any assistant, that is willing, out of one college into another, provided he be of the same degree and choice. But the last remaining vacant place in any college shall be filled up by the same choice, and out of the same degree of persons the assistant was of who is dead or removed. No place shall be vacant in any proprietor's court above six months. No place shall be vacant in any college longer than the next session of parliament.

Thirty-one. No man, being a member of the grand council, or of any of the seven colleges, shall be turned out but for misdemeanor, of which the grand council shall be judge; and the vacancy of the person so put out shall be filled, not by the election of the grand council, but by those who first chose him, and out of the same degree he was of who is expelled. But it is not hereby to be understood that the grand council hath any power to turn out any one of the lords proprietors or their deputies, the lords proprietors having in themselves an inherent original right.

Thirty-two. All elections in the parliament, in the several chambers of the parliament, and in the grand council, shall be passed by balloting.

Thirty-three. The palatine's court shall consist of the palatine and seven proprietors, wherein nothing shall be acted without the presence and consent of the palatine or his deputy, and three other of the proprietors or their deputies. This court shall have power to call parliaments, to pardon all offences, to make elections of all officers in the proprietor's dispose, and to nominate and appoint port towns; and also shall have power by their order to the treasurer to dispose of all public treasure, excepting money granted by the parliament, and by them directed to some particular public use; and also shall have a negative upon all acts, orders, votes, and judgments of the grand council and the parliament, except only as in sections six and twelve; and shall have all the powers granted to the lords proprietors, by their patent from our sovereign lord the King, except in such things as are limited by these fundamental constitutions.

Thirty-four. The palatine himself, when he in person shall be either in the army or any of the proprietors' courts, shall then have the power of general or of that proprietor in whose court he is then present, and the proprietor, in whose court the palatine then presides, shall, during his presence there, be but as one of the council.

Thirty-five. The councillor's court, consisting of one of the proprietors, and his six councillors, who shall be called vice-chancellors' shall have the custody of the seal of the palatine, under which charters of lands, or otherwise, commissions and grants of the palatine's court shall pass. And it shall not be lawful to put the seal of the palatinate to any writing which is not signed by the palatine or his deputy and three other proprietors or their deputies. To this court also belong all state matters, despatches, and treaties with the neighbor Indians. To this court also belong all invasions of the law, of liberty of conscience, and all invasions of the public peace, upon presence of religion, as also the license of printing. The twelve assistants belonging to this court shall be called recorders.

Thirty-six. Whatever passes under the seal of the palatinate, shall be registered in the proprietor's court to which the matter therein contained belongs.

Thirty-seven. The chancellor or his deputy shall be always speaker in parliament, and president of the grand council, and, in his and his deputy's absence, one of the vice-chancellors.

Thirty-eight. The chief justice's court, consisting of one of the proprietors and his six councillors, who shall be called justices of the bench, shall judge all appeals in cases both civil and criminal, except all such cases as shall be under the jurisdiction and cognizance of any other of the proprietor's courts, which shall be tried in those courts respectively. The government and regulation of registries of writings and contracts shall belong to the jurisdiction of this court. The twelve assistants of this court shall be called masters.

Thirty-nine. The constable's court, consisting of one of the proprietors and his six councillors, who shall be called marshals, shall order and determine of all military affairs by land, and all landforces, arms, ammunition, artillery, garrisons, forts, &c., and whatever belongs unto war. His twelve assistants shall be called lieutenant-generals.

Forty. In time of actual war the constable, while he is in the army, shall be general of the army, and the six councillors, or such of them as the palatine's court shall for that time or service appoint, shall be the immediate great officers under him, and the lieutenant-generals next to them.

Forty-one. The admiral's court, consisting of one of the proprietors and his six councillors, called consuls, shall have the care and inspection over all ports, moles, and navigable rivers, so far as the tide flows, and also all the public shipping of Carolina, and stores thereunto belonging, and all maritime affairs. This court also shall have the power of the court of admiralty; and shall have power to constitute judges in port-towns to try cases belonging to law-merchant, as shall be most convenient for trade. The twelve assistants belonging to this court shall be called proconsuls.

Forty-two. In time of actual war, the admiral, whilst he is at sea shall command in chief, and his six councillors, or such of them as the palatine's court shall for that time or service appoint, shall be the immediate great officers under him, and the proconsuls next to them.

Forty-three. The treasurer's court, consisting of a proprietor and his six councillors, called under-treasurers, shall take care of all matters that concern the public revenue and treasury. The twelve assistants shall be called auditors.

Forty-four. The high steward's court, consisting of a proprietor and his six councillors, called comptrollers, shall have the care of all foreign and domestic trade, manufactures, public buildings, workhouses, highways, passages by water above the flood of the tide, drains, sewers, and banks against inundation, bridges, posts, carriers, fairs, markets, corruption or infection of the common air or water, and all things in order to the public commerce and health; also setting out and surveying of lands; and also setting out and appointing places for towns to be built on in the precincts, and the prescribing and determining the figure and bigness of the said towns, according to such models as the said court shall order; contrary or differing from which models it shall not be lawful for any one to build in any town. This court shall have power also to make any public building, or any new highway, or enlarge any old highway, upon any man's land whatsoever; as also to make cuts, channels, banks, locks, and bridges, for making rivers navigable, or for draining fens, or any other public use. The damage the owner of such lands (on or through which any such public things shall be made) shall receive thereby shall be valued, and satisfaction made by such ways as the grand council shall appoint. The twelve assistants belonging to this court shall be called surveyors.

Forty-five. The chamberlain's court, consisting of a proprietor and six councillors, called vice-chamberlains, shall have the care of all ceremonies, precedency, heraldry, reception of public messengers, pedigrees, the registry of all births, burials, and marriages, legitimation, and all cases concerning matrimony, or arising from it; and shall also have power to regulate all fashions, habits, badges, games, and sports. To this court it shall also belong to convocate the grand council. The twelve assistants belonging to this court shall be called provosts.

Forty-six. All causes belonging to or under the jurisdiction of any of the proprietors' courts, shall in them respectively be tried, and ultimately determined, without any further appeal.

Forty-seven. The proprietors' courts have a power to mitigate all fines and suspend all execution in criminal causes, either before or after sentence, in any of the other inferior courts respectively.

Forty-eight. In all debates, hearings, or trials, in any of the proprietors' courts, the twelve assistants belonging to the said courts, respectively, shall have liberty to be present, but shall not interpose, unless their opinions be required, nor have any vote at all; but their business shall be, by the direction of the respective courts, to prepare such business as shall be committed to them; as also to bear such offices, and despatch such affairs, either where the court is kept or elsewhere, as the court shall think fit.

Forty-nine. In all the proprietors' courts, the proprietor, and any three of his councillors, shall make a quorum: Provided, always, That for the better despatch of business, it shall be in the power of the palatine's court to direct what sort of causes shall be heard and determined by a quorum of any three.

Fifty. The grand council shall consist of the palatine and seven proprietors, and the forty-two councillors of the several proprietors' courts, who shall have power to determine any controversy that may arise between any of the proprietors' courts, about their respective jurisdictions, or between the members of the same court, about their manner and methods of proceedings; to make peace and war, leagues, treaties, &c., with any of the neighbor Indians; to issue out their general orders to the constable's and admiral's courts, for the raising, disposing, or disbanding the forces, by land or by sea.

Fifty-one. The grand council shall prepare all matters to be proposed in parliament. Nor shall any matter whatsoever be proposed in parliament, but what has first passed the grand council; which, after having been read three several days in the parliament, shall by majority oft votes be passed or rejected;

Fifty-two. The grand council shall always be judges of all causes and appeals that concern the palatine, or any of the lords proprietors, or any councillor of any proprietor's court, in any cause, which should otherwise have been tried in the court of which the said councillor is judge himself.

Fifty-three. The grand council, by their warrants to the treasurer's court, shall dispose of all the money given by the parliament, and by them directed to any particular public use.

Fifty-four. The quorum of the grand council shall be thirteen, whereof a proprietor or his deputy shall be always one.

Fifty-five. The grand council shall meet the first Tuesday in every month, and as much oftener as either they shall think fit, or they shall be convocated by the chamberlain's court.

Fifty-six. The palatine, or any of the lords proprietors, shall have power, under hand and seal, to be registered in the grand council, to make a deputy, who shall have the same power to all intents and purposes as he himself who deputes him; except in confirming acts of parliament, as in section seventy-six, and except also in nominating and choosing landgraves and caziques, as in section ten. All such deputations shall cease and determine at the end of four years, and at any time shall be revocable at the pleasure of the deputator.

Fifty-seven. No deputy of any proprietor shall have any power whilst the deputator is in any part of Carolina, except the proprietor whose deputy he Is be a minor.

Fifty-eight. During the minority of any proprietor, his guardian shall have power to constitute and appoint his deputy.

Fifty-nine. The eldest of the lords proprietors, who shall be personally in Carolina, shall of course be the palatine's deputy, and if no proprietor be in Carolina, he shall choose his deputy out of the heirs apparent of any of the proprietors, if any such be there; and if there be no heir apparent of any of the lords proprietors above one-and-twenty years old in Carolina, then he shall choose for deputy any one of the landgraves of the grand council; till he have by deputation under hand and seal chosen any one of the forementioned heirs apparent or landgraves to be his deputy, the eldest man of the landgraves, and, for want of a landgrave, the eldest man of the caziques, who shall be personally in Carolina, shall of course be his deputy.

Sixty. Each proprietor's deputy shall be always one of his six councillors, respectively; and in case any of the proprietors hath not, in his absence out of Carolina, a deputy, commissioned under his hand and seal, the eldest nobleman of his court shall of course be his deputy.

Sixty-one. In every county there shall be a court, consisting of a sheriff, and four justices of the county, for every precinct one. The sheriff shall be an inhabitant of the county, and have at least five hundred acres of freehold within the said county; and the justices shall be inhabitants, and have each of them five hundred acres apiece freehold within the precinct for which they serve respectively. These five shall be chosen from time to time and commissioned by the palatine's court.

Sixty-two. For any personal causes exceeding the value of two hundred pounds sterling, or in title of land, or in any criminal cause, either party upon paying twenty pounds sterling to the lords proprietors' use, shall have liberty of appeal from the county court unto the respective proprietor's court.

Sixty-three. In every precinct there shall be a court, consisting of a steward and four justices of the precinct, being inhabitants and having three hundred acres of freehold within the said precinct, who shall judge all criminal causes; except for treason, murder, and any other offences punishable with death, and except all criminal causes of the nobility; and shall judge also all civil causes whatsoever; and in all personal actions not exceeding fifty pounds sterling, without appeal; but where the cause shall exceed that value, or concern a title of land, and in all criminal causes, there either party, upon paying five pounds sterling to the lords proprietors' use, shall have liberty of appeal to the county court.

Sixty-four. No cause shall be twice tried in any one court, upon any reason or presence whatsoever.

Sixty-five. For treason, murder, and all other offences punishable with death, there shall be a commission, twice a year at least, granted onto one or more members of the grand council or colleges; who shall come as itinerant judges to the several counties, and with the sheriff and four justices shall hold assizes to judge all such causes; but, upon paying of fifty pounds sterling to the lords proprietors' use, there shall be liberty of appeal to the respective proprietor's court.

Sixty-six. The grand jury at the several assizes shall, upon their oaths, and under their hands and seals, deliver in to their itinerant judges a presentment of such grievances, misdemeanors, exigencies, or defects, which they think necessary for the public good of the country; which presentments shall, by the itinerant judges, at the end of their circuit, be delivered in to the grand council at their next sitting. And whatsoever therein concerns the execution of laws already made, the several proprietors' courts, in the matters belonging to each of them, respectively, shall take cognizance of it, and give such order about it as shall be effectual for the due execution of the laws. But whatever concerns the making of any new law, shall be referred to the several respective courts to which that matter belongs, and be by them prepared and brought to the grand council.

Sixty-seven. For terms, there shall be quarterly such a certain number of days, not exceeding one-and-twenty at any one time, as the several respective courts shall appoint. The time for the beginning of the term, in the precinct court, shall be the first Monday in January, April, July, and October; in the county court, the first Monday in February, May, August, and November; and in the proprietors' courts the first Monday in March, June, September, and December.

Sixty-eight. In the precinct court no man shall be a juryman under fifty acres of freehold. In the county court, or at the assizes, no man shall be a grand-juryman under three hundred acres of freehold; and no man shall be a petty-juryman under two hundred acres of freehold. In the proprietors' courts no man shall be a juryman under five hundred acres of freehold.

Sixty-nine. Every jury shall consist of twelve men; and it shall not be necessary they should all agree, but the verdict shall be according to the consent of the majority.

Seventy. It shall be a base and vile thing to plead for money or reward; nor shall any one (except he be a near kinsman, not farther off than cousin-german to the party concerned) be permitted to plead another-man's cause, till, before the judge in open court, he hath taken an oath that he doth not plead for money or reward, nor hath nor will receive, nor directly nor indirectly bargained with the party whose cause he is going to plead, for money or any other reward for pleading his cause.

Seventy-one. There shall be a parliament, consisting of the proprietors or their deputies, the landgraves, and caziques, and one freeholder out of every precinct, to be chosen by the freeholders of the said precinct, respectively. They shall sit all together in one room, and have every member one vote.

Seventy-two. No man shall be chosen a member of parliament who has less than five hundred acres of freehold within the precinct for which he is chosen; nor shall any have a vote in choosing the said member that hath less than fifty acres of freehold within the said precinct.

Seventy-three. A new parliament shall be assembled the first Monday of the month of November every second year, and shall meet and sit in the town they last sat in, without any summons, unless by the palatine's court they be summoned to meet at any other place. And if there shall be any occasion of a parliament in these intervals, it shall be in the power of the palatine's court to assemble them in forty days' notice, and at such time and place as the said court shall think fit; and the palatine's court shall have power to dissolve the said parliament when they shall think fit.

Seventy-four. At the opening of every parliament, the first thing that shall be done shall be the reading of these fundamental constitutions, which the palatine and proprietors, and the rest of the members then present, shall subscribe. Nor shall any person whatsoever sit or vote in the parliament till he hath that session subscribed these fundamental constitutions, in a book kept for that purpose by the clerk of the parliament.

Seventy-five. In order to the due election of members for the biennial parliament, it shall be lawful for the freeholders of the respective precincts to meet the first Tuesday in September every two years in the same town or place that they last met in, to choose parliament men; and there choose those members that are to sit the next November following, unless the steward of the precinct shall, by sufficient notice thirty days before, appoint some other place for their meeting in order to the election.

Seventy-six. No act or order of parliament shall be of any force, unless it be ratified in open parliament, during the same session, by the palatine or his deputy, and three more of the lords proprietors or their deputies; and then not to continue longer in force but until the next biennial parliament, unless in the mean time it be ratified under the hands and seals of the palatine himself, and three more of the lords proprietors themselves, and by their order published at the next biennial parliament.

Seventy-seven. Any proprietor or his deputy may enter his protestation against any act of the parliament, before the palatine or his deputy's consent be given as aforesaid, if he shall conceive the said act to be contrary to this establishment, or any of these fundamental constitutions of the Government. And in such case, after full and free debate, the several estates shall retire into four several chambers; the palatine and proprietors into one; the landgraves into another; the caziques into another; and those chosen by the precincts into a fourth; and if the major part of any of the four estates shall vote that the law is not agreeable to this establishment, and these fundamental constitutions of the government, then it shall pass no farther, but be as if it had never been proposed.

Seventy-eight. The quorum of the parliament shall be one-half of those who are members and capable of sitting in the house that present session of parliament. The quorum of each of the chambers of parliament shall be one-half of the members of that chamber.

Seventy-nine. To avoid multiplicity of laws, which by degrees always change the right foundations of the original government, all acts of parliament whatsoever, in whatsoever form passed or enacted, shall, at the end of a hundred years after their enacting, respectively cease and determine of themselves, and without any repeal become null and void, as if no such acts or laws had ever been made.

Eighty. Since multiplicity of comments, as well as of laws, have great inconveniencies, and serve only to obscure and perplex, all manner of comments and expositions on any part of these fundamental constitutions, or on any part of the common or statute laws of Carolina, are absolutely prohibited.

Eighty-one. There shall be a registry in every precinct, wherein shall be enrolled all deeds, leases, judgments, mortgages, and other conveyances, which may concern any of the lands within the said precinct; and all such conveyances not so entered and registered shall not be of force against any person or party to the said contract or conveyance.

Eighty-two. No man shall be register of any precinct who hath not at least three hundred acres of freehold within the said precinct.

Eighty-three. The freeholders of every precinct shall nominate three men; out of which three the chief justice's court shall choose and commission one to be register of the said precinct, whilst he shall well behave himself.

Eighty-four. There shall be a registry in every signiory, barony, and colony, wherein shall be recorded all the births, marriages, and deaths that shall happen within the respective signiories, baronies, and colonies.

Eighty-five. No man shall be register of a colony that hath not above fifty acres of freehold within the said colony.

Eighty-six. The time of every one's age, that is born in Carolina, shall be reckoned from the day that his birth is entered in the registry, and not before.

Eighty-seven. No marriage shall be lawful, whatever contract and ceremony they have used, till both the parties mutually own it before the register of the place where they were married, and he register it, with the names of the father and mother of each party.

Eighty-eight. No man shall administer to the goods, or have a right to them, or enter upon the estate of any person deceased, till his death be registered in the respective registry.

Eighty-nine. He that doth not enter in the respective registry the birth or death of any person that is born or dies in his house or ground, shall pay to the said register one shilling per week for each such neglect, reckoning from the time of each birth or death, respectively, to the time of entering it in the register.

Ninety. In like manner, the births, marriages, and deaths of the lords proprietors, landgraves, and caziques shall be registered in the chamberlain's court.

Ninety-one. There shall be in every colony one constable, to be chosen annually, by the freeholders of the colony; his estate shall be above a hundred acres of freehold within the said colony, and such subordinate officers appointed for his assistance as the county court shall find requisite, and shall be established by the said county court. The election of the subordinate annual officers shall be also in the freeholders of the colony.

Ninety-two. All towns incorporate shall be governed by a mayor, twelve aldermen, and twenty-four of the common council. The said common council shall be chosen by the present householders of the said town; the aldermen shall be chosen out of the common council; and the mayor out of the aldermen, by the palatine's court.

Ninety-three. It being of great consequence to the plantation that port-towns should be built and preserved; therefore, whosoever shall lade or unlace any commodity at any other place than a port-town, shall forfeit to the lords proprietors, for each ton so laden or unladen, the sum of ten pounds sterling; except only such goods as the palatine's court shall license to be laden or unladen elsewhere.

Ninety-four. The first port-town upon every river shall be in a colony, and be a port-town forever.

Ninety-five. No man shall be permitted to be a freeman of Carolina, or to have any estate or habitation within it, that doth not acknowledge a (lod, and that God is publicly and solemnly to be worshipped.

Ninety-six. [As the country comes to be sufficiently planted and distributed into fit divisions, it shall belong to the parliament to take care for the building of churches, and the public maintenance of divines, to be employed in the exercise of religion, according to the Church of England; which being the only true and orthodox and the national religion of all the King's dominions, is so also of Carolina; and, therefore, it alone shall be allowed to receive public maintenance, by grant of parliament.](3)

Ninety-seven. But since the natives of that place, who will be concerned in our plantation, are utterly strangers to Christianity, whose idolatry, ignorance, or mistake gives us no right to expel or use them ill; and those who remove from other parts to plant there will unavoidably be of different opinions concerning matters of religion, the liberty whereof they will expect to have allowed them, and it will not be reasonable for us, on this account, to keep them out, that civil peace may be maintained amidst diversity of opinions, and our agreement and compact with all men may be duly and faithfully observed; the violation whereof, upon what presence soever, cannot be without great offence to Almighty God, and great scandal to the true religion which we profess; and also that Jews, heathens, and other dissenters from the purity of Christian religion may not be scared and kept at a distance from it, but, by having an opportunity of acquainting themselves with the truth and reasonableness of its doctrines, and the peaceableness and inoffensiveness of its professors, may, by good usage and persuasion, and all those convincing methods of gentleness and meekness, suitable to the rules and design of the gospel, be won ever to embrace and unfeignedly receive the truth; therefore, any seven or more persons agreeing in any religion, shall constitute a church or profession, to which they shall give some name, to distinguish it from others.

Ninety-eight. The terms of admittance and communion with any church or profession shall be written in a book, and therein be subscribed by all the members of the said church or profession; which book shall be kept by the public register of the precinct wherein they reside.

Ninety-nine. The time of every one's subscription and admittance shall be dated in the said book or religious record.

One hundred. In the terms of communion of every church or profession, these following shall be three; without which no agreement or assembly of men, upon presence of religion, shall be accounted a church or profession within these rules:

1st. "That there is a God."

II. "That God is publicly to be worshipped."

III. "That it is lawful and the duty of every man, being thereunto called by those that govern, to bear witness to truth; and that every church or profession shall, in their terms of communion, set down the external way whereby they witness a truth as in the presence of God, whether it be by laying hands on or kissing the bible, as in the Church of England, or by holding up the hand, or any other sensible way."

One hundred and one. No person above seventeen years of age shall have any benefit or protection of the law, or be capable of any place of profit or honor, who is not a member of some church or profession, having his name recorded in some one, and but one religious record at once.

One hundred and two. No person of any other church or profession shall disturb or molest any religious assembly.

One hundred and three. No person whatsoever shall speak anything in their religious assembly irreverently or seditiously of the government or governors, or of state matters.

One hundred and four. Any person subscribing the terms of communion, in the record of the said church or profession, before the precinct register, and any five members of the said church or profession, shall be thereby made a member of the said church or profession.

One hundred and five. Any person striking out his own name out of any religious record, or his name being struck out by any officer "hereunto authorized by each church or profession respectively, shall cease to be a member of that church or profession.

One hundred and six. No man shall use any reproachful, reviling, or abusive language against any religion of any church or profession; that being the certain way of disturbing the peace, and of hindering the conversion of any to the truth, by them in quarrels and animosities, to the hatred of the professors and that profession which otherwise they might be brought to assent to.

One hundred and seven. Since charity obliges us to wish well to the souls of all men, and religion ought to alter nothing in any man's civil estate or right, it shall be lawful for slaves, as well as others, to enter themselves, and be of what church or profession any of them shall think best, and, therefore, be as fully members as any freeman. But yet no slave shall hereby be exempted from that civil dominion his master hath over him, but be in all things in the same state and condition he was In before.

One hundred and eight. Assemblies, upon what presence soever of religion, not observing and performing the above said rules, shall not be esteemed as churches, but unlawful meetings, and be punished as other riots.

One hundred and nine. No person whatsover shall disturb, molest, or persecute another for his speculative opinions in religion, or his way of worship.

One hundred and ten. Every freeman of Carolina shall have absolute power and authority over his negro slaves, of what opinion or religion soever.

One hundred and eleven. No cause, whether civil or criminal, of any freeman, shall be tried in any court of judicature, without a jury of his peers.

One hundred and twelve. No person whatever shall hold or claim any land in Carolina by purchase or gift, or otherwise, from the natives, or any other whatsoever, but merely from and under the lords proprietors, upon pain of forfeiture of all his estate, movable or immovable, and perpetual banishment.

One hundred and thirteen. Whosoever shall possess any freehold in Carolina, upon what title or grant soever, shall, at the farthest, from and after the year one thousand six hundred and eighty-nine, pay yearly unto the lords proprietors, for each acre of land, English measure, as much fine silver as is at this present time in one English penny, or the value thereof, to be as a chief rent and acknowledgment to the lords proprietors, their heirs and successors, forever. And it shall be lawful for the palatine's court, by their officers, at any time to take a new survey of any man's land, not to oust him of any part of his possession, but that by such a survey the just number of acres he possesseth may be known, and the rent thereon due may be paid by him.

One hundred and fourteen. All wrecks, mines, minerals, quarries of gems, and precious stones, with pearl-fishing, whale-fishing, and one-half of all ambergris, by whomsoever found, shall wholly belong to the lords proprietors.

One hundred and fifteen. All revenues and profits belonging to the lords proprietors in common shall be divided into ten parts, whereof the palatine shall have three, and each proprietor one; but if the palatine shall govern by a deputy, the deputy shall have one of those three-tenths, and the palatine the other two-tenths.

One hundred and sixteen. All inhabitants and freemen of ()arolina above seventeen years of age, and under sixty, shall be bound to bear arms and serve as soldiers, whenever the grand council shall find it necessary.

One hundred and seventeen. A true copy of these fundamental constitutions shall be kept in a great book by the register of every precinct, to be subscribed before the said register. Nor shall any person, of what degree or condition soever, above seventeen years old, have any estate or possession in Carolina, or protection or benefit of the law there, who hath not, before a precinct register, subscribed these fundamental constitutions in this form:

" I, A. B., do promise to bear faith and true allegiance to our sovereign lord King Charles II, his heirs and successors; and will be true and faithful to the palatine and lords proprietors of Carolina, their heirs and successors; and with my utmost power will defend them, and maintain the government according to this establishment in these fundamental constitutions."

One hundred and eighteen. VVhatsoever alien shall, in this form, before any precinct register, subscribe these fundamental constitutions, shall be thereby naturalized.

One hundred and nineteen. In the same manner shall every person, at his admittance into any office, subscribe these flmdamental constitutions.

One hundred and twenty. These fundamental constitutions, in number a hundred and twenty, and every part thereof, shall be and remain the sacred and unalterable form and rule of government of Carolina forever. Witness our hands and seals, the first day of March, sixteen hundred and sixty-nine.

1 North Carolina Colonial records 187-205. Locke's Works [Eighth Edition] X. 175. Back

2 This form of government was framed by John Locke author of the Essay on the Human Understanding and amended by the Earl of Shaftesbury previously known as Anthony Ashley Cooper. It was only partially put into operation, and it was abrogated by the lords proprietors in April, 1693. Back

3 This article was not drawn up by Mr. Locke, but inserted by some of the chief of the proprietors, against his judgment; as Mr. Locke himself informed one of his friends, to whom he presented a copy of these constitutions.

A Letter Concerning Toleration

by John Locke

1689

Translated by William Popple

Honoured Sir,

Since you are pleased to inquire what are my thoughts about the mutual toleration of Christians in their different professions of religion, I must needs answer you freely that I esteem that toleration to be the chief characteristic mark of the true Church. For whatsoever some people boast of the antiquity of places and names, or of the pomp of their outward worship; others, of the reformation of their discipline; all, of the orthodoxy of their faith — for everyone is orthodox to himself — these things, and all others of this nature, are much rather marks of men striving for power and empire over one another than of the Church of Christ. Let anyone have never so true a claim to all these things, yet if he be destitute of charity, meekness, and good-will in general towards all mankind, even to those that are not Christians, he is certainly yet short of being a true Christian himself. "The kings of the Gentiles exercise leadership over them," said our Saviour to his disciples, "but ye shall not be so."[1] The business of true religion is quite another thing. It is not instituted in order to the erecting of an external pomp, nor to the obtaining of ecclesiastical dominion, nor to the exercising of compulsive force, but to the regulating of men's lives, according to the rules of virtue and piety. Whosoever will list himself under the banner of Christ, must, in the first place and above all things, make war upon his own lusts and vices. It is in vain for any man to unsurp the name of Christian, without holiness of life, purity of manners, benignity and meekness of spirit. "Let everyone that nameth the name of Christ, depart from iniquity."[2] "Thou, when thou art converted, strengthen thy brethren," said our Lord to Peter.[3] It would, indeed, be very hard for one that appears careless about his own salvation to persuade me that he were extremely concerned for mine. For it is impossible that those should sincerely and heartily apply themselves to make other people Christians, who have not really embraced the Christian religion in their own hearts. If the Gospel and the apostles may be credited, no man can be a Christian without charity and without that faith which works, not by force, but by love. Now, I appeal to the consciences of those that persecute, torment, destroy, and kill other men upon pretence of religion, whether they do it out of friendship and kindness towards them or no? And I shall then indeed, and not until then, believe they do so, when I shall see those fiery zealots correcting, in the same manner, their friends and familiar acquaintance for the manifest sins they commit against the precepts of the Gospel; when I shall see them persecute with fire and sword the members of their own communion that are tainted with enormous vices and without amendment are in danger of eternal perdition; and when I shall see them thus express their love and desire of the salvation of their souls by the infliction of torments and exercise of all manner of cruelties. For if it be out of a principle of charity, as they pretend, and love to men's souls that they deprive them of their estates, maim them with corporal punishments, starve and torment them in noisome prisons, and in the end even take away their lives — I say, if all this be done merely to make men Christians and procure their salvation, why then do they suffer whoredom, fraud, malice, and such-like enormities, which (according to the apostle)[4] manifestly relish of heathenish corruption, to predominate so much and abound amongst their flocks and people? These, and such-like things, are certainly more contrary to the glory of God, to the purity of the Church, and to the salvation of souls, than any conscientious dissent from ecclesiastical decisions, or separation from public worship, whilst accompanied with innocence of life. Why, then, does this burning zeal for God, for the Church, and for the salvation of souls — burning I say, literally, with fire and faggot — pass by those moral vices and wickednesses, without any chastisement, which are acknowledged by all men to be diametrically opposite to the profession of Christianity, and bend all its nerves either to the introducing of ceremonies, or to the establishment of opinions, which for the most part are about nice and intricate matters, that exceed the capacity of ordinary understandings? Which of the parties contending about these things is in the right, which of them is guilty of schism or heresy, whether those that domineer or those that suffer, will then at last be manifest when the causes of their separation comes to be judged of He, certainly, that follows Christ, embraces His doctrine, and bears His yoke, though he forsake both father and mother, separate from the public assemblies and ceremonies of his country, or whomsoever or whatsoever else he relinquishes, will not then be judged a heretic.

Now, though the divisions that are amongst sects should be allowed to be never so obstructive of the salvation of souls; yet, nevertheless, adultery, fornication, uncleanliness, lasciviousness, idolatry, and such-like things, cannot be denied to be works of the flesh, concerning which the apostle has expressly declared that "they who do them shall not inherit the kingdom of God."[5] Whosoever, therefore, is sincerely solicitous about the kingdom of God and thinks it his duty to endeavour the enlargement of it amongst men, ought to apply himself with no less care and industry to the rooting out of these immoralities than to the extirpation of sects. But if anyone do otherwise, and whilst he is cruel and implacable towards those that differ from him in opinion, he be indulgent to such iniquities and immoralities as are unbecoming the name of a Christian, let such a one talk never so much of the Church, he plainly demonstrates by his actions that it is another kingdom he aims at and not the advancement of the kingdom of God.

That any man should think fit to cause another man — whose salvation he heartily desires — to expire in torments, and that even in an unconverted state, would, I confess, seem very strange to me, and I think, to any other also. But nobody, surely, will ever believe that such a carriage can proceed from charity, love, or goodwill. If anyone maintain that men ought to be compelled by fire and sword to profess certain doctrines, and conform to this or that exterior worship, without any regard had unto their morals; if anyone endeavour to convert those that are erroneous unto the faith, by forcing them to profess things that they do not believe and allowing them to practise things that the Gospel does not permit, it cannot be doubted indeed but such a one is desirous to have a numerous assembly joined in the same profession with himself; but that he principally intends by those means to compose a truly Christian Church is altogether incredible. It is not, therefore, to be wondered at if those who do not really contend for the advancement of the true religion, and of the Church of Christ, make use of arms that do not belong to the Christian warfare. If, like the Captain of our salvation, they sincerely desired the good of souls, they would tread in the steps and follow the perfect example of that Prince of Peace, who sent out His soldiers to the subduing of nations, and gathering them into His Church, not armed with the sword, or other instruments of force, but prepared with the Gospel of peace and with the exemplary holiness of their conversation. This was His method. Though if infidels were to be converted by force, if those that are either blind or obstinate were to be drawn off from their errors by armed soldiers, we know very well that it was much more easy for Him to do it with armies of heavenly legions than for any son of the Church, how potent soever, with all his dragoons.

The toleration of those that differ from others in matters of religion is so agreeable to the Gospel of Jesus Christ, and to the genuine reason of mankind, that it seems monstrous for men to be so blind as not to perceive the necessity and advantage of it in so clear a light. I will not here tax the pride and ambition of some, the passion and uncharitable zeal of others. These are faults from which human affairs can perhaps scarce ever be perfectly freed; but yet such as nobody will bear the plain imputation of, without covering them with some specious colour; and so pretend to commendation, whilst they are carried away by their own irregular passions. But, however, that some may not colour their spirit of persecution and unchristian cruelty with a pretence of care of the public weal and observation of the laws; and that others, under pretence of religion, may not seek impunity for their libertinism and licentiousness; in a word, that none may impose either upon himself or others, by the pretences of loyalty and obedience to the prince, or of tenderness and sincerity in the worship of God; I esteem it above all things necessary to distinguish exactly the business of civil government from that of religion and to settle the just bounds that lie between the one and the other. If this be not done, there can be no end put to the controversies that will be always arising between those that have, or at least pretend to have, on the one side, a concernment for the interest of men's souls, and, on the other side, a care of the commonwealth.

The commonwealth seems to me to be a society of men constituted only for the procuring, preserving, and advancing their own civil interests.

Civil interests I call life, liberty, health, and indolency of body; and the possession of outward things, such as money, lands, houses, furniture, and the like.

It is the duty of the civil magistrate, by the impartial execution of equal laws, to secure unto all the people in general and to every one of his subjects in particular the just possession of these things belonging to this life. If anyone presume to violate the laws of public justice and equity, established for the preservation of those things, his presumption is to be checked by the fear of punishment, consisting of the deprivation or diminution of those civil interests, or goods, which otherwise he might and ought to enjoy. But seeing no man does willingly suffer himself to be punished by the deprivation of any part of his goods, and much less of his liberty or life, therefore, is the magistrate armed with the force and strength of all his subjects, in order to the punishment of those that violate any other man's rights.

Now that the whole jurisdiction of the magistrate reaches only to these civil concernments, and that all civil power, right and dominion, is bounded and confined to the only care of promoting these things; and that it neither can nor ought in any manner to be extended to the salvation of souls, these following considerations seem unto me abundantly to demonstrate.

First, because the care of souls is not committed to the civil magistrate, any more than to other men. It is not committed unto him, I say, by God; because it appears not that God has ever given any such authority to one man over another as to compel anyone to his religion. Nor can any such power be vested in the magistrate by the consent of the people, because no man can so far abandon the care of his own salvation as blindly to leave to the choice of any other, whether prince or subject, to prescribe to him what faith or worship he shall embrace. For no man can, if he would, conform his faith to the dictates of another. All the life and power of true religion consist in the inward and full persuasion of the mind; and faith is not faith without believing. Whatever profession we make, to whatever outward worship we conform, if we are not fully satisfied in our own mind that the one is true and the other well pleasing unto God, such profession and such practice, far from being any furtherance, are indeed great obstacles to our salvation. For in this manner, instead of expiating other sins by the exercise of religion, I say, in offering thus unto God Almighty such a worship as we esteem to be displeasing unto Him, we add unto the number of our other sins those also of hypocrisy and contempt of His Divine Majesty.

In the second place, the care of souls cannot belong to the civil magistrate, because his power consists only in outward force; but true and saving religion consists in the inward persuasion of the mind, without which nothing can be acceptable to God. And such is the nature of the understanding, that it cannot be compelled to the belief of anything by outward force. Confiscation of estate, imprisonment, torments, nothing of that nature can have any such efficacy as to make men change the inward judgement that they have framed of things.

It may indeed be alleged that the magistrate may make use of arguments, and, thereby; draw the heterodox into the way of truth, and procure their salvation. I grant it; but this is common to him with other men. In teaching, instructing, and redressing the erroneous by reason, he may certainly do what becomes any good man to do. Magistracy does not oblige him to put off either humanity or Christianity; but it is one thing to persuade, another to command; one thing to press with arguments, another with penalties. This civil power alone has a right to do; to the other, goodwill is authority enough. Every man has commission to admonish, exhort, convince another of error, and, by reasoning, to draw him into truth; but to give laws, receive obedience, and compel with the sword, belongs to none but the magistrate. And, upon this ground, I affirm that the magistrate's power extends not to the establishing of any articles of faith, or forms of worship, by the force of his laws. For laws are of no force at all without penalties, and penalties in this case are absolutely impertinent, because they are not proper to convince the mind. Neither the profession of any articles of faith, nor the conformity to any outward form of worship (as has been already said), can be available to the salvation of souls, unless the truth of the one and the acceptableness of the other unto God be thoroughly believed by those that so profess and practise. But penalties are no way capable to produce such belief. It is only light and evidence that can work a change in men's opinions; which light can in no manner proceed from corporal sufferings, or any other outward penalties.

In the third place, the care of the salvation of men's souls cannot belong to the magistrate; because, though the rigour of laws and the force of penalties were capable to convince and change men's minds, yet would not that help at all to the salvation of their souls. For there being but one truth, one way to heaven, what hope is there that more men would be led into it if they had no rule but the religion of the court and were put under the necessity to quit the light of their own reason, and oppose the dictates of their own consciences, and blindly to resign themselves up to the will of their governors and to the religion which either ignorance, ambition, or superstition had chanced to establish in the countries where they were born? In the variety and contradiction of opinions in religion, wherein the princes of the world are as much divided as in their secular interests, the narrow way would be much straitened; one country alone would be in the right, and all the rest of the world put under an obligation of following their princes in the ways that lead to destruction; and that which heightens the absurdity, and very ill suits the notion of a Deity, men would owe their eternal happiness or misery to the places of their nativity.

These considerations, to omit many others that might have been urged to the same purpose, seem unto me sufficient to conclude that all the power of civil government relates only to men's civil interests, is confined to the care of the things of this world, and hath nothing to do with the world to come.

Let us now consider what a church is. A church, then, I take to be a voluntary society of men, joining themselves together of their own accord in order to the public worshipping of God in such manner as they judge acceptable to Him, and effectual to the salvation of their souls.

I say it is a free and voluntary society. Nobody is born a member of any church; otherwise the religion of parents would descend unto children by the same right of inheritance as their temporal estates, and everyone would hold his faith by the same tenure he does his lands, than which nothing can be imagined more absurd. Thus, therefore, that matter stands. No man by nature is bound unto any particular church or sect, but everyone joins himself voluntarily to that society in which he believes he has found that profession and worship which is truly acceptable to God. The hope of salvation, as it was the only cause of his entrance into that communion, so it can be the only reason of his stay there. For if afterwards he discover anything either erroneous in the doctrine or incongruous in the worship of that society to which he has joined himself, why should it not be as free for him to go out as it was to enter? No member of a religious society can be tied with any other bonds but what proceed from the certain expectation of eternal life. A church, then, is a society of members voluntarily uniting to that end.

It follows now that we consider what is the power of this church and unto what laws it is subject.

Forasmuch as no society, how free soever, or upon whatsoever slight occasion instituted, whether of philosophers for learning, of merchants for commerce, or of men of leisure for mutual conversation and discourse, no church or company, I say, can in the least subsist and hold together, but will presently dissolve and break in pieces, unless it be regulated by some laws, and the members all consent to observe some order. Place and time of meeting must be agreed on; rules for admitting and excluding members must be established; distinction of officers, and putting things into a regular course, and suchlike, cannot be omitted. But since the joining together of several members into this church-society, as has already been demonstrated, is absolutely free and spontaneous, it necessarily follows that the right of making its laws can belong to none but the society itself; or, at least (which is the same thing), to those whom the society by common consent has authorised thereunto.

Some, perhaps, may object that no such society can be said to be a true church unless it have in it a bishop or presbyter, with ruling authority derived from the very apostles, and continued down to the present times by an uninterrupted succession.

To these I answer: In the first place, let them show me the edict by which Christ has imposed that law upon His Church. And let not any man think me impertinent, if in a thing of this consequence I require that the terms of that edict be very express and positive; for the promise He has made us,[6] that "wheresoever two or three are gathered together" in His name, He will be in the midst of them, seems to imply the contrary. Whether such an assembly want anything necessary to a true church, pray do you consider. Certain I am that nothing can be there wanting unto the salvation of souls, which is sufficient to our purpose.

Next, pray observe how great have always been the divisions amongst even those who lay so much stress upon the Divine institution and continued succession of a certain order of rulers in the Church. Now, their very dissension unavoidably puts us upon a necessity of deliberating and, consequently, allows a liberty of choosing that which upon consideration we prefer.

And, in the last place, I consent that these men have a ruler in their church, established by such a long series of succession as they judge necessary, provided I may have liberty at the same time to join myself to that society in which I am persuaded those things are to be found which are necessary to the salvation of my soul. In this manner ecclesiastical liberty will be preserved on all sides, and no man will have a legislator imposed upon him but whom himself has chosen.

But since men are so solicitous about the true church, I would only ask them here, by the way, if it be not more agreeable to the Church of Christ to make the conditions of her communion consist in such things, and such things only, as the Holy Spirit has in the Holy Scriptures declared, in express words, to be necessary to salvation; I ask, I say, whether this be not more agreeable to the Church of Christ than for men to impose their own inventions and interpretations upon others as if they were of Divine authority, and to establish by ecclesiastical laws, as absolutely necessary to the profession of Christianity, such things as the Holy Scriptures do either not mention, or at least not expressly command? Whosoever requires those things in order to ecclesiastical communion, which Christ does not require in order to life eternal, he may, perhaps, indeed constitute a society accommodated to his own opinion and his own advantage; but how that can be called the Church of Christ which is established upon laws that are not His, and which excludes such persons from its communion as He will one day receive into the Kingdom of Heaven, I understand not. But this being not a proper place to inquire into the marks of the true church, I will only mind those that contend so earnestly for the decrees of their own society, and that cry out continually, "The Church! the Church!" with as much noise, and perhaps upon the same principle, as the Ephesian silversmiths did for their Diana; this, I say, I desire to mind them of, that the Gospel frequently declares that the true disciples of Christ must suffer persecution; but that the Church of Christ should persecute others, and force others by fire and sword to embrace her faith and doctrine, I could never yet find in any of the books of the New Testament.

The end of a religious society (as has already been said) is the public worship of God and, by means thereof, the acquisition of eternal life. All discipline ought, therefore, to tend to that end, and all ecclesiastical laws to be thereunto confined. Nothing ought nor can be transacted in this society relating to the possession of civil and worldly goods. No force is here to be made use of upon any occasion whatsoever. For force belongs wholly to the civil magistrate, and the possession of all outward goods is subject to his jurisdiction.

But, it may be asked, by what means then shall ecclesiastical laws be established, if they must be thus destitute of all compulsive power? I answer: They must be established by means suitable to the nature of such things, whereof the external profession and observation — if not proceeding from a thorough conviction and approbation of the mind — is altogether useless and unprofitable. The arms by which the members of this society are to be kept within their duty are exhortations, admonitions, and advices. If by these means the offenders will not be reclaimed, and the erroneous convinced, there remains nothing further to be done but that such stubborn and obstinate persons, who give no ground to hope for their reformation, should be cast out and separated from the society. This is the last and utmost force of ecclesiastical authority. No other punishment can thereby be inflicted than that, the relation ceasing between the body and the member which is cut off. The person so condemned ceases to be a part of that church.

These things being thus determined, let us inquire, in the next place: How far the duty of toleration extends, and what is required from everyone by it?

And, first, I hold that no church is bound, by the duty of toleration, to retain any such person in her bosom as, after admonition, continues obstinately to offend against the laws of the society. For, these being the condition of communion and the bond of the society, if the breach of them were permitted without any animadversion the society would immediately be thereby dissolved. But, nevertheless, in all such cases care is to be taken that the sentence of excommunication, and the execution thereof, carry with it no rough usage of word or action whereby the ejected person may any wise be damnified in body or estate. For all force (as has often been said) belongs only to the magistrate, nor ought any private persons at any time to use force, unless it be in self-defence against unjust violence. Excommunication neither does, nor can, deprive the excommunicated person of any of those civil goods that he formerly possessed. All those things belong to the civil government and are under the magistrate's protection. The whole force of excommunication consists only in this: that, the resolution of the society in that respect being declared, the union that was between the body and some member comes thereby to be dissolved; and, that relation ceasing, the participation of some certain things which the society communicated to its members, and unto which no man has any civil right, comes also to cease. For there is no civil injury done unto the excommunicated person by the church minister's refusing him that bread and wine, in the celebration of the Lord's Supper, which was not bought with his but other men's money.

Secondly, no private person has any right in any manner to prejudice another person in his civil enjoyments because he is of another church or religion. All the rights and franchises that belong to him as a man, or as a denizen, are inviolably to be preserved to him. These are not the business of religion. No violence nor injury is to be offered him, whether he be Christian or Pagan. Nay, we must not content ourselves with the narrow measures of bare justice; charity, bounty, and liberality must be added to it. This the Gospel enjoins, this reason directs, and this that natural fellowship we are born into requires of us. If any man err from the right way, it is his own misfortune, no injury to thee; nor therefore art thou to punish him in the things of this life because thou supposest he will be miserable in that which is to come.

What I say concerning the mutual toleration of private persons differing from one another in religion, I understand also of particular churches which stand, as it were, in the same relation to each other as private persons among themselves: nor has any one of them any manner of jurisdiction over any other; no, not even when the civil magistrate (as it sometimes happens) comes to be of this or the other communion. For the civil government can give no new right to the church, nor the church to the civil government. So that, whether the magistrate join himself to any church, or separate from it, the church remains always as it was before — a free and voluntary society. It neither requires the power of the sword by the magistrate's coming to it, nor does it lose the right of instruction and excommunication by his going from it. This is the fundamental and immutable right of a spontaneous society — that it has power to remove any of its members who transgress the rules of its institution; but it cannot, by the accession of any new members, acquire any right of jurisdiction over those that are not joined with it. And therefore peace, equity, and friendship are always mutually to be observed by particular churches, in the same manner as by private persons, without any pretence of superiority or jurisdiction over one another.

That the thing may be made clearer by an example, let us suppose two churches — the one of Arminians, the other of Calvinists — residing in the city of Constantinople. Will anyone say that either of these churches has right to deprive the members of the other of their estates and liberty (as we see practised elsewhere) because of their differing from it in some doctrines and ceremonies, whilst the Turks, in the meanwhile, silently stand by and laugh to see with what inhuman cruelty Christians thus rage against Christians? But if one of these churches hath this power of treating the other ill, I ask which of them it is to whom that power belongs, and by what right? It will be answered, undoubtedly, that it is the orthodox church which has the right of authority over the erroneous or heretical. This is, in great and specious words, to say just nothing at all. For every church is orthodox to itself; to others, erroneous or heretical. For whatsoever any church believes, it believes to be true and the contrary unto those things it pronounce; to be error. So that the controversy between these churches about the truth of their doctrines and the purity of their worship is on both sides equal; nor is there any judge, either at Constantinople or elsewhere upon earth, by whose sentence it can be determined. The decision of that question belongs only to the Supreme judge of all men, to whom also alone belongs the punishment of the erroneous. In the meanwhile, let those men consider how heinously they sin, who, adding injustice, if not to their error, yet certainly to their pride, do rashly and arrogantly take upon them to misuse the servants of another master, who are not at all accountable to them.

Nay, further: if it could be manifest which of these two dissenting churches were in the right, there would not accrue thereby unto the orthodox any right of destroying the other. For churches have neither any jurisdiction in worldly matters, nor are fire and sword any proper instruments wherewith to convince men's minds of error, and inform them of the truth. Let us suppose, nevertheless, that the civil magistrate inclined to favour one of them and to put his sword into their hands that (by his consent) they might chastise the dissenters as they pleased. Will any man say that any right can be derived unto a Christian church over its brethren from a Turkish emperor? An infidel, who has himself no authority to punish Christians for the articles of their faith, cannot confer such an authority upon any society of Christians, nor give unto them a right which he has not himself. This would be the case at Constantinople; and the reason of the thing is the same in any Christian kingdom. The civil power is the same in every place. Nor can that power, in the hands of a Christian prince, confer any greater authority upon the Church than in the hands of a heathen; which is to say, just none at all.

Nevertheless, it is worthy to be observed and lamented that the most violent of these defenders of the truth, the opposers of errors, the exclaimers against schism do hardly ever let loose this their zeal for God, with which they are so warmed and inflamed, unless where they have the civil magistrate on their side. But so soon as ever court favour has given them the better end of the staff, and they begin to feel themselves the stronger, then presently peace and charity are to be laid aside. Otherwise they are religiously to be observed. Where they have not the power to carry on persecution and to become masters, there they desire to live upon fair terms and preach up toleration. When they are not strengthened with the civil power, then they can bear most patiently and unmovedly the contagion of idolatry, superstition, and heresy in their neighbourhood; of which on other occasions the interest of religion makes them to be extremely apprehensive. They do not forwardly attack those errors which are in fashion at court or are countenanced by the government. Here they can be content to spare their arguments; which yet (with their leave) is the only right method of propagating truth, which has no such way of prevailing as when strong arguments and good reason are joined with the softness of civility and good usage.

Nobody, therefore, in fine, neither single persons nor churches, nay, nor even commonwealths, have any just title to invade the civil rights and worldly goods of each other upon pretence of religion. Those that are of another opinion would do well to consider with themselves how pernicious a seed of discord and war, how powerful a provocation to endless hatreds, rapines, and slaughters they thereby furnish unto mankind. No peace and security, no, not so much as common friendship, can ever be established or preserved amongst men so long as this opinion prevails, that dominion is founded in grace and that religion is to be propagated by force of arms.

In the third place, let us see what the duty of toleration requires from those who are distinguished from the rest of mankind (from the laity, as they please to call us) by some ecclesiastical character and office; whether they be bishops, priests, presbyters, ministers, or however else dignified or distinguished. It is not my business to inquire here into the original of the power or dignity of the clergy. This only I say, that, whencesoever their authority be sprung, since it is ecclesiastical, it ought to be confined within the bounds of the Church, nor can it in any manner be extended to civil affairs, because the Church itself is a thing absolutely separate and distinct from the commonwealth. The boundaries on both sides are fixed and immovable. He jumbles heaven and earth together, the things most remote and opposite, who mixes these two societies, which are in their original, end, business, and in everything perfectly distinct and infinitely different from each other. No man, therefore, with whatsoever ecclesiastical office he be dignified, can deprive another man that is not of his church and faith either of liberty or of any part of his worldly goods upon the account of that difference between them in religion. For whatsoever is not lawful to the whole Church cannot by any ecclesiastical right become lawful to any of its members.

But this is not all. It is not enough that ecclesiastical men abstain from violence and rapine and all manner of persecution. He that pretends to be a successor of the apostles, and takes upon him the office of teaching, is obliged also to admonish his hearers of the duties of peace and goodwill towards all men, as well towards the erroneous as the orthodox; towards those that differ from them in faith and worship as well as towards those that agree with them therein. And he ought industriously to exhort all men, whether private persons or magistrates (if any such there be in his church), to charity, meekness, and toleration, and diligently endeavour to ally and temper all that heat and unreasonable averseness of mind which either any man's fiery zeal for his own sect or the craft of others has kindled against dissenters. I will not undertake to represent how happy and how great would be the fruit, both in Church and State, if the pulpits everywhere sounded with this doctrine of peace and toleration, lest I should seem to reflect too severely upon those men whose dignity I desire not to detract from, nor would have it diminished either by others or themselves. But this I say, that thus it ought to be. And if anyone that professes himself to be a minister of the Word of God, a preacher of the gospel of peace, teach otherwise, he either understands not or neglects the business of his calling and shall one day give account thereof unto the Prince of Peace. If Christians are to be admonished that they abstain from all manner of revenge, even after repeated provocations and multiplied injuries, how much more ought they who suffer nothing, who have had no harm done them, forbear violence and abstain from all manner of ill-usage towards those from whom they have received none! This caution and temper they ought certainly to use towards those. who mind only their own business and are solicitous for nothing but that (whatever men think of them) they may worship God in that manner which they are persuaded is acceptable to Him and in which they have the strongest hopes of eternal salvation. In private domestic affairs, in the management of estates, in the conservation of bodily health, every man may consider what suits his own convenience and follow what course he likes best. No man complains of the ill-management of his neighbour's affairs. No man is angry with another for an error committed in sowing his land or in marrying his daughter. Nobody corrects a spendthrift for consuming his substance in taverns. Let any man pull down, or build, or make whatsoever expenses he pleases, nobody murmurs, nobody controls him; he has his liberty. But if any man do not frequent the church, if he do not there conform his behaviour exactly to the accustomed ceremonies, or if he brings not his children to be initiated in the sacred mysteries of this or the other congregation, this immediately causes an uproar. The neighbourhood is filled with noise and clamour. Everyone is ready to be the avenger of so great a crime, and the zealots hardly have the patience to refrain from violence and rapine so long till the cause be heard and the poor man be, according to form, condemned to the loss of liberty, goods, or life. Oh, that our ecclesiastical orators of every sect would apply themselves with all the strength of arguments that they are able to the confounding of men's errors! But let them spare their persons. Let them not supply their want of reasons with the instruments of force, which belong to another jurisdiction and do ill become a Churchman's hands. Let them not call in the magistrate's authority to the aid of their eloquence or learning, lest perhaps, whilst they pretend only love for the truth, this their intemperate zeal, breathing nothing but fire and sword, betray their ambition and show that what they desire is temporal dominion. For it will be very difficult to persuade men of sense that he who with dry eyes and satisfaction of mind can deliver his brother to the executioner to be burnt alive, does sincerely and heartily concern himself to save that brother from the flames of hell in the world to come.

In the last place, let us now consider what is the magistrate's duty in the business of toleration, which certainly is very considerable.

We have already proved that the care of souls does not belong to the magistrate. Not a magisterial care, I mean (if I may so call it), which consists in prescribing by laws and compelling by punishments. But a charitable care, which consists in teaching, admonishing, and persuading, cannot be denied unto any man. The care, therefore, of every man's soul belongs unto himself and is to be left unto himself. But what if he neglect the care of his soul? I answer: What if he neglect the care of his health or of his estate, which things are nearlier related to the government of the magistrate than the other? Will the magistrate provide by an express law that such a one shall not become poor or sick? Laws provide, as much as is possible, that the goods and health of subjects be not injured by the fraud and violence of others; they do not guard them from the negligence or ill-husbandry of the possessors themselves. No man can be forced to be rich or healthful whether he will or no. Nay, God Himself will not save men against their wills. Let us suppose, however, that some prince were desirous to force his subjects to accumulate riches, or to preserve the health and strength of their bodies. Shall it be provided by law that they must consult none but Roman physicians, and shall everyone be bound to live according to their prescriptions? What, shall no potion, no broth, be taken, but what is prepared either in the Vatican, suppose, or in a Geneva shop? Or, to make these subjects rich, shall they all be obliged by law to become merchants or musicians? Or, shall everyone turn victualler, or smith, because there are some that maintain their families plentifully and grow rich in those professions? But, it may be said, there are a thousand ways to wealth, but one only way to heaven. It is well said, indeed, especially by those that plead for compelling men into this or the other way. For if there were several ways that led thither, there would not be so much as a pretence left for compulsion. But now, if I be marching on with my utmost vigour in that way which, according to the sacred geography, leads straight to Jerusalem, why am I beaten and ill-used by others because, perhaps, I wear not buskins; because my hair is not of the right cut; because, perhaps, I have not been dipped in the right fashion; because I eat flesh upon the road, or some other food which agrees with my stomach; because I avoid certain by-ways, which seem unto me to lead into briars or precipices; because, amongst the several paths that are in the same road, I choose that to walk in which seems to be the straightest and cleanest; because I avoid to keep company with some travellers that are less grave and others that are more sour than they ought to be; or, in fine, because I follow a guide that either is, or is not, clothed in white, or crowned with a mitre? Certainly, if we consider right, we shall find that, for the most part, they are such frivolous things as these that (without any prejudice to religion or the salvation of souls, if not accompanied with superstition or hypocrisy) might either be observed or omitted. I say they are such-like things as these which breed implacable enmities amongst Christian brethren, who are all agreed in the substantial and truly fundamental part of religion.

But let us grant unto these zealots, who condemn all things that are not of their mode, that from these circumstances are different ends. What shall we conclude from thence? There is only one of these which is the true way to eternal happiness: but in this great variety of ways that men follow, it is still doubted which is the right one. Now, neither the care of the commonwealth, nor the right enacting of laws, does discover this way that leads to heaven more certainly to the magistrate than every private man's search and study discovers it unto himself. I have a weak body, sunk under a languishing disease, for which (I suppose) there is one only remedy, but that unknown. Does it therefore belong unto the magistrate to prescribe me a remedy, because there is but one, and because it is unknown? Because there is but one way for me to escape death, will it therefore be safe for me to do whatsoever the magistrate ordains? Those things that every man ought sincerely to inquire into himself, and by meditation, study, search, and his own endeavours, attain the knowledge of, cannot be looked upon as the peculiar possession of any sort of men. Princes, indeed, are born superior unto other men in power, but in nature equal. Neither the right nor the art of ruling does necessarily carry along with it the certain knowledge of other things, and least of all of true religion. For if it were so, how could it come to pass that the lords of the earth should differ so vastly as they do in religious matters? But let us grant that it is probable the way to eternal life may be better known by a prince than by his subjects, or at least that in this incertitude of things the safest and most commodious way for private persons is to follow his dictates. You will say: "What then?" If he should bid you follow merchandise for your livelihood, would you decline that course for fear it should not succeed? I answer: I would turn merchant upon the prince's command, because, in case I should have ill-success in trade, he is abundantly able to make up my loss some other way. If it be true, as he pretends, that he desires I should thrive and grow rich, he can set me up again when unsuccessful voyages have broken me. But this is not the case in the things that regard the life to come; if there I take a wrong course, if in that respect I am once undone, it is not in the magistrate's power to repair my loss, to ease my suffering, nor to restore me in any measure, much less entirely, to a good estate. What security can be given for the Kingdom of Heaven?

Perhaps some will say that they do not suppose this infallible judgement, that all men are bound to follow in the affairs of religion, to be in the civil magistrate, but in the Church. What the Church has determined, that the civil magistrate orders to be observed; and he provides by his authority that nobody shall either act or believe in the business of religion otherwise than the Church teaches. So that the judgement of those things is in the Church; the magistrate himself yields obedience thereunto and requires the like obedience from others. I answer: Who sees not how frequently the name of the Church, which was venerable in time of the apostles, has been made use of to throw dust in the people's eyes in the following ages? But, however, in the present case it helps us not. The one only narrow way which leads to heaven is not better known to the magistrate than to private persons, and therefore I cannot safely take him for my guide, who may probably be as ignorant of the way as myself, and who certainly is less concerned for my salvation than I myself am. Amongst so many kings of the Jews, how many of them were there whom any Israelite, thus blindly following, had not fallen into idolatry and thereby into destruction? Yet, nevertheless, you bid me be of good courage and tell me that all is now safe and secure, because the magistrate does not now enjoin the observance of his own decrees in matters of religion, but only the decrees of the Church. Of what Church, I beseech you? of that, certainly, which likes him best. As if he that compels me by laws and penalties to enter into this or the other Church, did not interpose his own judgement in the matter. What difference is there whether he lead me himself, or deliver me over to be led by others? I depend both ways upon his will, and it is he that determines both ways of my eternal state. Would an Israelite that had worshipped Baal upon the command of his king have been in any better condition because somebody had told him that the king ordered nothing in religion upon his own head, nor commanded anything to be done by his subjects in divine worship but what was approved by the counsel of priests, and declared to be of divine right by the doctors of their Church? If the religion of any Church become, therefore, true and saving, because the head of that sect, the prelates and priests, and those of that tribe, do all of them, with all their might, extol and praise it, what religion can ever be accounted erroneous, false, and destructive? I am doubtful concerning the doctrine of the Socinians, I am suspicious of the way of worship practised by the Papists, or Lutherans; will it be ever a jot safer for me to join either unto the one or the other of those Churches, upon the magistrate's command, because he commands nothing in religion but by the authority and counsel of the doctors of that Church?

But, to speak the truth, we must acknowledge that the Church (if a convention of clergymen, making canons, must be called by that name) is for the most part more apt to be influenced by the Court than the Court by the Church. How the Church was under the vicissitude of orthodox and Arian emperors is very well known. Or if those things be too remote, our modern English history affords us fresh examples in the reigns of Henry VIII, Edward VI, Mary, and Elizabeth, how easily and smoothly the clergy changed their decrees, their articles of faith, their form of worship, everything according to the inclination of those kings and queens. Yet were those kings and queens of such different minds in point of religion, and enjoined thereupon such different things, that no man in his wits (I had almost said none but an atheist) will presume to say that any sincere and upright worshipper of God could, with a safe conscience, obey their several decrees. To conclude, it is the same thing whether a king that prescribes laws to another man's religion pretend to do it by his own judgement, or by the ecclesiastical authority and advice of others. The decisions of churchmen, whose differences and disputes are sufficiently known, cannot be any sounder or safer than his; nor can all their suffrages joined together add a new strength to the civil power. Though this also must be taken notice of — that princes seldom have any regard to the suffrages of ecclesiastics that are not favourers of their own faith and way of worship.

But, after all, the principal consideration, and which absolutely determines this controversy, is this: Although the magistrate's opinion in religion be sound, and the way that he appoints be truly Evangelical, yet, if I be not thoroughly persuaded thereof in my own mind, there will be no safety for me in following it. No way whatsoever that I shall walk in against the dictates of my conscience will ever bring me to the mansions of the blessed. I may grow rich by an art that I take not delight in; I may be cured of some disease by remedies that I have not faith in; but I cannot be saved by a religion that I distrust and by a worship that I abhor. It is in vain for an unbeliever to take up the outward show of another man's profession. Faith only and inward sincerity are the things that procure acceptance with God. The most likely and most approved remedy can have no effect upon the patient, if his stomach reject it as soon as taken; and you will in vain cram a medicine down a sick man's throat, which his particular constitution will be sure to turn into poison. In a word, whatsoever may be doubtful in religion, yet this at least is certain, that no religion which I believe not to be true can be either true or profitable unto me. In vain, therefore, do princes compel their subjects to come into their Church communion, under pretence of saving their souls. If they believe, they will come of their own accord, if they believe not, their coming will nothing avail them. How great soever, in fine, may be the pretence of good-will and charity, and concern for the salvation of men's souls, men cannot be forced to be saved whether they will or no. And therefore, when all is done, they must be left to their own consciences.

Having thus at length freed men from all dominion over one another in matters of religion, let us now consider what they are to do. All men know and acknowledge that God ought to be publicly worshipped; why otherwise do they compel one another unto the public assemblies? Men, therefore, constituted in this liberty are to enter into some religious society, that they meet together, not only for mutual edification, but to own to the world that they worship God and offer unto His Divine Majesty such service as they themselves are not ashamed of and such as they think not unworthy of Him, nor unacceptable to Him; and, finally, that by the purity of doctrine, holiness of life, and decent form of worship, they may draw others unto the love of the true religion, and perform such other things in religion as cannot be done by each private man apart.

These religious societies I call Churches; and these, I say, the magistrate ought to tolerate, for the business of these assemblies of the people is nothing but what is lawful for every man in particular to take care of — I mean the salvation of their souls; nor in this case is there any difference between the National Church and other separated congregations.

But as in every Church there are two things especially to be considered — the outward form and rites of worship, and the doctrines and articles of things must be handled each distinctly that so the whole matter of toleration may the more clearly be understood.

Concerning outward worship, I say, in the first place, that the magistrate has no power to enforce by law, either in his own Church, or much less in another, the use of any rites or ceremonies whatsoever in the worship of God. And this, not only because these Churches are free societies, but because whatsoever is practised in the worship of God is only so far justifiable as it is believed by those that practise it to be acceptable unto Him. Whatsoever is not done with that assurance of faith is neither well in itself, nor can it be acceptable to God. To impose such things, therefore, upon any people, contrary to their own judgment, is in effect to command them to offend God, which, considering that the end of all religion is to please Him, and that liberty is essentially necessary to that end, appears to be absurd beyond expression.

But perhaps it may be concluded from hence that I deny unto the magistrate all manner of power about indifferent things, which, if it be not granted, the whole subject-matter of law-making is taken away. No, I readily grant that indifferent things, and perhaps none but such, are subjected to the legislative power. But it does not therefore follow that the magistrate may ordain whatsoever he pleases concerning anything that is indifferent. The public good is the rule and measure of all law-making. If a thing be not useful to the commonwealth, though it be never so indifferent, it may not presently be established by law.

And further, things never so indifferent in their own nature, when they are brought into the Church and worship of God, are removed out of the reach of the magistrate's jurisdiction, because in that use they have no connection at all with civil affairs. The only business of the Church is the salvation of souls, and it no way concerns the commonwealth, or any member of it, that this or the other ceremony be there made use of. Neither the use nor the omission of any ceremonies in those religious assemblies does either advantage or prejudice the life, liberty, or estate of any man. For example, let it be granted that the washing of an infant with water is in itself an indifferent thing, let it be granted also that the magistrate understand such washing to be profitable to the curing or preventing of any disease the children are subject unto, and esteem the matter weighty enough to be taken care of by a law. In that case he may order it to be done. But will any one therefore say that a magistrate has the same right to ordain by law that all children shall be baptised by priests in the sacred font in order to the purification of their souls? The extreme difference of these two cases is visible to every one at first sight. Or let us apply the last case to the child of a Jew, and the thing speaks itself. For what hinders but a Christian magistrate may have subjects that are Jews? Now, if we acknowledge that such an injury may not be done unto a Jew as to compel him, against his own opinion, to practise in his religion a thing that is in its nature indifferent, how can we maintain that anything of this kind may be done to a Christian?

Again, things in their own nature indifferent cannot, by any human authority, be made any part of the worship of God — for this very reason: because they are indifferent. For, since indifferent things are not capable, by any virtue of their own, to propitiate the Deity, no human power or authority can confer on them so much dignity and excellency as to enable them to do it. In the common affairs of life that use of indifferent things which God has not forbidden is free and lawful, and therefore in those things human authority has place. But it is not so in matters of religion. Things indifferent are not otherwise lawful in the worship of God than as they are instituted by God Himself and as He, by some positive command, has ordained them to be made a part of that worship which He will vouchsafe to accept at the hands of poor sinful men. Nor, when an incensed Deity shall ask us, "Who has required these, or such-like things at your hands?" will it be enough to answer Him that the magistrate commanded them. If civil jurisdiction extend thus far, what might not lawfully be introduced into religion? What hodgepodge of ceremonies, what superstitious inventions, built upon the magistrate's authority, might not (against conscience) be imposed upon the worshippers of God? For the greatest part of these ceremonies and superstitions consists in the religious use of such things as are in their own nature indifferent; nor are they sinful upon any other account than because God is not the author of them. The sprinkling of water and the use of bread and wine are both in their own nature and in the ordinary occasions of life altogether indifferent. Will any man, therefore, say that these things could have been introduced into religion and made a part of divine worship if not by divine institution? If any human authority or civil power could have done this, why might it not also enjoin the eating of fish and drinking of ale in the holy banquet as a part of divine worship? Why not the sprinkling of the blood of beasts in churches, and expiations by water or fire, and abundance more of this kind? But these things, how indifferent soever they be in common uses, when they come to be annexed unto divine worship, without divine authority, they are as abominable to God as the sacrifice of a dog. And why is a dog so abominable? What difference is there between a dog and a goat, in respect of the divine nature, equally and infinitely distant from all affinity with matter, unless it be that God required the use of one in His worship and not of the other? We see, therefore, that indifferent things, how much soever they be under the power of the civil magistrate, yet cannot, upon that pretence, be introduced into religion and imposed upon religious assemblies, because, in the worship of God, they wholly cease to be indifferent. He that worships God does it with design to please Him and procure His favour. But that cannot be done by him who, upon the command of another, offers unto God that which he knows will be displeasing to Him, because not commanded by Himself. This is not to please God, or appease his wrath, but willingly and knowingly to provoke Him by a manifest contempt, which is a thing absolutely repugnant to the nature and end of worship.

But it will be here asked: "If nothing belonging to divine worship be left to human discretion, how is it then that Churches themselves have the power of ordering anything about the time and place of worship and the like?" To this I answer that in religious worship we must distinguish between what is part of the worship itself and what is but a circumstance. That is a part of the worship which is believed to be appointed by God and to be well-pleasing to Him, and therefore that is necessary. Circumstances are such things which, though in general they cannot be separated from worship, yet the particular instances or modifications of them are not determined, and therefore they are indifferent. Of this sort are the time and place of worship, habit and posture of him that worships. These are circumstances, and perfectly indifferent, where God has not given any express command about them. For example: amongst the Jews the time and place of their worship and the habits of those that officiated in it were not mere circumstances, but a part of the worship itself, in which, if anything were defective, or different from the institution, they could not hope that it would be accepted by God. But these, to Christians under the liberty of the Gospel, are mere circumstances of worship, which the prudence of every Church may bring into such use as shall be judged most subservient to the end of order, decency, and edification. But, even under the Gospel, those who believe the first or the seventh day to be set apart by God, and consecrated still to His worship, to them that portion of time is not a simple circumstance, but a real part of Divine worship, which can neither be changed nor neglected.

In the next place: As the magistrate has no power to impose by his laws the use of any rites and ceremonies in any Church, so neither has he any power to forbid the use of such rites and ceremonies as are already received, approved, and practised by any Church; because, if he did so, he would destroy the Church itself: the end of whose institution is only to worship God with freedom after its own manner.

You will say, by this rule, if some congregations should have a mind to sacrifice infants, or (as the primitive Christians were falsely accused) lustfully pollute themselves in promiscuous uncleanness, or practise any other such heinous enormities, is the magistrate obliged to tolerate them, because they are committed in a religious assembly? I answer: No. These things are not lawful in the ordinary course of life, nor in any private house; and therefore neither are they so in the worship of God, or in any religious meeting. But, indeed, if any people congregated upon account of religion should be desirous to sacrifice a calf, I deny that that ought to be prohibited by a law. Meliboeus, whose calf it is, may lawfully kill his calf at home, and burn any part of it that he thinks fit. For no injury is thereby done to any one, no prejudice to another man's goods. And for the same reason he may kill his calf also in a religious meeting. Whether the doing so be well-pleasing to God or no, it is their part to consider that do it. The part of the magistrate is only to take care that the commonwealth receive no prejudice, and that there be no injury done to any man, either in life or estate. And thus what may be spent on a feast may be spent on a sacrifice. But if peradventure such were the state of things that the interest of the commonwealth required all slaughter of beasts should be forborne for some while, in order to the increasing of the stock of cattle that had been destroyed by some extraordinary murrain, who sees not that the magistrate, in such a case, may forbid all his subjects to kill any calves for any use whatsoever? Only it is to be observed that, in this case, the law is not made about a religious, but a political matter; nor is the sacrifice, but the slaughter of calves, thereby prohibited.

By this we see what difference there is between the Church and the Commonwealth. Whatsoever is lawful in the Commonwealth cannot be prohibited by the magistrate in the Church. Whatsoever is permitted unto any of his subjects for their ordinary use, neither can nor ought to be forbidden by him to any sect of people for their religious uses. If any man may lawfully take bread or wine, either sitting or kneeling in his own house, the law ought not to abridge him of the same liberty in his religious worship; though in the Church the use of bread and wine be very different and be there applied to the mysteries of faith and rites of Divine worship. But those things that are prejudicial to the commonweal of a people in their ordinary use and are, therefore, forbidden by laws, those things ought not to be permitted to Churches in their sacred rites. Only the magistrate ought always to be very careful that he do not misuse his authority to the oppression of any Church, under pretence of public good.

It may be said: "What if a Church be idolatrous, is that also to be tolerated by the magistrate?" I answer: What power can be given to the magistrate for the suppression of an idolatrous Church, which may not in time and place be made use of to the ruin of an orthodox one? For it must be remembered that the civil power is the same everywhere, and the religion of every prince is orthodox to himself. If, therefore, such a power be granted unto the civil magistrate in spirituals as that at Geneva, for example, he may extirpate, by violence and blood, the religion which is there reputed idolatrous, by the same rule another magistrate, in some neighbouring country, may oppress the reformed religion and, in India, the Christian. The civil power can either change everything in religion, according to the prince's pleasure, or it can change nothing. If it be once permitted to introduce anything into religion by the means of laws and penalties, there can be no bounds put to it; but it will in the same manner be lawful to alter everything, according to that rule of truth which the magistrate has framed unto himself. No man whatsoever ought, therefore, to be deprived of his terrestrial enjoyments upon account of his religion. Not even Americans, subjected unto a Christian prince, are to be punished either in body or goods for not embracing our faith and worship. If they are persuaded that they please God in observing the rites of their own country and that they shall obtain happiness by that means, they are to be left unto God and themselves. Let us trace this matter to the bottom. Thus it is: An inconsiderable and weak number of Christians, destitute of everything, arrive in a Pagan country; these foreigners beseech the inhabitants, by the bowels of humanity, that they would succour them with the necessaries of life; those necessaries are given them, habitations are granted, and they all join together, and grow up into one body of people. The Christian religion by this means takes root in that country and spreads itself, but does not suddenly grow the strongest. While things are in this condition peace, friendship, faith, and equal justice are preserved amongst them. At length the magistrate becomes a Christian, and by that means their party becomes the most powerful. Then immediately all compacts are to be broken, all civil rights to be violated, that idolatry may be extirpated; and unless these innocent Pagans, strict observers of the rules of equity and the law of Nature and no ways offending against the laws of the society, I say, unless they will forsake their ancient religion and embrace a new and strange one, they are to be turned out of the lands and possessions of their forefathers and perhaps deprived of life itself. Then, at last, it appears what zeal for the Church, joined with the desire of dominion, is capable to produce, and how easily the pretence of religion, and of the care of souls, serves for a cloak to covetousness, rapine, and ambition.

Now whosoever maintains that idolatry is to be rooted out of any place by laws, punishments, fire, and sword, may apply this story to himself. For the reason of the thing is equal, both in America and Europe. And neither Pagans there, nor any dissenting Christians here, can, with any right, be deprived of their worldly goods by the predominating faction of a court-church; nor are any civil rights to be either changed or violated upon account of religion in one place more than another.

But idolatry, say some, is a sin and therefore not to be tolerated. If they said it were therefore to be avoided, the inference were good. But it does not follow that because it is a sin it ought therefore to be punished by the magistrate. For it does not belong unto the magistrate to make use of his sword in punishing everything, indifferently, that he takes to be a sin against God. Covetousness, uncharitableness, idleness, and many other things are sins by the consent of men, which yet no man ever said were to be punished by the magistrate. The reason is because they are not prejudicial to other men's rights, nor do they break the public peace of societies. Nay, even the sins of lying and perjury are nowhere punishable by laws; unless, in certain cases, in which the real turpitude of the thing and the offence against God are not considered, but only the injury done unto men's neighbours and to the commonwealth. And what if in another country, to a Mahometan or a Pagan prince, the Christian religion seem false and offensive to God; may not the Christians for the same reason, and after the same manner, be extirpated there?

But it may be urged farther that, by the law of Moses, idolaters were to be rooted out. True, indeed, by the law of Moses; but that is not obligatory to us Christians. Nobody pretends that everything generally enjoined by the law of Moses ought to be practised by Christians; but there is nothing more frivolous than that common distinction of moral, judicial, and ceremonial law, which men ordinarily make use of. For no positive law whatsoever can oblige any people but those to whom it is given. "Hear, O Israel," sufficiently restrains the obligations of the law of Moses only to that people. And this consideration alone is answer enough unto those that urge the authority of the law of Moses for the inflicting of capital punishment upon idolaters. But, however, I will examine this argument a little more particularly.

The case of idolaters, in respect of the Jewish commonwealth, falls under a double consideration. The first is of those who, being initiated in the Mosaical rites, and made citizens of that commonwealth, did afterwards apostatise from the worship of the God of Israel. These were proceeded against as traitors and rebels, guilty of no less than high treason. For the commonwealth of the Jews, different in that from all others, was an absolute theocracy; nor was there, or could there be, any difference between that commonwealth and the Church. The laws established there concerning the worship of One Invisible Deity were the civil laws of that people and a part of their political government, in which God Himself was the legislator.

Now, if any one can shew me where there is a commonwealth at this time, constituted upon that foundation, I will acknowledge that the ecclesiastical laws do there unavoidably become a part of the civil, and that the subjects of that government both may and ought to be kept in strict conformity with that Church by the civil power. But there is absolutely no such thing under the Gospel as a Christian commonwealth. There are, indeed, many cities and kingdoms that have embraced the faith of Christ, but they have retained their ancient form of government, with which the law of Christ hath not at all meddled. He, indeed, hath taught men how, by faith and good works, they may obtain eternal life; but He instituted no commonwealth. He prescribed unto His followers no new and peculiar form of government, nor put He the sword into any magistrate's hand, with commission to make use of it in forcing men to forsake their former religion and receive His.

Secondly, foreigners and such as were strangers to the commonwealth of Israel were not compelled by force to observe the rites of the Mosaical law; but, on the contrary, in the very same place where it is ordered that an Israelite that was an idolater should be put to death,[7] there it is provided that strangers should not be vexed nor oppressed. I confess that the seven nations that possessed the land which was promised to the Israelites were utterly to be cut off; but this was not singly because they were idolaters. For if that had been the reason, why were the Moabites and other nations to be spared? No: the reason is this. God being in a peculiar manner the King of the Jews, He could not suffer the adoration of any other deity (which was properly an act of high treason against Himself) in the land of Canaan, which was His kingdom. For such a manifest revolt could no ways consist with His dominion, which was perfectly political in that country. All idolatry was, therefore, to be rooted out of the bounds of His kingdom because it was an acknowledgment of another god, that is say, another king, against the laws of Empire. The inhabitants were also to be driven out, that the entire possession of the land might be given to the Israelites. And for the like reason the Emims and the Horims were driven out of their countries by the children of Esau and Lot; and their lands, upon the same grounds, given by God to the invaders.[8] But, though all idolatry was thus rooted out of the land of Canaan, yet every idolater was not brought to execution. The whole family of Rahab, the whole nation of the Gibeonites, articled with Joshua, and were allowed by treaty; and there were many captives amongst the Jews who were idolaters. David and Solomon subdued many countries without the confines of the Land of Promise and carried their conquests as far as Euphrates. Amongst so many captives taken, so many nations reduced under their obedience, we find not one man forced into the Jewish religion and the worship of the true God and punished for idolatry, though all of them were certainly guilty of it. If any one, indeed, becoming a proselyte, desired to be made a denizen of their commonwealth, he was obliged to submit to their laws; that is, to embrace their religion. But this he did willingly, on his own accord, not by constraint. He did not unwillingly submit, to show his obedience, but he sought and solicited for it as a privilege. And, as soon as he was admitted, he became subject to the laws of the commonwealth, by which all idolatry was forbidden within the borders of the land of Canaan. But that law (as I have said) did not reach to any of those regions, however subjected unto the Jews, that were situated without those bounds.

Thus far concerning outward worship. Let us now consider articles of faith.

The articles of religion are some of them practical and some speculative. Now, though both sorts consist in the knowledge of truth, yet these terminate simply in the understanding, those influence the will and manners. Speculative opinions, therefore, and articles of faith (as they are called) which are required only to be believed, cannot be imposed on any Church by the law of the land. For it is absurd that things should be enjoined by laws which are not in men's power to perform. And to believe this or that to be true does not depend upon our will. But of this enough has been said already. "But." will some say; "let men at least profess that they believe." A sweet religion, indeed, that obliges men to dissemble and tell lies, both to God and man, for the salvation of their souls! If the magistrate thinks to save men thus, he seems to understand little of the way of salvation. And if he does it not in order to save them, why is he so solicitous about the articles of faith as to enact them by a law?

Further, the magistrate ought not to forbid the preaching or professing of any speculative opinions in any Church because they have no manner of relation to the civil rights of the subjects. If a Roman Catholic believe that to be really the body of Christ which another man calls bread, he does no injury thereby to his neighbour. If a Jew do not believe the New Testament to be the Word of God, he does not thereby alter anything in men's civil rights. If a heathen doubt of both Testaments, he is not therefore to be punished as a pernicious citizen. The power of the magistrate and the estates of the people may be equally secure whether any man believe these things or no. I readily grant that these opinions are false and absurd. But the business of laws is not to provide for the truth of opinions, but for the safety and security of the commonwealth and of every particular man's goods and person. And so it ought to be. For the truth certainly would do well enough if she were once left to shift for herself. She seldom has received and, I fear, never will receive much assistance from the power of great men, to whom she is but rarely known and more rarely welcome. She is not taught by laws, nor has she any need of force to procure her entrance into the minds of men. Errors, indeed, prevail by the assistance of foreign and borrowed succours. But if Truth makes not her way into the understanding by her own light, she will be but the weaker for any borrowed force violence can add to her. Thus much for speculative opinions. Let us now proceed to practical ones.

A good life, in which consist not the least part of religion and true piety, concerns also the civil government; and in it lies the safety both of men's souls and of the commonwealth. Moral actions belong, therefore, to the jurisdiction both of the outward and inward court; both of the civil and domestic governor; I mean both of the magistrate and conscience. Here, therefore, is great danger, lest one of these jurisdictions intrench upon the other, and discord arise between the keeper of the public peace and the overseers of souls. But if what has been already said concerning the limits of both these governments be rightly considered, it will easily remove all difficulty in this matter.

Every man has an immortal soul, capable of eternal happiness or misery; whose happiness depending upon his believing and doing those things in this life which are necessary to the obtaining of God's favour, and are prescribed by God to that end. It follows from thence, first, that the observance of these things is the highest obligation that lies upon mankind and that our utmost care, application, and diligence ought to be exercised in the search and performance of them; because there is nothing in this world that is of any consideration in comparison with eternity. Secondly, that seeing one man does not violate the right of another by his erroneous opinions and undue manner of worship, nor is his perdition any prejudice to another man's affairs, therefore, the care of each man's salvation belongs only to himself. But I would not have this understood as if I meant hereby to condemn all charitable admonitions and affectionate endeavours to reduce men from errors, which are indeed the greatest duty of a Christian. Any one may employ as many exhortations and arguments as he pleases, towards the promoting of another man's salvation. But all force and compulsion are to be forborne. Nothing is to be done imperiously. Nobody is obliged in that matter to yield obedience unto the admonitions or injunctions of another, further than he himself is persuaded. Every man in that has the supreme and absolute authority of judging for himself. And the reason is because nobody else is concerned in it, nor can receive any prejudice from his conduct therein.

But besides their souls, which are immortal, men have also their temporal lives here upon earth; the state whereof being frail and fleeting, and the duration uncertain, they have need of several outward conveniences to the support thereof, which are to be procured or preserved by pains and industry. For those things that are necessary to the comfortable support of our lives are not the spontaneous products of nature, nor do offer themselves fit and prepared for our use. This part, therefore, draws on another care and necessarily gives another employment. But the pravity of mankind being such that they had rather injuriously prey upon the fruits of other men's labours than take pains to provide for themselves, the necessity of preserving men in the possession of what honest industry has already acquired and also of preserving their liberty and strength, whereby they may acquire what they farther want, obliges men to enter into society with one another, that by mutual assistance and joint force they may secure unto each other their properties, in the things that contribute to the comfort and happiness of this life, leaving in the meanwhile to every man the care of his own eternal happiness, the attainment whereof can neither be facilitated by another man's industry, nor can the loss of it turn to another man's prejudice, nor the hope of it be forced from him by any external violence. But, forasmuch as men thus entering into societies, grounded upon their mutual compacts of assistance for the defence of their temporal goods, may, nevertheless, be deprived of them, either by the rapine and fraud of their fellow citizens, or by the hostile violence of foreigners, the remedy of this evil consists in arms, riches, and multitude of citizens; the remedy of the other in laws; and the care of all things relating both to one and the other is committed by the society to the civil magistrate. This is the original, this is the use, and these are the bounds of the legislative (which is the supreme) power in every commonwealth. I mean that provision may be made for the security of each man's private possessions; for the peace, riches, and public commodities of the whole people; and, as much as possible, for the increase of their inward strength against foreign invasions.

These things being thus explained, it is easy to understand to what end the legislative power ought to be directed and by what measures regulated; and that is the temporal good and outward prosperity of the society; which is the sole reason of men's entering into society, and the only thing they seek and aim at in it. And it is also evident what liberty remains to men in reference to their eternal salvation, and that is that every one should do what he in his conscience is persuaded to be acceptable to the Almighty, on whose good pleasure and acceptance depends their eternal happiness. For obedience is due, in the first place, to God and, afterwards to the laws.

But some may ask: "What if the magistrate should enjoin anything by his authority that appears unlawful to the conscience of a private person?" I answer that, if government be faithfully administered and the counsels of the magistrates be indeed directed to the public good, this will seldom happen. But if, perhaps, it do so fall out, I say, that such a private person is to abstain from the action that he judges unlawful, and he is to undergo the punishment which it is not unlawful for him to bear. For the private judgement of any person concerning a law enacted in political matters, for the public good, does not take away the obligation of that law, nor deserve a dispensation. But if the law, indeed, be concerning things that lie not within the verge of the magistrate's authority (as, for example, that the people, or any party amongst them, should be compelled to embrace a strange religion, and join in the worship and ceremonies of another Church), men are not in these cases obliged by that law, against their consciences. For the political society is instituted for no other end, but only to secure every man's possession of the things of this life. The care of each man's soul and of the things of heaven, which neither does belong to the commonwealth nor can be subjected to it, is left entirely to every man's self. Thus the safeguard of men's lives and of the things that belong unto this life is the business of the commonwealth; and the preserving of those things unto their owners is the duty of the magistrate. And therefore the magistrate cannot take away these worldly things from this man or party and give them to that; nor change propriety amongst fellow subjects (no not even by a law), for a cause that has no relation to the end of civil government, I mean for their religion, which whether it be true or false does no prejudice to the worldly concerns of their fellow subjects, which are the things that only belong unto the care of the commonwealth.

But what if the magistrate believe such a law as this to be for the public good? I answer: As the private judgement of any particular person, if erroneous, does not exempt him from the obligation of law, so the private judgement (as I may call it) of the magistrate does not give him any new right of imposing laws upon his subjects, which neither was in the constitution of the government granted him, nor ever was in the power of the people to grant, much less if he make it his business to enrich and advance his followers and fellow-sectaries with the spoils of others. But what if the magistrate believe that he has a right to make such laws and that they are for the public good, and his subjects believe the contrary? Who shall be judge between them? I answer: God alone. For there is no judge upon earth between the supreme magistrate and the people. God, I say, is the only judge in this case, who will retribute unto every one at the last day according to his deserts; that is, according to his sincerity and uprightness in endeavouring to promote piety, and the public weal, and peace of mankind. But What shall be done in the meanwhile? I answer: The principal and chief care of every one ought to be of his own soul first, and, in the next place, of the public peace; though yet there are very few will think it is peace there, where they see all laid waste.

There are two sorts of contests amongst men, the one managed by law, the other by force; and these are of that nature that where the one ends, the other always begins. But it is not my business to inquire into the power of the magistrate in the different constitutions of nations. I only know what usually happens where controversies arise without a judge to determine them. You will say, then, the magistrate being the stronger will have his will and carry his point. Without doubt; but the question is not here concerning the doubtfulness of the event, but the rule of right.

But to come to particulars. I say, first, no opinions contrary to human society, or to those moral rules which are necessary to the preservation of civil society, are to be tolerated by the magistrate. But of these, indeed, examples in any Church are rare. For no sect can easily arrive to such a degree of madness as that it should think fit to teach, for doctrines of religion, such things as manifestly undermine the foundations of society and are, therefore, condemned by the judgement of all mankind; because their own interest, peace, reputation, everything would be thereby endangered.

Another more secret evil, but more dangerous to the commonwealth, is when men arrogate to themselves, and to those of their own sect, some peculiar prerogative covered over with a specious show of deceitful words, but in effect opposite to the civil right of the community. For example: we cannot find any sect that teaches, expressly and openly, that men are not obliged to keep their promise; that princes may be dethroned by those that differ from them in religion; or that the dominion of all things belongs only to themselves. For these things, proposed thus nakedly and plainly, would soon draw on them the eye and hand of the magistrate and awaken all the care of the commonwealth to a watchfulness against the spreading of so dangerous an evil. But, nevertheless, we find those that say the same things in other words. What else do they mean who teach that faith is not to be kept with heretics? Their meaning, forsooth, is that the privilege of breaking faith belongs unto themselves; for they declare all that are not of their communion to be heretics, or at least may declare them so whensoever they think fit. What can be the meaning of their asserting that kings excommunicated forfeit their crowns and kingdoms? It is evident that they thereby arrogate unto themselves the power of deposing kings, because they challenge the power of excommunication, as the peculiar right of their hierarchy. That dominion is founded in grace is also an assertion by which those that maintain it do plainly lay claim to the possession of all things. For they are not so wanting to themselves as not to believe, or at least as not to profess themselves to be the truly pious and faithful. These, therefore, and the like, who attribute unto the faithful, religious, and orthodox, that is, in plain terms, unto themselves, any peculiar privilege or power above other mortals, in civil concernments; or who upon pretence of religion do challenge any manner of authority over such as are not associated with them in their ecclesiastical communion, I say these have no right to be tolerated by the magistrate; as neither those that will not own and teach the duty of tolerating all men in matters of mere religion. For what do all these and the like doctrines signify, but that they may and are ready upon any occasion to seize the Government and possess themselves of the estates and fortunes of their fellow subjects; and that they only ask leave to be tolerated by the magistrate so long until they find themselves strong enough to effect it?

Again: That Church can have no right to be tolerated by the magistrate which is constituted upon such a bottom that all those who enter into it do thereby ipso facto deliver themselves up to the protection and service of another prince. For by this means the magistrate would give way to the settling of a foreign jurisdiction in his own country and suffer his own people to be listed, as it were, for soldiers against his own Government. Nor does the frivolous and fallacious distinction between the Court and the Church afford any remedy to this inconvenience; especially when both the one and the other are equally subject to the absolute authority of the same person, who has not only power to persuade the members of his Church to whatsoever he lists, either as purely religious, or in order thereunto, but can also enjoin it them on pain of eternal fire. It is ridiculous for any one to profess himself to be a Mahometan only in his religion, but in everything else a faithful subject to a Christian magistrate, whilst at the same time he acknowledges himself bound to yield blind obedience to the Mufti of Constantinople, who himself is entirely obedient to the Ottoman Emperor and frames the feigned oracles of that religion according to his pleasure. But this Mahometan living amongst Christians would yet more apparently renounce their government if he acknowledged the same person to be head of his Church who is the supreme magistrate in the state.

Lastly, those are not at all to be tolerated who deny the being of a God. Promises, covenants, and oaths, which are the bonds of human society, can have no hold upon an atheist. The taking away of God, though but even in thought, dissolves all; besides also, those that by their atheism undermine and destroy all religion, can have no pretence of religion whereupon to challenge the privilege of a toleration. As for other practical opinions, though not absolutely free from all error, if they do not tend to establish domination over others, or civil impunity to the Church in which they are taught, there can be no reason why they should not be tolerated.

It remains that I say something concerning those assemblies which, being vulgarly called and perhaps having sometimes been conventicles and nurseries of factions and seditions, are thought to afford against this doctrine of toleration. But this has not happened by anything peculiar unto the genius of such assemblies, but by the unhappy circumstances of an oppressed or ill-settled liberty. These accusations would soon cease if the law of toleration were once so settled that all Churches were obliged to lay down toleration as the foundation of their own liberty, and teach that liberty of conscience is every man's natural right, equally belonging to dissenters as to themselves; and that nobody ought to be compelled in matters of religion either by law or force. The establishment of this one thing would take away all ground of complaints and tumults upon account of conscience; and these causes of discontents and animosities being once removed, there would remain nothing in these assemblies that were not more peaceable and less apt to produce disturbance of state than in any other meetings whatsoever. But let us examine particularly the heads of these accusations.

You will say that assemblies and meetings endanger the public peace and threaten the commonwealth. I answer: If this be so, why are there daily such numerous meetings in markets and Courts of Judicature? Why are crowds upon the Exchange and a concourse of people in cities suffered? You will reply: "Those are civil assemblies, but these we object against are ecclesiastical." I answer: It is a likely thing, indeed, that such assemblies as are altogether remote from civil affairs should be most apt to embroil them. Oh, but civil assemblies are composed of men that differ from one another in matters of religion, but these ecclesiastical meetings are of persons that are all of one opinion. As if an agreement in matters of religion were in effect a conspiracy against the commonwealth; or as if men would not be so much the more warmly unanimous in religion the less liberty they had of assembling. But it will be urged still that civil assemblies are open and free for any one to enter into, whereas religious conventicles are more private and thereby give opportunity to clandestine machinations. I answer that this is not strictly true, for many civil assemblies are not open to everyone. And if some religious meetings be private, who are they (I beseech you) that are to be blamed for it, those that desire, or those that forbid their being public! Again, you will say that religious communion does exceedingly unite men's minds and affections to one another and is therefore the more dangerous. But if this be so, why is not the magistrate afraid of his own Church; and why does he not forbid their assemblies as things dangerous to his Government? You will say because he himself is a part and even the head of them. As if he were not also a part of the commonwealth, and the head of the whole people!

Let us therefore deal plainly. The magistrate is afraid of other Churches, but not of his own, because he is kind and favourable to the one, but severe and cruel to the other. These he treats like children, and indulges them even to wantonness. Those he uses as slaves and, how blamelessly soever they demean themselves, recompenses them no otherwise than by galleys, prisons, confiscations, and death. These he cherishes and defends; those he continually scourges and oppresses. Let him turn the tables. Or let those dissenters enjoy but the same privileges in civils as his other subjects, and he will quickly find that these religious meetings will be no longer dangerous. For if men enter into seditious conspiracies, it is not religion inspires them to it in their meetings, but their sufferings and oppressions that make them willing to ease themselves. Just and moderate governments are everywhere quiet, everywhere safe; but oppression raises ferments and makes men struggle to cast off an uneasy and tyrannical yoke. I know that seditions are very frequently raised upon pretence of religion, but it is as true that for religion subjects are frequently ill treated and live miserably. Believe me, the stirs that are made proceed not from any peculiar temper of this or that Church or religious society, but from the common disposition of all mankind, who when they groan under any heavy burthen endeavour naturally to shake off the yoke that galls their necks. Suppose this business of religion were let alone, and that there were some other distinction made between men and men upon account of their different complexions, shapes, and features, so that those who have black hair (for example) or grey eyes should not enjoy the same privileges as other citizens; that they should not be permitted either to buy or sell, or live by their callings; that parents should not have the government and education of their own children; that all should either be excluded from the benefit of the laws, or meet with partial judges; can it be doubted but these persons, thus distinguished from others by the colour of their hair and eyes, and united together by one common persecution, would be as dangerous to the magistrate as any others that had associated themselves merely upon the account of religion? Some enter into company for trade and profit, others for want of business have their clubs for claret. Neighbourhood joins some and religion others. But there is only one thing which gathers people into seditious commotions, and that is oppression.

You will say "What, will you have people to meet at divine service against the magistrate's will?" I answer: Why, I pray, against his will? Is it not both lawful and necessary that they should meet? Against his will, do you say? That is what I complain of; that is the very root of all the mischief. Why are assemblies less sufferable in a church than in a theatre or market? Those that meet there are not either more vicious or more turbulent than those that meet elsewhere. The business in that is that they are ill used, and therefore they are not to be suffered. Take away the partiality that is used towards them in matters of common right; change the laws, take away the penalties unto which they are subjected, and all things will immediately become safe and peaceable; nay, those that are averse to the religion of the magistrate will think themselves so much the more bound to maintain the peace of the commonwealth as their condition is better in that place than elsewhere; and all the several separate congregations, like so many guardians of the public peace, will watch one another, that nothing may be innovated or changed in the form of the government, because they can hope for nothing better than what they already enjoy — that is, an equal condition with their fellow-subjects under a just and moderate government. Now if that Church which agrees in religion with the prince be esteemed the chief support of any civil government, and that for no other reason (as has already been shown) than because the prince is kind and the laws are favourable to it, how much greater will be the security of government where all good subjects, of whatsoever Church they be, without any distinction upon account of religion, enjoying the same favour of the prince and the same benefit of the laws, shall become the common support and guard of it, and where none will have any occasion to fear the severity of the laws but those that do injuries to their neighbours and offend against the civil peace?

That we may draw towards a conclusion. The sum of all we drive at is that every man may enjoy the same rights that are granted to others. Is it permitted to worship God in the Roman manner? Let it be permitted to do it in the Geneva form also. Is it permitted to speak Latin in the market-place? Let those that have a mind to it be permitted to do it also in the Church. Is it lawful for any man in his own house to kneel, stand, sit, or use any other posture; and to clothe himself in white or black, in short or in long garments? Let it not be made unlawful to eat bread, drink wine, or wash with water in the church. In a word, whatsoever things are left free by law in the common occasions of life, let them remain free unto every Church in divine worship. Let no man's life, or body, or house, or estate, suffer any manner of prejudice upon these accounts. Can you allow of the Presbyterian discipline? Why should not the Episcopal also have what they like? Ecclesiastical authority, whether it be administered by the hands of a single person or many, is everywhere the same; and neither has any jurisdiction in things civil, nor any manner of power of compulsion, nor anything at all to do with riches and revenues.

Ecclesiastical assemblies and sermons are justified by daily experience and public allowance. These are allowed to people of some one persuasion; why not to all? If anything pass in a religious meeting seditiously and contrary to the public peace, it is to be punished in the same manner and no otherwise than as if it had happened in a fair or market. These meetings ought not to be sanctuaries for factious and flagitious fellows. Nor ought it to be less lawful for men to meet in churches than in halls; nor are one part of the subjects to be esteemed more blamable for their meeting together than others. Every one is to be accountable for his own actions, and no man is to be laid under a suspicion or odium for the fault of another. Those that are seditious, murderers, thieves, robbers, adulterers, slanderers, etc., of whatsoever Church, whether national or not, ought to be punished and suppressed. But those whose doctrine is peaceable and whose manners are pure and blameless ought to be upon equal terms with their fellow-subjects. Thus if solemn assemblies, observations of festivals, public worship be permitted to any one sort of professors, all these things ought to be permitted to the Presbyterians, Independents, Anabaptists, Arminians, Quakers, and others, with the same liberty. Nay, if we may openly speak the truth, and as becomes one man to another, neither Pagan nor Mahometan, nor Jew, ought to be excluded from the civil rights of the commonwealth because of his religion. The Gospel commands no such thing. The Church which "judgeth not those that are without"[9] wants it not. And the commonwealth, which embraces indifferently all men that are honest, peaceable, and industrious, requires it not. Shall we suffer a Pagan to deal and trade with us, and shall we not suffer him to pray unto and worship God? If we allow the Jews to have private houses and dwellings amongst us, why should we not allow them to have synagogues? Is their doctrine more false, their worship more abominable, or is the civil peace more endangered by their meeting in public than in their private houses? But if these things may be granted to Jews and Pagans, surely the condition of any Christians ought not to be worse than theirs in a Christian commonwealth.

You will say, perhaps: "Yes, it ought to be; because they are more inclinable to factions, tumults, and civil wars." I answer: Is this the fault of the Christian religion? If it be so, truly the Christian religion is the worst of all religions and ought neither to be embraced by any particular person, nor tolerated by any commonwealth. For if this be the genius, this the nature of the Christian religion, to be turbulent and destructive to the civil peace, that Church itself which the magistrate indulges will not always be innocent. But far be it from us to say any such thing of that religion which carries the greatest opposition to covetousness, ambition, discord, contention, and all manner of inordinate desires, and is the most modest and peaceable religion that ever was. We must, therefore, seek another cause of those evils that are charged upon religion. And, if we consider right, we shall find it to consist wholly in the subject that I am treating of. It is not the diversity of opinions (which cannot be avoided), but the refusal of toleration to those that are of different opinions (which might have been granted), that has produced all the bustles and wars that have been in the Christian world upon account of religion. The heads and leaders of the Church, moved by avarice and insatiable desire of dominion, making use of the immoderate ambition of magistrates and the credulous superstition of the giddy multitude, have incensed and animated them against those that dissent from themselves, by preaching unto them, contrary to the laws of the Gospel and to the precepts of charity, that schismatics and heretics are to be outed of their possessions and destroyed. And thus have they mixed together and confounded two things that are in themselves most different, the Church and the commonwealth. Now as it is very difficult for men patiently to suffer themselves to be stripped of the goods which they have got by their honest industry, and, contrary to all the laws of equity, both human and divine, to be delivered up for a prey to other men's violence and rapine; especially when they are otherwise altogether blameless; and that the occasion for which they are thus treated does not at all belong to the jurisdiction of the magistrate, but entirely to the conscience of every particular man for the conduct of which he is accountable to God only; what else can be expected but that these men, growing weary of the evils under which they labour, should in the end think it lawful for them to resist force with force, and to defend their natural rights (which are not forfeitable upon account of religion) with arms as well as they can? That this has been hitherto the ordinary course of things is abundantly evident in history, and that it will continue to be so hereafter is but too apparent in reason. It cannot indeed, be otherwise so long as the principle of persecution for religion shall prevail, as it has done hitherto, with magistrate and people, and so long as those that ought to be the preachers of peace and concord shall continue with all their art and strength to excite men to arms and sound the trumpet of war. But that magistrates should thus suffer these incendiaries and disturbers of the public peace might justly be wondered at if it did not appear that they have been invited by them unto a participation of the spoil, and have therefore thought fit to make use of their covetousness and pride as means whereby to increase their own power. For who does not see that these good men are, indeed, more ministers of the government than ministers of the Gospel and that, by flattering the ambition and favouring the dominion of princes and men in authority, they endeavour with all their might to promote that tyranny in the commonwealth which otherwise they should not be able to establish in the Church? This is the unhappy agreement that we see between the Church and State. Whereas if each of them would contain itself within its own bounds — the one attending to the worldly welfare of the commonwealth, the other to the salvation of souls — it is impossible that any discord should ever have happened between them. Sed pudet hoec opprobria. etc. God Almighty grant, I beseech Him, that the gospel of peace may at length be preached, and that civil magistrates, growing more careful to conform their own consciences to the law of God and less solicitous about the binding of other men's consciences by human laws, may, like fathers of their country, direct all their counsels and endeavours to promote universally the civil welfare of all their children, except only of such as are arrogant, ungovernable, and injurious to their brethren; and that all ecclesiastical men, who boast themselves to be the successors of the Apostles, walking peaceably and modestly in the Apostles' steps, without intermeddling with State Affairs, may apply themselves wholly to promote the salvation of souls.

FAREWELL.

PERHAPS it may not be amiss to add a few things concerning heresy and schism. A Turk is not, nor can be, either heretic or schismatic to a Christian; and if any man fall off from the Christian faith to Mahometism, he does not thereby become a heretic or schismatic, but an apostate and an infidel. This nobody doubts of; and by this it appears that men of different religions cannot be heretics or schismatics to one another.

We are to inquire, therefore, what men are of the same religion. Concerning which it is manifest that those who have one and the same rule of faith and worship are of the same religion; and those who have not the same rule of faith and worship are of different religions. For since all things that belong unto that religion are contained in that rule, it follows necessarily that those who agree in one rule are of one and the same religion, and vice versa. Thus Turks and Christians are of different religions, because these take the Holy Scriptures to be the rule of their religion, and those the Alcoran. And for the same reason there may be different religions also even amongst Christians. The Papists and Lutherans, though both of them profess faith in Christ and are therefore called Christians, yet are not both of the same religion, because these acknowledge nothing but the Holy Scriptures to be the rule and foundation of their religion, those take in also traditions and the decrees of Popes and of these together make the rule of their religion; and thus the Christians of St. John (as they are called) and the Christians of Geneva are of different religions, because these also take only the Scriptures, and those I know not what traditions, for the rule of their religion.

This being settled, it follows, first, that heresy is a separation made in ecclesiastical communion between men of the same religion for some opinions no way contained in the rule itself; and, secondly, that amongst those who acknowledge nothing but the Holy Scriptures to be their rule of faith, heresy is a separation made in their Christian communion for opinions not contained in the express words of Scripture. Now this separation may be made in a twofold manner:

1. When the greater part, or by the magistrate's patronage the stronger part, of the Church separates itself from others by excluding them out of her communion because they will not profess their belief of certain opinions which are not the express words of the Scripture. For it is not the paucity of those that are separated, nor the authority of the magistrate, that can make any man guilty of heresy, but he only is a heretic who divides the Church into parts, introduces names and marks of distinction, and voluntarily makes a separation because of such opinions.

2. When any one separates himself from the communion of a Church because that Church does not publicly profess some certain opinions which the Holy Scriptures do not expressly teach.

Both these are heretics because they err in fundamentals, and they err obstinately against knowledge; for when they have determined the Holy Scriptures to be the only foundation of faith, they nevertheless lay down certain propositions as fundamental which are not in the Scripture, and because others will not acknowledge these additional opinions of theirs, nor build upon them as if they were necessary and fundamental, they therefore make a separation in the Church, either by withdrawing themselves from others, or expelling the others from them. Nor does it signify anything for them to say that their confessions and symbols are agreeable to Scripture and to the analogy of faith; for if they be conceived in the express words of Scripture, there can be no question about them, because those things are acknowledged by all Christians to be of divine inspiration and therefore fundamental. But if they say that the articles which they require to be professed are consequences deduced from the Scripture, it is undoubtedly well done of them who believe and profess such things as seem unto them so agreeable to the rule of faith. But it would be very ill done to obtrude those things upon others unto whom they do not seem to be the indubitable doctrines of the Scripture; and to make a separation for such things as these, which neither are nor can be fundamental, is to become heretics; for I do not think there is any man arrived to that degree of madness as that he dare give out his consequences and interpretations of Scripture as divine inspirations and compare the articles of faith that he has framed according to his own fancy with the authority of Scripture. I know there are some propositions so evidently agreeable to Scripture that nobody can deny them to be drawn from thence, but about those, therefore, there can be no difference. This only I say — that however clearly we may think this or the other doctrine to be deduced from Scripture, we ought not therefore to impose it upon others as a necessary article of faith because we believe it to be agreeable to the rule of faith, unless we would be content also that other doctrines should be imposed upon us in the same manner, and that we should be compelled to receive and profess all the different and contradictory opinions of Lutherans, Calvinists, Remonstrants, Anabaptists, and other sects which the contrivers of symbols, systems, and confessions are accustomed to deliver to their followers as genuine and necessary deductions from the Holy Scripture. I cannot but wonder at the extravagant arrogance of those men who think that they themselves can explain things necessary to salvation more clearly than the Holy Ghost, the eternal and infinite wisdom of God.

Thus much concerning heresy, which word in common use is applied only to the doctrinal part of religion. Let us now consider schism, which is a crime near akin to it; for both these words seem unto me to signify an ill-grounded separation in ecclesiastical communion made about things not necessary. But since use, which is the supreme law in matter of language, has determined that heresy relates to errors in faith, and schism to those in worship or discipline, we must consider them under that distinction.

Schism, then, for the same reasons that have already been alleged, is nothing else but a separation made in the communion of the Church upon account of something in divine worship or ecclesiastical discipline that is not any necessary part of it. Now, nothing in worship or discipline can be necessary to Christian communion but what Christ our legislator, or the Apostles by inspiration of the Holy Spirit, have commanded in express words.

In a word, he that denies not anything that the Holy Scriptures teach in express words, nor makes a separation upon occasion of anything that is not manifestly contained in the sacred text — however he may be nicknamed by any sect of Christians and declared by some or all of them to be utterly void of true Christianity — yet in deed and in truth this man cannot be either a heretic or schismatic.

These things might have been explained more largely and more advantageously, but it is enough to have hinted at them thus briefly to a person of your parts.

Notes:

1. Luke 22. 25.

2. II Tim. 2. 19.

3. Luke 22. 32.

4. Rom. I.

5. Gal. 5.

6. Matt. 18. 20.

7. Exod. 22, 20, 21.

8. Deut. 2.

9. I Cor. 5. 12, 13.

Two Treatises on Government

Book I. Of Government

Chapter I. The Introduction

§. 1. SLAVERY is so vile and miserable an estate of man, and so directly opposite to the generous temper and courage of our nation; that it is hardly to be conceived, that an Englishman, much less a gentleman, should plead for it. And truly I should have taken Sir Robert Filmer's Patriarcha, as any other treatise, which would persuade all men, that they are slaves, and ought to be so, for such another exercise of wit, as was his who writ the encomium of Nero; rather than for a serious discourse meant in earnest, had not the gravity of the title and epistle, the picture in the front of the book, and the applause that followed it, required me to believe, that the author and publisher were both in earnest. I therefore took it into my hands with all the expectation, and read it through with all the attention due to a treatise that made such a noise at its coming abroad, and cannot but confess my self mightily surprised, that in a book, which was to provide chains for all mankind, I should find nothing but a rope of sand, useful perhaps to such, whose skill and business it is to raise a dust, and would blind the people, the better to mislead them; but in truth not of any force to draw those into bondage, who have their eyes open, and so much sense about them, as to consider, that chains are but an ill wearing, how much care soever hath been taken to file and polish them.

§. 2. If any one think I take too much liberty in speaking so freely of a man, who is the great champion of absolute power, and the idol of those who worship it; I beseech him to make this small allowance for once, to one, who, even after the reading of Sir Robert's book, cannot but think himself, as the laws allow him, a freeman: and I know no fault it is to do so, unless any one better skilled in the fate of it, than I, should have it revealed to him, that this treatise, which has lain dormant so long, was, when it appeared in the world, to carry, by strength of its arguments, all liberty out of it; and that from thenceforth our author's short model was to be the pattern in the mount, and the perfect standard of politics for the future. His system lies in a little compass, it is no more but this,
"That all government is absolute monarchy."
And the ground he builds on, is this,
"That no man is born free."

§. 3. In this last age a generation of men has sprung up amongst us, that would flatter princes with an opinion, that they have a divine right to absolute power, let the laws by which they are constituted, and are to govern, and the conditions under which they enter upon their authority, be what they will, and their engagements to observe them never so well ratified by solemn oaths and promises. To make way for this doctrine, they have denied mankind a right to natural freedom; whereby they have not only, as much as in them lies, exposed all subjects to the utmost misery of tyranny and oppression, but have also unsettled the titles, and shaken the thrones of princes: (for they too, by these men's system, except only one, are all born slaves, and by divine right are subjects to Adam's right heir;) as if they had designed to make war upon all government, and subvert the very foundations of human society, to serve their present turn.

§. 4. However we must believe them upon their own bare words, when they tell us, we are all born slaves, and we must continue so, there is no remedy for it; life and thraldom we enter'd into together, and can never be quit of the one, till we part with the other. Scripture or reason I am sure do not any where say so, notwithstanding the noise of divine right, as if divine authority hath subjected us to the unlimited will of another. An admirable state of mankind, and that which they have not had wit enough to find out till this latter age. For, however Sir Robert Filmer seems to condemn the novelty of the contrary opinion, Patr. p. 3. yet I believe it will be hard for him to find any other age, or country of the world, but this, which has asserted monarchy to be jure divino. And he confesses, Patr. p. 4. That Heyward, Blackwood, Barclay, and others, that have bravely vindicated the right of kings in most points, never thought of this, but with one consent admitted the natural liberty and equality of mankind.

§. 5. By whom this doctrine came at first to be broached, and brought in fashion amongst us, and what sad effects it gave rise to, I leave to historians to relate, or to the memory of those, who were contemporaries with Sibthorp and Manwering, to recollect. My business at present is only to consider what Sir Robert Filmer, who is allowed to have carried this argument farthest, and is supposed to have brought it to perfection, has said in it; for from him every one, who would be as fashionable as French was at court, has learned, and runs away with this short system of politics, viz. "Men are not born free, and therefore could never have the liberty to choose either governors, or forms of government." Princes have their power absolute, and by divine right; for slaves could never have a right to compact or consent. Adam was an absolute monarch, and so are all princes ever since.

Chapter II. Of Paternal and Regal Power

§. 6. SIR ROBERT FILMER'S great position is, that men are not naturally free. This is the foundation on which his absolute monarchy stands, and from which it erects itself to an height, that its power is above every power, caput inter nubila, so high above all earthly and human things, that thought can scarce reach it; that promises and oaths, which tye the infinite Deity, cannot confine it. But if this foundation fails, all his fabric falls with it, and governments must be left again to the old way of being made by contrivance, and the consent of men ([Greek]) making use of their reason to unite together into society. To prove this grand position of his, he tells us, p. 12. "Men are born in subjection to their parents," and therefore cannot be free. And this authority of parents, he calls royal authority, p. 12, 14. Fatherly authority, right of fatherhood, p. 12, 20. One would have thought he would, in the beginning of such a work as this, on which was to depend the authority of princes, and the obedience of subjects, have told us expressly, what that fatherly authority is, have defined it, though not limited it, because in some other treatises of his he tells us, it is unlimited, and unlimitable; 1 he should at least have given us such an account of it, that we might have had an entire notion of this fatherhood, or fatherly authority, whenever it came in our way in his writings: this I expected to have found in the first chapter of his Patriarcha. But instead thereof, having, 1. en passant, made his obeysance to the arcana imperii, p. 5.; 2. made his compliment to the rights and liberties of this, or any other nation, p. 6. which he is going presently to null and destroy; and, 3. made his leg to those learned men, who did not see so far into the matter as himself, p. 7. he comes to fall on Bellarmine, p. 8. and, by a victory over him, establishes his fatherly authority beyond any question. Bellarmine being routed by his own confession, p. 11. the day is clear got, and there is no more need of any forces: for having done that, I observe not that he states the question, or rallies up any arguments to make good his opinion, but rather tells us the story, as he thinks fit, of this strange kind of domineering phantom, called the fatherhood, which, whoever could catch, presently got empire, and unlimited absolute power. He assures us how this fatherhood began in Adam, continued its course, and kept the world in order all the time of the patriarchs till the flood, got out of the ark with Noah and his sons, made and supported all the kings of the earth till the captivity of the Israelites in Egypt, and then the poor fatherhood was under hatches, till God, by giving the Israelites kings, re-established the ancient and prime right of the lineal succession in paternal government. This is his business from p. 12, to p. 19. And then obviating an objection, and clearing a difficulty or two, with one half reason, p. 23. "to confirm the natural right of regal power," he ends the first chapter. I hope it is no injury to call an half quotation an half reason; for God says, "Honour thy father and mother;" but our author contents himself with half, leaves out thy mother quite, as little serviceable to his purpose. But of that more in another place.

§. 7. I do not think our author so little skilled in the way of writing discourses of this nature, nor so careless of the point in hand, that he by over-sight commits the fault, that he himself, in his Anarchy of a mixed Monarchy, p. 239, objects to Mr. Hunton in these words: "Where first I charge the author, that he hath not given us any definition, or description of Monarchy in general; for by the rules of method he should have first defined." And by the like rule of method Sir Robert should have told us, what his fatherhood or fatherly authority is, before he had told us, in whom it was to be found, and talked so much of it. But perhaps Sir Robert found, that this fatherly authority, this power of fathers, and of kings, for he makes them both the same, p. 24. would make a very odd and frightful figure, and very disagreeing with what either children imagine of their parents, or subjects of their kings, if he should have given us the whole draught together in that gigantic form, he had painted it in his own fancy; and therefore, like a wary physician, when he would have his patient swallow some harsh or corrosive liquor, he mingles it with a large quantity of that which may dilute it; that the scattered parts may go down with less feeling, and cause less aversion.

§. 8. Let us then endeavour to find what account he gives us of this fatherly authority, as it lies scattered in the several parts of his writings. And first, as it was vested in Adam, he says, "Not only Adam, but the succeeding patriarchs, had, by right of fatherhood, royal authority over their children," p. 12. "This lordship which Adam by command had over the whole world, and by right descending from him the patriarchs did enjoy, was as large and ample as the absolute dominion of any monarch, which hath been since the creation," p. 13. "Dominion of life and death, making war, and concluding peace," p. 13. "Adam and the patriarchs had absolute power of life and death," 35. "Kings, in the right of parents, succeed to the exercise of supreme jurisdiction," p. 19. "As kingly power is by the law of God, so it hath no inferior law to limit it; Adam was lord of all," p. 40. "The father of a family governs by no other law, than by his own will," p. 78. "The superiority of princes is above laws," p. 79. ""The unlimited jurisdiction of kings is so amply described by Samuel," p. 80. "Kings are above the laws," p. 93. And to this purpose see a great deal more which our author delivers in Bodin's words: "It is certain, that all laws, privileges, and grants of princes, have no force, but during their life; if they be not ratified by the express consent, or by sufferance of the prince following, especially privileges," Observations, p. 279. "The reason why laws have been also made by kings, was this; when kings were either busied with wars, or distracted with public cares, so that every private man could not have access to their persons, to learn their wills and pleasure, then were laws of necessity invented, that so every particular subject might find his prince's pleasure decyphered unto him in the tables of his laws," p. 92. "In a monarchy, the king must by necessity be above the laws," p. 100. "A perfect kingdom is that, wherein the king rules all things according to his own will," p. 100. "Neither common nor statute laws are, or can be, any diminution of that general power, which kings have over their people by right of fatherhood," p. 115. "Adam was the father, king, and lord over his family; a son, a subject, and a servant or slave, were one and the same thing at first. The father had power to dispose or sell his children or servants; whence we find, that the first reckoning up of goods in scripture, the man-servant and the maid-servant, are numbred among the possessions and substance of the owner, as other goods were," Observations, Pref. "God also hath given to the father a right or liberty, to alien his power over his children to any other; whence we find the sale and gift of children to have much been in use in the beginning of the world, when men had their servants for a possession and an inheritance, as well as other goods; whereupon we find the power of castrating and making eunuchs much in use in old times," Observations, p. 155. "Law is nothing else but the will of him that hath the power of the supreme father," Observations, p.

223. "It was God's ordinance that the supremacy should be unlimited in Adam, and as large as all the acts of his will; and as in him so in all others that have supreme power," Observations, p. 245.

§. 9. I have been fain to trouble my reader with these several quotations in our author's own words, that in them might be seen his own description of his fatherly authority, as it lies scattered up and down in his writings, which he supposes was first vested in Adam, and by right belongs to all princes ever since. This fatherly authority then, or right of fatherhood, in our author's sense, is a divine unalterable right of sovereignty, whereby a father or a prince hath an absolute, arbitrary, unlimited, and unlimitable power over the lives, liberties, and estates of his children and subjects; so that he may take or alienate their estates, sell, castrate, or use their persons as he pleases, they being all his slaves, and he lord or proprietor of every thing, and his unbounded will their law.

§. 10. Our author having placed such a mighty power in Adam, and upon that supposition sounded all government, and all power of princes, it is reasonable to expect, that he should have proved this with arguments clear and evident, suitable to the weightiness of the cause; that since men had nothing else left them, they might in slavery have such undeniable proofs of its necessity, that their consciences might be convinced, and oblige them to submit peaceably to that absolute dominion, which their governors had a right to exercise over them. Without this, what good could our author do, or pretend to do, by erecting such an unlimited power, but flatter the natural vanity and ambition of men, too apt of itself to grow and encrease with the possession of any power? and by persuading those, who, by the consent of their fellow-men, are advanced to great, but limited, degrees of it, that by that part which is given them, they have a right to all, that was not so; and therefore may do what they please, because they have authority to do more than others, and so tempt them to do what is neither for their own, nor the good of those under their care; whereby great mischiefs cannot but follow.

§. 11. The sovereignty of Adam, being that on which, as a sure basis, our author builds his mighty absolute monarchy, I expected, that in his Patriarcha, this his main supposition would have been proved, and established with all that evidence of arguments, that such a fundamental tenet required; and that this, on which the great stress of the business depends, would have been made out with reasons sufficient to justify the confidence with which it was assumed. But in all that treatise, I could find very little tending that way; the thing is there so taken for granted, without proof, that I could scarce believe myself, when, upon attentive reading that treatise, I found there so mighty a structure raised upon the bare supposition of this foundation: for it is scarce credible, that in a discourse, where he pretends to confute the erroneous principle of man's natural freedom, he should do it by a bare supposition of Adam's authority, without offering any proof for that authority. Indeed he confidently says, that "Adam had royal authority," p. 12, and 13; "absolute lordship and dominion of life and death," p. 13; "an universal monarchy," p. 33; "absolute power of life and death," p. 35. He is very frequent in such assertions; but, what is strange, in all his whole Patriarcha I find not one pretence of a reason to establish this his great foundation of government; not any thing that looks like an argument, but these words: "To confirm this natural right of regal power, we find in the Decalogue, that the law which enjoins obedience to kings, is delivered in the terms, Honour thy father, as if all power were originally in the father." And why may I not add as well, that in the Decalogue, the law that enjoins obedience to queens, is delivered in the terms of Honour thy mother, as if all power were originally in the mother? The argument, as Sir Robert puts it, will hold as well for one as the other: but of this, more in its due place.

§. 12. All that I take notice of here, is, that this is all our author says in this first, or any of the following chapters, to prove the absolute power of Adam, which is his great principle: and yet, as if he had there settled it upon sure demonstration, he begins his second chapter with these words, "By conferring these proofs and reasons, drawn from the authority of the scripture." Where those proofs and reasons for Adam's sovereignty are, bating that of Honour thy father, above mentioned, I confess, I cannot find; unless what he says, p. 11, "In these words we have an evident confession," viz. "of Bellarmine, that creation made man prince of his posterity," must be taken for proofs and reasons drawn from scripture, or for any sort of proof at all: though from thence by a new way of inference, in the words immediately following, he concludes, the royal authority of Adam sufficiently settled in him.

§. 13. If he has in that chapter, or any where in the whole treatise, given any other proofs of Adam's royal authority, other than by often repeating it, which, among some men, goes for argument, I desire any body for him to shew me the place and page, that I may be convinced of my mistake, and acknowledge my oversight. If no such arguments are to be found, I beseech those men, who have so much cried up this book, to consider, whether they do not give the world cause to suspect, that it is not the force of reason and argument, that makes them for absolute monarchy, but some other by interest, and therefore are resolved to applaud any author, that writes in favour of this doctrine, whether he support it with reason or no. But I hope they do not expect, that rational and indifferent men should be brought over to their opinion, because this their great doctor of it, in a discourse made on purpose, to set up the absolute monarchical power of Adam, in opposition to the natural freedom of mankind, has said so little to prove it, from whence it is rather naturally to be concluded, that there is little to be said.

§. 14. But that I might omit no care to inform myself in our author's full sense, I consulted his Observations on Aristotle, Hobbes, &c. to see whether in disputing with others he made use of any arguments for this his darling tenet of Adam's sovereignty; since in his treatise of the Natural Power of Kings, he hath been so sparing of them. In his Observations on Mr. Hobbes's Leviathan, I think he has put, in short, all those arguments for it together, which in his writings I find him any where to make use of: his words are these: "If God created only Adam, and of a piece of him made the woman, and if by generation from them two, as parts of them, all mankind be propagated: if also God gave to Adam not only the dominion over the woman and the children that should issue from them, but also over all the earth to subdue it, and over all the creatures on it, so that as long as Adam lived, no man could claim or enjoy any thing but by donation, assignation or permission from him, I wonder," &c. Observations, p. 165. Here we have the sum of all his arguments, for Adam's sovereignty and against natural freedom, which I find up and down in his other treatises: and they are these following; God's creation of Adam, the dominion he gave him over Eve, and the dominion he had as father over his children: all which I shall particularly consider.

Note 1. In grants and gifts that have their original from God or nature, as the power of the father hath, no inferior power of man can limit, nor make any law of prescription against them. Observations, 158.
The scripture teaches, that supreme power was originally the father, without any limitation. Observations, 245.

Chapter III. Of Adam's Title to Sovereignty by Creation

§. 15. SIR ROBERT, in his preface to his Observations on Aristotle's Politics, tells us, "A natural freedom of mankind cannot be supposed without the denial of the creation of Adam:" but how Adam's being created, which was nothing but his receiving a being immediately from omnipotence and the hand of God, gave Adam a sovereignty over any thing, I cannot see, nor consequently understand, how a supposition of natural freedom is a denial of Adam's creation, and would be glad any body else (since our author did not vouchsafe us the favour) would make it out for him: for I find no difficulty to suppose the freedom of mankind, though I have always believed the creation of Adam. He was created, or began to exist, by God's immediate power, without the intervention of parents or the pre-existence of any of the same species to beget him, when it pleased God he should; and so did the lion, the king of beasts, before him, by the same creating power of God: and if bare existence by that power, and in that way, will give dominion, without any more ado, our author, by this argument, will make the lion have as good a title to it, as he, and certainly the ancienter. No! for Adam had his title by the appointment of God, says our author in another place. Then bare creation gave him not dominion, and one might have supposed mankind free without the denying the creation of Adam, since it was God's appointment made him monarch.

§. 16. But let us see, how he puts his creation and this appointment together. "By the appointment of God," says Sir Robert, "as soon as Adam was created, he was monarch of the world, though he had no subjects; for though there could not be actual government till there were subjects, yet by the right of nature it was due to Adam to be governor of his posterity: though not in act, yet at least in habit, Adam was a king from his creation." I wish he had told us here, what he meant by God's appointment: for whatsoever Providence orders, or the law of nature directs, or positive revelation declares, may be said to be by God's appointment: but I suppose it cannot be meant here in the first sense, i. e. by Providence; because that would be to say no more, but that as soon as Adam was created he was de facto monarch, because by right of nature it was due to Adam, to be governor of his posterity. But he could not de facto be by Providence constituted the governor of the world, at a time when there was actually no government, no subjects to be governed, which our author here confesses. Monarch of the world is also differently used by our author; for sometimes he means by it a proprietor of all the world exclusive of the rest of mankind, and thus he does in the same page of his preface before cited: "Adam," says he, "being commanded to multiply and people the earth, and to subdue it, and having dominion given him over all creatures, was thereby the monarch of the whole world; none of his posterity had any right to possess any thing but by his grant or permission, or by succession from him." 2. Let us understand then by monarch proprietor of the world, and by appointment God's actual donation, and revealed positive grant made to Adam, Gen. i. 28. as we see Sir Robert himself does in this parallel place, and then his argument will stand thus: by the positive grant of God: as soon as Adam was created, he was proprietor of the world, because by the right of nature it was due to Adam to be governor of his posterity. In which way of arguing there are two manifest falsehoods. First, It is false, that God made that grant to Adam, as soon as he was created, since, though it stands in the text immediately after his creation, yet it is plain it could not be spoken to Adam, till after Eve was made and brought to him: and how then could he be monarch by appointment as soon as created, especially since he calls, if I mistake not, that which God says to Eve, Gen. iii. 16, the original grant of government, which not being till after the fall, when Adam was somewhat, at least in time, and very much distant in condition, from his creation, I cannot see, how our author can say in this sense, that by God's appointment, as soon as Adam was created, he was monarch of the world. Secondly, were it true that God's actual donation appointed Adam monarch of the world as soon as he was created, yet the reason here given for it would not prove it; but it would always be a false inference, that God, by a positive donation, appointed Adam monarch of the world, because by right of nature it was due to Adam to be governor of his posterity: for having given him the right of government by nature, there was no need of a positive donation; at least it will never be a proof of such a donation.

§. 17. On the other side the matter will not be much mended, if we understand by God's appointment the law of nature, (though it be a pretty harsh expression for it in this place) and by monarch of the world, sovereign ruler of mankind: for then the sentence under consideration must run thus: By the law of nature, as soon as Adam was created he was governor of mankind, for by right of nature it was due to Adam to be governor of his posterity; which amounts to this, he was governor by right of nature, because he was governor by right of nature: but supposing we should grant, that a man is by nature governor of his children, Adam could not hereby be monarch as soon as created: for this right of nature being founded in his being their father, how Adam could have a natural right to be governor, before he was a father, when by being a father only he had that right, is methinks, hard to conceive, unless he will have him to be a father before he was a father, and to have a title before he had it.

§. 18. To this foreseen objection, our author answers very logically, he was governor in habit, and not in act; a very pretty way of being a governor without government, a father without children, and a king without subjects. And thus Sir Robert was an author before he writ his book; not in act it is true, but in habit; for when he had once published it, it was due to him by the right of nature, to be an author, as much as it was to Adam to be governor of his children, when he had begot them: and if to be such a monarch of the world, an absolute monarch in habit, but not in act, will serve the turn, I should not much envy it to any of Sir Robert's friends, that he thought fit graciously to bestow it upon, though even this of act and habit, if it signified any thing but our author's skill in distinctions, be not to his purpose in this place. For the question is not here about Adam's actual exercise of government, but actually having a title to be governor. Government, says our author, was due to Adam by the right of nature: what is this right of nature? A right fathers have over their children by begetting them; generatione jus acquiritur parentibus in liberos, says our author out of Grotius, Observations, 223. The right then follows the begetting as arising from it; so that, according to this way of reasoning or distinguishing of our author, Adam, as soon as he was created, had a title only in habit, and not in act, which in plain English is, he had actually no title at all.

§. 19. To speak less learnedly, and more intelligibly, one may say of Adam, he was in a possibility of being governor, since it was possible he might beget children, and thereby acquire that right of nature, be it what it will, to govern them, that accrues from thence: but what connexion has this with Adam's creation, to make him say, that, as soon as he was created, he was monarch of the world? for it may be as well said of Noah, that as soon as he was born, he was monarch of the world, since he was in possibility (which in our author's sense is enough to make a monarch, a monarch in habit,) to outlive all mankind, but his own posterity. What such necessary connexion there is betwixt Adam's creation and his right to government, so that a natural freedom of mankind cannot be supposed without the denial of the creation of Adam, I confess for my part I do not see; nor how those words, by the appointment, &c. Observations, 254. however explained, can be put together, to make any tolerable sense, at least to establish this position, with which they end, viz. Adam was a king from his creation; a king, says our author, not in act, but in habit, i. e. actually no king at all.

§. 20. I fear I have tired my reader's patience, by dwelling longer on this passage, than the weightiness of any argument in it seems to require; but I have unavoidably been engaged in it by our author's way of writing, who, huddling several suppositions together, and that in doubtful and general terms, makes such a medly and confusion, that it is impossible to shew his mistakes, without examining the several senses wherein his words may be taken, and without seeing how, in any of these various meanings, they will consist together, and have any truth in them: for in this present passage before us, how can any one argue against this position of his, that Adam was a king from his creation, unless one examine, whether the words, from his creation, be to be taken, as they may, for the time of the commencement of his government, as the foregoing words import, as soon as he was created he was monarch; or, for the cause of it, as he says, p. 11. creation made man prince of his posterity? how farther can one judge of the truth of his being thus king, till one has examined whether king be to be taken, as the words in the beginning of this passage would persuade, on supposition of his private dominion, which was, by God's positive grant, monarch of the world by appointment; or king on supposition of his fatherly power over his offspring, which was by nature, due by the right of nature; whether, I say, king be to be taken in both, or one only of these two senses, or in neither of them, but only this, that creation made him prince, in a way different from both the other? For though this assertion, that Adam was king from his creation, be true in no sense, yet it stands here as an evident conclusion drawn from the preceding words, though in truth it be but a bare assertion joined to other assertions of the same kind, which confidently put together in words of undetermined and dubious meaning, look like a sort of arguing, when there is indeed neither proof nor connexion: a way very familiar with our author: of which having given the reader a taste here, I shall, as much as the argument will permit me, avoid touching on hereafter; and should not have done it here, were it not to let the world see, how incoherences in matter, and suppositions without proofs put handsomely together in good words and a plausible style, are apt to pass for strong reason and good sense, till they come to be looked into with attention.

Chapter IV. Of Adam's Title to Sovereignty by Donation, Gen. i. 28

§. 21. HAVING at last got through the foregoing passage, where we have been so long detained, not by the force of arguments and opposition, but the intricacy of the words, and the doubtfulness of the meaning; let us go on to his next argument, for Adam's sovereignty. Our author tells us in the words of Mr. Selden, that "Adam by donation from God," Gen. i. 28. "was made the general lord of all things, not without such a private dominion to himself, as without his grant did exclude his children. This determination of Mr. Selden," says our author, "is consonant to the history of the Bible, and natural reason," Observations, 210. And in his Pref. to his Observations on Aristotle, he says thus: "The first government in the world was monarchical in the father of all flesh, Adam being commanded to people and multiply the earth, and to subdue it, and having dominion given him over all creatures, was thereby the monarch of the whole world: none of his posterity had any right to possess any thing, but by his grant or permission, or by succession from him: The earth, saith the Psalmist, hath he given to the children of men, which shew the title comes from fatherhood."

§. 22. Before I examine this argument, and the text on which it is founded, it is necessary to desire the reader to observe, that our author, according to his usual method, begins in one sense, and concludes in another; he begins here with Adam's propriety, or private dominion, by donation; and his conclusion is, which shew the title comes from fatherhood.

§. 23. But let us see the argument. The words of the text are these: "and God blessed them, and God said unto them, be fruitful and multiply, and replenish the earth and subdue it, and have dominion over the fish of the sea, and over the fowl of the air, and over every living thing that moveth up the earth," Gen. i. 28. from whence our author concludes, that Adam, having here dominion given him over all creatures, was thereby the monarch of the whole world: whereby must be meant, that either this grant of God gave Adam property, or as our author calls it, private dominion over the earth, and all inferior or irrational creatures, and so consequently that he was thereby monarch: or 2dly, that it gave him rule and dominion over all earthly creatures whatsoever, and thereby over his children; and so he was monarch: for, as Mr. Selden has properly worded it, "Adam was made general lord of all things," one may very clearly understand him, that he means nothing to be granted to Adam here but property, and therefore he says not one word of Adam's monarchy. But our author says, Adam was hereby monarch of the world, which, properly speaking, signifies sovereign ruler of all the men in the world; and so Adam, by this grant, must be constituted such a ruler. If our author means otherwise, he might with much clearness have said, that Adam was hereby proprietor of the whole world. But he begs your pardon in that point: clear distinct speaking not serving every where to his purpose, you must not expect it in him, as in Mr. Selden, or other such writers.

§. 24. In opposition therefore to our author's doctrine, that Adam was monarch of the whole world, founded on this place, I shall shew,

1. That by this grant, Gen. i. 28. God gave no immediate power to Adam over men, over his children, over those of his own species; and so he was not made ruler, or monarch, by this charter.

2. That by this grant God gave him not private dominion over the inferior creatures, but right in common with all mankind; so neither was he monarch, upon the account of the property here given him.

§. 25. That this donation, Gen. i. 28. gave Adam no power over men, will appear if we consider the words of it: for since all positive grants convey no more than the express words they are made in will carry, let us see which of them here will comprehend mankind, or Adam's posterity; and those, I imagine, if any, must be these, every living thing that moveth: the words in Hebrew are, [Hebrew] i. e. Bestiam Reptantem, of which words the scripture itself is the best interpreter: God having created the fishes and fowls the fifth day, the beginning of the sixth he creates the irrational inhabitants of the dry land, which, v. 24. are described in these words, "let the earth bring forth the living creature after his kind; cattle and creeping things, and beasts of the earth, after his kind," v. 2. "And God made the beasts of the earth after his kind, and cattle after their kind, and every thing that creepeth on the earth after his kind:" here, in the creation of the brute inhabitants of the earth, he first speaks of them all under one general name, of living creatures, and then afterwards divides them into three ranks, 1. Cattle, or such creatures as were or might be tame, and so be the private possession of particular men; 2. [Hebrew] which, ver. 24 and 25. in our Bible, is translated beasts, and by the Septuagint [Greek], wild beasts, and is the same word, that here in our text, ver. 28. where we have this great charter to Adam, is translated living thing, and is also the same word used, Gen. ix. 2. where this grant is renewed to Noah, and there likewise translated beast. 3. The third rank were the creeping animals, which ver. 24. and 25. are comprised under the word [Hebrew], the same that is used here, ver. 28. and is translated moving, but in the former verses creeping, and by the Septuagint in all these places, [Greek], or reptils; from whence it appears, that the words which we translate here in God's donation, ver. 28. living creatures moving, are the same, which in the history of the creation, ver. 24, 25. signify two ranks of terrestrial creatures, viz. wild beasts and reptiles, and are so understood by the Septuagint.

§. 26. When God had made the irrational animals of the world, divided into three kinds, from the places of their habitation, viz. fishes of the sea, fowls of the air, and living creatures of the earth, and these again into cattle, wild beasts, and reptiles, he considers of making man, and the dominion he should have over the terrestrial world, ver. 26. and then he reckons up the inhabitants of these three kingdoms, but in the terrestrial leaves out the second rank [Hebrew] or wild beasts: but here, ver. 28. where he actually exercises this design, and gives him this dominion, the text mentions the fishes of the sea, and fowls of the air, and the terrestrial creatures in the words that signify the wild beasts and reptiles, though translated living thing that moveth, leaving out cattle. In both which places, though the word that signifies wild beasts be omitted in one, and that which signifies cattle in the other, yet, since God certainly executed in one place, what he declares he designed in the other, we cannot but understand the same in both places, and have here only an account, how the terrestrial irrational animals, which were already created and reckoned up at their creation, in three distinct ranks of cattle, wild beasts, and reptiles, were here, ver. 28. actually put under the dominion of man, as they were designed, ver. 26. nor do these words contain in them the least appearance of any thing that can be wrested to signify God's giving to one man dominion over another, to Adam over his posterity.

§. 27. And this further appears from Gen. ix. 2. where God renewing this charter to Noah and his sons, he gives them dominion over the fowls of the air, and the fishes of the sea, and the terrestrial creatures, expressed by [Hebrew] and [Hebrew] wild beasts and reptiles, the same words that in the text before us, Gen. i. 28. are translated every moving thing, that moveth on the earth, which by no means can comprehend man, the grant being made to Noah and his sons, all the men then living, and not to one part of men over another: which is yet more evident from the very next words, ver. 3. where God gives every [Hebrew] every moving thing, the very words used, chap. i. 28. to them for food. By all which it is plain that God's donation to Adam, chap. i. 28. and his designation, ver. 26. and his grant again to Noah and his sons, refer to and contain in them neither more nor less than the works of the creation the fifth day, and the beginning of the sixth, as they are set down from the 20th to the 26th ver. inclusively of the 1st chap. and so comprehend all the species of irrational animals of the terraqueous globe, though all the words, whereby they are expressed in the history of their creation, are no where used in any of the following grants, but some of them omitted in one, and some in another. From whence I think it is past all doubt, that man cannot be comprehended in this grant, nor any dominion over those of his own species be conveyed to Adam. All the terrestrial irrational creatures are enumerated at their creation, ver. 25. under the names beasts of the earth, cattle and creeping things; but man being not then created, was not contained under any of those names; and therefore, whether we understand the Hebrew words right or no, they cannot be supposed to comprehend man, in the very same history, and the very next verses following, especially since that Hebrew word [Hebrew] which, if any in this donation to Adam, chap. i. 28. must comprehend man, is so plainly used in contradistinction to him, as Gen. vi. 20. vii. 14, 21, 23. Gen. viii. 17, 19. And if God made all mankind slaves to Adam and his heirs by giving Adam dominion over every living thing that moveth on the earth, chap. i. 28. as our author would have it, methinks Sir Robert should have carried his monarchical power one step higher, and satisfied the world, that princes might eat their subjects too, since God gave as full power to Noah and his heirs, chap. ix. 2. to eat every living thing that moveth, as he did to Adam to have dominion over them, the Hebrew words in both places being the same.

§. 28. David, who might be supposed to understand the donation of God in this text, and the right of kings too, as well as our author in his comment on this place, as the learned and judicious Ainsworth calls it, in the 8th Psalm, finds here no such charter of monarchical power, his words are, "Thou hast made him," i. e. man, the son of man, "a little lower than the angels; thou madest him to have dominion over the works of thy hands; thou hast put all things under his feet, all sheep and oxen, and the beasts of the field, and the fowls of the air, and fish of the sea, and whatsover passeth through the paths of the sea." In which words, if any one can find out, that there is meant any monarchical power of one man over another, but only the dominion of the whole species of mankind, over the inferior species of creatures, he may, for aught I know, deserve to be one of Sir Robert's monarchs in habit, for the rareness of the discovery. And by this time I hope it is evident, that he that gave dominion over every living thing that moveth on the earth, gave Adam no monarchical power over those of his own species, which will yet appear more fully in the next thing I am to shew.

§. 29. 2. Whatever God gave by the words of this grant, Gen. i. 28. it was not to Adam in particular, exclusive of all other men: whatever dominion he had thereby, it was not a private dominion, but a dominion in common with the rest of mankind. That this donation was not made in particular to Adam, appears evidently from the words of the text, it being made to more than one; for it was spoken in the plural number, God blessed them, and said unto them, Have dominion. God says unto Adam and Eve, Have dominion; thereby, says our author, Adam was monarch of the world: but the grant being to them, i. e. spoke to Eve also, as many interpreters think with reason, that these words were not spoken till Adam had his wife, must not she thereby be lady, as well as he lord of the world? If it be said, that Eve was subjected to Adam, it seems she was not so subjected to him, as to hinder her dominion over the creatures, or property in them: for shall we say that God ever made a joint grant to two, and one only was to have the benefit of it?

§. 30. But perhaps it will be said, Eve was not made till afterward: grant it so, what advantage will our author get by it? The text will be only the more directly against him, and shew that God, in this donation, gave the world to mankind in common, and not to Adam in particular. The word them in the text must include the species of man, for it is certain them can by no means signify Adam alone. In the 26th verse, where God declares his intention to give this dominion, it is plain he meant, that he would make a species of creatures, that should have dominion over the other species of this terrestrial globe: the words are, "And God said, Let us make man in our image, after our likeness, and let them have dominion over the fish," &c. They then were to have dominion. Who? even those who were to have the image of God, the individuals of that species of man, that he was going to make; for that them should signify Adam singly, exclusive of the rest that should be in the world with him, is against both scripture and all reason: and it cannot possibly be made sense, if man in the former part of the verse do not signify the same with them in the latter; only man there, as is usual, is taken for the species, and them the individuals of that species: and we have a reason in the very text. God makes him in his own image, after his own likeness; makes him an intellectual creature, and so capable of dominion: for whereinsoever else the image of God consisted, the intellectual nature was certainly a part of it, and belonged to the whole species, and enabled them to have dominion over the inferior creatures; and therefore David says in the 8th Psalm above cited, "Thou hast made him little lower than the angels, thou hast made him to have dominion." It is not of Adam king David speaks here, for verse 4, it is plain, it is of man, and the son of man, of the species of mankind.

§. 31. And that this grant spoken to Adam was made to him, and the whole species of man, is clear from our author's own proof out of the Psalmist. "The earth," saith the Psalmist, "hath he given to the children of men; which shews the title comes from fatherhood." These are Sir Robert's words in the preface before cited, and a strange inference it is he makes; God hath given the earth to the children of men, ergo the title comes from fatherhood. It is pity the propriety of the Hebrew tongue had not used fathers of men, instead of children of men, to express mankind; then indeed our author might have had the countenance of the sound of the words, to have placed the title in the fatherhood. But to conclude, that the fatherhood had the right to the earth, because God gave it to the children of men, is a way of arguing peculiar to our author: and a man must have a great mind to go contrary to the sound as well as sense of the words before he could light on it. But the sense is yet harder, and more remote from our author's purpose: for as it stands in his preface, it is to prove Adam's being monarch, and his reasoning is thus, God gave the earth to the children of men, ergo Adam was monarch of the world. I defy any man to make a more pleasant conclusion than this, which cannot be excused from the most obvious absurdity, till it can be shewn, that by children of men, he who had no father, Adam alone is signified; but whatever our author does, the scripture speaks not nonsense.

§. 32. To maintain this property and private dominion of Adam, our author labours in the following page to destroy the community granted to Noah and his sons, in that parallel place,

Gen. ix. 1, 2, 3, and he endeavours to do it two ways.

1. Sir Robert would persuade us against the express words of the scripture, that what was here granted to Noah, was not granted to his sons in common with him. His words are, "As for the general community between Noah and his sons, which Mr. Selden will have to be granted to them, Gen. ix. 2. the text doth not warrant it." What warrant our author would have, when the plain express words of scripture, not capable of another meaning, will not satisfy him, who pretends to build wholly on scripture, is not easy to imagine. The text says, God blessed Noah and his sons, and said unto them, i. e. as our author would have it, unto him: for, faith he, although the sons are there mentioned with Noah in the blessing, yet it may best be understood, with a subordination or benediction in succession, Observations, 211. That indeed is best, for our author to be understood, which best serves to his purpose: but that truly may best be understood by any body else, which best agrees with the plain construction of the words, and arises from the obvious meaning of the place; and then with subordination and in succession, will not be best understood, in a grant of God, where he himself put them not, nor mentions any such limitation. But yet, our author has reasons, why it may be best understood so. "The blessing," says he, in the following words, "might truly be fulfilled, if the sons, either under or after their father, enjoyed a private dominion," Observations, 211. which is to say, that a grant, whose express words give a joint title in present (for the text says, into your hands they are delivered) may best be understood with a subordination or in succession; because it is possible, that in subordination, or in succession, it may be enjoyed. Which is all one as to say, that a grant of any thing in present possession may best be understood of reversion; because it is possible one may live to enjoy it in reversion. If the grant be indeed to a father and to his sons after him, who is so kind as to let his children enjoy it presently in common with him, one may truly say, as to the event one will be as good as the other; but it can never be true, that what the express words grant in possession, and in common, may best be understood, to be in reversion. The sum of all his reasoning amounts to this: God did not give to the sons of Noah the world in common with their father, because it was possible they might enjoy it under, or after him. A very good sort of argument against an express text of scripture: but God must not be believed, though he speaks it himself, when he says he does any thing, which will not consist with Sir Robert's hypothesis.

§. 33. For it is plain, however he would exclude them, that part of this benediction, as he would have it in succession, must needs be meant to the sons, and not to Noah himself at all: "Be fruitful, and multiply, and replenish the earth," says God, in this blessing. This part of the benediction, as appears by the sequel, concerned not Noah himself at all: for we read not of any children he had after the flood; and in the following chapter, where his posterity is reckoned up, there is no mention of any; and so this benediction in succession was not to take place till 350 years after: and to save our author's imaginary monarchy, the peopling of the world must be deferred 350 years; for this part of the benediction cannot be understood with subordination, unless our author will say, that they must ask leave of their father Noah to lie with their wives. But in this one point our author is constant to himself in all his discourses, he takes great care there should be monarchs in the world, but very little that there should be people; and indeed his way of government is not the way to people the world: for how much absolute monarchy helps to fulfil this great and primary blessing of God Almighty, "Be fruitful, and multiply, and replenish the earth," which contains in it the improvement too of arts and sciences, and the conveniences of life, may be seen in those large and rich countries which are happy under the Turkish government, where are not now to be found one-third, nay, in many, if not most parts of them, one-thirtieth, perhaps I might say not one-hundredth of the people, that were formerly, as will easily appear to any one, who will compare the accounts we have of it at this time, with antient history. But this by the by.

§. 34. The other parts of this benediction, or grant, are so expressed, that they must needs be understood to belong equally to them all; as much to Noah's sons as to Noah himself, and not to his sons with a subordination, or in succession. The fear of you, and the dread of you, says God, shall be upon every beast, &c. Will any body but our author say, that the creatures feared and stood in awe of Noah only, and not of his sons without his leave, or till after his death? And the following words, into your hands they are delivered, are they to be understood as our author says, if your father please, or they shall be delivered into your hands hereafter? If this be to argue from scripture, I know not what may not be proved by it; and I can scarce see how much this differs from that fiction and fansie, or how much a surer foundation it will prove, than the opinions of philosophers and poets, which our author so much condemns in his preface.

§. 35. But our author goes on to prove, that it may best be understood with a subordination, or a benediction in succession; for, says he, "it is not probable that the private dominion which God gave to Adam, and by his donation, assignation, or cession to his children, was abrogated, and a community of all things instituted between Noah and his sons.——Noah was left the sole heir of the world; why should it be thought that God would disinherit him of his birth-right, and make him of all men in the world the only tenant in common with his children?" Observations, 211.

§. 36. The prejudices of our own ill-grounded opinions, however by us called probable, cannot authorise us to understand scripture contrary to the direct and plain meaning of the words. I grant, it is not probable, that Adam's private dominion was here abrogated: because it is more than probable, (for it will never be proved) that ever Adam had any such private dominion: and since parallel places of scripture are most probable to make us know how they may be best understood, there needs but the comparing this blessing here to Noah and his sons after the flood, with that to Adam after the creation, Gen. i. 28. to assure any one that God gave Adam no such private dominion. It is probable, I confess, that Noah should have the same title, the same property and dominion after the flood, that Adam had before it: but since private dominion cannot consist with the blessing and grant God gave to him and his sons in common, it is a sufficient reason to conclude, that Adam had none, especially since in the donation made to him, there are no words that express it, or do in the least favour it; and then let my reader judge whether it may best be understood, when in the one place there is not one word for it, not to say what has been above proved, that the text itself proves the contrary; and in the other, the words and sense are directly against it.

§. 37. But our author says, "Noah was the sole heir of the world; why should it be thought that God would disinherit him of his birth-right?" Heir, indeed, in England, signifies the eldest son, who is by the law of England to have all his father's land; but where God ever appointed any such heir of the world, our author would have done well to have shewed us; and how God disinherited him of his birth-right, or what harm was done him if God gave his sons a right to make use of a part of the earth for the support of themselves and families, when the whole was not only more than Noah himself, but infinitely more than they all could make use of, and the possessions of one could not at all prejudice, or, as to any use, streighten that of the other.

§. 38. Our author probably foreseeing he might not be very successful in persuading people out of their senses, and, say what he could, men would be apt to believe the plain words of scripture, and think, as they saw, that the grant was spoken to Noah and his sons jointly; he endeavours to insinuate, as if this grant to Noah conveyed no property, no dominion; because, subduing the earth and dominion over the creatures are therein omitted, nor the earth once named. And therefore, says he, "there is a considerable difference between these two texts; the first blessing gave Adam a dominion over the earth and all creatures; the latter allows Noah liberty to use the living creatures for food: here is no alteration or diminishing of his title to a property of all things, but an enlargement only of his commons," Observations, 211. So that in our author's sense, all that was said here to Noah and his sons, gave them no dominion, no property, but only enlarged the commons; their commons, I should say, since God says, to you are they given, though our author says his; for as for Noah's sons, they, it seems, by Sir Robert's appointment, during their father's life-time, were to keep fasting days.

§. 39. Any one but our author would be mightily suspected to be blinded with prejudice, that in all this blessing to Noah and his sons, could see nothing but only an enlargement of commons: for as to dominion, which our author thinks omitted, the fear of you, and the dread of you, says God, shall be upon every beast, which I suppose expresses the dominion, or superiority was designed man over the living creatures, as fully as may be; for in that fear and dread seems chiefly to consist what was given to Adam over the inferior animals; who, as absolute a monarch as he was, could not make bold with a lark or rabbit to satisfy his hunger, and had the herbs but in common with the beasts, as is plain from Gen. i. 2, 9, and 30. In the next place, it is manifest that in this blessing to Noah and his sons, property is not only given in clear words, but in a larger extent than it was to Adam. Into your hands they are given, says God to Noah and his sons; which words, if they give not property, nay, property in possession, it will be hard to find words that can; since there is not a way to express a man's being possessed of any thing more natural, nor more certain, than to say, it is delivered into his hands. And ver. 3. to shew, that they had then given them the utmost property man is capable of, which is to have a right to destroy any thing by using it; "Every moving thing that liveth," saith God, "shall be meat for you;" which was not allowed to Adam in his charter. This our author calls, "a liberty of using them for food, and only an enlargement of commons, but no alteration of property," Observations, 211. What other property man can have in the creatures, but the liberty of using them, is hard to be understood: so that if the first blessing, as our author says, gave Adam dominion over the creatures, and the blessing to Noah and his sons, gave them such a liberty to use them, as Adam had not; it must needs give them something that Adam with all his sovereignty wanted, something that one would be apt to take for a greater property; for certainly he has no absolute dominion over even the brutal part of the creatures; and the property he has in them is very narrow and scanty, who cannot make that use of them, which is permitted to another. Should any one who is absolute lord of a country, have bidden our author subdue the earth, and given him dominion over the creatures in it, but not have permitted him to have taken a kid or a lamb out of the flock, to satisfy his hunger, I guess, he would scarce have thought himself lord or proprietor of that land, or the cattle on it; but would have found the difference between having dominion, which a shepherd may have, and having full property as an owner. So that, had it been his own case, Sir Robert, I believe, would have thought here was an alteration, nay, an enlarging of property; and that Noah and his children had by this grant, not only property given them, but such a property given them in the creatures, as Adam had not: for however, in respect of one another, men may be allowed to have propriety in their distinct portions of the creatures; yet in respect of God the maker of heaven and earth, who is sole lord and proprietor of the whole world, man's propriety in the creatures is nothing but that liberty to use them, which God has permitted; and so man's property may be altered and enlarged, as we see it was here, after the flood, when other uses of them are allowed, which before were not. From all which I suppose it is clear, that neither Adam, nor Noah, had any private dominion, any property in the creatures, exclusive of his posterity, as they should successively grow up into need of them, and come to be able to make use of them.

§. 40. Thus we have examined our author's argument for Adam's monarchy, founded on the blessing pronounced, Gen. i. 28. wherein I think it is impossible for any sober reader, to find any other but the setting of mankind above the other kinds of creatures, in this habitable earth of ours. It is nothing but the giving to man, the whole species of man, as the chief inhabitant, who is the image of his maker, the dominion over the other creatures. This lies so obvious in the plain words, that any one, but our author, would have thought it necessary to have shewn, how these words, that seemed to say the quite contrary, gave Adam monarchical absolute power over other men, or the sole property in all the creatures; and methinks in a business of this moment, and that whereon he builds all that follows, he should have done something more than barely cite words, which apparently make against him; for I confess, I cannot see any thing in them, tending to Adam's monarchy, or private dominion, but quite the contrary. And I the less deplore the dulness of my apprehension herein, since I find the apostle seems to have as little notion of any such private dominion of Adam as I, when he says, God gives us all things richly to enjoy, which he could not do, if it were all given away already, to monarch Adam, and the monarchs his heirs and successors. To conclude, this text is so far from proving Adam sole proprietor, that, on the contrary, it is a confirmation of the original community of all things amongst the sons of men, which appearing from this donation of God, as well as other places of scripture, the sovereignty of Adam, built upon his private dominion, must fall, not having any foundation to support it.

§. 41. But yet, if after all, any one will needs have it so, that by this donation of God, Adam was made sole proprietor of the whole earth, what will this be to his sovereignty? and how will it appear, that propriety in land gives a man power over the life of another? or how will the possession even of the whole earth, give any one a sovereign arbitrary authority over the persons of men? The most specious thing to be said, is, that he that is proprietor of the whole world, may deny all the rest of mankind food, and so at his pleasure starve them, if they will not acknowledge his sovereignty, and obey his will. If this were true, it would be a good argument to prove, that there never was any such property, that God never gave any such private dominion; since it is more reasonable to think, that God, who bid mankind increase and multiply, should rather himself give them all a right to make use of the food and raiment, and other conveniences of life, the materials whereof he had so plentifully provided for them; than to make them depend upon the will of a man for their subsistence, who should have power to destroy them all when he pleased, and who, being no better than other men, was in succession likelier, by want and the dependence of a scanty fortune, to tie them to hard service, than by liberal allowance of the conveniences of life to promote the great design of God, increase and multiply: he that doubts this, let him look into the absolute monarchies of the world, and see what becomes of the conveniences of life, and the multitudes of people.

§. 42. But we know God hath not left one man so to the mercy of another, that he may starve him if he please: God the Lord and Father of all, has given no one of his children such a property in his peculiar portion of the things of this world, but that he has given his needy brother a right to the surplusage of his goods; so that it cannot justly be denied him, when his pressing wants call for it: and therefore no man could ever have a just power over the life of another by right of property in land or possessions; since it would always be a sin, in any man of estate, to let his brother perish for want of affording him relief out of his plenty. As justice gives every man a title to the product of his honest industry, and the fair acquisitions of his ancestors descended to him; so charity gives every man a title to so much out of another's plenty, as will keep him from extreme want, where he has no means to subsist otherwise: and a man can no more justly make use of another's necessity, to force him to become his vassal, by with-holding that relief, God requires him to afford to the wants of his brother, than he that has more strength can seize upon a weaker, master him to his obedience, and with a dagger at his throat offer him death or slavery.

§. 43. Should any one make so perverse an use of God's blessings poured on him with a liberal hand; should any one be cruel and uncharitable to that extremity, yet all this would not prove that propriety in land, even in this case, gave any authority over the persons of men, but only that compact might; since the authority of the rich proprietor, and the subjection of the needy beggar, began not from the possession of the lord, but the consent of the poor man, who preferred being his subject to starving. And the man he thus submits to, can pretend to no more power over him, than he has consented to, upon compact. Upon this ground a man's having his stores filled in a time of scarcity, having money in his pocket, being in a vessel at sea, being able to swim, &c. may as well be the foundation of rule and dominion, as being possessor of all the land in the world; any of these being sufficient to enable me to save a man's life, who would perish if such assistance were denied him; and any thing, by this rule, that may be an occasion of working upon another's necessity, to save his life, or any thing dear to him, at the rate of his freedom, may be made a foundation of sovereignty, as well as property. From all which it is clear, that though God should have given Adam private dominion, yet that private dominion could give him no sovereignty; but we have already sufficiently proved, that God gave him no private dominion.

Chapter V. Of Adam's Title to sovereignty by the subjection of Eve

§. 44. THE NEXT place of scripture we find our author builds his monarchy of Adam on, is Gen. iii. 26. "And thy desire shall be to thy husband, and he shall rule over thee." Here we have (says he) the original grant of government, from whence he concludes, in the following part of the page, Observations, 244. "That the supreme power is settled in the fatherhood, and limited to one kind of government, that is, to monarchy." For let his premises be what they will, this is always the conclusion; let rule, in any text, be but once named, and presently absolute monarchy is by divine right established. If any one will but carefully read our author's own reasoning from these words, Observations, 244. and consider, among other things, the line and posterity of Adam, as he there brings them in, he will find some difficulty to make sense of what he says; but we will allow this at present to his peculiar way of writing, and consider the force of the text in hand. The words are the curse of God upon the woman for having been the first and forwardest in the disobedience; and if we will consider the occasion of what God says here to our first parents, that he was denouncing judgment, and declaring his wrath against them both, for their disobedience, we cannot suppose that this was the time, wherein God was granting Adam prerogatives and privileges, investing him with dignity and authority, elevating him to dominion and monarchy: for though, as a helper in the temptation, Eve was laid below him, and so he had accidentally a superiority over her, for her greater punishment; yet he too had his share in the fall, as well as the sin, and was laid lower, as may be seen in the following verses; and it would be hard to imagine, that God, in the same breath, should make him universal monarch over all mankind, and a day-labourer for his life; turn him out of paradise to till the ground, ver. 23, and at the same time advance him to a throne, and all the privileges and ease of absolute power.

§. 45. This was not a time, when Adam could expect any favours, any grant of privileges from his offended Maker. If this be the original grant of government, as our author tells us, and Adam was now made monarch, whatever Sir Robert would have him, it is plain, God made him but a very poor monarch, such an one as our author himself would have counted it no great privilege to be. God sets him to work for his living, and seems rather to give him a spade into his hand, to subdue the earth, than a sceptre to rule over its inhabitants. "In the sweat of thy face thou shalt eat thy bread," says God to him, ver. 19. This was unavoidable, may it perhaps be answered, because he was yet without subjects, and had nobody to work for him; but afterwards, living as he did above 900 years, he might have people enough, whom he might command to work for him; no, says God, not only whilst thou art without other help, save thy wife, but as long as thou livest shalt thou live by thy labour, "In the sweat of thy face shalt thou eat thy bread, till thou return unto the ground, for out of it wast thou taken; for dust thou art, and unto dust shalt thou return," ver. 19. It will perhaps be answered again in favour of our author, that these words are not spoken personally to Adam, but in him, as their representative, to all mankind, this being a curse upon mankind, because of the fall.

§. 46. God, I believe, speaks differently from men, because he speaks with more truth, more certainty; but when he vouchsafes to speak to men, I do not think he speaks differently from them, in crossing the rules of language in use amongst them: this would not be to condescend to their capacities, when he humbles himself to speak to them, but to lose his design in speaking what, thus spoken, they could not understand. And yet thus must we think of God, if the interpretations of scripture, necessary to maintain our author's doctrine, must be received for good; for, by the ordinary rules of language, it will be very hard to understand what God says, if what he speaks here, in the singular number, to Adam, must be understood to be spoken to all mankind, and what he says in the plural number, Gen. i. 26, and 28, must be understood of Adam alone, exclusive of all others, and what he says to Noah and his sons jointly, must be understood to be meant to Noah alone, Gen. ix.

§. 47. Farther it is to be noted, that these words here of Gen. iii. 16, which our author calls the original grant of government, were not spoken to Adam, neither indeed was there any grant in them made to Adam, but a punishment laid upon Eve: and if we will take them as they were directed in particular to her, or in her, as their representative to all other women, they will at most concern the female sex only, and import no more, but that subjection they should ordinarily be in to their husbands: but there is here no more law to oblige a woman to such a subjection, if the circumstances either of her condition, or contract with her husband, should exempt her from it, than there is, that she should bring forth her children in sorrow and pain, if there could be found a remedy for it, which is also a part of the same curse upon her; for the whole verse runs thus, "Unto the woman he said, I will greatly multiply thy sorrow and thy conception; in sorrow thou shalt bring forth children, and thy desire shall be to thy husband, and he shall rule over thee." It would, I think, have been a hard matter for any body, but our author, to have found out a grant of monarchical government to Adam in these words, which were neither spoke to, nor of him; neither will any one, I suppose, by these words, think the weaker sex, as by a law, so subjected to the curse contained in them, that it is their duty not to endeavour to avoid it. And will any one say, that Eve, or any other woman, sinned, if she were brought to bed without those multiplied pains God threatens her here with? or that either of our queens, Mary or Elizabeth, had they married any of their subjects, had been by this text, put into a political subjection to him? or that he thereby should have had monarchical rule over her? God, in this text, gives not, that I see, any authority to Adam over Eve, or to men over their wives, but only foretels what should be the woman's lot, how by his providence he would order it so, that she should be subject to her husband, as we see that generally the laws of mankind and customs of nations have ordered it so; and there is, I grant, a foundation in nature for it.

§. 48. Thus when God says of Jacob and Esau, that "the elder should serve the younger," Gen. xxv. 23, nobody supposes that God hereby made Jacob Esau's sovereign, but foretold what should de facto come to pass.

But if these words here spoke to Eve must needs be understood as a law to bind her and all other women to subjection, it can be no other subjection than what every wife owes her husband: and then if this be the original grant of government and the foundation of monarchical power, there will be as many monarchs as there are husbands: if therefore these words give any power to Adam, it can be only a conjugal power, not political; the power that every husband hath to order the things of private concernment in his family, as proprietor of the goods and land there, and to have his will take place before that of his wife in all things of their common concernment; but not a political power of life and death over her, much less over any body else.

§. 49. This I am sure: if our author will have this text to be a grant, the original grant of government, political government, he ought to have proved it by some better arguments than by barely saying, that thy desire shall be unto thy husband, was a law whereby Eve, and all that should come of her, were subjected to the absolute monarchical power of Adam and his heirs. Thy desire shall be to thy husband, is too doubtful an expression, of whose signification interpreters are not agreed, to build so confidently on, and in a matter of such moment, and so great and general concernment: but our author, according to his way of writing, having once named the text, concludes presently without any more ado, that the meaning is as he would have it. Let the words rule and subject be but found in the text or margent, and it immediately signifies the duty of a subject to his prince; the relation is changed, and though God says husband, Sir Robert will have it king; Adam has presently absolute monarchical power over Eve, and not only over Eve, but all that should come of her, though the scripture says not a word of it, nor our author a word to prove it. But Adam must for all that be an absolute monarch, and so down to the end of the chapter. And here I leave my reader to consider, whether my bare saying, without offering any reasons to evince it, that this text gave not Adam that absolute monarchical power, our author supposes, be not sufficient to destroy that power, as his bare assertion is to establish it, since the text mentions neither prince nor people, speaks nothing of absolute or monarchical power, but the subjection of Eve to Adam, a wife to her husband. And he that would trace our author so all through, would make a short and sufficient answer to the greatest part of the grounds he proceeds on, and abundantly consute them by barely denying; it being a sufficient answer to assertions without proof, to deny them without giving a reason. And therefore should I have said nothing but barely denied, that by this text the supreme power was settled and founded by God himself, in the fatherhood, limited to monarchy, and that to Adam's person and heirs, all which our author notably concludes from these words, as may be seen in the same page, Observations, 244. it had been a sufficient answer: should I have desired any sober man only to have read the text, and considered to whom, and on what occasion it was spoken, he would no doubt have wondered how our author found out monarchical absolute power in it, had he not had an exceeding good faculty to find it himself, where he could not shew it others. And thus we have examined the two places of scripture, all that I remember our author brings to prove Adam's sovereignty, that supremacy, which he says, it was God's ordinance should be unlimited in Adam, and as large as all the acts of his will, Observations, 254. viz. Gen. i. 28. and Gen. iii. 16. one whereof signifies only the subjection of the inferior ranks of creatures to mankind, and the other the subjection that is due from a wife to her husband, both far enough from that which subjects owe the governors of political societies.

Chapter VI. Of Adam's Title to Sovereignty by Fatherhood

§. 50. THERE is one thing more, and then I think I have given you all that our author brings for proof of Adam's sovereignty, and that is a supposition of a natural right of dominion over his children, by being their father: and this title of fatherhood he is so pleased with, that you will find it brought in almost in every page; particularly he says, "not only Adam, but the succeeding patriarchs had by right of fatherhood royal authority over their children," p. 12. And in the same page, "this subjection of children being the fountain of all regal authority," &c. This being, as one would think by his so frequent mentioning it, the main basis of all his frame, we may well expect clear and evident reason for it, since he lays it down as a position necessary to his purpose, that "every man that is born is so far from being free, that by his very birth he becomes a subject of him that begets him," Observations, 156. so that Adam being the only man created, and all ever since being begotten, nobody has been born free. If we ask how Adam comes by this power over his children, he tells us here it is by begetting them: and so again, Observations, 223. "this natural dominion of Adam," says he, "may be proved out of Grotius himself, who teacheth, that generatione jus acquiritur parentibus in liberos." And indeed the act of begetting being that which makes a man a father, his right of a father over his children can naturally arise from nothing else.

§. 51. Grotius tells us not here how far this jus in liberos, this power of parents over their children extends; but our author, always very clear in the point, assures us, it is supreme power, and like that of absolute monarchs over their slaves, absolute power of life and death. He that should demand of him, how, or for what reason it is, that begetting a child gives the father such an absolute power over him, will find him answer nothing: we are to take his word for this, as well as several other things; and by that the laws of nature and the constitutions of government must stand or fall. Had he been an absolute monarch, this way of talking might have suited well enough; pro ratione voluntas might have been of force in his mouth; but in the way of proof or argument is very unbecoming, and will little advantage his plea for absolute monarchy. Sir Robert has too much lessened a subject's authority to leave himself the hopes of establishing any thing by his bare saying it; one slave's opinion without proof is not of weight enough to dispose of the liberty and fortunes of all mankind. If all men are not, as I think they are, naturally equal, I am sure all slaves are; and then I may, without presumption, oppose my single opinion to his; and be confident that my saying, that begetting of children makes them not slaves to their fathers, as certainly sets all mankind free, as his affirming the contrary makes them all slaves. But that this position, which is the foundation of all their doctrine, who would have monarchy to be jure divino, may have all fair play, let us hear what reasons others give for it, since our author offers none.

§. 52. The argument, I have heard others make use of, to prove that fathers, by begetting them, come by an absolute power over their children, is this; that fathers have a power over the lives of their children, because they give them life and being, which is the only proof it is capable of: since there can be no reason, why naturally one man should have any claim or pretence of right over that in another, which was never his, which he bestowed not, but was received from the bounty of another. 1. I answer, that every one who gives another any thing, has not always thereby a right to take it away again. But, 2. They who say the father gives life to his children, are so dazzled with the thoughts of monarchy, that they do not, as they ought, remember God, who is the author and giver of life: it is in him alone we live, move, and have our being. How can he be thought to give life to another, that knows not wherein his own life consists? Philosophers are at a loss about it after their most diligent enquiries; and anatomists, after their whole lives and studies spent in dissections, and diligent examining the bodies of men, confess their ignorance in the structure and use of many parts of man's body, and in that operation wherein life consists in the whole. And doth the rude plough-man, or the more ignorant voluptuary, frame or fashion such an admirable engine as this is, and then put life and sense into it? Can any man say, he formed the parts that are necessary to the life of his child? or can he suppose himself to give the life, and yet not know what subject is fit to receive it, nor what actions or organs are necessary for its reception or preservation?

§. 53. To give life to that which has yet no being, is to frame and make a living creature, fashion the parts, and mould and suit them to their uses, and having proportioned and fitted them together, to put into them a living soul. He that could do this might indeed have some pretence to destroy his own workmanship. But is there any one so bold, that dares thus far arrogate to himself, the incomprehensible works of the Almighty? Who alone did at first, and still continues to make a living soul, he alone can breathe in the breath of life. If any one thinks himself an artist at this, let him number up the parts of his child's body which he hath made, tell me their uses and operations, and when the living and rational soul began to inhabit this curious structure, when sense began, and how this engine, which he has framed, thinks and reasons: if he made it, let him, when it is out of order, mend it, at least tell wherein the defects lie. "Shall he that made the eye, not see?" says the Psalmist, Psalm xciv. 9. See these men's vanities: the structure of that one part is sufficient to convince us of an all-wise contriver, and he has so visible a claim to us as his workmanship, that one of the ordinary appellations of God in scripture is, God our Maker, and the Lord our Maker. And therefore though our author, for the magnifying his fatherhood, be pleased to say, Observations, 159. "That even the power which God himself exerciseth over mankind is by right of fatherhood," yet this fatherhood is such an one as utterly excludes all pretence of title in earthly parents; for he is king, because he is indeed maker of us all, which no parents can pretend to be of their children.

§. 54. But had men skill and power to make their children, it is not so slight a piece of workmanship, that it can be imagined, they could make them without designing it. What father of a thousand, when he begets a child, thinks farther than the satisfying his present appetite? God in his infinite wisdom has put strong defires of copulation into the constitution of men, thereby to continue the race of mankind, which he doth most commonly without the intention, and often against the consent and will of the begetter. And indeed those who desire and design children, are but the occasions of their being, and when they design and wish to beget them, do little more towards their making, than Deucalion and his wife in the fable did towards the making of mankind, by throwing pebbles over their heads.

§. 55. But grant that the parents made their children, gave them life and being, and that hence there followed an absolute power. This would give the father but a joint dominion with the mother over them: for nobody can deny but that the woman hath an equal share, if not the greater, as nourishing the child a long time in her own body out of her own substance: there it is fashioned, and from her it receives the materials and principles of its constitution: and it is so hard to imagine the rational soul should presently inhabit the yet unformed embrio, as soon as the father has done his part in the act of generation, that if it must be supposed to derive any thing from the parents, it must certainly owe most to the mother. But be that as it will, the mother cannot be denied an equal share in begetting of the child, and so the absolute authority of the father will not arise from hence. Our author indeed is of another mind; for he says, "We know that God at the creation gave the sovereignty to the man over the woman, as being the nobler and principal agent in generation," Observations, 172. I remember not this in my Bible; and when the place is brought where God at the creation gave the sovereignty to man over the woman, and that for this reason, because he is the nobler and principal agent in generation, it will be time enough to consider, and answer it. But it is no new thing for our author to tell us his own fancies for certain and divine truths, though there be often a great deal of difference between his and divine revelations; for God in the scripture says, his father and his mother that begot him.

§. 56. They who alledge the practice of mankind, for exposing or selling their children, as a proof of their power over them, are with Sir Robert happy arguers; and cannot but recommend their opinion, by founding it on the most shameful action, and most unnatural murder, human nature is capable of. The dens of lions and nurseries of wolves know no such cruelty as this: these savage inhabitants of the desart obey God and nature in being tender and careful of their offspring: they will hunt, watch, fight, and almost starve for the preservation of their young; never part with them; never forsake them, till they are able to shift for themselves. And is it the privilege of man alone to act more contrary to nature than the wild and most untamed part of the creation? Doth God forbid us under the severest penalty, that of death, to take away the life of any man, a stranger, and upon provocation? and does he permit us to destroy those, he has given us the charge and care of; and by the dictates of nature and reason, as well as his revealed command, requires us to preserve? He has in all the parts of the creation taken a peculiar care to propagate and continue the several species of creatures, and makes the individuals act so strongly to this end, that they sometimes neglect their own private good for it, and seem to forget that general rule, which nature teaches all things, of self-preservation; and the preservation of their young, as the strongest principle in them, over-rules the constitution of their particular natures. Thus we see, when their young stand in need of it, the timorous become valiant, the fierce and savage kind, and the ravenous tender and liberal.

§. 57. But if the example of what hath been done, be the rule of what ought to be, history would have furnished our author with instances of this absolute fatherly power in its height and perfection, and he might have shewed us in Peru, people that begot children on purpose to fatten and eat them. The story is so remarkable, that I cannot but set it down in the author's words. "In some provinces," says he, "they were so liquorish after man's flesh, that they would not have the patience to stay till the breath was out of the body, but would suck the blood as it ran from the wounds of the dying man; they had public shambles of man's flesh, and their madness herein was to that degree, that they spared not their own children, which they had begot on strangers taken in war: for they made their captives their mistresses, and choicely nourished the children they had by them, till about thirteen years old they butchered and eat them; and they served the mothers after the same fashion, when they grew past childbearing, and ceased to bring them any more roasters," Garcilasso de la vega Hist. des Yncas de Peru, l. i. c. 12.

§. 58. Thus far can the busy mind of man carry him to a brutality below the level of beasts, when he quits his reason, which places him almost equal to angels. Nor can it be otherwise in a creature, whose thoughts are more than the sands, and wider than the ocean, where fancy and passion must needs run him into strange courses, if reason, which is his only star and compass, be not that he steers by. The imagination is always restless, and suggests variety of thoughts, and the will, reason being laid aside, is ready for every extravagant project; and in this state, he that goes farthest out of the way, is thought fittest to lead, and is sure of most followers: and when fashion hath once established what folly or craft began, custom makes it sacred, and it will be thought impudence, or madness, to contradict or question it. He that will impartially survey the nations of the world, will find so much of their religions, governments and manners, brought in and continued amongst them by these means, that he will have but little reverence for the practices which are in use and credit amongst men; and will have reason to think, that the woods and forests, where the irrational untaught inhabitants keep right by following nature, are fitter to give us rules, than cities and palaces, where those that call themselves civil and rational, go out of their way, by the authority of example. If precedents are sufficient to establish a rule in this case, our author might have found in holy writ children sacrificed by their parents, and this amongst the people of God themselves: the Psalmist tells us, Psal. cvi. 38. "They shed innocent blood, even the blood of their sons and of their daughters, whom they sacrificed unto the idols of Canaan." But God judged not of this by our author's rule, nor allowed of the authority of practice against his righteous law; but as it follows there, "the land was polluted with blood; therefore was the wrath of the Lord kindled against his people, insomuch that he abhorred his own inheritance." The killing of their children, though it were fashionable, was charged on them as innocent blood, and so had in the account of God the guilt of murder, as the offering them to idols had the guilt of idolatry.

§. 59. Be it then, as Sir Robert says, that anciently it was usual for men to sell and castrate their children, Observations, 155. Let it be, that they exposed them; add to it, if you please, for this is still greater power, that they begat them for their tables, to fat and eat them: if this proves a right to do so, we may, by the same argument, justify adultery, incest, and sodomy, for there are examples of these too, both ancient and modern; sins which, I suppose, have their principal aggravation from this, that they cross the main intention of nature, which willeth the increase of mankind, and the continuation of the species in the highest perfection, and the distinction of families, with the security of the marriage-bed, as necessary thereunto.

§. 60. In confirmation of this natural authority of the father, our author brings a lame proof from the positive command of God in scripture: his words are, "To confirm the natural right of regal power, we find in the Decalogue, that the law which enjoins obedience to kings, is delivered in the terms, Honour thy father," p. 23. "Whereas many confess, that government only in the abstract, is the ordinance of God, they are not able to prove any such ordinance in the scripture, but only in the fatherly power; and therefore we find the commandment, that enjoins obedience to superiors, given in the terms, Honour thy father; so that not only the power and right of government, but the form of the power governing, and the person having the power, are all the ordinances of God. The first father had not only simply power, but power monarchical, as he was father immediately from God," Observations, 254. To the same purpose, the same law is cited by our author in several other places, and just after the same fashion; that is, and mother, as apochryphal words, are always left out; a great argument of our author's ingenuity, and the goodness of his cause, which required in its defender zeal to a degree of warmth, able to warp the sacred rule of the word of God, to make it comply with his present occasion; a way of proceeding not unusual to those, who embrace not truths, because reason and revelation offer them, but espouse tenets and parties for ends different from truth, and then resolve at any rate to defend them; and so do with the words and sense of authors, they would fit to their purpose, just as Procrustes did with his guests, lop or stretch them, as may best fit them to the size of their notions: and they always prove like those so served, deformed, lame, and useless.

§. 61. For had our author set down this command without garbling, as God gave it, and joined mother to father, every reader would have seen, that it had made directly against him; and that it was so far from establishing the monarchical power of the father, that it set up the mother equal with him, and enjoined nothing but what was due in common, to both father and mother: for that is the constant tenor of the scripture, "Honour thy father and thy mother," Exod. xx. "He that smiteth his father or mother, shall surely be put to death," xxi. 15. "He that curseth his father or mother, shall surely be put to death," ver. 17. Repeated Lev. xx. 9. and by our Saviour, Matth. xv. 4. "Ye shall fear every man his mother and his father," Lev. xix. 3. "If a man have a rebellious son, which will not obey the voice of his father, or the voice of his mother; then shall his father and mother lay hold on him, and say, This our son is stubborn and rebellious, he will not obey our voice," Deut. xxi. 18, 19, 20, 21. "Cursed be he that setteth light by his father or his mother," xxviii. 16. "My son, hear the instructions of thy father, and forsake not the law of thy mother," are the words of Solomon, a king who was not ignorant of what belonged to him as a father or a king; and yet he joins father and mother together, in all the instructions he gives children quite through his book of Proverbs. "Woe unto him, that sayeth unto his father, What begettest thou? or to the woman, What hast thou brought forth?" Isa. xi. ver. 10. "In thee have they set light by father or mother," Ezek. xxviii. 2. "And it shall come to pass, that when any shall yet prophesy, then his father and his mother that begat him, shall say unto him, thou shalt not live, and his father and his mother that begat him, shall thrust him through when he prophesieth," Zech. xiii. 3. Here not the father only, but the father and mother jointly, had power in this case of life and death. Thus ran the law of the Old Testament, and in the New they are likewise joined, in the obedience of their children, Eph. vi. 1. The rule is, Children, obey your parents; and I do not remember, that I any where read, Children, obey your father, and no more: the scripture joins mother too in that homage, which is due from children; and had there been any text, where the honour or obedience of children had been directed to the father alone, it is not likely that our author, who pretends to build all upon scripture, would have omitted it: nay, the scripture makes the authority of father and mother, in respect of those they have begot, so equal, that in some places it neglects even the priority of order, which is thought due to the father, and the mother is put first, as Lev. xix. 3. from which so constantly joining father and mother together, as is found quite through the scripture, we may conclude that the honour they have a title to from their children, is one common right belonging so equally to them both, that neither can claim it wholly, neither can be excluded.

§. 62. One would wonder then how our author infers from the fifth commandment, that all power was originally in the father; how he finds monarchical power of government settled and fixed by the commandment, Honour thy father and thy mother. If all the honour due by the commandment, be it what it will, be the only right of the father, because he, as our author says, has the sovereignty over the woman, as being the nobler and principaler agent in generation, why did God afterwards all along join the mother with him, to share in his honour? can the father, by this sovereignty of his, discharge the child from paying this honour to his mother? The scripture gave no such licence to the Jews, and yet there were often breaches wide enough betwixt husband and wife, even to divorce and separation: and, I think, nobody will say a child may withhold honour from his mother, or, as the scripture terms it, set light by her, though his father should command him to do so; no more than the mother could dispense with him for neglecting to honour his father: whereby it is plain, that this command of God gives the father no sovereignty, no supremacy.

§. 63. I agree with our author that the title to this honour is vested in the parents by nature, and is a right which accrues to them by their having begotten their children, and God by many positive declarations has confirmed it to them: I also allow our author's rule, that in grants and gifts, that have their original from God and nature, as the power of the father, (let me add and mother, for whom God hath joined together, let no man put asunder) no inferior power of men can limit, nor make any law of prescription against them, Observations, 158. so that the mother having, by this law of God, a right to honour from her children, which is not subject to the will of her husband, we see this absolute monarchical power of the father can neither be founded on it, nor consist with it; and he has a power very far from monarchical, very far from that absoluteness our author contends; when another has over his subjects the same power he hath, and by the same title: and therefore he cannot forbear saying himself that he cannot see how any man's children can be free from subjection to their parents, p. 12. which, in common speech, I think, signifies mother as well as father; or if parents here signifies only father, it is the first time I ever yet knew it to do so, and by such an use of words one may say any thing.

§. 64. By our author's doctrine, the father having absolute jurisdiction over his children, has also the same over their issue; and the consequence is good, were it true, that the father had such a power: and yet I ask our author whether the grandfather, by his sovereignty, could discharge the grandchild from paying to his father the honour due to him by the fifth commandment. If the grandfather hath, by right of fatherhood, sole sovereign power in him, and that obedience which is due to the supreme magistrate, be commanded in these words, Honour thy father, it is certain the grandfather might dispense with the grandson's honouring his father, which since it is evident in common sense he cannot, it follows from hence, that Honour thy father and mother, cannot mean an absolute subjection to a sovereign power, but something else. The right therefore which parents have by nature, and which is confirmed to them by the fifth commandment, cannot be that political dominion, which our author would derive from it: for that being in every civil society supreme somewhere, can discharge any subject from any political obedience to any one of his fellow-subjects. But what law of the magistrate can give a child liberty, not to honour his father and mother? It is an eternal law, annexed purely to the relation of parents and children, and so contains nothing of the magistrate's power in it, nor is subjected to it.

§. 65. Our author says, "God hath given to a father a right or liberty to alien his power over his children to any other," Observations, 155. I doubt whether he can alien wholly the right of honour that is due from them; but be that as it will, this I am sure, he cannot alien, and retain the same power. If therefore the magistrate's sovereignty be, as our author would have it, nothing but the authority of a supreme father, p. 23. it is unavoidable, that if the magistrate hath all this paternal right, as he must have if fatherhood be the fountain of all authority; then the subjects, though fathers, can have no power over their children, no right to honour from them: for it cannot be all in another's hands, and a part remain with the parents. So that, according to our author's own doctrine, Honour thy father and mother cannot possibly be understood of political subjection and obedience; since the laws both in the Old and New Testament, that commanded children to honour and obey their parents, were given to such, whose fathers were under civil government, and fellow-subjects with them in political societies; and to have bid them honour and obey their parents, in our author's sense, had been to bid them be subjects to those who had no title to it; the right to obedience from subjects, being all vested in another; and instead of teaching obedience, this had been to foment sedition, by setting up powers that were not. If therefore this command, Honour thy father and mother, concern political dominion, it directly overthrows our author's monarchy; since it being to be paid by every child to his father, even in society, every father must necessarily have political dominion, and there will be as many sovereigns as there are fathers: besides that the mother too hath her title, which destroys the sovereignty of one supreme monarch. But if Honour thy father and mother mean something distinct from political power, as necessarily it must, it is besides our author's business, and serves nothing to his purpose.

§. 66. "The law that enjoins obedience to kings is delivered," says our author, "in the terms, Honour thy father, as if all power were originally in the father," Observations, 254. and that law is also delivered, say I, in the terms, Honour thy mother, as if all power were originally in the mother. I appeal whether the argument be not as good on one side as the other, father and mother being joined all along in the Old and New Testament wherever honour or obedience is enjoined children. Again our author tells us, Observations, 254. "that this command, Honour thy father, gives the right to govern, and makes the form of government monarchical." To which I answer, that if by Honour thy father be meant obedience to the political power of the magistrate, it concerns not any duty we owe to our natural fathers, who are subjects; because they, by our author's doctrine, are divested of all that power, it being placed wholly in the prince, and so being equally subjects and slaves with their children, can have no right, by that title, to any such honour or obedience, as contains in it political subjection: if Honour thy father and mother signifies the duty we owe our natural parents, as by our Saviour's interpretation, Matth. xv. 4. and all the other mentioned places, it is plain it does, then it cannot concern political obedience, but a duty that is owing to persons, who have no title to sovereignty, nor any political authority as magistrates over subjects. For the person of a private father, and a title to obedience, due to the supreme magistrate, are things inconsistent; and therefore this command, which must necessarily comprehend the persons of our natural fathers, must mean a duty we owe them distinct from our obedience to the magistrate, and from which the most absolute power of princes cannot absolve us. What this duty is, we shall in its due place examine.

§. 67. And thus we have at last got through all, that in our author looks like an argument for that absolute unlimited sovereignty described, Sect. 8. which he supposes in Adam; so that mankind ever since have been all born slaves, without any title to freedom. But if creation, which gave nothing but a being, made not Adam prince of his posterity: if Adam, Gen. i. 28. was not constituted lord of mankind, nor had a private dominion given him exclusive of his children, but only a right and power over the earth, and inferior creatures in common with the children of men; if also Gen. iii. 16. God gave not any political power to Adam over his wife and children, but only subjected Eve to Adam, as a punishment, or foretold the subjection of the weaker sex, in the ordering the common concernments of their families, but gave not thereby to Adam, as to the husband, power of life and death, which necessarily belongs to the magistrate: if fathers by begetting their children acquire no such power over them; and if the command, Honour thy father and mother, give it not, but only enjoins a duty owing to parents equally, whether subjects or not, and to the mother as well as the father; if all this be so, as I think, by what has been said, is very evident; then man has a natural freedom, notwithstanding all our author confidently says to the contrary; since all that share in the same common nature, faculties and powers, are in nature equal, and ought to partake in the same common rights and privileges, till the manifest appointment of God, who is Lord over all, blessed for ever, can be produced to shew any particular person's supremacy; or a man's own consent subjects him to a superior. This is so plain, that our author confesses, that Sir John Hayward, Blackwood and Barclay, the great vindicators of the right of kings, could not deny it, but admit with one consent the natural liberty and equality of mankind, for a truth unquestionable. And our author hath been so far from producing any thing, that may make good his great position, that Adam was absolute monarch, and so men are not naturally free, that even his own proofs make against him; so that to use his own way of arguing, the first erroneous principle failing, the whole fabric of this vast engine of absolute power and tyranny drops down of itself, and there needs no more to be said in answer to all that he builds upon so false and frail a foundation.

§. 68. But to save others the pains, were there any need, he is not sparing himself to shew, by his own contradictions, the weakness of his own doctrine. Adam's absolute and sole dominion is that, which he is every where full of, and all along builds on, and yet he tells us, p. 12. "that as Adam was lord of his children, so his children under him had a command and power over their own children." The unlimited and undivided sovereignty of Adam's fatherhood, by our author's computation, stood but a little while, only during the first generation, but as soon as he had grandchildren, Sir Robert could give but a very ill account of it. "Adam, as father of his children," faith he, "hath an absolute, unlimited royal power over them, and by virtue thereof over those that they begot, and so to all generations;" and yet his children, viz. Cain and Seth, have a paternal power over their children at the same time; so that they are at the same time absolute lords, and yet vassals and slaves; Adam has all the authority, as grandfather of the people, and they have a part of it as fathers of a part of them: he is absolute over them and their posterity, by having begotten them, and yet they are absolute over their own children by the same title. "No," says our author, "Adam's children under him had power over their own children, but still with subordination to the first parent." A good distinction that sounds well, and it is pity it signifies nothing, nor can it be reconciled with our author's words. I readily grant, that supposing Adam's absolute power over his posterity, any of his children might have from him a delegated, and so a subordinate power over a part, or all the rest: but that cannot be the power our author speaks of here; it is not a power by grant and commission, but the natural paternal power he supposes a father to have over his children. For 1. he says, "As Adam was lord of his children, so his children under him had a power over their own children:" they were then lords over their own children after the same manner, and by the same title, that Adam was, i. e. by right of generation, by right of fatherhood. 2. It is plain he means the natural power of fathers, because he limits it to be only over their own children; a delegated power has no such limitation, as only over their own children, it might be over others, as well as their own children. 3. If it were a delegated power, it must appear in scripture; but there is no ground in scripture to affirm, that Adam's children had any other power over theirs, than what they naturally had as fathers.

§. 69. But that he means here paternal power and no other, is past doubt, from the inference he makes in these words immediately following, "I see not then how the children of Adam, or of any man else, can be free from subjection to their parents." Whereby it appears that the power on one side, and the subjection on the other, our author here speaks of, is that natural power, and subjection between parents and children: for that which every man's children owed, could be no other; and that our author always affirms to be absolute and unlimited. This natural power of parents over their children, Adam had over his posterity, says our author; and this power of parents over their children, his children had over theirs in his life-time, says our author also; so that Adam, by a natural right of father, had an absolute unlimited power over all his posterity, and at the same time his children had by the same right absolute unlimited power over theirs. Here then are two absolute unlimited powers existing together, which I would have any body reconcile one to another, or to common sense. For the salvo he has put in of subordination, makes it more absurd: To have one absolute, unlimited, nay unlimitable power, in subordination to another, is so manifest a contradiction, that nothing can be more. Adam is absolute prince with the unlimited authority of fatherhood over all his posterity; all his posterity are then absolutely his subjects; and, as our author says, his slaves, children, and grandchildren, are equally in this state of subjection and slavery; and yet, says our author, the children of Adam have paternal, i. e. absolute unlimited power over their own children: which in plain English is, they are slaves and absolute princes at the same time, and in the same government; and one part of the subjects have an absolute unlimited power over the other by the natural right of parentage.

§. 70. If any one will suppose, in favour of our author, that he here meant, that parents, who are in subjection themselves to the absolute authority of their father, have yet some power over their children; I confess he is something nearer the truth: but he will not at all hereby help our author: for he no where speaking of the paternal power, but as an absolute unlimited authority, cannot be supposed to understand any thing else here, unless he himself had limited it, and shewed how far it reached. And that he means here paternal authority in that large extent, is plain from the immediately following words; "This subjection of children being," says he, "the foundation of all regal authority," p. 12. the subjection then that in the former line, he says, every man is in to his parents, and consequently what Adam's grandchildren were in to their parents, was that which was the fountain of all regal authority, i. e. according to our author, absolute unlimitable authority. And thus Adam's children had regal authority over their children, whilst they themselves were subjects to their father, and fellow-subjects with their children. But let him mean as he pleases, it is plain he allows Adam's children to have paternal power, p. 12. as also all other fathers to have paternal power over their children, Observations, 156. From whence one of these two things will necessarily follow, that either Adam's children, even in his life-time, had, and so all fathers have, as he phrases it, p. 12. "by right of fatherhood, royal authority over their children," or else, that "Adam, by right of fatherhood, had not royal authority." For it cannot be but that paternal power does, or does not, give royal authority to them that have it: if it does not, then Adam could not be sovereign by this title, nor any body else; and then there is an end of all our author's politics at once: if it does give royal authority, then every one that has paternal power has royal authority; and then by our author's patriarchal government, there will be as many kings as there are fathers.

§. 71. And thus what a monarchy he hath set up, let him and his disciples consider. Princes certainly will have great reason to thank him for these new politics, which set up as many absolute kings in every country as there are fathers of children. And yet who can blame our author for it, it lying unavoidably in the way of one discoursing upon our author's principles? For having placed an absolute power in fathers by right of begetting, he could not easily resolve how much of this power belonged to a son over the children he had begotten; and so it fell out to be a hard matter to give all the power, as he does, to Adam, and yet allow a part in his life-time to his children, when they were parents, and which he knew not well how to deny them. This makes him so doubtful in his expressions, and so uncertain where to place this absolute natural power, which he calls fatherhood. Sometimes Adam alone has it all, as p. 13. Observations, 244, 245. & Pref.

Sometimes parents have it, which word scarce signifies the father alone, p. 12, 19.
Sometimes children during their fathers' life-time, as p. 12.
Sometimes fathers of families, as p. 78, & 79.
Sometimes fathers indefinitely, Observations, 155.
Sometimes the heir to Adam, Observations, 253.
Sometimes the posterity of Adam, 244, 246.
Sometimes prime fathers, all sons or grandchildren of Noah, Observations, 244.
Sometimes the eldest parents, p. 12.
Sometimes all kings, p. 19.
Sometimes all that have supreme power, Observations, 245.
Sometimes heirs to those first progenitors, who were at first the natural parents of the whole people, p. 19.
Sometimes an elective king, p. 23.
Sometimes those, whether a few or a multitude, that govern the commonwealth, p. 23.
Sometimes he that can catch it, an usurper, p. 23. Observations, 155.
§. 72. Thus this new nothing, that is to carry with it all power, authority, and government; this fatherhood, which is to design the person, and establish the throne of monarchs, whom the people are to obey, may, according to Sir Robert, come into any hands, any how, and so by his politics give to democracy royal authority, and make an usurper a lawful prince. And if it will do all these fine feats, much good do our author and all his followers with their omnipotent fatherhood, which can serve for nothing but to unsettle and destroy all the lawful governments in the world, and to establish in their room disorder, tyranny, and usurpation.

Chapter VII. Of Fatherhood and Property considered together as Fountains of Sovereignty

§. 73. IN the foregoing chapters we have seen what Adam's monarchy was, in our author's opinion, and upon what titles he founded it. The foundations which he lays the chief stress on, as those from which he thinks he may best derive monarchical power to future princes, are two, viz. Fatherhood and property: and therefore the way he proposes to remove the absurdities and inconveniences of the doctrine of natural freedom, is, to maintain the natural and private dominion of Adam, Observations, 222. Conformable hereunto, he tells us, the "grounds and principles of government necessarily depend upon the original of property," Observations, 108. "The subjection of children to their parents is the fountain of all regal authority," p. 12. "And all power on earth is either derived or usurped from the fatherly power, there being no other original to be found of any power whatsoever," Observations, 158. I will not stand here to examine how it can be said without a contradiction, that the first grounds and principles of government necessarily depend upon the original of property, and yet, that there is no other original of any power whatsoever, but that of the father: it being hard to understand how there can be no other original but fatherhood, and yet that the grounds and principles of government depend upon the original of property; property and fatherhood being as far different as lord of a manor and father of children. Nor do I see how they will either of them agree with what our author says, Observations, 244. of God's sentence against Eve, Gen. iii. 16. That it is the original grant of government: so that if that were the original, government had not its original, by our author's own confession, either from property or fatherhood: and this text, which he brings as a proof of Adam's power over Eve, necessarily contradicts what he says of the fatherhood, that it is the sole fountain of all power: for if Adam had any such regal power over Eve, as our author contends for, it must be by some other title than that of begetting.

§. 74. But I leave him to reconcile these contradictions, as well as many others, which may plentifully be found in him by any one, who will but read him with a little attention; and shall come now to consider, how these two originals of government, Adam's natural and private dominion, will consist, and serve to make out and establish the titles of succeeding monarchs, who, as our author obliges them, must all derive their power from these fountains. Let us then suppose Adam made, by God's donation, lord and sole proprietor of the whole earth, in as large and ample a manner as Sir Robert could wish; let us suppose him also, by right of fatherhood, absolute ruler over his children with an unlimited supremacy; I ask then, upon Adam's death what becomes of both his natural and private dominion? and I doubt not it will be answered, that they descended to his next heir, as our author tells us in several places. But this way, it is plain, cannot possibly convey both his natural and private dominion to the same person: for should we allow, that all the property, all the estate of the father, ought to descend to the eldest son, (which will need some proof to establish it) and so he has by that title all the private dominion of the father, yet the father's natural dominion, the paternal power, cannot descend to him by inheritance: for it being a right that accrues to a man only by begetting, no man can have this natural dominion over any one he does not beget; unless it can be supposed, that a man can have a right to any thing, without doing that upon which that right is solely founded: for if a father by begetting, and no other title, has natural dominion over his children, he that does not beget them cannot have this natural dominion over them; and therefore be it true or false, that our author says, Observations, 156. "That every man that is born, by his very birth becomes subject to him that begets him," this necessarily follows, viz. That a man by his birth cannot become a subject to his brother, who did not beget him; unless it can be supposed that a man by the very same title can come to be under the natural and absolute dominion of two different men at once; or it be sense to say, that a man by birth is under the natural dominion of his father, only because he begat him, and a man by birth also is under the natural dominion of his eldest brother, though he did not beget him.

§. 75. If then the private dominion of Adam, i. e. his property in the creatures, descended at his death all entirely to his eldest son, his heir; (for, if it did not, there is presently an end of all Sir Robert's monarchy) and his natural dominion, the dominion a father has over his children by begetting them, belonged immediately, upon Adam's decease, equally to all his sons who had children, by the same title their father had it, the sovereignty founded upon property, and the sovereignty founded upon fatherhood, come to be divided; since Cain, as heir, had that or property alone; Seth, and the other sons, that of fatherhood equally with him. This is the best that can be made of our author's doctrine, and of the two titles of sovereignty he sets up in Adam: one of them will either signify nothing; or, if they both must stand, they can serve only to confound the rights of princes, and disorder government in his posterity: for by building upon two titles to dominion, which cannot descend together, and which he allows may be separated, (for he yields that "Adam's children had their distinct territories by right of private dominion," Observations, 210, p. 40.) he makes it perpetually a doubt upon his principles where the sovereignty is, or to whom we owe our obedience, since fatherhood and property are distinct titles, and began presently upon Adam's death to be in distinct persons. And which then was to give way to the other?

§. 76. Let us take the account of it, as he himself gives it us. He tells us out of Grotius, that "Adam's children by donation, assignation, or some kind of cession before he was dead, had their distinct territories by right of private dominion; Abel had his flocks and pastures for them: Cain had his fields for corn, and the land of Nod, where he built him a city," Observations, 210. Here it is obvious to demand, which of these two after Adam's death was sovereign? Cain, says our author, p. 19. By what title? "As heir; for heirs to progenitors, who were natural parents of their people, are not only lords of their own children, but also of their brethren," says our author, p. 19. What was Cain heir to? Not the entire possessions, not all that which Adam had private dominion in; for our author allows that Abel by a title derived from his father, had his distinct territory for pasture by right of private dominion. What then Abel had by private dominion, was exempt from Cain's dominion: for he could not have private dominion over that which was under the private dominion of another; and therefore his sovereignty over his brother is gone with this private dominion, and so there are presently two sovereigns, and his imaginary title of fatherhood is out of doors, and Cain is no prince over his brother: or else, if Cain retain his sovereignty over Abel, notwithstanding his private dominion, it will follow, that the first grounds and principles of government have nothing to do with property, whatever our author says to the contrary. It is true, Abel did not outlive his father Adam; but that makes nothing to the argument, which will hold good against Sir Robert in Abel's issue, or in Seth, or any of the posterity of Adam, not descended from Cain.

§. 77. The same inconvenience he runs into about the three sons of Noah, who, as he says, p. 13. "had the whole world divided amongst them by their father." I ask then, in which of the three shall we find the establishment of regal power after Noah's death? If in all three, as our author there seems to say; then it will follow, that regal power is founded in property of land, and follows private dominion, and not in paternal power, or natural dominion; and so there is an end of paternal power as the fountain of regal authority, and the so-much-magnified fatherhood quite vanishes. If the regal power descended to Shem as eldest, and heir to his father, then Noah's division of the world by lot, to his sons, or his ten years sailing about the Mediterranean, to appoint each son his part, which our author tells of, p. 15. was labour lost; his division of the world to them, was to ill, or to no purpose: for his grant to Cham and Japhet was little worth, if Shem, notwithstanding this grant, as soon as Noah was dead, was to be lord over them. Or, if this grant of private dominion to them, over their assigned territories, were good, here were set up two distinct sorts of power, not subordinate one to the other, with all those inconveniences which he musters up against the power of the people, Observations, 158. which I shall set down in his own words, only changing property for people. "All power on earth is either derived or usurped from the fatherly power, there being no other original to be found of any power whatsoever: for if there should be granted two sorts of power, without any subordination of one to the other, they would be in perpetual strife which should be supreme, for two supremes cannot agree: if the fatherly power be supreme, then the power grounded on private dominion must be subordinate, and depend on it; and if the power grounded on property be supreme, then the fatherly power must submit to it, and cannot be exercised without the licence of the proprietors, which must quite destroy the frame and course of nature." This is his own arguing against two distinct independent powers, which I have set down in his own words, only putting power rising from property, for power of the people; and when he has answered what he himself has urged here against two distinct powers, we shall be better able to see how, with any tolerable sense, he can derive all regal authority from the natural and private dominion of Adam, from fatherhood and property together, which are distinct titles, that do not always meet in the same person; and it is plain, by his own confession, presently separated as soon both as Adam's and Noah's death made way for succession: though our author frequently in his writings jumbles them together, and omits not to make use of either, where he thinks it will sound best to his purpose. But the absurdities of this will more fully appear in the next chapter, where we shall examine the ways of conveyance of the sovereignty of Adam, to princes that were to reign after him.

Chapter VIII. Of the Conveyance of Adam's Sovereign Monarchical Power

§. 78. SIR ROBERT, not having been very happy in any proof he brings for the sovereignty of Adam, is not much more fortunate in conveying it to future princes, who, if his politics be true, must all derive their titles from that first monarch. The ways he has assigned, as they lie scattered up and down in his writings, I will set down in his own words: in his preface he tells us, That "Adam being monarch of the whole world, none of his posterity had any right to possess any thing, but by his grant or permission, or by succession from him." Here he makes two ways of conveyance of any thing Adam stood possessed of; and those are grants or succession. Again he says, "All kings either are, or are to be reputed, the next heirs to those first progenitors, who were at first the natural parents of the whole people," p. 19. "There cannot be any multitude of men whatsoever, but that in it, considered by itself, there is one man amongst them, that in nature hath a right to be the king of all the rest, as being the next heir to Adam," Observations, 253. Here in these places inheritance is the only way he allows of conveying monarchical power to princes. In other places he tells us, Observations, 155. "All power on earth is either derived or usurped from the fatherly power," Observations, 158. "All kings that now are, or ever were, are or were either fathers of their people, or heirs of such fathers, or usurpers of the right of such fathers," Observations, 253. And here he makes inheritance or usurpation the only ways whereby kings come by this original power: but yet he tells us, "This fatherly empire, as it was of itself hereditary, so it was alienable by patent and seizable by an usurper," Observations, 190. So then here inheritance, grant, or usurpation, will convey it. And last of all, which is most admirable, he tells us, p. 100. "It skills not which way kings come by their power, whether by election, donation, succession, or by any other means; for it is still the manner of the government by supreme power, that makes them properly kings, and not the means of obtaining their crowns." Which I think is a full answer to all his whole hypothesis and discourse about Adam's royal authority, as the fountain from which all princes were to derive theirs: and he might have spared the trouble of speaking so much as he does, up and down, of heirs and inheritance, if to make any one properly a king, needs no more but governing by supreme power, and it matters not by what means he came by it.

§. 79. By this notable way, our author may make Oliver as properly king, as any one else he could think of: and had he had the happiness to live under Massanello's government, he could not by this his own rule have forborn to have done homage to him, with O king live for ever! since the manner of his government by supreme power, made him properly king, who was but the day before properly a fisherman. And if Don Quixote had taught his squire to govern with supreme authority, our author no doubt could have made a most loyal subject in Sancho Pancha's island; and he must needs have deserved some preferment in such governments, since I think he is the first politician, who, pretending to settle government upon its true basis, and to establish the thrones of lawful princes, ever told the world, That he was "properly a king, whose manner of government was by supreme power, by what means soever he obtained it:" which in plain English is to say, that regal and supreme power is properly and truly his, who can by any means seize upon it; and if this be to be properly a king, I wonder how he came to think of, or where he will find, an usurper.

§. 80. This is so strange a doctrine, that the surprise of it hath made me pass by, without their due reflection, the contradictions he runs into, by making sometimes inheritance alone, sometimes only grant or inheritance, sometimes only inheritance or usurpation, sometimes all these three, and at last election, or any other means, added to them, the ways whereby Adam's royal authority, that is, his right to supreme rule, could be conveyed down to future kings and governors, so as to give them a title to the obedience and subjection of the people. But these contradictions lie so open, that the very reading of our author's own words will discover them to any ordinary understanding; and though what I have quoted out of him (with abundance more of the same strain and coherence, which might be found in him) might well excuse me from any farther trouble in this argument, yet having proposed to myself, to examine the main parts of his doctrine, I shall a little more particularly consider how inheritance, grant, usurpation or election, can any way make out government in the world upon his principles; or derive to any one a right of empire from this regal authority of Adam, had it been never so well proved, that he had been absolute monarch, and lord of the whole world.

Chapter IX. Of Monarchy by Inheritance from Adam

§. 81. THOUGH it be never so plain, that there ought to be government in the world, nay, should all men be of our author's mind, that divine appointment had ordained it to be monarchical; yet, since men cannot obey any thing, that cannot command; and ideas of government in the fancy, though never so perfect, though never so right, cannot give laws, nor prescribe rules to the actions of men; it would be of no behoof for the settling of order, and establishment of government in its exercise and use amongst men, unless there were a way also taught how to know the person, to whom it belonged to have this power, and exercise this dominion over others. It is in vain then to talk of subjection and obedience without telling us whom we are to obey: for were I never so fully persuaded that there ought to be magistracy and rule in the world; yet I am never the less at liberty still, till it appears who is the person that hath right to my obedience; since, if there be no marks to know him by, and distinguish him that hath right to rule from other men, it may be myself, as well as any other. And therefore, though submission to government be every one's duty, yet since that signifies nothing but submitting to the direction and laws of such men as have authority to command, it is not enough to make a man a subject, to convince him that there is a regal power in the world; but there must be ways of designing, and knowing the person to whom this regal power of right belongs: and a man can never be obliged in conscience to submit to any power, unless he can be satisfied who is the person who has a right to exercise that power over him. If this were not so, there would be no distinction between pirates and lawful princes; he that has force is without any more ado to be obeyed, and crowns and sceptres would become the inheritance only of violence and rapine. Men too might as often and as innocently change their governors, as they do their physicians, if the person cannot be known who has a right to direct me, and whose prescriptions I am bound to follow. To settle therefore men's consciences, under an obligation to obedience, it is necessary that they know not only, that there is a power somewhere in the world, but the person who by right is vested with this power over them.

§. 82. How successful our author has been in his attempts, to set up a monarchical absolute power in Adam, the reader may judge by what has been already said; but were that absolute monarchy as clear as our author would desire it, as I presume it is the contrary, yet it could be of no use to the government of mankind now in the world, unless he also make out these two things.

First, That this power of Adam was not to end with him, but was upon his decease conveyed entire to some other person, and so on to posterity.

Secondly, That the princes and rulers now on earth are possessed of this power of Adam, by a right way of conveyance derived to them.

§. 83. If the first of these fail, the power of Adam, were it never so great, never so certain, will signify nothing to the present government and societies in the world; but we must seek out some other original of power for the government of politys than this of Adam, or else there will be none at all in the world. If the latter fail, it will destroy the authority of the present governors, and absolve the people from subjection to them, since they, having no better a claim than others to that power, which is alone the fountain of all authority, can have no title to rule over them.

§. 84. Our author, having fancied an absolute sovereignty in Adam, mentions several ways of its conveyance to princes, that were to be his successors; but that which he chiefly insists on, is that of inheritance, which occurs so often in his several discourses; and I having in the foregoing chapter quoted several of these passages, I shall not need here again to repeat them. This sovereignty he erects, as has been said, upon a double foundation, viz. that of property, and that of fatherhood. One was the right he was supposed to have in all creatures, a right to possess the earth with the beasts, and other inferior ranks of things in it, for his private use, exclusive of all other men. The other was the right he was supposed to have, to rule and govern men, all the rest of mankind.

§. 85. In both these rights, there being supposed an exclusion of all other men, it must be upon some reason peculiar to Adam, that they must both be founded.

That of his property our author supposes to arise from God's immediate donation, Gen. i. 28. and that of fatherhood from the act of begetting: now in all inheritance, if the heir succeed not to the reason upon which his father's right was founded, he cannot succeed to the right which followeth from it. For example, Adam had a right of property in the creatures upon the donation and grant of God almighty, who was lord and proprietor of them all: let this be so as our author tells us, yet upon his death his heir can have no title to them, no such right of property in them, unless the same reason, viz. God's donation, vested a right in the heir too: for if Adam could have had no property in, nor use of the creatures, without this positive donation from God, and this donation were only personally to Adam, his heir could have no right by it; but upon his death it must revert to God, the lord and owner again; for positive grants give no title farther than the express words convey it, and by which only it is held. And thus, if as our author himself contends, that donation, Gen. i. 28. were made only to Adam personally, his heir could not succeed to his property in the creatures; and if it were a donation to any but Adam, let it be shewn, that it was to his heir in our author's sense, i. e. to one of his children, exclusive of all the rest.

§. 86. But not to follow our author too far out of the way, the plain of the case is this. God having made man, and planted in him, as in all other animals, a strong desire of self-preservation; and furnished the world with things fit for food and raiment, and other necessaries of life, subservient to his design, that man should live and abide for some time upon the face of the earth, and not that so curious and wonderful a piece of workmanship, by his own negligence, or want of necessaries, should perish again, presently after a few moments continuance; God, I say, having made man and the world thus, spoke to him, (that is) directed him by his senses and reason, as he did the inferior animals by their sense and instinct, which were serviceable for his subsistence, and given him as the means of his preservation. And therefore I doubt not, but before these words were pronounced, Gen. i. 28, 29. (if they must be understood literally to have been spoken) and without any such verbal donation, man had a right to an use of the creatures, by the will and grant of God: for the desire, strong desire of preserving his life and being, having been planted in him as a principle of action by God himself, reason, which was the voice of God in him, could not but teach him and assure him, that pursuing that natural inclination he had to preserve his being, he followed the will of his Maker, and therefore had a right to make use of those creatures, which by his reason or senses he could discover would be serviceable thereunto. And thus man's property in the creatures was founded upon the right he had to make use of those things that were necessary or useful to his being.

§. 87. This being the reason and foundation of Adam's property, gave the same title, on the same ground, to all his children, not only after his death, but in his life-time: so that here was no privilege of his heir above his other children, which could exclude them from an equal right to the use of the inferior creatures, for the comfortable preservation of their beings, which is all the property man hath in them; and so Adam's sovereignty built on property, or, as our author calls it, private dominion, comes to nothing. Every man had a right to the creatures, by the same title Adam had, viz. by the right every one had to take care of, and provide for their subsistence: and thus men had a right in common, Adam's children in common with him. But if any one had began, and made himself a property in any particular thing, (which how he, or any one else, could do, shall be shewn in another place) that thing, that possession, if he disposed not otherwise of it by his positive grant, descended naturally to his children, and they had a right to succeed to it, and possess it.

§. 88. It might reasonably be asked here, how come children by this right of possessing, before any other, the properties of their parents upon their decease? for it being personally the parents, when they die, without actually transferring their right to another, why does it not return again to the common stock of mankind? It will perhaps be answered, that common consent hath disposed of it to their children. Common practice, we see indeed, does so dispose of it; but we cannot say, that it is the common consent of mankind; for that hath never been asked, nor actually given; and if common tacit consent hath established it, it would make but a positive, and not a natural right of children to inherit the goods of their parents: but where the practice is universal, it is reasonable to think the cause is natural. The ground then I think to be this. The first and strongest desire God planted in men, and wrought into the very principles of their nature, being that of self-preservation, that is the foundation of a right to the creatures for the particular support and use of each individual person himself. But, next to this, God planted in men a strong desire also of propagating their kind, and continuing themselves in their posterity; and this gives children a title to share in the property of their parents, and a right to inherit their possessions. Men are not proprietors of what they have, merely for themselves; their children have a title to part of it, and have their kind of right joined with their parents, in the possession which comes to be wholly theirs, when death, having put an end to their parents' use of it, hath taken them from their possessions; and this we call inheritance: men being by a like obligation bound to preserve what they have begotten, as to preserve themselves, their issue come to have a right in the goods they are possessed of. That children have such a right, is plain from the laws of God; and that men are convinced that children have such a right, is evident from the law of the land; both which laws require parents to provide for their children.

§. 89. For children being by the course of nature, born weak, and unable to provide for themselves, they have by the appointment of God himself, who hath thus ordered the course of nature, a right to be nourished and maintained by their parents; nay, a right not only to a bare subsistence, but to the conveniences and comforts of life, as far as the conditions of their parents can afford it. Hence it comes, that when their parents leave the world, and so the care due to their children ceases, the effects of it are to extend as far as possibly they can, and the provisions they have made in their life-time, are understood to be intended, as nature requires they should, for their children, whom, after themselves, they are bound to provide for: though the dying parents, by express words, declare nothing about them, nature appoints the descent of their property to their children, who thus come to have a title, and natural right of inheritance to their fathers' goods, which the rest of mankind cannot pretend to.

§. 90. Were it not for this right of being nourished and maintained by their parents, which God and nature has given to children, and obliged parents to as a duty, it would be reasonable, that the father should inherit the estate of his son, and be preferred in the inheritance before his grandchild: for to the grandfather there is due a long score of care and expences laid out upon the breeding and education of his son, which one would think in justice ought to be paid. But that having been done in obedience to the same law, whereby he received nourishment and education from his own parents; this score of education, received from a man's father, is paid by taking care, and providing for his own children; is paid, I say, as much as is required of payment by alteration of property, unless present necessity of the parents require a return of goods for their necessary support and subsistence: for we are not now speaking of that reverence, acknowledgment, respect and honour, that is always due from children to their parents; but of possessions and commodities of life valuable by money. But though it be incumbent on parents to bring up and provide for their children, yet this debt to their children does not quite cancel the score due to their parents; but only is made by nature preferable to it: for the debt a man owes his father takes place, and gives the father a right to inherit the son's goods, where, for want of issue, the right of children doth not exclude that title. And therefore a man having a right to be maintained by his children, where he needs it; and to enjoy also the comforts of life from them, when the necessary provision due to them and their children will afford it; if his son die without issue, the father has a right in nature to possess his goods, and inherit his estate, (whatever the municipal laws of some countries may absurdly direct otherwise); and so again his children and their issue from him; or, for want of such, his father and his issue. But where no such are to be found, i. e. no kindred, there we see the possessions of a private man revert to the community, and so in politic societies come into the hands of the public magistrate; but in the state of nature become again perfectly common, nobody having a right to inherit them: nor can any one have a property in them, otherwise than in other things common by nature; of which I shall speak in its due place.

§. 91. I have been the larger, in shewing upon what ground children have a right to succeed to the possession of their fathers' properties, not only because by it, it will appear, that if Adam had a property (a titular, insignificant, useless property; for it could be no better, for he was bound to nourish and maintain his children and posterity out of it) in the whole earth and its product, yet all his children coming to have, by the law of nature, and right of inheritance, a joint title, and right of property in it after his death, it could convey no right of sovereignty to any one of his posterity over the rest: since every one having a right of inheritance to his portion, they might enjoy their inheritance, or any part of it in common, or share it, or some parts of it, by division, as it best liked them. But no one could pretend to the whole inheritance, or any sovereignty supposed to accompany it; since a right of inheritance gave every one of the rest, as well as any one, a title to share in the goods of his father. Not only upon this account, I say, have I been so particular in examining the reason of children's inheriting the property of their fathers, but also because it will give us farther light in the inheritance of rule and power, which in countries where their particular municipal laws give the whole possession of land entirely to the first-born, and descent of power has gone so to men by this custom, some have been apt to be deceived into an opinion, that there was a natural or divine right of primogeniture, to both estate and power; and that the inheritance of both rule over men, and property in things, sprang from the same original, and were to descend by the same rules.

§. 92. Property, whose original is from the right a man has to use any of the inferior creatures, for the subsistence and comfort of his life, is for the benefit and sole advantage of the proprietor, so that he may even destroy the thing, that he has property in by his use of it, where need requires: but government being for the preservation of every man's right and property, by preserving him from the violence or injury of others, is for the good of the governed: for the magistrate's sword being for a terror to evil doers, and by that terror to inforce men to observe the positive laws of the society, made conformable to the laws of nature, for the public good, i. e. the good of every particular member of that society, as far as by common rules it can be provided for; the sword is not given the magistrate for his own good alone.

§. 93. Children therefore, as has been shewed, by the dependance they have on their parents for subsistence, have a right of inheritance to their fathers property, as that which belongs to them for their proper good and behoof, and therefore are fitly termed goods, wherein the first-born has not a sole or peculiar right by any law of God and nature, the younger children having an equal title with him, founded on that right they all have to maintenance, support, and comfort from their parents, and on nothing else. But government being for the benefit of the governed, and not the sole advantage of the governors, (but only for their's with the rest, as they make a part of that politic body, each of whose parts and members are taken care of, and directed in its peculiar functions for the good of the whole, by the laws of society) cannot be inherited by the same title, that children have to the goods of their father. The right a son has to be maintained and provided with the necessaries and conveniences of life out of his father's stock, gives him a right to succeed to his father's property for his own good; but this can give him no right to succeed also to the rule, which his father had over other men. All that a child has right to claim from his father is nourishment and education, and the things nature furnishes for the support of life: but he has no right to demand rule or dominion from him: he can subsist and receive from him the portion of good things, and advantages of education naturally due to him, without empire and dominion. That (if his father hath any) was vested in him, for the good and behoof of others: and therefore the son cannot claim or inherit it by a title, which is founded wholly on his own private good and advantage.

§. 94. We must know how the first ruler, from whom any one claims, came by his authority, upon what ground any one has empire, what his title is to it, before we can know who has a right to succeed him in it, and inherit it from him: if the agreement and consent of men first gave a sceptre into any one's hand, or put a crown on his head, that also must direct its descent and conveyance; for the same authority, that made the first a lawful ruler, must make the second too, and so give right of succession: in this case inheritance, or primogeniture, can in itself have no pretence to it, any farther than that consent, which established the form of the government, hath so settled the succession. And thus we see, the succession of crowns, in several countries, places it on different heads, and he comes by right of succession to be a prince in one place, who would be a subject in another.

§. 95. If God, by his positive grant and revealed declaration, first gave rule and dominion to any man, he that will claim by that title, must have the same positive grant of God for his succession: for if that has not directed the course of its descent and conveyance down to others, nobody can succeed to this title of the first ruler. Children have no right of inheritance in this; and primogeniture can lay no claim to it, unless God, the author of this constitution, hath so ordained it. Thus we see, the pretensions of Saul's family, who received his crown from the immediate appointment of God, ended with his reign; and David, by the same title that Saul reigned, viz. God's appointment, succeeded in his throne, to the exclusion of Jonathan, and all pretensions of paternal inheritance: and if Solomon had a right to succeed his father, it must be by some other title, than that of primogeniture. A cadet, or sister's son, must have the preference in succession, if he has the same title the first lawful prince had: and in dominion that has its foundation only in the positive appointment of God himself, Benjamin, the youngest, must have the inheritance of the crown, if God so direct, as well as one of that tribe had the first possession.

§. 96. If paternal right, the act of begetting, give a man rule and dominion, inheritance or primogeniture can give no title: for he that cannot succeed to his father's title, which was begetting, cannot succeed to that power over his brethren, which his father had by paternal right over them. But of this I shall have occasion to say more in another place. This is plain in the mean time, that any government, whether supposed to be at first founded in paternal right, consent of the people, or the positive appointment of God himself, which can supersede either of the other, and so begin a new government upon a new foundation; I say, any government began upon either of these, can by right of succession come to those only, who have the title of him they succeed to: power founded on contract can descend only to him, who has right by that contract: power founded on begetting, he only can have that begets; and power founded on the positive grant or donation of God, he only can have by right of succession, to whom that grant directs it.

§. 97. From what I have said, I think this is clear, that a right to the use of the creatures, being founded originally in the right a man has to subsist and enjoy the conveniences of life; and the natural right children have to inherit the goods of their parents, being founded in the right they have to the same subsistence and commodities of life, out of the stock of their parents, who are therefore taught by natural love and tenderness to provide for them, as a part of themselves; and all this being only for the good of the proprietor, or heir; it can be no reason for children's inheriting of rule and dominion, which has another original and a different end. Nor can primogeniture have any pretence to a right of solely inheriting either property or power, as we shall, in its due place, see more fully. It is enough to have shewed here, that Adam's property, or private dominion, could not convey any sovereignty or rule to his heir, who not having a right to inherit all his father's possessions, could not thereby come to have any sovereignty over his brethren: and therefore, if any sovereignty on account of his property had been vested in Adam, which in truth there was not, yet it would have died with him.

§. 98. As Adam's sovereignty, if, by virtue of being proprietor of the world, he had any authority over men, could not have been inherited by any of his children over the rest, because they had the same title to divide the inheritance, and every one had a right to a portion of his father's possessions; so neither could Adam's sovereignty by right of fatherhood, if any such he had, descend to any one of his children: for it being, in our author's account, a right acquired by begetting to rule over those he had begotten, it was not a power possible to be inherited, because the right being consequent to, and built on, an act perfectly personal, made that power so too, and impossible to be inherited: for paternal power, being a natural right rising only from the relation of father and son, is as impossible to be inherited as the relation itself; and a man may pretend as well to inherit the conjugal power the husband, whose heir he is, had over his wife, as he can to inherit the paternal power of a father over his children: for the power of the husband being founded on contract, and the power of the father on begetting, he may as well inherit the power obtained by the conjugal contract, which was only personal, as he may the power obtained by begetting, which could reach no farther than the person of the begetter, unless begetting can be a title to power in him that does not beget.

§. 99. Which makes it a reasonable question to ask, whether Adam, dying before Eve, his heir, (suppose Cain or Seth) should have by right of inheriting Adam's fatherhood, sovereign power over Eve his mother: for Adam's fatherhood being nothing but a right he had to govern his children, because he begot them, he that inherits Adam's fatherhood, inherits nothing, even in our author's sense, but the right Adam had to govern his children, because he begot them: so that the monarchy of the heir would not have taken in Eve; or if it did, it being nothing but the fatherhood of Adam descended by inheritance, the heir must have right to govern Eve, because Adam begot her; for fatherhood is nothing else.

§. 100. Perhaps it will be said with our author, that a man can alien his power over his child; and what may be transferred by compact, may be possessed by inheritance. I answer, a father cannot alien the power he has over his child: he may perhaps to some degrees forfeit it, but cannot transfer it; and if any other man acquire it, it is not by the father's grant, but by some act of his own. For example, a father, unnaturally careless of his child, sells or gives him to another man; and he again exposes him, a third man finding him, breeds up, cherishes, and provides for him as his own: I think in this case, nobody will doubt, but that the greatest part of filial duty and subjection was here owing, and to be paid to this foster-father; and if any thing could be demanded from the child, by either of the other, it could be only be due to his natural father, who perhaps might have forfeited his right to much of that duty comprehended in the command, Honour your parents, but could transfer none of it to another. He that purchased, and neglected the child, got by his purchase and grant of the father, no title to duty or honour from the child; but only he acquired it, who by his own authority, performing the office and care of a father, to the forlorn and perishing infant, made himself, by paternal care, a title to proportionable degrees of paternal power. This will be more easily admitted upon consideration of the nature of paternal power, for which I refer my reader to the second book.

§. 101. To return to the argument in hand; this is evident, That paternal power arising only from begetting, for in that our author places it alone, can neither be transferred nor inherited: and he that does not beget, can no more have paternal power, which arises from thence, than he can have a right to any thing, who performs not the condition, to which only it is annexed. If one should ask, by what law has a father power over his children? it will be answered, no doubt, by the law of nature, which gives such a power over them, to him that begets them. If one should ask likewise, by what law does our author's heir come by a right to inherit? I think it would be answered, by the law of nature too: for I find not that our author brings one word of scripture to prove the right of such an heir he speaks of. Why then the law of nature gives fathers paternal power over their children, because they did beget them; and the same law of nature gives the same paternal power to the heir over his brethren, who did not beget them: whence it follows, that either the father has not his paternal power by begetting, or else that the heir has it not at all; for it is hard to understand how the law of nature, which is the law of reason, can give the paternal power to the father over his children, for the only reason of begetting; and to the first-born over his brethren without this only reason, i. e. for no reason at all: and if the eldest, by the law of nature, can inherit this paternal power, without the only reason that gives a title to it, so may the youngest as well as he, and a stranger as well as either; for where there is no reason for any one, as there is not, but for him that begets, all have an equal title. I am sure our author offers no reason; and when any body does, we shall see whether it will hold or no.

§. 102. In the mean time it is as good sense to say, that by the law of nature a man has right to inherit the property of another, because he is of kin to him, and is known to be of his blood; and therefore, by the same law of nature, an utter stranger to his blood has right to inherit his estate; as to say that, by the law of nature, he that begets them has paternal power over his children, and therefore, by the law of nature, the heir that begets them not, has this paternal power over them; or supposing the law of the land gave absolute power over their children, to such only who nursed them, and fed their children themselves, could any body pretend, that this law gave any one, who did no such thing, absolute power over those, who were not his children?

§. 103. When therefore it can be shewed, that conjugal power can belong to him that is not an husband, it will also I believe be proved, that our author's paternal power, acquired by begetting, may be inherited by a son; and that a brother, as heir to his father's power, may have paternal power, over his brethren, and by the same rule conjugal power too: but till then, I think we may rest satisfied, that the paternal power of Adam, this sovereign authority of fatherhood, were there any such, could not descend to, nor be inherited by, his next heir. Fatherly power, I easily grant our author, if it will do him any good, can never be lost, because it will be as long in the world as there are fathers: but none of them will have Adam's paternal power, or derive their's from him; but every one will have his own, by the same title Adam had his, viz. by begetting, but not by inheritance, or succession, no more than husbands have their conjugal power by inheritance from Adam. And thus we see, as Adam had no such property, no such paternal power, as gave him sovereign jurisdiction over mankind; so likewise his sovereignty built upon either of these titles, if he had any such, could not have descended to his heir, but must have ended with him. Adam therefore, as has been proved, being neither monarch, nor his imaginary monarchy hereditable, the power which is now in the world, is not that which was Adam's, since all that Adam could have upon our author's grounds, either of property or fatherhood, necessarily died with him, and could not be conveyed to posterity by inheritance. In the next place we will consider, whether Adam had any such heir, to inherit his power, as our author talks of.

Chapter X. Of the Heir to Adam's Monarchical Power

§. 104. OUR author tells us, Observations, 253. "That it is a truth undeniable, that there cannot be any multitude of men whatsoever, either great or small, though gathered together from the several corners and remotest regions of the world, but that in the same multitude, considered by itself, there is one man amongst them, that in nature hath a right to be king of all the rest, as being the next heir to Adam: every man by nature is a king or a subject." And again, p. 20. "If Adam himself were still living, and now ready to die, it is certain that there is one man, and but one in the world, who is next heir." Let this multitude of men be, if our author pleases, all the princes upon the earth, there will then be, by our author's rule, one amongst them, that in nature hath a right to be king of all the rest, as being the right heir to Adam; an excellent way to establish the thrones of princes, and settle the obedience of their subjects, by setting up an hundred, or perhaps a thousand titles (if there be so many princes in the world) against any king now reigning, each as good, upon our author's grounds, as his who wears the crown. If this right of heir carry any weight with it, if it be the ordinance of God, as our author seems to tells us, Observations, 244. must not all be subject to it, from the highest to the lowest? Can those who wear the name of princes, without having the right of being heirs to Adam, demand obedience from their subjects by this title, and not be bound to pay it by the same law? Either governments in the world are not to be claimed, and held by this title of Adam's heir; and then the starting of it is to no purpose, the being or not being Adam's heir, signifies nothing as to the title of dominion: or if it really be, as our author says, the true title to government and sovereignty, the first thing to be done, is to find out this true heir of Adam, seat him in his throne, and then all the kings and princes of the world ought to come and resign up their crowns and sceptres to him, as things that belong no more to them, than to any of their subjects.

§. 105. For either this right in nature, of Adam's heir, to be king over all the race of men, (for all together they make one multitude) is a right not necessary to the making of a lawful king, and so there may be lawful kings without it, and then kings' titles and power depend not on it; or else all the kings in the world but one are not lawful kings, and so have no right to obedience: either this title of heir to Adam is that whereby kings hold their crowns, and have a right to subjection from their subjects, and then one only can have it, and the rest being subjects can require no obedience from other men, who are but their fellow-subjects; or else it is not the title whereby kings rule, and have a right to obedience from their subjects, and then kings are kings without it, and this dream of the natural sovereignty of Adam's heir is of no use to obedience and government: for if kings have a right to dominion, and the obedience of their subjects, who are not, nor can possibly be, heirs to Adam, what use is there of such a title, when we are obliged to obey without it? If kings, who are not heirs to Adam, have no right to sovereignty, we are all free, till our author, or any body for him, will shew us Adam's right heir. If there be but one heir of Adam, there can be but one lawful king in the world, and nobody in conscience can be obliged to obedience till it be resolved who that is; for it may be any one, who is not known to be of a younger house, and all others have equal titles. If there be more than one heir of Adam, every one is his heir, and so every one has regal power: for if two sons can be heirs together, then all the sons are equally heirs, and so all are heirs, being all sons, or sons' sons of Adam. Betwixt these two the right of heir cannot stand; for by it either but one only man, or all men are kings. Take which you please, it dissolves the bonds of government and obedience; since, if all men are heirs, they can owe obedience to nobody; if only one, nobody can be obliged to pay obedience to him, till he be known, and his title made out.

Chapter XI. Who Heir?

§. 106. THE GREAT question which in all ages has disturbed mankind, and brought on them the greatest part of those mischiefs which have ruined cities, depopulated countries, and disordered the peace of the world, has been, not whether there be power in the world, nor whence it came, but who should have it. The settling of this point being of no smaller moment than the security of princes, and the peace and welfare of their estates and kingdoms, a reformer of politics, one would think, should lay this sure, and be very clear in it: for if this remain disputable, all the rest will be to very little purpose; and the skill used in dressing up power with all the splendor and temptation absoluteness can add to it, without shewing who has a right to have it, will serve only to give a greater edge to man's natural ambition, which of itself is but too keen. What can this do but set men on the more eagerly to scramble, and so lay a sure and lasting foundation of endless contention and disorder, instead of that peace and tranquillity, which is the business of government, and the end of human society?

§. 107. This designation of the person our author is more than ordinary obliged to take care of, because he, affirming that the assignment of civil power is by divine institution, hath made the conveyance as well as the power itself sacred: so that no consideration, no act or art of man, can divert it from that person, to whom, by this divine right, it is assigned; no necessity or contrivance can substitute another person in his room: for if the assignment of civil power be by divine institution, and Adam's heir be he to whom it is thus assigned, as in the foregoing chapter our author tells us, it would be as much sacrilege for any one to be king, who was not Adam's heir, as it would have been amongst the Jews, for any one to have been priest, who had not been of Aaron's posterity: for not only the priesthood in general being by divine institution, but the assignment of it to the sole line and posterity of Aaron, made it impossible to be enjoyed or exercised by any one, but those persons who were the offspring of Aaron: whose succession therefore was carefully observed, and by that the persons who had a right to the priesthood certainly known.

§. 108. Let us see then what care our author has taken, to make us know who is this heir, who by divine institution has a right to be king over all men. The first account of him we meet with is, p. 12. in these words: "This subjection of children, being the fountain of all regal authority, by the ordination of God himself; it follows, that civil power, not only in general, is by divine institution, but even the assignment of it, specifically to the eldest parents." Matters of such consequence as this is, should be in plain words, as little liable, as might be, to doubt or equivocation; and I think, if language be capable of expressing any thing distinctly and clearly, that of kindred, and the several degrees of nearness of blood, is one. It were therefore to be wished, that our author had used a little more intelligible expressions here, that we might have better known who it is, to whom the assignment of civil power is made by divine institution; or at least would have told us what he meant by eldest parents: for I believe, if land had been assigned or granted to him, and the eldest parents of his family, he would have thought it had needed an interpreter; and it would scarce have been known to whom next it belonged.

§. 109. In propriety of speech, (and certainly propriety of speech is necessary in a discourse of this nature) eldest parents signifies either the eldest men and women that have had children, or those who have longest had issue; and then our author's assertion will be, that those fathers and mothers, who have been longest in the world, or longest fruitful, have by divine institution a right to civil power. If there be any absurdity in this, our author must answer for it: and if his meaning be different from my explication, he is to be blamed, that he would not speak it plainly. This I am sure, parents cannot signify heirs male, nor eldest parents an infant child: who yet may sometimes be the true heir, if there can be but one. And we are hereby still as much at a loss, who civil power belongs to, notwithstanding this assignment by divine institution, as if there had been no such assignment at all, or our author had said nothing of it. This of eldest parents leaving us more in the dark, who by divine institution has a right to civil power, than those who never heard any thing at all of heir, or descent, of which our author is so full. And though the chief matter of his writing be to teach obedience to those, who have a right to it, which he tells us is conveyed by descent, yet who those are, to whom this right by descent belongs, he leaves, like the philosopher's stone in politics, out of the reach of any one to discover from his writings.

§. 110. This obscurity cannot be imputed to want of language in so great a master of style as Sir Robert is, when he is resolved with himself what he would say: and therefore, I fear, finding how hard it would be to settle rules of descent by institution, and how little it would be to his purpose, or conduce to the clearing and establishing the titles of princes, if such rules of descent were settled, he chose rather to content himself with doubtful and general terms, which might make no ill sound in men's ears, who were willing to be pleased with them, rather than offer any clear rules of descent of this fatherhood of Adam, by which men's consciences might be satisfied to whom it descended, and know the persons who had a right to regal power, and with it to their obedience.

§. 111. How else is it possible, that laying so much stress, as he does, upon descent, and Adam's heir, next heir, true heir, he should never tell us what heir means, nor the way to know who the next or true heir is? This, I do not remember, he does any where expressly handle; but, where it comes in his way, very warily and doubtfully touches; though it be so necessary, that without it all discourses of government and obedience upon his principles would be to no purpose, and fatherly power, never so well made out, will be of no use to any body. Hence he tells us, Observations, 244. "That not only the constitution of power in general, but the limitation of it to one kind, (i. e.) monarchy, and the determination of it to the individual person and line of Adam, are all three ordinances of God; neither Eve nor her children could either limit Adam's power, or join others with him; and what was given unto Adam was given in his person to his posterity." Here again our author informs us, that the divine ordinance hath limited the descent of Adam's monarchical power. To whom? To Adam's line and posterity, says our author. A notable limitation, a limitation to all mankind: for if our author can find any one amongst mankind, that is not of the line and posterity of Adam, he may perhaps tell him, who this next heir of Adam is: but for us, I despair how this limitation of Adam's empire to his line and posterity will help us to find out one heir. This limitation indeed of our author will save those the labour, who would look for him amongst the race of brutes, if any such there were; but will very little contribute to the discovery of one next heir amongst men, though it make a short and easy determination of the question about the descent of Adam's regal power, by telling us, that the line and posterity of Adam is to have it, that is, in plain English, any one may have it, since there is no person living that hath not the title of being of the line and posterity of Adam; and while it keeps there, it keeps within our author's limitation by God's ordinance. Indeed, p. 19. he tells us, that "such heirs are not only lords of their own children, but of their brethren;" whereby, and by the words following, which we shall consider anon, he seems to insinuate, that the eldest son is heir; but he no where, that I know, says it in direct words, but by the instances of Cain and Jacob, that there follow, we may allow this to be so far his opinion concerning heirs, that where there are divers children, the eldest son has the right to be heir. That primogeniture cannot give any title to paternal power, we have already shewed. That a father may have a natural right to some kind of power over his children, is easily granted; but that an elder brother has so over his brethren, remains to be proved: God or nature has not any where, that I know, placed such jurisdiction in the first-born; nor can reason find any such natural superiority amongst brethren. The law of Moses gave a double portion of the goods and possessions to the eldest; but we find not any where that naturally, or by God's institution, superiority or dominion belonged to him, and the instances there brought by our author are but slender proofs of a right to civil power and dominion in the first-born, and do rather shew the contrary.

§. 112. His words are in the forecited place: "And therefore we find God told Cain of his brother Abel: his desire shall be subject unto thee, and thou shalt rule over him." To which I answer,

1. These words of God to Cain, are by many interpreters, with great reason, understood in a quite different sense than what our author uses them in.

2. Whatever was meant by them, it could not be, that Cain, as elder, had a natural dominion over Abel; for the words are conditional, If thou dost well: and so personal to Cain: and whatever was signified by them, did depend on his carriage, and not follow his birth-right; and therefore could by no means be an establishment of dominion in the first-born in general: for before this Abel had his distinct territories by right of private dominion, as our author himself confesses, Observations, 210. which he could not have had to the prejudice of the heir's title, if by divine institution, Cain as heir were to inherit all his father's dominion.

3. If this were intended by God as the charter of primogeniture, and the grant of dominion to elder brothers in general as such, by right of inheritance, we might expect it should have included all his brethren: for we may well suppose, Adam, from whom the world was to be peopled, had by this time, that these were grown up to be men, more sons than these two: whereas Abel himself is not so much as named; and the words in the original can scarce, with any good construction, be applied to him.

4. It is too much to build a doctrine of so mighty consequence upon so doubtful and obscure a place of scripture, which may be well, nay better, understood in a quite different sense, and so can be but an ill proof, being as doubtful as the thing to be proved by it; especially when there is nothing else in scripture or reason to be found, that favours or supports it.

§. 113. It follows, p. 19. "Accordingly when Jacob bought his brother's birth-right, Isaac blessed him thus; Be lord over thy brethren, and let the sons of thy mother bow before thee." Another instance, I take it, brought by our author to evince dominion due to birth-right, and an admirable one it is: for it must be no ordinary way of reasoning in a man, that is pleading for the natural power of kings, and against all compact, to bring for proof of it, an example, where his own account of it founds all the right upon compact, and settles empire in the younger brother, unless buying and selling be no compact; for he tells us, when Jacob bought his brother's birth-right. But passing by that, let us consider the history itself, what use our author makes of it, and we shall find these following mistakes about it.

1. That our author reports this, as if Isaac had given Jacob this blessing, immediately upon his purchasing the birth-right; for he says, when Jacob bought, Isaac blessed him; which is plainly otherwise in the scripture: for it appears, there was a distance of time between, and if we will take the story in the order it lies, it must be no small distance; all Isaac's sojourning in Gerar, and transactions with Abimelech, Gen. xxvi. coming between; Rebecca being then beautiful, and consequently young; but Isaac, when he blessed Jacob, was old and decrepit: and Esau also complains of Jacob, Gen. xxvii. 36. that two times he had supplanted him; He took away my birth-right, says he, and behold now he hath taken away my blessing; words that, I think, signify distance of time and difference of action.

2. Another mistake of our author's is, that he supposes Isaac gave Jacob the blessing, and bid him be lord over his brethren, because he had the birth-right; for our author brings this example to prove, that he that has the birth-right, has thereby a right to be lord over his brethren. But it is also manifest by the text, that Isaac had no consideration of Jacob's having bought the birth-right; for when he blessed him, he considered him not as Jacob, but took him for Esau. Nor did Esau understand any such connexion between birth-right and the blessing; for he says, He hath supplanted me these two times; he took away my birth-right, and behold now he hath taken away my blessing: whereas had the blessing, which was to be lord over his brethren, belonged to the birth-right, Esau could not have complained of this second, as a cheat, Jacob having got nothing but what Esau had sold him, when he sold him his birth-right; so that it is plain, dominion, if these words signify it, was not understood to belong to the birth-right.

§. 114. And that in those days of the patriarchs, dominion was not understood to be the right of the heir, but only a greater portion of goods, is plain from Gen. xxi. 10. for Sarah, taking Isaac to be heir, says, "Cast out this bondwoman and her son, for the son of this bondwoman shall not be heir with my son:" whereby could be meant nothing, but that he should not have a pretence to an equal share of his father's estate after his death, but should have his portion presently, and be gone. Accordingly we read, Gen. xxv. 5, 6. "That Abraham gave all that he had unto Isaac, but unto the sons of the concubines which Abraham had, Abraham gave gifts, and sent them away from Isaac his son, while he yet lived." That is, Abraham having given portions to all his other sons, and sent them away, that which he had reserved, being the greatest part of his substance, Isaac as heir possessed after his death: but by being heir, he had no right to be lord over his brethren; for if he had, why should Sarah endeavour to rob him of one of his subjects, or lessen the number of his slaves, by desiring to have Ishmael sent away?

§. 115. Thus, as under the law, the privilege of birth-right was nothing but a double portion: so we see that before Moses, in the patriarchs' time, from whence our author pretends to take his model, there was no knowledge, no thought, that birth-right gave rule or empire, paternal or kingly authority, to any one over his brethren. If this be not plain enough in the story of Isaac and Ishmael, he that will look into 1 Chron. v. 12. may read these words: "Reuben was the first-born; but forasmuch as he defiled his father's bed, his birth-right was given unto the sons of Joseph, the son of Israel: and the genealogy is not to be reckoned after the birth-right; for Judah prevailed above his brethren, and of him came the chief ruler; but the birth-right was Joseph's." What this birth-right was, Jacob blessing Joseph, Gen. xlviii. 22. telleth us in these words, "Moreover I have given thee one portion above thy brethren, which I took out of the hand of the Amorite, with my sword and with my bow." Whereby it is not only plain, that the birth-right was nothing but a double portion; but the text in Chronicles is express against our author's doctrine, and shews that dominion was no part of the birth-right; for it tells us, that

Joseph had the birth-right, but Judah the dominion. One would think our author were very fond of the very name of birth-right, when he brings this instance of Jacob and Esau, to prove that dominion belongs to the heir over his brethren.

§. 116. 1. Because it will be but an ill example to prove, that dominion by God's ordination belonged to the eldest son, because Jacob the youngest here had it, let him come by it how he would: for if it prove any thing, it can only prove, against our author, that the assignment of dominion to the eldest is not by divine institution, which would then be unalterable: for if by the law of God, or nature, absolute power and empire belongs to the eldest son and his heirs, so that they are supreme monarchs, and all the rest of their brethren slaves, our author gives us reason to doubt whether the eldest son has a power to part with it, to the prejudice of his posterity, since he tells us, Observations, 158. "That in grants and gifts that have their original from God or nature, no inferior power of man can limit or make any law of prescription against them."

§. 117. 2. Because this place, Gen. xxvii. 29. brought by our author, concerns not at all the dominion of one brother over the other, nor the subjection of Esau to Jacob: for it is plain in the history, that Esau was never subject to Jacob, but lived apart in mount Seir, where he founded a distinct people and government, and was himself prince over them, as much as Jacob was in his own family. This text, if considered, can never be understood of Esau himself, or the personal dominion of Jacob over him: for the words brethren and sons of thy mother, could not be used literally by Isaac, who knew Jacob had only one brother; and these words are so far from being true in a literal sense, or establishing any dominion in Jacob over Esau, that in the story we find the quite contrary, for Gen. xxxii. Jacob several times calls Esau lord, and himself his servant; and Gen. xxxiii. he bowed himself seven times to the ground to Esau. Whether Esau then were a subject and vassal (nay, as our author tells us, all subjects are slaves) to Jacob, and Jacob his sovereign prince by birth-right, I leave the reader to judge; and to believe if he can, that these words of Isaac, "Be lord over thy brethren, and let thy mother's sons bow down to thee," confirmed Jacob in a sovereignty over Esau, upon the account of the birth-right he had got from him.

§. 118. He that reads the story of Jacob and Esau, will find there was never any jurisdiction or authority, that either of them had over the other after their father's death: they lived with the friendship and equality of brethren, neither lord, neither slave to his brother; but independent each of other, were both heads of their distinct families, where they received no laws from one another, but lived separately, and were the roots out of which sprang two distinct people under two distinct governments. This blessing then of Isaac, whereon our author would build the dominion of the elder brother, signifies no more, but what Rebecca had been told from God, Gen. xxv. 23. "Two nations are in thy womb, and two manner of people shall be separated from thy bowels, and the one people shall be stronger than the other people, and the elder shall serve the younger; and so Jacob blessed Judah," Gen. xlix. and gave him the sceptre and dominion, from whence our author might have argued as well, that jurisdiction and dominion belongs to the third son over his brethren, as well as from this blessing of Isaac, that it belonged to Jacob: both these places contain only predictions of what should long after happen to their posterities, and not any declaration of the right of inheritance to dominion in either. And thus we have our author's two great and only arguments to prove, that heirs are lords over their brethren.

1. Because God tells Cain, Gen. iv. that however sin might set upon him, he ought or might be master of it: for the most learned interpreters understood the words of sin, and not of Abel, and give so strong reasons for it, that nothing can convincingly be inferred from so doubtful a text, to our author's purpose.

2. Because in this of Gen. xxvii. Isaac foretels that the Israelites, the posterity of Jacob, should have dominion over the Edomites, the posterity of Esau; therefore says our author, heirs are lords of their brethren: I leave any one to judge of the conclusion.

§. 119. And now we see how our author has provided for the descending, and conveyance down of Adam's monarchical power, or paternal dominion to posterity, by the inheritance of his heir, succeeding to all his father's authority, and becoming upon his death as much lord as his father was, not only over his own children, but over his brethren, and all descended from his father, and so in infinitum. But yet who this heir is, he does not once tell us; and all the light we have from him in this so fundamental a point, is only, that in his instance of Jacob, by using the word birth-right, as that which passed from Esau to Jacob, he leaves us to guess, that by heir, he means the eldest son; though I do not remember he any where mentions expressly the title of the first-born, but all along keeps himself under the shelter of the indefinite term heir. But taking it to be his meaning, that the eldest son is heir, (for if the eldest be not, there will be no pretence why the sons should not be all heirs alike) and so by right of primogeniture has dominion over his brethren; this is but one step towards the settlement of succession, and the difficulties remain still as much as ever, till he can shew us who is meant by right heir, in all those cases which may happen where the present possessor hath no son. This he silently passes over, and perhaps wisely too: for what can be wiser, after one has affirmed, that "the person having that power, as well as the power and form of government, is the ordinance of God, and by divine institution," vid. Observations, 254. p. 12. than to be careful, not to start any question concerning the person, the resolution whereof will certainly lead him into a confession, that God and nature hath determined nothing about him? And if our author cannot shew who by right of nature, or a clear positive law of God, has the next right to inherit the dominion of this natural monarch he has been at such pains about, when he died without a son, he might have spared his pains in all the rest, it being more necessary for the settling men's consciences, and determining their subjection and allegiance, to shew them who by original right, superior and antecedent to the will, or any act of men, hath a title to this paternal jurisdiction, than it is to shew that by nature there was such a jurisdiction; it being to no purpose for me to know there is such a paternal power, which I ought, and am disposed to obey, unless, where there are many pretenders, I also know the person that is rightfully invested and endowed with it.

§. 120. For the main matter in question being concerning the duty of my obedience, and the obligation of conscience I am under to pay it to him that is of right my lord and ruler, I must know the person that this right of paternal power resides in, and so impowers him to claim obedience from me: for let it be true what he says, p. 12. "That civil power not only in general is by divine institution, but even the assignment of it specially to the eldest parents;" and Observations, 254. "That not only the power, or right of government, but the form of the power of governing, and the person having that power, are all the ordinance of God;" yet unless he shew us in all cases, who is this person ordained by God, who is this eldest parent; all his abstract notions of monarchical power will signify just nothing, when they are to be reduced to practice, and men are conscientiously to pay their obedience: for paternal jurisdiction being not the thing to be obeyed, because it cannot command, but is only that which gives one man a right which another hath not, and if it come by inheritance, another man cannot have, to command and be obeyed; it is ridiculous to say, I pay obedience to the paternal power, when I obey him, to whom paternal power gives no right to my obedience: for he can have no divine right to my obedience, who cannot shew his divine right to the power of ruling over me, as well as that by divine right there is such a power in the world.

§. 121. And hence not being able to make out any prince's title to government, as heir to

Adam, which therefore is of no use, and had been better let alone, he is fain to resolve all into present possession, and makes civil obedience as due to an usurper, as to a lawful king; and thereby the usurper's title as good. His words are, Observations, 253. and they deserve to be remembered: "If an usurper dispossess the true heir, the subject's obedience to the fatherly power must go along, and wait upon God's providence." But I shall leave his title of usurpers to be examined in its due place, and desire my sober reader to consider what thanks princes owe such politics as this, which can suppose paternal power (i. e.) a right to government in the hands of a Cade, or a Cromwell; and so all obedience being due to paternal power, the obedience of subjects will be due to them, by the same right, and upon as good grounds, as it is to lawful princes; and yet this, as dangerous a doctrine as it is, must necessarily follow from making all political power to be nothing else, but Adam's paternal power by right and divine institution, descending from him without being able to shew to whom it descended, or who is heir to it.

§. 122. To settle government in the world, and to lay obligations to obedience on any man's conscience, it is necessary (supposing with our author that all power be nothing but the being possessed of Adam's fatherhood) to satisfy him, who has a right to this power, this fatherhood, when the possessor dies without sons to succeed immediately to it, as it was to tell him, that upon the death of the father, the eldest son had a right to it: for it is still to be remembered, that the great question is, (and that which our author would be thought to contend for, if he did not sometimes forget it) what persons have a right to be obeyed, and not whether there be a power in the world, which is to be called paternal, without knowing in whom it resides: for so it be a power, i. e. right to govern, it matters not, whether it be termed paternal or regal, natural or acquired; whether you call it supreme fatherhood, or supreme brotherhood, will be all one, provided we know who has it.

§. 123. I go on then to ask, whether in the inheriting of this paternal power, this supreme fatherhood, the grandson by a daughter hath a right before a nephew by a brother? Whether the grandson by the eldest son, being an infant, before the younger son, a man and able? Whether the daughter before the uncle? or any other man, descended by a male line? Whether a grandson by a younger daughter, before a grand-daughter by an elder daughter? Whether the elder son by a concubine, before a younger son by a wife? From whence also will arise many questions of legitimation, and what in nature is the difference betwixt a wife and a concubine? for as to the municipal or positive laws of men, they can signify nothing here. It may farther be asked, Whether the eldest son, being a fool, shall inherit this paternal power, before the younger, a wise man? and what degree of folly it must be that shall exclude him? and who shall be judge of it? Whether the son of a fool, excluded for his folly, before the son of his wise brother who reigned? Who has the paternal power whilst the widow-queen is with child by the deceased king, and nobody knows whether it will be a son or a daughter? Which shall be heir of the two male-twins, who by the dissection of the mother were laid open to the world? Whether a sister by the half blood, before a brother's daughter by the whole blood?

§. 124. These, and many more such doubts, might be proposed about the titles of succession, and the right of inheritance; and that not as idle speculations, but such as in history we shall find have concerned the inheritance of crowns and kingdoms; and if ours want them, we need not go farther for famous examples of it, than the other kingdom in this very island, which having been fully related by the ingenious and learned author of Patriarcha non Monarcha, I need say no more of. Till our author hath resolved all the doubts that may arise about the next heir, and shewed that they are plainly determined by the law of nature, or the revealed law of God, all his suppositions of a monarchical, absolute, supreme, paternal power in Adam, and the descent of that power to his heirs, would not be of the least use to establish the authority, or make out the title, of any one prince now on earth; but would rather unsettle and bring all into question: for let our author tell us as long as he pleases, and let all men believe it too, that Adam had a paternal, and thereby a monarchical power; that this (the only power in the world) descended to his heirs; and that there is no other power in the world but this: let this be all as clear demonstration, as it is manifest error, yet if it be not past doubt, to whom this paternal power descends, and whose now it is, nobody can be under any obligation of obedience, unless any one will say, that I am bound to pay obedience to paternal power in a man who has no more paternal power than I myself; which is all one as to say, I obey a man, because he has a right to govern; and if I be asked, how I know he has a right to govern, I should answer, it cannot be known, that he has any at all: for that cannot be the reason of my obedience, which I know not to be so; much less can that be a reason of my obedience, which nobody at all can know to be so.

§. 125. And therefore all this ado about Adam's fatherhood, the greatness of its power, and the necessity of its supposal, helps nothing to establish the power of those that govern, or to determine the obedience of subjects who are to obey, if they cannot tell whom they are to obey, or it cannot be known who are to govern, and who to obey. In the state the world is now, it is irrecoverably ignorant, who is Adam's heir. This fatherhood, this monarchical power of Adam, descending to his heirs, would be of no more use to the government of mankind, than it would be to the quieting of men's consciences, or securing their healths, if our author had assured them, that Adam had a power to forgive sins, or cure diseases, which by divine institution descended to his heir, whilst this heir is impossible to be known. And should not he do as rationally, who upon this assurance of our author went and confessed his sins, and expected a good absolution; or took physic with expectation of health, from any one who had taken on himself the name of priest or physician, or thrust himself into those employments, saying, I acquiesce in the absolving power descending from Adam, or I shall be cured by the medicinal power descending from Adam; as he who says, I submit to and obey the paternal power descending from Adam, when it is confessed all these powers descend only to his single heir, and that heir is unknown.

§. 126. It is true, the civil lawyers have pretended to determine some of these cases concerning the succession of princes; but by our author's principles, they have meddled in a matter that belongs not to them: for if all political power be derived only from Adam, and be to descend only to his successive heirs, by the ordinance of God and divine institution, this is a right antecedent and paramount to all government; and therefore the positive laws of men cannot determine that which is itself the foundation of all law and government, and is to receive its rule only from the law of God and nature. And that being silent in the case, I am apt to think there is no such right to be conveyed this way: I am sure it would be to no purpose if there were, and men would be more at a loss concerning government, and obedience to governors, than if there were no such right; since by positive laws and compact, which divine institution (if there be any) shuts out, all these endless inextricable doubts can be safely provided against: but it can never be understood, how a divine natural right, and that of such moment as is all order and peace in the world, should be conveyed down to posterity, without any plain, natural, or divine rule concerning it. And there would be an end of all civil government, if the assignment of civil power were by divine institution to the heir, and yet by that divine institution the person of the heir could not be known. This paternal regal power being by divine right only his, it leaves no room for human prudence, or consent, to place it any where else; for if only one man hath a divine right to the obedience of mankind, nobody can claim that obedience, but he that can shew that right; nor can men's consciences by any other pretence be obliged to it. And thus this doctrine cuts up all government by the roots.

§. 127. Thus we see how our author, laying it for a sure foundation, that the very person that is to rule, is the ordinance of God, and by divine institution, tells us at large, only that this person is the heir, but who this heir is, he leaves us to guess; and so this divine institution, which assigns it to a person whom we have no rule to know, is just as good as an assignment to nobody at all. But, whatever our author does, divine institution makes no such ridiculous assignments: nor can God be supposed to make it a sacred law, that one certain person should have a right to something, and yet not give rules to mark out, and know that person by, or give an heir a divine right to power, and yet not point out who that heir is. It is rather to be thought, that an heir had no such right by divine institution, than that God should give such a right to the heir, but yet leave it doubtful and undeterminable who such heir is.

§. 128. If God had given the land of Canaan to Abraham, and in general terms to somebody after him, without naming his seed, whereby it might be known who that somebody was, it would have been as good and useful an assignment to determine the right to the land of Canaan, as it would be the determining the right of crowns, to give empire to Adam and his successive heirs after him, without telling who his heir is: for the word heir, without a rule to know who it is, signifies no more than somebody, I know not whom. God making it a divine institution, that men should not marry those who were near of kin, thinks it not enough to say, None of you shall approach to any that is near of kin to him, to uncover their nakedness; but moreover, gives rules to know who are those near of kin, forbidden by divine institution; or else that law would have been of no use, it being to no purpose to lay restraint, or give privileges to men, in such general terms, as the particular person concerned cannot be known by. But God not having any where said, the next heir shall inherit all his father's estate or dominion, we are not to wonder, that he hath no where appointed who that heir should be; for never having intended any such thing, never designed any heir in that sense, we cannot expect he should any where nominate, or appoint any person to it, as we might, had it been otherwise. And therefore in scripture, though the word heir occur, yet there is no such thing as heir in our author's sense, one that was by right of nature to inherit all that his father had, exclusive of his brethren. Hence Sarah supposes, that if Ishmael staid in the house, to share in Abraham's estate after his death, this son of a bond-woman might be heir with Isaac; and therefore, says she, "cast out this bond-woman and her son, for the son of this bond-woman shall not be heir with my son:" but this cannot excuse our author, who telling us there is; in every number of men, one who is right and next heir to Adam, ought to have told us what the laws of descent are; but he having been so sparing to instruct us by rules, how to know who is heir, let us see in the next place, what his history out of scripture, on which he pretends wholly to build his government, gives us in this necessary and fundamental point.

§. 129. Our author, to make good the title of his book, p. 13. begins his history of the descent of Adam's regal power, p. 13. in these words: "This lordship which Adam by command had over the whole world, and by right descending from him, the patriarchs did enjoy, was a large," &c. How does he prove that the patriarch by descent did enjoy it? for "dominion of life and death," says he, "we find Judah the father pronounced sentence of death against Thamar his daughter-in-law for playing the harlot," p. 13. How does this prove that Judah had absolute and sovereign authority? he pronounced sentence of death. The pronouncing of sentence of death is not a certain mark of sovereignty, but usually the office of inferior magistrates. The power of making laws of life and death is indeed a mark of sovereignty, but pronouncing the sentence according to those laws may be done by others, and therefore this will but ill prove that he had sovereign authority: as if one should say, Judge Jefferies pronounced sentence of death in the late times, therefore Judge Jefferies had sovereign authority. But it will be said, Judah did it not by commission from another, and therefore did it in his own right. Who knows whether he had any right at all? Heat of passion might carry him to do that which he had no authority to do. Judah had dominion of life and death: how does that appear? He exercised it, he pronounced sentence of death against Thamar: our author thinks it is very good proof, that because he did it, therefore he had a right to do it: he lay with her also: by the same way of proof, he had a right to do that too. If the consequence be good from doing to a right of doing, Absalom too may be reckoned amongst our author's sovereigns, for he pronounced such a sentence of death against his brother Amnon, and much upon a like occasion, and had it executed too, if that be sufficient to prove a dominion of life and death.

But allowing this all to be clear demonstration of sovereign power, who was it that had this lordship by right descending to him from Adam, as large and ample as the absolutest dominion of any monarch? Judah, says our author, Judah, a younger son of Jacob, his father and elder brethren living; so that if our author's own proof be to be taken, a younger brother may, in the life of his father and elder brothers, by right of descent, enjoy Adam's monarchical power; and if one so qualified may be monarch by descent, why may not every man? If Judah, his father and elder brother living, were one of Adam's heirs, I know not who can be excluded from this inheritance; all men by inheritance may be monarchs as well as Judah.

§. 130. "Touching war, we see that Abraham commanded an army of three hundred and eighteen soldiers of his own family, and Esau met his brother Jacob with four hundred men at arms: for matter of peace, Abraham made a league with Abimelech," &c. p. 13. Is it not possible for a man to have three hundred and eighteen men in his family, without being heir to Adam? A planter in the West Indies has more, and might, if he pleased, (who doubts?) muster them up and lead them out against the Indians, to seek reparation upon any injury received from them; and all this without the absolute dominion of a monarch, descending to him from Adam. Would it not be an admirable argument to prove, that all power by God's institution descended from Adam by inheritance, and that the very person and power of this planter were the ordinance of God, because he had power in his family over servants, born in his house, and bought with his money? For this was just Abraham's case; those who were rich in the patriarch's days, as in the West Indies now, bought men and maid servants; and by their increase, as well as purchasing of new, came to have large and numerous families, which though they made use of in war or peace, can it be thought the power they had over them was an inheritance descended from Adam, when it was the purchase of their money? A man's riding in an expedition against an enemy, his horse bought in a fair, would be as good a proof that the owner enjoyed the lordship which Adam by command had over the whole world, by right of descending to him, as Abraham's leading out the servants of his family is, that the patriarchs enjoyed this lordship by descent from Adam: since the title to the power, the master had in both cases, whether over slaves or horses, was only from his purchase; and the getting a dominion over any thing by bargain and money, is a new way of proving one had it by descent and inheritance.

§. 131. But making war and peace are marks of sovereignty. Let it be so in politic societies: may not therefore a man in the West Indies, who hath with him sons of his own, friends, or companions, soldiers under pay, or slaves bought with money, or perhaps a band made up of all these, make war and peace, if there should be occasion, and ratify the articles too with an oath, without being a sovereign, an absolute king over those who went with him? He that says he cannot, must then allow many masters of ships, many private planters, to be absolute monarchs, for as much as this they have done. War and peace cannot be made for politic societies, but by the supreme power of such societies; because war and peace, giving a different motion to the force of such a politic body, none can make war or peace, but that which has the direction of the force of the whole body, and that in politic societies is only the supreme power. In voluntary societies for the time, he that has such a power by consent, may make war and peace, and so may a single man for himself, the state of war not consisting in the number of partisans, but the enmity of the parties, where they have no superior to appeal to.

§. 132. The actual making of war or peace, is no proof of any other power, but only of disposing those to exercise or cease acts of enmity for whom he makes it; and this power in many cases any one may have without any politic supremacy: and therefore the making of war or peace will not prove that every one that does so is a politic ruler, much less a king; for then commonwealths must be kings too, for they do as certainly make war and peace as monarchical government.

§. 133. But granting this a mark of sovereignty in Abraham, is it a proof of the descent to him of Adam's sovereignty over the whole world? If it be, it will surely be as good a proof of the descent of Adam's lordship to others too. And then commonwealths, as well as Abraham, will be heirs of Adam, for they make war and peace, as well as he. If you say, that the lordship of Adam doth not by right descend to commonwealths, though they make war and peace, the same say I of Abraham, and then there is an end of your argument: if you stand to your argument, and say those that do make war and peace, as commonwealths do without doubt, do inherit Adam's lordship, there is an end of your monarchy, unless you will say, that commonwealths by descent enjoying Adam's lordship are monarchies; and that indeed would be a new way of making all the governments in the world monarchical.

§. 134. To give our author the honour of this new invention, for I confess it is not I have first found it out by tracing his principles, and so charged it on him, it is fit my readers know that (as absurd as it may seem) he teaches it himself, p. 23. where he ingenuously says, "In all kingdoms and commonwealths in the world, whether the prince be the supreme father of the people, or but the true heir to such a father, or come to the crown by usurpation or election, or whether some few or a multitude govern the commonwealth; yet still the authority that is in any one, or in many, or in all these, is the only right, and natural authority of a supreme father;" which right of fatherhood, he often tells us, is regal and royal authority; as particularly, p. 12. the page immediately preceding this instance of Abraham. This regal authority, he says, those that govern commonwealths have; and if it be true, that regal and royal authority be in those that govern commonwealths, it is as true that commonwealths are governed by kings; for if regal authority be in him that governs, he that governs must needs be a king, and so all commonwealths are nothing but downright monarchies; and then what need any more ado about the matter? The governments of the world are as they should be, there is nothing but monarchy in it. This, without doubt, was the surest way our author could have found, to turn all other governments, but monarchical, out of the world.

§. 135. But all this scarce proves Abraham to have been a king as heir to Adam. If by inheritance he had been king, Lot, who was of the same family, must needs have been his subject, by that title, before the servants in his family; but we see they lived as friends and equals, and when their herdsmen could not agree, there was no pretence of jurisdiction or superiority between them, but they parted by consent, Gen. xiii. hence he is called both by Abraham, and by the text, Abraham's brother, the name of friendship and equality, and not of jurisdiction and authority, though he were really but his nephew. And if our author knows that Abraham was Adam's heir, and a king, it was more, it seems, than Abraham himself knew, or his servant whom he sent a wooing for his son; for when he sets out the advantages of the match, Gen. xxiv. 35. thereby to prevail with the young woman and her friends, he says, "I am Abraham's servant, and the Lord hath blessed my master greatly, and he is become great; and he hath given him flocks and herds, and silver and gold, and men-servants and maid-servants, and camels and asses: and Sarah, my master's wife, bare a son to my master when she was old, and unto him hath he given all he hath." Can one think that a discreet servant that was thus particular to set out his master's greatness would have omitted the crown Isaac was to have, if he had known of any such? Can it be imagined he should have neglected to have told them on such an occasion as this, that Abraham was a king, a name well known at that time, for he had nine of them his neighbours, if he or his master had thought any such thing, the likeliest matter of all the rest, to make his errand successful?

§. 136. But this discovery it seems was reserved for our author to make two or three thousand years after, and let him enjoy the credit of it; only he should have taken care that some of Adam's land should have descended to this his heir, as well as all Adam's lordship: for though this lordship which Abraham, (if we may believe our author) as well as the other patriarchs, by right descending to him did enjoy, was as large and ample as the absolutest dominion of any monarch which hath been since the creation; yet his estate, his territories, his dominions were very narrow and scanty, for he had not the possession of a foot of land, till he bought a field and a cave of the sons of Heth to bury Sarah in.

§. 137. The instance of Esau joined with this of Abraham, to prove that the lordship which Adam had over the whole world, by right descending from him, the patriarchs did enjoy, is yet more pleasant than the former. Esau met his brother Jacob with four hundred men at arms: he therefore was a king by right of heir to Adam. Four hundred armed men then, however got together, are enough to prove him that leads them, to be a king and Adam's heir. There have been tories in Ireland, (whatever there are in other countries) who would have thanked our author for so honourable an opinion of them, especially if there had been nobody near with a better title of five hundred armed men, to question their royal authority of four hundred. It is a shame for men to trifle so, to say no worse of it, in so serious an argument. Here Esau is brought as a proof that Adam's lordship, Adam's absolute dominion, as large as that of any monarch, descended by right to the patriarchs, and in this very chap. p. 19. Jacob is brought as an instance of one, that by birth-right was lord over his brethren. So we have here two brothers absolute monarchs by the same title, and at the same time heirs to Adam: the eldest, heir to Adam, because he met his brother with four hundred men; and the youngest, heir to Adam by birth-right. Esau enjoyed the lordship which Adam had over the whole world by right descending to him, in as large and ample manner, as the absolutest dominion of any monarch; and at the same time, Jacob lord over him, by the right heirs have to be lords over their brethren. Risum teneatis? I never, I confess, met with any man of parts so dexterous as Sir Robert at this way of arguing: but it was his misfortune to light upon an hypothesis, that could not be accommodated to the nature of things, and human affairs; his principles could not be made to agree with that constitution and order, which God had settled in the world, and therefore must needs often clash with common sense and experience.

§. 138. In the next section, he tells us, "This patriarchal power continued not only till the flood, but after it, as the name patriarch doth in part prove." The word patriarch doth more than in part prove, that patriarchal power continued in the world as long as there were patriarchs, for it is necessary that patriarchal power should be whilst there are patriarchs; as it is necessary there should be paternal or conjugal power whilst there are fathers or husbands; but this is but playing with names. That which he would fallaciously insinuate is the thing in question to be proved, viz. that the lordship which Adam had over the world, the supposed absolute universal dominion of Adam by right descending from him, the patriarchs did enjoy. If he affirms such an absolute monarchy continued to the flood, in the world, I would be glad to know what records he has it from; for I confess I cannot find a word of it in my Bible: if by patriarchal power he means any thing else, it is nothing to the matter in hand. And how the name patriarch in some part proves, that those, who are called by that name, had absolute monarchical power, I confess, I do not see, and therefore I think needs no answer till the argument from it be made out a little clearer.

§. 139. "The three sons of Noah had the world," says our author, "divided amongst them by their father, for of them was the whole world overspread," p. 14. The world might be overspread by the offspring of Noah's sons, though he never divided the world amongst them; for the earth might be replenished without being divided: so that all our author's argument here proves no such division. However, I allow it to him, and then ask, the world being divided amongst them, which of the three was Adam's heir? If Adam's lordship, Adam's monarchy, by right descended only to the eldest, then the other two could be but his subjects, his slaves: if by right it descended to all three brothers, by the same right, it will descend to all mankind; and then it will be impossible what he says, p. 19. that heirs are lords of their brethren, should be true; but all brothers, and consequently all men, will be equal and independent, all heirs to Adam's monarchy, and consequently all monarchs too, one as much as another. But it will be said, Noah their father divided the world amongst them; so that our author will allow more to Noah, than he will to God Almighty, for Observations, 211. he thought it hard, that God himself should give the world to Noah and his sons, to the prejudice of Noah's birth-right: his words are, "Noah was left sole heir to the world: why should it be thought that God would disinherit him of his birth-right, and make him, of all men in the world, the only tenant in common with his children?" and yet here he thinks it fit that Noah should disinherit Shem of his birth-right, and divide the world betwixt him and his brethren; so that this birth-right, when our author pleases, must, and when he pleases must not, be sacred and inviolable.

§. 140. If Noah did divide the world between his sons, and his assignment of dominions to them were good, there is an end of divine institution; all our author's discourse of Adam's heir, with whatsoever he builds on it, is quite out of doors; the natural power of kings falls to the ground; and then the form of the power governing, and the person having that power, will not be (as he says they are, Observations, 254.) the ordinance of God, but they will be ordinances of man: for if the right of the heir be the ordinance of God, a divine right, no man, father or not father, can alter it: if it be not a divine right, it is only human, depending on the will of man: and so where human institution gives it not, the first-born has no right at all above his brethren; and men may put government into what hands, and under what form, they please.

§. 141. He goes on, "Most of the civilest nations of the earth labour to fetch their original from some of the sons, or nephews of Noah," p. 14. How many do most of the civilest nations amount to? and who are they? I fear the Chinese, a very great and civil people, as well as several other people of the East, West, North and South, trouble not themselves much about this matter. All that believe the Bible, which I believe are our author's most of the civilest nations, must necessarily derive themselves from Noah: but for the rest of the world, they think little of his sons or nephews. But if the heralds and antiquaries of all nations, for it is these men generally that labour to find out the originals of nations, or all the nations themselves, should labour to fetch their original from some of the sons or nephews of Noah, what would this be to prove, that the lordship which Adam had over the whole world, by right descended to the patriarchs? Whoever, nations, or races of men, labour to fetch their original from, may be concluded to be thought by them, men of renown, famous to posterity, for the greatness of their virtues and actions; but beyond these they look not, nor consider who they were heirs to, but look on them as such as raised themselves, by their own virtue, to a degree that would give a lustre to those who in future ages could pretend to derive themselves from them. But if it were Ogyges, Hercules, Brama, Tamerlane, Pharamond; nay, if Jupiter and Saturn were the names from whence divers races of men, both ancient and modern, have laboured to derive their original; will that prove, that those men enjoyed the lordship of Adam, by right descending to them? If not, this is but a flourish of our author's to mislead his reader, that in itself signifies nothing.

§. 142. To as much purpose is what he tells us, p. 15. concerning this division of the world,

"That some say it was by Lot, and others that Noah sailed round the Mediterreanean in ten years, and divided the world into Asia, Afric and Europe, portions for his three sons. America then, it seems, was left to be his that could catch it. Why our author takes such pains to prove the division of the world by Noah to his sons, and will not leave out an imagination, though no better than a dream, that he can find any where to favour it, is hard to guess, since such a division, if it prove any thing, must necessarily take away the title of Adam's heir; unless three brothers can all together be heirs of Adam; and therefore the following words, "Howsoever the manner of this division be uncertain, yet it is most certain the division itself was by families from Noah and his children, over which the parents were heads and princes," p. 15. if allowed him to be true, and of any force to prove, that all the power in the world is nothing but the lordship of Adam's descending by right, they will only prove, that the fathers of the children are all heirs to this lordship of Adam: for if in those days Cham and Japhet, and other parents, besides the eldest son, were heads and princes over their families, and had a right to divide the earth by families, what hinders younger brothers, being fathers of families, from having the same right? If Cham and Japhet were princes by right descending to them, notwithstanding any title of heir in their eldest brother, younger brothers by the same right descending to them are princes now; and so all our author's natural power of kings will reach no farther than their own children, and no kingdom, by this natural right, can be bigger than a family: for either this lordship of Adam over the whole world, by right descends only to the eldest son, and then there can be but one heir, as our author says, p. 19. or else, it by right descends to all the sons equally, and then every father of a family will have it, as well as the three sons of Noah: take which you will, it destroys the present governments and kingdoms, that are now in the world, since whoever has this natural power of a king, by right descending to him, must have it, either as our author tells us Cain had it, and be lord over his brethren, and so be alone king of the whole world; or else, as he tells us here, Shem, Cham and Japhet had it, three brothers, and so be only prince of his own family, and all families independent one of another: all the world must be only one empire by the right of the next heir, or else every family be a distinct government of itself, by the lordship of Adam's descending to parents of families. And to this only tend all the proofs he here gives us of the descent of Adam's lordship: for continuing his story of this descent, he says,

§. 143. "In the dispersion of Babel, we must certainly find the establishment of royal power, throughout the kingdoms of the world," p. 14. If you must find it, pray do, and you will help us to a new piece of history: but you must shew it us before we shall be bound to believe, that regal power was established in the world upon your principles: for, that regal power was established in the kingdoms of the world, I think nobody will dispute; but that there should be kingdoms in the world, whose several kings enjoyed their crowns, by right descending to them from Adam, that we think not only Apocryphal, but also utterly impossible. If our author has no better foundation for his monarchy than a supposition of what was done at the dispersion of Babel, the monarchy he erects thereon, whose top is to reach to heaven to unite mankind, will serve only to divide and scatter them as that tower did; and, instead of establishing civil government and order in the world, will produce nothing but confusion.

§. 144. For he tells us, "the nations they were divided into, were distinct families, which had fathers for rulers over them; whereby it appears, that even in the confusion, God was careful to preserve the fatherly authority, by distributing the diversity of languages according to the diversity of families," p. 14. It would have been a hard matter for any one but our author to have found out so plainly, in the text he here brings, that all the nations in that dispersion were governed by fathers, and that God was careful to preserve the fatherly authority. The words of the text are; These are the sons of Shem after their families, after their tongues in their lands, after their nations; and the same thing is said of Cham and Japhet, after an enumeration of their posterities; in all which there is not one word said of their governors, or forms of government; of fathers, or fatherly authority. But our author, who is very quick sighted to spy out fatherhood, where nobody else could see any the least glimpses of it, tells us positively their rulers were fathers, and God was careful to preserve the fatherly authority; and why? Because those of the same family spoke the same language, and so of necessity in the division kept together. Just as if one should argue thus: Hanibal in his army, consisting of divers nations, kept those of the same language together; therefore fathers were captains of each band, and Hanibal was careful of the fatherly authority: or in peopling of Carolina, the English, French, Scotch and Welch that are there, plant themselves together, and by them the country is divided in their lands after their tongues, after their families, after their nations; therefore care was taken of the fatherly authority: or because, in many parts of America, every little tribe was a distinct people, with a different language, one should infer, that therefore God was careful to preserve the fatherly authority, or that therefore their rulers enjoyed Adam's lordship by right descending to them, though we know not who were their governors, nor what their form of government, but only that they were divided into little independent societies, speaking different languages.

§. 145. The scripture says not a word of their rulers or forms of government, but only gives an account, how mankind came to be divided into distinct languages and nations, and therefore it is not to argue from the authority of scripture, to tell us positively, fathers were their rulers, when the scripture says no such thing; but to set up fancies of one's own brain, when we confidently aver matter of fact, where records are utterly silent. Upon a like ground, i. e. none at all, he says, "That they were not confused multitudes without heads and governors, and at liberty to choose what governors or governments they pleased."

§. 146. For I demand, when mankind were all yet of one language, all congregated in the plain of Shinar, were they then all under one monarch, who enjoyed the lordship of Adam by right descending to him? If they were not, there were then no thoughts, it is plain, of Adam's heir, no right of government known then upon that title; no care taken, by God or man, of Adam's fatherly authority. If when mankind were but one people, dwelt all together, and were of one language, and were upon building a city together; and when it was plain, they could not but know the right heir, for Shem lived till Isaac's time, a long while after the division at Babel; if then, I say, they were not under the monarchical government of Adam's fatherhood, by right descending to the heir, it is plain there was no regard had to the fatherhood, no monarchy acknowledged due to Adam's heir, no empire of Shem's in Asia, and consequently no such division of the world by Noah, as our author has talked of. As far as we can conclude any thing from scripture in this matter, it seems from this place, that if they had any government, it was rather a commonwealth than an absolute monarchy: for the scripture tells us, Gen. xi. They said: it was not a prince commanded the building of this city and tower, it was not by the command of one monarch, but by the consultation of many, a free people; let us build us a city: they built it for themselves as free-men, not as slaves for their lord and master: that we be not scattered abroad; having a city once built, and fixed habitations to settle our abodes and families. This was the consultation and design of a people, that were at liberty to part asunder, but desired to keep in one body, and could not have been either necessary or likely in men tied together under the government of one monarch, who if they had been, as our author tells us, all slaves under the absolute dominion of a monarch, needed not have taken such care to hinder themselves from wandering out of the reach of his dominion. I demand whether this be not plainer in scripture than any thing of Adam's heir or fatherly authority?

§. 147. But if being, as God says, Gen. xi. 6. one people, they had one ruler, one king by natural right, absolute and supreme over them, what care had God to preserve the paternal authority of the supreme fatherhood, if on a sudden he suffer seventy-two (for so many our author talks of) distinct nations to be erected out of it, under distinct governors, and at once to withdraw themselves from the obedience of their sovereign? This is to intitle God's care how, and to what we please. Can it be sense to say, that God was careful to preserve the fatherly authority in those who had it not? for if these were subjects under a supreme prince, what authority had they? Was it an instance of God's care to preserve the fatherly authority, when he took away the true supreme fatherhood of the natural monarch? Can it be reason to say, that God, for the preservation of fatherly authority, lets several new governments with their governors start up, who could not all have fatherly authority? And is it not as much reason to say, that God is careful to destroy fatherly authority, when he suffers one, who is in possession of it, to have his government torn in pieces, and shared by several of his subjects? Would it not be an argument just like this, for monarchical government to say, when any monarchy was shattered to pieces, and divided amongst revolted subjects, that God was careful to preserve monarchical power, by rending a settled empire into a multitude of little governments? If any one will say, that what happens in providence to be preserved, God is careful to preserve as a thing therefore to be esteemed by men as necessary or useful, it is a peculiar propriety of speech, which every one will not think fit to imitate: but this I am sure is impossible to be either proper, or true speaking, that Shem, for example, (for he was then alive,) should have fatherly authority, or sovereignty by right of fatherhood, over that one people at Babel, and that the next moment, Shem yet living, seventy-two others should have fatherly authority, or sovereignty by right of fatherhood, over the same people, divided into so many distinct governments: either these seventy-two fathers actually were rulers, just before the confusion, and then they were not one people, but that God himself says they were; or else they were a commonwealth, and then where was monarchy? or else these seventy-two fathers had fatherly authority, but knew it not. Strange! that fatherly authority should be the only original of government amongst men, and yet all mankind not know it; and stranger yet, that the confusion of tongues should reveal it to them all of a sudden, that in an instant these seventy-two should know that they had fatherly power, and all others know that they were to obey it in them, and every one know that particular fatherly authority to which he was a subject. He that can think this arguing from scripture, may from thence make out what model of an Utopia will best suit with his fancy or interest; and this fatherhood, thus disposed of, will justify both a prince who claims an universal monarchy, and his subjects, who, being fathers of families, shall quit all subjection to him, and canton his empire into less governments for themselves; for it will always remain a doubt in which of these the fatherly authority resided, till our author resolves us, whether Shem, who was then alive, or these seventy-two new princes, beginning so many new empires in his dominions, and over his subjects, had right to govern, since our author tells us, that both one and the other had fatherly, which is supreme authority, and are brought in by him as instances of those who did enjoy the lordships of Adam by right descending to them, which was as large and ample as the absolutest dominion of any monarch. This at least is unavoidable, that if God was careful to preserve the fatherly authority, in the seventy-two new-erected nations, it necessarily follows, that he was as careful to destroy all pretences of Adam's heir; since he took care, and therefore did preserve the fatherly authority in so many, at least seventy-one, that could not possibly be Adam's heirs, when the right heir (if God had ever ordained any such inheritance) could not but be known, Shem then living, and they being all one people.

§. 148. Nimrod is his next instance of enjoying this patriarchal power, p. 16. but I know not for what reason our author seems a little unkind to him, and says, that he "against right enlarged his empire, by seizing violently on the rights of other lords of families." These lords of families here were called fathers of families, in his account of the dispersion at Babel: but it matters not how they were called, so we know who they are; for this fatherly authority must be in them, either as heirs to Adam, and so there could not be seventy-two, nor above one at once; or else as natural parents over their children, and so every father will have paternal authority over his children by the same right, and in as large extent as those seventy-two had, and so be independent princes over their own offspring. Taking his lords of families in this latter sense, (as it is hard to give those words any other sense in this place) he gives us a very pretty account of the original of monarchy, in these following words, p. 16. "And in this sense he may be said to be the author and founder of monarchy," viz. As against right seizing violently on the rights of fathers over their children; which paternal authority, if it be in them, by right of nature, (for else how could those seventy-two come by it?) nobody can take from them without their own consents; and then I desire our author and his friends to consider, how far this will concern other princes, and whether it will not, according to his conclusion of that paragraph, resolve all regal power of those, whose dominions extend beyond their families, either into tyranny and usurpation, or election and consent of fathers of families, which will differ very little from consent of the people.

§. 149. All his instances, in the next section, p. 17. of the twelve dukes of Edom, the nine kings in a little corner of Asia in Abraham's days, the thirty-one kings in Canaan destroyed by Joshua, and the care he takes to prove that these were all sovereign princes, and that every town in those days had a king, are so many direct proofs against him, that it was not the lordship of Adam by right descending to them, that made kings: for if they had held their royalties by that title, either there must have been but one sovereign over them all, or else every father of a family had been as good a prince, and had as good a claim to royalty, as these: for if all the sons of Esau had each of them, the younger as well as the eldest, the right of fatherhood, and so were sovereign princes after their father's death, the same right had their sons after them, and so on to all posterity; which will limit all the natural power of fatherhood, only to be over the issue of their own bodies, and their descendents; which power of fatherhood dies with the head of each family, and makes way for the like power of fatherhood to take place in each of his sons over their respective posterities: whereby the power of fatherhood will be preserved indeed, and is intelligible, but will not be at all to our author's purpose. None of the instances he brings are proofs of any power they had, as heirs of Adam's paternal authority by the title of his fatherhood descending to them; no, nor of any power they had by virtue of their own: for Adam's fatherhood being over all mankind, it could descend but to one at once, and from him to his right heir only, and so there could by that title be but one king in the world at a time: and by right of fatherhood, not descending from Adam, it must be only as they themselves were fathers, and so could be over none but their own posterity. So that if those twelve dukes of Edom; if Abraham and the nine kings his neighbours; if Jacob and Esau, and the thirty-one kings in Canaan, the seventy-two kings mutilated by Adonibeseck, the thirty-two kings that came to Benhadad, the seventy kings of Greece making war at Troy, were, as our author contends, all of them sovereign princes; it is evident that kings derived their power from some other original than fatherhood, since some of these had power over more than their own posterity; and it is demonstration, they could not be all heirs to Adam; for I challenge any man to make any pretence to power by right of fatherhood, either intelligible or possible in any one, otherwise than either as Adam's heir, or as progenitor over his own descendents, naturally sprung from him. And if our author could shew that any one of these princes, of which he gives us here so large a catalogue, had his authority by either of these titles, I think I might yield him the cause; though it is manifest they are all impertinent, and directly contrary to what he brings them to prove, viz. That the lordship which Adam had over the world by right descended to the patriarchs.

§. 150. Having told us, p. 16, "That the patriarchal government continued in Abraham, Isaac, and Jacob, until the Egyptian bondage," p. 17. he tells us, "By manifest footsteps we may trace this paternal government unto the Israelites coming into Egypt, where the exercise of supreme patriarchal government was intermitted, because they were in subjection to a stronger prince." What these footsteps are of paternal government, in our author's sense, i. e. of absolute monarchical power descending from Adam, and exercised by right of fatherhood, we have seen, that is for 2290 years no footsteps at all; since in all that time he cannot produce any one example of any person who claimed or exercised regal authority by right of fatherhood; or shew any one who being a king was Adam's heir: all that his proofs amount to, is only this, that there were fathers, patriarchs and kings, in that age of the world; but that the fathers and patriarchs had any absolute arbitrary power, or by what titles those kings had theirs, and of what extent it was, the scripture is wholly silent; it is manifest by right of fatherhood they neither did, nor could claim any title to dominion and empire.

§. 151. To say, "that the exercise of supreme patriarchal government was intermitted, because they were in subjection to a stronger prince," proves nothing but what I before suspected, viz. That patriarchal jurisdiction or government is a fallacious expression, and does not in our author signify (what he would yet insinuate by it) paternal and regal power, such an absolute sovereignty as he supposes was in Adam.

§. 152. For how can he say that patriarchal jurisdiction was intermitted in Egypt, where there was a king, under whose regal government the Israelites were, if patriarchal were absolute monarchical jurisdiction? And if it were not, but something else, why does he make such ado about a power not in question, and nothing to the purpose? The exercise of patriarchal jurisdiction, if patriarchal be regal, was not intermitted whilst the Israelites were in Egypt. It is true, the exercise of regal power was not then in the hands of any of the promised seed of Abraham, nor before neither that I know; but what is that to the intermission of regal authority, as descending from Adam, unless our author will have it, that this chosen line of Abraham had the right of inheritance to Adam's lordship? and then to what purpose are his instances of the seventy-two rulers, in whom the fatherly authority was preserved in the confusion at Babel? Why does he bring the twelve princes sons of Ishmael, and the dukes of Edom, and join them with Abraham, Isaac and Jacob, as examples of the exercise of true patriarchal government, if the exercise of patriarchal jurisdiction were intermitted in the world, whenever the heirs of Jacob had not supreme power? I fear, supreme patriarchal jurisdiction was not only intermitted, but from the time of the Egyptian bondage quite lost in the world, since it will be hard to find, from that time downwards, any one who exercised it as an inheritance descending to him from the patriarchs Abraham, Isaac and Jacob. I imagined monarchical government would have served his turn in the hands of Pharaoh, or any body. But one cannot easily discover in all places what his discourse tends to, as particularly in this place it is not obvious to guess what he drives at, when he says, the exercise of supreme patriarchal jurisdiction in Egypt, or how this serves to make out the descent of Adam's lordship to the patriarchs, or any body else.

§. 153. For I thought he had been giving us out of scripture, proofs and examples of monarchical government, founded on paternal authority, descending from Adam; and not an history of the Jews: amongst whom yet we find no kings, till many years after they were a people: and when kings were their rulers, there is not the least mention or room for a pretence that they were heirs to Adam, or kings by paternal authority. I expected, talking so much as he does of scripture, that he would have produced thence a series of monarchs, whose titles were clear to Adam's fatherhood, and who, as heirs to him, owned and exercised paternal jurisdiction over their subjects, and that this was the true patriarchical government; whereas he neither proves, that the patriarchs were kings; nor that either kings or patriarchs were heirs to Adam, or so much as pretended to it: and one may as well prove, that the patriarchs were all absolute monarchs; that the power both of patriarchs and kings was only paternal, and that this power descended to them from Adam: I say all these propositions may be as well proved by a confused account of a multitude of little kings in the West-Indies, out of Ferdinando Soto, or any of our late histories of the Northern America, or by our author's seventy kings of Greece, out of Homer, as by any thing he brings out of scripture, in that multitude of kings he has reckoned up.

§. 154. And methinks he should have let Homer and his wars of Troy alone, since his great zeal to truth or monarchy carried him to such a pitch of transport against philosophers and poets, that he tells us in his preface, that there "are too many in these days, who please themselves in running after the opinions of philosophers and poets, to find out such an original of government, as might promise them some title to liberty, to the great scandal of Christianity, and bringing in of atheism." And yet these heathens, philosopher Aristotle, and poet Homer, are not rejected by our zealous Christian politician, whenever they offer any thing that seems to serve his turn; whether to the great scandal of Christianity and bringing in of atheism, let him look. This I cannot but observe, in authors who it is visible write not for truth, how ready zeal for interest and party is to entitle Christianity to their designs, and to charge atheism on those who will not without examining submit to their doctrines, and blindly swallow their nonsense.

But to return to his scripture history, our author farther tells us, p. 18. that "after the return of the Israelites out of bondage, God, out of a special care of them, chose Moses and Joshua successively to govern as princes in the place and stead of the supreme fathers." If it be true, that they returned out of bondage; it must be into a state of freedom, and must imply that both before and after this bondage they were free, unless our author will say, that changing of masters is returning out of bondage; or that a slave returns out of bondage, when he is removed from one galley to another. If then they returned out of bondage, it is plain that in those days, whatever our author in his preface says to the contrary, there were difference between a son, a subject, and a slave; and that neither the patriarchs before, nor their rulers after this Egyptian bondage, numbered their sons or subjects amongst their possessions, and disposed of them with as absolute a dominion, as they did their other goods.

§. 155. This is evident in Jacob, to whom Reuben offered his two sons as pledges; and Judah was at last surety for Benjamin's safe return out of Egypt: which all had been vain, superfluous, and but a sort of mockery, if Jacob had had the same power over every one of his family as he had over his ox or his ass, as an owner over his substance; and the offers that Reuben or Judah made had been such a security for returning of Benjamin, as if a man should take two lambs out of his lord's flock, and offer one as security, that he will safely restore the other.

§. 156. When they were out of this bondage, what then? "God out of a special care of them, the Israelites." It is well that once in his book, he will allow God to have any care of the people; for in other places he speaks of mankind, as if God had no care of any part of them, but only of their monarchs, and that the rest of the people, the societies of men, were made as so many herds of cattle, only for the service, use, and pleasure of their princes.

§. 157. "Chose Moses and Joshua successively to govern as princes;" a shrewd argument our author has found out to prove God's care of the fatherly authority, and Adam's heirs, that here, as an expression of his care of his own people, he chooses those for princes over them, that had not the least pretence to either. The persons chosen were, Moses of the tribe of Levi, and Joshua of the tribe of Ephraim, neither of which had any title of fatherhood. But, says our author, they were in the place and stead of the supreme fathers. If God had any where as plainly declared his choice of such fathers to be rulers, as he did of Moses and Joshua, we might believe Moses and Joshua were in their place and stead: but that being the question in debate, till that be better proved, Moses being chosen by God to be ruler of his people, will no more prove that government belonged to Adam's heir, or to the fatherhood, than God's choosing Aaron of the tribe of Levi to be priest, will prove that the priesthood belonged to

Adam's heir, or the prime fathers; since God would choose Aaron to be priest, and Moses ruler in Israel, though neither of those offices were settled on Adam's heir, or the fatherhood.

§. 158. Our author goes on, "and after them likewise for a time he raised up judges, to defend his people in time of peril," p. 18. This proves fatherly authority to be the original of government, and that it descended from Adam to his heirs, just as well as what went before: only here our author seems to confess, that these judges, who were all the governors they then had, were only men of valour, whom they made their generals to defend them in time of peril; and cannot God raise up such men, unless fatherhood have a title to government?

But says our author, "when God gave the Israelites kings, he re-established the ancient and prime right of lineal succession to paternal government," p. 18.

§. 160. How did God re-establish it? by a law, a positive command? We find no such thing. Our author means then, that when God gave them a king, in giving them a king, he re-established the right, &c. To re-establish de facto the right of lineal succession to paternal government, is to put a man in possession of that government which his fathers did enjoy, and he by lineal succession had a right to: for, first, if it were another government than what his ancestors had, it was not succeeding to an ancient right, but beginning a new one: for if a prince should give a man, besides his antient patrimony, which for some ages his family had been disseized of, an additional estate, never before in the possession of his ancestors, he could not be said to re-establish the right of lineal succession to any more than what had been formerly enjoyed by his ancestors. If therefore the power the kings of Israel had, were any thing more than Isaac or Jacob had, it was not the re-establishing in them the right of succession to a power, but giving them a new power, however you please to call it, paternal or not: and whether Isaac and Jacob had the same power that the kings of Israel had, I desire any one, by what has been above said, to consider; and I do not think they will find, that either Abraham, Isaac, or Jacob, had any regal power at all.

§. 161. Next, there can be no re-establishment of the prime and ancient right of lineal succession to any thing, unless he, that is put in possession of it, has the right to succeed, and be the true and next heir to him he succeeds to. Can that be a re-establishment which begins in a new family? or that the re-establishment of an ancient right of lineal succession, when a crown is given to one, who has no right of succession to it, and who, if the lineal succession had gone on, had been out of all possibility of pretence to it? Saul, the first king God gave the Israelites, was of the tribe of Benjamin. Was the ancient and prime right of lineal succession re-established in him? The next was David, the youngest son of Jesse, of the posterity of Judah, Jacob's third son. Was the ancient and prime right of lineal succession to paternal government re-established in him? or in Solomon, his younger son and successor in the throne? or in Jereboam over the ten tribes? or in Athaliah, a woman who reigned six years an utter stranger to the royal blood? If the ancient and prime right of lineal succession to paternal government were re-established in any of these or their posterity, the ancient and prime right of lineal succession to paternal government belongs to younger brothers as well as elder, and may be re-established in any man living; for whatever younger brothers, by ancient and prime right of lineal succession, may have as well as the elder, that every living man may have a right to, by lineal succession, and Sir Robert as well as any other. And so what a brave right of lineal succession, to his paternal or regal government, our author has re-established, for the securing the rights and inheritance of crowns, where every one may have it, let the world consider.

§. 162. But says our author however, p. 19. "Whensoever God made choice of any special person to be king, he intended that the issue also should have benefit thereof, as being comprehended sufficiently in the person of the father, although the father was only named in the grant." This yet will not help out succession; for if, as our author says, the benefit of the grant be intended to the issue of the grantee, this will not direct the succession; since, if God give any thing to a man and his issue in general, the claim cannot be to any one of that issue in particular; every one that is of his race will have an equal right. If it be said our author meant heir, I believe our author was as willing as any body to have used that word, if it would have served his turn: but Solomon, who succeeded David in the throne, being no more his heir than Jeroboam, who succeeded him in the government of the ten tribes, was his issue, our author had reason to avoid saying, That God intended it to the heirs, when that would not hold in a succession, which our author could not except against; and so he has left his succession as undetermined, as if he had said nothing about it: for if the regal power be given by God to a man and his issue, as the land of Canaan was to Abraham and his seed, must they not all have a title to it, all share in it? And one may as well say, that by God's grant to Abraham and his seed, the land of Canaan was to belong only to one of his seed exclusive of all others, as by God's grant of dominion to a man and his issue, this dominion was to belong in peculiar to one of his issue exclusive of all others.

§. 163. But how will our author prove that whensoever God made choice of any special person to be a king, he intended that the (I suppose he means his) issue also should have benefit thereof? has he so soon forgot Moses and Joshua, whom in this very section, he says, God out of a special care chose to govern as princes, and the judges that God raised up? Had not these princes, having the authority of the supreme fatherhood, the same power that the kings had; and being specially chosen by God himself, should not their issue have the benefit of that choice, as well as David's or Solomon's? If these had the paternal authority put into their hands immediately by God, why had not their issue the benefit of this grant in a succession to this power? or if they had it as Adam's heirs, why did not their heirs enjoy it after them by right descending to them? for they could not be heirs to one another. Was the power the same, and from the same original, in Moses, Joshua, and the Judges, as it was in David and the Kings; and was it inheritable in one, and not in the other? If it was not paternal authority, then God's own people were governed by those that had not paternal authority, and those governors did well enough without it: if it were paternal authority, and God chose the persons that were to exercise it, our author's rule fails, that whensoever God makes choice of any person to be supreme ruler (for I suppose the name king has no spell in it, it is not the title, but the power makes the difference) he intends that the issue should have the benefit of it, since from their coming out of Egypt to David's time, four hundred years, the issue was never so sufficiently comprehended in the person of the father, as that any son, after the death of his father, succeeded to the government amongst all those judges that judged Israel. If, to avoid this, it be said, God always chose the person of the successor, and so, transferring the fatherly authority to him, excluded his issue from succeeding to it, that is manifestly not so in the story of Jephtha, where he articled with the people, and they made him judge over them, as is plain, Judges xi.

§. 164. It is in vain then to say, that whensoever God chooses any special person to have the exercise of paternal authority, (for if that be not to be king, I desire to know the difference between a king and one having the exercise of paternal authority) he intends the issue also should have the benefit of it, since we find the authority, the judges had, ended with them, and descended not to their issue; and if the judges had not paternal authority, I fear it will trouble our author, or any of the friends to his principles, to tell who had then the paternal authority, that is, the government and supreme power amongst the Israelites; and I suspect they must confess that the chosen people of God continued a people several hundreds of years, without any knowledge or thought of this paternal authority, or any appearance of monarchical government at all.

§. 165. To be satisfied of this, he need but read the story of the Levite, and the war thereupon with the Benjamites, in the three last chapters of Judges; and when he finds, that the Levite appeals to the people for justice, that it was the tribes and the congregation that debated, resolved, and directed all that was done on that occasion; he must conclude, either that God was not careful to preserve the fatherly authority amongst his own chosen people; or else that the fatherly authority may be preserved, where there is no monarchical government; if the latter, then it will follow, that though fatherly authority be never so well proved, yet it will not infer a necessity of monarchical government; if the former, it will seem very strange and improbable, that God should ordain fatherly authority to be so sacred amongst the sons of men, that there could be no power, or government without it, and yet that amongst his own people, even whilst he is providing a government for them, and therein prescribes rules to the several states and relations of men, this great and fundamental one, this most material and necessary of all the rest, should be concealed, and lie neglected for four hundred years after.

§. 166. Before I leave this, I must ask how our author knows that "whensoever God makes choice of any special person to be king, he intends that the issue should have the benefit thereof?" Does God by the law of nature or revelation say so? By the same law also he must say, which of his issue must enjoy the crown in succession, and so point out the heir, or else leave his issue to divide or scramble for the government: both alike absurd, and such as will destroy the benefit of such grant to the issue. When any such declaration of God's intention is produced, it will be our duty to believe God intends it so; but till that be done, our author must shew us some better warrant, before we shall be obliged to receive him as the authentic revealer of God's intentions.

§. 167. "The issue," says our author, "is comprehended sufficiently in the person of the father, although the father only was named in the grant:" and yet God, when he gave the land of Canaan to Abraham, Gen. xiii. 15. thought fit to put his seed into the grant too: so the priesthood was given to Aaron and his seed; and the crown God gave not only to David, but his seed also: and however our author assures us that "God intends, that the issue should have the benefit of it, when he chooses any person to be king," yet we see that the kingdom which he gave to Saul, without mentioning his seed after him, never came to any of his issue: and why, when God chose a person to be king, he should intend, that his issue should have the benefit of it, more than when he chose one to be judge in Israel, I would fain know a reason; or why does a grant of fatherly authority to a king more comprehend the issue, than when a like grant is made to a judge? Is paternal authority by right to descend to the issue of one, and not of the other? There will need some reason to be shewn of this difference, more than the name, when the thing given is the same fatherly authority, and the manner of giving it, God's choice of the person, the same too; for I suppose our author, when he says, God raised up judges, will by no means allow, they were chosen by the people.

§. 168. But since our author has so confidently assured us of the care of God to preserve the fatherhood, and pretends to build all he says upon the authority of the scripture, we may well expect that that people, whose law, constitution and history is chiefly contained in the scripture, should furnish him with the clearest instances of God's care of preserving the fatherly authority, in that people who it is agreed he had a most peculiar care of. Let us see then what state this paternal authority or government was in amongst the Jews, from their beginning to be a people. It was omitted, by our author's confession, from their coming into Egypt, till their return out of that bondage, above two hundred years: from thence till God gave the Israelites a king, about four hundred years more, our author gives but a very slender account of it; nor indeed all that time are there the least footsteps of paternal or regal government amongst them. But then, says our author, "God re-established the ancient and prime right of lineal succession to paternal government."

§. 169. What a lineal succession to paternal government was then established, we have already seen. I only now consider how long this lasted, and that was to their captivity, about five hundred years: from thence to their destruction by the Romans, above six hundred and fifty years after, the ancient and prime right of lineal succession to paternal government was again lost, and they continued a people in the promised land without it. So that of one thousand, seven hundred and fifty years that they were God's peculiar people, they had hereditary kingly government amongst them not one third of the time; and of that time there is not the least footstep of one moment of paternal government, nor the re-establishment of the ancient and prime right of lineal succession to it, whether we suppose it to be derived, as from its fountain, from David, Saul, Abraham, or, which upon our author's principles, is the only true, from Adam.

Book II. Of Civil Government

1764 EDITOR'S NOTE

The present Edition of this Book has not only been collated with the first three Editions, which were published during the Author's Life, but also has the Advantage of his last Corrections and Improvements, from a Copy delivered by him to Mr. Peter Coste, communicated to the Editor, and now lodged in Christ College, Cambridge.

PREFACE

Reader, thou hast here the beginning and end of a discourse concerning government; what fate has otherwise disposed of the papers that should have filled up the middle, and were more than all the rest, it is not worth while to tell thee. These, which remain, I hope are sufficient to establish the throne of our great restorer, our present King William; to make good his title, in the consent of the people, which being the only one of all lawful governments, he has more fully and clearly, than any prince in Christendom; and to justify to the world the people of England, whose love of their just and natural rights, with their resolution to preserve them, saved the nation when it was on the very brink of slavery and ruin. If these papers have that evidence, I flatter myself is to be found in them, there will be no great miss of those which are lost, and my reader may be satisfied without them: for I imagine, I shall have neither the time, nor inclination to repeat my pains, and fill up the wanting part of my answer, by tracing Sir Robert again, through all the windings and obscurities, which are to be met with in the several branches of his wonderful system. The king, and body of the nation, have since so thoroughly confuted his Hypothesis, that I suppose no body hereafter will have either the confidence to appear against our common safety, and be again an advocate for slavery; or the weakness to be deceived with contradictions dressed up in a popular stile, and well-turned periods: for if any one will be at the pains, himself, in those parts, which are here untouched, to strip Sir Robert's discourses of the flourish of doubtful expressions, and endeavour to reduce his words to direct, positive, intelligible propositions, and then compare them one with another, he will quickly be satisfied, there was never so much glib nonsense put together in well-sounding English. If he think it not worth while to examine his works all thro', let him make an experiment in that part, where he treats of usurpation; and let him try, whether he can, with all his skill, make Sir Robert intelligible, and consistent with himself, or common sense. I should not speak so plainly of a gentleman, long since past answering, had not the pulpit, of late years, publicly owned his doctrine, and made it the current divinity of the times. It is necessary those men, who taking on them to be teachers, have so dangerously misled others, should be openly shewed of what authority this their Patriarch is, whom they have so blindly followed, that so they may either retract what upon so ill grounds they have vented, and cannot be maintained; or else justify those principles which they preached up for gospel; though they had no better an author than an English courtier: for I should not have writ against Sir Robert, or taken the pains to shew his mistakes, inconsistencies, and want of (what he so much boasts of, and pretends wholly to build on) scripture-proofs, were there not men amongst us, who, by crying up his books, and espousing his doctrine, save me from the reproach of writing against a dead adversary. They have been so zealous in this point, that, if I have done him any wrong, I cannot hope they should spare me. I wish, where they have done the truth and the public wrong, they would be as ready to redress it, and allow its just weight to this reflection, viz. that there cannot be done a greater mischief to prince and people, than the propagating wrong notions concerning government; that so at last all times might not have reason to complain of the Drum Ecclesiastic. If any one, concerned really for truth, undertake the confutation of my

Hypothesis, I promise him either to recant my mistake, upon fair conviction; or to answer his difficulties. But he must remember two things.

First, That cavilling here and there, at some expression, or little incident of my discourse, is not an answer to my book.

Secondly, That I shall not take railing for arguments, nor think either of these worth my notice, though I shall always look on myself as bound to give satisfaction to any one, who shall appear to be conscientiously scrupulous in the point, and shall shew any just grounds for his scruples.

I have nothing more, but to advertise the reader, that Observations stands for Observations on Hobbs, Milton, &c. and that a bare quotation of pages always means pages of his Patriarcha, Edition 1680.

CHAP. I.

Sec. 1. It having been shewn in the foregoing discourse,

1. That Adam had not, either by natural right of fatherhood, or by positive donation from God, any such authority over his children, or dominion over the world, as is pretended:

2. That if he had, his heirs, yet, had no right to it:

3. That if his heirs had, there being no law of nature nor positive law of God that determines which is the right heir in all cases that may arise, the right of succession, and consequently of bearing rule, could not have been certainly determined:

4. That if even that had been determined, yet the knowledge of which is the eldest line of Adam's posterity, being so long since utterly lost, that in the races of mankind and families of the world, there remains not to one above another, the least pretence to be the eldest house, and to have the right of inheritance:

All these premises having, as I think, been clearly made out, it is impossible that the rulers now on earth should make any benefit, or derive any the least shadow of authority from that, which is held to be the fountain of all power, Adam's private dominion and paternal jurisdiction; so that he that will not give just occasion to think that all government in the world is the product only of force and violence, and that men live together by no other rules but that of beasts, where the strongest carries it, and so lay a foundation for perpetual disorder and mischief, tumult, sedition and rebellion, (things that the followers of that hypothesis so loudly cry out against) must of necessity find out another rise of government, another original of political power, and another way of designing and knowing the persons that have it, than what Sir Robert Filmer hath taught us.

Sec. 2. To this purpose, I think it may not be amiss, to set down what I take to be political power; that the power of a MAGISTRATE over a subject may be distinguished from that of a FATHER over his children, a MASTER over his servant, a HUSBAND over his wife, and a LORD over his slave. All which distinct powers happening sometimes together in the same man, if he be considered under these different relations, it may help us to distinguish these powers one from wealth, a father of a family, and a captain of a galley.

Sec. 3. POLITICAL POWER, then, I take to be a RIGHT of making laws with penalties of death, and consequently all less penalties, for the regulating and preserving of property, and of employing the force of the community, in the execution of such laws, and in the defence of the common-wealth from foreign injury; and all this only for the public good.

CHAP. II. Of the State of Nature.

Sec. 4. TO understand political power right, and derive it from its original, we must consider, what state all men are naturally in, and that is, a state of perfect freedom to order their actions, and dispose of their possessions and persons, as they think fit, within the bounds of the law of nature, without asking leave, or depending upon the will of any other man.

A state also of equality, wherein all the power and jurisdiction is reciprocal, no one having more than another; there being nothing more evident, than that creatures of the same species and rank, promiscuously born to all the same advantages of nature, and the use of the same faculties, should also be equal one amongst another without subordination or subjection, unless the lord and master of them all should, by any manifest declaration of his will, set one above another, and confer on him, by an evident and clear appointment, an undoubted right to dominion and sovereignty.

Sec. 5. This equality of men by nature, the judicious Hooker looks upon as so evident in itself, and beyond all question, that he makes it the foundation of that obligation to mutual love amongst men, on which he builds the duties they owe one another, and from whence he derives the great maxims of justice and charity. His words are,

"The like natural inducement hath brought men to know that it is no less their duty, to love others than themselves; for seeing those things which are equal, must needs all have one measure; if I cannot but wish to receive good, even as much at every man's hands, as any man can wish unto his own soul, how should I look to have any part of my desire herein satisfied, unless myself be careful to satisfy the like desire, which is undoubtedly in other men, being of one and the same nature? To have any thing offered them repugnant to this desire, must needs in all respects grieve them as much as me; so that if I do harm, I must look to suffer, there being no reason that others should shew greater measure of love to me, than they have by me shewed unto them: my desire therefore to be loved of my equals in nature as much as possible may be, imposeth upon me a natural duty of bearing to them-ward fully the like affection; from which relation of equality between ourselves and them that are as ourselves, what several rules and canons natural reason hath drawn, for direction of life, no man is ignorant, Eccl. Pol. Lib. 1."

Sec. 6. But though this be a state of liberty, yet it is not a state of licence: though man in that state have an uncontroulable liberty to dispose of his person or possessions, yet he has not liberty to destroy himself, or so much as any creature in his possession, but where some nobler use than its bare preservation calls for it. The state of nature has a law of nature to govern it, which obliges every one: and reason, which is that law, teaches all mankind, who will but consult it, that being all equal and independent, no one ought to harm another in his life, health, liberty, or possessions: for men being all the workmanship of one omnipotent, and infinitely wise maker; all the servants of one sovereign master, sent into the world by his order, and about his business; they are his property, whose workmanship they are, made to last during his, not one another's pleasure: and being furnished with like faculties, sharing all in one community of nature, there cannot be supposed any such subordination among us, that may authorize us to destroy one another, as if we were made for one another's uses, as the inferior ranks of creatures are for our's. Every one, as he is bound to preserve himself, and not to quit his station wilfully, so by the like reason, when his own preservation comes not in competition, ought he, as much as he can, to preserve the rest of mankind, and may not, unless it be to do justice on an offender, take away, or impair the life, or what tends to the preservation of the life, the liberty, health, limb, or goods of another.

Sec. 7. And that all men may be restrained from invading others rights, and from doing hurt to one another, and the law of nature be observed, which willeth the peace and preservation of all mankind, the execution of the law of nature is, in that state, put into every man's hands, whereby every one has a right to punish the transgressors of that law to such a degree, as may hinder its violation: for the law of nature would, as all other laws that concern men in this world 'be in vain, if there were no body that in the state of nature had a power to execute that law, and thereby preserve the innocent and restrain offenders. And if any one in the state of nature may punish another for any evil he has done, every one may do so: for in that state of perfect equality, where naturally there is no superiority or jurisdiction of one over another, what any may do in prosecution of that law, every one must needs have a right to do.

Sec. 8. And thus, in the state of nature, one man comes by a power over another; but yet no absolute or arbitrary power, to use a criminal, when he has got him in his hands, according to the passionate heats, or boundless extravagancy of his own will; but only to retribute to him, so far as calm reason and conscience dictate, what is proportionate to his transgression, which is so much as may serve for reparation and restraint: for these two are the only reasons, why one man may lawfully do harm to another, which is that we call punishment. In transgressing the law of nature, the offender declares himself to live by another rule than that of reason and common equity, which is that measure God has set to the actions of men, for their mutual security; and so he becomes dangerous to mankind, the tye, which is to secure them from injury and violence, being slighted and broken by him. Which being a trespass against the whole species, and the peace and safety of it, provided for by the law of nature, every man upon this score, by the right he hath to preserve mankind in general, may restrain, or where it is necessary, destroy things noxious to them, and so may bring such evil on any one, who hath transgressed that law, as may make him repent the doing of it, and thereby deter him, and by his example others, from doing the like mischief. And in the case, and upon this ground, EVERY MAN HATH A RIGHT TO PUNISH THE OFFENDER, AND BE EXECUTIONER OF THE LAW OF NATURE.

Sec. 9. I doubt not but this will seem a very strange doctrine to some men: but before they condemn it, I desire them to resolve me, by what right any prince or state can put to death, or punish an alien, for any crime he commits in their country. It is certain their laws, by virtue of any sanction they receive from the promulgated will of the legislative, reach not a stranger: they speak not to him, nor, if they did, is he bound to hearken to them. The legislative authority, by which they are in force over the subjects of that commonwealth, hath no power over him. Those who have the supreme power of making laws in England, France or Holland, are to an Indian, but like the rest of the world, men without authority: and therefore, if by the law of nature every man hath not a power to punish offences against it, as he soberly judges the case to require, I see not how the magistrates of any community can punish an alien of another country; since, in reference to him, they can have no more power than what every man naturally may have over another.

Sec. 10. Besides the crime which consists in violating the law, and varying from the right rule of reason, whereby a man so far becomes degenerate, and declares himself to quit the principles of human nature, and to be a noxious creature, there is commonly injury done to some person or other, and some other man receives damage by his transgression: in which case he who hath received any damage, has, besides the right of punishment common to him with other men, a particular right to seek reparation from him that has done it: and any other person, who finds it just, may also join with him that is injured, and assist him in recovering from the offender so much as may make satisfaction for the harm he has suffered.

Sec. 11. From these two distinct rights, the one of punishing the crime for restraint, and preventing the like offence, which right of punishing is in every body; the other of taking reparation, which belongs only to the injured party, comes it to pass that the magistrate, who by being magistrate hath the common right of punishing put into his hands, can often, where the public good demands not the execution of the law, remit the punishment of criminal offences by his own authority, but yet cannot remit the satisfaction due to any private man for the damage he has received. That, he who has suffered the damage has a right to demand in his own name, and he alone can remit: the damnified person has this power of appropriating to himself the goods or service of the offender, by right of self-preservation, as every man has a power to punish the crime, to prevent its being committed again, by the right he has of preserving all mankind, and doing all reasonable things he can in order to that end: and thus it is, that every man, in the state of nature, has a power to kill a murderer, both to deter others from doing the like injury, which no reparation can compensate, by the example of the punishment that attends it from every body, and also to secure men from the attempts of a criminal, who having renounced reason, the common rule and measure God hath given to mankind, hath, by the unjust violence and slaughter he hath committed upon one, declared war against all mankind, and therefore may be destroyed as a lion or a tyger, one of those wild savage beasts, with whom men can have no society nor security: and upon this is grounded that great law of nature, Whoso sheddeth man's blood, by man shall his blood be shed. And Cain was so fully convinced, that every one had a right to destroy such a criminal, that after the murder of his brother, he cries out, Every one that findeth me, shall slay me; so plain was it writ in the hearts of all mankind.

Sec. 12. By the same reason may a man in the state of nature punish the lesser breaches of that law. It will perhaps be demanded, with death? I answer, each transgression may be punished to that degree, and with so much severity, as will suffice to make it an ill bargain to the offender, give him cause to repent, and terrify others from doing the like. Every offence, that can be committed in the state of nature, may in the state of nature be also punished equally, and as far forth as it may, in a commonwealth: for though it would be besides my present purpose, to enter here into the particulars of the law of nature, or its measures of punishment; yet, it is certain there is such a law, and that too, as intelligible and plain to a rational creature, and a studier of that law, as the positive laws of commonwealths; nay, possibly plainer; as much as reason is easier to be understood, than the fancies and intricate contrivances of men, following contrary and hidden interests put into words; for so truly are a great part of the municipal laws of countries, which are only so far right, as they are founded on the law of nature, by which they are to be regulated and interpreted.

Sec. 13. To this strange doctrine, viz. That in the state of nature every one has the executive power of the law of nature, I doubt not but it will be objected, that it is unreasonable for men to be judges in their own cases, that selflove will make men partial to themselves and their friends: and on the other side, that ill nature, passion and revenge will carry them too far in punishing others; and hence nothing but confusion and disorder will follow, and that therefore God hath certainly appointed government to restrain the partiality and violence of men. I easily grant, that civil government is the proper remedy for the inconveniencies of the state of nature, which must certainly be great, where men may be judges in their own case, since it is easy to be imagined, that he who was so unjust as to do his brother an injury, will scarce be so just as to condemn himself for it: but I shall desire those who make this objection, to remember, that absolute monarchs are but men; and if government is to be the remedy of those evils, which necessarily follow from men's being judges in their own cases, and the state of nature is therefore not to be endured, I desire to know what kind of government that is, and how much better it is than the state of nature, where one man, commanding a multitude, has the liberty to be judge in his own case, and may do to all his subjects whatever he pleases, without the least liberty to any one to question or controul those who execute his pleasure and in whatsoever he doth, whether led by reason, mistake or passion, must be submitted to. Much better it is in the state of nature, wherein men are not bound to submit to the unjust will of another. And if he that judges, judges amiss in his own, or any other case, he is answerable for it to the rest of mankind.

Sec. 14. It is often asked as a mighty objection, where are, or ever were there any men in such a state of nature? To which it may suffice as an answer at present, that since all princes and rulers of independent governments all through the world, are in a state of nature, it is plain the world never was, nor ever will be, without numbers of men in that state. I have named all governors of independent communities, whether they are, or are not, in league with others: for it is not every compact that puts an end to the state of nature between men, but only this one of agreeing together mutually to enter into one community, and make one body politic; other promises, and compacts, men may make one with another, and yet still be in the state of nature. The promises and bargains for truck, &c. between the two men in the desert island, mentioned by Garcilasso de la Vega, in his history of Peru; or between a Swiss and an Indian, in the woods of America, are binding to them, though they are perfectly in a state of nature, in reference to one another: for truth and keeping of faith belongs to men, as men, and not as members of society.

Sec. 15. To those that say, there were never any men in the state of nature, I will not only oppose the authority of the judicious Hooker, Eccl. Pol. lib. i. sect. 10, where he says, The laws which have been hitherto mentioned, i.e. the laws of nature, do bind men absolutely, even as they are men, although they have never any settled fellowship, never any solemn agreement amongst themselves what to do, or not to do: but forasmuch as we are not by ourselves sufficient to furnish ourselves with competent store of things, needful for such a life as our nature doth desire, a life fit for the dignity of man; therefore to supply those defects and imperfections which are in us, as living single and solely by ourselves, we are naturally induced to seek communion and fellowship with others: this was the cause of men's uniting themselves at first in politic societies. But I moreover affirm, that all men are naturally in that state, and remain so, till by their own consents they make themselves members of some politic society; and I doubt not in the sequel of this discourse, to make it very clear.

CHAP. III. Of the State of War.

Sec. 16. THE state of war is a state of enmity and destruction: and therefore declaring by word or action, not a passionate and hasty, but a sedate settled design upon another man's life, puts him in a state of war with him against whom he has declared such an intention, and so has exposed his life to the other's power to be taken away by him, or any one that joins with him in his defence, and espouses his quarrel; it being reasonable and just, I should have a right to destroy that which threatens me with destruction: for, by the fundamental law of nature, man being to be preserved as much as possible, when all cannot be preserved, the safety of the innocent is to be preferred: and one may destroy a man who makes war upon him, or has discovered an enmity to his being, for the same reason that he may kill a wolf or a lion; because such men are not under the ties of the commonlaw of reason, have no other rule, but that of force and violence, and so may be treated as beasts of prey, those dangerous and noxious creatures, that will be sure to destroy him whenever he falls into their power.

Sec. 17. And hence it is, that he who attempts to get another man into his absolute power, does thereby put himself into a state of war with him; it being to be understood as a declaration of a design upon his life: for I have reason to conclude, that he who would get me into his power without my consent, would use me as he pleased when he had got me there, and destroy me too when he had a fancy to it; for no body can desire to have me in his absolute power, unless it be to compel me by force to that which is against the right of my freedom, i.e. make me a slave. To be free from such force is the only security of my preservation; and reason bids me look on him, as an enemy to my preservation, who would take away that freedom which is the fence to it; so that he who makes an attempt to enslave me, thereby puts himself into a state of war with me. He that, in the state of nature, would take away the freedom that belongs to any one in that state, must necessarily be supposed to have a foundation of all the rest; as he that in the state of society, would take away the freedom belonging to those of that society or commonwealth, must be supposed to design to take away from them every thing else, and so be looked on as in a state of war.

Sec. 18. This makes it lawful for a man to kill a thief, who has not in the least hurt him, nor declared any design upon his life, any farther than, by the use of force, so to get him in his power, as to take away his money, or what he pleases, from him; because using force, where he has no right, to get me into his power, let his pretence be what it will, I have no reason to suppose, that he, who would take away my liberty, would not, when he had me in his power, take away every thing else. And therefore it is lawful for me to treat him as one who has put himself into a state of war with me, i.e. kill him if I can; for to that hazard does he justly expose himself, whoever introduces a state of war, and is aggressor in it.

Sec. 19. And here we have the plain difference between the state of nature and the state of war, which however some men have confounded, are as far distant, as a state of peace, good will, mutual assistance and preservation, and a state of enmity, malice, violence and mutual destruction, are one from another. Men living together according to reason, without a common superior on earth, with authority to judge between them, is properly the state of nature. But force, or a declared design of force, upon the person of another, where there is no common superior on earth to appeal to for relief, is the state of war: and it is the want of such an appeal gives a man the right of war even against an aggressor, tho' he be in society and a fellow subject. Thus a thief, whom I cannot harm, but by appeal to the law, for having stolen all that I am worth, I may kill, when he sets on me to rob me but of my horse or coat; because the law, which was made for my preservation, where it cannot interpose to secure my life from present force, which, if lost, is capable of no reparation, permits me my own defence, and the right of war, a liberty to kill the aggressor, because the aggressor allows not time to appeal to our common judge, nor the decision of the law, for remedy in a case where the mischief may be irreparable. Want of a common judge with authority, puts all men in a state of nature: force without right, upon a man's person, makes a state of war, both where there is, and is not, a common judge.

Sec. 20. But when the actual force is over, the state of war ceases between those that are in society, and are equally on both sides subjected to the fair determination of the law; because then there lies open the remedy of appeal for the past injury, and to prevent future harm: but where no such appeal is, as in the state of nature, for want of positive laws, and judges with authority to appeal to, the state of war once begun, continues, with a right to the innocent party to destroy the other whenever he can, until the aggressor offers peace, and desires reconciliation on such terms as may repair any wrongs he has already done, and secure the innocent for the future; nay, where an appeal to the law, and constituted judges, lies open, but the remedy is denied by a manifest perverting of justice, and a barefaced wresting of the laws to protect or indemnify the violence or injuries of some men, or party of men, there it is hard to imagine any thing but a state of war: for wherever violence is used, and injury done, though by hands appointed to administer justice, it is still violence and injury, however coloured with the name, pretences, or forms of law, the end whereof being to protect and redress the innocent, by an unbiassed application of it, to all who are under it; wherever that is not bona fide done, war is made upon the sufferers, who having no appeal on earth to right them, they are left to the only remedy in such cases, an appeal to heaven.

Sec. 21. To avoid this state of war (wherein there is no appeal but to heaven, and wherein every the least difference is apt to end, where there is no authority to decide between the contenders) is one great reason of men's putting themselves into society, and quitting the state of nature: for where there is an authority, a power on earth, from which relief can be had by appeal, there the continuance of the state of war is excluded, and the controversy is decided by that power. Had there been any such court, any superior jurisdiction on earth, to determine the right between Jephtha and the Ammonites, they had never come to a state of war: but we see he was forced to appeal to heaven. The Lord the Judge (says he) be judge this day between the children of Israel and the children of Ammon, Judg. xi. 27. and then prosecuting, and relying on his appeal, he leads out his army to battle: and therefore in such controversies, where the question is put, who shall be judge? It cannot be meant, who shall decide the controversy; every one knows what Jephtha here tells us, that the Lord the Judge shall judge. Where there is no judge on earth, the appeal lies to God in heaven. That question then cannot mean, who shall judge, whether another hath put himself in a state of war with me, and whether I may, as Jephtha did, appeal to heaven in it? of that I myself can only be judge in my own conscience, as I will answer it, at the great day, to the supreme judge of all men.

CHAP. IV. Of Slavery.

Sec. 22. THE natural liberty of man is to be free from any superior power on earth, and not to be under the will or legislative authority of man, but to have only the law of nature for his rule. The liberty of man, in society, is to be under no other legislative power, but that established, by consent, in the commonwealth; nor under the dominion of any will, or restraint of any law, but what that legislative shall enact, according to the trust put in it. Freedom then is not what Sir Robert Filmer tells us, Observations, A. 55. a liberty for every one to do what he lists, to live as he pleases, and not to be tied by any laws: but freedom of men under government is, to have a standing rule to live by, common to every one of that society, and made by the legislative power erected in it; a liberty to follow my own will in all things, where the rule prescribes not; and not to be subject to the inconstant, uncertain, unknown, arbitrary will of another man: as freedom of nature is, to be under no other restraint but the law of nature.

Sec. 23. This freedom from absolute, arbitrary power, is so necessary to, and closely joined with a man's preservation, that he cannot part with it, but by what forfeits his preservation and life together: for a man, not having the power of his own life, cannot, by compact, or his own consent, enslave himself to any one, nor put himself under the absolute, arbitrary power of another, to take away his life, when he pleases. No body can give more power than he has himself; and he that cannot take away his own life, cannot give another power over it. Indeed, having by his fault forfeited his own life, by some act that deserves death; he, to whom he has forfeited it, may (when he has him in his power) delay to take it, and make use of him to his own service, and he does him no injury by it: for, whenever he finds the hardship of his slavery outweigh the value of his life, it is in his power, by resisting the will of his master, to draw on himself the death he desires.

Sec. 24. This is the perfect condition of slavery, which is nothing else, but the state of war continued, between a lawful conqueror and a captive: for, if once compact enter between them, and make an agreement for a limited power on the one side, and obedience on the other, the state of war and slavery ceases, as long as the compact endures: for, as has been said, no man can, by agreement, pass over to another that which he hath not in himself, a power over his own life.

I confess, we find among the Jews, as well as other nations, that men did sell themselves; but, it is plain, this was only to drudgery, not to slavery: for, it is evident, the person sold was not under an absolute, arbitrary, despotical power: for the master could not have power to kill him, at any time, whom, at a certain time, he was obliged to let go free out of his service; and the master of such a servant was so far from having an arbitrary power over his life, that he could not, at pleasure, so much as maim him, but the loss of an eye, or tooth, set him free, Exod. xxi.

CHAP. V. Of Property.

Sec. 25. Whether we consider natural reason, which tells us, that men, being once born, have a right to their preservation, and consequently to meat and drink, and such other things as nature affords for their subsistence: or revelation, which gives us an account of those grants God made of the world to Adam, and to Noah, and his sons, it is very clear, that God, as king David says, Psal. cxv. 16. has given the earth to the children of men; given it to mankind in common. But this being supposed, it seems to some a very great difficulty, how any one should ever come to have a property in any thing: I will not content myself to answer, that if it be difficult to make out property, upon a supposition that God gave the world to Adam, and his posterity in common, it is impossible that any man, but one universal monarch, should have any property upon a supposition, that God gave the world to Adam, and his heirs in succession, exclusive of all the rest of his posterity. But I shall endeavour to shew, how men might come to have a property in several parts of that which God gave to mankind in common, and that without any express compact of all the commoners.

Sec. 26. God, who hath given the world to men in common, hath also given them reason to make use of it to the best advantage of life, and convenience. The earth, and all that is therein, is given to men for the support and comfort of their being. And tho' all the fruits it naturally produces, and beasts it feeds, belong to mankind in common, as they are produced by the spontaneous hand of nature; and no body has originally a private dominion, exclusive of the rest of mankind, in any of them, as they are thus in their natural state: yet being given for the use of men, there must of necessity be a means to appropriate them some way or other, before they can be of any use, or at all beneficial to any particular man. The fruit, or venison, which nourishes the wild Indian, who knows no enclosure, and is still a tenant in common, must be his, and so his, i.e. a part of him, that another can no longer have any right to it, before it can do him any good for the support of his life.

Sec. 27. Though the earth, and all inferior creatures, be common to all men, yet every man has a property in his own person: this no body has any right to but himself. The labour of his body, and the work of his hands, we may say, are properly his. Whatsoever then he removes out of the state that nature hath provided, and left it in, he hath mixed his labour with, and joined to it something that is his own, and thereby makes it his property. It being by him removed from the common state nature hath placed it in, it hath by this labour something annexed to it, that excludes the common right of other men: for this labour being the unquestionable property of the labourer, no man but he can have a right to what that is once joined to, at least where there is enough, and as good, left in common for others.

Sec. 28. He that is nourished by the acorns he picked up under an oak, or the apples he gathered from the trees in the wood, has certainly appropriated them to himself. No body can deny but the nourishment is his. I ask then, when did they begin to be his? when he digested? or when he eat? or when he boiled? or when he brought them home? or when he picked them up? and it is plain, if the first gathering made them not his, nothing else could. That labour put a distinction between them and common: that added something to them more than nature, the common mother of all, had done; and so they became his private right. And will any one say, he had no right to those acorns or apples, he thus appropriated, because he had not the consent of all mankind to make them his? Was it a robbery thus to assume to himself what belonged to all in common? If such a consent as that was necessary, man had starved, notwithstanding the plenty God had given him. We see in commons, which remain so by compact, that it is the taking any part of what is common, and removing it out of the state nature leaves it in, which begins the property; without which the common is of no use. And the taking of this or that part, does not depend on the express consent of all the commoners. Thus the grass my horse has bit; the turfs my servant has cut; and the ore I have digged in any place, where I have a right to them in common with others, become my property, without the assignation or consent of any body. The labour that was mine, removing them out of that common state they were in, hath fixed my property in them.

Sec. 29. By making an explicit consent of every commoner, necessary to any one's appropriating to himself any part of what is given in common, children or servants could not cut the meat, which their father or master had provided for them in common, without assigning to every one his peculiar part. Though the water running in the fountain be every one's, yet who can doubt, but that in the pitcher is his only who drew it out? His labour hath taken it out of the hands of nature, where it was common, and belonged equally to all her children, and hath thereby appropriated it to himself.

Sec. 30. Thus this law of reason makes the deer that Indian's who hath killed it; it is allowed to be his goods, who hath bestowed his labour upon it, though before it was the common right of every one. And amongst those who are counted the civilized part of mankind, who have made and multiplied positive laws to determine property, this original law of nature, for the beginning of property, in what was before common, still takes place; and by virtue thereof, what fish any one catches in the ocean, that great and still remaining common of mankind; or what ambergrise any one takes up here, is by the labour that removes it out of that common state nature left it in, made his property, who takes that pains about it. And even amongst us, the hare that any one is hunting, is thought his who pursues her during the chase: for being a beast that is still looked upon as common, and no man's private possession; whoever has employed so much labour about any of that kind, as to find and pursue her, has thereby removed her from the state of nature, wherein she was common, and hath begun a property.

Sec. 31. It will perhaps be objected to this, that if gathering the acorns, or other fruits of the earth, &c. makes a right to them, then any one may ingross as much as he will. To which I answer, Not so. The same law of nature, that does by this means give us property, does also bound that property too. God has given us all things richly, 1 Tim. vi. 12. is the voice of reason confirmed by inspiration. But how far has he given it us? To enjoy. As much as any one can make use of to any advantage of life before it spoils, so much he may by his labour fix a property in: whatever is beyond this, is more than his share, and belongs to others. Nothing was made by God for man to spoil or destroy. And thus, considering the plenty of natural provisions there was a long time in the world, and the few spenders; and to how small a part of that provision the industry of one man could extend itself, and ingross it to the prejudice of others; especially keeping within the bounds, set by reason, of what might serve for his use; there could be then little room for quarrels or contentions about property so established.

Sec. 32. But the chief matter of property being now not the fruits of the earth, and the beasts that subsist on it, but the earth itself; as that which takes in and carries with it all the rest; I think it is plain, that property in that too is acquired as the former. As much land as a man tills, plants, improves, cultivates, and can use the product of, so much is his property. He by his labour does, as it were, inclose it from the common. Nor will it invalidate his right, to say every body else has an equal title to it; and therefore he cannot appropriate, he cannot inclose, without the consent of all his fellow-commoners, all mankind. God, when he gave the world in common to all mankind, commanded man also to labour, and the penury of his condition required it of him. God and his reason commanded him to subdue the earth, i.e. improve it for the benefit of life, and therein lay out something upon it that was his own, his labour. He that in obedience to this command of God, subdued, tilled and sowed any part of it, thereby annexed to it something that was his property, which another had no title to, nor could without injury take from him.

Sec. 33. Nor was this appropriation of any parcel of land, by improving it, any prejudice to any other man, since there was still enough, and as good left; and more than the yet unprovided could use. So that, in effect, there was never the less left for others because of his enclosure for himself: for he that leaves as much as another can make use of, does as good as take nothing at all. No body could think himself injured by the drinking of another man, though he took a good draught, who had a whole river of the same water left him to quench his thirst: and the case of land and water, where there is enough of both, is perfectly the same.

Sec. 34. God gave the world to men in common; but since he gave it them for their benefit, and the greatest conveniencies of life they were capable to draw from it, it cannot be supposed he meant it should always remain common and uncultivated. He gave it to the use of the industrious and rational, (and labour was to be his title to it;) not to the fancy or covetousness of the quarrelsome and contentious. He that had as good left for his improvement, as was already taken up, needed not complain, ought not to meddle with what was already improved by another's labour: if he did, it is plain he desired the benefit of another's pains, which he had no right to, and not the ground which God had given him in common with others to labour on, and whereof there was as good left, as that already possessed, and more than he knew what to do with, or his industry could reach to.

Sec. 35. It is true, in land that is common in England, or any other country, where there is plenty of people under government, who have money and commerce, no one can inclose or appropriate any part, without the consent of all his fellowcommoners; because this is left common by compact, i.e. by the law of the land, which is not to be violated. And though it be common, in respect of some men, it is not so to all mankind; but is the joint property of this country, or this parish. Besides, the remainder, after such enclosure, would not be as good to the rest of the commoners, as the whole was when they could all make use of the whole; whereas in the beginning and first peopling of the great common of the world, it was quite otherwise. The law man was under, was rather for appropriating. God commanded, and his wants forced him to labour. That was his property which could not be taken from him where-ever he had fixed it. And hence subduing or cultivating the earth, and having dominion, we see are joined together. The one gave title to the other. So that God, by commanding to subdue, gave authority so far to appropriate: and the condition of human life, which requires labour and materials to work on, necessarily introduces private possessions.

Sec. 36. The measure of property nature has well set by the extent of men's labour and the conveniencies of life: no man's labour could subdue, or appropriate all; nor could his enjoyment consume more than a small part; so that it was impossible for any man, this way, to intrench upon the right of another, or acquire to himself a property, to the prejudice of his neighbour, who would still have room for as good, and as large a possession (after the other had taken out his) as before it was appropriated. This measure did confine every man's possession to a very moderate proportion, and such as he might appropriate to himself, without injury to any body, in the first ages of the world, when men were more in danger to be lost, by wandering from their company, in the then vast wilderness of the earth, than to be straitened for want of room to plant in. And the same measure may be allowed still without prejudice to any body, as full as the world seems: for supposing a man, or family, in the state they were at first peopling of the world by the children of Adam, or Noah; let him plant in some inland, vacant places of America, we shall find that the possessions he could make himself, upon the measures we have given, would not be very large, nor, even to this day, prejudice the rest of mankind, or give them reason to complain, or think themselves injured by this man's incroachment, though the race of men have now spread themselves to all the corners of the world, and do infinitely exceed the small number was at the beginning. Nay, the extent of ground is of so little value, without labour, that I have heard it affirmed, that in Spain itself a man may be permitted to plough, sow and reap, without being disturbed, upon land he has no other title to, but only his making use of it. But, on the contrary, the inhabitants think themselves beholden to him, who, by his industry on neglected, and consequently waste land, has increased the stock of corn, which they wanted. But be this as it will, which I lay no stress on; this I dare boldly affirm, that the same rule of propriety, (viz.) that every man should have as much as he could make use of, would hold still in the world, without straitening any body; since there is land enough in the world to suffice double the inhabitants, had not the invention of money, and the tacit agreement of men to put a value on it, introduced (by consent) larger possessions, and a right to them; which, how it has done, I shall by and by shew more at large.

Sec. 37. This is certain, that in the beginning, before the desire of having more than man needed had altered the intrinsic value of things, which depends only on their usefulness to the life of man; or had agreed, that a little piece of yellow metal, which would keep without wasting or decay, should be worth a great piece of flesh, or a whole heap of corn; though men had a right to appropriate, by their labour, each one of himself, as much of the things of nature, as he could use: yet this could not be much, nor to the prejudice of others, where the same plenty was still left to those who would use the same industry. To which let me add, that he who appropriates land to himself by his labour, does not lessen, but increase the common stock of mankind: for the provisions serving to the support of human life, produced by one acre of inclosed and cultivated land, are (to speak much within compass) ten times more than those which are yielded by an acre of land of an equal richness lying waste in common. And therefore he that incloses land, and has a greater plenty of the conveniencies of life from ten acres, than he could have from an hundred left to nature, may truly be said to give ninety acres to mankind: for his labour now supplies him with provisions out of ten acres, which were but the product of an hundred lying in common. I have here rated the improved land very low, in making its product but as ten to one, when it is much nearer an hundred to one: for I ask, whether in the wild woods and uncultivated waste of America, left to nature, without any improvement, tillage or husbandry, a thousand acres yield the needy and wretched inhabitants as many conveniencies of life, as ten acres of equally fertile land do in Devonshire, where they are well cultivated?

Before the appropriation of land, he who gathered as much of the wild fruit, killed, caught, or tamed, as many of the beasts, as he could; he that so imployed his pains about any of the spontaneous products of nature, as any way to alter them from the state which nature put them in, by placing any of his labour on them, did thereby acquire a propriety in them: but if they perished, in his possession, without their due use; if the fruits rotted, or the venison putrified, before he could spend it, he offended against the common law of nature, and was liable to be punished; he invaded his neighbour's share, for he had no right, farther than his use called for any of them, and they might serve to afford him conveniencies of life.

Sec. 38. The same measures governed the possession of land too: whatsoever he tilled and reaped, laid up and made use of, before it spoiled, that was his peculiar right; whatsoever he enclosed, and could feed, and make use of, the cattle and product was also his. But if either the grass of his enclosure rotted on the ground, or the fruit of his planting perished without gathering, and laying up, this part of the earth, notwithstanding his enclosure, was still to be looked on as waste, and might be the possession of any other. Thus, at the beginning, Cain might take as much ground as he could till, and make it his own land, and yet leave enough to Abel's sheep to feed on; a few acres would serve for both their possessions. But as families increased, and industry inlarged their stocks, their possessions inlarged with the need of them;

but yet it was commonly without any fixed property in the ground they made use of, till they incorporated, settled themselves together, and built cities; and then, by consent, they came in time, to set out the bounds of their distinct territories, and agree on limits between them and their neighbours; and by laws within themselves, settled the properties of those of the same society: for we see, that in that part of the world which was first inhabited, and therefore like to be best peopled, even as low down as Abraham's time, they wandered with their flocks, and their herds, which was their substance, freely up and down; and this Abraham did, in a country where he was a stranger. Whence it is plain, that at least a great part of the land lay in common; that the inhabitants valued it not, nor claimed property in any more than they made use of. But when there was not room enough in the same place, for their herds to feed together, they by consent, as Abraham and Lot did, Gen. xiii. 5. separated and inlarged their pasture, where it best liked them. And for the same reason Esau went from his father, and his brother, and planted in mount Seir, Gen. xxxvi. 6.

Sec. 39. And thus, without supposing any private dominion, and property in Adam, over all the world, exclusive of all other men, which can no way be proved, nor any one's property be made out from it; but supposing the world given, as it was, to the children of men in common, we see how labour could make men distinct titles to several parcels of it, for their private uses; wherein there could be no doubt of right, no room for quarrel.

Sec. 40. Nor is it so strange, as perhaps before consideration it may appear, that the property of labour should be able to over-balance the community of land: for it is labour indeed that puts the difference of value on every thing; and let any one consider what the difference is between an acre of land planted with tobacco or sugar, sown with wheat or barley, and an acre of the same land lying in common, without any husbandry upon it, and he will find, that the improvement of labour makes the far greater part of the value. I think it will be but a very modest computation to say, that of the products of the earth useful to the life of man nine tenths are the effects of labour: nay, if we will rightly estimate things as they come to our use, and cast up the several expences about them, what in them is purely owing to nature, and what to labour, we shall find, that in most of them ninety-nine hundredths are wholly to be put on the account of labour.

Sec. 41. There cannot be a clearer demonstration of any thing, than several nations of the Americans are of this, who are rich in land, and poor in all the comforts of life; whom nature having furnished as liberally as any other people, with the materials of plenty, i.e. a fruitful soil, apt to produce in abundance, what might serve for food, raiment, and delight; yet for want of improving it by labour, have not one hundredth part of the conveniencies we enjoy: and a king of a large and fruitful territory there, feeds, lodges, and is clad worse than a day-labourer in England.

Sec. 42. To make this a little clearer, let us but trace some of the ordinary provisions of life, through their several progresses, before they come to our use, and see how much they receive of their value from human industry. Bread, wine and cloth, are things of daily use, and great plenty; yet notwithstanding, acorns, water and leaves, or skins, must be our bread, drink and cloathing, did not labour furnish us with these more useful commodities: for whatever bread is more worth than acorns, wine than water, and cloth or silk, than leaves, skins or moss, that is wholly owing to labour and industry; the one of these being the food and raiment which unassisted nature furnishes us with; the other, provisions which our industry and pains prepare for us, which how much they exceed the other in value, when any one hath computed, he will then see how much labour makes the far greatest part of the value of things we enjoy in this world: and the ground which produces the materials, is scarce to be reckoned in, as any, or at most, but a very small part of it; so little, that even amongst us, land that is left wholly to nature, that hath no improvement of pasturage, tillage, or planting, is called, as indeed it is, waste; and we shall find the benefit of it amount to little more than nothing.

This shews how much numbers of men are to be preferred to largeness of dominions; and that the increase of lands, and the right employing of them, is the great art of government: and that prince, who shall be so wise and godlike, as by established laws of liberty to secure protection and encouragement to the honest industry of mankind, against the oppression of power and narrowness of party, will quickly be too hard for his neighbours: but this by the by. To return to the argument in hand,

Sec. 43. An acre of land, that bears here twenty bushels of wheat, and another in America, which, with the same husbandry, would do the like, are, without doubt, of the same natural intrinsic value: but yet the benefit mankind receives from the one in a year, is worth 5l. and from the other possibly not worth a penny, if all the profit an Indian received from it were to be valued, and sold here; at least, I may truly say, not one thousandth. It is labour then which puts the greatest part of value upon land, without which it would scarcely be worth any thing: it is to that we owe the greatest part of all its useful products; for all that the straw, bran, bread, of that acre of wheat, is more worth than the product of an acre of as good land, which lies waste, is all the effect of labour: for it is not barely the plough-man's pains, the reaper's and thresher's toil, and the baker's sweat, is to be counted into the bread we eat; the labour of those who broke the oxen, who digged and wrought the iron and stones, who felled and framed the timber employed about the plough, mill, oven, or any other utensils, which are a vast number, requisite to this corn, from its being feed to be sown to its being made bread, must all be charged on the account of labour, and received as an effect of that: nature and the earth furnished only the almost worthless materials, as in themselves. It would be a strange catalogue of things, that industry provided and made use of, about every loaf of bread, before it came to our use, if we could trace them; iron, wood, leather, bark, timber, stone, bricks, coals, lime, cloth, dying drugs, pitch, tar, masts, ropes, and all the materials made use of in the ship, that brought any of the commodities made use of by any of the workmen, to any part of the work; all which it would be almost impossible, at least too long, to reckon up.

Sec. 44. From all which it is evident, that though the things of nature are given in common, yet man, by being master of himself, and proprietor of his own person, and the actions or labour of it, had still in himself the great foundation of property; and that, which made up the great part of what he applied to the support or comfort of his being, when invention and arts had improved the conveniencies of life, was perfectly his own, and did not belong in common to others.

Sec. 45. Thus labour, in the beginning, gave a right of property, wherever any one was pleased to employ it upon what was common, which remained a long while the far greater part, and is yet more than mankind makes use of. Men, at first, for the most part, contented themselves with what unassisted nature offered to their necessities: and though afterwards, in some parts of the world, (where the increase of people and stock, with the use of money, had made land scarce, and so of some value) the several communities settled the bounds of their distinct territories, and by laws within themselves regulated the properties of the private men of their society, and so, by compact and agreement, settled the property which labour and industry began; and the leagues that have been made between several states and kingdoms, either expresly or tacitly disowning all claim and right to the land in the others possession, have, by common consent, given up their pretences to their natural common right, which originally they had to those countries, and so have, by positive agreement, settled a property amongst themselves, in distinct parts and parcels of the earth; yet there are still great tracts of ground to be found, which (the inhabitants thereof not having joined with the rest of mankind, in the consent of the use of their common money) lie waste, and are more than the people who dwell on it do, or can make use of, and so still lie in common; tho' this can scarce happen amongst that part of mankind that have consented to the use of money.

Sec. 46. The greatest part of things really useful to the life of man, and such as the necessity of subsisting made the first commoners of the world look after, as it doth the Americans now, are generally things of short duration; such as, if they are not consumed by use, will decay and perish of themselves: gold, silver and diamonds, are things that fancy or agreement hath put the value on, more than real use, and the necessary support of life. Now of those good things which nature hath provided in common, every one had a right (as hath been said) to as much as he could use, and property in all that he could effect with his labour; all that his industry could extend to, to alter from the state nature had put it in, was his. He that gathered a hundred bushels of acorns or apples, had thereby a property in them, they were his goods as soon as gathered. He was only to look, that he used them before they spoiled, else he took more than his share, and robbed others. And indeed it was a foolish thing, as well as dishonest, to hoard up more than he could make use of. If he gave away a part to any body else, so that it perished not uselesly in his possession, these he also made use of. And if he also bartered away plums, that would have rotted in a week, for nuts that would last good for his eating a whole year, he did no injury; he wasted not the common stock; destroyed no part of the portion of goods that belonged to others, so long as nothing perished uselesly in his hands. Again, if he would give his nuts for a piece of metal, pleased with its colour; or exchange his sheep for shells, or wool for a sparkling pebble or a diamond, and keep those by him all his life he invaded not the right of others, he might heap up as much of these durable things as he pleased; the exceeding of the bounds of his just property not lying in the largeness of his possession, but the perishing of any thing uselesly in it.

Sec. 47. And thus came in the use of money, some lasting thing that men might keep without spoiling, and that by mutual consent men would take in exchange for the truly useful, but perishable supports of life.

Sec. 48. And as different degrees of industry were apt to give men possessions in different proportions, so this invention of money gave them the opportunity to continue and enlarge them: for supposing an island, separate from all possible commerce with the rest of the world, wherein there were but an hundred families, but there were sheep, horses and cows, with other useful animals, wholsome fruits, and land enough for corn for a hundred thousand times as many, but nothing in the island, either because of its commonness, or perishableness, fit to supply the place of money; what reason could any one have there to enlarge his possessions beyond the use of his family, and a plentiful supply to its consumption, either in what their own industry produced, or they could barter for like perishable, useful commodities, with others? Where there is not some thing, both lasting and scarce, and so valuable to be hoarded up, there men will not be apt to enlarge their possessions of land, were it never so rich, never so free for them to take: for I ask, what would a man value ten thousand, or an hundred thousand acres of excellent land, ready cultivated, and well stocked too with cattle, in the middle of the inland parts of America, where he had no hopes of commerce with other parts of the world, to draw money to him by the sale of the product? It would not be worth the enclosing, and we should see him give up again to the wild common of nature, whatever was more than would supply the conveniencies of life to be had there for him and his family.

Sec. 49. Thus in the beginning all the world was America, and more so than that is now; for no such thing as money was any where known. Find out something that hath the use and value of money amongst his neighbours, you shall see the same man will begin presently to enlarge his possessions.

Sec. 50. But since gold and silver, being little useful to the life of man in proportion to food, raiment, and carriage, has its value only from the consent of men, whereof labour yet makes, in great part, the measure, it is plain, that men have agreed to a disproportionate and unequal possession of the earth, they having, by a tacit and voluntary consent, found out, a way how a man may fairly possess more land than he himself can use the product of, by receiving in exchange for the overplus gold and silver, which may be hoarded up without injury to any one; these metals not spoiling or decaying in the hands of the possessor. This partage of things in an inequality of private possessions, men have made practicable out of the bounds of society, and without compact, only by putting a value on gold and silver, and tacitly agreeing in the use of money: for in governments, the laws regulate the right of property, and the possession of land is determined by positive constitutions.

Sec. 51. And thus, I think, it is very easy to conceive, without any difficulty, how labour could at first begin a title of property in the common things of nature, and how the spending it upon our uses bounded it. So that there could then be no reason of quarrelling about title, nor any doubt about the largeness of possession it gave. Right and conveniency went together; for as a man had a right to all he could employ his labour upon, so he had no temptation to labour for more than he could make use of. This left no room for controversy about the title, nor for encroachment on the right of others; what portion a man carved to himself, was easily seen; and it was useless, as well as dishonest, to carve himself too much, or take more than he needed.

CHAP. VI. Of Paternal Power.

Sec. 52. IT may perhaps be censured as an impertinent criticism, in a discourse of this nature, to find fault with words and names, that have obtained in the world: and yet possibly it may not be amiss to offer new ones, when the old are apt to lead men into mistakes, as this of paternal power probably has done, which seems so to place the power of parents over their children wholly in the father, as if the mother had no share in it; whereas, if we consult reason or revelation, we shall find, she hath an equal title. This may give one reason to ask, whether this might not be more properly called parental power? for whatever obligation nature and the right of generation lays on children, it must certainly bind them equal to both the concurrent causes of it. And accordingly we see the positive law of God every where joins them together, without distinction, when it commands the obedience of children, Honour thy father and thy mother, Exod. xx. 12. Whosoever curseth his father or his mother, Lev. xx. 9. Ye shall fear every man his mother and his father, Lev. xix. 3. Children, obey your parents, &c. Eph. vi. 1. is the stile of the Old and New Testament.

Sec. 53. Had but this one thing been well considered, without looking any deeper into the matter, it might perhaps have kept men from running into those gross mistakes, they have made, about this power of parents; which, however it might, without any great harshness, bear the name of absolute dominion, and regal authority, when under the title of paternal power it seemed appropriated to the father, would yet have founded but oddly, and in the very name shewn the absurdity, if this supposed absolute power over children had been called parental; and thereby have discovered, that it belonged to the mother too: for it will but very ill serve the turn of those men, who contend so much for the absolute power and authority of the fatherhood, as they call it, that the mother should have any share in it; and it would have but ill supported the monarchy they contend for, when by the very name it appeared, that that fundamental authority, from whence they would derive their government of a single person only, was not placed in one, but two persons jointly. But to let this of names pass.

Sec. 54. Though I have said above, Chap. II. That all men by nature are equal, I cannot be supposed to understand all sorts of equality: age or virtue may give men a just precedency: excellency of parts and merit may place others above the common level: birth may subject some, and alliance or benefits others, to pay an observance to those to whom nature, gratitude, or other respects, may have made it due: and yet all this consists with the equality, which all men are in, in respect of jurisdiction or dominion one over another; which was the equality I there spoke of, as proper to the business in hand, being that equal right, that every man hath, to his natural freedom, without being subjected to the will or authority of any other man.

Sec. 55. Children, I confess, are not born in this full state of equality, though they are born to it. Their parents have a sort of rule and jurisdiction over them, when they come into the world, and for some time after; but it is but a temporary one. The bonds of this subjection are like the swaddling clothes they art wrapt up in, and supported by, in the weakness of their infancy: age and reason as they grow up, loosen them, till at length they drop quite off, and leave a man at his own free disposal.

Sec. 56. Adam was created a perfect man, his body and mind in full possession of their strength and reason, and so was capable, from the first instant of his being to provide for his own support and preservation, and govern his actions according to the dictates of the law of reason which God had implanted in him. From him the world is peopled with his descendants, who are all born infants, weak and helpless, without knowledge or understanding: but to supply the defects of this imperfect state, till the improvement of growth and age hath removed them, Adam and Eve, and after them all parents were, by the law of nature, under an obligation to preserve, nourish, and educate the children they had begotten; not as their own workmanship, but the workmanship of their own maker, the Almighty, to whom they were to be accountable for them.

Sec. 57. The law, that was to govern Adam, was the same that was to govern all his posterity, the law of reason. But his offspring having another way of entrance into the world, different from him, by a natural birth, that produced them ignorant and without the use of reason, they were not presently under that law; for no body can be under a law, which is not promulgated to him; and this law being promulgated or made known by reason only, he that is not come to the use of his reason, cannot be said to be under this law; and Adam's children, being not presently as soon as born under this law of reason, were not presently free: for law, in its true notion, is not so much the limitation as the direction of a free and intelligent agent to his proper interest, and prescribes no farther than is for the general good of those under that law: could they be happier without it, the law, as an useless thing, would of itself vanish; and that ill deserves the name of confinement which hedges us in only from bogs and precipices. So that, however it may be mistaken, the end of law is not to abolish or restrain, but to preserve and enlarge freedom: for in all the states of created beings capable of laws, where there is no law, there is no freedom: for liberty is, to be free from restraint and violence from others; which cannot be, where there is no law: but freedom is not, as we are told, a liberty for every man to do what he lists: (for who could be free, when every other man's humour might domineer over him?) but a liberty to dispose, and order as he lists, his person, actions, possessions, and his whole property, within the allowance of those laws under which he is, and therein not to be subject to the arbitrary will of another, but freely follow his own.

Sec. 58. The power, then, that parents have over their children, arises from that duty which is incumbent on them, to take care of their off-spring, during the imperfect state of childhood. To inform the mind, and govern the actions of their yet ignorant nonage, till reason shall take its place, and ease them of that trouble, is what the children want, and the parents are bound to: for God having given man an understanding to direct his actions, has allowed him a freedom of will, and liberty of acting, as properly belonging thereunto, within the bounds of that law he is under. But whilst he is in an estate, wherein he has not understanding of his own to direct his will, he is not to have any will of his own to follow: he that understands for him, must will for him too; he must prescribe to his will, and regulate his actions; but when he comes to the estate that made his father a freeman, the son is a freeman too.

Sec. 59. This holds in all the laws a man is under, whether natural or civil. Is a man under the law of nature? What made him free of that law? what gave him a free disposing of his property, according to his own will, within the compass of that law? I answer, a state of maturity wherein he might be supposed capable to know that law, that so he might keep his actions within the bounds of it. When he has acquired that state, he is presumed to know how far that law is to be his guide, and how far he may make use of his freedom, and so comes to have it; till then, some body else must guide him, who is presumed to know how far the law allows a liberty. If such a state of reason, such an age of discretion made him free, the same shall make his son free too. Is a man under the law of England? What made him free of that law? that is, to have the liberty to dispose of his actions and possessions according to his own will, within the permission of that law? A capacity of knowing that law; which is supposed by that law, at the age of one and twenty years, and in some cases sooner. If this made the father free, it shall make the son free too. Till then we see the law allows the son to have no will, but he is to be guided by the will of his father or guardian, who is to understand for him. And if the father die, and fail to substitute a deputy in his trust; if he hath not provided a tutor, to govern his son, during his minority, during his want of understanding, the law takes care to do it; some other must govern him, and be a will to him, till he hath attained to a state of freedom, and his understanding be fit to take the government of his will. But after that, the father and son are equally free as much as tutor and pupil after nonage; equally subjects of the same law together, without any dominion left in the father over the life, liberty, or estate of his son, whether they be only in the state and under the law of nature, or under the positive laws of an established government.

Sec. 60. But if, through defects that may happen out of the ordinary course of nature, any one comes not to such a degree of reason, wherein he might be supposed capable of knowing the law, and so living within the rules of it, he is never capable of being a free man, he is never let loose to the disposure of his own will (because he knows no bounds to it, has not understanding, its proper guide) but is continued under the tuition and government of others, all the time his own understanding is uncapable of that charge. And so lunatics and ideots are never set free from the government of their parents; children, who are not as yet come unto those years whereat they may have; and innocents which are excluded by a natural defect from ever having; thirdly, madmen, which for the present cannot possibly have the use of right reason to guide themselves, have for their guide, the reason that guideth other men which are tutors over them, to seek and procure their good for them, says Hooker, Eccl. Pol. lib. i. sec. 7. All which seems no more than that duty, which God and nature has laid on man, as well as other creatures, to preserve their offspring, till they can be able to shift for themselves, and will scarce amount to an instance or proof of parents regal authority.

Sec. 61. Thus we are born free, as we are born rational; not that we have actually the exercise of either: age, that brings one, brings with it the other too. And thus we see how natural freedom and subjection to parents may consist together, and are both founded on the same principle. A child is free by his father's title, by his father's understanding, which is to govern him till he hath it of his own. The freedom of a man at years of discretion, and the subjection of a child to his parents, whilst yet short of that age, are so consistent, and so distinguishable, that the most blinded contenders for monarchy, by right of fatherhood, cannot miss this difference; the most obstinate cannot but allow their consistency: for were their doctrine all true, were the right heir of Adam now known, and by that title settled a monarch in his throne, invested with all the absolute unlimited power Sir Robert Filmer talks of; if he should die as soon as his heir were born, must not the child, notwithstanding he were never so free, never so much sovereign, be in subjection to his mother and nurse, to tutors and governors, till age and education brought him reason and ability to govern himself and others? The necessities of his life, the health of his body, and the information of his mind, would require him to be directed by the will of others, and not his own; and yet will any one think, that this restraint and subjection were inconsistent with, or spoiled him of that liberty or sovereignty he had a right to, or gave away his empire to those who had the government of his nonage? This government over him only prepared him the better and sooner for it. If any body should ask me, when my son is of age to be free? I shall answer, just when his monarch is of age to govern. But at what time, says the judicious Hooker, Eccl. Pol. l. i. sect. 6. a man may be said to have attained so far forth the use of reason, as sufficeth to make him capable of those laws whereby he is then bound to guide his actions: this is a great deal more easy for sense to discern, than for any one by skill and learning to determine.

Sec. 62. Common-wealths themselves take notice of, and allow, that there is a time when men are to begin to act like free men, and therefore till that time require not oaths of fealty, or allegiance, or other public owning of, or submission to the government of their countries.

Sec. 63. The freedom then of man, and liberty of acting according to his own will, is grounded on his having reason, which is able to instruct him in that law he is to govern himself by, and make him know how far he is left to the freedom of his own will. To turn him loose to an unrestrained liberty, before he has reason to guide him, is not the allowing him the privilege of his nature to be free; but to thrust him out amongst brutes, and abandon him to a state as wretched, and as much beneath that of a man, as their's. This is that which puts the authority into the parents hands to govern the minority of their children. God hath made it their business to employ this care on their offspring, and hath placed in them suitable inclinations of tenderness and concern to temper this power, to apply it, as his wisdom designed it, to the children's good, as long as they should need to be under it.

Sec. 64. But what reason can hence advance this care of the parents due to their off-spring into an absolute arbitrary dominion of the father, whose power reaches no farther, than by such a discipline, as he finds most effectual, to give such strength and health to their bodies, such vigour and rectitude to their minds, as may best fit his children to be most useful to themselves and others; and, if it be necessary to his condition, to make them work, when they are able, for their own subsistence. But in this power the mother too has her share with the father.

Sec. 65. Nay, this power so little belongs to the father by any peculiar right of nature, but only as he is guardian of his children, that when he quits his care of them, he loses his power over them, which goes along with their nourishment and education, to which it is inseparably annexed; and it belongs as much to the foster-father of an exposed child, as to the natural father of another. So little power does the bare act of begetting give a man over his issue; if all his care ends there, and this be all the title he hath to the name and authority of a father. And what will become of this paternal power in that part of the world, where one woman hath more than one husband at a time? or in those parts of America, where, when the husband and wife part, which happens frequently, the children are all left to the mother, follow her, and are wholly under her care and provision? If the father die whilst the children are young, do they not naturally every where owe the same obedience to their mother, during their minority, as to their father were he alive? and will any one say, that the mother hath a legislative power over her children? that she can make standing rules, which shall be of perpetual obligation, by which they ought to regulate all the concerns of their property, and bound their liberty all the course of their lives? or can she inforce the observation of them with capital punishments? for this is the proper power of the magistrate, of which the father hath not so much as the shadow. His command over his children is but temporary, and reaches not their life or property: it is but a help to the weakness and imperfection of their nonage, a discipline necessary to their education: and though a father may dispose of his own possessions as he pleases, when his children are out of danger of perishing for want, yet his power extends not to the lives or goods, which either their own industry, or another's bounty has made their's; nor to their liberty neither, when they are once arrived to the infranchisement of the years of discretion. The father's empire then ceases, and he can from thence forwards no more dispose of the liberty of his son, than that of any other man: and it must be far from an absolute or perpetual jurisdiction, from which a man may withdraw himself, having license from divine authority to leave father and mother, and cleave to his wife.

Sec. 66. But though there be a time when a child comes to be as free from subjection to the will and command of his father, as the father himself is free from subjection to the will of any body else, and they are each under no other restraint, but that which is common to them both, whether it be the law of nature, or municipal law of their country; yet this freedom exempts not a son from that honour which he ought, by the law of God and nature, to pay his parents. God having made the parents instruments in his great design of continuing the race of mankind, and the occasions of life to their children; as he hath laid on them an obligation to nourish, preserve, and bring up their offspring; so he has laid on the children a perpetual obligation of honouring their parents, which containing in it an inward esteem and reverence to be shewn by all outward expressions, ties up the child from any thing that may ever injure or affront, disturb or endanger, the happiness or life of those from whom he received his; and engages him in all actions of defence, relief, assistance and comfort of those, by whose means he entered into being, and has been made capable of any enjoyments of life: from this obligation no state, no freedom can absolve children. But this is very far from giving parents a power of command over their children, or an authority to make laws and dispose as they please of their lives or liberties. It is one thing to owe honour, respect, gratitude and assistance; another to require an absolute obedience and submission. The honour due to parents, a monarch in his throne owes his mother; and yet this lessens not his authority, nor subjects him to her government.

Sec. 67. The subjection of a minor places in the father a temporary government, which terminates with the minority of the child: and the honour due from a child, places in the parents a perpetual right to respect, reverence, support and compliance too, more or less, as the father's care, cost, and kindness in his education, has been more or less. This ends not with minority, but holds in all parts and conditions of a man's life. The want of distinguishing these two powers, viz. that which the father hath in the right of tuition, during minority, and the right of honour all his life, may perhaps have caused a great part of the mistakes about this matter: for to speak properly of them, the first of these is rather the privilege of children, and duty of parents, than any prerogative of paternal power. The nourishment and education of their children is a charge so incumbent on parents for their children's good, that nothing can absolve them from taking care of it: and though the power of commanding and chastising them go along with it, yet God hath woven into the principles of human nature such a tenderness for their off-spring, that there is little fear that parents should use their power with too much rigour; the excess is seldom on the severe side, the strong byass of nature drawing the other way. And therefore God almighty when he would express his gentle dealing with the Israelites, he tells them, that though he chastened them, he chastened them as a man chastens his son, Deut. viii. 5. i.e. with tenderness and affection, and kept them under no severer discipline than what was absolutely best for them, and had been less kindness to have slackened. This is that power to which children are commanded obedience, that the pains and care of their parents may not be increased, or ill rewarded.

Sec. 68. On the other side, honour and support, all that which gratitude requires to return for the benefits received by and from them, is the indispensable duty of the child, and the proper privilege of the parents. This is intended for the parents advantage, as the other is for the child's; though education, the parents duty, seems to have most power, because the ignorance and infirmities of childhood stand in need of restraint and correction; which is a visible exercise of rule, and a kind of dominion. And that duty which is comprehended in the word honour, requires less obedience, though the obligation be stronger on grown, than younger children: for who can think the command, Children obey your parents, requires in a man, that has children of his own, the same submission to his father, as it does in his yet young children to him; and that by this precept he were bound to obey all his father's commands, if, out of a conceit of authority, he should have the indiscretion to treat him still as a boy?

Sec. 69. The first part then of paternal power, or rather duty, which is education, belongs so to the father, that it terminates at a certain season; when the business of education is over, it ceases of itself, and is also alienable before: for a man may put the tuition of his son in other hands; and he that has made his son an apprentice to another, has discharged him, during that time, of a great part of his obedience both to himself and to his mother. But all the duty of honour, the other part, remains never the less entire to them; nothing can cancel that: it is so inseparable from them both, that the father's authority cannot dispossess the mother of this right, nor can any man discharge his son from honouring her that bore him. But both these are very far from a power to make laws, and enforcing them with penalties, that may reach estate, liberty, limbs and life. The power of commanding ends with nonage; and though, after that, honour and respect, support and defence, and whatsoever gratitude can oblige a man to, for the highest benefits he is naturally capable of, be always due from a son to his parents; yet all this puts no scepter into the father's hand, no sovereign power of commanding. He has no dominion over his son's property, or actions; nor any right, that his will should prescribe to his son's in all things; however it may become his son in many things, not very inconvenient to him and his family, to pay a deference to it.

Sec. 70. A man may owe honour and respect to an ancient, or wise man; defence to his child or friend; relief and support to the distressed; and gratitude to a benefactor, to such a degree, that all he has, all he can do, cannot sufficiently pay it: but all these give no authority, no right to any one, of making laws over him from whom they are owing. And it is plain, all this is due not only to the bare title of father; not only because, as has been said, it is owing to the mother too; but because these obligations to parents, and the degrees of what is required of children, may be varied by the different care and kindness, trouble and expence, which is often employed upon one child more than another.

Sec. 71. This shews the reason how it comes to pass, that parents in societies, where they themselves are subjects, retain a power over their children, and have as much right to their subjection, as those who are in the state of nature. Which could not possibly be, if all political power were only paternal, and that in truth they were one and the same thing: for then, all paternal power being in the prince, the subject could naturally have none of it. But these two powers, political and paternal, are so perfectly distinct and separate; are built upon so different foundations, and given to so different ends, that every subject that is a father, has as much a paternal power over his children, as the prince has over his: and every prince, that has parents, owes them as much filial duty and obedience, as the meanest of his subjects do to their's; and can therefore contain not any part or degree of that kind of dominion, which a prince or magistrate has over his subject.

Sec. 72. Though the obligation on the parents to bring up their children, and the obligation on children to honour their parents, contain all the power on the one hand, and submission on the other, which are proper to this relation, yet there is another power ordinarily in the father, whereby he has a tie on the obedience of his children; which tho' it be common to him with other men, yet the occasions of shewing it, almost consich tho' it be common to him with other men, yet the occasions of shewing it, almost constantly happening to fathers in their private families, and the instances of it elsewhere being rare, and less taken notice of, it passes in the world for a part of paternal jurisdiction. And this is the power men generally have to bestow their estates on those who please them best; the possession of the father being the expectation and inheritance of the children, ordinarily in certain proportions, according to the law and custom of each country; yet it is commonly in the father's power to bestow it with a more sparing or liberal hand, according as the behaviour of this or that child hath comported with his will and humour.

Sec. 73. This is no small tie on the obedience of children: and there being always annexed to the enjoyment of land, a submission to the government of the country, of which that land is a part; it has been commonly supposed, that a father could oblige his posterity to that government, of which he himself was a subject, and that his compact held them; whereas, it being only a necessary condition annexed to the land, and the inheritance of an estate which is under that government, reaches only those who will take it on that condition, and so is no natural tie or engagement, but a voluntary submission: for every man's children being by nature as free as himself, or any of his ancestors ever were, may, whilst they are in that freedom, choose what society they will join themselves to, what common-wealth they will put themselves under. But if they will enjoy the inheritance of their ancestors, they must take it on the same terms their ancestors had it, and submit to all the conditions annexed to such a possession. By this power indeed fathers oblige their children to obedience to themselves, even when they are past minority, and most commonly too subject them to this or that political power: but neither of these by any peculiar right of fatherhood, but by the reward they have in their hands to inforce and recompence such a compliance; and is no more power than what a French man has over an English man, who by the hopes of an estate he will leave him, will certainly have a strong tie on his obedience: and if, when it is left him, he will enjoy it, he must certainly take it upon the conditions annexed to the possession of land in that country where it lies, whether it be France or England.

Sec. 74. To conclude then, tho' the father's power of commanding extends no farther than the minority of his children, and to a degree only fit for the discipline and government of that age; and tho' that honour and respect, and all that which the Latins called piety, which they indispensably owe to their parents all their life-time, and in all estates, with all that support and defence is due to them, gives the father no power of governing, i.e. making laws and enacting penalties on his children; though by all this he has no dominion over the property or actions of his son: yet it is obvious to conceive how easy it was, in the first ages of the world, and in places still, where the thinness of people gives families leave to separate into unpossessed quarters, and they have room to remove or plant themselves in yet vacant habitations, for the father of the family to become the prince of* it; he had been a ruler from the beginning of the infancy of his children: and since without some government it would be hard for them to live together, it was likeliest it should, by the express or tacit consent of the children when they were grown up, be in the father, where it seemed without any change barely to continue; when indeed nothing more was required to it, than the permitting the father to exercise alone, in his family, that executive power of the law of nature, which every free man naturally hath, and by that permission resigning up to him a monarchical power, whilst they remained in it. But that this was not by any paternal right, but only by the consent of his children, is evident from hence, that no body doubts, but if a stranger, whom chance or business had brought to his family, had there killed any of his children, or committed any other fact, he might condemn and put him to death, or other-wise have punished him, as well as any of his children; which it was impossible he should do by virtue of any paternal authority over one who was not his child, but by virtue of that executive power of the law of nature, which, as a man, he had a right to: and he alone could punish him in his family, where the respect of his children had laid by the exercise of such a power, to give way to the dignity and authority they were willing should remain in him, above the rest of his family.

(*It is no improbable opinion therefore, which the archphilosopher was of, that the chief person in every houshold was always, as it were, a king: so when numbers of housholds joined themselves in civil societies together, kings were the first kind of governors amongst them, which is also, as it seemeth, the reason why the name of fathers continued still in them, who, of fathers, were made rulers; as also the ancient custom of governors to do as Melchizedec, and being kings, to exercise the office of priests, which fathers did at the first, grew perhaps by the same occasion. Howbeit, this is not the only kind of regiment that has been received in the world. The inconveniences of one kind have caused sundry others to be devised; so that in a word, all public regiment, of what kind soever, seemeth evidently to have risen from the deliberate advice, consultation and composition between men, judging it convenient and behoveful; there being no impossibility in nature considered by itself, but that man might have lived without any public regiment, Hooker's Eccl. Pol. lib. i. sect. 10.)

Sec. 75. Thus it was easy, and almost natural for children, by a tacit, and scarce avoidable consent, to make way for the father's authority and government. They had been accustomed in their childhood to follow his direction, and to refer their little differences to him, and when they were men, who fitter to rule them? Their little properties, and less covetousness, seldom afforded greater controversies; and when any should arise, where could they have a fitter umpire than he, by whose care they had every one been sustained and brought up, and who had a tenderness for them all? It is no wonder that they made no distinction betwixt minority and full age; nor looked after one and twenty, or any other age that might make them the free disposers of themselves and fortunes, when they could have no desire to be out of their pupilage: the government they had been under, during it, continued still to be more their protection than restraint; and they could no where find a greater security to their peace, liberties, and fortunes, than in the rule of a father.

Sec. 76. Thus the natural fathers of families, by an insensible change, became the politic monarchs of them too: and as they chanced to live long, and leave able and worthy heirs, for several successions, or otherwise; so they laid the foundations of hereditary, or elective kingdoms, under several constitutions and mannors, according as chance, contrivance, or occasions happened to mould them. But if princes have their titles in their fathers right, and it be a sufficient proof of the natural right of fathers to political authority, because they commonly were those in whose hands we find, de facto, the exercise of government: I say, if this argument be good, it will as strongly prove, that all princes, nay princes only, ought to be priests, since it is as certain, that in the beginning, the father of the family was priest, as that he was ruler in his own houshold.

CHAP. VII. Of Political or Civil Society.

Sec. 77. GOD having made man such a creature, that in his own judgment, it was not good for him to be alone, put him under strong obligations of necessity, convenience, and inclination to drive him into society, as well as fitted him with understanding and language to continue and enjoy it. The first society was between man and wife, which gave beginning to that between parents and children; to which, in time, that between master and servant came to be added: and though all these might, and commonly did meet together, and make up but one family, wherein the master or mistress of it had some sort of rule proper to a family; each of these, or all together, came short of political society, as we shall see, if we consider the different ends, ties, and bounds of each of these.

Sec. 78. Conjugal society is made by a voluntary compact between man and woman; and tho' it consist chiefly in such a communion and right in one another's bodies as is necessary to its chief end, procreation; yet it draws with it mutual support and assistance, and a communion of interests too, as necessary not only to unite their care and affection, but also necessary to their common off-spring, who have a right to be nourished, and maintained by them, till they are able to provide for themselves.

Sec. 79. For the end of conjunction, between male and female, being not barely procreation, but the continuation of the species; this conjunction betwixt male and female ought to last, even after procreation, so long as is necessary to the nourishment and support of the young ones, who are to be sustained even after procreation, so long as is necessary to the nourishment and support of the young ones, who are to be sustained by those that got them, till they are able to shift and provide for themselves. This rule, which the infinite wise maker hath set to the works of his hands, we find the inferior creatures steadily obey. In those viviparous animals which feed on grass, the conjunction between male and female lasts no longer than the very act of copulation; because the teat of the dam being sufficient to nourish the young, till it be able to feed on grass, the male only begets, but concerns not himself for the female or young, to whose sustenance he can contribute nothing. But in beasts of prey the conjunction lasts longer: because the dam not being able well to subsist herself, and nourish her numerous off-spring by her own prey alone, a more laborious, as well as more dangerous way of living, than by feeding on grass, the assistance of the male is necessary to the maintenance of their common family, which cannot subsist till they are able to prey for themselves, but by the joint care of male and female. The same is to be observed in all birds, (except some domestic ones, where plenty of food excuses the cock from feeding, and taking care of the young brood) whose young needing food in the nest, the cock and hen continue mates, till the young are able to use their wing, and provide for themselves.

Sec. 80. And herein I think lies the chief, if not the only reason, why the male and female in mankind are tied to a longer conjunction than other creatures, viz. because the female is capable of conceiving, and de facto is commonly with child again, and brings forth too a new birth, long before the former is out of a dependency for support on his parents help, and able to shift for himself, and has all the assistance is due to him from his parents: whereby the father, who is bound to take care for those he hath begot, is under an obligation to continue in conjugal society with the same woman longer than other creatures, whose young being able to subsist of themselves, before the time of procreation returns again, the conjugal bond dissolves of itself, and they are at liberty, till Hymen at his usual anniversary season summons them again to chuse new mates. Wherein one cannot but admire the wisdom of the great Creator, who having given to man foresight, and an ability to lay up for the future, as well as to supply the present necessity, hath made it necessary, that society of man and wife should be more lasting, than of male and female amongst other creatures; that so their industry might be encouraged, and their interest better united, to make provision and lay up goods for their common issue, which uncertain mixture, or easy and frequent solutions of conjugal society would mightily disturb.

Sec. 81. But tho'these are ties upon mankind, which make the conjugal bonds more firm and lasting in man, than the other species of animals; yet it would give one reason to enquire, why this compact, where procreation and education are secured, and inheritance taken care for, may not be made determinable, either by consent, or at a certain time, or upon certain conditions, as well as any other voluntary compacts, there being no necessity in the nature of the thing, nor to the ends of it, that it should always be for life; I mean, to such as are under no restraint of any positive law, which ordains all such contracts to be perpetual.

Sec. 82. But the husband and wife, though they have but one common concern, yet having different understandings, will unavoidably sometimes have different wills too; it therefore being necessary that the last determination, i. e. the rule, should be placed somewhere; it naturally falls to the man's share, as the abler and the stronger. But this reaching but to the things of their common interest and property, leaves the wife in the full and free possession of what by contract is her peculiar right, and gives the husband no more power over her life than she has over his; the power of the husband being so far from that of an absolute monarch, that the wife has in many cases a liberty to separate from him, where natural right, or their contract allows it; whether that contract be made by themselves in the state of nature, or by the customs or laws of the country they live in; and the children upon such separation fall to the father or mother's lot, as such contract does determine.

Sec. 83. For all the ends of marriage being to be obtained under politic government, as well as in the state of nature, the civil magistrate doth not abridge the right or power of either naturally necessary to those ends, viz. procreation and mutual support and assistance whilst they are together; but only decides any controversy that may arise between man and wife about them. If it were otherwise, and that absolute sovereignty and power of life and death naturally belonged to the husband, and were necessary to the society between man and wife, there could be no matrimony in any of those countries where the husband is allowed no such absolute authority. But the ends of matrimony requiring no such power in the husband, the condition of conjugal society put it not in him, it being not at all necessary to that state. Conjugal society could subsist and attain its ends without it; nay, community of goods, and the power over them, mutual assistance and maintenance, and other things belonging to conjugal society, might be varied and regulated by that contract which unites man and wife in that society, as far as may consist with procreation and the bringing up of children till they could shift for themselves; nothing being necessary to any society, that is not necessary to the ends for which it is made.

Sec. 84. The society betwixt parents and children, and the distinct rights and powers belonging respectively to them, I have treated of so largely, in the foregoing chapter, that I shall not here need to say any thing of it. And I think it is plain, that it is far different from a politic society.

Sec. 85. Master and servant are names as old as history, but given to those of far different condition; for a freeman makes himself a servant to another, by selling him, for a certain time, the service he undertakes to do, in exchange for wages he is to receive: and though this commonly puts him into the family of his master, and under the ordinary discipline thereof; yet it gives the master but a temporary power over him, and no greater than what is contained in the contract between them. But there is another sort of servants, which by a peculiar name we call slaves, who being captives taken in a just war, are by the right of nature subjected to the absolute dominion and arbitrary power of their masters. These men having, as I say, forfeited their lives, and with it their liberties, and lost their estates; and being in the state of slavery, not capable of any property, cannot in that state be considered as any part of civil society; the chief end whereof is the preservation of property.

Sec. 86. Let us therefore consider a master of a family with all these subordinate relations of wife, children, servants, and slaves, united under the domestic rule of a family; which, what resemblance soever it may have in its order, offices, and number too, with a little common-wealth, yet is very far from it, both in its constitution, power and end: or if it must be thought a monarchy, and the paterfamilias the absolute monarch in it, absolute monarchy will have but a very shattered and short power, when it is plain, by what has been said before, that the master of the family has a very distinct and differently limited power, both as to time and extent, over those several persons that are in it; for excepting the slave (and the family is as much a family, and his power as paterfamilias as great, whether there be any slaves in his family or no) he has no legislative power of life and death over any of them, and none too but what a mistress of a family may have as well as he. And he certainly can have no absolute power over the whole family, who has but a very limited one over every individual in it. But how a family, or any other society of men, differ from that which is properly political society, we shall best see, by considering wherein political society itself consists.

Sec. 87. Man being born, as has been proved, with a title to perfect freedom, and an uncontrouled enjoyment of all the rights and privileges of the law of nature, equally with any other man, or number of men in the world, hath by nature a power, not only to preserve his property, that is, his life, liberty and estate, against the injuries and attempts of other men; but to judge of, and punish the breaches of that law in others, as he is persuaded the offence deserves, even with death itself, in crimes where the heinousness of the fact, in his opinion, requires it. But because no political society can be, nor subsist, without having in itself the power to preserve the property, and in order thereunto, punish the offences of all those of that society; there, and there only is political society, where every one of the members hath quitted this natural power, resigned it up into the hands of the community in all cases that exclude him not from appealing for protection to the law established by it. And thus all private judgment of every particular member being excluded, the community comes to be umpire, by settled standing rules, indifferent, and the same to all parties; and by men having authority from the community, for the execution of those rules, decides all the differences that may happen between any members of that society concerning any matter of right; and punishes those offences which any member hath committed against the society, with such penalties as the law has established: whereby it is easy to discern, who are, and who are not, in political society together. Those who are united into one body, and have a common established law and judicature to appeal to, with authority to decide controversies between them, and punish offenders, are in civil society one with another: but those who have no such common appeal, I mean on earth, are still in the state of nature, each being, where there is no other, judge for himself, and executioner; which is, as I have before shewed it, the perfect state of nature.

Sec. 88. And thus the common-wealth comes by a power to set down what punishment shall belong to the several transgressions which they think worthy of it, committed amongst the members of that society, (which is the power of making laws) as well as it has the power to punish any injury done unto any of its members, by any one that is not of it, (which is the power of war and peace;) and all this for the preservation of the property of all the members of that society, as far as is possible. But though every man who has entered into civil society, and is become a member of any commonwealth, has thereby quitted his power to punish offences, against the law of nature, in prosecution of his own private judgment, yet with the judgment of offences, which he has given up to the legislative in all cases, where he can appeal to the magistrate, he has given a right to the common-wealth to employ his force, for the execution of the judgments of the common-wealth, whenever he shall be called to it; which indeed are his own judgments, they being made by himself, or his representative. And herein we have the original of the legislative and executive power of civil society, which is to judge by standing laws, how far offences are to be punished, when committed within the common-wealth; and also to determine, by occasional judgments founded on the present circumstances of the fact, how far injuries from without are to be vindicated; and in both these to employ all the force of all the members, when there shall be need.

Sec. 89. Where-ever therefore any number of men are so united into one society, as to quit every one his executive power of the law of nature, and to resign it to the public, there and there only is a political, or civil society. And this is done, where-ever any number of men, in the state of nature, enter into society to make one people, one body politic, under one supreme government; or else when any one joins himself to, and incorporates with any government already made: for hereby he authorizes the society, or which is all one, the legislative thereof, to make laws for him, as the public good of the society shall require; to the execution whereof, his own assistance (as to his own decrees) is due. And this puts men out of a state of nature into that of a common-wealth, by setting up a judge on earth, with authority to determine all the controversies, and redress the injuries that may happen to any member of the commonwealth; which judge is the legislative, or magistrates appointed by it. And where-ever there are any number of men, however associated, that have no such decisive power to appeal to, there they are still in the state of nature.

Sec. 90. Hence it is evident, that absolute monarchy, which by some men is counted the only government in the world, is indeed inconsistent with civil society, and so can be no form of civil-government at all: for the end of civil society, being to avoid, and remedy those inconveniencies of the state of nature, which necessarily follow from every man's being judge in his own case, by setting up a known authority, to which every one of that society may appeal upon any injury received, or controversy that may arise, and which every one of the* society ought to obey; where-ever any persons are, who have not such an authority to appeal to, for the decision of any difference between them, there those persons are still in the state of nature; and so is every absolute prince, in respect of those who are under his dominion.

(* The public power of all society is above every soul contained in the same society; and the principal use of that power is, to give laws unto all that are under it, which laws in such cases we must obey, unless there be reason shewed which may necessarily inforce, that the law of reason, or of God, doth enjoin the contrary, Hook. Eccl. Pol. l. i. sect. 16.)

Sec. 91. For he being supposed to have all, both legislative and executive power in himself alone, there is no judge to be found, no appeal lies open to any one, who may fairly, and indifferently, and with authority decide, and from whose decision relief and redress may be expected of any injury or inconviency, that may be suffered from the prince, or by his order: so that such a man, however intitled, Czar, or Grand Seignior, or how you please, is as much in the state of nature, with all under his dominion, as he is with therest of mankind: for where-ever any two men are, who have no standing rule, and common judge to appeal to on earth, for the determination of controversies of right betwixt them, there they are still in the state of* nature, and under all the inconveniencies of it, with only this woful difference to the subject, or rather slave of an absolute prince: that whereas, in the ordinary state of nature, he has a liberty to judge of his right, and according to the best of his power, to maintain it; now, whenever his property is invaded by the will and order of his monarch, he has not only no appeal, as those in society ought to have, but as if he were degraded from the common state of rational creatures, is denied a liberty to judge of, or to defend his right; and so is exposed to all the misery and inconveniencies, that a man can fear from one, who being in the unrestrained state of nature, is yet corrupted with flattery, and armed with power.

(* To take away all such mutual grievances, injuries and wrongs, i.e. such as attend men in the state of nature, there was no way but only by growing into composition and agreement amongst themselves, by ordaining some kind of government public, and by yielding themselves subject thereunto, that unto whom they granted authority to rule and govern, by them the peace, tranquillity and happy estate of the rest might be procured. Men always knew that where force and injury was offered, they might be defenders of themselves; they knew that however men may seek their own commodity, yet if this were done with injury unto others, it was not to be suffered, but by all men, and all good means to be withstood. Finally, they knew that no man might in reason take upon him to determine his own right, and according to his own determination proceed in maintenance thereof, in as much as every man is towards himself, and them whom he greatly affects, partial; and therefore that strifes and troubles would be endless, except they gave their common consent, all to be ordered by some, whom they should agree upon, without which consent there would be no reason that one man should take upon him to be lord or judge over another, Hooker's Eccl. Pol. l. i. sect. 10.)

Sec. 92. For he that thinks absolute power purifies men's blood, and corrects the baseness of human nature, need read but the history of this, or any other age, to be convinced of the contrary. He that would have been insolent and injurious in the woods of America, would not probably be much better in a throne; where perhaps learning and religion shall be found out to justify all that he shall do to his subjects, and the sword presently silence all those that dare question it: for what the protection of absolute monarchy is, what kind of fathers of their countries it makes princes to be and to what a degree of happiness and security it carries civil society, where this sort of government is grown to perfection, he that will look into the late relation of Ceylon, may easily see.

Sec. 93. In absolute monarchies indeed, as well as other governments of the world, the subjects have an appeal to the law, and judges to decide any controversies, and restrain any violence that may happen betwixt the subjects themselves, one amongst another. This every one thinks necessary, and believes he deserves to be thought a declared enemy to society and mankind, who should go about to take it away. But whether this be from a true love of mankind and society, and such a charity as we owe all one to another, there is reason to doubt: for this is no more than what every man, who loves his own power, profit, or greatness, may and naturally must do, keep those animals from hurting, or destroying one another, who labour and drudge only for his pleasure and advantage; and so are taken care of, not out of any love the master has for them, but love of himself, and the profit they bring him: for if it be asked, what security, what fence is there, in such a state, against the violence and oppression of this absolute ruler? the very question can scarce be borne. They are ready to tell you, that it deserves death only to ask after safety. Betwixt subject and subject, they will grant, there must be measures, laws and judges, for their mutual peace and security: but as for the ruler, he ought to be absolute, and is above all such circumstances; because he has power to do more hurt and wrong, it is right when he does it. To ask how you may be guarded from harm, or injury, on that side where the strongest hand is to do it, is presently the voice of faction and rebellion: as if when men quitting the state of nature entered into society, they agreed that all of them but one, should be under the restraint of laws, but that he should still retain all the liberty of the state of nature, increased with power, and made licentious by impunity. This is to think, that men are so foolish, that they take care to avoid what mischiefs may be done them by pole-cats, or foxes; but are content, nay, think it safety, to be devoured by lions.

Sec. 94. But whatever flatterers may talk to amuse people's understandings, it hinders not men from feeling; and when they perceive, that any man, in what station soever, is out of the bounds of the civil society which they are of, and that they have no appeal on earth against any harm, they may receive from him, they are apt to think themselves in the state of nature, in respect of him whom they find to be so; and to take care, as soon as they can, to have that safety and security in civil society, for which it was first instituted, and for which only they entered into it. And therefore, though perhaps at first , (as shall be shewed more at large hereafter in the following part of this discourse) some one good and excellent man having got a pre -eminency amongst the rest, had this deference paid to his goodness and virtue, as to a kind of natural authority, that the chief rule, with arbitration of their differences, by a tacit consent devolved into his hands, without any other caution, but the assurance they had of his uprightness and wisdom; yet when time, giving authority, and (as some men would persuade us) sacredness of customs, which the negligent, and unforeseeing innocence of the first ages began, had brought in successors of another stamp, the people finding their properties not secure under the government, as then it was, (whereas government has no other end but the preservation of * property) could never be safe nor at rest, nor think themselves in civil society, till the legislature was placed in collective bodies of men, call them senate, parliament, or what you please. By which means every single person became subject, equally with other the meanest men, to those laws, which he himself, as part of the legislative, had established; nor could any one, by his own authority; avoid the force of the law, when once made; nor by any pretence of superiority plead exemption, thereby to license his own, or the miscarriages of any of his dependents.** No man in civil society can be exempted from the laws of it: for if any man may do what he thinks fit, and there be no appeal on earth, for redress or security against any harm he shall do; I ask, whether he be not perfectly still in the state of nature, and so can be no part or member of that civil society; unless any one will say, the state of nature and civil society are one and the same thing, which I have never yet found any one so great a patron of anarchy as to affirm.

(* At the first, when some certain kind of regiment was once appointed, it may be that nothing was then farther thought upon for the manner of governing, but all permitted unto their wisdom and discretion, which were to rule, till by experience they found this for all parts very inconvenient, so as the thing which they had devised for a remedy, did indeed but increase the sore, which it should have cured. They saw, that to live by one man's will, became the cause of all men's misery. This constrained them to come unto laws, wherein all men might see their duty beforehand, and know the penalties of transgressing them. Hooker's Eccl. Pol. l. i. sect. 10.)

(** Civil law being the act of the whole body politic, doth therefore over-rule each several part of the same body. Hooker, ibid.)

CHAP. VIII.Of the Beginning of Political Societies.

Sec. 95. MEN being, as has been said, by nature, all free, equal, and independent, no one can be put out of this estate, and subjected to the political power of another, without his own consent. The only way whereby any one divests himself of his natural liberty, and puts on the bonds of civil society, is by agreeing with other men to join and unite into a community for their comfortable, safe, and peaceable living one amongst another, in a secure enjoyment of their properties, and a greater security against any, that are not of it. This any number of men may do, because it injures not the freedom of the rest; they are left as they were in the liberty of the state of nature. When any number of men have so consented to make one community or government, they are thereby presently incorporated, and make one body politic, wherein the majority have a right to act and conclude the rest.

Sec. 96. For when any number of men have, by the consent of every individual, made a community, they have thereby made that community one body, with a power to act as one body, which is only by the will and determination of the majority: for that which acts any community, being only the consent of the individuals of it, and it being necessary to that which is one body to move one way; it is necessary the body should move that way whither the greater force carries it, which is the consent of the majority: or else it is impossible it should act or continue one body, one community, which the consent of every individual that united into it, agreed that it should; and so every one is bound by that consent to be concluded by the majority. And therefore we see, that in assemblies, impowered to act by positive laws, where no number is set by that positive law which impowers them, the act of the majority passes for the act of the whole, and of course determines, as having, by the law of nature and reason, the power of the whole.

Sec. 97. And thus every man, by consenting with others to make one body politic under one government, puts himself under an obligation, to every one of that society, to submit to the determination of the majority, and to be concluded by it; or else this original compact, whereby he with others incorporates into one society, would signify nothing, and be no compact, if he be left free, and under no other ties than he was in before in the state of nature. For what appearance would there be of any compact? what new engagement if he were no farther tied by any decrees of the society, than he himself thought fit, and did actually consent to? This would be still as great a liberty, as he himself had before his compact, or any one else in the state of nature hath, who may submit himself, and consent to any acts of it if he thinks fit.

Sec. 98. For if the consent of the majority shall not, in reason, be received as the act of the whole, and conclude every individual; nothing but the consent of every individual can make any thing to be the act of the whole: but such a consent is next to impossible ever to be had, if we consider the infirmities of health, and avocations of business, which in a number, though much less than that of a common-wealth, will necessarily keep many away from the public assembly. To which if we add the variety of opinions, and contrariety of interests, which unavoidably happen in all collections of men, the coming into society upon such terms would be only like Cato's coming into the theatre, only to go out again. Such a constitution as this would make the mighty Leviathan of a shorter duration, than the feeblest creatures, and not let it outlast the day it was born in: which cannot be supposed, till we can think, that rational creatures should desire and constitute societies only to be dissolved: for where the majority cannot conclude the rest, there they cannot act as one body, and consequently will be immediately dissolved again.

Sec. 99. Whosoever therefore out of a state of nature unite into a community, must be understood to give up all the power, necessary to the ends for which they unite into society, to the majority of the community, unless they expresly agreed in any number greater than the majority. And this is done by barely agreeing to unite into one political society, which is all the compact that is, or needs be, between the individuals, that enter into, or make up a commonwealth. And thus that, which begins and actually constitutes any political society, is nothing but the consent of any number of freemen capable of a majority to unite and incorporate into such a society. And this is that, and that only, which did, or could give beginning to any lawful government in the world.

Sec. 100. To this I find two objections made.

First, That there are no instances to be found in story, of a company of men independent, and equal one amongst another, that met together, and in this way began and set up a government.

Secondly, It is impossible of right, that men should do so, because all men being born under government, they are to submit to that, and are not at liberty to begin a new one.

Sec. 101. To the first there is this to answer, That it is not at all to be wondered, that history gives us but a very little account of men, that lived together in the state of nature. The inconveniences of that condition, and the love and want of society, no sooner brought any number of them together, but they presently united and incorporated, if they designed to continue together. And if we may not suppose men ever to have been in the state of nature, because we hear not much of them in such a state, we may as well suppose the armies of Salmanasser or Xerxes were never children, because we hear little of them, till they were men, and imbodied in armies. Government is every where antecedent to records, and letters seldom come in amongst a people till a long continuation of civil society has, by other more necessary arts, provided for their safety, ease, and plenty: and then they begin to look after the history of their founders, and search into their original, when they have outlived the memory of it: for it is with commonwealths as with particular persons, they are commonly ignorant of their own births and infancies: and if they know any thing of their original, they are beholden for it, to the accidental records that others have kept of it. And those that we have, of the beginning of any polities in the world, excepting that of the Jews, where God himself immediately interposed, and which favours not at all paternal dominion, are all either plain instances of such a beginning as I have mentioned, or at least have manifest footsteps of it.

Sec. 102. He must shew a strange inclination to deny evident matter of fact, when it agrees not with his hypothesis, who will not allow, that shew a strange inclination to deny evident matter of fact, when it agrees not with his hypothesis, who will not allow, that the beginning of Rome and Venice were by the uniting together of several men free and independent one of another, amongst whom there was no natural superiority or subjection. And if Josephus Acosta's word may be taken, he tells us, that in many parts of America there was no government at all. There are great and apparent conjectures, says he, that these men, speaking of those of Peru, for a long time had neither kings nor commonwealths, but lived in troops, as they do this day in Florida, the Cheriquanas, those of Brazil, and many other nations, which have no certain kings, but as occasion is offered, in peace or war, they choose their captains as they please, 1. i. c. 25. If it be said, that every man there was born subject to his father, or the head of his family; that the subjection due from a child to a father took not away his freedom of uniting into what political society he thought fit, has been already proved. But be that as it will, these men, it is evident, were actually free; and whatever superiority some politicians now would place in any of them, they themselves claimed it not, but by consent were all equal, till by the same consent they set rulers over themselves. So that their politic societies all began from a voluntary union, and the mutual agreement of men freely acting in the choice of their governors, and forms of government.

Sec. 103. And I hope those who went away from Sparta with Palantus, mentioned by Justin, 1. iii. c. 4. will be allowed to have been freemen independent one of another, and to have set up a government over themselves, by their own consent. Thus I have given several examples, out of history, of people free and in the state of nature, that being met together incorporated and began a commonwealth. And if the want of such instances be an argument to prove that government were not, nor could not be so begun, I suppose the contenders for paternal empire were better let it alone, than urge it against natural liberty: for if they can give so many instances, out of history, of governments begun upon paternal right, I think (though at best an argument from what has been, to what should of right be, has no great force) one might, without any great danger, yield them the cause. But if I might advise them in the case, they would do well not to search too much into the original of governments, as they have begun de facto, lest they should find, at the foundation of most of them, something very little favourable to the design they promote, and such a power as they contend for.

Sec. 104. But to conclude, reason being plain on our side, that men are naturally free, and the examples of history shewing, that the governments of the world, that were begun in peace, had their beginning laid on that foundation, and were made by the consent of the people; there can be little room for doubt, either where the right is, or what has been the opinion, or practice of mankind, about the first erecting of governments.

Sec. 105. I will not deny, that if we look back as far as history will direct us, towards the original of commonwealths, we shall generally find them under the government and administration of one man. And I am also apt to believe, that where a family was numerous enough to subsist by itself, and continued entire together, without mixing with others, as it often happens, where there is much land, and few people, the government commonly began in the father: for the father having, by the law of nature, the same power with every man else to punish, as he thought fit, any offences against that law, might thereby punish his transgressing children, even when they were men, and out of their pupilage; and they were very likely to submit to his punishment, and all join with him against the offender, in their turns, giving him thereby power to execute his sentence against any transgression, and so in effect make him the law-maker, and governor over all that remained in conjunction with his family. He was fittest to be trusted; paternal affection secured their property and interest under his care; and the custom of obeying him, in their childhood, made it easier to submit to him, rather than to any other. If therefore they must have one to rule them, as government is hardly to be avoided amongst men that live together; who so likely to be the man as he that was their common father; unless negligence, cruelty, or any other defect of mind or body made him unfit for it? But when either the father died, and left his next heir, for want of age, wisdom, courage, or any other qualities, less fit for rule; or where several families met, and consented to continue together; there, it is not to be doubted, but they used their natural freedom, to set up him, whom they judged the ablest, and most likely, to rule well over them. Conformable hereunto we find the people of America, who (living out of the reach of the conquering swords, and spreading domination of the two great empires of Peru and Mexico) enjoyed their own natural freedom, though, caeteris paribus, they commonly prefer the heir of their deceased king; yet if they find him any way weak, or uncapable, they pass him by, and set up the stoutest and bravest man for their ruler.

Sec. 106. Thus, though looking back as far as records give us any account of peopling the world, and the history of nations, we commonly find the government to be in one hand; yet it destroys not that which I affirm, viz. that the beginning of politic society depends upon the consent of the individuals, to join into, and make one society; who, when they are thus incorporated, might set up what form of government they thought fit. But this having given occasion to men to mistake, and think, that by nature government was monarchical, and belonged to the father, it may not be amiss here to consider, why people in the beginning generally pitched upon this form, which though perhaps the father's pre-eminency might, in the first institution of some commonwealths, give a rise to, and place in the beginning, the power in one hand; yet it is plain that the reason, that continued the form of government in a single person, was not any regard, or respect to paternal authority; since all petty monarchies, that is, almost all monarchies, near their original, have been commonly, at least upon occasion, elective.

Sec. 107. First then, in the beginning of things, the father's government of the childhood of those sprung from him, having accustomed them to the rule of one man, and taught them that where it was exercised with care and skill, with affection and love to those under it, it was sufficient to procure and preserve to men all the political happiness they sought for in society. It was no wonder that they should pitch upon, and naturally run into that form of government, which from their infancy they had been all accustomed to; and which, by experience, they had found both easy and safe. To which, if we add, that monarchy being simple, and most obvious to men, whom neither experience had instructed in forms of government, nor the ambition or insolence of empire had taught to beware of the encroachments of prerogative, or the inconveniences of absolute power, which monarchy in succession was apt to lay claim to, and bring upon them, it was not at all strange, that they should not much trouble themselves to think of methods of restraining any exorbitances of those to whom they had given the authority over them, and of balancing the power of government, by placing several parts of it in different hands. They had neither felt the oppression of tyrannical dominion, nor did the fashion of the age, nor their possessions, or way of living, (which afforded little matter for covetousness or ambition) give them any reason to apprehend or provide against it; and therefore it is no wonder they put themselves into such a frame of government, as was not only, as I said, most obvious and simple, but also best suited to their present state and condition; which stood more in need of defence against foreign invasions and injuries, than of multiplicity of laws. The equality of a simple poor way of living, confining their desires within the narrow bounds of each man's small property, made few controversies, and so no need of many laws to decide them, or variety of officers to superintend the process, or look after the execution of justice, where there were but few trespasses, and few offenders. Since then those, who like one another so well as to join into society, cannot but be supposed to have some acquaintance and friendship together, and some trust one in another; they could not but have greater apprehensions of others, than of one another: and therefore their first care and thought cannot but be supposed to be, how to secure themselves against foreign force. It was natural for them to put themselves under a frame of government which might best serve to that end, and chuse the wisest and bravest man to conduct them in their wars, and lead them out against their enemies, and in this chiefly be their ruler.

Sec. 108. Thus we see, that the kings of the Indians in America, which is still a pattern of the first ages in Asia and Europe, whilst the inhabitants were too few for the country, and want of people and money gave men no temptation to enlarge their possessions of land, or contest for wider extent of ground, are little more than generals of their armies; and though they command absolutely in war, yet at home and in time of peace they exercise very little dominion, and have but a very moderate sovereignty, the resolutions of peace and war being ordinarily either in the people, or in a council. Tho' the war itself, which admits not of plurality of governors, naturally devolves the command into the king's sole authority.

Sec. 109. And thus in Israel itself, the chief business of their judges, and first kings, seems to have been to be captains in war, and leaders of their armies; which (besides what is signified by going out and in before the people, which was, to march forth to war, and home again in the heads of their forces) appears plainly in the story of Iephtha. The Ammonites making war upon Israel, the Gileadites in fear send to Iephtha, a bastard of their family whom they had cast off, and article with him, if he will assist them against the Ammonites, to make him their ruler; which they do in these words, And the people made him head and captain over them, Judg. xi. ii. which was, as it seems, all one as to be judge. And he judged Israel, judg. xii. 7. that is, was their captain-general six years. So when Iotham upbraids the Shechemites with the obligation they had to Gideon, who had been their judge and ruler, he tells them, He fought for you, and adventured his life far, and delivered you out of the hands of Midian, Judg. ix. 17. Nothing mentioned of him but what he did as a general: and indeed that is all is found in his history, or in any of the rest of the judges. And Abimelech particularly is called king, though at most he was but their general. And when, being weary of the ill conduct of Samuel's sons, the children of Israel desired a king, like all the nations to judge them, and to go out before them, and to fight their battles, I. Sam viii. 20. God granting their desire, says to Samuel, I will send thee a man, and thou shalt anoint him to be captain over my people Israel, that he may save my people out of the hands of the Philistines, ix. 16. As if the only business of a king had been to lead out their armies, and fight in their defence; and accordingly at his inauguration pouring a vial of oil upon him, declares to Saul, that the Lord had anointed him to be captain over his inheritance, x. 1. And therefore those, who after Saul's being solemnly chosen and saluted king by the tribes at Mispah, were unwilling to have him their king, made no other objection but this, How shall this man save us? v. 27. as if they should have said, this man is unfit to be our king, not having skill and conduct enough in war, to be able to defend us. And when God resolved to transfer the government to David, it is in these words, But now thy kingdom shall not continue: the Lord hath sought him a man after his own heart, and the Lord hath commanded him to be captain over his people, xiii. 14. As if the whole kingly authority were nothing else but to be their general: and therefore the tribes who had stuck to Saul's family, and opposed David's reign, when they came to Hebron with terms of submission to him, they tell him, amongst other arguments they had to submit to him as to their king, that he was in effect their king in Saul's time, and therefore they had no reason but to receive him as their king now. Also (say they) in time past, when Saul was king over us, thou wast he that reddest out and broughtest in Israel, and the Lord said unto thee, Thou shalt feed my people Israel, and thou shalt be a captain over Israel.

Sec. 110. Thus, whether a family by degrees grew up into a common-wealth, and the fatherly authority being continued on to the elder son, every one in his turn growing up under it, tacitly submitted to it, and the easiness and equality of it not offending any one, every one acquiesced, till time seemed to have confirmed it, and settled a right of succession by prescription: or whether several families, or the descendants of several families, whom chance, neighbourhood, or business brought together, uniting into society, the need of a general, whose conduct might defend them against their enemies in war, and the great confidence the innocence and sincerity of that poor but virtuous age, (such as are almost all those which begin governments, that ever come to last in the world) gave men one of another, made the first beginners of commonwealths generally put the rule into one man's hand, without any other express limitation or restraint, but what the nature of the thing, and the end of government required: which ever of those it was that at first put the rule into the hands of a single person, certain it is no body was intrusted with it but for the public good and safety, and to those ends, in the infancies of commonwealths, those who had it commonly used it. And unless they had done so, young societies could not have subsisted; without such nursing fathers tender and careful of the public weal, all governments would have sunk under the weakness and infirmities of their infancy, and the prince and the people had soon perished together.

Sec. 111. But though the golden age (before vain ambition, and amor sceleratus habendi, evil concupiscence, had corrupted men's minds into a mistake of true power and honour) had more virtue, and consequently better governors, as well as less vicious subjects, and there was then no stretching prerogative on the one side, to oppress the people; nor consequently on the other, any dispute about privilege, to lessen or restrain the power of the magistrate, and so no contest betwixt rulers and people about governors or goveernment: yet, when ambition and luxury in future ages* would retain and increase the power, without doing the business for which it was given; and aided by flattery, taught princes to have distinct and separate interests from their people, men found it necessary to examine more carefully the original and rights of government; and to find out ways to restrain the exorbitances, and prevent the abuses of that power, which they having intrusted in another's hands only for their own good, they found was made use of to hurt them.

(* At first, when some certain kind of regiment was once approved, it may be nothing was then farther thought upon for the manner of governing, but all permitted unto their wisdom and discretion which were to rule, till by experience they found this for all parts very inconvenient, so as the thing which they had devised for a remedy, did indeed but increase the sore which it should have cured. They saw, that to live by one man's will, became the cause of all men's misery. This constrained them to come unto laws wherein all men might see their duty before hand, and know the penalties of transgressing them. Hooker's Eccl. Pol. l. i. sect. 10.)

Sec. 112. Thus we may see how probable it is, that people that were naturally free, and by their own consent either submitted to the government of their father, or united together out of different families to make a government, should generally put the rule into one man's hands, and chuse to be under the conduct of a single person, without so much as by express conditions limiting or regulating his power, which they thought safe enough in his honesty and prudence; though they never dreamed of monarchy being Iure Divino, which we never heard of among mankind, till it was revealed to us by the divinity of this last age; nor ever allowed paternal power to have a right to dominion, or to be the foundation of all government. And thus much may suffice to shew, that as far as we have any light from history, we have reason to conclude, that all peaceful beginnings of government have been laid in the consent of the people. I say peaceful, because I shall have occasion in another place to speak of conquest, which some esteem a way of beginning of governments.

The other objection I find urged against the beginning of polities, in the way I have mentioned, is this, viz.

Sec. 113. That all men being born under government, some or other, it is impossible any of them should ever be free, and at liberty to unite together, and begin a new one, or ever be able to erect a lawful government.

If this argument be good; I ask, how came so many lawful monarchies into the world? for if any body, upon this supposition, can shew me any one man in any age of the world free to begin a lawful monarchy, I will be bound to shew him ten other free men at liberty, at the same time to unite and begin a new government under a regal, or any other form; it being demonstration, that if any one, born under the dominion of another, may be so free as to have a right to command others in a new and distinct empire, every one that is born under the dominion of another may be so free too, and may become a ruler, or subject, of a distinct separate government. And so by this their own principle, either all men, however born, are free, or else there is but one lawful prince, one lawful government in the world. And then they have nothing to do, but barely to shew us which that is; which when they have done, I doubt not but all mankind will easily agree to pay obedience to him.

Sec. 114. Though it be a sufficient answer to their objection, to shew that it involves them in the same difficulties that it doth those they use it against; yet I shall endeavour to discover the weakness of this argument a little farther. All men, say they, are born under government, and therefore they cannot be at liberty to begin a new one. Every one is born a subject to his father, or his prince, and is therefore under the perpetual tie of subjection and allegiance. It is plain mankind never owned nor considered any such natural subjection that they were born in, to one or to the other that tied them, without their own consents, to a subjection to them and their heirs.

Sec. 115. For there are no examples so frequent in history, both sacred and profane, as those of men withdrawing themselves, and their obedience, from the jurisdiction they were born under, and the family or community they were bred up in, and setting up new governments in other places; from whence sprang all that number of petty commonwealths in the beginning of ages, and which always multiplied, as long as there was room enough, till the stronger, or more fortunate, swallowed the weaker; and those great ones again breaking to pieces, dissolved into lesser dominions. All which are so many testimonies against paternal sovereignty, and plainly prove, that it was not the natural right of the father descending to his heirs, that made governments in the beginning, since it was impossible, upon that ground, there should have been so many little kingdoms; all must have been but only one universal monarchy, if men had not been at liberty to separate themselves from their families, and the government, be it what it will, that was set up in it, and go and make distinct commonwealths and other governments, as they thought fit.

Sec. 116. This has been the practice of the world from its first beginning to this day; nor is it now any more hindrance to the freedom of mankind, that they are born under constituted and ancient polities, that have established laws, and set forms of government, than if they were born in the woods, amongst the unconfined inhabitants, that run loose in them: for those, who would persuade us, that by being born under any government, we are naturally subjects to it, and have no more any title or pretence to the freedom of the state of nature, have no other reason (bating that of paternal power, which we have already answered) to produce for it, but only, because our fathers or progenitors passed away their natural liberty, and thereby bound up themselves and their posterity to a perpetual subjection to the government, which they themselves submitted to. It is true, that whatever engagements or promises any one has made for himself, he is under the obligation of them, but cannot, by any compact whatsoever, bind his children or posterity: for his son, when a man, being altogether as free as the father, any act of the father can no more give away the liberty of the son, than it can of any body else: he may indeed annex such conditions to the land, he enjoyed as a subject of any common-wealth, as may oblige his son to be of that community, if he will enjoy those possessions which were his father's; because that estate being his father's property, he may dispose, or settle it, as he pleases.

Sec. 117. And this has generally given the occasion to mistake in this matter; because commonwealths not permitting any part of their dominions to be dismembered, nor to be enjoyed by any but those of their community, the son cannot ordinarily enjoy the possessions of his father, but under the same terms his father did, by becoming a member of the society; whereby he puts himself presently under the government he finds there established, as much as any other subject of that common-wealth. And thus the consent of freemen, born under government, which only makes them members of it, being given separately in their turns, as each comes to be of age, and not in a multitude together; people take no notice of it, and thinking it not done at all, or not necessary, conclude they are naturally subjects as they are men.

Sec. 118. But, it is plain, governments themselves understand it otherwise; they claim no power over the son, because of that they had over the father; nor look on children as being their subjects, by their fathers being so. If a subject of England have a child, by an English woman in France, whose subject is he? Not the king of England's; for he must have leave to be admitted to the privileges of it: nor the king of France's; for how then has his father a liberty to bring him away, and breed him as he pleases? and who ever was judged as a traytor or deserter, if he left, or warred against a country, for being barely born in it of parents that were aliens there? It is plain then, by the practice of governments themselves, as well as by the law of right reason, that a child is born a subject of no country or government. He is under his father's tuition and authority, till he comes to age of discretion; and then he is a freeman, at liberty what government he will put himself under, what body politic he will unite himself to: for if an Englishman's son, born in France, be at liberty, and may do so, it is evident there is no tie upon him by his father's being a subject of this kingdom; nor is he bound up by any compact of his ancestors. And why then hath not his son, by the same reason, the same liberty, though he be born any where else? Since the power that a father hath naturally over his children, is the same, where-ever they be born, and the ties of natural obligations, are not bounded by the positive limits of kingdoms and commonwealths.

Sec. 119. Every man being, as has been shewed, naturally free, and nothing being able to put him into subjection to any earthly power, but only his own consent; it is to be considered, what shall be understood to be a sufficient declaration of a man's consent, to make him subject to the laws of any government. There is a common distinction of an express and a tacit consent, which will concern our present case. No body doubts but an express consent, of any man entering into any society, makes him a perfect member of that society, a subject of that government. The difficulty is, what ought to be looked upon as a tacit consent, and how far it binds, i.e. how far any one shall be looked on to have consented, and thereby submitted to any government, where he has made no expressions of it at all. And to this I say, that every man, that hath any possessions, or enjoyment, of any part of the dominions of any government, doth thereby give his tacit consent, and is as far forth obliged to obedience to the laws of that government, during such enjoyment, as any one under it; whether this his possession be of land, to him and his heirs for ever, or a lodging only for a week; or whether it be barely travelling freely on the highway; and in effect, it reaches as far as the very being of any one within the territories of that government.

Sec. 120. To understand this the better, it is fit to consider, that every man, when he at first incorporates himself into any commonwealth, he, by his uniting himself thereunto, annexed also, and submits to the community, those possessions, which he has, or shall acquire, that do not already belong to any other government: for it would be a direct contradiction, for any one to enter into society with others for the securing and regulating of property; and yet to suppose his land, whose property is to be regulated by the laws of the society, should be exempt from the jurisdiction of that government, to which he himself, the proprietor of the land, is a subject. By the same act therefore, whereby any one unites his person, which was before free, to any common-wealth, by the same he unites his possessions, which were before free, to it also; and they become, both of them, person and possession, subject to the government and dominion of that common-wealth, as long as it hath a being. VVhoever therefore, from thenceforth, by inheritance, purchase, permission, or otherways, enjoys any part of the land, so annexed to, and under the government of that common-wealth, must take it with the condition it is under; that is, of submitting to the government of the common-wealth, under whose jurisdiction it is, as far forth as any subject of it.

Sec. 121. But since the government has a direct jurisdiction only over the land, and reaches the possessor of it, (before he has actually incorporated himself in the society) only as he dwells upon, and enjoys that; the obligation any one is under, by virtue of such enjoyment, to submit to the government, begins and ends with the enjoyment; so that whenever the owner, who has given nothing but such a tacit consent to the government, will, by donation, sale, or otherwise, quit the said possession, he is at liberty to go and incorporate himself into any other common-wealth; or to agree with others to begin a new one, in vacuis locis, in any part of the world, they can find free and unpossessed: whereas he, that has once, by actual agreement, and any express declaration, given his consent to be of any commonwealth, is perpetually and indispensably obliged to be, and remain unalterably a subject to it, and can never be again in the liberty of the state of nature; unless, by any calamity, the government he was under comes to be dissolved; or else by some public act cuts him off from being any longer a member of it.

Sec. 122. But submitting to the laws of any country, living quietly, and enjoying privileges and protection under them, makes not a man a member of that society: this is only a local protection and homage due to and from all those, who, not being in a state of war, come within the territories belonging to any government, to all parts whereof the force of its laws extends. But this no more makes a man a member of that society, a perpetual subject of that common-wealth, than it would make a man a subject to another, in whose family he found it convenient to abide for some time; though, whilst he continued in it, he were obliged to comply with the laws, and submit to the government he found there. And thus we see, that foreigners, by living all their lives under another government, and enjoying the privileges and protection of it, though they are bound, even in conscience, to submit to its administration, as far forth as any denison; yet do not thereby come to be subjects or members of that commonwealth. Nothing can make any man so, but his actually entering into it by positive engagement, and express promise and compact. This is that, which I think, concerning the beginning of political societies, and that consent which makes any one a member of any common-wealth.

CHAP. IX.Of the Ends of Political Society and Government.

Sec. 123. IF man in the state of nature be so free, as has been said; if he be absolute lord of his own person and possessions, equal to the greatest, and subject to no body, why will he part with his freedom? why will he give up this empire, and subject himself to the dominion and controul of any other power? To which it is obvious to answer, that though in the state of nature he hath such a right, yet the enjoyment of it is very uncertain, and constantly exposed to the invasion of others: for all being kings as much as he, every man his equal, and the greater part no strict observers of equity and justice, the enjoyment of the property he has in this state is very unsafe, very unsecure. This makes him willing to quit a condition, which, however free, is full of fears and continual dangers: and it is not without reason, that he seeks out, and is willing to join in society with others, who are already united, or have a mind to unite, for the mutual preservation of their lives, liberties and estates, which I call by the general name, property.

Sec. 124. The great and chief end, therefore, of men's uniting into commonwealths, and putting themselves under government, is the preservation of their property. To which in the state of nature there are many things wanting.

First, There wants an established, settled, known law, received and allowed by common consent to be the standard of right and wrong, and the common measure to decide all controversies between them: for though the law of nature be plain and intelligible to all rational creatures; yet men being biassed by their interest, as well as ignorant for want of study of it, are not apt to allow of it as a law binding to them in the application of it to their particular cases.

Sec. 125. Secondly, In the state of nature there wants a known and indifferent judge, with authority to determine all differences according to the established law: for every one in that state being both judge and executioner of the law of nature, men being partial to themselves, passion and revenge is very apt to carry them too far, and with too much heat, in their own cases; as well as negligence, and unconcernedness, to make them too remiss in other men's.

Sec. 126. Thirdly, In the state of nature there often wants power to back and support the sentence when right, and to give it due execution, They who by any injustice offended, will seldom fail, where they are able, by force to make good their injustice; such resistance many times makes the punishment dangerous, and frequently destructive, to those who attempt it.

Sec. 127. Thus mankind, notwithstanding all the privileges of the state of nature, being but in an ill condition, while they remain in it, are quickly driven into society. Hence it comes to pass, that we seldom find any number of men live any time together in this state. The inconveniencies that they are therein exposed to, by the irregular and uncertain exercise of the power every man has of punishing the transgressions of others, make them take sanctuary under the established laws of government, and therein seek the preservation of their property. It is this makes them so willingly give up every one his single power of punishing, to be exercised by such alone, as shall be appointed to it amongst them; and by such rules as the community, or those authorized by them to that purpose, shall agree on. And in this we have the original right and rise of both the legislative and executive power, as well as of the governments and societies themselves.

Sec. 128. For in the state of nature, to omit the liberty he has of innocent delights, a man has two powers.

The first is to do whatsoever he thinks fit for the preservation of himself, and others within the permission of the law of nature: by which law, common to them all, he and all the rest of mankind are one community, make up one society, distinct from all other creatures. And were it not for the corruption and vitiousness of degenerate men, there would be no need of any other; no necessity that men should separate from this great and natural community, and by positive agreements combine into smaller and divided associations.

The other power a man has in the state of nature, is the power to punish the crimes committed against that law. Both these he gives up, when he joins in a private, if I may so call it, or particular politic society, and incorporates into any common-wealth, separate from the rest of mankind.

Sec. 129. The first power, viz. of doing whatsoever he thought for the preservation of himself, and the rest of mankind, he gives up to be regulated by laws made by the society, so far forth as the preservation of himself, and the rest of that society shall require; which laws of the society in many things confine the liberty he had by the law of nature.

Sec. 130. Secondly, The power of punishing he wholly gives up, and engages his natural force, (which he might before employ in the execution of the law of nature, by his own single authority, as he thought fit) to assist the executive power of the society, as the law thereof shall require: for being now in a new state, wherein he is to enjoy many conveniencies, from the labour, assistance, and society of others in the same community, as well as protection from its whole strength; he is to part also with as much of his natural liberty, in providing for himself, as the good, prosperity, and safety of the society shall require; which is not only necessary, but just, since the other members of the society do the like.

Sec. 131. But though men, when they enter into society, give up the equality, liberty, and executive power they had in the state of nature, into the hands of the society, to be so far disposed of by the legislative, as the good of the society shall require; yet it being only with an intention in every one the better to preserve himself, his liberty and property; (for no rational creature can be supposed to change his condition with an intention to be worse) the power of the society, or legislative constituted by them, can never be supposed to extend farther, than the common good; but is obliged to secure every one's property, by providing against those three defects above mentioned, that made the state of nature so unsafe and uneasy. And so whoever has the legislative or supreme power of any common-wealth, is bound to govern by established standing laws, promulgated and known to the people, and not by extemporary decrees; by indifferent and upright judges, who are to decide controversies by those laws; and to employ the force of the community at home, only in the execution of such laws, or abroad to prevent or redress foreign injuries, and secure the community from inroads and invasion. And all this to be directed to no other end, but the peace, safety, and public good of the people.

CHAP. X. Of the Forms of a Common-wealth.

Sec. 132. THE majority having, as has been shewed, upon men's first uniting into society, the whole power of the community naturally in them, may employ all that power in making laws for the community from time to time, and executing those laws by officers of their own appointing; and then the form of the government is a perfect democracy: or else may put the power of making laws into the hands of a few select men, and their heirs or successors; and then it is an oligarchy: or else into the hands of one man, and then it is a monarchy: if to him and his heirs, it is an hereditary monarchy: if to him only for life, but upon his death the power only of nominating a successor to return to them; an elective monarchy. And so accordingly of these the community may make compounded and mixed forms of government, as they think good. And if the legislative power be at first given by the majority to one or more persons only for their lives, or any limited time, and then the supreme power to revert to them again; when it is so reverted, the community may dispose of it again anew into what hands they please, and so constitute a new form of government: for the form of government depending upon the placing the supreme power, which is the legislative, it being impossible to conceive that an inferior power should prescribe to a superior, or any but the supreme make laws, according as the power of making laws is placed, such is the form of the common-wealth.

Sec. 133. By common-wealth, I must be understood all along to mean, not a democracy, or any form of government, but any independent community, which the Latines signified by the word civitas, to which the word which best answers in our language, is common-wealth, and most properly expresses such a society of men, which community or city in English does not; for there may be subordinate communities in a government; and city amongst us has a quite different notion from common-wealth: and therefore, to avoid ambiguity, I crave leave to use the word common-wealth in that sense, in which I find it used by king James the first; and I take it to be its genuine signification; which if any body dislike, I consent with him to change it for a better.

CHAP. XI. Of the Extent of the Legislative Power.

Sec. 134. THE great end of men's entering into society, being the enjoyment of their properties in peace and safety, and the great instrument and means of that being the laws established in that society; the first and fundamental positive law of all commonwealths is the establishing of the legislative power; as the first and fundamental natural law, which is to govern even the legislative itself, is the preservation of the society, and (as far as will consist with the public good) of every person in it. This legislative is not only the supreme power of the common-wealth, but sacred and unalterable in the hands where the community have once placed it; nor can any edict of any body else, in what form soever conceived, or by what power soever backed, have the force and obligation of a law, which has not its sanction from that legislative which the public has chosen and appointed: for without this the law could not have that, which is absolutely necessary to its being a law,* the consent of the society, over whom no body can have a power to make laws, but by their own consent, and by authority received from them; and therefore all the obedience, which by the most solemn ties any one can be obliged to pay, ultimately terminates in this supreme power, and is directed by those laws which it enacts: nor can any oaths to any foreign power whatsoever, or any domestic subordinate power, discharge any member of the society from his obedience to the legislative, acting pursuant to their trust; nor oblige him to any obedience contrary to the laws so enacted, or farther than they do allow; it being ridiculous to imagine one can be tied ultimately to obey any power in the society, which is not the supreme.

(* The lawful power of making laws to command whole politic societies of men, belonging so properly unto the same intire societies, that for any prince or potentate of what kind soever upon earth, to exercise the same of himself, and not by express commission immediately and personally received from God, or else by authority derived at the first from their consent, upon whose persons they impose laws, it is no better than mere tyranny. Laws they are not therefore which public approbation hath not made so. Hooker's Eccl. Pol. l. i. sect. 10. Of this point therefore we are to note, that sith men naturally have no full and perfect power to command whole politic multitudes of men, therefore utterly without our consent, we could in such sort be at no man's commandment living. And to be commanded we do consent, when that society, whereof we be a part, hath at any time before consented, without revoking the same after by the like universal agreement.

Laws therefore human, of what kind so ever, are available by consent. Ibid.)

Sec. 135. Though the legislative, whether placed in one or more, whether it be always in being, or only by intervals, though it be the supreme power in every common-wealth; yet,

First, It is not, nor can possibly be absolutely arbitrary over the lives and fortunes of the people: for it being but the joint power of every member of the society given up to that person, or assembly, which is legislator; it can be no more than those persons had in a state of nature before they entered into society, and gave up to the community: for no body can transfer to another more power than he has in himself; and no body has an absolute arbitrary power over himself, or over any other, to destroy his own life, or take away the life or property of another. A man, as has been proved, cannot subject himself to the arbitrary power of another; and having in the state of nature no arbitrary power over the life, liberty, or possession of another, but only so much as the law of nature gave him for the preservation of himself, and the rest of mankind; this is all he doth, or can give up to the common-wealth, and by it to the legislative power, so that the legislative can have no more than this. Their power, in the utmost bounds of it, is limited to the public good of the society. It is a power, that hath no other end but preservation, and therefore can never* have a right to destroy, enslave, or designedly to impoverish the subjects. The obligations of the law of nature cease not in society, but only in many cases are drawn closer, and have by human laws known penalties annexed to them, to inforce their observation. Thus the law of nature stands as an eternal rule to all men, legislators as well as others. The rules that they make for other men's actions, must, as well as their own and other men's actions, be conformable to the law of nature, i.e. to the will of God, of which that is a declaration, and the fundamental law of nature being the preservation of mankind, no human sanction can be good, or valid against it.

(* Two foundations there are which bear up public societies; the one a natural inclination, whereby all men desire sociable life and fellowship; the other an order, expressly or secretly agreed upon, touching the manner of their union in living together: the latter is that which we call the law of a commonweal, the very soul of a politic body, the parts whereof are by law animated, held together, and set on work in such actions as the common good requireth. Laws politic, ordained for external order and regiment amongst men, are never framed as they should be, unless presuming the will of man to be inwardly obstinate, rebellious, and averse from all obedience to the sacred laws of his nature; in a word, unless presuming man to be, in regard of his depraved mind, little better than a wild beast, they do accordingly provide, notwithstanding, so to frame his outward actions, that they be no hindrance unto the common good, for which societies are instituted. Unless they do this, they are not perfect. Hooker's Eccl. Pol. l. i. sect. 10.)

Sec. 136. Secondly,* The legislative, or supreme authority, cannot assume to its self a power to rule by extemporary arbitrary decrees, but is bound to dispense justice, and decide the rights of the subject by promulgated standing laws, and known authorized judges: for the law of nature being unwritten, and so no where to be found but in the minds of men, they who through passion or interest shall miscite, or misapply it, cannot so easily be convinced of their mistake where there is no established judge: and so it serves not, as it ought, to determine the rights, and fence the properties of those that live under it, especially where every one is judge, interpreter, and executioner of it too, and that in his own case: and he that has right on his side, having ordinarily but his own single strength, hath not force enough to defend himself from injuries, or to punish delinquents. To avoid these inconveniences, which disorder men's propperties in the state of nature, men unite into societies, that they may have the united strength of the whole society to secure and defend their properties, and may have standing rules to bound it, by which every one may know what is his. To this end it is that men give up all their natural power to the society which they enter into, and the community put the legislative power into such hands as they think fit, with this trust, that they shall be governed by declared laws, or else their peace, quiet, and property will still be at the same uncertainty, as it was in the state of nature.

(* Human laws are measures in respect of men whose actions they must direct, howbeit such measures they are as have also their higher rules to be measured by, which rules are two, the law of God, and the law of nature; so that laws human must be made according to the general laws of nature, and without contradiction to any positive law of scripture, otherwise they are ill made. Hooker's Eccl. Pol. l. iii. sect. 9.

To constrain men to any thing inconvenient doth seem unreasonable. Ibid. l. i. sect. 10.)

Sec. 137. Absolute arbitrary power, or governing without settled standing laws, can neither of them consist with the ends of society and government, which men would not quit the freedom of the state of nature for, and tie themselves up under, were it not to preserve their lives, liberties and fortunes, and by stated rules of right and property to secure their peace and quiet.

It cannot be supposed that they should intend, had they a power so to do, to give to any one, or more, an absolute arbitrary power over their persons and estates, and put a force into the magistrate's hand to execute his unlimited will arbitrarily upon them. This were to put themselves into a worse condition than the state of nature, wherein they had a liberty to defend their right against the injuries of others, and were upon equal terms of force to maintain it, whether invaded by a single man, or many in combination. Whereas by supposing they have given up themselves to the absolute arbitrary power and will of a legislator, they have disarmed themselves, and armed him, to make a prey of them when he pleases; he being in a much worse condition, who is exposed to the arbitrary power of one man, who has the command of 100,000, than he that is exposed to the arbitrary power of 100,000 single men; no body being secure, that his will, who has such a command, is better than that of other men, though his force be 100,000 times stronger. And therefore, whatever form the common-wealth is under, the ruling power ought to govern by declared and received laws, and not by extemporary dictates and undetermined resolutions: for then mankind will be in a far worse condition than in the state of nature, if they shall have armed one, or a few men with the joint power of a multitude, to force them to obey at pleasure the exorbitant and unlimited decrees of their sudden thoughts, or unrestrained, and till that moment unknown wills, without having any measures set down which may guide and justify their actions: for all the power the government has, being only for the good of the society, as it ought not to be arbitrary and at pleasure, so it ought to be exercised by established and promulgated laws; that both the people may know their duty, and be safe and secure within the limits of the law; and the rulers too kept within their bounds, and not be tempted, by the power they have in their hands, to employ it to such purposes, and by such measures, as they would not have known, and own not willingly.

Sec. 138. Thirdly, The supreme power cannot take from any man any part of his property without his own consent: for the preservation of property being the end of government, and that for which men enter into society, it necessarily supposes and requires, that the people should have property, without which they must be supposed to lose that, by entering into society, which was the end for which they entered into it; too gross an absurdity for any man to own. Men therefore in society having property, they have such a right to the goods, which by the law of the community are their's, that no body hath a right to take their substance or any part of it from them, without their own consent: without this they have no property at all; for I have truly no property in that, which another can by right take from me, when he pleases, against my consent. Hence it is a mistake to think, that the supreme or legislative power of any commonwealth, can do what it will, and dispose of the estates of the subject arbitrarily, or take any part of them at pleasure. This is not much to be feared in governments where the legislative consists, wholly or in part, in assemblies which are variable, whose members, upon the dissolution of the assembly, are subjects under the common laws of their country, equally with the rest. But in governments, where the legislative is in one lasting assembly always in being, or in one man, as in absolute monarchies, there is danger still, that they will think themselves to have a distinct interest from the rest of the community; and so will be apt to increase their own riches and power, by taking what they think fit from the people: for a man's property is not at all secure, tho' there be good and equitable laws to set the bounds of it between him and his fellow subjects, if he who commands those subjects have power to take from any private man, what part he pleases of his property, and use and dispose of it as he thinks good.

Sec. 139. But government, into whatsoever hands it is put, being, as I have before shewed, intrusted with this condition, and for this end, that men might have and secure their properties; the prince, or senate, however it may have power to make laws, for the regulating of property between the subjects one amongst another, yet can never have a power to take to themselves the whole, or any part of the subjects property, without their own consent: for this would be in effect to leave them no property at all. And to let us see, that even absolute power, where it is necessary, is not arbitrary by being absolute, but is still limited by that reason, and confined to those ends, which required it in some cases to be absolute, we need look no farther than the common practice of martial discipline: for the preservation of the army, and in it of the whole common-wealth, requires an absolute obedience to the command of every superior officer, and it is justly death to disobey or dispute the most dangerous or unreasonable of them; but yet we see, that neither the serjeant, that could command a soldier to march up to the mouth of a cannon, or stand in a breach, where he is almost sure to perish, can command that soldier to give him one penny of his money; nor the general, that can condemn him to death for deserting his post, or for not obeying the most desperate orders, can yet, with all his absolute power of life and death, dispose of one farthing of that soldier's estate, or seize one jot of his goods; whom yet he can command any thing, and hang for the least disobedience; because such a blind obedience is necessary to that end, for which the commander has his power, viz. the preservation of the rest; but the disposing of his goods has nothing to do with it.

Sec. 140. It is true, governments cannot be supported without great charge, and it is fit every one who enjoys his share of the protection, should pay out of his estate his proportion for the maintenance of it. But still it must be with his own consent, i.e. the consent of the majority, giving it either by themselves, or their representatives chosen by them: for if any one shall claim a power to lay and levy taxes on the people, by his own authority, and without such consent of the people, he thereby invades the fundamental law of property, and subverts the end of government: for what property have I in that, which another may by right take, when he pleases, to himself?

Sec. 141. Fourthly, The legislative cannot transfer the power of making laws to any other hands: for it being but a delegated power from the people, they who have it cannot pass it over to others. The people alone can appoint the form of the common-wealth, which is by constituting the legislative, and appointing in whose hands that shall be. And when the people have said, We will submit to rules, and be governed by laws made by such men, and in such forms, no body else can say other men shall make laws for them; nor can the people be bound by any laws, but such as are enacted by those whom they have chosen, and authorized to make laws for them. The power of the legislative, being derived from the people by a positive voluntary grant and institution, can be no other than what that positive grant conveyed, which being only to make laws, and not to make legislators, the legislative can have no power to transfer their authority of making laws, and place it in other hands.

Sec. 142. These are the bounds which the trust, that is put in them by the society, and the law of God and nature, have set to the legislative power of every common-wealth, in all forms of government.

First, They are to govern by promulgated established laws, not to be varied in particular cases, but to have one rule for rich and poor, for the favourite at court, and the country man at plough.

Secondly, These laws also ought to be designed for no other end ultimately, but the good of the people.

Thirdly, They must not raise taxes on the property of the people, without the consent of the people, given by themselves, or their deputies. And this properly concerns only such governments where the legislative is always in being, or at least where the people have not reserved any part of the legislative to deputies, to be from time to time chosen by themselves.

Fourthly, The legislative neither must nor can transfer the power of making laws to any body else, or place it any where, but where the people have.

CHAP. XII. Of the Legislative, Executive, and Federative Power of the Common-wealth.

Sec. 143. THE legislative power is that, which has a right to direct how the force of the common-wealth shall be employed for preserving the community and the members of it. But because those laws which are constantly to be executed, and whose force is always to continue, may be made in a little time; therefore there is no need, that the legislative should be always in being, not having always business to do. And because it may be too great a temptation to human frailty, apt to grasp at power, for the same persons, who have the power of making laws, to have also in their hands the power to execute them, whereby they may exempt themselves from obedience to the laws they make, and suit the law, both in its making, and execution, to their own private advantage, and thereby come to have a distinct interest from the rest of the community, contrary to the end of society and government: therefore in well ordered commonwealths, where the good of the whole is so con sidered, as it ought, the legislative power is put into the hands of divers persons, who duly assembled, have by themselves, or jointly with others, a power to make laws, which when they have done, being separated again, they are themselves subject to the laws they have made; which is a new and near tie upon them, to take care, that they make them for the public good.

Sec. 144. But because the laws, that are at once, and in a short time made, have a constant and lasting force, and need a perpetual execution, or an attendance thereunto; therefore it is necessary there should be a power always in being, which should see to the execution of the laws that are made, and remain in force. And thus the legislative and executive power come often to be separated.

Sec. 145. There is another power in every common-wealth, which one may call natural, because it is that which answers to the power every man naturally had before he entered into society: for though in a common-wealth the members of it are distinct persons still in reference to one another, and as such as governed by the laws of the society; yet in reference to the rest of mankind, they make one body, which is, as every member of it before was, still in the state of nature with the rest of mankind. Hence it is, that the controversies that happen between any man of the society with those that are out of it, are managed by the public; and an injury done to a member of their body, engages the whole in the reparation of it. So that under this consideration, the whole community is one body in the state of nature, in respect of all other states or persons out of its community.

Sec. 146. This therefore contains the power of war and peace, leagues and alliances, and all the transactions, with all persons and communities without the common-wealth, and may be called federative, if any one pleases. So the thing be understood, I am indifferent as to the name.

Sec. 147. These two powers, executive and federative, though they be really distinct in themselves, yet one comprehending the execution of the municipal laws of the society within its self, upon all that are parts of it; the other the management of the security and interest of the public without, with all those that it may receive benefit or damage from, yet they are always almost united. And though this federative power in the well or ill management of it be of great moment to the common-wealth, yet it is much less capable to be directed by antecedent, standing, positive laws, than the executive; and so must necessarily be left to the prudence and wisdom of those, whose hands it is in, to be managed for the public good: for the laws that concern subjects one amongst another, being to direct their actions, may well enough precede them. But what is to be done in reference to foreigners, depending much upon their actions, and the variation of designs and interests, must be left in great part to the prudence of those, who have this power committed to them, to be managed by the best of their skill, for the advantage of the common-wealth.

Sec. 148. Though, as I said, the executive and federative power of every community be really distinct in themselves, yet they are hardly to be separated, and placed at the same time, in the hands of distinct persons: for both of them requiring the force of the society for their exercise, it is almost impracticable to place the force of the common-wealth in distinct, and not subordinate hands; or that the executive and federative power should be placed in persons, that might act separately, whereby the force of the public would be under different commands: which would be apt some time or other to cause disorder and ruin.

CHAP. XIII.Of the Subordination of the Powers of the Common-wealth.

Sec. 149. THOUGH in a constituted common-wealth, standing upon its own basis, and acting according to its own nature, that is, acting for the preservation of the community, there can be but one supreme power, which is the legislative, to which all the rest are and must be subordinate, yet the legislative being only a fiduciary power to act for certain ends, there remains still in the people a supreme power to remove or alter the legislative, when they find the legislative act contrary to the trust reposed in them: for all power given with trust for the attaining an end, being limited by that end, whenever that end is manifestly neglected, or opposed, the trust must necessarily be forfeited, and the power devolve into the hands of those that gave it, who may place it anew where they shall think best for their safety and security. And thus the community perpetually retains a supreme power of saving themselves from the attempts and designs of any body, even of their legislators, whenever they shall be so foolish, or so wicked, as to lay and carry on designs against the liberties and properties of the subject: for no man or society of men, having a power to deliver up their preservation, or consequently the means of it, to the absolute will and arbitrary dominion of another; when ever any one shall go about to bring them into such a slavish condition, they will always have a right to preserve, what they have not a power to part with; and to rid themselves of those, who invade this fundamental, sacred, and unalterable law of self-preservation, for which they entered into society. And thus the community may be said in this respect to be always the supreme power, but not as considered under any form of government, because this power of the people can never take place till the government be dissolved.

Sec. 150. In all cases, whilst the government subsists, the legislative is the supreme power: for what can give laws to another, must needs be superior to him; and since the legislative is no otherwise legislative of the society, but by the right it has to make laws for all the parts, and for every member of the society, prescribing rules to their actions, and giving power of execution, where they are transgressed, the legislative must needs be the supreme, and all other powers, in any members or parts of the society, derived from and subordinate to it.

Sec. 151. In some commonwealths, where the legislative is not always in being, and the executive is vested in a single person, who has also a share in the legislative; there that single person in a very tolerable sense may also be called supreme: not that he has in himself all the supreme power, which is that of law-making; but because he has in him the supreme execution, from whom all inferior magistrates derive all their several subordinate powers, or at least the greatest part of them: having also no legislative superior to him, there being no law to be made without his consent, which cannot be expected should ever subject him to the other part of the legislative, he is properly enough in this sense supreme. But yet it is to be observed, that tho' oaths of allegiance and fealty are taken to him, it is not to him as supreme legislator, but as supreme executor of the law, made by a joint power of him with others; allegiance being nothing but an obedience according to law, which when he violates, he has no right to obedience, nor can claim it otherwise than as the public person vested with the power of the law, and so is to be considered as the image, phantom, or representative of the common-wealth, acted by the will of the society, declared in its laws; and thus he has no will, no power, but that of the law. But when he quits this representation, this public will, and acts by his own private will, he degrades himself, and is but a single private person without power, and without will, that has any right to obedience; the members owing no obedience but to the public will of the society.

Sec. 152. The executive power, placed any where but in a person that has also a share in the legislative, is visibly subordinate and accountable to it, and may be at pleasure changed and displaced; so that it is not the supreme executive power, that is exempt from subordination, but the supreme executive power vested in one, who having a share in the legislative, has no distinct superior legislative to be subordinate and accountable to, farther than he himself shall join and consent; so that he is no more subordinate than he himself shall think fit, which one may certainly conclude will be but very little. Of other ministerial and subordinate powers in a commonwealth, we need not speak, they being so multiplied with infinite variety, in the different customs and constitutions of distinct commonwealths, that it is impossible to give a particular account of them all. Only thus much, which is necessary to our present purpose, we may take notice of concerning them, that they have no manner of authority, any of them, beyond what is by positive grant and commission delegated to them, and are all of them accountable to some other power in the common-wealth.

Sec. 153. It is not necessary, no, nor so much as convenient, that the legislative should be always in being; but absolutely necessary that the executive power should, because there is not always need of new laws to be made, but always need of execution of the laws that are made. When the legislative hath put the execution of the laws, they make, into other hands, they have a power still to resume it out of those hands, when they find cause, and to punish for any maladministration against the laws. The same holds also in regard of the federative power, that and the executive being both ministerial and subordinate to the legislative, which, as has been shewed, in a constituted common-wealth is the supreme. The legislative also in this case being supposed to consist of several persons, (for if it be a single person, it cannot but be always in being, and so will, as supreme, naturally have the supreme executive power, together with the legislative) may assemble, and exercise their legislature, at the times that either their original constitution, or their own adjournment, appoints, or when they please; if neither of these hath appointed any time, or there be no other way prescribed to convoke them: for the supreme power being placed in them by the people, it is always in them, and they may exercise it when they please, unless by their original constitution they are limited to certain seasons, or by an act of their supreme power they have adjourned to a certain time; and when that time comes, they have a right to assemble and act again.

Sec. 154. If the legislative, or any part of it, be made up of representatives chosen for that time by the people, which afterwards return into the ordinary state of subjects, and have no share in the legislature but upon a new choice, this power of chusing must also be exercised by the people, either at certain appointed seasons, or else when they are summoned to it; and in this latter case ' the power of convoking the legislative is ordinarily placed in the executive, and has one of these two limitations in respect of time: that either the original constitution requires their assembling and acting at certain intervals, and then the executive power does nothing but ministerially issue directions for their electing and assembling, according to due forms; or else it is left to his prudence to call them by new elections, when the occasions or exigencies of the public require the amendment of old, or making of new laws, or the redress or prevention of any inconveniencies, that lie on, or threaten the people.

Sec. 155. It may be demanded here, What if the executive power, being possessed of the force of the common-wealth, shall make use of that force to hinder the meeting and acting of the legislative, when the original constitution, or the public exigencies require it? I say, using force upon the people without authority, and contrary to the trust put in him that does so, is a state of war with the people, who have a right to reinstate their legislative in the exercise of their power: for having erected a legislative, with an intent they should exercise the power of making laws, either at certain set times, or when there is need of it, when they are hindered by any force from what is so necessary to the society, and wherein the safety and preservation of the people consists, the people have a right to remove it by force. In all states and conditions, the true remedy of force without authority, is to oppose force to it. The use of force without authority, always puts him that uses it into a state of war, as the aggressor, and renders him liable to be treated accordingly.

Sec. 156. The power of assembling and dismissing the legislative, placed in the executive, gives not the executive a superiority over it, but is a fiduciary trust placed in him, for the safety of the people, in a case where the uncertainty and variableness of human affairs could not bear a steady fixed rule: for it not being possible, that the first framers of the government should, by any foresight, be so much masters of future events, as to be able to prefix so just periods of return and duration to the assemblies of the legislative, in all times to come, that might exactly answer all the exigencies of the commonwealth; the best remedy could be found for this defect, was to trust this to the prudence of one who was always to be present, and whose business it was to watch over the public good. Constant frequent meetings of the legislative, and long continuations of their assemblies, without necessary occasion, could not but be burdensome to the people, and must necessarily in time produce more dangerous inconveniencies, and yet the quick turn of affairs might be sometimes such as to need their present help: any delay of their convening might endanger the public; and sometimes too their business might be so great, that the limited time of their sitting might be too short for their work, and rob the public of that benefit which could be had only from their mature deliberation. What then could be done in this case to prevent the community from being exposed some time or other to eminent hazard, on one side or the other, by fixed intervals and periods, set to the meeting and acting of the legislative, but to intrust it to the prudence of some, who being present, and acquainted with the state of public affairs, might make use of this prerogative for the public good? and where else could this be so well placed as in his hands, who was intrusted with the execution of the laws for the same end? Thus supposing the regulation of times for the assembling and sitting of the legislative, not settled by the original constitution, it naturally fell into the hands of the executive, not as an arbitrary power depending on his good pleasure, but with this trust always to have it exercised only for the public weal, as the occurrences of times and change of affairs might require. Whether settled periods of their convening, or a liberty left to the prince for convoking the legislative, or perhaps a mixture of both, hath the least inconvenience attending it, it is not my business here to inquire, but only to shew, that though the executive power may have the prerogative of convoking and dissolving such conventions of the legislative, yet it is not thereby superior to it.

Sec. 157. Things of this world are in so constant a flux, that nothing remains long in the same state. Thus people, riches, trade, power, change their stations, flourishing mighty cities come to ruin, and prove in times neglected desolate corners, whilst other unfrequented places grow into populous countries, filled with wealth and inhabitants. But things not always changing equally, and private interest often keeping up customs and privileges, when the reasons of them are ceased, it often comes to pass, that in governments, where part of the legislative consists of representatives chosen by the people, that in tract of time this representation becomes very unequal and disproportionate to the reasons it was at first established upon. To what gross absurdities the following of custom, when reason has left it, may lead, we may be satisfied, when we see the bare name of a town, of which there remains not so much as the ruins, where scarce so much housing as a sheepcote, or more inhabitants than a shepherd is to be found, sends as many representatives to the grand assembly of law-makers, as a whole county numerous in people, and powerful in riches. This strangers stand amazed at, and every one must confess needs a remedy; tho' most think it hard to find one, because the constitution of the legislative being the original and supreme act of the society, antecedent to all positive laws in it, and depending wholly on the people, no inferior power can alter it. And therefore the people, when the legislative is once constituted, having, in such a government as we have been speaking of, no power to act as long as the government stands; this inconvenience is thought incapable of a remedy.

Sec. 158. Salus populi suprema lex, is certainly so just and fundamental a rule, that he, who sincerely follows it, cannot dangerously err. If therefore the executive, who has the power of convoking the legislative, observing rather the true proportion, than fashion of representation, regulates, not by old custom, but true reason, the number of members, in all places that have a right to be distinctly represented, which no part of the people however incorporated can pretend to, but in proportion to the assistance which it affords to the public, it cannot be judged to have set up a new legislative, but to have restored the old and true one, and to have rectified the disorders which succession of time had insensibly, as well as inevitably introduced: For it being the interest as well as intention of the people, to have a fair and equal representative; whoever brings it nearest to that, is an undoubted friend to, and establisher of the government, and cannot miss the consent and approbation of the community; prerogative being nothing but a power, in the hands of the prince, to provide for the public good, in such cases, which depending upon unforeseen and uncertain occurrences, certain and unalterable laws could not safely direct; whatsoever shall be done manifestly for the good of the people, and the establishing the government upon its true foundations, is, and always will be, just prerogative. The power of erecting new corporations, and therewith new representatives, carries with it a supposition, that in time the measures of representation might vary, and those places have a just right to be represented which before had none; and by the same reason, those cease to have a right, and be too inconsiderable for such a privilege, which before had it. 'Tis not a change from the present state, which perhaps corruption or decay has introduced, that makes an inroad upon the government, but the tendency of it to injure or oppress the people, and to set up one part or party, with a distinction from, and an unequal subjection of the rest. Whatsoever cannot but be acknowledged to be of advantage to the society, and people in general, upon just and lasting measures, will always, when done, justify itself; and whenever the people shall chuse their representatives upon just and undeniably equal measures, suitable to the original frame of the government, it cannot be doubted to be the will and act of the society, whoever permitted or caused them so to do.

CHAP. XIV. Of Prerogative.

Sec. 159. WHERE the legislative and executive power are in distinct hands, (as they are in all moderated monarchies, and well-framed governments) there the good of the society requires, that several things should be left to the discretion of him that has the executive power: for the legislators not being able to foresee, and provide by laws, for all that may be useful to the community, the executor of the laws having the power in his hands, has by the common law of nature a right to make use of it for the good of the society, in many cases, where the municipal law has given no direction, till the legislative can conveniently be assembled to provide for it. Many things there are, which the law can by no means provide for; and those must necessarily be left to the discretion of him that has the executive power in his hands, to be ordered by him as the public good and advantage shall require: nay, it is fit that the laws themselves should in some cases give way to the executive power, or rather to this fundamental law of nature and government, viz. That as much as may be, all the members of the society are to be preserved: for since many accidents may happen, wherein a strict and rigid observation of the laws may do harm; (as not to pull down an innocent man's house to stop the fire, when the next to it is burning) and a man may come sometimes within the reach of the law, which makes no distinction of persons, by an action that may deserve reward and pardon; 'tis fit the ruler should have a power, in many cases, to mitigate the severity of the law, and pardon some offenders: for the end of government being the preservation of all, as much as may be, even the guilty are to be spared, where it can prove no prejudice to the innocent.

Sec. 160. This power to act according to discretion, for the public good, without the prescription of the law, and sometimes even against it, is that which is called prerogative: for since in some governments the lawmaking power is not always in being, and is usually too numerous, and so too slow, for the dispatch requisite to execution; and because also it is impossible to foresee, and so by laws to provide for, all accidents and necessities that may concern the public, or to make such laws as will do no harm, if they are executed with an inflexible rigour, on all occasions, and upon all persons that may come in their way; therefore there is a latitude left to the executive power, to do many things of choice which the laws do not prescribe.

Sec. 161. This power, whilst employed for the benefit of the community, and suitably to the trust and ends of the government, is undoubted prerogative, and never is questioned: for the people are very seldom or never scrupulous or nice in the point; they are far from examining prerogative, whilst it is in any tolerable degree employed for the use it was meant, that is, for the good of the people, and not manifestly against it: but if there comes to be a question between the executive power and the people, about a thing claimed as a prerogative; the tendency of the exercise of such prerogative to the good or hurt of the people, will easily decide that question.

Sec. 162. It is easy to conceive, that in the infancy of governments, when commonwealths differed little from families in number of people, they differed from them too but little in number of laws: and the governors, being as the fathers of them, watching over them for their good, the government was almost all prerogative. A few established laws served the turn, and the discretion and care of the ruler supplied the rest. But when mistake or flattery prevailed with weak princes to make use of this power for private ends of their own, and not for the public good, the people were fain by express laws to get prerogative determined in those points wherein they found disadvantage from it: and thus declared limitations of prerogative were by the people found necessary in cases which they and their ancestors had left, in the utmost latitude, to the wisdom of those princes who made no other but a right use of it, that is, for the good of their people.

Sec. 163. And therefore they have a very wrong notion of government, who say, that the people have encroached upon the prerogative, when they have got any part of it to be defined by positive laws: for in so doing they have not pulled from the prince any thing that of right belonged to him, but only declared, that that power which they indefinitely left in his or his ancestors hands, to be exercised for their good, was not a thing which they intended him when he used it otherwise: for the end of government being the good of the community, whatsoever alterations are made in it, tending to that end, cannot be an encroachment upon any body, since no body in government can have a right tending to any other end: and those only are encroachments which prejudice or hinder the public good. Those who say otherwise, speak as if the prince had a distinct and separate interest from the good of the community, and was not made for it; the root and source from which spring almost all those evils and disorders which happen in kingly governments. And indeed, if that be so, the people under his government are not a society of rational creatures, entered into a community for their mutual good; they are not such as have set rulers over themselves, to guard, and promote that good; but are to be looked on as an herd of inferior creatures under the dominion of a master, who keeps them and works them for his own pleasure or profit. If men were so void of reason, and brutish, as to enter into society upon such terms, prerogative might indeed be, what some men would have it, an arbitrary power to do things hurtful to the people.

Sec. 164. But since a rational creature cannot be supposed, when free, to put himself into subjection to another, for his own harm; (though, where he finds a good and wise ruler, he may not perhaps think it either necessary or useful to set precise bounds to his power in all things) prerogative can be nothing but the people's permitting their rulers to do several things, of their own free choice, where the law was silent, and sometimes too against the direct letter of the law, for the public good; and their acquiescing in it when so done: for as a good prince, who is mindful of the trust put into his hands, and careful of the good of his people, cannot have too much prerogative, that is, power to do good; so a weak and ill prince, who would claim that power which his predecessors exercised without the direction of the law, as a prerogative belonging to him by right of his office, which he may exercise at his pleasure, to make or promote an interest distinct from that of the public, gives the people an occasion to claim their right, and limit that power, which, whilst it was exercised for their good, they were content should be tacitly allowed. Sec. 165. And therefore he that will look into the history of England, will find, that prerogative was always largest in the hands of our wisest and best princes; because the people, observing the whole tendency of their actions to be the public good, contested not what was done without law to that end: or, if any human frailty or mistake (for princes are but men, made as others) appeared in some small declinations from that end; yet 'twas visible, the main of their conduct tended to nothing but the care of the public. The people therefore, finding reason to be satisfied with these princes, whenever they acted without, or contrary to the letter of the law, acquiesced in what they did, and, without the least complaint, let them inlarge their prerogative as they pleased, judging rightly, that they did nothing herein to the prejudice of their laws, since they acted conformable to the foundation and end of all laws, the public good.

Sec. 166. Such god-like princes indeed had some title to arbitrary power by that argument, that would prove absolute monarchy the best government, as that which God himself governs the universe by; because such kings partake of his wisdom and goodness. Upon this is founded that saying, That the reigns of good princes have been always most dangerous to the liberties of their people: for when their successors, managing the government with different thoughts, would draw the actions of those good rulers into precedent, and make them the standard of their prerogative, as if what had been done only for the good of the people was a right in them to do, for the harm of the people, if they so pleased; it has often occasioned contest, and sometimes public disorders, before the people could recover their original right, and get that to be declared not to be prerogative, which truly was never so; since it is impossible that any body in the society should ever have a right to do the people harm; though it be very possible, and reasonable, that the people should not go about to set any bounds to the prerogative of those kings, or rulers, who themselves transgressed not the bounds of the public good: for prerogative is nothing but the power of doing public good without a rule.

Sec. 167. The power of calling parliaments in England, as to precise time, place, and duration, is certainly a prerogative of the king, but still with this trust, that it shall be made use of for the good of the nation, as the exigencies of the times, and variety of occasions, shall require: for it being impossible to foresee which should always be the fittest place for them to assemble in, and what the best season; the choice of these was left with the executive power, as might be most subservient to the public good, and best suit the ends of parliaments.

Sec. 168. The old question will be asked in this matter of prerogative, But who shall be judge when this power is made a right use of ? 1 answer: between an executive power in being, with such a prerogative, and a legislative that depends upon his will for their convening, there can be no judge on earth; as there can be none between the legislative and the people, should either the executive, or the legislative, when they have got the power in their hands, design, or go about to enslave or destroy them. The people have no other remedy in this, as in all other cases where they have no judge on earth, but to appeal to heaven: for the rulers, in such attempts, exercising a power the people never put into their hands, (who can never be supposed to consent that any body should rule over them for their harm) do that which they have not a right to do. And where the body of the people, or any single man, is deprived of their right, or is under the exercise of a power without right, and have no appeal on earth, then they have a liberty to appeal to heaven, whenever they judge the cause of sufficient moment. And therefore, though the people cannot be judge, so as to have, by the constitution of that society, any superior power, to determine and give effective sentence in the case; yet they have, by a law antecedent and paramount to all positive laws of men, reserved that ultimate determination to themselves which belongs to all mankind, where there lies no appeal on earth, viz. to judge, whether they have just cause to make their appeal to heaven. And this judgment they cannot part with, it being out of a man's power so to submit himself to another, as to give him a liberty to destroy him; God and nature never allowing a man so to abandon himself, as to neglect his own preservation: and since he cannot take away his own life, neither can he give another power to take it. Nor let any one think, this lays a perpetual foundation for disorder; for this operates not, till the inconveniency is so great, that the majority feel it, and are weary of it, and find a necessity to have it amended. But this the executive power, or wise princes, never need come in the danger of: and it is the thing, of all others, they have most need to avoid, as of all others the most perilous.

CHAP. XV. Of Paternal, Political, and Despotical Power, considered together.

Sec. 169. THOUGH I have had occasion to speak of these separately before, yet the great mistakes of late about government, having, as I suppose, arisen from confounding these distinct powers one with another, it may not, perhaps, be amiss to consider them here together.

Sec. 170. First, then, Paternal or parental power is nothing but that which parents have over their children, to govern them for the children's good, till they come to the use of reason, or a state of knowledge, wherein they may be supposed capable to understand that rule, whether it be the law of nature, or the municipal law of their country, they are to govern themselves by: capable, I say, to know it, as well as several others, who live as freemen under that law. The affection and tenderness which God hath planted in the breast of parents towards their children, makes it evident, that this is not intended to be a severe arbitrary government, but only for the help, instruction, and preservation of their offspring. But happen it as it will, there is, as I have proved, no reason why it should be thought to extend to life and death, at any time, over their children, more than over any body else; neither can there be any pretence why this parental power should keep the child, when grown to a man, in subjection to the will of his parents, any farther than having received life and education from his parents, obliges him to respect, honour, gratitude, assistance and support, all his life, to both father and mother. And thus, 'tis true, the paternal is a natural government, but not at all extending itself to the ends and jurisdictions of that which is political. The power of the father doth not reach at all to the property of the child, which is only in his own disposing.

Sec. 171. Secondly, Political power is that power, which every man having in the state of nature, has given up into the hands of the society, and therein to the governors, whom the society hath set over itself, with this express or tacit trust, that it shall be employed for their good, and the preservation of their property: now this power, which every man has in the state of nature, and which he parts with to the society in all such cases where the society can secure him, is to use such means, for the preserving of his own property, as he thinks good, and nature allows him; and to punish the breach of the law of nature in others, so as (according to the best of his reason) may most conduce to the preservation of himself, and the rest of mankind. So that the end and measure of this power, when in every man's hands in the state of nature, being the preservation of all of his society, that is, all mankind in general, it can have no other end or measure, when in the hands of the magistrate, but to preserve the members of that society in their lives, liberties, and possessions; and so cannot be an absolute, arbitrary power over their lives and fortunes, which are as much as possible to be preserved; but a power to make laws, and annex such penalties to them, as may tend to the preservation of the whole, by cutting off those parts, and those only, which are so corrupt, that they threaten the sound and healthy, without which no severity is lawful. And this power has its original only from compact and agreement, and the mutual consent of those who make up the community.

Sec. 172. Thirdly, Despotical power is an absolute, arbitrary power one man has over another, to take away his life, whenever he pleases. This is a power, which neither nature gives, for it has made no such distinction between one man and another; nor compact can convey: for man not having such an arbitrary power over his own life, cannot give another man such a power over it; but it is the effect only of forfeiture, which the aggressor makes of his own life, when he puts himself into the state of war with another: for having quitted reason, which God hath given to be the rule betwixt man and man, and the common bond whereby human kind is united into one fellowship and society; and having renounced the way of peace which that teaches, and made use of the force of war, to compass his unjust ends upon another, where he has no right; and so revolting from his own kind to that of beasts, by making force, which is their's, to be his rule of right, he renders himself liable to be destroyed by the injured person, and the rest of mankind, that will join with him in the execution of justice, as any other wild beast, or noxious brute, with whom mankind can have neither society nor security*. And thus captives, taken in a just and lawful war, and such only, are subject to a despotical power, which, as it arises not from compact, so neither is it capable of any, but is the state of war continued: for what compact can be made with a man that is not master of his own life? what condition can he perform? and if he be once allowed to be master of his own life, the despotical, arbitrary power of his master ceases. He that is master of himself, and his own life, has a right too to the means of preserving it; so that as soon as compact enters, slavery ceases, and he so far quits his absolute power, and puts an end to the state of war, who enters into conditions with his captive.

(* Another copy corrected by Mr. Locke, has it thus, Noxious brute that is destructive to their being.)

Sec. 173. Nature gives the first of these, viz. paternal power to parents for the benefit of their children during their minority, to supply their want of ability, and understanding how to manage their property. (By property I must be understood here, as in other places, to mean that property which men have in their persons as well as goods.) Voluntary agreement gives the second, viz. political power to governors for the benefit of their subjects, to secure them in the possession and use of their properties. And forfeiture gives the third despotical power to lords for their own benefit, over those who are stripped of all property.

Sec. 174. He, that shall consider the distinct rise and extent, and the different ends of these several powers, will plainly see, that paternal power comes as far short of that of the magistrate, as despotical exceeds it; and that absolute dominion, however placed, is so far from being one kind of civil society, that it is as inconsistent with it, as slavery is with property. Paternal power is only where minority makes the child incapable to manage his property; political, where men have property in their own disposal; and despotical, over such as have no property at all.

CHAP. XVI.Of Conquest.

Sec. 175. THOUGH governments can originally have no other rise than that before mentioned, nor polities be founded on any thing but the consent of the people; yet such have been the disorders ambition has filled the world with, that in the noise of war, which makes so great a part of the history of mankind, this consent is little taken notice of: and therefore many have mistaken the force of arms for the consent of the people, and reckon conquest as one of the originals of government. But conquest is as far from setting up any government, as demolishing an house is from building a new one in the place. Indeed, it often makes way for a new frame of a common-wealth, by destroying the former; but, without the consent of the people, can never erect a new one.

Sec. 176. That the aggressor, who puts himself into the state of war with another, and unjustly invades another man's right, can, by such an unjust war, never come to have a right over the conquered, will be easily agreed by all men, who will not think, that robbers and pyrates have a right of empire over whomsoever they have force enough to master; or that men are bound by promises, which unlawful force extorts from them. Should a robber break into my house, and with a dagger at my throat make me seal deeds to convey my estate to him, would this give him any title? Just such a title, by his sword, has an unjust conqueror, who forces me into submission. The injury and the crime is equal, whether committed by the wearer of a crown, or some petty villain. The title of the offender, and the number of his followers, make no difference in the offence, unless it be to aggravate it. The only difference is, great robbers punish little ones, to keep them in their obedience; but the great ones are rewarded with laurels and triumphs, because they are too big for the weak hands of justice in this world, and have the power in their own possession, which should punish offenders. What is my remedy against a robber, that so broke into my house? Appeal to the law for justice. But perhaps justice is denied, or I am crippled and cannot stir, robbed and have not the means to do it. If God has taken away all means of seeking remedy, there is nothing left but patience. But my son, when able, may seek the relief of the law, which I am denied: he or his son may renew his appeal, till he recover his right. But the conquered, or their children, have no court, no arbitrator on earth to appeal to. Then they may appeal, as Jephtha did, to heaven, and repeat their appeal till they have recovered the native right of their ancestors, which was, to have such a legislative over them, as the majority should approve, and freely acquiesce in. If it be objected, This would cause endless trouble; I answer, no more than justice does, where she lies open to all that appeal to her. He that troubles his neighbour without a cause, is punished for it by the justice of the court he appeals to: and he that appeals to heaven must be sure he has right on his side; and a right too that is worth the trouble and cost of the appeal, as he will answer at a tribunal that cannot be deceived, and will be sure to retribute to every one according to the mischiefs he hath created to his fellow subjects; that is, any part of mankind: from whence it is plain, that he that conquers in an unjust war can thereby have no title to the subjection and obedience of the conquered.

Sec. 177. But supposing victory favours the right side, let us consider a conqueror in a lawful war, and see what power he gets, and over whom.

First, It is plain he gets no power by his conquest over those that conquered with him. They that fought on his side cannot suffer by the conquest, but must at least be as much freemen as they were before. And most commonly they serve upon terms, and on condition to share with their leader, and enjoy a part of the spoil, and other advantages that attend the conquering sword; or at least have a part of the subdued country bestowed upon them. And the conquering people are not, I hope, to be slaves by conquest, and wear their laurels only to shew they are sacrifices to their leaders triumph. They that found absolute monarchy upon the title of the sword, make their heroes, who are the founders of such monarchies, arrant Draw-can-sirs, and forget they had any officers and soldiers that fought on their side in the battles they won, or assisted them in the subduing, or shared in possessing, the countries they mastered. We are told by some, that the English monarchy is founded in the Norman conquest, and that our princes have thereby a title to absolute dominion: which if it were true, (as by the history it appears otherwise) and that William had a right to make war on this island; yet his dominion by conquest could reach no farther than to the Saxons and Britons, that were then inhabitants of this country. The Normans that came with him, and helped to conquer, and all descended from them, are freemen, and no subjects by conquest; let that give what dominion it will. And if I, or any body else, shall claim freedom, as derived from them, it will be very hard to prove the contrary: and it is plain, the law, that has made no distinction between the one and the other, intends not there should be any difference in their freedom or privileges.

Sec. 178. But supposing, which seldom happens, that the conquerors and conquered never incorporate into one people, under the same laws and freedom; let us see next what power a lawful conqueror has over the subdued: and that I say is purely despotical. He has an absolute power over the lives of those who by an unjust war have forfeited them; but not over the lives or fortunes of those who engaged not in the war, nor over the possessions even of those who were actually engaged in it.

Sec. 179. Secondly, I say then the conqueror gets no power but only over those who have actually assisted, concurred, or consented to that unjust force that is used against him: for the people having given to their governors no power to do an unjust thing, such as is to make an unjust war, (for they never had such a power in themselves) they ought not to be charged as guilty of the violence and unjustice that is committed in an unjust war, any farther than they actually abet it; no more than they are to be thought guilty of any violence or oppression their governors should use upon the people themselves, or any part of their fellow subjects, they having empowered them no more to the one than to the other. Conquerors, it is true, seldom trouble themselves to make the distinction, but they willingly permit the confusion of war to sweep all together: but yet this alters not the right; for the conquerors power over the lives of the conquered, being only because they have used force to do, or maintain an injustice, he can have that power only over those who have concurred in that force; all the rest are innocent; and he has no more title over the people of that country, who have done him no injury, and so have made no forfeiture of their lives, than he has over any other, who, without any injuries or provocations, have lived upon fair terms with him.

Sec. 180. Thirdly, The power a conqueror gets over those he overcomes in a just war, is perfectly despotical: he has an absolute power over the lives of those, who, by putting themselves in a state of war, have forfeited them; but he has not thereby a right and title to their possessions. This I doubt not, but at first sight will seem a strange doctrine, it being so quite contrary to the practice of the world; there being nothing more familiar in speaking of the dominion of countries, than to say such an one conquered it; as if conquest, without any more ado, conveyed a right of possession. But when we consider, that the practice of the strong and powerful, how universal soever it may be, is seldom the rule of right, however it be one part of the subjection of the conquered, not to argue against the conditions cut out to them by the conquering sword.

Sec. 181. Though in all war there be usually a complication of force and damage, and the aggressor seldom fails to harm the estate, when he uses force against the persons of those he makes war upon; yet it is the use of force only that puts a man into the state of war: for whether by force he begins the injury, or else having quietly, and by fraud, done the injury, he refuses to make reparation, and by force maintains it, (which is the same thing, as at first to have done it by force) it is the unjust use of force that makes the war: for he that breaks open my house, and violently turns me out of doors; or having peaceably got in, by force keeps me out, does in effect the same thing; supposing we are in such a state, that we have no common judge on earth, whom I may appeal to, and to whom we are both obliged to submit: for of such I am now speaking. It is the unjust use of force then, that puts a man into the state of war with another; and thereby he that is guilty of it makes a forfeiture of his life: for quitting reason, which is the rule given between man and man, and using force, the way of beasts, he becomes liable to be destroyed by him he uses force against, as any savage ravenous beast, that is dangerous to his being.

Sec. 182. But because the miscarriages of the father are no faults of the children, and they may be rational and peaceable, notwithstanding the brutishness and injustice of the father; the father, by his miscarriages and violence, can forfeit but his own life, but involves not his children in his guilt or destruction. His goods, which nature, that willeth the preservation of all mankind as much as is possible, hath made to belong to the children to keep them from perishing, do still continue to belong to his children: for supposing them not to have joined in the war, either thro'infancy, absence, or choice, they have done nothing to forfeit them: nor has the conqueror any right to take them away, by the bare title of having subdued him that by force attempted his destruction; though perhaps he may have some right to them, to repair the damages he has sustained by the war, and the defence of his own right; which how far it reaches to the possessions of the conquered, we shall see by and by. So that he that by conquest has a right over a man's person to destroy him if he pleases, has not thereby a right over his estate to possess and enjoy it: for it is the brutal force the aggressor has used, that gives his adversary a right to take away his life, and destroy him if he pleases, as a noxious creature; but it is damage sustained that alone gives him title to another man's goods: for though I may kill a thief that sets on me in the highway, yet I may not (which seems less) take away his money, and let him go: this would be robbery on my side. His force, and the state of war he put himself in, made him forfeit his life, but gave me no title to his goods. The right then of conquest extends only to the lives of those who joined in the war, not to their estates, but only in order to make reparation for the damages received, and the charges of the war, and that too with reservation of the right of the innocent wife and children.

Sec. 183. Let the conqueror have as much justice on his side, as could be supposed, he has no right to seize more than the vanquished could forfeit: his life is at the victor's mercy; and his service and goods he may appropriate, to make himself reparation; but he cannot take the goods of his wife and children; they too had a title to the goods he enjoyed, and their shares in the estate he possessed: for example, I in the state of nature (and all commonwealths are in the state of nature one with another) have injured another man, and refusing to give satisfaction, it comes to a state of war, wherein my defending by force what I had gotten unjustly, makes me the aggressor. I am conquered: my life, it is true, as forfeit, is at mercy, but not my wife's and children's. They made not the war, nor assisted in it. I could not forfeit their lives; they were not mine to forfeit. My wife had a share in my estate; that neither could I forfeit. And my children also, being born of me, had a right to be maintained out of my labour or substance. Here then is the case: the conqueror has a title to reparation for damages received, and the children have a title to their father's estate for their subsistence: for as to the wife's share, whether her own labour, or compact, gave her a title to it, it is plain, her husband could not forfeit what was her's. What must be done in the case? I answer; the fundamental law of nature being, that all, as much as may be, should be preserved, it follows, that if there be not enough fully to satisfy both, viz, for the conqueror's losses, and children's maintenance, he that hath, and to spare, must remit something of his full satisfaction, and give way to the pressing and preferable title of those who are in danger to perish without it.

Sec. 184. But supposing the charge and damages of the war are to be made up to the conqueror, to the utmost farthing; and that the children of the vanquished, spoiled of all their father's goods, are to be left to starve and perish; yet the satisfying of what shall, on this score, be due to the conqueror, will scarce give him a title to any country he shall conquer: for the damages of war can scarce amount to the value of any considerable tract of land, in any part of the world, where all the land is possessed, and none lies waste. And if I have not taken away the conqueror's land, which, being vanquished, it is impossible I should; scarce any other spoil I have done him can amount to the value of mine, supposing it equally cultivated, and of an extent any way coming near what I had overrun of his. The destruction of a year's product or two (for it seldom reaches four or five) is the utmost spoil that usually can be done: for as to money, and such riches and treasure taken away, these are none of nature's goods, they have but a fantastical imaginary value: nature has put no such upon them: they are of no more account by her standard, than the wampompeke of the Americans to an European prince, or the silver money of Europe would have been formerly to an American. And five years product is not worth the perpetual inheritance of land, where all is possessed, and none remains waste, to be taken up by him that is disseized: which will be easily granted, if one do but take away the imaginary value of money, the disproportion being more than between five and five hundred; though, at the same time, half a year's product is more worth than the inheritance, where there being more land than the inhabitants possess and make use of, any one has liberty to make use of the waste: but there conquerors take little care to possess themselves of the lands of the vanquished, No damage therefore, that men in the state of nature (as all princes and governments are in reference to one another) suffer from one another, can give a conqueror power to dispossess the posterity of the vanquished, and turn them out of that inheritance, which ought to be the possession of them and their descendants to all generations. The conqueror indeed will be apt to think himself master: and it is the very condition of the subdued not to be able to dispute their right. But if that be all, it gives no other title than what bare force gives to the stronger over the weaker: and, by this reason, he that is strongest will have a right to whatever he pleases to seize on.

Sec. 185. Over those then that joined with him in the war, and over those of the subdued country that opposed him not, and the posterity even of those that did, the conqueror, even in a just war, hath, by his conquest, no right of dominion: they are free from any subjection to him, and if their former government be dissolved, they are at liberty to begin and erect another to themselves.

Sec. 186. The conqueror, it is true, usually, by the force he has over them, compels them, with a sword at their breasts, to stoop to his conditions, and submit to such a government as he pleases to afford them; but the enquiry is, what right he has to do so? If it be said, they submit by their own consent, then this allows their own consent to be necessary to give the conqueror a title to rule over them. It remains only to be considered, whether promises extorted by force, without right, can be thought consent, and how far they bind. To which I shall say, they bind not at all; because whatsoever another gets from me by force, I still retain the right of, and he is obliged presently to restore. He that forces my horse from me, ought presently to restore him, and I have still a right to retake him. By the same reason, he that forced a promise from me, ought presently to restore it, i.e. quit me of the obligation of it; or I may resume it myself, i.e. chuse whether I will perform it: for the law of nature laying an obligation on me only by the rules she prescribes, cannot oblige me by the violation of her rules: such is the extorting any thing from me by force. Nor does it at all alter the case to say, I gave my promise, no more than it excuses the force, and passes the right, when I put my hand in my pocket, and deliver my purse myself to a thief, who demands it with a pistol at my breast.

Sec. 187. From all which it follows, that the government of a conqueror, imposed by force on the subdued, against whom he had no right of war, or who joined not in the war against him, where he had right, has no obligation upon them.

Sec. 188. But let us suppose, that all the men of that community, being all members of the same body politic, may be taken to have joined in that unjust war wherein they are subdued, and so their lives are at the mercy of the conqueror.

Sec. 189. I say, this concerns not their children who are in their minority: for since a father hath not, in himself, a power over the life or liberty of his child, no act of his can possibly forfeit it. So that the children, whatever may have happened to the fathers, are freemen, and the absolute power of the conqueror reaches no farther than the persons of the men that were subdued by him, and dies with them: and should he govern them as slaves, subjected to his absolute arbitrary power, he has no such right of dominion over their children. He can have no power over them but by their own consent, whatever he may drive them to say or do; and he has no lawfull authority, whilst force, and not choice, compels them to submission.

Sec. 190. Every man is born with a double right: first, a right of freedom to his person, which no other man has a power over, but the free disposal of it lies in himself. Secondly, a right, before any other man, to inherit with his brethren his father's goods.

Sec. 191. By the first of these, a man is naturally free from subjection to any government, tho' he be born in a place under its jurisdiction; but if he disclaim the lawful government of the country he was born in, he must also quit the right that belonged to him by the laws of it, and the possessions there descending to him from his ancestors, if it were a government made by their consent.

Sec. 192. By the second, the inhabitants of any country, who are descended, and derive a title to their estates from those who are subdued, and had a government forced upon them against their free consents, retain a right to the possession of their ancestors, though they consent not freely to the government, whose hard conditions were by force imposed on the possessors of that country: for the first conqueror never having had a title to the land of that country, the people who are the descendants of, or claim under those who were forced to submit to the yoke of a government by constraint, have always a right to shake it off, and free themselves from the usurpation or tyranny which the sword hath brought in upon them, till their rulers put them under such a frame of government as they willingly and of choice consent to. Who doubts but the Grecian Christians, descendants of the ancient possessors of that country, may justly cast off the Turkish yoke, which they have so long groaned under, whenever they have an opportunity to do it? For no government can have a right to obedience from a people who have not freely consented to it; which they can never be supposed to do, till either they are put in a full state of liberty to chuse their government and governors, or at least till they have such standing laws, to which they have by themselves or their representatives given their free consent, and also till they are allowed their due property, which is so to be proprietors of what they have, that no body can take away any part of it without their own consent, without which, men under any government are not in the state of freemen, but are direct slaves under the force of war.

Sec. 193. But granting that the conqueror in a just war has a right to the estates, as well as power over the persons, of the conquered; which, it is plain, he hath not: nothing of absolute power will follow from hence, in the continuance of the government; because the descendants of these being all freemen, if he grants them estates and possessions to inhabit his country, (without which it would be worth nothing) whatsoever he grants them, they have, so far as it is granted, property in. The nature whereof is, that without a man's own consent it cannot be taken from him.

Sec. 194. Their persons are free by a native right, and their properties, be they more or less, are their own, and at their own dispose, and not at his; or else it is no property. Supposing the conqueror gives to one man a thousand acres, to him and his heirs for ever; to another he lets a thousand acres for his life, under the rent of 50l. or 500l. per arm. has not the one of these a right to his thousand acres for ever, and the other, during his life, paying the said rent? and hath not the tenant for life a property in all that he gets over and above his rent, by his labour and industry during the said term, supposing it be double the rent? Can any one say, the king, or conqueror, after his grant, may by his power of conqueror take away all, or part of the land from the heirs of one, or from the other during his life, he paying the rent? or can he take away from either the goods or money they have got upon the said land, at his pleasure? If he can, then all free and voluntary contracts cease, and are void in the world; there needs nothing to dissolve them at any time, but power enough: and all the grants and promises of men in power are but mockery and collusion: for can there be any thing more ridiculous than to say, I give you and your's this for ever, and that in the surest and most solemn way of conveyance can be devised; and yet it is to be understood, that I have right, if I please, to take it away from you again to morrow?

Sec. 195. I will not dispute now whether princes are exempt from the laws of their country; but this I am sure, they owe subjection to the laws of God and nature. No body, no power, can exempt them from the obligations of that eternal law. Those are so great, and so strong, in the case of promises, that omnipotency itself can be tied by them. Grants, promises, and oaths, are bonds that hold the Almighty: whatever some flatterers say to princes of the world, who all together, with all their people joined to them, are, in comparison of the great God, but as a drop of the bucket, or a dust on the balance, inconsiderable, nothing!

Sec. 196. The short of the case in conquest is this: the conqueror, if he have a just cause, has a despotical right over the persons of all, that actually aided, and concurred in the war against him, and a right to make up his damage and cost out of their labour and estates, so he injure not the right of any other. Over the rest of the people, if there were any that consented not to the war, and over the children of the captives themselves, or the possessions of either, he has no power; and so can have, by virtue of conquest, no lawful title himself to dominion over them, or derive it to his posterity; but is an aggressor, if he attempts upon their properties, and thereby puts himself in a state of war against them, and has no better a right of principality, he, nor any of his successors, than Hingar, or Hubba, the Danes, had here in England; or Spartacus, had he conquered Italy, would have had; which is to have their yoke cast off, as soon as God shall give those under their subjection courage and opportunity to do it. Thus, notwithstanding whatever title the kings of Assyria had over Judah, by the sword, God assisted Hezekiah to throw off the dominion of that conquering empire. And the lord was with Hezekiah, and he prospered; wherefore he went forth, and he rebelled against the king of Assyria, and served him not, 2 Kings xviii. 7. Whence it is plain, that shaking off a power, which force, and not right, hath set over any one, though it hath the name of rebellion, yet is no offence before God, but is that which he allows and countenances, though even promises and covenants, when obtained by force, have intervened: for it is very probable, to any one that reads the story of Ahaz and Hezekiah attentively, that the Assyrians subdued Ahaz, and deposed him, and made Hezekiah king in his father's lifetime; and that Hezekiah by agreement had done him homage, and paid him tribute all this time.

CHAP. XVII. Of Usurpation.

Sec. 197. AS conquest may be called a foreign usurpation, so usurpation is a kind of domestic conquest, with this difference, that an usurper can never have right on his side, it being no usurpation, but where one is got into the possession of what another has right to. This, so far as it is usurpation, is a change only of persons, but not of the forms and rules of the government: for if the usurper extend his power beyond what of right belonged to the lawful princes, or governors of the commonwealth, it is tyranny added to usurpation.

Sec. 198. In all lawful governments, the designation of the persons, who are to bear rule, is as natural and necessary a part as the form of the government itself, and is that which had its establishment originally from the people; the anarchy being much alike, to have no form of government at all, or to agree that it shall be monarchical, but to appoint no way to design the person that shall have the power, and be the monarch. Hence all commonwealths, with the form of government established, have rules also of appointing those who are to have any share in the public authority, and settled methods of conveying the right to them. Whoever gets into the exercise of any part of the power, by other ways than what the laws of the community have prescribed, hath no right to be obeyed, though the form of the commonwealth be still preserved; since he is not the person the laws have appointed, and consequently not the person the people have consented to. Nor can such an usurper, or any deriving from him, ever have a title, till the people are both at liberty to consent, and have actually consented to allow, and confirm in him the power he hath till then usurped.

CHAP. XVIII. Of Tyranny.

Sec. 199. AS usurpation is the exercise of power, which another hath a right to; so tyranny is the exercise of power beyond right, which no body can have a right to. And this is making use of the power any one has in his hands, not for the good of those who are under it, but for his own private separate advantage. When the governor, however intitled, makes not the law, but his will, the rule; and his commands and actions are not directed to the preservation of the properties of his people, but the satisfaction of his own ambition, revenge, covetousness, or any other irregular passion.

Sec. 200. If one can doubt this to be truth, or reason, because it comes from the obscure hand of a subject, I hope the authority of a king will make it pass with him. King James the first, in his speech to the parliament, 1603, tells them thus, I will ever prefer the weal of the public, and of the whole commonwealth, in making of good laws and constitutions, to any particular and private ends of mine; thinking ever the wealth and weal of the commonwealth to be my greatest weal and worldly felicity; a point wherein a lawful king doth directly differ from a tyrant: for I do acknowledge, that the special and greatest point of difference that is between a rightful king and an usurping tyrant, is this, that whereas the proud and ambitious tyrant doth think his kingdom and people are only ordained for satisfaction of his desires and unreasonable appetites, the righteous and just king doth by the contrary acknowledge himself to be ordained for the procuring of the wealth and property of his people, And again, in his speech to the parliament, 1609, he hath these words, The king binds himself by a double oath, to the observation of the fundamental laws of his kingdom; tacitly, as by being a king, and so bound to protect as well the people, as the laws of his kingdom; and expressly, by his oath at his coronation, so as every just king, in a settled kingdom, is bound to observe that paction made to his people, by his laws, in framing his government agreeable thereunto, according to that paction which God made with Noah after the deluge. Hereafter, seed-time and harvest, and cold and heat, and summer and winter, and day and night, shall not cease while the earth remaineth. And therefore a king governing in a settled kingdom, leaves to be a king, and degenerates into a tyrant, as soon as he leaves off to rule according to his laws, And a little after, Therefore all kings that are not tyrants, or perjured, will be glad to bound themselves within the limits of their laws; and they that persuade them the contrary, are vipers, and pests both against them and the commonwealth. Thus that learned king, who well understood the notion of things, makes the difference betwixt a king and a tyrant to consist only in this, that one makes the laws the bounds of his power, and the good of the public, the end of his government; the other makes all give way to his own will and appetite.

Sec. 201. It is a mistake, to think this fault is proper only to monarchies; other forms of government are liable to it, as well as that: for wherever the power, that is put in any hands for the government of the people, and the preservation of their properties, is applied to other ends, and made use of to impoverish, harass, or subdue them to the arbitrary and irregular commands of those that have it; there it presently becomes tyranny, whether those that thus use it are one or many. Thus we read of the thirty tyrants at Athens, as well as one at Syracuse; and the intolerable dominion of the Decemviri at Rome was nothing better.

Sec. 202. Where-ever law ends, tyranny begins, if the law be transgressed to another's harm; and whosoever in authority exceeds the power given him by the law, and makes use of the force he has under his command, to compass that upon the subject, which the law allows not, ceases in that to be a magistrate; and, acting without authority, may be opposed, as any other man, who by force invades the right of another. This is acknowledged in subordinate magistrates. He that hath authority to seize my person in the street, may be opposed as a thief and a robber, if he endeavours to break into my house to execute a writ, notwithstanding that I know he has such a warrant, and such a legal authority, as will impower him to arrest me abroad. And why this should not hold in the highest, as well as in the most inferior magistrate, I would gladly be informed. Is it reasonable, that the eldest brother, because he has the greatest part of his father's estate, should thereby have a right to take away any of his younger brothers portions? or that a rich man, who possessed a whole country, should from thence have a right to seize, when he pleased, the cottage and garden of his poor neighbour? The being rightfully possessed of great power and riches, exceedingly beyond the greatest part of the sons of Adam, is so far from being an excuse, much less a reason, for rapine and oppression, which the endamaging another without authority is, that it is a great aggravation of it: for the exceeding the bounds of authority is no more a right in a great, than in a petty officer; no more justifiable in a king than a constable; but is so much the worse in him, in that he has more trust put in him, has already a much greater share than the rest of his brethren, and is supposed, from the advantages of his education, employment, and counsellors, to be more knowing in the measures of right and wrong.

Sec. 203. May the commands then of a prince be opposed? may he be resisted as often as any one shall find himself aggrieved, and but imagine he has not right done him? This will unhinge and overturn all polities, and, instead of government and order, leave nothing but anarchy and confusion.

Sec. 204. To this I answer, that force is to be opposed to nothing, but to unjust and unlawful force; whoever makes any opposition in any other case, draws on himself a just condemnation both from God and man; and so no such danger or confusion will follow, as is often suggested: for,

Sec. 205. First, As, in some countries, the person of the prince by the law is sacred; and so, whatever he commands or does, his person is still free from all question or violence, not liable to force, or any judicial censure or condemnation. But yet opposition may be made to the illegal acts of any inferior officer, or other commissioned by him; unless he will, by actually putting himself into a state of war with his people, dissolve the government, and leave them to that defence which belongs to every one in the state of nature: for of such things who can tell what the end will be? and a neighbour kingdom has shewed the world an odd example. In all other cases the sacredness of the person exempts him from all inconveniencies, whereby he is secure, whilst the government stands, from all violence and harm whatsoever; than which there cannot be a wiser constitution: for the harm he can do in his own person not being likely to happen often, nor to extend itself far; nor being able by his single strength to subvert the laws, nor oppress the body of the people, should any prince have so much weakness, and ill nature as to be willing to do it, the inconveniency of some particular mischiefs, that may happen sometimes, when a heady prince comes to the throne, are well recompensed by the peace of the public, and security of the government, in the person of the chief magistrate, thus set out of the reach of danger: it being safer for the body, that some few private men should be sometimes in danger to suffer, than that the head of the republic should be easily, and upon slight occasions, exposed.

Sec. 206. Secondly, But this privilege, belonging only to the king's person, hinders not, but they may be questioned, opposed, and resisted, who use unjust force, though they pretend a commission from him, which the law authorizes not; as is plain in the case of him that has the king's writ to arrest a man, which is a full commission from the king; and yet he that has it cannot break open a man's house to do it, nor execute this command of the king upon certain days, nor in certain places, though this commission have no such exception in it; but they are the limitations of the law, which if any one transgress, the king's commission excuses him not:

for the king's authority being given him only by the law, he cannot impower any one to act against the law, or justify him, by his commission, in so doing; the commission, or command of any magistrate, where he has no authority, being as void and insignificant, as that of any private man; the difference between the one and the other, being that the magistrate has some authority so far, and to such ends, and the private man has none at all: for it is not the commission, but the authority, that gives the right of acting; and against the laws there can be no authority. But, notwithstanding such resistance, the king's person and authority are still both secured, and so no danger to governor or government.

Sec. 207. Thirdly, Supposing a government wherein the person of the chief magistrate is not thus sacred; yet this doctrine of the lawfulness of resisting all unlawful exercises of his power, will not upon every slight occasion indanger him, or imbroil the government: for where the injured party may be relieved, and his damages repaired by appeal to the law, there can be no pretence for force, which is only to be used where a man is intercepted from appealing to the law: for nothing is to be accounted hostile force, but where it leaves not the remedy of such an appeal; and it is such force alone, that puts him that uses it into a state of war, and makes it lawful to resist him. A man with a sword in his hand demands my purse in the high-way, when perhaps I have not twelve pence in my pocket: this man I may lawfully kill. To another I deliver 100l. to hold only whilst I alight, which he refuses to restore me, when I am got up again, but draws his sword to defend the possession of it by force, if I endeavour to retake it. The mischief this man does me is a hundred, or possibly a thousand times more than the other perhaps intended me (whom I killed before he really did me any); and yet I might lawfully kill the one, and cannot so much as hurt the other lawfully. The reason whereof is plain; because the one using force, which threatened my life, I could not have time to appeal to the law to secure it: and when it was gone, it was too late to appeal. The law could not restore life to my dead carcass: the loss was irreparable; which to prevent, the law of nature gave me a right to destroy him, who had put himself into a state of war with me, and threatened my destruction. But in the other case, my life not being in danger, I may have the benefit of appealing to the law, and have reparation for my 100l. that way.

Sec. 208. Fourthly, But if the unlawful acts done by the magistrate be maintained (by the power he has got), and the remedy which is due by law, be by the same power obstructed; yet the right of resisting, even in such manifest acts of tyranny, will not suddenly, or on slight occasions, disturb the government: for if it reach no farther than some private men's cases, though they have a right to defend themselves, and to recover by force what by unlawful force is taken from them; yet the right to do so will not easily engage them in a contest, wherein they are sure to perish; it being as impossible for one, or a few oppressed men to disturb the government, where the body of the people do not think themselves concerned in it, as for a raving mad-man, or heady malcontent to overturn a well settled state; the people being as little apt to follow the one, as the other.

Sec. 209. But if either these illegal acts have extended to the majority of the people; or if the mischief and oppression has lighted only on some few, but in such cases, as the precedent, and consequences seem to threaten all; and they are persuaded in their consciences, that their laws, and with them their estates, liberties, and lives are in danger, and perhaps their religion too; how they will be hindered from resisting illegal force, used against them, I cannot tell. This is an inconvenience, I confess, that attends all governments whatsoever, when the governors have brought it to this pass, to be generally suspected of their people; the most dangerous state which they can possibly put themselves in. wherein they are the less to be pitied, because it is so easy to be avoided; it being as impossible for a governor, if he really means the good of his people, and the preservation of them, and their laws together, not to make them see and feel it, as it is for the father of a family, not to let his children see he loves, and takes care of them.

Sec. 210. But if all the world shall observe pretences of one kind, and actions of another; arts used to elude the law, and the trust of prerogative (which is an arbitrary power in some things left in the prince's hand to do good, not harm to the people) employed contrary to the end for which it was given: if the people shall find the ministers and subordinate magistrates chosen suitable to such ends, and favoured, or laid by, proportionably as they promote or oppose them: if they see several experiments made of arbitrary power, and that religion underhand favoured, (tho' publicly proclaimed against) which is readiest to introduce it; and the operators in it supported, as much as may be; and when that cannot be done, yet approved still, and liked the better: if a long train of actions shew the councils all tending that way; how can a man any more hinder himself from being persuaded in his own mind, which way things are going; or from casting about how to save himself, than he could from believing the captain of the ship he was in, was carrying him, and the rest of the company, to Algiers, when he found him always steering that course, though cross winds, leaks in his ship, and want of men and provisions did often force him to turn his course another way for some time, which he steadily returned to again, as soon as the wind, weather, and other circumstances would let him?

CHAP. XIX.Of the Dissolution of Government.

Sec. 211. HE that will with any clearness speak of the dissolution of government, ought in the first place to distinguish between the dissolution of the society and the dissolution of the government. That which makes the community, and brings men out of the loose state of nature, into one politic society, is the agreement which every one has with the rest to incorporate, and act as one body, and so be one distinct commonwealth. The usual, and almost only way whereby this union is dissolved, is the inroad of foreign force making a conquest upon them: for in that case, (not being able to maintain and support themselves, as one intire and independent body) the union belonging to that body which consisted therein, must necessarily cease, and so every one return to the state he was in before, with a liberty to shift for himself, and provide for his own safety, as he thinks fit, in some other society. Whenever the society is dissolved, it is certain the government of that society cannot remain. Thus conquerors swords often cut up governments by the roots, and mangle societies to pieces, separating the subdued or scattered multitude from the protection of, and dependence on, that society which ought to have preserved them from violence. The world is too well instructed in, and too forward to allow of, this way of dissolving of governments, to need any more to be said of it; and there wants not much argument to prove, that where the society is dissolved, the government cannot remain; that being as impossible, as for the frame of an house to subsist when the materials of it are scattered and dissipated by a whirl-wind, or jumbled into a confused heap by an earthquake.

Sec. 212. Besides this over-turning from without, governments are dissolved from within,

First, When the legislative is altered. Civil society being a state of peace, amongst those who are of it, from whom the state of war is excluded by the umpirage, which they have provided in their legislative, for the ending all differences that may arise amongst any of them, it is in their legislative, that the members of a commonwealth are united, and combined together into one coherent living body. This is the soul that gives form, life, and unity, to the common-wealth: from hence the several members have their mutual influence, sympathy, and connexion: and therefore, when the legislative is broken, or dissolved, dissolution and death follows: for the essence and union of the society consisting in having one will, the legislative, when once established by the majority, has the declaring, and as it were keeping of that will. The constitution of the legislative is the first and fundamental act of society, whereby provision is made for the continuation of their union, under the direction of persons, and bonds of laws, made by persons authorized thereunto, by the consent and appointment of the people, without which no one man, or number of men, amongst them, can have authority of making laws that shall be binding to the rest. When any one, or more, shall take upon them to make laws, whom the people have not appointed so to do, they make laws without authority, which the people are not therefore bound to obey; by which means they come again to be out of subjection, and may constitute to themselves a new legislative, as they think best, being in full liberty to resist the force of those, who without authority would impose any thing upon them. Every one is at the disposure of his own will, when those who had, by the delegation of the society, the declaring of the public will, are excluded from it, and others usurp the place, who have no such authority or delegation.

Sec. 213. This being usually brought about by such in the commonwealth who misuse the power they have; it is hard to consider it aright, and know at whose door to lay it, without knowing the form of government in which it happens. Let us suppose then the legislative placed in the concurrence of three distinct persons.

1. A single hereditary person, having the constant, supreme, executive power, and with it the power of convoking and dissolving the other two within certain periods of time.

2. An assembly of hereditary nobility.

3. An assembly of representatives chosen, pro tempore, by the people. Such a form of government supposed, it is evident,

Sec. 214. First, That when such a single person, or prince, sets up his own arbitrary will in place of the laws, which are the will of the society, declared by the legislative, then the legislative is changed: for that being in effect the legislative, whose rules and laws are put in execution, and required to be obeyed; when other laws are set up, and other rules pretended, and inforced, than what the legislative, constituted by the society, have enacted, it is plain that the legislative is changed. Whoever introduces new laws, not being thereunto authorized by the fundamental appointment of the society, or subverts the old, disowns and overturns the power by which they were made, and so sets up a new legislative.

Sec. 215. Secondly, When the prince hinders the legislative from assembling in its due time, or from acting freely, pursuant to those ends for which it was constituted, the legislative is altered: for it is not a certain number of men, no, nor their meeting, unless they have also freedom of debating, and leisure of perfecting, what is for the good of the society, wherein the legislative consists: when these are taken away or altered, so as to deprive the society of the due exercise of their power, the legislative is truly altered; for it is not names that constitute governments, but the use and exercise of those powers that were intended to accompany them; so that he, who takes away the freedom, or hinders the acting of the legislative in its due seasons, in effect takes away the legislative, and puts an end to the government.

Sec. 216. Thirdly, When, by the arbitrary power of the prince, the electors, or ways of election, are altered, without the consent, and contrary to the common interest of the people, there also the legislative is altered: for, if others than those whom the society hath authorized thereunto, do chuse, or in another way than what the society hath prescribed, those chosen are not the legislative appointed by the people.

Sec. 217. Fourthly, The delivery also of the people into the subjection of a foreign power, either by the prince, or by the legislative, is certainly a change of the legislative, and so a dissolution of the government: for the end why people entered into society being to be preserved one intire, free, independent society, to be governed by its own laws; this is lost, whenever they are given up into the power of another.

Sec. 218. Why, in such a constitution as this, the dissolution of the government in these cases is to be imputed to the prince, is evident; because he, having the force, treasure and offices of the state to employ, and often persuading himself, or being flattered by others, that as supreme magistrate he is uncapable of controul; he alone is in a condition to make great advances toward such changes, under pretence of lawful authority, and has it in his hands to terrify or suppress opposers, as factious, seditious, and enemies to the government: whereas no other part of the legislative, or people, is capable by themselves to attempt any alteration of the legislative, without open and visible rebellion, apt enough to be taken notice of, which, when it prevails, produces effects very little different from foreign conquest. Besides, the prince in such a form of government, having the power of dissolving the other parts of the legislative, and thereby rendering them private persons, they can never in opposition to him, or without his concurrence, alter the legislative by a law, his consent being necessary to give any of their decrees that sanction. But yet, so far as the other parts of the legislative any way contribute to any attempt upon the government, and do either promote, or not, what lies in them, hinder such designs, they are guilty, and partake in this, which is certainly the greatest crime which men can partake of one towards another.

Sec. 219. There is one way more whereby such a government may be dissolved, and that is: When he who has the supreme executive power neglects and abandons that charge, so that the laws already made can no longer be put in execution; this is demonstratively to reduce all to anarchy, and so effectively to dissolve the government. For laws not being made for themselves, but to be, by their execution, the bonds of the society to keep every part of the body politic in its due place and function. When that totally ceases, the government visibly ceases, and the people become a confused multitude without order or connection. Where there is no longer the administration of justice for the securing of menâ€²s rights, nor any remaining power within the community to direct the force, or provide for the necessities of the public, there certainly is no government left. Where the laws cannot be executed it is all one as if there were no laws, and a government without laws is, I suppose, a mystery in politics inconceivable to human capacity, and inconsistent with human society.

Sec. 220. In these and the like cases, when the government is dissolved, the people are at liberty to provide for themselves, by erecting a new legislative, differing from the other, by the change of persons, or form, or both, as they shall find it most for their safety and good: for the society can never, by the fault of another, lose the native and original right it has to preserve itself, which can only be done by a settled legislative, and a fair and impartial execution of the laws made by it. But the state of mankind is not so miserable that they are not capable of using this remedy, till it be too late to look for any. To tell people they may provide for themselves, by erecting a new legislative, when by oppression, artifice, or being delivered over to a foreign power, their old one is gone, is only to tell them, they may expect relief when it is too late, and the evil is past cure. This is in effect no more than to bid them first be slaves, and then to take care of their liberty; and when their chains are on, tell them, they may act like freemen. This, if barely so, is rather mockery than relief; and men can never be secure from tyranny, if there be no means to escape it till they are perfectly under it: and therefore it is, that they have not only a right to get out of it, but to prevent it.

Sec. 221. There is therefore, secondly, another way whereby governments are dissolved, and that is, when the legislative, or the prince, either of them, act contrary to their trust. First, The legislative acts against the trust reposed in them, when they endeavour to invade the property of the subject, and to make themselves, or any part of the community, masters, or arbitrary disposers of the lives, liberties, or fortunes of the people.

Sec. 222. The reason why men enter into society, is the preservation of their property; and the end why they chuse and authorize a legislative, is, that there may be laws made, and rules set, as guards and fences to the properties of all the members of the society, to limit the power, and moderate the dominion, of every part and member of the society: for since it can never be supposed to be the will of the society, that the legislative should have a power to destroy that which every one designs to secure, by entering into society, and for which the people submitted themselves to legislators of their own making; whenever the legislators endeavour to take away, and destroy the property of the people, or to reduce them to slavery under arbitrary power, they put themselves into a state of war with the people, who are thereupon absolved from any farther obedience, and are left to the common refuge, which God hath provided for all men, against force and violence. Whensoever therefore the legislative shall transgress this fundamental rule of society; and either by ambition, fear, folly or corruption, endeavour to grasp themselves, or put into the hands of any other, an absolute power over the lives, liberties, and estates of the people; by this breach of trust they forfeit the power the people had put into their hands for quite contrary ends, and it devolves to the people, who. have a right to resume their original liberty, and, by the establishment of a new legislative, (such as they shall think fit) provide for their own safety and security, which is the end for which they are in society. What I have said here, concerning the legislative in general, holds true also concerning the supreme executor, who having a double trust put in him, both to have a part in the legislative, and the supreme execution of the law, acts against both, when he goes about to set up his own arbitrary will as the law of the society. He acts also contrary to his trust, when he either employs the force, treasure, and offices of the society, to corrupt the representatives, and gain them to his purposes; or openly preengages the electors, and prescribes to their choice, such, whom he has, by sollicitations, threats, promises, or otherwise, won to his designs; and employs them to bring in such, who have promised before-hand what to vote, and what to enact. Thus to regulate candidates and electors, and new-model the ways of election, what is it but to cut up the government by the roots, and poison the very fountain of public security? for the people having reserved to themselves the choice of their representatives, as the fence to their properties, could do it for no other end, but that they might always be freely chosen, and so chosen, freely act, and advise, as the necessity of the common-wealth, and the public good should, upon examination, and mature debate, be judged to require. This, those who give their votes before they hear the debate, and have weighed the reasons on all sides, are not capable of doing. To prepare such an assembly as this, and endeavour to set up the declared abettors of his own will, for the true representatives of the people, and the law-makers of the society, is certainly as great a breach of trust, and as perfect a declaration of a design to subvert the government, as is possible to be met with. To which, if one shall add rewards and punishments visibly employed to the same end, and all the arts of perverted law made use of, to take off and destroy all that stand in the way of such a design, and will not comply and consent to betray the liberties of their country, it will be past doubt what is doing. What power they ought to have in the society, who thus employ it contrary to the trust went along with it in its first institution, is easy to determine; and one cannot but see, that he, who has once attempted any such thing as this, cannot any longer be trusted.

Sec. 223. To this perhaps it will be said, that the people being ignorant, and always discontented, to lay the foundation of government in the unsteady opinion and uncertain humour of the people, is to expose it to certain ruin; and no government will be able long to subsist, if the people may set up a new legislative, whenever they take offence at the old one. To this I answer, Quite the contrary. People are not so easily got out of their old forms, as some are apt to suggest. They are hardly to be prevailed with to amend the acknowledged faults in the frame they have been accustomed to. And if there be any original defects, or adventitious ones introduced by time, or corruption; it is not an easy thing to get them changed, even when all the world sees there is an opportunity for it. This slowness and aversion in the people to quit their old constitutions, has, in the many revolutions which have been seen in this kingdom, in this and former ages, still kept us to, or, after some interval of fruitless attempts, still brought us back again to our old legislative of king, lords and commons: and whatever provocations have made the crown be taken from some of our princes heads, they never carried the people so far as to place it in another line.

Sec. 224. But it will be said, this hypothesis lays a ferment for frequent rebellion. To which I answer,

First, No more than any other hypothesis: for when the people are made miserable, and find themselves exposed to the ill usage of arbitrary power, cry up their governors, as much as you will, for sons of Jupiter; let them be sacred and divine, descended, or authorized from heaven; give them out for whom or what you please, the same will happen. The people generally ill treated, and contrary to right, will be ready upon any occasion to ease themselves of a burden that sits heavy upon them. They will wish, and seek for the opportunity, which in the change, weakness and accidents of human affairs, seldom delays long to offer itself. He must have lived but a little while in the world, who has not seen examples of this in his time; and he must have read very little, who cannot produce examples of it in all sorts of governments in the world.

Sec. 225. Secondly, I answer, such revolutions happen not upon every little mismanagement in public affairs. Great mistakes in the ruling part, many wrong and inconvenient laws, and all the slips of human frailty, will be born by the people without mutiny or murmur. But if a long train of abuses, prevarications and artifices, all tending the same way, make the design visible to the people, and they cannot but feel what they lie under, and see whither they are going; it is not to be wondered, that they should then rouze themselves, and endeavour to put the rule into such hands which may secure to them the ends for which government was at first erected; and without which, ancient names, and specious forms, are so far from being better, that they are much worse, than the state of nature, or pure anarchy; the inconveniencies being all as great and as near, but the remedy farther off and more difficult.

Sec. 226. Thirdly, I answer, that this doctrine of a power in the people of providing for their safety a-new, by a new legislative, when their legislators have acted contrary to their trust, by invading their property, is the best fence against rebellion, and the probablest means to hinder it: for rebellion being an opposition, not to persons, but authority, which is founded only in the constitutions and laws of the government; those, whoever they be, who by force break through, and by force justify their violation of them, are truly and properly rebels: for when men, by entering into society and civil-government, have excluded force, and introduced laws for the preservation of property, peace, and unity amongst themselves, those who set up force again in opposition to the laws, do rebellare, that is, bring back again the state of war, and are properly rebels: which they who are in power, (by the pretence they have to authority, the temptation of force they have in their hands, and the flattery of those about them) being likeliest to do; the properest way to prevent the evil, is to shew them the danger and injustice of it, who are under the greatest temptation to run into it.

Sec. 227. In both the fore-mentioned cases, when either the legislative is changed, or the legislators act contrary to the end for which they were constituted; those who are guilty are guilty of rebellion: for if any one by force takes away the established legislative of any society, and the laws by them made, pursuant to their trust, he thereby takes away the umpirage, which every one had consented to, for a peaceable decision of all their controversies, and a bar to the state of war amongst them. They, who remove, or change the legislative, take away this decisive power, which no body can have, but by the appointment and consent of the people; and so destroying the authority which the people did, and no body else can set up, and introducing a power which the people hath not authorized, they actually introduce a state of war, which is that of force without authority: and thus, by removing the legislative established by the society, (in whose decisions the people acquiesced and united, as to that of their own will) they untie the knot, and expose the people a-new to the state of war, And if those, who by force take away the legislative, are rebels, the legislators themselves, as has been shewn, can be no less esteemed so; when they, who were set up for the protection, and preservation of the people, their liberties and properties, shall by force invade and endeavour to take them away; and so they putting themselves into a state of war with those who made them the protectors and guardians of their peace, are properly, and with the greatest aggravation, rebellantes, rebels.

Sec. 228. But if they, who say it lays a foundation for rebellion, mean that it may occasion civil wars, or intestine broils, to tell the people they are absolved from obedience when illegal attempts are made upon their liberties or properties, and may oppose the unlawful violence of those who were their magistrates, when they invade their properties contrary to the trust put in them; and that therefore this doctrine is not to be allowed, being so destructive to the peace of the world: they may as well say, upon the same ground, that honest men may not oppose robbers or pirates, because this may occasion disorder or bloodshed. If any mischief come in such cases, it is not to be charged upon him who defends his own right, but on him that invades his neighbours. If the innocent honest man must quietly quit all he has, for peace sake, to him who will lay violent hands upon it, I desire it may be considered, what a kind of peace there will be in the world, which consists only in violence and rapine; and which is to be maintained only for the benefit of robbers and oppressors. VVho would not think it an admirable peace betwix the mighty and the mean, when the lamb, without resistance, yielded his throat to be torn by the imperious wolf? Polyphemus's den gives us a perfect pattern of such a peace, and such a government, wherein Ulysses and his companions had nothing to do, but quietly to suffer themselves to be devoured. And no doubt Ulysses, who was a prudent man, preached up passive obedience, and exhorted them to a quiet submission, by representing to them of what concernment peace was to mankind; and by shewing the inconveniences might happen, if they should offer to resist Polyphemus, who had now the power over them.

Sec. 229. The end of government is the good of mankind; and which is best for mankind, that the people should be always exposed to the boundless will of tyranny, or that the rulers should be sometimes liable to be opposed, when they grow exorbitant in the use of their power, and employ it for the destruction, and not the preservation of the properties of their people?

Sec. 230. Nor let any one say, that mischief can arise from hence, as often as it shall please a busy head, or turbulent spirit, to desire the alteration of the government. It is true, such men may stir, whenever they please; but it will be only to their own just ruin and perdition: for till the mischief be grown general, and the ill designs of the rulers become visible, or their attempts sensible to the greater part, the people, who are more disposed to suffer than right themselves by resistance, are not apt to stir. The examples of particular injustice, or oppression of here and there an unfortunate man, moves them not. But if they universally have a persuasion, grounded upon manifest evidence, that designs are carrying on against their liberties, and the general course and tendency of things cannot but give them strong suspicions of the evil intention of their governors, who is to be blamed for it? Who can help it, if they, who might avoid it, bring themselves into this suspicion? Are the people to be blamed, if they have the sense of rational creatures, and can think of things no otherwise than as they find and feel them? And is it not rather their fault, who put things into such a posture, that they would not have them thought to be as they are? I grant, that the pride, ambition, and turbulency of private men have sometimes caused great disorders in commonwealths, and factions have been fatal to states and kingdoms. But whether the mischief hath oftener begun in the peoples wantonness, and a desire to cast off the lawful authority of their rulers, or in the rulers insolence, and endeavours to get and exercise an arbitrary power over their people; whether oppression, or disobedience, gave the first rise to the disorder, I leave it to impartial history to determine. This I am sure, whoever, either ruler or subject, by force goes about to invade the rights of either prince or people, and lays the foundation for overturning the constitution and frame of any just government, is highly guilty of the greatest crime, I think, a man is capable of, being to answer for all those mischiefs of blood, rapine, and desolation, which the breaking to pieces of governments bring on a country. And he who does it, is justly to be esteemed the common enemy and pest of mankind, and is to be treated accordingly.

Sec. 231. That subjects or foreigners, attempting by force on the properties of any people, may be resisted with force, is agreed on all hands. But that magistrates, doing the same thing, may be resisted, hath of late been denied: as if those who had the greatest privileges and advantages by the law, had thereby a power to break those laws, by which alone they were set in a better place than their brethren: whereas their offence is thereby the greater, both as being ungrateful for the greater share they have by the law, and breaking also that trust, which is put into their hands by their brethren.

Sec. 232. Whosoever uses force without right, as every one does in society, who does it without law, puts himself into a state of war with those against whom he so uses it; and in that state all former ties are cancelled, all other rights cease, and every one has a right to defend himself, and to resist the aggressor. This is so evident, that Barclay himself, that great assertor of the power and sacredness of kings, is forced to confess, That it is lawful for the people, in some cases, to resist their king; and that too in a chapter, wherein he pretends to shew, that the divine law shuts up the people from all manner of rebellion. Whereby it is evident, even by his own doctrine, that, since they may in some cases resist, all resisting of princes is not rebellion. His words are these.

Quod siquis dicat, Ergone populus tyrannicae crudelitati & furori jugulum semper praebebit? Ergone multitude civitates suas fame, ferro, & flamma vastari, seque, conjuges, & liberos fortunae ludibrio & tyranni libidini exponi, inque omnia vitae pericula omnesque miserias & molestias a rege deduci patientur? Num illis quod omni animantium generi est a natura tributum, denegari debet, ut sc. vim vi repellant, seseq; ab injuria, tueantur? Huic breviter responsum sit, Populo universo negari defensionem, quae juris naturalis est, neque ultionem quae praeter naturam est adversus regem concedi debere. Quapropter si rex non in singulares tantum personas aliquot privatum odium exerceat, sed corpus etiam reipublicae, cujus ipse caput est, i.e. totum populum, vel insignem aliquam ejus partem immani & intoleranda saevitia seu tyrannide divexet; populo, quidem hoc casu resistendi ac tuendi se ab injuria potestas competit, sed tuendi se tantum, non enim in principem invadendi: & restituendae injuriae illatae, non recedendi a debita reverentia propter acceptam injuriam. Praesentem denique impetum propulsandi non vim praeteritam ulciscenti jus habet. Horum enim alterum a natura est, ut vitam scilicet corpusque tueamur. Alterum vero contra naturam, ut inferior de superiori supplicium sumat. Quod itaque populus malum, antequam factum sit, impedire potest, ne fiat, id postquam factum est, in regem authorem sceleris vindicare non potest: populus igitur hoc amplius quam privatus quispiam habet: quod huic, vel ipsis adversariis judicibus, excepto Buchanano, nullum nisi in patientia remedium superest. Cum ille si intolerabilis tyrannus est (modicum enim ferre omnino debet) resistere cum reverentia possit, Barclay contra Monarchom. l. iii. c. 8.

In English thus:

Sec. 233. But if any one should ask, Must the people then always lay themselves open to the cruelty and rage of tyranny? Must they see their cities pillaged, and laid in ashes, their wives and children exposed to the tyrant's lust and fury, and themselves and families reduced by their king to ruin, and all the miseries of want and oppression, and yet sit still? Must men alone be debarred the common privilege of opposing force with force, which nature allows so freely to all other creatures for their preservation from injury? I answer: Self-defence is a part of the law of nature; nor can it be denied the community, even against the king himself: but to revenge themselves upon him, must by no means be allowed them; it being not agreeable to that law. Wherefore if the king shall shew an hatred, not only to some particular persons, but sets himself against the body of the common-wealth, whereof he is the head, and shall, with intolerable ill usage, cruelly tyrannize over the whole, or a considerable part of the people, in this case the people have a right to resist and defend themselves from injury: but it must be with this caution, that they only defend themselves, but do not attack their prince: they may repair the damages received, but must not for any provocation exceed the bounds of due reverence and respect. They may repulse the present attempt, but must not revenge past violences: for it is natural for us to defend life and limb, but that an inferior should punish a superior, is against nature. The mischief which is designed them, the people may prevent before it be done; but when it is done, they must not revenge it on the king, though author of the villany. This therefore is the privilege of the people in general, above what any private person hath; that particular men are allowed by our adversaries themselves (Buchanan only excepted) to have no other remedy but patience; but the body of the people may with respect resist intolerable tyranny; for when it is but moderate, they ought to endure it.

Sec. 234. Thus far that great advocate of monarchical power allows of resistance.

Sec. 235. It is true, he has annexed two limitations to it, to no purpose:

First, He says, it must be with reverence.

Secondly, It must be without retribution, or punishment; and the reason he gives is, because an inferior cannot punish a superior.

First, How to resist force without striking again, or how to strike with reverence, will need some skill to make intelligible. He that shall oppose an assault only with a shield to receive the blows, or in any more respectful posture, without a sword in his hand, to abate the confidence and force of the assailant, will quickly be at an end of his resistance, and will find such a defence serve only to draw on himself the worse usage. This is as ridiculous a way of resisting, as juvenal thought it of fighting; ubi tu pulsas, ego vapulo tantum. And the success of the combat will be unavoidably the same he there describes it:

— Libertas pauperis haec est:
Pulsatus rogat, & pugnis concisus, adorat,
Ut liceat paucis cum dentibus inde reverti.

This will always be the event of such an imaginary resistance, where men may not strike again. He therefore who may resist, must be allowed to strike. And then let our author, or any body else, join a knock on the head, or a cut on the face, with as much reverence and respect as he thinks fit. He that can reconcile blows and reverence, may, for aught I know, desire for his pains, a civil, respectful cudgeling where-ever he can meet with it.

Secondly, As to his second, An inferior cannot punish a superior; that is true, generally speaking, whilst he is his superior. But to resist force with force, being the state of war that levels the parties, cancels all former relation of reverence, respect, and superiority: and then the odds that remains, is, that he, who opposes the unjust agressor, has this superiority over him, that he has a right, when he prevails, to punish the offender, both for the breach of the peace, and all the evils that followed upon it. Barclay therefore, in another place, more coherently to himself, denies it to be lawful to resist a king in any case. But he there assigns two cases, whereby a king may un-king himself. His words are,

Quid ergo, nulline casus incidere possunt quibus populo sese erigere atque in regem impotentius dominantem arma capere & invadere jure suo suaque authoritate liceat? Nulli certe quamdiu rex manet. Semper enim ex divinis id obstat, Regem honorificato; & qui potestati resistit, Dei ordinationi resisit: non alias igitur in eum populo potestas est quam si id committat propter quod ipso jure rex esse desinat. Tunc enim se ipse principatu exuit atque in privatis constituit liber: hoc modo populus & superior efficitur, reverso ad eum sc. jure illo quod ante regem inauguratum in interregno habuit. At sunt paucorum generum commissa ejusmodi quae hunc effectum pariunt. At ego cum plurima animo perlustrem, duo tantum invenio, duos, inquam, casus quibus rex ipso facto ex rege non regem se facit & omni honore & dignitate regali atque in subditos potestate destituit; quorum etiam meminit Winzerus. Horum unus est, Si regnum disperdat, quemadmodum de Nerone fertur, quod is nempe senatum populumque Romanum, atque adeo urbem ipsam ferro flammaque vastare, ac novas sibi sedes quaerere decrevisset. Et de Caligula, quod palam denunciarit se neque civem neque principem senatui amplius fore, inque animo habuerit interempto utriusque ordinis electissimo quoque Alexandriam commigrare, ac ut populum uno ictu interimeret, unam ei cervicem optavit. Talia cum rex aliquis meditator & molitur serio, omnem regnandi curam & animum ilico abjicit, ac proinde imperium in subditos amittit, ut dominus servi pro derelicto habiti dominium.

Sec. 236. Alter casus est, Si rex in alicujus clientelam se contulit, ac regnum quod liberum a majoribus & populo traditum accepit, alienae ditioni mancipavit. Nam tunc quamvis forte non ea mente id agit populo plane ut incommodet: tamen quia quod praecipuum est regiae dignitatis amifit, ut summus scilicet in regno secundum Deum sit, & solo Deo inferior, atque populum etiam totum ignorantem vel invitum, cujus libertatem sartam & tectam conservare debuit, in alterius gentis ditionem & potestatem dedidit; hac velut quadam regni ab alienatione effecit, ut nec quod ipse in regno imperium habuit retineat, nec in eum cui collatum voluit, juris quicquam transferat; atque ita eo facto liberum jam & suae potestatis populum relinquit, cujus rei exemplum unum annales Scotici suppeditant. Barclay contra Monarchom. 1. iii. c. 16.

Which in English runs thus:

Sec. 237. What then, can there no case happen wherein the people may of right, and by their own authority, help themselves, take arms, and set upon their king, imperiously domineering over them? None at all, whilst he remains a king. Honour the king, and he that resists the power, resists the ordinance of God; are divine oracles that will never permit it, The people therefore can never come by a power over him, unless he does something that makes him cease to be a king: for then he divests himself of his crown and dignity, and returns to the state of a private man, and the people become free and superior, the power which they had in the interregnum, before they crowned him king, devolving to them again. But there are but few miscarriages which bring the matter to this state. After considering it well on all sides, I can find but two. Two cases there are, I say, whereby a king, ipso facto, becomes no king, and loses all power and regal authority over his people; which are also taken notice of by Winzerus.

The first is, If he endeavour to overturn the government, that is, if he have a purpose and design to ruin the kingdom and commonwealth, as it is recorded of Nero, that he resolved to cut off the senate and people of Rome, lay the city waste with fire and sword, and then remove to some other place. And of Caligula, that he openly declared, that he would be no longer a head to the people or senate, and that he had it in his thoughts to cut off the worthiest men of both ranks, and then retire to Alexandria: and he wisht that the people had but one neck, that he might dispatch them all at a blow, Such designs as these, when any king harbours in his thoughts, and seriously promotes, he immediately gives up all care and thought of the common-wealth; and consequently forfeits the power of governing his subjects, as a master does the dominion over his slaves whom he hath abandoned.

Sec. 238. The other case is, When a king makes himself the dependent of another, and subjects his kingdom which his ancestors left him, and the people put free into his hands, to the dominion of another: for however perhaps it may not be his intention to prejudice the people;

yet because he has hereby lost the principal part of regal dignity, viz. to be next and immediately under God, supreme in his kingdom; and also because he betrayed or forced his people, whose liberty he ought to have carefully preserved, into the power and dominion of a foreign nation. By this, as. it were, alienation of his kingdom, he himself loses the power he had in it before, without transferring any the least right to those on whom he would have bestowed it; and so by this act sets the people free, and leaves them at their own disposal. One example of this is to be found in the Scotch Annals.

Sec. 239. In these cases Barclay, the great champion of absolute monarchy, is forced to allow, that a king may be resisted, and ceases to be a king. That is, in short, not to multiply cases, in whatsoever he has no authority, there he is no king, and may be resisted: for wheresoever the authority ceases, the king ceases too, and becomes like other men who have no authority. And these two cases he instances in, differ little from those above mentioned, to be destructive to governments, only that he has omitted the principle from which his doctrine flows: and that is, the breach of trust, in not preserving the form of government agreed on, and in not intending the end of government itself, which is the public good and preservation of property. When a king has dethroned himself, and put himself in a state of war with his people, what shall hinder them from prosecuting him who is no king, as they would any other man, who has put himself into a state of war with them, Barclay, and those of his opinion, would do well to tell us. This farther I desire may be taken notice of out of Barclay, that he says, The mischief that is designed them, the people may prevent before it be clone: whereby he allows resistance when tyranny is but in design. Such designs as these (says he) when any king harbours in his thoughts and seriously promotes, he immediately gives up all care and thought of the common-wealth; so that, according to him, the neglect of the public good is to be taken as an evidence of such design, or at least for a sufficient cause of resistance. And the reason of all, he gives in these words, Because he betrayed or forced his people, whose liberty he ought carefully to have preserved. What he adds, into the power and dominion of a foreign nation, signifies nothing, the fault and forfeiture lying in the loss of their liberty, which he ought to have preserved, and not in any distinction of the persons to whose dominion they were subjected. The peoples right is equally invaded, and their liberty lost, whether they are made slaves to any of their own, or a foreign nation; and in this lies the injury, and against this only have they the right of defence. And there are instances to be found in all countries, which shew, that it is not the change of nations in the persons of their governors, but the change of government, that gives the offence. Bilson, a bishop of our church, and a great stickler for the power and prerogative of princes, does, if I mistake not, in his treatise of Christian subjection, acknowledge, that princes may forfeit their power, and their title to the obedience of their subjects; and if there needed authority in a case where reason is so plain, I could send my reader to Bracton, Fortescue, and the author of the Mirrour, and others, writers that cannot be suspected to be ignorant of our government, or enemies to it. But I thought Hooker alone might be enough to satisfy those men, who relying on him for their ecclesiastical polity, are by a strange fate carried to deny those principles upon which he builds it. Whether they are herein made the tools of cunninger workmen, to pull down their own fabric, they were best look. This I am sure, their civil policy is so new, so dangerous, and so destructive to both rulers and people, that as former ages never could bear the broaching of it; so it may be hoped, those to come, redeemed from the impositions of these Egyptian under-task-masters, will abhor the memory of such servile flatterers, who, whilst it seemed to serve their turn, resolved all government into absolute tyranny, and would have all men born to, what their mean souls fitted them for, slavery.

Sec. 240. Here, it is like, the common question will be made, Who shall be judge, whether the prince or legislative act contrary to their trust? This, perhaps, ill-affected and factious men may spread amongst the people, when the prince only makes use of his due prerogative. To this I reply, The people shall be judge; for who shall be judge whether his trustee or deputy acts well, and according to the trust reposed in him, but he who deputes him, and must, by having deputed him, have still a power to discard him, when he fails in his trust? If this be reasonable in particular cases of private men, why should it be otherwise in that of the greatest moment, where the welfare of millions is concerned, and also where the evil, if not prevented, is greater, and the redress very difficult, dear, and dangerous?

Sec. 241. But farther, this question, (Who shall be judge?) cannot mean, that there is no judge at all: for where there is no judicature on earth, to decide controversies amongst men, God in heaven is judge. He alone, it is true, is judge of the right. But every man is judge for himself, as in all other cases, so in this, whether another hath put himself into a state of war with him, and whether he should appeal to the Supreme Judge, as leptha did.

Sec. 242. If a controversy arise betwixt a prince and some of the people, in a matter where the law is silent, or doubtful, and the thing be of great consequence, I should think the proper umpire, in such a case, should be the body of the people: for in cases where the prince hath a trust reposed in him, and is dispensed from the common ordinary rules of the law; there, if any men find themselves aggrieved, and think the prince acts contrary to, or beyond that trust, who so proper to judge as the body of the people, (who, at first, lodged that trust in him) how far they meant it should extend? But if the prince, or whoever they be in the administration, decline that way of determination, the appeal then lies no where but to heaven; force between either persons, who have no known superior on earth, or which permits no appeal to a judge on earth, being properly a state of war, wherein the appeal lies only to heaven; and in that state the injured party must judge for himself, when he will think fit to make use of that appeal, and put himself upon it.

Sec. 243. To conclude, The power that every individual gave the society, when he entered into it, can never revert to the individuals again, as long as the society lasts, but will always remain in the community; because without this there can be no community, no common-wealth, which is contrary to the original agreement: so also when the society hath placed the legislative in any assembly of men, to continue in them and their successors, with direction and authority for providing such successors, the legislative can never revert to the people whilst that government lasts; because having provided a legislative with power to continue for ever, they have given up their political power to the legislative, and cannot resume it. But if they have set limits to the duration of their legislative, and made this supreme power in any person, or assembly, only temporary; or else, when by the miscarriages of those in authority, it is forfeited; upon the forfeiture, or at the determination of the time set, it reverts to the society, and the people have a right to act as supreme, and continue the legislative in themselves; or erect a new form, or under the old form place it in new hands, as they think good.

FINIS.

An Essay Concerning Human Understanding

TO THE RIGHT HONOURABLE
LORD THOMAS, EARL OF PEMBROKE AND MONTGOMERY,
BARRON HERBERT OF CARDIFF, LORD ROSS, OF KENDAL, PAR, FITZHUGH,
MARMION, ST. QUINTIN, AND SHURLAND; LORD PRESIDENT OF HIS MAJESTY'S
MOST HONOURABLE PRIVY COUNCIL; AND LORD LIEUTENANT OF THE
COUNTY OF WILTS, AND OF SOUTH WALES.

MY LORD,

THIS Treatise, which is grown up under your lordship's eye, and has ventured into the world by your order, does now, by a natural kind of right, come to your lordship for that protection which you several years since promised it. It is not that I think any name, how great soever, set at the beginning of a book, will be able to cover the faults that are to be found in it. Things in print must stand and fall by their own worth, or the reader's fancy. But there being nothing more to be desired for truth than a fair unprejudiced hearing, nobody is more likely to procure me that than your lordship, who are allowed to have got so intimate an acquaintance with her, in her more retired recesses. Your lordship is known to have so far advanced your speculations in the most abstract and general knowledge of things, beyond the ordinary reach or common methods, that your allowance and approbation of the design of this Treatise will at least preserve it from being condemned without reading, and will prevail to have those parts a little weighted, which might otherwise perhaps be thought to deserve no consideration, for being somewhat out of the common road. The imputation of Novelty is a terrible charge amongst those who judge of men's heads, as they do of their perukes, by the fashion, and can allow none to be right but the received doctrines. Truth scarce ever yet carried it by vote anywhere at its first appearance: new opinions are always suspected, and usually opposed, without any other reason but because they are not already common. But truth, like gold, is not the less so for being newly brought out of the mine. It is trial and examination must give it price, and not any antique fashion; and though it be not yet current by the public stamp, yet it may, for all that, be as old as nature, and is certainly not the less genuine. Your lordship can give great and convincing instances of this, whenever you please to oblige the public with some of those large and comprehensive discoveries you have made of truths hitherto unknown, unless to some few, from whom your lordship has been pleased not wholly to conceal them. This alone were a sufficient reason, were there no other, why I should dedicate this Essay to your lordship; and its having some little correspondence with some parts of that nobler and vast system of the sciences your lordship has made so new, exact, and instructive a draught of, I think it glory enough, if your lordship permit me to boast, that here and there I have fallen into some thoughts not wholly different from yours. If your lordship think fit that, by your encouragement, this should appear in the world, I hope it may be a reason, some time or other, to lead your lordship further; and you will allow me to say, that you here give the world an earnest of something that, if they can bear with this, will be truly worth their expectation. This, my lord, shows what a present I here make to your lordship; just such as the poor man does to his rich and great neighbour, by whom the basket of flowers or fruit is not ill taken, though he has more plenty of his own growth, and in much greater perfection. Worthless things receive a value when they are made the offerings of respect, esteem, and gratitude: these you have given me so mighty and peculiar reasons to have, in the highest degree, for your lordship, that if they can add a price to what they go along with, proportionable to their own greatness, I can with confidence brag, I here make your lordship the richest present you ever received. This I am sure, I am under the greatest obligations to seek all occasions to acknowledge a long train of favours I have received from your lordship; favours, though great and important in themselves, yet made much more so by the forwardness, concern, and kindness, and other obliging circumstances, that never failed to accompany them. To all this you are pleased to add that which gives yet more weight and relish to all the rest: you vouchsafe to continue me in some degrees of your esteem, and allow me a place in your good thoughts, I had almost said friendship. This, my lord, your words and actions so constantly show on all occasions, even to others when I am absent, that it is not vanity in me to mention what everybody knows: but it would be want of good manners not to acknowledge what so many are witnesses of, and every day tell me I am indebted to your lordship for. I wish they could as easily assist my gratitude, as they convince me of the great and growing engagements it has to your lordship. This I am sure, I should write of the Understanding without having any, if I were not extremely sensible of them, and did not lay hold on this opportunity to testify to the world how much I am obliged to be, and how much I am,

MY LORD,

Your Lordship's most humble and most obedient servant,

JOHN LOCKE

Dorset Court,

24th of May, 1689

EPISTLE TO THE READER

I HAVE put into thy hands what has been the diversion of some of my idle and heavy hours. If it has the good luck to prove so of any of thine, and thou hast but half so much pleasure in reading as I had in writing it, thou wilt as little think thy money, as I do my pains, ill bestowed. Mistake not this for a commendation of my work; nor conclude, because I was pleased with the doing of it, that therefore I am fondly taken with it now it is done. He that hawks at larks and sparrows has no less sport, though a much less considerable quarry, than he that flies at nobler game: and he is little acquainted with the subject of this treatise — the UNDERSTANDING— who does not know that, as it is the most elevated faculty of the soul, so it is employed with a greater and more constant delight than any of the other. Its searches after truth are a sort of hawking and hunting, wherein the very pursuit makes a great part of the pleasure. Every step the mind takes in its progress towards Knowledge makes some discovery, which is not only new, but the best too, for the time at least.

For the understanding, like the eye, judging of objects only by its own sight, cannot but be pleased with what it discovers, having less regret for what has escaped it, because it is unknown. Thus he who has raised himself above the alms-basket, and, not content to live lazily on scraps of begged opinions, sets his own thoughts on work, to find and follow truth, will (whatever he lights on) not miss the hunter's satisfaction; every moment of his pursuit will reward his pains with some delight; and he will have reason to think his time not ill spent, even when he cannot much boast of any great acquisition.

This, Reader, is the entertainment of those who let loose their own thoughts, and follow them in writing; which thou oughtest not to envy them, since they afford thee an opportunity of the like diversion, if thou wilt make use of thy own thoughts in reading. It is to them, if they are thy own, that I refer myself: but if they are taken upon trust from others, it is no great matter what they are; they are not following truth, but some meaner consideration; and it is not worth while to be concerned what he says or thinks, who says or thinks only as he is directed by another. If thou judgest for thyself I know thou wilt judge candidly, and then I shall not be harmed or offended, whatever be thy censure. For though it be certain that there is nothing in this Treatise of the truth whereof I am not fully persuaded, yet I consider myself as liable to mistakes as I can think thee, and know that this book must stand or fall with thee, not by any opinion I have of it, but thy own. If thou findest little in it new or instructive to thee, thou art not to blame me for it. It was not meant for those that had already mastered this subject, and made a thorough acquaintance with their own understandings; but for my own information, and the satisfaction of a few friends, who acknowledged themselves not to have sufficiently considered it.

Were it fit to trouble thee with the history of this Essay, I should tell thee, that five or six friends meeting at my chamber, and discoursing on a subject very remote from this, found themselves quickly at a stand, by the difficulties that rose on every side. After we had awhile puzzled ourselves, without coming any nearer a resolution of those doubts which perplexed us, it came into my thoughts that we took a wrong course; and that before we set ourselves upon inquiries of that nature, it was necessary to examine our own abilities, and see what objects our understandings were, or were not, fitted to deal with. This I proposed to the company, who all readily assented; and thereupon it was agreed that this should be our first inquiry. Some hasty and undigested thoughts, on a subject I had never before considered, which I set down against our next meeting, gave the first entrance into this Discourse; which having been thus begun by chance, was continued by intreaty; written by incoherent parcels; and after long intervals of neglect, resumed again, as my humour or occasions permitted; and at last, in a retirement where an attendance on my health gave me leisure, it was brought into that order thou now seest it.

This discontinued way of writing may have occasioned, besides others, two contrary faults, viz., that too little and too much may be said in it. If thou findest anything wanting, I shall be glad that what I have written gives thee any desire that I should have gone further. If it seems too much to thee, thou must blame the subject; for when I put pen to paper, I thought all I should have to say on this matter would have been contained in one sheet of paper; but the further I went the larger prospect I had; new discoveries led me still on, and so it grew insensibly to the bulk it now appears in. I will not deny, but possibly it might be reduced to a narrower compass than it is, and that some parts of it might be contracted, the way it has been writ in, by catches, and many long intervals of interruption, being apt to cause some repetitions. But to confess the truth, I am now too lazy, or too busy, to make it shorter.

I am not ignorant how little I herein consult my own reputation, when I knowingly let it go with a fault, so apt to disgust the most judicious, who are always the nicest readers. But they who know sloth is apt to content itself with any excuse, will pardon me if mine has prevailed on me, where I think I have a very good one. I will not therefore allege in my defence, that the same notion, having different respects, may be convenient or necessary to prove or illustrate several parts of the same discourse, and that so it has happened in many parts of this: but waiving that, I shall frankly avow that I have sometimes dwelt long upon the same argument, and expressed it different ways, with a quite different design. I pretend not to publish this Essay for the information of men of large thoughts and quick apprehensions; to such masters of knowledge I profess myself a scholar, and therefore warn them beforehand not to expect anything here, but what, being spun out of my own coarse thoughts, is fitted to men of my own size, to whom, perhaps, it will not be unacceptable that I have taken some pains to make plain and familiar to their thoughts some truths which established prejudice, or the abstractedness of the ideas themselves, might render difficult. Some objects had need be turned on every side; and when the notion is new, as I confess some of these are to me; or out of the ordinary road, as I suspect they will appear to others, it is not one simple view of it that will gain it admittance into every understanding, or fix it there with a clear and lasting impression. There are few, I believe, who have not observed in themselves or others, that what in one way of proposing was very obscure, another way of expressing it has made very clear and intelligible; though afterwards the mind found little difference in the phrases, and wondered why one failed to be understood more than the other. But everything does not hit alike upon every man's imagination. We have our understandings no less different than our palates; and he that thinks the same truth shall be equally relished by every one in the same dress, may as well hope to feast every one with the same sort of cookery: the meat may be the same, and the nourishment good, yet every one not be able to receive it with that seasoning; and it must be dressed another way, if you will have it go down with some, even of strong constitutions. The truth is, those who advised me to publish it, advised me, for this reason, to publish it as it is: and since I have been brought to let it go abroad, I desire it should be understood by whoever gives himself the pains to read it. I have so little affection to be in print, that if I were not flattered this Essay might be of some use to others, as I think it has been to me, I should have confined it to the view of some friends, who gave the first occasion to it. My appearing therefore in print being on purpose to be as useful as I may, I think it necessary to make what I have to say as easy and intelligible to all sorts of readers as I can. And I had much rather the speculative and quick-sighted should complain of my being in some parts tedious, than that any one, not accustomed to abstract speculations, or prepossessed with different notions, should mistake or not comprehend my meaning.

It will possibly be censured as a great piece of vanity or insolence in me, to pretend to instruct this our knowing age; it amounting to little less, when I own, that I publish this Essay with hopes it may be useful to others. But, if it may be permitted to speak freely of those who with a feigned modesty condemn as useless what they themselves write, methinks it savours much more of vanity or insolence to publish a book for any other end; and he fails very much of that respect he owes the public, who prints, and consequently expects men should read, that wherein he intends not they should meet with anything of use to themselves or others: and should nothing else be found allowable in this Treatise, yet my design will not cease to be so;

and the goodness of my intention ought to be some excuse for the worthlessness of my present. It is that chiefly which secures me from the fear of censure, which I expect not to escape more than better writers. Men's principles, notions, and relishes are so different, that it is hard to find a book which pleases or displeases all men. I acknowledge the age we live in is not the least knowing, and therefore not the most easy to be satisfied. If I have not the good luck to please, yet nobody ought to be offended with me. I plainly tell all my readers, except half a dozen, this Treatise was not at first intended for them; and therefore they need not be at the trouble to be of that number. But yet if any one thinks fit to be angry and rail at it, he may do it securely, for I shall find some better way of spending my time than in such kind of conversation. I shall always have the satisfaction to have aimed sincerely at truth and usefulness, though in one of the meanest ways. The commonwealth of learning is not at this time without master-builders, whose mighty designs, in advancing the sciences, will leave lasting monuments to the admiration of posterity: but every one must not hope to be a Boyle or a Sydenham; and in an age that produces such masters as the great Huygenius and the incomparable Mr. Newton, with some others of that strain, it is ambition enough to be employed as an under-labourer in clearing the ground a little, and removing some of the rubbish that lies in the way to knowledge;— which certainly had been very much more advanced in the world, if the endeavours of ingenious and industrious men had not been much cumbered with the learned but frivolous use of uncouth, affected, or unintelligible terms, introduced into the sciences, and there made an art of, to that degree that Philosophy, which is nothing but the true knowledge of things, was thought unfit or incapable to be brought into well-bred company and polite conversation. Vague and insignificant forms of speech, and abuse of language, have so long passed for mysteries of science; and hard and misapplied words, with little or no meaning, have, by prescription, such a right to be mistaken for deep learning and height of speculation, that it will not be easy to persuade either those who speak or those who hear them, that they are but the covers of ignorance, and hindrance of true knowledge. To break in upon the sanctuary of vanity and ignorance will be, I suppose, some service to human understanding; though so few are apt to think they deceive or are deceived in the use of words; or that the language of the sect they are of has any faults in it which ought to be examined or corrected, that I hope I shall be pardoned if I have in the Third Book dwelt long on this subject, and endeavoured to make it so plain, that neither the inveterateness of the mischief, nor the prevalency of the fashion, shall be any excuse for those who will not take care about the meaning of their own words, and will not suffer the significancy of their expressions to be inquired into.

I have been told that a short Epitome of this Treatise, which was printed in 1688, was by some condemned without reading, because innate ideas were denied in it; they too hastily concluding, that if innate ideas were not supposed, there would be little left either of the notion or proof of spirits. If any one take the like offence at the entrance of this Treatise, I shall desire him to read it through; and then I hope he will be convinced, that the taking away false foundations is not to the prejudice but advantage of truth, which is never injured or endangered so much as when mixed with, or built on, falsehood.

In the Second Edition I added as followeth:—

The bookseller will not forgive me if I say nothing of this New Edition, which he has promised, by the correctness of it, shall make amends for the many faults committed in the former. He desires too, that it should be known that it has one whole new chapter concerning Identity, and many additions and amendments in other places. These I must inform my reader are not all new matter, but most of them either further confirmation of what I had said, or explications, to prevent others being mistaken in the sense of what was formerly printed, and not any variation in me from it.

I must only except the alterations I have made in Book II. chap. xxi.

What I had there written concerning Liberty and the Will, I thought deserved as accurate a view as I am capable of; those subjects having in all ages exercised the learned part of the world with questions and difficulties, that have not a little perplexed morality and divinity, those parts of knowledge that men are most concerned to be clear in. Upon a closer inspection into the working of men's minds, and a stricter examination of those motives and views they are turned by, I have found reason somewhat to alter the thoughts I formerly had concerning that which gives the last determination to the Will in all voluntary actions. This I cannot forbear to acknowledge to the world with as much freedom and readiness as I at first published what then seemed to me to be right; thinking myself more concerned to quit and renounce any opinion of my own, than oppose that of another, when truth appears against it. For it is truth alone I seek, and that will always be welcome to me, when or from whencesoever it comes. But what forwardness soever I have to resign any opinion I have, or to recede from anything I have writ, upon the first evidence of any error in it; yet this I must own, that I have not had the good luck to receive any light from those exceptions I have met with in print against any part of my book, nor have, from anything that has been urged against it, found reason to alter my sense in any of the points that have been questioned. Whether the subject I have in hand requires often more thought and attention than cursory readers, at least such as are prepossessed, are willing to allow; or whether any obscurity in my expressions casts a cloud over it, and these notions are made difficult to others' apprehensions in my way of treating them; so it is, that my meaning, I find, is often mistaken, and I have not the good luck to be everywhere rightly understood.

Of this the ingenious author of the Discourse Concerning the Nature of Man has given me a late instance, to mention no other. For the civility of his expressions, and the candour that belongs to his order, forbid me to think that he would have closed his Preface with an insinuation, as if in what I had said, Book II. ch. xxvii, concerning the third rule which men refer their actions to, I went about to make virtue vice and vice virtue unless he had mistaken my meaning; which he could not have done if he had given himself the trouble to consider what the argument was I was then upon, and what was the chief design of that chapter, plainly enough set down in the fourth section and those following. For I was there not laying down moral rules, but showing the original and nature of moral ideas, and enumerating the rules men make use of in moral relations, whether these rules were true or false: and pursuant thereto I tell what is everywhere called virtue and vice; which "alters not the nature of things," though men generally do judge of and denominate their actions according to the esteem and fashion of the place and sect they are of.

If he had been at the pains to reflect on what I had said, Bk. I. ch. ii. sect. 18, and Bk. II. ch. xxviii. sects. 13, 14, 15 and 20, he would have known what I think of the eternal and unalterable nature of right and wrong, and what I call virtue and vice. And if he had observed that in the place he quotes I only report as a matter of fact what others call virtue and vice, he would not have found it liable to any great exception. For I think I am not much out in saying that one of the rules made use of in the world for a ground or measure of a moral relation is — that esteem and reputation which several sorts of actions find variously in the several societies of men, according to which they are there called virtues or vices. And whatever authority the learned Mr. Lowde places in his Old English Dictionary, I daresay it nowhere tells him (if I should appeal to it) that the same action is not in credit, called and counted a virtue, in one place, which, being in disrepute, passes for and under the name of vice in another. The taking notice that men bestow the names of "virtue" and "vice" according to this rule of Reputation is all I have done, or can be laid to my charge to have done, towards the making vice virtue or virtue vice. But the good man does well, and as becomes his calling, to be watchful in such points, and to take the alarm even at expressions, which, standing alone by themselves, might sound ill and be suspected.

'Tis to this zeal, allowable in his function, that I forgive his citing as he does these words of mine (ch. xxviii. sect. II): "Even the exhortations of inspired teachers have not feared to appeal to common repute, Philip. iv. 8"; without taking notice of those immediately preceding, which introduce them, and run thus: "Whereby even in the corruption of manners, the true boundaries of the law of nature, which ought to be the rule of virtue and vice, were pretty well preserved. So that even the exhortations of inspired teachers," &c. By which words, and the rest of that section, it is plain that I brought that passage of St. Paul, not to prove that the general measure of what men called virtue and vice throughout the world was, the reputation and fashion of each particular society within itself; but to show that, though it were so, yet, for reasons I there give, men, in that way of denominating their actions, did not for the most part much stray from the Law of Nature; which is that standing and unalterable rule by which they ought to judge of the moral rectitude and gravity of their actions, and accordingly denominate them virtues or vices. Had Mr. Lowde considered this, he would have found it little to his purpose to have quoted this passage in a sense I used it not; and would I imagine have spared the application he subjoins to it, as not very necessary. But I hope this Second Edition will give him satisfaction on the point, and that this matter is now so expressed as to show him there was no cause for scruple.

Though I am forced to differ from him in these apprehensions he has expressed, in the latter end of his preface, concerning what I had said about virtue and vice, yet we are better agreed than he thinks in what he says in his third chapter (p. 78) concerning "natural inscription and innate notions." I shall not deny him the privilege he claims (p. 52), to state the question as he pleases, especially when he states it so as to leave nothing in it contrary to what I have said. For, according to him, "innate notions, being conditional things, depending upon the concurrence of several other circumstances in order to the soul's exerting them," all that he says for "innate, imprinted, impressed notions" (for of innate ideas he says nothing at all), amounts at last only to this — that there are certain propositions which, though the soul from the beginning, or when a man is born, does not know, yet "by assistance from the outward senses, and the help of some previous cultivation," it may afterwards come certainly to know the truth of; which is no more than what I have affirmed in my First Book. For I suppose by the "soul's exerting them," he means its beginning to know them; or else the soul's "exerting of notions" will be to me a very unintelligible expression; and I think at best is a very unfit one in this, it misleading men's thoughts by an insinuation, as if these notions were in the mind before the "soul exerts them," i.e. before they are known;— whereas truly before they are known, there is nothing of them in the mind but a capacity to know them, when the "concurrence of those circumstances," which this ingenious author thinks necessary "in order to the soul's exerting them," brings them into our knowledge.

P. 52 I find him express it thus: "These natural notions are not so imprinted upon the soul as that they naturally and necessarily exert themselves (even in children and idiots) without any assistance from the outward senses, or without the help of some previous cultivation." Here, he says, they exert themselves, as p. 78, that the "soul exerts them." When he has explained to himself or others what he means by "the soul's exerting innate notions," or their "exerting themselves"; and what that "previous cultivation and circumstances" in order to their being exerted are — he will I suppose find there is so little of controversy between him and me on the point, bating that he calls that "exerting of notions" which I in a more vulgar style call "knowing," that I have reason to think he brought in my name on this occasion only out of the pleasure he has to speak civilly of me; which I must gratefully acknowledge he has done everywhere he mentions me, not without conferring on me, as some others have done, a title I have no right to.

There are so many instances of this, that I think it justice to my reader and myself to conclude, that either my book is plainly enough written to be rightly understood by those who peruse it with that attention and indifference, which every one who will give himself the pains to read ought to employ in reading; or else that I have written mine so obscurely that it is in vain to go about to mend it. Whichever of these be the truth, it is myself only am affected thereby; and therefore I shall be far from troubling my reader with what I think might be said in answer to those several objections I have met with, to passages here and there of my book; since I persuade myself that he who thinks them of moment enough to be concerned whether they are true or false, will be able to see that what is said is either not well founded, or else not contrary to my doctrine, when I and my opposer come both to be well understood.

If any other authors, careful that none of their good thoughts should be lost, have published their censures of my Essay, with this honour done to it, that they will not suffer it to be an essay, I leave it to the public to value the obligation they have to their critical pens, and shall not waste my reader's time in so idle or ill-natured an employment of mine, as to lessen the satisfaction any one has in himself, or gives to others, in so hasty a confutation of what I have written.

The booksellers preparing for the Fourth Edition of my Essay, gave me notice of it, that I might, if I had leisure, make any additions or alterations I should think fit. Whereupon I thought it convenient to advertise the reader, that besides several corrections I had made here and there, there was one alteration which it was necessary to mention, because it ran through the whole book, and is of consequence to be rightly understood. What I thereupon said was this:—

Clear and distinct ideas are terms which, though familiar and frequent in men's mouths, I have reason to think every one who uses does not perfectly understand. And possibly 'tis but here and there one who gives himself the trouble to consider them so far as to know what he himself or others precisely mean by them. I have therefore in most places chose to put determinate or determined, instead of clear and distinct, as more likely to direct men's thoughts to my meaning in this matter. By those denominations, I mean some object in the mind, and consequently determined, i.e. such as it is there seen and perceived to be. This, I think, may fitly be called a determinate or determined idea, when such as it is at any time objectively in the mind, and so determined there, it is annexed, and without variation determined, to a name or articulate sound, which is to be steadily the sign of that very same object of the mind, or determinate idea.

To explain this a little more particularly. By determinate, when applied to a simple idea, I mean that simple appearance which the mind has in its view, or perceives in itself, when that idea is said to be in it: by determined, when applied to a complex idea, I mean such an one as consists of a determinate number of certain simple or less complex ideas, joined in such a proportion and situation as the mind has before its view, and sees in itself, when that idea is present in it, or should be present in it, when a man gives a name to it. I say should be, because it is not every one, nor perhaps any one, who is so careful of his language as to use no word till he views in his mind the precise determined idea which he resolves to make it the sign of The want of this is the cause of no small obscurity and confusion in men's thoughts and discourses. I know there are not words enough in any language to answer all the variety of ideas that enter into men's discourses and reasonings. But this hinders not but that when any one uses any term, he may have in his mind a determined idea, which he makes it the sign of, and to which he should keep it steadily annexed during that present discourse. Where he does not, or cannot do this, he in vain pretends to clear or distinct ideas: it is plain his are not so; and therefore there can be expected nothing but obscurity and confusion, where such terms are made use of which have not such a precise determination.

Upon this ground I have thought determined ideas a way of speaking less liable to mistakes, than clear and distinct: and where men have got such determined ideas of all that they reason, inquire, or argue about, they will find a great part of their doubts and disputes at an end; the greatest part of the questions and controversies that perplex mankind depending on the doubtful and uncertain use of words, or (which is the same) indetermined ideas, which they are made to stand for. I have made choice of these terms to signify, (1) Some immediate object of the mind, which it perceives and has before it, distinct from the sound it uses as a sign of it. (2) That this idea, thus determined, i.e. which the mind has in itself, and knows, and sees there, be determined without any change to that name, and that name determined to that precise idea. If men had such determined ideas in their inquiries and discourses, they would both discern how far their own inquiries and discourses went, and avoid the greatest part of the disputes and wranglings they have with others.

Besides this, the bookseller will think it necessary I should advertise the reader that there is an addition of two chapters wholly new; the one of the Association of Ideas, the other of Enthusiasm. These, with some other larger additions never before printed, he has engaged to print by themselves, after the same manner, and for the same purpose, as was done when this Essay had the second impression.

In the Sixth Edition there is very little added or altered. The greatest part of what is new is contained in the twenty-first chapter of the second book, which any one, if he thinks it worth while, may, with a very little labour, transcribe into the margin of the former edition.

BOOK I.Neither Principles nor Ideas are Innate

As thou knowest not what is the way of the Spirit, nor how the bones do grow in the womb of her that is with child: even so thou knowest not the works of God, who maketh all things.— Eccles. 11. 5.

Quam bellum est velle confiteri potius nescire quod nescias, quam ista effutientem nauseare, atque ipsum sibi displicere.— Cicero, de Natur. Deor. l. i.

INTRODUCTION

1. An Inquiry into the understanding, pleasant and useful. Since it is the understanding that sets man above the rest of sensible beings, and gives him all the advantage and dominion which he has over them; it is certainly a subject, even for its nobleness, worth our labour to inquire into. The understanding, like the eye, whilst it makes us see and perceive all other things, takes no notice of itself; and it requires art and pains to set it at a distance and make it its own object. But whatever be the difficulties that lie in the way of this inquiry; whatever it be that keeps us so much in the dark to ourselves; sure I am that all the light we can let in upon our minds, all the acquaintance we can make with our own understandings, will not only be very pleasant, but bring us great advantage, in directing our thoughts in the search of other things.

2. Design. This, therefore, being my purpose — to inquire into the original, certainty, and extent of human knowledge, together with the grounds and degrees of belief, opinion, and assent;— I shall not at present meddle with the physical consideration of the mind; or trouble myself to examine wherein its essence consists; or by what motions of our spirits or alterations of our bodies we come to have any sensation by our organs, or any ideas in our understandings; and whether those ideas do in their formation, any or all of them, depend on matter or not. These are speculations which, however curious and entertaining, I shall decline, as lying out of my way in the design I am now upon. It shall suffice to my present purpose, to consider the discerning faculties of a man, as they are employed about the objects which they have to do with. And I shall imagine I have not wholly misemployed myself in the thoughts I shall have on this occasion, if, in this historical, plain method, I can give any account of the ways whereby our understandings come to attain those notions of things we have; and can set down any measures of the certainty of our knowledge; or the grounds of those persuasions which are to be found amongst men, so various, different, and wholly contradictory; and yet asserted somewhere or other with such assurance and confidence, that he that shall take a view of the opinions of mankind, observe their opposition, and at the same time consider the fondness and devotion wherewith they are embraced, the resolution and eagerness wherewith they are maintained, may perhaps have reason to suspect, that either there is no such thing as truth at all, or that mankind hath no sufficient means to attain a certain knowledge of it.

3. Method. It is therefore worth while to search out the bounds between opinion and knowledge; and examine by what measures, in things whereof we have no certain knowledge, we ought to regulate our assent and moderate our persuasion. In order whereunto I shall pursue this following method:—

First, I shall inquire into the original of those ideas, notions, or whatever else you please to call them, which a man observes, and is conscious to himself he has in his mind; and the ways whereby the understanding comes to be furnished with them.

Secondly, I shall endeavour to show what knowledge the understanding hath by those ideas; and the certainty, evidence, and extent of it.

Thirdly, I shall make some inquiry into the nature and grounds of faith or opinion: whereby I mean that assent which we give to any proposition as true, of whose truth yet we have no certain knowledge. And here we shall have occasion to examine the reasons and degrees of assent.

4. Useful to know the extent of our comprehension. If by this inquiry into the nature of the understanding, I can discover the powers thereof; how far they reach; to what things they are in any degree proportionate; and where they fail us, I suppose it may be of use to prevail with the busy mind of man to be more cautious in meddling with things exceeding its comprehension; to stop when it is at the utmost extent of its tether; and to sit down in a quiet ignorance of those things which, upon examination, are found to be beyond the reach of our capacities. We should not then perhaps be so forward, out of an affectation of an universal knowledge, to raise questions, and perplex ourselves and others with disputes about things to which our understandings are not suited; and of which we cannot frame in our minds any clear or distinct perceptions, or whereof (as it has perhaps too often happened) we have not any notions at all. If we can find out how far the understanding can extend its view; how far it has faculties to attain certainty; and in what cases it can only judge and guess, we may learn to content ourselves with what is attainable by us in this state.

5. Our capacity suited to our state and concerns. For though the comprehension of our understandings comes exceeding short of the vast extent of things, yet we shall have cause enough to magnify the bountiful Author of our being, for that proportion and degree of knowledge he has bestowed on us, so far above all the rest of the inhabitants of this our mansion. Men have reason to be well satisfied with what God hath thought fit for them, since he hath given them (as St. Peter says) pana pros zoen kaieusebeian, whatsoever is necessary for the conveniences of life and information of virtue; and has put within the reach of their discovery, the comfortable provision for this life, and the way that leads to a better. How short soever their knowledge may come of an universal or perfect comprehension of whatsoever is, it yet secures their great concernments, that they have light enough to lead them to the knowledge of their Maker, and the sight of their own duties. Men may find matter sufficient to busy their heads, and employ their hands with variety, delight, and satisfaction, if they will not boldly quarrel with their own constitution, and throw away the blessings their hands are filled with, because they are not big enough to grasp everything. We shall not have much reason to complain of the narrowness of our minds, if we will but employ them about what may be of use to us; for of that they are very capable. And it will be an unpardonable, as well as childish peevishness, if we undervalue the advantages of our knowledge, and neglect to improve it to the ends for which it was given us, because there are some things that are set out of the reach of it. It will be no excuse to an idle and untoward servant, who would not attend his business by candle light, to plead that he had not broad sunshine. The Candle that is set up in us shines bright enough for all our purposes. The discoveries we can make with this ought to satisfy us; and we shall then use our understandings right, when we entertain all objects in that way and proportion that they are suited to our faculties, and upon those grounds they are capable of being proposed to us; and not peremptorily or intemperately require demonstration, and demand certainty, where probability only is to be had, and which is sufficient to govern all our concernments. If we will disbelieve everything, because we cannot certainly know all things, we shall do muchwhat as wisely as he who would not use his legs, but sit still and perish, because he had no wings to fly.

6. Knowledge of our capacity a cure of scepticism and idleness. When we know our own strength, we shall the better know what to undertake with hopes of success; and when we have well surveyed the powers of our own minds, and made some estimate what we may expect from them, we shall not be inclined either to sit still, and not set our thoughts on work at all, in despair of knowing anything; nor on the other side, question everything, and disclaim all knowledge, because some things are not to be understood. It is of great use to the sailor to know the length of his line, though he cannot with it fathom all the depths of the ocean. It is well he knows that it is long enough to reach the bottom, at such places as are necessary to

direct his voyage, and caution him against running upon shoals that may ruin him. Our business here is not to know all things, but those which concern our conduct. If we can find out those measures, whereby a rational creature, put in that state in which man is in this world, may and ought to govern his opinions, and actions depending thereon, we need not to be troubled that some other things escape our knowledge.

7. Occasion of this essay. This was that which gave the first rise to this Essay concerning the understanding. For I thought that the first step towards satisfying several inquiries the mind of man was very apt to run into, was, to take a survey of our own understandings, examine our own powers, and see to what things they were adapted. Till that was done I suspected we began at the wrong end, and in vain sought for satisfaction in a quiet and sure possession of truths that most concerned us, whilst we let loose our thoughts into the vast ocean of Being; as if all that boundless extent were the natural and undoubted possession of our understandings, wherein there was nothing exempt from its decisions, or that escaped its comprehension. Thus men, extending their inquiries beyond their capacities, and letting their thoughts wander into those depths where they can find no sure footing, it is no wonder that they raise questions and multiply disputes, which, never coming to any clear resolution, are proper only to continue and increase their doubts, and to confirm them at last in perfect scepticism. Whereas, were the capacities of our understandings well considered, the extent of our knowledge once discovered, and the horizon found which sets the bounds between the enlightened and dark parts of things; between what is and what is not comprehensible by us, men would perhaps with less scruple acquiesce in the avowed ignorance of the one, and employ their thoughts and discourse with more advantage and satisfaction in the other.

8. What "Idea" stands for. Thus much I thought necessary to say concerning the occasion of this Inquiry into human Understanding. But, before I proceed on to what I have thought on this subject, I must here in the entrance beg pardon of my reader for the frequent use of the word idea, which he will find in the following treatise. It being that term which, I think, serves best to stand for whatsoever is the object of the understanding when a man thinks, I have used it to express whatever is meant by phantasm, notion, species, or whatever it is which the mind can be employed about in thinking; and I could not avoid frequently using it.

I presume it will be easily granted me, that there are such ideas in men's minds: every one is conscious of them in himself; and men's words and actions will satisfy him that they are in others.

Our first inquiry then shall be,— how they come into the mind.

Chapter II.No Innate Speculative Principles

1. The way shown how we come by any knowledge, sufficient to prove it not innate. It is an established opinion amongst some men, that there are in the understanding certain innate principles; some primary notions, koinai ennoiai, characters, as it were stamped upon the mind of man; which the soul receives in its very first being, and brings into the world with it. It would be sufficient to convince unprejudiced readers of the falseness of this supposition, if I should only show (as I hope I shall in the following parts of this Discourse) how men, barely by the use of their natural faculties, may attain to all the knowledge they have, without the help of any innate impressions; and may arrive at certainty, without any such original notions or principles. For I imagine any one will easily grant that it would be impertinent to suppose the ideas of colours innate in a creature to whom God hath given sight, and a power to receive them by the eyes from external objects: and no less unreasonable would it be to attribute several truths to the impressions of nature, and innate characters, when we may observe in ourselves faculties fit to attain as easy and certain knowledge of them as if they were originally imprinted on the mind.

But because a man is not permitted without censure to follow his own thoughts in the search of truth, when they lead him ever so little out of the common road, I shall set down the reasons that made me doubt of the truth of that opinion, as an excuse for my mistake, if I be in one; which I leave to be considered by those who, with me, dispose themselves to embrace truth wherever they find it.

2. General assent the great argument. There is nothing more commonly taken for granted than that there are certain principles, both speculative and practical, (for they speak of both), universally agreed upon by all mankind: which therefore, they argue, must needs be the constant impressions which the souls of men receive in their first beings, and which they bring into the world with them, as necessarily and really as they do any of their inherent faculties.

3. Universal consent proves nothing innate. This argument, drawn from universal consent, has this misfortune in it, that if it were true in matter of fact, that there were certain truths wherein all mankind agreed, it would not prove them innate, if there can be any other way shown how men may come to that universal agreement, in the things they do consent in, which I presume may be done.

4. "What is, is," and "It is impossible for the same thing to be and not to be," not universally assented to. But, which is worse, this argument of universal consent, which is made use of to prove innate principles, seems to me a demonstration that there are none such: because there are none to which all mankind give an universal assent. I shall begin with the speculative, and instance in those magnified principles of demonstration, "Whatsoever is, is," and "It is impossible for the same thing to be and not to be"; which, of all others, I think have the most allowed title to innate. These have so settled a reputation of maxims universally received, that it will no doubt be thought strange if any one should seem to question it. But yet I take liberty to say, that these propositions are so far from having an universal assent, that there are a great part of mankind to whom they are not so much as known.

5. Not on the mind naturally imprinted, because not known to children, idiots, &c. For, first, it is evident, that all children and idiots have not the least apprehension or thought of them. And the want of that is enough to destroy that universal assent which must needs be the necessary concomitant of all innate truths: it seeming to me near a contradiction to say, that there are truths imprinted on the soul, which it perceives or understands not: imprinting, if it signify anything, being nothing else but the making certain truths to be perceived. For to imprint anything on the mind without the mind's perceiving it, seems to me hardly intelligible. If therefore children and idiots have souls, have minds, with those impressions upon them, they must unavoidably perceive them, and necessarily know and assent to these truths; which since they do not, it is evident that there are no such impressions. For if they are not notions naturally imprinted, how can they be innate? and if they are notions imprinted, how can they be unknown? To say a notion is imprinted on the mind, and yet at the same time to say, that the mind is ignorant of it, and never yet took notice of it, is to make this impression nothing. No proposition can be said to be in the mind which it never yet knew, which it was never yet conscious of. For if any one may, then, by the same reason, all propositions that are true, and the mind is capable ever of assenting to, may be said to be in the mind, and to be imprinted: since, if any one can be said to be in the mind, which it never yet knew, it must be only because it is capable of knowing it; and so the mind is of all truths it ever shall know. Nay, thus truths may be imprinted on the mind which it never did, nor ever shall know; for a man may live long, and die at last in ignorance of many truths which his mind was capable of knowing, and that with certainty. So that if the capacity of knowing be the natural impression contended for, all the truths a man ever comes to know will, by this account, be every one of them innate; and this great point will amount to no more, but only to a very improper way of speaking; which, whilst it pretends to assert the contrary, says nothing different from those who deny innate principles. For nobody, I think, ever denied that the mind was capable of knowing several truths. The capacity, they say, is innate; the knowledge acquired. But then to what end such contest for certain innate maxims? If truths can be imprinted on the understanding without being perceived, I can see no difference there can be between any truths

the mind is capable of knowing in respect of their original: they must all be innate or all adventitious: in vain shall a man go about to distinguish them. He therefore that talks of innate notions in the understanding, cannot (if he intend thereby any distinct sort of truths) mean such truths to be in the understanding as it never perceived, and is yet wholly ignorant of. For if these words "to be in the understanding" have any propriety, they signify to be understood. So that to be in the understanding, and not to be understood; to be in the mind and never to be perceived, is all one as to say anything is and is not in the mind or understanding. If therefore these two propositions, "Whatsoever is, is," and "It is impossible for the same thing to be and not to be," are by nature imprinted, children cannot be ignorant of them: infants, and all that have souls, must necessarily have them in their understandings, know the truth of them, and assent to it.

6. That men know them when they come to the use of reason, answered. To avoid this, it is usually answered, that all men know and assent to them, when they come to the use of reason; and this is enough to prove them innate. I answer:

7. Doubtful expressions, that have scarce any signification, go for clear reasons to those who, being prepossessed, take not the pains to examine even what they themselves say. For, to apply this answer with any tolerable sense to our present purpose, it must signify one of these two things: either that as soon as men come to the use of reason these supposed native inscriptions come to be known and observed by them; or else, that the use and exercise of men's reason, assists them in the discovery of these principles, and certainly makes them known to them.

8. If reason discovered them, that would not prove them innate. If they mean, that by the use of reason men may discover these principles, and that this is sufficient to prove them innate; their way of arguing will stand thus, viz. that whatever truths reason can certainly discover to us, and make us firmly assent to, those are all naturally imprinted on the mind; since that universal assent, which is made the mark of them, amounts to no more but this,— that by the use of reason we are capable to come to a certain knowledge of and assent to them; and, by this means, there will be no difference between the maxims of the mathematicians, and theorems they deduce from them: all must be equally allowed innate; they being all discoveries made by the use of reason, and truths that a rational creature may certainty come to know, if he apply his thoughts rightly that way.

9. It is false that reason discovers them. But how can these men think the use of reason necessary to discover principles that are supposed innate, when reason (if we may believe them) is nothing else but the faculty of deducing unknown truths from principles or propositions that are already known? That certainly can never be thought innate which we have need of reason to discover; unless, as I have said, we will have all the certain truths that reason ever teaches us, to be innate. We may as well think the use of reason necessary to make our eyes discover visible objects, as that there should be need of reason, or the exercise thereof, to make the understanding see what is originally engraven on it, and cannot be in the understanding before it be perceived by it. So that to make reason discover those truths thus imprinted, is to say, that the use of reason discovers to a man what he knew before: and if men have those innate impressed truths originally, and before the use of reason, and yet are always ignorant of them till they come to the use of reason, it is in effect to say, that men know and know them not at the same time.

10. No use made of reasoning in the discovery of these two maxims. It will here perhaps be said that mathematical demonstrations, and other truths that are not innate, are not assented to as soon as proposed, wherein they are distinguished from these maxims and other innate truths. I shall have occasion to speak of assent upon the first proposing, more particularly by and by. I shall here only, and that very readily, allow, that these maxims and mathematical demonstrations are in this different: that the one have need of reason, using of proofs, to make them out and to gain our assent; but the other, as soon as understood, are, without any the least reasoning, embraced and assented to. But I withal beg leave to observe, that it lays open the

weakness of this subterfuge, which requires the use of reason for the discovery of these general truths: since it must be confessed that in their discovery there is no use made of reasoning at all. And I think those who give this answer will not be forward to affirm that the knowledge of this maxim, "That it is impossible for the same thing to be and not to be," is a deduction of our reason. For this would be to destroy that bounty of nature they seem so fond of, whilst they make the knowledge of those principles to depend on the labour of our thoughts. For all reasoning is search, and casting about, and requires pains and application. And how can it with any tolerable sense be supposed, that what was imprinted by nature, as the foundation and guide of our reason, should need the use of reason to discover it?

11. And if there were, this would prove them not innate. Those who will take the pains to reflect with a little attention on the operations of the understanding, will find that this ready assent of the mind to some truths, depends not, either on native inscription, or the use of reason, but on a faculty of the mind quite distinct from both of them, as we shall see hereafter. Reason, therefore, having nothing to do in procuring our assent to these maxims, if by saying, that "men know and assent to them, when they come to the use of reason," be meant, that the use of reason assists us in the knowledge of these maxims, it is utterly false; and were it true, would prove them not to be innate.

12. The coming to the use of reason not the time we come to know these maxims. If by knowing and assenting to them "when we come to the use of reason," be meant, that this is the time when they come to be taken notice of by the mind; and that as soon as children come to the use of reason, they come also to know and assent to these maxims; this also is false and frivolous. First, it is false; because it is evident these maxims are not in the mind so early as the use of reason; and therefore the coming to the use of reason is falsely assigned as the time of their discovery. How many instances of the use of reason may we observe in children, a long time before they have any knowledge of this maxim, "That it is impossible for the same thing to be and not to be?" And a great part of illiterate people and savages pass many years, even of their rational age, without ever thinking on this and the like general propositions. I grant, men come not to the knowledge of these general and more abstract truths, which are thought innate, till they come to the use of reason; and I add, nor then neither. Which is so, because, till after they come to the use of reason, those general abstract ideas are not framed in the mind, about which those general maxims are, which are mistaken for innate principles, but are indeed discoveries made and verities introduced and brought into the mind by the same way, and discovered by the same steps, as several other propositions, which nobody was ever so extravagant as to suppose innate. This I hope to make plain in the sequel of this Discourse. I allow therefore, a necessity that men should come to the use of reason before they get the knowledge of those general truths; but deny that men's coming to the use of reason is the time of their discovery.

13. By this they are not distinguished from other knowable truths. In the mean time it is observable, that this saying, that men know and assent to these maxims "when they come to the use of reason," amounts in reality of fact to no more but this,— that they are never known nor taken notice of before the use of reason, but may possibly be assented to some time after, during a man's life; but when is uncertain. And so may all other knowable truths, as well as these; which therefore have no advantage nor distinction from others by this note of being known when we come to the use of reason; nor are thereby proved to be innate, but quite the contrary.

14. If coming to the use of reason were the time of their discovery it would not prove them innate. But, secondly, were it true that the precise time of their being known and assented to were, when men come to the use of reason; neither would that prove them innate. This way of arguing is as frivolous as the supposition itself is false. For, by what kind of logic will it appear that any notion is originally by nature imprinted in the mind in its first constitution, because it comes first to be observed and assented to when a faculty of the mind, which has quite a distinct province, begins to exert itself? And therefore the coming to the use of speech,

if it were supposed the time that these maxims are first assented to, (which it may be with as much truth as the time when men come to the use of reason,) would be as good a proof that they were innate, as to say they are innate because men assent to them when they come to the use of reason. I agree then with these men of innate principles, that there is no knowledge of these general and self-evident maxims in the mind, till it comes to the exercise of reason: but I deny that the coming to the use of reason is the precise time when they are first taken notice of, and if that were the precise time, I deny that it would prove them innate. All that can with any truth be meant by this proposition, that men "assent to them when they come to the use of reason," is no more but this,— that the making of general abstract ideas, and the understanding of general names, being a concomitant of the rational faculty, and growing up with it, children commonly get not those general ideas, nor learn the names that stand for them, till, having for a good while exercised their reason about familiar and more particular ideas, they are, by their ordinary discourse and actions with others, acknowledged to be capable of rational conversation. If assenting to these maxims, when men come to the use of reason, can be true in any other sense, I desire it may be shown; or at least, how in this, or any other sense, it proves them innate.

15. The steps by which the mind attains several truths. The senses at first let in particular ideas, and furnish the yet empty cabinet, and the mind by degrees growing familiar with some of them, they are lodged in the memory, and names got to them. Afterwards, the mind proceeding further, abstracts them, and by degrees learns the use of general names. In this manner the mind comes to be furnished with ideas and language, the materials about which to exercise its discursive faculty. And the use of reason becomes daily more visible, as these materials that give it employment increase. But though the having of general ideas and the use of general words and reason usually grow together, yet I see not how this any way proves them innate. The knowledge of some truths, I confess, is very early in the mind but in a way that shows them not to be innate. For, if we will observe, we shall find it still to be about ideas, not innate, but acquired; it being about those first which are imprinted by external things, with which infants have earliest to do, which make the most frequent impressions on their senses. In ideas thus got, the mind discovers that some agree and others differ, probably as soon as it has any use of memory; as soon as it is able to retain and perceive distinct ideas. But whether it be then or no, this is certain, it does so long before it has the use of words; or comes to that which we commonly call "the use of reason." For a child knows as certainly before it can speak the difference between the ideas of sweet and bitter (i.e. that sweet is not bitter), as it knows afterwards (when it comes to speak) that wormwood and sugarplums are not the same thing.

16. Assent to supposed innate truths depends on having clear and distinct ideas of what their terms mean, and not on their innateness. A child knows not that three and four are equal to seven, till he comes to be able to count seven, and has got the name and idea of equality; and then, upon explaining those words, he presently assents to, or rather perceives the truth of that proposition. But neither does he then readily assent because it is an innate truth, nor was his assent wanting till then because he wanted the use of reason; but the truth of it appears to him as soon as he has settled in his mind the clear and distinct ideas that these names stand for. And then he knows the truth of that proposition upon the same grounds and by the same means, that he knew before that a rod and a cherry are not the same thing; and upon the same grounds also that he may come to know afterwards "That it is impossible for the same thing to be and not to be," as shall be more fully shown hereafter. So that the later it is before any one comes to have those general ideas about which those maxims are; or to know the signification of those general terms that stand for them; or to put together in his mind the ideas they stand for; the later also will it be before he comes to assent to those maxims;— whose terms, with the ideas they stand for, being no more innate than those of a cat or a weasel, he must stay till time and observation have acquainted him with them; and then he will be in a capacity to know the truth of these maxims, upon the first occasion that shall make him put together those

ideas in his mind, and observe whether they agree or disagree, according as is expressed in those propositions. And therefore it is that a man knows that eighteen and nineteen are equal to thirty-seven, by the same self-evidence that he knows one and two to be equal to three: yet a child knows this not so soon as the other; not for want of the use of reason, but because the ideas the words eighteen, nineteen, and thirty-seven stand for, are not so soon got, as those which are signified by one, two, and three.

17. Assenting as soon as proposed and understood, proves them not innate. This evasion therefore of general assent when men come to the use of reason, failing as it does, and leaving no difference between those suppose innate and other truths that are afterwards acquired and learnt, men have endeavoured to secure an universal assent to those they call maxims, by saying, they are generally assented to as soon as proposed, and the terms they are proposed in understood: seeing all men, even children, as soon as they hear and understand the terms, assent to these propositions, they think it is sufficient to prove them innate. For since men never fail after they have once understood the words, to acknowledge them for undoubted truths, they would infer, that certainly these propositions were first lodged in the understanding, which, without any teaching, the mind, at the very first proposal immediately closes with and assents to, and after that never doubts again.

18. If such an assent be a mark of innate, then "that one and two are equal to three, that sweetness is not bitterness," and a thousand the like, must be innate. In answer to this, I demand whether ready assent given to a proposition, upon first hearing and understanding the terms, be a certain mark of an innate principle? If it be not, such a general assent is in vain urged as a proof of them: if it be said that it is a mark of innate, they must then allow all such propositions to be innate which are generally assented to as soon as heard, whereby they will find themselves plentifully stored with innate principles. For upon the same ground, viz. of assent at first hearing and understanding the terms, that men would have those maxims pass for innate, they must also admit several propositions about numbers to be innate; and thus, that one and two are equal to three, that two and two are equal to four, and a multitude of other the like propositions in numbers, that everybody assents to at first hearing and understanding the terms, must have a place amongst these innate axioms. Nor is this the prerogative of numbers alone, and propositions made about several of them; but even natural philosophy, and all the other sciences, afford propositions which are sure to meet with assent as soon as they are understood. That "two bodies cannot be in the same place" is a truth that nobody any more sticks at than at these maxims, that "it is impossible for the same thing to be and not to be," that "white is not black," that "a square is not a circle," that "bitterness is not sweetness." These and a million of such other propositions, as many at least as we have distinct ideas of, every man in his wits, at first hearing, and knowing what the names stand for, must necessarily assent to. If these men will be true to their own rule, and have assent at first hearing and understanding the terms to be a mark of innate, they must allow not only as many innate propositions as men have distinct ideas, but as many as men can make propositions wherein different ideas are denied one of another. Since every proposition wherein one different idea is denied of another, will as certainly find assent at first hearing and understanding the terms as this general one, "It is impossible for the same thing to be and not to be," or that which is the foundation of it, and is the easier understood of the two, "The same is not different"; by which account they will have legions of innate propositions of this one sort, without mentioning any other. But, since no proposition can be innate unless the ideas about which it is be innate, this will be to suppose all our ideas of colours, sounds, tastes, figure, &c., innate, than which there cannot be anything more opposite to reason and experience. Universal and ready assent upon hearing and understanding the terms is, I grant, a mark of self-evidence; but self-evidence, depending not on innate impressions, but on something else, (as we shall show hereafter,) belongs to several propositions which nobody was yet so extravagant as to pretend to be innate.

19. Such less general propositions known before these universal maxims. Nor let it be said,

that those more particular self-evident propositions, which are assented to at first hearing, as that "one and two are equal to three," that "green is not red," &c., are received as the consequences of those more universal propositions which are looked on as innate principles; since any one, who will but take the pains to observe what passes in the understanding, will certainly find that these, and the like less general propositions, are certainly known, and firmly assented to by those who are utterly ignorant of those more general maxims; and so, being earlier in the mind than those (as they are called) first principles, cannot owe to them the assent wherewith they are received at first hearing.

20. "One and one equal to Two, &c., not general nor useful," answered. If it be said, that these propositions, viz. "two and two are equal to four," "red is not blue," &c., are not general maxims, nor of any great use, I answer, that makes nothing to the argument of universal assent upon hearing and understanding. For, if that be the certain mark of innate, whatever proposition can be found that receives general assent as soon as heard and understood, that must be admitted for an innate proposition, as well as this maxim, "That it is impossible for the same thing to be and not to be," they being upon this ground equal. And as to the difference of being more general, that makes this maxim more remote from being innate; those general and abstract ideas being more strangers to our first apprehensions than those of more particular self-evident propositions; and therefore it is longer before they are admitted and assented to by the growing understanding. And as to the usefulness of these magnified maxims, that perhaps will not be found so great as is generally conceived, when it comes in its due place to be more fully considered.

21. These maxims not being known sometimes till proposed, proves them not innate. But we have not yet done with "assenting to propositions at first hearing and understanding their terms." It is fit we first take notice that this, instead of being a mark that they are innate, is a proof of the contrary; since it supposes that several, who understand and know other things, are ignorant of these principles till they are proposed to them; and that one may be unacquainted with these truths till he hears them from others. For, if they were innate, what need they be proposed in order to gaining assent, when, by being in the understanding, by a natural and original impression, (if there were any such,) they could not but be known before? Or doth the proposing them print them clearer in the mind than nature did? If so, then the consequence will be, that a man knows them better after he has been thus taught them than he did before. Whence it will follow that these principles may be made more evident to us by others' teaching than nature has made them by impression: which will ill agree with the opinion of innate principles, and give but little authority to them; but, on the contrary, makes them unfit to be the foundations of all our other knowledge; as they are pretended to be. This cannot be denied, that men grow first acquainted with many of these self-evident truths upon their being proposed: but it is clear that whosoever does so, finds in himself that he then begins to know a proposition, which he knew not before, and which from thenceforth he never questions; not because it was innate, but because the consideration of the nature of the things contained in those words would not suffer him to think otherwise, how, or whensoever he is brought to reflect on them. And if whatever is assented to at first hearing and understanding the terms must pass for an innate principle, every well-grounded observation, drawn from particulars into a general rule, must be innate. When yet it is certain that not all, but only sagacious heads, light at first on these observations, and reduce them into general propositions: not innate, but collected from a preceding acquaintance and reflection on particular instances. These, when observing men have made them, unobserving men, when they are proposed to them, cannot refuse their assent to.

22. Implicitly known before proposing, signifies that the mind is capable of understanding them, or else signifies nothing. If it be said, the understanding hath an implicit knowledge of these principles, but not an explicit, before this first hearing (as they must who will say "that they are in the understanding before they are known,") it will be hard to conceive what is meant by a principle imprinted on the understanding implicitly, unless it be this,— that the

mind is capable of understanding and assenting firmly to such propositions. And thus all mathematical demonstrations, as well as first principles, must be received as native impressions on the mind; which I fear they will scarce allow them to be, who find it harder to demonstrate a proposition than assent to it when demonstrated. And few mathematicians will be forward to believe, that all the diagrams they have drawn were but copies of those innate characters which nature had engraven upon their minds.

23. The argument of assenting on first hearing, is upon a false supposition of no precedent teaching. There is, I fear, this further weakness in the foregoing argument, which would persuade us that therefore those maxims are to be thought innate, which men admit at first hearing; because they assent to propositions which they are not taught, nor do receive from the force of any argument or demonstration, but a bare explication or understanding of the terms. Under which there seems to me to lie this fallacy, that men are supposed not to be taught nor to learn anything de novo; when, in truth, they are taught, and do learn something they were ignorant of before. For, first, it is evident that they have learned the terms, and their signification; neither of which was born with them. But this is not all the acquired knowledge in the case: the ideas themselves, about which the proposition is, are not born with them, no more than their names, but got afterwards. So that in all propositions that are assented to at first hearing, the terms of the proposition, their standing for such ideas, and the ideas themselves that they stand for, being neither of them innate, I would fain know what there is remaining in such propositions that is innate. For I would gladly have any one name that proposition whose terms or ideas were either of them innate. We by degrees get ideas and names, and learn their appropriated connexion one with another; and then to propositions made in such terms, whose signification we have learnt, and wherein the agreement or disagreement we can perceive in our ideas when put together is expressed, we at first hearing assent; though to other propositions, in themselves as certain and evident, but which are concerning ideas not so soon or so easily got, we are at the same time no way capable of assenting. For, though a child quickly assents to this proposition, "That an apple is not fire," when by familiar acquaintance he has got the ideas of those two different things distinctly imprinted on his mind, and has learnt that the names apple and fire stand for them; yet it will be some years after, perhaps, before the same child will assent to this proposition, "That it is impossible for the same thing to be and not to be"; because that, though perhaps the words are as easy to be learnt, yet the signification of them being more large, comprehensive, and abstract than of the names annexed to those sensible things the child hath to do with, it is longer before he learns their precise meaning, and it requires more time plainly to form in his mind those general ideas they stand for. Till that be done, you will in vain endeavour to make any child assent to a proposition made up of such general terms; but as soon as ever he has got those ideas, and learned their names, he forwardly closes with the one as well as the other of the forementioned propositions: and with both for the same reason; viz. because he finds the ideas he has in his mind to agree or disagree, according as the words standing for them are affirmed or denied one of another in the proposition. But if propositions be brought to him in words which stand for ideas he has not yet in his mind, to such propositions, however evidently true or false in themselves, he affords neither assent nor dissent, but is ignorant. For words being but empty sounds, any further than they are signs of our ideas, we cannot but assent to them as they correspond to those ideas we have, but no further than that. But the showing by what steps and ways knowledge comes into our minds; and the grounds of several degrees of assent, being the business of the following Discourse, it may suffice to have only touched on it here, as one reason that made me doubt of those innate principles.

24. Not innate, because not universally assented to. To conclude this argument of universal consent, I agree with these defenders of innate principles,— that if they are innate, they must needs have universal assent. For that a truth should be innate and yet not assented to, is to me as unintelligible as for a man to know a truth and be ignorant of it at the same time. But then, by these men's own confession, they cannot be innate; since they are not assented to by those

who understand not the terms; nor by a great part of those who do understand them, but have yet never heard nor thought of those propositions; which, I think, is at least one half of mankind. But were the number far less, it would be enough to destroy universal assent, and thereby show these propositions not to be innate, if children alone were ignorant of them.

25. These maxims not the first known. But that I may not be accused to argue from the thoughts of infants, which are unknown to us, and to conclude from what passes in their understandings before they express it; I say next, that these two general propositions are not the truths that first possess the minds of children, nor are antecedent to all acquired and adventitious notions: which, if they were innate, they must needs be. Whether we can determine it or no, it matters not, there is certainly a time when children begin to think, and their words and actions do assure us that they do so. When therefore they are capable of thought, of knowledge, of assent, can it rationally be supposed they can be ignorant of those notions that nature has imprinted, were there any such? Can it be imagined, with any appearance of reason, that they perceive the impressions from things without, and be at the same time ignorant of those characters which nature itself has taken care to stamp within? Can they receive and assent to adventitious notions, and be ignorant of those which are supposed woven into the very principles of their being, and imprinted there in indelible characters, to be the foundation and guide of all their acquired knowledge and future reasonings? This would be to make nature take pains to no purpose; or at least to write very ill; since its characters could not be read by those eyes which saw other things very well: and those are very ill supposed the clearest parts of truth, and the foundations of all our knowledge, which are not first known, and without which the undoubted knowledge of several other things may be had. The child certainly knows, that the nurse that feeds it is neither the cat it plays with, nor the blackmoor it is afraid of: that the wormseed or mustard it refuses, is not the apple or sugar it cries for: this it is certainly and undoubtedly assured of: but will any one say, it is by virtue of this principle, "That it is impossible for the same thing to be and not to be," that it so firmly assents to these and other parts of its knowledge? Or that the child has any notion or apprehension of that proposition at an age, wherein yet, it is plain, it knows a great many other truths? He that will say, children join in these general abstract speculations with their sucking-bottles and their rattles, may perhaps, with justice, be thought to have more passion and zeal for his opinion, but less sincerity and truth, than one of that age.

26. And so not innate. Though therefore there be several general propositions that meet with constant and ready assent, as soon as proposed to men grown up, who have attained the use of more general and abstract ideas, and names standing for them; yet they not being to be found in those of tender years, who nevertheless know other things, they cannot pretend to universal assent of intelligent persons, and so by no means can be supposed innate;— it being impossible that any truth which is innate (if there were any such) should be unknown, at least to any one who knows anything else. Since, if they are innate truths, they must be innate thoughts: there being nothing a truth in the mind that it has never thought on. Whereby it is evident, if there by any innate truths, they must necessarily be the first of any thought on; the first that appear.

27. Not innate, because they appear least where what is innate shows itself clearest. That the general maxims we are discoursing of are not known to children, idiots, and a great part of mankind, we have already sufficiently proved: whereby it is evident they have not an universal assent, nor are general impressions. But there is this further argument in it against their being innate: that these characters, if they were native and original impressions, should appear fairest and clearest in those persons in whom yet we find no footsteps of them; and it is, in my opinion, a strong presumption that they are not innate, since they are least known to those in whom, if they were innate, they must needs exert themselves with most force and vigour. For children, idiots, savages, and illiterate people, being of all others the least corrupted by custom, or borrowed opinions; learning and education having not cast their native thoughts into new moulds; nor by super-inducing foreign and studied doctrines, confounded those fair

characters nature had written there; one might reasonably imagine that in their minds these innate notions should lie open fairly to every one's view, as it is certain the thoughts of children do. It might very well be expected that these principles should be perfectly known to naturals; which being stamped immediately on the soul, (as these men suppose,) can have no dependence on the constitution or organs of the body, the only confessed difference between them and others. One would think, according to these men's principles, that all these native beams of light (were there any such) should, in those who have no reserves, no arts of concealment, shine out in their full lustre, and leave us in no more doubt of their being there, than we are of their love of pleasure and abhorrence of pain. But alas, amongst children, idiots, savages, and the grossly illiterate, what general maxims are to be found? What universal principles of knowledge? Their notions are few and narrow, borrowed only from those objects they have had most to do with, and which have made upon their senses the frequentest and strongest impressions. A child knows his nurse and his cradle, and by degrees the playthings of a little more advanced age; and a young savage has, perhaps, his head filled with love and hunting, according to the fashion of his tribe. But he that from a child untaught, or a wild inhabitant of the woods, will expect these abstract maxims and reputed principles of science, will, I fear, find himself mistaken. Such kind of general propositions are seldom mentioned in the huts of Indians: much less are they to be found in the thoughts of children, or any impressions of them on the minds of naturals. They are the language and business of the schools and academies of learned nations, accustomed to that sort of conversation or learning, where disputes are frequent; these maxims being suited to artificial argumentation and useful for conviction, but not much conducing to the discovery of truth or advancement of knowledge. But of their small use for the improvement of knowledge I shall have occasion to speak more at large, 1. 4, c. 7.

28. Recapitulation. I know not how absurd this may seem to the masters of demonstration. And probably it will hardly go down with anybody at first hearing. I must therefore beg a little truce with prejudice, and the forbearance of censure, till I have been heard out in the sequel of this Discourse, being very willing to submit to better judgments. And since I impartially search after truth, I shall not be sorry to be convinced, that I have been too fond of my own notions; which I confess we are all apt to be, when application and study have warmed our heads with them.

Upon the whole matter, I cannot see any ground to think these two speculative Maxims innate: since they are not universally assented to; and the assent they so generally find is no other than what several propositions, not allowed to be innate, equally partake in with them: and since the assent that is given them is produced another way, and comes not from natural inscription, as I doubt not but to make appear in the following Discourse. And if these "first principles" of knowledge and science are found not to be innate, no other speculative maxims can (I suppose), with better right pretend to be so.

Chapter III.No Innate Practical Principles

1. No moral principles so clear and so generally received as the forementioned speculative maxims. If those speculative Maxims, whereof we discoursed in the foregoing chapter, have not an actual universal assent from all mankind, as we there proved, it is much more visible concerning practical Principles, that they come short of an universal reception: and I think it will be hard to instance any one moral rule which can pretend to so general and ready an assent as, "What is, is"; or to be so manifest a truth as this, that "It is impossible for the same thing to be and not to be." Whereby it is evident that they are further removed from a title to be innate; and the doubt of their being native impressions on the mind is stronger against those moral principles than the other. Not that it brings their truth at all in question. They are equally true, though not equally evident. Those speculative maxims carry their own evidence with

them: but moral principles require reasoning and discourse, and some exercise of the mind, to discover the certainty of their truth. They lie not open as natural characters engraven on the mind; which, if any such were, they must needs be visible by themselves, and by their own light be certain and known to everybody. But this is no derogation to their truth and certainty; no more than it is to the truth or certainty of the three angles of a triangle being equal to two right ones: because it is not so evident as "the whole is bigger than a part," nor so apt to be assented to at first hearing. It may suffice that these moral rules are capable of demonstration: and therefore it is our own faults if we come not to a certain knowledge of them. But the ignorance wherein many men are of them, and the slowness of assent wherewith others receive them, are manifest proofs that they are not innate, and such as offer themselves to their view without searching.

2. Faith and justice not owned as principles by all men. Whether there be any such moral principles, wherein all men do agree, I appeal to any who have been but moderately conversant in the history of mankind, and looked abroad beyond the smoke of their own chimneys. Where is that practical truth that is universally received, without doubt or question, as it must be if innate? Justice, and keeping of contracts, is that which most men seem to agree in. This is a principle which is thought to extend itself to the dens of thieves, and the confederacies of the greatest villains; and they who have gone furthest towards the putting off of humanity itself, keep faith and rules of justice one with another. I grant that outlaws themselves do this one amongst another: but it is without receiving these as the innate laws of nature. They practise them as rules of convenience within their own communities: but it is impossible to conceive that he embraces justice as a practical principle, who acts fairly with his fellow-highwayman, and at the same time plunders or kills the next honest man he meets with. Justice and truth are the common ties of society; and therefore even outlaws and robbers, who break with all the world besides, must keep faith and rules of equity amongst themselves; or else they cannot hold together. But will any one say, that those that live by fraud or rapine have innate principles of truth and justice which they allow and assent to?

3. Objection: "though men deny them in their practice, yet they admit them in their thoughts," answered. Perhaps it will be urged, that the tacit assent of their minds agrees to what their practice contradicts. I answer, first, I have always thought the actions of men the best interpreters of their thoughts. But, since it is certain that most men's practices, and some men's open professions, have either questioned or denied these principles, it is impossible to establish an universal consent, (though we should look for it only amongst grown men,) without which it is impossible to conclude them innate. Secondly, it is very strange and unreasonable to suppose innate practical principles, that terminate only in contemplation. Practical principles, derived from nature, are there for operation, and must produce conformity of action, not barely speculative assent to their truth, or else they are in vain distinguished from speculative maxims. Nature, I confess, has put into man a desire of happiness and an aversion to misery: these indeed are innate practical principles which (as practical principles ought) do continue constantly to operate and influence all our actions without ceasing: these may be observed in all persons and all ages, steady and universal; but these are inclinations of the appetite to good, not impressions of truth on the understanding. I deny not that there are natural tendencies imprinted on the minds of men; and that from the very first instances of sense and perception, there are some things that are grateful and others unwelcome to them; some things that they incline to and others that they fly: but this makes nothing for innate characters on the mind, which are to be the principles of knowledge regulating our practice. Such natural impressions on the understanding are so far from being confirmed hereby, that this is an argument against them; since, if there were certain characters imprinted by nature on the understanding, as the principles of knowledge, we could not but perceive them constantly operate in us and influence our knowledge, as we do those others on the will and appetite; which never cease to be the constant springs and motives of all our actions, to which we perpetually feel them strongly impelling us.

4. Moral rules need a proof, ergo not innate. Another reason that makes me doubt of any innate practical principles is, that I think there cannot any one moral rule be proposed whereof a man may not justly demand a reason: which would be perfectly ridiculous and absurd if they were innate; or so much as self-evident, which every innate principle must needs be, and not need any proof to ascertain its truth, nor want any reason to gain it approbation. He would be thought void of common sense who asked on the one side, or on the other side went to give a reason why "it is impossible for the same thing to be and not to be." It carries its own light and evidence with it, and needs no other proof: he that understands the terms assents to it for its own sake or else nothing will ever be able to prevail with him to do it. But should that most unshaken rule of morality and foundation of all social virtue, "That one should do as he would be done unto," be proposed to one who never heard of it before, but yet is of capacity to understand its meaning; might he not without any absurdity ask a reason why? And were not he that proposed it bound to make out the truth and reasonableness of it to him? Which plainly shows it not to be innate; for if it were it could neither want nor receive any proof; but must needs (at least as soon as heard and understood) be received and assented to as an unquestionable truth, which a man can by no means doubt of. So that the truth of all these moral rules plainly depends upon some other antecedent to them, and from which they must be deduced; which could not be if either they were innate or so much as self-evident.

5. Instance in keeping compacts. That men should keep their compacts is certainly a great and undeniable rule in morality. But yet, if a Christian, who has the view of happiness and misery in another life, be asked why a man must keep his word, he will give this as a reason:— Because God, who has the power of eternal life and death, requires it of us. But if a Hobbist be asked why? he will answer:— Because the public requires it, and the Leviathan will punish you if you do not. And if one of the old philosophers had been asked, he would have answered:— Because it was dishonest, below the dignity of a man, and opposite to virtue, the highest perfection of human nature, to do otherwise.

6. Virtue generally approved, not because innate, but because profitable. Hence naturally flows the great variety of opinions concerning moral rules which are to be found among men, according to the different sorts of happiness they have a prospect of, or propose to themselves; which could not be if practical principles were innate, and imprinted in our minds immediately by the hand of God. I grant the existence of God is so many ways manifest, and the obedience we owe him so congruous to the light of reason, that a great part of mankind give testimony to the law of nature: but yet I think it must be allowed that several moral rules may receive from mankind a very general approbation, without either knowing or admitting the true ground of morality; which can only be the will and law of a God, who sees men in the dark, has in his hand rewards and punishments and power enough to call to account the proudest offender. For, God having, by an inseparable connexion, joined virtue and public happiness together, and made the practice thereof necessary to the preservation of society, and visibly beneficial to all with whom the virtuous man has to do; it is no wonder that every one should not only allow, but recommend and magnify those rules to others, from whose observance of them he is sure to reap advantage to himself He may, out of interest as well as conviction, cry up that for sacred, which, if once trampled on and profaned, he himself cannot be safe nor secure. This, though it takes nothing from the moral and eternal obligation which these rules evidently have, yet it shows that the outward acknowledgment men pay to them in their words proves not that they are innate principles: nay, it proves not so much as that men assent to them inwardly in their own minds, as the inviolable rules of their own practice; since we find that self-interest, and the conveniences of this life, make many men own an outward profession and approbation of them, whose actions sufficiently prove that they very little consider the Lawgiver that prescribed these rules; nor the hell that he has ordained for the punishment of those that transgress them.

7. Men's actions convince us that the rule of virtue is not their internal principle. For, if we will not in civility allow too much sincerity to the professions of most men, but think their

actions to be the interpreters of their thoughts, we shall find that they have no such internal veneration for these rules, nor so full a persuasion of their certainty and obligation. The great principle of morality, "To do as one would be done to," is more commended than practised. But the breach of this rule cannot be a greater vice, than to teach others, that it is no moral rule, nor obligatory, would be thought madness, and contrary to that interest men sacrifice to, when they break it themselves. Perhaps conscience will be urged as checking us for such breaches, and so the internal obligation and establishment of the rule be preserved.

8. Conscience no proof of any innate moral rule. To which I answer, that I doubt not but, without being written on their hearts, many men may, by the same way that they come to the knowledge of other things, come to assent to several moral rules, and be convinced of their obligation. Others also may come to be of the same mind, from their education, company, and customs of their country; which persuasion, however got, will serve to set conscience on work; which is nothing else but our own opinion or judgment of the moral rectitude or pravity of our own actions; and if conscience be a proof of innate principles, contraries may be innate principles; since some men with the same bent of conscience prosecute what others avoid.

9. Instances of enormities practised without remorse. But I cannot see how any men should ever transgress those moral rules, with confidence and serenity, were they innate, and stamped upon their minds. View but an army at the sacking of a town, and see what observation or sense of moral principles, or what touch of conscience for all the outrages they do. Robberies, murders, rapes, are the sports of men set at liberty from punishment and censure. Have there not been whole nations, and those of the most civilized people, amongst whom the exposing their children, and leaving them in the fields to perish by want or wild beasts has been the practice; as little condemned or scrupled as the begetting them? Do they not still, in some countries, put them into the same graves with their mothers, if they die in childbirth; or despatch them, if a pretended astrologer declares them to have unhappy stars? And are there not places where, at a certain age, they kill or expose their parents, without any remorse at all? In a part of Asia, the sick, when their case comes to be thought desperate, are carried out and laid on the earth before they are dead; and left there, exposed to wind and weather, to perish without assistance or pity. It is familiar among the Mingrelians, a people professing Christianity, to bury their children alive without scruple. There are places where they eat their own children. The Caribbees were wont to geld their children, on purpose to fat and eat them. And Garcilasso de la Vega tells us of a people in Peru which were wont to fat and eat the children they got on their female captives, whom they kept as concubines for that purpose, and when they were past breeding, the mothers themselves were killed too and eaten. The virtues whereby the Tououpinambos believed they merited paradise, were revenge, and eating abundance of their enemies. They have not so much as a name for God, and have no religion, no worship. The saints who are canonized amongst the Turks, lead lives which one cannot with modesty relate. A remarkable passage to this purpose, out of the voyage of Baumgarten, which is a book not every day to be met with, I shall set down at large, in the language it is published in. Ibi (sc. prope Belbes in AEgypto) vidimus sanctum unum Saracenicum inter arenarum cumulos, ita ut ex utero matris prodiit nudum sedentem. Mos est, ut didicimus, Mahometistis, ut eos, qui amentes et sine ratione sunt, prosanctis colant et venerentur. Insuper et eos, qui cum diu vitam egerint inquinatissimam, voluntariam demum poenitentiam et paupertatem, sanctitate venerandos deputant. Ejusmodi vero genus hominum libertatem quandam effrenem habent, domos quos volunt intrandi, edendi, bibendi, et quod majus est, concumbendi; ex quo concubitu, si proles secuta fuerit, sancta similiter habetur. His ergo hominibus dum vivunt, magnos exhibent honores; mortuis vero vel templa vel monumenta extruunt amplissima, eosque contingere ac sepelire maximae fortunae ducunt loco. Audivimus haec dicta et dicenda per interpretem a Mucrelo nostro. Insuper sanctum illum, quem eo loco vidimus, publicitus apprime commendari, eum esse hominem sanctum, divinum ac integritate praecipuum; eo quod, nec foeminarum unquam esset, nec puerorum, sed tantummodo asellarum concubitor atque mularum. (Peregr. Baumgarten, l. ii. c. I. p. 73.) More of the same

kind concerning these precious saints amongst the Turks may be seen in Pietro della Valle, in his letter of the 25th of January, 1616.

Where then are those innate principles of justice, piety, gratitude, equity, chastity? Or where is that universal consent that assures us there are such inbred rules? Murders in duels, when fashion has made them honourable, are committed without remorse of conscience: nay, in many places innocence in this case is the greatest ignominy. And if we look abroad to take a view of men as they are, we shall find that they have remorse, in one place, for doing or omitting that which others, in another place, think they merit by.

10. Men have contrary practical principles. He that will carefully peruse the history of mankind, and look abroad into the several tribes of men, and with indifferency survey their actions, will be able to satisfy himself, that there is scarce that principle of morality to be named, or rule of virtue to be thought on, (those only excepted that are absolutely necessary to hold society together, which commonly too are neglected betwixt distinct societies,) which is not, somewhere or other, slighted and condemned by the general fashion of whole societies of men, governed by practical opinions and rules of living quite opposite to others.

11. Whole nations reject several moral rules. Here perhaps it will be objected, that it is no argument that the rule is not known, because it is broken. I grant the objection good where men, though they transgress, yet disown not the law; where fear of shame, censure, or punishment carries the mark of some awe it has upon them. But it is impossible to conceive that a whole nation of men should all publicly reject and renounce what every one of them certainly and infallibly knew to be a law; for so they must who have it naturally imprinted on their minds. It is possible men may sometimes own rules of morality which in their private thoughts they do not believe to be true, only to keep themselves in reputation and esteem amongst those who are persuaded of their obligation. But it is not to be imagined that a whole society of men should publicly and professedly disown and cast off a rule which they could not in their own minds but be infallibly certain was a law; nor be ignorant that all men they should have to do with knew it to be such: and therefore must every one of them apprehend from others all the contempt and abhorrence due to one who professes himself void of humanity: and one who, confounding the known and natural measures of right and wrong, cannot but be looked on as the professed enemy of their peace and happiness. Whatever practical principle is innate, cannot but be known to every one to be just and good. It is therefore little less than a contradiction to suppose, that whole nations of men should, both in their professions and practice, unanimously and universally give the lie to what, by the most invincible evidence, every one of them knew to be true, right, and good. This is enough to satisfy us that no practical rule which is anywhere universally, and with public approbation or allowance, transgressed, can be supposed innate.— But I have something further to add in answer to this objection.

12. The generally allowed breach of a rule, proof that it is not innate. The breaking of a rule, say you, is no argument that it is unknown. I grant it: but the generally allowed breach of it anywhere, I say, is a proof that it is not innate. For example: let us take any of these rules, which, being the most obvious deductions of human reason, and comfortable to the natural inclination of the greatest part of men, fewest people have had the impudence to deny or inconsideration to doubt of. If any can be thought to be naturally imprinted, none, I think, can have a fairer pretence to be innate than this: "Parents, preserve and cherish your children." When, therefore, you say that this is an innate rule, what do you mean? Either that it is an innate principle which upon all occasions excites and directs the actions of all men; or else, that it is a truth which all men have imprinted on their minds, and which therefore they know and assent to. But in neither of these senses is it innate. First, that it is not a principle which influences all men's actions, is what I have proved by the examples before cited: nor need we seek so far as Mingrelia or Peru to find instances of such as neglect, abuse, nay, and destroy their children; or look on it only as the more than brutality of some savage and barbarous nations, when we remember that it was a familiar and uncondemned practice amongst the

Greeks and Romans to expose, without pity or remorse, their innocent infants. Secondly, that it is an innate truth, known to all men, is also false. For, "Parents preserve your children," is so far from an innate truth, that it is no truth at all: it being a command, and not a proposition, and so not capable of truth or falsehood. To make it capable of being assented to as true, it must be reduced to some such proposition as this: "It is the duty of parents to preserve their children." But what duty is, cannot be understood without a law; nor a law be known or supposed without a lawmaker, or without reward and punishment; so that it is impossible that this, or any other, practical principle should be innate, i.e. be imprinted on the mind as a duty, without supposing the ideas of God, of law, of obligation, of punishment, of a life after this, innate: for that punishment follows not in this life the breach of this rule, and consequently that it has not the force of a law in countries where the generally allowed practice runs counter to it, is in itself evident. But these ideas (which must be all of them innate, if anything as a duty be so) are so far from being innate, that it is not every studious or thinking man, much less every one that is born, in whom they are to be found clear and distinct; and that one of them, which of all others seems most likely to be innate, is not so, (I mean the idea of God,) I think, in the next chapter, will appear very evident to any considering man.

13. If men can be ignorant of what is innate, certainty is not described by innate principles. From what has been said, I think we may safely conclude, that whatever practical rule is in any place generally and with allowance broken, cannot be supposed innate; it being impossible that men should, without shame or fear, confidently and serenely, break a rule which they could not but evidently know that God had set up, and would certainly punish the breach of, (which they must, if it were innate,) to a degree to make it a very ill bargain to the transgressor. Without such a knowledge as this, a man can never be certain that anything is his duty. Ignorance or doubt of the law, hopes to escape the knowledge or power of the law-maker, or the like, may make men give way to a present appetite; but let any one see the fault, and the rod by it, and with the transgression, a fire ready to punish it; a pleasure tempting, and the hand of the Almighty visibly held up and prepared to take vengeance, (for this must be the case where any duty is imprinted on the mind,) and then tell me whether it be possible for people with such a prospect, such a certain knowledge as this, wantonly, and without scruple, to offend against a law which they carry about them in indelible characters, and that stares them in the face whilst they are breaking it? Whether men, at the same time that they feel in themselves the imprinted edicts of an Omnipotent Law-maker, can, with assurance and gaiety, slight and trample underfoot his most sacred injunctions? And lastly, whether it be possible that whilst a man thus openly bids defiance to this innate law and supreme Lawgiver, all the bystanders, yea, even the governors and rulers of the people, full of the same sense both of the law and Law-maker, should silently connive, without testifying their dislike or laying the least blame on it? Principles of actions indeed there are lodged in men's appetites; but these are so far from being innate moral principles, that if they were left to their full swing they would carry men to the overturning of all morality. Moral laws are set as a curb and restraint to these exorbitant desires, which they cannot be but by rewards and punishments that will overbalance the satisfaction any one shall propose to himself in the breach of the law. If, therefore, anything be imprinted on the minds of all men as a law, all men must have a certain and unavoidable knowledge that certain and unavoidable punishment will attend the breach of it. For if men can be ignorant or doubtful of what is innate, innate principles are insisted on, and urged to no purpose; truth and certainty (the things pretended) are not at all secured by them; but men are in the same uncertain floating estate with as without them. An evident indubitable knowledge of unavoidable punishment, great enough to make the transgression very uneligible, must accompany an innate law; unless with an innate law they can suppose an innate Gospel too. I would not here be mistaken, as if, because I deny an innate law, I thought there were none but positive laws. There is a great deal of difference between an innate law, and a law of nature; between something imprinted on our minds in their very original, and something that we, being ignorant of, may attain to the knowledge of, by the use and due

application of our natural faculties. And I think they equally forsake the truth who, running into contrary extremes, either affirm an innate law, or deny that there is a law knowable by the light of nature, i.e. without the help of positive revelation.

14. Those who maintain innate practical principles tell us not what they are. The difference there is amongst men in their practical principles is so evident that I think I need say no more to evince, that it will be impossible to find any innate moral rules by this mark of general assent; and it is enough to make one suspect that the supposition of such innate principles is but an opinion taken up at pleasure; since those who talk so confidently of them are so sparing to tell us which they are. This might with justice be expected from those men who lay stress upon this opinion; and it gives occasion to distrust either their knowledge or charity, who, declaring that God has imprinted on the minds of men the foundations of knowledge and the rules of living, are yet so little favourable to the information of their neighbours, or the quiet of mankind, as not to point out to them which they are, in the variety men are distracted with. But, in truth, were there any such innate principles there would be no need to teach them. Did men find such innate propositions stamped on their minds, they would easily be able to distinguish them from other truths that they afterwards learned and deduced from them; and there would be nothing more easy than to know what, and how many, they were. There could be no more doubt about their number than there is about the number of our fingers; and it is like then every system would be ready to give them us by tale. But since nobody, that I know, has ventured yet to give a catalogue of them, they cannot blame those who doubt of these innate principles; since even they who require men to believe that there are such innate propositions, do not tell us what they are. It is easy to foresee, that if different men of different sects should go about to give us a list of those innate practical principles, they would set down only such as suited their distinct hypotheses, and were fit to support the doctrines of their particular schools or churches; a plain evidence that there are no such innate truths. Nay, a great part of men are so far from finding any such innate moral principles in themselves, that, by denying freedom to mankind, and thereby making men no other than bare machines, they take away not only innate, but all moral rules whatsoever, and leave not a possibility to believe any such, to those who cannot conceive how anything can be capable of a law that is not a free agent. And upon that ground they must necessarily reject all principles of virtue, who cannot put morality and mechanism together, which are not very easy to be reconciled or made consistent.

15. Lord Herbert's innate principles examined. When I had written this, being informed that my Lord Herbert had, in his book De Veritate, assigned these innate principles, I presently consulted him, hoping to find in a man of so great parts, something that might satisfy me in this point, and put an end to my inquiry. In his chapter De Instinctu Naturali, p. 72, ed. 1656, I met with these six marks of his Notitiae, Communes:— 1. Prioritas. 2. Independentia. 3. Universalitas. 4. Certitudo. 5. Necessitas, i.e. as he explains it, faciunt ad hominis conservationem. 6. Modus conformationis, i.e. Assensus mulla interposita mora. And at the latter end of his little treatise De Religione Laici, he says this of these innate principles: Adeo ut non uniuscujusvis religionis confinio arctentur quae ubique vigent veritates. Sunt enim in ipsa mente caelitus descriptae, nullisque traditionibus, sive scriptis, sive non scriptis, obnoxiae, p. 3. And Veritates nostrae catholicae, quae tanquam indubia Dei emata inforo interiori descriptae.

Thus, having given the marks of the innate principles or common notions, and asserted their being imprinted on the minds of men by the hand of God, he proceeds to set them down, and they are these: 1. Esse aliquod supremum numen. 2. Numen illud coli debere. 3. Virtutem cum pietate conjunctam optimam esse rationem cultus divini. 4. Resipiscendum esse a peccatis. 5. Dari praemium vel paenam post hanc vitam transactam. Though I allow these to be clear truths, and such as, if rightly explained, a rational creature can hardly avoid giving his assent to, yet I think he is far from proving them innate impressions in foro interiori descriptae. For I must take leave to observe:—

16. These five either not all, or more than all, if there are any. First, that these five propositions are either not all, or more than all, those common notions written on our minds by the finger of God; if it were reasonable to believe any at all to be so written. Since there are other propositions which, even by his own rules, have as just a pretence to such an original, and may be as well admitted for innate principles, as at least some of these five he enumerates, viz. "Do as thou wouldst be done unto." And perhaps some hundreds of others, when well considered.

17. The supposed marks wanting. Secondly, that all his marks are not to be found in each of his five propositions, viz. his first, second, and third marks agree perfectly to neither of them; and the first, second, third, fourth, and sixth marks agree but ill to his third, fourth, and fifth propositions. For, besides that we are assured from history of many men, nay whole nations, who doubt or disbelieve some or all of them, I cannot see how the third, viz. "That virtue joined with piety is the best worship of God," can be an innate principle, when the name or sound virtue, is so hard to be understood; liable to so much uncertainty in its signification; and the thing it stands for so much contended about and difficult to be known. And therefore this cannot be but a very uncertain rule of human practice, and serve but very little to the conduct of our lives, and is therefore very unfit to be assigned as an innate practical principle.

18. Of little use if they were innate. For let us consider this proposition as to its meaning, (for it is the sense, and not sound, that is and must be the principle or common notion,) viz. "Virtue is the best worship of God," i.e. is most acceptable to him; which, if virtue be taken, as most commonly it is, for those actions which, according to the different opinions of several countries, are accounted laudable, will be a proposition so far from being certain, that it will not be true. If virtue be taken for actions conformable to God's will, or to the rule prescribed by God — which is the true and only measure of virtue when virtue is used to signify what is in its own nature right and good — then this proposition, "That virtue is the best worship of God," will be most true and certain, but of very little use in human life: since it will amount to no more but this, viz. "That God is pleased with the doing of what he commands;"— which a man may certainly know to be true, without knowing what it is that God doth command; and so be as far from any rule or principle of his actions as he was before. And I think very few will take a proposition which amounts to no more than this, viz. "That God is pleased with the doing of what he himself commands," for an innate moral principle written on the minds of all men, (however true and certain it may be,) since it teaches so little. Whosoever does so will have reason to think hundreds of propositions innate principles; since there are many which have as good a title as this to be received for such, which nobody yet ever put into that rank of innate principles.

19. Scarce possible that God should engrave principles in words of uncertain meaning. Nor is the fourth proposition (viz."Men must repent of their sins") much more instructive, till what those actions are that are meant by sins be set down. For the word peccata, or sins, being put, as it usually is, to signify in general ill actions that will draw punishment upon the doers, what great principle of morality can that be to tell us we should be sorry, and cease to do that which will bring mischief upon us; without knowing what those particular actions are that will do so? Indeed this is a very true proposition, and fit to be incated on and received by those who are supposed to have been taught what actions in all kinds are sins: but neither this nor the former can be imagined to be innate principles; nor to be of any use if they were innate, unless the particular measures and bounds of all virtues and vices were engraven in men's minds, and were innate principles also, which I think is very much to be doubted. And, therefore, I imagine, it will scarcely seem possible that God should engrave principles in men's minds, in words of uncertain signification, such as virtues and sins, which amongst different men stand for different things: nay, it cannot be supposed to be in words at all, which, being in most of these principles very general, names, cannot be understood but by knowing the particulars comprehended under them. And in the practical instances, the measures must be taken from the knowledge of the actions themselves, and the rules of them,— abstracted from words, and antecedent to the knowledge of names; which rules a man must know, what language soever

he chance to learn, whether English or Japan, or if he should learn no language at all, or never should understand the use of words, as happens in the case of dumb and deaf men. When it shall be made out that men ignorant of words, or untaught by the laws and customs of their country, know that it is part of the worship of God, not to kill another man; not to know more women than one; not to procure abortion; not to expose their children; not to take from another what is his, though we want it ourselves, but on the contrary, relieve and supply his wants; and whenever we have done the contrary we ought to repent, be sorry, and resolve to do so no more;— when I say, all men shall be proved actually to know and allow all these and a thousand other such rules, all of which come under these two general words made use of above, viz. virtutes et peccata, virtues and sins, there will be more reason for admitting these and the like, for common notions and practical principles. Yet, after all, universal consent (were there any in moral principles) to truths, the knowledge whereof may be attained otherwise, would scarce prove them to be innate; which is all I contend for.

20. Objection, "innate principles may be corrupted," answered. Nor will it be of much moment here to offer that very ready but not very material answer, viz. that the innate principles of morality may, by education, and custom, and the general opinion of those amongst whom we converse, be darkened, and at last quite worn out of the minds of men. Which assertion of theirs, if true, quite takes away the argument of universal consent, by which this opinion of innate principles is endeavoured to be proved; unless those men will think it reasonable that their private persuasions, or that of their party, should pass for universal consent;— a thing not unfrequently done, when men, presuming themselves to be the only masters of right reason, cast by the votes and opinions of the rest of mankind as not worthy the reckoning. And then their argument stands thus:—"The principles which all mankind allow for true, are innate; those that men of right reason admit, are the principles allowed by all mankind; we, and those of our mind, are men of reason; therefore, we agreeing, our principles are innate;"— which is a very pretty way of arguing, and a short cut to infallibility. For otherwise it will be very hard to understand how there be some principles which all men do acknowledge and agree in; and yet there are none of those principles which are not, by depraved custom and ill education, blotted out of the minds of many men: which is to say, that all men admit, but yet many men do deny and dissent from them. And indeed the supposition of such first principles will serve us to very little purpose; and we shall be as much at a loss with as without them, if they may, by any human power — such as the will of our teachers, or opinions of our companions — be altered or lost in us: and notwithstanding all this boast of first principles and innate light, we shall be as much in the dark and uncertainty as if there were no such thing at all: it being all one to have no rule, and one that will warp any way; or amongst various and contrary rules, not to know which is the right. But concerning innate principles, I desire these men to say, whether they can or cannot, by education and custom, be blurred and blotted out; if they cannot, we must find them in all mankind alike, and they must be clear in everybody; and if they may suffer variation from adventitious notions, we must then find them clearest and most perspicuous nearest the fountain, in children and illiterate people, who have received least impression from foreign opinions. Let them take which side they please, they will certainly find it inconsistent with visible matter of fact and daily observation.

21. Contrary principles in the world. I easily grant that there are great numbers of opinions which, by men of different countries, educations, and tempers, are received and embraced as first and unquestionable principles; many whereof, both for their absurdity as well as oppositions to one another, it is impossible should be true. But yet all those propositions, how remote soever from reason, are so sacred somewhere or other, that men even of good understanding in other matters, will sooner part with their lives, and whatever is dearest to them, than suffer themselves to doubt, or others to question, the truth of them.

22. How men commonly come by their principles. This, however strange it may seem, is that which every day's experience confirms; and will not, perhaps, appear so wonderful, if we consider the ways and steps by which it is brought about; and how really it may come to pass,

that doctrines that have been derived from no better original than the superstition of a nurse, or the authority of an old woman, may, by length of time and consent of neighbours, grow up to the dignity of principles in religion or morality. For such, who are careful (as they call it) to principle children well, (and few there be who have not a set of those principles for them, which they believe in,) instil into the unwary, and as yet unprejudiced, understanding, (for white paper receives any characters,) those doctrines they would have them retain and profess. These being taught them as soon as they have any apprehension; and still as they grow up confirmed to them, either by the open profession or tacit consent of all they have to do with; or at least by those of whose wisdom, knowledge, and piety they have an opinion, who never suffer those propositions to be otherwise mentioned but as the basis and foundation on which they build their religion and manners, come, by these means, to have the reputation of unquestionable, self-evident, and innate truths.

23. Principles supposed innate because we do not remember when we began to hold them. To which we may add, that when men so instructed are grown up, and reflect on their own minds, they cannot find anything more ancient there than those opinions, which were taught them before their memory began to keep a register of their actions, or date the time when any new thing appeared to them; and therefore make no scruple to conclude, that those propositions of whose knowledge they can find in themselves no original, were certainly the impress of God and nature upon their minds, and not taught them by any one else. These they entertain and submit to, as many do to their parents with veneration; not because it is natural; nor do children do it where they are not so taught; but because, having been always so educated, and having no remembrance of the beginning of this respect, they think it is natural.

24. How such principles come to be held. This will appear very likely, and almost unavoidable to come to pass, if we consider the nature of mankind and the constitution of human affairs; wherein most men cannot live without employing their time in the daily labours of their callings; nor be at quiet in their minds without some foundation or principle to rest their thoughts on. There is scarcely any one so floating and superficial in his understanding, who hath not some reverenced propositions, which are to him the principles on which he bottoms his reasonings, and by which he judgeth of truth and falsehood, right and wrong; which some, wanting skill and leisure, and others the inclination, and some being taught that they ought not to examine, there are few to be found who are not exposed by their ignorance, laziness, education, or precipitancy, to take them upon trust.

25. Further explained. This is evidently the case of all children and young folk; and custom, a greater power than nature, seldom failing to make them worship for divine what she hath inured them to bow their minds and submit their understandings to, it is no wonder that grown men, either perplexed in the necessary affairs of life, or hot in the pursuit of pleasures, should not seriously sit down to examine their own tenets; especially when one of their principles is, that principles ought not to be questioned. And had men leisure, parts, and will, who is there almost that dare shake the foundations of all his past thoughts and actions, and endure to bring upon himself the shame of having been a long time wholly in mistake and error? Who is there hardy enough to contend with the reproach which is everywhere prepared for those who dare venture to dissent from the received opinions of their country or party? And where is the man to be found that can patiently prepare himself to bear the name of whimsical, sceptical, or atheist; which he is sure to meet with, who does in the least scruple any of the common opinions? And he will be much more afraid to question those principles, when he shall think them, as most men do, the standards set up by God in his mind, to be the rule and touchstone of all other opinions. And what can hinder him from thinking them sacred, when he finds them the earliest of all his own thoughts, and the most reverenced by others?

26. A worship of idols. It is easy to imagine how, by these means, it comes to pass than men worship the idols that have been set up in their minds; grow fond of the notions they have been long acquainted with there; and stamp the characters of divinity upon absurdities and errors; become zealous votaries to bulls and monkeys, and contend too, fight, and die in defence of

their opinions. Dum solos credit habendos esse deos, quos ipse colit. For, since the reasoning faculties of the soul, which are almost constantly, though not always warily nor wisely employed, would not know how to move, for want of a foundation and footing, in most men, who through laziness or avocation do not, or for want of time, or true helps, or for other causes, cannot penetrate into the principles of knowledge, and trace truth to its fountain and original, it is natural for them, and almost unavoidable, to take up with some borrowed principles; which being reputed and presumed to be the evident proofs of other things, are thought not to need any other proof themselves. Whoever shall receive any of these into his mind, and entertain them there with the reverence usually paid to principles, never venturing to examine them, but accustoming himself to believe them, because they are to be believed, may take up, from his education and the fashions of his country, any absurdity for innate principles; and by long poring on the same objects, so dim his sight as to take monsters lodged in his own brain for the images of the Deity, and the workmanship of his hands.

27. Principles must be examined. By this progress, how many there are who arrive at principles which they believe innate may be easily observed, in the variety of opposite principles held and contended for by all sorts and degrees of men. And he that shall deny this to be the method wherein most men proceed to the assurance they have of the truth and evidence of their principles, will perhaps find it a hard matter any other way to account for the contrary tenets, which are firmly believed, confidently asserted, and which great numbers are ready at any time to seal with their blood. And, indeed, if it be the privilege of innate principles to be received upon their own authority, without examination, I know not what may not be believed, or how any one's principles can be questioned. If they may and ought to be examined and tried, I desire to know how first and innate principles can be tried; or at least it is reasonable to demand the marks and characters whereby the genuine innate principles may be distinguished from others: that so, amidst the great variety of pretenders, I may be kept from mistakes in so material a point as this. When this is done, I shall be ready to embrace such welcome and useful propositions; and till then I may with modesty doubt; since I fear universal consent, which is the only one produced, will scarcely prove a sufficient mark to direct my choice, and assure me of any innate principles.

From what has been said, I think it past doubt, that there are no practical principles wherein all men agree; and therefore none innate.

Chapter IV. Other considerations concerning Innate Principles, both Speculative and Practical

1. Principles not innate, unless their ideas be innate. Had those who would persuade us that there are innate principles not taken them together in gross, but considered separately the parts out of which those propositions are made, they would not, perhaps, have been so forward to believe they were innate. Since, if the ideas which made up those truths were not, it was impossible that the propositions made up of them should be innate, or our knowledge of them be born with us. For, if the ideas be not innate, there was a time when the mind was without those principles; and then they will not be innate, but be derived from some other original. For, where the ideas themselves are not, there can be no knowledge, no assent, no mental or verbal propositions about them.

2. Ideas, especially those belonging to principles, not born with children. If we will attentively consider new-born children, we shall have little reason to think that they bring many ideas into the world with them. For, bating perhaps some faint ideas of hunger, and thirst, and warmth, and some pains, which they may have felt in the womb, there is not the least appearance of any settled ideas at all in them; especially of ideas answering the terms which make up those universal propositions that are esteemed innate principles. One may perceive how, by degrees, afterwards, ideas come into their minds; and that they get no more, nor other, than what

experience, and the observation of things that come in their way, furnish them with; which might be enough to satisfy us that they are not original characters stamped on the mind.

3. "Impossibility" and "identity" not innate ideas. "It is impossible for the same thing to be, and not to be," is certainly (if there be any such) an innate principle. But can any one think, or will any one say, that "impossibility" and "identity" are two innate ideas? Are they such as all mankind have, and bring into the world with them? And are they those which are the first in children, and antecedent to all acquired ones? If they are innate, they must needs be so. Hath a child an idea of impossibility and identity, before it has of white or black, sweet or bitter? And is it from the knowledge of this principle that it concludes, that wormwood rubbed on the nipple hath not the same taste that it used to receive from thence? Is it the actual knowledge of impossible est idem esse, et non esse, that makes a child distinguish between its mother and a stranger; or that makes it fond of the one and flee the other? Or does the mind regulate itself and its assent by ideas that it never yet had? Or the understanding draw conclusions from principles which it never yet knew or understood? The names impossibility and identity stand for two ideas, so far from being innate, or born with us, that I think it requires great care and attention to form them right in our understandings. They are so far from being brought into the world with us, so remote from the thoughts of infancy and childhood, that I believe, upon examination it will be found that many grown men want them.

4. "Identity," an idea not innate. If identity (to instance that alone) be a native impression, and consequently so clear and obvious to us that we must needs know it even from our cradles, I would gladly be resolved by any one of seven, or seventy years old, whether a man, being a creature consisting of soul and body, be the same man when his body is changed? Whether Euphorbus and Pythagoras, having had the same soul, were the same men, though they lived several ages asunder? Nay, whether the cock too, which had the same soul, were not the same with both of them? Whereby, perhaps, it will appear that our idea of sameness is not so settled and clear as to deserve to be thought innate in us. For if those innate ideas are not clear and distinct, so as to be universally known and naturally agreed on, they cannot be subjects of universal and undoubted truths, but will be the unavoidable occasion of perpetual uncertainty. For, I suppose every one's idea of identity will not be the same that Pythagoras and thousands of his followers have. And which then shall be true? Which innate? Or are there two different ideas of identity, both innate?

5. What makes the same man? Nor let any one think that the questions I have here proposed about the identity of man are bare empty speculations; which, if they were, would be enough to show, that there was in the understandings of men no innate idea of identity. He that shall with a little attention reflect on the resurrection, and consider that divine justice will bring to judgment, at the last day, the very same persons, to be happy or miserable in the other, who did well or ill in this life, will find it perhaps not easy to resolve with himself, what makes the same man, or wherein identity consists; and will not be forward to think he, and every one, even children themselves, have naturally a clear idea of it.

6. Whole and part, not innate ideas. Let us examine that principle of mathematics, viz. that the whole is bigger than a part. This, I take it, is reckoned amongst innate principles. I am sure it has as good a title as any to be thought so; which yet nobody can think it to be, when he considers [that] the ideas it comprehends in it, whole and part, are perfectly relative; but the positive ideas to which they properly and immediately belong are extension and number, of which alone whole and part are relations. So that if whole and part are innate ideas, extension and number must be so too; it being impossible to have an idea of a relation, without having any at all of the thing to which it belongs, and in which it is founded. Now, whether the minds of men have naturally imprinted on them the ideas of extension and number, I leave to be considered by these who are the patrons of innate principles.

7. Idea of worship not innate. That God is to be worshipped, is, without doubt, as great a truth as any that can enter into the mind of man, and deserves the first place amongst all practical principles. But yet it can by no means be thought innate, unless the ideas of God and worship

are innate. That the idea the term worship stands for is not in the understanding of children, and a character stamped on the mind in its first original, I think will be easily granted, by any one that considers how few there be amongst grown men who have a clear and distinct notion of it. And, I suppose, there cannot be anything more ridiculous than to say, that children have this practical principle innate, "That God is to be worshipped," and yet that they know not what that worship of God is, which is their duty. But to pass by this.

8. Idea of God not innate. If any idea can be imagined innate, the idea of God may, of all others, for many reasons, be thought so; since it is hard to conceive how there should be innate moral principles, without an innate idea of a Deity. Without a notion of a law-maker, it is impossible to have a notion of a law, and an obligation to observe it. Besides the atheists taken notice of amongst the ancients, and left branded upon the records of history, hath not navigation discovered, in these later ages, whole nations, at the bay of Soldania, in Brazil, [in Boranday,] and in the Caribbee islands, &c., amongst whom there was to be found no notion of a God, no religion? Nicholaus del Techo, in Literis ex Paraquaria, de Caiguarum Conversione, has these words: Reperi eam gentem nullum nomen habere quod Deum, et hominis animam significet; nulla sacra habet, nulla idola. These are instances of nations where uncultivated nature has been left to itself, without the help of letters and discipline, and the improvements of arts and sciences. But there are others to be found who have enjoyed these in a very great measure, who yet, for want of a due application of their thoughts this way, want the idea and knowledge of God. It will, I doubt not, be a surprise to others, as it was to me, to find the Siamites of this number. But for this, let them consult the King of France's late envoy thither, who gives no better account of the Chinese themselves. And if we will not believe La Loubere, the missionaries of China, even the Jesuits themselves, the great encomiasts of the Chinese, do all to a man agree, and will convince us, that the sect of the literari, or learned, keeping to the old religion of China, and the ruling party there, are all of them atheists. Vid. Navarette, in the Collection of Voyages, vol. i., and Historia Cultus Sinensium. And perhaps, if we should with attention mind the lives and discourses of people not so far off, we should have too much reason to fear, that many, in more civilized countries, have no very strong and clear impressions of a Deity upon their minds, and that the complaints of atheism made from the pulpit are not without reason. And though only some profligate wretches own it too barefacedly now; yet perhaps we should hear more than we do of it from others, did not the fear of the magistrate's sword, or their neighbour's censure, tie up people's tongues; which, were the apprehensions of punishment or shame taken away, would as openly proclaim their atheism as their lives do.

9. The name of God not universal or obscure in meaning. But had all mankind everywhere a notion of a God, (whereof yet history tells us the contrary,) it would not from thence follow, that the idea of him was innate. For, though no nation were to be found without a name, and some few dark notions of him, yet that would not prove them to be natural impressions on the mind; no more than the names of fire, or the sun, heat, or number, do prove the ideas they stand for to be innate; because the names of those things, and the ideas of them, are so universally received and known amongst mankind. Nor, on the contrary, is the want of such a name, or the absence of such a notion out of men's minds, any argument against the being of a God; any more than it would be a proof that there was no loadstone in the world, because a great part of mankind had neither a notion of any such thing nor a name for it; or be any show of argument to prove that there are no distinct and various species of angels, or intelligent beings above us, because we have no ideas of such distinct species, or names for them. For, men being furnished with words, by the common language of their own countries, can scarce avoid having some kind of ideas of those things whose names those they converse with have occasion frequently to mention to them. And if they carry with it the notion of excellency, greatness, or something extraordinary; if apprehension and concernment accompany it; if the fear of absolute and irresistible power set it on upon the mind,— the idea is likely to sink the deeper, and spread the further; especially if it be such an idea as is agreeable to the common

light of reason, and naturally deducible from every part of our knowledge, as that of a God is. For the visible marks of extraordinary wisdom and power appear so plainly in all the works of the creation, that a rational creature, who will but seriously reflect on them, cannot miss the discovery of a Deity. And the influence that the discovery of such a Being must necessarily have on the minds of all that have but once heard of it is so great, and carries such a weight of thought and communication with it, that it seems stranger to me that a whole nation of men should be anywhere found so brutish as to want the notion of a God, than that they should be without any notion of numbers, or fire.

10. Ideas of God and idea of fire. The name of God being once mentioned in any part of the world, to express a superior, powerful, wise, invisible Being, the suitableness of such a notion to the principles of common reason, and the interest men will always have to mention it often, must necessarily spread it far and wide; and continue it down to all generations: though yet the general reception of this name, and some imperfect and unsteady notions conveyed thereby to the unthinking part of mankind, prove not the idea to be innate; but only that they who made the discovery had made a right use of their reason, thought maturely of the causes of things, and traced them to their original; from whom other less considering people having once received so important a notion, it could not easily be lost again.

11. Idea of God not innate. This is all could be inferred from the notion of a God, were it to be found universally in all the tribes of mankind, and generally acknowledged, by men grown to maturity in all countries. For the generality of the acknowledging of a God, as I imagine, is extended no further than that; which, if it be sufficient to prove the idea of God innate, will as well prove the idea of fire innate; since I think it may be truly said, that there is not a person in the world who has a notion of a God, who has not also the idea of fire. I doubt not but if a colony of young children should be placed in an island where no fire was, they would certainly neither have any notion of such a thing, nor name for it, how generally soever it were received and known in all the world besides; and perhaps too their apprehensions would be as far removed from any name, or notion, of a God, till some one amongst them had employed his thoughts to inquire into the constitution and causes of things, which would easily lead him to the notion of a God; which having once taught to others, reason, and the natural propensity of their own thoughts, would afterwards propagate, and continue amongst them.

12. Suitable to God's goodness, that all men should have an idea of Him, therefore naturally imprinted by Him, answered. Indeed it is urged, that it is suitable to the goodness of God, to imprint upon the minds of men characters and notions of himself, and not to leave them in the dark and doubt in so grand a concernment; and also, by that means, to secure to himself the homage and veneration due from so intelligent a creature as man; and therefore he has done it. This argument, if it be of any force, will prove much more than those who use it in this case expect from it. For, if we may conclude that God hath done for men all that men shall judge is best for them, because it is suitable to his goodness so to do, it will prove, not only that God has imprinted on the minds of men an idea of himself, but that he hath plainly stamped there, in fair characters, all that men ought to know or believe of him; all that they ought to do in obedience to his will; and that he hath given them a will and affections conformable to it. This, no doubt, every one will think better for men, than that they should, in the dark, grope after knowledge, as St. Paul tells us all nations did after God (Acts 17. 27); than that their wills should clash with their understandings, and their appetites cross their duty. The Romanists say it is best for men, and so suitable to the goodness of God, that there should be an infallible judge of controversies on earth; and therefore there is one. And I, by the same reason, say it is better for men that every man himself should be infallible. I leave them to consider, whether, by the force of this argument, they shall think that every man is so. I think it a very good argument to say,— the infinitely wise God hath made it so; and therefore it is best. But it seems to me a little too much confidence of our own wisdom to say,—"I think it best; and therefore God hath made it so." And in the matter in hand, it will be in vain to argue from such a topic, that God hath done so, when certain experience shows us that he hath not. But the

goodness of God hath not been wanting to men, without such original impressions of knowledge or ideas stamped on the mind; since he hath furnished man with those faculties which will serve for the sufficient discovery of all things requisite to the end of such a being; and I doubt not but to show, that a man, by the right use of his natural abilities, may, without any innate principles, attain a knowledge of a God, and other things that concern him. God having endued man with those faculties of knowledge which he hath, was no more obliged by his goodness to plant those innate notions in his mind, than that, having given him reason, hands, and materials, he should build him bridges or houses,— which some people in the world, however of good parts, do either totally want, or are but ill provided of, as well as others are wholly without ideas of God and principles of morality, or at least have but very ill ones; the reason in both cases, being, that they never employed their parts, faculties, and powers industriously that way, but contented themselves with the opinions, fashions, and things of their country, as they found them, without looking any further. Had you or I been born at the Bay of Soldania, possibly our thoughts and notions had not exceeded those brutish ones of the Hottentots that inhabit there. And had the Virginia king Apochancana been educated in England, he had been perhaps as knowing a divine, and as good a mathematician as any in it; the difference between him and a more improved Englishman lying barely in this, that the exercise of his faculties was bounded within the ways, modes, and notions of his own country, and never directed to any other or further inquiries. And if he had not any idea of a God, it was only because he pursued not those thoughts that would have led him to it.

13. Ideas of God various in different men. I grant that if there were any ideas to be found imprinted on the minds of men, we have reason to expect it should be the notion of his Maker, as a mark God set on his own workmanship, to mind man of his dependence and duty; and that herein should appear the first instances of human knowledge. But how late is it before any such notion is discoverable in children? And when we find it there, how much more does it resemble the opinion and notion of the teacher, than represent the true God? He that shall observe in children the progress whereby their minds attain the knowledge they have, will think that the objects they do first and most familiarly converse with are those that make the first impressions on their understandings; nor will he find the least footsteps of any other. It is easy to take notice how their thoughts enlarge themselves, only as they come to be acquainted with a greater variety of sensible objects; to retain the ideas of them in their memories; and to get the skill to compound and enlarge them, and several ways put them together. How, by these means, they come to frame in their minds an idea men have of a Deity, I shall hereafter show.

14. Contrary and inconsistent ideas of God under the same name. Can it be thought that the ideas men have of God are the characters and marks of himself, engraven in their minds by his own finger, when we see that, in the same country, under one and the same name, men have far different, nay often contrary and inconsistent ideas and conceptions of him? Their agreeing in a name, or sound, will scarce prove an innate notion of him.

15. Gross ideas of God. What true or tolerable notion of a Deity could they have, who acknowledged and worshipped hundreds? Every deity that they owned above one was an infallible evidence of their ignorance of Him, and a proof that they had no true notion of God, where unity, infinity, and eternity were excluded. To which, if we add their gross conceptions of corporeity, expressed in their images and representations of their deities; the amours, marriages, copulations, lusts, quarrels, and other mean qualities attributed by them to their gods; we shall have little reason to think that the heathen world, i.e. the greatest part of mankind, had such ideas of God in their minds as he himself, out of care that they should not be mistaken about him, was author of. And this universality of consent, so much argued, if it prove any native impressions, it will be only this:— that God imprinted on the minds of all men speaking the same language, a name for himself, but not any idea; since those people who agreed in the name, had, at the same time, far different apprehensions about the thing signified. If they say that the variety of deities worshipped by the heathen world were but

figurative ways of expressing the several attributes of that incomprehensible Being, or several parts of his providence, I answer: what they might be in the original I will not here inquire; but that they were so in the thoughts of the vulgar I think nobody will affirm. And he that will consult the voyage of the Bishop of Beryte, c. 13, (not to mention other testimonies,) will find that the theology of the Siamites professedly owns a plurality of gods: or, as the Abbe de Choisy more judiciously remarks in his Journal du Voyage de Siam, 107/177, it consists properly in acknowledging no God at all.

16. Idea of God not innate although wise men of all nations come to have it. If it be said, that wise men of all nations came to have true conceptions of the unity and infinity of the Deity, I grant it. But then this,

First, excludes universality of consent in anything but the name; for those wise men being very few, perhaps one of a thousand, this universality is very narrow.

Secondly, it seems to me plainly to prove, that the truest and best notions men have of God were not imprinted, but acquired by thought and meditation, and a right use of their faculties: since the wise and considerate men of the world, by a right and careful employment of their thoughts and reason, attained true notions in this as well as other things; whilst the lazy and inconsiderate part of men, making far the greater number, took up their notions by chance, from common tradition and vulgar conceptions, without much beating their heads about them. And if it be a reason to think the notion of God innate, because all wise men had it, virtue too must be thought innate; for that also wise men have always had.

17. Odd, low, and pitiful ideas of God common among men. This was evidently the case of all Gentilism. Nor hath even amongst Jews, Christians, and Mahometans, who acknowledged but one God, this doctrine, and the care taken in those nations to teach men to have true notions of a God, prevailed so far as to make men to have the same and the true ideas of him. How many even amongst us, will be found upon inquiry to fancy him in the shape of a man sitting in heaven; and to have many other absurd and unfit conceptions of him? Christians as well as Turks have had whole sects owning and contending earnestly for it,— that the Deity was corporeal, and of human shape: and though we find few now amongst us who profess themselves Anthropomorphites, (though some I have met with that own it,) yet I believe he that will make it his business may find amongst the ignorant and uninstructed Christians many of that opinion. Talk but with country people, almost of any age, or young people almost of any condition, and you shall find that, though the name of God be frequently in their mouths, yet the notions they apply this name to are so odd, low, and pitiful, that nobody can imagine they were taught by a rational man; much less that they were characters written by the finger of God himself. Nor do I see how it derogates more from the goodness of God, that he has given us minds unfurnished with these ideas of himself, than that he hath sent us into the world with bodies unclothed; and that there is no art or skill born with us. For, being fitted with faculties to attain these, it is want of industry and consideration in us, and not of bounty in him, if we have them not. It is as certain that there is a God, as that the opposite angles made by the intersection of two straight lines are equal. There was never any rational creature that set himself sincerely to examine the truth of these propositions that could fail to assent to them; though yet it be past doubt that there are many men, who, having not applied their thoughts that way, are ignorant both of the one and the other. If any one think fit to call this (which is the utmost of its extent) universal consent, such an one I easily allow; but such an universal consent as this proves not the idea of God, any more than it does the idea of such angles, innate.

18. If the idea of God be not innate, no other can be supposed innate. Since then though the knowledge of a God be the most natural discovery of human reason, yet the idea of him is not innate, as I think is evident from what has been said; I imagine there will be scarce any other idea found that can pretend to it. Since if God hath set any impression, any character, on the understanding of men, it is most reasonable to expect it should have been some clear and uniform idea of Himself; as far as our weak capacities were capable to receive so

incomprehensible and infinite an object. But our minds being at first void of that idea which we are most concerned to have, it is a strong presumption against all other innate characters. I must own, as far as I can observe, I can find none, and would be glad to be informed by any other.

19. Idea of substance not innate. I confess there is another idea which would be of general use for mankind to have, as it is of general talk as if they had it; and that is the idea of substance; which we neither have nor can have by sensation or reflection. If nature took care to provide us any ideas, we might well expect they should be such as by our own faculties we cannot procure to ourselves; but we see, on the contrary, that since, by those ways whereby other ideas are brought into our minds, this is not, we have no such clear idea at all; and therefore signify nothing by the word substance but only an uncertain supposition of we know not what, i.e. of something whereof we have no [particular distinct positive] idea, which we take to be the substratum, or support, of those ideas we do know.

20. No propositions can be innate, since no ideas are innate. Whatever then we talk of innate, either speculative or practical, principles, it may with as much probability be said, that a man hath L100 sterling in his pocket, and yet denied that he hath there either penny, shilling, crown, or other coin out of which the sum is to be made up; as to think that certain propositions are innate when the ideas about which they are can by no means be supposed to be so. The general reception and assent that is given doth not at all prove, that the ideas expressed in them are innate; for in many cases, however the ideas came there, the assent to words expressing the agreement or disagreement of such ideas, will necessarily follow. Every one that hath a true idea of God and worship, will assent to this proposition, "That God is to be worshipped," when expressed in a language he understands; and every rational man that hath not thought on it to-day, may be ready to assent to this proposition to-morrow; and yet millions of men may be well supposed to want one or both those ideas to-day. For, if we will allow savages, and most country people, to have ideas of God and worship, (which conversation with them will not make one forward to believe,) yet I think few children can be supposed to have those ideas, which therefore they must begin to have some time or other; and then they will also begin to assent to that proposition, and make very little question of it ever after. But such an assent upon hearing, no more proves the ideas to be innate, than it does that one born blind (with cataracts which will be couched to-morrow) had the innate ideas of the sun, or light, or saffron, or yellow; because, when his sight is cleared, he will certainly assent to this proposition, "That the sun is lucid, or that saffron is yellow." And therefore, if such an assent upon hearing cannot prove the ideas innate, it can much less the propositions made up of those ideas. If they have any innate ideas, I would be glad to be told what, and how many, they are.

21. No innate ideas in the memory. To which let me add: if there be any innate ideas, any ideas in the mind which the mind does not actually think on, they must be lodged in the memory; and from thence must be brought into view by remembrance; i.e. must be known, when they are remembered, to have been perceptions in the mind before; unless remembrance can be without remembrance. For, to remember is to perceive anything with memory, or with a consciousness that it was perceived or known before. Without this, whatever idea comes into the mind is new, and not remembered; this consciousness of its having been in the mind before, being that which distinguishes remembering from all other ways of thinking. Whatever idea was never perceived by the mind was never in the mind. Whatever idea is in the mind, is, either an actual perception, or else, having been an actual perception, is so in the mind that, by the memory, it can be made an actual perception again. Whenever there is the actual perception of any idea without memory, the idea appears perfectly new and unknown before to the understanding. Whenever the memory brings any idea into actual view, it is with a consciousness that it had been there before, and was not wholly a stranger to the mind. Whether this be not so, I appeal to every one's observation. And then I desire an instance of an idea, pretended to be innate, which (before any impression of it by ways hereafter to be

mentioned) any one could revive and remember, as an idea he had formerly known; without which consciousness of a former perception there is no remembrance; and whatever idea comes into the mind without that consciousness is not remembered, or comes not out of the memory, nor can be said to be in the mind before that appearance. For what is not either actually in view or in the memory, is in the mind no way at all, and is all one as if it had never been there. Suppose a child had the use of his eyes till he knows and distinguishes colours; but then cataracts shut the windows, and he is forty or fifty years perfectly in the dark; and in that time perfectly loses all memory of the ideas of colours he once had. This was the case of a blind man I once talked with, who lost his sight by the small-pox when he was a child, and had no more notion of colours than one born blind. I ask whether any one can say this man had then any ideas of colours in his mind, any more than one born blind? And I think nobody will say that either of them had in his mind any ideas of colours at all. His cataracts are couched, and then he has the ideas (which he remembers not) of colours, de novo, by his restored sight, conveyed to his mind, and that without any consciousness of a former acquaintance. And these now he can revive and call to mind in the dark. In this case all these ideas of colours, which, when out of view, can be revived with a consciousness of a former acquaintance, being thus in the memory, are said to be in the mind. The use I make of this is,— that whatever idea, being not actually in view, is in the mind, is there only by being in the memory; and if it be not in the memory, it is not in the mind; and if it be in the memory, it cannot by the memory be brought into actual view without a perception that it comes out of the memory; which is this, that it had been known before, and is now remembered. If therefore there be any innate ideas, they must be in the memory, or else nowhere in the mind; and if they be in the memory, they can be revived without any impression from without; and whenever they are brought into the mind they are remembered, i.e. they bring with them a perception of their not being wholly new to it. This being a constant and distinguishing difference between what is, and what is not in the memory, or in the mind;— that what is not in the memory, whenever it appears there, appears perfectly new and unknown before; and what is in the memory, or in the mind, whenever it is suggested by the memory, appears not to be new, but the mind finds it in itself, and knows it was there before. By this it may be tried whether there be any innate ideas in the mind before impression from sensation or reflection. I would fain meet with the man who, when he came to the use of reason, or at any other time, remembered any of them; and to whom, after he was born, they were never new. If any one will say, there are ideas in the mind that are not in the memory, I desire him to explain himself, and make what he says intelligible.

22. Principles not innate, because of little use or little certainty. Besides what I have already said, there is another reason why I doubt that neither these nor any other principles are innate. I that am fully persuaded that the infinitely wise God made all things in perfect wisdom, cannot satisfy myself why he should be supposed to print upon the minds of men some universal principles; whereof those that are pretended innate, and concern speculation, are of no great use; and those that concern practice, not self-evident; and neither of them distinguishable from some other truths not allowed to be innate. For, to what purpose should characters be graven on the mind by the finger of God, which are not clearer there than those which are afterwards introduced, or cannot be distinguished from them? If any one thinks there are such innate ideas and propositions, which by their clearness and usefulness are distinguishable from all that is adventitious in the mind and acquired, it will not be a hard matter for him to tell us which they are; and then every one will be a fit judge whether they be so or no. Since if there be such innate ideas and impressions, plainly different from all other perceptions and knowledge, every one will find it true in himself of the evidence of these supposed innate maxims, I have spoken already: of their usefulness I shall have occasion to speak more hereafter.

23. Difference of men's discoveries depends upon the different application of their faculties. To conclude: some ideas forwardly offer themselves to all men's understanding; and some sorts of truths result from any ideas, as soon as the mind puts them into propositions: other

truths require a train of ideas placed in order, a due comparing of them, and deductions made with attention, before they can be discovered and assented to. Some of the first sort, because of their general and easy reception, have been mistaken for innate: but the truth is, ideas and notions are no more born with us than arts and sciences; though some of them indeed offer themselves to our faculties more readily than others; and therefore are more generally received: though that too be according as the organs of our bodies and powers of our minds happen to be employed; God having fitted men with faculties and means to discover, receive, and retain truths, according as they are employed. The great difference that is to be found in the notions of mankind is, from the different use they put their faculties to. Whilst some (and those the most) taking things upon trust, misemploy their power of assent, by lazily enslaving their minds to the dictates and dominion of others, in doctrines which it is their duty carefully to examine, and not blindly, with an implicit faith, to swallow; others, employing their thoughts only about some few things, grow acquainted sufficiently with them, attain great degrees of knowledge in them, and are ignorant of all other, having never let their thoughts loose in the search of other inquiries. Thus, that the three angles of a triangle are quite equal to two right ones is a truth as certain as anything can be, and I think more evident than many of those propositions that go for principles; and yet there are millions, however expert in other things, who know not this at all, because they never set their thoughts on work about such angles. And he that certainly knows this proposition may yet be utterly ignorant of the truth of other propositions, in mathematics itself, which are as clear and evident as this; because, in his search of those mathematical truths, he stopped his thoughts short and went not so far. The same may happen concerning the notions we have of the being of a Deity. For, though there be no truth which a man may more evidently make out to himself than the existence of a God, yet he that shall content himself with things as he finds them in this world, as they minister to his pleasures and passions, and not make inquiry a little further into their causes, ends, and admirable contrivances, and pursue the thoughts thereof with diligence and attention, may live long without any notion of such a Being. And if any person hath by talk put such a notion into his head, he may perhaps believe it; but if he hath never examined it, his knowledge of it will be no perfecter than his, who having been told, that the three angles of a triangle are equal to two right ones, takes it upon trust, without examining the demonstration; and may yield his assent as a probable opinion, but hath no knowledge of the truth of it; which yet his faculties, if carefully employed, were able to make clear and evident to him. But this only, by the by, to show how much our knowledge depends upon the right use of those powers nature hath bestowed upon us, and how little upon such innate principles as are in vain supposed to be in all mankind for their direction; which all men could not but know if they were there, or else they would be there to no purpose. And which since all men do not know, nor can distinguish from other adventitious truths, we may well conclude there are no such.

24. Men must think and know for themselves. What censure doubting thus of innate principles may deserve from men, who will be apt to call it pulling up the old foundations of knowledge and certainty, I cannot tell;— I persuade myself at least that the way I have pursued, being conformable to truth, lays those foundations surer. This I am certain, I have not made it my business either to quit or follow any authority in the ensuing Discourse. Truth has been my only aim; and wherever that has appeared to lead, my thoughts have impartially followed, without minding whether the footsteps of any other lay that way or not. Not that I want a due respect to other men's opinions; but, after all, the greatest reverence is due to truth: and I hope it will not be thought arrogance to say, that perhaps we should make greater progress in the discovery of rational and contemplative knowledge, if we sought it in the fountain, in the consideration of things themselves; and made use rather of our own thoughts than other men's to find it. For I think we may as rationally hope to see with other men's eyes, as to know by other men's understandings. So much as we ourselves consider and comprehend of truth and reason, so much we possess of real and true knowledge. The floating of other men's opinions in our brains, makes us not one jot the more knowing, though they happen to be true. What in

them was science, is in us but opiniatrety; whilst we give up our assent only to reverend names, and do not, as they did, employ our own reason to understand those truths which gave them reputation. Aristotle was certainly a knowing man, but nobody ever thought him so because he blindly embraced, and confidently vented the opinions of another. And if the taking up of another's principles, without examining them, made not him a philosopher, I suppose it will hardly make anybody else so. In the sciences, every one has so much as he really knows and comprehends. What he believes only, and takes upon trust, are but shreds; which, however well in the whole piece, make no considerable addition to his stock who gathers them. Such borrowed wealth, like fairy money, though it were gold in the hand from which he received it, will be but leaves and dust when it comes to use.

25. Whence the opinion of innate principles. When men have found some general propositions that could not be doubted of as soon as understood, it was, I know, a short and easy way to conclude them innate. This being once received, it eased the lazy from the pains of search, and stopped the inquiry of the doubtful concerning all that was once styled innate. And it was of no small advantage to those who affected to be masters and teachers, to make this the principle of principles,— that principles must not be questioned. For, having once established this tenet,— that there are innate principles, it put their followers upon a necessity of receiving some doctrines as such; which was to take them off from the use of their own reason and judgment, and put them on believing and taking them upon trust without further examination: in which posture of blind credulity, they might be more easily governed by, and made useful to some sort of men, who had the skill and office to principle and guide them. Nor is it a small power it gives one man over another, to have the authority to be the dictator of principles, and teacher of unquestionable truths; and to make a man swallow that for an innate principle which may serve to his purpose who teacheth them. Whereas had they examined the ways whereby men came to the knowledge of many universal truths, they would have found them to result in the minds of men from the being of things themselves, when duly considered; and that they were discovered by the application of those faculties that were fitted by nature to receive and judge of them, when duly employed about them.

26. Conclusion. To show how the understanding proceeds herein is the design of the following Discourse; which I shall proceed to when I have first premised, that hitherto,— to clear my way to those foundations which I conceive are the only true ones, whereon to establish those notions we can have of our own knowledge,— it hath been necessary for me to give an account of the reasons I had to doubt of innate principles. And since the arguments which are against them do, some of them, rise from common received opinions, I have been forced to take several things for granted; which is hardly avoidable to any one, whose task is to show the falsehood or improbability of any tenet;— it happening in controversial discourses as it does in assaulting of towns; where, if the ground be but firm whereon the batteries are erected, there is no further inquiry of whom it is borrowed, nor whom it belongs to, so it affords but a fit rise for the present purpose. But in the future part of this Discourse, designing to raise an edifice uniform and consistent with itself, as far as my own experience and observation will assist me, I hope to erect it on such a basis that I shall not need to shore it up with props and buttresses, leaning on borrowed or begged foundations: or at least, if mine prove a castle in the air, I will endeavour it shall be all of a piece and hang together. Wherein I warn the reader not to expect undeniable cogent demonstrations, unless I may be allowed the privilege, not seldom assumed by others, to take my principles for granted; and then, I doubt not, but I can demonstrate too. All that I shall say for the principles I proceed on is, that I can only appeal to men's own unprejudiced experience and observation whether they be true or not; and this is enough for a man who professes no more than to lay down candidly and freely his own conjectures, concerning a subject lying somewhat in the dark, without any other design than an unbiased inquiry after truth.

BOOK II. Of Ideas

Chapter I.Of Ideas in general, and their Original

1. Idea is the object of thinking. Every man being conscious to himself that he thinks; and that which his mind is applied about whilst thinking being the ideas that are there, it is past doubt that men have in their minds several ideas,— such as are those expressed by the words whiteness, hardness, sweetness, thinking, motion, man, elephant, army, drunkenness, and others: it is in the first place then to be inquired, How he comes by them?
I know it is a received doctrine, that men have native ideas, and original characters, stamped upon their minds in their very first being. This opinion I have at large examined already; and, I suppose what I have said in the foregoing Book will be much more easily admitted, when I have shown whence the understanding may get all the ideas it has; and by what ways and degrees they may come into the mind;— for which I shall appeal to every one's own observation and experience.
2. All ideas come from sensation or reflection. Let us then suppose the mind to be, as we say, white paper, void of all characters, without any ideas:— How comes it to be furnished? Whence comes it by that vast store which the busy and boundless fancy of man has painted on it with an almost endless variety? Whence has it all the materials of reason and knowledge? To this I answer, in one word, from EXPERIENCE. In that all our knowledge is founded; and from that it ultimately derives itself. Our observation employed either, about external sensible objects, or about the internal operations of our minds perceived and reflected on by ourselves, is that which supplies our understandings with all the materials of thinking. These two are the fountains of knowledge, from whence all the ideas we have, or can naturally have, do spring.
3. The objects of sensation one source of ideas. First, our Senses, conversant about particular sensible objects, do convey into the mind several distinct perceptions of things, according to those various ways wherein those objects do affect them. And thus we come by those ideas we have of yellow, white, heat, cold, soft, hard, bitter, sweet, and all those which we call sensible qualities; which when I say the senses convey into the mind, I mean, they from external objects convey into the mind what produces there those perceptions. This great source of most of the ideas we have, depending wholly upon our senses, and derived by them to the understanding, I call SENSATION.
4. The operations of our minds, the other source of them. Secondly, the other fountain from which experience furnisheth the understanding with ideas is,— the perception of the operations of our own mind within us, as it is employed about the ideas it has got;— which operations, when the soul comes to reflect on and consider, do furnish the understanding with another set of ideas, which could not be had from things without. And such are perception, thinking, doubting, believing, reasoning, knowing, willing, and all the different actings of our own minds;— which we being conscious of, and observing in ourselves, do from these receive into our understandings as distinct ideas as we do from bodies affecting our senses. This source of ideas every man has wholly in himself; and though it be not sense, as having nothing to do with external objects, yet it is very like it, and might properly enough be called internal sense. But as I call the other SENSATION, so I Call this REFLECTION, the ideas it affords being such only as the mind gets by reflecting on its own operations within itself. By reflection then, in the following part of this discourse, I would be understood to mean, that notice which the mind takes of its own operations, and the manner of them, by reason whereof there come to be ideas of these operations in the understanding. These two, I say, viz. external material things, as the objects of SENSATION, and the operations of our own minds within, as the objects of REFLECTION, are to me the only originals from whence all our ideas take their beginnings. The term operations here I use in a large sense, as comprehending not barely the

actions of the mind about its ideas, but some sort of passions arising sometimes from them, such as is the satisfaction or uneasiness arising from any thought.

5. All our ideas are of the one or the other of these. The understanding seems to me not to have the least glimmering of any ideas which it doth not receive from one of these two. External objects furnish the mind with the ideas of sensible qualities, which are all those different perceptions they produce in us; and the mind furnishes the understanding with ideas of its own operations.

These, when we have taken a full survey of them, and their several modes, combinations, and relations, we shall find to contain all our whole stock of ideas; and that we have nothing in our minds which did not come in one of these two ways. Let any one examine his own thoughts, and thoroughly search into his understanding; and then let him tell me, whether all the original ideas he has there, are any other than of the objects of his senses, or of the operations of his mind, considered as objects of his reflection. And how great a mass of knowledge soever he imagines to be lodged there, he will, upon taking a strict view, see that he has not any idea in his mind but what one of these two have imprinted;— though perhaps, with infinite variety compounded and enlarged by the understanding, as we shall see hereafter.

6. Observable in children. He that attentively considers the state of a child, at his first coming into the world, will have little reason to think him stored with plenty of ideas, that are to be the matter of his future knowledge. It is by degrees he comes to be furnished with them. And though the ideas of obvious and familiar qualities imprint themselves before the memory begins to keep a register of time or order, yet it is often so late before some unusual qualities come in the way, that there are few men that cannot recollect the beginning of their acquaintance with them. And if it were worth while, no doubt a child might be so ordered as to have but a very few, even of the ordinary ideas, till he were grown up to a man. But all that are born into the world, being surrounded with bodies that perpetually and diversely affect them, variety of ideas, whether care be taken of it or not, are imprinted on the minds of children. Light and colours are busy at hand everywhere, when the eye is but open; sounds and some tangible qualities fail not to solicit their proper senses, and force an entrance to the mind;— but yet, I think, it will be granted easily, that if a child were kept in a place where he never saw any other but black and white till he were a man, he would have no more ideas of scarlet or green, than he that from his childhood never tasted an oyster, or a pine-apple, has of those particular relishes.

7. Men are differently furnished with these, according to the different objects they converse with. Men then come to be furnished with fewer or more simple ideas from without, according as the objects they converse with afford greater or less variety; and from the operations of their minds within, according as they more or less reflect on them. For, though he that contemplates the operations of his mind, cannot but have plain and clear ideas of them; yet, unless he turn his thoughts that way, and considers them attentively, he will no more have clear and distinct ideas of all the operations of his mind, and all that may be observed therein, than he will have all the particular ideas of any landscape, or of the parts and motions of a clock, who will not turn his eyes to it, and with attention heed all the parts of it. The picture, or clock may be so placed, that they may come in his way every day; but yet he will have but a confused idea of all the parts they are made up of, till he applies himself with attention, to consider them each in particular.

8. Ideas of reflection later, because they need attention. And hence we see the reason why it is pretty late before most children get ideas of the operations of their own minds; and some have not any very clear or perfect ideas of the greatest part of them all their lives. Because, though they pass there continually, yet, like floating visions, they make not deep impressions enough to leave in their mind clear, distinct, lasting ideas, till the understanding turns inward upon itself, reflects on its own operations, and makes them the objects of its own contemplation. Children when they come first into it, are surrounded with a world of new things, which, by a constant solicitation of their senses, draw the mind constantly to them; forward to take notice

of new, and apt to be delighted with the variety of changing objects. Thus the first years are usually employed and diverted in looking abroad. Men's business in them is to acquaint themselves with what is to be found without; and so growing up in a constant attention to outward sensations, seldom make any considerable reflection on what passes within them, till they come to be of riper years; and some scarce ever at all.

9. The soul begins to have ideas when it begins to perceive. To ask, at what time a man has first any ideas, is to ask, when he begins to perceive;— having ideas, and perception, being the same thing. I know it is an opinion, that the soul always thinks, and that it has the actual perception of ideas in itself constantly, as long as it exists; and that actual thinking is as inseparable from the soul as actual extension is from the body; which if true, to inquire after the beginning of a man's ideas is the same as to inquire after the beginning of his soul. For, by this account, soul and its ideas, as body and its extension, will begin to exist both at the same time.

10. The soul thinks not always; for this wants proofs. But whether the soul be supposed to exist antecedent to, or coeval with, or some time after the first rudiments of organization, or the beginnings of life in the body, I leave to be disputed by those who have better thought of that matter. I confess myself to have one of those dull souls, that doth not perceive itself always to contemplate ideas; nor can conceive it any more necessary for the soul always to think, than for the body always to move: the perception of ideas being (as I conceive) to the soul, what motion is to the body; not its essence, but one of its operations. And therefore, though thinking be supposed never so much the proper action of the soul, yet it is not necessary to suppose that it should be always thinking, always in action. That, perhaps, is the privilege of the infinite Author and Preserver of all things, who "never slumbers nor sleeps;" but is not competent to any finite being, at least not to the soul of man. We know certainly, by experience, that we sometimes think; and thence draw this infallible consequence,— that there is something in us that has a power to think. But whether that substance perpetually thinks or no, we can be no further assured than experience informs us. For, to say that actual thinking is essential to the soul, and inseparable from it, is to beg what is in question, and not to prove it by reason;— which is necessary to be done, if it be not a self-evident proposition. But whether this, "That the soul always thinks," be a self-evident proposition, that everybody assents to at first hearing, I appeal to mankind. It is doubted whether I thought at all last night or no. The question being about a matter of fact, it is begging it to bring, as a proof for it, an hypothesis, which is the very thing in dispute: by which way one may prove anything, and it is but supposing that all watches, whilst the balance beats, think, and it is sufficiently proved, and past doubt, that my watch thought all last night. But he that would not deceive himself, ought to build his hypothesis on matter of fact, and make it out by sensible experience, and not presume on matter of fact, because of his hypothesis, that is, because he supposes it to be so; which way of proving amounts to this, that I must necessarily think all last night, because another supposes I always think, though I myself cannot perceive that I always do so.

But men in love with their opinions may not only suppose what is in question, but allege wrong matter of fact. How else could any one make it an inference of mine, that a thing is not, because we are not sensible of it in our sleep? I do not say there is no soul in a man, because he is not sensible of it in his sleep; but I do say, he cannot think at any time, waking or sleeping: without being sensible of it. Our being sensible of it is not necessary to anything but to our thoughts; and to them it is; and to them it always will be necessary, till we can think without being conscious of it.

11. It is not always conscious of it. I grant that the soul, in a waking man, is never without thought, because it is the condition of being awake. But whether sleeping without dreaming be not an affection of the whole man, mind as well as body, may be worth a waking man's consideration; it being hard to conceive that anything should think and not be conscious of it. If the soul doth think in a sleeping man without being conscious of it, I ask whether, during such thinking, it has any pleasure or pain, or be capable of happiness or misery? I am sure the

man is not; no more than the bed or earth he lies on. For to be happy or miserable without being conscious of it, seems to me utterly inconsistent and impossible. Or if it be possible that the soul can, whilst the body is sleeping, have its thinking, enjoyments, and concerns, its pleasures or pain, apart, which the man is not conscious of nor partakes in,— it is certain that Socrates asleep and Socrates awake is not the same person; but his soul when he sleeps, and Socrates the man, consisting of body and soul, when he is waking, are two persons: since waking Socrates has no knowledge of, or concernment for that happiness or misery of his soul, which it enjoys alone by itself whilst he sleeps, without perceiving anything of it; no more than he has for the happiness or misery of a man in the Indies, whom he knows not. For, if we take wholly away all consciousness of our actions and sensations, especially of pleasure and pain, and the concernment that accompanies it, it will be hard to know wherein to place personal identity.

12. If a sleeping man thinks without knowing it, the sleeping and waking man are two persons. The soul, during sound sleep, thinks, say these men. Whilst it thinks and perceives, it is capable certainly of those of delight or trouble, as well as any other perceptions; and it must necessarily be conscious of its own perceptions. But it has all this apart: the sleeping man, it is plain, is conscious of nothing of all this. Let us suppose, then, the soul of Castor, while he is sleeping, retired from his body; which is no impossible supposition for the men I have here to do with, who so liberally allow life, without a thinking soul, to all other animals. These men cannot then judge it impossible, or a contradiction, that the body should live without the soul; nor that the soul should subsist and think, or have perception, even perception of happiness or misery, without the body. Let us then, I say, suppose the soul of Castor separated during his sleep from his body, to think apart. Let us suppose, too, that it chooses for its scene of thinking the body of another man, v.g. Pollux, who is sleeping without a soul. For, if Castor's soul can think, whilst Castor is asleep, what Castor is never conscious of, it is no matter what place it chooses to think in. We have here, then, the bodies of two men with only one soul between them, which we will suppose to sleep and wake by turns; and the soul still thinking in the waking man, whereof the sleeping man is never conscious, has never the least perception. I ask, then, whether Castor and Pollux, thus with only one soul between them, which thinks and perceives in one what the other is never conscious of, nor is concerned for, are not two as distinct persons as Castor and Hercules, or as Socrates and Plato were? And whether one of them might not be very happy, and the other very miserable? Just by the same reason, they make the soul and the man two persons, who make the soul think apart what the man is not conscious of. For, I suppose nobody will make identity of persons to consist in the soul's being united to the very same numerical particles of matter. For if that be necessary to identity, it will be impossible, in that constant flux of the particles of our bodies, that any man should be the same person two days, or two moments, together.

13. Impossible to convince those that sleep without dreaming, that they think. Thus, methinks, every drowsy nod shakes their doctrine, who teach that the soul is always thinking. Those, at least, who do at any time sleep without dreaming, can never be convinced that their thoughts are sometimes for four hours busy without their knowing of it; and if they are taken in the very act, waked in the middle of that sleeping contemplation, can give no manner of account of it.

14. That men dream without remembering it, in vain urged. It will perhaps be said,— That the soul thinks even in the soundest sleep, but the memory retains it not. That the soul in a sleeping man should be this moment busy a thinking, and the next moment in a waking man not remember nor be able to recollect one jot of all those thoughts, is very hard to be conceived, and would need some better proof than bare assertion to make it be believed. For who can without any more ado, but being barely told so, imagine that the greatest part of men do, during all their lives, for several hours every day, think of something, which if they were asked, even in the middle of these thoughts, they could remember nothing at all of? Most men, I think, pass a great part of their sleep without dreaming. I once knew a man that was bred a scholar, and had no bad memory, who told me he had never dreamed in his life, till he had that

fever he was then newly recovered of, which was about the five or six and twentieth year of his age. I suppose the world affords more such instances: at least every one's acquaintance will furnish him with examples enough of such as pass most of their nights without dreaming.

15. Upon this hypothesis, the thoughts of a sleeping man ought to be most rational. To think often, and never to retain it so much as one moment, is a very useless sort of thinking; and the soul, in such a state of thinking, does very little, if at all, excel that of a looking-glass, which constantly receives variety of images, or ideas, but retains none; they disappear and vanish, and there remain no footsteps of them; the looking-glass is never the better for such ideas, nor the soul for such thoughts. Perhaps it will be said, that in a waking man the materials of the body are employed, and made use of, in thinking; and that the memory of thoughts is retained by the impressions that are made on the brain, and the traces there left after such thinking; but that in the thinking of the soul, which is not perceived in a sleeping man, there the soul thinks apart, and making no use of the organs of the body, leaves no impressions on it, and consequently no memory of such thoughts. Not to mention again the absurdity of two distinct persons, which follows from this supposition, I answer, further,— That whatever ideas the mind can receive and contemplate without the help of the body, it is reasonable to conclude it can retain without the help of the body too; or else the soul, or any separate spirit, will have but little advantage by thinking. If it has no memory of its own thoughts; if it cannot lay them up for its own use, and be able to recall them upon occasion; if it cannot reflect upon what is past, and make use of its former experiences, reasonings, and contemplations, to what purpose does it think? They who make the soul a thinking thing, at this rate, will not make it a much more noble being than those do whom they condemn, for allowing it to be nothing but the subtilist parts of matter. Characters drawn on dust, that the first breath of wind effaces; or impressions made on a heap of atoms, or animal spirits, are altogether as useful, and render the subject as noble, as the thoughts of a soul that perish in thinking; that, once out of sight, are gone forever, and leave no memory of themselves behind them. Nature never makes excellent things for mean or no uses: and it is hardly to be conceived that our infinitely wise Creator should make so admirable a faculty which comes nearest the excellency of his own incomprehensible being, to be so idly and uselessly employed, at least a fourth part of its time here, as to think constantly, without remembering any of those thoughts, without doing any good to itself or others, or being any way useful to any other part of the creation, If we will examine it, we shall not find, I suppose, the motion of dull and senseless matter, any where in the universe, made so little use of and so wholly thrown away.

16. On this hypothesis, the soul must have ideas not derived from sensation or reflection, of which there is no appearance. It is true, we have sometimes instances of perception whilst we are asleep, and retain the memory of those thoughts: but how extravagant and incoherent for the most part they are; how little conformable to the perfection and order of a rational being, those who are acquainted with dreams need not be told. This I would willingly be satisfied in,— whether the soul, when it thinks thus apart, and as it were separate from the body, acts less rationally than when conjointly with it, or no. If its separate thoughts be less rational, then these men must say, that the soul owes the perfection of rational thinking to the body: if it does not, it is a wonder that our dreams should be, for the most part, so frivolous and irrational; and that the soul should retain none of its more rational soliloquies and meditations.

17. If I think when I know it not, nobody else can know it. Those who so confidently tell us that the soul always actually thinks, I would they would also tell us, what those ideas are that are in the soul of a child, before or just at the union with the body, before it hath received any by sensation. The dreams of sleeping men are, as I take it, all made up of the waking man's ideas; though for the most part oddly put together. It is strange, if the soul has ideas of its own that it derived not from sensation or reflection, (as it must have, if it thought before it received any impressions from the body,) that it should never, in its private thinking, (so private, that the man himself perceives it not,) retain any of them the very moment it wakes out of them, and then make the man glad with new discoveries. Who can find it reason that the soul should,

in its retirement during sleep, have so many hours' thoughts, and yet never light on any of those ideas it borrowed not from sensation or reflection; or at least preserve the memory of none but such, which, being occasioned from the body, must needs be less natural to a spirit? It is strange the soul should never once in a man's whole life recall over any of its pure native thoughts, and those ideas it had before it borrowed anything from the body; never bring into the waking man's view any other ideas but what have a tang of the cask, and manifestly derive their original from that union. If it always thinks, and so had ideas before it was united, or before it received any from the body, it is not to be supposed but that during sleep it recollects its native ideas; and during that retirement from communicating with the body, whilst it thinks by itself, the ideas it is busied about should be, sometimes at least, those more natural and congenial ones which it had in itself, underived from the body, or its own operations about them: which, since the waking man never remembers, we must from this hypothesis conclude either that the soul remembers something that the man does not; or else that memory belongs only to such ideas as are derived from the body, or the mind's operations about them.

18. How knows any one that the soul always thinks? For if it be not a self-evident proposition, it needs proof. I would be glad also to learn from these men who so confidently pronounce that the human soul, or, which is all one, that a man always thinks, how they come to know it; nay, how they come to know that they themselves think when they themselves do not perceive it. This, I am afraid, is to be sure without proofs, and to know without perceiving. It is, I suspect, a confused notion, taken up to serve an hypothesis; and none of those clear truths, that either their own evidence forces us to admit, or common experience makes it impudence to deny. For the most that can be said of it is, that it is possible the soul may always think, but not always retain it in memory. And I say, it is as possible that the soul may not always think; and much more probable that it should sometimes not think, than that it should often think, and that a long while together, and not be conscious to itself, the next moment after, that it had thought.

19. "That a man should be busy in thinking, and yet not retain it the next moment," very improbable. To suppose the soul to think, and the man not to perceive it, is, as has been said, to make two persons in one man. And if one considers well these men's way of speaking, one should be led into a suspicion that they do so. For they who tell us that the soul always thinks, do never, that I remember, say that a man always thinks. Can the soul think, and not the man? Or a man think, and not be conscious of it? This, perhaps, would be suspected of jargon in others. If they say the man thinks always, but is not always conscious of it, they may as well say his body is extended without having parts. For it is altogether as intelligible to say that a body is extended without parts, as that anything thinks without being conscious of it, or perceiving that it does so. They who talk thus may, with as much reason, if it be necessary to their hypothesis, say that a man is always hungry, but that he does not always feel it; whereas hunger consists in that very sensation, as thinking consists in being conscious that one thinks. If they say that a man is always conscious to himself of thinking, I ask, How they know it? Consciousness is the perception of what passes in a man's own mind. Can another man perceive that I am conscious of anything, when I perceive it not myself? No man's knowledge here can go beyond his experience. Wake a man out of a sound sleep, and ask him what he was that moment thinking of. If he himself be conscious of nothing he then thought on, he must be a notable diviner of thoughts that can assure him that he was thinking. May he not, with more reason, assure him he was not asleep? This is something beyond philosophy; and it cannot be less than revelation, that discovers to another thoughts in my mind, when I can find none there myself. And they must needs have a penetrating sight who can certainly see that I think, when I cannot perceive it myself, and when I declare that I do not; and yet can see that dogs or elephants do not think, when they give all the demonstration of it imaginable, except only telling us that they do so. This some may suspect to be a step beyond the Rosicrucians; it seeming easier to make one's self invisible to others, than to make another's thoughts visible to me, which are not visible to himself. But it is but defining the soul to be "a substance that always thinks," and the business is done. If such definition be of any authority, I know not

what it can serve for but to make many men suspect that they have no souls at all; since they find a good part of their lives pass away without thinking. For no definitions that I know, no suppositions of any sect, are of force enough to destroy constant experience; and perhaps it is the affectation of knowing beyond what we perceive, that makes so much useless dispute and noise in the world.

20. No ideas but from sensation and reflection, evident, if we observe children. I see no reason, therefore, to believe that the soul thinks before the senses have furnished it with ideas to think on; and as those are increased and retained, so it comes, by exercise, to improve its faculty of thinking in the several parts of it; as well as, afterwards, by compounding those ideas, and reflecting on its own operations, it increases its stock, as well as facility in remembering, imagining, reasoning, and other modes of thinking.

21. State of a child in the mother's womb. He that will suffer himself to be informed by observation and experience, and not make his own hypothesis the rule of nature, will find few signs of a soul accustomed to much thinking in a new-born child, and much fewer of any reasoning at all. And yet it is hard to imagine that the rational soul should think so much, and not reason at all. And he that will consider that infants newly come into the world spend the greatest part of their time in sleep, and are seldom awake but when either hunger calls for the teat, or some pain (the most importunate of all sensations), or some other violent impression on the body, forces the mind to perceive and attend to it;— he, I say, who considers this, will perhaps find reason to imagine that a foetus in the mother's womb differs not much from the state of a vegetable, but passes the greatest part of its time without perception or thought; doing very little but sleep in a place where it needs not seek for food, and is surrounded with liquor, always equally soft, and near of the same temper; where the eyes have no light, and the ears so shut up are not very susceptible of sounds; and where there is little or no variety, or change of objects, to move the senses.

22. The mind thinks in proportion to the matter it gets from experience to think about. Follow a child from its birth, and observe the alterations that time makes, and you shall find, as the mind by the senses comes more and more to be furnished with ideas, it comes to be more and more awake; thinks more, the more it has matter to think on. After some time it begins to know the objects which, being most familiar with it, have made lasting impressions. Thus it comes by degrees to know the persons it daily converses with, and distinguishes them from strangers; which are instances and effects of its coming to retain and distinguish the ideas the senses convey to it. And so we may observe how the mind, by degrees, improves in these; and advances to the exercise of those other faculties of enlarging, compounding, and abstracting its ideas, and of reasoning about them, and reflecting upon all these; of which I shall have occasion to speak more hereafter.

23. A man begins to have ideas when he first has sensation. What sensation is. If it shall be demanded then, when a man begins to have any ideas, I think the true answer is,— when he first has any sensation. For, since there appear not to be any ideas in the mind before the senses have conveyed any in, I conceive that ideas in the understanding are coeval with sensation; which is such an impression or motion made in some part of the body, as produces some perception in the understanding. It is about these impressions made on our senses by outward objects that the mind seems first to employ itself, in such operations as we call perception, remembering, consideration, reasoning, &c.

24. The original of all our knowledge. In time the mind comes to reflect on its own operations about the ideas got by sensation, and thereby stores itself with a new set of ideas, which I call ideas of reflection. These are the impressions that are made on our senses by outward objects that are extrinsical to the mind; and its own operations, proceeding from powers intrinsical and proper to itself, which, when reflected on by itself, become also objects of its contemplation — are, as I have said, the original of all knowledge. Thus the first capacity of human intellect is,— that the mind is fitted to receive the impressions made on it; either through the senses by outward objects, or by its own operations when it reflects on them. This is the first step a man

makes towards the discovery of anything, and the groundwork whereon to build all those notions which ever he shall have naturally in this world. All those sublime thoughts which tower above the clouds, and reach as high as heaven itself, take their rise and footing here: in all that great extent wherein the mind wanders, in those remote speculations it may seem to be elevated with, it stirs not one jot beyond those ideas which sense or reflection have offered for its contemplation.

25. In the reception of simple ideas, the understanding is for the most part passive. In this part the understanding is merely passive; and whether or no it will have these beginnings, and as it were materials of knowledge, is not in its own power. For the objects of our senses do, many of them, obtrude their particular ideas upon our minds whether we will or not; and the operations of our minds will not let us be without, at least, some obscure notions of them. No man can be wholly ignorant of what he does when he thinks. These simple ideas, when offered to the mind, the understanding can no more refuse to have, nor alter when they are imprinted, nor blot them out and make new ones itself, than a mirror can refuse, alter, or obliterate the images or ideas which the objects set before it do therein produce. As the bodies that surround us do diversely affect our organs, the mind is forced to receive the impressions; and cannot avoid the perception of those ideas that are annexed to them.

Chapter II.Of Simple Ideas

1. Uncompounded appearances. The better to understand the nature, manner, and extent of our knowledge, one thing is carefully to be observed concerning the ideas we have; and that is, that some of them are simple and some complex.

Though the qualities that affect our senses are, in the things themselves, so united and blended, that there is no separation, no distance between them; yet it is plain, the ideas they produce in the mind enter by the senses simple and unmixed. For, though the sight and touch often take in from the same object, at the same time, different ideas;— as a man sees at once motion and colour; the hand feels softness and warmth in the same piece of wax: yet the simple ideas thus united in the same subject, are as perfectly distinct as those that come in by different senses. The coldness and hardness which a man feels in a piece of ice being as distinct ideas in the mind as the smell and whiteness of a lily; or as the taste of sugar, and smell of a rose. And there is nothing can be plainer to a man than the clear and distinct perception he has of those simple ideas; which, being each in itself uncompounded, contains in it nothing but one uniform appearance, or conception in the mind, and is not distinguishable into different ideas.

2. The mind can neither make nor destroy them. These simple ideas, the materials of all our knowledge, are suggested and furnished to the mind only by those two ways above mentioned, viz. sensation and reflection. When the understanding is once stored with these simple ideas, it has the power to repeat, compare, and unite them, even to an almost infinite variety, and so can make at pleasure new complex ideas. But it is not in the power of the most exalted wit, or enlarged understanding, by any quickness or variety of thought, to invent or frame one new simple idea in the mind, not taken in by the ways before mentioned: nor can any force of the understanding destroy those that are there. The dominion of man, in this little world of his own understanding being muchwhat the same as it is in the great world of visible things; wherein his power, however managed by art and skill, reaches no farther than to compound and divide the materials that are made to his hand; but can do nothing towards the making the least particle of new matter, or destroying one atom of what is already in being. The same inability will every one find in himself, who shall go about to fashion in his understanding one simple idea, not received in by his senses from external objects, or by reflection from the operations of his own mind about them. I would have any one try to fancy any taste which had never affected his palate; or frame the idea of a scent he had never smelt: and when he can do this, I will also conclude that a blind man hath ideas of colours, and a deaf man true distinct notions

of sounds.

3. Only the qualities that affect the senses are imaginable. This is the reason why — though we cannot believe it impossible to God to make a creature with other organs, and more ways to convey into the understanding the notice of corporeal things than those five, as they are usually counted, which he has given to man — yet I think it is not possible for any man to imagine any other qualities in bodies, howsoever constituted, whereby they can be taken notice of, besides sounds, tastes, smells, visible and tangible qualities. And had mankind been made but with four senses, the qualities then which are the objects of the fifth sense had been as far from our notice, imagination, and conception, as now any belonging to a sixth, seventh, or eighth sense can possibly be;— which, whether yet some other creatures, in some other parts of this vast and stupendous universe, may not have, will be a great presumption to deny. He that will not set himself proudly at the top of all things, but will consider the immensity of this fabric, and the great variety that is to be found in this little and inconsiderable part of it which he has to do with, may be apt to think that, in other mansions of it, there may be other and different intelligent beings, of whose faculties he has as little knowledge or apprehension as a worm shut up in one drawer of a cabinet hath of the senses or understanding of a man; such variety and excellency being suitable to the wisdom and power of the Maker. I have here followed the common opinion of man's having but five senses; though, perhaps, there may be justly counted more;— but either supposition serves equally to my present purpose.

Chapter III.Of Simple Ideas of Sense

1. Division of simple ideas. The better to conceive the ideas we receive from sensation, it may not be amiss for us to consider them, in reference to the different ways whereby they make their approaches to our minds, and make themselves perceivable by us.

First, then, There are some which come into our minds by one sense only.

Secondly, There are others that convey themselves into the mind by more senses than one.

Thirdly, Others that are had from reflection only.

Fourthly, There are some that make themselves way, and are suggested to the mind by all the ways of sensation and reflection.

We shall consider them apart under these several heads.

Ideas of one sense. There are some ideas which have admittance only through one sense, which is peculiarly adapted to receive them. Thus light and colours, as white, red, yellow, blue; with their several degrees or shades and mixtures, as green, scarlet, purple, sea-green, and the rest, come in only by the eyes. All kinds of noises, sounds, and tones, only by the ears. The several tastes and smells, by the nose and palate. And if these organs, or the nerves which are the conduits to convey them from without to their audience in the brain,— the mind's presence-room (as I may so call it)— are any of them so disordered as not to perform their functions, they have no postern to be admitted by; no other way to bring themselves into view, and be perceived by the understanding.

The most considerable of those belonging to the touch, are heat and cold, and solidity: all the rest, consisting almost wholly in the sensible configuration, as smooth and rough; or else, more or less firm adhesion of the parts, as hard and soft, tough and brittle, are obvious enough.

2. Few simple ideas have names. I think it will be needless to enumerate all the particular simple ideas belonging to each sense. Nor indeed is it possible if we would; there being a great many more of them belonging to most of the senses than we have names for. The variety of smells, which are as many almost, if not more, than species of bodies in the world, do most of them want names. Sweet and stinking commonly serve our turn for these ideas, which in effect is little more than to call them pleasing or displeasing; though the smell of a rose and violet, both sweet, are certainly very distinct ideas. Nor are the different tastes, that by our palates we receive ideas of, much better provided with names. Sweet, bitter, sour, harsh, and salt are

almost all the epithets we have to denominate that numberless variety of relishes, which are to be found distinct, not only in almost every sort of creatures, but in the different parts of the same plant, fruit, or animal. The same may be said of colours and sounds. I shall, therefore, in the account of simple ideas I am here giving, content myself to set down only such as are most material to our present purpose, or are in themselves less apt to be taken notice of though they are very frequently the ingredients of our complex ideas; amongst which, I think, I may well account solidity, which therefore I shall treat of in the next chapter.

Chapter IV.Idea of Solidity

1. We receive this idea from touch. The idea of solidity we receive by our touch: and it arises from the resistance which we find in body to the entrance of any other body into the place it possesses, till it has left it. There is no idea which we receive more constantly from sensation than solidity. Whether we move or rest, in what posture soever we are, we always feel something under us that support us, and hinders our further sinking downwards; and the bodies which we daily handle make us perceive that, whilst they remain between them, they do, by an insurmountable force, hinder the approach of the parts of our hands that press them. That which thus hinders the approach of two bodies, when they are moved one towards another, I call solidity. I will not dispute whether this acceptation of the word solid be nearer to its original signification than that which mathematicians use it in. It suffices that I think the common notion of solidity will allow, if not justify, this use of it; but if any one think it better to call it impenetrability, he has my consent. Only I have thought the term solidity the more proper to express this idea, not only because of its vulgar use in that sense, but also because it carries something more of positive in it than impenetrability; which is negative, and is perhaps more a consequence of solidity, than solidity itself. This, of all other, seems the idea most intimately connected with, and essential to body; so as nowhere else to be found or imagined, but only in matter. And though our senses take no notice of it, but in masses of matter, of a bulk sufficient to cause a sensation in us: yet the mind, having once got this idea from such grosser sensible bodies, traces it further, and considers it, as well as figure, in the minutest particle of matter that can exist; and finds it inseparably inherent in body, wherever or however modified.

2. Solidity fills space. This is the idea which belongs to body, whereby we conceive it to fill space. The idea of which filling of space is,— that where we imagine any space taken up by a solid substance, we conceive it so to possess it, that it excludes all other solid substances; and will for ever hinder any other two bodies, that move towards one another in a straight line, from coming to touch one another, unless it removes from between them in a line not parallel to that which they move in. This idea of it, the bodies which we ordinarily handle sufficiently furnish us with.

3. Distinct from space. This resistance, whereby it keeps other bodies out of the space which it possesses, is so great, that no force, how great soever, can surmount it. All the bodies in the world, pressing a drop of water on all sides, will never be able to overcome the resistance which it will make, soft as it is, to their approaching one another, till it be removed out of their way: whereby our idea of solidity is distinguished both from pure space, which is capable neither of resistance nor motion; and from the ordinary idea of hardness. For a man may conceive two bodies at a distance, so as they may approach one another, without touching or displacing any solid thing, till their superficies come to meet; whereby, I think, we have the clear idea of space without solidity. For (not to go so far as annihilation of any particular body) I ask, whether a man cannot have the idea of the motion of one single body alone, without any other succeeding immediately into its place? I think it is evident he can: the idea of motion in one body no more including the idea of motion in another, than the idea of a square figure in one body includes the idea of a square figure in another. I do not ask, whether

bodies do so exist, that the motion of one body cannot really be without the motion of another. To determine this either way, is to beg the question for or against a vacuum. But my question is,— whether one cannot have the idea of one body moved, whilst others are at rest? And I think this no one will deny. If so, then the place it deserted gives us the idea of pure space without solidity; whereinto any other body may enter, without either resistance or protrusion of anything. When the sucker in a pump is drawn, the space it filled in the tube is certainly the same whether any other body follows the motion of the sucker or not: nor does it imply a contradiction that, upon the motion of one body, another that is only contiguous to it should not follow it. The necessity of such a motion is built only on the supposition that the world is full; but not on the distinct ideas of space and solidity, which are as different as resistance and not resistance, protrusion and not protrusion. And that men have ideas of space without a body, their very disputes about a vacuum plainly demonstrate, as is shown in another place.

4. From hardness. Solidity is hereby also differenced from hardness, in that solidity consists in repletion, and so an utter exclusion of other bodies out of the space it possesses: but hardness, in a firm cohesion of the parts of matter, making up masses of a sensible bulk, so that the whole does not easily change its figure. And indeed, hard and soft are names that we give to things only in relation to the constitutions of our own bodies; that being generally called hard by us, which will put us to pain sooner than change figure by the pressure of any part of our bodies; and that, on the contrary, soft, which changes the situation of its parts upon an easy and unpainful touch.

But this difficulty of changing the situation of the sensible parts amongst themselves, or of the figure of the whole, gives no more solidity to the hardest body in the world than to the softest; nor is an adamant one jot more solid than water. For, though the two flat sides of two pieces of marble will more easily approach each other, between which there is nothing but water or air, than if there be a diamond between them; yet it is not that the parts of the diamond are more solid than those of water, or resist more; but because the parts of water, being more easily separable from each other, they will, by a side motion, be more easily removed, and give way to the approach of the two pieces of marble. But if they could be kept from making place by that side motion, they would eternally hinder the approach of these two pieces of marble, as much as the diamond; and it would be as impossible by any force to surmount their resistance, as to surmount the resistance of the parts of a diamond. The softest body in the world will as invincibly resist the coming together of any other two bodies, if it be not put out of the way, but remain between them, as the hardest that can be found or imagined. He that shall fill a yielding soft body well with air or water, will quickly find its resistance. And he that thinks that nothing but bodies that are hard can keep his hands from approaching one another, may be pleased to make a trial, with the air inclosed in a football. The experiment, I have been told, was made at Florence, with a hollow globe of gold filled with water, and exactly closed; which further shows the solidity of so soft a body as water. For the golden globe thus filled, being put into a press, which was driven by the extreme force of screws, the water made itself way through the pores of that very close metal, and finding no room for a nearer approach of its particles within, got to the outside, where it rose like a dew, and so fell in drops, before the sides of the globe could be made to yield to the violent compression of the engine that squeezed it.

5. On solidity depend impulse, resistance, and protrusion. By this idea of solidity is the extension of body distinguished from the extension of space:— the extension of body being nothing but the cohesion or continuity of solid, separable, movable parts; and the extension of space, the continuity of unsolid, inseparable, and immovable parts. Upon the solidity of bodies also depend their mutual impulse, resistance, and protrusion. Of pure space then, and solidity, there are several (amongst which I confess myself one) who persuade themselves they have clear and distinct ideas; and that they can think on space, without anything in it that resists or is protruded by body. This is the idea of pure space, which they think they have as clear as any idea they can have of the extension of body: the idea of the distance between the opposite parts

of a concave superficies being equally as clear without as with the idea of any solid parts between: and on the other side, they persuade themselves that they have, distinct from that of pure space, the idea of something that fills space, that can be protruded by the impulse of other bodies, or resist their motion. If there be others that have not these two ideas distinct, but confound them, and make but one of them, I know not how men, who have the same idea under different names, or different ideas under the same name, can in that case talk with one another; any more than a man who, not being blind or deaf, has distinct ideas of the colour of scarlet and the sound of a trumpet, could discourse concerning scarlet colour with the blind man I mentioned in another place, who fancied that the idea of scarlet was like the sound of a trumpet.

6. What solidity is. If any one ask me, What this solidity is, I send him to his senses to inform him. Let him put a flint or a football between his hands, and then endeavour to join them, and he will know. If he thinks this not a sufficient explication of solidity, what it is, and wherein it consists; I promise to tell him what it is, and wherein it consists, when he tells me what thinking is, or wherein it consists; or explains to me what extension or motion is, which perhaps seems much easier. The simple ideas we have, are such as experience teaches them us; but if, beyond that, we endeavour by words to make them clearer in the mind, we shall succeed no better than if we went about to clear up the darkness of a blind man's mind by talking; and to discourse into him the ideas of light and colours. The reason of this I shall show in another place.

Chapter V.Of Simple Ideas of Divers Senses

Ideas received both by seeing and touching. The ideas we get by more than one sense are, of space or extension, figure, rest, and motion. For these make perceivable impressions, both on the eyes and touch; and we can receive and convey into our minds the ideas of the extension, figure, motion, and rest of bodies, both by seeing and feeling. But having occasion to speak more at large of these in another place, I here only enumerate them.

Chapter VI.Of Simple Ideas of Reflection

1. Simple ideas are the operations of mind about its other ideas. The mind receiving the ideas mentioned in the foregoing chapters from without, when it turns its view inward upon itself, and observes its own actions about those ideas it has, takes from thence other ideas, which are as capable to be the objects of its contemplation as any of those it received from foreign things.

2. The idea of perception, and idea of willing, we have from reflection. The two great and principal actions of the mind, which are most frequently considered, and which are so frequent that every one that pleases may take notice of them in himself, are these two:— Perception, or Thinking; and Volition, or Willing.

The power of thinking is called the Understanding, and the power of volition is called the Will; and these two powers or abilities in the mind are denominated faculties.

Of some of the modes of these simple ideas of reflection, such as are remembrance, discerning, reasoning, judging, knowledge, faith, &c., I shall have occasion to speak hereafter.

Chapter VII.Of Simple Ideas of both Sensation and Reflection

1. Ideas of pleasure and pain. There be other simple ideas which convey themselves into the

mind by all the ways of sensation and reflection, viz. pleasure or delight, and its opposite, pain, or uneasiness; power; existence; unity.

2. Mix with almost all our other ideas. Delight or uneasiness, one or other of them, join themselves to almost all our ideas both of sensation and reflection: and there is scarce any affection of our senses from without, any retired thought of our mind within, which is not able to produce in us pleasure or pain. By pleasure and pain, I would be understood to signify, whatsoever delights or molests us; whether it arises from the thoughts of our minds, or anything operating on our bodies. For, whether we call it satisfaction, delight, pleasure, happiness, &c., on the one side, or uneasiness, trouble, pain, torment, anguish, misery, &c., on the other, they are still but different degrees of the same thing, and belong to the ideas of pleasure and pain, delight or uneasiness; which are the names I shall most commonly use for those two sorts of ideas.

3. As motives of our actions. The infinite wise Author of our being, having given us the power over several parts of our bodies, to move or keep them at rest as we think fit; and also. by the motion of them, to move ourselves and other contiguous bodies, in which consist all the actions of our body: having also given a power to our minds, in several instances, to choose, amongst its ideas, which it will think on, and to pursue the inquiry of this or that subject with consideration and attention, to excite us to these actions of thinking and motion that we are capable of,— has been pleased to join to several thoughts, and several sensations a perception of delight. If this were wholly separated from all our outward sensations, and inward thoughts, we should have no reason to prefer one thought or action to another; negligence to attention, or motion to rest. And so we should neither stir our bodies, nor employ our minds, but let our thoughts (if I may so call it) run adrift, without any direction or design, and suffer the ideas of our minds, like unregarded shadows, to make their appearances there, as it happened, without attending to them. In which state man, however furnished with the faculties of understanding and will, would be a very idle, inactive creature, and pass his time only in a lazy, lethargic dream. It has therefore pleased our wise Creator to annex to several objects, and the ideas which we receive from them, as also to several of our thoughts, a concomitant pleasure, and that in several objects, to several degrees, that those faculties which he had endowed us with might not remain wholly idle and unemployed by us.

4. An end and use of pain. Pain has the same efficacy and use to set us on work that pleasure has, we being as ready to employ our faculties to avoid that, as to pursue this: only this is worth our consideration, that pain is often produced by the same objects and ideas that produce pleasure in us. This their near conjunction, which makes us often feel pain in the sensations where we expected pleasure, gives us new occasion of admiring the wisdom and goodness of our Maker, who, designing the preservation of our being, has annexed pain to the application of many things to our bodies, to warn us of the harm that they will do, and as advices to withdraw from them. But he, not designing our preservation barely, but the preservation of every part and organ in its perfection, hath in many cases annexed pain to those very ideas which delight us. Thus heat, that is very agreeable to us in one degree, by a little greater increase of it proves no ordinary torment: and the most pleasant of all sensible objects, light itself, if there be too much of it, if increased beyond a due proportion to our eyes, causes a very painful sensation. Which is wisely and favourably so ordered by nature, that when any object does, by the vehemency of its operation, disorder the instruments of sensation, whose structures cannot but be very nice and delicate, we might, by the pain, be warned to withdraw, before the organ be quite put out of order, and so be unfitted for its proper function for the future. The consideration of those objects that produce it may well persuade us, that this is the end or use of pain. For, though great light be insufferable to our eyes, yet the highest degree of darkness does not at all disease them: because that, causing no disorderly motion in it, leaves that curious organ unharmed in its natural state. But yet excess of cold as well as heat pains us: because it is equally destructive to that temper which is necessary to the preservation of life, and the exercise of the several functions of the body, and

which consists in a moderate degree of warmth; or, if you please, a motion of the insensible parts of our bodies, confined within certain bounds.

5. Another end. Beyond all this, we may find another reason why God hath scattered up and down several degrees of pleasure and pain, in all the things that environ and affect us; and blended them together in almost all that our thoughts and senses have to do with;— that we, finding imperfection, dissatisfaction, and want of complete happiness, in all the enjoyments which the creatures can afford us, might be led to seek it in the enjoyment of Him with whom there is fullness of joy, and at whose right hand are pleasures for evermore.

6. Goodness of God in annexing pleasure and pain to our other ideas. Though what I have here said may not, perhaps, make the ideas of pleasure and pain clearer to us than our own experience does, which is the only way that we are capable of having them; yet the consideration of the reason why they are annexed to so many other ideas, serving to give us due sentiments of the wisdom and goodness of the Sovereign Disposer of all things, may not be unsuitable to the main end of these inquiries: the knowledge and veneration of him being the chief end of all our thoughts, and the proper business of all understandings.

7. Ideas of existence and unity. Existence and Unity are two other ideas that are suggested to the understanding by every object without, and every idea within. When ideas are in our minds, we consider them as being actually there, as well as we consider things to be actually without us;— which is, that they exist, or have existence. And whatever we can consider as one thing, whether a real being or idea, suggests to the understanding the idea of unity.

8. Idea of power. Power also is another of those simple ideas which we receive from sensation and reflection. For, observing in ourselves that we do and can think, and that we can at pleasure move several parts of our bodies which were at rest; the effects, also, that natural bodies are able to produce in one another, occurring every moment to our senses,— we both these ways get the idea of power.

9. Idea of succession. Besides these there is another idea, which, though suggested by our senses, yet is more constantly offered to us by what passes in our minds; and that is the idea of succession. For if we look immediately into ourselves, and reflect on what is observable there, we shall find our ideas always, whilst we are awake, or have any thought, passing in train, one going and another coming, without intermission.

10. Simple ideas the materials of all our knowledge. These, if they are not all, are at least (as I think) the most considerable of those simple ideas which the mind has, and out of which is made all its other knowledge; all which it receives only by the two forementioned ways of sensation and reflection.

Nor let any one think these too narrow bounds for the capacious mind of man to expatiate in, which takes its flight further than the stars, and cannot be confined by the limits of the world; that extends its thoughts often even beyond the utmost expansion of Matter, and makes excursions into that incomprehensible Inane. I grant all this, but desire any one to assign any simple idea which is not received from one of those inlets before mentioned, or any complex idea not made out of those simple ones. Nor will it be so strange to think these few simple ideas sufficient to employ the quickest thought, or largest capacity; and to furnish the materials of all that various knowledge, and more various fancies and opinions of all mankind, if we consider how many words may be made out of the various composition of twenty-four letters; or if, going one step further, we will but reflect on the variety of combinations that may be made with barely one of the above-mentioned ideas, viz. number, whose stock is inexhaustible and truly infinite: and what a large and immense field doth extension alone afford the mathematicians?

Chapter VIII.Some further considerations concerning our Simple Ideas of Sensation

1. Positive ideas from privative causes. Concerning the simple ideas of Sensation, it is to be considered,— that whatsoever is so constituted in nature as to be able, by affecting our senses, to cause any perception in the mind, doth thereby produce in the understanding a simple idea; which, whatever be the external cause of it, when it comes to be taken notice of by our discerning faculty, it is by the mind looked on and considered there to be a real positive idea in the understanding, as much as any other whatsoever; though, perhaps, the cause of it be but a privation of the subject.

2. Ideas in the mind distinguished from that in things which gives rise to them. Thus the ideas of heat and cold, light and darkness, white and black, motion and rest, are equally clear and positive ideas in the mind; though, perhaps, some of the causes which produce them are barely privations, in those subjects from whence our senses derive those ideas. These the understanding, in its view of them, considers all as distinct positive ideas, without taking notice of the causes that produce them: which is an inquiry not belonging to the idea, as it is in the understanding, but to the nature of the things existing without us. These are two very different things, and carefully to be distinguished; it being one thing to perceive and know the idea of white or black, and quite another to examine what kind of particles they must be, and how ranged in the superficies, to make any object appear white or black.

3. We may have the ideas when we are ignorant of their physical causes. A painter or dyer who never inquired into their causes hath the ideas of white and black, and other colours, as clearly, perfectly, and distinctly in his understanding, and perhaps more distinctly, than the philosopher who hath busied himself in considering their natures, and thinks he knows how far either of them is, in its cause, positive or privative; and the idea of black is no less positive in his mind than that of white, however the cause of that colour in the external object may be only a privation.

4. Why a privative cause in nature may occasion a positive idea. If it were the design of my present undertaking to inquire into the natural causes and manner of perception, I should offer this as a reason why a privative cause might, in some cases at least, produce a positive idea; viz. that all sensation being produced in us only by different degrees and modes of motion in our animal spirits, variously agitated by external objects, the abatement of any former motion must as necessarily produce a new sensation as the variation or increase of it; and so introduce a new idea, which depends only on a different motion of the animal spirits in that organ.

5. Negative names need not be meaningless. But whether this be so or not I will not here determine, but appeal to every one's own experience, whether the shadow of a man, though it consists of nothing but the absence of light (and the more the absence of light is, the more discernible is the shadow) does not, when a man looks on it, cause as clear and positive idea in his mind as a man himself, though covered over with clear sunshine? And the picture of a shadow is a positive thing. Indeed, we have negative names, which stand not directly for positive ideas, but for their absence, such as insipid, silence, nihil, &c.; which words denote positive ideas, v.g. taste, sound, being, with a signification of their absence.

6. Whether any ideas are due to causes really privative. And thus one may truly be said to see darkness. For, supposing a hole perfectly dark, from whence no light is reflected, it is certain one may see the figure of it, or it may be painted; or whether the ink I write with makes any other idea, is a question. The privative causes I have here assigned of positive ideas are according to the common opinion; but, in truth, it will be hard to determine whether there be really any ideas from a privative cause, till it be determined, whether rest be any more a privation than motion.

7. Ideas in the mind, qualities in bodies. To discover the nature of our ideas the better, and to discourse of them intelligibly, it will be convenient to distinguish them as they are ideas or perceptions in our minds; and as they are modifications of matter in the bodies that cause such perceptions in us: that so we may not think (as perhaps usually is done) that they are exactly the images and resemblances of something inherent in the subject; most of those of sensation being in the mind no more the likeness of something existing without us, than the names that

stand for them are the likeness of our ideas, which yet upon hearing they are apt to excite in us.

8. Our ideas and the qualities of bodies. Whatsoever the mind perceives in itself, or is the immediate object of perception, thought, or understanding, that I call idea; and the power to produce any idea in our mind, I call quality of the subject wherein that power is. Thus a snowball having the power to produce in us the ideas of white, cold, and round,— the power to produce those ideas in us, as they are in the snowball, I call qualities; and as they are sensations or perceptions in our understandings, I call them ideas; which ideas, if I speak of sometimes as in the things themselves, I would be understood to mean those qualities in the objects which produce them in us.

9. Primary qualities of bodies. Qualities thus considered in bodies are,
First, such as are utterly inseparable from the body, in what state soever it be; and such as in all the alterations and changes it suffers, all the force can be used upon it, it constantly keeps; and such as sense constantly finds in every particle of matter which has bulk enough to be perceived; and the mind finds inseparable from every particle of matter, though less than to make itself singly be perceived by our senses: v.g. Take a grain of wheat, divide it into two parts; each part has still solidity, extension, figure, and mobility: divide it again, and it retains still the same qualities; and so divide it on, till the parts become insensible; they must retain still each of them all those qualities. For division (which is all that a mill, or pestle, or any other body, does upon another, in reducing it to insensible parts) can never take away either solidity, extension, figure, or mobility from any body, but only makes two or more distinct separate masses of matter, of that which was but one before; all which distinct masses, reckoned as so many distinct bodies, after division, make a certain number. These I call original or primary qualities of body, which I think we may observe to produce simple ideas in us, viz. solidity, extension, figure, motion or rest, and number.

10. Secondary qualities of bodies. Secondly, such qualities which in truth are nothing in the objects themselves but power to produce various sensations in us by their primary qualities, i.e. by the bulk, figure, texture, and motion of their insensible parts, as colours, sounds, tastes, &c. These I call secondary qualities. To these might be added a third sort, which are allowed to be barely powers; though they are as much real qualities in the subject as those which I, to comply with the common way of speaking, call qualities, but for distinction, secondary qualities. For the power in fire to produce a new colour, or consistency, in wax or clay,— by its primary qualities, is as much a quality in fire, as the power it has to produce in me a new idea or sensation of warmth or burning, which I felt not before,— by the same primary qualities, viz. the bulk, texture, and motion of its insensible parts.

11. How bodies produce ideas in us. The next thing to be considered is, how bodies produce ideas in us; and that is manifestly by impulse, the only way which we can conceive bodies to operate in.

12. By motions, external, and in our organism. If then external objects be not united to our minds when they produce ideas therein; and yet we perceive these original qualities in such of them as singly fall under our senses, it is evident that some motion must be thence continued by our nerves, or animal spirits, by some parts of our bodies, to the brains or the seat of sensation, there to produce in our minds the particular ideas we have of them. And since the extension, figure, number, and motion of bodies of an observable bigness, may be perceived at a distance by the sight, it is evident some singly imperceptible bodies must come from them to the eyes, and thereby convey to the brain some motion; which produces these ideas which we have of them in us.

13. How secondary qualities produce their ideas. After the same manner, that the ideas of these original qualities are produced in us, we may conceive that the ideas of secondary qualities are also produced, viz. by the operation of insensible particles on our senses. For, it being manifest that there are bodies and good store of bodies, each whereof are so small, that we cannot by any of our senses discover either their bulk, figure, or motion,— as is evident in

the particles of the air and water, and others extremely smaller than those; perhaps as much smaller than the particles of air and water, as the particles of air and water are smaller than peas or hail-stones;— let us suppose at present that the different motions and figures, bulk and number, of such particles, affecting the several organs of our senses, produce in us those different sensations which we have from the colours and smells of bodies; v.g. that a violet, by the impulse of such insensible particles of matter, of peculiar figures and bulks, and in different degrees and modifications of their motions, causes the ideas of the blue colour, and sweet scent of that flower to be produced in our minds. It being no more impossible to conceive that God should annex such ideas to such motions, with which they have no similitude, than that he should annex the idea of pain to the motion of a piece of steel dividing our flesh, with which that idea hath no resemblance.

14. They depend on the primary qualities. What I have said concerning colours and smells may be understood also of tastes and sounds, and other the like sensible qualities; which, whatever reality we by mistake attribute to them, are in truth nothing in the objects themselves, but powers to produce various sensations in us; and depend on those primary qualities, viz. bulk, figure, texture, and motion of parts as I have said.

15. Ideas of primary qualities are resemblances; of secondary, not. From whence I think it easy to draw this observation,— that the ideas of primary qualities of bodies are resemblances of them, and their patterns do really exist in the bodies themselves, but the ideas produced in us by these secondary qualities have no resemblance of them at all. There is nothing like our ideas, existing in the bodies themselves. They are, in the bodies we denominate from them, only a power to produce those sensations in us: and what is sweet, blue, or warm in idea, is but the certain bulk, figure, and motion of the insensible parts, in the bodies themselves, which we call so.

16. Examples. Flame is denominated hot and light; snow, white and cold; and manna, white and sweet, from the ideas they produce in us. Which qualities are commonly thought to be the same in those bodies that those ideas are in us, the one the perfect resemblance of the other, as they are in a mirror, and it would by most men be judged very extravagant if one should say otherwise. And yet he that will consider that the same fire that, at one distance produces in us the sensation of warmth, does, at a nearer approach, produce in us the far different sensation of pain, ought to bethink himself what reason he has to say — that this idea of warmth, which was produced in him by the fire, is actually in the fire; and his idea of pain, which the same fire produced in him the same way, is not in the fire. Why are whiteness and coldness in snow, and pain not, when it produces the one and the other idea in us; and can do neither, but by the bulk, figure, number, and motion of its solid parts?

17. The ideas of the primary alone really exist. The particular bulk, number, figure, and motion of the parts of fire or snow are really in them,— whether any one's senses perceive them or no: and therefore they may be called real qualities, because they really exist in those bodies. But light, heat, whiteness, or coldness, are no more really in them than sickness or pain is in manna. Take away the sensation of them; let not the eyes see light or colours, nor the ears hear sounds; let the palate not taste, nor the nose smell, and all colours, tastes, odours, and sounds, as they are such particular ideas, vanish and cease, and are reduced to their causes, i.e. bulk, figure, and motion of parts.

18. The secondary exist in things only as modes of the primary. A piece of manna of a sensible bulk is able to produce in us the idea of a round or square figure; and by being removed from one place to another, the idea of motion. This idea of motion represents it as it really is in manna moving: a circle or square are the same, whether in idea or existence, in the mind or in the manna. And this, both motion and figure, are really in the manna, whether we take notice of them or no: this everybody is ready to agree to. Besides, manna, by tie bulk, figure, texture, and motion of its parts, has a power to produce the sensations of sickness, and sometimes of acute pains or gripings in us. That these ideas of sickness and pain are not in the manna, but effects of its operations on us, and are nowhere when we feel them not; this also every one

readily agrees to. And yet men are hardly to be brought to think that sweetness and whiteness are not really in manna; which are but the effects of the operations of manna, by the motion, size, and figure of its particles, on the eyes and palate: as the pain and sickness caused by manna are confessedly nothing but the effects of its operations on the stomach and guts, by the size, motion, and figure of its insensible parts, (for by nothing else can a body operate, as has been proved): as if it could not operate on the eyes and palate, and thereby produce in the mind particular distinct ideas, which in itself it has not, as well as we allow it can operate on the guts and stomach, and thereby produce distinct ideas, which in itself it has not. These ideas, being all effects of the operations of manna on several parts of our bodies, by the size, figure number, and motion of its parts;— why those produced by the eyes and palate should rather be thought to be really in the manna, than those produced by the stomach and guts; or why the pain and sickness, ideas that are the effect of manna, should be thought to be nowhere when they are not felt; and yet the sweetness and whiteness, effects of the same manna on other parts of the body, by ways equally as unknown, should be thought to exist in the manna, when they are not seen or tasted, would need some reason to explain.

19. Examples. Let us consider the red and white colours in porphyry. Hinder light from striking on it, and its colours vanish; it no longer produces any such ideas in us: upon the return of light it produces these appearances on us again. Can any one think any real alterations are made in the porphyry by the presence or absence of light; and that those ideas of whiteness and redness are really in porphyry in. the light, when it is plain it has no colour in the dark? It has, indeed, such a configuration of particles, both night and day, as are apt, by the rays of light rebounding from some parts of that hard stone, to produce in us the idea of redness, and from others the idea of whiteness; but whiteness or redness are not in it at any time, but such a texture that hath the power to produce such a sensation in us.

20. Pound an almond, and the clear white colour will be altered into a dirty one, and the sweet taste into an oily one. What real alteration can the beating of the pestle make in any body, but an alteration of the texture of it?

21. Explains how water felt as cold by one hand may be warm to the other. Ideas being thus distinguished and understood, we may be able to give an account how the same water, at the same time, may produce the idea of cold by one hand and of heat by the other: whereas it is impossible that the same water, if those ideas were really in it, should at the same time be both hot and cold. For, if we imagine warmth, as it is in our hands, to be nothing but a certain sort and degree of motion in the minute particles of our nerves or animal spirits, we may understand how it is possible that the same water may, at the same time, produce the sensations of heat in one hand and cold in the other; which yet figure never does, that never producing — the idea of a square by one hand which has produced the idea of a globe by another. But if the sensation of heat and cold be nothing but the increase or diminution of the motion of the minute parts of our bodies, caused by the corpuscles of any other body, it is easy to be understood, that if that motion be greater in one hand than in the other; if a body be applied to the two hands, which has in its minute particles a greater motion than in those of one of the hands, and a less than in those of the other, it will increase the motion of the one hand and lessen it in the other; and so cause the different sensations of heat and cold that depend thereon.

22. An excursion into natural philosophy. I have in what just goes before been engaged in physical inquiries a little further than perhaps I intended. But, it being necessary to make the nature of sensation a little understood; and to make the difference between the qualities in bodies, and the ideas produced by them in the mind, to be distinctly conceived, without which it were impossible to discourse intelligibly of them;— I hope I shall be pardoned this little excursion into natural philosophy; it being necessary in our present inquiry to distinguish the primary and real qualities of bodies, which are always in them (viz. solidity, extension, figure, number, and motion, or rest, and are sometimes perceived by us, viz. when the bodies they are in are big enough singly to be discerned), from those secondary and imputed qualities, which

are but the powers of several combinations of those primary ones, when they operate without being distinctly discerned;— whereby we may also come to know what ideas are, and what are not, resemblances of something really existing in the bodies we denominate from them.

23. Three sorts of qualities in bodies. The qualities, then, that are in bodies, rightly considered, are of three sorts:—

First, The bulk, figure, number, situation, and motion or rest of their solid parts. Those are in them, whether we perceive them or not; and when they are of that size that we can discover them, we have by these an idea of the thing as it is in itself; as is plain in artificial things. These I call primary qualities.

Secondly, The power that is in any body, by reason of its insensible primary qualities, to operate after a peculiar manner on any of our senses, and thereby produce in us the different ideas of several colours, sounds, smells, tastes, &c. These are usually called sensible qualities.

Thirdly, The power that is in any body, by reason of the particular constitution of its primary qualities, to make such a change in the bulk, figure, texture, and motion of another body, as to make it operate on our senses differently from what it did before. Thus the sun has a power to make wax white, and fire to make lead fluid. These are usually called powers.

The first of these, as has been said, I think may be properly called real, original, or primary qualities; because they are in the things themselves, whether they are perceived or not: and upon their different modifications it is that the secondary qualities depend.

The other two are only powers to act differently upon other things: which powers result from the different modifications of those primary qualities.

24. The first are resemblances; the second thought to be resemblances, but are not; the third neither are nor are thought so. But, though the two latter sorts of qualities are powers barely, and nothing but powers, relating to several other bodies, and resulting from the different modifications of the original qualities, yet they are generally otherwise thought of. For the second sort, viz, the powers to produce several ideas in us, by our senses, are looked upon as real qualities in the things thus affecting us: but the third sort are called and esteemed barely powers. v.g. The idea of heat or light, which we receive by our eyes, or touch, from the sun, are commonly thought real qualities existing in the sun, and something more than mere powers in it. But when we consider the sun in reference to wax, which it melts or blanches, we look on the whiteness and softness produced in the wax, not as qualities in the sun, but effects produced by powers in it. Whereas, if rightly considered, these qualities of light and warmth, which are perceptions in me when I am warmed or enlightened by the sun, are no otherwise in the sun, than the changes made in the wax, when it is blanched or melted, are in the sun. They are all of them equally powers in the sun, depending on its primary qualities; whereby it is able, in the one case, so to alter the bulk, figure, texture, or motion of some of the insensible parts of my eyes or hands, as thereby to produce in me the idea of light or heat; and in the other, it is able so to alter the bulk, figure, texture, or motion of the insensible parts of the wax, as to make them fit to produce in me the distinct ideas of white and fluid.

25. Why the secondary are ordinarily taken for real qualities, and not for bare powers. The reason why the one are ordinarily taken for real qualities, and the other only for bare powers, seems to be, because the ideas we have of distinct colours, sounds, &c., containing nothing at all in them of bulk, figure, or motion, we are not apt to think them the effects of these primary qualities; which appear not, to our senses, to operate in their production, and with which they have not any apparent congruity or conceivable connexion. Hence it is that we are so forward to imagine, that those ideas are the resemblances of something really existing in the objects themselves: since sensation discovers nothing of bulk, figure, or motion of parts in their production; nor can reason show how bodies, by their bulk, figure, and motion, should produce in the mind the ideas of blue or yellow, &c. But, in the other case, in the operations of bodies changing the qualities one of another, we plainly discover that the quality produced hath commonly no resemblance with anything in the thing producing it; wherefore we look on it as a bare effect of power. For, through receiving the idea of heat or light from the sun, we

are apt to think it is a perception and resemblance of such a quality in the sun; yet when we see wax, or a fair face, receive change of colour from the sun, we cannot imagine that to be the reception or resemblance of anything in the sun, because we find not those different colours in the sun itself. For, our senses being able to observe a likeness or unlikeness of sensible qualities in two different external objects, we forwardly enough conclude the production of any sensible quality in any subject to be an effect of bare power, and not the communication of any quality which was really in the efficient, when we find no such sensible quality in the thing that produced it. But our senses, not being able to discover any unlikeness between the idea produced in us, and the quality of the object producing it, we are apt to imagine that our ideas are resemblances of something in the objects, and not the effects of certain powers placed in the modification of their primary qualities, with which primary qualities the ideas produced in us have no resemblance.

26. Secondary qualities twofold; first, immediately perceivable; secondly, mediately perceivable. To conclude. Besides those before-mentioned primary qualities in bodies, viz. bulk, figure, extension, number, and motion of their solid parts; all the rest, whereby we take notice of bodies, and distinguish them one from another, are nothing else but several powers in them, depending on those primary qualities; whereby they are fitted, either by immediately operating on our bodies to produce several different ideas in us; or else, by operating on other bodies, so to change their primary qualities as to render them capable of producing ideas in us different from what before they did. The former of these, I think, may be called secondary qualities immediately perceivable: the latter, secondary qualities, mediately perceivable.

Chapter IX.Of Perception

1. Perception the first simple idea of reflection. PERCEPTION, as it is the first faculty of the mind exercised about our ideas; so it is the first and simplest idea we have from reflection, and is by some called thinking in general. Though thinking, in the propriety of the English tongue, signifies that sort of operation in the mind about its ideas, wherein the mind is active; where it, with some degree of voluntary attention, considers anything. For in bare naked perception, the mind is, for the most part, only passive; and what it perceives, it cannot avoid perceiving.

2. Reflection alone can give us the idea of what perception is. What perception is, every one will know better by reflecting on what he does himself, when he sees, hears, feels, &c., or thinks, than by any discourse of mine. Whoever reflects on what passes in his own mind cannot miss it. And if he does not reflect, all the words in the world cannot make him have any notion of it.

3. Arises in sensation only when the mind notices the organic impression. This is certain, that whatever alterations are made in the body, if they reach not the mind; whatever impressions are made on the outward parts, if they are not taken notice of within, there is no perception. Fire may burn our bodies with no other effect than it does a billet, unless the motion be continued to the brain, and there the sense of heat, or idea of pain, be produced in the mind; wherein consists actual perception.

4. Impulse on the organ insufficient. How often may a man observe in himself, that whilst his mind is intently employed in the contemplation of some objects, and curiously surveying some ideas that are there, it takes no notice of impressions of sounding bodies made upon the organ of hearing, with the same alteration that uses to be for the producing the idea of sound? A sufficient impulse there may be on the organ; but it not reaching the observation of the mind, there follows no perception: and though the motion that uses to produce the idea of sound be made in the ear, yet no sound is heard. Want of sensation, in this case, is not through any defect in the organ, or that the man's ears are less affected than at other times when he does hear: but that which uses to produce the idea, though conveyed in by the usual organ, not being taken notice of in the understanding, and so imprinting no idea in the mind, there

follows no sensation. So that wherever there is sense or perception, there some idea is actually produced, and present in the understanding.

5. Children, though they may have ideas in the womb, have none innate. Therefore I doubt not but children, by the exercise of their senses about objects that affect them in the womb, receive some few ideas before they are born, as the unavoidable effects, either of the bodies that environ them, or else of those wants or diseases they suffer; amongst which (if one may conjecture concerning things not very capable of examination) I think the ideas of hunger and warmth are two: which probably are some of the first that children have, and which they scarce ever part with again.

6. The effects of sensation in the womb. But though it be reasonable to imagine that children receive some ideas before they come into the world, yet these simple ideas are far from those innate principles which some contend for, and we, above, have rejected. These here mentioned, being the effects of sensation, are only from some affections of the body, which happen to them there, and so depend on something exterior to the mind; no otherwise differing in their manner of production from other ideas derived from sense, but only in the precedency of time. Whereas those innate principles are supposed to be quite of another nature; not coming into the mind by any accidental alterations in, or operations on the body; but, as it were, original characters impressed upon it, in the very first moment of its being and constitution.

7. Which ideas appear first, is not evident, nor important. As there are some ideas which we may reasonably suppose may be introduced into the minds of children in the womb, subservient to the necessities of their life and being there: so, after they are born, those ideas are the earliest imprinted which happen to be the sensible qualities which first occur to them; amongst which light is not the least considerable, nor of the weakest efficacy. And how covetous the mind is to be furnished with all such ideas as have no pain accompanying them, may be a little guessed by what is observable in children new-born; who always turn their eyes to that part from whence the light comes, lay them how you please. But the ideas that are most familiar at first, being various according to the divers circumstances of children's first entertainment in the world, the order wherein the several ideas come at first into the mind is very various, and uncertain also; neither is it much material to know it.

8. Sensations often changed by the judgment. We are further to consider concerning perception, that the ideas we receive by sensation are often, in grown people, altered by the judgment, without our taking notice of it. When we set before our eyes a round globe of any uniform colour, v.g. gold, alabaster, or jet, it is certain that the idea thereby imprinted on our mind is of a flat circle, variously shadowed, with several degrees of light and brightness coming to our eyes. But we having, by use, been accustomed to perceive what kind of appearance convex bodies are wont to make in us; what alterations are made in the reflections of light by the difference of the sensible figures of bodies;— the judgment presently, by an habitual custom, alters the appearances into their causes. So that from that which is truly variety of shadow or colour, collecting the figure, it makes it pass for a mark of figure, and frames to itself the perception of a convex figure and an uniform colour; when the idea we receive from thence is only a plane variously coloured, as is evident in painting. To which purpose I shall here insert a problem of that very ingenious and studious promoter of real knowledge, the learned and worthy Mr. Molyneux, which he was pleased to send me in a letter some months since; and it is this:—"Suppose a man born blind, and now adult, and taught by his touch to distinguish between a cube and a sphere of the same metal, and nighly of the same bigness, so as to tell, when he felt one and the other, which is the cube, which the sphere. Suppose then the cube and sphere placed on a table, and the blind man be made to see: quaere, whether by his sight, before he touched them, he could now distinguish and tell which is the globe, which the cube?" To which the acute and judicious proposer answers, "Not. For, though he has obtained the experience of how a globe, how a cube affects his touch, yet he has not yet obtained the experience, that what affects his touch so or so, must affect his sight so or so; or

that a protuberant angle in the cube, that pressed his hand unequally, shall appear to his eye as it does in the cube."— I agree with this thinking gentleman, whom I am proud to call my friend, in his answer to this problem; and am of opinion that the blind man, at first sight, would not be able with certainty to say which was the globe, which the cube, whilst he only saw them; though he could unerringly name them by his touch, and certainly distinguish them by the difference of their figures felt. This I have set down, and leave with my reader, as an occasion for him to consider how much he may be beholden to experience, improvement, and acquired notions, where he thinks he had not the least use of, or help from them. And the rather, because this observing gentleman further adds, that "having, upon the occasion of my book, proposed this to divers very ingenious men, he hardly ever met with one that at first gave the answer to it which he thinks true, till by hearing his reasons they were convinced."

9. This judgment apt to be mistaken for direct perception. But this is not, I think, usual in any of our ideas, but those received by sight. Because sight, the most comprehensive of all our senses, conveying to our minds the ideas of light and colours, which are peculiar only to that sense; and also the far different ideas of space, figure, and motion, the several varieties whereof change the appearances of its proper object, viz. light and colours; we bring ourselves by use to judge of the one by the other. This, in many cases by a settled habit,— in things whereof we have frequent experience, is performed so constantly and so quick, that we take that for the perception of our sensation which is an idea formed by our judgment; so that one, viz. that of sensation, serves only to excite the other, and is scarce taken notice of itself;— as a man who reads or hears with attention and understanding, takes little notice of the characters or sounds, but of the ideas that are excited in him by them.

10. How, by habit, ideas of sensation are unconsciously changed into ideas of judgment. Nor need we wonder that this is done with so little notice, if we consider how quick the actions of the mind are performed. For, as itself is thought to take up no space, to have no extension; so its actions seem to require no time, but many of them seem to be crowded into an instant. I speak this in comparison to the actions of the body. Any one may easily observe this in his own thoughts, who will take the pains to reflect on them. How, as it were in an instant, do our minds, with one glance, see all the parts of a demonstration, which may very well be called a long one, if we consider the time it will require to put it into words, and step by step show it another? Secondly, we shall not be so much surprised that this is done in us with so little notice, if we consider how the facility which we get of doing things, by a custom of doing, makes them often pass in us without our notice. Habits, especially such as are begun very early, come at last to produce actions in us, which often escape our observation. How frequently do we, in a day, cover our eyes with our eyelids, without perceiving that we are at all in the dark! Men that, by custom, have got the use of a by-word, do almost in every sentence pronounce sounds which, though taken notice of by others, they themselves neither hear nor observe. And therefore it is not so strange, that our mind should often change the idea of its sensation into that of its judgment, and make one serve only to excite the other, without our taking notice of it.

11. Perception puts the difference between animals and vegetables. This faculty of perception seems to me to be, that which puts the distinction betwixt the animal kingdom and the inferior parts of nature. For, however vegetables have, many of them, some degrees of motion, and upon the different application of other bodies to them, do very briskly alter their figures and motions, and so have obtained the name of sensitive plants, from a motion which has some resemblance to that which in animals follows upon sensation: yet I suppose it is all bare mechanism; and no otherwise produced than the turning of a wild oat-beard, by the insinuation of the particles of moisture, or the shortening of a rope, by the affusion of water. All which is done without any sensation in the subject, or the having or receiving any ideas.

12. Perception in all animals. Perception, I believe, is, in some degree, in all sorts of animals; though in some possibly the avenues provided by nature for the reception of sensations are so few, and the perception they are received with so obscure and dull, that it comes extremely

short of the quickness and variety of sensation which is in other animals; but yet it is sufficient for, and wisely adapted to, the state and condition of that sort of animals who are thus made. So that the wisdom and goodness of the Maker plainly appear in all the parts of this stupendous fabric, and all the several degrees and ranks of creatures in it.

13. According to their condition. We may, I think, from the make of an oyster or cockle, reasonably conclude that it has not so many, nor so quick senses as a man, or several other animals; nor if it had, would it, in that state and incapacity of transferring itself from one place to another, be bettered by them. What good would sight and hearing do to a creature that cannot move itself to or from the objects wherein at a distance it perceives good or evil? And would not quickness of sensation be an inconvenience to an animal that must lie still where chance has once placed it, and there receive the afflux of colder or warmer, clean or foul water, as it happens to come to it?

14. Decay of perception in old age. But yet I cannot but think there is some small dull perception, whereby they are distinguished from perfect insensibility. And that this may be so, we have plain instances, even in mankind itself. Take one in whom decrepit old age has blotted out the memory of his past knowledge, and clearly wiped out the ideas his mind was formerly stored with, and has, by destroying his sight, hearing, and smell quite, and his taste to a great degree, stopped up almost all the passages for new ones to enter; or if there be some of the inlets yet half open, the impressions made are scarcely perceived, or not at all retained. How far such an one (notwithstanding all that is boasted of innate principles) is in his knowledge and intellectual faculties above the condition of a cockle or an oyster, I leave to be considered. And if a man had passed sixty years in such a state, as it is possible he might, as well as three days, I wonder what difference there would be, in any intellectual perfections, between him and the lowest degree of animals.

15. Perception the inlet of all materials of knowledge. Perception then being the first step and degree towards knowledge, and the inlet of all the materials of it; the fewer senses any man, as well as any other creature, hath; and the fewer and duller the impressions are that are made by them, and the duller the faculties are that are employed about them,— the more remote are they from that knowledge which is to be found in some men. But this being in great variety of degrees (as may be perceived amongst men) cannot certainly be discovered in the several species of animals, much less in their particular individuals. It suffices me only to have remarked here,— that perception is the first operation of all our intellectual faculties, and the inlet of all knowledge in our minds. And I am apt too to imagine, that it is perception, in the lowest degree of it, which puts the boundaries between animals and the inferior ranks of creatures. But this I mention only as my conjecture by the by; it being indifferent to the matter in hand which way the learned shall determine of it.

Chapter X.Of Retention

1. Contemplation. The next faculty of the mind, whereby it makes a further progress towards knowledge, is that which I call retention; or the keeping of those simple ideas which from sensation or reflection it hath received. This is done two ways.

First, by keeping the idea which is brought into it, for some time actually in view, which is called contemplation.

2. Memory. The other way of retention is, the power to revive again in our minds those ideas which, after imprinting, have disappeared, or have been as it were laid aside out of sight. And thus we do, when we conceive heat or light, yellow or sweet,— the object being removed. This is memory, which is as it were the storehouse of our ideas. For, the narrow mind of man not being capable of having many ideas under view and consideration at once, it was necessary to have a repository, to lay up those ideas which, at another time, it might have use of. But, our ideas being nothing but actual perceptions in the mind, which cease to be anything

when there is no perception of them; this laying up of our ideas in the repository of the memory signifies no more but this,— that the mind has a power in many cases to revive perceptions which it has once had, with this additional perception annexed to them, that it has had them before. And in this sense it is that our ideas are said to be in our memories, when indeed they are actually nowhere;— but only there is an ability in the mind when it will to revive them again, and as it were paint them anew on itself, though some with more, some with less difficulty; some more lively, and others more obscurely. And thus it is, by the assistance of this faculty, that we are said to have all those ideas in our understandings which, though we do not actually contemplate, yet we can bring in sight, and make appear again, and be the objects of our thoughts, without the help of those sensible qualities which first imprinted them there.

3. Attention, repetition, pleasure and pain, fix ideas. Attention and repetition help much to the fixing any ideas in the memory. But those which naturally at first make the deepest and most lasting impressions, are those which are accompanied with pleasure or pain. The great business of the senses being, to make us take notice of what hurts or advantages the body, it is wisely ordered by nature, as has been shown, that pain should accompany the reception of several ideas; which, supplying the place of consideration and reasoning in children, and acting quicker than consideration in grown men, makes both the old and young avoid painful objects with that haste which is necessary for their preservation; and in both settles in the memory a caution for the future.

4. Ideas fade in the memory. Concerning the several degrees of lasting, wherewith ideas are imprinted on the memory, we may observe,— that some of them have been produced in the understanding by an object affecting the senses once only, and no more than once; others, that have more than once offered themselves to the senses, have yet been little taken notice of: the mind, either heedless, as in children, or otherwise employed, as in men intent only on one thing; not setting the stamp deep into itself. And in some, where they are set on with care and repeated impressions, either through the temper of the body, or some other fault, the memory is very weak. In all these cases, ideas in the mind quickly fade, and often vanish quite out of the understanding, leaving no more footsteps or remaining characters of themselves than shadows do flying over fields of corn, and the mind is as void of them as if they had never been there.

5. Causes of oblivion. Thus many of those ideas which were produced in the minds of children, in the beginning of their sensation, (some of which perhaps, as of some pleasures and pains, were before they were born, and others in their infancy,) if the future course of their lives they are not repeated again, are quite lost, without the least glimpse remaining of them. This may be observed in those who by some mischance have lost their sight when they were very young; in whom the ideas of colours having been but slightly taken notice of, and ceasing to be repeated, do quite wear out; so that some years after, there is no more notion nor memory of colours left in their minds, than in those of people born blind. The memory of some men, it is true, is very tenacious, even to a miracle. But yet there seems to be a constant decay of all our ideas, even of those which are struck deepest, and in minds the most retentive; so that if they be not sometimes renewed, by repeated exercise of the senses, or reflection on those kinds of objects which at first occasioned them, the print wears out, and at last there remains nothing to be seen. Thus the ideas, as well as children, of our youth, often die before us: and our minds represent to us those tombs to which we are approaching; where, though the brass and marble remain, yet the inscriptions are effaced by time, and the imagery moulders away. The pictures drawn in our minds are laid in fading colours; and if not sometimes refreshed, vanish and disappear. How much the constitution of our bodies and the make of our animal spirits are concerned in this; and whether the temper of the brain makes this difference, that in some it retains the characters drawn on it like marble, in others like freestone, and in others little better than sand, I shall not here inquire; though it may seem probable that the constitution of the body does sometimes influence the memory, since we oftentimes find a

disease quite strip the mind of all its ideas, and the flames of a fever in a few days calcine all those images to dust and confusion, which seemed to be as lasting as if graved in marble.

6. Constantly repeated ideas can scarce be lost. But concerning the ideas themselves, it is easy to remark, that those that are oftenest refreshed (amongst which are those that are conveyed into the mind by more ways than one) by a frequent return of the objects or actions that produce them, fix themselves best in the memory, and remain clearest and longest there; and therefore those which are of the original qualities of bodies, vis. solidity, extension, figure, motion, and rest; and those that almost constantly affect our bodies, as heat and cold; and those which are the affections of all kinds of beings, as existence, duration, and number, which almost every object that affects our senses, every thought which employs our minds, bring along with them;— these, I say, and the like ideas, are seldom quite lost, whilst the mind retains any ideas at all.

7. In remembering, the mind is often active. In this secondary perception, as I may so call it, or viewing again the ideas that are lodged in the memory, the mind is oftentimes more than barely passive; the appearance of those dormant pictures depending sometimes on the will. The mind very often sets itself on work in search of some hidden idea, and turns as it were the eye of the soul upon it; though sometimes too they start up in our minds of their own accord, and offer themselves to the understanding; and very often are roused and tumbled out of their dark cells into open daylight, by turbulent and tempestuous passions; our affections bringing ideas to our memory, which had otherwise lain quiet and unregarded. This further is to be observed, concerning ideas lodged in the memory, and upon occasion revived by the mind, that they are not only (as the word revive imports) none of them new ones, but also that the mind takes notice of them as of a former impression, and renews its acquaintance with them, as with ideas it had known before. So that though ideas formerly imprinted are not all constantly in view, yet in remembrance they are constantly known to be such as have been formerly imprinted; i.e. in view, and taken notice of before, by the understanding.

8. Two defects in the memory, oblivion and slowness. Memory, in an intellectual creature, is necessary in the next degree to perception. It is of so great moment, that, where it is wanting, all the rest of our faculties are in a great measure useless. And we in our thoughts, reasonings, and knowledge, could not proceed beyond present objects, were it not for the assistance of our memories; wherein there may be two defects:—

First, That it loses the idea quite, and so far it produces perfect ignorance. For, since we can know nothing further than we have the idea of it, when that is gone, we are in perfect ignorance.

Secondly, That it moves slowly, and retrieves not the ideas that it has, and are laid up in store, quick enough to serve the mind upon occasion. This, if it be to a great degree, is stupidity; and he who, through this default in his memory, has not the ideas that are really preserved there, ready at hand when need and occasion calls for them, were almost as good be without them quite, since they serve him to little purpose. The dull man, who loses the opportunity, whilst he is seeking in his mind for those ideas that should serve his turn, is not much more happy in his knowledge than one that is perfectly ignorant. It is the business therefore of the memory to furnish to the mind those dormant ideas which it has present occasion for; in the having them ready at hand on all occasions, consists that which we call invention, fancy, and quickness of parts.

9. A defect which belongs to the memory of man, as finite. These are defects we may observe in the memory of one man compared with another. There is another defect which we may conceive to be in the memory of man in general;— compared with some superior created intellectual beings, which in this faculty may so far excel man, that they may have constantly in view the whole scene of all their former actions, wherein no one of the thoughts they have ever had may slip out of their sight. The omniscience of God, who knows all things, past, present, and to come, and to whom the thoughts of men's hearts always lie open, may satisfy us of the possibility of this. For who can doubt but God may communicate to those glorious

spirits, his immediate attendants, any of his perfections; in what proportions he pleases, as far as created finite beings can be capable? It is reported of that prodigy of parts, Monsieur Pascal, that till the decay of his health had impaired his memory, he forgot nothing of what he had done, read, or thought, in any part of his rational age. This is a privilege so little known to most men, that it seems almost incredible to those who, after the ordinary way, measure all others by themselves; but yet, when considered, may help us to enlarge our thoughts towards greater perfections of it, in superior ranks of spirits. For this of Monsieur Pascal was still with the narrowness that human minds are confined to here,— of having great variety of ideas only by succession, not all at once. Whereas the several degrees of angels may probably have larger views; and some of them be endowed with capacities able to retain together, and constantly set before them, as in one picture, all their past knowledge at once. This, we may conceive, would be no small advantage to the knowledge of a thinking man,— if all his past thoughts and reasonings could be always present to him. And therefore we may suppose it one of those ways, wherein the knowledge of separate spirits may exceedingly surpass ours.

10. Brutes have memory. This faculty of laying up and retaining the ideas that are brought into the mind, several other animals seem to have to a great degree, as well as man. For, to pass by other instances, birds learning of tunes, and the endeavours one may observe in them to hit the notes right, put it past doubt with me, that they have perception, and retain ideas in their memories, and use them for patterns. For it seems to me impossible that they should endeavour to conform their voices to notes (as it is plain they do) of which they had no ideas. For, though I should grant sound may mechanically cause a certain motion of the animal spirits in the brains of those birds, whilst the tune is actually playing; and that motion may be continued on to the muscles of the wings, and so the bird mechanically be driven away by certain noises, because this may tend to the bird's preservation; yet that can never be supposed a reason why it should cause mechanically — either whilst the tune is playing, much less after it has ceased — such a motion of the organs in the bird's voice as should conform it to the notes of a foreign sound, which imitation can be of no use to the bird's preservation. But, which is more, it cannot with any appearance of reason be supposed (much less proved) that birds, without sense and memory, can approach their notes nearer and nearer by degrees to a tune played yesterday; which if they have no idea of in their memory, is now nowhere, nor can be a pattern for them to imitate, or which any repeated essays can bring them nearer to. Since there is no reason why the sound of a pipe should leave traces in their brains, which, not at first, but by their after-endeavours, should produce the like sounds; and why the sounds they make themselves, should not make traces which they should follow, as well as those of the pipe, is impossible to conceive.

Chapter XI. Of Discerning, and other operations of the Mind

1. No knowledge without discernment. Another faculty we may take notice of in our minds is that of discerning and distinguishing between the several ideas it has. It is not enough to have a confused perception of something in general. Unless the mind had a distinct perception of different objects and their qualities, it would be capable of very little knowledge, though the bodies that affect us were as busy about us as they are now, and the mind were continually employed in thinking. On this faculty of distinguishing one thing from another depends the evidence and certainty of several, even very general, propositions, which have passed for innate truths;— because men, overlooking the true cause why those propositions find universal assent, impute it wholly to native uniform impressions; whereas it in truth depends upon this clear discerning faculty of the mind, whereby it perceives two ideas to be the same, or different. But of this more hereafter.

2. The difference of wit and judgment. How much the imperfection of accurately discriminating ideas one from another lies, either in the dulness or faults of the organs of

sense; or want of acuteness, exercise, or attention in the understanding; or hastiness and precipitancy, natural to some tempers, I will not here examine: it suffices to take notice, that this is one of the operations that the mind may reflect on and observe in itself It is of that consequence to its other knowledge, that so far as this faculty is in itself dull, or not rightly made use of, for the distinguishing one thing from another,— so far our notions are confused, and our reason and judgment disturbed or misled. If in having our ideas in the memory ready at hand consists quickness of parts; in this, of having them unconfused, and being able nicely to distinguish one thing from another, where there is but the least difference, consists, in a great measure, the exactness of judgment, and clearness of reason, which is to be observed in one man above another. And hence perhaps may be given some reason of that common observation,— that men who have a great deal of wit, and prompt memories, have not always the clearest judgment or deepest reason. For wit lying most in the assemblage of ideas, and putting those together with quickness and variety, wherein can be found any resemblance or congruity, thereby to make up pleasant pictures and agreeable visions in the fancy; judgment, on the contrary, lies quite on the other side, in separating carefully, one from another, ideas wherein can be found the least difference, thereby to avoid being misled by similitude, and by affinity to take one thing for another. This is a way of proceeding quite contrary to metaphor and allusion; wherein for the most part lies that entertainment and pleasantry of wit, which strikes so lively on the fancy, and therefore is so acceptable to all people, because its beauty appears at first sight, and there is required no labor of thought to examine what truth or reason there is in it. The mind, without looking any further, rests satisfied with the agreeableness of the picture and the gaiety of the fancy. And it is a kind of affront to go about to examine it, by the severe rules of truth and good reason; whereby it appears that it consists in something that is not perfectly conformable to them.

3. Clearness done hinders confusion. To the well distinguishing our ideas, it chiefly contributes that they be clear and determinate. And when they are so, it will not breed any confusion or mistake about them, though the senses should (as sometimes they do) convey them from the same object differently on different occasions, and so seem to err. For, though a man in a fever should from sugar have a bitter taste, which at another time would produce a sweet one, yet the idea of bitter in that man's mind would be as clear and distinct from the idea of sweet as if he had tasted only gall. Nor does it make any more confusion between the two ideas of sweet and bitter, that the same sort of body produces at one time one, and at another time another idea by the taste, than it makes a confusion in two ideas of white and sweet, or white and round, that the same piece of sugar produces them both in the mind at the same time. And the ideas of orange-colour and azure, that are produced in the mind by the same parcel of the infusion of lignum nephriticum, are no less distinct ideas than those of the same colours taken from two very different bodies.

4. Comparing. The COMPARING them one with another, in respect of extent, degrees, time, place, or any other circumstances, is another operation of the mind about its ideas, and is that upon which depends all that large tribe of ideas comprehended under relation; which, of how vast an extent it is, I shall have occasion to consider hereafter.

5. Brutes compare but imperfectly. How far brutes partake in this faculty, is not easy to determine. I imagine they have it not in any great degree: for, though they probably have several ideas distinct enough, yet it seems to me to be the prerogative of human understanding, when it has sufficiently distinguished any ideas, so as to perceive them to be perfectly different, and so consequently two, to cast about and consider in what circumstances they are capable to be compared. And therefore, I think, beasts compare not their ideas further than some sensible circumstances annexed to the objects themselves. The other power of comparing, which may be observed in men, belonging to general ideas, and useful only to abstract reasonings, we may probably conjecture beasts have not.

6. Compounding. The next operation we may observe in the mind about its ideas is COMPOSITION; whereby it puts together several of those simple ones it has received from

sensation and reflection, and combines them into complex ones. Under this of composition may be reckoned also that of enlarging, wherein, though the composition does not so much appear as in more complex ones, yet it is nevertheless a putting several ideas together, though of the same kind. Thus, by adding several units together, we make the idea of a dozen; and putting together the repeated ideas of several perches, we frame that of a furlong.

7. Brutes compound but little. In this also, I suppose, brutes come far short of man. For, though they take in, and retain together, several combinations of simple ideas, as possibly the shape, smell, and voice of his master make up the complex idea a dog has of him, or rather are so many distinct marks whereby he knows him; yet I do not think they do of themselves ever compound them and make complex ideas. And perhaps even where we think they have complex ideas, it is only one simple one that directs them in the knowledge of several things, which possibly they distinguish less by their sight than we imagine. For I have been credibly informed that a bitch will nurse, play with, and be fond of young foxes, as much as, and in place of her puppies, if you can but get them once to suck her so long that her milk may go through them. And those animals which have a numerous brood of young ones at once, appear not to have any knowledge of their number; for though they are mightily concerned for any of their young that are taken from them whilst they are in sight or hearing, yet if one or two of them be stolen from them in their absence, or without noise, they appear not to miss them, or to have any sense that their number is lessened.

8. Naming. When children have, by repeated sensations, got ideas fixed in their memories, they begin by degrees to learn the use of signs. And when they have got the skill to apply the organs of speech to the framing of articulate sounds, they begin to make use of words, to signify their ideas to others. These verbal signs they sometimes borrow from others, and sometimes make themselves, as one may observe among the new and unusual names children often give to things in the first use of language.

9. Abstraction. The use of words then being to stand as outward marks of our internal ideas, and those ideas being taken from particular things, if every particular idea that we take in should have a distinct name, names must be endless. To prevent this, the mind makes the particular ideas received from particular objects to become general; which is done by considering them as they are in the mind such appearances,— separate from all other existences, and the circumstances of real existence, as time, place, or any other concomitant ideas. This is called ABSTRACTION, whereby ideas taken from particular beings become general representatives of all of the same kind; and their names general names, applicable to whatever exists conformable to such abstract ideas. Such precise, naked appearances in the mind, without considering how, whence, or with what others they came there, the understanding lays up (with names commonly annexed to them) as the standards to rank real existences into sorts, as they agree with these patterns, and to denominate them accordingly. Thus the same colour being observed to-day in chalk or snow, which the mind yesterday received from milk, it considers that appearance alone, makes it a representative of all of that kind; and having given it the name whiteness, it by that sound signifies the same quality wheresoever to be imagined or met with; and thus universals, whether ideas or terms, are made.

10. Brutes abstract not. If it may be doubted whether beasts compound and enlarge their ideas that way to any degree; this, I think, I may be positive in,— that the power of abstracting is not at all in them; and that the having of general ideas is that which puts a perfect distinction betwixt man and brutes, and is an excellency which the faculties of brutes do by no means attain to. For it is evident we observe no footsteps in them of making use of general signs for universal ideas; from which we have reason to imagine that they have not the faculty of abstracting, or making general ideas, since they have no use of words, or any other general signs.

11. Brutes abstract not, yet are not bare machines. Nor can it be imputed to their want of fit organs to frame articulate sounds, that they have no use or knowledge of general words; since

many of them, we find, can fashion such sounds, and pronounce words distinctly enough, but never with any such application. And, on the other side, men who, through some defect in the organs, want words, yet fail not to express their universal ideas by signs, which serve them instead of general words, a faculty which we see beasts come short in. And, therefore, I think, we may suppose, that it is in this that the species of brutes are discriminated from man: and it is that proper difference wherein they are wholly separated, and which at last widens to so vast a distance. For if they have any ideas at all, and are not bare machines, (as some would have them,) we cannot deny them to have some reason. It seems as evident to me, that they do some of them in certain instances reason, as that they have sense; but it is only in particular ideas, just as they received them from their senses. They are the best of them tied up within those narrow bounds, and have not (as I think) the faculty to enlarge them by any kind of abstraction.

12. Idiots and madmen. How far idiots are concerned in the want or weakness of any, or all of the foregoing faculties, an exact observation of their several ways of faultering would no doubt discover. For those who either perceive but dully, or retain the ideas that come into their minds but ill, who cannot readily excite or compound them, will have little matter to think on. Those who cannot distinguish, compare, and abstract, would hardly be able to understand and make use of language, or judge or reason to any tolerable degree; but only a little and imperfectly about things present, and very familiar to their senses. And indeed any of the forementioned faculties, if wanting, or out of order, produce suitable defects in men's understandings and knowledge.

13. Difference between idiots and madmen. In fine, the defect in naturals seems to proceed from want of quickness, activity, and motion in the intellectual faculties, whereby they are deprived of reason; whereas madmen, on the other side, seem to suffer by the other extreme. For they do not appear to me to have lost the faculty of reasoning, but having joined together some ideas very wrongly, they mistake them for truths; and they err as men do that argue right from wrong principles. For, by the violence of their imaginations, having taken their fancies for realities, they make right deductions from them. Thus you shall find a distracted man fancying himself a king, with a right inference require suitable attendance, respect, and obedience: others who have thought themselves made of glass, have used the caution necessary to preserve such brittle bodies. Hence it comes to pass that a man who is very sober, and of a right understanding in all other things, may in one particular be as frantic as any in Bedlam; if either by any sudden very strong impression, or long fixing his fancy upon one sort of thoughts, incoherent ideas have been cemented together so powerfully, as to remain united. But there are degrees of madness, as of folly; the disorderly jumbling ideas together is in some more, and some less. In short, herein seems to lie the difference between idiots and madmen: that madmen put wrong ideas together, and so make wrong propositions, but argue and reason right from them; but idiots make very few or no propositions, and reason scarce at all.

14. Method followed in this explication of faculties. These, I think, are the first faculties and operations of the mind, which it makes use of in understanding; and though they are exercised about all its ideas in general, yet the instances I have hitherto given have been chiefly in simple ideas. And I have subjoined the explication of these faculties of the mind to that of simple ideas, before I come to what I have to say concerning complex ones, for these following reasons:—

First, Because several of these faculties being exercised at first principally about simple ideas, we might, by following nature in its ordinary method, trace and discover them, in their rise, progress, and gradual improvements.

Secondly, Because observing the faculties of the mind, how they operate about simple ideas,— which are usually, in most men's minds, much more clear, precise, and distinct than complex ones,— we may the better examine and learn how the mind extracts, denominates, compares, and exercises, in its other operations about those which are complex, wherein we are much more liable to mistake.

Thirdly, Because these very operations of the mind about ideas received from sensations, are themselves, when reflected on, another set of ideas, derived from that other source of our knowledge, which I call reflection; and therefore fit to be considered in this place after the simple ideas of sensation. Of compounding, comparing, abstracting, &c., I have but just spoken, having occasion to treat of them more at large in other places.

15. The true beginning of human knowledge. And thus I have given a short, and, I think, true history of the first beginnings of human knowledge;— whence the mind has its first objects; and by what steps it makes its progress to the laying in and storing up those ideas, out of which is to be framed all the knowledge it is capable of: wherein I must appeal to experience and observation whether I am in the right: the best way to come to truth being to examine things as really they are, and not to conclude they are, as we fancy of ourselves, or have been taught by others to imagine.

16. Appeal to experience. To deal truly, this is the only way that I can discover, whereby the ideas of things are brought into the understanding. If other men have either innate ideas or infused principles, they have reason to enjoy them; and if they are sure of it, it is impossible for others to deny them the privilege that they have above their neighbours. I can speak but of what I find in myself, and is agreeable to those notions, which, if we will examine the whole course of men in their several ages, countries, and educations, seem to depend on those foundations which I have laid, and to correspond with this method in all the parts and degrees thereof.

17. Dark room. I pretend not to teach, but to inquire; and therefore cannot but confess here again,— that external and internal sensation are the only passages I can find of knowledge to the understanding. These alone, as far as I can discover, are the windows by which light is let into this dark room. For, methinks, the understanding is not much unlike a closet wholly shut from light, with only some little openings left, to let in external visible resemblances, or ideas of things without: would the pictures coming into such a dark room but stay there, and lie so orderly as to be found upon occasion, it would very much resemble the understanding of a man, in reference to all objects of sight, and the ideas of them.

These are my guesses concerning the means whereby the understanding comes to have and retain simple ideas, and the modes of them, with some other operations about them.

I proceed now to examine some of these simple ideas and their modes a little more particularly.

Chapter XII. Of Complex Ideas

1. Made by the mind out of simple ones. We have hitherto considered those ideas, in the reception whereof the mind is only passive, which are those simple ones received from sensation and reflection before mentioned, whereof the mind cannot make one to itself, nor have any idea which does not wholly consist of them. But as the mind is wholly passive in the reception of all its simple ideas, so it exerts several acts of its own, whereby out of its simple ideas, as the materials and foundations of the rest, the others are framed. The acts of the mind, wherein it exerts its power over its simple ideas, are chiefly these three: (1) Combining several simple ideas into one compound one; and thus all complex ideas are made. (2) The second is bringing two ideas, whether simple or complex, together, and setting them by one another, so as to take a view of them at once, without uniting them into one; by which way it gets all its ideas of relations. (3) The third is separating them from all other ideas that accompany them in their real existence: this is called abstraction: and thus all its general ideas are made. This shows man's power, and its ways of operation, to be much the same in the material and intellectual world. For the materials in both being such as he has no power over, either to make or destroy, all that man can do is either to unite them together, or to set them by one another,

or wholly separate them. I shall here begin with the first of these in the consideration of complex ideas, and come to the other two in their due places. As simple ideas are observed to exist in several combinations united together, so the mind has a power to consider several of them united together as one idea; and that not only as they are united in external objects, but as itself has joined them together. Ideas thus made up of several simple ones put together, I call complex;— such as are beauty, gratitude, a man, an army, the universe; which, though complicated of various simple ideas, or complex ideas made up of simple ones, yet are, when the mind pleases, considered each by itself, as one entire thing, and signified by one name.

2. Made voluntarily. In this faculty of repeating and joining together its ideas, the mind has great power in varying and multiplying the objects of its thoughts, infinitely beyond what sensation or reflection furnished it with: but all this still confined to those simple ideas which it received from those two sources, and which are the ultimate materials of all its compositions. For simple ideas are all from things themselves, and of these the mind can have no more, nor other than what are suggested to it. It can have no other ideas of sensible qualities than what come from without by the senses; nor any ideas of other kind of operations of a thinking substance, than what it finds in itself But when it has once got these simple ideas, it is not confined barely to observation, and what offers itself from without; it can, by its own power, put together those ideas it has, and make new complex ones, which it never received so united.

3. Complex ideas are either of modes, substances, or relations. COMPLEX IDEAS, however compounded and decompounded, though their number be infinite, and the variety endless, wherewith they fill and entertain the thoughts of men; yet I think they may be all reduced under these three heads:— 1. MODES. 2. SUBSTANCES. 3. RELATIONS.

4. Ideas of modes. First, Modes I call such complex ideas which, however compounded, contain not in them the supposition of subsisting by themselves, but are considered as dependences on, or affections of substances;— such as are the ideas signified by the words triangle, gratitude, murder, &c. And if in this I use the word mode in somewhat a different sense from its ordinary signification, I beg pardon; it being unavoidable in discourses, differing from the ordinary received notions, either to make new words, or to use old words in somewhat a new signification; the later whereof, in our present case, is perhaps the more tolerable of the two.

5. Simple and mixed modes of simple ideas. Of these modes, there are two sorts which deserve distinct consideration:

First, there are some which are only variations, or different combinations of the same simple idea, without the mixture of any other;— as a dozen, or score; which are nothing but the ideas of so many distinct units added together, and these I call simple modes as being contained within the bounds of one simple idea.

Secondly, there are others compounded of simple ideas of several kinds, put together to make one complex one;— v.g. beauty, consisting of a certain composition of colour and figure, causing delight to the beholder; theft, which being the concealed change of the possession of anything, without the consent of the proprietor, contains, as is visible, a combination of several ideas of several kinds: and these I call mixed modes.

6. Ideas of substances, single or collective. Secondly, the ideas of Substances are such combinations of simple ideas as are taken to represent distinct particular things subsisting by themselves; the supposed or confused idea of substance, such as it is, is always the first and chief Thus if to substance be joined the simple idea of a certain dull whitish colour, with certain degrees of weight, hardness, ductility, and fusibility, we have the idea of lead; and a combination of the ideas of a certain sort of figure, with the powers of motion, thought and reasoning, joined to substance, the ordinary idea of a man. Now of substances also, there are two sorts of ideas:— one of single substances, as they exist separately, as of a man or a sheep; the other of several of those put together, as an army of men, or flock of sheep — which collective ideas of several substances thus put together are as much each of them one single

idea as that of a man or an unit.

7. Ideas of relation. Thirdly, the last sort of complex ideas is that we call Relation, which consists in the consideration and comparing one idea with another.

Of these several kinds we shall treat in their order.

8. The abstrusest ideas we can have are all from two sources. If we trace the progress of our minds, and with attention observe how it repeats, adds together, and unites its simple ideas received from sensation or reflection, it will lead us further than at first perhaps we should have imagined. And, I believe, we shall find, if we warily observe the originals of our notions, that even the most abstruse ideas, how remote soever they may seem from sense, or from any operations of our own minds, are yet only such as the understanding frames to itself, by repeating and joining together ideas that it had either from objects of sense, or from its own operations about them: so that those even large and abstract ideas are derived from sensation or reflection, being no other than what the mind, by the ordinary use of its own faculties, employed about ideas received from objects of sense, or from the operations it observes in itself about them, may, and does, attain unto.

This I shall endeavour to show in the ideas we have of space, time, and infinity, and some few others that seem the most remote, from those originals.

Chapter XIII.Complex Ideas of Simple Modes:— and First, of the Simple Modes of the Idea of Space

1. Simple modes of simple ideas. Though in the foregoing part I have often mentioned simple ideas, which are truly the materials of all our knowledge; yet having treated of them there, rather in the way that they come into the mind, than as distinguished from others more compounded, it will not be perhaps amiss to take a view of some of them again under this consideration, and examine those different modifications of the same idea; which the mind either finds in things existing, or is able to make within itself without the help of any extrinsical object, or any foreign suggestion.

Those modifications of any one simple idea (which, as has been said, I call simple modes) are as perfectly different and distinct ideas in the mind as those of the greatest distance or contrariety. For the idea of two is as distinct from that of one, as blueness from heat, or either of them from any number: and yet it is made up only of that simple idea of an unit repeated; and repetitions of this kind joined together make those distinct simple modes, of a dozen, a gross, a million.

2. Idea of Space. I shall begin with the simple idea of space. I have showed above, chap. V, that we get the idea of space, both by our sight and touch; which, I think, is so evident, that it would be as needless to go to prove that men perceive, by their sight, a distance between bodies of different colours, or between the parts of the same body, as that they see colours themselves: nor is it less obvious, that they can do so in the dark by feeling and touch.

3. Space and extension. This space, considered barely in length between any two beings, without considering anything else between them, is called distance: if considered in length, breadth, and thickness, I think it may be called capacity. (The term extension is usually applied to it in what manner soever considered.)

4. Immensity. Each different distance is a different modification of space; and each idea of any different distance, or space, is a simple mode of this idea. Men, for the use and by the custom of measuring, settle in their minds the ideas of certain stated lengths,— such as are an inch, foot, yard, fathom, mile, diameter of the earth, &c., which are so many distinct ideas made up only of space. When any such stated lengths or measures of space are made familiar to men's thoughts, they can, in their minds, repeat them as often as they will, without mixing or joining to them the idea of body, or anything else; and frame to themselves the ideas of long, square, or cubic feet, yards or fathoms, here amongst the bodies of the universe, or else beyond the

utmost bounds of all bodies; and, by adding these still one to another, enlarge their ideas of space as much as they please. The power of repeating or doubling any idea we have of any distance and adding it to the former as often as we will, without being ever able to come to any stop or stint, let us enlarge it as much as we will, is that which gives us the idea of immensity.

5. Figure. There is another modification of this idea, which is nothing but the relation which the parts of the termination of extension, or circumscribed space, have amongst themselves. This the touch discovers in sensible bodies, whose extremities come within our reach; and the eye takes both from bodies and colours, whose boundaries are within its view: where, observing how the extremities terminate,— either in straight lines which meet at discernible angles, or in crooked lines wherein no angles can be perceived; by considering these as they relate to one another, in all parts of the extremities of any body or space, it has that idea we call figure, which affords to the mind infinite variety. For, besides the vast number of different figures that do really exist, in the coherent masses of matter, the stock that the mind has in its power, by varying the idea of space, and thereby making still new compositions, by repeating its own ideas, and joining them as it pleases, is perfectly inexhaustible. And so it can multiply figures in infinitum.

6. Endless variety of figures. For the mind having a power to repeat the idea of any length directly stretched out, and join it to another in the same direction, which is to double the length of that straight line; or else join another with what inclination it thinks fit, and so make what sort of angle it pleases: and being able also to shorten any line it imagines, by taking from it one half, one fourth, or what part it pleases, without being able to come to an end of any such divisions, it can make an angle of any bigness. So also the lines that are its sides, of what length it pleases, which joining again to other lines, of different lengths, and at different angles, till it has wholly enclosed any space, it is evident that it can multiply figures, both in their shape and capacity, in infinitum; all which are but so many different simple modes of space.

The same that it can do with straight lines, it can also do with crooked, or crooked and straight together; and the same it can do in lines, it can also in superficies; by which we may be led into farther thoughts of the endless variety of figures that the mind has a power to make, and thereby to multiply the simple modes of space.

7. Place. Another idea coming under this head, and belonging to this tribe, is that we call place. As in simple space, we consider the relation of distance between any two bodies or points; so in our idea of place, we consider the relation of distance betwixt anything, and any two or more points, which are considered as keeping the same distance one with another, and so considered as at rest. For when we find anything at the same distance now which it was yesterday, from any two or more points, which have not since changed their distance one with another, and with which we then compared it, we say it hath kept the same place: but if it hath sensibly altered its distance with either of those points, we say it hath changed its place: though, vulgarly speaking, in the common notion of place, we do not always exactly observe the distance from these precise points, but from larger portions of sensible objects, to which we consider the thing placed to bear relation, and its distance from which we have some reason to observe.

8. Place relative to particular bodies. Thus, a company of chess-men, standing on the same squares of the chess-board where we left them, we say they are all in the same place, or unmoved, though perhaps the chess-board hath been in the mean time carried out of one room into another; because we compared them only to the parts of the chess-board, which keep the same distance one with another. The chess-board, we also say, is in the same place it was, if it remain in the same part of the cabin, though perhaps the ship which it is in sails all the while. And the ship is said to be in the same place, supposing it kept the same distance with the parts of the neighbouring land; though perhaps the earth hath turned round, and so both chess-men, and board, and ship, have every one changed place, in respect of remoter bodies, which have kept the same distance one with another. But yet the distance from certain parts of the board

being that which determines the place of the chessmen; and the distance from the fixed parts of the cabin (with which we made the comparison) being that which determined the place of the chess-board; and the fixed parts of the earth that by which we determined the place of the ship,— these things may be said to be in the same place in those respects: though their distance from some other things, which in this matter we did not consider, being varied, they have undoubtedly changed place in that respect; and we ourselves shall think so, when we have occasion to compare them with those other.

9. Place relative to a present purpose. But this modification of distance we call place, being made by men for their common use, that by it they might be able to design the particular position of things, where they had occasion for such designation; men consider and determine of this place by reference to those adjacent things which best served to their present purpose, without considering other things which, to another purpose, would better determine the place of the same thing. Thus in the chess-board, the use of the designation of the place of each chess-man being determined only within that chequered piece of wood, it would cross that purpose to measure it by anything else; but when these very chess-men are put up in a bag, if any one should ask where the black king is, it would be proper to determine the place by the part of the room it was in, and not by the chess-board; there being another use of designing the place it is now in, than when in play it was on the chess-board, and so must be determined by other bodies. So if any one should ask, in what place are the verses which report the story of Nisus and Euryalus, it would be very improper to determine this place, by saying, they were in such a part of the earth, or in Bodley's library: but the right designation of the place would be by the parts of Virgil's works; and the proper answer would be, that these verses were about the middle of the ninth book of his AEneids, and that they have been always constantly in the same place ever since Virgil was printed: which is true, though the book itself hath moved a thousand times, the use of the idea of place here being, to know in what part of the book that story is, that so, upon occasion, we may know where to find it, and have recourse to it for use.

10. Place of the universe. That our idea of place is nothing else but such a relative position of anything as I have before mentioned, I think is plain, and will be easily admitted, when we consider that we can have no idea of the place of the universe, though we can of all the parts of it; because beyond that we have not the idea of any fixed, distinct, particular beings, in reference to which we can imagine it to have any relation of distance; but all beyond it is one uniform space or expansion, wherein the mind finds no variety, no marks. For to say that the world is somewhere, means no more than that it does exist; this, though a phrase borrowed from place, signifying only its existence, not location: and when one can find out, and frame in his mind, clearly and distinctly, the place of the universe, he will be able to tell us whether it moves or stands still in the undistinguishable inane of infinite space: though it be true that the word place has sometimes a more confused sense, and stands for that space which anybody takes up; and so the universe is in a place.

The idea, therefore, of place we have by the same means that we get the idea of space, (whereof this is but a particular limited consideration,) viz. by our sight and touch; by either of which we receive into our minds the ideas of extension or distance.

11. Extension and body not the same. There are some that would persuade us, that body and extension are the same thing, who either change the signification of words, which I would not suspect them of,— they having so severely condemned the philosophy of others, because it hath been too much placed in the uncertain meaning, or deceitful obscurity of doubtful or insignificant terms. If, therefore, they mean by body and extension the same that other people do, viz. by body something that is solid and extended, whose parts are separable and movable different ways; and by extension, only the space that lies between the extremities of those solid coherent parts, and which is possessed by them,— they confound very different ideas one with another; for I appeal to every man's own thoughts whether the idea of space be not as distinct from that of solidity, as it is from the idea of scarlet colour? It is true, solidity cannot exist without extension, neither can scarlet colour exist without extension, but this hinders not,

but that they are distinct ideas. Many ideas require others, as necessary to their existence or conception, which yet are very distinct ideas. Motion can neither be, nor be conceived, without space; and yet motion is not space, nor space motion; space can exist without it, and they are very distinct ideas; and so, I think, are those of space and solidity. Solidity is so inseparable an idea from body, that upon that depends its filling of space, its contact, impulse, and communication of motion upon impulse. And if it be a reason to prove that spirit is different from body, because thinking includes not the idea of extension in it; the same reason will be as valid, I suppose, to prove that space is not body, because it includes not the idea of solidity in it; space and solidity being as distinct ideas as thinking and extension, and as wholly separable in the mind one from another. Body then and extension, it is evident, are two distinct ideas. For,

12. Extension not solidity. First, Extension includes no solidity, nor resistance to the motion of body, as body does.

13. The parts of space inseparable, both really and mentally. Secondly, The parts of pure space are inseparable one from the other; so that the continuity cannot be separated, neither really nor mentally. For I demand of any one to remove any part of it from another, with which it is continued, even so much as in thought. To divide and separate actually is, as I think, by removing the parts one from another, to make two superficies, where before there was a continuity: and to divide mentally is, to make in the mind two superficies, where before there was a continuity, and consider them as removed one from the other; which can only be done in things considered by the mind as capable of being separated; and by separation, of acquiring new distinct superficies, which they then have not, but are capable of But neither of these ways of separation, whether real or mental, is, as I think, compatible to pure space.

It is true, a man may consider so much of such a space as is answerable or commensurate to a foot, without considering the rest, which is, indeed, a partial consideration, but not so much as mental separation or division; since a man can no more mentally divide, without considering two superficies separate one from the other, than he can actually divide, without making two superficies disjoined one from the other: but a partial consideration is not separating. A man may consider light in the sun without its heat, or mobility in body without its extension, without thinking of their separation. One is only a partial consideration, terminating in one alone; and the other is a consideration of both, as existing separately.

14. The parts of space, immovable. Thirdly, The parts of pure space are immovable, which follows from their inseparability; motion being nothing but change of distance between any two things; but this cannot be between parts that are inseparable, which, therefore, must needs be at perpetual rest one amongst another.

Thus the determined idea of simple space distinguishes it plainly and sufficiently from body; since its parts are inseparable, immovable, and without resistance to the motion of body.

15. The definition of extension explains it not. If any one ask me what this space I speak of is, I will tell him when he tells me what his extension is. For to say, as is usually done, that extension is to have partes extra partes, is to say only, that extension is extension. For what am I the better informed in the nature of extension, when I am told that extension is to have parts that are extended, exterior to parts that are extended, i.e. extension consists of extended parts? As if one, asking what a fibre was, I should answer him,— that it was a thing made up of several fibres. Would he thereby be enabled to understand what a fibre was better than he did before? Or rather, would he not have reason to think that my design was to make sport with him, rather than seriously to instruct him?

16. Division of beings into bodies and spirits proves not space and body the same. Those who contend that space and body are the same, bring this dilemma:— either this space is something or nothing; if nothing be between two bodies, they must necessarily touch; if it be allowed to be something, they ask, Whether it be body or spirit? To which I answer by another question, Who told them that there was, or could be, nothing but solid beings, which could not think, and thinking beings that were not extended?— which is all they mean by the terms body and

spirit.

17. Substance which we know not, no proof against space without body. If it be demanded (as usually it is) whether this space, void of body, be substance or accident, I shall readily answer I know not; nor shall be ashamed to own my ignorance, till they that ask show me a clear distinct idea of substance.

18. Different meanings of substance. I endeavour as much as I can to deliver myself from those fallacies which we are apt to put upon ourselves, by taking words for things. It helps not our ignorance to feign a knowledge where we have none, by making a noise with sounds, without clear and distinct significations. Names made at pleasure, neither alter the nature of things, nor make us understand them, but as they are signs of and stand for determined ideas. And I desire those who lay so much stress on the sound of these two syllables, substance, to consider whether applying it, as they do, to the infinite, incomprehensible God, to finite spirits, and to body, it be in the same sense; and whether it stands for the same idea, when each of those three so different beings are called substances. If so, whether it will thence follow — that God, spirits, and body, agreeing in the same common nature of substance, differ not any otherwise than in a bare different modification of that substance; as a tree and a pebble, being in the same sense body, and agreeing in the common nature of body, differ only in a bare modification of that common matter, which will be a very harsh doctrine. If they say, that they apply it to God, finite spirit, and matter, in three different significations and that it stands for one idea when God is said to be a substance; for another when the soul is called substance; and for a third when body is called so;— if the name substance stands for three several distinct ideas, they would do well to make known those distinct ideas, or at least to give three distinct names to them, to prevent in so important a notion the confusion and errors that will naturally follow from the promiscuous use of so doubtful a term; which is so far from being suspected to have three distinct, that in ordinary use it has scarce one clear distinct signification. And if they can thus make three distinct ideas of substance, what hinders why another may not make a fourth?

19. Substance and accidents of little use in philosophy. They who first ran into the notion of accidents, as a sort of real beings that needed something to inhere in, were forced to find out the word substance to support them. Had the poor Indian philosopher (who imagined that the earth also wanted something to bear it up) but thought of this word substance, he needed not to have been at the trouble to find an elephant to support it, and a tortoise to support his elephant: the word substance would have done it effectually. And he that inquired might have taken it for as good an answer from an Indian philosopher,— that substance, without knowing what it is, is that which supports the earth, as we take it for a sufficient answer and good doctrine from our European philosophers,— that substance, without knowing what it is, is that which supports accidents. So that of substance, we have no idea of what it is, but only a confused, obscure one of what it does.

20. Sticking on and under-propping. Whatever a learned man may do here, an intelligent American, who inquired into the nature of things, would scarce take it for a satisfactory account, if, desiring to learn our architecture, he should be told that a pillar is a thing supported by a basis, and a basis something that supported a pillar. Would he not think himself mocked, instead of taught, with such an account as this? And a stranger to them would be very liberally instructed in the nature of books, and the things they contained, if he should be told that all learned books consisted of paper and letters, and that letters were things inhering in paper, and paper a thing that held forth letters: a notable way of having clear ideas of letters and paper. But were the Latin words, inhaerentia and substantio, put into the plain English ones that answer them, and were called sticking on and under-propping, they would better discover to us the very great clearness there is in the doctrine of substance and accidents, and show of what use they are in deciding of questions in philosophy.

21. A vacuum beyond the utmost bounds of body. But to return to our idea of space. If body be not supposed infinite, (which I think no one will affirm), I would ask, whether, if God

placed a man at the extremity of corporeal beings, he could not stretch his hand beyond his body? If he could, then he would put his arm where there was before space without body; and if there he spread his fingers, there would still be space between them without body. If he could not stretch out his hand, it must be because of some external hindrance; (for we suppose him alive, with such a power of moving the parts of his body that he hath now, which is not in itself impossible, if God so pleased to have it; or at least it is not impossible for God so to move him): and then I ask,— whether that which hinders his hand from moving outwards be substance or accident, something or nothing? And when they have resolved that, they will be able to resolve themselves,— what that is, which is or may be between two bodies at a distance, that is not body, and has no solidity. In the mean time, the argument is at least as good, that, where nothing hinders, (as beyond the utmost bounds of all bodies), a body put in motion may move on, as where there is nothing between, there two bodies must necessarily touch. For pure space between is sufficient to take away the necessity of mutual contact; but bare space in the way is not sufficient to stop motion. The truth is, these men must either own that they think body infinite, though they are loth to speak it out, or else affirm that space is not body. For I would fain meet with that thinking man that can in his thoughts set any bounds to space, more than he can to duration; or by thinking hope to arrive at the end of either. And therefore, if his idea of eternity be infinite, so is his idea of immensity; they are both finite or infinite alike.

22. The power of annihilation proves a vacuum. Farther, those who assert the impossibility of space existing without matter, must not only make body infinite, but must also deny a power in God to annihilate any part of matter. No one, I suppose, will deny that God can put an end to all motion that is in matter, and fix all the bodies of the universe in a perfect quiet and rest, and continue them so long as he pleases. Whoever then will allow that God can, during such a general rest, annihilate either this book or the body of him that reads it, must necessarily admit the possibility of a vacuum. For, it is evident that the space that was filled by the parts of the annihilated body will still remain, and be a space without body. For the circumambient bodies being in perfect rest, are a wall of adamant, and in that state make it a perfect impossibility for any other body to get into that space. And indeed the necessary motion of one particle of matter into the place from whence another particle of matter is removed, is but a consequence from the supposition of plenitude; which will therefore need some better proof than a supposed matter of fact, which experiment can never make out;— our own clear and distinct ideas plainly satisfying us, that there is no necessary connexion between space and solidity, since we can conceive the one without the other. And those who dispute for or against a vacuum, do thereby confess they have distinct ideas of vacuum and plenum, i.e. that they have an idea of extension void of solidity, though they deny its existence; or else they dispute about nothing at all. For they who so much alter the signification of words, as to call extension body, and consequently make the whole essence of body to be nothing but pure extension without solidity, must talk absurdly whenever they speak of vacuum; since it is impossible for extension to be without extension. For vacuum, whether we affirm or deny its existence, signifies space without body; whose very existence no one can deny to be possible, who will not make matter infinite, and take from God a power to annihilate any particle of it.

23. Motion proves a vacuum. But not to go so far as beyond the utmost bounds of body in the universe, nor appeal to God's omnipotency to find a vacuum, the motion of bodies that are in our view and neighbourhood seems to me plainly to evince it. For I desire any one so to divide a solid body, of any dimension he pleases, as to make it possible for the solid parts to move up and down freely every way within the bounds of that superficies, if there be not left in it a void space as big as the least part into which he has divided the said solid body. And if, where the least particle of the body divided is as big as a mustard-seed, a void space equal to the bulk of a mustard-seed be requisite to make room for the free motion of the parts of the divided body within the bounds of its superficies, where the particles of matter are 100,000,000 less than a mustard-seed, there must also be a space void of solid matter as big as 100,000,000 part of a

mustard-seed; for if it hold in the one it will hold in the other, and so on in infinitum. And let this void space be as little as it will, it destroys the hypothesis of plenitude. For if there can be a space void of body equal to the smallest separate particle of matter now existing in nature, it is still space without body; and makes as great a difference between space and body as if it were mega chasma, a distance as wide as any in nature. And therefore, if we suppose not the void space necessary to motion equal to the least parcel of the divided solid matter, but to 1/10 or 1/1000 of it, the same consequence will always follow of space without matter.

24. The ideas of space and body distinct. But the question being here,— Whether the idea of space or extension be the same with the idea of body? it is not necessary to prove the real existence of a vacuum, but the idea of it; which it is plain men have when they inquire and dispute whether there be a vacuum or no. For if they had not the idea of space without body, they could not make a question about its existence: and if their idea of body did not include in it something more than the bare idea of space, they could have no doubt about the plenitude of the world; and it would be as absurd to demand, whether there were space without body, as whether there were space without space, or body without body, since these were but different names of the same idea.

25. Extension being inseparable from body, proves it not the same. It is true, the idea of extension joins itself so inseparably with all visible, and most tangible qualities, that it suffers us to see no one, or feel very few external objects, without taking in impressions of extension too. This readiness of extension to make itself be taken notice of so constantly with other ideas, has been the occasion, I guess, that some have made the whole essence of body to consist in extension; which is not much to be wondered at, since some have had their minds, by their eyes and touch, (the busiest of all our senses,) so filled with the idea of extension, and, as it were, wholly possessed with it, that they allowed no existence to anything that had not extension. I shall not now argue with those men, who take the measure and possibility of all being only from their narrow and gross imaginations: but having here to do only with those who conclude the essence of body to be extension, because they say they cannot imagine any sensible quality of any body without extension,— I shall desire them to consider, that, had they reflected on their ideas of tastes and smells as much as on those of sight and touch; nay, had they examined their ideas of hunger and thirst, and several other pains, they would have found that they included in them no idea of extension at all, which is but an affection of body, as well as the rest, discoverable by our senses, which are scarce acute enough to look into the pure essences of things.

26. Essences of things. If those ideas which are constantly joined to all others, must therefore be concluded to be the essence of those things which have constantly those ideas joined to them, and are inseparable from them; then unity is without doubt the essence of everything. For there is not any object of sensation or reflection which does not carry with it the idea of one: but the weakness of this kind of argument we have already shown sufficiently.

27. Ideas of space and solidity distinct. To conclude: whatever men shall think concerning the existence of a vacuum, this is plain to me — that we have as clear an idea of space distinct from solidity, as we have of solidity distinct from motion, or motion from space. We have not any two more distinct ideas; and we can as easily conceive space without solidity, as we can conceive body or space without motion, though it be never so certain that neither body nor motion can exist without space. But whether any one will take space to be only a relation resulting from the existence of other beings at a distance; or whether they will think the words of the most knowing King Solomon, "The heaven, and the heaven of heavens, cannot contain thee"; or those more emphatical ones of the inspired philosopher St. Paul, "In him we live, move, and have our being," are to be understood in a literal sense, I leave every one to consider: only our idea of space is, I think, such as I have mentioned, and distinct from that of body. For, whether we consider, in matter itself, the distance of its coherent solid parts, and call it, in respect of those solid parts, extension; or whether, considering it as lying between the

extremities of any body in its several dimensions, we call it length, breadth, and thickness; or else, considering it as lying between any two bodies or positive beings, without any consideration whether there be any matter or not between, we call it distance;— however named or considered, it is always the same uniform simple idea of space, taken from objects about which our senses have been conversant; whereof, having settled ideas in our minds, we can revive, repeat, and add them one to another as often as we will, and consider the space or distance so imagined, either as filled with solid parts, so that another body cannot come there without displacing and thrusting out the body that was there before; or else as void of solidity, so that a body of equal dimensions to that empty or pure space may be placed in it, without the removing or expulsion of anything that was there. But, to avoid confusion in discourses concerning this matter, it were possibly to be wished that the name extension were applied only to matter, or the distance of the extremities of particular bodies; and the term expansion to space in general, with or without solid matter possessing it,— so as to say space is expanded and body extended. But in this every one has his liberty: I propose it only for the more clear and distinct way of speaking.

28. Men differ little in clear, simple ideas. The knowing precisely what our words stand for, would, I imagine, in this as well as a great many other cases, quickly end the dispute. For I am apt to think that men, when they come to examine them, find their simple ideas all generally to agree, though in discourse with one another they perhaps confound one another with different names. I imagine that men who abstract their thoughts, and do well examine the ideas of their own minds, cannot much differ in thinking; however they may perplex themselves with words, according to the way of speaking to the several schools or sects they have been bred up in: though amongst unthinking men, who examine not scrupulously and carefully their own ideas, and strip them not from the marks men use for them, but confound them with words, there must be endless dispute, wrangling, and jargon; especially if they be learned, bookish men, devoted to some sect, and accustomed to the language of it, and have learned to talk after others. But if it should happen that any two thinking men should really have different ideas, I do not see how they could discourse or argue with another. Here I must not be mistaken, to think that every floating imagination in men's brains is presently of that sort of ideas I speak of. It is not easy for the mind to put off those confused notions and prejudices it has imbibed from custom, inadvertency, and common conversation. It requires pains and assiduity to examine its ideas, till it resolves them into those clear and distinct simple ones, out of which they are compounded; and to see which, amongst its simple ones, have or have not a necessary connexion and dependence one upon another. Till a man doth this in the primary and original notions of things, he builds upon floating and uncertain principles, and will often find himself at a loss.

Chapter XIV.Idea of Duration and its Simple Modes

1. Duration is fleeting extension. There is another sort of distance, or length, the idea whereof we get not from the permanent parts of space, but from the fleeting and perpetually perishing parts of succession. This we call duration; the simple modes whereof are any different lengths of it whereof we have distinct ideas, as hours, days, years, &c., time and eternity.

2. Its idea from reflection on the train of our ideas. The answer of a great man, to one who asked what time was: Si non rogas intelligo, (which amounts to this; The more I set myself to think of it, the less I understand it,) might perhaps persuade one that time, which reveals all other things, is itself not to be discovered. Duration, time, and eternity, are, not without reason, thought to have something very abstruse in their nature. But however remote these may seem from our comprehension, yet if we trace them right to their originals, I doubt not but one of those sources of all our knowledge, viz. sensation and reflection, will be able to furnish us with these ideas, as clear and distinct as many others which are thought much less obscure;

and we shall find that the idea of eternity itself is derived from the same common original with the rest of our ideas.

3. Nature and origin of the idea of duration. To understand time and eternity aright, we ought with attention to consider what idea it is we have of duration, and how we came by it. It is evident to any one who will but observe what passes in his own mind, that there is a train of ideas which constantly succeed one another in his understanding, as long as he is awake. Reflection on these appearances of several ideas one after another in our minds, is that which furnishes us with the idea of succession: and the distance between any parts of that succession, or between the appearance of any two ideas in our minds, is that we call duration. For whilst we are thinking, or whilst we receive successively several ideas in our minds, we know that we do exist; and so we call the existence, or the continuation of the existence of ourselves, or anything else, commensurate to the succession of any ideas in our minds, the duration of ourselves, or any such other thing co-existent with our thinking.

4. Proof that its idea is got from reflection on the train of our ideas. That we have our notion of succession and duration from this original, viz. from reflection on the train of ideas, which we find to appear one after another in our own minds, seems plain to me, in that we have no perception of duration but by considering the train of ideas that take their turns in our understandings. When that succession of ideas ceases, our perception of duration ceases with it; which every one clearly experiments in himself, whilst he sleeps soundly, whether an hour or a day, a month or a year; of which duration of things, while he sleeps or thinks not, he has no perception at all, but it is quite lost to him; and the moment wherein he leaves off to think, till the moment he begins to think again, seems to him to have no distance. And so I doubt not it would be to a waking man, if it were possible for him to keep only one idea in his mind, without variation and the succession of others. And we see, that one who fixes his thoughts very intently on one thing, so as to take but little notice of the succession of ideas that pass in his mind, whilst he is taken up with that earnest contemplation, lets slip out of his account a good part of that duration, and thinks that time shorter than it is. But if sleep commonly unites the distant parts of duration, it is because during that time we have no succession of ideas in our minds. For if a man, during his sleep, dreams, and variety of ideas make themselves perceptible in his mind one after another, he hath then, during such dreaming, a sense of duration, and of the length of it. By which it is to me very clear, that men derive their ideas of duration from their reflections on the train of the ideas they observe to succeed one another in their own understandings; without which observation they can have no notion of duration, whatever may happen in the world.

5. The idea of duration applicable to things whilst we sleep. Indeed a man having, from reflecting on the succession and number of his own thoughts, got the notion or idea of duration, he can apply that notion to things which exist while he does not think; as he that has got the idea of extension from bodies by his sight or touch, can apply it to distances, where no body is seen or felt. And therefore, though a man has no perception of the length of duration which passed whilst he slept or thought not; yet, having observed the revolution of days and nights, and found the length of their duration to be in appearance regular and constant, he can, upon the supposition that that revolution has proceeded after the same manner whilst he was asleep or thought not, as it used to do at other times, he can, I say, imagine and make allowance for the length of duration whilst he slept. But if Adam and Eve, (when they were alone in the world), instead of their ordinary night's sleep, had passed the whole twenty-four hours in one continued sleep, the duration of that twenty-four hours had been irrecoverably lost to them, and been for ever left out of their account of time.

6. The idea of succession not from motion. Thus by reflecting on the appearing of various ideas one after another in our understandings, we get the notion of succession; which, if any one should think we did rather get from our observation of motion by our senses, he will perhaps be of my mind when he considers, that even motion produces in his mind an idea of succession no otherwise than as it produces there a continued train of distinguishable ideas.

For a man looking upon a body really moving, perceives yet no motion at all unless that motion produces a constant train of successive ideas: v.g. a man becalmed at sea, out of sight of land, in a fair day, may look on the sun, or sea, or ship, a whole hour together, and perceive no motion at all in either; though it be certain that two, and perhaps all of them, have moved during that time a great way. But as soon as he perceives either of them to have changed distance with some other body, as soon as this motion produces any new idea in him, then he perceives that there has been motion. But wherever a man is, with all things at rest about him, without perceiving any motion at all,— if during this hour of quiet he has been thinking, he will perceive the various ideas of his own thoughts in his own mind, appearing one after another, and thereby observe and find succession where he could observe no motion.

7. Very slow motions unperceived. And this, I think, is the reason why motions very slow, though they are constant, are not perceived by us; because in their remove from one sensible part towards another, their change of distance is so slow, that it causes no new ideas in us, but a good while one after another. And so not causing a constant train of new ideas to follow one another immediately in our minds, we have no perception of motion; which consisting in a constant succession, we cannot perceive that succession without a constant succession of varying ideas arising from it.

8. Very swift motions unperceived. On the contrary, things that move so swift as not to affect the senses distinctly with several distinguishable distances of their motion, and so cause not any train of ideas in the mind, are not also perceived. For anything that moves round about in a circle, in less times than our ideas are wont to succeed one another in our minds, is not perceived to move; but seems to be a perfect entire circle of that matter or colour, and not a part of a circle in motion.

9. The train of ideas has a certain degree of quickness. Hence I leave it to others to judge, whether it be not probable that our ideas do, whilst we are awake, succeed one another in our minds at certain distances; not much unlike the images in the inside of a lantern, turned round by the heat of a candle. This appearance of theirs in train, though perhaps it may be sometimes faster and sometimes slower, yet, I guess, varies not very much in a waking man: there seem to be certain bounds to the quickness and slowness of the succession of those ideas one to another in our minds, beyond which they can neither delay nor hasten.

10. Real succession in swift motions without sense of succession. The reason I have for this odd conjecture is, from observing that, in the impressions made upon any of our senses, we can but to a certain degree perceive any succession; which, if exceeding quick, the sense of succession is lost, even in cases where it is evident that there is a real succession. Let a cannon-bullet pass through a room, and in its way take with it any limb, or fleshy parts of a man, it is as clear as any demonstration can be, that it must strike successively the two sides of the room: it is also evident that it must touch one part of the flesh first, and another after, and so in succession: and yet, I believe, nobody who ever felt the pain of such a shot, or heard the blow against the two distant walls, could perceive any succession either in the pain or sound of so swift a stroke. Such a part of duration as this, wherein we perceive no succession, is that which we call an instant, and is that which takes up the time of only one idea in our minds, without the succession of another; wherein, therefore, we perceive no succession at all.

11. In slow motions. This also happens where the motion is so slow as not to supply a constant train of fresh ideas to the senses, as fast as the mind is capable of receiving new ones into it; and so other ideas of our own thoughts, having room to come into our minds between those offered to our senses by the moving body, there the sense of motion is lost; and the body, though it really moves, yet, not changing perceivable distance with some other bodies as fast as the ideas of our own minds do naturally follow one another in train, the thing seems to stand still; as is evident in the hands of clocks, and shadows of sun-dials, and other constant but slow motions, where, though, after certain intervals, we perceive, by the change of distance, that it hath moved, yet the motion itself we perceive not.

12. This train, the measure of other successions. So that to me it seems, that the constant and

regular succession of ideas in a waking man, is, as it were, the measure and standard of all other successions. Whereof, if any one either exceeds the pace of our ideas, as where two sounds or pains, &c., take up in their succession the duration of but one idea; or else where any motion or succession is so slow, as that it keeps not pace with the ideas in our minds, or the quickness in which they take their turns, as when any one or more ideas in their ordinary course come into our mind, between those which are offered to the sight by the different perceptible distances of a body in motion, or between sounds or smells following one another,— there also the sense of a constant continued succession is lost, and we perceive it not, but with certain gaps of rest between.

13. The mind cannot fix long on one invariable idea. If it be so, that the ideas of our minds, whilst we have any there, do constantly change and shift in a continual succession, it would be impossible, may any one say, for a man to think long of any one thing. By which, if it be meant that a man may have one self-same single idea a long time alone in his mind, without any variation at all, I think, in matter of fact, it is not possible. For which (not knowing how the ideas of our minds are framed, of what materials they are made, whence they have their light, and how they come to make their appearances) I can give no other reason but experience: and I would have any one try, whether he can keep one unvaried single idea in his mind, without any other, for any considerable time together.

14. Proof. For trial, let him take any figure, any degree of light or whiteness, or what other he pleases, and he will, I suppose, find it difficult to keep all other ideas out of his mind; but that some, either of another kind, or various considerations of that idea, (each of which considerations is a new idea), will constantly succeed one another in his thoughts, let him be as wary as he can.

15. The extent of our power over the succession of our ideas. All that is in a man's power in this case, I think, is only to mind and observe what the ideas are that take their turns in his understanding; or else to direct the sort, and call in such as he hath a desire or use of: but hinder the constant succession of fresh ones, I think he cannot, though he may commonly choose whether he will heedfully observe and consider them.

16. Ideas, however made, include no sense of motion. Whether these several ideas in a man's mind be made by certain motions, I will not here dispute; but this I am sure, that they include no idea of motion in their appearance; and if a man had not the idea of motion otherwise, I think he would have none at all, which is enough to my present purpose; and sufficiently shows that the notice we take of the ideas of our own minds, appearing there one after another, is that which gives us the idea of succession and duration, without which we should have no such ideas at all. It is not then motion, but the constant train of ideas in our minds whilst we are waking, that furnishes us with the idea of duration; whereof motion no otherwise gives us any perception than as it causes in our minds a constant succession of ideas, as I have before showed: and we have as clear an idea of succession and duration, by the train of other ideas succeeding one another in our minds, without the idea of any motion, as by the train of ideas caused by the uninterrupted sensible change of distance between two bodies, which we have from motion; and therefore we should as well have the idea of duration were there no sense of motion at all.

17. Time is duration set out by measures. Having thus got the idea of duration, the next thing natural for the mind to do, is to get some measure of this common duration, whereby it might judge of its different lengths, and consider the distinct order wherein several things exist; without which a great part of our knowledge would be confused, and a great part of history be rendered very useless. This consideration of duration, as set out by certain periods, and marked by certain measures or epochs, is that, I think, which most properly we call time.

18. A good measure of time must divide its whole duration into equal periods. In the measuring of extension, there is nothing more required but the application of the standard or measure we make use of to the thing of whose extension we would be informed. But in the measuring of duration this cannot be done, because no two different parts of succession can be

put together to measure one another. And nothing being a measure of duration but duration, as nothing is of extension but extension, we cannot keep by us any standing, unvarying measure of duration, which consists in a constant fleeting succession, as we can of certain lengths of extension, as inches, feet, yards, &c., marked out in permanent parcels of matter. Nothing then could serve well for a convenient measure of time, but what has divided the whole length of its duration into apparently equal portions, by constantly repeated periods. What portions of duration are not distinguished, or considered as distinguished and measured, by such periods, come not so properly under the notion of time; as appears by such phrases as these, viz. "Before all time," and "When time shall be no more."

19. The revolutions of the sun and moon, the properest measures of time for mankind. The diurnal and annual revolutions of the sun, as having been, from the beginning of nature, constant, regular, and universally observable by all mankind, and supposed equal to one another, have been with reason made use of for the measure of duration. But the distinction of days and years having depended on the motion of the sun, it has brought this mistake with it, that it has been thought that motion and duration were the measure one of another. For men, in the measuring of the length of time, having been accustomed to the ideas of minutes, hours, days, months, years, &c., which they found themselves upon any mention of time or duration presently to think on, all which portions of time were measured out by the motion of those heavenly bodies, they were apt to confound time and motion; or at least to think that they had a necessary connexion one with another. Whereas any constant periodical appearance, or alteration of ideas, in seemingly equidistant spaces of duration, if constant and universally observable, would have as well distinguished the intervals of time, as those that have been made use of. For, supposing the sun, which some have taken to be a fire, had been lighted up at the same distance of time that it now every day comes about to the same meridian, and then gone out again about twelve hours after, and that in the space of an annual revolution it had sensibly increased in brightness and heat, and so decreased again,— would not such regular appearances serve to measure out the distances of duration to all that could observe it, as well without as with motion? For if the appearances were constant, universally observable, in equidistant periods, they would serve mankind for measure of time as well were the motion away.

20. But not by their motion, but periodical appearances. For the freezing of water, or the blowing of a plant, returning at equidistant periods in all parts of the earth, would as well serve men to reckon their years by as the motions of the sun: and in effect we see, that some people in America counted their years by the coming of certain birds amongst them at their certain seasons, and leaving them at others. For a fit of an ague; the sense of hunger or thirst; a smell or a taste; or any other idea returning constantly at equidistant periods, and making itself universally be taken notice of, would not fail to measure out the course of succession, and distinguish the distances of time. Thus we see that men born blind count time well enough by years, whose revolutions yet they cannot distinguish by motions that they perceive not. And I ask whether a blind man, who distinguished his years either by the heat of summer, or cold of winter; by the smell of any flower of the spring, or taste of any fruit of the autumn, would not have a better measure of time than the Romans had before the reformation of their calendar by Julius Caesar, or many other people whose years, notwithstanding the motion of the sun, which they pretended to make use of, are very irregular? And it adds no small difficulty to chronology, that the exact lengths of the years that several nations counted by, are hard to be known, they differing very much one from another, and I think I may say all of them from the precise motion of the sun. And if the sun moved from the creation to the flood constantly in the equator, and so equally dispersed its light and heat to all the habitable parts of the earth, in days all of the same length, without its annual variations to the tropics, as a late ingenious author supposes, I do not think it very easy to imagine, that (notwithstanding the motion of the sun) men should in the antediluvian world, from the beginning, count by years, or measure their time by periods that had no sensible marks very obvious to distinguish them by.

21. No two parts of duration can be certainly known to be equal. But perhaps it will be said,—without a regular motion, such as of the sun, or some other, how could it ever be known that such periods were equal? To which I answer,— the equality of any other returning appearances might be known by the same way that that of days was known, or presumed to be so at first; which was only by judging of them by the train of ideas which had passed in men's minds in the intervals; by which train of ideas discovering inequality in the natural days, but none in the artificial days, the artificial days, or nuchtheerha, were guessed to be equal, which was sufficient to make them serve for a measure; though exacter search has since discovered inequality in the diurnal revolutions of the sun, and we know not whether the annual also be not unequal. These yet, by their presumed and apparent equality, serve as well to reckon time by (though not to measure the parts of duration exactly) as if they could be proved to be exactly equal. We must, therefore, carefully distinguish betwixt duration itself, and the measures we make use of to judge of its length. Duration, in itself, is to be considered as going on in one constant, equal, uniform course: but none of the measures of it which we make use of can be known to do so, nor can we be assured that their assigned parts or periods are equal in duration one to another; for two successive lengths of duration, however measured, can never be demonstrated to be equal. The motion of the sun, which the world used so long and so confidently for an exact measure of duration, has, as I said, been found in its several parts unequal. And though men have, of late, made use of a pendulum, as a more steady and regular motion than that of the sun, or, (to speak more truly), of the earth;— yet if any one should be asked how he certainly knows that the two successive swings of a pendulum are equal, it would be very hard to satisfy him that they are infallibly so; since we cannot be sure that the cause of that motion, which is unknown to us, shall always operate equally; and we are sure that the medium in which the pendulum moves is not constantly the same: either of which varying, may alter the equality of such periods, and thereby destroy the certainty and exactness of the measure by motion, as well as any other periods of other appearances; the notion of duration still remaining clear, though our measures of it cannot (any of them) be demonstrated to be exact. Since then no two portions of succession can be brought together, it is impossible ever certainly to know their equality. All that we can do for a measure of time is, to take such as have continual successive appearances at seemingly equidistant periods; of which seeming equality we have no other measure, but such as the train of our own ideas have lodged in our memories, with the concurrence of other probable reasons, to persuade us of their equality.
22. Time not the measure of motion. One thing seems strange to me,— that whilst all men manifestly measured time by the motion of the great and visible bodies of the world, time yet should be defined to be the "measure of motion": whereas it is obvious to every one who reflects ever so little on it, that to measure motion, space is as necessary to be considered as time; and those who look a little farther will find also the bulk of the thing moved necessary to be taken into the computation, by any one who will estimate or measure motion so as to judge right of it. Nor indeed does motion any otherwise conduce to the measuring of duration, than as it constantly brings about the return of certain sensible ideas, in seeming equidistant periods. For if the motion of the sun were as unequal as of a ship driven by unsteady winds, sometimes very slow, and at others irregularly very swift; or if, being constantly equally swift, it yet was not circular, and produced not the same appearances,— it would not at all help us to measure time, any more than the seeming unequal motion of a comet does.
23. Minutes, hours, days, and years not necessary measures of duration. Minutes, hours, days, and years are, then, no more necessary to time or duration, than inches, feet, yards, and miles, marked out in any matter, are to extension. For, though we in this part of the universe, by the constant use of them, as of periods set out by the revolutions of the sun, or as known parts of such periods, have fixed the ideas of such lengths of duration in our minds, which we apply to all parts of time whose lengths we would consider; yet there may be other parts of the universe, where they no more use there measures of ours, than in Japan they do our inches, feet, or miles; but yet something analogous to them there must be. For without some regular

periodical returns, we could not measure ourselves, or signify to others, the length of any duration; though at the same time the world were as full of motion as it is now, but no part of it disposed into regular and apparently equidistant revolutions. But the different measures that may be made use of for the account of time, do not at all alter the notion of duration, which is the thing to be measured; no more than the different standards of a foot and a cubit alter the notion of extension to those who make use of those different measures.

24. Our measure of time applicable to duration before time. The mind having once got such a measure of time as the annual revolution of the sun, can apply that measure to duration wherein that measure itself did not exist, and with which, in the reality of its being, it had nothing to do. For should one say, that Abraham was born in the two thousand seven hundred and twelfth year of the Julian period, it is altogether as intelligible as reckoning from the beginning of the world, though there were so far back no motion of the sun, nor any motion at all. For, though the Julian period be supposed to begin several hundred years before there were really either days, nights, or years, marked out by any revolutions of the sun,— yet we reckon as right, and thereby measure durations as well, as if really at that time the sun had existed, and kept the same ordinary motion it doth now. The idea of duration equal to an annual revolution of the sun, is as easily applicable in our thoughts to duration, where no sun or motion was, as the idea of a foot or yard, taken from bodies here, can be applied in our thoughts to duration, where no sun or motion was, as the idea of a foot or yard, taken from bodies here, can be applied in our thoughts to distances beyond the confines of the world, where are no bodies at all.

25. As we can measure space in our thoughts where there is no body. For supposing it were 5639 miles, or millions of miles, from this place to the remotest body of the universe, (for being finite, it must be at a certain distance), as we suppose it to be 5639 years from this time to the first existence of any body in the beginning of the world;— we can, in our thoughts, apply this measure of a year to duration before the creation, or beyond the duration of bodies or motion, as we can this measure of a mile to space beyond the utmost bodies; and by the one measure duration, where there was no motion, as well as by the other measure space in our thoughts, where there is no body.

26. The assumption that the world is neither boundless nor eternal. If it be objected to me here, that, in this way of explaining of time, I have begged what I should not, viz. that the world is neither eternal nor infinite; I answer, That to my present purpose it is not needful, in this place, to make use of arguments to evince the world to be finite both in duration and extension. But it being at least as conceivable as the contrary, I have certainly the liberty to suppose it, as well as any one hath to suppose the contrary; and I doubt not, but that every one that will go about it, may easily conceive in his mind the beginning of motion, though not of all duration, and so may come to a step and non ultra in his consideration of motion. So also, in his thoughts, he may set limits to body, and the extension belonging to it; but not to space, where no body is, the utmost bounds of space and duration being beyond the reach of thought, as well as the utmost bounds of number are beyond the largest comprehension of the mind; and all for the same reason, as we shall see in another place.

27. Eternity. By the same means, therefore, and from the same original that we come to have the idea of time, we have also that idea which we call Eternity; viz. having got the idea of succession and duration, by reflecting on the train of our own ideas, caused in us either by the natural appearances of those ideas coming constantly of themselves into our waking thoughts, or else caused by external objects successively affecting our senses; and having from the revolutions of the sun got the ideas of certain lengths of duration,— we can in our thoughts add such lengths of duration to one another, as often as we please, and apply them, so added, to durations past or to come. And this we can continue to do on, without bounds or limits, and proceed in infinitum, and apply thus the length of the annual motion of the sun to duration, supposed before the sun's or any other motion had its being; which is no more difficult or absurd, than to apply the notion I have of the moving of a shadow one hour to-day upon the

sun-dial to the duration of something last night, v.g. the burning of a candle, which is now absolutely separate from all actual motion; and it is as impossible for the duration of that flame for an hour last night to co-exist with any motion that now is, or for ever shall be, as for any part of duration, that was before the beginning of the world, to co-exist with the motion of the sun now. But yet this hinders not but that, having the idea of the length of the motion of the shadow on a dial between the marks of two hours, I can as distinctly measure in my thoughts the duration of that candle-light last night, as I can the duration of anything that does now exist: and it is no more than to think, that, had the sun shone then on the dial, and moved after the same rate it doth now, the shadow on the dial would have passed from one hour-line to another whilst that flame of the candle lasted.

28. Our measures of duration dependent on our ideas. The notion of an hour, day, or year, being only the idea I have of the length of certain periodical regular motions, neither of which motions do ever all at once exist, but only in the ideas I have of them in my memory derived from my senses or reflection; I can with the same ease, and for the same reason, apply it in my thoughts to duration antecedent to all manner of motion, as well as to anything that is but a minute or a day antecedent to the motion that at this very moment the sun is in. All things past are equally and perfectly at rest; and to this way of consideration of them are all one, whether they were before the beginning of the world, or but yesterday: the measuring of any duration by some motion depending not at all on the real co-existence of that thing to that motion, or any other periods of revolution, but the having a clear idea of the length of some periodical known motion, or other interval of duration, in my mind, and applying that to the duration of the thing I would measure.

29. The duration of anything need not be co-existent with the motion we measure it by. Hence we see that some men imagine the duration of the world, from its first existence to this present year 1689, to have been 5639 years, or equal to 5639 annual revolutions of the sun, and others a great deal more; as the Egyptians of old, who in the time of Alexander counted 23,000 years from the reign of the sun; and the Chinese now, who account the world 3,269,000 years old, or more; which longer duration of the world, according to their computation, though I should not believe to be true, yet I can equally imagine it with them, and as truly understand, and say one is longer than the other, as I understand, that Methusalem's life was longer than Enoch's. And if the common reckoning Of 5639 should be true, (as it may be as well as any other assigned,) it hinders not at all my imagining what others mean, when they make the world one thousand years older, since every one may with the same facility imagine (I do not say believe) the world to be 50,000 years old, as 5639; and may as well conceive the duration of 50,000 years as 5639. Whereby it appears that, to the measuring the duration of anything by time, it is not requisite that that thing should be co-existent to the motion we measure by, or any other periodical revolution; but it suffices to this purpose, that we have the idea of the length of any regular periodical appearances, which we can in our minds apply to duration, with which the motion or appearance never co-existed.

30. Infinity in duration. For, as in the history of the creation delivered by Moses, I can imagine that light existed three days before the sun was, or had any motion, barely by thinking that the duration of light before the sun was created was so long as (if the sun had moved then as it doth now) would have been equal to three of his diurnal revolutions; so by the same way I can have an idea of the chaos, or angels, being created before there was either light or any continued motion, a minute, an hour, a day, a year, or one thousand years. For, if I can but consider duration equal to one minute, before either the being or motion of any body, I can add one minute more till I come to sixty; and by the same way of adding minutes, hours, or years (i.e. such or such parts of the sun's revolutions, or any other period whereof I have the idea) proceed in infinitum, and suppose a duration exceeding as many such periods as I can reckon, let me add whilst I will, which I think is the notion we have of eternity; of whose infinity we have no other notion than we have of the infinity of number, to which we can add for ever without end.

31. Origin of our ideas of duration, and of the measures of it. And thus I think it is plain, that from those two fountains of all knowledge before mentioned, viz. reflection and sensation, we got the ideas of duration, and the measures of it.

For, First, by observing what passes in our minds, how our ideas there in train constantly some vanish and others begin to appear, we come by the idea of succession.

Secondly, by observing a distance in the parts of this succession, we get the idea of duration.

Thirdly, by sensation observing certain appearances, at certain regular and seeming equidistant periods, we get the ideas of certain lengths or measures of duration, as minutes, hours, days, years, &c.

Fourthly, by being able to repeat those measures of time, or ideas of stated length of duration, in our minds, as often as we will, we can come to imagine duration, where nothing does really endure or exist; and thus we imagine to-morrow, next year, or seven years hence.

Fifthly, by being able to repeat ideas of any length of time, as of a minute, a year, or an age, as often as we will in our own thoughts, and adding them one to another, without ever coming to the end of such addition, any nearer than we can to the end of number, to which we can always add; we come by the idea of eternity, as the future eternal duration of our souls, as well as the eternity of that infinite Being which must necessarily have always existed.

Sixthly, by considering any part of infinite duration, as set out by periodical measures, we come by the idea of what we call time in general.

Chapter XV.Ideas of Duration and Expansion, considered together

1. Both capable of greater and less. Though we have in the precedent chapters dwelt pretty long on the considerations of space and duration, yet, they being ideas of general concernment, that have something very abstruse and peculiar in their nature, the comparing them one with another may perhaps be of use for their illustration; and we may have the more clear and distinct conception of them by taking a view of them together. Distance or space, in its simple abstract conception, to avoid confusion, I call expansion, to distinguish it from extension, which by some is used to express this distance only as it is in the solid parts of matter, and so includes, or at least intimates, the idea of body: whereas the idea of pure distance includes no such thing. I prefer also the word expansion to space, because space is often applied to distance of fleeting successive parts, which never exist together, as well as to those which are permanent. In both these (viz. expansion and duration) the mind has this common idea of continued lengths, capable of greater or less quantities. For a man has as clear an idea of the difference of the length of an hour and a day, as of an inch and a foot.

2. Expansion not bounded by matter. The mind, having got the idea of the length of any part of expansion, let it be a span, or a pace, or what length you will, can, as has been said, repeat that idea, and so, adding it to the former, enlarge its idea of length, and make it equal to two spans, or two paces; and so, as often as it will, till it equals the distance of any parts of the earth one from another, and increase thus till it amounts to the distance of the sun or remotest star. By such a progression as this, setting out from the place where it is, or any other place, it can proceed and pass beyond all those lengths, and find nothing to stop its going on, either in or without body. It is true, we can easily in our thoughts come to the end of solid extension; the extremity and bounds of all body we have no difficulty to arrive at: but when the mind is there, it finds nothing to hinder its progress into this endless expansion; of that it can neither find nor conceive any end. Nor let any one say, that beyond the bounds of body, there is nothing at all; unless he will confine God within the limits of matter. Solomon, whose understanding was filled and enlarged with wisdom, seems to have other thoughts when he says, "Heaven, and the heaven of heavens, cannot contain thee." And he, I think, very much magnifies to himself the capacity of his own understanding, who persuades himself that he can extend his thoughts

further than God exists, or imagine any expansion where He is not.

3. Nor duration by motion. Just so is it in duration. The mind having got the idea of any length of duration, can double, multiply, and enlarge it, not only beyond its own, but beyond the existence of all corporeal beings, and all the measures of time, taken from the great bodies of all the world and their motions. But yet every one easily admits, that, though we make duration boundless, as certainly it is, we cannot yet extend it beyond all being. God, every one easily allows, fills eternity; and it is hard to find a reason why any one should doubt that He likewise fills immensity. His infinite being is certainly as boundless one way as another; and methinks it ascribes a little too much to matter to say, where there is no body, there is nothing.

4. Why men more easily admit infinite duration than infinite expansion. Hence I think we may learn the reason why every one familiarly and without the least hesitation speaks of and supposes Eternity, and sticks not to ascribe infinity to duration; but it is with more doubting and reserve that many admit or suppose the infinity of space. The reason whereof seems to me to be this,— That duration and extension being used as names of affections belonging to other beings, we easily conceive in God infinite duration, and we cannot avoid doing so: but, not attributing to Him extension, but only to matter, which is finite, we are apter to doubt of the existence of expansion without matter; of which alone we commonly suppose it an attribute. And, therefore, when men pursue their thoughts of space, they are apt to stop at the confines of body: as if space were there at an end too, and reached no further. Or if their ideas, upon consideration, carry them further, yet they term what is beyond the limits of the universe, imaginary space: as if it were nothing, because there is no body existing in it. Whereas duration, antecedent to all body, and to the motions which it is measured by, they never term imaginary: because it is never supposed void of some other real existence. And if the names of things may at all direct our thoughts towards the original of men's ideas, (as I am apt to think they may very much,) one may have occasion to think by the name duration, that the continuation of existence, with a kind of resistance to any destructive force, and the continuation of solidity (which is apt to be confounded with, and if we will look into the minute anatomical parts of matter, is little different from, hardness) were thought to have some analogy, and gave occasion to words so near of kin as durare and durum esse. And that durare is applied to the idea of hardness, as well as that of existence, we see in Horace, Epod. xvi. ferro duravit secula. But, be that as it will, this is certain, that whoever pursues his own thoughts, will find them sometimes launch out beyond the extent of body, into the infinity of space or expansion; the idea whereof is distinct and separate from body and all other things: which may, (to those who please), be a subject of further meditation.

5. Time to duration is as place to expansion. Time in general is to duration as place to expansion. They are so much of those boundless oceans of eternity and immensity as is set out and distinguished from the rest, as it were by landmarks; and so are made use of to denote the position of finite real beings, in respect one to another, in those uniform infinite oceans of duration and space. These, rightly considered, are only ideas of determinate distances from certain known points, fixed in distinguishable sensible things, and supposed to keep the same distance one from another. From such points fixed in sensible beings we reckon, and from them we measure our portions of those infinite quantities; which, so considered, are that which we call time and place. For duration and space being in themselves uniform and boundless, the order and position of things, without such known settled points, would be lost in them; and all things would lie jumbled in an incurable confusion.

6. Time and place are taken for so much of either as are set out by the existence and motion of bodies. Time and place, taken thus for determinate distinguishable portions of those infinite abysses of space and duration, set out or supposed to be distinguished from the rest, by marks and known boundaries, have each of them a twofold acceptation.

First, Time in general is commonly taken for so much of infinite duration as is measured by, and co-existent with, the existence and motions of the great bodies of the universe, as far as we know anything of them: and in this sense time begins and ends with the frame of this sensible world, as in these phrases before mentioned, "Before all time," or, "When time shall be no more." Place likewise is taken sometimes for that portion of infinite space which is possessed by and comprehended within the material world; and is thereby distinguished from the rest of expansion; though this may be more properly called extension than place. Within these two are confined, and by the observable parts of them are measured and determined, the particular time or duration, and the particular extension and place, of all corporeal beings.

7. Sometimes for so much of either as we design by measures taken from the bulk or motion of bodies. Secondly, sometimes the word time is used in a larger sense, and is applied to parts of that infinite duration, not that were really distinguished and measured out by this real existence, and periodical motions of bodies, that were appointed from the beginning to be for signs and for seasons and for days and years, and are accordingly our measures of time; but such other portions too of that infinite uniform duration, which we upon any occasion do suppose equal to certain lengths of measured time; and so consider them as bounded and determined. For, if we should suppose the creation, or fall of the angels, was at the beginning of the Julian period, we should speak properly enough, and should be understood if we said, it is a longer time since the creation of angels than the creation of the world, by 7640 years: whereby we would mark out so much of that undistinguished duration as we suppose equal to, and would have admitted, 7640 annual revolutions of the sun, moving at the rate it now does. And thus likewise we sometimes speak of place, distance, or bulk, in the great inane, beyond the confines of the world, when we consider so much of that space as is equal to, or capable to receive, a body of any assigned dimensions, as a cubic foot; or do suppose a point in it, at such a certain distance from any part of the universe.

8. They belong to all finite beings. Where and when are questions belonging to all finite existences, and are by us always reckoned from some known parts of this sensible world, and from some certain epochs marked out to us by the motions observable in it. Without some such fixed parts or periods, the order of things would be lost, to our finite understandings, in the boundless invariable oceans of duration and expansion, which comprehend in them all finite beings, and in their full extent belong only to the Deity. And therefore we are not to wonder that we comprehend them not, and do so often find our thoughts at a loss, when we would consider them, either abstractly in themselves, or as any way attributed to the first incomprehensible Being. But when applied to any particular finite beings, the extension of any body is so much of that infinite space as the bulk of the body takes up. And place is the position of any body, when considered at a certain distance from some other. As the idea of the particular duration of anything is, an idea of that portion of infinite duration which passes during the existence of that thing; so the time when the thing existed is, the idea of that space of duration which passed between some known and fixed period of duration, and the being of that thing. One shows the distance of the extremities of the bulk or existence of the same thing, as that it is a foot square, or lasted two years; the other shows the distance of it in place, or existence from other fixed points of space or duration, as that it was in the middle of Lincoln's Inn Fields, or the first degree of Taurus, and in the year of our Lord 1671, or the 1000th year of the Julian period. All which distances we measure by preconceived ideas of certain lengths of space and duration,— as inches, feet, miles, and degrees, and in the other, minutes, days, and years, &c.

9. All the parts of extension are extension, and all the parts of duration are duration. There is one thing more wherein space and duration have a great conformity, and that is, though they are justly reckoned amongst our simple ideas, yet none of the distinct ideas we have of either is without all manner of composition: it is the very nature of both of them to consist of parts: but their parts being all of the same kind, and without the mixture of any other idea, hinder them not from having a place amongst simple ideas. Could the mind, as in number, come to so small a part of extension or duration as excluded divisibility, that would be, as it were, the indivisible unit or idea; by repetition of which, it would make its more enlarged ideas of extension and duration. But, since the mind is not able to frame an idea of any space without

parts, instead thereof it makes use of the common measures, which, by familiar use in each country, have imprinted themselves on the memory (as inches and feet; or cubits and parasangs; and so seconds, minutes, hours, days, and years in duration);— the mind makes use, I say, of such ideas as these, as simple ones: and these are the component parts of larger ideas, which the mind upon occasion makes by the addition of such known lengths which it is acquainted with. On the other side, the ordinary smallest measure we have of either is looked on as an unit in number, when the mind by division would reduce them into less fractions. Though on both sides, both in addition and division, either of space or duration, when the idea under consideration becomes very big or very small its precise bulk becomes very obscure and confused; and it is the number of its repeated additions or divisions that alone remains clear and distinct; as will easily appear to any one who will let his thoughts loose in the vast expansion of space, or divisibility of matter. Every part of duration is duration too; and every part of extension is extension, both of them capable of addition or division in infinitum. But the least portions of either of them, whereof we have clear and distinct ideas, may perhaps be fittest to be considered by us, as the simple ideas of that kind out of which our complex modes of space, extension, and duration are made up, and into which they can again be distinctly resolved. Such a small part in duration may be called a moment, and is the time of one idea in our minds, in the train of their ordinary succession there. The other, wanting a proper name, I know not whether I may be allowed to call a sensible point, meaning thereby the least particle of matter or space we can discern, which is ordinarily about a minute, and to the sharpest eyes seldom less than thirty seconds of a circle, whereof the eye is the centre.

10. Their parts inseparable. Expansion and duration have this further agreement, that, though they are both considered by us as having parts, yet their parts are not separable one from another, no not even in thought: though the parts of bodies from whence we take our measure of the one; and the parts of motion, or rather the succession of ideas in our minds, from whence we take the measure of the other, may be interrupted and separated; as the one is often by rest, and the other is by sleep, which we call rest too.

11. Duration is as a line, expansion as a solid. But there is this manifest difference between them,— That the ideas of length which we have of expansion are turned every way, and so make figure, and breadth, and thickness; but duration is but as it were the length of one straight line, extended in infinitum, not capable of multiplicity, variation, or figure; but is one common measure of all existence whatsoever, wherein all things, whilst they exist, equally partake. For this present moment is common to all things that are now in being, and equally comprehends that part of their existence, as much as if they were all but one single being; and we may truly say, they all exist in the same moment of time. Whether angels and spirits have any analogy to this, in respect to expansion, is beyond my comprehension: and perhaps for us, who have understandings and comprehensions suited to our own preservation, and the ends of our own being, but not to the reality and extent of all other beings, it is near as hard to conceive any existence, or to have an idea of any real being, with a perfect negation of all manner of expansion, as it is to have the idea of any real existence with a perfect negation of all manner of duration. And therefore, what spirits have to do with space, or how they communicate in it, we know not. All that we know is, that bodies do each singly possess its proper portion of it, according to the extent of solid parts; and thereby exclude all other bodies from having any share in that particular portion of space, whilst it remains there.

12. Duration has never two parts together, expansion altogether. Duration, and time which is a part of it, is the idea we have of perishing distance, of which no two parts exist together, but follow each other in succession; an expansion is the idea of lasting distance, all whose parts exist together, and are not capable of succession. And therefore, though we cannot conceive any duration without succession, nor can put it together in our thoughts that any being does now exist tomorrow, or possess at once more than the present moment of duration; yet we can conceive the eternal duration of the Almighty far different from that of man, or any other finite being. Because man comprehends not in his knowledge or power all past and future things: his

thoughts are but of yesterday, and he knows not what tomorrow will bring forth. What is once past he can never recall; and what is yet to come he cannot make present. What I say of man, I say of all finite beings; who, though they may far exceed man in knowledge and power, yet are no more than the meanest creature, in comparison with God himself Finite or any magnitude holds not any proportion to infinite. God's infinite duration, being accompanied with infinite knowledge and infinite power, He sees all things, past and to come; and they are no more distant from His knowledge, no further removed from His sight, than the present: they all lie under the same view: and there is nothing which He cannot make exist each moment He pleases. For the existence of all things, depending upon His good pleasure, all things exist every moment that He thinks fit to have them exist. To conclude: expansion and duration do mutually embrace and comprehend each other; every part of space being in every part of duration, and every part of duration in every part of expansion. Such a combination of two distinct ideas is, I suppose, scarce to be found in all that great variety we do or can conceive, and may afford matter to further speculation.

Chapter XVI. Idea of Number

1. Number the simplest and most universal idea. Amongst all the ideas we have, as there is none suggested to the mind by more ways, so there is none more simple, than that of unity, or one: it has no shadow of variety or composition in it: every object our senses are employed about; every idea in our understandings; every thought of our minds, brings this idea along with it. And therefore it is the most intimate to our thoughts, as well as it is, in its agreement to all other things, the most universal idea we have. For number applies itself to men, angels, actions, thoughts; everything that either doth exist, or can be imagined.

2. Its modes made by addition. By repeating this idea in our minds, and adding the repetitions together, we come by the complex ideas of the modes of it. Thus, by adding one to one, we have the complex idea of a couple; by putting twelve units together, we have the complex idea of a dozen; and so of a score, or a million, or any other number.

3. Each mode distinct. The simple modes of number are of all other the most distinct; every the least variation, which is an unit, making each combination as clearly different from that which approacheth nearest to it, as the most remote; two being as distinct from one, as two hundred; and the idea of two as distinct from the idea of three, as the magnitude of the whole earth is from that of a mite. This is not so in other simple modes, in which it is not so easy, nor perhaps possible for us to distinguish betwixt two approaching ideas, which yet are really different. For who will undertake to find a difference between the white of this paper and that of the next degree to it: or can form distinct ideas of every the least excess in extension?

4. Therefore demonstrations in numbers the most precise. The clearness and distinctness of each mode of number from all others, even those that approach nearest, makes me apt to think that demonstrations in numbers, if they are not more evident and exact than in extension, yet they are more general in their use, and more determinate in their application. Because the ideas of numbers are more precise and distinguishable than in extension; where every equality and excess are not so easy to be observed or measured; because our thoughts cannot in space arrive at any determined smallness beyond which it cannot go, as an unit; and therefore the quantity or proportion of any the least excess cannot be discovered; which is clear otherwise in number, where, as has been said, 91 is as distinguishable from go as from 9000, though 91 be the next immediate excess to 90. But it is not so in extension, where, whatsoever is more than just a foot or an inch, is not distinguishable from the standard of a foot or an inch; and in lines which appear of an equal length, one may be longer than the other by innumerable parts: nor can any one assign an angle, which shall be the next biggest to a right one.

5. Names necessary to numbers. By the repeating, as has been said, the idea of an unit, and joining it to another unit, we make thereof one collective idea, marked by the name two. And

whosoever can do this, and proceed on, still adding one more to the last collective idea which he had of any number, and gave a name to it, may count, or have ideas, for several collections of units, distinguished one from another, as far as he hath a series of names for following numbers, and a memory to retain that series, with their several names: all numeration being but still the adding of one unit more, and giving to the whole together, as comprehended in one idea, a new or distinct name or sign, whereby to know it from those before and after, and distinguish it from every smaller or greater multitude of units. So that he that can add one to one, and so to two, and so go on with his tale, taking still with him the distinct names belonging to every progression; and so again, by subtracting an unit from each collection, retreat and lessen them, is capable of all the ideas of numbers within the compass of his language, or for which he hath names, though not perhaps of more. For, the several simple modes of numbers being in our minds but so many combinations of units, which have no variety, nor are capable of any other difference but more or less, names or marks for each distinct combination seem more necessary than in any other sort of ideas. For, without such names or marks, we can hardly well make use of numbers in reckoning, especially where the combination is made up of any great multitude of units; which put together, without a name or mark to distinguish that precise collection, will hardly be kept from being a heap in confusion.

6. Another reason for the necessity of names to numbers. This I think to be the reason why some Americans I have spoken with, (who were otherwise of quick and rational parts enough,) could not, as we do, by any means count to 1000; nor had any distinct idea of that number, though they could reckon very well to 20. Because their language being scanty, and accommodated only to the few necessaries of a needy, simple life, unacquainted either with trade or mathematics, had no words in it to stand for 1000; so that when they were discoursed with of those greater numbers, they would show the hairs of their head, to express a great multitude, which they could not number; which inability, I suppose, proceeded from their want of names. The Tououpinambos had no names for numbers above 5; any number beyond that they made out by showing their fingers, and the fingers of others who were present. And I doubt not but we ourselves might distinctly number in words a great deal further than we usually do, would we find out but some fit denominations to signify them by; whereas, in the way we take now to name them, by millions of millions of millions, &c., it is hard to go beyond eighteen, or at most, four and twenty, decimal progressions, without confusion. But to show how much distinct names conduce to our well reckoning, or having useful ideas of numbers, let us see all these following figures in one continued line, as the marks of one number: v. g.

Nonillions Octillions Septillions Sextillions Quintrillions 857324 162486 345896 437918 423147

Quartrillions Trillions Billions Millions Units 248106 235421 261734 368149 623137

The ordinary way of naming this number in English, will be the often repeating of millions, of millions, of millions, of millions, of millions, of millions, of millions, of millions, (which is the denomination of the second six figures). In which way, it will be very hard to have any distinguishing notions of this number. But whether, by giving every six figures a new and orderly denomination, these, and perhaps a great many more figures in progression, might not easily be counted distinctly, and ideas of them both got more easily to ourselves, and more plainly signified to others, I leave it to be considered. This I mention only to show how necessary distinct names are to numbering, without pretending to introduce new ones of my invention.

7. Why children number not earlier. Thus children, either for want of names to mark the several progressions of numbers, or not having yet the faculty to collect scattered ideas into complex ones, and range them in a regular order, and so retain them in their memories, as is necessary to reckoning, do not begin to number very early, nor proceed in it very far or steadily, till a good while after they are well furnished with good store of other ideas: and one may often observe them discourse and reason pretty well, and have very clear conceptions of

several other things, before they can tell twenty. And some, through the default of their memories, who cannot retain the several combinations of numbers, with their names, annexed in their distinct orders, and the dependence of so long a train of numeral progressions, and their relation one to another, are not able all their lifetime to reckon, or regularly go over any moderate series of numbers. For he that will count twenty, or have any idea of that number, must know that nineteen went before, with the distinct name or sign of every one of them, as they stand marked in their order; for wherever this fails, a gap is made, the chain breaks, and the progress in numbering can go no further. So that to reckon right, it is required, (1) That the mind distinguish carefully two ideas, which are different one from another only by the addition or subtraction of one unit: (2) That it retain in memory the names or marks of the several combinations, from an unit to that number; and that not confusedly, and at random, but in that exact order that the numbers follow one another. In either of which, if it trips, the whole business of numbering will be disturbed, and there will remain only the confused idea of multitude, but the ideas necessary to distinct numeration will not be attained to.

8. Number measures all measureables. This further is observable in number, that it is that which the mind makes use of in measuring all things that by us are measurable, which principally are expansion and duration; and our idea of infinity, even when applied to those, seems to be nothing but the infinity of number. For what else are our ideas of Eternity and Immensity, but the repeated additions of certain ideas of imagined parts of duration and expansion, with the infinity of number; in which we can come to no end of addition? For such an inexhaustible stock, number (of all other our ideas) most clearly furnishes us with, as is obvious to every one. For let a man collect into one sum as great a number as he pleases, this multitude, how great soever, lessens not one jot the power of adding to it, or brings him any nearer the end of the inexhaustible stock of number; where still there remains as much to be added, as if none were taken out. And this endless addition or addibility (if any one like the word better) of numbers, so apparent to the mind, is that, I think, which gives us the clearest and most distinct idea of infinity: of which more in the following chapter.

Chapter XVII.Of Infinity

1. Infinity, in its original intention, attributed to space, duration, and number. He that would know what kind of idea it is to which we give the name of infinity, cannot do it better than by considering to what infinity is by the mind more immediately attributed; and then how the mind comes to frame it.

Finite and infinite seem to me to be looked upon by the mind as the modes of quantity, and to be attributed primarily in their first designation only to those things which have parts, and are capable of increase or diminution by the addition or subtraction of any the least part: and such are the ideas of space, duration, and number, which we have considered in the foregoing chapters. It is true, that we cannot but be assured, that the great God, of whom and from whom are all things, is incomprehensibly infinite: but yet, when we apply to that first and supreme Being our idea of infinite, in our weak and narrow thoughts, we do it primarily in respect to his duration and ubiquity; and, I think, more figuratively to his power, wisdom, and goodness, and other attributes, which are properly inexhaustible and incomprehensible, &c. For, when we call them infinite, we have no other idea of this infinity but what carries with it some reflection on, and imitation of, that number or extent of the acts or objects of God's power, wisdom, and goodness, which can never be supposed so great, or so many, which these attributes will not always surmount and exceed, let us multiply them in our thoughts as far as we can, with all the infinity of endless number. I do not pretend to say how these attributes are in God, who is infinitely beyond the reach of our narrow capacities: they do, without doubt, contain in them all possible perfection: but this, I say, is our way of conceiving them, and these our ideas of their infinity.

2. The idea of finite easily got. Finite then, and infinite, being by the mind looked on as modifications of expansion and duration, the next thing to be considered, is,— How the mind comes by them. As for the idea of finite, there is no great difficulty. The obvious portions of extension that affect our senses, carry with them into the mind the idea of finite: and the ordinary periods of succession, whereby we measure time and duration, as hours, days, and years, are bounded lengths. The difficulty is, how we come by those boundless ideas of eternity and immensity; since the objects we converse with come so much short of any approach or proportion to that largeness.

3. How we come by the idea of infinity. Every one that has any idea of any stated lengths of space, as a foot, finds that he can repeat that idea; and joining it to the former, make the idea of two feet; and by the addition of a third, three feet; and so on, without ever coming to an end of his additions, whether of the same idea of a foot, or, if he pleases, of doubling it, or any other idea he has of any length, as a mile, or diameter of the earth, or of the orbis magnus: for whichever of these he takes, and how often soever he doubles, or any otherwise multiplies it, he finds, that, after he has continued his doubling in his thoughts, and enlarged his idea as much as he pleases, he has no more reason to stop, nor is one jot nearer the end of such addition, than he was at first setting out: the power of enlarging his idea of space by further additions remaining still the same, he hence takes the idea of infinite space.

4. Our idea of space boundless. This, I think, is the way whereby the mind gets the idea of infinite space. It is a quite different consideration, to examine whether the mind has the idea of such a boundless space actually existing; since our ideas are not always proofs of the existence of things: but yet, since this comes here in our way, I suppose I may say, that we are apt to think that space in itself is actually boundless, to which imagination the idea of space or expansion of itself naturally leads us. For, it being considered by us, either as the extension of body, or as existing by itself, without any solid matter taking it up, (for of such a void space we have not only the idea, but I have proved, as I think, from the motion of body, its necessary existence), it is impossible the mind should be ever able to find or suppose any end of it, or be stopped anywhere in its progress in this space, how far soever it extends its thoughts. Any bounds made with body, even adamantine walls, are so far from putting a stop to the mind in its further progress in space and extension that it rather facilitates and enlarges it. For so far as that body reaches, so far no one can doubt of extension; and when we are come to the utmost extremity of body, what is there that can there put a stop, and satisfy the mind that it is at the end of space, when it perceives that it is not; nay, when it is satisfied that body itself can move into it? For, if it be necessary for the motion of body, that there should be an empty space, though ever so little, here amongst bodies; and if it be possible for body to move in or through that empty space;— nay, it is impossible for any particle of matter to move but into an empty space; the same possibility of a body's moving into a void space, beyond the utmost bounds of body, as well as into a void space interspersed amongst bodies, will always remain clear and evident: the idea of empty pure space, whether within or beyond the confines of all bodies, being exactly the same, differing not in nature, though in bulk; and there being nothing to hinder body from moving into it. So that wherever the mind places itself by any thought, either amongst, or remote from all bodies, it can, in this uniform idea of space, nowhere find any bounds, any end; and so must necessarily conclude it, by the very nature and idea of each part of it, to be actually infinite.

5. And so of duration. As, by the power we find in ourselves of repeating, as often as we will, any idea of space, we get the idea of immensity; so, by being able to repeat the idea of any length of duration we have in our minds, with all the endless addition of number, we come by the idea of eternity. For we find in ourselves, we can no more come to an end of such repeated ideas than we can come to the end of number; which every one perceives he cannot. But here again it is another question, quite different from our having an idea of eternity, to know whether there were any real being, whose duration has been eternal. And as to this, I say, he that considers something now existing, must necessarily come to Something eternal. But

having spoke of this in another place, I shall say here no more of it, but proceed on to some other considerations of our idea of infinity.

6. Why other ideas are not capable of infinity. If it be so, that our idea of infinity be got from the power we observe in ourselves of repeating, without end, our own ideas, it may be demanded,— Why we do not attribute infinity to other ideas, as well as those of space and duration; since they may be as easily, and as often, repeated in our minds as the other: and yet nobody ever thinks of infinite sweetness, or infinite whiteness, though he can repeat the idea of sweet or white, as frequently as those of a yard or a day? To which I answer,— All the ideas that are considered as having parts, and are capable of increase by the addition of any equal or less parts, afford us, by their repetition, the idea of infinity; because, with this endless repetition, there is continued an enlargement of which there can be no end. But in other ideas it is not so. For to the largest idea of extension or duration that I at present have, the addition of any the least part makes an increase; but to the perfectest idea I have of the whitest whiteness, if I add another of a less or equal whiteness, (and of a whiter than I have, I cannot add the idea), it makes no increase, and enlarges not my idea at all; and therefore the different ideas of whiteness, &c. are called degrees. For those ideas that consist of parts are capable of being augmented by every addition of the least part; but if you take the idea of white, which one parcel of snow yielded yesterday to our sight, and another idea of white from another parcel of snow you see to-day, and put them together in your mind, they embody, as it were, and run into one, and the idea of whiteness is not at all increased; and if we add a less degree of whiteness to a greater, we are so far from increasing, that we diminish it. Those ideas that consist not of parts cannot be augmented to what proportion men please, or be stretched beyond what they have received by their senses; but space, duration, and number, being capable of increase by repetition, leave in the mind an idea of endless room for more; nor can we conceive anywhere a stop to a further addition or progression: and so those ideas alone lead our minds towards the thought of infinity.

7. Difference between infinity of space, and space infinite. Though our idea of infinity arise from the contemplation of quantity, and the endless increase the mind is able to make in quantity, by the repeated additions of what portions thereof it pleases; yet I guess we cause great confusion in our thoughts, when we join infinity to any supposed idea of quantity the mind can be thought to have, and so discourse or reason about an infinite quantity, as an infinite space, or an infinite duration. For, as our idea of infinity being, as I think, an endless growing idea, but the idea of any quantity the mind has, being at that time terminated in that idea, (for be it as great as it will, it can be no greater than it is,)— to join infinity to it, is to adjust a standing measure to a growing bulk; and therefore I think it is not an insignificant subtilty, if I say, that we are carefully to distinguish between the idea of the infinity of space, and the idea of a space infinite. The first is nothing but a supposed endless progression of the mind, over what repeated ideas of space it pleases; but to have actually in the mind the idea of a space infinite, is to suppose the mind already passed over, and actually to have a view of all those repeated ideas of space which an endless repetition can never totally represent to it; which carries in it a plain contradiction.

8. We have no idea of infinite space. This, perhaps, will be a little plainer, if we consider it in numbers. The infinity of numbers, to the end of whose addition every one perceives there is no approach, easily appears to any one that reflects on it. But, how clear soever this idea of the infinity of number be, there is nothing yet more evident than the absurdity of the actual idea of an infinite number. Whatsoever positive ideas we have in our minds of any space, duration, or number, let them be ever so great, they are still finite; but when we suppose an inexhaustible remainder, from which we remove all bounds, and wherein we allow the mind an endless progression of thought, without ever completing the idea, there we have our idea of infinity: which, though it seems to be pretty clear when we consider nothing else in it but the negation of an end, yet, when we would frame in our minds the idea of an infinite space or duration, that idea is very obscure and confused, because it is made up of two parts, very different, if not

inconsistent. For, let a man frame in his mind an idea of any space or number, as great as he will; it is plain the mind rests and terminates in that idea, which is contrary to the idea of infinity, which consists in a supposed endless progression. And therefore I think it is that we are so easily confounded, when we come to argue and reason about infinite space or duration, &c. Because the parts of such an idea not being perceived to be, as they are, inconsistent, the one side or other always perplexes, whatever consequences we draw from the other; as an idea of motion not passing on would perplex any one who should argue from such an idea, which is not better than an idea of motion at rest. And such another seems to me to be the idea of a space, or (which is the same thing) a number infinite, i.e. of a space or number which the mind actually has, and so views and terminates in; and of a space or number, which, in a constant and endless enlarging and progression, it can in thought never attain to. For, how large soever an idea of space I have in my mind, it is no larger than it is that instant that I have it, though I be capable the next instant to double it, and so on in infinitum; for that alone is infinite which has no bounds; and that the idea of infinity, in which our thoughts can find none.

9. Number affords us the clearest idea of infinity. But of all other ideas, it is number, as I have said, which I think furnishes us with the clearest and most distinct idea of infinity we are capable of. For, even in space and duration, when the mind pursues the idea of infinity, it there makes use of the ideas and repetitions of numbers, as of millions and millions of miles, or years, which are so many distinct ideas,— kept best by number from running into a confused heap, wherein the mind loses itself; and when it has added together as many millions, &c., as it pleases, of known lengths of space or duration, the clearest idea it can get of infinity, is the confused incomprehensible remainder of endless addible numbers, which affords no prospect of stop or boundary.

10. Our different conceptions of the infinity of number contrasted with those of duration and expansion. It will, perhaps, give us a little further light into the idea we have of infinity, and discover to us, that it is nothing but the infinity of number applied to determinate parts, of which we have in our minds the distinct ideas, if we consider that number is not generally thought by us infinite, whereas duration and extension are apt to be so; which arises from hence,— that in number we are at one end, as it were: for there being in number nothing less than an unit, we there stop, and are at an end; but in addition, or increase of number, we can set no bounds: and so it is like a line, whereof one end terminating with us, the other is extended still forwards, beyond all that we can conceive. But in space and duration it is otherwise. For in duration we consider it as if this line of number were extended both ways — to an unconceivable, undeterminate, and infinite length; which is evident to any one that will but reflect on what consideration he hath of Eternity; which, I suppose, will find to be nothing else but the turning this infinity of number both ways, a parte ante, and a parte post, as they speak. For, when we would consider eternity, a parte ante, what do we but, beginning from ourselves and the present time we are in, repeat in our minds the ideas of years, or ages, or any other assignable portion of duration past, with a prospect of proceeding in such addition with all the infinity of number: and when we would consider eternity, a parte post, we just after the same rate begin from ourselves, and reckon by multiplied periods yet to come, still extending that line of number as before. And these two being put together, are that infinite duration we call Eternity: which, as we turn our view either way, forwards or backwards, appears infinite, because we still turn that way the infinite end of number, i.e. the power still of adding more.

11. How we conceive the infinity of space. The same happens also in space, wherein, conceiving ourselves to be, as it were, in the centre, we do on all sides pursue those indeterminable lines of number; and reckoning any way from ourselves, a yard, mile, diameter of the earth, or orbis magnus,— by the infinity of number, we add others to them, as often as we will. And having no more reason to set bounds to those repeated ideas than we have to set bounds to number, we have that indeterminable idea of immensity.

12. Infinite divisibility. And since in any bulk of matter our thoughts can never arrive at the utmost divisibility, therefore there is an apparent infinity to us also in that, which has the

infinity also of number; but with this difference,— that, in the former considerations of the infinity of space and duration, we only use addition of numbers; whereas this is like the division of an unit into its fractions, wherein the mind also can proceed in infinitum, as well as in the former additions; it being indeed but the addition still of new numbers: though in the addition of the one, we can have no more the positive idea of a space infinitely great, than, in the division of the other, we can have the [positive] idea of a body infinitely little;— our idea of infinity being, as I may say, a growing or fugitive idea, still in a boundless progression, that can stop nowhere.

13. No positive idea of infinity. Though it be hard, I think, to find anyone so absurd as to say he has the positive idea of an actual infinite number;— the infinity whereof lies only in a power still of adding any combination of units to any former number, and that as long and as much as one will; the like also being in the infinity of space and duration, which power leaves always to the mind room for endless additions;— yet there be those who imagine they have positive ideas of infinite duration and space. It would, I think, be enough to destroy any such positive idea of infinite, to ask him that has it,— whether he could add to it or no; which would easily show the mistake of such a positive idea. We can, I think, have no positive idea of any space or duration which is not made up of, and commensurate to, repeated numbers of feet or yards, or days and years; which are the common measures, whereof we have the ideas in our minds, and whereby we judge of the greatness of this sort of quantities. And therefore, since an infinite idea of space or duration must needs be made up of infinite parts, it can have no other infinity than that of number capable still of further addition; but not an actual positive idea of a number infinite. For, I think it is evident, that the addition of finite things together (as are all lengths whereof we have the positive ideas) can never otherwise produce the idea of infinite than as number does; which, consisting of additions of finite units one to another, suggests the idea of infinite, only by a power we find we have of still increasing the sum, and adding more of the same kind; without coming one jot nearer the end of such progression.

14. How we cannot have a positive idea of infinity in quantity. They who would prove their idea of infinite to be positive, seem to me to do it by a pleasant argument, taken from the negation of an end; which being negative, the negation of it is positive. He that considers that the end is, in body, but the extremity or superficies of that body, will not perhaps be forward to grant that the end is a bare negative: and he that perceives the end of his pen is black or white, will be apt to think that the end is something more than a pure negation. Nor is it, when applied to duration, the bare negation of existence, but more properly the last moment of it. But if they will have the end to be nothing but the bare negation of existence, I am sure they cannot deny but the beginning is the first instant of being, and is not by any body conceived to be a bare negation; and therefore, by their own argument, the idea of eternal, a parte ante, or of a duration without a beginning, is but a negative idea.

15. What is positive, what negative, in our idea of infinite. The idea of infinite has, I confess, something of positive in all those things we apply to it. When we would think of infinite space or duration, we at first step usually make some very large idea, as perhaps of millions of ages, or miles, which possibly we double and multiply several times. All that we thus amass together in our thoughts is positive, and the assemblage of a great number of positive ideas of space or duration. But what still remains beyond this we have no more a positive distinct notion of than a mariner has of the depth of the sea; where, having let down a large portion of his sounding-line, he reaches no bottom. Whereby he knows the depth to be so many fathoms, and more; but how much the more is, he hath no distinct notion at all: and could he always supply new line, and find the plummet always sink, without ever stopping, he would be something in the posture of the mind reaching after a complete and positive idea of infinity. In which case, let this line be ten, or ten thousand fathoms long, it equally discovers what is beyond it, and gives only this confused and comparative idea, that this is not all, but one may yet go farther. So much as the mind comprehends of any space, it has a positive idea of: but in endeavouring to make it infinite,— it being always enlarging, always advancing,— the idea is

still imperfect and incomplete. So much space as the mind takes a view of in its contemplation of greatness, is a clear picture, and positive in the understanding: but infinite is still greater. 1. Then the idea of so much is positive and clear. 2. The idea of greater is also clear; but it is but a comparative idea, the idea of so much greater as cannot be comprehended. 3. And this is plainly negative: not positive. For he has no positive clear idea of the largeness of any extension, (which is that sought for in the idea of infinite), that has not a comprehensive idea of the dimensions of it: and such, nobody, I think, pretends to in what is infinite. For to say a man has a positive clear idea of any quantity, without knowing how great it is, is as reasonable as to say, he has the positive clear idea of the number of the sands on the sea-shore, who knows not how many there be, but only that they are more than twenty. For just such a perfect and positive idea has he of an infinite space or duration, who says it is larger than the extent or duration of ten, one hundred, one thousand, or any other number of miles, or years, whereof he has or can have a positive idea; which is all the idea, I think, we have of infinite. So that what lies beyond our positive idea towards infinity, lies in obscurity, and has the indeterminate confusion of a negative idea, wherein I know I neither do nor can comprehend all I would, it being too large for a finite and narrow capacity. And that cannot but be very far from a positive complete idea, wherein the greatest part of what I would comprehend is left out, under the undeterminate intimation of being still greater. For to say, that, having in any quantity measured so much, or gone so far, you are not yet at the end, is only to say that that quantity is greater. So that the negation of an end in any quantity is, in other words, only to say that it is bigger; and a total negation of an end is but carrying this bigger still with you, in all the progressions of your thoughts shall make in quantity; and adding this idea of still greater to all the ideas you have, or can be supposed to have, of quantity. Now, whether such an idea as that be positive, I leave any one to consider.

16. We have no positive idea of an infinite duration. I ask those who say they have a positive idea of eternity, whether their idea of duration includes in it succession, or not? If it does not, they ought to show the difference of their notion of duration, when applied to an eternal Being, and to a finite; since, perhaps, there may be others as well as I, who will own to them their weakness of understanding in this point, and acknowledge that the notion they have of duration forces them to conceive, that whatever has duration, is of a longer continuance to-day than it was yesterday. If, to avoid succession in external existence, they return to the punctum stans of the schools, I suppose they will thereby very little mend the matter, or help us to a more clear and positive idea of infinite duration; there being nothing more inconceivable to me than duration without succession. Besides, that punctum stans, if it signify anything, being not quantum, finite or infinite cannot belong to it. But, if our weak apprehensions cannot separate succession from any duration whatsoever, our idea of eternity can be nothing but of infinite succession of moments of duration wherein anything does exist; and whether any one has, or can have, a positive idea of an actual infinite number, I leave him to consider, till his infinite number be so great that he himself can add no more to it; and as long as he can increase it, I doubt he himself will think the idea he hath of it a little too scanty for positive infinity.

17. No complete idea of eternal being. I think it unavoidable for every considering, rational creature, that will but examine his own or any other existence, to have the notion of an eternal, wise Being, who had no beginning: and such an idea of infinite duration I am sure I have. But this negation of a beginning, being but the negation of a positive thing, scarce gives me a positive idea of infinity; which, whenever I endeavour to extend my thoughts to, I confess myself at a loss, and I find I cannot attain any clear comprehension of it.

18. No positive idea of infinite space. He that thinks he has a positive idea of infinite space, will, when he considers it, find that he can no more have a positive idea of the greatest, than he has of the least space. For in this latter, which seems the easier of the two, and more within our comprehension, we are capable only of a comparative idea of smallness, which will always be less than any one whereof we have the positive idea. All our positive ideas of any quantity, whether great or little, have always bounds, though our comparative idea, whereby we can

always add to the one, and take from the other, hath no bounds. For that which remains, either great or little, not being comprehended in that positive idea which we have, lies in obscurity; and we have no other idea of it, but of the power of enlarging the one and diminishing the other, without ceasing. A pestle and mortar will as soon bring any particle of matter to indivisibility, as the acutest thought of a mathematician; and a surveyor may as soon with his chain measure out infinite space, as a philosopher by the quickest flight of mind reach it, or by thinking comprehend it; which is to have a positive idea of it. He that thinks on a cube of an inch diameter, has a clear and positive idea of it in his mind, and so can frame one of 1/2, 1/4, 1/8, and so on, till he has the idea in his thoughts of something very little; but yet reaches not the idea of that incomprehensible littleness which division can produce. What remains of smallness is as far from his thoughts as when he first began; and therefore he never comes at all to have a clear and positive idea of that smallness which is consequent to infinite divisibility.

19. What is positive, what negative, in our idea of infinite. Every one that looks towards infinity does, as I have said, at first glance make some very large idea of that which he applies it to, let it be space or duration; and possibly he wearies his thoughts, by multiplying in his mind that first large idea: but yet by that he comes no nearer to the having a positive clear idea of what remains to make up a positive infinite, than the country fellow had of the water which was yet to come, and pass the channel of the river where he stood: Rusticus expectat dum defluat amnis, at ille Labitur, et labetur in omne volubilis oevum.

20. Some think they have a positive idea of eternity, and not of infinite space. There are some I have met that put so much difference between infinite duration and infinite space, that they persuade themselves that they have a positive idea of eternity, but that they have not, nor can have any idea of infinite space. The reason of which mistake I suppose to be this — that finding, by a due contemplation of causes and effects, that it is necessary to admit some Eternal Being, and so to consider the real existence of that Being as taken up and commensurate to their idea of eternity; but, on the other side, not finding it necessary, but, on the contrary, apparently absurd, that body should be infinite, they forwardly conclude that they can have no idea of infinite space, because they can have no idea of infinite matter. Which consequence, I conceive, is very ill collected, because the existence of matter is no ways necessary to the existence of space, no more than the existence of motion, or the sun, is necessary to duration, though duration used to be measured by it. And I doubt not but that a man may have the idea of ten thousand miles square, without any body so big, as well as the idea of ten thousand years, without any body so old. It seems as easy to me to have the idea of space empty of body, as to think of the capacity of a bushel without corn, or the hollow of a nut-shell without a kernel in it: it being no more necessary that there should be existing a solid body, infinitely extended, because we have an idea of the infinity of space, than it is necessary that the world should be eternal, because we have an idea of infinite duration. And why should we think our idea of infinite space requires the real existence of matter to support it, when we find that we have as clear an idea of an infinite duration to come, as we have of infinite duration past? Though I suppose nobody thinks it conceivable that anything does or has existed in that future duration. Nor is it possible to join our idea of future duration with present or past existence, any more than it is possible to make the ideas of yesterday, to-day, and to-morrow to be the same; or bring ages past and future together, and make them contemporary. But if these men are of the mind, that they have clearer ideas of infinite duration than of infinite space, because it is past doubt that God has existed from all eternity, but there is no real matter co-extended with infinite space; yet those philosophers who are of opinion that infinite space is possessed by God's infinite omnipresence, as well as infinite duration by his eternal existence, must be allowed to have as clear an idea of infinite space as of infinite duration; though neither of them, I think, has any positive idea of infinity in either case. For whatsoever positive ideas a man has in his mind of any quantity, he can repeat it, and add it to the former, as easy as he can add together the ideas of two days, or two paces, which are

positive ideas of lengths he has in his mind, and so on as long as he pleases: whereby, if a man had a positive idea of infinite, either duration or space, he could add two infinities together; nay, make one infinite infinitely bigger than another — absurdities too gross to be confuted.

21. Supposed positive ideas of infinity, cause of mistakes. But yet if after all this, there be men who persuade themselves that they have clear positive comprehensive ideas of infinity, it is fit they enjoy their privilege: and I should be very glad (with some others that I know, who acknowledge they have none such) to be better informed by their communication. For I have been hitherto apt to think that the great and inextricable difficulties which perpetually involve all discourses concerning infinity,— whether of space, duration, or divisibility, have been the certain marks of a defect in our ideas of infinity, and the disproportion the nature thereof has to the comprehension of our narrow capacities. For, whilst men talk and dispute of infinite space or duration, as if they had as complete and positive ideas of them as they have of the names they use for them, or as they have of a yard, or an hour, or any other determinate quantity; it is no wonder if the incomprehensible nature of the thing they discourse of, or reason about, leads them into perplexities and contradictions, and their minds be overlaid by an object too large and mighty to be surveyed and managed by them.

22. All these are modes of ideas got from sensation and reflection. If I have dwelt pretty long on the consideration of duration, space, and number, and what arises from the contemplation of them,— Infinity, it is possibly no more than the matter requires; there being few simple ideas whose modes give more exercise to the thoughts of men than those do. I pretend not to treat of them in their full latitude. It suffices to my design to show how the mind receives them, such as they are, from sensation and reflection; and how even the idea we have of infinity, how remote soever it may seem to be from any object of sense, or operation of our mind, has, nevertheless, as all our other ideas, its original there. Some mathematicians perhaps, of advanced speculations, may have other ways to introduce into their minds ideas of infinity. But this hinders not but that they themselves, as well as all other men, got the first ideas which they had of infinity from sensation and reflection, in the method we have here set down.

Chapter XVIII.Other Simple Modes

1. Other simple modes of simple ideas of sensation. Though I have, in the foregoing chapters, shown how, from simple ideas taken in by sensation, the mind comes to extend itself even to infinity; which, however it may of all others seem most remote from any sensible perception, yet at last hath nothing in it but what is made out of simple ideas: received into the mind by the senses, and afterwards there put together, by the faculty the mind has to repeat its own ideas;— Though, I say, these might be instances enough of simple modes of the simple ideas of sensation, and suffice to show how the mind comes by them, yet I shall, for method's sake, though briefly, give an account of some few more, and then proceed to more complex ideas.

2. Simple modes of motion. To slide, roll, tumble, walk, creep, run, dance, leap, skip, and abundance of others that might be named, are words which are no sooner heard but every one who understands English has presently in his mind distinct ideas, which are all but the different modifications of motion. Modes of motion answer those of extension; swift and slow are two different ideas of motion, the measures whereof are made of the distances of time and space put together; so they are complex ideas, comprehending time and space with motion.

3. Modes of sounds. The like variety have we in sounds. Every articulate word is a different modification of sound; by which we see that, from the sense of hearing, by such modifications, the mind may be furnished with distinct ideas, to almost an infinite number. Sounds also, besides the distinct cries of birds and beasts, are modified by diversity of notes of different length put together, which make that complex idea called a tune, which a musician may have in his mind when he hears or makes no sound at all, by reflecting on the ideas of those sounds,

so put together silently in his own fancy.

4. Modes of colours. Those of colours are also very various: some we take notice of as the different degrees, or as they were termed shades, of the same colour. But since we very seldom make assemblages of colours, either for use or delight, but figure is taken in also, and has its part in it, as in painting, weaving, needleworks, &c.; those which are taken notice of do most commonly belong to mixed modes, as being made up of ideas of divers kinds, viz. figure and colour, such as beauty, rainbow, &c.

5. Modes of tastes. All compounded tastes and smells are also modes, made up of the simple ideas of those senses. But they, being such as generally we have no names for, are less taken notice of, and cannot be set down in writing; and therefore must be left without enumeration to the thoughts and experience of my reader.

6. Some simple modes have no names. In general it may be observed, that those simple modes which are considered but as different degrees of the same simple idea, though they are in themselves many of them very distinct ideas, yet have ordinarily no distinct names, nor are much taken notice of, as distinct ideas, where the difference is but very small between them. Whether men have neglected these modes, and given no names to them, as wanting measures nicely to distinguish them; or because, when they were so distinguished, that knowledge would not be of general or necessary use, I leave it to the thoughts of others. It is sufficient to my purpose to show, that all our simple ideas come to our minds only by sensation and reflection; and that when the mind has them, it can variously repeat and compound them, and so make new complex ideas. But, though white, red, or sweet, &c. have not been modified, or made into complex ideas, by several combinations, so as to be named, and thereby ranked into species; yet some others of the simple ideas, viz. those of unity, duration, and motion, &c., above instanced in, as also power and thinking, have been thus modified to a great variety of complex ideas, with names belonging to them.

7. Why some modes have, and others have not, names. The reason whereof, I suppose, has been this,— That the great concernment of men being with men one amongst another, the knowledge of men, and their actions, and the signifying of them to one another, was most necessary; and therefore they made ideas of actions very nicely modified, and gave those complex ideas names, that they might the more easily record and discourse of those things they were daily conversant in, without long ambages and circumlocutions; and that the things they were continually to give and receive information about might be the easier and quicker understood. That this is so, and that men in framing different complex ideas, and giving them names, have been much governed by the end of speech in general, (which is a very short and expedite way of conveying their thoughts one to another), is evident in the names which in several arts have been found out, and applied to several complex ideas of modified actions, belonging to their several trades, for dispatch sake, in their direction or discourses about them. Which ideas are not generally framed in the minds of men not conversant about these operations. And thence the words that stand for them, by the greatest part of men of the same language, are not understood: v.g. coltshire, drilling, filtration, cohobation, are words standing for certain complex ideas, which being seldom in the minds of any but those few whose particular employments do at every turn suggest them to their thoughts, those names of them are not generally understood but by smiths and chymists; who, having framed the complex ideas which these words stand for, and having given names to them, or received them from others, upon hearing of these names in communication, readily conceive those ideas in their minds;— as by cohobation all the simple ideas of distilling, and the pouring the liquor distilled from anything back upon the remaining matter, and distilling it again. Thus we see that there are great varieties of simple ideas, as of tastes and smells, which have no names; and of modes many more; which either not having been generally enough observed, or else not being of any great use to be taken notice of in the affairs and converse of men, they have not had names given to them, and so pass not for species. This we shall have occasion hereafter to consider more at large, when we come to speak of words.

Chapter XIX. Of the Modes of Thinking

1. Sensation, remembrance, contemplation, &c., modes of thinking. When the mind turns its view inwards upon itself, and contemplates its own actions, thinking is the first that occurs. In it the mind observes a great variety of modifications, and from thence receives distinct ideas. Thus the perception or thought which actually accompanies, and is annexed to, any impression on the body, made by an external object, being distinct from all other modifications of thinking, furnishes the mind with a distinct idea, which we call sensation;— which is, as it were, the actual entrance of any idea into the understanding by the senses. The same idea, when it again recurs without the operation of the like object on the external sensory, is remembrance: if it be sought after by the mind, and with pain and endeavour found, and brought again in view, it is recollection: if it be held there long under attentive consideration, it is contemplation: when ideas float in our mind, without any reflection or regard of the understanding, it is that which the French call reverie; our language has scarce a name for it: when the ideas that offer themselves (for, as I have observed in another place, whilst we are awake, there will always be a train of ideas succeeding one another in our minds) are taken notice of, and, as it were, registered in the memory, it is attention: when the mind with great earnestness, and of choice, fixes its view on any idea, considers it on all sides, and will not be called off by the ordinary solicitation of other ideas, it is that we call intention or study: sleep, without dreaming, is rest from all these: and dreaming itself is the having of ideas (whilst the outward senses are stopped, so that they receive not outward objects with their usual quickness) in the mind, not suggested by any external objects, or known occasion; nor under any choice or conduct of the understanding at all: and whether that which we call ecstasy be not dreaming with the eyes open, I leave to be examined.

2. Other modes of thinking. These are some few instances of those various modes of thinking, which the mind may observe in itself, and so have as distinct ideas of as it hath of white and red, a square or a circle. I do not pretend to enumerate them all, nor to treat at large of this set of ideas, which are got from reflection: that would be to make a volume. It suffices to my present purpose to have shown here, by some few examples, of what sort these ideas are, and how the mind comes by them; especially since I shall have occasion hereafter to treat more at large of reasoning, judging, volition, and knowledge, which are some of the most considerable operations of the mind, and modes of thinking.

3. The various degrees of attention in thinking. But perhaps it may not be an unpardonable digression, nor wholly impertinent to our present design, if we reflect here upon the different state of the mind in thinking, which those instances of attention, reverie, and dreaming, &c., before mentioned, naturally enough suggest. That there are ideas, some or other, always present in the mind of a waking man, every one's experience convinces him; though the mind employs itself about them with several degrees of attention. Sometimes the mind fixes itself with so much earnestness on the contemplation of some objects, that it turns their ideas on all sides; marks their relations and circumstances; and views every part so nicely and with such intention, that it shuts out all other thoughts, and takes no notice of the ordinary impressions made then on the senses, which at another season would produce very sensible perceptions: at other times it barely observes the train of ideas that succeed in the understanding, without directing and pursuing any of them: and at other times it lets them pass almost quite unregarded, as faint shadows that make no impression.

4. Hence it is probable that thinking is the action, not the essence of the soul. This difference of intention, and remission of the mind in thinking, with a great variety of degrees between earnest study and very near minding nothing at all, every one, I think, has experimented in himself. Trace it a little further, and you find the mind in sleep retired as it were from the senses, and out of the reach of those motions made on the organs of sense, which at other

times produce very vivid and sensible ideas. I need not, for this, instance in those who sleep out whole stormy nights, without hearing the thunder, or seeing the lightning, or feeling the shaking of the house, which are sensible enough to those who are waking. But in this retirement of the mind from the senses, it often retains a yet more loose and incoherent manner of thinking, which we call dreaming. And, last of all, sound sleep closes the scene quite, and puts an end to all appearances. This, I think almost every one has experience of in himself, and his own observation without difficulty leads him thus far. That which I would further conclude from hence is, that since the mind can sensibly put on, at several times, several degrees of thinking, and be sometimes, even in a waking man, so remiss, as to have thoughts dim and obscure to that degree that they are very little removed from none at all; and at last, in the dark retirements of sound sleep, loses the sight perfectly of all ideas whatsoever: since, I say, this is evidently so in matter of fact and constant experience, I ask whether it be not probable, that thinking is the action and not the essence of the soul? Since the operations of agents will easily admit of intention and remission: but the essences of things are not conceived capable of any such variation. But this by the by.

Chapter XX.Of Modes of Pleasure and Pain

1. Pleasure and pain, simple ideas. Amongst the simple ideas which we receive both from sensation and reflection, pain and pleasure are two very considerable ones. For as in the body there is sensation barely in itself, or accompanied with pain or pleasure, so the thought or perception of the mind is simply so, or else accompanied also with pleasure or pain, delight or trouble, call it how you please. These, like other simple ideas, cannot be described, nor their names defined; the way of knowing them is, as of the simple ideas of the senses, only by experience. For, to define them by the presence of good or evil, is no otherwise to make them known to us than by making us reflect on what we feel in ourselves, upon the several and various operations of good and evil upon our minds, as they are differently applied to or considered by us.

2. Good and evil, what. Things then are good or evil, only in reference to pleasure or pain. That we call good, which is apt to cause or increase pleasure, or diminish pain in us; or else to procure or preserve us the possession of any other good or absence of any evil. And, on the contrary, we name that evil which is apt to produce or increase any pain, or diminish any pleasure in us: or else to procure us any evil, or deprive us of any good. By pleasure and pain, I must be understood to mean of body or mind, as they are commonly distinguished; though in truth they be only different constitutions of the mind, sometimes occasioned by disorder in the body, sometimes by thoughts of the mind.

3. Our passions moved by good and evil. Pleasure and pain and that which causes them,— good and evil, are the hinges on which our passions turn. And if we reflect on ourselves, and observe how these, under various considerations, operate in us; what modifications or tempers of mind, what internal sensations (if I may so call them) they produce in us we may thence form to ourselves the ideas of our passions.

4. Love. Thus any one reflecting upon the thought he has of the delight which any present or absent thing is apt to produce in him, has the idea we call love. For when a man declares in autumn when he is eating them, or in spring when there are none, that he loves grapes, it is no more but that the taste of grapes delights him: let an alteration of health or constitution destroy the delight of their taste, and he then can be said to love grapes no longer.

5. Hatred. On the contrary, the thought of the pain which anything present or absent is apt to produce in us, is what we call hatred. Were it my business here to inquire any further than into the bare ideas of our passions, as they depend on different modifications of pleasure and pain, I should remark, that our love and hatred of inanimate insensible beings is commonly founded on that pleasure and pain which we receive from their use and application any way to our

senses, though with their destruction. But hatred or love, to beings capable of happiness or misery, is often the uneasiness or delight which we find in ourselves, arising from a consideration of their very being or happiness. Thus the being and welfare of a man's children or friends, producing constant delight in him, he is said constantly to love them. But it suffices to note, that our ideas of love and hatred are but the dispositions of the mind, in respect of pleasure and pain in general, however caused in us.

6. Desire. The uneasiness a man finds in himself upon the absence of anything whose present enjoyment carries the idea of delight with it, is that we call desire; which is greater or less, as that uneasiness is more or less vehement. Where, by the by, it may perhaps be of some use to remark, that the chief, if not only spur to human industry and action is uneasiness. For whatsoever good is proposed, if its absence carries no displeasure or pain with it, if a man be easy and content without it, there is no desire of it, nor endeavour after it; there is no more but a bare velleity, the term used to signify the lowest degree of desire, and that which is next to none at all, when there is so little uneasiness in the absence of anything, that it carries a man no further than some faint wishes for it, without any more effectual or vigorous use of the means to attain it. Desire also is stopped or abated by the opinion of the impossibility or unattainableness of the good proposed, as far as the uneasiness is cured or allayed by that consideration. This might carry our thoughts further, were it seasonable in this place.

7. Joy is a delight of the mind, from the consideration of the present or assured approaching possession of a good; and we are then possessed of any good, when we have it so in our power that we can use it when we please. Thus a man almost starved has joy at the arrival of relief, even before he has the pleasure of using it: and a father, in whom the very well-being of his children causes delight, is always, as long as his children are in such a state, in the possession of that good; for he needs but to reflect on it, to have that pleasure.

8. Sorrow is uneasiness in the mind, upon the thought of a good lost, which might have been enjoyed longer; or the sense of a present evil.

9. Hope is that pleasure in the mind, which every one finds in himself, upon the thought of a probable future enjoyment of a thing which is apt to delight him.

10. Fear is an uneasiness of the mind, upon the thought of future evil likely to befal us.

11. Despair is the thought of the unattainableness of any good, which works differently in men's minds, sometimes producing uneasiness or pain, sometimes rest and indolency.

12. Anger is uneasiness or discomposure of the mind, upon the receipt of any injury, with a present purpose of revenge.

13. Envy is an uneasiness of the mind, caused by the consideration of a good we desire obtained by one we think should not have had it before us.

14. What passions all men have. These two last, envy and anger, not being caused by pain and pleasure simply in themselves, but having in them some mixed considerations of ourselves and others, are not therefore to be found in all men, because those other parts, of valuing their merits, or intending revenge, is wanting in them. But all the rest, terminating purely in pain and pleasure, are, I think, to be found in all men. For we love, desire, rejoice, and hope, only in respect of pleasure; we hate, fear, and grieve, only in respect of pain ultimately. In fine, all these passions are moved by things, only as they appear to be the causes of pleasure and pain, or to have pleasure or pain some way or other annexed to them. Thus we extend our hatred usually to the subject (at least, if a sensible or voluntary agent) which has produced pain in us; because the fear it leaves is a constant pain: but we do not so constantly love what has done us good; because pleasure operates not so strongly on us as pain, and because we are not so ready to have hope it will do so again. But this by the by.

15. Pleasure and pain, what. By pleasure and pain, delight and uneasiness, I must all along be understood (as I have above intimated) to mean not only bodily pain and pleasure, but whatsoever delight or uneasiness is felt by us, whether arising from any grateful or unacceptable sensation or reflection.

16. Removal or lessening of either. It is further to be considered, that, in reference to the

passions, the removal or lessening of a pain is considered, and operates, as a pleasure: and the loss or diminishing of a pleasure, as a pain.

17. Shame. The passions too have most of them, in most persons, operations on the body, and cause various changes in it; which not being always sensible, do not make a necessary part of the idea of each passion. For shame, which is an uneasiness of the mind upon the thought of having done something which is indecent, or will lessen the valued esteem which others have for us, has not always blushing accompanying it.

18. These instances to show how our ideas of the passions are got from sensation and reflection. I would not be mistaken here, as if I meant this as a Discourse of the Passions; they are many more than those I have here named: and those I have taken notice of would each of them require a much larger and more accurate discourse. I have only mentioned these here, as so many instances of modes of pleasure and pain resulting in our minds from various considerations of good and evil. I might perhaps have instanced in other modes of pleasure and pain, more simple than these; as the pain of hunger and thirst, and the pleasure of eating and drinking to remove them: the pain of teeth set on edge; the pleasure of music; pain from captious uninstructive wrangling, and the pleasure of rational conversation with a friend, or of well-directed study in the search and discovery of truth. But the passions being of much more concernment to us, I rather made choice to instance in them, and show how the ideas we have of them are derived from sensation or reflection.

Chapter XXI.Of Power

1. This idea how got. The mind being every day informed, by the senses, of the alteration of those simple ideas it observes in things without; and taking notice how one comes to an end, and ceases to be, and another begins to exist which was not before; reflecting also on what passes within itself, and observing a constant change of its ideas, sometimes by the impression of outward objects on the senses, and sometimes by the determination of its own choice; and concluding from what it has so constantly observed to have been, that the like changes will for the future be made in the same things, by like agents, and by the like ways,— considers in one thing the possibility of having any of its simple ideas changed, and in another the possibility of making that change; and so comes by that idea which we call power. Thus we say, Fire has a power to melt gold, i.e. to destroy the consistency of its insensible parts, and consequently its hardness, and make it fluid; and gold has a power to be melted; that the sun has a power to blanch wax, and wax a power to be blanched by the sun, whereby the yellowness is destroyed, and whiteness made to exist in its room. In which, and the like cases, the power we consider is in reference to the change of perceivable ideas. For we cannot observe any alteration to be made in, or operation upon anything, but by the observable change of its sensible ideas; nor conceive any alteration to be made, but by conceiving a change of some of its ideas.

2. Power, active and passive. Power thus considered is two-fold, viz. as able to make, or able to receive any change. The one may be called active, and the other passive power. Whether matter be not wholly destitute of active power, as its author, God, is truly above all passive power; and whether the intermediate state of created spirits be not that alone which is capable of both active and passive power, may be worth consideration. I shall not now enter into that inquiry, my present business being not to search into the original of power, but how we come by the idea of it. But since active powers make so great a part of our complex ideas of natural substances, (as we shall see hereafter,) and I mention them as such, according to common apprehension; yet they being not, perhaps, so truly active powers as our hasty thoughts are apt to represent them, I judge it not amiss, by this intimation, to direct our minds to the consideration of God and spirits, for the clearest idea of active power.

3. Power includes relation. I confess power includes in it some kind of relation, (a relation to action or change,) as indeed which of our ideas, of what kind soever, when attentively

considered, does not? For, our ideas of extension, duration, and number, do they not all contain in them a secret relation of the parts? Figure and motion have something relative in them much more visibly. And sensible qualities, as colours and smells, &c., what are they but the powers of different bodies, in relation to our perception, &c.? And, if considered in the things themselves, do they not depend on the bulk, figure, texture, and motion of the parts? All which include some kind of relation in them. Our idea therefore of power, I think, may well have a place amongst other simple ideas, and be considered as one of them; being one of those that make a principal ingredient in our complex ideas of substances, as we shall hereafter have occasion to observe.

4. The clearest idea of active power had from spirit. We are abundantly furnished with the idea of passive power by almost all sorts of sensible things. In most of them we cannot avoid observing their sensible qualities, nay, their very substances, to be in a continual flux. And therefore with reason we look on them as liable still to the same change. Nor have we of active power (which is the more proper signification of the word power) fewer instances. Since whatever change is observed, the mind must collect a power somewhere able to make that change, as well as a possibility in the thing itself to receive it. But yet, if we will consider it attentively, bodies, by our senses, do not afford us so clear and distinct an idea of active power, as we have from reflection on the operations of our minds. For all power relating to action, and there being but two sorts of action whereof we have an idea, viz. thinking and motion, let us consider whence we have the clearest ideas of the powers which produce these actions. (1) Of thinking, body affords us no idea at all; it is only from reflection that we have that. (2) Neither have we from body any idea of the beginning of motion. A body at rest affords us no idea of any active power to move; and when it is set in motion itself, that motion is rather a passion than an action in it. For, when the ball obeys the motion of a billiard-stick, it is not any action of the ball, but bare passion. Also when by impulse it sets another ball in motion that lay in its way, it only communicates the motion it had received from another, and loses in itself so much as the other received: which gives us but a very obscure idea of an active power of moving in body, whilst we observe it only to transfer, but not produce any motion. For it is but a very obscure idea of power which reaches not the production of the action, but the continuation of the passion. For so is motion in a body impelled by another; the continuation of the alteration made in it from rest to motion being little more an action, than the continuation of the alteration of its figure by the same blow is an action. The idea of the beginning of motion we have only from reflection on what passes in ourselves; where we find by experience, that, barely by willing it, barely by a thought of the mind, we can move the parts of our bodies, which were before at rest. So that it seems to me, we have, from the observation of the operation of bodies by our senses, but a very imperfect obscure idea of active power; since they afford us not any idea in themselves of the power to begin any action, either motion or thought. But if, from the impulse bodies are observed to make one upon another, any one thinks he has a clear idea of power, it serves as well to my purpose; sensation being one of those ways whereby the mind comes by its ideas: only I thought it worth while to consider here, by the way, whether the mind doth not receive its idea of active power clearer from reflection on its own operations, than it doth from any external sensation.

5. Will and understanding two powers in mind or spirit. This, at least, I think evident,— That we find in ourselves a power to begin or forbear, continue or end several actions of our minds, and motions of our bodies, barely by a thought or preference of the mind ordering, or as it were commanding, the doing or not doing such or such a particular action. This power which the mind has thus to order the consideration of any idea, or the forbearing to consider it; or to prefer the motion of any part of the body to its rest, and vice versa, in any particular instance, is that which we call the Will. The actual exercise of that power, by directing any particular action, or its forbearance, is that which we call volition or willing. The forbearance of that action, consequent to such order or command of the mind, is called voluntary. And whatsoever action is performed without such a thought of the mind, is called involuntary. The power of

perception is that which we call the Understanding. Perception, which we make the act of the understanding, is of three sorts:— 1. The perception of ideas in our minds. 2. The perception of the signification of signs. 3. The perception of the connexion or repugnancy, agreement or disagreement, that there is between any of our ideas. All these are attributed to the understanding, or perceptive power, though it be the two latter only that use allows us to say we understand.

6. Faculties, not real beings. These powers of the mind, viz. of perceiving, and of preferring, are usually called by another name. And the ordinary way of speaking is, that the understanding and will are two faculties of the mind; a word proper enough, if it be used, as all words should be, so as not to breed any confusion in men's thoughts, by being supposed (as I suspect it has been) to stand for some real beings in the soul that performed those actions of understanding and volition. For when we say the will is the commanding and superior faculty of the soul; that it is or is not free; that it determines the inferior faculties; that it follows the dictates of the understanding, &c.,— though these and the like expressions, by those that carefully attend to their own ideas, and conduct their thoughts more by the evidence of things than the sound of words, may be understood in a clear and distinct sense — yet I suspect, I say, that this way of speaking of faculties has misled many into a confused notion of so many distinct agents in us, which had their several provinces and authorities, and did command, obey, and perform several actions, as so many distinct beings; which has been no small occasion of wrangling, obscurity, and uncertainty, in questions relating to them.

7. Whence the ideas of liberty and necessity. Every one, I think, finds in himself a power to begin or forbear, continue or put an end to several actions in himself. From the consideration of the extent of this power of the mind over the actions of the man, which everyone finds in himself, arise the ideas of liberty and necessity.

8. Liberty, what. All the actions that we have any idea of reducing themselves, as has been said, to these two, viz. thinking and motion; so far as a man has power to think or not to think, to move or not to move, according to the preference or direction of his own mind, so far is a man free. Wherever any performance or forbearance are not equally in a man's power; wherever doing or not doing will not equally follow upon the preference of his mind directing it, there he is not free, though perhaps the action may be voluntary. So that the idea of liberty is, the idea of a power in any agent to do or forbear any particular action, according to the determination or thought of the mind, whereby either of them is preferred to the other: where either of them is not in the power of the agent to be produced by him according to his volition, there he is not at liberty; that agent is under necessity. So that liberty cannot be where there is no thought, no volition, no will; but there may be thought, there may be will, there may be volition, where there is no liberty. A little consideration of an obvious instance or two may make this clear.

9. Supposes understanding and will. A tennis-ball, whether in motion by the stroke of a racket, or lying still at rest, is not by any one taken to be a free agent. If we inquire into the reason, we shall find it is because we conceive not a tennis-ball to think, and consequently not to have any volition, or preference of motion to rest, or vice versa; and therefore has not liberty, is not a free agent; but all its both motion and rest come under our idea of necessary, and are so called. Likewise a man falling into the water, (a bridge breaking under him), has not herein liberty, is not a free agent. For though he has volition, though he prefers his not falling to falling; yet the forbearance of that motion not being in his power, the stop or cessation of that motion follows not upon his volition; and therefore therein he is not free. So a man striking himself, or his friend, by a convulsive motion of his arm, which it is not in his power, by volition or the direction of his mind, to stop or forbear, nobody thinks he has in this liberty; every one pities him, as acting by necessity and constraint.

10. Belongs not to volition. Again: suppose a man be carried, whilst fast asleep, into a room where is a person he longs to see and speak with; and be there locked fast in, beyond his power to get out: he awakes, and is glad to find himself in so desirable company, which he

stays willingly in, i.e. prefers his stay to going away. I ask, is not this stay voluntary? I think nobody will doubt it: and yet, being locked fast in, it is evident he is not at liberty not to stay, he has not freedom to be gone. So that liberty is not an idea belonging to volition, or preferring; but to the person having the power of doing, or forbearing to do, according as the mind shall choose or direct. Our idea of liberty reaches as far as that power, and no farther. For wherever restraint comes to check that power, or compulsion takes away that indifferency of ability to act, or to forbear acting, there liberty, and our notion of it, presently ceases.

11. Voluntary opposed to involuntary, not to necessary. We have instances enough, and often more than enough, in our own bodies. A man's heart beats, and the blood circulates, which it is not in his power by any thought or volition to stop; and therefore in respect of these motions, where rest depends not on his choice, nor would follow the determination of his mind, if it should prefer it, he is not a free agent. Convulsive motions agitate his legs, so that though he wills it ever so much, he cannot by any power of his mind stop their motion, (as in that odd disease called chorea sancti viti), but he is perpetually dancing; he is not at liberty in this action, but under as much necessity of moving, as a stone that falls, or a tennis-ball struck with a racket. On the other side, a palsy or the stocks hinder his legs from obeying the determination of his mind, if it would thereby transfer his body to another place. In all these there is want of freedom; though the sitting still, even of a paralytic, whilst he prefers it to a removal, is truly voluntary. Voluntary, then, is not opposed to necessary, but to involuntary. For a man may prefer what he can do, to what he cannot do; the state he is in, to its absence or change; though necessity has made it in itself unalterable.

12. Liberty, what. As it is in the motions of the body, so it is in the thoughts of our minds: where any one is such, that we have power to take it up, or lay it by, according to the preference of the mind, there we are at liberty. A waking man, being under the necessity of having some ideas constantly in his mind, is not at liberty to think or not to think; no more than he is at liberty, whether his body shall touch any other or no: but whether he will remove his contemplation from one idea to another is many times in his choice; and then he is, in respect of his ideas, as much at liberty as he is in respect of bodies he rests on; he can at pleasure remove himself from one to another. But yet some ideas to the mind, like some motions to the body, are such as in certain circumstances it cannot avoid, nor obtain their absence by the utmost effort it can use. A man on the rack is not at liberty to lay by the idea of pain, and divert himself with other contemplations: and sometimes a boisterous passion hurries our thoughts, as a hurricane does our bodies, without leaving us the liberty of thinking on other things, which we would rather choose. But as soon as the mind regains the power to stop or continue, begin or forbear, any of these motions of the body without, or thoughts within, according as it thinks fit to prefer either to the other, we then consider the man as a free agent again.

13. Necessity, what. Wherever thought is wholly wanting, or the power to act or forbear according to the direction of thought, there necessity takes place. This, in an agent capable of volition, when the beginning or continuation of any action is contrary to that preference of his mind, is called compulsion; when the hindering or stopping any action is contrary to his volition, it is called restraint. Agents that have no thought, no volition at all, are in everything necessary agents.

14. Liberty belongs not to the will. If this be so, (as I imagine it is,) I leave it to be considered, whether it may not help to put an end to that long agitated, and, I think, unreasonable, because unintelligible question, viz. Whether man's will be free or no? For if I mistake not, it follows from what I have said, that the question itself is altogether improper; and it is as insignificant to ask whether man's will be free, as to ask whether his sleep be swift, or his virtue square: liberty being as little applicable to the will, as swiftness of motion is to sleep, or squareness to virtue. Every one would laugh at the absurdity of such a question as either of these: because it is obvious that the modifications of motion belong not to sleep, nor the difference of figure to virtue; and when one well considers it, I think he will as plainly perceive that liberty, which is

but a power, belongs only to agents, and cannot be an attribute or modification of the will, which is also but a power.

15. Volition. Such is the difficulty of explaining and giving clear notions of internal actions by sounds, that I must here warn my reader, that ordering, directing, choosing, preferring, &c., which I have made use of, will not distinctly enough express volition, unless he will reflect on what he himself does when he wills. For example, preferring, which seems perhaps best to express the act of volition, does it not precisely. For though a man would prefer flying to walking, yet who can say he ever wills it? Volition, it is plain, is an act of the mind knowingly exerting that dominion it takes itself to have over any part of the man, by employing it in, or withholding it from, any particular action. And what is the will, but the faculty to do this? And is that faculty anything more in effect than a power; the power of the mind to determine its thought, to the producing, continuing, or stopping any action, as far as it depends on us? For can it be denied that whatever agent has a power to think on its own actions, and to prefer their doing or omission either to other, has that faculty called will? Will, then, is nothing but such a power. Liberty, on the other side, is the power a man has to do or forbear doing any particular action according as its doing or forbearance has the actual preference in the mind; which is the same thing as to say, according as he himself wills it.

16. Powers, belonging to agents. It is plain then that the will is nothing but one power or ability, and freedom another power or ability so that, to ask, whether the will has freedom, is to ask whether one power has another power, one ability another ability; a question at first sight too grossly absurd to make a dispute, or need an answer. For, who is it that sees not that powers belong only to agents, and are attributes only of substances, and not of powers themselves? So that this way of putting the question (viz. whether the will be free) is in effect to ask, whether the will be a substance, an agent, or at least to suppose it, since freedom can properly be attributed to nothing else. If freedom can with any propriety of speech be applied to power, it may be attributed to the power that is in a man to produce, or forbear producing, motion in parts of his body, by choice or preference; which is that which denominates him free, and is freedom itself. But if any one should ask, whether freedom were free, he would be suspected not to understand well what he said; and he would be thought to deserve Midas's ears, who, knowing that rich was a denomination for the possession of riches, should demand whether riches themselves were rich.

17. How the will, instead of the man, is called free. However, the name faculty, which men have given to this power called the will, and whereby they have been led into a way of talking of the will as acting, may, by an appropriation that disguises its true sense, serve a little to palliate the absurdity; yet the will, in truth, signifies nothing but a power or ability to prefer or choose: and when the will, under the name of a faculty, is considered as it is, barely as an ability to do something, the absurdity in saying it is free, or not free, will easily discover itself For, if it be reasonable to suppose and talk of faculties as distinct beings that can act, (as we do, when we say the will orders, and the will is free,) it is fit that we should make a speaking faculty, and a walking faculty, and a dancing faculty, by which these actions are produced, which are but several modes of motion; as well as we make the will and understanding to be faculties, by which the actions of choosing and perceiving are produced, which are but several modes of thinking. And we may as properly say that it is the singing faculty sings, and the dancing faculty dances, as that the will chooses, or that the understanding conceives; or, as is usual, that the will directs the understanding, or the understanding obeys or obeys not the will: it being altogether as proper and intelligible to say that the power of speaking directs the power of singing, or the power of singing obeys or disobeys the power of speaking.

18. This way of talking causes confusion of thought. This way of talking, nevertheless, has prevailed, and, as I guess, produced great confusion. For these being all different powers in the mind, or in the man, to do several actions, he exerts them as he thinks fit: but the power to do one action is not operated on by the power of doing another action. For the power of thinking operates not on the power of choosing, nor the power of choosing on the power of thinking; no

more than the power of dancing operates on the power of singing, or the power of singing on the power of dancing, as any one who reflects on it will easily perceive. And yet this is it which we say when we thus speak, that the will operates on the understanding, or the understanding on the will.

19. Powers are relations, not agents. I grant, that this or that actual thought may be the occasion of volition, or exercising the power a man has to choose; or the actual choice of the mind, the cause of actual thinking on this or that thing: as the actual singing of such a tune may be the cause of dancing such a dance, and the actual dancing of such a dance the occasion of singing such a tune. But in all these it is not one power that operates on another: but it is the mind that operates, and exerts these powers; it is the man that does the action; it is the agent that has power, or is able to do. For powers are relations, not agents: and that which has the power or not the power to operate, is that alone which is or is not free, and not the power itself For freedom, or not freedom, can belong to nothing but what has or has not a power to act.

20. Liberty belongs not to the will. The attributing to faculties that which belonged not to them, has given occasion to this way of talking: but the introducing into discourses concerning the mind, with the name of faculties, a notion of their operating, has, I suppose, as little advanced our knowledge in that part of ourselves, as the great use and mention of the like invention of faculties, in the operations of the body, has helped us in the knowledge of physic. Not that I deny there are faculties, both in the body and mind: they both of them have their powers of operating, else neither the one nor the other could operate. For nothing can operate that is not able to operate; and that is not able to operate that has no power to operate. Nor do I deny that those words, and the like, are to have their place in the common use of languages that have made them current. It looks like too much affectation wholly to lay them by: and philosophy itself, though it likes not a gaudy dress, yet, when it appears in public, must have so much complacency as to be clothed in the ordinary fashion and language of the country, so far as it can consist with truth and perspicuity. But the fault has been, that faculties have been spoken of and represented as so many distinct agents. For, it being asked, what it was that digested the meat in our stomachs? it was a ready and very satisfactory answer to say, that it was the digestive faculty. What was it that made anything come out of the body? the expulsive faculty. What moved? the motive faculty. And so in the mind, the intellectual faculty, or the understanding, understood; and the elective faculty, or the will, willed or commanded. This is, in short, to say, that the ability to digest, digested; and the ability to move, moved; and the ability to understand, understood. For faculty, ability, and power, I think, are but different names of the same things: which ways of speaking, when put into more intelligible words, will, I think, amount to thus much;— That digestion is performed by something that is able to digest, motion by something able to move, and understanding by something able to understand. And, in truth, it would be very strange if it should be otherwise; as strange as it would be for a man to be free without being able to be free.

21. But to the agent, or man. To return, then, to the inquiry about liberty, I think the question is not proper, whether the will be free, but whether a man be free. Thus, I think,

First, That so far as any one can, by the direction or choice of his mind, preferring the existence of any action to the non-existence of that action, and vice versa, make it to exist or not exist, so far he is free. For if I can, by a thought directing the motion of my finger, make it move when it was at rest, or vice versa, it is evident, that in respect of that I am free: and if I can, by a like thought of my mind, preferring one to the other, produce either words or silence, I am at liberty to speak or hold my peace: and as far as this power reaches, of acting or not acting, by the determination of his own thought preferring either, so far is a man free. For how can we think any one freer, than to have the power to do what he will? And so far as any one can, by preferring any action to its not being, or rest to any action, produce that action or rest, so far can he do what he will. For such a preferring of action to its absence, is the willing of it: and we can scarce tell how to imagine any being freer, than to be able to do what he wills. So that in respect of actions within the reach of such a power in him, a man seems as free as it is possible for freedom to make him.

22. In respect of willing, a man is not free. But the inquisitive mind of man, willing to shift off from himself, as far as he can, all thoughts of guilt, though it be by putting himself into a worse state than that of fatal necessity, is not content with this: freedom, unless it reaches further than this, will not serve the turn: and it passes for a good plea, that a man is not free at all, if he be not as free to will as he is to act what he wills. Concerning a man's liberty, there yet, therefore, is raised this further question, Whether a man be free to will? Which I think is what is meant, when it is disputed whether the will be free. And as to that I imagine.

23. How a man cannot be free to will. Secondly, That willing, or volition, being an action, and freedom consisting in a power of acting or not acting, a man in respect of willing or the act of volition, when any action in his power is once proposed to his thoughts, as presently to be done, cannot be free. The reason whereof is very manifest. For, it being unavoidable that the action depending on his will should exist or not exist, and its existence or not existence following perfectly the determination and preference of his will, he cannot avoid willing the existence or non-existence of that action; it is absolutely necessary that he will the one or the other; i.e. prefer the one to the other: since one of them must necessarily follow; and that which does follow follows by the choice and determination of his mind; that is, by his willing it: for if he did not will it, it would not be. So that, in respect of the act of willing, a man in such a case is not free: liberty consisting in a power to act or not to act; which, in regard of volition, a man, upon such a proposal has not. For it is unavoidably necessary to prefer the doing or forbearance of an action in a man's power, which is once so proposed to his thoughts; a man must necessarily will the one or the other of them; upon which preference or volition, the action or its forbearance certainly follows, and is truly voluntary. But the act of volition, or preferring one of the two, being that which he cannot avoid, a man, in respect of that act of willing, is under a necessity, and so cannot be free; unless necessity and freedom can consist together, and a man can be free and bound at once. Besides to make a man free after this manner, by making the action of willing to depend on his will, there must be another antecedent will, to determine the acts of this will, and another to determine that, and so in infinitum: for wherever one stops, the actions of the last will cannot be free. Nor is any being, as far I can comprehend beings above me, capable of such a freedom of will, that it can forbear to will, i.e. to prefer the being or not being of anything in its power, which it has once considered as such.

24. Liberty is freedom to execute what is willed. This, then, is evident, That a man is not at liberty to will, or not to will, anything in his power that he once considers of: liberty consisting in a power to act or to forbear acting, and in that only. For a man that sits still is said yet to be at liberty; because he can walk if he wills it. A man that walks is at liberty also, not because he walks or moves; but because he can stand still if he wills it. But if a man sitting still has not a power to remove himself, he is not at liberty; so likewise a man falling down a precipice, though in motion, is not at liberty, because he cannot stop that motion if he would. This being so, it is plain that a man that is walking, to whom it is proposed to give off walking, is not at liberty, whether he will determine himself to walk, or give off walking or not: he must necessarily prefer one or the other of them; walking or not walking. And so it is in regard of all other actions in our power so proposed, which are the far greater number. For, considering the vast number of voluntary actions that succeed one another every moment that we are awake in the course of our lives, there are but few of them that are thought on or proposed to the will, till the time they are to be done; and in all such actions, as I have shown, the mind, in respect of willing, has not a power to act or not to act, wherein consists liberty. The mind, in that case, has not a power to forbear willing; it cannot avoid some determination concerning them, let the consideration be as short, the thought as quick as it will, it either leaves the man in the state he was before thinking, or changes it; continues the action, or puts an end to it. Whereby it is manifest, that it orders and directs one, in preference to, or with neglect of the other, and thereby either the continuation or change becomes unavoidably voluntary.

25. The will determined by something without it. Since then it is plain that, in most cases, a man is not at liberty, whether he will or no, (for, when an action in his power is proposed to his thoughts, he cannot forbear volition; he must determine one way or the other); the next thing demanded is,— Whether a man be at liberty to will which of the two he pleases, motion or rest? This question carries the absurdity of it so manifestly in itself, that one might thereby sufficiently be convinced that liberty concerns not the will. For, to ask whether a man be at liberty to will either motion or rest, speaking or silence, which he pleases, is to ask whether a man can will what he wills, or be pleased with what he is pleased with? A question which, I think, needs no answer: and they who can make a question of it must suppose one will to determine the acts of another, and another to determine that, and so on in infinitum.

26. The ideas of liberty and volition must be defined. To avoid these and the like absurdities, nothing can be of greater use than to establish in our minds determined ideas of the things under consideration. If the ideas of liberty and volition were well fixed in our understandings, and carried along with us in our minds, as they ought, through all the questions that are raised about them, I suppose a great part of the difficulties that perplex men's thoughts, and entangle their understandings, would be much easier resolved; and we should perceive where the confused signification of terms, or where the nature of the thing caused the obscurity.

27. Freedom. First, then, it is carefully to be remembered, That freedom consists in the dependence of the existence, or not existence of any action, upon our volition of it; and not in the dependence of any action, or its contrary, on our preference. A man standing on a cliff, is at liberty to leap twenty yards downwards into the sea, not because he has a power to do the contrary action, which is to leap twenty yards upwards, for that he cannot do; but he is therefore free, because he has a power to leap or not to leap. But if a greater force than his, either holds him fast, or tumbles him down, he is no longer free in that case; because the doing or forbearance of that particular action is no longer in his power. He that is a close prisoner in a room twenty feet square, being at the north side of his chamber, is at liberty to walk twenty feet southward, because he can walk or not walk it; but is not, at the same time, at liberty to do the contrary, i.e. to walk twenty feet northward.

In this, then, consists freedom, viz. in our being able to act or not to act, according as we shall choose or will.

28. What volition and action mean. Secondly, we must remember, that volition or willing is an act of the mind directing its thought to the production of any action, and thereby exerting its power to produce it. To avoid multiplying of words, I would crave leave here, under the word action, to comprehend the forbearance too of any action proposed: sitting still, or holding one's peace, when walking or speaking are proposed, though mere forbearances, requiring as much the determination of the will, and being as often weighty in their consequences, as the contrary actions, may, on that consideration, well enough pass for actions too: but this I say, that I may not be mistaken, if (for brevity's sake) I speak thus.

29. What determines the will. Thirdly, the will being nothing but a power in the mind to direct the operative faculties of a man to motion or rest, as far as they depend on such direction; to the question, What is it determines the will? the true and proper answer is, The mind. For that which determines the general power of directing, to this or that particular direction, is nothing but the agent itself exercising the power it has that particular way. If this answer satisfies not, it is plain the meaning of the question, What determines the will? is this,— What moves the mind, in every particular instance, to determine its general power of directing, to this or that particular motion or rest? And to this I answer,— The motive for continuing in the same state or action, is only the present satisfaction in it; the motive to change is always some uneasiness: nothing setting us upon the change of state, or upon any new action, but some uneasiness. This is the great motive that works on the mind to put it upon action, which for shortness' sake we will call determining of the will, which I shall more at large explain.

30. Will and desire must not be confounded. But, in the way to it, it will be necessary to premise, that, though I have above endeavoured to express the act of volition, by choosing,

preferring, and the like terms, that signify desire as well as volition, for want of other words to mark that act of the mind whose proper name is willing or volition; yet, it being a very simple act, whosoever desires to understand what it is, will better find it by reflecting on his own mind, and observing what it does when it wills, than by any variety of articulate sounds whatsoever. This caution of being careful not to be misled by expressions that do not enough keep up the difference between the will and several acts of the mind that are quite distinct from it, I think the more necessary, because I find the will often confounded with several of the affections, especially desire, and one put for the other; and that by men who would not willingly be thought not to have had very distinct notions of things, and not to have writ very clearly about them. This, I imagine, has been no small occasion of obscurity and mistake in this matter; and therefore is, as much as may be, to be avoided. For he that shall turn his thoughts inwards upon what passes in his mind when he wills, shall see that the will or power of volition is conversant about nothing but our own actions; terminates there; and reaches no further; and that volition is nothing but that particular determination of the mind, whereby, barely by a thought the mind endeavours to give rise, continuation, or stop, to any action which it takes to be in its power. This, well considered, plainly shows that the will is perfectly distinguished from desire; which, in the very same action, may have a quite contrary tendency from that which our will sets us upon. A man, whom I cannot deny, may oblige me to use persuasions to another, which, at the same time I am speaking, I may wish may not prevail on him. In this case, it is plain the will and desire run counter. I will the action; that tends one way, whilst my desire tends another, and that the direct contrary way. A man who, by a violent fit of the gout in his limbs, finds a doziness in his head, or a want of appetite in his stomach removed, desires to be eased too of the pain of his feet or hands, (for wherever there is pain, there is a desire to be rid of it), though yet, whilst he apprehends that the removal of the pain may translate the noxious humour to a more vital part, his will is never determined to any one action that may serve to remove this pain. Whence it is evident that desiring and willing are two distinct acts of the mind; and consequently, that the will, which is but the power of volition, is much more distinct from desire.

31. Uneasiness determines the will. To return, then, to the inquiry, what is it that determines the will in regard to our actions? And that, upon second thoughts, I am apt to imagine is not, as is generally supposed, the greater good in view; but some (and for the most part the most pressing) uneasiness a man is at present under. This is that which successively determines the will, and sets us upon those actions we perform. This uneasiness we may call, as it is, desire; which is an uneasiness of the mind for want of some absent good. All pain of the body, of what sort soever, and disquiet of the mind, is uneasiness: and with this is always joined desire, equal to the pain or uneasiness felt; and is scarce distinguishable from it. For desire being nothing but an uneasiness in the want of an absent good, in reference to any pain felt, ease is that absent good; and till that ease be attained, we may call it desire; nobody feeling pain that he wishes not to be eased of, with a desire equal to that pain, and inseparable from it. Besides this desire of ease from pain, there is another of absent positive good; and here also the desire and uneasiness are equal. As much as we desire any absent good, so much are we in pain for it. But here all absent good does not, according to the greatness it has, or is acknowledged to have, cause pain equal to that greatness; as all pain causes desire equal to itself: because the absence of good is not always a pain, as the presence of pain is. And therefore absent good may be looked on and considered without desire. But so much as there is anywhere of desire, so much there is of uneasiness.

32. Desire is uneasiness. That desire is a state of uneasiness, every one who reflects on himself will quickly find. Who is there that has not felt in desire what the wise man says of hope, (which is not much different from it), that it being "deferred makes the heart sick"; and that still proportionable to the greatness of the desire, which sometimes raises the uneasiness to that pitch, that it makes people cry out, "Give me children." give me the thing desired, "or I die." Life itself, and all its enjoyments, is a burden cannot be borne under the lasting and

unremoved pressure of such an uneasiness.

33. The uneasiness of desire determines the will. Good and evil, present and absent, it is true, work upon the mind. But that which immediately determines the will, from time to time, to every voluntary action, is the uneasiness of desire, fixed on some absent good: either negative, as indolence to one in pain; or positive, as enjoyment of pleasure. That it is this uneasiness that determines the will to the successive voluntary actions, whereof the greatest part of our lives is made up, and by which we are conducted through different courses to different ends, I shall endeavour to show, both from experience, and the reason of the thing.

34. This is the spring of action. When a man is perfectly content with the state he is in — which is when he is perfectly without any uneasiness — what industry, what action, what will is there left, but to continue in it? Of this every man's observation will satisfy him. And thus we see our all-wise Maker, suitably to our constitution and frame, and knowing what it is that determines the will, has put into man the uneasiness of hunger and thirst, and other natural desires, that return at their seasons, to move and determine their wills, for the preservation of themselves, and the continuation of their species. For I think we may conclude, that, if the bare contemplation of these good ends to which we are carried by these several uneasinesses had been sufficient to determine the will, and set us on work, we should have had none of these natural pains, and perhaps in this world little or no pain at all. "It is better to marry than to burn," says St. Paul, where we may see what it is that chiefly drives men into the enjoyments of a conjugal life. A little burning felt pushes us more powerfully than greater pleasures in prospect draw or allure.

35. The greatest positive good determines not the will, but present uneasiness alone. It seems so established and settled a maxim, by the general consent of all mankind, that good, the greater good, determines the will, that I do not at all wonder that, when I first published my thoughts on this subject I took it for granted; and I imagine that, by a great many, I shall be thought more excusable for having then done so, than that now I have ventured to recede from so received an opinion. But yet, upon a stricter inquiry, I am forced to conclude that good, the greater good, though apprehended and acknowledged to be so, does not determine the will, until our desire, raised proportionably to it, makes us uneasy in the want of it. Convince a man never so much, that plenty has its advantages over poverty; make him see and own, that the handsome conveniences of life are better than nasty penury: yet, as long as he is content with the latter, and finds no uneasiness in it, he moves not; his will never is determined to any action that shall bring him out of it. Let a man be ever so well persuaded of the advantages of virtue, that it is as necessary to a man who has any great aims in this world, or hopes in the next, as food to life: yet, till he hungers or thirsts after righteousness, till he feels an uneasiness in the want of it, his will will not be determined to any action in pursuit of this confessed greater good; but any other uneasiness he feels in himself shall take place, and carry his will to other actions. On the other side, let a drunkard see that his health decays, his estate wastes; discredit and diseases, and the want of all things, even of his beloved drink, attends him in the course he follows: yet the returns of uneasiness to miss his companions, the habitual thirst after his cups at the usual time, drives him to the tavern, though he has in his view the loss of health and plenty, and perhaps of the joys of another life: the least of which is no inconsiderable good, but such as he confesses is far greater than the tickling of his palate with a glass of wine, or the idle chat of a soaking club. It is not want of viewing the greater good: for he sees and acknowledges it, and, in the intervals of his drinking hours, will take resolutions to pursue the greater good; but when the uneasiness to miss his accustomed delight returns, the great acknowledged good loses its hold, and the present uneasiness determines the will to the accustomed action; which thereby gets stronger footing to prevail against the next occasion, though he at the same time makes secret promises to himself that he will do so no more; this is the last time he will act against the attainment of those greater goods. And thus he is, from time to time, in the state of that unhappy complainer, Video meliora, proboque, deteriora sequor: which sentence, allowed for true, and made good by constant experience,

may in this, and possibly no other way, be easily made intelligible.

36. Because the removal of uneasiness is the first step to happiness. If we inquire into the reason of what experience makes so evident in fact, and examine, why it is uneasiness alone operates on the will, and determines it in its choice, we shall find that, we being capable but of one determination of the will to one action at once, the present uneasiness that we are under does naturally determine the will, in order to that happiness which we all aim at in all our actions. For, as much as whilst we are under any uneasiness, we cannot apprehend ourselves happy, or in the way to it; pain and uneasiness being, by every one, concluded and felt to be inconsistent with happiness, spoiling the relish even of those good things which we have: a little pain serving to mar all the pleasure we rejoiced in. And, therefore, that which of course determines the choice of our will to the next action will always be — the removing of pain, as long as we have any left, as the first and necessary step towards happiness.

37. Because uneasiness alone is present. Another reason why it is uneasiness alone determines the will, is this: because that alone is present and, it is against the nature of things, that what is absent should operate where it is not. It may be said that absent good may, by contemplation, be brought home to the mind and made present. The idea of it indeed may be in the mind, and viewed as present there; but nothing will be in the mind as a present good, able to counterbalance the removal of any uneasiness which we are under, till it raises our desire; and the uneasiness of that has the prevalency in determining the will. Till then, the idea in the mind of whatever is good is there only, like other ideas, the object of bare unactive speculation; but operates not on the will, nor sets us on work; the reason whereof I shall show by and by. How many are to be found that have had lively representations set before their minds of the unspeakable joys of heaven, which they acknowledge both possible and probable too, who yet would be content to take up with their happiness here? And so the prevailing uneasiness of their desires, let loose after the enjoyments of this life, take their turns in the determining their wills; and all that while they take not one step, are not one jot moved, towards the good things of another life, considered as ever so great.

38. Because all who allow the joys of heaven possible, pursue them not. Were the will determined by the views of good, as it appears in contemplation greater or less to the understanding, which is the state of all absent good, and that which, in the received opinion, the will is supposed to move to, and to be moved by,— I do not see how it could ever get loose from the infinite eternal joys of heaven, once proposed and considered as possible. For, all absent good, by which alone, barely proposed, and coming in view, the will is thought to be determined, and so to set us on action, being only possible, but not infallibly certain, it is unavoidable that the infinitely greater possible good should regularly and constantly determine the will in all the successive actions it directs; and then we should keep constantly and steadily in our course towards heaven, without ever standing still, or directing our actions to any other end: the eternal condition of a future state infinitely outweighing the expectation of riches, or honour, or any other worldly pleasure which we can propose to ourselves, though we should grant these the more probable to be obtained: for nothing future is yet in possession, and so the expectation even of these may deceive us. If it were so that the greater good in view determines the will, so great a good, once proposed, could not but seize the will, and hold it fast to the pursuit of this infinitely greatest good, without ever letting it go again: for the will having a power over, and directing the thoughts, as well as other actions, would, if it were so, hold the contemplation of the mind fixed to that good.

39. But any great uneasiness is never neglected. This would be the state of the mind, and regular tendency of the will in all its determinations, were it determined by that which is considered and in view the greater good. But that it is not so, is visible in experience; the infinitely greatest confessed good being often neglected, to satisfy the successive uneasiness of our desires pursuing trifles. But, though the greatest allowed, even ever-lasting unspeakable, good, which has sometimes moved and affected the mind, does not stedfastly hold the will, yet we see any very great and prevailing uneasiness having once laid hold on the will, let it not go;

by which we may be convinced, what it is that determines the will. Thus any vehement pain of the body; the ungovernable passion of a man violently in love; or the impatient desire of revenge, keeps the will steady and intent; and the will, thus determined, never lets the understanding lay by the object, but all the thoughts of the mind and powers of the body are uninterruptedly employed that way, by the determination of the will, influenced by that topping uneasiness, as long as it lasts; whereby it seems to me evident, that the will, or power of setting us upon one action in preference to all others, is determined in us by uneasiness: and whether this be not so, I desire every one to observe in himself.

40. Desire accompanies all uneasiness. I have hitherto chiefly instanced in the uneasiness of desire, as that which determines the will: because that is the chief and most sensible; and the will seldom orders any action, nor is there any voluntary action performed, without some desire accompanying it; which I think is the reason why the will and desire are so often confounded. But yet we are not to look upon the uneasiness which makes up, or at least accompanies, most of the other passions, as wholly excluded in the case. Aversion, fear, anger, envy, shame, &c. have each their uneasinesses too, and thereby influence the will. These passions are scarce any of them, in life and practice, simple and alone, and wholly unmixed with others; though usually, in discourse and contemplation, that carries the name which operates strongest, and appears most in the present state of the mind. Nay, there is, I think, scarce any of the passions to be found without desire joined with it. I am sure wherever there is uneasiness, there is desire. For we constantly desire happiness; and whatever we feel of uneasiness, so much it is certain we want of happiness; even in our own opinion, let our state and condition otherwise be what it will. Besides, the present moment not being our eternity, whatever our enjoyment be, we look beyond the present, and desire goes with our foresight, and that still carries the will with it. So that even in joy itself, that which keeps up the action whereon the enjoyment depends, is the desire to continue it, and fear to lose it: and whenever a greater uneasiness than that takes place in the mind, the will presently is by that determined to some new action, and the present delight neglected.

41. The most pressing uneasiness naturally determines the will. But we being in this world beset with sundry uneasinesses, distracted with different desires, the next inquiry naturally will be,— Which of them has the precedency in determining the will to the next action? and to that the answer is,— That ordinarily which is the most pressing of those that are judged capable of being then removed. For, the will being the power of directing our operative faculties to some action, for some end, cannot at any time be moved towards what is judged at that time unattainable: that would be to suppose an intelligent being designedly to act for an end, only to lose its labour; for so it is to act for what is judged not attainable; and therefore very great uneasinesses move not the will, when they are judged not capable of a cure: they in that case put us not upon endeavours. But, these set apart, the most important and urgent uneasiness we at that time feel, is that which ordinarily determines the will, successively, in that train of voluntary actions which makes up our lives. The greatest present uneasiness is the spur to action, that is constantly most felt, and for the most part determines the will in its choice of the next action. For this we must carry along with us, that the proper and only object of the will is some action of ours, and nothing else. For we producing nothing by our willing it, but some action in our power, it is there the will terminates, and reaches no further.

42. All desire happiness. If it be further asked,— What it is moves desire? I answer,— happiness, and that alone. Happiness and misery are the names of two extremes, the utmost bounds whereof we know not; it is what "eye hath not seen, ear hath not heard, nor hath it entered into the heart of man to conceive." But of some degrees of both we have very lively impressions; made by several instances of delight and joy on the one side, and torment and sorrow on the other; which, for shortness' sake, I shall comprehend under the names of pleasure and pain; there being pleasure and pain of the mind as well as the body,-"With him is fulness of joy, and pleasure for evermore." Or, to speak truly, they are all of the mind; though some have their rise in the mind from thought, others in the body from certain modifications of

motion.

43. Happiness and misery, good and evil, what they are. Happiness, then, in its full extent, is the utmost pleasure we are capable of, and misery the utmost pain; and the lowest degree of what can be called happiness is so much ease from all pain, and so much present pleasure, as without which any one cannot be content. Now, because pleasure and pain are produced in us by the operation of certain objects, either on our minds or our bodies, and in different degrees; therefore, what has an aptness to produce pleasure in us is that we call good, and what is apt to produce pain in us we call evil; for no other reason but for its aptness to produce pleasure and pain in us, wherein consists our happiness and misery. Further, though what is apt to produce any degree of pleasure be in itself good; and what is apt to produce any degree of pain be evil; yet it often happens that we do not call it so when it comes in competition with a greater of its sort; because, when they come in competition, the degrees also of pleasure and pain have justly a preference. So that if we will rightly estimate what we call good and evil, we shall find it lies much in comparison: for the cause of every less degree of pain, as well as every greater degree of pleasure, has the nature of good, and vice versa.

44. What good is desired, what not. Though this be that which is called good and evil, and all good be the proper object of desire in general; yet all good, even seen and confessed to be so, does not necessarily move every particular man's desire; but only that part, or so much of it as is considered and taken to make a necessary part of his happiness. All other good, however great in reality or appearance, excites not a man's desires who looks not on it to make a part of that happiness wherewith he, in his present thoughts, can satisfy himself. Happiness, under this view, every one constantly pursues, and desires what makes any part of it: other things, acknowledged to be good, he can look upon without desire, pass by, and be content without. There is nobody, I think, so senseless as to deny that there is pleasure in knowledge: and for the pleasures of sense, they have too many followers to let it be questioned whether men are taken with them or no. Now, let one man place his satisfaction in sensual pleasures, another in the delight of knowledge: though each of them cannot but confess, there is great pleasure in what the other pursues; yet, neither of them making the other's delight a part of his happiness, their desires are not moved, but each is satisfied without what the other enjoys; and so his will is not determined to the pursuit of it. But yet, as soon as the studious man's hunger and thirst make him uneasy, he, whose will was never determined to any pursuit of good cheer, poignant sauces, delicious wine, by the pleasant taste he has found in them, is, by the uneasiness of hunger and thirst, presently determined to eating and drinking, though possibly with great indifferency, what wholesome food comes in his way. And, on the other side, the epicure buckles to study, when shame, or the desire to recommend himself to his mistress, shall make him uneasy in the want of any sort of knowledge. Thus, how much soever men are in earnest and constant in pursuit of happiness, yet they may have a clear view of good, great and confessed good, without being concerned for it, or moved by it, if they think they can make up their happiness without it. Though as to pain, that they are always concerned for; they can feel no uneasiness without being moved. And therefore, being uneasy in the want of whatever is judged necessary to their happiness, as soon as any good appears to make a part of their portion of happiness, they begin to desire it.

45. Why the greatest good is not always desired. This, I think, any one may observe in himself and others,— That the greater visible good does not always raise men's desires in proportion to the greatness it appears, and is acknowledged, to have: though every little trouble moves us, and sets us on work to get rid of it. The reason whereof is evident from the nature of our happiness and misery itself. All present pain, whatever it be, makes a part of our present misery. but all absent good does not at any time make a necessary part of our present happiness, nor the absence of it make a part of our misery. If it did, we should be constantly and infinitely miserable; there being infinite degrees of happiness which are not in our possession. All uneasiness therefore being removed, a moderate portion of good serves at present to content men; and a few degrees of pleasure, in a succession of ordinary enjoyments,

make up a happiness wherein they can be satisfied. If this were not so, there could be no room for those indifferent and visibly trifling actions, to which our wills are so often determined, and wherein we voluntarily waste so much of our lives; which remissness could by no means consist with a constant determination of will or desire to the greatest apparent good. That this is so, I think few people need go far from home to be convinced. And indeed in this life there are not many whose happiness reaches so far as to afford them a constant train of moderate mean pleasures, without any mixture of uneasiness; and yet they could be content to stay here for ever: though they cannot deny, but that it is possible there may be a state of eternal durable joys after this life, far surpassing all the good that is to be found here. Nay, they cannot but see that it is more possible than the attainment and continuation of that pittance of honour, riches, or pleasure which they pursue, and for which they neglect that eternal state. But yet, in full view of this difference, satisfied of the possibility of a perfect, secure, and lasting happiness in a future state, and under a clear conviction that it is not to be had here,— whilst they bound their happiness within some little enjoyment or aim of this life, and exclude the joys of heaven from making any necessary part of it,— their desires are not moved by this greater apparent good, nor their wills determined to any action, or endeavour for its attainment.

46. Why not being desired, it moves not the will. The ordinary necessities of our lives fill a great part of them with the uneasinesses of hunger, thirst, heat, cold, weariness, with labour, and sleepiness, in their constant returns, &c. To which, if, besides accidental harms, we add the fantastical uneasiness (as itch after honour, power, or riches, &c.) which acquired habits, by fashion, example, and education, have settled in us, and a thousand other irregular desires, which custom has made natural to us, we shall find that a very little part of our life is so vacant from these uneasinesses, as to leave us free to the attraction of remoter absent good. We are seldom at ease, and free enough from the solicitation of our natural or adopted desires, but a constant succession of uneasinesses out of that stock which natural wants or acquired habits have heaped up, take the will in their turns; and no sooner is one action dispatched, which by such a determination of the will we are set upon, but another uneasiness is ready to set us on work. For, the removing of the pains we feel, and are at present pressed with, being the getting out of misery, and consequently the first thing to be done in order to happiness,— absent good, though thought on, confessed, and appearing to be good, not making any part of this unhappiness in its absence, is justled out, to make way for the removal of those uneasinesses we feel; till due and repeated contemplation has brought it nearer to our mind, given some relish of it, and raised in us some desire: which then beginning to make a part of our present uneasiness, stands upon fair terms with the rest to be satisfied, and so, according to its greatness and pressure, comes in its turn to determine the will.

47. Due consideration raises desire. And thus, by a due consideration, and examining any good proposed, it is in our power to raise our desires in a due proportion to the value of that good, whereby in its turn and place it may come to work upon the will, and be pursued. For good, though appearing and allowed ever so great, yet till it has raised desires in our minds, and thereby made us uneasy in its want, it reaches not our wills; we are not within the sphere of its activity, our wills being under the determination only of those uneasinesses which are present to us, which (whilst we have any) are always soliciting, and ready at hand to give the will its next determination. The balancing, when there is any in the mind, being only, which desire shall be next satisfied, which uneasiness first removed. Whereby it comes to pass that, as long as any uneasiness, any desire, remains in our mind, there is no room for good, barely as such, to come at the will, or at all to determine it. Because, as has been said, the first step in our endeavours after happiness being to get wholly out of the confines of misery, and to feel no part of it, the will can be at leisure for nothing else, till every uneasiness we feel be perfectly removed. which, in the multitude of wants and desires we are beset with in this imperfect state, we are not like to be ever freed from in this world.

48. The power to suspend the prosecution of any desire makes way for consideration. There being in us a great many uneasinesses, always soliciting and ready to determine the will, it is

natural, as I have said, that the greatest and most pressing should determine the will to the next action; and so it does for the most part, but not always. For, the mind having in most cases, as is evident in experience, a power to suspend the execution and satisfaction of any of its desires; and so all, one after another; is at liberty to consider the objects of them, examine them on all sides, and weigh them with others. In this lies the liberty man has; and from the not using of it right comes all that variety of mistakes, errors, and faults which we run into in the conduct of our lives, and our endeavours after happiness; whilst we precipitate the determination of our wills, and engage too soon, before due examination. To prevent this, we have a power to suspend the prosecution of this or that desire; as every one daily may experiment in himself. This seems to me the source of all liberty; in this seems to consist that which is (as I think improperly) called free-will. For, during this suspension of any desire, before the will be determined to action, and the action (which follows that determination) done, we have opportunity to examine, view, and judge of the good or evil of what we are going to do; and when, upon due examination, we have judged, we have done our duty, all that we can, or ought to do, in pursuit of our happiness; and it is not a fault, but a perfection of our nature, to desire, will, and act according to the last result of a fair examination.

49. To be determined by our own judgment, is no restraint to liberty. This is so far from being a restraint or diminution of freedom, that it is the very improvement and benefit of it; it is not an abridgment, it is the end and use of our liberty; and the further we are removed from such a determination, the nearer we are to misery and slavery. A perfect indifference in the mind, not determinable by its last judgment of the good or evil that is thought to attend its choice, would be so far from being an advantage and excellency of any intellectual nature, that it would be as great an imperfection, as the want of indifference. to act, or not to act, till determined by the will, would be an imperfection on the other side. A man is at liberty to lift up his hand to his head, or let it rest quiet: he is perfectly indifferent in either; and it would be an imperfection in him, if he wanted that power, if he were deprived of that indifferency. But it would be as great an imperfection, if he had the same indifferency, whether he would prefer the lifting up his hand, or its remaining in rest, when it would save his head or eyes from a blow he sees coming: it is as much a perfection, that desire, or the power of preferring, should be determined by good, as that the power of acting should be determined by the will; and the certainer such determination is, the greater is the perfection. Nay, were we determined by anything but the last result of our own minds, judging of the good or evil of any action, we were not free; the very end of our freedom being, that we may attain the good we choose. And therefore, every man is put under a necessity, by his constitution as an intelligent being, to be determined in willing by his own thought and judgment what is best for him to do: else he would be under the determination of some other than himself, which is want of liberty. And to deny that a man's will, in every determination, follows his own judgment, is to say, that a man wills and acts for an end that he would not have, at the time that he wills and acts for it. For if he prefers it in his present thoughts before any other, it is plain he then thinks better of it, and would have it before any other; unless he can have and not have it, will and not will it, at the same time; a contradiction too manifest to be admitted.

50. The freest agents are so determined. If we look upon those superior beings above us, who enjoy perfect happiness, we shall have reason to judge that they are more steadily determined in their choice of good than we; and yet we have no reason to think they are less happy, or less free, than we are. And if it were fit for such poor finite creatures as we are to pronounce what infinite wisdom and goodness could do, I think we might say, that God himself cannot choose what is not good; the freedom of the Almighty hinders not his being determined by what is best.

51. A constant determination to a pursuit of happiness no abridgment of liberty. But to give a right view of this mistaken part of liberty let me ask,— Would any one be a changeling, because he is less determined by wise considerations than a wise man? Is it worth the name of freedom to be at liberty to play the fool, and draw shame and misery upon a man's self? If to

break loose from the conduct of reason, and to want that restraint of examination and judgment which keeps us from choosing or doing the worse, be liberty, true liberty, madmen and fools are the only freemen: but yet, I think, nobody would choose to be mad for the sake of such liberty, but he that is mad already. The constant desire of happiness, and the constraint it puts upon us to act for it, nobody, I think, accounts an abridgment of liberty, or at least an abridgment of liberty to be complained of. God Almighty himself is under the necessity of being happy; and the more any intelligent being is so, the nearer is its approach to infinite perfection and happiness. That, in this state of ignorance, we short-sighted creatures might not mistake true felicity, we are endowed with a power to suspend any particular desire, and keep it from determining the will, and engaging us in action. This is standing still, where we are not sufficiently assured of the way: examination is consulting a guide. The determination of the will upon inquiry, is following the direction of that guide: and he that has a power to act or not to act, according as such determination directs, is a free agent: such determination abridges not that power wherein liberty consists. He that has his chains knocked off, and the prison doors set open to him, is perfectly at liberty, because he may either go or stay, as he best likes; though his preference be determined to stay, by the darkness of the night, or illness of the weather, or want of other lodging. He ceases not to be free; though the desire of some convenience to be had there absolutely determines his preference, and makes him stay in his prison.

52. The necessity of pursuing true happiness the foundation of liberty. As therefore the highest perfection of intellectual nature lies in a careful and constant pursuit of true and solid happiness; so the care of ourselves, that we mistake not imaginary for real happiness, is the necessary foundation of our liberty. The stronger ties we have to an unalterable pursuit of happiness in general, which is our greatest good, and which, as such, our desires always follow, the more are we free from any necessary determination of our will to any particular action, and from a necessary compliance with our desire, set upon any particular, and then appearing preferable good, till we have duly examined whether it has a tendency to, or be inconsistent with, our real happiness: and therefore, till we are as much informed upon this inquiry as the weight of the matter, and the nature of the case demands, we are, by the necessity of preferring and pursuing true happiness as our greatest good, obliged to suspend the satisfaction of our desires in particular cases.

53. Power to suspend. This is the hinge on which turns the liberty of intellectual beings, in their constant endeavours after, and a steady prosecution of true felicity,— That they can suspend this prosecution in particular cases, till they have looked before them, and informed themselves whether that particular thing which is then proposed or desired lie in the way to their main end, and make a real part of that which is their greatest good. For, the inclination and tendency of their nature to happiness is an obligation and motive to them, to take care not to mistake or miss it; and so necessarily puts them upon caution, deliberation, and wariness, in the direction of their particular actions, which are the means to obtain it. Whatever necessity determines to the pursuit of real bliss, the same necessity, with the same force, establishes suspense, deliberation, and scrutiny of each successive desire, whether the satisfaction of it does not interfere with our true happiness, and mislead us from it. This, as seems to me, is the great privilege of finite intellectual beings; and I desire it may be well considered, whether the great inlet and exercise of all the liberty men have, are capable of, or can be useful to them, and that whereon depends the turn of their actions, does not lie in this,— That they can suspend their desires, and stop them from determining their wills to any action, till they have duly and fairly examined the good and evil of it, as far forth as the weight of the thing requires. This we are able to do; and when we have done it, we have done our duty, and all that is in our power; and indeed all that needs. For, since the will supposes knowledge to guide its choice, all that we can do is to hold our wills undetermined, till we have examined the good and evil of what we desire. What follows after that, follows in a chain of consequences, linked one to another, all depending on the last determination of the judgment, which, whether it shall

be upon a hasty and precipitate view, or upon a due and mature examination, is in our power; experience showing us, that in most cases, we are able to suspend the present satisfaction of any desire.

54. Government of our passions the right improvement of liberty. But if any extreme disturbance (as sometimes it happens) possesses our whole mind, as when the pain of the rack, an impetuous uneasiness, as of love, anger, or any other violent passion, running away with us, allows us not the liberty of thought, and we are not masters enough of our own minds to consider thoroughly and examine fairly;— God, who knows our frailty, pities our weakness, and requires of us no more than we are able to do, and sees what was and what was not in our power, will judge as a kind and merciful Father. But the forbearance of a too hasty compliance with our desires, the moderation and restraint of our passions, so that our understandings may be free to examine, and reason unbiased give its judgment, being that whereon a right direction of our conduct to true happiness depends; it is in this we should employ our chief care and endeavours. In this we should take pains to suit the relish of our minds to the true intrinsic good or ill that is in things; and not permit an allowed or supposed possible great and weighty good to slip out of our thoughts, without leaving any relish, any desire of itself there, till, by a due consideration of its true worth, we have formed appetites in our minds suitable to it, and made ourselves uneasy in the want of it, or in the fear of losing it. And how much this is in every one's power, by making resolutions to himself, such as he may keep, is easy for every one to try. Nor let any one say, he cannot govern his passions, nor hinder them from breaking out, and carrying him into action; for what he can do before a prince or a great man, he can do alone, or in the presence of God, if he will.

55. How men come to pursue different, and often evil, courses. From what has been said, it is easy to give an account how it comes to pass, that, though all men desire happiness, yet their wills carry them so contrarily; and consequently some of them to what is evil. And to this I say, that the various and contrary choices that men make in the world do not argue that they do not all pursue good; but that the same thing is not good to every man alike. This variety of pursuits shows, that every one does not place his happiness in the same thing, or choose the same way to it. Were all the concerns of man terminated in this life, why one followed study and knowledge, and another hawking and hunting: why one chose luxury and debauchery, and another sobriety and riches, would not be because every one of these did not aim at his own happiness; but because their happiness was placed in different things. And therefore it was a right answer of the physician to his patient that had sore eyes:— If you have more pleasure in the taste of wine than in the use of your sight, wine is good for you; but if the pleasure of seeing be greater to you than that of drinking, wine is naught.

56. All men seek happiness, but not of the same sort. The mind has a different relish, as well as the palate; and you will as fruitlessly endeavour to delight all men with riches or glory (which yet some men place their happiness in) as you would to satisfy all men's hunger with cheese or lobsters; which, though very agreeable and delicious fare to some, are to others extremely nauseous and offensive: and many persons would with reason prefer the griping of an hungry belly to those dishes which are a feast to others. Hence it was, I think, that the philosophers of old did in vain inquire, whether summum bonum consisted in riches, or bodily delights, or virtue, or contemplation: and they might have as reasonably disputed, whether the best relish were to be found in apples, plums, or nuts, and have divided themselves into sects upon it. For, as pleasant tastes depend not on the things themselves, but on their agreeableness to this or that particular palate, wherein there is great variety; so the greatest happiness consists in the having those things which produce the greatest pleasure, and in the absence of those which cause any disturbance, any pain. Now these, to different men, are very different things. If, therefore, men in this life only have hope; if in this life only they can enjoy, it is not strange nor unreasonable, that they should seek their happiness by avoiding all things that disease them here, and by pursuing all that delight them; wherein it will be no wonder to find variety and difference. For if there be no prospect beyond the grave, the inference is certainly

right —"Let us eat and drink," let us enjoy what we "for to-morrow we shall die." This, I think, may serve to show us the reason, why, though all men's desires tend to happiness, yet they are not moved by the same object. Men may choose different things, and yet all choose right; supposing them only like a company of poor insects; whereof some are bees, delighted with flowers and their sweetness; others beetles, delighted with other kinds of viands, which having enjoyed for a season, they would cease to be, and exist no more for ever.

57. Power to suspend volition explains responsibility for ill choice. These things, duly weighed, will give us, as I think, a clear view into the state of human liberty. Liberty, it is plain, consists in a power to do, or not to do; to do, or forbear doing, as we will. This cannot be denied. But this seeming to comprehend only the actions of a man consecutive to volition, it is further inquired,— Whether he be at liberty to will or no? And to this it has been answered, that, in most cases, a man is not at liberty to forbear the act of volition: he must exert an act of his will, whereby the action proposed is made to exist or not to exist. But yet there is a case wherein a man is at liberty in respect of willing; and that is the choosing of a remote good as an end to be pursued. Here a man may suspend the act of his choice from being determined for or against the thing proposed, till he has examined whether it be really of a nature, in itself and consequences, to make him happy or not. For, when he has once chosen it, and thereby it is become a part of his happiness, it raises desire, and that proportionably gives him uneasiness; which determines his will, and sets him at work in pursuit of his choice on all occasions that offer. And here we may see how it comes to pass that a man may justly incur punishment, though it be certain that, in all the particular actions that he wills, he does, and necessarily does, will that which he then judges to be good. For, though his will be always determined by that which is judged good by his understanding, yet it excuses him not; because, by a too hasty choice of his own making, he has imposed on himself wrong measures of good and evil; which, however false and fallacious, have the same influence on all his future conduct, as if they were true and right. He has vitiated his own palate, and must be answerable to himself for the sickness and death that follows from it. The eternal law and nature of things must not be altered to comply with his ill-ordered choice. If the neglect or abuse of the liberty he had, to examine what would really and truly make for his happiness, misleads him, the miscarriages that follow on it must be imputed to his own election. He had a power to suspend his determination; it was given him, that he might examine, and take care of his own happiness, and look that he were not deceived. And he could never judge, that it was better to be deceived than not, in a matter of so great and near concernment.

58. Why men choose what makes them miserable. What has been said may also discover to us the reason why men in this world prefer different things, and pursue happiness by contrary courses. But yet, since men are always constant and in earnest in matters of happiness and misery, the question still remains, How men come often to prefer the worse to the better; and to choose that, which, by their own confession, has made them miserable?

59. The causes of this. To account for the various and contrary ways men take, though all aim at being happy, we must consider whence the various uneasinesses that determine the will, in the preference of each voluntary action, have their rise:

(1) From bodily pain. Some of them come from causes not in our power; such as are often the pains of the body from want, disease, or outward injuries, as the rack, &c.; which, when present and violent, operate for the most part forcibly on the will, and turn the courses of men's lives from virtue, piety, and religion, and what before they judged to lead to happiness; every one not endeavouring, or, through disuse, not being able, by the contemplation of remote and future good, to raise in himself desires of them strong enough to counterbalance the uneasiness he feels in those bodily torments, and to keep his will steady in the choice of those actions which lead to future happiness. A neighbouring country has been of late a tragical theatre from which we might fetch instances, if there needed any, and the world did not in all countries and ages furnish examples enough to confirm that received observation, Necessitas cogit ad turpia; and therefore there is great reason for us to pray, "Lead us not into

temptation."

(2) From wrong desires arising from wrong judgments. Other uneasinesses arise from our desires of absent good; which desires always bear proportion to, and depend on, the judgment we make, and the relish we have of any absent good; in both which we are apt to be variously misled, and that by our own fault.

60. Our judgment of present good or evil always right. In the first place, I shall consider the wrong judgments men make of future good and evil, whereby their desires are misled. For, as to present happiness and misery, when that alone comes into consideration, and the consequences are quite removed, a man never chooses amiss: he knows what best pleases him, and that he actually prefers. Things in their present enjoyment are what they seem: the apparent and real good are, in this case, always the same. For, the pain or pleasure being just so great and no greater than it is felt, the present good or evil is really so much as it appears. And therefore were every action of ours concluded within itself, and drew no consequences after it, we should undoubtedly never err in our choice of good: we should always infallibly prefer the best. Were the pains of honest industry, and of starving with hunger and cold set together before us, nobody would be in doubt which to choose: were the satisfaction of a lust and the joys of heaven offered at once to any one's present possession, he would not balance, or err in the determination of his choice.

61. Our wrong judgments have regard to future good and evil only. But since our voluntary actions carry not all the happiness and misery that depend on them along with them in their present performance, but are the precedent causes of good and evil, which they draw after them, and bring upon us, when they themselves are past and cease to be; our desires look beyond our present enjoyments, and carry the mind out to absent good, according to the necessity which we think there is of it, to the making or increase of our happiness. It is our opinion of such a necessity that gives it its attraction: without that, we are not moved by absent good. For, in this narrow scantling of capacity which we are accustomed to and sensible of here, wherein we enjoy but one pleasure at once, which, when all uneasiness is away, is, whilst it lasts, sufficient to make us think ourselves happy, it is not all remote and even apparent good that affects us. Because the indolency and enjoyment we have, sufficing for our present happiness, we desire not to venture the change; since we judge that we are happy already, being content, and that is enough. For who is content is happy. But as soon as any new uneasiness comes in, this happiness is disturbed, and we are set afresh on work in the pursuit of happiness.

62. From a wrong judgment of what makes a necessary part of their happiness. Their aptness therefore to conclude that they can be happy without it, is one great occasion that men often are not raised to the desire of the greatest absent good. For, whilst such thoughts possess them, the joys of a future state move them not; they have little concern or uneasiness about them; and the will, free from the determination of such desires, is left to the pursuit of nearer satisfactions, and to the removal of those uneasinesses which it then feels, in its want of and longings after them. Change but a man's view of these things; let him see that virtue and religion are necessary to his happiness; let him look into the future state of bliss or misery, and see there God, the righteous judge, ready to "render to every man according to his deeds; to them who by patient continuance in well-doing seek for glory, and honour, and immortality, eternal life; but unto every soul that doth evil, indignation and wrath, tribulation and anguish." To him, I say, who hath a prospect of the different state of perfect happiness or misery that attends all men after this life, depending on their behaviour here, the measures of good and evil that govern his choice are mightily changed. For, since nothing of pleasure and pain in this life can bear any proportion to the endless happiness or exquisite misery of an immortal soul hereafter, actions in his power will have their preference, not according to the transient pleasure or pain that accompanies or follows them here, but as they serve to secure that perfect durable happiness hereafter.

63. A more particular account of wrong judgments. But, to account more particularly for the

misery that men often bring on themselves, notwithstanding that they do all in earnest pursue happiness, we must consider how things come to be represented to our desires under deceitful appearances: and that is by the judgment pronouncing wrongly concerning them. To see how far this reaches, and what are the causes of wrong judgment, we must remember that things are judged good or bad in a double sense:—

First, That which is properly good or bad, is nothing but barely pleasure or pain.

Secondly, But because not only present pleasure and pain, but that also which is apt by its efficacy or consequences to bring it upon us at a distance, is a proper object of our desires, and apt to move a creature that has foresight; therefore things also that draw after them pleasure and pain, are considered as good and evil.

64. No one chooses misery willingly, but only by wrong judgment. The wrong judgment that misleads us, and makes the will often fasten on the worse side, lies in misreporting upon the various comparisons of these. The wrong judgment I am here speaking of is not what one man may think of the determination of another, but what every man himself must confess to be wrong. For, since I lay it for a certain ground, that every intelligent being really seeks happiness, which consists in the enjoyment of pleasure, without any considerable mixture of uneasiness; it is impossible anyone should willingly put into his own draught any bitter ingredient, or leave out anything in his power that would tend to his satisfaction, and the completing of his happiness, but only by a wrong judgment. I shall not here speak of that mistake which is the consequence of invincible error, which scarce deserves the name of wrong judgment; but of that wrong judgment which every man himself must confess to be so.

65. Men may err in comparing present and future. (1) Therefore, as to present pleasure and pain, the mind, as has been said, never mistakes that which is really good or evil; that which is the greater pleasure, or the greater pain, is really just as it appears. But, though present pleasure and pain show their difference and degrees so plainly as not to leave room to mistake; yet, when we compare present pleasure or pain with future, (which is usually the case in most important determinations of the will,) we often make wrong judgments of them; taking our measures of them in different positions of distance. Objects near our view are apt to be thought greater than those of a larger size that are more remote. And so it is with pleasures and pains: the present is apt to carry it; and those at a distance have the disadvantage in the comparison. Thus most men, like spendthrift heirs, are apt to judge a little in hand better than a great deal to come; and so, for small matters in possession, part with greater ones in reversion. But that this is a wrong judgment every one must allow, let his pleasure consist in whatever it will: since that which is future will certainly come to be present; and then, having the same advantage of nearness, will show itself in its full dimensions, and discover his wilful mistake who judged of it by unequal measures. Were the pleasure of drinking accompanied, the very moment a man takes off his glass, with that sick stomach and aching head which, in some men, are sure to follow not many hours after, I think nobody, whatever pleasure he had in his cups, would, on these conditions, ever let wine touch his lips; which yet he daily swallows, and the evil side comes to be chosen only by the fallacy of a little difference in time. But, if pleasure or pain can be so lessened only by a few hours' removal, how much more will it be so by a further distance, to a man that will not, by a right judgment, do what time will, i.e. bring it home upon himself, and consider it as present, and there take its true dimensions? This is the way we usually impose on ourselves, in respect of bare pleasure and pain, or the true degrees of happiness or misery: the future loses its just proportion, and what is present obtains the preference as the greater. I mention not here the wrong judgment, whereby the absent are not only lessened, but reduced to perfect nothing; when men enjoy what they can in present, and make sure of that, concluding amiss that no evil will thence follow. For that lies not in comparing the greatness of future good and evil, which is that we are here speaking of; but in another sort of wrong judgment, which is concerning good or evil, as it is considered to be the cause and procurement of pleasure or pain that will follow from it.

66. Causes of our judging amiss when we compare present pleasure and pain with future. The

cause of our judging amiss, when we compare our present pleasure or pain with future, seems to me to be the weak and narrow constitution of our minds. We cannot well enjoy two pleasures at once; much less any pleasure almost, whilst pain possesses us. The present pleasure, if it be not very languid, and almost none at all, fills our narrow souls, and so takes up the whole mind that it scarce leaves any thought of things absent: or if among our pleasures there are some which are not strong enough to exclude the consideration of things at a distance, yet we have so great an abhorrence of pain, that a little of it extinguishes all our pleasures. A little bitter mingled in our cup, leaves no relish of the sweet. Hence it comes that, at any rate, we desire to be rid of the present evil, which we are apt to think nothing absent can equal; because, under the present pain, we find not ourselves capable of any the least degree of happiness. Men's daily complaints are a loud proof of this: the pain that any one actually feels is still of all other the worst; and it is with anguish they cry out,—"Any rather than this: nothing can be so intolerable as what I now suffer." And therefore our whole endeavours and thoughts are intent to get rid of the present evil, before all things, as the first necessary condition to our happiness; let what will follow. Nothing, as we passionately think, can exceed, or almost equal, the uneasiness that sits so heavy upon us. And because the abstinence from a present pleasure that offers itself is a pain, nay, oftentimes a very great one, the desire being inflamed by a near and tempting object, it is no wonder that that operates after the same manner pain does, and lessens in our thoughts what is future; and so forces us, as it were blindfold, into its embraces.

67. Absent good unable to counterbalance present uneasiness. Add to this, that absent good, or, which is the same thing, future pleasure,— especially if of a sort we are unacquainted with,— seldom is able to counterbalance any uneasiness, either of pain or desire, which is present. For, its greatness being no more than what shall be really tasted when enjoyed, men are apt enough to lessen that; to make it give place to any present desire; and conclude with themselves that, when it comes to trial, it may possibly not answer the report or opinion that generally passes of it: they having often found that, not only what others have magnified, but even what they themselves have enjoyed with great pleasure and delight at one time, has proved insipid or nauseous at another; and therefore they see nothing in it for which they should forego a present enjoyment. But that this is a false way of judging, when applied to the happiness of another life, they must confess; unless they will say, God cannot make those happy he designs to be so. For that being intended for a state of happiness, it must certainly be agreeable to everyone's wish and desire: could we suppose their relishes as different there as they are here, yet the manna in heaven will suit every one's palate. Thus much of the wrong judgment we make of present and future pleasure and pain, when they are compared together, and so the absent considered as future.

68. Wrong judgment in considering consequences of actions. (II) As to things good or bad in their consequences, and by the aptness that is in them to procure us good or evil in the future, we judge amiss several ways.

1. When we judge that so much evil does not really depend on them as in truth there does.

2. When we judge that, though the consequence be of that moment, yet it is not of that certainty, but that it may otherwise fall out, or else by some means be avoided; as by industry, address, change, repentance, &c.

That these are wrong ways of judging, were easy to show in every particular, if I would examine them at large singly: but I shall only mention this in general, viz. that it is a very wrong and irrational way of proceeding, to venture a greater good for a less, upon uncertain guesses; and before a due examination be made, proportionable to the weightiness of the matter, and the concernment it is to us not to mistake. This I think every one must confess, especially if he considers the usual cause of this wrong judgment, whereof these following are some:—

69. Causes of this. (i) Ignorance: He that judges without informing himself to the utmost that he is capable, cannot acquit himself of judging amiss.

(ii) Inadvertency: When a man overlooks even that which he does know. This is an affected and present ignorance, which misleads our judgments as much as the other. Judging is, as it were, balancing an account, and determining on which side the odds lie. If therefore either side be huddled up in haste, and several of the sums that should have gone into the reckoning be overlooked and left out, this precipitancy causes as wrong a judgment as if it were a perfect ignorance. That which most commonly causes this is, the prevalency of some present pleasure or pain, heightened by our feeble passionate nature, most strongly wrought on by what is present. To check this precipitancy, our understanding and reason were given us, if we will make a right use of them, to search and see, and then judge thereupon. Without liberty, the understanding would be to no purpose: and without understanding, liberty (if it could be) would signify nothing. If a man sees what would do him good or harm, what would make him happy or miserable, without being able to move himself one step towards or from it, what is he the better for seeing? And he that is at liberty to ramble in perfect darkness, what is his liberty better than if he were driven up and down as a bubble by the force of the wind? The being acted by a blind impulse from without, or from within, is little odds. The first, therefore, and great use of liberty is to hinder blind precipitancy; the principal exercise of freedom is to stand still, open the eyes, look about, and take a view of the consequence of what we are going to do, as much as the weight of the matter requires. How much sloth and negligence, heat and passion, the prevalency of fashion or acquired indispositions do severally contribute, on occasion, to these wrong judgments, I shall not here further inquire. I shall only add one other false judgment, which I think necessary to mention, because perhaps it is little taken notice of, though of great influence.

70. Wrong judgment of what is necessary to our happiness. All men desire happiness, that is past doubt: but, as has been already observed, when they are rid of pain, they are apt to take up with any pleasure at hand, or that custom has endeared to them; to rest satisfied in that; and so being happy, till some new desire, by making them uneasy, disturbs that happiness, and shows them that they are not so, they look no further; nor is the will determined to any action in pursuit of any other known or apparent good. For since we find that we cannot enjoy all sorts of good, but one excludes another; we do not fix our desires on every apparent greater good, unless it be judged to be necessary to our happiness: if we think we can be happy without it, it moves us not. This is another occasion to men of judging wrong; when they take not that to be necessary to their happiness which really is so. This mistake misleads us, both in the choice of the good we aim at, and very often in the means to it, when it is a remote good. But, which way ever it be, either by placing it where really it is not, or by neglecting the means as not necessary to it;— when a man misses his great end, happiness, he will acknowledge he judged not right. That which contributes to this mistake is the real or supposed unpleasantness of the actions which are the way to this end; it seeming so preposterous a thing to men, to make themselves unhappy in order to happiness, that they do not easily bring themselves to it.

71. We can change the agreeableness or disagreeableness in things. The last inquiry, therefore, concerning this matter is,— Whether it be in a man's power to change the pleasantness and unpleasantness that accompanies any sort of action? And as to that, it is plain, in many cases he can. Men may and should correct their palates, and give relish to what either has, or they suppose has none. The relish of the mind is as various as that of the body, and like that too may be altered; and it is a mistake to think that men cannot change the displeasingness or indifferency that is in actions into pleasure and desire, if they will do but what is in their power. A due consideration will do it in some cases; and practice, application, and custom in most. Bread or tobacco may be neglected where they are shown to be useful to health, because of an indifferency or disrelish to them; reason and consideration at first recommends, and begins their trial, and use finds, or custom makes them pleasant. That this is so in virtue too, is very certain. Actions are pleasing or displeasing, either in themselves, or considered as a means to a greater and more desirable end. The eating of a well-seasoned dish, suited to a man's palate, may move the mind by the delight itself that accompanies the eating, without

reference to any other end; to which the consideration of the pleasure there is in health and strength (to which that meat is subservient) may add a new gusto, able to make us swallow an ill-relished potion. In the latter of these, any action is rendered more or less pleasing, only by the contemplation of the end, and the being more or less persuaded of its tendency to it, or necessary connexion with it: but the pleasure of the action itself is best acquired or increased by use and practice. Trials often reconcile us to that, which at a distance we looked on with aversion; and by repetitions wear us into a liking of what possibly, in the first essay, displeased us. Habits have powerful charms, and put so strong attractions of easiness and pleasure into what we accustom ourselves to, that we cannot forbear to do, or at least be easy in the omission of, actions, which habitual practice has suited, and thereby recommends to us. Though this be very visible, and every one's experience shows him he can do so; yet it is a part in the conduct of men towards their happiness, neglected to a degree, that it will be possibly entertained as a paradox, if it be said, that men can make things or actions more or less pleasing to themselves; and thereby remedy that, to which one may justly impute a great deal of their wandering. Fashion and the common opinion having settled wrong notions, and education and custom ill habits, the just values of things are misplaced, and the palates of men corrupted. Pains should be taken to rectify these; and contrary habits change our pleasures, and give a relish to that which is necessary or conducive to our happiness. This every one must confess he can do; and when happiness is lost, and misery overtakes him, he will confess he did amiss in neglecting it, and condemn himself for it; and I ask every one, whether he has not often done so?

72. Preference of vice to virtue a manifest wrong judgment. I shall not now enlarge any further on the wrong judgments and neglect of what is in their power, whereby men mislead themselves. This would make a volume, and is not my business. But whatever false notions, or shameful neglect of what is in their power, may put men out of their way to happiness, and distract them, as we see, into so different courses of life, this yet is certain, that morality, established upon its true foundations, cannot but determine the choice in any one that will but consider: and he that will not be so far a rational creature as to reflect seriously upon infinite happiness and misery, must needs condemn himself as not making that use of his understanding he should. The rewards and punishments of another life, which the Almighty has established, as the enforcements of his law, are of weight enough to determine the choice, against whatever pleasure or pain this life can show, when the eternal state is considered but in its bare possibility, which nobody can make any doubt of. He that will allow exquisite and endless happiness to be but the possible consequence of a good life here, and the contrary state the possible reward of a bad one, must own himself to judge very much amiss if he does not conclude,— That a virtuous life, with the certain expectation of everlasting bliss, which may come, is to be preferred to a vicious one, with the fear of that dreadful state of misery, which it is very possible may overtake the guilty; or, at best, the terrible uncertain hope of annihilation. This is evidently so, though the virtuous life here had nothing but pain, and the vicious continual pleasure: which yet is, for the most part, quite otherwise, and wicked men have not much the odds to brag of, even in their present possession; nay, all things rightly considered, have, I think, even the worse part here. But when infinite happiness is put into one scale, against infinite misery in the other; if the worst that comes to the pious man, if he mistakes, be the best that the wicked can attain to, if he be in the right, who can without madness run the venture? Who in his wits would choose to come within a possibility of infinite misery; which if he miss, there is yet nothing to be got by that hazard? Whereas, on the other side, the sober man ventures nothing against infinite happiness to be got, if his expectation comes not to pass. If the good man be in the right, he is eternally happy; if he mistakes, he's not miserable, he feels nothing. On the other side, if the wicked man be in the right, he is not happy; if he mistakes, he is infinitely miserable. Must it not be a most manifest wrong judgment that does not presently see to which side, in this case, the preference is to be given? I have forborne to mention anything of the certainty or probability of a future state, designing here to show the

wrong judgment that any one must allow he makes, upon his own principles, laid how he pleases, who prefers the short pleasures of a vicious life upon any consideration, whilst he knows, and cannot but be certain, that a future life is at least possible.

73. Recapitulation — liberty of indifferency. To conclude this inquiry into human liberty, which, as it stood before, I myself from the beginning fearing, and a very judicious friend of mine, since the publication, suspecting to have some mistake in it, though he could not particularly show it me, I was put upon a stricter review of this chapter. Wherein lighting upon a very easy and scarce observable slip I had made, in putting one seemingly indifferent word for another that discovery opened to me this present view, which here, in this second edition, I submit to the learned world, and which, in short, is this: Liberty is a power to act or not to act, according as the mind directs. A power to direct the operative faculties to motion or rest in particular instances is that which we call the will. That which in the train of our voluntary actions determines the will to any change of operation is some present uneasiness, which is, or at least is always accompanied with that of desire. Desire is always moved by evil, to fly it: because a total freedom from pain always makes a necessary part of our happiness: but every good, nay, every greater good, does not constantly move desire, because it may not make, or may not be taken to make, part of our happiness. For all that we desire, is only to be happy. But, though this general desire of happiness operates constantly and invariably, yet the satisfaction of any particular desire can be suspended from determining the will to any subservient action, till we have maturely examined whether the particular apparent good which we then desire makes a part of our real happiness, or be consistent or inconsistent with it. The result of our judgment upon that examination is what ultimately determines the man; who could not be free if his will were determined by anything but his own desire, guided by his own judgment. I know that liberty, by some, is placed in an indifferency of the man; antecedent to the determination of his will. I wish they who lay so much stress on such an antecedent indifferency, as they call it, had told us plainly, whether this supposed indifferency be antecedent to the thought and judgment of the understanding, as well as to the decree of the will. For it is pretty hard to state it between them, i.e. immediately after the judgment of the understanding, and before the determination of the will: because the determination of the will immediately follows the judgment of the understanding: and to place liberty in an indifferency, antecedent to the thought and judgment of the understanding, seems to me to place liberty in a state of darkness, wherein we can neither see nor say anything of it; at least it places it in a subject incapable of it, no agent being allowed capable of liberty, but in consequence of thought and judgment. I am not nice about phrases, and therefore consent to say with those that love to speak so, that liberty is placed in indifferency, but it is an indifferency which remains after the judgment of the understanding, yea, even after the determination of the will: and that is an indifferency not of the man, (for after he has once judged which is best, viz. to do or forbear, he is no longer indifferent,) but an indifferency of the operative powers of the man, which remaining equally able to operate or to forbear operating after as before the decree of the will, are in a state, which, if one pleases, may be called indifferency; and as far as this indifferency reaches, a man is free, and no further: v.g. I have the ability to move my hand, or to let it rest; that operative power is indifferent to move or not to move my hand. I am then, in that respect perfectly free; my will determines that operative power to rest: I am yet free, because the indifferency of that my operative power to act, or not to act, still remains; the power of moving my hand is not at all impaired by the determination of my will, which at present orders rest; the indifferency of that power to act, or not to act, is just as it was before, as will appear, if the will puts it to the trial, by ordering the contrary. But if, during the rest of my hand, it be seized with a sudden palsy, the indifferency of that operative power is gone, and with it my liberty; I have no longer freedom in that respect, but am under a necessity of letting my hand rest. On the other side, if my hand be put into motion by a convulsion, the indifferency of that operative faculty is taken away by that motion; and my liberty in that case is lost, for I am under a necessity of having my hand move.

I have added this, to show in what sort of indifferency liberty seems to me to consist, and not in any other, real or imaginary.

74. Active and passive power, in motions and in thinking. True notions concerning the nature and extent of liberty are of so great importance, that I hope I shall be pardoned this digression, which my attempt to explain it has led me into. The ideas of will, volition, liberty, and necessity, in this Chapter of Power, came naturally in my way. In a former edition of this Treatise I gave an account of my thoughts concerning them, according to the light I then had. And now, as a lover of truth, and not a worshipper of my own doctrines, I own some change of my opinion; which I think I have discovered ground for. In what I first writ, I with an unbiased indifferency followed truth, whither I thought she led me. But neither being so vain as to fancy infallibility, nor so disingenuous as to dissemble my mistakes for fear of blemishing my reputation, I have, with the same sincere design for truth only, not been ashamed to publish what a severer inquiry has suggested. It is not impossible but that some may think my former notions right; and some (as I have already found) these latter; and some neither. I shall not at all wonder at this variety in men's opinions: impartial deductions of reason in controverted points being so rare, and exact ones in abstract notions not so very easy, especially if of any length. And, therefore, I should think myself not a little beholden to any one, who would, upon these or any other grounds, fairly clear this subject of liberty from any difficulties that may yet remain.

Before I close this chapter, it may perhaps be to our purpose, and help to give us clearer conceptions about power, if we make our thoughts take a little more exact survey of action. I have said above, that we have ideas but of two sorts of action, viz. motion and thinking. These, in truth, though called and counted actions, yet, if nearly considered, will not be found to be always perfectly so. For, if I mistake not, there are instances of both kinds, which, upon due consideration, will be found rather passions than actions; and consequently so far the effects barely of passive powers in those subjects, which yet on their accounts are thought agents. For, in these instances, the substance that hath motion or thought receives the impression, whereby it is put into that action, purely from without, and so acts merely by the capacity it has to receive such an impression from some external agent; and such power is not properly an active power, but a mere passive capacity in the subject. Sometimes the substance or agent puts itself into action by its own power, and this is properly active power. Whatsoever modification a substance has, whereby it produces any effect, that is called action: v.g. a solid substance, by motion, operates on or alters the sensible ideas of another substance, and therefore this modification of motion we call action. But yet this motion in that solid substance is, when rightly considered, but a passion, if it received it only from some external agent. So that the active power of motion is in no substance which cannot begin motion in itself or in another substance when at rest. So likewise in thinking, a power to receive ideas or thoughts from the operation of any external substance is called a power of thinking: but this is but a passive power, or capacity. But to be able to bring into view ideas out of sight at one's own choice, and to compare which of them one thinks fit, this is an active power. This reflection may be of some use to preserve us from mistakes about powers and actions, which grammar, and the common frame of languages, may be apt to lead us into. Since what is signified by verbs that grammarians call active, does not always signify action: v.g. this proposition: I see the moon, or a star, or I feel the heat of the sun, though expressed by a verb active, does not signify any action in me, whereby I operate on those substances, but only the reception of the ideas of light, roundness, and heat; wherein I am not active, but barely passive, and cannot, in that position of my eyes or body, avoid receiving them. But when I turn my eyes another way, or remove my body out of the sunbeams, I am properly active; because of my own choice, by a power within myself, I put myself into that motion. Such an action is the product of active power.

75. Summary of our original ideas. And thus I have, in a short draught, given a view of our original ideas, from whence all the rest are derived, and of which they are made up; which, if I

would consider as a philosopher, and examine on what causes they depend, and of what they are made, I believe they all might be reduced to these very few primary and original ones, viz. Extension, Solidity, Mobility, or the power of being moved; which by our senses we receive from body: Perceptivity, or the power of perception, or thinking; Motivity, or the power of moving: which by reflection we receive from our minds.

I crave leave to make use of these two new words, to avoid the danger of being mistaken in the use of those which are equivocal.

To which if we add Existence, Duration, Number, which belong both to the one and the other, we have, perhaps, all the original ideas on which the rest depend. For by these, I imagine, might be explained the nature of colours, sounds, tastes, smells, and all other ideas we have, if we had but faculties acute enough to perceive the severally modified extensions and motions of these minute bodies, which produce those several sensations in us. But my present purpose being only to inquire into the knowledge the mind has of things, by those ideas and appearances which God has fitted it to receive from them, and how the mind comes by that knowledge; rather than into their causes or manner of production, I shall not, contrary to the design of this Essay, set myself to inquire philosophically into the peculiar constitution of bodies, and the configuration of parts, whereby they have the power to produce in us the ideas of their sensible qualities. I shall not enter any further into that disquisition; it sufficing to my purpose to observe, that gold or saffron has a power to produce in us the idea of yellow, and snow or milk, the idea of white, which we can only have by our sight; without examining the texture of the parts of those bodies, or the particular figures or motion of the particles which rebound from them, to cause in us that particular sensation: though, when we go beyond the bare ideas in our minds, and would inquire into their causes, we cannot conceive anything else to be in any sensible object, whereby it produces different ideas in us, but the different bulk, figure, number, texture, and motion of its insensible parts.

Chapter XXII.Of Mixed Modes

1. Mixed modes, what. Having treated of simple modes in the foregoing chapters, and given several instances of some of the most considerable of them, to show what they are, and how we come by them; we are now in the next place to consider those we call mixed modes; such are the complex ideas we mark by the names obligation, drunkenness, a lie, &c.; which consisting of several combinations of simple ideas of different kinds, I have called mixed modes, to distinguish them from the more simple modes, which consist only of simple ideas of the same kind. These mixed modes, being also such combinations of simple ideas as are not looked upon to be characteristical marks of any real beings that have a steady existence, but scattered and independent ideas put together by the mind, are thereby distinguished from the complex ideas of substances.

2. Made by the mind. That the mind, in respect of its simple ideas, is wholly passive, and receives them all from the existence and operations of things, such as sensation or reflection offers them, without being able to make any one idea, experience shows us. But if we attentively consider these ideas I call mixed modes, we are now speaking of, we shall find their original quite different. The mind often exercises an active power in making these several combinations. For, it being once furnished with simple ideas, it can put them together in several compositions, and so make variety of complex ideas, without examining whether they exist so together in nature. And hence I think it is that these ideas are called notions: as if they had their original, and constant existence, more in the thoughts of men, than in the reality of things; and to form such ideas, it sufficed that the mind put the parts of them together, and that they were consistent in the understanding, without considering whether they had any real being: though I do not deny but several of them might be taken from observation, and the existence of several simple ideas so combined, as they are put together in the understanding.

For the man who first framed the idea of hypocrisy, might have either taken it at first from the observation of one who made show of good qualities which he had not; or else have framed that idea in his mind without having any such pattern to fashion it by. For it is evident that, in the beginning of languages and societies of men, several of those complex ideas, which were consequent to the constitutions established amongst them, must needs have been in the minds of men, before they existed anywhere else; and that many names that stood for such complex ideas were in use, and so those ideas framed, before the combinations they stood for ever existed.

3. Sometimes got by the explication of their names. Indeed, now that languages are made, and abound with words standing for such combinations, an usual way of getting these complex ideas is, by the explication of those terms that stand for them. For, consisting of a company of simple ideas combined, they may, by words standing for those simple ideas, be represented to the mind of one who understands those words, though that complex combination of simple ideas were never offered to his mind by the real existence of things. Thus a man may come to have the idea of sacrilege or murder, by enumerating to him the simple ideas which these words stand for; without ever seeing either of them committed.

4. The name ties the parts of mixed modes into one idea. Every mixed mode consisting of many distinct simple ideas, it seems reasonable to inquire, Whence it has its unity; and how such a precise multitude comes to make but one idea; since that combination does not always exist together in nature? To which I answer, it is plain it has its unity from an act of the mind, combining those several simple ideas together, and considering them as one complex one, consisting of those parts; and the mark of this union, or that which is looked on generally to complete it, is one name given to that combination. For it is by their names that men commonly regulate their account of their distinct species of mixed modes, seldom allowing or considering any number of simple ideas to make one complex one, but such collections as there be names for. Thus, though the killing of an old man be as fit in nature to be united into one complex idea, as the killing a man's father; yet, there being no name standing precisely for the one, as there is the name of parricide to mark the other, it is not taken for a particular complex idea, nor a distinct species of actions from that of killing a young man, or any other man.

5. The cause of making mixed modes. If we should inquire a little further, to see what it is that occasions men to make several combinations of simple ideas into distinct, and, as it were, settled modes, and neglect others, which in the nature of things themselves, have as much an aptness to be combined and make distinct ideas, we shall find the reason of it to be the end of language; which being to mark, or communicate men's thoughts to one another with all the dispatch that may be, they usually make such collections of ideas into complex modes, and affix names to them, as they have frequent use of in their way of living and conversation, leaving others, which they have but seldom an occasion to mention, loose and without names that tie them together: they rather choosing to enumerate (when they have need) such ideas as make them up, by the particular names that stand for them, than to trouble their memories by multiplying of complex ideas with names to them, which they seldom or never have any occasion to make use of.

6. Why words in one language have none answering in another. This shows us how it comes to pass that there are in every language many particular words which cannot be rendered by any one single word of another. For the several fashions, customs, and manners of one nation, making several combinations of ideas familiar and necessary in one, which another people have had never an occasion to make, or perhaps so much as take notice of, names come of course to be annexed to them, to avoid long periphrases in things of daily conversation; and so they become so many distinct complex ideas in their minds. Thus ostrhakismos amongst the Greeks, and proscriptio amongst the Romans, were words which other languages had no names that exactly answered; because they stood for complex ideas which were not in the minds of the men of other nations. Where there was no such custom, there was no notion of

any such actions; no use of such combinations of ideas as were united, and, as it were, tied together, by those terms: and therefore in other countries there were no names for them.

7. And languages change. Hence also we may see the reason, why languages constantly change, take up new and lay by old terms. Because change of customs and opinions bringing with it new combinations of ideas, which it is necessary frequently to think on and talk about, new names, to avoid long descriptions, are annexed to them; and so they become new species of complex modes. What a number of different ideas are by this means wrapped up in one short sound, and how much of our time and breath is thereby saved, any one will see, who will but take the pains to enumerate all the ideas that either reprieve or appeal stand for; and instead of either of those names, use a periphrasis, to make any one understand their meaning.

8. Mixed modes, where they exist. Though I shall have occasion to consider this more at large when I come to treat of Words and their use, yet I could not avoid to take this much notice here of the names of mixed modes; which being fleeting and transient combinations of simple ideas, which have but a short existence anywhere but in the minds of men, and there too have no longer any existence than whilst they are thought on, have not so much anywhere the appearance of a constant and lasting existence as in their names: which are therefore, in this sort of ideas, very apt to be taken for the ideas themselves. For, if we should inquire where the idea of a triumph or apotheosis exists, it is evident they could neither of them exist altogether anywhere in the things themselves, being actions that required time to their performance, and so could never all exist together; and as to the minds of men, where the ideas of these actions are supposed to be lodged, they have there too a very uncertain existence: and therefore we are apt to annex them to the names that excite them in us.

9. How we get the ideas of mixed modes. There are therefore three ways whereby we get these complex ideas of mixed modes:—(1) By experience and observation of things themselves: thus, by seeing two men wrestle or fence, we get the idea of wrestling or fencing. (2) By invention, or voluntary putting together of several simple ideas in our own minds: so he that first invented printing or etching, had an idea of it in his mind before it ever existed. (3) Which is the most usual way, by explaining the names of actions we never saw, or motions we cannot see; and by enumerating, and thereby, as it were, setting before our imaginations all those ideas which go to the making them up, and are the constituent parts of them. For, having by sensation and reflection stored our minds with simple ideas, and by use got the names that stand for them, we can by those means represent to another any complex idea we would have him conceive; so that it has in it no simple ideas but what he knows, and has with us the same name for. For all our complex ideas are ultimately resolvable into simple ideas, of which they are compounded and originally made up, though perhaps their immediate ingredients, as I may so say, are also complex ideas. Thus, the mixed mode which the word lie stands for is made of these simple ideas:—(1) Articulate sounds. (2) Certain ideas in the mind of the speaker. (3) Those words the signs of those ideas. (4) Those signs put together, by affirmation or negation, otherwise than the ideas they stand for are in the mind of the speaker. I think I need not go any further in the analysis of that complex idea we call a lie: what I have said is enough to show that it is made up of simple ideas. And it could not be but an offensive tediousness to my reader, to trouble him with a more minute enumeration of every particular simple idea that goes to this complex one; which, from what has been said, he cannot but be able to make out to himself. The same may be done in all our complex ideas whatsoever; which, however compounded and decompounded, may at last be resolved into simple ideas, which are all the materials of knowledge or thought we have, or can have. Nor shall we have reason to fear that the mind is hereby stinted to too scanty a number of ideas, if we consider what an inexhaustible stock of simple modes number and figure alone afford us. How far then mixed modes, which admit of the various combinations of different simple ideas, and their infinite modes, are from being few and scanty, we may easily imagine. So that, before we have done, we shall see that nobody need be afraid he shall not have scope and compass enough for his thoughts to range in, though they be, as I pretend, confined only to simple ideas, received from

sensation or reflection, and their several combinations.

10. Motion, thinking, and power have been most modified. It is worth our observing, which of all our simple ideas have been most modified, and had most mixed ideas made out of them, with names given to them. And those have been these three:— thinking and motion (which are the two ideas which comprehend in them all action,) and power, from whence these actions are conceived to flow. These simple ideas, I say, of thinking, motion, and power, have been those which have been most modified; and out of whose modifications have been made most complex modes, with names to them. For action being the great business of mankind, and the whole matter about which all laws are conversant, it is no wonder that the several modes of thinking and motion should be taken notice of, the ideas of them observed, and laid up in the memory, and have names assigned to them; without which laws could be but ill made, or vice and disorders repressed. Nor could any communication be well had amongst men without such complex ideas, with names to them: and therefore men have settled names, and supposed settled ideas in their minds, of modes of actions, distinguished by their causes, means, objects, ends, instruments, time, place, and other circumstances; and also of their powers fitted for those actions: v.g. boldness is the power to speak or do what we intend, before others, without fear or disorder; and the Greeks call the confidence of speaking by a peculiar name, parrhesia: which power or ability in man of doing anything, when it has been acquired by frequent doing the same thing, is that idea we name habit; when it is forward, and ready upon every occasion to break into action, we call it disposition. Thus, testiness is a disposition or aptness to be angry.

To conclude: Let us examine any modes of action, v.g. consideration and assent, which are actions of the mind; running and speaking, which are actions of the body; revenge and murder, which are actions of both together, and we shall find them but so many collections of simple ideas, which, together, make up the complex ones signified by those names.

11. Several words seeming to signify action, signify but the effect. Power being the source from whence all action proceeds, the substances wherein these powers are, when they exert this power into act, are called causes, and the substances which thereupon are produced, or the simple ideas which are introduced into any subject by the exerting of that power, are called effects. The efficacy whereby the new substance or idea is produced is called, in the subject exerting that power, action; but in the subject wherein any simple idea is changed or produced, it is called passion: which efficacy, however various, and the effects almost infinite, yet we can, I think, conceive it, in intellectual agents, to be nothing else but modes of thinking and willing; in corporeal agents, nothing else but modifications of motion. I say, I think we cannot conceive it to be any other but these two. For whatever sort of action besides these produce any effects, I confess myself to have no notion nor idea of; and so it is quite remote from my thoughts, apprehensions, and knowledge; and as much in the dark to me as five other senses, or as the ideas of colours to a blind man. And therefore many words which seem to express some action, signify nothing of the action or modus operandi at all, but barely the effect, with some circumstances of the subject wrought on, or cause operating: v.g. creation, annihilation, contain in them no idea of the action or manner whereby they are produced, but barely of the cause, and the thing done. And when a countryman says the cold freezes water, though the word freezing seems to import some action, yet truly it signifies nothing but the effect, viz. that water that was before fluid is become hard and consistent, without containing any idea of the action whereby it is done.

12. Mixed modes made also of other ideas than those of power and action. I think I shall not need to remark here that, though power and action make the greatest part of mixed modes, marked by names, and familiar in the minds and mouths of men, yet other simple ideas, and their several combinations, are not excluded: much less, I think, will it be necessary for me to enumerate all the mixed modes which have been settled, with names to them. That would be to make a dictionary of the greatest part of the words made use of in divinity, ethics, law, and politics, and several other sciences. All that is requisite to my present design, is to show what

sort of ideas those are which I call mixed modes; how the mind comes by them; and that they are compositions made up of simple ideas got from sensation and reflection; which I suppose I have done.

Chapter XXIII.Of our Complex Ideas of Substances

1. Ideas of particular substances, how made. The mind being, as I have declared, furnished with a great number of the simple ideas, conveyed in by the senses as they are found in exterior things, or by reflection on its own operations, takes notice also that a certain number of these simple ideas go constantly together; which being presumed to belong to one thing, and words being suited to common apprehensions, and made use of for quick dispatch, are called, so united in one subject, by one name; which, by inadvertency, we are apt afterward to talk of and consider as one simple idea, which indeed is a complication of many ideas together: because, as I have said, not imagining how these simple ideas can subsist by themselves, we accustom ourselves to suppose some substratum wherein they do subsist, and from which they do result, which therefore we call substance.

2. Our obscure idea of substance in general. So that if any one will examine himself concerning his notion of pure substance in general, he will find he has no other idea of it at all, but only a supposition of he knows not what support of such qualities which are capable of producing simple ideas in us; which qualities are commonly called accidents. If any one should be asked, what is the subject wherein colour or weight inheres, he would have nothing to say, but the solid extended parts; and if he were demanded, what is it that solidity and extension adhere in, he would not be in a much better case than the Indian before mentioned who, saying that the world was supported by a great elephant, was asked what the elephant rested on; to which his answer was — a great tortoise: but being again pressed to know what gave support to the broad-backed tortoise, replied — something, he knew not what. And thus here, as in all other cases where we use words without having clear and distinct ideas, we talk like children: who, being questioned what such a thing is, which they know not, readily give this satisfactory answer, that it is something: which in truth signifies no more, when so used, either by children or men, but that they know not what; and that the thing they pretend to know, and talk of, is what they have no distinct idea of at all, and so are perfectly ignorant of it, and in the dark. The idea then we have, to which we give the general name substance, being nothing but the supposed, but unknown, support of those qualities we find existing, which we imagine cannot subsist sine re substante, without something to support them, we call that support substantia; which, according to the true import of the word, is, in plain English, standing under or upholding.

3. Of the sorts of substances. An obscure and relative idea of substance in general being thus made we come to have the ideas of particular sorts of substances, by collecting such combinations of simple ideas as are, by experience and observation of men's senses, taken notice of to exist together; and are therefore supposed to flow from the particular internal constitution, or unknown essence of that substance. Thus we come to have the ideas of a man, horse, gold, water, &c.; of which substances, whether any one has any other clear idea, further than of certain simple ideas co-existent together, I appeal to every one's own experience. It is the ordinary qualities observable in iron, or a diamond, put together, that make the true complex idea of those substances, which a smith or a jeweller commonly knows better than a philosopher; who, whatever substantial forms he may talk of, has no other idea of those substances, than what is framed by a collection of those simple ideas which are to be found in them: only we must take notice, that our complex ideas of substances, besides all those simple ideas they are made up of, have always the confused idea of something to which they belong, and in which they subsist: and therefore when we speak of any sort of substance, we say it is a thing having such or such qualities; as body is a thing that is extended, figured, and capable of

motion; spirit, a thing capable of thinking; and so hardness, friability, and power to draw iron, we say, are qualities to be found in a loadstone. These, and the like fashions of speaking, intimate that the substance is supposed always something besides the extension, figure, solidity, motion, thinking, or other observable ideas, though we know not what it is.

4. No clear or distinct idea of substance in general. Hence, when we talk or think of any particular sort of corporeal substances, as horse, stone, &c., though the idea we have of either of them be but the complication or collection of those several simple ideas of sensible qualities, which we used to find united in the thing called horse or stone; yet, because we cannot conceive how they should subsist alone, nor one in another, we suppose them existing in and supported by some common subject; which support we denote by the name substance, though it be certain we have no clear or distinct idea of that thing we suppose a support.

5. As clear an idea of spiritual substance as of corporeal substance. The same thing happens concerning the operations of the mind, viz. thinking, reasoning, fearing, &c., which we concluding not to subsist of themselves, nor apprehending how they can belong to body, or be produced by it, we are apt to think these the actions of some other substance, which we call spirit; whereby yet it is evident that, having no other idea or notion of matter, but something wherein those many sensible qualities which affect our senses do subsist; by supposing a substance wherein thinking, knowing, doubting, and a power of moving, &c., do subsist, we have as clear a notion of the substance of spirit, as we have of body; the one being supposed to be (without knowing what it is) the substratum to those simple ideas we have from without; and the other supposed (with a like ignorance of what it is) to be the substratum to those operations we experiment in ourselves within. It is plain then, that the idea of corporeal substance in matter is as remote from our conceptions and apprehensions, as that of spiritual substance, or spirit: and therefore, from our not having any notion of the substance of spirit, we can no more conclude its non-existence, than we can, for the same reason, deny the existence of body; it being as rational to affirm there is no body, because we have no clear and distinct idea of the substance of matter, as to say there is no spirit, because we have no clear and distinct idea of the substance of a spirit.

6. Our ideas of particular sorts of substances. Whatever therefore be the secret abstract nature of substance in general, all the ideas we have of particular distinct sorts of substances are nothing but several combinations of simple ideas, coexisting in such, though unknown, cause of their union, as makes the whole subsist of itself It is by such combinations of simple ideas, and nothing else, that we represent particular sorts of substances to ourselves; such are the ideas we have of their several species in our minds; and such only do we, by their specific names, signify to others, v.g. man, horse, sun, water, iron: upon hearing which words, every one who understands the language, frames in his mind a combination of those several simple ideas which he has usually observed, or fancied to exist together under that denomination; all which he supposes to rest in and be, as it were, adherent to that unknown common subject, which inheres not in anything else. Though, in the meantime, it be manifest, and every one, upon inquiry into his own thoughts, will find, that he has no other idea of any substance, v.g. let it be gold, horse, iron, man, vitriol, bread, but what he has barely of those sensible qualities, which he supposes to inhere; with a supposition of such a substratum as gives, as it were, a support to those qualities or simple ideas, which he has observed to exist united together. Thus, the idea of the sun,— what is it but an aggregate of those several simple ideas, bright, hot, roundish, having a constant regular motion, at a certain distance from us, and perhaps some other: as he who thinks and discourses of the sun has been more or less accurate in observing those sensible qualities, ideas, or properties, which are in that thing which he calls the sun.

7. Their active and passive powers a great part of our complex ideas of substances. For he has the perfectest idea of any of the particular sorts of substances, who has gathered, and put together, most of those simple ideas which do exist in it; among which are to be reckoned its

active powers, and passive capacities, which, though not simple ideas, yet in this respect, for brevity's sake, may conveniently enough be reckoned amongst them. Thus, the power of drawing iron is one of the ideas of the complex one of that substance we call a loadstone; and a power to be so drawn is a part of the complex one we call iron: which powers pass for inherent qualities in those subjects. Because every substance, being as apt, by the powers we observe in it, to change some sensible qualities in other subjects, as it is to produce in us those simple ideas which we receive immediately from it, does, by those new sensible qualities introduced into other subjects, discover to us those powers which do thereby mediately affect our senses, as regularly as its sensible qualities do it immediately: v.g. we immediately by our senses perceive in fire its heat and colour; which are, if rightly considered, nothing but powers in it to produce those ideas in us: we also by our senses perceive the colour and brittleness of charcoal, whereby we come by the knowledge of another power in fire, which it has to change the colour and consistency of wood. By the former, fire immediately, by the latter, it mediately discovers to us these several powers; which therefore we look upon to be a part of the qualities of fire, and so make them a part of the complex idea of it. For all those powers that we take cognizance of, terminating only in the alteration of some sensible qualities in those subjects on which they operate, and so making them exhibit to us new sensible ideas, therefore it is that I have reckoned these powers amongst the simple ideas which make the complex ones of the sort? of substances; though these powers considered in themselves, are truly complex ideas. And in this looser sense I crave leave to be understood, when I name any of these potentialities among the simple ideas which we recollect in our minds when we think of particular substances. For the powers that are severally in them are necessary to be considered, if we will have true distinct notions of the several sorts of substances.

8. And why. Nor are we to wonder that powers make a great part of our complex ideas of substances; since their secondary qualities are those which in most of them serve principally to distinguish substances one from another, and commonly make a considerable part of the complex idea of the several sorts of them. For, our senses failing us in the discovery of the bulk, texture, and figure of the minute parts of bodies, on which their real constitutions and differences depend, we are fain to make use of their secondary qualities as the characteristical notes and marks whereby to frame ideas of them in our minds, and distinguish them one from another: all which secondary qualities, as has been shown, are nothing but bare powers. For the colour and taste of opium are, as well as its soporific or anodyne virtues, mere powers, depending on its primary qualities, whereby it is fitted to produce different operations on different parts of our bodies.

9. Three sorts of ideas make our complex ones of corporeal substances. The ideas that make our complex ones of corporeal substances, are of these three sorts. First, the ideas of the primary qualities of things, which are discovered by our senses, and are in them even when we perceive them not; such are the bulk, figure, number, situation, and motion of the parts of bodies; which are really in them, whether we take notice of them or not. Secondly, the sensible secondary qualities, which, depending on these, are nothing but the powers those substances have to produce several ideas in us by our senses; which ideas are not in the things themselves, otherwise than as anything is in its cause. Thirdly, the aptness we consider in any substance, to give or receive such alterations of primary qualities, as that the substance so altered should produce in us different ideas from what it did before; these are called active and passive powers: all which powers, as far as we have any notice or notion of them, terminate only in sensible simple ideas. For whatever alteration a loadstone has the power to make in the minute particles of iron, we should have no notion of any power it had at all to operate on iron, did not its sensible motion discover it: and I doubt not, but there are a thousand changes, that bodies we daily handle have a power to use in one another, which we never suspect, because they never appear in sensible effects.

10. Powers thus make a great part of our complex ideas of particular substances. Powers therefore justly make a great part of our complex ideas of substances. He that will examine his

complex idea of gold, will find several of its ideas that make it up to be only powers; as the power of being melted, but of not spending itself in the fire; of being dissolved in aqua regia, are ideas as necessary to make up our complex idea of gold, as its colour and weight: which, if duly considered, are also nothing but different powers. For, to speak truly, yellowness is not actually in gold, but is a power in gold to produce that idea in us by our eyes, when placed in a due light: and the heat, which we cannot leave out of our ideas of the sun, is no more really in the sun, than the white colour it introduces into wax. These are both equally powers in the sun, operating, by the motion and figure of its sensible parts, so on a man, as to make him have the idea of heat; and so on wax, as to make it capable to produce in a man the idea of white.

11. The now secondary qualities of bodies would disappear, if we could discover the primary ones of their minute parts. Had we senses acute enough to discern the minute particles of bodies, and the real constitution on which their sensible qualities depend, I doubt not but they would produce quite different ideas in us: and that which is now the yellow colour of gold, would then disappear, and instead of it we should see an admirable texture of parts, of a certain size and figure. This microscopes plainly discover to us; for what to our naked eyes produces a certain colour, is, by thus augmenting the acuteness of our senses, discovered to be quite a different thing; and the thus altering, as it were, the proportion of the bulk of the minute parts of a coloured object to our usual sight, produces different ideas from what it did before. Thus, sand or pounded glass, which is opaque, and white to the naked eye, is pellucid in a microscope; and a hair seen in this way, loses its former colour, and is, in a great measure, pellucid, with a mixture of some bright sparkling colours, such as appear from the refraction of diamonds, and other pellucid bodies. Blood, to the naked eye, appears all red; but by a good microscope, wherein its lesser parts appear, shows only some few globules of red, swimming in a pellucid liquor, and how these red globules would appear, if glasses could be found that could yet magnify them a thousand or ten thousand times more, is uncertain.

12. Our faculties for discovery of the qualities and powers of substances suited to our state. The infinite wise Contriver of us, and all things about us, hath fitted our senses, faculties, and organs, to the conveniences of life, and the business we have to do here. We are able, by our senses, to know and distinguish things: and to examine them so far as to apply them to our uses, and several ways to accommodate the exigences of this life. We have insight enough into their admirable contrivances and wonderful effects, to admire and magnify the wisdom, power, and goodness of their Author. Such a knowledge as this, which is suited to our present condition, we want not faculties to attain. But it appears not that God intended we should have a perfect, clear, and adequate knowledge of them: that perhaps is not in the comprehension of any finite being. We are furnished with faculties (dull and weak as they are) to discover enough in the creatures to lead us to the knowledge of the Creator, and the knowledge of our duty; and we are fitted well enough with abilities to provide for the conveniences of living: these are our business in this world. But were our senses altered, and made much quicker and acuter, the appearance and outward scheme of things would have quite another face to us; and, I am apt to think, would be inconsistent with our being, or at least well-being, in this part of the universe which we inhabit. He that considers how little our constitution is able to bear a remove into parts of this air, not much higher than that we commonly breath in, will have reason to be satisfied, that in this globe of earth allotted for our mansion, the all-wise Architect has suited our organs, and the bodies that are to affect them, one to another. If our sense of hearing were but a thousand times quicker than it is, how would a perpetual noise distract us. And we should in the quietest retirement be less able to sleep or meditate than in the middle of a sea-fight. Nay, if that most instructive of our senses, seeing, were in any man a thousand or a hundred thousand times more acute than it is by the best microscope, things several millions of times less than the smallest object of his sight now would then be visible to his naked eyes, and so he would come nearer to the discovery of the texture and motion of the minute parts of corporeal things; and in many of them, probably get ideas of their internal constitutions: but then he would be in a quite different world from other people: nothing would appear the same

to him and others: the visible ideas of everything would be different. So that I doubt, whether he and the rest of men could discourse concerning the objects of sight, or have any communication about colours, their appearances being so wholly different. And perhaps such a quickness and tenderness of sight could not endure bright sunshine, or so much as open daylight; nor take in but a very small part of any object at once, and that too only at a very near distance. And if by the help of such microscopical eyes (if I may so call them) a man could penetrate further than ordinary into the secret composition and radical texture of bodies, he would not make any great advantage by the change, if such an acute sight would not serve to conduct him to the market and exchange; if he could not see things he was to avoid, at a convenient distance; nor distinguish things he had to do with by those sensible qualities others do. He that was sharp-sighted enough to see the configuration of the minute particles of the spring of a clock, and observe upon what peculiar structure and impulse its elastic motion depends, would no doubt discover something very admirable: but if eyes so framed could not view at once the hand, and the characters of the hour-plate, and thereby at a distance see what o'clock it was, their owner could not be much benefited by that acuteness; which, whilst it discovered the secret contrivance of the parts of the machine, made him lose its use.

13. Conjecture about the corporeal organs of some spirits. And here give me leave to propose an extravagant conjecture of mine, viz. That since we have some reason (if there be any credit to be given to the report of things that our philosophy cannot account for) to imagine, that Spirits can assume to themselves bodies of different bulk, figure, and conformation of parts — whether one great advantage some of them have over us may not lie in this, that they can so frame and shape to themselves organs of sensation or perception, as to suit them to their present design, and the circumstances of the object they would consider. For how much would that man exceed all others in knowledge, who had but the faculty so to alter the structure of his eyes, that one sense, as to make it capable of all the several degrees of vision which the assistance of glasses (casually at first lighted on) has taught us to conceive? What wonders would he discover, who could so fit his eyes to all sorts of objects, as to see when he pleased the figure and motion of the minute particles in the blood, and other juices of animals, as distinctly as he does, at other times, the shape and motion of the animals themselves? But to us, in our present state, unalterable organs, so contrived as to discover the figure and motion of the minute parts of bodies, whereon depend those sensible qualities we now observe in them, would perhaps be of no advantage. God has no doubt made them so as is best for us in our present condition. He hath fitted us for the neighbourhood of the bodies that surround us, and we have to do with; and though we cannot, by the faculties we have, attain to a perfect knowledge of things, yet they will serve us well enough for those ends above-mentioned, which are our great concernment. I beg my reader's pardon for laying before him so wild a fancy concerning the ways of perception of beings above us; but how extravagant soever it be, I doubt whether we can imagine anything about the knowledge of angels but after this manner, some way or other in proportion to what we find and observe in ourselves. And though we cannot but allow that the infinite power and wisdom of God may frame creatures with a thousand other faculties and ways of perceiving things without them than what we have, yet our thoughts can go no further than our own: so impossible it is for us to enlarge our very guesses beyond the ideas received from our own sensation and reflection. The supposition, at least, that angels do sometimes assume bodies, needs not startle us; since some of the most ancient and most learned Fathers of the church seemed to believe that they had bodies: and this is certain, that their state and way of existence is unknown to us.

14. Our specific ideas of substances. But to return to the matter in hand,— the ideas we have of substances, and the ways we come by them. I say, our specific ideas of substances are nothing else but a collection of a certain number of simple ideas, considered as united in one thing. These ideas of substances, though they are commonly simple apprehensions, and the names of them simple terms, yet in effect are complex and compounded. Thus the idea which an Englishman signifies by the name swan, is white colour, long neck, red beak, black legs,

and whole feet, and all these of a certain size, with a power of swimming in the water, and making a certain kind of noise, and perhaps, to a man who has long observed this kind of birds, some other properties: which all terminate in sensible simple ideas, all united in one common subject.

15. Our ideas of spiritual substances, as clear as of bodily substances. Besides the complex ideas we have of material sensible substances, of which I have last spoken,— by the simple ideas we have taken from those operations of our own minds, which we experiment daily in ourselves, as thinking, understanding, willing, knowing, and power of beginning motion, &c., co-existing in some substance, we are able to frame the complex idea of an immaterial spirit. And thus, by putting together the ideas of thinking, perceiving, liberty, and power of moving themselves and other things, we have as clear a perception and notion of immaterial substances as we have of material. For putting together the ideas of thinking and willing, or the power of moving or quieting corporeal motion, joined to substance, of which we have no distinct idea, we have the idea of an immaterial spirit; and by putting together the ideas of coherent solid parts, and a power of being moved, joined with substance, of which likewise we have no positive idea, we have the idea of matter. The one is as clear and distinct an idea as the other: the idea of thinking, and moving a body, being as clear and distinct ideas as the ideas of extension, solidity, and being moved. For our idea of substance is equally obscure, or none at all, in both; it is but a supposed I know not what, to support those ideas we call accidents. It is for want reflection that we are apt to think that our senses show us nothing but material things. Every act of sensation, when duly considered, gives us an equal view of both parts of nature, the corporeal and spiritual. For whilst I know, by seeing or hearing, &c., that there is some corporeal being without me, the object of that sensation, I do more certainly know, that there is some spiritual being within me that sees and hears. This, I must be convinced, cannot be the action of bare insensible matter; nor ever could be, without an immaterial thinking being.

16. No idea of abstract substance either in body or spirit. By the complex idea of extended, figured, coloured, and all other sensible qualities, which is all that we know of it, we are as far from the idea of the substance of body, as if we knew nothing at all: nor after all the acquaintance and familiarity which we imagine we have with matter, and the many qualities men assure themselves they perceive and know in bodies, will it perhaps upon examination be found, that they have any more or clearer primary ideas belonging to body, than they have belonging to immaterial spirit.

17. Cohesion of solid parts and impulse, the primary ideas peculiar to body. The primary ideas we have peculiar to body, as contradistinguished to spirit, are the cohesion of solid, and consequently separable, parts, and a power of communicating motion by impulse. These, I think, are the original ideas proper and peculiar to body; for figure is but the consequence of finite extension.

18. Thinking and motivity the primary ideas peculiar to spirit. The ideas we have belonging and peculiar to spirit, are thinking, and will, or a power of putting body into motion by thought, and, which is consequent to it, liberty. For, as body cannot but communicate its motion by impulse to another body, which it meets with at rest, so the mind can put bodies into motion, or forbear to do so, as it pleases. The ideas of existence, duration, and mobility, are common to them both.

19. Spirits capable of motion. There is no reason why it should be thought strange, that I make mobility belong to spirit; for having no other idea of motion, but change of distance with other beings that are considered as at rest; and finding that spirits, as well as bodies, cannot operate but where they are; and that spirits do operate at several times in several places, I cannot but attribute change of place to all finite spirits: (for of the Infinite Spirit I speak not here). For my soul, being a real being as well as my body, is certainly as capable of changing distance with any other body, or being, as body itself; and so is capable of motion. And if a mathematician can consider a certain distance, or a change of that distance between two points, one may

certainly conceive a distance, and a change of distance, between two spirits; and so conceive their motion, their approach or removal, one from another.

20. Proof of this. Every one finds in himself that his soul can think, will, and operate on his body in the place where that is, but cannot operate on a body, or in a place, an hundred miles distant from it. Nobody can imagine that his soul can think or move a body at Oxford, whilst he is at London; and cannot but know, that, being united to his body, it constantly changes place all the whole journey between Oxford and London, as the coach or horse does that carries him, and I think may be said to be truly all that while in motion: or if that will not be allowed to afford us a clear idea enough of its motion, its being separated from the body in death, I think, will; for to consider it as going out of the body, or leaving it, and yet to have no idea of its motion, seems to me impossible.

21. God immoveable, because infinite. If it be said by any one that it cannot change place, because it hath none, for the spirits are not in loco, but ubi; I suppose that way of talking will not now be of much weight to many, in an age that is not much disposed to admire, or suffer themselves to be deceived by such unintelligible ways of speaking. But if any one thinks there is any sense in that distinction, and that it is applicable to our present purpose, I desire him to put it into intelligible English; and then from thence draw a reason to show that immaterial spirits are not capable of motion. Indeed motion cannot be attributed to God; not because he is an immaterial, but because he is an infinite spirit.

22. Our complex idea of an immaterial spirit and our complex idea of body compared. Let us compare, then, our complex idea of an immaterial spirit with our complex idea of body, and see whether there be any more obscurity in one than in the other, and in which most. Our idea of body, as I think, is an extended solid substance, capable of communicating motion by impulse: and our idea of soul, as an immaterial spirit, is of a substance that thinks, and has a power of exciting motion in body, by willing, or thought. These, I think, are our complex ideas of soul and body, as contradistinguished; and now let us examine which has most obscurity in it, and difficulty to be apprehended. I know that people whose thoughts are immersed in matter, and have so subjected their minds to their senses that they seldom reflect on anything beyond them, are apt to say, they cannot comprehend a thinking thing, which perhaps is true: but I affirm, when they consider it well, they can no more comprehend an extended thing.

23. Cohesion of solid parts in body as hard to be conceived as thinking in a soul. If any one says he knows not what it is thinks in him, he means he knows not what the substance is of that thinking thing: No more, say I, knows he what the substance is of that solid thing. Further, if he says he knows not how he thinks, I answer, Neither knows he how he is extended, how the solid parts of body are united, or cohere together to make extension. For though the pressure of the particles of air may account for the cohesion of several parts of matter that are grosser than the particles of air, and have pores less than the corpuscles of air, yet the weight or pressure of the air will not explain, nor can be a cause of the coherence of the particles of air themselves. And if the pressure of the aether, or any subtiler matter than the air, may unite, and hold fast together, the parts of a particle of air, as well as other bodies, yet it cannot make bonds for itself, and hold together the parts that make up every the least corpuscle of that materia subtilis. So that that hypothesis, how ingeniously soever explained, by showing that the parts of sensible bodies are held together by the pressure of other external insensible bodies, reaches not the parts of the aether itself; and by how much the more evident it proves, that the parts of other bodies are held together by the external pressure of the aether, and can have no other conceivable cause of their cohesion and union, by so much the more it leaves us in the dark concerning the cohesion of the parts of the corpuscles of the aether itself: which we can neither conceive without parts, they being bodies, and divisible, nor yet how their parts cohere, they wanting that cause of cohesion which is given of the cohesion of the parts of all other bodies.

24. Not explained by an ambient fluid. But, in truth, the pressure of any ambient fluid, how great soever, can be no intelligible cause of the cohesion of the solid parts of matter. For,

though such a pressure may hinder the avulsion of two polished superficies, one from another, in a line perpendicular to them, as in the experiment of two polished marbles; yet it can never in the least hinder the separation by a motion, in a line parallel to those surfaces. Because the ambient fluid, having a full liberty to succeed in each point of space, deserted by a lateral motion, resists such a motion of bodies, so joined, no more than it would resist the motion of that body were it on all sides environed by that fluid, and touched no other body; and therefore, if there were no other cause of cohesion, all parts of bodies must be easily separable by such a lateral sliding motion. For if the pressure of the aether be the adequate cause of cohesion, wherever that cause operates not, there can be no cohesion. And since it cannot operate against a lateral separation, (as has been shown), therefore in every imaginary plane, intersecting any mass of matter, there could be no more cohesion than of two polished surfaces, which will always, notwithstanding any imaginable pressure of a fluid, easily slide one from another. So that perhaps, how clear an idea soever we think we have of the extension of body, which is nothing but the cohesion of solid parts, he that shall well consider it in his mind, may have reason to conclude, That it is as easy for him to have a clear idea how the soul thinks as how body is extended. For, since body is no further, nor otherwise, extended, than by the union and cohesion of its solid parts, we shall very ill comprehend the extension of body, without understanding wherein consists the union and cohesion of its parts; which seems to me as incomprehensible as the manner of thinking, and how it is performed.

25. We can as little understand how the parts cohere in extension, as how our spirits perceive or move. I allow it is usual for most people to wonder how any one should find a difficulty in what they think they every day observe. Do we not see (will they be ready to say) the parts of bodies stick firmly together? Is there anything more common? And what doubt can there be made of it? And the like, I say, concerning thinking and voluntary motion. Do we not every moment experiment it in ourselves, and therefore can it be doubted? The matter of fact is clear, I confess; but when we would a little nearer look into it, and consider how it is done, there I think we are at a loss, both in the one and the other; and can as little understand how the parts of body cohere, as how we ourselves perceive or move. I would have any one intelligibly explain to me, how the parts of gold, or brass, (that but now in fusion were as loose from one another as the particles of water, or the sands of an hour-glass), come in a few moments to be so united, and adhere so strongly one to another, that the utmost force of men's arms cannot separate them? A considering man will, I suppose, be here at a loss to satisfy his own, or another man's understanding.

26. The cause of coherence of atoms in extended substances incomprehensible. The little bodies that compose that fluid we call water, are so extremely small, that I have never heard of any one, who, by a microscope, (and yet I have heard of some that have magnified to ten thousand; nay, to much above a hundred thousand times), pretended to perceive their distinct bulk, figure, or motion; and the particles of water are also so perfectly loose one from another, that the least force sensibly separates them. Nay, if we consider their perpetual motion, we must allow them to have no cohesion one with another; and yet let but a sharp cold come, and they unite, they consolidate; these little atoms cohere, and are not, without great force, separable. He that could find the bonds that tie these heaps of loose little bodies together so firmly; he that could make known the cement that makes them stick so fast one to another, would discover a great and yet unknown secret: and yet when that was done, would he be far enough from making the extension of body (which is the cohesion of its solid parts) intelligible, till he could show wherein consisted the union, or consolidation of the parts of those bonds, or of that cement, or of the least particle of matter that exists. Whereby it appears that this primary and supposed obvious quality of body will be found, when examined, to be as incomprehensible as anything belonging to our minds, and a solid extended substance as hard to be conceived as a thinking immaterial one, whatever difficulties some would raise against it.

27. The supposed pressure brought to explain cohesion is unintelligible. For, to extend our

thoughts a little further, that pressure which is brought to explain the cohesion of bodies is as unintelligible as the cohesion itself. For if matter be considered, as no doubt it is, finite, let any one send his contemplation to the extremities of the universe, and there see what conceivable hoops, what bond he can imagine to hold this mass of matter in so close a pressure together; from whence steel has its firmness, and the parts of a diamond their hardness and indissolubility. If matter be finite, it must have its extremes; and there must be something to hinder it from scattering asunder. If, to avoid this difficulty, any one will throw himself into the supposition and abyss of infinite matter, let him consider what light he thereby brings to the cohesion of body, and whether he be ever the nearer making it intelligible, by resolving it into a supposition the most absurd and most incomprehensible of all other: so far is our extension of body (which is nothing but the cohesion of solid parts) from being clearer, or more distinct, when we would inquire into the nature, cause, or manner of it, than the idea of thinking.

28. Communication of motion by impulse, or by thought, equally unintelligible. Another idea we have of body is, the power of communication of motion by impulse; and of our souls, the power of exciting motion by thought. These ideas, the one of body, the other of our minds, every day's experience clearly furnishes us with: but if here again we inquire how this is done, we are equally in the dark. For, in the communication of motion by impulse, wherein as much motion is lost to one body as is got to the other, which is the ordinariest case, we can have no other conception, but of the passing of motion out of one body into another; which, I think, is as obscure and inconceivable as how our minds move or stop our bodies by thought, which we every moment find they do. The increase of motion by impulse, which is observed or believed sometimes to happen, is yet harder to be understood. We have by daily experience clear evidence of motion produced both by impulse and by thought; but the manner how, hardly comes within our comprehension: we are equally at a loss in both. So that, however we consider motion, and its communication, either from body or spirit, the idea which belongs to spirit is at least as clear as that which belongs to body. And if we consider the active power of moving, or, as I may call it, motivity, it is much clearer in spirit than body; since two bodies, placed by one another at rest, will never afford us the idea of a power in the one to move the other, but by a borrowed motion: whereas the mind every day affords us ideas of an active power of moving of bodies; and therefore it is worth our consideration, whether active power be not the proper attribute of spirits, and passive power of matter. Hence may be conjectured that created spirits are not totally separate from matter, because they are both active and passive. Pure spirit, viz. God, is only active; pure matter is only passive; those beings that are both active and passive, we may judge to partake of both. But be that as it will, I think, we have as many and as clear ideas belonging to spirit as we have belonging to body, the substance of each being equally unknown to us; and the idea of thinking in spirit, as clear as of extension in body; and the communication of motion by thought, which we attribute to spirit, is as evident as that by impulse, which we ascribe to body. Constant experience makes us sensible of both these, though our narrow understandings can comprehend neither. For, when the mind would look beyond those original ideas we have from sensation or reflection, and penetrate into their causes, and manner of production, we find still it discovers nothing but its own short-sightedness.

29. Summary. To conclude. Sensation convinces us that there are solid extended substances; and reflection, that there are thinking ones: experience assures us of the existence of such beings, and that the one hath a power to move body by impulse, the other by thought; this we cannot doubt of. Experience, I say, every moment furnishes us with the clear ideas both of the one and the other. But beyond these ideas, as received from their proper sources, our faculties will not reach. If we would inquire further into their nature, causes, and manner, we perceive not the nature of extension clearer than we do of thinking. If we would explain them any further, one is as easy as the other; and there is no more difficulty to conceive how a substance we know not should, by thought, set body into motion, than how a substance we know not

should, by impulse, set body into motion. So that we are no more able to discover wherein the ideas belonging to body consist, than those belonging to spirit. From whence it seems probable to me, that the simple ideas we receive from sensation and reflection are the boundaries of our thoughts; beyond which the mind, whatever efforts it would make, is not able to advance one jot; nor can it make any discoveries, when it would pry into the nature and hidden causes of those ideas.

30. Our idea of spirit and our idea of body compared. So that, in short, the idea we have of spirit, compared with the idea we have of body, stands thus: the substance of spirits is unknown to us; and so is the substance of body equally unknown to us. Two primary qualities or properties of body, viz. solid coherent parts and impulse, we have distinct clear ideas of: so likewise we know, and have distinct clear ideas, of two primary qualities or properties of spirit, viz. thinking, and a power of action; i.e. a power of beginning or stopping several thoughts or motions. We have also the ideas of several qualities inherent in bodies, and have the clear distinct ideas of them; which qualities are but the various modifications of the extension of cohering solid parts, and their motion. We have likewise the ideas of the several modes of thinking viz. believing, doubting, intending, fearing, hoping; all which are but the several modes of thinking. We have also the ideas of willing, and moving the body consequent to it, and with the body itself too; for, as has been shown, spirit is capable of motion.

31. The notion of spirit involves no more difficulty in it than that of body. Lastly, if this notion of immaterial spirit may have, perhaps, some difficulties in it not easily to be explained, we have therefore no more reason to deny or doubt the existence of such spirits, than we have to deny or doubt the existence of body; because the notion of body is cumbered with some difficulties very hard, and perhaps impossible to be explained or understood by us. For I would fain have instanced anything in our notion of spirit more perplexed, or nearer a contradiction, than the very notion of body includes in it; the divisibility in infinitum of any finite extension involving us, whether we grant or deny it, in consequences impossible to be explicated or made in our apprehensions consistent; consequences that carry greater difficulty, and more apparent absurdity, than anything can follow from the notion of an immaterial knowing substance.

32. We know nothing of things beyond our simple ideas of them. Which we are not at all to wonder at, since we having but some few superficial ideas of things, discovered to us only by the senses from without, or by the mind, reflecting on what it experiments in itself within, have no knowledge beyond that, much less of the internal constitution, and true nature of things, being destitute of faculties to attain it. And therefore experimenting and discovering in ourselves knowledge, and the power of voluntary motion, as certainly as we experiment, or discover in things without us, the cohesion and separation of solid parts, which is the extension and motion of bodies; we have as much reason to be satisfied with our notion of immaterial spirit, as with our notion of body, and the existence of the one as well as the other. For it being no more a contradiction that thinking should exist separate and independent from solidity, than it is a contradiction that solidity should exist separate and independent from thinking, they being both but simple ideas, independent one from another: and having as clear and distinct ideas in us of thinking, as of solidity, I know not why we may not as well allow a thinking thing without solidity, i.e. immaterial, to exist, as a solid thing without thinking, i.e. matter, to exist; especially since it is not harder to conceive how thinking should exist without matter, than how matter should think. For whensoever we would proceed beyond these simple ideas we have from sensation and reflection, and dive further into the nature of things, we fall presently into darkness and obscurity, perplexedness and difficulties, and can discover nothing further but our own blindness and ignorance. But whichever of these complex ideas be clearest, that of body, or immaterial spirit, this is evident, that the simple ideas that make them up are no other than what we have received from sensation or reflection: and so is it of all our other ideas of substances, even of God himself.

33. Our complex idea of God. For if we examine the idea we have of the incomprehensible

Supreme Being, we shall find that we come by it the same way; and that the complex ideas we have both of God, and separate spirits, are made of the simple ideas we receive from reflection: v.g. having, from what we experiment in ourselves, got the ideas of existence and duration; of knowledge and power; of pleasure and happiness; and of several other qualities and powers, which it is better to have than to be without; when we would frame an idea the most suitable we can to the Supreme Being, we enlarge every one of these with our idea of infinity; and so putting them together, make our complex idea of God. For that the mind has such a power of enlarging some of its ideas, received from sensation and reflection, has been already shown.

34. Our complex idea of God as infinite. If I find that I know some few things, and some of them, or all, perhaps imperfectly, I can frame an idea of knowing twice as many; which I can double again, as often as I can add to number; and thus enlarge my idea of knowledge, by extending its comprehension to all things existing, or possible. The same also I can do of knowing them more perfectly; i.e. all their qualities, powers, causes, consequences, and relations, &c., till all be perfectly known that is in them, or can any way relate to them: and thus frame the idea of infinite or boundless knowledge. The same may also be done of power, till we come to that we call infinite; and also of the duration of existence, without beginning or end, and so frame the idea of an eternal being. The degrees or extent wherein we ascribe existence, power, wisdom, and all other perfections (which we can have any ideas of) to that sovereign Being, which we call God, being all boundless and infinite, we frame the best idea of him our minds are capable of: all which is done, I say, by enlarging those simple ideas we have taken from the operations of our own minds, by reflection; or by our senses, from exterior things, to that vastness to which infinity can extend them.

35. God in his own essence incognisable. For it is infinity, which, joined to our ideas of existence, power, knowledge, &c., makes that complex idea, whereby we represent to ourselves, the best we can, the Supreme Being. For, though in his own essence (which certainly we do not know, not knowing the real essence of a pebble, or a fly, or of our own selves) God be simple and uncompounded; yet I think I may say we have no other idea of him, but a complex one of existence, knowledge, power, happiness, &c., infinite and eternal: which are all distinct ideas, and some of them, being relative, are again compounded of others: all which being, as has been shown, originally got from sensation and reflection, go to make up the idea or notion we have of God.

36. No ideas in our complex ideas of spirits, but those got from sensation or reflection. This further is to be observed, that there is no idea we attribute to God, bating infinity, which is not also a part of our complex idea of other spirits. Because, being capable of no other simple ideas, belonging to anything but body, but those which by reflection we receive from the operation of our own minds, we can attribute to spirits no other but what we receive from thence: and all the difference we can put between them, in our contemplation of spirits, is only in the several extents and degrees of their knowledge, power, duration, happiness, &c. For that in our ideas, as well of spirits as of other things, we are restrained to those we receive from sensation and reflection, is evident from hence,— That, in our ideas of spirits, how much soever advanced in perfection beyond those of bodies, even to that of infinite, we cannot yet have any idea of the manner wherein they discover their thoughts one to another: though we must necessarily conclude that separate spirits, which are beings that have perfecter knowledge and greater happiness than we, must needs have also a perfecter way of communicating their thoughts than we have, who are fain to make use of corporeal signs, and particular sounds; which are therefore of most general use, as being the best and quickest we are capable of. But of immediate communication having no experiment in ourselves, and consequently no notion of it at all, we have no idea how spirits, which use not words, can with quickness, or much less how spirits that have no bodies can be masters of their own thoughts, and communicate or conceal them at pleasure, though we cannot but necessarily suppose they have such a power.

37. Recapitulation. And thus we have seen what kind of ideas we have of substances of all kinds, wherein they consist, and how we came by them. From whence, I think, it is very evident,

First, That all our ideas of the several sorts of substances are nothing but collections of simple ideas: with a supposition of something to which they belong, and in which they subsist: though of this supposed something we have no clear distinct idea at all.

Secondly, That all the simple ideas, that thus united in one common substratum, make up our complex ideas of several sorts of substances, are no other but such as we have received from sensation or reflection. So that even in those which we think we are most intimately acquainted with, and that come nearest the comprehension of our most enlarged conceptions, we cannot go beyond those simple ideas. And even in those which seem most remote from all we have to do with, and do infinitely surpass anything we can perceive in ourselves by reflection; or discover by sensation in other things, we can attain to nothing but those simple ideas, which we originally received from sensation or reflection; as is evident in the complex ideas we have of angels, and particularly of God himself.

Thirdly, That most of the simple ideas that make up our complex ideas of substances, when truly considered, are only powers, however we are apt to take them for positive qualities; v.g. the greatest part of the ideas that make our complex idea of gold are yellowness, great weight, ductility, fusibility, and solubility in aqua regia, &c., all united together in an unknown substratum: all which ideas are nothing else but so many relations to other substances; and are not really in the gold, considered barely in itself, though they depend on those real and primary qualities of its internal constitution, whereby it has a fitness differently to operate, and be operated on by several other substances.

Chapter XXIV.Of Collective Ideas of Substances

1. A collective idea is one idea. Besides these complex ideas of several single substances, as of man, horse, gold, violet, apple, &c., the mind hath also complex collective ideas of substances; which I so call, because such ideas are made up of many particular substances considered together, as united into one idea, and which so joined are looked on as one; v.g. the idea of such a collection of men as make an army, though consisting of a great number of distinct substances, is as much one idea as the idea of a man: and the great collective idea of all bodies whatsoever, signified by the name world, is as much one idea as the idea of any the least particle of matter in it; it sufficing to the unity of any idea, that it be considered as one representation or picture, though made up of ever so many particulars.

2. Made by the power of composing in the mind. These collective ideas of substances the mind makes, by its power of composition, and uniting severally either simple or complex ideas into one, as it does, by the same faculty, make the complex ideas of particular substances, consisting of an aggregate of divers simple ideas, united in one substance. And as the mind, by putting together the repeated ideas of unity, makes the collective mode, or complex idea, of any number, as a score, or a gross, &c.,— so, by putting together several particular substances, it makes collective ideas of substances, as a troop, an army, a swarm, a city, a fleet; each of which every one finds that he represents to his own mind by one idea, in one view; and so under that notion considers those several things as perfectly one, as one ship, or one atom. Nor is it harder to conceive how an army of ten thousand men should make one idea, than how a man should make one idea; it being as easy to the mind to unite into one the idea of a great number of men, and consider it as one, as it is to unite into one particular all the distinct ideas that make up the composition of a man, and consider them all together as one.

3. Artificial things that are made up of distinct substances are our collective ideas. Amongst such kind of collective ideas are to be counted most part of artificial things, at least such of them as are made up of distinct substances: and, in truth, if we consider all these collective

ideas aright, as army, constellation, universe, as they are united into so many single ideas, they are but the artificial draughts of the mind; bringing things very remote, and independent on one another, into one view, the better to contemplate and discourse of them, united into one conception, and signified by one name. For there are no things so remote, nor so contrary, which the mind cannot, by this art of composition, bring into one idea; as is visible in that signified by the name universe.

Chapter XXV.Of Relation

1. Relation, what. Besides the ideas, whether simple or complex, that the mind has of things as they are in themselves, there are others it gets from their comparison one with another. The understanding, in the consideration of anything, is not confined to that precise object: it can carry an idea as it were beyond itself, or at least look beyond it, to see how it stands in conformity to any other. When the mind so considers one thing, that it does as it were bring it to, and set it by another, and carries its view from one to the other — this is, as the words import, relation and respect; and the denominations given to positive things, intimating that respect, and serving as marks to lead the thoughts beyond the subject itself denominated to something distinct from it, are what we call relatives; and the things so brought together, related. Thus, when the mind considers Caius as such a positive being, it takes nothing into that idea but what really exists in Caius; v.g. when I consider him as a man, I have nothing in my mind but the complex idea of the species, man. So likewise, when I say Caius is a white man, I have nothing but the bare consideration of a man who hath that white colour. But when I give Caius the name husband, I intimate some other person; and when I give him the name whiter, I intimate some other thing: in both cases my thought is led to something beyond Caius, and there are two things brought into consideration. And since any idea, whether simple or complex, may be the occasion why the mind thus brings two things together, and as it were takes a view of them at once, though still considered as distinct: therefore any of our ideas may be the foundation of relation. As in the above-mentioned instance, the contract and ceremony of marriage with Sempronia is the occasion of the denomination and relation of husband; and the colour white the occasion why he is said to be whiter than free-stone.
2. Ideas of relations without correlative terms, not easily apprehended. These and the like relations, expressed by relative terms that have others answering them, with a reciprocal intimation, as father and son, bigger and less, cause and effect, are very obvious to every one, and everybody at first sight perceives the relation. For father and son, husband and wife, and such other correlative terms, seem so nearly to belong one to another, and, through custom, do so readily chime and answer one another in people's memories, that, upon the naming of either of them, the thoughts are presently carried beyond the thing so named; and nobody overlooks or doubts of a relation, where it is so plainly intimated. But where languages have failed to give correlative names, there the relation is not always so easily taken notice of. Concubine is, no doubt, a relative name, as well as a wife: but in languages where this and the like words have not a correlative term, there people are not so apt to take them to be so, as wanting that evident mark of relation which is between correlatives, which seem to explain one another, and not to be able to exist, but together. Hence it is, that many of those names, which, duly considered, do include evident relations, have been called external denominations. But all names that are more than empty sounds must signify some idea, which is either in the thing to which the name is applied, and then it is positive, and is looked on as united to and existing in the thing to which the denomination is given; or else it arises from the respect the mind finds in it to something distinct from it, with which it considers it, and then it includes a relation.
3. Some seemingly absolute terms contain relations. Another sort of relative terms there is, which are not looked on to be either relative, or so much as external denominations: which yet, under the form and appearance of signifying something absolute in the subject, do conceal a

tacit, though less observable, relation. Such are the seemingly positive terms of old, great, imperfect, &c., whereof I shall have occasion to speak more at large in the following chapters.
4. Relation different from the things related. This further may be observed, That the ideas of relation may be the same in men who have far different ideas of the things that are related, or that are thus compared: v.g. those who have far different ideas of a man, may yet agree in the notion of a father; which is a notion superinduced to the substance, or man, and refers only to an act of that thing called man whereby he contributed to the generation of one of his own kind, let man be what it will.
5. Change of relation may be without any change in the things related. The nature therefore of relation consists in the referring or comparing two things one to another; from which comparison one or both comes to be denominated. And if either of those things be removed, or cease to be, the relation ceases, and the denomination consequent to it, though the other receive in itself no alteration at all: v.g. Caius, whom I consider to-day as a father, ceases to be so to-morrow, only by the death of his son, without any alteration made in himself. Nay, barely by the mind's changing the object to which it compares anything, the same thing is capable of having contrary denominations at the same time: v.g. Caius, compared to several persons, may be truly be said to be older and younger, stronger and weaker, &c.
6. Relation only betwixt two things. Whatsoever doth or can exist, or be considered as one thing is positive: and so not only simple ideas and substances, but modes also, are positive beings: though the parts of which they consist are very often relative one to another: but the whole together considered as one thing, and producing in us the complex idea of one thing, which idea is in our minds, as one picture, though an aggregate of divers parts, and under one name, it is a positive or absolute thing, or idea. Thus a triangle, though the parts thereof compared one to another be relative, yet the idea of the whole is a positive absolute idea. The same may be said of a family, a tune, &c.; for there can be no relation but betwixt two things considered as two things. There must always be in relation two ideas or things, either in themselves really separate, or considered as distinct, and then a ground or occasion for their comparison.
7. All things capable of relation. Concerning relation in general, these things may be considered:
First, That there is no one thing, whether simple idea, substance, mode, or relation, or name of either of them, which is not capable of almost an infinite number of considerations in reference to other things: and therefore this makes no small part of men's thoughts and words: v.g. one single man may at once be concerned in, and sustain all these following relations, and many more, viz. father, brother, son, grandfather, grandson, father-in-law, son-in-law, husband, friend, enemy, subject, general, judge, patron, client, professor, European, Englishman, islander, servant, master, possessor, captain, superior, inferior, bigger, less, older, younger, contemporary, like, unlike, &c., to an almost infinite number: he being capable of as many relations as there can be occasions of comparing him to other things, in any manner of agreement, disagreement, or respect whatsoever. For, as I said, relation is a way of comparing or considering two things together, and giving one or both of them some appellation from that comparison; and sometimes giving even the relation itself a name.
8. Our ideas of relations often clearer than of the subjects related. Secondly, This further may be considered concerning relation, that though it be not contained in the real existence of things, but something extraneous and superinduced, yet the ideas which relative words stand for are often clearer and more distinct than of those substances to which they do belong. The notion we have of a father or brother is a great deal clearer and more distinct than that we have of a man; or, if you will, paternity is a thing whereof it is easier to have a clear idea, than of humanity; and I can much easier conceive what a friend is, than what God; because the knowledge of one action, or one simple idea, is oftentimes sufficient to give me the notion of a relation; but to the knowing of any substantial being, an accurate collection of sundry ideas is necessary. A man, if he compares two things together, can hardly be supposed not to know

what it is wherein he compares them: so that when he compares any things together, he cannot but have a very clear idea of that relation. The ideas, then, of relations, are capable at least of being more perfect and distinct in our minds than those of substances. Because it is commonly hard to know all the simple ideas which are really in any substance, but for the most part easy enough to know the simple ideas that make up any relation I think on, or have a name for: v.g. comparing two men in reference to one common parent, it is very easy to frame the ideas of brothers, without having yet the perfect idea of a man. For significant relative words, as well as others, standing only for ideas; and those being all either simple, or made up of simple ones, it suffices for the knowing the precise idea the relative term stands for, to have a clear conception of that which is the foundation of the relation; which may be done without having a perfect and clear idea of the thing it is attributed to. Thus, having the notion that one laid the egg out of which the other was hatched, I have a clear idea of the relation of dam and chick between the two cassiowaries in St. James's Park; though perhaps I have but a very obscure and imperfect idea of those birds themselves.

9. Relations all terminate in simple ideas. Thirdly, Though there be a great number of considerations wherein things may be compared one with another, and so a multitude of relations, yet they all terminate in, and are concerned about those simple ideas, either of sensation or reflection, which I think to be the whole materials of all our knowledge. To clear this, I shall show it in the most considerable relations that we have any notion of; and in some that seem to be the most remote from sense or reflection: which yet will appear to have their ideas from thence, and leave it past doubt that the notions we have of them are but certain simple ideas, and so originally derived from sense or reflection.

10. Terms leading the mind beyond the subject denominated, are relative. Fourthly, That relation being the considering of one thing with another which is extrinsical to it, it is evident that all words that necessarily lead the mind to any other ideas than are supposed really to exist in that thing to which the words are applied are relative words: v.g. a man, black, merry, thoughtful, thirsty, angry, extended; these and the like are all absolute, because they neither signify nor intimate anything but what does or is supposed really to exist in the man thus denominated; but father, brother, king, husband, blacker, merrier, &c., are words which, together with the thing they denominate, imply also something else separate and exterior to the existence of that thing.

11. All relatives made up of simple ideas. Having laid down these premises concerning relation in general, I shall now proceed to show, in some instances, how all the ideas we have of relation are made up, as the others are, only of simple ideas; and that they all, how refined or remote from sense soever they seem, terminate at last in simple ideas. I shall begin with the most comprehensive relation, wherein all things that do, or can exist, are concerned, and that is the relation of cause and effect: the idea whereof, how derived from the two fountains of all our knowledge, sensation and reflection, I shall in the next place consider.

Chapter XXVI. Of Cause and Effect, and other Relations

1. Whence the ideas of cause and effect got. In the notice that our senses take of the constant vicissitude of things, we cannot but observe that several particular, both qualities and substances, begin to exist; and that they receive this their existence from the due application and operation of some other being. From this observation we get our ideas of cause and effect. That which produces any simple or complex idea we denote by the general name, cause, and that which is produced, effect. Thus, finding that in that substance which we call wax, fluidity, which is a simple idea that was not in it before, is constantly produced by the application of a certain degree of heat we call the simple idea of heat, in relation to fluidity in wax, the cause of it, and fluidity the effect. So also, finding that the substance, wood, which is a certain collection of simple ideas so called, by the application of fire, is turned into another substance,

called ashes; i.e., another complex idea, consisting of a collection of simple ideas, quite different from that complex idea which we call wood; we consider fire, in relation to ashes, as cause, and the ashes, as effect. So that whatever is considered by us to conduce or operate to the producing any particular simple idea, or collection of simple ideas, whether substance or mode, which did not before exist, hath thereby in our minds the relation of a cause, and so is denominated by us.

2. Creation, generation, making, alteration. Having thus, from what our senses are able to discover in the operations of bodies on one another, got the notion of cause and effect, viz. that a cause is that which makes any other thing, either simple idea, substance, or mode, begin to be; and an effect is that which had its beginning from some other thing; the mind finds no great difficulty to distinguish the several originals of things into two sorts:—

First, When the thing is wholly made new, so that no part thereof did ever exist before; as when a new particle of matter doth begin to exist, in rerum natura, which had before no being, and this we call creation.

Secondly, When a thing is made up of particles, which did all of them before exist; but that very thing, so constituted of pre-existing particles, which, considered all together, make up such a collection of simple ideas, had not any existence before, as this man, this egg, rose, or cherry, &c. And this, when referred to a substance, produced in the ordinary course of nature by internal principle, but set on work by, and received from, some external agent, or cause, and working by insensible ways which we perceive not, we call generation. When the cause is extrinsical, and the effect produced by a sensible separation, or juxta-position of discernible parts, we call it making; and such are all artificial things. When any simple idea is produced, which was not in that subject before, we call it alteration. Thus a man is generated, a picture made; and either of them altered, when any new sensible quality or simple idea is produced in either of them, which was not there before: and the things thus made to exist, which were not there before, are effects; and those things which operated to the existence, causes. In which, and all other cases, we may observe, that the notion of cause and effect has its rise from ideas received by sensation or reflection; and that this relation, how comprehensive soever, terminates at last in them. For to have the idea of cause and effect, it suffices to consider any simple idea or substance, as beginning to exist, by the operation of some other, without knowing the manner of that operation.

3. Relations of time. Time and place are also the foundations of very large relations; and all finite beings at least are concerned in them. But having already shown in another place how we get those ideas, it may suffice here to intimate, that most of the denominations of things received from time are only relations. Thus, when any one says that Queen Elizabeth lived sixty-nine, and reigned forty-five years, these words import only the relation of that duration to some other, and mean no more but this, That the duration of her existence was equal to sixty-nine, and the duration of her government to forty-five annual revolutions of the sun; and so are all words, answering, How Long? Again, William the Conqueror invaded England about the year 1066; which means this, That, taking the duration from our Saviour's time till now for one entire great length of time, it shows at what distance this invasion was from the two extremes; and so do all words of time answering to the question, When, which show only the distance of any point of time from the period of a longer duration, from which we measure, and to which we thereby consider it as related.

4. Some ideas of time supposed positive and found to be relative. There are yet, besides those, other words of time, that ordinarily are thought to stand for positive ideas, which yet will, when considered, be found to be relative; such as are, young, old, &c., which include and intimate the relation anything has to a certain length of duration, whereof we have the idea in our minds. Thus, having settled in our thoughts the idea of the ordinary duration of a man to be seventy years, when we say a man is young, we mean that his age is yet but a small part of that which usually men attain to; and when we denominate him old, we mean that his duration is run out almost to the end of that which men do not usually exceed. And so it is but

comparing the particular age or duration of this or that man, to the idea of that duration which we have in our minds, as ordinarily belonging to that sort of animals: which is plain in the application of these names to other things; for a man is called young at twenty years, and very young at seven years old: but yet a horse we call old at twenty, and a dog at seven years, because in each of these we compare their age to different ideas of duration, which are settled in our minds as belonging to these several sorts of animals, in the ordinary course of nature. But the sun and stars, though they have outlasted several generations of men, we call not old, because we do not know what period God hath set to that sort of beings. This term belonging properly to those things which we can observe in the ordinary course of things, by a natural decay, to come to an end in a certain period of time; and so have in our minds, as it were, a standard to which we can compare the several parts of their duration; and, by the relation they bear thereunto, call them young or old; which we cannot, therefore, do to a ruby or a diamond, things whose usual periods we know not.

5. Relations of place and extension. The relation also that things have to one another in their places and distances is very obvious to observe; as above, below, a mile distant from Charing-cross, in England, and in London. But as in duration, so in extension and bulk, there are some ideas that are relative which we signify by names that are thought positive; as great and little are truly relations. For here also, having, by observation, settled in our minds the ideas of the bigness of several species of things from those we have been most accustomed to, we make them as it were the standards, whereby to denominate the bulk of others. Thus we call a great apple, such a one as is bigger than the ordinary sort of those we have been used to; and a little horse, such a one as comes not up to the size of that idea which we have in our minds to belong ordinarily to horses; and that will be a great horse to a Welchman, which is but a little one to a Fleming; they two having, from the different breed of their countries, taken several-sized ideas to which they compare, and in relation to which they denominate their great and their little.

6. Absolute terms often stand for relations. So likewise weak and strong are but relative denominations of power, compared to some ideas we have at that time of greater or less power. Thus, when we say a weak man, we mean one that has not so much strength or power to move as usually men have, or usually those of his size have; which is a comparing his strength to the idea we have of the usual strength of men, or men of such a size. The like when we say the creatures are all weak things; weak there is but a relative term, signifying the disproportion there is in the power of God and the creatures. And so abundance of words, in ordinary speech, stand only for relations (and perhaps the greatest part) which at first sight seem to have no such signification: v.g. the ship has necessary stores. Necessary and stores are both relative words; one having a relation to the accomplishing the voyage intended, and the other to future use. All which relations, how they are confined to, and terminate in ideas derived from sensation or reflection, is too obvious to need any explication.

Chapter XXVII.Of Identity and Diversity

1. Wherein identity consists. Another occasion the mind often takes of comparing, is the very being of things, when, considering anything as existing at any determined time and place, we compare it with itself existing at another time, and thereon form the ideas of identity and diversity. When we see anything to be in any place in any instant of time, we are sure (be it what it will) that it is that very thing, and not another which at that same time exists in another place, how like and undistinguishable soever it may be in all other respects: and in this consists identity, when the ideas it is attributed to vary not at all from what they were that moment wherein we consider their former existence, and to which we compare the present. For we never finding, nor conceiving it possible, that two things of the same kind should exist in the same place at the same time, we rightly conclude, that, whatever exists anywhere at any

time, excludes all of the same kind, and is there itself alone. When therefore we demand whether anything be the same or no, it refers always to something that existed such a time in such a place, which it was certain, at that instant, was the same with itself, and no other. From whence it follows, that one thing cannot have two beginnings of existence, nor two things one beginning; it being impossible for two things of the same kind to be or exist in the same instant, in the very same place; or one and the same thing in different places. That, therefore, that had one beginning, is the same thing; and that which had a different beginning in time and place from that, is not the same, but diverse. That which has made the difficulty about this relation has been the little care and attention used in having precise notions of the things to which it is attributed.

2. Identity of substances. We have the ideas but of three sorts of substances: 1. God. 2. Finite intelligences. 3. Bodies.

First, God is without beginning, eternal, unalterable, and everywhere, and therefore concerning his identity there can be no doubt.

Secondly, Finite spirits having had each its determinate time and place of beginning to exist, the relation to that time and place will always determine to each of them its identity, as long as it exists.

Thirdly, The same will hold of every particle of matter, to which no addition or subtraction of matter being made, it is the same. For, though these three sorts of substances, as we term them, do not exclude one another out of the same place, yet we cannot conceive but that they must necessarily each of them exclude any of the same kind out of the same place: or else the notions and names of identity and diversity would be in vain, and there could be no such distinctions of substances, or anything else one from another. For example: could two bodies be in the same place at the same time; then those two parcels of matter must be one and the same, take them great or little; nay, all bodies must be one and the same. For, by the same reason that two particles of matter may be in one place, all bodies may be in one place: which, when it can be supposed, takes away the distinction of identity and diversity of one and more, and renders it ridiculous. But it being a contradiction that two or more should be one, identity and diversity are relations and ways of comparing well founded, and of use to the understanding.

Identity of modes and relations. All other things being but modes or relations ultimately terminated in substances, the identity and diversity of each particular existence of them too will be by the same way determined: only as to things whose existence is in succession, such as are the actions of finite beings, v.g. motion and thought, both which consist in a continued train of succession, concerning their diversity there can be no question: because each perishing the moment it begins, they cannot exist in different times, or in different places, as permanent beings can at different times exist in distant places; and therefore no motion or thought, considered as at different times, can be the same, each part thereof having a different beginning of existence.

3. Principium Individuationis. From what has been said, it is easy to discover what is so much inquired after, the principium individuationis; and that, it is plain, is existence itself; which determines a being of any sort to a particular time and place, incommunicable to two beings of the same kind. This, though it seems easier to conceive in simple substances or modes; yet, when reflected on, is not more difficult in compound ones, if care be taken to what it is applied: v.g. let us suppose an atom, i.e. a continued body under one immutable superficies, existing in a determined time and place; it is evident, that, considered in any instant of its existence, it is in that instant the same with itself. For, being at that instant what it is, and nothing else, it is the same, and so must continue as long as its existence is continued; for so long it will be the same, and no other. In like manner, if two or more atoms be joined together into the same mass, every one of those atoms will be the same, by the foregoing rule: and whilst they exist united together, the mass, consisting of the same atoms, must be the same mass, or the same body, let the parts be ever so differently jumbled. But if one of these atoms

be taken away, or one new one added, it is no longer the same mass or the same body. In the state of living creatures, their identity depends not on a mass of the same particles, but on something else. For in them the variation of great parcels of matter alters not the identity: an oak growing from a plant to a great tree, and then lopped, is still the same oak; and a colt grown up to a horse, sometimes fat, sometimes lean, is all the while the same horse: though, in both these cases, there may be a manifest change of the parts; so that truly they are not either of them the same masses of matter, though they be truly one of them the same oak, and the other the same horse. The reason whereof is, that, in these two cases — a mass of matter and a living body — identity is not applied to the same thing.

4. Identity of vegetables. We must therefore consider wherein an oak differs from a mass of matter, and that seems to me to be in this, that the one is only the cohesion of particles of matter any how united, the other such a disposition of them as constitutes the parts of an oak; and such an organization of those parts as is fit to receive and distribute nourishment, so as to continue and frame the wood, bark, and leaves, &c., of an oak, in which consists the vegetable life. That being then one plant which has such an organization of parts in one coherent body, partaking of one common life, it continues to be the same plant as long as it partakes of the same life, though that life be communicated to new particles of matter vitally united to the living plant, in a like continued organization conformable to that sort of plants. For this organization, being at any one instant in any one collection of matter, is in that particular concrete distinguished from all other, and is that individual life, which existing constantly from that moment both forwards and backwards, in the same continuity of insensibly succeeding parts united to the living body of the plant, it has that identity which makes the same plant, and all the parts of it, parts of the same plant, during all the time that they exist united in that continued organization, which is fit to convey that common life to all the parts so united.

5. Identity of animals. The case is not so much different in brutes but that any one may hence see what makes an animal and continues it the same. Something we have like this in machines, and may serve to illustrate it. For example, what is a watch? It is plain it is nothing but a fit organization or construction of parts to a certain end, which, when a sufficient force is added to it, it is capable to attain. If we would suppose this machine one continued body, all whose organized parts were repaired, increased, or diminished by a constant addition or separation of insensible parts, with one common life, we should have something very much like the body of an animal; with this difference, That, in an animal the fitness of the organization, and the motion wherein life consists, begin together, the motion coming from within; but in machines the force coming sensibly from without, is often away when the organ is in order, and well fitted to receive it.

6. The identity of man. This also shows wherein the identity of the same man consists; viz. in nothing but a participation of the same continued life, by constantly fleeting particles of matter, in succession vitally united to the same organized body. He that shall place the identity of man in anything else, but, like that of other animals, in one fitly organized body, taken in any one instant, and from thence continued, under one organization of life, in several successively fleeting particles of matter united to it, will find it hard to make an embryo, one of years, mad and sober, the same man, by any supposition, that will not make it possible for Seth, Ismael, Socrates, Pilate, St. Austin, and Caesar Borgia, to be the same man. For if the identity of soul alone makes the same man; and there be nothing in the nature of matter why the same individual spirit may not be united to different bodies, it will be possible that those men, living in distant ages, and of different tempers, may have been the same man: which way of speaking must be from a very strange use of the word man, applied to an idea out of which body and shape are excluded. And that way of speaking would agree yet worse with the notions of those philosophers who allow of transmigration, and are of opinion that the souls of men may, for their miscarriages, be detruded into the bodies of beasts, as fit habitations, with organs suited to the satisfaction of their brutal inclinations. But yet I think nobody, could he be

sure that the soul of Heliogabalus were in one of his hogs, would yet say that hog were a man or Heliogabalus.

7. Idea of identity suited to the idea it is applied to. It is not therefore unity of substance that comprehends all sorts of identity, or will determine it in every case; but to conceive and judge of it aright, we must consider what idea the word it is applied to stands for: it being one thing to be the same substance, another the same man, and a third the same person, if person, man, and substance, are three names standing for three different ideas;— for such as is the idea belonging to that name, such must be the identity; which, if it had been a little more carefully attended to, would possibly have prevented a great deal of that confusion which often occurs about this matter, with no small seeming difficulties, especially concerning personal identity, which therefore we shall in the next place a little consider.

8. Same man. An animal is a living organized body; and consequently the same animal, as we have observed, is the same continued life communicated to different particles of matter, as they happen successively to be united to that organized living body. And whatever is talked of other definitions, ingenious observation puts it past doubt, that the idea in our minds, of which the sound man in our mouths is the sign, is nothing else but of an animal of such a certain form. Since I think I may be confident, that, whoever should see a creature of his own shape or make, though it had no more reason all its life than a cat or a parrot, would call him still a man; or whoever should hear a cat or a parrot discourse, reason, and philosophize, would call or think it nothing but a cat or a parrot; and say, the one was a dull irrational man, and the other a very intelligent rational parrot. A relation we have in an author of great note, is sufficient to countenance the supposition of a rational parrot.

His words are: "I had a mind to know, from Prince Maurice's own mouth, the account of a common, but much credited story, that I had heard so often from many others, of an old parrot he had in Brazil, during his government there, that spoke, and asked, and answered common questions, like a reasonable creature: so that those of his train there generally concluded it to be witchery or possession; and one of his chaplains, who lived long afterwards in Holland, would never from that time endure a parrot, but said they all had a devil in them. I had heard many particulars of this story, and as severed by people hard to be discredited, which made me ask Prince Maurice what there was of it. He said, with his usual plainness and dryness in talk, there was something true, but a great deal false of what had been reported. I desired to know of him what there was of the first. He told me short and coldly, that he had heard of such an old parrot when he had been at Brazil; and though he believed nothing of it, and it was a good way off, yet he had so much curiosity as to send for it: that it was a very great and a very old one; and when it came first into the room where the prince was, with a great many Dutchmen about him, it said presently, What a company of white men are here! They asked it, what it thought that man was, pointing to the prince. It answered, Some General or other. When they brought it close to him, he asked it, D'ou venez-vous? It answered, De Marinnan. The Prince, A qui estes-vous? The Parrot, A un Portugais. The Prince, Que fais-tu la? Parrot, Je garde les poulles. The Prince laughed, and said, Vous gardez les poulles? The Parrot answered, Oui, moi; et je scai bien faire; and made the chuck four or five times that people use to make to chickens when they call them. I set down the words of this worthy dialogue in French, just as Prince Maurice said them to me. I asked him in what language the parrot spoke, and he said in Brazilian. I asked whether he understood Brazilian; he said No, but he had taken care to have two interpreters by him, the one a Dutchman that spoke Brazilian, and the other a Brazilian that spoke Dutch; that he asked them separately and privately, and both of them agreed in telling him just the same thing that the parrot had said. I could not but tell this odd story, because it is so much out of the way, and from the first hand, and what may pass for a good one; for I dare say this Prince at least believed himself in all he told me, having ever passed for a very honest and pious man: I leave it to naturalists to reason, and to other men to believe, as they please upon it; however, it is not, perhaps, amiss to relieve or enliven a busy scene sometimes with such digressions, whether to the purpose or no."

I have taken care that the reader should have the story at large in the author's own words, because he seems to me not to have thought it incredible; for it cannot be imagined that so able a man as he, who had sufficiency enough to warrant all the testimonies he gives of himself, should take so much pains, in a place where it had nothing to do, to pin so close, not only on a man whom he mentions as his friend, but on a Prince in whom he acknowledges very great honesty and piety, a story which, if he himself thought incredible, he could not but also think ridiculous. The Prince, it is plain, who vouches this story, and our author, who relates it from him, both of them call this talker a parrot: and I ask any one else who thinks such a story fit to be told, whether, if this parrot, and all of its kind, had always talked, as we have a prince's word for it this one did,— whether, I say, they would not have passed for a race of rational animals; but yet, whether, for all that, they would have been allowed to be men, and not parrots? For I presume it is not the idea of a thinking or rational being alone that makes the idea of a man in most people's sense: but of a body, so and so shaped, joined to it: and if that be the idea of a man, the same successive body not shifted all at once, must, as well as the same immaterial spirit, go to the making of the same man.

9. Personal identity. This being premised, to find wherein personal identity consists, we must consider what person stands for;— which, I think, is a thinking intelligent being, that has reason and reflection, and can consider itself as itself, the same thinking thing, in different times and places; which it does only by that consciousness which is inseparable from thinking, and, as it seems to me, essential to it: it being impossible for any one to perceive without perceiving that he does perceive. When we see, hear, smell, taste, feel, meditate, or will anything, we know that we do so. Thus it is always as to our present sensations and perceptions: and by this every one is to himself that which he calls self:— it not being considered, in this case, whether the same self be continued in the same or divers substances. For, since consciousness always accompanies thinking, and it is that which makes every one to be what he calls self, and thereby distinguishes himself from all other thinking things, in this alone consists personal identity, i.e. the sameness of a rational being: and as far as this consciousness can be extended backwards to any past action or thought, so far reaches the identity of that person; it is the same self now it was then; and it is by the same self with this present one that now reflects on it, that that action was done.

10. Consciousness makes personal identity. But it is further inquired, whether it be the same identical substance. This few would think they had reason to doubt of, if these perceptions, with their consciousness, always remained present in the mind, whereby the same thinking thing would be always consciously present, and, as would be thought, evidently the same to itself. But that which seems to make the difficulty is this, that this consciousness being interrupted always by forgetfulness, there being no moment of our lives wherein we have the whole train of all our past actions before our eyes in one view, but even the best memories losing the sight of one part whilst they are viewing another; and we sometimes, and that the greatest part of our lives, not reflecting on our past selves, being intent on our present thoughts, and in sound sleep having no thoughts at all, or at least none with that consciousness which remarks our waking thoughts,— I say, in all these cases, our consciousness being interrupted, and we losing the sight of our past selves, doubts are raised whether we are the same thinking thing, i.e. the same substance or no. Which, however reasonable or unreasonable, concerns not personal identity at all. The question being what makes the same person; and not whether it be the same identical substance, which always thinks in the same person, which, in this case, matters not at all: different substances, by the same consciousness (where they do partake in it) being united into one person, as well as different bodies by the same life are united into one animal, whose identity is preserved in that change of substances by the unity of one continued life. For, it being the same consciousness that makes a man be himself to himself, personal identity depends on that only, whether it be annexed solely to one individual substance, or can be continued in a succession of several substances. For as far as any intelligent being can repeat the idea of any past action with the same consciousness it had

of it at first, and with the same consciousness it has of any present action; so far it is the same personal self For it is by the consciousness it has of its present thoughts and actions, that it is self to itself now, and so will be the same self, as far as the same consciousness can extend to actions past or to come. and would be by distance of time, or change of substance, no more two persons, than a man be two men by wearing other clothes to-day than he did yesterday, with a long or a short sleep between: the same consciousness uniting those distant actions into the same person, whatever substances contributed to their production.

11. Personal identity in change of substance. That this is so, we have some kind of evidence in our very bodies, all whose particles, whilst vitally united to this same thinking conscious self, so that we feel when they are touched, and are affected by, and conscious of good or harm that happens to them, as a part of ourselves; i.e. of our thinking conscious self. Thus, the limbs of his body are to every one a part of Himself; he sympathizes and is concerned for them. Cut off a hand, and thereby separate it from that consciousness he had of its heat, cold, and other affections, and it is then no longer a part of that which is himself, any more than the remotest part of matter. Thus, we see the substance whereof personal self consisted at one time may be varied at another, without the change of personal identity; there being no question about the same person, though the limbs which but now were a part of it, be cut off.

12. Personality in change of substance. But the question is, Whether if the same substance which thinks be changed, it can be the same person; or, remaining the same, it can be different persons?

And to this I answer: First, This can be no question at all to those who place thought in a purely material animal constitution, void of an immaterial substance. For, whether their supposition be true or no, it is plain they conceive personal identity preserved in something else than identity of substance; as animal identity is preserved in identity of life, and not of substance. And therefore those who place thinking in an immaterial substance only, before they can come to deal with these men, must show why personal identity cannot be preserved in the change of immaterial substances, or variety of particular immaterial substances, as well as animal identity is preserved in the change of material substances, or variety of particular bodies: unless they will say, it is one immaterial spirit that makes the same life in brutes, as it is one immaterial spirit that makes the same person in men; which the Cartesians at least will not admit, for fear of making brutes thinking things too.

13. Whether in change of thinking substances there can be one person. But next, as to the first part of the question, Whether, if the same thinking substance (supposing immaterial substances only to think) be changed, it can be the same person? I answer, that cannot be resolved but by those who know what kind of substances they are that do think; and whether the consciousness of past actions can be transferred from one thinking substance to another. I grant were the same consciousness the same individual action it could not: but it being a present representation of a past action, why it may not be possible, that that may be represented to the mind to have been which really never was, will remain to be shown. And therefore how far the consciousness of past actions is annexed to any individual agent, so that another cannot possibly have it, will be hard for us to determine, till we know what kind of action it is that cannot be done without a reflex act of perception accompanying it, and how performed by thinking substances, who cannot think without being conscious of it. But that which we call the same consciousness, not being the same individual act, why one intellectual substance may not have represented to it, as done by itself, what it never did, and was perhaps done by some other agent — why, I say, such a representation may not possibly be without reality of matter of fact, as well as several representations in dreams are, which yet whilst dreaming we take for true — will be difficult to conclude from the nature of things. And that it never is so, will by us, till we have clearer views of the nature of thinking substances, be best resolved into the goodness of God; who, as far as the happiness or misery of any of his sensible creatures is concerned in it, will not, by a fatal error of theirs, transfer from one to another that consciousness which draws reward or punishment with it. How far this may be an

argument against those who would place thinking in a system of fleeting animal spirits, I leave to be considered. But yet, to return to the question before us, it must be allowed, that, if the same consciousness (which, as has been shown, is quite a different thing from the same numerical figure or motion in body) can be transferred from one thinking substance to another, it will be possible that two thinking substances may make but one person. For the same consciousness being preserved, whether in the same or different substances, the personal identity is preserved.

14. Whether, the same immaterial substance remaining, there can be two persons. As to the second part of the question, Whether the same immaterial substance remaining, there may be two distinct persons; which question seems to me to be built on this,— Whether the same immaterial being, being conscious of the action of its past duration, may be wholly stripped of all the consciousness of its past existence, and lose it beyond the power of ever retrieving it again: and so as it were beginning a new account from a new period, have a consciousness that cannot reach beyond this new state. All those who hold pre-existence are evidently of this mind; since they allow the soul to have no remaining consciousness of what it did in that pre-existent state, either wholly separate from body, or informing any other body; and if they should not, it is plain experience would be against them. So that personal identity, reaching no further than consciousness reaches, a pre-existent spirit not having continued so many ages in a state of silence, must needs make different persons. Suppose a Christian Platonist or a Pythagorean should, upon God's having ended all his works of creation the seventh day, think his soul hath existed ever since; and should imagine it has revolved in several human bodies; as I once met with one, who was persuaded his had been the soul of Socrates (how reasonably I will not dispute; this I know, that in the post he filled, which was no inconsiderable one, he passed for a very rational man, and the press has shown that he wanted not parts or learning;)— would any one say, that he, being not conscious of any of Socrates's actions or thoughts, could be the same person with Socrates? Let any one reflect upon himself, and conclude that he has in himself an immaterial spirit, which is that which thinks in him, and, in the constant change of his body keeps him the same: and is that which he calls himself: let him also suppose it to be the same soul that was in Nestor or Thersites, at the siege of Troy, (for souls being, as far as we know anything of them, in their nature indifferent to any parcel of matter, the supposition has no apparent absurdity in it), which it may have been, as well as it is now the soul of any other man: but he now having no consciousness of any of the actions either of Nestor or Thersites, does or can he conceive himself the same person with either of them? Can he be concerned in either of their actions? attribute them to himself, or think them his own, more than the actions of any other men that ever existed? So that this consciousness, not reaching to any of the actions of either of those men, he is no more one self with either of them than if the soul or immaterial spirit that now informs him had been created, and began to exist, when it began to inform his present body; though it were never so true, that the same spirit that informed Nestor's or Thersites' body were numerically the same that now informs his. For this would no more make him the same person with Nestor, than if some of the particles of matter that were once a part of Nestor were now a part of this man; the same immaterial substance, without the same consciousness, no more making the same person, by being united to any body, than the same particle of matter, without consciousness, united to any body, makes the same person. But let him once find himself conscious of any of the actions of Nestor, he then finds himself the same person with Nestor.

15. The body, as well as the soul, goes to the making of a man. And thus may we be able, without any difficulty, to conceive the same person at the resurrection, though in a body not exactly in make or parts the same which he had here,— the same consciousness going along with the soul that inhabits it. But yet the soul alone, in the change of bodies, would scarce to any one but to him that makes the soul the man, be enough to make the same man. For should the soul of a prince, carrying with it the consciousness of the prince's past life, enter and inform the body of a cobbler, as soon as deserted by his own soul, every one sees he would be

the same person with the prince, accountable only for the prince's actions: but who would say it was the same man? The body too goes to the making the man, and would, I guess, to everybody determine the man in this case, wherein the soul, with all its princely thoughts about it, would not make another man: but he would be the same cobbler to every one besides himself. I know that, in the ordinary way of speaking, the same person, and the same man, stand for one and the same thing. And indeed every one will always have a liberty to speak as he pleases, and to apply what articulate sounds to what ideas he thinks fit, and change them as often as he pleases. But yet, when we will inquire what makes the same spirit, man, or person, we must fix the ideas of spirit, man, or person in our minds; and having resolved with ourselves what we mean by them, it will not be hard to determine, in either of them, or the like, when it is the same, and when not.

16. Consciousness alone unites actions into the same person. But though the same immaterial substance or soul does not alone, wherever it be, and in whatsoever state, make the same man; yet it is plain, consciousness, as far as ever it can be extended — should it be to ages past — unites existences and actions very remote in time into the same person, as well as it does the existences and actions of the immediately preceding moment: so that whatever has the consciousness of present and past actions, is the same person to whom they both belong. Had I the same consciousness that I saw the ark and Noah's flood, as that I saw an overflowing of the Thames last winter, or as that I write now, I could no more doubt that I who write this now, that saw' the Thames overflowed last winter, and that viewed the flood at the general deluge, was the same self,— place that self in what substance you please — than that I who write this am the same myself now whilst I write (whether I consist of all the same substance, material or immaterial, or no) that I was yesterday. For as to this point of being the same self, it matters not whether this present self be made up of the same or other substances — I being as much concerned, and as justly accountable for any action that was done a thousand years since, appropriated to me now by this self-consciousness, as I am for what I did the last moment.

17. Self depends on consciousness, not on substance. Self is that conscious thinking thing,— whatever substance made up of, (whether spiritual or material, simple or compounded, it matters not)— which is sensible or conscious of pleasure and pain, capable of happiness or misery, and so is concerned for itself, as far as that consciousness extends. Thus every one finds that, whilst comprehended under that consciousness, the little finger is as much a part of himself as what is most so. Upon separation of this little finger, should this consciousness go along with the little finger, and leave the rest of the body, it is evident the little finger would be the person, the same person; and self then would have nothing to do with the rest of the body. As in this case it is the consciousness that goes along with the substance, when one part is separate from another, which makes the same person, and constitutes this inseparable self: so it is in reference to substances remote in time. That with which the consciousness of this present thinking thing can join itself, makes the same person, and is one self with it, and with nothing else; and so attributes to itself, and owns all the actions of that thing, as its own, as far as that consciousness reaches, and no further; as every one who reflects will perceive.

18. Persons, not substances, the objects of reward and punishment. In this personal identity is founded all the right and justice of reward and punishment; happiness and misery being that for which every one is concerned for himself, and not mattering what becomes of any substance, not joined to, or affected with that consciousness. For, as it is evident in the instance I gave but now, if the consciousness went along with the little finger when it was cut off, that would be the same self which was concerned for the whole body yesterday, as making part of itself, whose actions then it cannot but admit as its own now. Though, if the same body should still live, and immediately from the separation of the little finger have its own peculiar consciousness, whereof the little finger knew nothing, it would not at all be concerned for it, as a part of itself, or could own any of its actions, or have any of them imputed to him.

19. Which shows wherein personal identity consists. This may show us wherein personal identity consists: not in the identity of substance, but, as I have said, in the identity of

consciousness, wherein if Socrates and the present mayor of Queinborough agree, they are the same person: if the same Socrates waking and sleeping do not partake of the same consciousness, Socrates waking and sleeping is not the same person. And to punish Socrates waking for what sleeping Socrates thought, and waking Socrates was never conscious of, would be no more of right, than to punish one twin for what his brother-twin did, whereof he knew nothing, because their outsides were so like, that they could not be distinguished; for such twins have been seen.

20. Absolute oblivion separates what is thus forgotten from the person, but not from the man. But yet possibly it will still be objected,— Suppose I wholly lose the memory of some parts of my life, beyond a possibility of retrieving them, so that perhaps I shall never be conscious of them again; yet am I not the same person that did those actions, had those thoughts that I once was conscious of, though I have now forgot them? To which I answer, that we must here take notice what the word I is applied to; which, in this case, is the man only. And the same man being presumed to be the same person, I is easily here supposed to stand also for the same person. But if it be possible for the same man to have distinct incommunicable consciousness at different times, it is past doubt the same man would at different times make different persons; which, we see, is the sense of mankind in the solemnest declaration of their opinions, human laws not punishing the mad man for the sober man's actions, nor the sober man for what the mad man did,— thereby making them two persons: which is somewhat explained by our way of speaking in English when we say such an one is "not himself," or is "beside himself"; in which phrases it is insinuated, as if those who now, or at least first used them, thought that self was changed; the selfsame person was no longer in that man.

21. Difference between identity of man and of person. But yet it is hard to conceive that Socrates, the same individual man, should be two persons. To help us a little in this, we must consider what is meant by Socrates, or the same individual man.

First, it must be either the same individual, immaterial, thinking substance; in short, the same numerical soul, and nothing else.

Secondly, or the same animal, without any regard to an immaterial soul.

Thirdly, or the same immaterial spirit united to the same animal.

Now, take which of these suppositions you please, it is impossible to make personal identity to consist in anything but consciousness; or reach any further than that does.

For, by the first of them, it must be allowed possible that a man born of different women, and in distant times, may be the same man. A way of speaking which, whoever admits, must allow it possible for the same man to be two distinct persons, as any two that have lived in different ages without the knowledge of one another's thoughts.

By the second and third, Socrates, in this life and after it, cannot be the same man any way, but by the same consciousness; and so making human identity to consist in the same thing wherein we place personal identity, there will be no difficulty to allow the same man to be the same person. But then they who place human identity in consciousness only, and not in something else, must consider how they will make the infant Socrates the same man with Socrates after the resurrection. But whatsoever to some men makes a man, and consequently the same individual man, wherein perhaps few are agreed, personal identity can by us be placed in nothing but consciousness, (which is that alone which makes what we call self,) without involving us in great absurdities.

22. But is not a man drunk and sober the same person? why else is he punished for the fact he commits when drunk, though he be never afterwards conscious of it? Just as much the same person as a man that walks, and does other things in his sleep, is the same person, and is answerable for any mischief he shall do in it. Human laws punish both, with a justice suitable to their way of knowledge;— because, in these cases, they cannot distinguish certainly what is real, what counterfeit: and so the ignorance in drunkenness or sleep is not admitted as a plea. For, though punishment be annexed to personality, and personality to consciousness, and the drunkard perhaps be not conscious of what he did, yet human judicatures justly punish him;

because the fact is proved against him, but want of consciousness cannot be proved for him. But in the Great Day, wherein the secrets of all hearts shall be laid open, it may be reasonable to think, no one shall be made to answer for what he knows nothing of, but shall receive his doom, his conscience accusing or excusing him.

23. Consciousness alone unites remote existences into one person. Nothing but consciousness can unite remote existences into the same person: the identity of substance will not do it; for whatever substance there is, however framed, without consciousness there is no person: and a carcass may be a person, as well as any sort of substance be so, without consciousness. Could we suppose two distinct incommunicable consciousnesses acting the same body, the one constantly by day, the other by night; and, on the other side, the same consciousness, acting by intervals, two distinct bodies: I ask, in the first case, whether the day and the night — man would not be two as distinct persons as Socrates and Plato? And whether, in the second case, there would not be one person in two distinct bodies, as much as one man is the same in two distinct clothings? Nor is it at all material to say, that this same, and this distinct consciousness, in the cases above mentioned, is owing to the same and distinct immaterial substances, bringing it with them to those bodies; which, whether true or no, alters not the case: since it is evident the personal identity would equally be determined by the consciousness, whether that consciousness were annexed to some individual immaterial substance or no. For, granting that the thinking substance in man must be necessarily supposed immaterial, it is evident that immaterial thinking thing may sometimes part with its past consciousness, and be restored to it again: as appears in the forgetfulness men often have of their past actions; and the mind many times recovers the memory of a past consciousness, which it had lost for twenty years together. Make these intervals of memory and forgetfulness to take their turns regularly by day and night, and you have two persons with the same immaterial spirit, as much as in the former instance two persons with the same body. So that self is not determined by identity or diversity of substance, which it cannot be sure of, but only by identity of consciousness.

24. Not the substance with which the consciousness may be united. Indeed it may conceive the substance whereof it is now made up to have existed formerly, united in the same conscious being: but, consciousness removed, that substance is no more itself, or makes no more a part of it, than any other substance; as is evident in the instance we have already given of a limb cut off, of whose heat, or cold, or other affections, having no longer any consciousness, it is no more of a man's self than any other matter of the universe. In like manner it will be in reference to any immaterial substance, which is void of that consciousness whereby I am myself to myself: if there be any part of its existence which I cannot upon recollection join with that present consciousness whereby I am now myself, it is, in that part of its existence, no more myself than any other immaterial being. For, whatsoever any substance has thought or done, which I cannot recollect, and by my consciousness make my own thought and action, it will no more belong to me, whether a part of me thought or did it, than if it had been thought or done by any other immaterial being anywhere existing.

25. Consciousness unites substances, material or spiritual, with the same personality. I agree, the more probable opinion is, that this consciousness is annexed to, and the affection of, one individual immaterial substance.

But let men, according to their diverse hypotheses, resolve of that as they please. This every intelligent being, sensible of happiness or misery, must grant — that there is something that is himself, that he is concerned for, and would have happy; that this self has existed in a continued duration more than one instant, and therefore it is possible may exist, as it has done, months and years to come, without any certain bounds to be set to its duration; and may be the same self, by the same consciousness continued on for the future. And thus, by this consciousness he finds himself to be the same self which did such and such an action some years since, by which he comes to be happy or miserable now. In all which account of self, the same numerical substance is not considered as making the same self, but the same continued consciousness, in which several substances may have been united, and again separated from it, which, whilst they continued in a vital union with that wherein this consciousness then resided, made a part of that same self. Thus any part of our bodies, vitally united to that which is conscious in us, makes a part of ourselves: but upon separation from the vital union by which that consciousness is communicated, that which a moment since was part of ourselves, is now no more so than a part of another man's self is a part of me: and it is not impossible but in a little time may become a real part of another person. And so we have the same numerical substance become a part of two different persons; and the same person preserved under the change of various substances. Could we suppose any spirit wholly stripped of all its memory or consciousness of past actions, as we find our minds always are of a great part of ours, and sometimes of them all; the union or separation of such a spiritual substance would make no variation of personal identity, any more than that of any particle of matter does. Any substance vitally united to the present thinking being is a part of that very same self which now is; anything united to it by a consciousness of former actions, makes also a part of the same self, which is the same both then and now.

26. "Person" a forensic term. Person, as I take it, is the name for this self. Wherever a man finds what he calls himself, there, I think, another may say is the same person. It is a forensic term, appropriating actions and their merit; and so belongs only to intelligent agents, capable of a law, and happiness, and misery. This personality extends itself beyond present existence to what is past, only by consciousness,— whereby it becomes concerned and accountable; owns and imputes to itself past actions, just upon the same ground and for the same reason as it does the present. All which is founded in a concern for happiness, the unavoidable concomitant of consciousness; that which is conscious of pleasure and pain, desiring that that self that is conscious should be happy. And therefore whatever past actions it cannot reconcile or appropriate to that present self by consciousness, it can be no more concerned in than if they had never been done: and to receive pleasure or pain, i.e. reward or punishment, on the account of any such action, is all one as to be made happy or miserable in its first being, without any demerit at all. For, supposing a man punished now for what he had done in another life, whereof he could be made to have no consciousness at all, what difference is there between that punishment and being created miserable? And therefore, conformable to this, the apostle tells us, that, at the great day, when every one shall "receive according to his doings, the secrets of all hearts shall be laid open." The sentence shall be justified by the consciousness all persons shall have, that they themselves, in what bodies soever they appear, or what substances soever that consciousness adheres to, are the same that committed those actions, and deserve that punishment for them.

27. Suppositions that look strange are pardonable in our ignorance. I am apt enough to think I have, in treating of this subject, made some suppositions that will look strange to some readers, and possibly they are so in themselves. But yet, I think they are such as are pardonable, in this ignorance we are in of the nature of that thinking thing that is in us, and which we look on as ourselves. Did we know what it was, or how it was tied to a certain system of fleeting animal spirits; or whether it could or could not perform its operations of thinking and memory out of a body organized as ours is; and whether it has pleased God that no one such spirit shall ever be united to any but one such body, upon the right constitution of whose organs its memory should depend; we might see the absurdity of some of those suppositions I have made. But taking, as we ordinarily now do (in the dark concerning these matters), the soul of a man for an immaterial substance, independent from matter, and indifferent alike to it all; there can, from the nature of things, be no absurdity at all to suppose that the same soul may at different times be united to different bodies, and with them make up for that time one man: as well as we suppose a part of a sheep's body yesterday should be a part of a man's body to-morrow, and in that union make a vital part of Meliboeus himself, as well as it did of his ram.

28. The difficulty from ill use of names. To conclude: Whatever substance begins to exist, it

must, during its existence, necessarily be the same: whatever compositions of substances begin to exist, during the union of those substances, the concrete must be the same: whatsoever mode begins to exist, during its existence it is the same: and so if the composition be of distinct substances and different modes, the same rule holds. Whereby it will appear, that the difficulty or obscurity that has been about this matter rather rises from the names ill-used, than from any obscurity in things themselves. For whatever makes the specific idea to which the name is applied, if that idea be steadily kept to, the distinction of anything into the same and divers will easily be conceived, and there can arise no doubt about it.

29. Continuance of that which we have made to he our complex idea of man makes the same man. For, supposing a rational spirit be the idea of a man, it is easy to know what is the same man, viz. the same spirit — whether separate or in a body — will be the same man. Supposing a rational spirit vitally united to a body of a certain conformation of parts to make a man; whilst that rational spirit, with that vital conformation of parts, though continued in a fleeting successive body, remains, it will be the same man. But if to any one the idea of a man be but the vital union of parts in a certain shape; as long as that vital union and shape remain in a concrete, no otherwise the same but by a continued succession of fleeting particles, it will be the same man. For, whatever be the composition whereof the complex idea is made, whenever existence makes it one particular thing under any denomination the same existence continued preserves it the same individual under the same denomination.

Chapter XXVIII.Of Other Relations

1. Ideas of proportional relations. Besides the before-mentioned occasions of time, place, and causality of comparing or referring things one to another, there are, as I have said, infinite others, some whereof I shall mention.

First, The first I shall name is some one simple idea, which, being capable of parts or degrees, affords an occasion of comparing the subjects wherein it is to one another, in respect of that simple idea, v.g. whiter, sweeter, equal, more, &c. These relations depending on the equality and excess of the same simple idea, in several subjects, may be called, if one will, proportional; and that these are only conversant about those simple ideas received from sensation or reflection is so evident that nothing need be said to evince it.

2. Natural relation. Secondly, Another occasion of comparing things together, or considering one thing, so as to include in that consideration some other thing, is the circumstances of their origin or beginning; which being not afterwards to be altered, make the relations depending thereon as lasting as the subjects to which they belong, v.g. father and son, brothers, cousin-germans, &c., which have their relations by one community of blood, wherein they partake in several degrees: countrymen, i.e. those who were born in the same country or tract of ground; and these I call natural relations: wherein we may observe, that mankind have fitted their notions and words to the use of common life, and not to the truth and extent of things. For it is certain, that, in reality, the relation is the same betwixt the begetter and the begotten, in the several races of other animals as well as men; but yet it is seldom said, this bull is the grandfather of such a calf, or that two pigeons are cousin-germans. It is very convenient that, by distinct names, these relations should be observed and marked out in mankind, there being occasion, both in laws and other communications one with another, to mention and take notice of men under these relations: from whence also arise the obligations of several duties amongst men: whereas, in brutes, men having very little or no cause to mind these relations, they have not thought fit to give them distinct and peculiar names. This, by the way, may give us some light into the different state and growth of languages; which being suited only to the convenience of communication, are proportioned to the notions men have, and the commerce of thoughts familiar amongst them; and not to the reality or extent of things, nor to the various respects might be found among them; nor the different abstract considerations might be

framed about them. Where they had no philosophical notions, there they had no terms to express them: and it is no wonder men should have framed no names for those things they found no occasion to discourse of. From whence it is easy to imagine why, as in some countries, they may have not so much as the name for a horse; and in others, where they are more careful of the pedigrees of their horses, than of their own, that there they may have not only names for particular horses, but also of their several relations of kindred one to another.

3. Ideas of instituted or voluntary relations. Thirdly, Sometimes the foundation of considering things, with reference to one another, is some act whereby any one comes by a moral right, power, or obligation to do something. Thus, a general is one that hath power to command an army; and an army under a general is a collection of armed men, obliged to obey one man. A citizen, or a burgher, is one who has a right to certain privileges in this or that place. All this sort depending upon men's wills, or agreement in society, I call instituted, or voluntary; and may be distinguished from the natural, in that they are most, if not all of them, some way or other alterable, and separable from the persons to whom they have sometimes belonged, though neither of the substances, so related, be destroyed. Now, though these are all reciprocal, as well as the rest, and contain in them a reference of two things one to the other; yet, because one of the two things often wants a relative name, importing that reference, men usually take no notice of it, and the relation is commonly overlooked: v.g. a patron and client ire easily allowed to be relations, but a constable or dictator are not so readily at first hearing considered as such. Because there is no peculiar name for those who are under the command of a dictator or constable, expressing a relation to either of them; though it be certain that either of them hath a certain power over some others, and so is so far related to them, as well as a patron is to his client, or general to his army.

4. Ideas of moral relations. Fourthly, There is another sort of relation, which is the conformity or disagreement men's voluntary actions have to a rule to which they are referred, and by which they are judged of; which, I think, may be called moral relation, as being that which denominates our moral actions, and deserves well to be examined; there being no part of knowledge wherein we should be more careful to get determined ideas, and avoid, as much as may be, obscurity and confusion. Human actions, when with their various ends, objects, manners, and circumstances, they are framed into distinct complex ideas, are, as has been shown so many mixed modes, a great part whereof have names annexed to them. Thus, supposing gratitude to be a readiness to acknowledge and return kindness received; polygamy to be the having more wives than one at once: when we frame these notions thus in our minds, we have there so many determined ideas of mixed modes. But this is not all that concerns our actions: it is not enough to have determined ideas of them, and to know what names belong to such and such combinations of ideas. We have a further and greater concernment, and that is, to know whether such actions, so made up, are morally good or bad.

5. Moral good and evil. Good and evil, as hath been shown, (Bk. II. chap. xx. SS 2, and chap. xxi. SS 43,) are nothing but pleasure or pain, or that which occasions or procures pleasure or pain to us. Moral good and evil, then, is only the conformity or disagreement of our voluntary actions to some law, whereby good or evil is drawn on us, from the will and power of the law-maker; which good and evil, pleasure or pain, attending our observance or breach of the law by the decree of the lawmaker, is that we call reward and punishment.

6. Moral rules. Of these moral rules or laws, to which men generally refer, and by which they judge of the rectitude or pravity of their actions, there seem to me to be three sorts, with their three different enforcements, or rewards and punishments. For, since it would be utterly in vain to suppose a rule set to the free actions of men, without annexing to it some enforcement of good and evil to determine his will, we must, wherever we suppose a law, suppose also some reward or punishment annexed to that law. It would be in vain for one intelligent being to set a rule to the actions of another, if he had it not in his power to reward the compliance with, and punish deviation from his rule, by some good and evil, that is not the natural product and consequence of the action itself For that, being a natural convenience or inconvenience,

would operate of itself, without a law. This, if I mistake not, is the true nature of all law, properly so called.

7. Laws. The laws that men generally refer their actions to, to judge of their rectitude or obliquity, seem to me to be these three:— 1. The divine law. 2. The civil law. 3. The law of opinion or reputation, if I may so call it. By the relation they bear to the first of these, men judge whether their actions are sins or duties; by the second, whether they be criminal or innocent; and by the third, whether they be virtues or vices.

8. Divine law the measure of sin and duty. First, the divine law, whereby that law which God has set to the actions of men,— whether promulgated to them by the light of nature, or the voice of revelation. That God has given a rule whereby men should govern themselves, I think there is nobody so brutish as to deny. He has a right to do it; we are his creatures: he has goodness and wisdom to direct our actions to that which is best: and he has power to enforce it by rewards and punishments of infinite weight and duration in another life; for nobody can take us out of his hands. This is the only true touchstone of moral rectitude; and, by comparing them to this law, it is that men judge of the most considerable moral good or evil of their actions; that is, whether, as duties or sins, they are like to procure them happiness or misery from the hands of the ALMIGHTY.

9. Civil law the measure of crimes and innocence. Secondly, the civil law — the rule set by the commonwealth to the actions of those who belong to it — is another rule to which men refer their actions; to judge whether they be criminal or no. This law nobody overlooks: the rewards and punishments that enforce it being ready at hand, and suitable to the power that makes it: which is the force of the Commonwealth, engaged to protect the lives, liberties, and possessions of those who live according to its laws, and has power to take away life, liberty, or goods, from him who disobeys; which is the punishment of offences committed against his law.

10. Philosophical law the measure of virtue and vice. Thirdly, the law of opinion or reputation. Virtue and vice are names pretended and supposed everywhere to stand for actions in their own nature right and wrong: and as far as they really are so applied, they so far are coincident with the divine law above mentioned. But yet, whatever is pretended, this is visible, that these names, virtue and vice, in the particular instances of their application, through the several nations and societies of men in the world, are constantly attributed only to such actions as in each country and society are in reputation or discredit. Nor is it to be thought strange, that men everywhere should give the name of virtue to those actions, which amongst them are judged praiseworthy; and call that vice, which they account blamable: since otherwise they would condemn themselves, if they should think anything right, to which they allowed not commendation, anything wrong, which they let pass without blame. Thus the measure of what is everywhere called and esteemed virtue and vice is this approbation or dislike, praise or blame, which, by a secret and tacit consent, establishes itself in the several societies, tribes, and clubs of men in the world: whereby several actions come to find credit or disgrace amongst them, according to the judgment, maxims, or fashion of that place. For, though men uniting into politic societies, have resigned up to the public the disposing of all their force, so that they cannot employ it against any fellow-citizens any further than the law of the country directs: yet they retain still the power of thinking well or ill, approving or disapproving of the actions of those whom they live amongst, and converse with: and by this approbation and dislike they establish amongst themselves what they will call virtue and vice.

11. The measure that men commonly apply to determine what they call virtue and vice. That this is the common measure of virtue and vice, will appear to any one who considers, that, though that passes for vice in one country which is counted a virtue, or at least not vice, in another, yet everywhere virtue and praise, vice and blame, go together. Virtue is everywhere, that which is thought praiseworthy; and nothing else but that which has the allowance of public esteem is called virtue. Virtue and praise are so united, that they are called often by the same name. Sunt sua praemia laudi, says Virgil; and so Cicero, Nihil habet natura praestantius,

quam honestatem, quam laudem, quam dignitatem, quam decus, which he tells you are all names for the same thing. This is the language of the heathen philosophers, who well understood wherein their notions of virtue and vice consisted. And though perhaps, by the different temper, education, fashion, maxims, or interest of different sorts of men, it fell out, that what was thought praiseworthy in one place, escaped not censure in another; and so in different societies, virtues and vices were changed: yet, as to the main, they for the most part kept the same everywhere. For, since nothing can be more natural than to encourage with esteem and reputation that wherein every one finds his advantage, and to blame and discountenance the contrary; it is no wonder that esteem and discredit, virtue and vice, should, in a great measure, everywhere correspond with the unchangeable rule of right and wrong, which the law of God hath established; there being nothing that so directly and visibly secures and advances the general good of mankind in this world, as obedience to the laws he has set them, and nothing that breeds such mischiefs and confusion, as the neglect of them. And therefore men, without renouncing all sense and reason, and their own interest, which they are so constantly true to, could not generally mistake, in placing their commendation and blame on that side that really deserved it not. Nay, even those men whose practice was otherwise, failed not to give their approbation right, few being depraved to that degree as not to condemn, at least in others, the faults they themselves were guilty of; whereby, even in the corruption of manners, the true boundaries of the law of nature, which ought to be the rule of virtue and vice, were pretty well preferred. So that even the exhortations of inspired teachers, have not feared to appeal to common repute: "Whatsoever is lovely, whatsoever is of good report, if there be any virtue, if there be any praise," &c. (Phil. 4. 8.)

12. Its enforcement is commendation and discredit. If any one shall imagine that I have forgot my own notion of a law, when I make the law, whereby men judge of virtue and vice, to be nothing else but the consent of private men, who have not authority enough to make a law: especially wanting that which is so necessary and essential to a law, a power to enforce it: I think I may say, that he who imagines commendation and disgrace not to be strong motives to men to accommodate themselves to the opinions and rules of those with whom they converse, seems little skilled in the nature or history of mankind: the greatest part whereof we shall find to govern themselves chiefly, if not solely, by this law of fashion; and so they do that which keeps them in reputation with their company, little regard the laws of God, or the magistrate. The penalties that attend the breach of God's laws some, nay perhaps most men, seldom seriously reflect on: and amongst those that do, many, whilst they break the law, entertain thoughts of future reconciliation, and making their peace for such breaches. And as to the punishments due from the laws of the commonwealth, they frequently flatter themselves with the hopes of impunity. But no man escapes the punishment of their censure and dislike, who offends against the fashion and opinion of the company he keeps, and would recommend himself to. Nor is there one of ten thousand, who is stiff and insensible enough, to bear up under the constant dislike and condemnation of his own club. He must be of a strange and unusual constitution, who can content himself to live in constant disgrace and disrepute with his own particular society. Solitude many men have sought, and been reconciled to: but nobody that has the least thought or sense of a man about him, can live in society under the constant dislike and ill opinion of his familiars, and those he converses with. This is a burden too heavy for human sufferance: and he must be made up of irreconcilable contradictions, who can take pleasure in company, and yet be insensible of contempt and disgrace from his companions.

13. These three laws the rules of moral good and evil. These three then, first, the law of God; secondly, the law of politic societies; thirdly, the law of fashion, or private censure, are those to which men variously compare their actions: and it is by their conformity to one of these laws that they take their measures, when they would judge of their moral rectitude, and denominate their actions good or bad.

14. Morality is the relation of voluntary actions to these rules. Whether the rule to which, as to

a touchstone, we bring our voluntary actions, to examine them by, and try their goodness, and accordingly to name them, which is, as it were, the mark of the value we set upon them: whether, I say, we take that rule from the fashion of the country, or the will of a law-maker, the mind is easily able to observe the relation any action hath to it, and to judge whether the action agrees or disagrees with the rule; and so hath a notion of moral goodness or evil, which is either conformity or not conformity of any action to that rule: and therefore is often called moral rectitude. This rule being nothing but a collection of several simple ideas, the conformity thereto is but so ordering the action, that the simple ideas belonging to it may correspond to those which the law requires. And thus we see how moral beings and notions are founded on, and terminated in, these simple ideas we have received from sensation or reflection. For example: let us consider the complex idea we signify by the word murder: and when we have taken it asunder, and examined all the particulars, we shall find them to amount to a collection of simple ideas derived from reflection or sensation, viz. First, from reflection on the operations of our own minds, we have the ideas of willing, considering, purposing beforehand, malice, or wishing ill to another; and also of life, or perception, and self-motion. Secondly, from sensation we have the collection of those simple sensible ideas which are to be found in a man, and of some action, whereby we put an end to perception and motion in the man; all which simple ideas are comprehended in the word murder. This collection of simple ideas, being found by me to agree or disagree with the esteem of the country I have been bred in, and to be held by most men there worthy praise or blame, I call the action virtuous or vicious: if I have the will of a supreme invisible Lawgiver for my rule, then, as I supposed the action commanded or forbidden by God, I call it good or evil, sin or duty: and if I compare it to the civil law, the rule made by the legislative power of the country, I call it lawful or unlawful, a crime or no crime. So that whencesoever we take the rule of moral actions; or by what standard soever we frame in our minds the ideas of virtues or vices, they consist only, and are made up of collections of simple ideas, which we originally received from sense or reflection: and their rectitude or obliquity consists in the agreement or disagreement with those patterns prescribed by some law.

15. Moral actions may be regarded either absolutely, or as ideas of relation. To conceive rightly of moral actions, we must take notice of them under this two-fold consideration. First, as they are in themselves, each made up of such a collection of simple ideas. Thus drunkenness, or lying, signify such or such a collection of simple ideas, which I call mixed modes: and in this sense they are as much positive absolute ideas, as the drinking of a horse, or speaking of a parrot. Secondly, our actions are considered as good, bad, or indifferent; and in this respect they are relative, it being their conformity to, or disagreement with some rule that makes them to be regular or irregular, good or bad; and so, as far as they are compared with a rule, and thereupon denominated, they come under relation. Thus the challenging and fighting with a man, as it is a certain positive mode, or particular sort of action, by particular ideas, distinguished from all others, is called duelling: which, when considered in relation to the law of God, will deserve the name of sin; to the law of fashion, in some countries, valour and virtue; and to the municipal laws of some governments, a capital crime. In this case, when the positive mode has one name, and another name as it stands in relation to the law, the distinction may as easily be observed as it is in substances, where one name, v.g. man, is used to signify the thing; another, v.g. father, to signify the relation.

16. The denominations of actions often mislead us. But because very frequently the positive idea of the action, and its moral relation, are comprehended together under one name, and the same word made use of to express both the mode or action, and its moral rectitude or obliquity: therefore the relation itself is less taken notice of; and there is often no distinction made between the positive idea of the action, and the reference it has to a rule. By which confusion of these two distinct considerations under one term, those who yield too easily to the impressions of sounds, and are forward to take names for things, are often misled in their judgment of actions. Thus, the taking from another what is his, without his knowledge or

allowance, is properly called stealing: but that name, being commonly understood to signify also the moral pravity of the action, and to denote its contrariety to the law, men are apt to condemn whatever they hear called stealing, as an ill action, disagreeing with the rule of right. And yet the private taking away his sword from a madman, to prevent his doing mischief, though it be properly denominated stealing, as the name of such a mixed mode; yet when compared to the law of God, and considered in its relation to that supreme rule, it is no sin or transgression, though the name stealing ordinarily carries such an intimation with it.

17. Relations innumerable, and only the most considerable here mentioned. And thus much for the relation of human actions to a law, which, therefore, I call moral relations.

It would make a volume to go over all sorts of relations: it is not, therefore, to be expected that I should here mention them all. It suffices to our present purpose to show by these, what the ideas are we have of this comprehensive consideration called relation. Which is so various, and the occasions of it so many, (as many as there can be of comparing things one to another,) that it is not very easy to reduce it to rules, or under just heads. Those I have mentioned, I think, are some of the most considerable; and such as may serve to let us see from whence we get our ideas of relations, and wherein they are founded. But before I quit this argument, from what has been said give me leave to observe:

18. All relations terminate in simple ideas. First, That it is evident, that all relation terminates in, and is ultimately founded on, those simple ideas we have got from sensation or reflection: so that all we have in our thoughts ourselves, (if we think of anything, or have any meaning), or would signify to others, when we use words standing for relations, is nothing but some simple ideas, or collections of simple ideas, compared one with another. This is so manifest in that sort called proportional, that nothing can be more. For when a man says "honey is sweeter than wax," it is plain that his thoughts in this relation terminate in this simple idea, sweetness; which is equally true of all the rest: though, where they are compounded, or decompounded, the simple ideas they are made up of, are, perhaps, seldom taken notice of: v.g. when the word father is mentioned: first, there is meant that particular species, or collective idea, signified by the word man; secondly, those sensible simple ideas, signified by the word generation; and, thirdly, the effects of it, and all the simple ideas signified by the word child. So the word friend, being taken for a man who loves and is ready to do good to another, has all these following ideas to the making of it up: first, all the simple ideas, comprehended in the word man, or intelligent being; secondly, the idea of love; thirdly, the idea of readiness or disposition; fourthly, the idea of action, which is any kind of thought or motion; fifthly, the idea of good, which signifies anything that may advance his happiness, and terminates at last, if examined, in particular simple ideas, of which the word good in general signifies any one: but, if removed from all simple ideas quite, it signifies nothing at all. And thus also all moral words terminate at last, though perhaps more remotely, in a collection of simple ideas: the immediate signification of relative words, being very often other supposed known relations; which, if traced one to another, still end in simple ideas.

19. We have ordinarily as clear a notion of the relation, as of the simple ideas in things on which it is founded. Secondly, That in relations, we have for the most part, if not always, as clear a notion of the relation as we have of those simple ideas wherein it is founded: agreement or disagreement, whereon relation depends, being things whereof we have commonly as clear ideas as of any other whatsoever; it being but the distinguishing simple ideas, or their degrees one from another, without which we could have no distinct knowledge at all. For, if I have a clear idea of sweetness, light, or extension, I have, too, of equal, or more, or less, of each of these: if I know what it is for one man to be born of a woman, viz. Sempronia, I know what it is for another man to be born of the same woman Sempronia; and so have as clear a notion of brothers as of births, and perhaps clearer. For if I believed that Sempronia digged Titus out of the parsley-bed, (as they used to tell children), and thereby became his mother; and that afterwards, in the same manner, she digged Caius out of the parsley-bed, I had as clear a notion of the relation of brothers between them, as if I had all the skill of a midwife: the notion

that the same woman contributed, as mother, equally to their births, (though I were ignorant or mistaken in the manner of it), being that on which I grounded the relation; and that they agreed in that circumstance of birth, let it be what it will. The comparing them then in their descent from the same person, without knowing the particular circumstances of that descent, is enough to found my notion of their having, or not having the relation of brothers. But though the ideas of particular relations are capable of being as clear and distinct in the minds of those who will duly consider them as those of mixed modes, and more determinate than those of substances: yet the names belonging to relation are often of as doubtful and uncertain signification as those of substances or mixed modes; and much more than those of simple ideas. Because relative words, being the marks of this comparison, which is made only by men's thoughts, and is an idea only in men's minds, men frequently apply them to different comparisons of things, according to their own imaginations; which do not always correspond with those of others using the same name.

20. The notion of relation is the same, whether the rule any action is compared to be true or false. Thirdly, That in these I call moral relations, I have a true notion of relation, by comparing the action with the rule, whether the rule be true or false. For if I measure anything by a yard, I know whether the thing I measure be longer or shorter than that supposed yard, though perhaps the yard I measure by be not exactly the standard: which indeed is another inquiry. For though the rule be erroneous, and I mistaken in it; yet the agreement or disagreement observable in that which I compare with, makes me perceive the relation. Though, measuring by a wrong rule, I shall thereby be brought to judge amiss of its moral rectitude; because I have tried it by that which is not the true rule: yet I am not mistaken in the relation which that action bears to that rule I compare it to, which is agreement or disagreement.

Chapter XXIX. Of Clear and Obscure, Distinct and Confused Ideas

1. Ideas, some clear and distinct, others obscure and confused. Having shown the original of our ideas, and taken a view of their several sorts; considered the difference between the simple and the complex; and observed how the complex ones are divided into those of modes, substances, and relations — all which, I think, is necessary to be done by any one who would acquaint himself thoroughly with the progress of the mind, in its apprehension and knowledge of things — it will, perhaps, be thought I have dwelt long enough upon the examination of ideas. I must nevertheless, crave leave to offer some few other considerations concerning them.

The first is, that some are clear and others obscure; some distinct and others confused.

2. Clear and obscure explained by sight. The perception of the mind being most aptly explained by words relating to the sight, we shall best understand what is meant by clear and obscure in our ideas, by reflecting on what we call clear and obscure in the objects of sight. Light being that which discovers to us visible objects, we give the name of obscure to that which is not placed in a light sufficient to discover minutely to us the figure and colours which are observable in it, and which, in a better light, would be discernible. In like manner, our simple ideas are clear, when they are such as the objects themselves from whence they were taken did or might, in a well-ordered sensation or perception, present them. Whilst the memory retains them thus, and can produce them to the mind whenever it has occasion to consider them, they are clear ideas. So far as they either want anything of the original exactness, or have lost any of their first freshness, and are, as it were, faded or tarnished by time, so far are they obscure. Complex ideas, as they are made up of simple ones, so they are clear, when the ideas that go to their composition are clear, and the number and order of those simple ideas that are the ingredients of any complex one is determinate and certain.

3. Causes of obscurity. The causes of obscurity, in simple ideas, seem to be either dull organs; or very slight and transient impressions made by the objects; or else a weakness in the memory, not able to retain them as received. For to return again to visible objects, to help us to apprehend this matter. If the organs, or faculties of perception, like wax over-hardened with cold, will not receive the impression of the seal, from the usual impulse wont to imprint it; or, like wax of a temper too soft, will not hold it well, when well imprinted; or else supposing the wax of a temper fit, but the seal not applied with a sufficient force to make a clear impression: in any of these cases, the print left by the seal will be obscure. This, I suppose, needs no application to make it plainer.

4. Distinct and confused, what. As a clear idea is that whereof the mind has such a full and evident perception, as it does receive from an outward object operating duly on a well-disposed organ, so a distinct idea is that wherein the mind perceives a difference from all other; and a confused idea is such an one as is not sufficiently distinguishable from another, from which it ought to be different.

5. Objection. If no idea be confused, but such as is not sufficiently distinguishable from another from which it should be different, it will be hard, may any one say, to find anywhere a confused idea. For, let any idea be as it will, it can be no other but such as the mind perceives it to be; and that very perception sufficiently distinguishes it from all other ideas, which cannot be other, i.e. different, without being perceived to be so. No idea, therefore, can be undistinguishable from another from which it ought to be different, unless you would have it different from itself: for from all other it is evidently different.

6. Confusion of ideas is in reference to their names. To remove this difficulty, and to help us to conceive aright what it is that makes the confusion ideas are at any time chargeable with, we must consider, that things ranked under distinct names are supposed different enough to be distinguished, that so each sort by its peculiar name may be marked, and discoursed of apart upon any occasion: and there is nothing more evident, than that the greatest part of different names are supposed to stand for different things. Now every idea a man has, being visibly what it is, and distinct from all other ideas but itself; that which makes it confused, is, when it is such that it may as well be called by another name as that which it is expressed by; the difference which keeps the things (to be ranked under those two different names) distinct, and makes some of them belong rather to the one and some of them to the other of those names, being left out; and so the distinction, which was intended to be kept up by those different names, is quite lost.

7. Defaults which make this confusion. The defaults which usually occasion this confusion, I think, are chiefly these following:

Complex Ideas made up of too few simple ones. First, when any complex idea (for it is complex ideas that are most liable to confusion) is made up of too small a number of simple ideas, and such only as are common to other things, whereby the differences that make it deserve a different name, are left out. Thus, he that has an idea made up of barely the simple ones of a beast with spots, has but a confused idea of a leopard; it not being thereby sufficiently distinguished from a lynx, and several other sorts of beasts that are spotted. So that such an idea, though it hath the peculiar name leopard, is not distinguishable from those designed by the names lynx or panther, and may as well come under the name lynx as leopard. How much the custom of defining of words by general terms contributes to make the ideas we would express by them confused and undetermined, I leave others to consider. This is evident, that confused ideas are such as render the use of words uncertain, and take away the benefit of distinct names. When the ideas, for which we use different terms, have not a difference answerable to their distinct names, and so cannot be distinguished by them, there it is that they are truly confused.

8. Their simple ones jumbled disorderly together. Secondly, Another fault which makes our ideas confused is, when, though the particulars that make up any idea are in number enough, yet they are so jumbled together, that it is not easily discernible whether it more belongs to the

name that is given it than to any other. There is nothing properer to make us conceive this confusion than a sort of pictures, usually shown as surprising pieces of art, wherein the colours, as they are laid by the pencil on the table itself, mark out very odd and unusual figures, and have no discernible order in their position. This draught, thus made up of parts wherein no symmetry nor order appears, is in itself no more a confused thing, than the picture of a cloudy sky; wherein, though there be as little order of colours or figures to be found, yet nobody thinks it a confused picture. What is it, then, that makes it be thought confused, since the want of symmetry does not? As it is plain it does not: for another draught made barely in imitation of this could not be called confused. I answer, That which makes it be thought confused is, the applying it to some name to which it does no more discernibly belong than to some other: v.g. when it is said to be the picture of a man, or Caesar, then any one with reason counts it confused; because it is not discernible in that state to belong more to the name man, or Caesar, than to the name baboon, or Pompey: which are supposed to stand for different ideas from those signified by man, or Caesar. But when a cylindrical mirror, placed right, had reduced those irregular lines on the table into their due order and proportion, then the confusion ceases, and the eye presently sees that it is a man, or Caesar; i.e. that it belongs to those names; and that it is sufficiently distinguishable from a baboon, or Pompey; i.e. from the ideas signified by those names. Just thus it is with our ideas, which are as it were the pictures of things. No one of these mental draughts, however the parts are put together, can be called confused (for they are plainly discernible as they are) till it be ranked under some ordinary name to which it cannot be discerned to belong, any more than it does to some other name of an allowed different signification.

9. Their simple ones mutable and undetermined. Thirdly, A third defect that frequently gives the name of confused to our ideas, is, when any one of them is uncertain and undetermined. Thus we may observe men who, not forbearing to use the ordinary words of their language till they have learned their precise signification, change the idea they make this or that term stand for, almost as often as they use it. He that does this out of uncertainty of what he should leave out, or put into his idea of church, or idolatry, every time he thinks of either, and holds not steady to any one precise combination of ideas that makes it up, is said to have a confused idea of idolatry or the church: though this be still for the same reason as the former, viz. because a mutable idea (if we will allow it to be one idea) cannot belong to one name rather than another, and so loses the distinction that distinct names are designed for.

10. Confusion without reference to names, hardly conceivable. By what has been said, we may observe how much names, as supposed steady signs of things, and by their difference to stand for, and keep things distinct that in themselves are different, are the occasion of denominating ideas distinct or confused, by a secret and unobserved reference the mind makes of its ideas to such names. This perhaps will be fuller understood, after what I say of Words in the third Book has been read and considered. But without taking notice of such a reference of ideas to distinct names, as the signs of distinct things, it will be hard to say what a confused idea is. And therefore when a man designs, by any name, a sort of things, or any one particular thing, distinct from all others, the complex idea he annexes to that name is the more distinct, the more particular the ideas are, and the greater and more determinate the number and order of them is, whereof it is made up. For, the more it has of these, the more it has still of the perceivable differences, whereby it is kept separate and distinct from all ideas belonging to other names, even those that approach nearest to it, and thereby all confusion with them is avoided.

11. Confusion concerns always two ideas. Confusion making it a difficulty to separate two things that should be separated, concerns always two ideas; and those most which most approach one another. Whenever, therefore, we suspect any idea to be confused, we must examine what other it is in danger to be confounded with, or which it cannot easily be separated from; and that will always be found an idea belonging to another name, and so should be a different thing, from which yet it is not sufficiently distinct: being either the same

with it, or making a part of it, or at least as properly called by that name as the other it is ranked under; and so keeps not that difference from that other idea which the different names import.

12. Causes of confused ideas. This, I think, is the confusion proper to ideas; which still carries with it a secret reference to names. At least, if there be any other confusion of ideas, this is that which most of all disorders men's thoughts and discourses: ideas, as ranked under names, being those that for the most part men reason of within themselves, and always those which they commune about with others. And therefore where there are supposed two different ideas, marked by two different names, which are not as distinguishable as the sounds that stand for them, there never fails to be confusion; and where any ideas are distinct as the ideas of those two sounds they are marked by, there can be between them no confusion. The way to prevent it is to collect and unite into one complex idea, as precisely as is possible, all those ingredients whereby it is differenced from others; and to them, so united in a determinate number and order, apply steadily the same name. But this neither accommodating men's ease or vanity, nor serving any design but that of naked truth, which is not always the thing aimed at, such exactness is rather to be wished than hoped for. And since the loose application of names, to undetermined, variable, and almost no ideas, serves both to cover our own ignorance, as well as to perplex and confound others, which goes for learning and superiority in knowledge, it is no wonder that most men should use it themselves, whilst they complain of it in others.

Though I think no small part of the confusion to be found in the notions of men might, by care and ingenuity, be avoided, yet I am far from concluding it everywhere wilful. Some ideas are so complex, and made up of so many parts, that the memory does not easily retain the very same precise combination of simple ideas under one name: much less are we able constantly to divine for what precise complex idea such a name stands in another man's use of it. From the first of these, follows confusion in a man's own reasonings and opinions within himself; from the latter, frequent confusion in discoursing and arguing with others. But having more at large treated of Words, their defects, and abuses, in the following Book, I shall here say no more of it.

13. Complex ideas may be distinct in one part, and confused in another. Our complex ideas, being made up of collections, and so variety of simple ones, may accordingly be very clear and distinct in one part, and very obscure and confused in another. In a man who speaks of a chiliaedron, or a body of a thousand sides, the ideas of the figure may be very confused, though that of the number be very distinct; so that he being able to discourse and demonstrate concerning that part of his complex idea which depends upon the number of thousand, he is apt to think he has a distinct idea of a chiliaedron; though it be plain he has no precise idea of its figure, so as to distinguish it, by that, from one that has but 999 sides: the not observing whereof causes no small error in men's thoughts, and confusion in their discourses.

14. This, if not heeded, causes confusion in our arguings. He that thinks he has a distinct idea of the figure of a chiliaedron, let him for trial sake take another parcel of the same uniform matter, viz. gold or wax of an equal bulk, and make it into a figure of 999 sides. He will, I doubt not, be able to distinguish these two ideas one from another, by the number of sides; and reason and argue distinctly about them, whilst he keeps his thoughts and reasoning to that part only of these ideas which is contained in their numbers; as that the sides of the one could be divided into two equal numbers, and of the others not, &c. But when he goes about to distinguish them by their figure, he will there be presently at a loss, and not be able, I think, to frame in his mind two ideas, one of them distinct from the other, by the bare figure of these two pieces of gold; as he could, if the same parcels of gold were made one into a cube, the other a figure of five sides. In which incomplete ideas, we are very apt to impose on ourselves, and wrangle with others, especially where they have particular and familiar names. For, being satisfied in that part of the idea which we have clear; and the name which is familiar to us, being applied to the whole, containing that part also which is imperfect and obscure, we are apt to use it for that confused part, and draw deductions from it in the obscure part of its

signification, as confidently as we do from the other.

15. Instance in eternity. Having frequently in our mouths the name Eternity, we are apt to think we have a positive comprehensive idea of it, which is as much as to say, that there is no part of that duration which is not clearly contained in our idea. It is true that he that thinks so may have a clear idea of duration; he may also have a clear idea of a very great length of duration; he may also have a clear idea of the comparison of that great one with still a greater: but it not being possible for him to include in his idea of any duration, let it be as great as it will, the whole extent together of a duration, where he supposes no end, that part of his idea, which is still beyond the bounds of that large duration he represents to his own thoughts, is very obscure and undetermined. And hence it is that in disputes and reasonings concerning eternity, or any other infinite, we are very apt to blunder, and involve ourselves in manifest absurdities.

16. Infinite divisibility of matter. In matter, we have no clear ideas of the smallness of parts much beyond the smallest that occur to any of our senses: and therefore, when we talk of the divisibility of matter in infinitum, though we have clear ideas of division and divisibility, and have also clear ideas of parts made out of a whole by division; yet we have but very obscure and confused ideas of corpuscles, or minute bodies, so to be divided, when, by former divisions, they are reduced to a smallness much exceeding the perception of any of our senses; and so all that we have clear and distinct ideas of is of what division in general or abstractedly is, and the relation of totum and pars: but of the bulk of the body, to be thus infinitely divided after certain progressions, I think, we have no clear nor distinct idea at all. For I ask any one, whether, taking the smallest atom of dust he ever saw, he has any distinct idea (bating still the number, which concerns not extension) betwixt the 1,000,000th and the 1,000,000,000th part of it. Or if he think he can refine his ideas to that degree, without losing sight of them, let him add ten cyphers to each of those numbers. Such a degree of smallness is not unreasonable to be supposed; since a division carried on so far brings it no nearer the end of infinite division, than the first division into two halves does. I must confess, for my part, I have no clear distinct ideas of the different bulk or extension of those bodies, having but a very obscure one of either of them. So that, I think, when we talk of division of bodies in infinitum, our idea of their distinct bulks, which is the subject and foundation of division, comes, after a little progression, to be confounded, and almost lost in obscurity. For that idea which is to represent only bigness must be very obscure and confused, which we cannot distinguish from one ten times as big, but only by number: so that we have clear distinct ideas, we may say, of ten and one, but no distinct ideas of two such extensions. It is plain from hence, that, when we talk of infinite divisibility of body or extension, our distinct and clear ideas are only of numbers: but the clear distinct ideas of extension after some progress of division, are quite lost; and of such minute parts we have no distinct ideas at all; but it returns, as all our ideas of infinite do, at last to that of number always to be added; but thereby never amounts to any distinct idea of actual infinite parts. We have, it is true, a clear idea of division, as often as we think of it; but thereby we have no more a clear idea of infinite parts in matter, than we have a clear idea of an infinite number, by being able still to add new numbers to any assigned numbers we have: endless divisibility giving us no more a clear and distinct idea of actually infinite parts, than endless addibility (if I may so speak) gives us a clear and distinct idea of an actually infinite number: they both being only in a power still of increasing the number, be it already as great as it will. So that of what remains to be added (wherein consists the infinity) we have but an obscure, imperfect, and confused idea; from or about which we can argue or reason with no certainty or clearness, no more than we can in arithmetic, about a number of which we have no such distinct idea as we have of 4 or 100; but only this relative obscure one, that, compared to any other, it is still bigger: and we have no more a clear positive idea of it, when we say or conceive it is bigger, or more than 400,000,000, than if we should say it is bigger than 40 or 4: 400,000,000 having no nearer a proportion to the end of addition or number than 4. For he that adds only 4 to 4, and so proceeds, shall as soon come to the end of all addition, as he that adds

400,000,000 to 400,000,000. And so likewise in eternity; he that has an idea of but four years, has as much a positive complete idea of eternity, as he that has one of 400,000,000 of years: for what remains of eternity beyond either of these two numbers of years, is as clear to the one as the other; i.e. neither of them has any clear positive idea of it at all. For he that adds only 4 years to 4, and so on, shall as soon reach eternity as he that adds 400,000,000 of years, and so on; or, if he please, doubles the increase as often as he will: the remaining abyss being still as far beyond the end of all these progressions as it is from the length of a day or an hour. For nothing finite bears any proportion to infinite; and therefore our ideas, which are all finite, cannot bear any. Thus it is also in our idea of extension, when we increase it by addition, as well as when we diminish it by division, and would enlarge our thoughts to infinite space. After a few doublings of those ideas of extension, which are the largest we are accustomed to have, we lose the clear distinct idea of that space: it becomes a confusedly great one, with a surplus of still greater; about which, when we would argue or reason, we shall always find ourselves at a loss; confused ideas, in our arguings and deductions from that part of them which is confused, always leading us into confusion.

Chapter XXX. Of Real and Fantastical Ideas

1. Ideas considered in reference to their archetypes. Besides what we have already mentioned concerning ideas, other considerations belong to them, in reference to things from whence they are taken, or which they may be supposed to represent; and thus, I think, they may come under a three-fold distinction, and are:—
First, either real or fantastical;
Secondly, adequate or inadequate;
Thirdly, true or false.
First, by real ideas, I mean such as have a foundation in nature; such as have a conformity with the real being and existence of things, or with their archetypes. Fantastical or chimerical, I call such as have no foundation in nature, nor have any conformity with that reality of being to which they are tacitly referred, as to their archetypes. If we examine the several sorts of ideas before mentioned, we shall find that,
2. Simple ideas are all real appearances of things. First, Our simple ideas are all real, all agree to the reality of things: not that they are all of them the images or representations of what does exist; the contrary whereof, in all but the primary qualities of bodies, hath been already shown. But, though whiteness and coldness are no more in snow than pain is; yet those ideas of whiteness and coldness, pain, &c., being in us the effects of powers in things without us, ordained by our Maker to produce in us such sensations; they are real ideas in us, whereby we distinguish the qualities that are really in things themselves. For, these several appearances being designed to be the mark whereby we are to know and distinguish things which we have to do with, our ideas do as well serve us to that purpose, and are as real distinguishing characters, whether they be only constant effects, or else exact resemblances of something in the things themselves: the reality lying in that steady correspondence they have with the distinct constitutions of real beings. But whether they answer to those constitutions, as to causes or patterns, it matters not; it suffices that they are constantly produced by them. And thus our simple ideas are all real and true, because they answer and agree to those powers of things which produce them in our minds; that being all that is requisite to make them real, and not fictions at pleasure. For in simple ideas (as has been shown) the mind is wholly confined to the operation of things upon it, and can make to itself no simple idea, more than what it has received.
3. Complex ideas are voluntary combinations. Though the mind be wholly passive in respect of its simple ideas; yet, I think, we may say it is not so in respect of its complex ideas. For those being combinations of simple ideas put together, and united under one general name, it

is plain that the mind of man uses some kind of liberty in forming those complex ideas: how else comes it to pass that one man's idea of gold, or justice, is different from another's, but because he has put in, or left out of his, some simple idea which the other has not? The question then is, Which of these are real, and which barely imaginary combinations? What collections agree to the reality of things, and what not? And to this I say that,

4. Mixed modes and relations, made of consistent ideas, are real. Secondly, Mixed modes and relations, having no other reality but what they have in the minds of men, there is nothing more required to this kind of ideas to make them real, but that they be so framed, that there be a possibility of existing conformable to them. These ideas themselves, being archetypes, cannot differ from their archetypes, and so cannot be chimerical, unless any one will jumble together in them inconsistent ideas. Indeed, as any of them have the names of a known language assigned to them, by which he that has them in his mind would signify them to others, so bare possibility of existing is not enough; they must have a conformity to the ordinary signification of the name that is given them, that they may not be thought fantastical: as if a man would give the name of justice to that idea which common use calls liberality. But this fantasticalness relates more to propriety of speech, than reality of ideas. For a man to be undisturbed in danger, sedately to consider what is fittest to be done, and to execute it steadily, is a mixed mode, or a complex idea of an action which may exist. But to be undisturbed in danger, without using one's reason or industry, is what is also possible to be; and so is as real an idea as the other. Though the first of these, having the name courage given to it, may, in respect of that name, be a right or wrong idea; but the other, whilst it has not a common received name of any known language assigned to it, is not capable of any deformity, being made with no reference to anything but itself.

5. Complex ideas of substances are real, when they agree with the existence of things. Thirdly, Our complex ideas of substances, being made all of them in reference to things existing without us, and intended to be representations of substances as they really are, are no further real than as they are such combinations of simple ideas as are really united, and co-exist in things without us. On the contrary, those are fantastical which are made up of such collections of simple ideas as were really never united, never were found together in any substance: v.g. a rational creature, consisting of a horse's head, joined to a body of human shape, or such as the centaurs are described: or, a body yellow, very malleable, fusible, and fixed, but lighter than common water: or an uniform, unorganized body, consisting, as to sense, all of similar parts, with perception and voluntary motion joined to it. Whether such substances as these can possibly exist or no, it is probable we do not know: but be that as it will, these ideas of substances, being made conformable to no pattern existing that we know; and consisting of such collections of ideas as no substance ever showed us united together, they ought to pass with us for barely imaginary: but much more are those complex ideas so, which contain in them any inconsistency or contradiction of their parts.

Chapter XXXI.Of Adequate and Inadequate Ideas

1. Adequate ideas are such as perfectly represent their archetypes. Of our real ideas, some are adequate, and some are inadequate. Those I call adequate, which perfectly represent those archetypes which the mind supposes them taken from: which it intends them to stand for, and to which it refers them. Inadequate ideas are such, which are but a partial or incomplete representation of those archetypes to which they are referred. Upon which account it is plain,

2. Simple ideas all adequate. First, that all our simple ideas are adequate. Because, being nothing but the effects of certain powers in things, fitted and ordained by God to produce such sensations in us, they cannot but be correspondent and adequate to those powers: and we are sure they agree to the reality of things. For, if sugar produce in us the ideas which we call whiteness and sweetness, we are sure there is a power in sugar to produce those ideas in our

minds, or else they could not have been produced by it. And so each sensation answering the power that operates on any of our senses, the idea so produced is a real idea, (and not a fiction of the mind, which has no power to produce any simple idea); and cannot but be adequate, since it ought only to answer that power: and so all simple ideas are adequate. It is true, the things producing in us these simple ideas are but few of them denominated by us, as if they were only the causes of them; but as if those ideas were real beings in them. For, though fire be called painful to the touch, whereby is signified the power of producing in us the idea of pain, yet it is denominated also light and hot; as if light and heat were really something in the fire, more than a power to excite these ideas in us; and therefore are called qualities in or of the fire. But these being nothing, in truth, but powers to excite such ideas in us, I must in that sense be understood, when I speak of secondary qualities as being in things; or of their ideas as being the objects that excite them in us. Such ways of speaking, though accommodated to the vulgar notions, without which one cannot be well understood, yet truly signify nothing but those powers which are in things to excite certain sensations or ideas in us. Since were there no fit organs to receive the impressions fire makes on the sight and touch, nor a mind joined to those organs to receive the ideas of light and heat by those impressions from the fire or sun, there would yet be no more light or heat in the world than there would be pain if there were no sensible creature to feel it, though the sun should continue just as it is now, and Mount AEtna flame higher than ever it did. Solidity and extension, and the termination of it, figure, with motion and rest, whereof we have the ideas, would be really in the world as they are, whether there were any sensible being to perceive them or no: and therefore we have reason to look on those as the real modifications of matter, and such as are the exciting causes of all our various sensations from bodies. But this being an inquiry not belonging to this place, I shall enter no further into it, but proceed to show what complex ideas are adequate, and what not.

3. Modes are all adequate. Secondly, our complex ideas of modes, being voluntary collections of simple ideas, which the mind puts together, without reference to any real archetypes, or standing patterns, existing anywhere, are and cannot but be adequate ideas. Because they, not being intended for copies of things really existing, but for archetypes made by the mind, to rank and denominate things by, cannot want anything; they having each of them that combination of ideas, and thereby that perfection, which the mind intended they should: so that the mind acquiesces in them, and can find nothing wanting. Thus, by having the idea of a figure with three sides meeting at three angles, I have a complete idea, wherein I require nothing else to make it perfect. That the mind is satisfied with the perfection of this its idea is plain, in that it does not conceive that any understanding hath, or can have, a more complete or perfect idea of that thing it signifies by the word triangle, supposing it to exist, than itself has, in that complex idea of three sides and three angles, in which is contained all that is or can be essential to it, or necessary to complete it, wherever or however it exists. But in our ideas of substances it is otherwise. For there, desiring to copy things as they really do exist, and to represent to ourselves that constitution on which all their properties depend, we perceive our ideas attain not that perfection we intend: we find they still want something we should be glad were in them; and so are all inadequate. But mixed modes and relations, being archetypes without patterns, and so having nothing to represent but themselves, cannot but be adequate, everything being so to itself. He that at first put together the idea of danger perceived, absence of disorder from fear, sedate consideration of what was justly to be done, and executing that without disturbance, or being deterred by the danger of it, had certainly in his mind that complex idea made up of that combination: and intending it to be nothing else but what is, nor to have in it any other simple ideas but what it hath, it could not also but be an adequate idea: and laying this up in his memory, with the name courage annexed to it, to signify to others, and denominate from thence any action he should observe to agree with it, had thereby a standard to measure and denominate actions by, as they agreed to it. This idea, thus made and laid up for a pattern, must necessarily be adequate, being referred to nothing else but itself, nor made by any other original but the good liking and will of him that first made this

combination.

4. Modes, in reference to settled names, may be inadequate. Indeed another coming after, and in conversation learning from him the word courage, may make an idea, to which he gives the name courage, different from what the first author applied it to, and has in his mind when he uses it. And in this case, if he designs that his idea in thinking should be conformable to the other's idea, as the name he uses in speaking is conformable in sound to his from whom he learned it, his idea may be very wrong and inadequate: because in this case, making the other man's idea the pattern of his idea in thinking, as the other man's word or sound is the pattern of his in speaking, his idea is so far defective and inadequate, as it is distant from the archetype and pattern he refers it to, and intends to express and signify by the name he uses for it; which name he would have to be a sign of the other man's idea, (to which, in its proper use, it is primarily annexed), and of his own, as agreeing to it: to which if his own does not exactly correspond, it is faulty and inadequate.

5. Because then meant, in propriety of speech, to correspond to the ideas in some other mind. Therefore these complex ideas of modes, which they are referred by the mind, and intended to correspond to the ideas in the mind of some other intelligent being, expressed by the names we apply to them, they may be very deficient, wrong, and inadequate; because they agree not to that which the mind designs to be their archetype and pattern: in which respect only any idea of modes can be wrong, imperfect, or inadequate. And on this account our ideas of mixed modes are the most liable to be faulty of any other; but this refers more to proper speaking than knowing right.

6. Ideas of substances, as referred to real essences, not adequate. Thirdly, what ideas we have of substances, I have above shown. Now, those ideas have in the mind a double reference: 1. Sometimes they are referred to a supposed real essence of each species of things. 2. Sometimes they are only designed to be pictures and representations in the mind of things that do exist, by ideas of those qualities that are discoverable in them. In both which ways these copies of those originals and archetypes are imperfect and inadequate.

First, it is usual for men to make the names of substances stand for things as supposed to have certain real essences, whereby they are of this or that species: and names standing for nothing but the ideas that are in men's minds, they must constantly refer their ideas to such real essences, as to their archetypes. That men (especially such as have been bred up in the learning taught in this part of the world) do suppose certain specific essences of substances, which each individual in its several kinds is made conformable to and partakes of, is so far from needing proof that it will be thought strange if any one should do otherwise. And thus they ordinarily apply the specific names they rank particular substances under, to things as distinguished by such specific real essences. Who is there almost, who would not take it amiss if it should be doubted whether he called himself a man, with any other meaning than as having the real essence of a man? And yet if you demand what those real essences are, it is plain men are ignorant, and know them not. From whence it follows, that the ideas they have in their minds, being referred to real essences, as to archetypes which are unknown, must be so far from being adequate that they cannot be supposed to be any representation of them at all. The complex ideas we have of substances are, as it has been shown, certain collections of simple ideas that have been observed or supposed constantly to exist together. But such a complex idea cannot be the real essence of any substance; for then the properties we discover in that body would depend on that complex idea, and be deducible from it, and their necessary connexion with it be known; as all properties of a triangle depend on, and, as far as they are discoverable, are deducible from the complex idea of three lines including a space. But it is plain that in our complex ideas of substances are not contained such ideas, on which all the other qualities that are to be found in them do depend. The common idea men have of iron is, a body of a certain colour, weight, and hardness; and a property that they look on as belonging to it, is malleableness. But yet this property has no necessary connexion with that complex idea, or any part of it: and there is no more reason to think that malleableness depends on that colour, weight, and hardness, than that colour or that weight depends on its malleableness. And yet, though we know nothing of these real essences, there is nothing more ordinary than that men should attribute the sorts of things to such essences. The particular parcel of matter which makes the ring I have on my finger is forwardly by most men supposed to have a real essence, whereby it is gold; and from whence those qualities flow which I find in it, viz. its peculiar colour, weight, hardness, fusibility, fixedness, and change of colour upon a slight touch of mercury, &c. This essence, from which all these properties flow, when I inquire into it and search after it, I plainly perceive I cannot discover: the furthest I can go is, only to presume that, it being nothing but body, its real essence or internal constitution, on which these qualities depend, can be nothing but the figure, size, and connexion of its solid parts; of neither of which having any distinct perception at all can I have any idea of its essence: which is the cause that it has that particular shining yellowness; a greater weight than anything I know of the same bulk; and a fitness to have its colour changed by the touch of quicksilver. If any one will say, that the real essence and internal constitution, on which these properties depend, is not the figure, size, and arrangement or connexion of its solid parts, but something else, called its particular form, I am further from having any idea of its real essence than I was before. For I have an idea of figure, size, and situation of solid parts in general, though I have none of the particular figure, size, or putting together of parts, whereby the qualities above mentioned are produced; which qualities I find in that particular parcel of matter that is on my finger, and not in another parcel of matter, with which I cut the pen I write with. But, when I am told that something besides the figure, size, and posture of the solid parts of that body in its essence, something called substantial form, of that I confess I have no idea at all, but only of the sound form; which is far enough from an idea of its real essence or constitution. The like ignorance as I have of the real essence of this particular substance, I have also of the real essence of all other natural ones: of which essences I confess I have no distinct ideas at all; and, I am apt to suppose, others, when they examine their own knowledge, will find in themselves, in this one point, the same sort of ignorance.

7. Because men know not the real essences of substances. Now, then, when men apply to this particular parcel of matter on my finger a general name already in use, and denominate it gold, do they not ordinarily, or are they not understood to give it that name, as belonging to a particular species of bodies, having a real internal essence; by having of which essence this particular substance comes to be of that species, and to be called by that name? If it be so, as it is plain it is, the name by which things are marked as having that essence must be referred primarily to that essence; and consequently the idea to which that name is given must be referred also to that essence, and be intended to represent it. Which essence, since they who so use the names know not, their ideas of substances must be all inadequate in that respect, as not containing in them that real essence which the mind intends they should.

8. Ideas of substances, when regarded as collections of their qualities, are all inadequate. Secondly, those who, neglecting that useless supposition of unknown real essences, whereby they are distinguished, endeavour to copy the substances that exist in the world, by putting together the ideas of those sensible qualities which are found coexisting in them, though they come much nearer a likeness of them than those who imagine they know not what real specific essences: yet they arrive not at perfectly adequate ideas of those substances they would thus copy into the their minds: nor do those copies exactly and fully contain all that is to be found in their archetypes. Because those qualities and powers of substances, whereof we make their complex ideas, are so many and various, that no man's complex idea contains them all. That our complex ideas of substances do not contain in them all the simple ideas that are united in the things themselves is evident, in that men do rarely put into their complex idea of any substance all the simple ideas they do know to exist in it. Because, endeavouring to make the signification of their names as clear and as little cumbersome as they can, they make their specific ideas of the sorts of substance, for the most part, of a few of those simple ideas which are to be found in them: but these having no original precedency, or right to be put in, and

make the specific idea, more than others that are left out, it is plain that both these ways our ideas of substances are deficient and inadequate. The simple ideas whereof we make our complex ones of substances are all of them (bating only the figure and bulk of some sorts) powers; which being relations to other substances, we can never be sure that we know all the powers that are in any one body, till we have tried what changes it is fitted to give to or receive from other substances in their several ways of application: which being impossible to be tried upon any one body, much less upon all, it is impossible we should have adequate ideas of any substance made up of a collection of all its properties.

9. Their powers usually make up our complex ideas of substances. Whosoever first lighted on a parcel of that sort of substance we denote by the word gold, could not rationally take the bulk and figure he observed in that lump to depend on its real essence, or internal constitution. Therefore those never went into his idea of that species of body; but its peculiar colour, perhaps, and weight, were the first he abstracted from it, to make the complex idea of that species. Which both are but powers; the one to affect our eyes after such a manner, and to produce in us that idea we call yellow; and the other to force upwards any other body of equal bulk, they being put into a pair of equal scales, one against another. Another perhaps added to these the ideas of fusibility and fixedness, two other passive powers, in relation to the operation of fire upon it; another, its ductility and solubility in aqua regia, two other powers, relating to the operation of other bodies, in changing its outward figure, or separation of it into insensible parts. These, or parts of these, put together, usually make the complex idea in men's minds of that sort of body we call gold.

10. Substances have innumerable powers not contained in our complex ideas of them. But no one who hath considered the properties of bodies in general, or this sort in particular, can doubt that this, called gold, has infinite other properties not contained in that complex idea. Some who have examined this species more accurately could, I believe, enumerate ten times as many properties in gold, all of them as inseparable from its internal constitution, as its colour or weight: and it is probable, if any one knew all the properties that are by divers men known of this metal, there would be an hundred times as many ideas go to the complex idea of gold as any one man yet has in his; and yet perhaps that not be the thousandth part of what is to be discovered in it. The changes that that one body is apt to receive, and make in other bodies, upon a due application, exceeding far not only what we know, but what we are apt to imagine. Which will not appear so much a paradox to any one who will but consider how far men are yet from knowing all the properties of that one, no very compound figure, a triangle; though it be no small number that are already by mathematicians discovered of it.

11. Ideas of substances, being got only by collecting their qualities, are all inadequate. So that all our complex ideas of substances are imperfect and inadequate. Which would be so also in mathematical figures, if we were to have our complex ideas of them, only by collecting their properties in reference to other figures. How uncertain and imperfect would our ideas be of an ellipsis, if we had no other idea of it, but some few of its properties? Whereas, having in our plain idea the whole essence of that figure, we from thence discover those properties, and demonstratively see how they flow, and are inseparable from it.

12. Simple ideas, ektupa, and adequate. Thus the mind has three sorts of abstract ideas or nominal essences:

First, simple ideas, which are ektupa or copies; but yet certainly adequate. Because, being intended to express nothing but the power in things to produce in the mind such a sensation, that sensation when it is produced, cannot but be the effect of that power. So the paper I write on, having the power in the light (I speak according to the common notion of light) to produce in men the sensation which I call white, it cannot but be the effect of such a power in something without the mind; since the mind has not the power to produce any such idea in itself: and being meant for nothing else but the effect of such a power, that simple idea is real and adequate; the sensation of white, in my mind, being the effect of that power which is in the paper to produce it, is perfectly adequate to that power; or else that power would produce a different idea.

13. Ideas of substances are ektupa, and inadequate. Secondly, the complex ideas of substances are ectypes, copies too; but not perfect ones, not adequate: which is very evident to the mind, in that it plainly perceives, that whatever collection of simple ideas it makes of any substance that exists, it cannot be sure that it exactly answers all that are in that substance. Since, not having tried all the operations of all other substances upon it, and found all the alterations it would receive from, or cause in, other substances, it cannot have an exact adequate collection of all its active and passive capacities; and so not have an adequate complex idea of the powers of any substance existing, and its relations; which is that sort of complex idea of substances we have. And, after all, if we would have, and actually had, in our complex idea, an exact collection of all the secondary qualities or powers of any substance, we should not yet thereby have an idea of the essence of that thing. For, since the powers or qualities that are observable by us are not the real essence of that substance, but depend on it, and flow from it, any collection whatsoever of these qualities cannot be the real essence of that thing. Whereby it is plain, that our ideas of substances are not adequate; are not what the mind intends them to be. Besides, a man has no idea of substance in general, nor knows what substance is in itself.

14. Ideas of modes and relations are archetypes and cannot be adequate. Thirdly, complex ideas of modes and relations are originals, and archetypes; are not copies, nor made after the pattern of any real existence, to which the mind intends them to be conformable, and exactly to answer. These being such collections of simple ideas that the mind itself puts together, and such collections that each of them contains in it precisely all that the mind intends that it should, they are archetypes and essences of modes that may exist; and so are designed only for, and belong only to such modes as, when they do exist, have an exact conformity with those complex ideas. The ideas, therefore, of modes and relations cannot but be adequate.

Chapter XXXII.Of True and False Ideas

1. Truth and falsehood properly belong to propositions, not to ideas. Though truth and falsehood belong, in propriety of speech, only to propositions: yet ideas are oftentimes termed true or false (as what words are there that are not used with great latitude, and with some deviation from their strict and proper significations?) Though I think that when ideas themselves are termed true or false, there is still some secret or tacit proposition, which is the foundation of that denomination: as we shall see, if we examine the particular occasions wherein they come to be called true or false. In all which we shall find some kind of affirmation or negation, which is the reason of that denomination. For our ideas, being nothing but bare appearances, or perceptions in our minds, cannot properly and simply in themselves be said to be true or false, no more than a single name of anything can be said to be true or false.

2. Ideas and words may be said to be true, inasmuch as they really are ideas and words. Indeed both ideas and words may be said to be true, in a metaphysical sense of the word truth; as all other things that any way exist are said to be true, i.e. really to be such as they exist. Though in things called true, even in that sense, there is perhaps a secret reference to our ideas, looked upon as the standards of that truth; which amounts to a mental proposition, though it be usually not taken notice of.

3. No idea, as an appearance in the mind, either true or false. But it is not in that metaphysical sense of truth which we inquire here, when we examine, whether our ideas are capable of being true or false, but in the more ordinary acceptation of those words: and so I say that the ideas in our minds, being only so many perceptions or appearances there, none of them are false; the idea of a centaur having no more falsehood in it when it appears in our minds, than the name centaur has falsehood in it, when it is pronounced by our mouths, or written on paper. For truth or falsehood lying always in some affirmation or negation, mental or verbal,

our ideas are not capable, any of them, of being false, till the mind passes some judgment on them; that is, affirms or denies something of them.

4. Ideas referred to anything extraneous to them may be true or false. Whenever the mind refers any of its ideas to anything extraneous to them, they are then capable to be called true or false. Because the mind, in such a reference, makes a tacit supposition of their conformity to that thing; which supposition, as it happens to be true or false, so the ideas themselves come to be denominated. The most usual cases wherein this happens, are these following:

5. Other men's ideas; real existence; and supposed real essences, are what men usually refer their ideas to. First, when the mind supposes any idea it has conformable to that in other men's minds, called by the same common name; v.g. when the mind intends or judges its ideas of justice, temperance, religion, to be the same with what other men give those names to.

Secondly, when the mind supposes any idea it has in itself to be conformable to some real existence. Thus the two ideas of a man and a centaur, supposed to be the ideas of real substances, are the one true and the other false; the one having a conformity to what has really existed, the other not.

Thirdly, when the mind refers any of its ideas to that real constitution and essence of anything, whereon all its properties depend: and thus the greatest part, if not all our ideas of substances, are false.

6. The cause of such reference. These suppositions the mind is very apt tacitly to make concerning its own ideas. But yet, if we will examine it, we shall find it is chiefly, if not only, concerning its abstract complex ideas. For the natural tendency of the mind being towards knowledge; and finding that, if it should proceed by and dwell upon only particular things, its progress would be very slow, and its work endless; therefore, to shorten its way to knowledge, and make each perception more comprehensive, the first thing it does, as the foundation of the easier enlarging its knowledge, either by contemplation of the things themselves that it would know, or conference with others about them, is to bind them into bundles, and rank them so into sorts, that what knowledge it gets of any of them it may thereby with assurance extend to all of that sort; and so advance by larger steps in that which is its great business, knowledge. This, as I have elsewhere shown, is the reason why we collect things under comprehensive ideas, with names annexed to them, into genera and species; i.e. into kinds and sorts.

7. Names of things supposed to carry in them knowledge of their essences. If therefore we will warily attend to the motions of the mind, and observe what course it usually takes in its way to knowledge, we shall I think find, that the mind having got an idea which it thinks it may have use of either in contemplation or discourse, the first thing it does is to abstract it, and then get a name to it; and so lay it up in its storehouse, the memory, as containing the essence of a sort of things, of which that name is always to be the mark. Hence it is, that we may often observe that, when any one sees a new thing of a kind that he knows not, he presently asks, what it is; meaning by that inquiry nothing but the name. As if the name carried with it the knowledge of the species, or the essence of it; whereof it is indeed used as the mark, and is generally supposed annexed to it.

8. How men suppose that their ideas must correspond to things, and to the customary meanings of names. But this abstract idea, being something in the mind, between the thing that exists, and the name that is given to it; it is in our ideas that both the rightness of our knowledge, and the propriety and intelligibleness of our speaking, consists. And hence it is that men are so forward to suppose, that the abstract ideas they have in their minds are such as agree to the things existing without them, to which they are referred; and are the same also to which the names they give them do by the use and propriety of that language belong. For without this double conformity of their ideas, they find they should both think amiss of things in themselves, and talk of them unintelligibly to others.

9. Simple ideas may be false, in reference to others of the same name, but are least liable to be so. First, then, I say, that when the truth of our ideas is judged of by the conformity they have to the ideas which other men have, and commonly signify by the same name, they may be any

of them false. But yet simple ideas are least of all liable to be so mistaken. Because a man, by his senses and every day's observation, may easily satisfy himself what the simple ideas are which their several names that are in common use stand for; they being but few in number, and such as, if he doubts or mistakes in, he may easily rectify by the objects they are to be found in. Therefore it is seldom that any one mistakes in his names of simple ideas, or applies the name red to the idea green, or the name sweet to the idea bitter: mush less are men apt to confound the names of ideas belonging to different senses, and call a colour by the name of a taste, &c. Whereby it is evident that the simple ideas they call by any name are commonly the same that others have and mean when they use the same names.

10. Ideas of mixed modes most liable to be false in this sense. Complex ideas are much more liable to be false in this respect; and the complex ideas of mixed modes, much more than those of substances; because in substances (especially those which the common and unborrowed names of any language are applied to) some remarkable sensible qualities, serving ordinarily to distinguish one sort from another, easily preserve those who take any care in the use of their words, from applying them to sorts of substances to which they do not at all belong. But in mixed modes we are much more uncertain; it being not so easy to determine of several actions, whether they are to be called justice or cruelly, liberality or prodigality. And so in referring our ideas to those of other men, called by the same names, ours may be false; and the idea in our minds, which we express by the word justice, may perhaps be that which ought to have another name.

11. Or at least to be thought false. But whether or no our ideas of mixed modes are more liable than any sort to be different from those of other men, which are marked by the same names, this at least is certain, That this sort of falsehood is much more familiarly attributed to our ideas of mixed modes than to any other. When a man is thought to have a false idea of justice, or gratitude, or glory, it is for no other reason, but that his agrees not with the ideas which each of those names are the signs of in other men.

12. And why. The reason whereof seems to me to be this: That the abstract ideas of mixed modes, being men's voluntary combinations of such a precise collection of simple ideas, and so the essence of each species being made by men alone, whereof we have no other sensible standard existing anywhere but the name itself, or the definition of that name; we having nothing else to refer these our ideas of mixed modes to, as a standard to which we would conform them, but the ideas of those who are thought to use those names in their most proper significations; and, so as our ideas conform or differ from them, they pass for true or false. And thus much concerning the truth and falsehood of our ideas, in reference to their names.

13. As referred to real existence, none of our ideas can be false but those of substances. Secondly, as to the truth and falsehood of our ideas, in reference to the real existence of things. When that is made the standard of their truth, none of them can be termed false but only our complex ideas of substances.

14. Simple ideas in this sense not false, and why. First, our simple ideas, being barely such perceptions as God has fitted us to receive, and given power to external objects to produce in us by established laws and ways, suitable to his wisdom and goodness, though incomprehensible to us, their truth consists in nothing else but in such appearances as are produced in us, and must be suitable to those powers he has placed in external objects or else they could not be produced in us: and thus answering those powers, they are what they should be, true ideas. Nor do they become liable to any imputation of falsehood, if the mind (as in most men I believe it does) judges these ideas to be in the things themselves. For God in his wisdom having set them as marks of distinction in things, whereby we may be able to discern one thing from another, and so choose any of them for our uses as we have occasion; it alters not the nature of our simple idea, whether we think that the idea of blue be in the violet itself, or in our mind only; and only the power of producing it by the texture of its parts, reflecting the particles of light after a certain manner, to be in the violet itself. For that texture in the object, by a regular and constant operation producing the same idea of blue in us, it serves us

to distinguish, by our eyes, that from any other thing; whether that distinguishing mark, as it is really in the violet, be only a peculiar texture of parts, or else that very colour, the idea whereof (which is in us) is the exact resemblance. And it is equally from that appearance to be denominated blue, whether it be that real colour, or only a peculiar texture in it, that causes in us that idea: since the name, blue, notes properly nothing but that mark of distinction that is in a violet, discernible only by our eyes, whatever it consists in; that being beyond our capacities distinctly to know, and perhaps would be of less use to us, if we had faculties to discern.

15. Though one man's idea of blue should be different from another's. Neither would it carry any imputation of falsehood to our simple ideas, if by the different structure of our organs it were so ordered, that the same object should produce in several men's minds different ideas at the same time; v.g. if the idea that a violet produced in one man's mind by his eyes were the same that a marigold produced in another man's, and vice versa. For, since this could never be known, because one man's mind could not pass into another man's body, to perceive what appearances were produced by those organs; neither the ideas hereby, nor the names, would be at all confounded, or any falsehood be in either. For all things that had the texture of a violet, producing constantly the idea that he called blue, and those which had the texture of a marigold, producing constantly the idea which he as constantly called yellow, whatever those appearances were in his mind; he would be able as regularly to distinguish things for his use by those appearances, and understand and signify those distinctions marked by the name blue and yellow, as if the appearances or ideas in his mind received from those two flowers were exactly the same with the ideas in other men's minds. I am nevertheless very apt to think that the sensible ideas produced by any object in different men's minds, are most commonly very near and undiscernibly alike. For which opinion, I think, there might be many reasons offered: but that being besides my present business, I shall not trouble my reader with them; but only mind him, that the contrary supposition, if it could be proved, is of little use, either for the improvement of our knowledge, or conveniency of life, and so we need not trouble ourselves to examine it.

16. Simple ideas can none of them be false in respect of real existence. From what has been said concerning our simple ideas, I think it evident that our simple ideas can none of them be false in respect of things existing without us. For the truth of these appearances or perceptions in our minds consisting, as has been said, only in their being answerable to the powers in external objects to produce by our senses such appearances in us, and each of them being in the mind such as it is, suitable to the power that produced it, and which alone it represents, it cannot upon that account, or as referred to such a pattern, be false. Blue and yellow, bitter or sweet, can never be false ideas: these perceptions in the mind are just such as they are there, answering the powers appointed by God to produce them; and so are truly what they are, and are intended to be. Indeed the names may be misapplied, but that in this respect makes no falsehood in the ideas; as if a man ignorant in the English tongue should call purple scarlet.

17. Modes not false cannot be false in reference to essences of things. Secondly, neither can our complex ideas of modes, in reference to the essence of anything really existing, be false; because whatever complex ideas I have of any mode, it hath no reference to any pattern existing, and made by nature; it is not supposed to contain in it any other ideas than what it hath; nor to represent anything but such a complication of ideas as it does. Thus, when I have the idea of such an action of a man who forbears to afford himself such meat, drink, and clothing, and other conveniences of life, as his riches and estate will be sufficient to supply and his station requires, I have no false idea; but such an one as represents an action, either as I find or imagine it, and so is capable of neither truth nor falsehood. But when I give the name frugality or virtue to this action, then it may be called a false idea, if thereby it be supposed to agree with that idea to which, in propriety of speech, the name of frugality doth belong, or to be conformable to that law which is the standard of virtue and vice.

18. Ideas of substances may be false in reference to existing things. Thirdly, our complex ideas of substances, being all referred to patterns in things themselves, may be false. That they are

all false, when looked upon as the representations of the unknown essences of things, is so evident that there needs nothing to be said of it. I shall therefore pass over that chimerical supposition, and consider them as collections of simple ideas in the mind, taken from combinations of simple ideas existing together constantly in things, of which patterns they are the supposed copies; and in this reference of them to the existence of things, they are false ideas:—(1) When they put together simple ideas, which in the real existence of things have no union; as when to the shape and size that exist together in a horse, is joined in the same complex idea the power of barking like a dog: which three ideas, however put together into one in the mind, were never united in nature; and this, therefore, may be called a false idea of a horse. (2) Ideas of substances are, in this respect, also false, when, from any collection of simple ideas that do always exist together, there is separated, by a direct negation, any other simple idea which is constantly joined with them. Thus, if to extension, solidity, fusibility, the peculiar weightiness, and yellow colour of gold, any one join in his thoughts the negation of a greater degree of fixedness than is in lead or copper, he may be said to have a false complex idea, as well as when he joins to those other simple ones the idea of perfect absolute fixedness. For either way, the complex idea of gold being made up of such simple ones as have no union in nature, may be termed false. But, if he leave out of this his complex idea that of fixedness quite, without either actually joining to or separating it from the rest in his mind, it is, I think, to be looked on as an inadequate and imperfect idea, rather than a false one; since, though it contains not all the simple ideas that are united in nature, yet it puts none together but what do really exist together.

19. Truth or falsehood always supposes affirmation or negation. Though, in compliance with the ordinary way of speaking, I have shown in what sense and upon what ground our ideas may be sometimes called true or false; yet if we will look a little nearer into the matter, in all cases where any idea is called true or false, it is from some judgment that the mind makes, or is supposed to make, that is true or false. For truth or falsehood, being never without some affirmation or negation, express or tacit, it is not to be found but where signs are joined or separated, according to the agreement or disagreement of the things they stand for. The signs we chiefly use are either ideas or words; wherewith we make either mental or verbal propositions. Truth lies in so joining or separating these representatives, as the things they stand for do in themselves agree or disagree; and falsehood in the contrary, as shall be more fully shown hereafter.

20. Ideas in themselves neither true nor false. Any idea, then, which we have in our minds, whether conformable or not to the existence of things, or to any idea in the minds of other men, cannot properly for this alone be called false. For these representations, if they have nothing in them but what is really existing in things without, cannot be thought false, being exact representations of something: nor yet if they have anything in them differing from the reality of things, can they properly be said to be false representations, or ideas of things they do not represent. But the mistake and falsehood is:

21. But are false — when judged agreeable to another man's idea, without being so. First, when the mind having any idea, it judges and concludes it the same that is in other men's minds, signified by the same name; or that it is conformable to the ordinary received signification or definition of that word, when indeed it is not: which is the most usual mistake in mixed modes, though other ideas also are liable to it.

22. When judged to agree to real existence, when they do not. (2) When it having a complex idea made up of such a collection of simple ones as nature never puts together, it judges it to agree to a species of creatures really existing; as when it joins the weight of tin to the colour, fusibility, and fixedness of gold.

23. When judged adequate, without being so. (3) When in its complex idea it has united a certain number of simple ideas that do really exist together in some sort of creatures, but has also left out others as much inseparable, it judges this to be a perfect complete idea of a sort of things which really it is not; v.g. having joined the ideas of substance, yellow, malleable, most

heavy, and fusible, it takes that complex idea to be the complete idea of gold, when yet its peculiar fixedness, and solubility in aqua regia, are as inseparable from those other ideas, or qualities, of that body as they are one from another.

24. When judged to represent the real essence. (4) The mistake is yet greater, when I judge that this complex idea contains in it the real essence of any body existing; when at least it contains but some few of those properties which flow from its real essence and constitution. I say only some few of those properties; for those properties consisting mostly in the active and passive powers it has in reference to other things, all that are vulgarly known of any one body, of which the complex idea of that kind of things is usually made, are but a very few, in comparison of what a man that has several ways tried and examined it knows of that one sort of things; and all that the most expert man knows are but a few, in comparison of what are really in that body, and depend on its internal or essential constitution. The essence of a triangle lies in a very little compass, consists in a very few ideas: three lines including a space make up that essence: but the properties that flow from this essence are more than can be easily known or enumerated. So I imagine it is in substances; their real essences lie in a little compass, though the properties flowing from that internal constitution are endless.

25. Ideas, when called false. To conclude, a man having no notion of anything without him, but by the idea he has of it in his mind, (which idea he has a power to call by what name he pleases), he may indeed make an idea neither answering the reason of things, nor agreeing to the idea commonly signified by other people's words; but cannot make a wrong or false idea of a thing which is no otherwise known to him but by the idea he has of it: v.g. when I frame an idea of the legs, arms, and body of a man, and join to this a horse's head and neck, I do not make a false idea of anything; because it represents nothing without me. But when I call it a man or Tartar, and imagine it to represent some real being without me, or to be the same idea that others call by the same name; in either of these cases I may err. And upon this account it is that it comes to be termed a false idea; though indeed the falsehood lies not in the idea, but in that tacit mental proposition, wherein a conformity and resemblance is attributed to it which it has not. But yet, if, having framed such an idea in my mind without thinking either that existence, or the name man or Tartar, belongs to it, I will call it man or Tartar, I may be justly thought fantastical in the naming; but not erroneous in my judgment; nor the idea any way false.

26. More properly to be called right or wrong. Upon the whole, matter, I think that our ideas, as they are considered by the mind,— either in reference to the proper signification of their names; or in reference to the reality of things,— may very fitly be called right or wrong ideas, according as they agree or disagree to those patterns to which they are referred. But if any one had rather call them true or false, it is fit he use a liberty, which every one has, to call things by those names he thinks best; though, in propriety of speech, truth or falsehood will, I think, scarce agree to them, but as they, some way or other, virtually contain in them some mental proposition. The ideas that are in a man's mind, simply considered, cannot be wrong; unless complex ones, wherein inconsistent parts are jumbled together. All other ideas are in themselves right, and the knowledge about them right and true knowledge; but when we come to refer them to anything, as to their patterns and archetypes, then they are capable of being wrong, as far as they disagree with such archetypes.

Chapter XXXIII.Of the Association of Ideas

1. Something unreasonable in most men. There is scarce any one that does not observe something that seems odd to him, and is in itself really extravagant, in the opinions, reasonings, and actions of other men. The least flaw of this kind, if at all different from his own, every one is quick-sighted enough to espy in another, and will by the authority of reason forwardly condemn; though he be guilty of much greater unreasonableness in his own tenets

and conduct, which he never perceives, and will very hardly, if at all, be convinced of.

2. Not wholly from self-love. This proceeds not wholly from self-love, though that has often a great hand in it. Men of fair minds, and not given up to the overweening of self-flattery, are frequently guilty of it; and in many cases one with amazement hears the arguings, and is astonished at the obstinacy of a worthy man, who yields not to the evidence of reason, though laid before him as clear as daylight.

3. Not from education. This sort of unreasonableness is usually imputed to education and prejudice, and for the most part truly enough, though that reaches not the bottom of the disease, nor shows distinctly enough whence it rises, or wherein it lies. Education is often rightly assigned for the cause, and prejudice is a good general name for the thing itself: but yet, I think, he ought to look a little further, who would trace this sort of madness to the root it springs from, and so explain it, as to show whence this flaw has its original in very sober and rational minds, and wherein it consists.

4. A degree of madness found in most men. I shall be pardoned for calling it by so harsh a name as madness, when it is considered that opposition to reason deserves that name, and is really madness; and there is scarce a man so free from it, but that if he should always, on all occasions, argue or do as in some cases he constantly does, would not be thought fitter for Bedlam than civil conversation. I do not here mean when he is under the power of an unruly passion, but in the steady calm course of his life. That which will yet more apologize for this harsh name, and ungrateful imputation on the greatest part of mankind, is, that, inquiring a little by the bye into the nature of madness (Bk. ii. ch. xi. SS 13), I found it to spring from the very same root, and to depend on the very same cause we are here speaking of. This consideration of the thing itself, at a time when I thought not the least on the subject which I am now treating of, suggested it to me. And if this be a weakness to which all men are so liable, if this be a taint which so universally infects mankind, the greater care should be taken to lay it open under its due name, thereby to excite the greater care in its prevention and cure.

5. From a wrong connexion of ideas. Some of our ideas have a natural correspondence and connexion one with another: it is the office and excellency of our reason to trace these, and hold them together in that union and correspondence which is founded in their peculiar beings. Besides this, there is another connexion of ideas wholly owing to chance or custom. Ideas that in themselves are not all of kin, come to be so united in some men's minds, that it is very hard to separate them; they always keep in company, and the one no sooner at any time comes into the understanding, but its associate appears with it; and if they are more than two which are thus united, the whole gang, always inseparable, show themselves together.

6. This connexion made by custom. This strong combination of ideas, not allied by nature, the mind makes in itself either voluntarily or by chance; and hence it comes in different men to be very different, according to their different inclinations, education, interests, &c. Custom settles habits of thinking in the understanding, as well as of determining in the will, and of motions in the body: all which seems to be but trains of motions in the animal spirits, which, once set a going, continue in the same steps they have used to; which, by often treading, are worn into a smooth path, and the motion in it becomes easy, and as it were natural. As far as we can comprehend thinking, thus ideas seem to be produced in our minds; or, if they are not, this may serve to explain their following one another in an habitual train, when once they are put into their track, as well as it does to explain such motions of the body. A musician used to any tune will find that, let it but once begin in his head, the ideas of the several notes of it will   · follow one another orderly in his understanding, without any care or attention, as regularly as his fingers move orderly over the keys of the organ to play out the tune he has begun, though his unattentive thoughts be elsewhere a wandering. Whether the natural cause of these ideas, as well as of that regular dancing of his fingers be the motion of his animal spirits, I will not determine, how probable soever, by this instance, it appears to be so: but this may help us a little to conceive of intellectual habits, and of the tying together of ideas.

7. Some antipathies an effect of it. That there are such associations of them made by custom,

in the minds of most men, I think nobody will question, who has well considered himself or others; and to this, perhaps, might be justly attributed most of the sympathies and antipathies observable in men, which work as strongly, and produce as regular effects as if they were natural; and are therefore called so, though they at first had no other original but the accidental connexion of two ideas, which either the strength of the first impression, or future indulgence so united, that they always afterwards kept company together in that man's mind, as if they were but one idea. I say most of the antipathies, I do not say all; for some of them are truly natural, depend upon our original constitution, and are born with us; but a great part of those which are counted natural, would have been known to be from unheeded, though perhaps early, impressions, or wanton fancies at first, which would have been acknowledged the original of them, if they had been warily observed. A grown person surfeiting with honey no sooner hears the name of it, but his fancy immediately carries sickness and qualms to his stomach, and he cannot bear the very idea of it; other ideas of dislike, and sickness, and vomiting, presently accompany it, and he is disturbed; but he knows from whence to date this weakness, and can tell how he got this indisposition. Had this happened to him by an over-dose of honey when a child, all the same effects would have followed; but the cause would have been mistaken, and the antipathy counted natural.

8. Influence of association to be watched educating young children. I mention this, not out of any great necessity there is in this present argument to distinguish nicely between natural and acquired antipathies; but I take notice of it for another purpose, viz. that those who have children, or the charge of their education, would think it worth their while diligently to watch, and carefully to prevent the undue connexion of ideas in the minds of young people. This is the time most susceptible of lasting impressions; and though those relating to the health of the body are by discreet people minded and fenced against, yet I am apt to doubt, that those which relate more peculiarly to the mind, and terminate in the understanding or passions, have been much less heeded than the thing deserves: nay, those relating purely to the understanding, have, as I suspect, been by most men wholly overlooked.

9. Wrong connexion of ideas a great cause of errors. This wrong connexion in our minds of ideas in themselves loose and independent of one another, has such an influence, and is of so great force to set us awry in our actions, as well moral as natural, passions, reasonings, and notions themselves, that perhaps there is not any one thing that deserves more to be looked after.

10. An instance. The ideas of goblins and sprites have really no more to do with darkness than light: yet let but a foolish maid inculcate these often on the mind of a child, and raise them there together, possibly he shall never be able to separate them again so long as he lives, but darkness shall ever afterwards bring with it those frightful ideas, and they shall be so joined, that he can no more bear the one than the other.

11. Another instance. A man receives a sensible injury from another, thinks on the man and that action over and over, and by ruminating on them strongly, or much, in his mind, so cements those two ideas together, that he makes them almost one; never thinks on the man, but the pain and displeasure he suffered comes into his mind with it, so that he scarce distinguishes them, but has as much an aversion for the one as the other. Thus hatreds are often begotten from slight and innocent occasions, and quarrels propagated and continued in the world.

12. A third instance. A man has suffered pain or sickness in any place; he saw his friend die in such a room: though these have in nature nothing to do one with another, yet when the idea of the place occurs to his mind, it brings (the impression being once made) that of the pain and displeasure with it: he confounds them in his mind, and can as little bear the one as the other.

13. Why time cures some disorders in the mind, which reason cannot cure. When this combination is settled, and while it lasts, it is not in the power of reason to help us, and relieve us from the effects of it. Ideas in our minds, when they are there, will operate according to their natures and circumstances. And here we see the cause why time cures certain affections,

which reason, though in the right, and allowed to be so, has not power over, nor is able against them to prevail with those who are apt to hearken to it in other cases. The death of a child that was the daily delight of its mother's eyes, and joy of her soul, rends from her heart the whole comfort of her life, and gives her all the torment imaginable: use the consolations of reason in this case, and you were as good preach ease to one on the rack, and hope to allay, by rational discourses, the pain of his joints tearing asunder. Till time has by disuse separated the sense of that enjoyment and its loss, from the idea of the child returning to her memory, all representations, though ever so reasonable, are in vain; and therefore some in whom the union between these ideas is never dissolved, spend their lives in mourning, and carry an incurable sorrow to their graves.

14. Another instance of the effect of the association of ideas. A friend of mine knew one perfectly cured of madness by a very harsh and offensive operation. The gentleman who was thus recovered, with great sense of gratitude and acknowledgment owned the cure all his life after, as the greatest obligation he could have received; but, whatever gratitude and reason suggested to him, he could never bear the sight of the operator: that image brought back with it the idea of that agony which he suffered from his hands, which was too mighty and intolerable for him to endure.

15. More instances. Many children, imputing the pain they endured at school to their books they were corrected for, so join those ideas together, that a book becomes their aversion, and they are never reconciled to the study and use of them all their lives after; and thus reading becomes a torment to them, which otherwise possibly they might have made the great pleasure of their lives. There are rooms convenient enough, that some men cannot study in, and fashions of vessels, which, though ever so clean and commodious, they cannot drink out of, and that by reason of some accidental ideas which are annexed to them, and make them offensive; and who is there that hath not observed some man to flag at the appearance, or in the company of some certain person not otherwise superior to him, but because, having once on some occasion got the ascendant, the idea of authority and distance goes along with that of the person, and he that has been thus subjected, is not able to separate them.

16. A curious instance. Instances of this kind are so plentiful everywhere, that if I add one more, it is only for the pleasant oddness of it. It is of a young gentleman, who, having learnt to dance, and that to great perfection, there happened to stand an old trunk in the room where he learnt. The idea of this remarkable piece of household stuff had so mixed itself with the turns and steps of all his dances, that though in that chamber he could dance excellently well, yet it was only whilst that trunk was there; nor could he perform well in any other place, unless that or some such other trunk had its due position in the room. If this story shall be suspected to be dressed up with some comical circumstances, a little beyond precise nature, I answer for myself that I had it some years since from a very sober and worthy man, upon his own knowledge, as I report it; and I dare say there are very few inquisitive persons who read this, who have not met with accounts, if not examples, of this nature, that may parallel, or at least justify this.

17. Influence of association on intellectual habits. Intellectual habits and defects this way contracted, are not less frequent and powerful, though less observed. Let the ideas of being and matter be strongly joined, either by education or much thought; whilst these are still combined in the mind, what notions, what reasonings, will there be about separate spirits? Let custom from the very childhood have joined figure and shape to the idea of God, and what absurdities will that mind be liable to about the Deity? Let the idea of infallibility be inseparably joined to any person, and these two constantly together possess the mind; and then one body in two places at once, shall unexamined be swallowed for a certain truth, by an implicit faith, whenever that imagined infallible person dictates and demands assent without inquiry.

18. Observable in the opposition between different sects of philosophy and of religion. Some such wrong and unnatural combinations of ideas will be found to establish the irreconcilable

opposition between different sects of philosophy and religion; for we cannot imagine every one of their followers to impose wilfully on himself, and knowingly refuse truth offered by plain reason. Interest, though it does a great deal in the case, yet cannot be thought to work whole societies of men to so universal a perverseness, as that every one of them to a man should knowingly maintain falsehood: some at least must be allowed to do what all pretend to, i.e. to pursue truth sincerely; and therefore there must be something that blinds their understandings, and makes them not see the falsehood of what they embrace for real truth. That which thus captivates their reasons, and leads men of sincerity blindfold from common sense, will, when examined, be found to be what we are speaking of: some independent ideas, of no alliance to one another, are, by education, custom, and the constant din of their party, so coupled in their minds, that they always appear there together; and they can no more separate them in their thoughts than if they were but one idea, and they operate as if they were so. This gives sense to jargon, demonstration to absurdities, and consistency to nonsense, and is the foundation of the greatest, I had almost said of all the errors in the world; or, if it does not reach so far, it is at least the most dangerous one, since, so far as it obtains, it hinders men from seeing and examining. When two things, in themselves disjoined, appear to the sight constantly united; if the eye sees these things riveted which are loose, where will you begin to rectify the mistakes that follow in two ideas that they have been accustomed so to join in their minds as to substitute one for the other, and, as I am apt to think, often without perceiving it themselves? This, whilst they are under the deceit of it, makes them incapable of conviction, and they applaud themselves as zealous champions for truth, when indeed they are contending for error; and the confusion of two different ideas, which a customary connexion of them in their minds hath to them made in effect but one, fills their heads with false views, and their reasonings with false consequences.

19. Conclusion. Having thus given an account of the original, sorts, and extent of our IDEAS, with several other considerations about these (I know not whether I may say) instruments, or materials of our knowledge, the method I at first proposed to myself would now require that I should immediately proceed to show, what use the understanding makes of them, and what KNOWLEDGE we have by them. This was that which, in the first general view I had of this subject, was all that I thought I should have to do: but, upon a nearer approach, I find that there is so close a connexion between ideas and WORDS, and our abstract ideas and general words have so constant a relation one to another, that it is impossible to speak clearly and distinctly of our knowledge, which all consists in propositions, without considering, first, the nature, use, and signification of Language; which, therefore, must be the business of the next Book.

BOOK III.Of Words

Chapter I.Of Words or Language in General

1. Man fitted to form articulate sounds. God, having designed man for a sociable creature, made him not only with an inclination, and under a necessity to have fellowship with those of his own kind, but furnished him also with language, which was to be the great instrument and common tie of society. Man, therefore, had by nature his organs so fashioned, as to be fit to frame articulate sounds, which we call words. But this was not enough to produce language; for parrots, and several other birds, will be taught to make articulate sounds distinct enough, which yet by no means are capable of language.

2. To use these sounds as signs of ideas. Besides articulate sounds, therefore, it was further necessary that he should be able to use these sounds as signs of internal conceptions; and to make them stand as marks for the ideas within his own mind, whereby they might be made

known to others, and the thoughts of men's minds be conveyed from one to another.
3. To make them general signs. But neither was this sufficient to make words so useful as they ought to be. It is not enough for the perfection of language, that sounds can be made signs of ideas, unless those signs can be so made use of as to comprehend several particular things: for the multiplication of words would have perplexed their use, had every particular thing need of a distinct name to be signified by. To remedy this inconvenience, language had yet a further improvement in the use of general terms, whereby one word was made to mark a multitude of particular existences: which advantageous use of sounds was obtained only by the difference of the ideas they were made signs of: those names becoming general, which are made to stand for general ideas, and those remaining particular, where the ideas they are used for are particular.
4. To make them signify the absence of positive ideas. Besides these names which stand for ideas, there be other words which men make use of, not to signify any idea, but the want or absence of some ideas, simple or complex, or all ideas together; such as are nihil in Latin, and in English, ignorance and barrenness. All which negative or privative words cannot be said properly to belong to, or signify no ideas: for then they would be perfectly insignificant sounds; but they relate to positive ideas, and signify their absence.
5. Words ultimately derived from such as signify sensible ideas. It may also lead us a little towards the original of all our notions and knowledge, if we remark how great a dependence our words have on common sensible ideas; and how those which are made use of to stand for actions and notions quite removed from sense, have their rise from thence, and from obvious sensible ideas are transferred to more abstruse significations, and made to stand for ideas that come not under the cognizance of our senses; v.g. to imagine, apprehend, comprehend, adhere, conceive, instil, disgust, disturbance, tranquillity, &c., are all words taken from the operations of sensible things, and applied to certain modes of thinking. Spirit, in its primary signification, is breath; angel, a messenger: and I doubt not but, if we could trace them to their sources, we should find, in all languages, the names which stand for things that fall not under our senses to have had their first rise from sensible ideas. By which we may give some kind of guess what kind of notions they were, and whence derived, which filled their minds who were the first beginners of languages, and how nature, even in the naming of things, unawares suggested to men the originals and principles of all their knowledge: whilst, to give names that might make known to others any operations they felt in themselves, or any other ideas that came not under their senses, they were fain to borrow words from ordinary known ideas of sensation, by that means to make others the more easily to conceive those operations they experimented in themselves, which made no outward sensible appearances; and then, when they had got known and agreed names to signify those internal operations of their own minds, they were sufficiently furnished to make known by words all their other ideas; since they could consist of nothing but either of outward sensible perceptions, or of the inward operations of their minds about them; we having, as has been proved, no ideas at all, but what originally come either from sensible objects without, or what we feel within ourselves, from the inward workings of our own spirits, of which we are conscious to ourselves within.
6. Distribution of subjects to be treated of. But to understand better the use and force of Language, as subservient to instruction and knowledge, it will be convenient to consider:
First, To what it is that names, in the use of language, are immediately applied.
Secondly, Since all (except proper) names are general, and so stand not particularly for this or that single thing, but for sorts and ranks of things, it will be necessary to consider, in the next place, what the sorts and kinds, or, if you rather like the Latin names, what the Species and Genera of things are, wherein they consist, and how they come to be made. These being (as they ought) well looked into, we shall the better come to find the right use of words; the natural advantages and defects of language; and the remedies that ought to be used, to avoid the inconveniences of obscurity or uncertainty in the signification of words: without which it is impossible to discourse with any clearness or order concerning knowledge: which, being

conversant about propositions, and those most commonly universal ones, has greater connexion with words than perhaps is suspected.

These considerations, therefore, shall be the matter of the following chapters.

Chapter II.Of the Signification of Words

1. Words are sensible signs, necessary for communication of ideas. Man, though he have great variety of thoughts, and such from which others as well as himself might receive profit and delight; yet they are all within his own breast, invisible and hidden from others, nor can of themselves be made to appear. The comfort and advantage of society not being to be had without communication of thoughts, it was necessary that man should find out some external sensible signs, whereof those invisible ideas, which his thoughts are made up of, might be made known to others. For this purpose nothing was so fit, either for plenty or quickness, as those articulate sounds, which with so much ease and variety he found himself able to make. Thus we may conceive how words, which were by nature so well adapted to that purpose, came to be made use of by men as the signs of their ideas; not by any natural connexion that there is between particular articulate sounds and certain ideas, for then there would be but one language amongst all men; but by a voluntary imposition, whereby such a word is made arbitrarily the mark of such an idea. The use, then, of words, is to be sensible marks of ideas; and the ideas they stand for are their proper and immediate signification.

2. Words, in their immediate signification, are the sensible signs of his ideas who uses them. The use men have of these marks being either to record their own thoughts, for the assistance of their own memory or, as it were, to bring out their ideas, and lay them before the view of others: words, in their primary or immediate signification, stand for nothing but the ideas in the mind of him that uses them, how imperfectly soever or carelessly those ideas are collected from the things which they are supposed to represent. When a man speaks to another, it is that he may be understood: and the end of speech is, that those sounds, as marks, may make known his ideas to the hearer. That then which words are the marks of are the ideas of the speaker: nor can any one apply them as marks, immediately, to anything else but the ideas that he himself hath: for this would be to make them signs of his own conceptions, and yet apply them to other ideas; which would be to make them signs and not signs of his ideas at the same time, and so in effect to have no signification at all. Words being voluntary signs, they cannot be voluntary signs imposed by him on things he knows not. That would be to make them signs of nothing, sounds without signification. A man cannot make his words the signs either of qualities in things, or of conceptions in the mind of another, whereof he has none in his own. Till he has some ideas of his own, he cannot suppose them to correspond with the conceptions of another man; nor can he use any signs for them of another man; nor can he use any signs for them: for thus they would be the signs of he knows not what, which is in truth to be the signs of nothing. But when he represents to himself other men's ideas by some of his own, if he consent to give them the same names that other men do, it is still to his own ideas; to ideas that he has, and not to ideas that he has not.

3. Examples of this. This is so necessary in the use of language, that in this respect the knowing and the ignorant, the learned and the unlearned, use the words they speak (with any meaning) all alike. They, in every man's mouth, stand for the ideas he has, and which he would express by them. A child having taken notice of nothing in the metal he hears called gold, but the bright shining yellow colour, he applies the word gold only to his own idea of that colour, and nothing else; and therefore calls the same colour in a peacock's tail gold. Another that hath better observed, adds to shining yellow great weight: and then the sound gold, when he uses it, stands for a complex idea of a shining yellow and a very weighty substance. Another adds to those qualities fusibility: and then the word gold signifies to him a body, bright, yellow, fusible, and very heavy. Another adds malleability. Each of these uses

equally the word gold, when they have occasion to express the idea which they have applied it to: but it is evident that each can apply it only to his own idea; nor can he make it stand as a sign of such a complex idea as he has not.

4. Words are often secretly referred first to the ideas supposed to be in other men's minds. But though words, as they are used by men, can properly and immediately signify nothing but the ideas that are in the mind of the speaker; yet they in their thoughts give them a secret reference to two other things.

First, They suppose their words to be marks of the ideas in the minds also of other men, with whom they communicate: for else they should talk in vain, and could not be understood, if the sounds they applied to one idea were such as by the hearer were applied to another, which is to speak two languages. But in this men stand not usually to examine, whether the idea they, and those they discourse with have in their minds be the same: but think it enough that they use the word, as they imagine, in the common acceptation of that language; in which they suppose that the idea they make it a sign of is precisely the same to which the understanding men of that country apply that name.

5. To the reality of things. Secondly, Because men would not be thought to talk barely of their own imagination, but of things as really they are; therefore they often suppose the words to stand also for the reality of things. But this relating more particularly to substances and their names, as perhaps the former does to simple ideas and modes, we shall speak of these two different ways of applying words more at large, when we come to treat of the names of mixed modes and substances in particular: though give me leave here to say, that it is a perverting the use of words, and brings unavoidable obscurity and confusion into whenever we make them stand for anything but those ideas we have in our own minds.

6. Words by use readily excite ideas of their objects. Concerning words, also, it is further to be considered:

First, that they being immediately the signs of men's ideas, and by that means the instruments whereby men communicate their conceptions, and express to one another those thoughts and imaginations they have within their own their own breasts; there comes, by constant use, to be such a connexion between certain sounds and the ideas they stand for, that the names heard, almost as readily excite certain ideas as if the objects themselves, which are apt to produce them, did actually affect the senses. Which is manifestly so in all obvious sensible qualities, and in all substances that frequently and familiarly occur to us.

7. Words are often used without signification, and why. Secondly, That though the proper and immediate signification of words are ideas in the mind of the speaker, yet, because by familiar use from our cradles, we come to learn certain articulate sounds very perfectly, and have them readily on our tongues, and always at hand in our memories, but yet are not always careful to examine or settle their significations perfectly; it often happens that men, even when they would apply themselves to an attentive consideration, do set their thoughts more on words than things. Nay, because words are many of them learned before the ideas are known for which they stand: therefore some, not only children but men, speak several words no otherwise than parrots do, only because they have learned them, and have been accustomed to those sounds. But so far as words are of use and signification, so far is there a constant connexion between the sound and the idea, and a designation that the one stands for the other; without which application of them, they are nothing but so much insignificant noise.

8. Their signification perfectly arbitrary, not the consequence of a natural connexion. Words, by long and familiar use, as has been said, come to excite in men certain ideas so constantly and readily, that they are apt to suppose a natural connexion between them. But that they signify only men's peculiar ideas, and that by a perfect arbitrary imposition, is evident, in that they often fail to excite in others (even that use the same language) the same ideas we take them to be signs of: and every man has so inviolable a liberty to make words stand for what ideas he pleases, that no one hath the power to make others have the same ideas in their minds that he has, when they use the same words that he does. And therefore the great Augustus

himself, in the possession of that power which ruled the world, acknowledged he could not make a new Latin word: which was as much as to say, that he could not arbitrarily appoint what idea any sound should be a sign of, in the mouths and common language of his subjects. It is true, common use, by a tacit consent, appropriates certain sounds to certain ideas in all languages, which so far limits the signification of that sound, that unless a man applies it to the same idea, he does not speak properly: and let me add, that unless a man's words excite the same ideas in the hearer which he makes them stand for in speaking, he does not speak intelligibly. But whatever be the consequence of any man's using of words differently, either from their general meaning, or the particular sense of the person to whom he addresses them; this is certain, their signification, in his use of them, is limited to his ideas, and they can be signs of nothing else.

Chapter III.Of General Terms

1. The greatest part of words are general terms. All things that exist being particulars, it may perhaps be thought reasonable that words, which ought to be conformed to things, should be so too,— I mean in their signification: but yet we find quite the contrary. The far greatest part of words that make all languages are general terms: which has not been the effect of neglect or chance, but of reason and necessity.
2. That every particular thing should have a name for itself is impossible. First, It is impossible that every particular thing should have a distinct peculiar name. For, the signification and use of words depending on that connexion which the mind makes between its ideas and the sounds it uses as signs of them, it is necessary, in the application of names to things, that the mind should have distinct ideas of the things, and retain also the particular name that belongs to every one, with its peculiar appropriation to that idea. But it is beyond the power of human capacity to frame and retain distinct ideas of all the particular things we meet with: every bird and beast men saw; every tree and plant that affected the senses, could not find a place in the most capacious understanding. If it be looked on as an instance of a prodigious memory, that some generals have been able to call every soldier in their army by his proper name, we may easily find a reason why men have never attempted to give names to each sheep in their flock, or crow that flies over their heads; much less to call every leaf of plants, or grain of sand that came in their way, by a peculiar name.
3. And would be useless, if it were possible. Secondly, If it were possible, it would yet be useless; because it would not serve to the chief end of language. Men would in vain heap up names of particular things, that would not serve them to communicate their thoughts. Men learn names, and use them in talk with others, only that they may be understood: which is then only done when, by use or consent, the sound I make by the organs of speech, excites in another man's mind who hears it, the idea I apply it to in mine, when I speak it. This cannot be done by names applied to particular things; whereof I alone having the ideas in my mind, the names of them could not be significant or intelligible to another, who was not acquainted with all those very particular things which had fallen under my notice.
4. A distinct name for every particular thing, not fitted for enlargement of knowledge. Thirdly, But yet, granting this also feasible, (which I think is not), yet a distinct name for every particular thing would not be of any great use for the improvement of knowledge: which, though founded in particular things, enlarges itself by general views; to which things reduced into sorts, under general names, are properly subservient. These, with the names belonging to them, come within some compass, and do not multiply every moment, beyond what either the mind can contain, or use requires. And therefore, in these, men have for the most part stopped: but yet not so as to hinder themselves from distinguishing particular things by appropriated names, where convenience demands it. And therefore in their own species, which they have most to do with, and wherein they have often occasion to mention particular persons, they

make use of proper names; and there distinct individuals have distinct denominations.

5. What things have proper names, and why. Besides persons, countries also, cities, rivers, mountains, and other the like distinctions of place have usually found peculiar names, and that for the same reason; they being such as men have often an occasion to mark particularly, and, as it were, set before others in their discourses with them. And I doubt not but, if we had reason to mention particular horses as often as we have to mention particular men, we should have proper names for the one, as familiar as for the other, and Bucephalus would be a word as much in use as Alexander. And therefore we see that, amongst jockeys, horses have their proper names to be known and distinguished by, as commonly as their servants: because, amongst them, there is often occasion to mention this or that particular horse when he is out of sight.

6. How general words are made. The next thing to be considered is,— How general words come to be made. For, since all things that exist are only particulars, how come we by general terms; or where find we those general natures they are supposed to stand for? Words become general by being made the signs of general ideas: and ideas become general, by separating from them the circumstances of time and place, and any other ideas that may determine them to this or that particular existence. By this way of abstraction they are made capable of representing more individuals than one; each of which having in it a conformity to that abstract idea, is (as we call it) of that sort.

7. Shown by the way we enlarge our complex ideas from infancy. But, to deduce this a little more distinctly, it will not perhaps be amiss to trace our notions and names from their beginning, and observe by what degrees we proceed, and by what steps we enlarge our ideas from our first infancy. There is nothing more evident, than that the ideas of the persons children converse with (to instance in them alone) are, like the persons themselves, only particular. The ideas of the nurse and the mother are well framed in their minds; and, like pictures of them there, represent only those individuals. The names they first gave to them are confined to these individuals; and the names of nurse and mamma, the child uses, determine themselves to those persons. Afterwards, when time and a larger acquaintance have made them observe that there are a great many other things in the world, that in some common agreements of shape, and several other qualities, resemble their father and mother, and those persons they have been used to, they frame an idea, which they find those many particulars do partake in; and to that they give, with others, the name man, for example. And thus they come to have a general name, and a general idea. Wherein they make nothing new; but only leave out of the complex idea they had of Peter and James, Mary and Jane, that which is peculiar to each, and retain only what is common to them all.

8. And further enlarge our complex ideas, by still leaving out properties contained in them. By the same way that they come by the general name and idea of man, they easily advance to more general names and notions. For, observing that several things that differ from their idea of man, and cannot therefore be comprehended under that name, have yet certain qualities wherein they agree with man, by retaining only those qualities, and uniting them into one idea, they have again another and more general idea; to which having given a name they make a term of a more comprehensive extension: which new idea is made, not by any new addition, but only as before, by leaving out the shape, and some other properties signified by the name man, and retaining only a body, with life, sense, and spontaneous motion, comprehended under the name animal.

9. General natures are nothing but abstract and partial ideas of more complex ones. That this is the way whereby men first formed general ideas, and general names to them, I think is so evident, that there needs no other proof of it but the considering of a man's self, or others, and the ordinary proceedings of their minds in knowledge. And he that thinks general natures or notions are anything else but such abstract and partial ideas of more complex ones, taken at first from particular existences, will, I fear, be at a loss where to find them. For let any one effect, and then tell me, wherein does his idea of man differ from that of Peter and Paul, or his

idea of horse from that of Bucephalus, but in the leaving out something that is peculiar to each individual, and retaining so much of those particular complex ideas of several particular existences as they are found to agree in? Of the complex ideas signified by the names man and horse, leaving out but those particulars wherein they differ, and retaining only those wherein they agree, and of those making a new distinct complex idea, and giving the name animal to it, one has a more general term, that comprehends with man several other creatures. Leave out of the idea of animal, sense and spontaneous motion, and the remaining complex idea, made up of the remaining simple ones of body, life, and nourishment, becomes a more general one, under the more comprehensive term, vivens. And, not to dwell longer upon this particular, so evident in itself; by the same way the mind proceeds to body, substance, and at last to being, thing, and such universal terms, which stand for any of our ideas whatsoever. To conclude: this whole mystery of genera and species, which make such a noise in the schools, and are with justice so little regarded out of them, is nothing else but abstract ideas, more or less comprehensive, with names annexed to them. In all which this is constant and unvariable, That every more general term stands for such an idea, and is but a part of any of those contained under it.

10. Why the genus is ordinarily made use of in definitions. This may show us the reason why, in the defining of words, which is nothing but declaring their signification, we make use of the genus, or next general word that comprehends it. Which is not out of necessity, but only to save the labour of enumerating the several simple ideas which the next general word or genus stands for; or, perhaps, sometimes the shame of not being able to do it. But though defining by genus and differentia (I crave leave to use these terms of art, though originally Latin, since they most properly suit those notions they are applied to), I say, though defining by the genus be the shortest way, yet I think it may be doubted whether it be the best. This I am sure, it is not the only, and so not absolutely necessary. For, definition being nothing but making another understand by words what idea the term defined stands for, a definition is best made by enumerating those simple ideas that are combined in the signification of the term defined: and if, instead of such an enumeration, men have accustomed themselves to use the next general term, it has not been out of necessity, or for greater clearness, but for quickness and dispatch sake. For I think that, to one who desired to know what idea the word man stood for; if it should be said, that man was a solid extended substance, having life, sense, spontaneous motion, and the faculty of reasoning, I doubt not but the meaning of the term man would be as well understood, and the idea it stands for be at least as clearly made known, as when it is defined to be a rational animal: which, by the several definitions of animal, vivens, and corpus, resolves itself into those enumerated ideas. I have, in explaining the term man, followed here the ordinary definition of the schools; which, though perhaps not the most exact, yet serves well enough to my present purpose. And one may, in this instance, see what gave occasion to the rule, that a definition must consist of genus and differentia; and it suffices to show us the little necessity there is of such a rule, or advantage in the strict observing of it. For, definitions, as has been said, being only the explaining of one word by several others, so that the meaning or idea it stands for may be certainly known; languages are not always so made according to the rules of logic, that every term can have its signification exactly and clearly expressed by two others. Experience sufficiently satisfies us to the contrary; or else those who have made this rule have done ill, that they have given us so few definitions conformable to it. But of definitions more in the next chapter.

11. General and universal are creatures of the understanding, and belong not to the real existence of things. To return to general words: it is plain, by what has been said, that general and universal belong not to the real existence of things; but are the inventions and creatures of the understanding, made by it for its own use, and concern only signs, whether words or ideas. Words are general, as has been said, when used for signs of general ideas, and so are applicable indifferently to many particular things; and ideas are general when they are set up as the representatives of many particular things: but universality belongs not to things

themselves, which are all of them particular in their existence, even those words and ideas which in their signification are general. When therefore we quit particulars, the generals that rest are only creatures of our own making; their general nature being nothing but the capacity they are put into, by the understanding, of signifying or representing many particulars. For the signification they have is nothing but a relation that, by the mind of man, is added to them.

12. Abstract ideas are the essences of genera and species. The next thing therefore to be considered is, What kind of signification it is that general words have. For, as it is evident that they do not signify barely one particular thing; for then they would not be general terms, but proper names, so, on the other side, it is as evident they do not signify a plurality; for man and men would then signify the same; and the distinction of numbers (as the grammarians call them) would be superfluous and useless. That then which general words signify is a sort of things; and each of them does that, by being a sign of an abstract idea in the mind; to which idea, as things existing are found to agree, so they come to be ranked under that name, or, which is all one, be of that sort. Whereby it is evident that the essences of the sorts, or, if the Latin word pleases better, species of things, are nothing else but these abstract ideas. For the having the essence of any species, being that which makes anything to be of that species; and the conformity to the idea to which the name is annexed being that which gives a right to that name; the having the essence, and the having that conformity, must needs be the same thing: since to be of any species, and to have a right to the name of that species, is all one. As, for example, to be a man, or of the species man, and to have right to the name man, is the same thing. Again, to be a man, or of the species man, and have the essence of a man, is the same thing. Now, since nothing can be a man, or have a right to the name man, but what has a conformity to the abstract idea the name man stands for, nor anything be a man, or have a right to the species man, but what has the essence of that species; it follows, that the abstract idea for which the name stands, and the essence of the species, is one and the same. From whence it is easy to observe, that the essences of the sorts of things, and, consequently, the sorting of things, is the workmanship of the understanding that abstracts and makes those general ideas.

13. They are the workmanship of the understanding, but have their foundation in the similitude of things. I would not here be thought to forget, much less to deny, that Nature, in the production of things, makes several of them alike: there is nothing more obvious, especially in the race of animals, and all things propagated by seed. But yet I think we may say, the sorting of them under names is the workmanship of the understanding, taking occasion, from the similitude it observes amongst them, to make abstract general ideas, and set them up in the mind, with names annexed to them, as patterns or forms, (for, in that sense, the word form has a very proper signification,) to which as particular things existing are found to agree, so they come to be of that species, have that denomination, or are put into that classis. For when we say this is a man, that a horse; this justice, that cruelty; this a watch, that a jack; what do we else but rank things under different specific names, as agreeing to those abstract ideas, of which we have made those names the signs? And what are the essences of those species set out and marked by names, but those abstract ideas in the mind; which are, as it were, the bonds between particular things that exist, and the names they are to be ranked under? And when general names have any connexion with particular beings, these abstract ideas are the medium that unites them: so that the essences of species, as distinguished and denominated by us, neither are nor can be anything but those precise abstract ideas we have in our minds. And therefore the supposed real essences of substances, if different from our abstract ideas, cannot be the essences of the species we rank things into. For two species may be one, as rationally as two different essences be the essence of one species: and I demand what are the alterations [which] may, or may not be made in a horse or lead, without making either of them to be of another species? In determining the species of things by our abstract ideas, this is easy to resolve: but if any one will regulate himself herein by supposed real essences, he will, I suppose, be at a loss: and he will never be able to know when anything precisely ceases to be of the species of a horse or lead.

14. Each distinct abstract idea is a distinct essence. Nor will any one wonder that I say these essences, or abstract ideas (which are the measures of name, and the boundaries of species) are the workmanship of the understanding, who considers that at least the complex ones are often, in several men, different collections of simple ideas; and therefore that is covetousness to one man, which is not so to another. Nay, even in substances, where their abstract ideas seem to be taken from the things themselves, they are not constantly the same; no, not in that species which is most familiar to us, and with which we have the most intimate acquaintance: it having been more than once doubted, whether the foetus born of a woman were a man, even so far as that it hath been debated, whether it were or were not to be nourished and baptized: which could not be, if the abstract idea or essence to which the name man belonged were of nature's making; and were not the uncertain and various collection of simple ideas, which the understanding put together, and then, abstracting it, affixed a name to it. So that, in truth, every distinct abstract idea is a distinct essence; and the names that stand for such distinct ideas are the names of things essentially different. Thus a circle is as essentially different from an oval as a sheep from a goat; and rain is as essentially different from snow as water from earth: that abstract idea which is the essence of one being impossible to be communicated to the other. And thus any two abstract ideas, that in any part vary one from another, with two distinct names annexed to them, constitute two distinct sorts, or, if you please, species, as essentially different as any two of the most remote or opposite in the world.

15. Several significations of the word "essence." But since the essences of things are thought by some (and not without reason) to be wholly unknown, it may not be amiss to consider the several significations of the word essence.

Real essences. First, Essence may be taken for the very being of anything, whereby it is what it is. And thus the real internal, but generally (in substances) unknown constitution of things, whereon their discoverable qualities depend, may be called their essence. This is the proper original signification of the word, as is evident from the formation of it; essentia, in its primary notation, signifying properly, being. And in this sense it is still used, when we speak of the essence of particular things, without giving them any name.

Nominal essences. Secondly, The learning and disputes of the schools having been much busied about genus and species, the word essence has almost lost its primary signification: and, instead of the real constitution of things, has been almost wholly applied to the artificial constitution of genus and species. It is true, there is ordinarily supposed a real constitution of the sorts of things; and it is past doubt there must be some real constitution, on which any collection of simple ideas co-existing must depend. But, it being evident that things are ranked under names into sorts or species, only as they agree to certain abstract ideas, to which we have annexed those names, the essence of each genus, or sort, comes to be nothing but that abstract idea which the general, or sortal (if I may have leave so to call it from sort, as I do general from genus), name stands for. And this we shall find to be that which the word essence imports in its most familiar use.

These two sorts of essences, I suppose, may not unfitly be termed, the one the real, the other nominal essence.

16. Constant connexion between the name and nominal essence. Between the nominal essence and the name there is so near a connexion, that the name of any sort of things cannot be attributed to any particular being but what has this essence, whereby it answers that abstract idea whereof that name is the sign.

17. Supposition, that species are distinguished by their real essences, useless. Concerning the real essences of corporeal substances (to mention these only) there are, if I mistake not, two opinions. The one is of those who, using the word essence for they know not what, suppose a certain number of those essences, according to which all natural things are made, and wherein they do exactly every one of them partake, and so become of this or that species. The other and more rational opinion is of those who look on all natural things to have a real, but unknown, constitution of their insensible parts; from which flow those sensible qualities which

serve us to distinguish them one from another, according as we have occasion to rank them into sorts, under common denominations. The former of these opinions, which supposes these essences as a certain number of forms or moulds, wherein all natural things that exist are cast, and do equally partake, has, I imagine, very much perplexed the knowledge of natural things. The frequent productions of monsters, in all the species of animals, and of changelings, and other strange issues of human birth, carry with them difficulties, not possible to consist with this hypothesis; since it is as impossible that two things partaking exactly of the same real essence should have different properties, as that two figures partaking of the same real essence of a circle should have different properties. But were there no other reason against it, yet the supposition of essences that cannot be known; and the making of them, nevertheless, to be that which distinguishes the species of things, is so wholly useless and unserviceable to any part of our knowledge, that that alone were sufficient to make us lay it by, and content ourselves with such essences of the sorts or species of things as come within the reach of our knowledge: which, when seriously considered, will be found, as I have said, to be nothing else but, those abstract complex ideas to which we have annexed distinct general names.

18. Real and nominal essence the same in simple ideas and modes, different in substances. Essences being thus distinguished into nominal and real, we may further observe, that, in the species of simple ideas and modes, they are always the same; but in substances always quite different. Thus, a figure including a space between three lines, is the real as well as nominal essence of a triangle; it being not only the abstract idea to which the general name is annexed, but the very essentia or being of the thing itself; that foundation from which all its properties flow, and to which they are all inseparably annexed. But it is far otherwise concerning that parcel of matter which makes the ring on my finger; wherein these two essences are apparently different. For, it is the real constitution of its insensible parts, on which depend all those properties of colour, weight, fusibility, fixedness, &c., which are to be found in it; which constitution we know not, and so, having no particular idea of, having no name that is the sign of it. But yet it is its colour, weight, fusibility, fixedness, &c., which makes it to be gold, or gives it a right to that name, which is therefore its nominal essence. Since nothing can be called gold but what has a conformity of qualities to that abstract complex idea to which that name is annexed. But this distinction of essences, belonging particularly to substances, we shall, when we come to consider their names, have an occasion to treat of more fully.
19. Essences ingenerable and incorruptible. That such abstract ideas, with names to them, as we have been speaking of are essences, may further appear by what we are told concerning essences, viz. that they are all ingenerable and incorruptible. Which cannot be true of the real constitutions of things, which begin and perish with them. All things that exist, besides their Author, are all liable to change; especially those things we are acquainted with, and have ranked into bands under distinct names or ensigns. Thus, that which was grass to-day is to-morrow the flesh of a sheep; and, within a few days after, becomes part of a man: in all which and the like changes, it is evident their real essence — i.e. that constitution whereon the properties of these several things depended — is destroyed, and perishes with them. But essences being taken for ideas established in the mind, with names annexed to them, they are supposed to remain steadily the same, whatever mutations the particular substances are liable to. For, whatever becomes of Alexander and Bucephalus, the ideas to which man and horse are annexed, are supposed nevertheless to remain the same; and so the essences of those species are preserved whole and undestroyed, whatever changes happen to any or all of the individuals of those species. By this means the essence of a species rests safe and entire, without the existence of so much as one individual of that kind. For, were there now no circle existing anywhere in the world, (as perhaps that figure exists not anywhere exactly marked out), yet the idea annexed to that name would not cease to be what it is; nor cease to be as a pattern to determine which of the particular figures we meet with have or have not a right to the name circle, and so to show which of them, by having that essence, was of that species. And though

there neither were nor had been in nature such a beast as an unicorn, or such a fish as a mermaid; yet, supposing those names to stand for complex abstract ideas that contained no inconsistency in them, the essence of a mermaid is as intelligible as that of a man; and the idea of an unicorn as certain, steady, and permanent as that of a horse. From what has been said, it is evident, that the doctrine of the immutability of essences proves them to be only abstract ideas; and is founded on the relation established between them and certain sounds as signs of them; and will always be true, as long as the same name can have the same signification.

20. Recapitulation. To conclude. This is that which in short I would say, viz. that all the great business of genera and species, and their essences, amounts to no more but this:— That men making abstract ideas, and settling them in their minds with names annexed to them, do thereby enable themselves to consider things, and discourse of them, as it were in bundles, for the easier and readier improvement and communication of their knowledge, which would advance but slowly were their words and thoughts confined only to particulars.

Chapter III.Of General Terms

1. The greatest part of words are general terms. All things that exist being particulars, it may perhaps be thought reasonable that words, which ought to be conformed to things, should be so too,— I mean in their signification: but yet we find quite the contrary. The far greatest part of words that make all languages are general terms: which has not been the effect of neglect or chance, but of reason and necessity.

2. That every particular thing should have a name for itself is impossible. First, It is impossible that every particular thing should have a distinct peculiar name. For, the signification and use of words depending on that connexion which the mind makes between its ideas and the sounds it uses as signs of them, it is necessary, in the application of names to things, that the mind should have distinct ideas of the things, and retain also the particular name that belongs to every one, with its peculiar appropriation to that idea. But it is beyond the power of human capacity to frame and retain distinct ideas of all the particular things we meet with: every bird and beast men saw; every tree and plant that affected the senses, could not find a place in the most capacious understanding. If it be looked on as an instance of a prodigious memory, that some generals have been able to call every soldier in their army by his proper name, we may easily find a reason why men have never attempted to give names to each sheep in their flock, or crow that flies over their heads; much less to call every leaf of plants, or grain of sand that came in their way, by a peculiar name.

3. And would be useless, if it were possible. Secondly, If it were possible, it would yet be useless; because it would not serve to the chief end of language. Men would in vain heap up names of particular things, that would not serve them to communicate their thoughts. Men learn names, and use them in talk with others, only that they may be understood: which is then only done when, by use or consent, the sound I make by the organs of speech, excites in another man's mind who hears it, the idea I apply it to in mine, when I speak it. This cannot be done by names applied to particular things; whereof I alone having the ideas in my mind, the names of them could not be significant or intelligible to another, who was not acquainted with all those very particular things which had fallen under my notice.

4. A distinct name for every particular thing, not fitted for enlargement of knowledge. Thirdly, But yet, granting this also feasible, (which I think is not), yet a distinct name for every particular thing would not be of any great use for the improvement of knowledge: which, though founded in particular things, enlarges itself by general views; to which things reduced into sorts, under general names, are properly subservient. These, with the names belonging to them, come within some compass, and do not multiply every moment, beyond what either the mind can contain, or use requires. And therefore, in these, men have for the most part stopped: but yet not so as to hinder themselves from distinguishing particular things by appropriated

names, where convenience demands it. And therefore in their own species, which they have most to do with, and wherein they have often occasion to mention particular persons, they make use of proper names; and there distinct individuals have distinct denominations.

5. What things have proper names, and why. Besides persons, countries also, cities, rivers, mountains, and other the like distinctions of place have usually found peculiar names, and that for the same reason; they being such as men have often an occasion to mark particularly, and, as it were, set before others in their discourses with them. And I doubt not but, if we had reason to mention particular horses as often as we have to mention particular men, we should have proper names for the one, as familiar as for the other, and Bucephalus would be a word as much in use as Alexander. And therefore we see that, amongst jockeys, horses have their proper names to be known and distinguished by, as commonly as their servants: because, amongst them, there is often occasion to mention this or that particular horse when he is out of sight.

6. How general words are made. The next thing to be considered is,— How general words come to be made. For, since all things that exist are only particulars, how come we by general terms; or where find we those general natures they are supposed to stand for? Words become general by being made the signs of general ideas: and ideas become general, by separating from them the circumstances of time and place, and any other ideas that may determine them to this or that particular existence. By this way of abstraction they are made capable of representing more individuals than one; each of which having in it a conformity to that abstract idea, is (as we call it) of that sort.

7. Shown by the way we enlarge our complex ideas from infancy. But, to deduce this a little more distinctly, it will not perhaps be amiss to trace our notions and names from their beginning, and observe by what degrees we proceed, and by what steps we enlarge our ideas from our first infancy. There is nothing more evident, than that the ideas of the persons children converse with (to instance in them alone) are, like the persons themselves, only particular. The ideas of the nurse and the mother are well framed in their minds; and, like pictures of them there, represent only those individuals. The names they first gave to them are confined to these individuals; and the names of nurse and mamma, the child uses, determine themselves to those persons. Afterwards, when time and a larger acquaintance have made them observe that there are a great many other things in the world, that in some common agreements of shape, and several other qualities, resemble their father and mother, and those persons they have been used to, they frame an idea, which they find those many particulars do partake in; and to that they give, with others, the name man, for example. And thus they come to have a general name, and a general idea. Wherein they make nothing new; but only leave out of the complex idea they had of Peter and James, Mary and Jane, that which is peculiar to each, and retain only what is common to them all.

8. And further enlarge our complex ideas, by still leaving out properties contained in them. By the same way that they come by the general name and idea of man, they easily advance to more general names and notions. For, observing that several things that differ from their idea of man, and cannot therefore be comprehended under that name, have yet certain qualities wherein they agree with man, by retaining only those qualities, and uniting them into one idea, they have again another and more general idea; to which having given a name they make a term of a more comprehensive extension: which new idea is made, not by any new addition, but only as before, by leaving out the shape, and some other properties signified by the name man, and retaining only a body, with life, sense, and spontaneous motion, comprehended under the name animal.

9. General natures are nothing but abstract and partial ideas of more complex ones. That this is the way whereby men first formed general ideas, and general names to them, I think is so evident, that there needs no other proof of it but the considering of a man's self, or others, and the ordinary proceedings of their minds in knowledge. And he that thinks general natures or notions are anything else but such abstract and partial ideas of more complex ones, taken at

first from particular existences, will, I fear, be at a loss where to find them. For let any one effect, and then tell me, wherein does his idea of man differ from that of Peter and Paul, or his idea of horse from that of Bucephalus, but in the leaving out something that is peculiar to each individual, and retaining so much of those particular complex ideas of several particular existences as they are found to agree in? Of the complex ideas signified by the names man and horse, leaving out but those particulars wherein they differ, and retaining only those wherein they agree, and of those making a new distinct complex idea, and giving the name animal to it, one has a more general term, that comprehends with man several other creatures. Leave out of the idea of animal, sense and spontaneous motion, and the remaining complex idea, made up of the remaining simple ones of body, life, and nourishment, becomes a more general one, under the more comprehensive term, vivens. And, not to dwell longer upon this particular, so evident in itself; by the same way the mind proceeds to body, substance, and at last to being, thing, and such universal terms, which stand for any of our ideas whatsoever. To conclude: this whole mystery of genera and species, which make such a noise in the schools, and are with justice so little regarded out of them, is nothing else but abstract ideas, more or less comprehensive, with names annexed to them. In all which this is constant and unvariable, That every more general term stands for such an idea, and is but a part of any of those contained under it.

10. Why the genus is ordinarily made use of in definitions. This may show us the reason why, in the defining of words, which is nothing but declaring their signification, we make use of the genus, or next general word that comprehends it. Which is not out of necessity, but only to save the labour of enumerating the several simple ideas which the next general word or genus stands for; or, perhaps, sometimes the shame of not being able to do it. But though defining by genus and differentia (I crave leave to use these terms of art, though originally Latin, since they most properly suit those notions they are applied to), I say, though defining by the genus be the shortest way, yet I think it may be doubted whether it be the best. This I am sure, it is not the only, and so not absolutely necessary. For, definition being nothing but making another understand by words what idea the term defined stands for, a definition is best made by enumerating those simple ideas that are combined in the signification of the term defined: and if, instead of such an enumeration, men have accustomed themselves to use the next general term, it has not been out of necessity, or for greater clearness, but for quickness and dispatch sake. For I think that, to one who desired to know what idea the word man stood for; if it should be said, that man was a solid extended substance, having life, sense, spontaneous motion, and the faculty of reasoning, I doubt not but the meaning of the term man would be as well understood, and the idea it stands for be at least as clearly made known, as when it is defined to be a rational animal: which, by the several definitions of animal, vivens, and corpus, resolves itself into those enumerated ideas. I have, in explaining the term man, followed here the ordinary definition of the schools; which, though perhaps not the most exact, yet serves well enough to my present purpose. And one may, in this instance, see what gave occasion to the rule, that a definition must consist of genus and differentia; and it suffices to show us the little necessity there is of such a rule, or advantage in the strict observing of it. For, definitions, as has been said, being only the explaining of one word by several others, so that the meaning or idea it stands for may be certainly known; languages are not always so made according to the rules of logic, that every term can have its signification exactly and clearly expressed by two others. Experience sufficiently satisfies us to the contrary; or else those who have made this rule have done ill, that they have given us so few definitions conformable to it. But of definitions more in the next chapter.

11. General and universal are creatures of the understanding, and belong not to the real existence of things. To return to general words: it is plain, by what has been said, that general and universal belong not to the real existence of things; but are the inventions and creatures of the understanding, made by it for its own use, and concern only signs, whether words or ideas. Words are general, as has been said, when used for signs of general ideas, and so are

applicable indifferently to many particular things; and ideas are general when they are set up as the representatives of many particular things: but universality belongs not to things themselves, which are all of them particular in their existence, even those words and ideas which in their signification are general. When therefore we quit particulars, the generals that rest are only creatures of our own making; their general nature being nothing but the capacity they are put into, by the understanding, of signifying or representing many particulars. For the signification they have is nothing but a relation that, by the mind of man, is added to them.

12. Abstract ideas are the essences of genera and species. The next thing therefore to be considered is, What kind of signification it is that general words have. For, as it is evident that they do not signify barely one particular thing; for then they would not be general terms, but proper names, so, on the other side, it is as evident they do not signify a plurality; for man and men would then signify the same; and the distinction of numbers (as the grammarians call them) would be superfluous and useless. That then which general words signify is a sort of things; and each of them does that, by being a sign of an abstract idea in the mind; to which idea, as things existing are found to agree, so they come to be ranked under that name, or, which is all one, be of that sort. Whereby it is evident that the essences of the sorts, or, if the Latin word pleases better, species of things, are nothing else but these abstract ideas. For the having the essence of any species, being that which makes anything to be of that species; and the conformity to the idea to which the name is annexed being that which gives a right to that name; the having the essence, and the having that conformity, must needs be the same thing: since to be of any species, and to have a right to the name of that species, is all one. As, for example, to be a man, or of the species man, and to have right to the name man, is the same thing. Again, to be a man, or of the species man, and have the essence of a man, is the same thing. Now, since nothing can be a man, or have a right to the name man, but what has a conformity to the abstract idea the name man stands for, nor anything be a man, or have a right to the species man, but what has the essence of that species; it follows, that the abstract idea for which the name stands, and the essence of the species, is one and the same. From whence it is easy to observe, that the essences of the sorts of things, and, consequently, the sorting of things, is the workmanship of the understanding that abstracts and makes those general ideas.

13. They are the workmanship of the understanding, but have their foundation in the similitude of things. I would not here be thought to forget, much less to deny, that Nature, in the production of things, makes several of them alike: there is nothing more obvious, especially in the race of animals, and all things propagated by seed. But yet I think we may say, the sorting of them under names is the workmanship of the understanding, taking occasion, from the similitude it observes amongst them, to make abstract general ideas, and set them up in the mind, with names annexed to them, as patterns or forms, (for, in that sense, the word form has a very proper signification,) to which as particular things existing are found to agree, so they come to be of that species, have that denomination, or are put into that classis. For when we say this is a man, that a horse; this justice, that cruelty; this a watch, that a jack; what do we else but rank things under different specific names, as agreeing to those abstract ideas, of which we have made those names the signs? And what are the essences of those species set out and marked by names, but those abstract ideas in the mind; which are, as it were, the bonds between particular things that exist, and the names they are to be ranked under? And when general names have any connexion with particular beings, these abstract ideas are the medium that unites them: so that the essences of species, as distinguished and denominated by us, neither are nor can be anything but those precise abstract ideas we have in our minds. And therefore the supposed real essences of substances, if different from our abstract ideas, cannot be the essences of the species we rank things into. For two species may be one, as rationally as two different essences be the essence of one species: and I demand what are the alterations [which] may, or may not be made in a horse or lead, without making either of them to be of another species? In determining the species of things by our abstract ideas, this is easy to resolve: but if any one will regulate himself herein by supposed real essences, he will, I

suppose, be at a loss: and he will never be able to know when anything precisely ceases to be of the species of a horse or lead.

14. Each distinct abstract idea is a distinct essence. Nor will any one wonder that I say these essences, or abstract ideas (which are the measures of name, and the boundaries of species) are the workmanship of the understanding, who considers that at least the complex ones are often, in several men, different collections of simple ideas; and therefore that is covetousness to one man, which is not so to another. Nay, even in substances, where their abstract ideas seem to be taken from the things themselves, they are not constantly the same; no, not in that species which is most familiar to us, and with which we have the most intimate acquaintance: it having been more than once doubted, whether the foetus born of a woman were a man, even so far as that it hath been debated, whether it were or were not to be nourished and baptized: which could not be, if the abstract idea or essence to which the name man belonged were of nature's making; and were not the uncertain and various collection of simple ideas, which the understanding put together, and then, abstracting it, affixed a name to it. So that, in truth, every distinct abstract idea is a distinct essence; and the names that stand for such distinct ideas are the names of things essentially different. Thus a circle is as essentially different from an oval as a sheep from a goat; and rain is as essentially different from snow as water from earth: that abstract idea which is the essence of one being impossible to be communicated to the other. And thus any two abstract ideas, that in any part vary one from another, with two distinct names annexed to them, constitute two distinct sorts, or, if you please, species, as essentially different as any two of the most remote or opposite in the world.

15. Several significations of the word "essence." But since the essences of things are thought by some (and not without reason) to be wholly unknown, it may not be amiss to consider the several significations of the word essence.

Real essences. First, Essence may be taken for the very being of anything, whereby it is what it is. And thus the real internal, but generally (in substances) unknown constitution of things, whereon their discoverable qualities depend, may be called their essence. This is the proper original signification of the word, as is evident from the formation of it; essentia, in its primary notation, signifying properly, being. And in this sense it is still used, when we speak of the essence of particular things, without giving them any name.

Nominal essences. Secondly, The learning and disputes of the schools having been much busied about genus and species, the word essence has almost lost its primary signification: and, instead of the real constitution of things, has been almost wholly applied to the artificial constitution of genus and species. It is true, there is ordinarily supposed a real constitution of the sorts of things; and it is past doubt there must be some real constitution, on which any collection of simple ideas co-existing must depend. But, it being evident that things are ranked under names into sorts or species, only as they agree to certain abstract ideas, to which we have annexed those names, the essence of each genus, or sort, comes to be nothing but that abstract idea which the general, or sortal (if I may have leave so to call it from sort, as I do general from genus), name stands for. And this we shall find to be that which the word essence imports in its most familiar use.

These two sorts of essences, I suppose, may not unfitly be termed, the one the real, the other nominal essence.

16. Constant connexion between the name and nominal essence. Between the nominal essence and the name there is so near a connexion, that the name of any sort of things cannot be attributed to any particular being but what has this essence, whereby it answers that abstract idea whereof that name is the sign.

17. Supposition, that species are distinguished by their real essences, useless. Concerning the real essences of corporeal substances (to mention these only) there are, if I mistake not, two opinions. The one is of those who, using the word essence for they know not what, suppose a certain number of those essences, according to which all natural things are made, and wherein they do exactly every one of them partake, and so become of this or that species. The other

and more rational opinion is of those who look on all natural things to have a real, but unknown, constitution of their insensible parts; from which flow those sensible qualities which serve us to distinguish them one from another, according as we have occasion to rank them into sorts, under common denominations. The former of these opinions, which supposes these essences as a certain number of forms or moulds, wherein all natural things that exist are cast, and do equally partake, has, I imagine, very much perplexed the knowledge of natural things. The frequent productions of monsters, in all the species of animals, and of changelings, and other strange issues of human birth, carry with them difficulties, not possible to consist with this hypothesis; since it is as impossible that two things partaking exactly of the same real essence should have different properties, as that two figures partaking of the same real essence of a circle should have different properties. But were there no other reason against it, yet the supposition of essences that cannot be known; and the making of them, nevertheless, to be that which distinguishes the species of things, is so wholly useless and unserviceable to any part of our knowledge, that that alone were sufficient to make us lay it by, and content ourselves with such essences of the sorts or species of things as come within the reach of our knowledge: which, when seriously considered, will be found, as I have said, to be nothing else but, those abstract complex ideas to which we have annexed distinct general names.

18. Real and nominal essence the same in simple ideas and modes, different in substances. Essences being thus distinguished into nominal and real, we may further observe, that, in the species of simple ideas and modes, they are always the same; but in substances always quite different. Thus, a figure including a space between three lines, is the real as well as nominal essence of a triangle; it being not only the abstract idea to which the general name is annexed, but the very essentia or being of the thing itself; that foundation from which all its properties flow, and to which they are all inseparably annexed. But it is far otherwise concerning that parcel of matter which makes the ring on my finger; wherein these two essences are apparently different. For, it is the real constitution of its insensible parts, on which depend all those properties of colour, weight, fusibility, fixedness, &c., which are to be found in it; which constitution we know not, and so, having no particular idea of, having no name that is the sign of it. But yet it is its colour, weight, fusibility, fixedness, &c., which makes it to be gold, or gives it a right to that name, which is therefore its nominal essence. Since nothing can be called gold but what has a conformity of qualities to that abstract complex idea to which that name is annexed. But this distinction of essences, belonging particularly to substances, we shall, when we come to consider their names, have an occasion to treat of more fully.
19. Essences ingenerable and incorruptible. That such abstract ideas, with names to them, as we have been speaking of are essences, may further appear by what we are told concerning essences, viz. that they are all ingenerable and incorruptible. Which cannot be true of the real constitutions of things, which begin and perish with them. All things that exist, besides their Author, are all liable to change; especially those things we are acquainted with, and have ranked into bands under distinct names or ensigns. Thus, that which was grass to-day is to-morrow the flesh of a sheep; and, within a few days after, becomes part of a man: in all which and the like changes, it is evident their real essence — i.e. that constitution whereon the properties of these several things depended — is destroyed, and perishes with them. But essences being taken for ideas established in the mind, with names annexed to them, they are supposed to remain steadily the same, whatever mutations the particular substances are liable to. For, whatever becomes of Alexander and Bucephalus, the ideas to which man and horse are annexed, are supposed nevertheless to remain the same; and so the essences of those species are preserved whole and undestroyed, whatever changes happen to any or all of the individuals of those species. By this means the essence of a species rests safe and entire, without the existence of so much as one individual of that kind. For, were there now no circle existing anywhere in the world, (as perhaps that figure exists not anywhere exactly marked out), yet the idea annexed to that name would not cease to be what it is; nor cease to be as a pattern to

determine which of the particular figures we meet with have or have not a right to the name circle, and so to show which of them, by having that essence, was of that species. And though there neither were nor had been in nature such a beast as an unicorn, or such a fish as a mermaid; yet, supposing those names to stand for complex abstract ideas that contained no inconsistency in them, the essence of a mermaid is as intelligible as that of a man; and the idea of an unicorn as certain, steady, and permanent as that of a horse. From what has been said, it is evident, that the doctrine of the immutability of essences proves them to be only abstract ideas; and is founded on the relation established between them and certain sounds as signs of them; and will always be true, as long as the same name can have the same signification.

20. Recapitulation. To conclude. This is that which in short I would say, viz. that all the great business of genera and species, and their essences, amounts to no more but this:— That men making abstract ideas, and settling them in their minds with names annexed to them, do thereby enable themselves to consider things, and discourse of them, as it were in bundles, for the easier and readier improvement and communication of their knowledge, which would advance but slowly were their words and thoughts confined only to particulars.

Chapter IV. Of the Names of Simple Ideas

1. Names of simple ideas, modes, and substances, have each something peculiar. Though all words, as I have shown, signify nothing immediately but the ideas in the mind of the speaker; yet, upon a nearer survey, we shall find the names of simple ideas, mixed modes (under which I comprise relations too), and natural substances, have each of them something peculiar and different from the other. For example:

2. Names of simple ideas, and of substances intimate real existence. First, the names of simple ideas and substances, with the abstract ideas in the mind which they immediately signify, intimate also some real existence, from which was derived their original pattern. But the names of mixed modes terminate in the idea that is in the mind, and lead not the thoughts any further; as we shall see more at large in the following chapter.

3. Names of simple ideas and modes signify always both real and nominal essences. Secondly, The names of simple ideas and modes signify always the real as well as nominal essence of their species. But the names of natural substances signify rarely, if ever, anything but barely the nominal essences of those species; as we shall show in the chapter that treats of the names of substances in particular.

4. Names of simple ideas are undefinable. Thirdly, The names of simple ideas are not capable of any definition; the names of all complex ideas are. It has not, that I know, been yet observed by anybody what words are, and what are not, capable of being defined; the want whereof is (as I am apt to think) not seldom the occasion of great wrangling and obscurity in men's discourses, whilst some demand definitions of terms that cannot be defined; and others think they ought not to rest satisfied in an explication made by a more general word, and its restriction, (or to speak in terms of art, by a genus and difference), when, even after such definition, made according to rule, those who hear it have often no more a clear conception of the meaning of the word than they had before. This at least I think, that the showing what words are, and what are not, capable of definitions, and wherein consists a good definition, is not wholly besides our present purpose; and perhaps will afford so much light to the nature of these signs and our ideas, as to deserve a more particular consideration.

5. If all names were definable, it would be a process in infinitum. I will not here trouble myself to prove that all terms are not definable, from that progress in infinitum, which it will visibly lead us into, if we should allow that all names could be defined. For, if the terms of one definition were still to be defined by another, where at last should we stop? But I shall, from the nature of our ideas, and the signification of our words, show why some names can, and others cannot be defined; and which they are.

6. What a definition is. I think it is agreed, that a definition is nothing else but the showing the meaning of one word by several other not synonymous terms. The meaning of words being only the ideas they are made to stand for by him that uses them, the meaning of any term is then showed, or the word is defined, when, by other words, the idea it is made the sign of, and annexed to, in the mind of the speaker, is as it were represented, or set before the view of another; and thus its signification is ascertained. This is the only use and end of definitions; and therefore the only measure of what is, or is not a good definition.

7. Simple ideas, why undefinable. This being premised, I say that the names of simple ideas, and those only, are incapable of being defined. The reason whereof is this, That the several terms of a definition, signifying several ideas, they can all together by no means represent an idea which has no composition at all: and therefore a definition, which is properly nothing but the showing the meaning of one word by several others not signifying each the same thing, can in the names of simple ideas have no place.

8. Instances: scholastic definitions of motion. The not observing this difference in our ideas, and their names, has produced that eminent trifling in the schools, which is so easy to be observed in the definitions they give us of some few of these simple ideas. For, as to the greatest part of them, even those masters of definitions were fain to leave them untouched, merely by the impossibility they found in it. What more exquisite jargon could the wit of man invent, than this definition:—"The act of a being in power, as far forth as in power"; which would puzzle any rational man, to whom it was not already known by its famous absurdity, to guess what word it could ever be supposed to be the explication of. If Tully, asking a Dutchman what beweeginge was, should have received this explication in his own language, that it was "actus entis in potentia quatenus in potentia"; I ask whether any one can imagine he could thereby have understood what the word beweeginge signified, or have guessed what idea a Dutchman ordinarily had in his mind, and would signify to another, when he used that sound?

9. Modern definitions of motion. Nor have the modern philosophers, who have endeavoured to throw off the jargon of the schools, and speak intelligibly, much better succeeded in defining simple ideas, whether by explaining their causes, or any otherwise. The atomists, who define motion to be "a passage from one place to another," what do they more than put one synonymous word for another? For what is passage other than motion? And if they were asked what passage was, how would they better define it than by motion? For is it not at least as proper and significant to say, Passage is a motion from one place to another, as to say, Motion is a passage, &c.? This is to translate, and not to define, when we change two words of the same signification one for another; which, when one is better understood than the other, may serve to discover what idea the unknown stands for; but is very far from a definition, unless we will say every English word in the dictionary is the definition of the Latin word it answers, and that motion is a definition of motus. Nor will the "successive application of the parts of the superficies of one body to those of another," which the Cartesians give us, prove a much better definition of motion, when well examined.

10. Definitions of light. "The act of perspicuous, as far forth as perspicuous," is another Peripatetic definition of a simple idea; which, though not more absurd than the former of motion, yet betrays its uselessness and insignificancy more plainly; because experience will easily convince any one that it cannot make the meaning of the word light (which it pretends to define) at all understood by a blind man, but the definition of motion appears not at first sight so useless, because it escapes this way of trial. For this simple idea, entering by the touch as well as sight, it is impossible to show an example of any one who has no other way to get the idea of motion, but barely by the definition of that name. Those who tell us that light is a great number of little globules, striking briskly on the bottom of the eye, speak more intelligibly than the Schools: but yet these words never so well understood would make the idea the word light stands for no more known to a man that understands it not before, than if one should tell him that light was nothing but a company of little tennis-balls, which fairies all

day long struck with rackets against some men's foreheads, whilst they passed by others. For granting this explication of the thing to be true, yet the idea of the cause of light, if we had it never so exact, would no more give us the idea of light itself, as it is such a particular perception in us, than the idea of the figure and motion of a sharp piece of steel would give us the idea of that pain which it is able to cause in us. For the cause of any sensation, and the sensation itself, in all the simple ideas of one sense, are two ideas; and two ideas so different and distant one from another, that no two can be more so. And therefore, should Descartes's globules strike never so long on the retina of a man who was blind by a gutta serena, he would thereby never have any idea of light, or anything approaching it, though he understood never so well what little globules were, and what striking on another body was. And therefore the Cartesians very well distinguish between that light which is the cause of that sensation in us, and the idea which is produced in us by it, and is that which is properly light.

11. Simple ideas, why undefinable, further explained. Simple ideas, as has been shown, are only to be got by those impressions objects themselves make on our minds, by the proper inlets appointed to each sort. If they are not received this way, all the words in the world, made use of to explain or define any of their names, will never be able to produce in us the idea it stands for. For, words being sounds, can produce in us no other simple ideas than of those very sounds; nor excite any in us, but by that voluntary connexion which is known to be between them and those simple ideas which common use has made them the signs of. He that thinks otherwise, let him try if any words can give him the taste of a pine-apple, and make him have the true idea of the relish of that celebrated delicious fruit. So far as he is told it has a resemblance with any tastes whereof he has the ideas already in his memory, imprinted there by sensible objects, not strangers to his palate, so far may he approach that resemblance in his mind. But this is not giving us that idea by a definition, but exciting in us other simple ideas by their known names; which will be still very different from the true taste of that fruit itself. In light and colours, and all other simple ideas, it is the same thing: for the signification of sounds is not natural, but only imposed and arbitrary. And no definition of light or redness is more fitted or able to produce either of those ideas in us, than the sound light or red, by itself. For, to hope to produce an idea of light or colour by a sound, however formed, is to expect that sounds should be visible, or colours audible; and to make the ears do the office of all the other senses. Which is all one as to say, that we might taste, smell, and see by the ears: a sort of philosophy worthy only of Sancho Panza, who had the faculty to see Dulcinea by hearsay. And therefore he that has not before received into his mind, by the proper inlet, the simple idea which any word stands for, can never come to know the signification of that word by any other words or sounds whatsoever, put together according to any rules of definition. The only way is, by applying to his senses the proper object; and so producing that idea in him, for which he has learned the name already. A studious blind man, who had mightily beat his head about visible objects, and made use of the explication of his books and friends, to understand those names of light and colours which often came in his way, bragged one day, That he now understood what scarlet signified. Upon which, his friend demanding what scarlet was? The blind man answered, It was like the sound of a trumpet. Just such an understanding of the name of any other simple idea will he have, who hopes to get it only from a definition, or other words made use of to explain it.

12. The contrary shown in complex ideas, by instances of a statue and rainbow. The case is quite otherwise in complex ideas; which, consisting of several simple ones, it is in the power of words, standing for the several ideas that make that composition, to imprint complex ideas in the mind which were never there before, and so make their names be understood. In such collections of ideas, passing under one name, definition, or the teaching the signification of one word by several others, has place, and may make us understand the names of things which never came within the reach of our senses; and frame ideas suitable to those in other men's minds, when they use those names: provided that none of the terms of the definition stand for any such simple ideas, which he to whom the explication is made has never yet had in his

thought. Thus the word statue may be explained to a blind man by other words, when picture cannot; his senses having given him the idea of figure, but not of colours, which therefore words cannot excite in him. This gained the prize to the painter against the statuary: each of which contending for the excellency of his art, and the statuary bragging that his was to be preferred, because it reached further, and even those who had lost their eyes could yet perceive the excellency of it. The painter agreed to refer himself to the judgment of a blind man; who being brought where there was a statue made by the one, and a picture drawn by the other; he was first led to the statue, in which he traced with his hands all the lineaments of the face and body, and with great admiration applauded the skill of the workman. But being led to the picture, and having his hands laid upon it, was told, that now he touched the head, and then the forehead, eyes, nose, &c., as his hand moved over the parts of the picture on the cloth, without finding any the least distinction: whereupon he cried out, that certainly that must needs be a very admirable and divine piece of workmanship, which could represent to them all those parts, where he could neither feel nor perceive anything.

13. Colours indefinable to the born-blind. He that should use the word rainbow to one who knew all those colours, but yet had never seen that phenomenon, would, by enumerating the figure, largeness, position, and order of the colours, so well define that word that it might be perfectly understood. But yet that definition, how exact and perfect soever, would never make a blind man understand it; because several of the simple ideas that make that complex one, being such as he never received by sensation and experience, no words are able to excite them in his mind.

14. Complex ideas definable only when the simple ideas of which they consist have been got from experience. Simple ideas, as has been shown, can only be got by experience from those objects which are proper to produce in us those perceptions. When, by this means, we have our minds stored with them, and know the names for them, then we are in a condition to define, and by definition to understand, the names of complex ideas that are made up of them. But when any term stands for a simple idea that a man has never yet had in his mind, it is impossible by any words to make known its meaning to him. When any term stands for an idea a man is acquainted with, but is ignorant that that term is the sign of it, then another name of the same idea, which he has been accustomed to, may make him understand its meaning. But in no case whatsoever is any name of any simple idea capable of a definition.

15. Names of simple ideas of less doubtful meaning than those of mixed modes and substances. Fourthly, But though the names of simple ideas have not the help of definition to determine their signification, yet that hinders not but that they are generally less doubtful and uncertain than those of mixed modes and substances; because they, standing only for one simple perception, men for the most part easily and perfectly agree in their signification; and there is little room for mistake and wrangling about their meaning. He that knows once that whiteness is the name of that colour he has observed in snow or milk, will not be apt to misapply that word, as long as he retains that idea; which when he has quite lost, he is not apt to mistake the meaning of it, but perceives he understands it not. There is neither a multiplicity of simple ideas to be put together, which makes the doubtfulness in the names of mixed modes; nor a supposed, but an unknown, real essence, with properties depending thereon, the precise number whereof is also unknown, which makes the difficulty in the names of substances. But, on the contrary, in simple ideas the whole signification of the name is known at once, and consists not of parts, whereof more or less being put in, the idea may be varied, and so the signification of name be obscure, or uncertain.

16. Simple ideas have few ascents in linea praedicamentali. Fifthly, This further may be observed concerning simple ideas and their names, that they have but few ascents in linea praedicamentali, (as they call it,) from the lowest species to the summum genus. The reason whereof is, that the lowest species being but one simple idea, nothing can be left out of it, that so the difference being taken away, it may agree with some other thing in one idea common to them both; which, having one name, is the genus of the other two: v.g. there is nothing that

can be left out of the idea of white and red to make them agree in one common appearance, and so have one general name; as rationality being left out of the complex idea of man, makes it agree with brute in the more general idea and name of animal. And therefore when, to avoid unpleasant enumerations, men would comprehend both white and red, and several other such simple ideas, under one general name, they have been fain to do it by a word which denotes only the way they get into the mind. For when white, red, and yellow are all comprehended under the genus or name colour, it signifies no more but such ideas as are produced in the mind only by the sight, and have entrance only through the eyes. And when they would frame yet a more general term to comprehend both colours and sounds, and the like simple ideas, they do it by a word that signifies all such as come into the mind only by one sense. And so the general term quality, in its ordinary acceptation, comprehends colours, sounds, tastes, smells, and tangible qualities, with distinction from extension, number, motion, pleasure, and pain, which make impressions on the mind and introduce their ideas by more senses than one.

17. Names of simple ideas not arbitrary, but perfectly taken from the existence of things. Sixthly, The names of simple ideas, substances, and mixed modes have also this difference: that those of mixed modes stand for ideas perfectly arbitrary; those of substances are not perfectly so, but refer to a pattern, though with some latitude; and those of simple ideas are perfectly taken from the existence of things, and are not arbitrary at an. Which, what difference it makes in the significations of their names, we shall see in the following chapters. Simple modes. The names of simple modes differ little from those of simple ideas.

Chapter V. Of the Names of Mixed Modes and Relations

1. Mixed modes stand for abstract ideas, as other general names. The names of mixed modes, being general, they stand, as has been shewed, for sorts or species of things, each of which has its peculiar essence. The essences of these species also, as has been shewed, are nothing but the abstract ideas in the mind, to which the name is annexed. Thus far the names and essences of mixed modes have nothing but what is common to them with other ideas: but if we take a little nearer survey of them, we shall find that they have something peculiar, which perhaps may deserve our attention.

2. First, The abstract ideas they stand for are made by the understanding. The first particularity I shall observe in them, is, that the abstract ideas, or, if you please, the essences, of the several species of mixed modes, are made by the understanding, wherein they differ from those of simple ideas: in which sort the mind has no power to make any one, but only receives such as are presented to it by the real existence of things operating upon it.

3. Secondly, made arbitrarily, and without patterns. In the next place, these essences of the species of mixed modes are not only made by the mind, but made very arbitrarily, made without patterns, or reference to any real existence. Wherein they differ from those of substances, which carry with them the supposition of some real being, from which they are taken, and to which they are comformable. But, in its complex ideas of mixed modes, the mind takes a liberty not to follow the existence of things exactly. It unites and retains certain collections, as so many distinct specific ideas; whilst others, that as often occur in nature, and are as plainly suggested by outward things, pass neglected, without particular names or specifications. Nor does the mind, in these of mixed modes, as in the complex idea of substances, examine them by the real existence of things; or verify them by patterns containing such peculiar compositions in nature. To know whether his idea of adultery or incest be right, will a man seek it anywhere amongst things existing? Or is it true because any one has been witness to such an action? No: but it suffices here, that men have put together such a collection into one complex idea, that makes the archetype and specific idea, whether ever any such action were committed in rerum natura or no.

4. How this is done. To understand this right, we must consider wherein this making of these

complex ideas consists; and that is not in the making any new idea, but putting together those which the mind had before. Wherein the mind does these three things: First, It chooses a certain number; Secondly, It gives them connexion, and makes them into one idea; Thirdly, It ties them together by a name. If we examine how the mind proceeds in these, and what liberty it takes in them, we shall easily observe how these essences of the species of mixed modes are the workmanship of the mind; and, consequently, that the species themselves are of men's making. Evidently arbitrary, in that the idea is often before the existence. Nobody can doubt but that these ideas of mixed modes are made by a voluntary collection of ideas, put together in the mind, independent from any original patterns in nature, who will but reflect that this sort of complex ideas may be made, abstracted, and have names given them, and so a species be constituted, before any one individual of that species ever existed. Who can doubt but the ideas of sacrilege or adultery might be framed in the minds of men, and have names given them, and so these species of mixed modes be constituted, before either of them was ever committed; and might be as well discoursed of and reasoned about, and as certain truths discovered of them, whilst yet they had no being but in the understanding, as well as now, that they have but too frequently a real existence? Whereby it is plain how much the sorts of mixed modes are the creatures of the understanding, where they have a being as subservient to all the ends of real truth and knowledge, as when they really exist. And we cannot doubt but law-makers have often made laws about species of actions which were only the creatures of their own understandings; beings that had no other existence but in their own minds. And I think nobody can deny but that the resurrection was a species of mixed modes in the mind, before it really existed.

6. Instances: murder, incest, stabbing. To see how arbitrarily these essences of mixed modes are made by the mind, we need but take a view of almost any of them. A little looking into them will satisfy us, that it is the mind that combines several scattered independent ideas into one complex one; and, by the common name it gives them, makes them the essence of a certain species, without regulating itself by any connexion they have in nature. For what greater connexion in nature has the idea of a man than the idea of a sheep with killing, that this is made a particular species of action, signified by the word murder, and the other not? Or what union is there in nature between the idea of the relation of a father with killing than that of a son or neighbour, that those are combined into one complex idea, and thereby made the essence of the distinct species parricide, whilst the other makes no distinct species at all? But, though they have made killing a man's father or mother a distinct species from killing his son or daughter, yet, in some other cases, son and daughter are taken in too, as well as father and mother: and they are all equally comprehended in the same species, as in that of incest. Thus the mind in mixed modes arbitrarily unites into complex ideas such as it finds convenient; whilst others that have altogether as much union in nature are left loose, and never combined into one idea, because they have no need of one name. It is evident then that the mind, by its free choice, gives a connexion to a certain number of ideas, which in nature have no more union with one another than others that it leaves out: why else is the part of the weapon the beginning of the wound is made with taken notice of, to make the distinct species called stabbing, and the figure and matter of the weapon left out? I do not say this is done without reason, as we shall see more by and by; but this I say, that it is done by the free choice of the mind, pursuing its own ends; and that, therefore, these species of mixed modes are the workmanship of the understanding. And there is nothing more evident than that, for the most part, in the framing of these ideas, the mind searches not its patterns in nature, nor refers the ideas it makes to the real existence of things, but puts such together as may best serve its own purposes, without tying itself to a precise imitation of anything that really exists.

7. But still subservient to the end of language, and not made at random. But, though these complex ideas or essences of mixed modes depend on the mind, and are made by it with great liberty, yet they are not made at random, and jumbled together without any reason at all. Though these complex ideas be not always copied from nature, yet they are always suited to

the end for which abstract ideas are made: and though they be combinations made of ideas that are loose enough, and have as little union in themselves as several others to which the mind never gives a connexion that combines them into one idea; yet they are always made for the convenience of communication, which is the chief end of language. The use of language is, by short sounds, to signify with ease and dispatch general conceptions; wherein not only abundance of particulars may be contained, but also a great variety of independent ideas collected into one complex one. In the making therefore of the species of mixed modes, men have had regard only to such combinations as they had occasion to mention one to another. Those they have combined into distinct complex ideas, and given names to; whilst others, that in nature have as near a union, are left loose and unregarded. For, to go no further than human actions themselves, if they would make distinct abstract ideas of all the varieties which might be observed in them, the number must be infinite, and the memory confounded with the plenty, as well as overcharged to little purpose. It suffices that men make and name so many complex ideas of these mixed modes as they find they have occasion to have names for, in the ordinary occurrence of their affairs. If they join to the idea of killing the idea of father or mother, and so make a distinct species from killing a man's son or neighbour, it is because of the different heinousness of the crime, and the distinct punishment is, due to the murdering a man's father and mother, different to what ought to be inflicted on the murderer of a son or neighbour; and therefore they find it necessary to mention it by a distinct name, which is the end of making that distinct combination. But though the ideas of mother and daughter are so differently treated, in reference to the idea of killing, that the one is joined with it to make a distinct abstract idea with a name, and so a distinct species, and the other not; yet, in respect of carnal knowledge, they are both taken in under incest: and that still for the same convenience of expressing under one name, and reckoning of one species, such unclean mixtures as have a peculiar turpitude beyond others; and this to avoid circumlocutions and tedious descriptions.
8. Whereof the intranslatable words of divers languages are a proof. A moderate skill in different languages will easily satisfy one of the truth of this, it being so obvious to observe great store of words in one language which have not any that answer them in another. Which plainly shows that those of one country, by their customs and manner of life, have found occasion to make several complex ideas, and given names to them, which others never collected into specific ideas. This could not have happened if these species were the steady workmanship of nature, and not collections made and abstracted by the mind, in order to naming, and for the convenience of communication. The terms of our law, which are not empty sounds, will hardly find words that answer them in the Spanish or Italian, no scanty languages; much less, I think, could any one translate them into the Caribbee or Westoe tongues: and the versura of the Romans, or corban of the Jews, have no words in other languages to answer them; the reason whereof is plain, from what has been said. Nay, if we look a little more nearly into this matter, and exactly compare different languages, we shall find that, though they have words which in translations and dictionaries are supposed to answer one another, yet there is scarce one of ten amongst the names of complex ideas, especially of mixed modes, that stands for the same precise idea which the word does that in dictionaries it is rendered by. There are no ideas more common and less compounded than the measures of time, extension and weight; and the Latin names, hora, pes, libra, are without difficulty rendered by the English names, hour, foot, and pound: but yet there is nothing more evident than that the ideas a Roman annexed to these Latin names, were very far different from those which an Englishman expresses by those English ones. And if either of these should make use of the measures that those of the other language designed by their names, he would be quite out in his account. These are too sensible proofs to be doubted; and we shall find this much more so in the names of more abstract and compounded ideas, such as are the greatest part of those which make up moral discourses: whose names, when men come curiously to compare with those they are translated into, in other languages, they will find very few of them exactly to correspond in the whole extent of their significations.

9. This shows species to be made for communication. The reason why I take so particular notice of this is, that we may not be mistaken about genera and species, and their essences, as if they were things regularly and constantly made by nature, and had a real existence in things; when they appear, upon a more wary survey, to be nothing else but an artifice of the understanding, for the easier signifying such collections of ideas as it should often have occasion to communicate by one general term; under which divers particulars, as far forth as they agreed to that abstract idea, might be comprehended. And if the doubtful signification of the word species may make it sound harsh to some, that I say the species of mixed modes are "made by the understanding"; yet, I think, it can by nobody be denied that it is the mind makes those abstract complex ideas to which specific names are given. And if it be true, as it is, that the mind makes the patterns for sorting and naming of things, I leave it to be considered who makes the boundaries of the sort or species; since with me species and sort have no other difference than that of a Latin and English idiom.

10. In mixed modes it is the name that ties the combination of simple ideas together, and makes it a species. The near relation that there is between species, essences, and their general name, at least in mixed modes, will further appear when we consider, that it is the name that seems to preserve those essences, and give them their lasting duration. For, the connexion between the loose parts of those complex ideas being made by the mind, this union, which has no particular foundation in nature, would cease again, were there not something that did, as it were, hold it together, and keep the parts from scattering. Though therefore it be the mind that makes the collection, it is the name which is as it were the knot that ties them fast together. What a vast variety of different ideas does the word triumphus hold together, and deliver to us as one species! Had this name been never made, or quite lost, we might, no doubt, have had descriptions of what passed in that solemnity: but yet, I think, that which holds those different parts together, in the unity of one complex idea, is that very word annexed to it; without which the several parts of that would no more be thought to make one thing, than any other show, which having never been made but once, had never been united into one complex idea, under one denomination. How much, therefore, in mixed modes, the unity necessary to any essence depends on the mind; and how much the continuation and fixing of that unity depends on the name in common use annexed to it, I leave to be considered by those who look upon essences and species as real established things in nature.

11. Suitable to this, we find that men speaking of mixed modes, seldom imagine or take any other for species of them, but such as are set out by name: because they, being of man's making only, in order to naming, no such species are taken notice of, or supposed to be, unless a name be joined to it, as the sign of man's having combined into one idea several loose ones; and by that name giving a lasting union to the parts which would otherwise cease to have any, as soon as the mind laid by that abstract idea, and ceased actually to think on it. But when a name is once annexed to it, wherein the parts of that complex idea have a settled and permanent union, then is the essence, as it were, established, and the species looked on as complete. For to what purpose should the memory charge itself with such compositions, unless it were by abstraction to make them general? And to what purpose make them general, unless it were that they might have general names for the convenience of discourse and communication? Thus we see, that killing a man with a sword or a hatchet are looked on as no distinct species of action; but if the point of the sword first enter the body, it passes for a distinct species, where it has a distinct name, as in England, in whose language it is called stabbing: but in another country, where it has not happened to be specified under a peculiar name, it passes not for a distinct species. But in the species of corporeal substances, though it be the mind that makes the nominal essence, yet, since those ideas which are combined in it are supposed to have an union in nature whether the mind joins them or not, therefore those are looked on as distinct species, without any operation of the mind, either abstracting, or giving a name to that complex idea.

12. For the originals of our mixed modes, we look no further than the mind; which also shows

them to he the workmanship of the understanding. Conformable also to what has been said concerning the essences of the species of mixed modes, that they are the creatures of the understanding rather than the works of nature; conformable, I say, to this, we find that their names lead our thoughts to the mind, and no further. When we speak of justice, or gratitude, we frame to ourselves no imagination of anything existing, which we would conceive; but our thoughts terminate in the abstract ideas of those virtues, and look not further; as they do when we speak of a horse, or iron, whose specific ideas we consider not as barely in the mind, but as in things themselves, which afford the original patterns of those ideas. But in mixed modes, at least the most considerable parts of them, which are moral beings, we consider the original patterns as being in the mind, and to those we refer for the distinguishing of particular beings under names. And hence I think it is that these essences of the species of mixed modes are by a more particular name called notions; as, by a peculiar right, appertaining to the understanding.

13. Their being made by the understanding without patterns, shows the reason why they are so compounded. Hence, likewise, we may learn why the complex ideas of mixed modes are commonly more compounded and decompounded than those of natural substances. Because they being the workmanship of the understanding, pursuing only its own ends, and the conveniency of expressing in short those ideas it would make known to another, it does with great liberty unite often into one abstract idea things that, in their nature, have no coherence; and so under one term bundle together a great variety of compounded and decompounded ideas. Thus the name of procession: what a great mixture of independent ideas of persons, habits, tapers, orders, motions, sounds, does it contain in that complex one, which the mind of man has arbitrarily put together, to express by that one name? Whereas the complex ideas of the sorts of substances are usually made up of only a small number of simple ones; and in the species of animals, these two, viz. shape and voice, commonly make the whole nominal essence.

14. Names of mixed modes stand always for their real essences, which are the workmanship of our minds. Another thing we may observe from what has been said is, That the names of mixed modes always signify (when they have any determined signification) the real essences of their species. For, these abstract ideas being the workmanship of the mind, and not referred to the real existence of things, there is no supposition of anything more signified by that name, but barely that complex idea the mind itself has formed; which is all it would have expressed by it; and is that on which all the properties of the species depend, and from which alone they all flow: and so in these the real and nominal essence is the same; which, of what concernment it is to the certain knowledge of general truth, we shall see hereafter.

15. Why their names are usually got before their ideas. This also may show us the reason why for the most part the names of fixed modes are got before the ideas they stand for are perfectly known. Because there being no species of these ordinarily taken notice of but what have names, and those species, or rather their essences, being abstract complex ideas, made arbitrarily by the mind, it is convenient, if not necessary, to know the names, before one endeavour to frame these complex ideas: unless a man will fill his head with a company of abstract complex ideas, which, others having no names for, he has nothing to do with, but to lay by and forget again. I confess that, in the beginning of languages, it was necessary to have the idea before one gave it the name: and so it is still, where, making a new complex idea, one also, by giving it a new name, makes a new word. But this concerns not languages made, which have generally pretty well provided for ideas which men have frequent occasion to have and communicate; and in such, I ask whether it be not the ordinary method, that children learn the names of mixed modes before they have their ideas? What one of a thousand ever frames the abstract ideas of glory and ambition, before he has heard the names of them? In simple ideas and substances I grant it is otherwise, which, being such ideas as have a real existence and union in nature, the ideas and names are got one before the other, as it happens.

16. Reason of my being so large on this subject. What has been said here of mixed modes is,

with very little difference, applicable also to relations; which, since every man himself may observe, I may spare myself the pains to enlarge on: especially, since what I have here said concerning Words in this third Book, will possibly be thought by some to be much more than what so slight a subject required. I allow it might be brought into a narrower compass; but I was willing to stay my reader on an argument that appears to me new and a little out of the way, (I am sure it is one I thought not of when I began to write,) that, by searching it to the bottom, and turning it on every side, some part or other might meet with every one's thoughts, and give occasion to the most averse or negligent to reflect on a general miscarriage, which, though of great consequence, is little taken notice of. When it is considered what a pudder is made about essences, and how much all sorts of knowledge, discourse, and conversation are pestered and disordered by the careless and confused use and application of words, it will perhaps be thought worth while thoroughly to lay it open. And I shall be pardoned if I have dwelt long on an argument which I think, therefore, needs to be inculcated, because the faults men are usually guilty of in this kind, are not only the greatest hindrances of true knowledge, but are so well thought of as to pass for it. Men would often see what a small pittance of reason and truth, or possibly none at all, is mixed with those huffing opinions they are swelled with; if they would but look beyond fashionable sounds, and observe what ideas are or are not comprehended under those words with which they are so armed at all points, and with which they so confidently lay about them. I shall imagine I have done some service to truth, peace, and learning, if, by any enlargement on this subject, I can make men reflect on their own use of language; and give them reason to suspect, that, since it is frequent for others, it may also be possible for them, to have sometimes very good and approved words in their mouths and writings, with very uncertain, little, or no signification. And therefore it is not unreasonable for them to be wary herein themselves, and not to be unwilling to have them examined by others. With this design, therefore, I shall go on with what I have further to say concerning this matter.

Chapter VI. Of the Names of Substances

1. The common names of substances stand for sorts. The common names of substances, as well as other general terms, stand for sorts: which is nothing else but the being made signs of such complex ideas wherein several particular substances do or might agree, by virtue of which they are capable of being comprehended in one common conception, and signified by one name. I say do or might agree: for though there be but one sun existing in the world, yet the idea of it being abstracted, so that more substances (if there were several) might each agree in it, it is as much a sort as if there were as many suns as there are stars. They want not their reasons who think there are, and that each fixed star would answer the idea the name sun stands for, to one who was placed in a due distance: which, by the way, may show us how much the sorts, or, if you please, genera and species of things (for those Latin terms signify to me no more than the English word sort) depend on such collections of ideas as men have made, and not on the real nature of things; since it is not impossible but that, in propriety of speech, that might be a sun to one which is a star to another.

2. The essence of each sort of substance is our abstract idea to which the name is annexed. The measure and boundary of each sort or species, whereby it is constituted that particular sort, and distinguished from others, is that we call its essence, which is nothing but that abstract idea to which the name is annexed; so that everything contained in that idea is essential to that sort. This, though it be all the essence of natural substances that we know, or by which we distinguish them into sorts, yet I call it by a peculiar name, the nominal essence, to distinguish it from the real constitution of substances, upon which depends this nominal essence, and all the properties of that sort; which, therefore, as has been said, may be called the real essence: v.g. the nominal essence of gold is that complex idea the word gold stands for, let it be, for

instance, a body yellow, of a certain weight, malleable, fusible, and fixed. But the real essence is the constitution of the insensible parts of that body, on which those qualities and all the other properties of gold depend. How far these two are different, though they are both called essence, is obvious at first sight to discover.

3. The nominal and real essence different. For, though perhaps voluntary motion, with sense and reason, joined to a body of a certain shape, be the complex idea to which I and others annex the name man, and so be the nominal essence of the species so called: yet nobody will say that complex idea is the real essence and source of all those operations which are to be found in any individual of that sort. The foundation of all those qualities which are the ingredients of our complex idea, is something quite different: and had we such a knowledge of that constitution of man, from which his faculties of moving, sensation, and reasoning, and other powers flow, and on which his so regular shape depends, as it is possible angels have, and it is certain his Maker has, we should have a quite other idea of his essence than what now is contained in our definition of that species, be it what it will: and our idea of any individual man would be as far different from what it is now, as is his who knows all the springs and wheels and other contrivances within of the famous clock at Strasburg, from that which a gazing countryman has of it, who barely sees the motion of the hand, and hears the clock strike, and observes only some of the outward appearances.

4. Nothing essential to individuals. That essence, in the ordinary use of the word, relates to sorts, and that it is considered in particular beings no further than as they are ranked into sorts, appears from hence: that, take but away the abstract ideas by which we sort individuals, and rank them under common names, and then the thought of anything essential to any of them instantly vanishes: we have no notion of the one without the other, which plainly shows their relation. It is necessary for me to be as I am; God and nature has made me so: but there is nothing I have is essential to me. An accident or disease may very much alter my colour or shape; a fever or fall may take away my reason or memory, or both; and an apoplexy leave neither sense, nor understanding, no, nor life. Other creatures of my shape may be made with more and better, or fewer and worse faculties than I have; and others may have reason and sense in a shape and body very different from mine. None of these are essential to the one or the other, or to any individual whatever, till the mind refers it to some sort or species of things; and then presently, according to the abstract idea of that sort, something is found essential. Let any one examine his own thoughts, and he will find that as soon as he supposes or speaks of essential, the consideration of some species, or the complex idea signified by some general name, comes into his mind; and it is in reference to that that this or that quality is said to be essential. So that if it be asked, whether it be essential to me or any other particular corporeal being, to have reason? I say, no; no more than it is essential to this white thing I write on to have words in it. But if that particular being be to be counted of the sort man, and to have the name man given it, then reason is essential to it; supposing reason to be a part of the complex idea the name man stands for: as it is essential to this thing I write on to contain words, if I will give it the name treatise, and rank it under that species. So that essential and not essential relate only to our abstract ideas, and the names annexed to them; which amounts to no more than this, That whatever particular thing has not in it those qualities which are contained in the abstract idea which any general term stands for, cannot be ranked under that species, nor be called by that name; since that abstract idea is the very essence of that species.

5. The only essences perceived by us in individual substances are those qualities which entitle them to receive their names. Thus, if the idea of body with some people be bare extension or space, then solidity is not essential to body: if others make the idea to which they give the name body to be solidity and extension, then solidity is essential to body. That therefore, and that alone, is considered as essential, which makes a part of the complex idea the name of a sort stands for: without which no particular thing can be reckoned of that sort, nor be entitled to that name. Should there be found a parcel of matter that had all the other qualities that are in iron, but wanted obedience to the loadstone, and would neither be drawn by it nor receive

direction from it, would any one question whether it wanted anything essential? It would be absurd to ask, Whether a thing really existing wanted anything essential to it. Or could it be demanded, Whether this made an essential or specific difference or no, since we have no other measure of essential or specific but our abstract ideas? And to talk of specific differences in nature, without reference to general ideas in names, is to talk unintelligibly. For I would ask any one, What is sufficient to make an essential difference in nature between any two particular beings, without any regard had to some abstract idea, which is looked upon as the essence and standard of a species? All such patterns and standards being quite laid aside, particular beings, considered barely in themselves, will be found to have all their qualities equally essential; and everything in each individual will be essential to it; or, which is more, nothing at all. For, though it may be reasonable to ask, Whether obeying the magnet be essential to iron? yet I think it is very improper and insignificant to ask, whether it be essential to the particular parcel of matter I cut my pen with; without considering it under the name, iron, or as being of a certain species. And if, as has been said, our abstract ideas, which have names annexed to them, are the boundaries of species, nothing can be essential but what is contained in those ideas.

6. Even the real essences of individual substances imply potential sorts. It is true, I have often mentioned a real essence, distinct in substances from those abstract ideas of them, which I call their nominal essence. By this real essence I mean, that real constitution of anything, which is the foundation of all those properties that are combined in, and are constantly found to co-exist with the nominal essence; that particular constitution which everything has within itself, without any relation to anything without it. But essence, even in this sense, relates to a sort, and supposes a species. For, being that real constitution on which the properties depend, it necessarily supposes a sort of things, properties belonging only to species, and not to individuals: v.g. supposing the nominal essence of gold to be a body of such a peculiar colour and weight, with malleability and fusibility, the real essence is that constitution of the parts of matter on which these qualities and their union depend; and is also the foundation of its solubility in aqua regia and other properties, accompanying that complex idea. Here are essences and properties, but all upon supposition of a sort or general abstract idea, which is considered as immutable; but there is no individual parcel of matter to which any of these qualities are so annexed as to be essential to it or inseparable from it. That which is essential belongs to it as a condition whereby it is of this or that sort: but take away the consideration of its being ranked under the name of some abstract idea, and then there is nothing necessary to it, nothing inseparable from it. Indeed, as to the real essences of substances, we only suppose their being, without precisely knowing what they are; but that which annexes them still to the species is the nominal essence, of which they are the supposed foundation and cause.

7. The nominal essence bounds the species for us. The next thing to be considered is, by which of those essences it is that substances are determined into sorts or species; and that, it is evident, is by the nominal essence. For it is that alone that the name, which is the mark of the sort, signifies. It is impossible, therefore, that anything should determine the sorts of things, which we rank under general names, but that idea which that name is designed as a mark for; which is that, as has been shown, which we call nominal essence. Why do we say this is a horse, and that a mule; this is an animal, that an herb? How comes any particular thing to be of this or that sort, but because it has that nominal essence; or, which is all one, agrees to that abstract idea, that name is annexed to? And I desire any one but to reflect on his own thoughts, when he hears or speaks any of those or other names of substances, to know what sort of essences they stand for.

8. The nature of species, as formed by us. And that the species of things to us are nothing but the ranking them under distinct names, according to the complex ideas in us, and not according to precise, distinct, real essences in them, is plain from hence:— That we find many of the individuals that are ranked into one sort, called by one common name, and so received as being of one species, have yet qualities, depending on their real constitutions, as far

different one from another as from others from which they are accounted to differ specifically. This, as it is easy to be observed by all who have to do with natural bodies, so chemists especially are often, by sad experience, convinced of it, when they, sometimes in vain, seek for the same qualities in one parcel of sulphur, antimony, or vitriol, which they have found in others. For, though they are bodies of the same species, having the same nominal essence, under the same name, yet do they often, upon severe ways of examination, betray qualities so different one from another, as to frustrate the expectation and labour of very wary chemists. But if things were distinguished into species, according to their real essences, it would be as impossible to find different properties in any two individual substances of the same species, as it is to find different properties in two circles, or two equilateral triangles. That is properly the essence to us, which determines every particular to this or that classis; or, which is the same thing, to this or that general name: and what can that be else, but that abstract idea to which that name is annexed; and so has, in truth, a reference, not so much to the being of particular things, as to their general denominations?

9. Not the real essence, or texture of parts, which we know not. Nor indeed can we rank and sort things, and consequently (which is the end of sorting) denominate them, by their real essences; because we know them not. Our faculties carry us no further towards the knowledge and distinction of substances, than a collection of those sensible ideas which we observe in them; which, however made with the greatest diligence and exactness we are capable of, yet is more remote from the true internal constitution from which those qualities flow, than, as I said, a countryman's idea is from the inward contrivance of that famous clock at Strasburg, whereof he only sees the outward figure and motions. There is not so contemptible a plant or animal, that does not confound the most enlarged understanding. Though the familiar use of things about us take off our wonder, yet it cures not our ignorance. When we come to examine the stones we tread on, or the iron we daily handle, we presently find we know not their make; and can give no reason of the different qualities we find in them. It is evident the internal constitution, whereon their properties depend, is unknown to us: for to go no further than the grossest and most obvious we can imagine amongst them, What is that texture of parts, that real essence, that makes lead and antimony fusible, wood and stones not? What makes lead and iron malleable, antimony and stones not? And yet how infinitely these come short of the fine contrivances and inconceivable real essences of plants or animals, every one knows. The workmanship of the all-wise and powerful God in the great fabric of the universe, and every part thereof, further exceeds the capacity and comprehension of the most inquisitive and intelligent man, than the best contrivance of the most ingenious man doth the conceptions of the most ignorant of rational creatures. Therefore we in vain pretend to range things into sorts, and dispose them into certain classes under names, by their real essences, that are so far from our discovery or comprehension. A blind man may as soon sort things by their colours, and he that has lost his smell as well distinguish a lily and a rose by their odours, as by those internal constitutions which he knows not. He that thinks he can distinguish sheep and goats by their real essences, that are unknown to him, may be pleased to try his skill in those species called cassiowary and querechinchio; and by their internal real essences determine the boundaries of those species, without knowing the complex idea of sensible qualities that each of those names stand for, in the countries where those animals are to be found.

10. Not the substantial form, which we know less. Those, therefore, who have been taught that the several species of substances had their distinct internal substantial forms, and that it was those forms which made the distinction of substances into their true species and genera, were led yet further out of the way by having their minds set upon fruitless inquiries after "substantial forms"; wholly unintelligible, and whereof we have scarce so much as any obscure or confused conception in general.

11. That the nominal essence is that only whereby we distinguish species of substances, further evident, from our ideas of finite spirits and of God. That our ranking and distinguishing natural substances into species consists in the nominal essences the mind makes, and not in the

real essences to be found in the things themselves, is further evident from our ideas of spirits. For the mind getting, only by reflecting on its own operations, those simple ideas which it attributes to spirits, it hath or can have no other notion of spirit but by attributing all those operations it finds in itself to a sort of beings; without consideration of matter. And even the most advanced notion we have of GOD is but attributing the same simple ideas which we have got from reflection on what we find in ourselves, and which we conceive to have more perfection in them than would be in their absence; attributing, I say, those simple ideas to Him in an unlimited degree. Thus, having got from reflecting on ourselves the idea of existence, knowledge, power and pleasure — each of which we find it better to have than to want; and the more we have of each the better — joining all these together, with infinity to each of them, we have the complex idea of an eternal, omniscient, omnipotent, infinitely wise and happy being. And though we are told that there are different species of angels; yet we know not how to frame distinct specific ideas of them: not out of any conceit that the existence of more species than one of spirits is impossible; but because having no more simple ideas (nor being able to frame more) applicable to such beings, but only those few taken from ourselves, and from the actions of our own minds in thinking, and being delighted, and moving several parts of our bodies; we can no otherwise distinguish in our conceptions the several species of spirits, one from another, but by attributing those operations and powers we find in ourselves to them in a higher or lower degree; and so have no very distinct specific ideas of spirits, except only of GOD, to whom we attribute both duration and all those other ideas with infinity; to the other spirits, with limitation: nor, as I humbly conceive, do we, between GOD and them in our ideas, put any difference, by any number of simple ideas which we have of one and not of the other, but only that of infinity. All the particular ideas of existence, knowledge, will, power, and motion, &c., being ideas derived from the operations of our minds, we attribute all of them to all sorts of spirits, with the difference only of degrees; to the utmost we can imagine, even infinity, when we would frame as well as we can an idea of the First Being; who yet, it is certain, is infinitely more remote, in the real excellency of his nature, from the highest and perfectest of all created beings, than the greatest man, nay, purest seraph, is from the most contemptible part of matter; and consequently must infinitely exceed what our narrow understandings can conceive of Him.

12. Of finite spirits there are probably numberless species, in a continuous series or gradation. It is not impossible to conceive, nor repugnant to reason, that there may be many species of spirits, as much separated and diversified one from another by distinct properties whereof we have no ideas, as the species of sensible things are distinguished one from another by qualities which we know and observe in them. That there should be more species of intelligent creatures above us, than there are of sensible and material below us, is probable to me from hence: that in all the visible corporeal world, we see no chasms or gaps. All quite down from us the descent is by easy steps, and a continued series of things, that in each remove differ very little one from the other. There are fishes that have wings, and are not strangers to the airy region: and there are some birds that are inhabitants of the water, whose blood is cold as fishes, and their flesh so like in taste that the scrupulous are allowed them on fish-days. There are animals so near of kin both to birds and beasts that they are in the middle between both: amphibious animals link the terrestrial and aquatic together; seals live at land and sea, and porpoises have the warm blood and entrails of a hog; not to mention what is confidently reported of mermaids, or sea-men. There are some brutes that seem to have as much knowledge and reason as some that are called men: and the animal and vegetable kingdoms are so nearly joined, that, if you will take the lowest of one and the highest of the other, there will scarce be perceived any great difference between them: and so on, till we come to the lowest and the most inorganical parts of matter, we shall find everywhere that the several species are linked together, and differ but in almost insensible degrees. And when we consider the infinite power and wisdom of the Maker, we have reason to think that it is suitable to the magnificent harmony of the universe, and the great design and infinite goodness of the

Architect, that the species of creatures should also, by gentle degrees, ascend upward from us toward his infinite perfection, as we see they gradually descend from us downwards: which if it be probable, we have reason then to be persuaded that there are far more species of creatures above us than there are beneath; we being, in degrees of perfection, much more remote from the infinite being of GOD than we are from the lowest state of being, and that which approaches nearest to nothing. And yet of all those distinct species, for the reasons above said, we have no clear distinct ideas.

13. The nominal essence that of the species, as conceived by us, proved from water and ice. But to return to the species of corporeal substances. If I should ask any one whether ice and water were two distinct species of things, I doubt not but I should be answered in the affirmative: and it cannot be denied but he that says they are two distinct species is in the right. But if an Englishman bred in Jamaica, who perhaps had never seen nor heard of ice, coming into England in the winter, find the water he put in his basin at night in a great part frozen in the morning, and, not knowing any peculiar name it had, should call it hardened water; I ask whether this would be a new species to him, different from water? And I think it would be answered here, It would not be to him a new species, no more than congealed jelly, when it is cold, is a distinct species from the same jelly fluid and warm; or than liquid gold in the furnace is a distinct species from hard gold in the hands of a workman. And if this be so, it is plain that our distinct species are nothing but distinct complex ideas, with distinct names annexed to them. It is true every substance that exists has its peculiar constitution, whereon depend those sensible qualities and powers we observe in it; but the ranking of things into species (which is nothing but sorting them under several titles) is done by us according to the ideas that we have of them: which, though sufficient to distinguish them by names, so that we may be able to discourse of them when we have them not present before us; yet if we suppose it to be done by their real internal constitutions, and that things existing are distinguished by nature into species, by real essences, according as we distinguish them into species by names, we shall be liable to great mistakes.

14. Difficulties in the supposition of a certain number of real essences. To distinguish substantial beings into species, according to the usual supposition, that there are certain precise essences or forms of things, whereby all the individuals existing are, by nature distinguished into species, these things are necessary:—

15. A crude supposition. First, To be assured that nature, in the production of things, always designs them to partake of certain regulated established essences, which are to be the models of all things to be produced. This, in that crude sense it is usually proposed, would need some better explication, before it can fully be assented to.

16. Monstrous births. Secondly, It would be necessary to know whether nature always attains that essence it designs in the production of things. The irregular and monstrous births, that in divers sorts of animals have been observed, will always give us reason to doubt of one or both of these.

17. Are monsters really a distinct species? Thirdly, It ought to be determined whether those we call monsters be really a distinct species, according to the scholastic notion of the word species; since it is certain that everything that exists has its particular constitution. And yet we find that some of these monstrous productions have few or none of those qualities which are supposed to result from, and accompany, the essence of that species from whence, they derive their originals, and to which, by their descent, they seem to belong.

18. Men can have no ideas of real essences. Fourthly, The real essences of those things which we distinguish into species, and as so distinguished we name, ought to be known; i.e. we ought to have ideas of them. But since we are ignorant in these four points, the supposed real essences of things stand us not in stead for the distinguishing substances into species.

19. Our nominal essences of substances not perfect collections of the properties that flow from their real essences. Fifthly, The only imaginable help in this case would be, that, having framed perfect complex ideas of the properties of things flowing from their different real

essences, we should thereby distinguish them into species. But neither can this be done. For, being ignorant of the real essence itself, it is impossible to know all those properties that flow from it, and are so annexed to it, that any one of them being away, we may certainly conclude that that essence is not there, and so the thing is not of that species. We can never know what is the precise number of properties depending on the real essence of gold, any one of which failing, the real essence of gold, and consequently gold, would not be there, unless we knew the real essence of gold itself, and by that determined that species. By the word gold here, I must be understood to design a particular piece of matter; v.g. the last guinea that was coined. For, if it should stand here, in its ordinary signification, for that complex idea which I or any one else calls gold, i.e. for the nominal essence of gold, it would be jargon. So hard is it to show the various meaning and imperfection of words, when we have nothing else but words to do it by.

20. Hence names independent of real essences. By all which it is clear, that our distinguishing substances into species by names, is not at all founded on their real essences; nor can we pretend to range and determine them exactly into species, according to internal essential differences.

21. But stand for such a collection of simple substances, as we have made the name stand for. But since, as has been remarked, we have need of general words, though we know not the real essences of things; all we can do is, to collect such a number of simple ideas as, by examination, we find to be united together in things existing, and thereof to make one complex idea. Which, though it be not the real essence of any substance that exists, is yet the specific essence to which our name belongs, and is convertible with it; by which we may at least try the truth of these nominal essences. For example: there be that say that the essence of body is extension; if it be so, we can never mistake in putting the essence of anything for the thing itself. Let us then in discourse put extension for body, and when we would say that body moves, let us say that extension moves, and see how ill it will look. He that should say that one extension by impulse moves another extension, would, by the bare expression, sufficiently show the absurdity of such a notion. The essence of anything in respect of us, is the whole complex idea comprehended and marked by that name; and in substances, besides the several distinct simple ideas that make them up, the confused one of substance, or of an unknown support and cause of their union, is always a part: and therefore the essence of body is not bare extension, but an extended solid thing; and so to say, an extended solid thing moves, or impels another, is all one, and as intelligible, as to say, body moves or impels. Likewise, to say that a rational animal is capable of conversation, is all one as to say a man; but no one will say that rationality is capable of conversation, because it makes not the whole essence to which we give the name man.

22. Our abstract ideas are to us the measures of the species we make: instance in that of man. There are creatures in the world that have shapes like ours, but are hairy, and want language and reason. There are naturals amongst us that have perfectly our shape, but want reason, and some of them language too. There are creatures, as it is said, (sit fides penes authorem, but there appears no contradiction that there should be such), that, with language and reason and a shape in other things agreeing with ours, have hairy tails; others where the males have no beards, and others where the females have. If it be asked whether these be all men or no, all of human species? it is plain, the question refers only to the nominal essence: for those of them to whom the definition of the word man, or the complex idea signified by the name, agrees, are men, and the other not. But if the inquiry be made concerning the supposed real essence; and whether the internal constitution and frame of these several creatures be specifically different, it is wholly impossible for us to answer, no part of that going into our specific idea: only we have reason to think, that where the faculties or outward frame so much differs, the internal constitution is not exactly the same. But what difference in the real internal constitution makes a specific difference it is in vain to inquire; whilst our measures of species be, as they are, only our abstract ideas, which we know; and not that internal constitution, which makes no part of

them. Shall the difference of hair only on the skin be a mark of a different internal specific constitution between a changeling and a drill, when they agree in shape, and want of reason and speech? And shall not the want of reason and speech be a sign to us of different real constitutions and species between a changeling and a reasonable man? And so of the rest, if we pretend that distinction of species or sorts is fixedly established by the real frame and secret constitutions of things.

23. Species in animals not distinguished by generation. Nor let any one say, that the power of propagation in animals by the mixture of male and female, and in plants by seeds, keeps the supposed real species distinct and entire. For, granting this to be true, it would help us in the distinction of the species of things no further than the tribes of animals and vegetables. What must we do for the rest? But in those too it is not sufficient: for if history lie not, women have conceived by drills; and what real species, by that measure, such a production will be in nature will be a new question: and we have reason to think this is not impossible, since mules and jumarts, the one from the mixture of an ass and a mare, the other from the mixture of a bull and a mare, are so frequent in the world. I once saw a creature that was the issue of a cat and a rat, and had the plain marks of both about it; wherein nature appeared to have followed the pattern of neither sort alone, but to have jumbled them both together. To which he that shall add the monstrous productions that are so frequently to be met with in nature, will find it hard, even in the race of animals, to determine by the pedigree of what species every animal's issue is; and be at a loss about the real essence, which he thinks certainly conveyed by generation, and has alone a right to the specific name. But further, if the species of animals and plants are to be distinguished only by propagation, must I go to the Indies to see the sire and dam of the one, and the plant from which the seed was gathered that produced the other, to know whether this be a tiger or that tea?

24. Not by substantial forms. Upon the whole matter, it is evident that it is their own collections of sensible qualities that men make the essences of their several sorts of substances; and that their real internal structures are not considered by the greatest part of men in the sorting them. Much less were any substantial forms ever thought on by any but those who have in this one part of the world learned the language of the schools: and yet those ignorant men, who pretend not any insight into the real essences, nor trouble themselves about substantial forms, but are content with knowing things one from another by their sensible qualities, are often better acquainted with their differences; can more nicely distinguish them from their uses; and better know what they expect from each, than those learned quick-sighted men, who look so deep into them, and talk so confidently of something more hidden and essential.

25. The specific essences that are commonly made by men. But supposing that the real essences of substances were discoverable by those that would severely apply themselves to that inquiry, yet we could not reasonably think that the ranking of things under general names was regulated by those internal real constitutions, or anything else but their obvious appearances; since languages, in all countries, have been established long before sciences. So that they have not been philosophers or logicians, or such who have troubled themselves about forms and essences, that have made the general names that are in use amongst the several nations of men: but those more or less comprehensive terms have, for the most part, in all languages, received their birth and signification from ignorant and illiterate people, who sorted and denominated things by those sensible qualities they found in them; thereby to signify them, when absent, to others, whether they had an occasion to mention a sort or a particular thing.

26. Therefore very various and uncertain in the ideas of different men. Since then it is evident that we sort and name substances by their nominal and not by their real essences, the next thing to be considered is how, and by whom these essences come to be made. As to the latter, it is evident they are made by the mind, and not by nature: for were they Nature's workmanship, they could not be so various and different in several men as experience tells us

they are. For if we will examine it, we shall not find the nominal essence of any one species of substances in all men the same: no, not of that which of all others we are the most intimately acquainted with. It could not possibly be that the abstract idea to which the name man is given should be different in several men, if it were of Nature's making; and that to one it should be animal rationale, and to another, animal implume bipes latis unguibus. He that annexes the name to a complex idea, made up of sense and spontaneous motion, joined to a body of such a shape, has thereby one essence of the species man; and he that, upon further examination, adds rationality, has another essence of the species he calls man: by which means the same individual will be a true man to the one which is not so to the other. I think there is scarce any one will allow this upright figure, so well known, to be the essential difference of the species man; and yet how far men determine of the sorts of animals rather by their shape than descent, is very visible; since it has been more than once debated, whether several human foetuses should be preserved or received to baptism or no, only because of the difference of their outward configuration from the ordinary make of children, without knowing whether they were not as capable of reason as infants cast in another mould: some whereof, though of an approved shape, are never capable of as much appearance of reason all their lives as is to be found in an ape, or an elephant, and never give any signs of being acted by a rational soul. Whereby it is evident, that the outward figure, which only was found wanting, and not the faculty of reason, which nobody could know would be wanting in its due season, was made essential to the human species. The learned divine and lawyer must, on such occasions, renounce his sacred definition of animal rationale, and substitute some other essence of the human species. Monsieur Menage furnishes us with an example worth the taking notice of on this occasion: "When the abbot of Saint Martin," says he, "was born, he had so little of the figure of a man, that it bespake him rather a monster. It was for some time under deliberation, whether he should be baptized or no. However, he was baptized, and declared a man provisionally till time should show what he would prove. Nature had moulded him so untowardly, that he was called all his life the Abbot Malotru; i.e. ill-shaped. He was of Caen." (Menagiana, 278, 430.) This child, we see, was very near being excluded out of the species of man, barely by his shape. He escaped very narrowly as he was; and it is certain, a figure a little more oddly turned had cast him, and he had been executed, as a thing not to be allowed to pass for a man. And yet there can be no reason given why, if the lineaments of his face had been a little altered, a rational soul could not have been lodged in him; why a visage somewhat longer, or a nose flatter, or a wider mouth, could not have consisted, as well as the rest of his ill figure, with such a soul, such parts, as made him, disfigured as he was, capable to be a dignitary in the church.

27. Nominal essences of particular substances are undetermined by nature, and therefore various as men vary. Wherein, then, would I gladly know, consist the precise and unmovable boundaries of that species? It is plain, if we examine, there is no such thing made by Nature, and established by her amongst men. The real essence of that or any other sort of substances, it is evident, we know not; and therefore are so undetermined in our nominal essences, which we make ourselves, that, if several men were to be asked concerning some oddly shaped foetus, as soon as born, whether it were a man or no, it is past doubt one should meet with different answers. Which could not happen, if the nominal essences, whereby we limit and distinguish the species of substances, were not made by man with some liberty; but were exactly copied from precise boundaries set by nature, whereby it distinguished all substances into certain species. Who would undertake to resolve what species that monster was of which is mentioned by Licetus (Bk. i. c. 3), with a man's head and hog's body? Or those other which to the bodies of men had the heads of beasts, as dogs, horses, &c. If any of these creatures had lived, and could have spoke, it would have increased the difficulty. Had the upper part to the middle been of human shape, and all below swine, had it been murder to destroy it? Or must the bishop have been consulted, whether it were man enough to be admitted to the font or no? As I have been told it happened in France some years since, in somewhat a like case. So uncertain are

the boundaries of species of animals to us, who have no other measures than the complex ideas of our own collecting: and so far are we from certainly knowing what a man is; though perhaps it will be judged great ignorance to make any doubt about it. And yet I think I may say, that the certain boundaries of that species are so far from being determined, and the precise number of simple ideas which make the nominal essence so far from being settled and perfectly known, that very material doubts may still arise about it. And I imagine none of the definitions of the word man which we yet have, nor descriptions of that sort of animal, are so perfect and exact as to satisfy a considerate inquisitive person; much less to obtain a general consent, and to be that which men would everywhere stick by, in the decision of cases, and determining of life and death, baptism or no baptism, in productions that might happen.

28. But not so arbitrary as mixed modes. But though these nominal essences of substances are made by the mind, they are not yet made so arbitrarily as those of mixed modes. To the making of any nominal essence, it is necessary, First, that the ideas whereof it consists have such a union as to make but one idea, how compounded soever. Secondly, that the particular ideas so united be exactly the same, neither more nor less. For if two abstract complex ideas differ either in number or sorts of their component parts, they make two different, and not one and the same essence. In the first of these, the mind, in making its complex ideas of substances, only follows nature; and puts none together which are not supposed to have a union in nature. Nobody joins the voice of a sheep with the shape of a horse; nor the colour of lead with the weight and fixedness of gold, to be the complex ideas of any real substances; unless he has a mind to fill his head with chimeras, and his discourse with unintelligible words. Men observing certain qualities always joined and existing together, therein copied nature; and of ideas so united made their complex ones of substances. For, though men may make what complex ideas they please, and give what names to them they will; yet, if they will be understood when they speak of things really existing, they must in some degree conform their ideas to the things they would speak of; or else men's language will be like that of Babel; and every man's words, being intelligible only to himself, would no longer serve to conversation and the ordinary affairs of life, if the ideas they stand for be not some way answering the common appearances and agreement of substances as they really exist.

29. Our nominal essences of substances usually consist of a few obvious qualities observed in things. Secondly, Though the mind of man, in making its complex ideas of substances, never puts any together that do not really, or are not supposed to, co-exist; and so it truly borrows that union from nature: yet the number it combines depends upon the various care, industry, or fancy of him that makes it. Men generally content themselves with some few sensible obvious qualities; and often, if not always, leave out others as material and as firmly united as those that they take. Of sensible substances there are two sorts: one of organized bodies, which are propagated by seed; and in these the shape is that which to us is the leading quality, and most characteristical part, that determines the species. And therefore in vegetables and animals, an extended solid substance of such a certain figure usually serves the turn. For however some men seem to prize their definition of animal rationale, yet should there a creature be found that had language and reason, but partaked not of the usual shape of a man, I believe it would hardly pass for a man, how much soever it were animal rationale. And if Balaam's ass had all his life discoursed as rationally as he did once with his master, I doubt yet whether any one would have thought him worthy the name man, or allowed him to be of the same species with himself. As in vegetables and animals it is the shape, so in most other bodies, not propagated by seed, it is the colour we must fix on, and are most led by. Thus where we find the colour of gold, we are apt to imagine all the other qualities comprehended in our complex idea to be there also: and we commonly take these two obvious qualities, viz. shape and colour, for so presumptive ideas of several species, that in a good picture, we readily say, this is a lion, and that a rose; this is a gold, and that a silver goblet, only by the different figures and colours represented to the eye by the pencil.

30. Yet, imperfect as they thus are, they serve for common converse. But though this serves

well enough for gross and confused conceptions, and inaccurate ways of talking and thinking; yet men are far enough from having agreed on the precise number of simple ideas or qualities belonging to any sort of things, signified by its name. Nor is it a wonder; since it requires much time, pains, and skill, strict inquiry, and long examination to find out what, and how many, those simple ideas are, which are constantly and inseparably united in nature, and are always to be found together in the same subject. Most men, wanting either time, inclination, or industry enough for this, even to some tolerable degree, content themselves with some few obvious and outward appearances of things, thereby readily to distinguish and sort them for the common affairs of life: and so, without further examination, give them names, or take up the names already in use. Which, though in common conversation they pass well enough for the signs of some few obvious qualities co-existing, are yet far enough from comprehending, in a settled signification, a precise number of simple ideas, much less all those which are united in nature. He that shall consider, after so much stir about genus and species, and such a deal of talk of specific differences, how few words we have yet settled definitions of, may with reason imagine, that those forms which there hath been so much noise made about are only chimeras, which give us no light into the specific natures of things. And he that shall consider how far the names of substances are from having significations wherein all who use them do agree, will have reason to conclude that, though the nominal essences of substances are all supposed to be copied from nature, yet they are all, or most of them, very imperfect. Since the composition of those complex ideas are, in several men, very different: and therefore that these boundaries of species are as men, and not as Nature, makes them, if at least there are in nature any such prefixed bounds. It is true that many particular substances are so made by Nature, that they have agreement and likeness one with another, and so afford a foundation of being ranked into sorts. But the sorting of things by us, or the making of determinate species, being in order to naming and comprehending them under general terms, I cannot see how it can be properly said, that Nature sets the boundaries of the species of things: or, if it be so, our boundaries of species are not exactly conformable to those in nature. For we, having need of general names for present use, stay not for a perfect discovery of all those qualities which would best show us their most material differences and agreements; but we ourselves divide them, by certain obvious appearances, into species, that we may the easier under general names communicate our thoughts about them. For, having no other knowledge of any substance but of the simple ideas that are united in it; and observing several particular things to agree with others in several of those simple ideas; we make that collection our specific idea, and give it a general name; that in recording our thoughts, and in our discourse with others, we may in one short word designate all the individuals that agree in that complex idea, without enumerating the simple ideas that make it up; and so not waste our time and breath in tedious descriptions: which we see they are fain to do who would discourse of any new sort of things they have not yet a name for.

31. Essences of species under the same name very different in different minds. But however these species of substances pass well enough in ordinary conversation, it is plain that this complex idea, wherein they observe several individuals to agree, is by different men made very differently; by some more, and others less accurately. In some, this complex idea contains a greater, and in others a smaller number of qualities; and so is apparently such as the mind makes it. The yellow shining colour makes gold to children; others add weight, malleableness, and fusibility; and others yet other qualities, which they find joined with that yellow colour, as constantly as its weight and fusibility. For in all these and the like qualities, one has as good a right to be put into the complex idea of that substance wherein they are all joined as another. And therefore different men, leaving out or putting in several simple ideas which others do not, according to their various examination, skill, or observation of that subject, have different essences of gold, which must therefore be of their own and not of nature's making.

32. The more general our ideas of substances are, the more incomplete and partial they are. If the number of simple ideas that make the nominal essence of the lowest species, or first

sorting, of individuals, depends on the mind of man, variously collecting them, it is much more evident that they do so in the more comprehensive classes, which, by the masters of logic, are called genera. These are complex ideas designedly imperfect: and it is visible at first sight, that several of those qualities that are to be found in the things themselves are purposely left out of generical ideas. For, as the mind, to make general ideas comprehending several particulars, leaves out those of time and place, and such other, that make them incommunicable to more than one individual; so to make other yet more general ideas, that may comprehend different sorts, it leaves out those qualities that distinguish them, and puts into its new collection only such ideas as are common to several sorts. The same convenience that made men express several parcels of yellow matter coming from Guinea and Peru under one name, sets them also upon making of one name that may comprehend both gold and silver, and some other bodies of different sorts. This is done by leaving out those qualities, which are peculiar to each sort, and retaining a complex idea made up of those that are common to them all. To which the name metal being annexed, there is a genus constituted; the essence whereof being that abstract idea, containing only malleableness and fusibility, with certain degrees of weight and fixedness, wherein some bodies of several kinds agree, leaves out the colour and other qualities peculiar to gold and silver, and the other sorts comprehended under the name metal. Whereby it is plain that men follow not exactly the patterns set them by nature, when they make their general ideas of substances; since there is no body to be found which has barely malleableness and fusibility in it, without other qualities as inseparable as those. But men, in making their general ideas, seeking more the convenience of language, and quick dispatch by short and comprehensive signs, than the true and precise nature of things as they exist, have, in the framing their abstract ideas, chiefly pursued that end; which was to be furnished with store of general and variously comprehensive names. So that in this whole business of genera and species, the genus, or more comprehensive, is but a partial conception of what is in the species; and the species but a partial idea of what is to be found in each individual. If therefore any one will think that a man, and a horse, and an animal, and a plant, &c., are distinguished by real essences made by nature, he must think nature to be very liberal of these real essences, making one for body, another for an animal, and another for a horse; and all these essences liberally bestowed upon Bucephalus. But if we would rightly consider what is done in all these genera and species, or sorts, we should find that there is no new thing made; but only more or less comprehensive signs, whereby we may be enabled to express in a few syllables great numbers of particular things, as they agree in more or less general conceptions, which we have framed to that purpose. In all which we may observe, that the more general term is always the name of a less complex idea; and that each genus is but a partial conception of the species comprehended under it. So that if these abstract general ideas be thought to be complete, it can only be in respect of a certain established relation between them and certain names which are made use of to signify them; and not in respect of anything existing, as made by nature.

33. This all accommodated to the end of speech. This is adjusted to the true end of speech, which is to be the easiest and shortest way of communicating our notions. For thus he that would discourse of things, as they agreed in the complex idea of extension and solidity, needed but use the word body to denote all such. He that to these would join others, signified by the words life, sense, and spontaneous motion, needed but use the word animal to signify all which partaked of those ideas, and he that had made a complex idea of a body, with life, sense, and motion, with the faculty of reasoning, and a certain shape joined to it, needed but use the short monosyllable man, to express all particulars that correspond to that complex idea. This is the proper business of genus and species: and this men do without any consideration of real essences, or substantial forms; which come not within the reach of our knowledge when we think of those things, nor within the signification of our words when we discourse with others.

34. Instance in Cassowaries. Were I to talk with any one of a sort of birds I lately saw in St.

James's Park, about three or four feet high, with a covering of something between feathers and hair, of a dark brown colour, without wings, but in the place thereof two or three little branches coming down like sprigs of Spanish broom, long great legs, with feet only of three claws, and without a tail; I must make this description of it, and so may make others understand me. But when I am told that the name of it is cassuaris, I may then use that word to stand in discourse for all my complex idea mentioned in that description; though by that word, which is now become a specific name, I know no more of the real essence or constitution of that sort of animals than I did before; and knew probably as much of the nature of that species of birds before I learned the name, as many Englishmen do of swans or herons, which are specific names, very well known, of sorts of birds common in England.

35. Men determine the sorts of substances, which may be sorted variously. From what has been said, it is evident that men make sorts of things. For, it being different essences alone that make different species, it is plain that they who make those abstract ideas which are the nominal essences do thereby make the species, or sort. Should there be a body found, having all the other qualities of gold except malleableness, it would no doubt be made a question whether it were gold or not, i.e. whether it were of that species. This could be determined only by that abstract idea to which every one annexed the name gold: so that it would be true gold to him, and belong to that species, who included not malleableness in his nominal essence, signified by the sound gold; and on the other side it would not be true gold, or of that species, to him who included malleableness in his specific idea. And who, I pray, is it that makes these diverse species, even under one and the same name, but men that make two different abstract ideas, consisting not exactly of the same collection of qualities? Nor is it a mere supposition to imagine that a body may exist wherein the other obvious qualities of gold may be without malleableness; since it is certain that gold itself will be sometimes so eager, (as artists call it), that it will as little endure the hammer as glass itself. What we have said of the putting in, or leaving out of malleableness, in the complex idea the name gold is by any one annexed to, may be said of its peculiar weight, fixedness, and several other the like qualities: for whatever is left out, or put in, it is still the complex idea to which that name is annexed that makes the species: and as any particular parcel of matter answers that idea, so the name of the sort belongs truly to it; and it is of that species. And thus anything is true gold, perfect metal. All which determination of the species, it is plain, depends on the understanding of man, making this or that complex idea.

36. Nature makes the similitudes of substances. This, then, in short, is the case: Nature makes many particular things, which do agree one with another in many sensible qualities, and probably too in their internal frame and constitution: but it is not this real essence that distinguishes them into species; it is men who, taking occasion from the qualities they find united in them, and wherein they observe often several individuals to agree, range them into sorts, in order to their naming, for the convenience of comprehensive signs; under which individuals, according to their conformity to this or that abstract idea, come to be ranked as under ensigns: so that this is of the blue, that the red regiment; this is a man, that a drill: and in this, I think, consists the whole business of genus and species.

37. The manner of sorting particular beings the work of fallible men, though nature makes things alike. I do not deny but nature, in the constant production of particular beings, makes them not always new and various, but very much alike and of kin one to another: but I think it nevertheless true, that the boundaries of the species, whereby men sort them, are made by men; since the essences of the species, distinguished by different names, are, as has been proved, of man's making, and seldom adequate to the internal nature of the things they are taken from. So that we may truly say, such a manner of sorting of things is the workmanship of men.

38. Each abstract idea, with a name to it, makes a nominal essence. One thing I doubt not but will seem very strange in this doctrine, which is, that from what has been said it will follow, that each abstract idea, with a name to it, makes a distinct species. But who can help it, if truth

will have it so? For so it must remain till somebody can show us the species of things limited and distinguished by something else; and let us see that general terms signify not our abstract ideas, but something different from them. I would fain know why a shock and a hound are not as distinct species as a spaniel and an elephant. We have no other idea of the different essence of an elephant and a spaniel, than we have of the different essence of a shock and a hound; all the essential difference, whereby we know and distinguish them one from another, consisting only in the different collection of simple ideas, to which we have given those different names.

39. How genera and species are related to naming. How much the making of species and genera is in order to general names; and how much general names are necessary, if not to the being, yet at least to the completing of a species, and making it pass for such, will appear, besides what has been said above concerning ice and water, in a very familiar example. A silent and a striking watch are but one species to those who have but one name for them: but he that has the name watch for one, and clock for the other, and distinct complex ideas to which those names belong, to him they are different species. It will be said perhaps, that the inward contrivance and constitution is different between these two, which the watchmaker has a clear idea of. And yet it is plain they are but one species to him, when he has but one name for them. For what is sufficient in the inward contrivance to make a new species? There are some watches that are made with four wheels, others with five; is this a specific difference to the workman? Some have strings and physies, and others none; some have the balance loose, and others regulated by a spiral spring, and others by hogs' bristles. Are any or all of these enough to make a specific difference to the workman, that knows each of these and several other different contrivances in the internal constitutions of watches? It is certain each of these hath a real difference from the rest; but whether it be an essential, a specific difference or no, relates only to the complex idea to which the name watch is given: as long as they all agree in the idea which that name stands for, and that name does not as a generical name comprehend different species under it, they are not essentially nor specifically different. But if any one will make minuter divisions, from differences that he knows in the internal frame of watches, and to such precise complex ideas give names that shall prevail; they will then be new species, to them who have those ideas with names to them, and can by those differences distinguish watches into these several sorts; and then watch will be a generical name. But yet they would be no distinct species to men ignorant of clock-work, and the inward contrivances of watches, who had no other idea but the outward shape and bulk, with the marking of the hours by the hand. For to them all those other names would be but synonymous terms for the same idea, and signify no more, nor no other thing but a watch. Just thus I think it is in natural things. Nobody will doubt that the wheels or springs (if I may so say) within, are different in a rational man and a changeling; no more than that there is a difference in the frame between a drill and a changeling. But whether one or both these differences be essential or specifical, is only to be known to us by their agreement or disagreement with the complex idea that the name man stands for: for by that alone can it be determined whether one, or both, or neither of those be a man.

40. Species of artificial things less confused than natural. From what has been before said, we may see the reason why, in the species of artificial things, there is generally less confusion and uncertainty than in natural. Because an artificial thing being a production of man, which the artificer designed, and therefore well knows the idea of, the name of it is supposed to stand for no other idea, nor to import any other essence, than what is certainly to be known, and easy enough to be apprehended. For the idea or essence of the several sorts of artificial things, consisting for the most part in nothing but the determinate figure of sensible parts, and sometimes motion depending thereon, which the artificer fashions in matter, such as he finds for his turn; it is not beyond the reach of our faculties to attain a certain idea thereof; and so settle the signification of the names whereby the species of artificial things are distinguished, with less doubt, obscurity, and equivocation than we can in things natural, whose differences and operations depend upon contrivances beyond the reach of our discoveries.

41. Artificial things of distinct species. I must be excused here if I think artificial things are of distinct species as well as natural: since I find they are as plainly and orderly ranked into sorts, by different abstract ideas, with general names annexed to them, as distinct one from another as those of natural substances. For why should we not think a watch and pistol as distinct species one from another, as a horse and a dog; they being expressed in our minds by distinct ideas, and to others by distinct appellations?

42. Substances alone, of all our several sorts of ideas, have proper names. This is further to be observed concerning substances, that they alone of all our several sorts of ideas have particular or proper names, whereby one only particular thing is signified. Because in simple ideas, modes, and relations, it seldom happens that men have occasion to mention often this or that particular when it is absent. Besides, the greatest part of mixed modes, being actions which perish in their birth, are not capable of a lasting duration, as substances which are the actors; and wherein the simple ideas that make up the complex ideas designed by the name have a lasting union.

43. Difficult to lead another by words into the thoughts of things stripped of those abstract ideas we give them. I must beg pardon of my reader for having dwelt so long upon this subject, and perhaps with some obscurity. But I desire it may be considered, how difficult it is to lead another by words into the thoughts of things, stripped of those specifical differences we give them: which things, if I name not, I say nothing; and if I do name them, I thereby rank them into some sort or other, and suggest to the mind the usual abstract idea of that species; and so cross my purpose. For, to talk of a man, and to lay by, at the same time, the ordinary signification of the name man, which is our complex idea usually annexed to it; and bid the reader consider man, as he is in himself, and as he is really distinguished from others in his internal constitution, or real essence, that is, by something he knows not what, looks like trifling: and yet thus one must do who would speak of the supposed real essences and species of things, as thought to be made by nature, if it be but only to make it understood, that there is no such thing signified by the general names which substances are called by. But because it is difficult by known familiar names to do this, give me leave to endeavour by an example to make the different consideration the mind has of specific names and ideas a little more clear; and to show how the complex ideas of modes are referred sometimes to archetypes in the minds of other intelligent beings, or, which is the same, to the signification annexed by others to their received names; and sometimes to no archetypes at all. Give me leave also to show how the mind always refers its ideas of substances, either to the substances themselves, or to the signification of their names, as to the archetypes; and also to make plain the nature of species or sorting of things, as apprehended and made use of by us; and of the essences belonging to those species: which is perhaps of more moment to discover the extent and certainty of our knowledge than we at first imagine.

44. Instances of mixed modes named kinneah and niouph. Let us suppose Adam, in the state of a grown man, with a good understanding, but in a strange country, with all things new and unknown about him; and no other faculties to attain the knowledge of them but what one of this age has now. He observes Lamech more melancholy than usual, and imagines it to be from a suspicion he has of his wife Adah, (whom he most ardently loved) that she had too much kindness for another man. Adam discourses these his thoughts to Eve, and desires her to take care that Adah commit not folly: and in these discourses with Eve he makes use of these two new words kinneah and niouph. In time, Adam's mistake appears, for he finds Lamech's trouble proceeded from having killed a man: but yet the two names kinneah and niouph, (the one standing for suspicion in a husband of his wife's disloyalty to him; and the other for the act of committing disloyalty), lost not their distinct significations. It is plain then, that here were two distinct complex ideas of mixed modes, with names to them, two distinct species of actions essentially different; I ask wherein consisted the essences of these two distinct species of actions? And it is plain it consisted in a precise combination of simple ideas, different in one from the other. I ask, whether the complex idea in Adam's mind, which he called kinneah,

were adequate or not? And it is plain it was; for it being a combination of simple ideas, which he, without any regard to any archetype, without respect to anything as a pattern, voluntarily put together, abstracted, and gave the name kinneah to, to express in short to others, by that one sound, all the simple ideas contained and united in that complex one; it must necessarily follow that it was an adequate idea. His own choice having made that combination, it had all in it he intended it should, and so could not but be perfect, could not but be adequate; it being referred to no other archetype which it was supposed to represent.

45. These words, kinneah and niouph, by degrees grew into common use, and then the case was somewhat altered. Adam's children had the same faculties, and thereby the same power that he had, to make what complex ideas of mixed modes they pleased in their own minds; to abstract them, and make what sounds they pleased the signs of them: but the use of names being to make our ideas within us known to others, that cannot be done, but when the same sign stands for the same idea in two who would communicate their thoughts and discourse together. Those, therefore, of Adam's children, that found these two words, kinneah and niouph, in familiar use, could not take them for insignificant sounds, but must needs conclude they stood for something; for certain ideas, abstract ideas. they being general names; which abstract ideas were the essences of the species distinguished by those names. If, therefore, they would use these words as names of species already established and agreed on, they were obliged to conform the ideas in their minds, signified by these names, to the ideas that they stood for in other men's minds, as to their patterns and archetypes; and then indeed their ideas of these complex modes were liable to be inadequate, as being very apt (especially those that consisted of combinations of many simple ideas) not to be exactly conformable to the ideas in other men's minds, using the same names; though for this there be usually a remedy at hand, which is to ask the meaning of any word we understand not of him that uses it: it being as impossible to know certainly what the words jealousy and adultery stand for in another man's mind, with whom I would discourse about them; as it was impossible, in the beginning of language, to know what kinneah and niouph stood for in another man's mind, without explication; they being voluntary signs in every one.

46. Instances of a species of substance named Zahab. Let us now also consider, after the same manner, the names of substances in their first application. One of Adam's children, roving in the mountains, lights on a glittering substance which pleases his eye. Home he carries it to Adam, who, upon consideration of it, finds it to be hard, to have a bright yellow colour, and an exceeding great weight. These perhaps, at first, are all the qualities he takes notice of in it; and abstracting this complex idea, consisting of a substance having that peculiar bright yellowness, and a weight very great in proportion to its bulk, he gives the name zahab, to denominate and mark all substances that have these sensible qualities in them. It is evident now, that, in this case, Adam acts quite differently from what he did before, in forming those ideas of mixed modes to which he gave the names kinneah and niouph. For there he put ideas together only by his own imagination, not taken from the existence of anything; and to them he gave names to denominate all things that should happen to agree to those his abstract ideas, without considering whether any such thing did exist or not; the standard there was of his own making. But in the forming his idea of this new substance, he takes the quite contrary course; here he has a standard made by nature; and therefore, being to represent that to himself, by the idea he has of it, even when it is absent, he puts in no simple idea into his complex one, but what he has the perception of from the thing itself. He takes care that his idea be conformable to this archetype, and intends the name should stand for an idea so conformable.

47. This piece of matter, thus denominated zahab by Adam, being quite different from any he had seen before, nobody, I think, will deny to be a distinct species, and to have its peculiar essence: and that the name zahab is the mark of the species, and a name belonging to all things partaking in that essence. But here it is plain the essence Adam made the name zahab stand for was nothing but a body hard, shining, yellow, and very heavy. But the inquisitive mind of man, not content with the knowledge of these, as I may say, superficial qualities, puts Adam

upon further examination of this matter. He therefore knocks, and beats it with flints, to see what was discoverable in the inside: he finds it yield to blows, but not easily separate into pieces: he finds it will bend without breaking. Is not now ductility to be added to his former idea, and made part of the essence of the species that name Zahab stands for? Further trials discover fusibility and fixedness. Are not they also, by the same reason that any of the others were, to be put into the complex idea signified by the name zahab? If not, what reason will there be shown more for the one than the other? If these must, then all the other properties, which any further trials shall discover in this matter, ought by the same reason to make a part of the ingredients of the complex idea which the name zahab stands for, and so be the essence of the species marked by that name. Which properties, because they are endless, it is plain that the idea made after this fashion, by this archetype, will be always inadequate.

48. The abstract ideas of substances always imperfect, and therefore various. But this is not all. It would also follow that the names of substances would not only have, as in truth they have, but would also be supposed to have different significations, as used by different men, which would very much cumber the use of language. For if every distinct quality that were discovered in any matter by any one were supposed to make a necessary part of the complex idea signified by the common name given to it, it must follow, that men must suppose the same word to signify different things in different men: since they cannot doubt but different men may have discovered several qualities, in substances of the same denomination, which others know nothing of.

49. Therefore to fix their nominal species, a real essense is supposed. To avoid this therefore, they have supposed a real essence belonging to every species, from which these properties all flow, and would have their name of the species stand for that. But they, not having any idea of that real essence in substances, and their words signifying nothing but the ideas they have, that which is done by this attempt is only to put the name or sound in the place and stead of the thing having that real essence, without knowing what the real essence is, and this is that which men do when they speak of species of things, as supposing them made by nature, and distinguished by real essences.

50. Which supposition is of no use. For, let us consider, when we affirm that "all gold is fixed," either it means that fixedness is a part of the definition, i.e., part of the nominal essence the word gold stands for; and so this affirmation, "all gold is fixed," contains nothing but the signification of the term gold. Or else it means, that fixedness, not being a part of the definition of the gold, is a property of that substance itself: in which case it is plain that the word gold stands in the place of a substance, having the real essence of a species of things made by nature. In which way of substitution it has so confused and uncertain a signification, that, though this proposition —"gold is fixed"— be in that sense an affirmation of something real; yet it is a truth will always fail us in its particular application, and so is of no real use or certainty. For let it be ever so true, that all gold, i.e. all that has the real essence of gold, is fixed, what serves this for, whilst we know not, in this sense, what is or is not gold? For if we know not the real essence of gold, it is impossible we should know what parcel of matter has that essence, and so whether it be true gold or no.

51. Conclusion. To conclude: what liberty Adam had at first to make any complex ideas of mixed modes by no other pattern but by his own thoughts, the same have all men ever since had. And the same necessity of conforming his ideas of substances to things without him, as to archetypes made by nature, that Adam was under, if he would not wilfully impose upon himself, the same are all men ever since under too. The same liberty also that Adam had of affixing any new name to any idea, the same has any one still, (especially the beginners of languages, if we can imagine any such); but only with this difference, that, in places where men in society have already established a language amongst them, the significations of words are very warily and sparingly to be altered. Because men being furnished already with names for their ideas, and common use having appropriated known names to certain ideas, an affected misapplication of them cannot but be very ridiculous. He that hath new notions will

perhaps venture sometimes on the coining of new terms to express them: but men think it a boldness, and it is uncertain whether common use will ever make them pass for current. But in communication with others, it is necessary that we conform the ideas we make the vulgar words of any language stand for to their known proper significations, (which I have explained at large already), or else to make known that new signification we apply them to.

Chapter VII. Of Particles

1. Particles connect parts, or whole sentences together. Besides words which are names of ideas in the mind, there are a great many others that are made use of to signify the connexion that the mind gives to ideas, or to propositions, one with another. The mind, in communicating its thoughts to others, does not only need signs of the ideas it has then before it, but others also, to show or intimate some particular action of its own, at that time, relating to those ideas. This it does several ways; as Is, and Is not, are the general marks, of the mind, affirming or denying. But besides affirmation or negation, without which there is in words no truth or falsehood, the mind does, in declaring its sentiments to others, connect not only the parts of propositions, but whole sentences one to another, with their several relations and dependencies, to make a coherent discourse.
2. In right use of particles consists the art of well-speaking. The words whereby it signifies what connexion it gives to the several affirmations and negations, that it unites in one continued reasoning or narration, are generally called particles: and it is in the right use of these that more particularly consists the clearness and beauty of a good style. To think well, it is not enough that a man has ideas clear and distinct in his thoughts, nor that he observes the agreement or disagreement of some of them; but he must think in train, and observe the dependence of his thoughts and reasonings upon one another. And to express well such methodical and rational thoughts, he must have words to show what connexion, restriction, distinction, opposition, emphasis &c., he gives to each respective part of his discourse. To mistake in any of these, is to puzzle instead of informing his hearer: and therefore it is, that those words which are not truly by themselves the names of any ideas are of such constant and indispensable use in language, and do much contribute to men's well expressing themselves.
3. They show what relation the mind gives to its own thoughts. This part of grammar has been perhaps as much neglected as some others over-diligently cultivated. It is easy for men to write, one after another, of cases and genders, moods and tenses, gerunds and supines: in these and the like there has been great diligence used; and particles themselves, in some languages, have been, with great show of exactness, ranked into their several orders. But though prepositions and conjunctions, &c., are names well known in grammar, and the particles contained under them carefully ranked into their distinct subdivisions; yet he who would show the right use of particles, and what significancy and force they have, must take a little more pains, enter into his own thoughts, and observe nicely the several postures of his mind in discoursing.
4. They are all marks of some action or intimation of the mind. Neither is it enough, for the explaining of these words, to render them, as is usual in dictionaries, by words of another tongue which come nearest to their signification: for what is meant by them is commonly as hard to be understood in one as another language. They are all marks of some action or intimation of the mind; and therefore to understand them rightly, the several views, postures, stands, turns, limitations, and exceptions, and several other thoughts of the mind, for which we have either none or very deficient names, are diligently to be studied. Of these there is a great variety, much exceeding the number of particles that most languages have to express them by: and therefore it is not to be wondered that most of these particles have divers and sometimes almost opposite significations. In the Hebrew tongue there is a particle consisting of but one single letter, of which there are reckoned up, as I remember, seventy, I am sure above fifty,

several significations.

5. Instance in "but." "But" is a particle, none more familiar in our language: and he that says it is a discretive conjunction, and that it answers to sed Latin, or mais in French, thinks he has sufficiently explained it. But yet it seems to me to intimate several relations the mind gives to the several propositions or parts of them which it joins by this monosyllable.

First, "But to say no more": here it intimates a stop of the mind in the course it was going, before it came quite to the end of it.

Secondly, "I saw but two plants"; here it shows that the mind limits the sense to what is expressed, with a negation of all other.

Thirdly, "You pray; but it is not that God would bring you to the true religion."

Fourthly, "But that he would confirm you in your own." The first of these buts intimates a supposition in the mind of something otherwise than it should be: the latter shows that the mind makes a direct opposition between that and what goes before it.

Fifthly, "All animals have sense, but a dog is an animal": here it signifies little more but that the latter proposition is joined to the former, as the minor of a syllogism.

6. This matter of the use of particles but lightly touched here. To these, I doubt not, might be added a great many other significations of this particle, if it were my business to examine it in its full latitude, and consider it in all the places it is to be found: which if one should do, I doubt whether in all those manners it is made use of, it would deserve the title of discretive, which grammarians give to it. But I intend not here a full explication of this sort of signs. The instances I have given in this one may give occasion to reflect on their use and force in language, and lead us into the contemplation of several actions of our minds in discoursing, which it has found a way to intimate to others by these particles, some whereof constantly, and others in certain constructions, have the sense of a whole sentence contained in them.

Chapter VIII. Of Abstract and Concrete Terms

1. Abstract terms not predictable one of another, and why. The ordinary words of language, and our common use of them, would have given us light into the nature of our ideas, if they had been but considered with attention. The mind, as has been shown, has a power to abstract its ideas, and so they become essences, general essences, whereby the sorts of things are distinguished. Now each abstract idea being distinct, so that of any two the one can never be the other, the mind will, by its intuitive knowledge, perceive their difference, and therefore in propositions no two whole ideas can ever be affirmed one of another. This we see in the common use of language, which permits not any two abstract words, or names of abstract ideas, to be affirmed one of another. For how near of kin soever they may seem to be, and how certain soever it is that man is an animal, or rational, or white, yet every one at first hearing perceives the falsehood of these propositions: humanity is animality, or rationality, or whiteness: and this is as evident as any of the most allowed maxims. All our affirmations then are only in concrete, which is the affirming, not one abstract idea to be another, but one abstract idea to be joined to another; which abstract ideas, in substances, may be of any sort; in all the rest are little else but of relations; and in substances the most frequent are of powers: v.g. "a man is white," signifies that the thing that has the essence of a man has also in it the essence of whiteness, which is nothing but a power to produce the idea of whiteness in one whose eyes can discover ordinary objects: or, "a man is rational," signifies that the same thing that hath the essence of a man hath also in it the essence of rationality, i.e. a power of reasoning.

2. They show the difference of our ideas. This distinction of names shows us also the difference of our ideas: for if we observe them, we shall find that our simple ideas have all abstract as well as concrete names: the one whereof is (to speak the language of grammarians) a substantive, the other an adjective; as whiteness, white; sweetness, sweet. The like also holds

in our ideas of modes and relations; as justice, just; equality, equal: only with this difference, that some of the concrete names of relations amongst men chiefly are substantives; as, paternitas, pater; whereof it were easy to render a reason. But as to our ideas of substances, we have very few or no abstract names at all. For though the Schools have introduced animalitas, humanitas, corporietas, and some others; yet they hold no proportion with that infinite number of names of substances, to which they never were ridiculous enough to attempt the coining of abstract ones: and those few that the schools forged, and put into the mouths of their scholars, could never yet get admittance into common use, or obtain the license of public approbation. Which seems to me at least to intimate the confession of all mankind, that they have no ideas of the real essences of substances, since they have not names for such ideas: which no doubt they would have had, had not their consciousness to themselves of their ignorance of them kept them from so idle an attempt. And therefore, though they had ideas enough to distinguish gold from a stone, and metal from wood; yet they but timorously ventured on such terms, as aurietas and saxietas, metallietas and lignietas, or the like names, which should pretend to signify the real essences of those substances whereof they knew they had no ideas. And indeed it was only the doctrine of substantial forms, and the confidence of mistaken pretenders to a knowledge that they had not, which first coined and then introduced animalitas and humanitas, and the like; which yet went very little further than their own Schools, and could never get to be current amongst understanding men. Indeed, humanitas was a word in familiar use amongst the Romans; but in a far different sense, and stood not for the abstract essence of any substance; but was the abstracted name of a mode, and its concrete humanus, not homo.

Chapter IX. Of the Imperfection of Words

1. Words are used for recording and communicating our thoughts. From what has been said in the foregoing chapters, it is easy to perceive what imperfection there is in language, and how the very nature of words makes it almost unavoidable for many of them to be doubtful and uncertain in their significations. To examine the perfection or imperfection of words, it is necessary first to consider their use and end: for as they are more or less fitted to attain that, so they are more or less perfect. We have, in the former part of this discourse often, upon occasion, mentioned a double use of words.
First, One for the recording of our own thoughts.
Secondly, The other for the communicating of our thoughts to others.
2. Any words will serve for recording. As to the first of these, for the recording our own thoughts for the help of our own memories, whereby, as it were, we talk to ourselves, any words will serve the turn. For since sounds are voluntary and indifferent signs of any ideas, a man may use what words he pleases to signify his own ideas to himself: and there will be no imperfection in them, if he constantly use the same sign for the same idea: for then he cannot fail of having his meaning understood, wherein consists the right use and perfection of language.
3. Communication by words either for civil or philosophical purposes. Secondly, As to communication by words, that too has a double use. I. Civil.
II. Philosophical.
First, by their civil use, I mean such a communication of thoughts and ideas by words, as may serve for the upholding common conversation and commerce, about the ordinary affairs and conveniences of civil life, in the societies of men, one amongst another.
Secondly, By the philosophical use of words, I mean such a use of them as may serve to convey the precise notions of things, and to express in general propositions certain and undoubted truths, which the mind may rest upon and be satisfied with in its search after true knowledge. These two uses are very distinct; and a great deal less exactness will serve in the one than in the other, as we shall see in what follows.

4. The imperfection of words is the doubtfulness or ambiguity of their signification, which is caused by the sort of ideas they stand for. The chief end of language in communication being to be understood, words serve not well for that end, neither in civil nor philosophical discourse, when any word does not excite in the hearer the same idea which it stands for in the mind of the speaker. Now, since sounds have no natural connexion with our ideas, but have all their signification from the arbitrary imposition of men, the doubtfulness and uncertainty of their signification, which is the imperfection we here are speaking of, has its cause more in the ideas they stand for than in any incapacity there is in one sound more than in another to signify any idea: for in that regard they are all equally perfect.

That then which makes doubtfulness and uncertainty in the signification of some more than other words, is the difference of ideas they stand for.

5. Natural causes of their imperfection, especially in those that stand for mixed modes, and for our ideas of substances. Words having naturally no signification, the idea which each stands for must be learned and retained, by those who would exchange thoughts, and hold intelligible discourse with others, in any language. But this is the hardest to be done where,

First, The ideas they stand for are very complex, and made up of a great number of ideas put together.

Secondly, Where the ideas they stand for have no certain connexion in nature; and so no settled standard anywhere in nature existing, to rectify and adjust them by.

Thirdly, When the signification of the word is referred to a standard, which standard is not easy to be known.

Fourthly, Where the signification of the word and the real essence of the thing are not exactly the same.

These are difficulties that attend the signification of several words that are intelligible. Those which are not intelligible at all, such as names standing for any simple ideas which another has not organs or faculties to attain; as the names of colours to a blind man, or sounds to a deaf man, need not here be mentioned.

In all these cases we shall find an imperfection in words; which I shall more at large explain, in their particular application to our several sorts of ideas: for if we examine them, we shall find that the names of Mixed Modes are most liable to doubtfulness and imperfection, for the two first of these reasons; and the names of Substances chiefly for the two latter.

6. The names of mixed modes doubtful. First, because the ideas they stand for are so complex. First, The names of mixed modes are, many of them, liable to great uncertainty and obscurity in their signification

I. Because of that great composition these complex ideas are often made up of. To make words serviceable to the end of communication, it is necessary, as has been said, that they excite in the hearer exactly the same idea they stand for in the mind of the speaker. Without this, men fill one another's heads with noise and sounds; but convey not thereby their thoughts, and lay not before one another their ideas, which is the end of discourse and language. But when a word stands for a very complex idea that is compounded and decompounded, it is not easy for men to form and retain that idea so exactly, as to make the name in common use stand for the same precise idea, without any the least variation. Hence it comes to pass that men's names of very compound ideas, such as for the most part are moral words, have seldom in two different men the same precise signification; since one man's complex idea seldom agrees with another's, and often differs from his own — from that which he had yesterday, or will have to-morrow.

7. Secondly, because they have no standards in nature. Because the names of mixed modes for the most part want standards in nature, whereby men may rectify and adjust their significations, therefore they are very various and doubtful. They are assemblages of ideas put together at the pleasure of the mind, pursuing its own ends of discourse, and suited to its own notions, whereby it designs not to copy anything really existing, but to denominate and rank things as they come to agree with those archetypes or forms it has made. He that first brought

the word sham, or wheedle, or banter, in use, put together as he thought fit those ideas he made it stand for; and as it is with any new names of modes that are now brought into any language, so it was with the old ones when they were first made use of. Names, therefore, that stand for collections of ideas which the mind makes at pleasure must needs be of doubtful signification, when such collections are nowhere to be found constantly united in nature, nor any patterns to be shown whereby men may adjust them. What the word murder, or sacrilege, &c., signifies can never be known from things themselves: there be many of the parts of those complex ideas which are not visible in the action itself; the intention of the mind, or the relation of holy things, which make a part of murder or sacrilege, have no necessary connexion with the outward and visible action of him that commits either: and the pulling the trigger of the gun with which the murder is committed, and is all the action that perhaps is visible, has no natural connexion with those other ideas that make up the complex one named murder. They have their union and combination only from the understanding which unites them under one name: but, uniting them without any rule or pattern, it cannot be but that the signification of the name that stands for such voluntary collections should be often various in the minds of different men, who have scarce any standing rule to regulate themselves and their notions by, in such arbitrary ideas.

8. Common use, or propriety not a sufficient remedy. It is true, common use, that is, the rule of propriety may be supposed here to afford some aid, to settle the signification of language; and it cannot be denied but that in some measure it does. Common use regulates the meaning of words pretty well for common conversation; but nobody having an authority to establish the precise signification of words, nor determine to what ideas any one shall annex them, common use is not sufficient to adjust them to Philosophical Discourses; there being scarce any name of any very complex idea (to say nothing of others) which, in common use, has not a great latitude, and which, keeping within the bounds of propriety, may not be made the sign of far different ideas. Besides, the rule and measure of propriety itself being nowhere established, it is often matter of dispute, whether this or that way of using a word be propriety of speech or no. From all which it is evident, that the names of such kind of very complex ideas are naturally liable to this imperfection, to be of doubtful and uncertain signification; and even in men that have a mind to understand one another, do not always stand for the same idea in speaker and hearer. Though the names glory and gratitude be the same in every man's mouth through a whole country, yet the complex collective idea which every one thinks on or intends by that name, is apparently very different in men using the same language.

9. The way of learning these names contributes also to their doubtfulness. The way also wherein the names of mixed modes are ordinarily learned, does not a little contribute to the doubtfulness of their signification. For if we will observe how children learn languages, we shall find that, to make them understand what the names of simple ideas or substances stand for, people ordinarily show them the thing whereof they would have them have the idea; and then repeat to them the name that stands for it; as white, sweet, milk, sugar, cat, dog. But as for mixed modes, especially the most material of them, moral words, the sounds are usually learned first; and then, to know what complex ideas they stand for, they are either beholden to the explication of others, or (which happens for the most part) are left to their own observation and industry; which being little laid out in the search of the true and precise meaning of names, these moral words are in most men's mouths little more than bare sounds; or when they have any, it is for the most part but a very loose and undetermined, and, consequently, obscure and confused signification. And even those themselves who have with more attention settled their notions, do yet hardly avoid the inconvenience to have them stand for complex ideas different from those which other, even intelligent and studious men, make them the signs of. Where shall one find any, either controversial debate, or familiar discourse, concerning honour, faith, grace, religion, church, &c., wherein it is not easy to observe the different notions men have of them? Which is nothing but this, that they are not agreed in the signification of those words, nor have in their minds the same complex ideas which they make

them stand for, and so all the contests that follow thereupon are only about the meaning of a sound. And hence we see that, in the interpretation of laws, whether divine or human, there is no end; comments beget comments, and explications make new matter for explications; and of limiting, distinguishing, varying the signification of these moral words there is no end. These ideas of men's making are, by men still having the same power, multiplied in infinitum. Many a man who was pretty well satisfied of the meaning of a text of Scripture, or clause in the code, at first reading, has, by consulting commentators, quite lost the sense of it, and by these elucidations given rise or increase to his doubts, and drawn obscurity upon the place. I say not this that I think commentaries needless; but to show how uncertain the names of mixed modes naturally are, even in the mouths of those who had both the intention and the faculty of speaking as clearly as language was capable to express their thoughts.

10. Hence unavoidable obscurity in ancient authors. What obscurity this has unavoidably brought upon the writings of men who have lived in remote ages, and different countries, it will be needless to take notice. Since the numerous volumes of learned men, employing their thoughts that way, are proofs more than enough, to show what attention, study, sagacity, and reasoning are required to find out the true meaning of ancient authors. But, there being no writings we have any great concernment to be very solicitous about the meaning of, but those that contain either truths we are required to believe, or laws we are to obey, and draw inconveniences on us when we mistake or transgress, we may be less anxious about the sense of other authors; who, writing but their own opinions, we are under no greater necessity to know them, than they to know ours. Our good or evil depending not on their decrees, we may safely be ignorant of their notions: and therefore in the reading of them, if they do not use their words with a due clearness and perspicuity, we may lay them aside, and without any injury done them, resolve thus with ourselves, Si non vis intelligi, debes negligi.

11. Names of substances of doubtful signification, because the ideas they stand for relate to the reality of things. If the signification of the names of mixed modes be uncertain, because there be no real standards existing in nature to which those ideas are referred, and by which they may be adjusted, the names of substances are of a doubtful signification, for a contrary reason, viz. because the ideas they stand for are supposed conformable to the reality of things, and are referred to as standards made by Nature. In our ideas of substances we have not the liberty, as in mixed modes, to frame what combinations we think fit, to be the characteristical notes to rank and denominate things by. In these we must follow Nature, suit our complex ideas to real existences, and regulate the signification of their names by the things themselves, if we will have our names to be signs of them, and stand for them. Here, it is true, we have patterns to follow; but patterns that will make the signification of their names very uncertain: for names must be of a very unsteady and various meaning, if the ideas they stand for be referred to standards without us, that either cannot be known at all, or can be known but imperfectly and uncertainly.

12. Names of substances referred, to real essences that cannot be known. The names of substances have, as has been shown, a double reference in their ordinary use.

First, Sometimes they are made to stand for, and so their signification is supposed to agree to, the real constitution of things, from which all their properties flow, and in which they all centre. But this real constitution, or (as it is apt to be called) essence, being utterly unknown to us, any sound that is put to stand for it must be very uncertain in its application; and it will be impossible to know what things are or ought to be called a horse, or antimony, when those words are put for real essences that we have no ideas of at all. And therefore in this supposition, the names of substances being referred to standards that cannot be known, their significations can never be adjusted and established by those standards.

13. To co-existing qualities, which are known but imperfectly. Secondly, The simple ideas that are found to co-exist in substances being that which their names immediately signify, these, as united in the several sorts of things, are the proper standards to which their names are referred, and by which their significations may be best rectified. But neither will these archetypes so

well serve to this purpose as to leave these names without very various and uncertain significations. Because these simple ideas that co-exist, and are united in the same subject, being very numerous, and having all an equal right to go into the complex specific idea which the specific name is to stand for, men, though they propose to themselves the very same subject to consider, yet frame very different ideas about it; and so the name they use for it unavoidably comes to have, in several men, very different significations. The simple qualities which make up the complex ideas, being most of them powers, in relation to changes which they are apt to make in, or receive from other bodies, are almost infinite. He that shall but observe what a great variety of alterations any one of the baser metals is apt to receive, from the different application only of fire; and how much a greater number of changes any of them will receive in the hands of a chymist, by the application of other bodies, will not think it strange that I count the properties of any sort of bodies not easy to be collected, and completely known, by the ways of inquiry which our faculties are capable of. They being therefore at least so many, that no man can know the precise and definite number, they are differently discovered by different men, according to their various skill, attention, and ways of handling; who therefore cannot choose but have different ideas of the same substance, and therefore make the signification of its common name very various and uncertain. For the complex ideas of substances, being made up of such simple ones as are supposed to co-exist in nature, every one has a right to put into his complex idea those qualities he has found to be united together. For, though in the substance of gold one satisfies himself with colour and weight, yet another thinks solubility in aqua regia as necessary to be joined with that colour in his idea of gold, as any one does its fusibility; solubility in aqua regia being a quality as constantly joined with its colour and weight as fusibility or any other; others put into it ductility or fixedness, &c., as they have been taught by tradition or experience. Who of all these has established the right signification of the word, gold? Or who shall be the judge to determine? Each has his standard in nature, which he appeals to, and with reason thinks he has the same right to put into his complex idea signified by the word gold, those qualities, which, upon trial, he has found united; as another who has not so well examined has to leave them out; or a third, who has made other trials, has to put in others. For the union in nature of these qualities being the true ground of their union in one complex idea, who can say one of them has more reason to be put in or left out than another? From hence it will unavoidably follow, that the complex ideas of substances in men using the same names for them, will be very various, and so the significations of those names very uncertain.

14. Thirdly, to co-existing qualities which are known but imperfectly. Besides, there is scarce any particular thing existing, which, in some of its simple ideas, does not communicate with a greater, and in others a less number of particular beings: who shall determine in this case which are those that are to make up the precise collection that is to be signified by the specific name? or can with any just authority prescribe, which obvious or common qualities are to be left out; or which more secret, or more particular, are to be put into the signification of the name of any substance? All which together, seldom or never fall to produce that various and doubtful signification in the names of substances, which causes such uncertainty, disputes, or mistakes, when we come to a philosophical use of them.

15. With this imperfection, they may serve for civil, but not well for philosophical use. It is true, as to civil and common conversation, the general names of substances, regulated in their ordinary signification by some obvious qualities, (as by the shape and figure in things of known seminal propagation, and in other substances, for the most part by colour, joined with some other sensible qualities), do well enough to design the things men would be understood to speak of: and so they usually conceive well enough the substances meant by the word gold or apple, to distinguish the one from the other. But in philosophical inquiries and debates, where general truths are to be established, and consequences drawn from positions laid down, there the precise signification of the names of substances will be found not only not to be well established, but also very hard to be so. For example: he that shall make malleability, or a

certain degree of fixedness, a part of his complex idea of gold, may make propositions concerning gold, and draw consequences from them, that will truly and clearly follow from gold, taken in such a signification: but yet such as another man can never be forced to admit, nor be convinced of their truth, who makes not malleableness, or the same degree of fixedness, part of that complex idea that the name gold, in his use of it, stands for.

16. Instance, liquor. This is a natural and almost unavoidable imperfection in almost all the names of substances, in all languages whatsoever, which men will easily find when, once passing from confused or loose notions, they come to more strict and close inquiries. For then they will be convinced how doubtful and obscure those words are in their signification, which in ordinary use appeared very clear and determined. I was once in a meeting of very learned and ingenious physicians, where by chance there arose a question, whether any liquor passed through the filaments of the nerves. The debate having been managed a good while, by variety of arguments on both sides, I (who had been used to suspect, that the greatest part of disputes were more about the signification of words than a real difference in the conception of things) desired, that, before they went any further on in this dispute, they would first examine and establish amongst them, what the word liquor signified. They at first were a little surprised at the proposal; and had they been persons less ingenious, they might perhaps have taken it for a very frivolous or extravagant one: since there was no one there that thought not himself to understand very perfectly what the word liquor stood for; which I think, too, none of the most perplexed names of substances. However, they were pleased to comply with my motion; and upon examination found that the signification of that word was not so settled or certain as they had all imagined; but that each of them made it a sign of a different complex idea. This made them perceive that the main of their dispute was about the signification of that term; and that they differed very little in their opinions concerning some fluid and subtle matter, passing through the conduits of the nerves; though it was not so easy to agree whether it was to be called liquor or no, a thing, which, when considered, they thought it not worth the contending about.

17. Instance, gold. How much this is the case in the greatest part of disputes that men are engaged so hotly in, I shall perhaps have an occasion in another place to take notice. Let us only here consider a little more exactly the forementioned instance of the word gold, and we shall see how hard it is precisely to determine its signification. I think all agree to make it stand for a body of a certain yellow shining colour; which being the idea to which children have annexed that name, the shining yellow part of a peacock's tail is properly to them gold. Others finding fusibility joined with that yellow colour in certain parcels of matter, make of that combination a complex idea to which they give the name gold, to denote a sort of substances; and so exclude from being gold all such yellow shining bodies as by fire will be reduced to ashes; and admit to be of that species, or to be comprehended under that name gold, only such substances as, having that shining yellow colour, will by fire be reduced to fusion, and not to ashes. Another, by the same reason, adds the weight, which, being a quality as straightly joined with that colour as its fusibility, he thinks has the same reason to be joined in its idea, and to be signified by its name: and therefore the other made up of body, of such a colour and fusibility, to be imperfect; and so on of all the rest: wherein no one can show a reason why some of the inseparable qualities, that are always united in nature, should be put into the nominal essence, and others left out: or why the word gold, signifying that sort of body the ring on his finger is made of, should determine that sort rather by its colour, weight, and fusibility, than by its colour, weight, and solubility in aqua regia: since the dissolving it by that liquor is as inseparable from it as the fusion by fire; and they are both of them nothing but the relation which that substance has to two other bodies, which have a power to operate differently upon it. For by what right is it that fusibility comes to be a part of the essence signified by the word gold, and solubility but a property of it? Or why is its colour part of the essence, and its malleableness but a property? That which I mean is this, That these being all but properties, depending on its real constitution, and nothing but powers, either active or

passive, in reference to other bodies, no one has authority to determine the signification of the word gold (as referred to such a body existing in nature) more to one collection of ideas to be found in that body than to another: whereby the signification of that name must unavoidably be very uncertain. Since, as has been said, several people observe several properties in the same substance; and I think I may say nobody all. And therefore we have but very imperfect descriptions of things, and words have very uncertain significations.

18. The names of simple ideas the least doubtful. From what has been said, it is easy to observe what has been before remarked, viz. that the names of simple ideas are, of all others, the least liable to mistakes, and that for these reasons. First, Because the ideas they stand for, being each but one single perception, are much easier got, and more clearly retained, than the more complex ones, and therefore are not liable to the uncertainty which usually attends those compounded ones of substances and mixed modes, in which the precise number of simple ideas that make them up are not easily agreed, so readily kept in mind. And, Secondly, Because they are never referred to any other essence, but barely that perception they immediately signify: which reference is that which renders the signification of the names of substances naturally so perplexed, and gives occasion to so many disputes. Men that do not perversely use their words, or on purpose set themselves to cavil, seldom mistake, in any language which they are acquainted with, the use and signification of the name of simple ideas. White and sweet, yellow and bitter, carry a very obvious meaning with them, which every one precisely comprehends, or easily perceives he is ignorant of, and seeks to be informed. But what precise collection of simple ideas modesty or frugality stand for, in another's use, is not so certainly known. And however we are apt to think we well enough know what is meant by gold or iron; yet the precise complex idea others make them the signs of is not so certain: and I believe it is very seldom that, in speaker and hearer, they stand for exactly the same collection. Which must needs produce mistakes and disputes, when they are made use of in discourses, wherein men have to do with universal propositions, and would settle in their minds universal truths, and consider the consequences that follow from them.

19. And next to them, simple modes. By the same rule, the names of simple modes are, next to those of simple ideas, least liable to doubt and uncertainty; especially those of figure and number, of which men have so clear and distinct ideas. Who ever that had a mind to understand them mistook the ordinary meaning of seven, or a triangle? And in general the least compounded ideas in every kind have the least dubious names.

20. The most doubtful are the names of very compounded mixed modes and substances. Mixed modes, therefore, that are made up but of a few and obvious simple ideas, have usually names of no very uncertain signification. But the names of mixed modes which comprehend a great number of simple ideas, are commonly of a very doubtful and undetermined meaning, as has been shown. The names of substances, being annexed to ideas that are neither the real essences, nor exact representations of the patterns they are referred to, are liable to yet greater imperfection and uncertainty, especially when we come to a philosophical use of them.

21. Why this imperfection charged upon words. The great disorder that happens in our names of substances, proceeding, for the most part, from our want of knowledge, and inability to penetrate into their real constitutions, it may probably be wondered why I charge this as an imperfection rather upon our words than understandings. This exception has so much appearance of justice, that I think myself obliged to give a reason why I have followed this method. I must confess, then, that, when I first began this Discourse of the Understanding, and a good while after, I had not the least thought that any consideration of words was at all necessary to it. But when, having passed over the original and composition of our ideas, I began to examine the extent and certainty of our knowledge, I found it had so near a connexion with words, that, unless their force and manner of signification were first well observed, there could be very little said clearly and pertinently concerning knowledge: which being conversant about truth, had constantly to do with propositions. And though it terminated in things, yet it was for the most part so much by the intervention of words, that they seemed

scarce separable from our general knowledge. At least they interpose themselves so much between our understandings, and the truth which it would contemplate and apprehend, that, like the medium through which visible objects pass, the obscurity and disorder do not seldom cast a mist before our eyes, and impose upon our understandings. If we consider, in the fallacies men put upon themselves, as well as others, and the mistakes in men's disputes and notions, how great a part is owing to words, and their uncertain or mistaken significations, we shall have reason to think this no small obstacle in the way to knowledge; which I conclude we are the more carefully to be warned of, because it has been so far from being taken notice of as an inconvenience, that the arts of improving it have been made the business of men's study, and obtained the reputation of learning and subtilty, as we shall see in the following chapter. But I am apt to imagine, that, were the imperfections of language, as the instrument of knowledge, more thoroughly weighed, a great many of the controversies that make such a noise in the world, would of themselves cease; and the way to knowledge, and perhaps peace too, lie a great deal opener than it does.

22. This should teach us moderation in imposing our own sense of old authors. Sure I am that the signification of words in all languages, depending very much on the thoughts, notions, and ideas of him that uses them, must unavoidably be of great uncertainty to men of the same language and country. This is so evident in the Greek authors, that he that shall peruse their writings will find in almost every one of them, a distinct language, though the same words. But when to this natural difficulty in every country, there shall be added different countries and remote ages, wherein the speakers and writers had very different notions, tempers, customs, ornaments, and figures of speech, &c., every one of which influenced the signification of their words then, though to us now they are lost and unknown; it would become us to be charitable one to another in our interpretations or misunderstandings of those ancient writings; which, though of great concernment to be understood, are liable to the unavoidable difficulties of speech, which (if we except the names of simple ideas, and some very obvious things) is not capable, without a constant defining the terms, of conveying the sense and intention of the speaker, without any manner of doubt and uncertainty to the hearer. And in discourses of religion, law, and morality, as they are matters of the highest concernment, so there will be the greatest difficulty.

23. Especially of the Old and New Testament Scriptures. The volumes of interpreters and commentators on the Old and New Testament are but too manifest proofs of this. Though everything said in the text be infallibly true, yet the reader may be, nay, cannot choose but be, very fallible in the understanding of it. Nor is it to be wondered, that the will of God, when clothed in words, should be liable to that doubt and uncertainty which unavoidably attends that sort of conveyance, when even his Son, whilst clothed in flesh, was subject to all the frailties and inconveniences of human nature, sin excepted. And we ought to magnify his goodness, that he hath spread before all the world such legible characters of his works and providence, and given all mankind so sufficient a light of reason, that they to whom this written word never came, could not (whenever they set themselves to search) either doubt of the being of a God, or of the obedience due to him. Since then the precepts of Natural Religion are plain, and very intelligible to all mankind, and seldom come to be controverted; and other revealed truths, which are conveyed to us by books and languages, are liable to the common and natural obscurities and difficulties incident to words; methinks it would become us to be more careful and diligent in observing the former, and less magisterial, positive, and imperious, in imposing our own sense and interpretations of the latter.

Chapter X. Of the Abuse of Words

1. Woeful abuse of words. Besides the imperfection that is naturally in language, and the obscurity and confusion that is so hard to be avoided in the use of words, there are several

wilful faults and neglects which men are guilty of in this way of communication, whereby they render these signs less clear and distinct in their signification than naturally they need to be. 2. Words are often employed without any, or without clear ideas. First, In this kind the first and most palpable abuse is, the using of words without clear and distinct ideas; or, which is worse, signs without anything signified. Of these there are two sorts:—

I. Some words introduced without clear ideas annexed to them, even in their first original. One may observe, in all languages, certain words that, if they be examined, will be found in their first original, and their appropriated use, not to stand for any clear and distinct ideas. These, for the most part, the several sects of philosophy and religion have introduced. For their authors or promoters, either affecting something singular, and out of the way of common apprehensions, or to support some strange opinions, or cover some weakness of their hypothesis, seldom fail to coin new words, and such as, when they come to be examined, may justly be called insignificant terms. For, having either had no determinate collection of ideas annexed to them when they were first invented; or at least such as, if well examined, will be found inconsistent, it is no wonder, if, afterwards, in the vulgar use of the same party, they remain empty sounds, with little or no signification, amongst those who think it enough to have them often in their mouths, as the distinguishing characters of their Church or School, without much troubling their heads to examine what are the precise ideas they stand for. I shall not need here to heap up instances; every man's reading and conversation will sufficiently furnish him. Or if he wants to be better stored, the great mintmasters of this kind of terms, I mean the Schoolmen and Metaphysicians (under which I think the disputing natural and moral philosophers of these latter ages may be comprehended) have wherewithal abundantly to content him.

3. II. Other words, to which ideas were annexed at first, used afterwards without distinct meanings. Others there be who extend this abuse yet further, who take so little care to lay by words, which, in their primary notation have scarce any clear and distinct ideas which they are annexed to, that, by an unpardonable negligence, they familiarly use words which the propriety of language has affixed to very important ideas, without any distinct meaning at all. Wisdom, glory, grace, &c., are words frequent enough in every man's mouth; but if a great many of those who use them should be asked what they mean by them, they would be at a stand, and not know what to answer: a plain proof, that, though they have learned those sounds, and have them ready at their tongues ends, yet there are no determined ideas laid up in their minds, which are to be expressed to others by them.

4. This occasioned by men learning names before they have the ideas the names belong to. Men having been accustomed from their cradles to learn words which are easily got and retained, before they knew or had framed the complex ideas to which they were annexed, or which were to be found in the things they were thought to stand for, they usually continue to do so all their lives; and without taking the pains necessary to settle in their minds determined ideas, they use their words for such unsteady and confused notions as they have, contenting themselves with the same words other people use; as if their very sound necessarily carried with it constantly the same meaning. This, though men make a shift with in the ordinary occurrences of life, where they find it necessary to be understood, and therefore they make signs till they are so; yet this insignificancy in their words, when they come to reason concerning either their tenets or interest, manifestly fills their discourse with abundance of empty unintelligible noise and jargon, especially in moral matters, where the words for the most part standing for arbitrary and numerous collections of ideas, not regularly and permanently united in nature, their bare sounds are often only thought on, or at least very obscure and uncertain notions annexed to them. Men take the words they find in use amongst their neighbors; and that they may not seem ignorant what they stand for, use them confidently, without much troubling their heads about a certain fixed meaning; whereby, besides the ease of it, they obtain this advantage, That, as in such discourses they seldom are in the right, so they are as seldom to be convinced that they are in the wrong; it being all one

to go about to draw those men out of their mistakes who have no settled notions, as to dispossess a vagrant of his habitation who has no settled abode. This I guess to be so; and every one may observe in himself and others whether it be so or not.

5. Unsteady application of them. Secondly, Another great abuse of words is inconstancy in the use of them. It is hard to find a discourse written on any subject, especially of controversy, wherein one shall not observe, if he read with attention, the same words (and those commonly the most material in the discourse, and upon which the argument turns) used sometimes for one collection of simple ideas, and sometimes for another; which is a perfect abuse of language. Words being intended for signs of my ideas, to make them known to others, not by any natural signification, but by a voluntary imposition, it is plain cheat and abuse, when I make them stand sometimes for one thing and sometimes for another; the wilful doing whereof can be imputed to nothing but great folly, or greater dishonesty. And a man, in his accounts with another may, with as much fairness make the characters of numbers stand sometimes for one and sometimes for another collection of units: v.g. this character 3, stand sometimes for three, sometimes for four, and sometimes for eight, as in his discourse or reasoning make the same words stand for different collections of simple ideas. If men should do so in their reckonings, I wonder who would have to do with them? One who would speak thus in the affairs and business of the world, and call 8 sometimes seven, and sometimes nine, as best served his advantage, would presently have clapped upon him, one of the two names men are commonly disgusted with. And yet in arguings and learned contests, the same sort of proceedings passes commonly for wit and learning; but to me it appears a greater dishonesty than the misplacing of counters in the casting up a debt; and the cheat the greater, by how much truth is of greater concernment and value than money.

6. III. Affected obscurity, as in the Peripatetick and other sects of philosophy. Thirdly, Another abuse of language is an affected obscurity; by either applying old words to new and unusual significations; or introducing new and ambiguous terms, without defining either; or else putting them so together, as may confound their ordinary meaning. Though the Peripatetick philosophy has been most eminent in this way, yet other sects have not been wholly clear of it. There are scarce any of them that are not cumbered with some difficulties (such is the imperfection of human knowledge,) which they have been fain to cover with obscurity of terms, and to confound the signification of words, which, like a mist before people's eyes, might hinder their weak parts from being discovered. That body and extension in common use, stand for two distinct ideas, is plain to any one that will but reflect a little. For were their signification precisely the same, it would be as proper, and as intelligible to say, "the body of an extension," as the "extension of a body"; and yet there are those who find it necessary to confound their signification. To this abuse, and the mischiefs of confounding the signification of words, logic, and the liberal sciences as they have been handled in the schools, have given reputation; and the admired Art of Disputing hath added much to the natural imperfection of languages, whilst it has been made use of and fitted to perplex the signification of words, more than to discover the knowledge and truth of things: and he that will look into that sort of learned writings, will find the words there much more obscure, uncertain, and undetermined in their meaning, than they are in ordinary conversation.

7. Logic and dispute have much contributed to this. This is unavoidably to be so, where men's parts and learning are estimated by their skill in disputing. And if reputation and reward shall attend these conquests, which depend mostly on the fineness and niceties of words, it is no wonder if the wit of man so employed, should perplex, involve, and subtilize the signification of sounds, so as never to want something to say in opposing or defending any question; the victory being adjudged not to him who had truth on his side, but the last word in the dispute.

8. Calling it "subtlety." This, though a very useless skin, and that which I think the direct opposite to the ways of knowledge, hath yet passed hitherto under the laudable and esteemed names of subtlety and acuteness, and has had the applause of the schools, and encouragement of one part of the learned men of the world. And no wonder, since the philosophers of old, (the

disputing and wrangling philosophers I mean, such as Lucian wittily and with reason taxes), and the Schoolmen since, aiming at glory and esteem, for their great and universal knowledge, easier a great deal to be pretended to than really acquired, found this a good expedient to cover their ignorance, with a curious and inexplicable web of perplexed words, and procure to themselves the admiration of others, by unintelligible terms, the apter to produce wonder because they could not be understood: whilst it appears in all history, that these profound doctors were no wiser nor more useful than their neighbours, and brought but small advantage to human life or the societies wherein they lived: unless the coining of new words, where they produced no new things to apply them to, or the perplexing or obscuring the signification of old ones, and so bringing all things into question and dispute, were a thing profitable to the life of man, or worthy commendation and reward.

9. This learning very little benefits society. For, notwithstanding these learned disputants, these all-knowing doctors, it was to the unscholastic statesman that the governments of the world owed their peace, defence, and liberties; and from the illiterate and contemned mechanic (a name of disgrace) that they received the improvements of useful arts. Nevertheless, this artificial ignorance, and learned gibberish, prevailed mightily in these last ages, by the interest and artifice of those who found no easier way to that pitch of authority and dominion they have attained, than by amusing the men of business, and ignorant, with hard words, or employing the ingenious and idle in intricate disputes about unintelligible terms, and holding them perpetually entangled in that endless labyrinth. Besides, there is no such way to gain admittance, or give defence to strange and absurd doctrines, as to guard them round about with legions of obscure, doubtful, and undefined words. Which yet make these retreats more like the dens of robbers, or holes of foxes, than the fortresses of fair warriors: which, if it be hard to get them out of, it is not for the strength that is in them, but the briars and thorns, and the obscurity of the thickets they are beset with. For untruth being unacceptable to the mind of man, there is no other defence left for absurdity but obscurity.

10. But destroys the instruments of knowledge and communication. Thus learned ignorance, and this art of keeping even inquisitive men from true knowledge, hath been propagated in the world, and hath much perplexed, whilst it pretended to inform the understanding. For we see that other well-meaning and wise men, whose education and parts had not acquired that acuteness, could intelligibly express themselves to one another; and in its plain use make a benefit of language. But though unlearned men well enough understood the words white and black, &c., and had constant notions of the ideas signified by those words; yet there were philosophers found who had learning and subtlety enough to prove that snow was black; i.e. to prove that white was black. Whereby they had the advantage to destroy the instruments and means of discourse, conversation, instruction, and society; whilst, with great art and subtlety, they did no more but perplex and confound the signification of words, and thereby render language less useful than the real defects of it had made it; a gift which the illiterate had not attained to.

11. As useful as to confound the sounds that the letters of the alphabet stand for. These learned men did equally instruct men's understandings, and profit their lives, as he who should alter the signification of known characters, and, by a subtle device of learning, far surpassing the capacity of the illiterate, dull, and vulgar, should in his writing show that he could put A for B, and D for E, &c., to the no small admiration and benefit of his reader. It being as senseless to put black, which is a word agreed on to stand for one sensible idea, to put it, I say, for another, or the contrary idea; i.e. to call snow black, as to put this mark A, which is a character agreed on to stand for one modification of sound, made by a certain motion of the organs of speech, for B, which is agreed on to stand for another modification of sound, made by another certain mode of the organs of speech.

12. This art has perplexed religion and justice. Nor hath this mischief stopped in logical niceties, or curious empty speculations; it hath invaded the great concernments of human life and society; obscured and perplexed the material truths of law and divinity; brought confusion,

disorder, and uncertainty into the affairs of mankind; and if not destroyed, yet in a great measure rendered useless, these two great rules, religion and justice. What have the greatest part of the comments and disputes upon the laws of God and man served for, but to make the meaning more doubtful, and perplex the sense? What have been the effect of those multiplied curious distinctions, and acute niceties, but obscurity and uncertainty, leaving the words more unintelligible, and the reader more at a loss? How else comes it to pass that princes, speaking or writing to their servants, in their ordinary commands are easily understood; speaking to their people, in their laws, are not so? And, as I remarked before, doth it not often happen that a man of an ordinary capacity very well understands a text, or a law, that he reads, till he consults an expositor, or goes to counsel; who, by that time he hath done explaining them, makes the words signify either nothing at all, or what he pleases.

13 And ought not to pass for learning. Whether any by-interests of these professions have occasioned this, I will not here examine; but I leave it to be considered, whether it would not be well for mankind, whose concernment it is to know things as they are, and to do what they ought, and not to spend their lives in talking about them, or tossing words to and fro;—whether it would not be well, I say, that the use of words were made plain and direct; and that language, which was given us for the improvement of knowledge and bond of society, should not be employed to darken truth and unsettle people's rights; to raise mists, and render unintelligible both morality and religion? Or that at least, if this will happen, it should not be thought learning or knowledge to do so?

14. IV. By taking words for things. Fourthly, Another great abuse of words, is the taking them for things. This, though it in some degree concerns all names in general, yet more particularly affects those of substances. To this abuse those men are most subject who most confine their thoughts to anyone system, and give themselves up into a firm belief of the perfection of any received hypothesis: whereby they come to be persuaded that the terms of that sect are so suited to the nature of things, that they perfectly correspond with their real existence. Who is there that has been bred up in the Peripatetick philosophy, who does not think the Ten Names, under which are ranked the Ten Predicaments, to be exactly conformable to the nature of things? Who is there of that school that is not persuaded that substantial forms, vegetative souls, abhorrence of a vacuum, intentional species, &c., are something real? These words men have learned from their very entrance upon knowledge, and have found their masters and systems lay great stress upon them: and therefore they cannot quit the opinion, that they are conformable to nature, and are the representations of something that really exists. The Platonists have their soul of the world, and the Epicureans their endeavour towards motion in their atoms when at rest. There is scarce any sect in philosophy has not a distinct set of terms that others understand not. But yet this gibberish, which, in the weakness of human understanding, serves so well to palliate men's ignorance, and cover their errors, comes, by familiar use amongst those of the same tribe, to seem the most important part of language, and of all other the terms the most significant: and should aerial and aetherial vehicles come once, by the prevalency of that doctrine, to be generally received anywhere, no doubt those terms would make impressions on men's minds, so as to establish them in the persuasion of the reality of such things, as much as Peripatetick forms and intentional species have heretofore done.

15. Instance, in matter. How much names taken for things are apt to mislead the understanding, the attentive reading of philosophical writers would abundantly discover; and that perhaps in words little suspected of any such misuse. I shall instance in one only, and that a very familiar one. How many intricate disputes have there been about matter, as if there were some such thing really in nature, distinct from body; as it is evident the word matter stands for an idea distinct from the idea of body? For if the ideas these two terms stood for were precisely the same, they might indifferently in all places be put for one another. But we see that though it be proper to say, There is one matter of all bodies, one cannot say, There is one body of all matters: we familiarly say one body is bigger than another; but it sounds harsh (and

I think is never used) to say one matter is bigger than another. Whence comes this, then? Viz. from hence: that, though matter and body be not really distinct, but wherever there is the one there is the other; yet matter and body stand for two different conceptions, whereof the one is incomplete, and but a part of the other. For body stands for a solid extended figured substance, whereof matter is but a partial and more confused conception; it seeming to me to be used for the substance and solidity of body, without taking in its extension and figure: and therefore it is that, speaking of matter, we speak of it always as one, because in truth it expressly contains nothing but the idea of a solid substance, which is everywhere the same, everywhere uniform. This being our idea of matter, we no more conceive or speak of different matters in the world than we do of different solidities; though we both conceive and speak of different bodies, because extension and figure are capable of variation. But, since solidity cannot exist without extension and figure, the taking matter to be the name of something really existing under that precision, has no doubt produced those obscure and unintelligible discourses and disputes, which have filled the heads and books of philosophers concerning materia prima; which imperfection or abuse, how far it may concern a great many other general terms I leave to be considered. This, I think, I may at least say, that we should have a great many fewer disputes in the world, if words were taken for what they are, the signs of our ideas only; and not for things themselves. For, when we argue about matter, or any the like term, we truly argue only about the idea we express by that sound, whether that precise idea agree to anything really existing in nature or no. And if men would tell what ideas they make their words stand for, there could not be half that obscurity or wrangling in the search or support of truth that there is.

16. This makes errors lasting. But whatever inconvenience follows from this mistake of words, this I am sure, that, by constant and familiar use, they charm men into notions far remote from the truth of things. It would be a hard matter to persuade any one that the words which his father, or schoolmaster, the parson of the parish, or such a reverend doctor used, signified nothing that really existed in nature: which perhaps is none of the least causes that men are so hardly drawn to quit their mistakes, even in opinions purely philosophical, and where they have no other interest but truth. For the words they have a long time been used to, remaining firm in their minds, it is no wonder that the wrong notions annexed to them should not be removed.

17. V. By setting them in the place of what they cannot signify. Fifthly Another abuse of words is the setting them in the place of things which they do or can by no means signify. We may observe that in the general names of substances whereof the nominal essences are only known to us when we put them into propositions, and affirm or deny anything about them, we do most commonly tacitly suppose or intend, they should stand for the real essence of a certain sort of substances. For, when a man says gold is malleable, he means and would insinuate something more than this. That what I call gold is malleable, (though truly it amounts to no more,) but would have this understood, viz. That gold, i.e. what has the real essence of gold, is malleable; which amounts to thus much, that malleableness depends on, and is inseparable from the real essence of gold. But a man, not knowing wherein that real essence consists, the connexion in his mind of malleableness is not truly with an essence he knows not, but only with the sound gold he puts for it. Thus, when we say that animal rationale is, and animal implume bipes latis unguibus is not a good definition of a man; it is plain we suppose the name man in this case to stand for the real essence of a species, and would signify that "a rational animal" better described that real essence than "a two-legged animal with broad nails, and without feathers." For else, why might not Plato as properly make the word anthropos, or man, stand for his complex idea, made up of the idea of a body, distinguished from others by a certain shape and other outward appearances, as Aristotle make the complex idea to which he gave the name anthropos, or man, of body and the faculty of reasoning joined together; unless the name anthropos, or man, were supposed to stand for something else than what it signifies; and to be put in the place of some other thing than the idea a man professes he would express

by it?

18. V.g. Putting them for the real essences of substances. It is true the names of substances would be much more useful, and propositions made in them much more certain, were the real essences of substances the ideas in our minds which those words signified. And it is for want of those real essences that our words convey so little knowledge or certainty in our discourses about them; and therefore the mind, to remove that imperfection as much as it can, makes them, by a secret supposition, to stand for a thing having that real essence, as if thereby it made some nearer approaches to it. For, though the word man or gold signify nothing truly but a complex idea of properties united together in one sort of substances; yet there is scarce anybody, in the use of these words, but often supposes each of those names to stand for a thing having the real essence on which these properties depend. Which is so far from diminishing the imperfection of our words, that by a plain abuse it adds to it, when we would make them stand for something, which, not being in our complex idea, the name we use can no ways be the sign of.

19. Hence we think change of our complex ideas of substances not to change their species. This shows us the reason why in mixed modes any of the ideas that make the composition of the complex one being left out or changed, it is allowed to be another thing, i.e. to be of another species, as is plain in chance-medley, manslaughter, murder, parricide, &c. The reason whereof is, because the complex idea signified by that name is the real as well as nominal essence; and there is no secret reference of that name to any other essence but that. But in substances, it is not so. For though in that called gold, one puts into his complex idea what another leaves out, and vice versa: yet men do not usually think that therefore the species is changed: because they secretly in their minds refer that name, and suppose it annexed to a real immutable essence of a thing existing, on which those properties depend. He that adds to his complex idea of gold that of fixedness and solubility in aqua regia, which he put not in it before, is not thought to have changed the species; but only to have a more perfect idea, by adding another simple idea, which is always in fact joined with those other, of which his former complex idea consisted. But this reference of the name to a thing, whereof we have not the idea, is so far from helping at all, that it only serves the more to involve us in difficulties. For by this tacit reference to the real essence of that species of bodies, the word gold (which, by standing for a more or less perfect collection of simple ideas, serves to design that sort of body well enough in civil discourse) comes to have no signification at all, being put for somewhat whereof we have no idea at all, and so can signify nothing at all, when the body itself is away. For however it may be thought all one, yet, if well considered, it will be found a quite different thing, to argue about gold in name, and about a parcel in the body itself, v.g. a piece of leaf-gold laid before us; though in discourse we are fain to substitute the name for the thing.

20. The cause of this abuse, a supposition of nature's working always regularly, in setting boundaries to species. That which I think very much disposes men to substitute their names for the real essences of species, is the supposition before mentioned, that nature works regularly in the production of things, and sets the boundaries to each of those species, by giving exactly the same real internal constitution to each individual which we rank under one general name. Whereas anyone who observes their different qualities can hardly doubt, that many of the individuals, called by the same name, are, in their internal constitution, as different one from another as several of those which are ranked under different specific names. This supposition, however, that the same precise and internal constitution goes always with the same specific name, makes men forward to take those names for the representatives of those real essences; though indeed they signify nothing but the complex ideas they have in their minds when they use them. So that, if I may so say, signifying one thing, and being supposed for, or put in the place of another, they cannot but, in such a kind of use, cause a great deal of uncertainty in men's discourses; especially in those who have thoroughly imbibed the doctrine of substantial forms, whereby they firmly imagine the several species of things to be determined and

distinguished.

21. This abuse contains two false suppositions. But however preposterous and absurd it be to make our names stand for ideas we have not, or (which is all one) essences that we know not, it being in effect to make our words the signs of nothing; yet it is evident to any one who ever so little reflects on the use men make of their words, that there is nothing more familiar. When a man asks whether this or that thing he sees, let it be a drill, or a monstrous foetus, be a man or no; it is evident the question is not, Whether that particular thing agree to his complex idea expressed by the name man: but whether it has in it the real essence of a species of things which he supposes his name man to stand for. In which way of using the names of substances, there are these false suppositions contained:—

First, that there are certain precise essences according to which nature makes all particular things, and by which they are distinguished into species. That everything has a real constitution, whereby it is what it is, and on which its sensible qualities depend, is past doubt: but I think it has been proved that this makes not the distinction of species as we rank them, nor the boundaries of their names.

Secondly, this tacitly also insinuates, as if we had ideas of these proposed essences. For to what purpose else is it, to inquire whether this or that thing have the real essence of the species man, if we did not suppose that there were such a specific essence known? Which yet is utterly false. And therefore such application of names as would make them stand for ideas which we have not, must needs cause great disorder in discourses and reasonings about them, and be a great inconvenience in our communication by words.

22. VI. By proceeding upon the supposition that the words we use have a certain and evident signification which other men cannot but understand. Sixthly, there remains yet another more general, though perhaps less observed, abuse of words; and that is, that men having by a long and familiar use annexed to them certain ideas, they are apt to imagine so near and necessary a connexion between the names and the signification they use them in, that they forwardly suppose one cannot but understand what their meaning is; and therefore one ought to acquiesce in the words delivered, as if it were past doubt that, in the use of those common received sounds, the speaker and hearer had necessarily the same precise ideas. Whence presuming, that when they have in discourse used any term, they have thereby, as it were, set before others the very thing they talked of. And so likewise taking the words of others as naturally standing for just what they themselves have been accustomed to apply them to, they never trouble themselves to explain their own, or understand clearly others' meaning. From whence commonly proceeds noise, and wrangling, without improvement or information; whilst men take words to be the constant regular marks of agreed notions, which in truth are no more but the voluntary and unsteady signs of their own ideas. And yet men think it strange, if in discourse, or (where it is often absolutely necessary) in dispute, one sometimes asks the meaning of their terms: though the arguings one may every day observe in conversation make it evident, that there are few names of complex ideas which any two men use for the same just precise collection. It is hard to name a word which is hard to name a word which will not be a clear instance of this. Life is a term, none more familiar. Any one almost would take it for an affront to be asked what he meant by it. And yet if it comes in question, whether a plant that lies ready formed in the seed have life; whether the embryo in an egg before incubation, or a man in a swoon without sense or motion, be alive or no; it is easy to perceive that a clear, distinct, settled idea does not always accompany the use of so known a word as that of life is. Some gross and confused conceptions men indeed ordinarily have, to which they apply the common words of their language; and such a loose use of their words serves them well enough in their ordinary discourses or affairs. But this is not sufficient for philosophical inquiries. Knowledge and reasoning require precise determinate ideas. And though men will not be so importunately dull as not to understand what others say, without demanding an explication of their terms; nor so troublesomely critical as to correct others in the use of the words they receive from them: yet, where truth and knowledge are concerned in the case, I know not what

fault it can be, to desire the explication of words whose sense seems dubious; or why a man should be ashamed to own his ignorance in what sense another man uses his words; since he has no other way of certainly knowing it but by being informed. This abuse of taking words upon trust has nowhere spread so far, nor with so ill effects, as amongst men of letters. The multiplication and obstinacy of disputes, which have so laid waste the intellectual world, is owing to nothing more than to this ill use of words. For though it be generally believed that there is great diversity of opinions in the volumes and variety of controversies the world is distracted with; yet the most I can find that the contending learned men of different parties do, in their arguings one with another, is, that they speak different languages. For I am apt to imagine, that when any of them, quitting terms, think upon things, and know what they think, they think all the same: though perhaps what they would have be different.

23. The ends of language: First, to convey our ideas. To conclude this consideration of the imperfection and abuse of language. The ends of language in our discourse with others being chiefly these three: First, to make known one man's thoughts or ideas to another; Secondly, to do it with as much ease and quickness as possible; and, Thirdly, thereby to convey the knowledge of things: language is either abused of deficient, when it fails of any of these three. First, Words fail in the first of these ends, and lay not open one man's ideas to another's view: 1. When men have names in their mouths without any determinate ideas in their minds, whereof they are the signs: or, 2. When they apply the common received names of any language to ideas, to which the common use of that language does not apply them: or, 3. When they apply them very unsteadily, making them stand, now for one, and by and by for another idea.

24. To do it with quickness. Secondly, Men fail of conveying their thoughts with all the quickness and ease that may be, when they have complex ideas without having any distinct names for them. This is sometimes the fault of the language itself, which has not in it a sound yet applied to such a signification; and sometimes the fault of the man, who has not yet learned the name for that idea he would show another.

25. Therewith to convey the knowledge of things. Thirdly, There is no knowledge of things conveyed by men's words, when their ideas agree not to the reality of things. Though it be a defect that has its original in our ideas, which are not so conformable to the nature of things as attention, study, and application might make them, yet it fails not to extend itself to our words too, when we use them as signs of real beings, which yet never had any reality or existence.

26. How men's words fail in all these: First, when used without any ideas. First, He that hath words of any language, without distinct ideas in his mind to which he applies them, does, so far as he uses them in discourse, only make a noise without any sense or signification; and how learned soever he may seem, by the use of hard words or learned terms, is not much more advanced thereby in knowledge, than he would be in learning, who had nothing in his study but the bare titles of books, without possessing the contents of them. For all such words, however put into discourse, according to the right construction of grammatical rules, or the harmony of well-turned periods, do yet amount to nothing but bare sounds, and nothing else.

27. When complex ideas are without names annexed to them. Secondly, He that has complex ideas, without particular names for them, would be in no better case than a bookseller, who had in his warehouse volumes that lay there unbound, and without titles, which he could therefore make known to others only by showing the loose sheets, and communicate them only by tale. This man is hindered in his discourse, for want of words to communicate his complex ideas, which he is therefore forced to make known by an enumeration of the simple ones that compose them; and so is fain often to use twenty words, to express what another man signifies in one.

28. When the same sign is not put for the same idea. Thirdly, He that puts not constantly the same sign for the same idea, but uses the same words sometimes in one and sometimes in another signification, ought to pass in the schools and conversation for as fair a man, as he does in the market and exchange, who sells several things under the same name.

29. When words are diverted from their common use. Fourthly, He that applies the words of any language to ideas different from those to which the common use of that country applies them, however his own understanding may be filled with truth and light, will not by such words be able to convey much of it to others, without defining his terms. For however the sounds are such as are familiarly known, and easily enter the ears of those who are accustomed to them; yet standing for other ideas than those they usually are annexed to, and are wont to excite in the mind of the hearers, they cannot make known the thoughts of him who thus uses them.

30. When they are names of fantastical imaginations. Fifthly, He that imagined to himself substances such as never have been, and filled his head with ideas which have not any correspondence with the real nature of things, to which yet he gives settled and defined names, may fill his discourse, and perhaps another man's head with the fantastical imaginations of his own brain, but will be very far from advancing thereby one jot in real and true knowledge.

31. Summary. He that hath names without ideas, wants meaning in his words, and speaks only empty sounds. He that hath complex ideas without names for them, wants liberty and dispatch in his expressions, and is necessitated to use periphrases. He that uses his words loosely and unsteadily will either be not minded or not understood. He that applies his names to ideas different from their common use, wants propriety in his language, and speaks gibberish. And he that hath the ideas of substances disagreeing with the real existence of things, so far wants the materials of true knowledge in his understanding, and hath instead thereof chimeras.

32. How men's words fail when they stand for substances. In our notions concerning Substances, we are liable to all the former inconveniences: v.g. he that uses the word tarantula, without having any imagination or idea of what it stands for, pronounces a good word; but so long means nothing at all by it. 2. He that, in a newly-discovered country, shall see several sorts of animals and vegetables, unknown to him before, may have as true ideas of them, as of a horse or a stag; but can speak of them only by a description, till he shall either take the names the natives call them by, or give them names himself. 3. He that uses the word body sometimes for pure extension, and sometimes for extension and solidity together, will talk very fallaciously. 4. He that gives the name horse to that idea which common usage calls mule, talks improperly, and will not be understood. 5. He that thinks the name centaur stands for some real being, imposes on himself, and mistakes words for things.

33. How when they stand for modes and relations. In Modes and Relations generally, we are liable only to the four first of these inconveniences; viz. 1. I may have in my memory the names of modes, as gratitude or charity, and yet not have any precise ideas annexed in my thoughts to those names. 2. I may have ideas, and not know the names that belong to them: v.g. I may have the idea of a man's drinking till his colour and humour be altered, till his tongue trips, and his eyes look red, and his feet fail him; and yet not know that it is to be called drunkenness. 3. I may have the ideas of virtues or vices, and names also, but apply them amiss: v.g. when I apply the name frugality to that idea which others call and signify by this sound, covetousness. 4. I may use any of those names with inconstancy. 5. But, in modes and relations, I cannot have ideas disagreeing to the existence of things: for modes being complex ideas, made by the mind at pleasure, and relation being but by way of considering or comparing two things together, and so also an idea of my own making, these ideas can scarce be found to disagree with anything existing; since they are not in the mind as the copies of things regularly made by nature, nor as properties inseparably flowing from the internal constitution or essence of any substance; but, as it were, patterns lodged in my memory, with names annexed to them, to denominate actions and relations by, as they come to exist. But the mistake is commonly in my giving a wrong name to my conceptions; and so using words in a different sense from other people: I am not understood, but am thought to have wrong ideas of them, when I give wrong names to them. Only if I put in my ideas of mixed modes or relations any inconsistent ideas together, I fill my head also with chimeras; since such ideas, if well examined, cannot so much as exist in the mind, much less any real being ever be denominated

from them.

34. Seventhly, language is often abused by figurative speech. Since wit and fancy find easier entertainment in the world than dry truth and real knowledge, figurative speeches and allusion in language will hardly be admitted as an imperfection or abuse of it. I confess, in discourses where we seek rather pleasure and delight than information and improvement, such ornaments as are borrowed from them can scarce pass for faults. But yet if we would speak of things as they are, we must allow that all the art of rhetoric, besides order and clearness; all the artificial and figurative application of words eloquence hath invented, are for nothing else but to insinuate wrong ideas, move the passions, and thereby mislead the judgment; and so indeed are perfect cheats: and therefore, however laudable or allowable oratory may render them in harangues and popular addresses, they are certainly, in all discourses that pretend to inform or instruct, wholly to be avoided; and where truth and knowledge are concerned, cannot but be thought a great fault, either of the language or person that makes use of them. What and how various they are, will be superfluous here to take notice; the books of rhetoric which abound in the world, will instruct those who want to be informed: only I cannot but observe how little the preservation and improvement of truth and knowledge is the care and concern of mankind; since the arts of fallacy are endowed and preferred. It is evident how much men love to deceive and be deceived, since rhetoric, that powerful instrument of error and deceit, has its established professors, is publicly taught, and has always been had in great reputation: and I doubt not but it will be thought great boldness, if not brutality, in me to have said thus much against it. Eloquence, like the fair sex, has too prevailing beauties in it to suffer itself ever to be spoken against. And it is in vain to find fault with those arts of deceiving, wherein men find pleasure to be deceived.

Chapter XI. Of the Remedies of the Foregoing Imperfections and Abuses of Words

1. Remedies are worth seeking The natural and improved imperfections of languages we have seen above at large: and speech being the great bond that holds society together, and the common conduit, whereby the improvements of knowledge are conveyed from one man and one generation to another, it would well deserve our most serious thoughts to consider, what remedies are to be found for the inconveniences above mentioned.

2. Are not easy to find. I am not so vain as to think that any one can pretend to attempt the perfect reforming the languages of the world, no not so much as of his own country, without rendering himself ridiculous. To require that men should use their words constantly in the same sense, and for none but determined and uniform ideas, would be to think that all men should have the same notions, and should talk of nothing but what they have clear and distinct ideas of: which is not to be expected by any one who hath not vanity enough to imagine he can prevail with men to be very knowing or very silent And he must be very little skilled in the world, who thinks that a voluble tongue shall accompany only a good understanding; or that men's talking much or little should hold proportion only to their knowledge.

3. But yet necessary to those who search after truth. But though the market and exchange must be left to their own ways of talking, and gossipings not be robbed of their ancient privilege: though the schools, and men of argument would perhaps take it amiss to have anything offered, to abate the length or lessen the number of their disputes; yet methinks those who pretend seriously to search after or maintain truth, should think themselves obliged to study how they might deliver themselves without obscurity, doubtfulness, or equivocation, to which men's words are naturally liable, if care be not taken.

4. Misuse of words the great cause of errors. For he that shall well consider the errors and obscurity, the mistakes and confusion, that are spread in the world by an ill use of words, will find some reason to doubt whether language, as it has been employed, has contributed more to

the improvement or hindrance of knowledge amongst mankind. How many are there, that, when they would think on things, fix their thoughts only on words, especially when they would apply their minds to moral matters? And who then can wonder if the result of such contemplations and reasonings, about little more than sounds, whilst the ideas they annex to them are very confused and very unsteady, or perhaps none at all; who can wonder, I say, that such thoughts and reasonings end in nothing but obscurity and mistake, without any clear judgment or knowledge?

5. Has made men more conceited and obstinate. This inconvenience, in an ill use of words, men suffer in their own private meditations: but much more manifest are the disorders which follow from it, in conversation, discourse, and arguings with others. For language being the great conduit, whereby men convey their discoveries, reasonings, and knowledge, from one to another, he that makes an ill use of it, though he does not corrupt the fountains of knowledge, which are in things themselves, yet he does, as much as in him lies, break or stop the pipes whereby it is distributed to the public use and advantage of mankind. He that uses words without any clear and steady meaning, what does he but lead himself and others into errors? And he that designedly does it, ought to be looked on as an enemy to truth and knowledge. And yet who can wonder that all the sciences and parts of knowledge have been so overcharged with obscure and equivocal terms, and insignificant and doubtful expressions, capable to make the most attentive or quick-sighted very little, or not at all, the more knowing or orthodox: since subtlety, in those who make profession to teach or defend truth, hath passed so much for a virtue: a virtue, indeed, which, consisting for the most part in nothing but the fallacious and illusory use of obscure or deceitful terms, is only fit to make men more conceited in their ignorance, and more obstinate in their errors.

6. Addicted to wrangling about sounds. Let us look into the books of controversy of any kind, there we shall see that the effect of obscure, unsteady, or equivocal terms is nothing but noise and wrangling about sounds, without convincing or bettering a man's understanding. For if the idea be not agreed on, betwixt the speaker and hearer, for which the words stand, the argument is not about things, but names. As often as such a word whose signification is not ascertained betwixt them, comes in use, their understandings have no other object wherein they agree, but barely the sound; the things that they think on at that time, as expressed by that word, being quite different.

7. Instance, bat and bird. Whether a bat be a bird or no, is not a question, Whether a bat be another thing than indeed it is, or have other qualities than indeed it has; for that would be extremely absurd to doubt of. But the question is, (1) Either between those that acknowledged themselves to have but imperfect ideas of one or both of this sort of things, for which these names are supposed to stand. And then it is a real inquiry concerning the nature of a bird or a bat, to make their yet imperfect ideas of it more complete; by examining whether all the simple ideas to which, combined together, they both give the name bird, be all to be found in a bat: but this is a question only of inquirers (not disputers) who neither affirm nor deny, but examine: Or, (2) It is a question between disputants; whereof the one affirms, and the other denies that a bat is a bird. And then the question is barely about the signification of one or both these words; in that they not having both the same complex ideas to which they give these two names, one holds and the other denies, that these two names may be affirmed one of another. Were they agreed in the signification of these two names, it were impossible they should dispute about them. For they would presently and clearly see (were that adjusted between them), whether all the simple ideas of the more general name bird were found in the complex idea of a bat or no; and so there could be no doubt whether a bat were a bird or no. And here I desire it may be considered, and carefully examined, whether the greatest part of the disputes in the world are not merely verbal, and about the signification of words; and whether, if the terms they are made in were defined, and reduced in their signification (as they must be where they signify anything) to determined collections of the simple ideas they do or should stand for, those disputes would not end of themselves, and immediately vanish. I leave it then to be

considered, what the learning of disputation is, and how well they are employed for the advantage of themselves or others, whose business is only the vain ostentation of sounds; i.e. those who spend their lives in disputes and controversies. When I shall see any of those combatants strip all his terms of ambiguity and obscurity, (which every one may do in the words he uses himself), I shall think him a champion for knowledge, truth, and peace, and not the slave of vain-glory, ambition, or a party.

8. Remedies. To remedy the defects of speech before mentioned to some degree, and to prevent the inconveniences that follow from them, I imagine the observation of these following rules may be of use, till somebody better able shall judge it worth his while to think more maturely on this matter, and oblige the world with his thoughts on it.

First remedy: To use no word without an idea annexed to it. First, A man shall take care to use no word without a signification, no name without an idea for which he makes it stand. This rule will not seem altogether needless to any one who shall take the pains to recollect how often he has met with such words as instinct, sympathy, and antipathy, &c., in the discourse of others, so made use of as he might easily conclude that those that used them had no ideas in their minds to which they applied them, but spoke them only as sounds, which usually served instead of reasons on the like occasions. Not but that these words, and the like, have very proper significations in which they may be used; but there being no natural connexion between any words and any ideas, these, and any other, may be learned by rote, and pronounced or writ by men who have no ideas in their minds to which they have annexed them, and for which they make them stand; which is necessary they should, if men would speak intelligibly even to themselves alone.

9. Second remedy: To have distinct, determinate ideas annexed to words, especially in mixed modes. Secondly, It is not enough a man uses his words as signs of some ideas: those he annexes them to, if they be simple, must be clear and distinct; if complex, must be determinate, i.e. the precise collection of simple ideas settled in the mind, with that sound annexed to it, as the sign of that precise determined collection, and no other. This is very necessary in names of modes, and especially moral words; which, having no settled objects in nature, from whence their ideas are taken, as from their original, are apt to be very confused. Justice is a word in every man's mouth, but most commonly with a very undertermined, loose signification; which will always be so, unless a man has in his mind a distinct comprehension of the component parts that complex idea consists of: and if it be decompounded, must be able to resolve it still on, till he at last comes to the simple ideas that make it up: and unless this be done, a man makes an ill use of the word, let it be justice, for example, or any other. I do not say, a man needs stand to recollect, and make this analysis at large, every time the word justice comes in his way: but this at least is necessary, that he have so examined the signification of that name, and settled the idea of all its parts in his mind, that he can do it when he pleases. If any one who makes his complex idea of justice to be, such a treatment of the person or goods of another as is according to law, hath not a clear and distinct idea what law is, which makes a part of his complex idea of justice, it is plain his idea of justice itself will be confused and imperfect. This exactness will, perhaps, be judged very troublesome; and therefore most men will think they may be excused from settling the complex ideas of mixed modes so precisely in their minds. But yet I must say, till this be done, it must not be wondered, that they have a great deal of obscurity and confusion in their own minds, and a great deal of wrangling in their discourse with others.

10. And distinct and conformable ideas in words that stand for substances. In the names of substances, for a right use of them, something more is required than barely determined ideas. In these the names must also be conformable to things as they exist; but of this I shall have occasion to speak more at large by and by. This exactness is absolutely necessary in inquiries after philosophical knowledge, and in controversies about truth. And though it would be well, too, if it extended itself to common conversation and the ordinary affairs of life; yet I think that is scarce to be expected. Vulgar notions suit vulgar discourses: and both, though confused

enough, yet serve pretty well the market and the wake. Merchants and lovers, cooks and tailors, have words wherewithal to dispatch their ordinary affairs: and so, I think, might philosophers and disputants too, if they had a mind to understand, and to be clearly understood.

11. Third remedy: To apply words to such ideas as common use has annexed them to. Thirdly, it is not enough that men have ideas, determined ideas, for which they make these signs stand; but they must also take care to apply their words as near as may be to such ideas as common use has annexed them to. For words, especially of languages already framed, being no man's private possession, but the common measure of commerce and communication, it is not for any one at pleasure to change the stamp they are current in, nor alter the ideas they are affixed to; or at least, when there is a necessity to do so, he is bound to give notice of it. Men's intentions in speaking are, or at least should be, to be understood; which cannot be without frequent explanations, demands, and other the like incommodious interruptions, where men do not follow common use. Propriety of speech is that which gives our thoughts entrance into other men's minds with the greatest ease and advantage: and therefore deserves some part of our care and study, especially in the names of moral words. The proper signification and use of terms is best to be learned from those who in their writings and discourses appear to have had the clearest notions, and applied to them their terms with the exactest choice and fitness. This way of using a man's words, according to the propriety of the language, though it have not always the good fortune to be understood; yet most commonly leaves the blame of it on him who is so unskilful in the language he speaks, as not to understand it when made use of as it ought to be.

12. Fourth remedy: To declare the meaning in which we use them. Fourthly, But, because common use has not so visibly annexed any signification to words, as to make men know always certainly what they precisely stand for: and because men in the improvement of their knowledge, come to have ideas different from the vulgar and ordinary received ones, for which they must either make new words, (which men seldom venture to do, for fear of being though guilty of affectation or novelty), or else must use old ones in a new signification: therefore, after the observation of the foregoing rules, it is sometimes necessary, for the ascertaining the signification of words, to declare their meaning; where either common use has left it uncertain and loose, (as it has in most names of very complex ideas); or where the term, being very material in the discourse, and that upon which it chiefly turns, is liable to any doubtfulness or mistake.

13. And that in three ways. As the ideas men's words stand for are of different sorts, so the way of making known the ideas they stand for, when there is occasion, is also different. For though defining be thought the proper way to make known the proper signification of words; yet there are some words that will not be defined, as there are others whose precise meaning cannot be made known but by definition: and perhaps a third, which partake somewhat of both the other, as we shall see in the names of simple ideas, modes, and substances.

14. I. In simple ideas, either by synonymous terms, or by showing examples. First, when a man makes use of the name of any simple idea, which he perceives is not understood, or is in danger to be mistaken, he is obliged, by the laws of ingenuity and the end of speech, to declare his meaning, and make known what idea he makes it stand for. This, as has been shown, cannot be done by definition: and therefore, when a synonymous word fails to do it, there is but one of these ways left. First, Sometimes the naming the subject wherein that simple idea is to be found, will make its name to be understood by those who are acquainted with that subject, and know it by that name. So to make a countryman understand what feuillemorte colour signifies, it may suffice to tell him, it is the colour of withered leaves falling in autumn. Secondly, but the only sure way of making known the signification of the name of any simple idea, is by presenting to his senses that subject which may produce it in his mind, and make him actually have the idea that word stands for.

15. II. In mixed modes, by definition. Secondly, Mixed modes, especially those belonging to

morality, being most of them such combinations of ideas as the mind puts together of its own choice, and whereof there are not always standing patterns to be found existing, the signification of their names cannot be made known, as those of simple ideas, by any showing: but, in recompense thereof, may be perfectly and exactly defined. For they being combinations of several ideas that the mind of man has arbitrarily put together, without reference to any archetypes, men may, if they please, exactly know the ideas that go to each composition, and so both use these words in a certain and undoubted signification, and perfectly declare, when there is occasion, what they stand for. This, if well considered, would lay great blame on those who make not their discourses about moral things very clear and distinct. For since the precise signification of the names of mixed modes, or, which is all one, the real essence of each species is to be known, they being not of nature's, but man's making, it is a great negligence and perverseness to discourse of moral things with uncertainty and obscurity; which is more pardonable in treating of natural substances, where doubtful terms are hardly to be avoided, for a quite contrary reason, as we shall see by and by.

16. Morality capable of demonstration. Upon this ground it is that I am bold to think that morality is capable of demonstration, as well as mathematics: since the precise real essence of the things moral words stand for may be perfectly known, and so the congruity and incongruity of the things themselves be certainly discovered; in which consists perfect knowledge. Nor let any one object, that the names of substances are often to be made use of in morality, as well as those of modes, from which will arise obscurity. For, as to substances, when concerned in moral discourses, their divers natures are not so much inquired into as supposed: v.g. when we say that man is subject to law, we mean nothing by man but a corporeal rational creature: what the real essence or other qualities of that creature are in this case is no way considered. And, therefore, whether a child or changeling be a man, in a physical sense, may amongst the naturalists be as disputable as it will, it concerns not at all the moral man, as I may call him, which is this immovable, unchangeable idea, a corporeal rational being. For, were there a monkey, or any other creature, to be found that had the use of reason to such a degree, as to be able to understand general signs, and to deduce consequences about general ideas, he would no doubt be subject to law, and in that sense be a man, how much soever he differed in shape from others of that name. The names of substances, if they be used in them as they should, can no more disturb moral than they do mathematical discourses; where, if the mathematician speaks of a cube or globe of gold, or of any other body, he has his clear, settled idea, which varies not, though it may by mistake be applied to a particular body to which it belongs not.

17. Definitions can make moral discourses clear. This I have here mentioned, by the by, to show of what consequence it is for men, in their names of mixed modes, and consequently in all their moral discourses, to define their words when there is occasion: since thereby moral knowledge may be brought to so great clearness and certainty. And it must be great want of ingenuousness (to say no worse of it) to refuse to do it: since a definition is the only way whereby the precise meaning of moral words can be known; and yet a way whereby their meaning may be known certainly, and without leaving any room for any contest about it. And therefore the negligence or perverseness of mankind cannot be excused, if their discourses in morality be not much more clear than those in natural philosophy: since they are about ideas in the mind, which are none of them false or disproportionate; they having no external beings for the archetypes which they are referred to and must correspond with. It is far easier for men to frame in their minds an idea, which shall be the standard to which they will give the name justice; with which pattern so made, all actions that agree shall pass under that denomination, than, having seen Aristides, to frame an idea that shall in all things be exactly like him; who is as he is, let men make what idea they please of him. For the one, they need but know the combination of ideas that are put together in their own minds; for the other, they must inquire into the whole nature, and abstruse hidden constitution, and various qualities of a thing existing without them.

18. And is the only way in which the meaning of mixed modes can be made known. Another reason that makes the defining of mixed modes so necessary, especially of moral words, is what I mentioned a little before, viz. that it is the only way whereby the signification of the most of them can be known with certainty. For the ideas they stand for, being for the most part such whose component parts nowhere exist together, but scattered and mingled with others, it is the mind alone that collects them, and gives them the union of one idea: and it is only by words enumerating the several simple ideas which the mind has united, that we can make known to others what their names stand for; the assistance of the senses in this case not helping us, by the proposal of sensible objects, to show the ideas which our names of this kind stand for, as it does often in the names of sensible simple ideas, and also to some degree in those of substances.

19. III. In substances, both by showing and by defining. Thirdly, for the explaining the signification of the names of substances, as they stand for the ideas we have of their distinct species, both the forementioned ways, viz. of showing and defining, are requisite, in many cases, to be made use of. For, there being ordinarily in each sort some leading qualities, to which we suppose the other ideas which make up our complex idea of that species annexed, we forwardly give the specific name to that thing wherein that characteristical mark is found, which we take to be the most distinguishing idea of that species. These leading or characteristical (as I may call them) ideas, in the sorts of animals and vegetables, are (as has been before remarked, ch. vi. SS 29, and ch. ix. SS 15) mostly figure; and in inanimate bodies, colour; and in some, both together. Now,

20. Ideas of the leading qualities of substances are best got by showing. These leading sensible qualities are those which make the chief ingredients of our specific ideas, and consequently the most observable and invariable part in the definitions of our specific names, as attributed to sorts of substances coming under our knowledge. For though the sound man, in its own nature, be as apt to signify a complex idea made up of animality and rationality, united in the same subject, as to signify any other combination; yet, used as a mark to stand for a sort of creatures we count of our own kind, perhaps the outward shape is as necessary to be taken into our complex idea, signified by the word man, as any other we find in it: and therefore, why Plato's animal implume bipes latis unguibus should not be a good definition of the name man, standing for that sort of creatures, will not be easy to show: for it is the shape, as the leading quality, that seems more to determine that species, than a faculty of reasoning, which appears not at first, and in some never. And if this be not allowed to be so, I do not know how they can be excused from murder who kill monstrous births, (as we call them), because of an unordinary shape, without knowing whether they have a rational soul or no; which can be no more discerned in a well-formed than ill-shaped infant, as soon as born. And who is it has informed us that a rational soul can inhabit no tenement, unless it has just such a sort of frontispiece; or can join itself to, and inform no sort of body, but one that is just of such an outward structure?

21. And can hardly be made known otherwise. Now these leading qualities are best made known by showing, and can hardly be made known otherwise. For the shape of a horse or cassowary will be but rudely and imperfectly imprinted on the mind by words; the sight of the animals doth it a thousand times better. And the idea of the particular colour of gold is not to be got by any description of it, but only by the frequent exercise of the eyes about it; as is evident in those who are used to this metal, who will frequently distinguish true from counterfeit, pure from adulterate, by the sight, where others (who have as good eyes, but yet by use have not got the precise nice idea of that peculiar yellow) shall not perceive any difference. The like may be said of those other simple ideas, peculiar in their kind to any substance; for which precise ideas there are no peculiar names. The particular ringing sound there is in gold, distinct from the sound of other bodies, has no particular name annexed to it, no more than the particular yellow that belongs to that metal.

22. The Ideas of the powers of substances are best known by definition. But because many of

the simple ideas that make up our specific ideas of substances are powers which lie not obvious to our senses in the things as they ordinarily appear; therefore, in the signification of our names of substances, some part of the signification will be better made known by enumerating those simple ideas, than by showing the substance itself. For, he that to the yellow shining colour of gold, got by sight, shall, from my enumerating them, have the ideas of great ductility, fusibility, fixedness, and solubility in aqua regia, will have a perfecter idea of gold than he can have by seeing a piece of gold, and thereby imprinting in his mind only its obvious qualities. But if the formal constitution of this shining, heavy, ductile thing, (from whence all these its properties flow), lay open to our senses, as the formal constitution or essence of a triangle does, the signification of the word gold might as easily be ascertained as that of triangle.

23. A reflection on the knowledge of corporeal things possessed by spirits separate from bodies. Hence we may take notice, how much the foundation of all our knowledge of corporeal things lies in our senses. For how spirits, separate from bodies, (whose knowledge and ideas of these things are certainly much more perfect than ours), know them, we have no notion, no idea at all. The whole extent of our knowledge or imagination reaches not beyond our own ideas limited to our ways of perception. Though yet it be not to be doubted that spirits of a higher rank than those immersed in flesh may have as clear ideas of the radical constitution of substances as we have of a triangle, and so perceive how all their properties and operations flow from thence: but the manner how they come by that knowledge exceeds our conceptions.

24. IV Ideas of substances must be conformable to things. Fourthly, But, though definitions will serve to explain the names of substances as they stand for our ideas, yet they leave them not without great imperfection as they stand for things. For our names of substances being not put barely for our ideas, but being made use of ultimately to represent things, and so are put in their place, their signification must agree with the truth of things as well as with men's ideas. And therefore, in substances, we are not always to rest in the ordinary complex idea commonly received as the signification of that word, but must go a little further, and inquire into the nature and properties of the things themselves, and thereby perfect, as much as we can, our ideas of their distinct species; or else learn them from such as are used to that sort of things, and are experienced in them. For, since it is intended their names should stand for such collections of simple ideas as do really exist in things themselves, as well as for the complex idea in other men's minds, which in their ordinary acceptation they stand for, therefore, to define their names right, natural history is to be inquired into, and their properties are, with care and examination, to be found out. For it is not enough, for the avoiding inconveniences in discourse and arguings about natural bodies and substantial things, to have learned, from the propriety of the language, the common, but confused, or very imperfect, idea to which each word is applied, and to keep them to that idea in our use of them; but we must, by acquainting ourselves with the history of that sort of things, rectify and settle our complex idea belonging to each specific name; and in discourse with others, (if we find them mistake us), we ought to tell what the complex idea is that we make such a name stand for. This is the more necessary to be done by all those who search after knowledge and philosophical verity, in that children, being taught words, whilst they have but imperfect notions of things, apply them at random, and without much thinking, and seldom frame determined ideas to be signified by them. Which custom (it being easy, and serving well enough for the ordinary affairs of life and conversation) they are apt to continue when they are men: and so begin at the wrong end, learning words first and perfectly, but make the notions to which they apply those words afterwards very overtly. By this means it comes to pass, that men speaking the language of their country, i.e. according to grammar rules of that language, do yet speak very improperly of things themselves; and, by their arguing one with another, make but small progress in the discoveries of useful truths, and the knowledge of things, as they are to be found in themselves, and not in our imaginations; and it matters not much for the improvement of our

knowledge how they are called.

25. Not easy to be made so. It were therefore to be wished, That men versed in physical inquiries, and acquainted with the several sorts of natural bodies, would set down those simple ideas wherein they observe the individuals of each sort constantly to agree. This would remedy a great deal of that confusion which comes from several persons applying the same name to a collection of a smaller or greater number of sensible qualities, proportionably as they have been more or less acquainted with, or accurate in examining, the qualities of any sort of things which come under one denomination. But a dictionary of this sort, containing, as it were, a natural history, requires too many hands as well as too much time, cost, pains, and sagacity ever to be hoped for; and till that be done, we must content ourselves with such definitions of the names of substances as explain the sense men use them in. And it would be well, where there is occasion, if they would afford us so much. This yet is not usually done; but men talk to one another, and dispute in words, whose meaning is not agreed between them, out of a mistake that the significations of common words are certainly established, and the precise ideas they stand for perfectly known; and that it is a shame to be ignorant of them. Both which suppositions are false; no names of complex ideas having so settled determined significations, that they are constantly used for the same precise ideas. Nor is it a shame for a man not to have a certain knowledge of anything, but by the necessary ways of attaining it; and so it is no discredit not to know what precise idea any sound stands for in another man's mind, without he declare it to me by some other way than barely using that sound, there being no other way, without such a declaration, certainly to know it. Indeed the necessity of communication by language brings men to an agreement in the signification of common words, within some tolerable latitude, that may serve for ordinary conversation: and so a man cannot be supposed wholly ignorant of the ideas which are annexed to words by common use, in a language familiar to him. But common use being but a very uncertain rule, which reduces itself at last to the ideas of particular men, proves often but a very variable standard. But though such a Dictionary as I have above mentioned will require too much time, cost, and pains to be hoped for in this age; yet methinks it is not unreasonable to propose, that words standing for things which are known and distinguished by their outward shapes should be expressed by little draughts and prints made of them. A vocabulary made after this fashion would perhaps with more ease, and in less time, teach the true signification of many terms, especially in languages of remote countries or ages, and settle truer ideas in men's minds of several things, whereof we read the names in ancient authors, than all the large and laborious comments of learned critics. Naturalists, that treat of plants and animals, have found the benefit of this way: and he that has had occasion to consult them will have reason to confess that he has a clearer idea of apium or ibex, from a little print of that herb or beast, than he could have from a long definition of the names of either of them. And so no doubt he would have of strigil and sistrum, if, instead of currycomb and cymbal, (which are the English names dictionaries render them by,) he could see stamped in the margin small pictures of these instruments, as they were in use amongst the ancients. Toga, tunica, pallium, are words easily translated by gown, coat, and cloak; but we have thereby no more true ideas of the fashion of those habits amongst the Romans, than we have of the faces of the tailors who made them. Such things as these, which the eye distinguishes by their shapes, would be best let into the mind by draughts made of them, and more determine the signification of such words, than any other words set for them, or made use of to define them. But this is only by the bye.

26. V. Fifth remedy: To use the same word constantly in the same sense. Fifthly, If men will not be at the pains to declare the meaning of their words, and definitions of their terms are not to be had, yet this is the least that can be expected, that, in all discourses wherein one man pretends to instruct or convince another, he should use the same word constantly in the same sense. If this were done, (which nobody can refuse without great disingenuity,) many of the books extant might be spared; many of the controversies in dispute would be at an end; several of those great volumes, swollen with ambiguous words, now used in one sense, and by and by

in another, would shrink into a very narrow compass; and many of the philosophers, (to mention no other) as well as poets works, might be contained in a nutshell.

27. When not so used, the variation is to he explained. But after all, the provision of words is so scanty in respect to that infinite variety of thoughts, that men, wanting terms to suit their precise notions, will, notwithstanding their utmost caution, be forced often to use the same word in somewhat different senses. And though in the continuation of a discourse, or the pursuit of an argument, there can be hardly room to digress into a particular definition, as often as a man varies the signification of any term; yet the import of the discourse will, for the most part, if there be no designed fallacy, sufficiently lead candid and intelligent readers into the true meaning of it; but where there is not sufficient to guide the reader, there it concerns the writer to explain his meaning, and show in what sense he there uses that term.

BOOK IV.Of Knowledge and Probability

Chapter I.Of Knowledge in General

1. Our knowledge conversant about our ideas only. Since the mind, in all its thoughts and reasonings, hath no other immediate object but its own ideas, which it alone does or can contemplate, it is evident that our knowledge is only conversant about them.

2. Knowledge is the perception of the agreement or disagreement of two ideas. Knowledge then seems to me to be nothing but the perception of the connexion of and agreement, or disagreement and repugnancy of any of our ideas. In this alone it consists. Where this perception is, there is knowledge, and where it is not, there, though we may fancy, guess, or believe, yet we always come short of knowledge. For when we know that white is not black, what do we else but perceive, that these two ideas do not agree? When we possess ourselves with the utmost security of the demonstration, that the three angles of a triangle are equal to two right ones, what do we more but perceive, that equality to two right ones does necessarily agree to, and is inseparable from, the three angles of a triangle?

3. This agreement or disagreement may be any of four sorts. But to understand a little more distinctly wherein this agreement or disagreement consists, I think we may reduce it all to these four sorts: I. Identity, or diversity. II. Relation.
III. Co-existence, or necessary connexion. IV. Real existence.

4. Of identity, or diversity in ideas. First, As to the first sort of agreement or disagreement, viz. identity or diversity. It is the first act of the mind, when it has any sentiments or ideas at all, to perceive its ideas; and so far as it perceives them, to know each what it is, and thereby also to perceive their difference, and that one is not another. This is so absolutely necessary, that without it there could be no knowledge, no reasoning, no imagination, no distinct thoughts at all. By this the mind clearly and infallibly perceives each idea to agree with itself, and to be what it is; and all distinct ideas to disagree, i.e. the one not to be the other: and this it does without pains, labour, or deduction; but at first view, by its natural power of perception and distinction. And though men of art have reduced this into those general rules, What is, is, and It is impossible for the same thing to be and not to be, for ready application in all cases, wherein there may be occasion to reflect on it: yet it is certain that the first exercise of this faculty is about particular ideas. A man infallibly knows, as soon as ever he has them in his mind, that the ideas he calls white and round are the very ideas they are; and that they are not other ideas which he calls red or square. Nor can any maxim or proposition in the world make him know it clearer or surer than he did before, and without any such general rule. This then is the first agreement or disagreement which the mind perceives in its ideas; which it always

perceives at first sight: and if there ever happen any doubt about it, it will always be found to be about the names, and not the ideas themselves, whose identity and diversity will always be perceived, as soon and clearly as the ideas themselves are; nor can it possibly be otherwise.

5. Of abstract relations between ideas. Secondly, the next sort of agreement or disagreement the mind perceives in any of its ideas may, I think, be called relative, and is nothing but the perception of the relation between any two ideas, of what kind soever, whether substances, modes, or any other. For, since all distinct ideas must eternally be known not to be the same, and so be universally and constantly denied one of another, there could be no room for any positive knowledge at all, if we could not perceive any relation between our ideas, and find out the agreement or disagreement they have one with another, in several ways the mind takes of comparing them.

6. Of their necessary co-existence in substances. Thirdly, The third sort of agreement or disagreement to be found in our ideas, which the perception of the mind is employed about, is co-existence or non-co-existence in the same subject; and this belongs particularly to substances. Thus when we pronounce concerning gold, that it is fixed, our knowledge of this truth amounts to no more but this, that fixedness, or a power to remain in the fire unconsumed, is an idea that always accompanies and is joined with that particular sort of yellowness, weight, fusibility, malleableness, and solubility in aqua regia, which make our complex idea signified by the word gold,

7. Of real existence agreeing to any idea. Fourthly, The fourth and last sort is that of actual real existence agreeing to any idea.

Within these four sorts of agreement or disagreement is, I suppose, contained all the knowledge we have, or are capable of For all the inquiries we can make concerning any of our ideas, all that we know or can affirm concerning any of them, is, That it is, or is not, the same with some other; that it does or does not always coexist with some other idea in the same subject; that it has this or that relation with some other idea; or that it has a real existence without the mind. Thus, "blue is not yellow," is of identity. "Two triangles upon equal bases between two parallels are equal," is of relation. "Iron is susceptible of magnetical impressions," is of co-existence. "God is," is of real existence. Though identity and co-existence are truly nothing but relations, yet they are such peculiar ways of agreement or disagreement of our ideas, that they deserve well to be considered as distinct heads, and not under relation in general; since they are so different grounds of affirmation and negation, as will easily appear to any one, who will but reflect on what is said in several places of this Essay.

I should now proceed to examine the several degrees of our knowledge, but that it is necessary first, to consider the different acceptations of the word knowledge.

8. Knowledge is either actual or habitual. There are several ways wherein the mind is possessed of truth; each of which is called knowledge.

I. There is actual knowledge, which is the present view the mind has of the agreement or disagreement of any of its ideas, or of the relation they have one to another.

II. A man is said to know any proposition, which having been once laid before his thoughts, he evidently perceived the agreement or disagreement of the ideas whereof it consists; and so lodged it in his memory, that whenever that proposition comes again to be reflected on, he, without doubt or hesitation, embraces the right side, assents to, and is certain of the truth of it. This, I think, one may call habitual knowledge. And thus a man may be said to know all those truths which are lodged in his memory, by a foregoing clear and full perception, whereof the mind is assured past doubt as often as it has occasion to reflect on them. For our finite understandings being able to think clearly and distinctly but on one thing at once, if men had no knowledge of any more than what they actually thought on, they would all be very ignorant: and he that knew most, would know but one truth, that being all he was able to think on at one time.

9. Habitual knowledge is of two degrees. Of habitual knowledge there are, also, vulgarly

speaking, two degrees:

First, The one is of such truths laid up in the memory as, whenever they occur to the mind, it actually perceives the relation is between those ideas. And this is in all those truths whereof we have an intuitive knowledge; where the ideas themselves, by an immediate view, discover their agreement or disagreement one with another.

Secondly, The other is of such truths whereof the mind having been convinced, it retains the memory of the conviction, without the proofs. Thus, a man that remembers certainly that he once perceived the demonstration, that the three angles of a triangle are equal to two right ones, is certain that he knows it, because he cannot doubt the truth of it. In his adherence to a truth, where the demonstration by which it was at first known is forgot, though a man may be thought rather to believe his memory than really to know, and this way of entertaining a truth seemed formerly to me like something between opinion and knowledge; a sort of assurance which exceeds bare belief, for that relies on the testimony of another;— yet upon a due examination I find it comes not short of perfect certainty, and is in effect true knowledge. That which is apt to mislead our first thoughts into a mistake in this matter is, that the agreement or disagreement of the ideas in this case is not perceived, as it was at first, by an actual view of all the intermediate ideas whereby the agreement or disagreement of those in the proposition was at first perceived; but by other intermediate ideas, that show the agreement or disagreement of the ideas contained in the proposition whose certainty we remember. For example: in this proposition, that "the three angles of a triangle are equal to two right ones," one who has seen and clearly perceived the demonstration of this truth knows it to be true, when that demonstration is gone out of his mind; so that at present it is not actually in view, and possibly cannot be recollected: but he knows it in a different way from what he did before. The agreement of the two ideas joined in that proposition is perceived; but it is by the intervention of other ideas than those which at first produced that perception. He remembers, i.e. he knows (for remembrance is but the reviving of some past knowledge) that he was once certain of the truth of this proposition, that the three angles of a triangle are equal to two right ones. The immutability of the same relations between the same immutable things is now the idea that shows him, that if the three angles of a triangle were once equal to two right ones, they will always be equal to two right ones. And hence he comes to be certain, that what was once true in the case, is always true; what ideas once agreed will always agree; and consequently what he once knew to be true, he will always know to be true; as long as he can remember that he once knew it. Upon this ground it is, that particular demonstrations in mathematics afford general knowledge. If then the perception, that the same ideas will eternally have the same habitudes and relations, be not a sufficient ground of knowledge, there could be no knowledge of general propositions in mathematics; for no mathematical demonstration would be any other than particular: and when a man had demonstrated any proposition concerning one triangle or circle, his knowledge would not reach beyond that particular diagram. If he would extend it further, he must renew his demonstration in another instance, before he could know it to be true in another like triangle, and so on: by which means one could never come to the knowledge of any general propositions. Nobody, I think, can deny, that Mr. Newton certainly knows any proposition that he now at any time reads in his book to be true; though he has not in actual view that admirable chain of intermediate ideas whereby he at first discovered it to be true. Such a memory as that, able to retain such a train of particulars, may be well thought beyond the reach of human faculties, when the very discovery, perception, and laying together that wonderful connexion of ideas, is found to surpass most readers' comprehension. But yet it is evident the author himself knows the proposition to be true, remembering he once saw the connexion of those ideas; as certainly as he knows such a man wounded another, remembering that he saw him run him through. But because the memory is not always so clear as actual perception, and does in all men more or less decay in length of time, this, amongst other differences, is one which shows that demonstrative knowledge is much more imperfect than intuitive, as we shall see in the following chapter.

Chapter II.Of the Degrees of our Knowledge

1. Of the degrees, or differences in clearness, of our knowledge: 1. Intuitive. All our knowledge consisting, as I have said, in the view the mind has of its own ideas, which is the utmost light and greatest certainty we, with our faculties, and in our way of knowledge, are capable of, it may not be amiss to consider a little the degrees of its evidence. The different clearness of our knowledge seems to me to lie in the different way of perception the mind has of the agreement or disagreement of any of its ideas. For if we will reflect on our own ways of thinking, we will find, that sometimes the mind perceives the agreement or disagreement of two ideas immediately by themselves, without the intervention of any other: and this I think we may call intuitive knowledge. For in this the mind is at no pains of proving or examining, but perceives the truth as the eye doth light, only by being directed towards it. Thus the mind perceives that white is not black, that a circle is not a triangle, that three are more than two and equal to one and two. Such kinds of truths the mind perceives at the first sight of the ideas together, by bare intuition; without the intervention of any other idea: and this kind of knowledge is the clearest and most certain that human frailty is capable of. This part of knowledge is irresistible, and, like bright sunshine, forces itself immediately to be perceived, as soon as ever the mind turns its view that way; and leaves no room for hesitation, doubt, or examination, but the mind is presently filled with the clear light of it. It is on this intuition that depends all the certainty and evidence of all our knowledge; Which certainty every one finds to be so great, that he cannot imagine, and therefore not require a greater: for a man cannot conceive himself capable of a greater certainty than to know that any idea in his mind is such as he perceives it to be; and that two ideas, wherein he perceives a difference, are different and not precisely the same. He that demands a greater certainty than this, demands he knows not what, and shows only that he has a mind to be a sceptic, without being able to be so. Certainty depends so wholly on this intuition, that, in the next degree of knowledge which I call demonstrative, this intuition is necessary in all the connexions of the intermediate ideas, without which we cannot attain knowledge and certainty.

2. II. Demonstrative. The next degree of knowledge is, where the mind perceives the agreement or disagreement of any ideas, but not immediately. Though wherever the mind perceives the agreement or disagreement of any of its ideas, there be certain knowledge; yet it does not always happen, that the mind sees that agreement or disagreement, which there is between them, even where it is discoverable; and in that case remains in ignorance, and at most gets no further than a probable conjecture. The reason why the mind cannot always perceive presently the agreement or disagreement of two ideas, is, because those ideas, concerning whose agreement or disagreement the inquiry is made, cannot by the mind be so put together as to show it. In this case then, when the mind cannot so bring its ideas together as by their immediate comparison, and as it were juxta-position or application one to another, to perceive their agreement or disagreement, it is fain, by the intervention of other ideas (one or more, as it happens) to discover the agreement or disagreement which it searches; and this is that which we call reasoning. Thus, the mind being willing to know the agreement or disagreement in bigness between the three angles of a triangle and two right ones, cannot by an immediate view and comparing them do it: because the three angles of a triangle cannot be brought at once, and be compared with any other one, or two, angles; and so of this the mind has no immediate, no intuitive knowledge. In this case the mind is fain to find out some other angles, to which the three angles of a triangle have an equality; and, finding those equal to two right ones. comes to know their equality to two right ones.

3. Demonstration depends on clearly perceived proofs. Those intervening ideas, which serve to show the agreement of any two others, are called proofs; and where the agreement and

disagreement is by this means plainly and clearly perceived, it is called demonstration; it being shown to the understanding, and the mind made to see that it is so. A quickness in the mind to find out these intermediate ideas, (that shall discover the agreement or disagreement of any other,) and to apply them right, is, I suppose, that which is called sagacity.

4. As certain, but not so easy and ready as intuitive knowledge. This knowledge, by intervening proofs, though it be certain, yet the evidence of it is not altogether so clear and bright, nor the assent so ready, as in intuitive knowledge. For, though in demonstration the mind does at last perceive the agreement or disagreement of the ideas it considers; yet it is not without pains and attention: there must be more than one transient view to find it. A steady application and pursuit are required to this discovery: and there must be a progression by steps and degrees, before the mind can in this way arrive at certainty, and come to perceive the agreement or repugnancy between two ideas that need proofs and the use of reason to show it.

5. The demonstrated conclusion not without doubt, precedent to the demonstration. Another difference between intuitive and demonstrative knowledge is, that, though in the latter all doubt be removed when, by the intervention of the intermediate ideas, the agreement or disagreement is perceived, yet before the demonstration there was a doubt; which in intuitive knowledge cannot happen to the mind that has its faculty of perception left to a degree capable of distinct ideas; no more than it can be a doubt to the eye (that can distinctly see white and black), Whether this ink and this paper be all of a colour. If there be sight in the eyes, it will, at first glimpse, without hesitation, perceive the words printed on this paper different from the colour of the paper: and so if the mind have the faculty of distinct perception, it will perceive the agreement or disagreement of those ideas that produce intuitive knowledge. If the eyes have lost the faculty of seeing, or the mind of perceiving, we in vain inquire after the quickness of sight in one, or clearness of perception in the other.

6. Not so clear as intuitive knowledge. It is true, the perception produced by demonstration is also very clear; yet it is often with a great abatement of that evident lustre and full assurance that always accompany that which I call intuitive: like a face reflected by several mirrors one to another, where, as long as it retains the similitude and agreement with the object, it produces a knowledge; but it is still, in every successive reflection, with a lessening of that perfect clearness and distinctness which is in the first; till at last, after many removes, it has a great mixture of dimness, and is not at first sight so knowable, especially to weak eyes. Thus it is with knowledge made out by a long train of proof.

7. Each step in demonstrated knowledge must have intuitive evidence. Now, in every step reason makes in demonstrative knowledge, there is an intuitive knowledge of that agreement or disagreement it seeks with the next intermediate idea which it uses as a proof: for if it were not so, that yet would need a proof; since without the perception of such agreement or disagreement, there is no knowledge produced: if it be perceived by itself, it is intuitive knowledge: if it cannot be perceived by itself, there is need of some intervening idea, as a common measure, to show their agreement or disagreement. By which it is plain that every step in reasoning that produces knowledge, has intuitive certainty; which when the mind perceives, there is no more required but to remember it, to make the agreement or disagreement of the ideas concerning which we inquire visible and certain. So that to make anything a demonstration, it is necessary to perceive the immediate agreement of the intervening ideas, whereby the agreement or disagreement of the two ideas under examination (whereof the one is always the first, and the other the last in the account) is found. This intuitive perception of the agreement or disagreement of the intermediate ideas, in each step and progression of the demonstration, must also be carried exactly in the mind, and a man must be sure that no part is left out: which, because in long deductions, and the use of many proofs, the memory does not always so readily and exactly retain; therefore it comes to pass, that this is more imperfect than intuitive knowledge, and men embrace often falsehood for demonstrations.

8. Hence the mistake, ex praecognitis, et praeconcessis. The necessity of this intuitive

knowledge, in each step of scientifical or demonstrative reasoning, gave occasion, I imagine, to that mistaken axiom, That all reasoning was ex pracognitis et praeconcessis: which, how far it is a mistake, I shall have occasion to show more at large, when I come to consider propositions, and particularly those propositions which are called maxims, and to show that it is by a mistake that they are supposed to be the foundations of all our knowledge and reasonings.

9. Demonstration not limited to ideas of mathematical quantity. It has been generally taken for granted, that mathematics alone are capable of demonstrative certainty: but to have such an agreement or disagreement as may intuitively be perceived, being, as I imagine, not the privilege of the ideas of number, extension, and figure alone, it may possibly be the want of due method and application in us, and not of sufficient evidence in things, that demonstration has been thought to have so little to do in other parts of knowledge, and been scarce so much as aimed at by any but mathematicians. For whatever ideas we have wherein the mind can perceive the immediate agreement or disagreement that is between them, there the mind is capable of intuitive knowledge; and where it can perceive the agreement or disagreement of any two ideas, by an intuitive perception of the agreement or disagreement they have with any intermediate ideas, there the mind is capable of demonstration: which is not limited to ideas of extension, figure, number, and their modes.

10. Why it has been thought to be so limited. The reason why it has been generally sought for, and supposed to be only in those, I imagine has been, not only the general usefulness of those sciences: but because, in comparing their equality or excess, the modes of numbers have every the least difference very clear and perceivable: and though in extension every the least excess is not so perceptible, yet the mind has found out ways to examine, and discover demonstratively, the just equality of two angles, or extensions, or figures: and both these, i.e. numbers and figures, can be set down by visible and lasting marks, wherein the ideas under consideration are perfectly determined; which for the most part they are not, where they are marked only by names and words.

11. Modes of qualities not demonstrable like modes of quantity. But in other simple ideas, whose modes and differences are made and counted by degrees, and not quantity, we have not so nice and accurate a distinction of their differences as to perceive, or find ways to measure, their just equality, or the least differences. For those other simple ideas, being appearances of sensations produced in us, by the size, figure, number, and motion of minute corpuscles singly insensible; their different degrees also depend upon the variation of some or of all those causes: which, since it cannot be observed by us, in particles of matter whereof each is too subtile to be perceived, it is impossible for us to have any exact measures of the different degrees of these simple ideas. For, supposing the sensation or idea we name whiteness be produced in us by a certain number of globules, which, having a verticity about their own centres, strike upon the retina of the eye, with a certain degree of rotation, as well as progressive swiftness; it will hence easily follow, that the more the superficial parts of any body are so ordered as to reflect the greater number of globules of light, and to give them the proper rotation, which is fit to produce this sensation of white in us, the more white will that body appear, that from an equal space sends to the retina the greater number of such corpuscles, with that peculiar sort of motion. I do not say that the nature of light consists in very small round globules; nor of whiteness in such a texture of parts as gives a certain rotation to these globules when it reflects them: for I am not now treating physically of light or colours. But this I think I may say, that I cannot (and I would be glad any one would make intelligible that he did), conceive how bodies without us can any ways affect our senses, but by the immediate contact of the sensible bodies themselves, as in tasting and feeling, or the impulse of some sensible particles coming from them, as in seeing, hearing, and smelling; by the different impulse of which parts, caused by their different size, figure, and motion, the variety of sensations is produced in us.

12. Particles of light and simple ideas of colour. Whether then they be globules or no; or

whether they have a verticity about their own centres that produces the idea of whiteness in us; this is certain, that the more particles of light are reflected from a body, fitted to give them that peculiar motion which produces the sensation of whiteness in us; and possibly too, the quicker that peculiar motion is,— the whiter does the body appear from which the greatest number are reflected, as is evident in the same piece of paper put in the sunbeams, in the shade, and in a dark hole; in each of which it will produce in us the idea of whiteness in far different degrees.

13. The secondary qualities of things not discovered by demonstration. Not knowing, therefore, what number of particles, nor what motion of them, is fit to produce any precise degree of whiteness, we cannot demonstrate the certain equality of any two degrees of whiteness; because we have no certain standard to measure them by, nor means to distinguish every the least real difference, the only help we have being from our senses, which in this point fail us. But where the difference is so great as to produce in the mind clearly distinct ideas, whose differences can be perfectly retained, there these ideas or colours, as we see in different kinds, as blue and red, are as capable of demonstration as ideas of number and extension. What I have here said of whiteness and colours, I think holds true in all secondary qualities and their modes.

14. Sensitive knowledge of the particular existence of finite beings without us. These two, viz. intuition and demonstration, are the degrees of our knowledge; whatever comes short of one of these, with what assurance soever embraced, is but faith or opinion, but not knowledge, at least in all general truths. There is, indeed, another perception of the mind, employed about the particular existence of finite beings without us, which, going beyond bare probability, and yet not reaching perfectly to either of the foregoing degrees of certainty, passes under the name of knowledge. There can be nothing more certain than that the idea we receive from an external object is in our minds: this is intuitive knowledge. But whether there be anything more than barely that idea in our minds; whether we can thence certainly infer the existence of anything without us, which corresponds to that idea, is that whereof some men think there may be a question made; because men may have such ideas in their minds, when no such thing exists, no such object affects their senses. But yet here I think we are provided with an evidence that puts us past doubting. For I ask any one, Whether he be not invincibly conscious to himself of a different perception, when he looks on the sun by day, and thinks on it by night; when he actually tastes wormwood, or smells a rose, or only thinks on that savour or odour? We as plainly find the difference there is between any idea revived in our minds by our own memory, and actually coming into our minds by our senses, as we do between any two distinct ideas. If any one say, a dream may do the same thing, and all these ideas may be produced in us without any external objects; he may please to dream that I make him this answer:— 1. That it is no great matter, whether I remove his scruple or no: where all is but dream, reasoning and arguments are of no use, truth and knowledge nothing. 2. That I believe he will allow a very manifest difference between dreaming of being in the fire, and being actually in it. But yet if he be resolved to appear so sceptical as to maintain, that what I call being actually in the fire is nothing but a dream; and that we cannot thereby certainly know, that any such thing as fire actually exists without us: I answer, That we certainly finding that pleasure or pain follows upon the application of certain objects to us, whose existence we perceive, or dream that we perceive, by our senses; this certainty is as great as our happiness or misery, beyond which we have no concernment to know or to be. So that, I think, we may add to the two former sorts of knowledge this also, of the existence of particular external objects, by that perception and consciousness we have of the actual entrance of ideas from them, and allow these three degrees of knowledge, viz. intuitive, demonstrative, and sensitive: in each of which there are different degrees and ways of evidence and certainty.

15. Knowledge not always clear, where the ideas that enter into it are clear. But since our knowledge is founded on and employed about our ideas only, will it not follow from thence that it is conformable to our ideas; and that where our ideas are clear and distinct, or obscure and confused, our knowledge will be so too? To which I answer, No: for our knowledge

consisting in the perception of the agreement or disagreement of any two ideas, its clearness or obscurity consists in the clearness or obscurity of that perception, and not in the clearness or obscurity of the ideas themselves: v.g. a man that has as clear ideas of the angles of a triangle, and of equality to two right ones, as any mathematician in the world, may yet have but a very obscure perception of their agreement, and so have but a very obscure knowledge of it. But ideas which, by reason of their obscurity or otherwise, are confused, cannot produce any clear or distinct knowledge; because, as far as any ideas are confused, so far the mind cannot perceive clearly whether they agree or disagree. Or to express the same thing in a way less apt to be misunderstood: he that hath not determined ideas to the words he uses, cannot make propositions of them of whose truth he can be certain.

Chapter III.Of the Extent of Human Knowledge

1. Extent of our knowledge. Knowledge, as has been said, lying in the perception of the agreement or disagreement of any of our ideas, it follows from hence That,
It extends no further than we have ideas. First, we can have knowledge no further than we have ideas.
2. It extends no further than we can perceive their agreement or disagreement. Secondly, That we can have no knowledge further than we can have perception of that agreement or disagreement. Which perception being: 1. Either by intuition, or the immediate comparing any two ideas; or, 2. By reason, examining the agreement or disagreement of two ideas, by the intervention of some others; or, 3. By sensation, perceiving the existence of particular things: hence it also follows:
3. Intuitive knowledge extends itself not to all the relations of all our ideas. Thirdly, That we cannot have an intuitive knowledge that shall extend itself to all our ideas, and all that we would know about them; because we cannot examine and perceive all the relations they have one to another, by juxta-position, or an immediate comparison one with another. Thus, having the ideas of an obtuse and an acute angled triangle, both drawn from equal bases, and between parallels, I can, by intuitive knowledge, perceive the one not to be the other, but cannot that way know whether they be equal or no; because their agreement or disagreement in equality can never be perceived by an immediate comparing them: the difference of figure makes their parts incapable of an exact immediate application; and therefore there is need of some intervening qualities to measure them by, which is demonstration, or rational knowledge.
4. Nor does demonstrative knowledge. Fourthly, It follows, also, from what is above observed, that our rational knowledge cannot reach to the whole extent of our ideas: because between two different ideas we would examine, we cannot always find such mediums as we can connect one to another with an intuitive knowledge in all the parts of the deduction; and wherever that fails, we come short of knowledge and demonstration.
5. Sensitive knowledge narrower than either. Fifthly, Sensitive knowledge reaching no further than the existence of things actually present to our senses, is yet much narrower than either of the former.
6. Our knowledge, therefore, narrower than our ideas. Sixthly, From all which it is evident, that the extent of our knowledge comes not only short of the reality of things, but even of the extent of our own ideas. Though our knowledge be limited to our ideas, and cannot exceed them either in extent or perfection; and though these be very narrow bounds, in respect of the extent of All-being, and far short of what we may justly imagine to be in some even created understandings, not tied down to the dull and narrow information that is to be received from some few, and not very acute, ways of perception, such as are our senses; yet it would be well with us if our knowledge were but as large as our ideas, and there were not many doubts and inquiries concerning the ideas we have, whereof we are not, nor I believe ever shall be in this world resolved. Nevertheless I do not question but that human knowledge, under the present

circumstances of our beings and constitutions, may be carried much further than it has hitherto been, if men would sincerely, and with freedom of mind, employ all that industry and labour of thought, in improving the means of discovering truth, which they do for the colouring or support of falsehood, to maintain a system, interest, or party they are once engaged in. But yet after all, I think I may, without injury to human perfection, be confident, that our knowledge would never reach to all we might desire to know concerning those ideas we have; nor be able to surmount all the difficulties, and resolve all the questions that might arise concerning any of them. We have the ideas of a square, a circle, and equality; and yet, perhaps, shall never be able to find a circle equal to a square, and certainly know that it is so. We have the ideas of matter and thinking, but possibly shall never be able to know whether any mere material being thinks or no; it being impossible for us, by the contemplation of our own ideas, without revelation, to discover whether Omnipotency has not given to some systems of matter, fitly disposed, a power to perceive and think, or else joined and fixed to matter, so disposed, a thinking immaterial substance: it being, in respect of our notions, not much more remote from our comprehension to conceive that GOD can, if he pleases, superadd to matter a faculty of thinking, than that he should superadd to it another substance with a faculty of thinking; since we know not wherein thinking consists, nor to what sort of substances the Almighty has been pleased to give that power, which cannot be in any created being, but merely by the good pleasure and bounty of the Creator.

Whether Matter may not be made by God to think is more than man can know. For I see no contradiction in it, that the first Eternal thinking Being, or Omnipotent Spirit, should, if he pleased, give to certain systems of created senseless matter, put together as he thinks fit, some degrees of sense, perception, and thought: though, as I think I have proved, Bk. iv. ch. 10, SS 14, &c., it is no less than a contradiction to suppose matter (which is evidently in its own nature void of sense and thought) should be that Eternal first-thinking Being. What certainty of knowledge can any one have, that some perceptions, such as, v.g., pleasure and pain, should not be in some bodies themselves, after a certain manner modified and moved, as well as that they should be in an immaterial substance, upon the motion of the parts of body: Body, as far as we can conceive, being able only to strike and affect body, and motion, according to the utmost reach of our ideas, being able to produce nothing but motion; so that when we allow it to produce pleasure or pain, or the idea of a colour or sound, we are fain to quit our reason, go beyond our ideas, and attribute it wholly to the good pleasure of our Maker. For, since we must allow He has annexed effects to motion which we can no way conceive motion able to produce, what reason have we to conclude that He could not order them as well to be produced in a subject we cannot conceive capable of them, as well as in a subject we cannot conceive the motion of matter can any way operate upon? I say not this, that I would any way lessen the belief of the soul's immateriality: I am not here speaking of probability, but knowledge; and I think not only that it becomes the modesty of philosophy not to pronounce magisterially, where we want that evidence that can produce knowledge; but also, that it is of use to us to discern how far our knowledge does reach; for the state we are at present in, not being that of vision, we must in many things content ourselves with faith and probability: and in the present question, about the Immateriality of the Soul, if our faculties cannot arrive at demonstrative certainty, we need not think it strange. All the great ends of morality and religion are well enough secured, without philosophical proofs of the soul's immateriality; since it is evident, that he who made us at the beginning to subsist here, sensible intelligent beings, and for several years continued us in such a state, can and will restore us to the like state of sensibility in another world, and make us capable there to receive the retribution he has designed to men, according to their doings in this life. And therefore it is not of such mighty necessity to determine one way or the other, as some, over-zealous for or against the immateriality of the soul, have been forward to make the world believe. Who, either on the one side, indulging too much their thoughts immersed altogether in matter, can allow no existence to what is not material: or who, on the other side, finding not cogitation within the natural powers of matter, examined over and over again by the utmost intention of mind, have the confidence to conclude — That Omnipotency itself cannot give perception and thought to a substance which has the modification of solidity. He that considers how hardly sensation is, in our thoughts, reconcilable to extended matter; or existence to anything that has no extension at all, will confess that he is very far from certainly knowing what his soul is. It is a point which seems to me to be put out of the reach of our knowledge: and he who will give himself leave to consider freely, and look into the dark and intricate part of each hypothesis, will scarce find his reason able to determine him fixedly for or against the soul's materiality. Since, on which side soever he views it, either as an unextended substance, or as a thinking extended matter, the difficulty to conceive either will, whilst either alone is in his thoughts, still drive him to the contrary side. An unfair way which some men take with themselves: who, because of the inconceivableness of something they find in one, throw themselves violently into the contrary hypothesis, though altogether as unintelligible to an unbiassed understanding. This serves not only to show the weakness and the scantiness of our knowledge, but the insignificant triumph of such sort of arguments; which, drawn from our own views, may satisfy us that we can find no certainty on one side of the question: but do not at all thereby help us to truth by running into the opposite opinion; which, on examination, will be found clogged with equal difficulties. For what safety, what advantage to any one is it, for the avoiding the seeming absurdities, and to him unsurmountable rubs, he meets with in one opinion, to take refuge in the contrary, which is built on something altogether as inexplicable, and as far remote from his comprehension? It is past controversy, that we have in us something that thinks; our very doubts about what it is, confirm the certainty of its being, though we must content ourselves in the ignorance of what kind of being it is: and it is in vain to go about to be sceptical in this, as it is unreasonable in most other cases to be positive against the being of anything, because we cannot comprehend its nature. For I would fain know what substance exists, that has not something in it which manifestly baffles our understandings. Other spirits, who see and know the nature and inward constitution of things, how much must they exceed us in knowledge? To which, if we add larger comprehension, which enables them at one glance to see the connexion and agreement of very many ideas, and readily supplies to them the intermediate proofs, which we by single and slow steps, and long poring in the dark, hardly at last find out, and are often ready to forget one before we have hunted out another; we may guess at some part of the happiness of superior ranks of spirits, who have a quicker and more penetrating sight, as well as a larger field of knowledge.

But to return to the argument in hand: our knowledge, I say, is not only limited to the paucity and imperfections of the ideas we have, and which we employ it about, but even comes short of that too: but how far it reaches, let us now inquire.

7. How far our knowledge reaches. The affirmations or negations we make concerning the ideas we have, may, as I have before intimated in general, be reduced to these four sorts, viz. identity, co-existence, relation, and real existence. I shall examine how far our knowledge extends in each of these:

8. Our knowledge of identity and diversity in ideas extends as far as our ideas themselves. First, as to identity and diversity. In this way of agreement or disagreement of our ideas, our intuitive knowledge is as far extended as our ideas themselves: and there can be no idea in the mind, which it does not, presently, by an intuitive knowledge, perceive to be what it is, and to be different from any other.

9. Of their co-existence, extends only a very little way. Secondly, as to the second sort, which is the agreement or disagreement of our ideas in co-existence, in this our knowledge is very short; though in this consists the greatest and most material part of our knowledge concerning substances. For our ideas of the species of substances being, as I have showed, nothing but certain collections of simple ideas united in one subject, and so co-existing together; v.g. our idea of flame is a body hot, luminous, and moving upward; of gold, a body heavy to a certain degree, yellow, malleable, and fusible: for these, or some such complex ideas as these, in

men's minds, do these two names of the different substances, flame and gold, stand for. When we would know anything further concerning these, or any other sort of substances, what do we inquire, but what other qualities or powers these substances have or have not? Which is nothing else but to know what other simple ideas do, or do not co-exist with those that make up that complex idea?

10. Because the connexion between simple ideas in substances is for the most part unknown. This, how weighty and considerable a part soever of human science, is yet very narrow, and scarce any at all. The reason whereof is, that the simple ideas whereof our complex ideas of substances are made up are, for the most part, such as carry with them, in their own nature, no visible necessary connexion or inconsistency with any other simple ideas, whose co-existence with them we would inform ourselves about.

11. Especially of the secondary qualities of bodies. The ideas that our complex ones of substances are made up of, and about which our knowledge concerning substances is most employed, are those of their secondary qualities; which depending all (as has been shown) upon the primary qualities of their minute and insensible parts; or, if not upon them, upon something yet more remote from our comprehension; it is impossible we should know which have a necessary union or inconsistency one with another. For, not knowing the root they spring from, not knowing what size, figure, and texture of parts they are, on which depend, and from which result those qualities which make our complex idea of gold, it is impossible we should know what other qualities result from, or are incompatible with, the same constitution of the insensible parts of gold; and so consequently must always co-exist with that complex idea we have of it, or else are inconsistent with it.

12. Because necessary connexion between any secondary and the primary qualities is undiscoverable by us. Besides this ignorance of the primary qualities of the insensible parts of bodies, on which depend all their secondary qualities, there is yet another and more incurable part of ignorance, which sets us more remote from a certain knowledge of the co-existence or inco-existence (if I may so say) of different ideas in the same subject; and that is, that there is no discoverable connexion between any secondary quality and those primary qualities which it depends on.

13. We have no perfect knowledge of their primary qualities. That the size, figure, and motion of one body should cause a change in the size, figure, and motion of another body, is not beyond our conception; the separation of the parts of one body upon the intrusion of another; and the change from rest to motion upon impulse; these and the like seem to have some connexion one with another. And if we knew these primary qualities of bodies, we might have reason to hope we might be able to know a great deal more of these operations of them one upon another: but our minds not being able to discover any connexion betwixt these primary qualities of bodies and the sensations that are produced in us by them, we can never be able to establish certain and undoubted rules of the consequence or co-existence of any secondary qualities, though we could discover the size, figure, or motion of those invisible parts which immediately produce them. We are so far from knowing what figure, size, or motion of parts produce a yellow colour, a sweet taste, or a sharp sound, that we can by no means conceive how any size, figure, or motion of any particles, can possibly produce in us the idea of any colour, taste, or sound whatsoever: there is no conceivable connexion between the one and the other.

14. And seek in vain for certain and universal knowledge of unperceived qualities in substances. In vain, therefore, shall we endeavour to discover by our ideas (the only true way of certain and universal knowledge) what other ideas are to be found constantly joined with that of our complex idea of any substance: since we neither know the real constitution of the minute parts on which their qualities do depend; nor, did we know them, could we discover any necessary connexion between them and any of the secondary qualities: which is necessary to be done before we can certainly know their necessary co-existence. So, that, let our complex idea of any species of substances be what it will, we can hardly, from the simple

ideas contained in it, certainly determine the necessary co-existence of any other quality whatsoever. Our knowledge in all these inquiries reaches very little further than our experience. Indeed some few of the primary qualities have a necessary dependence and visible connexion one with another, as figure necessarily supposes extension; receiving or communicating motion by impulse, supposes solidity. But though these, and perhaps some others of our ideas have: yet there are so few of them that have a visible connexion one with another, that we can by intuition or demonstration discover the co-existence of very few of the qualities that are to be found united in substances: and we are left only to the assistance of our senses to make known to us what qualities they contain. For of all the qualities that are co-existent in any subject, without this dependence and evident connexion of their ideas one with another, we cannot know certainly any two to co-exist, any further than experience, by our senses, informs us. Thus, though we see the yellow colour, and, upon trial, find the weight, malleableness, fusibility, and fixedness that are united in a piece of gold, yet; because no one of these ideas has any evident dependence or necessary connexion with the other, we cannot certainly know that where any four of these are, the fifth will be there also, how highly probable soever it may be; because the highest probability amounts not to certainty, without which there can be no true knowledge. For this co-existence can be no further known than it is perceived; and it cannot be perceived but either in particular subjects, by the observation of our senses, or, in general, by the necessary connexion of the ideas themselves.

15. Of repugnancy to co-exist, our knowledge is larger. As to the incompatibility or repugnancy to coexistence, we may know that any subject may have of each sort of primary qualities but one particular at once: v.g. each particular extension, figure, number of parts, motion, excludes all other of each kind. The like also is certain of all sensible ideas peculiar to each sense; for whatever of each kind is present in any subject, excludes all other of that sort: v.g. no one subject can have two smells or two colours at the same time. To this, perhaps will be said, Has not an opal, or the infusion of lignum nephriticum, two colours at the same time? To which I answer, that these bodies, to eyes differently placed, may at the same time afford different colours: but I take liberty also to say, to eyes differently placed, it is different parts of the object that reflect the particles of light: and therefore it is not the same part of the object, and so not the very same subject, which at the same time appears both yellow and azure. For, it is as impossible that the very same particle of any body should at the same time differently modify or reflect the rays of light, as that it should have two different figures and textures at the same time.

16. Our knowledge of the co-existence of powers in bodies extends but a very little way. But as to the powers of substances to change the sensible qualities of other bodies, which make a great part of our inquiries about them, and is no inconsiderable branch of our knowledge; I doubt as to these, whether our knowledge reaches much further than our experience; or whether we can come to the discovery of most of these powers, and be certain that they are in any subject, by the connexion with any of those ideas which to us make its essence. Because the active and passive powers of bodies, and their ways of operating, consisting in a texture and motion of parts which we cannot by any means come to discover; it is but in very few cases we can be able to perceive their dependence on, or repugnance to, any of those ideas which make our complex one of that sort of things. I have here instanced in the corpuscularian hypothesis, as that which is thought to go furthest in an intelligible explication of those qualities of bodies; and I fear the weakness of human understanding is scarce able to substitute another, which will afford us a fuller and clearer discovery of the necessary connexion and coexistence of the powers which are to be observed united in several sorts of them. This at least is certain, that, whichever hypothesis be clearest and truest, (for of that it is not my business to determine,) our knowledge concerning corporeal substances will be very little advanced by any of them, till we are made to see what qualities and powers of bodies have a necessary connexion or repugnancy one with another; which in the present state of philosophy I think we know but to a very small degree: and I doubt whether, with those faculties we have,

we shall ever be able to carry our general knowledge (I say not particular experience) in this part much further. Experience is that which in this part we must depend on. And it were to be wished that it were more improved. We find the advantages some men's generous pains have this way brought to the stock of natural knowledge. And if others, especially the philosophers by fire, who pretend to it, had been so wary in their observations, and sincere in their reports as those who call themselves philosophers ought to have been, our acquaintance with the bodies here about us, and our insight into their powers and operations had been yet much greater.

17. Of the powers that co-exist in spirits yet narrower. If we are at a loss in respect of the powers and operations of bodies, I think it is easy to conclude we are much more in the dark in reference to spirits; whereof we naturally have no ideas but what we draw from that of our own, by reflecting on the operations of our own souls within us, as far as they can come within our observation. But how inconsiderable a rank the spirits that inhabit our bodies hold amongst those various and possibly innumerable kinds of nobler beings; and how far short they come of the endowments and perfections of cherubim and seraphim, and infinite sorts of spirits above us, is what by a transient hint in another place I have offered to my reader's consideration.

18. Of relations between abstracted ideas it is not easy to say how far our knowledge extends. Thirdly, As to the third sort of our knowledge, viz. the agreement or disagreement of any of our ideas in any other relation: this, as it is the largest field of our knowledge, so it is hard to determine how far it may extend: because the advances that are made in this part of knowledge, depending on our sagacity in finding intermediate ideas, that may show the relations and habitudes of ideas whose co-existence is not considered, it is a hard matter to tell when we are at an end of such discoveries; and when reason has all the helps it is capable of, for the finding of proofs or examining the agreement or disagreement of remote ideas. They that are ignorant of Algebra cannot imagine the wonders in this kind are to be done by it: and what further improvements and helps advantageous to other parts of knowledge the sagacious mind of man may yet find out, it is not easy to determine. This at least I believe, that the ideas of quantity are not those alone that are capable of demonstration and knowledge; and that other, and perhaps more useful, parts of contemplation, would afford us certainty, if vices, passions, and domineering interest did not oppose or menace such endeavours.

Morality capable of demonstration. The idea of a supreme Being, infinite in power, goodness, and wisdom, whose workmanship we are, and on whom we depend; and the idea of ourselves, as understanding, rational creatures, being such as are clear in us, would, I suppose, if duly considered and pursued, afford such foundations of our duty and rules of action as might place morality amongst the sciences capable of demonstration: wherein I doubt not but from self-evident propositions, by necessary consequences, as incontestible as those in mathematics, the measures of right and wrong might be made out, to any one that will apply himself with the same indifferency and attention to the one as he does to the other of these sciences. The relation of other modes may certainly be perceived, as well as those of number and extension: and I cannot see why they should not also be capable of demonstration, if due methods were thought on to examine or pursue their agreement or disagreement. "Where there is no property there is no injustice," is a proposition as certain as any demonstration in Euclid: for the idea of property being a right to anything, and the idea to which the name "injustice" is given being the invasion or violation of that right, it is evident that these ideas, being thus established, and these names annexed to them, I can as certainly know this proposition to be true, as that a triangle has three angles equal to two right ones. Again: "No government allows absolute liberty." The idea of government being the establishment of society upon certain rules or laws which require conformity to them; and the idea of absolute liberty being for any one to do whatever he pleases; I am as capable of being certain of the truth of this proposition as of any in the mathematics.

19. Two things have made moral ideas to be thought incapable of demonstration: their unfitness for sensible representation, and their complexedness. That which in this respect has

given the advantage to the ideas of quantity, and made them thought more capable of certainty and demonstration, is,

First, That they can be set down and represented by sensible marks, which have a greater and nearer correspondence with them than any words or sounds whatsoever. Diagrams drawn on paper are copies of the ideas in the mind, and not liable to the uncertainty that words carry in their signification. An angle, circle, or square, drawn in lines, lies open to the view, and cannot be mistaken: it remains unchangeable, and may at leisure be considered and examined, and the demonstration be revised, and all the parts of it may be gone over more than once, without any danger of the least change in the ideas. This cannot be thus done in moral ideas: we have no sensible marks that resemble them, whereby we can set them down; we have nothing but words to express them by; which, though when written they remain the same, yet the ideas they stand for may change in the same man; and it is very seldom that they are not different in different persons.

Secondly, Another thing that makes the greater difficulty in ethics is, That moral ideas are commonly more complex than those of the figures ordinarily considered in mathematics. From whence these two inconveniences follow:— First, that their names are of more uncertain signification, the precise collection of simple ideas they stand for not being so easily agreed on; and so the sign that is used for them in communication always, and in thinking often, does not steadily carry with it the same idea. Upon which the same disorder, confusion, and error follow, as would if a man, going to demonstrate something of an heptagon, should, in the diagram he took to do it, leave out one of the angles, or by oversight make the figure with one angle more than the name ordinarily imported, or he intended it should when at first he thought of his demonstration. This often happens, and is hardly avoidable in very complex moral ideas, where the same name being retained, one angle, i.e. one simple idea, is left out, or put in the complex one (still called by the same name) more at one time than another.

Secondly, From the complexedness of these moral ideas there follows another inconvenience, viz. that the mind cannot easily retain those precise combinations so exactly and perfectly as is necessary in the examination of the habitudes and correspondences, agreements or disagreements, of several of them one with another; especially where it is to be judged of by long deductions, and the intervention of several other complex ideas to show the agreement or disagreement of two remote ones.

The great help against this which mathematicians find in diagrams and figures, which remain unalterable in their draughts, is very apparent, and the memory would often have great difficulty otherwise to retain them so exactly, whilst the mind went over the parts of them step by step to examine their several correspondences. And though in casting up a long sum either in addition, multiplication, or division, every part be only a progression of the mind taking a view of its own ideas, and considering their agreement or disagreement, and the resolution of the question be nothing but the result of the whole, made up of such particulars, whereof the mind has a clear perception: yet, without setting down the several parts by marks, whose precise significations are known, and by marks that last, and remain in view when the memory had let them go, it would be almost impossible to carry so many different ideas in the mind, without confounding or letting slip some parts of the reckoning, and thereby making all our reasonings about it useless. In which case the cyphers or marks help not the mind at all to perceive the agreement of any two or more numbers, their equalities or proportions; that the mind has only by intuition of its own ideas of the numbers themselves. But the numerical characters are helps to the memory, to record and retain the several ideas about which the demonstration is made, whereby a man may know how far his intuitive knowledge in surveying several of the particulars has proceeded; that so he may without confusion go on to what is yet unknown; and at last have in one view before him the result of all his perceptions and reasonings.

20. Remedies of our difficulties in dealing demonstratively with moral ideas. One part of these disadvantages in moral ideas which has made them be thought not capable of demonstration,

may in a good measure be remedied by definitions, setting down that collection of simple ideas, which every term shall stand for: and then using the terms steadily and constantly for that precise collection. And what methods algebra, or something of that kind, may hereafter suggest, to remove the other difficulties, it is not easy to foretell. Confident I am, that, if men would in the same method, and with the same indifferency, search after moral as they do mathematical truths, they would find them have a stronger connexion one with another, and a more necessary consequence from our clear and distinct ideas, and to come nearer perfect demonstration than is commonly imagined. But much of this is not to be expected, whilst the desire of esteem, riches, or power makes men espouse the well-endowed opinions in fashion, and then seek arguments either to make good their beauty, or varnish over and cover their deformity. Nothing being so beautiful to the eye as truth is to the mind; nothing so deformed and irreconcilable to the understanding as a lie. For though many a man can with satisfaction enough own a no very handsome wife to in his bosom; yet who is bold enough openly to avow that he has espoused a falsehood, and received into his breast so ugly a thing as a lie? Whilst the parties of men cram their tenets down all men's throats whom they can get into their power, without permitting them to examine their truth or falsehood; and will not let truth have fair play in the world, nor men the liberty to search after it: what improvements can be expected of this kind? What greater light can be hoped for in the moral sciences? The subject part of mankind in most places might, instead thereof, with Egyptian bondage, expect Egyptian darkness, were not the candle of the Lord set up by himself in men's minds, which it is impossible for the breath or power of man wholly to extinguish.

21. Of the three real existences of which we have certain knowledge. Fourthly, As to the fourth sort of our knowledge, viz. of the real actual existence of things, we have an intuitive knowledge of our own existence, and a demonstrative knowledge of the existence of a God: of the existence of anything else, we have no other but a sensitive knowledge; which extends not beyond the objects present to our senses.

22. Our ignorance great. Our knowledge being so narrow, as I have shown, it will perhaps give us some light into the present state of our minds if we look a little into the dark side, and take a view of our ignorance; which, being infinitely larger than our knowledge, may serve much to the quieting of disputes, and improvement of useful knowledge; if, discovering how far we have clear and distinct ideas, we confine our thoughts within the contemplation of those things that are within the reach of our understandings, and launch not out into that abyss of darkness, (where we have not eyes to see, nor faculties to perceive anything), out of a presumption that nothing is beyond our comprehension. But to be satisfied of the folly of such a conceit, we need not go far. He that knows anything, knows this, in the first place, that he need not seek long for instances of his ignorance. The meanest and most obvious things that come in our way have dark sides, that the quickest sight cannot penetrate into. The clearest and most enlarged understandings of thinking men find themselves puzzled and at a loss in every particle of matter. We shall the less wonder to find it so, when we consider the causes of our ignorance; which, from what has been said, I suppose will be found to be these three:—
Its causes. First, Want of ideas.
Secondly, Want of a discoverable connexion between the ideas we have.
Thirdly, Want of tracing and examining our ideas.

23. One cause of our ignorance want of ideas. First, There are some things, and those not a few, that we are ignorant of, for want of ideas.
I. Want of simple ideas that other creatures in other parts of the universe may have. First, all the simple ideas we have are confined (as I have shown) to those we receive from corporeal objects by sensation, and from the operations of our own minds as the objects of reflection. But how much these few and narrow inlets are disproportionate to the vast whole extent of all beings, will not be hard to persuade those who are not so foolish as to think their span the measure of all things. What other simple ideas it is possible the creatures in other parts of the universe may have, by the assistance of senses and faculties more or perfecter than we have, or

different from ours, it is not for us to determine. But to say or think there are no such, because we conceive nothing of them, is no better an argument than if a blind man should be positive in it, that there was no such thing as sight and colours, because he had no manner of idea of any such thing, nor could by any means frame to himself any notions about seeing. The ignorance and darkness that is in us no more hinders nor confines the knowledge that is in others, than the blindness of a mole is an argument against the quicksightedness of an eagle. He that will consider the infinite power, wisdom, and goodness of the Creator of all things will find reason to think it was not all laid out upon so inconsiderable, mean, and impotent a creature as he will find man to be; who in all probability is one of the lowest of all intellectual beings. What faculties, therefore, other species of creatures have to penetrate into the nature and inmost constitutions of things; what ideas they may receive of them far different from ours, we know not. This we know and certainly find, that we want several other views of them besides those we have, to make discoveries of them more perfect. And we may be convinced that the ideas we can attain to by our faculties are very disproportionate to things themselves, when a positive, clear, distinct one of substance itself, which is the foundation of all the rest, is concealed from us. But want of ideas of this kind, being a part as well as cause of our ignorance, cannot be described. Only this I think I may confidently say of it, That the intellectual and sensible world are in this perfectly alike: that that part which we see of either of them holds no proportion with what we see not; and whatsoever we can reach with our eyes or our thoughts of either of them is but a point, almost nothing in comparison of the rest.

24. Want of simple ideas that men are capable of having, but have not, because of their remoteness. Secondly, Another great cause of ignorance is the want of ideas we are capable of. As the want of ideas which our faculties are not able to give us shuts us wholly from those views of things which it is reasonable to think other beings, perfecter than we, have, of which we know nothing; so the want of ideas I now speak of keeps us in ignorance of things we conceive capable of being known to us. Bulk, figure, and motion we have ideas of. But though we are not without ideas of these primary qualities of bodies in general, yet not knowing what is the particular bulk, figure, and motion, of the greatest part of the bodies of the universe, we are ignorant of the several powers, efficacies, and ways of operation, whereby the effects which we daily see are produced. These are hid from us, in some things by being too remote, and in others by being too minute. When we consider the vast distance of the known and visible parts of the world, and the reasons we have to think that what lies within our ken is but a small part of the universe, we shall then discover a huge abyss of ignorance. What are the particular fabrics of the great masses of matter which make up the whole stupendous frame of corporeal beings; how far they are extended; what is their motion, and how continued or communicated; and what influence they have one upon another, are contemplations that at first glimpse our thoughts lose themselves in. If we narrow our contemplations, and confine our thoughts to this little canton — I mean this system of our sun, and the grosser masses of matter that visibly move about it, What several sorts of vegetables, animals, and intellectual corporeal beings, infinitely different from those of our little spot of earth, may there probably be in the other planets, to the knowledge of which, even of their outward figures and parts, we can no way attain whilst we are confined to this earth; there being no natural means, either by sensation or reflection, to convey their certain ideas into our minds? They are out of the reach of those inlets of all our knowledge: and what sorts of furniture and inhabitants those mansions contain in them we cannot so much as guess, much less have clear and distinct ideas of them.

25. Because of their minuteness. If a great, nay, far the greatest part of the several ranks of bodies in the universe escape our notice by their remoteness, there are others that are no less concealed from us by their minuteness. These insensible corpuscles, being the active parts of matter, and the great instruments of nature, on which depend not only all their secondary qualities, but also most of their natural operations, our want of precise distinct ideas of their primary qualities keeps us in an incurable ignorance of what we desire to know about them. I doubt not but if we could discover the figure, size, texture, and motion of the minute

constituent parts of any two bodies, we should know without trial several of their operations one upon another; as we do now the properties of a square or a triangle. Did we know the mechanical affections of the particles of rhubarb, hemlock, opium, and a man, as a watchmaker does those of a watch, whereby it performs its operations; and of a file, which by rubbing on them will alter the figure of any of the wheels; we should be able to tell beforehand that rhubarb will purge, hemlock kill, and opium make a man sleep: as well as a watchmaker can, that a little piece of paper laid on the balance will keep the watch from going till it be removed; or that, some small part of it being rubbed by a file, the machine would quite lose its motion, and the watch go no more. The dissolving of silver in aqua fortis, and gold in aqua regia, and not vice versa, would be then perhaps no more difficult to know than it is to a smith to understand why the turning of one key will open a lock, and not the turning of another. But whilst we are destitute of senses acute enough to discover the minute particles of bodies, and to give us ideas of their mechanical affections, we must be content to be ignorant of their properties and ways of operation; nor can we be assured about them any further than some few trials we make are able to reach. But whether they will succeed again another time, we cannot be certain. This hinders our certain knowledge of universal truths concerning natural bodies: and our reason carries us herein very little beyond particular matter of fact.

26. Hence no science of bodies within our reach. And therefore I am apt to doubt that, how far soever human industry may advance useful and experimental philosophy in physical things, scientifical will still be out of our reach: because we want perfect and adequate ideas of those very bodies which are nearest to us, and most under our command. Those which we have ranked into classes under names, and we think ourselves best acquainted with, we have but very imperfect and incomplete ideas of. Distinct ideas of the several sorts of bodies that fall under the examination of our senses perhaps we may have: but adequate ideas, I suspect, we have not of any one amongst them. And though the former of these will serve us for common use and discourse, yet whilst we want the latter, we are not capable of scientifical knowledge; nor shall ever be able to discover general, instructive, unquestionable truths concerning them. Certainty and demonstration are things we must not, in these matters, pretend to. By the colour, figure, taste, and smell, and other sensible qualities, we have as clear and distinct ideas of sage and hemlock, as we have of a circle and a triangle: but having no ideas of the particular primary qualities of the minute parts of either of these plants, nor of other bodies which we would apply them to, we cannot tell what effects they will produce; nor when we see those effects can we so much as guess, much less know, their manner of production. Thus, having no ideas of the particular mechanical affections of the minute parts of bodies that are within our view and reach, we are ignorant of their constitutions, powers, and operations: and of bodies more remote we are yet more ignorant, not knowing so much as their very outward shapes, or the sensible and grosser parts of their constitutions.

27. Much less a science of unembodied spirits. This at first will show us how disproportionate our knowledge is to the whole extent even of material beings; to which if we add the consideration of that infinite number of spirits that may be, and probably are, which are yet more remote from our knowledge, whereof we have no cognizance, nor can frame to ourselves any distinct ideas of their several ranks and sorts, we shall find this cause of ignorance conceal from us, in an impenetrable obscurity, almost the whole intellectual world; a greater certainty, and more beautiful world than the material. For, bating some very few, and those, if I may so call them, superficial ideas of spirit, which by reflection we get of our own, and from thence the best we can collect of the Father of all spirits, the eternal independent Author of them, and us, and all things, we have no certain information, so much as of the existence of other spirits, but by revelation. Angels of all sorts are naturally beyond our discovery; and all those intelligences, whereof it is likely there are more orders than of corporeal substances, are things whereof our natural faculties give us no certain account at all. That there are minds and thinking beings in other men as well as himself, every man has a reason, from their words and actions, to be satisfied: and the knowledge of his own mind cannot suffer a man that considers,

to be ignorant that there is a God. But that there are degrees of spiritual beings between us and the great God, who is there, that, by his own search and ability, can come to know? Much less have we distinct ideas of their different natures, conditions, states, powers, and several constitutions wherein they agree or differ from one another and from us. And, therefore, in what concerns their different species and properties we are in absolute ignorance.

28. Another cause, want of a discoverable connexion between ideas we have. Secondly, What a small part of the substantial beings that are in the universe the want of ideas leaves open to our knowledge, we have seen. In the next place, another cause of ignorance, of no less moment, is a want of a discoverable connexion between those ideas we have. For wherever we want that, we are utterly incapable of universal and certain knowledge; and are, in the former case, left only to observation and experiment: which, how narrow and confined it is, how far from general knowledge we need not be told. I shall give some few instances of this cause of our ignorance, and so leave it. It is evident that the bulk, figure, and motion of several bodies about us produce in us several sensations, as of colours, sounds, tastes, smells, pleasure, and pain, &c. These mechanical affections of bodies having no affinity at all with those ideas they produce in us, (there being no conceivable connexion between any impulse of any sort of body and any perception of a colour or smell which we find in our minds,) we can have no distinct knowledge of such operations beyond our experience; and can reason no otherwise about them, than as effects produced by the appointment of an infinitely Wise Agent, which perfectly surpass our comprehensions. As the ideas of sensible secondary qualities which we have in our minds, can by us be no way deduced from bodily causes, nor any correspondence or connexion be found between them and those primary qualities which (experience shows us) produce them in us; so, on the other side, the operation of our minds upon our bodies is as inconceivable. How any thought should produce a motion in body is as remote from the nature of our ideas, as how any body should produce any thought in the mind. That it is so, if experience did not convince us, the consideration of the things themselves would never be able in the least to discover to us. These, and the like, though they have a constant and regular connexion in the ordinary course of things; yet that connexion being not discoverable in the ideas themselves, which appearing to have no necessary dependence one on another, we can attribute their connexion to nothing else but the arbitrary determination of that All-wise Agent who has made them to be, and to operate as they do, in a way wholly above our weak understandings to conceive.

29. Instances. In some of our ideas there are certain relations, habitudes, and connexions, so visibly included in the nature of the ideas themselves, that we cannot conceive them separable from them by any power whatsoever. And in these only we are capable of certain and universal knowledge. Thus the idea of a right-lined triangle necessarily carries with it an equality of its angles to two right ones. Nor can we conceive this relation, this connexion of these two ideas, to be possibly mutable, or to depend on any arbitrary power, which of choice made it thus, or could make it otherwise. But the coherence and continuity of the parts of matter; the production of sensation in us of colours and sounds, &c., by impulse and motion; nay, the original rules and communication of motion being such, wherein we can discover no natural connexion with any ideas we have, we cannot but ascribe them to the arbitrary will and good pleasure of the Wise Architect. I need not, I think, here mention the resurrection of the dead, the future state of this globe of earth, and such other things, which are by every one acknowledged to depend wholly on the determination of a free agent. The things that, as far as our observation reaches, we constantly find to proceed regularly, we may conclude do act by a law set them; but yet by a law that we know not: whereby, though causes work steadily, and effects constantly flow from them, yet their connexions and dependencies being not discoverable in our ideas, we can have but an experimental knowledge of them. From all which it is easy to perceive what a darkness we are involved in, how little it is of Being, and the things that are, that we are capable to know. And therefore we shall do no injury to our knowledge, when we modestly think with ourselves, that we are so far from being able to

comprehend the whole nature of the universe and all the things contained in it, that we are not capable of a philosophical knowledge of the bodies that are about us, and make a part of us: concerning their secondary qualities, powers, and operations, we can have no universal certainty. Several effects come every day within the notice of our senses, of which we have so far sensitive knowledge: but the causes, manner, and certainty of their production, for the two foregoing reasons, we must be content to be very ignorant of. In these we can go no further than particular experience informs us matter of fact, and by analogy to guess what effects the like bodies are, upon other trials, like to produce. But as to a perfect science of natural bodies, (not to mention spiritual beings,) we are, I think, so far from being capable of any such thing, that I conclude it lost labour to seek after it.

30. A third cause, want of tracing our ideas. Thirdly, Where we have adequate ideas, and where there is a certain and discoverable connexion between them, yet we are often ignorant, for want of tracing those ideas which we have or may have; and for want of finding out those intermediate ideas, which may show us what habitude of agreement or disagreement they have one with another. And thus many are ignorant of mathematical truths, not out of any imperfection of their faculties, or uncertainty in the things themselves, but for want of application in acquiring, examining, and by due ways comparing those ideas. That which has most contributed to hinder the due tracing of our ideas, and finding out their relations, and agreements or disagreements, one with another, has been, I suppose, the ill use of words. It is impossible that men should ever truly seek or certainly discover the agreement or disagreement of ideas themselves, whilst their thoughts flutter about, or stick only in sounds of doubtful and uncertain significations. Mathematicians abstracting their thoughts from names, and accustoming themselves to set before their minds the ideas themselves that they would consider, and not sounds instead of them, have avoided thereby a great part of that perplexity, puddering, and confusion, which has so much hindered men's progress in other parts of knowledge. For whilst they stick in words of undetermined and uncertain signification, they are unable to distinguish true from false, certain from probable, consistent from inconsistent, in their own opinions. This having been the fate or misfortune of a great part of men of letters, the increase brought into the stock of real knowledge has been very little, in proportion to the schools, disputes, and writings, the world has been filled with; whilst students, being lost in the great wood of words, knew not whereabouts they were, how far their discoveries were advanced, or what was wanting in their own, or the general stock of knowledge. Had men, in the discoveries of the material, done as they have in those of the intellectual world, involved all in the obscurity of uncertain and doubtful ways of talking, volumes writ of navigation and voyages, theories and stories of zones and tides, multiplied and disputed; nay, ships built, and fleets sent out, would never have taught us the way beyond the line; and the Antipodes would be still as much unknown, as when it was declared heresy to hold there were any. But having spoken sufficiently of words, and the ill or careless use that is commonly made of them, I shall not say anything more of it here.

31. Extent of human knowledge in respect to its universality. Hitherto we have examined the extent of our knowledge, in respect of the several sorts of beings that are. There is another extent of it, in respect of universality, which will also deserve to be considered; and in this regard, our knowledge follows the nature of our ideas. If the ideas are abstract, whose agreement or disagreement we perceive, our knowledge is universal. For what is known of such general ideas, will be true of every particular thing in whom that essence, i.e. that abstract idea, is to be found: and what is once known of such ideas, will be perpetually and for ever true. So that as to all general knowledge we must search and find it only in our minds; and it is only the examining of our own ideas that furnisheth us with that. Truths belonging to essences of things (that is, to abstract ideas) are eternal; and are to be found out by the contemplation only of those essences: as the existence of things is to be known only from experience. But having more to say of this in the chapters where I shall speak of general and real knowledge, this may here suffice as to the universality of our knowledge in general.

Chapter IV.Of the Reality of Knowledge

1. Objection. "Knowledge placed in our ideas may be all unreal or chimerical." I doubt not but my reader, by this time, may be apt to think that I have been all this while only building a castle in the air; and be ready to say to me:

"To what purpose all this stir? Knowledge, say you, is only the perception of the agreement or disagreement of our own ideas: but who knows what those ideas may be? Is there anything so extravagant as the imaginations of men's brains? Where is the head that has no chimeras in it? Or if there be a sober and a wise man, what difference will there be, by your rules, between his knowledge and that of the most extravagant fancy in the world? They both have their ideas, and perceive their agreement and disagreement one with another. If there be any difference between them, the advantage will be on the warm-headed man's side, as having the more ideas, and the more lively. And so, by your rules, he will be the more knowing. If it be true, that all knowledge lies only in the perception of the agreement or disagreement of our own ideas, the visions of an enthusiast and the reasonings of a sober man will be equally certain. It is no matter how things are: so a man observe but the agreement of his own imaginations, and talk conformably, it is all truth, all certainty. Such castles in the air will be as strongholds of truth, as the demonstrations of Euclid. That an harpy is not a centaur is by this way as certain knowledge, and as much a truth, as that a square is not a circle."

"But of what use is all this fine knowledge of men's own imaginations, to a man that inquires after the reality of things? It matters not what men's fancies are, it is the knowledge of things that is only to be prized: it is this alone gives a value to our reasonings, and preference to one man's knowledge over another's, that it is of things as they really are, and not of dreams and fancies."

2. Answer: "Not so, where ideas agree with things." To which I answer, That if our knowledge of our ideas terminate in them, and reach no further, where there is something further intended, our most serious thoughts will be of little more use than the reveries of a crazy brain; and the truths built thereon of no more weight than the discourses of a man who sees things clearly in a dream, and with great assurance utters them. But I hope, before I have done, to make it evident, that this way of certainty, by the knowledge of our own ideas, goes a little further than bare imagination: and I believe it will appear that all the certainty of general truths a man has lies in nothing else.

3. But what shall be the criterion of this agreement? It is evident the mind knows not things immediately, but only by the intervention of the ideas it has of them. Our knowledge, therefore is real only so far as there is a conformity between our ideas and the reality of things. But what shall be here the criterion? How shall the mind, when it perceives nothing but its own ideas, know that they agree with things themselves? This, though it seems not to want difficulty, yet, I think, there be two sorts of ideas that we may be assured agree with things.

4. As all simple ideas are really conformed to things. First, The first are simple ideas, which since the mind, as has been shown, can by no means make to itself, must necessarily be the product of things operating on the mind, in a natural way, and producing therein those perceptions which by the Wisdom and Will of our Maker they are ordained and adapted to. From whence it follows, that simple ideas are not fictions of our fancies, but the natural and regular productions of things without us, really operating upon us; and so carry with them all the conformity which is intended; or which our state requires: for they represent to us things under those appearances which they are fitted to produce in us: whereby we are enabled to distinguish the sorts of particular substances, to discern the states they are in, and so to take them for our necessities, and apply them to our uses. Thus the idea of whiteness, or bitterness, as it is in the mind, exactly answering that power which is in any body to produce it there, has

all the real conformity it can or ought to have, with things without us. And this conformity between our simple ideas and the existence of things, is sufficient for real knowledge.

5. All complex ideas, except ideas of substances, are their own archetypes. Secondly, All our complex ideas, except those of substances, being archetypes of the mind's own making, not intended to be the copies of anything, nor referred to the existence of anything, as to their originals, cannot want any conformity necessary to real knowledge. For that which is not designed to represent anything but itself, can never be capable of a wrong representation, nor mislead us from the true apprehension of anything, by its dislikeness to it: and such, excepting those of substances, are all our complex ideas. Which, as I have shown in another place, are combinations of ideas, which the mind, by its free choice, puts together, without considering any connexion they have in nature. And hence it is, that in all these sorts the ideas themselves are considered as the archetypes, and things no otherwise regarded, but as they are conformable to them. So that we cannot but be infallibly certain, that all the knowledge we attain concerning these ideas is real, and reaches things themselves. Because in all our thoughts, reasonings, and discourses of this kind, we intend things no further than as they are conformable to our ideas. So that in these we cannot miss of a certain and undoubted reality.

6. Hence the reality of mathematical knowledge. I doubt not but it will be easily granted, that the knowledge we have of mathematical truths is not only certain, but real knowledge; and not the bare empty vision of vain, insignificant chimeras of the brain: and yet, if we will consider, we shall find that it is only of our own ideas. The mathematician considers the truth and properties belonging to a rectangle or circle only as they are in idea in his own mind. For it is possible he never found either of them existing mathematically, i.e. precisely true, in his life. But yet the knowledge he has of any truths or properties belonging to a circle, or any other mathematical figure, are nevertheless true and certain, even of real things existing: because real things are no further concerned, nor intended to be meant by any such propositions, than as things really agree to those archetypes in his mind. Is it true of the idea of a triangle, that its three angles are equal to two right ones? It is true also of a triangle, wherever it really exists. Whatever other figure exists, that it is not exactly answerable to that idea of a triangle in his mind, is not at all concerned in that proposition. And therefore it is certain all his knowledge concerning such ideas is real knowledge: because, intending things no further than they agree with those his ideas, he is sure what he knows concerning those figures, when they have barely an ideal existence in his mind, will hold true of them also when they have a real existence in matter: his consideration being barely of those figures, which are the same wherever or however they exist.

7. And of moral. And hence it follows that moral knowledge is as capable of real certainty as mathematics. For certainty being but the perception of the agreement or disagreement of our ideas, and demonstration nothing but the perception of such agreement, by the intervention of other ideas or mediums; our moral ideas, as well as mathematical, being archetypes themselves, and so adequate and complete ideas; all the agreement or disagreement which we shall find in them will produce real knowledge, as well as in mathematical figures.

8. Existence not required to make abstract knowledge real. For the attaining of knowledge and certainty, it is requisite that we have determined ideas: and, to make our knowledge real, it is requisite that the ideas answer their archetypes. Nor let it be wondered, that I place the certainty of our knowledge in the consideration of our ideas, with so little care and regard (as it may seem) to the real existence of things: since most of those discourses which take up the thoughts and engage the disputes of those who pretend to make it their business to inquire after truth and certainty, will, I presume, upon examination, be found to be general propositions, and notions in which existence is not at all concerned. All the discourses of the mathematicians about the squaring of a circle, conic sections, or any other part of mathematics, concern not the existence of any of those figures: but their demonstrations, which depend on their ideas, are the same, whether there be any square or circle existing in the world or no. In the same manner, the truth and certainty of moral discourses abstracts from the

lives of men, and the existence of those virtues in the world whereof they treat: nor are Tully's Offices less true, because there is nobody in the world that exactly practises his rules, and lives up to that pattern of a virtuous man which he has given us, and which existed nowhere when he writ but in idea. If it be true in speculation, i.e. in idea, that murder deserves death, it will also be true in reality of any action that exists conformable to that idea of murder. As for other actions, the truth of that proposition concerns them not. And thus it is of all other species of things, which have no other essences but those ideas which are in the minds of men.

9. Nor will it be less true or certain, because moral ideas are of our own making and naming. But it will here be said, that if moral knowledge be placed in the contemplation of our own moral ideas, and those, as other modes, be of our own making, What strange notions will there be of justice and temperance? What confusion of virtues and vice, if every one may make what ideas of them he pleases? No confusion or disorder in the things themselves, nor the reasonings about them; no more than (in mathematics) there would be a disturbance in the demonstration, or a change in the properties of figures, and their relations one to another, if a man should make a triangle with four corners, or a trapezium with four right angles: that is, in plain English, change the names of the figures, and call that by one name, which mathematicians call ordinarily by another. For, let a man make to himself the idea of a figure with three angles, whereof one is a right one, and call it, if he please, equilaterum or trapezium, or anything else; the properties of, and demonstrations about that idea will be the same as if he called it a rectangular triangle. I confess the change of the name, by the impropriety of speech, will at first disturb him who knows not what idea it stands for: but as soon as the figure is drawn, the consequences and demonstrations are plain and clear. Just the same is it in moral knowledge: let a man have the idea of taking from others, without their consent, what their honest industry has possessed them of, and call this justice if he please. He that takes the name here without the idea put to it will be mistaken, by joining another idea of his own to that name: but strip the idea of that name, or take it such as it is in the speaker's mind, and the same things will agree to it, as if you called it injustice. Indeed, wrong names in moral discourses breed usually more disorder, because they are not so easily rectified as in mathematics, where the figure, once drawn and seen, makes the name useless and of no force. For what need of a sign, when the thing signified is present and in view? But in moral names, that cannot be so easily and shortly done, because of the many decompositions that go to the making up the complex ideas of those modes. But yet for all this, the miscalling of any of those ideas, contrary to the usual signification of the words of that language, hinders not but that we may have certain and demonstrative knowledge of their several agreements and disagreements, if we will carefully, as in mathematics, keep to the same precise ideas, and trace them in their several relations one to another, without being led away by their names. If we but separate the idea under consideration from the sign that stands for it, our knowledge goes equally on in the discovery of real truth and certainty, whatever sounds we make use of.

10. Misnaming disturbs not the certainty of the knowledge. One thing more we are to take notice of, That where God or any other law-maker, hath defined any moral names, there they have made the essence of that species to which that name belongs; and there it is not safe to apply or use them otherwise: but in other cases it is bare impropriety of speech to apply them contrary to the common usage of the country. But yet even this too disturbs not the certainty of that knowledge, which is still to be had by a due contemplation and comparing of those even nicknamed ideas.

11. Our complex ideas of substances have their archetypes without us; and here knowledge comes short. Thirdly, There is another sort of complex ideas, which, being referred to archetypes without us, may differ from them, and so our knowledge about them may come short of being real. Such are our ideas of substances, which, consisting of a collection of simple ideas, supposed taken from the works of nature, may yet vary from them; by having more or different ideas united in them than are to be found united in the things themselves. From whence it comes to pass, that they may, and often do, fail of being exactly conformable

to things themselves.

12. So far as our complex ideas agree with those archetypes without us, so far our knowledge concerning substances is real. I say, then, that to have ideas of substances which, by being conformable to things, may afford us real knowledge, it is not enough, as in modes, to put together such ideas as have no inconsistence, though they did never before so exist: v.g. the ideas of sacrilege or perjury, &c., were as real and true ideas before, as after the existence of any such fact. But our ideas of substances, being supposed copies, and referred to archetypes without us, must still be taken from something that does or has existed: they must not consist of ideas put together at the pleasure of our thoughts, without any real pattern they were taken from, though we can perceive no inconsistence in such a combination. The reason whereof is, because we, knowing not what real constitution it is of substances whereon our simple ideas depend, and which really is the cause of the strict union of some of them one with another, and the exclusion of others there are very few of them that we can be sure are or are not inconsistent in nature, any further than experience and sensible observation reach. Herein, therefore, is founded the reality of our knowledge concerning substances — That all our complex ideas of them must be such, and such only, as are made up of such simple ones as have been discovered to co-exist in nature. And our ideas being thus true, though not perhaps very exact copies, are yet the subjects of real (as far as we have any) knowledge of them. Which (as has been already shown) will not be found to reach very far: but so far as it does, it will still be real knowledge. Whatever ideas we have, the agreement we find they have with others will still be knowledge. If those ideas be abstract, it will be general knowledge. But to make it real concerning substances, the ideas must be taken from the real existence of things. Whatever simple ideas have been found to co-exist in any substance, these we may with confidence join together again, and so make abstract ideas of substances. For whatever have once had an union in nature, may be united again.

13. In our inquiries about substances, we must consider ideas, and not confine our thoughts to names or species supposed set out by names. This, if we rightly consider, and confine not our thoughts and abstract ideas to names, as if there were, or could be no other sorts of things than what known names had already determined, and, as it were, set out, we should think of things with greater freedom and less confusion than perhaps we do. It would possibly be thought a bold paradox, if not a very dangerous falsehood, if I should say that some changelings, who have lived forty years together, without any appearance of reason, are something between a man and a beast: which prejudice is founded upon nothing else but a false supposition, that these two names, man and beast, stand for distinct species so set out by real essences, that there can come no other species between them: whereas if we will abstract from those names, and the supposition of such specific essences made by nature, wherein all things of the same denominations did exactly and equally partake; if we would not fancy that there were a certain number of these essences, wherein all things, as in moulds, were cast and formed; we should find that the idea of the shape, motion, and life of a man without reason, is as much a distinct idea, and makes as much a distinct sort of things from man and beast, as the idea of the shape of an ass with reason would be different from either that of man or beast, and be a species of an animal between, or distinct from both.

14. Objection against a changeling being something between a man and beast, answered. Here everybody will be ready to ask, If changelings may be supposed something between man and beast, pray what are they? I answer, changelings; which is as good a word to signify something different from the signification of man or beast, as the names man and beast are to have significations different one from the other. This, well considered, would resolve this matter, and show my meaning without any more ado. But I am not so unacquainted with the zeal of some men, which enables them to spin consequences, and to see religion threatened, whenever any one ventures to quit their forms of speaking, as not to foresee what names such a proposition as this is like to be charged with: and without doubt it will be asked, If changelings are something between man and beast, what will become of them in the other

world? To which I answer, I. It concerns me not to know or inquire. To their own master they stand or fall. It will make their state neither better nor worse, whether we determine anything of it or no. They are in the hands of a faithful Creator and a bountiful Father, who disposes not of his creatures according to our narrow thoughts or opinions, nor distinguishes them according to names and species of our contrivance. And we that know so little of this present world we are in, may, I think, content ourselves without being peremptory in defining the different states which creatures shall come into when they go off this stage. It may suffice us, that He hath made known to all those who are capable of instruction, discoursing, and reasoning, that they shall come to an account, and receive according to what they have done in this body.

15. What will become of changelings in a future state? But, Secondly, I answer, The force of these men's question (viz. Will you deprive changelings of a future state?) is founded on one of these two suppositions, which are both false. The first is, That all things that have the outward shape and appearance of a man must necessarily be designed to an immortal future being after this life: or, secondly, That whatever is of human birth must be so. Take away these imaginations, and such questions will be groundless and ridiculous. I desire then those who think there is no more but an accidental difference between themselves and changelings, the essence in both being exactly the same, to consider, whether they can imagine immortality annexed to any outward shape of the body; the very proposing it is, I suppose, enough to make them disown it. No one yet, that ever I heard of, how much soever immersed in matter, allowed that excellency to any figure of the gross sensible outward parts, as to affirm eternal life due to it, or a necessary consequence of it; or that any mass of matter should, after its dissolution here, be again restored hereafter to an everlasting state of sense, perception, and knowledge, only because it was moulded into this or that figure, and had such a particular frame of its visible parts. Such an opinion as this, placing immortality in a certain superficial figure, turns out of doors all consideration of soul or spirit; upon whose account alone some corporeal beings have hitherto been concluded immortal, and others not. This is to attribute more to the outside than inside of things; and to place the excellency of a man more in the external shape of his body, than internal perfections of his soul: which is but little better than to annex the great and inestimable advantage of immortality and life everlasting, which he has above other material beings, to annex it, I say, to the cut of his beard, or the fashion of his coat. For this or that outward mark of our bodies no more carries with it the hope of an eternal duration, than the fashion of a man's suit gives him reasonable grounds to imagine it will never wear out, or that it will make him immortal. It will perhaps be said, that nobody thinks that the shape makes anything immortal, but it is the shape is the sign of a rational soul within, which is immortal. I wonder who made it the sign of any such thing: for barely saying it, will not make it so. It would require some proofs to persuade one of it. No figure that I know speaks any such language. For it may as rationally be concluded, that the dead body of a man, wherein there is to be found no more appearance or action of life than there is in a statue, has yet nevertheless a living soul in it, because of its shape; as that there is a rational soul in a changeling, because he has the outside of a rational creature, when his actions carry far less marks of reason with them, in the whole course of his life, than what are to be found in many a beast.

16. Monsters. But it is the issue of rational parents, and must therefore be concluded to have a rational soul. I know not by what logic you must so conclude. I am sure this is a conclusion that men nowhere allow of. For if they did, they would not make bold, as everywhere they do, to destroy ill-formed and mis-shaped productions. Ay, but these are monsters. Let them be so: what will your drivelling, unintelligent, intractable changeling be? Shall a defect in the body make a monster; a defect in the mind (the far more noble, and, in the common phrase, the far more essential part) not? Shall the want of a nose, or a neck, make a monster, and put such issue out of the rank of men; the want of reason and understanding, not? This is to bring all back again to what was exploded just now: this is to place all in the shape, and to take the

measure of a man only by his outside. To show that according to the ordinary way of reasoning in this matter, people do lay the whole stress on the figure, and resolve the whole essence of the species of man (as they make it) into the outward shape, how unreasonable soever it be, and how much soever they disown it, we need but trace their thoughts and practice a little further, and then it will plainly appear. The well-shaped changeling is a man, has a rational soul, though it appear not: this is past doubt, say you: make the ears a little longer, and more pointed, and the nose a little flatter than ordinary, and then you begin to boggle: make the face yet narrower, flatter, and longer, and then you are at a stand: add still more and more of the likeness of a brute to it, and let the head be perfectly that of some other animal, then presently it is a monster; and it is demonstration with you that it hath no rational soul, and must be destroyed. Where now (I ask) shall be the just measure; which the utmost bounds of that shape, that carries with it a rational soul? For, since there have been human foetuses produced, half beast and half man; and others three parts one, and one part the other; and so it is possible they may be in all the variety of approaches to the one or the other shape, and may have several degrees of mixture of the likeness of a man, or a brute;— I would gladly know what are those precise lineaments, which, according to this hypothesis, are or are not capable of a rational soul to be joined to them. What sort of outside is the certain sign that there is or is not such an inhabitant within? For till that be done, we talk at random of man: and shall always, I fear, do so, as long as we give ourselves up to certain sounds, and the imaginations of settled and fixed species in nature, we know not what. But, after all, I desire it may be considered, that those who think they have answered the difficulty, by telling us, that a mis-shaped foetus is a monster, run into the same fault they are arguing against; by constituting a species between man and beast. For what else, I pray, is their monster in the case, (if the word monster signifies anything at all,) but something neither man nor beast, but partaking somewhat of either? And just so is the changeling before mentioned. So necessary is it to quit the common notion of species and essences, if we will truly look into the nature of things, and examine them by what our faculties can discover in them as they exist, and not by groundless fancies that have been taken up about them.

17. Words and species. I have mentioned this here, because I think we cannot be too cautious that words and species, in the ordinary notions which we have been used to of them, impose not on us. For I am apt to think therein lies one great obstacle to our clear and distinct knowledge, especially in reference to substances: and from thence has risen a great part of the difficulties about truth and certainty. Would we accustom ourselves to separate our contemplations and reasonings from words, we might in a great measure remedy this inconvenience within our own thoughts: but yet it would still disturb us in our discourse with others, as long as we retained the opinion, that species and their essences were anything else but our abstract ideas (such as they are) with names annexed to them, to be the signs of them.

18. Recapitulation. Wherever we perceive the agreement or disagreement of any of our ideas, there is certain knowledge: and wherever we are sure those ideas agree with the reality of things, there is certain real knowledge. Of which agreement of our ideas with the reality of things, having here given the marks, I think, I have shown wherein it is that certainty, real certainty, consists. Which, whatever it was to others, was, I confess, to me heretofore, one of those desiderata which I found great want of.

Chapter V.Of Truth in General

1. What truth is. What is truth? was an inquiry many ages since; and it being that which all mankind either do, or pretend to search after, it cannot but be worth our while carefully to examine wherein it consists, and so acquaint ourselves with the nature of it, as to observe how the mind distinguishes it from falsehood.

2. A right joining or separating of signs, i.e. either ideas or words. Truth, then, seems to me, in

the proper import of the word, to signify nothing but the joining or separating of Signs, as the Things signified by them do agree or disagree one with another. The joining or separating of signs here meant, is what by another name we call proposition. So that truth properly belongs only to propositions: whereof there are two sorts, viz. mental and verbal; as there are two sorts of signs commonly made use of, viz. ideas and words.

3. Which make mental or verbal propositions. To form a clear notion of truth, it is very necessary to consider truth of thought, and truth of words, distinctly one from another: but yet it is very difficult to treat of them asunder. Because it is unavoidable, in treating of mental propositions, to make use of words: and then the instances given of mental propositions cease immediately to be barely mental, and become verbal. For a mental proposition being nothing but a bare consideration of the ideas, as they are in our minds, stripped of names, they lose the nature of purely mental propositions as soon as they are put into words.

4. Mental propositions are very hard to he treated of. And that which makes it yet harder to treat of mental and verbal propositions separately is, that most men, if not all, in their thinking and reasonings within themselves, make use of words instead of ideas; at least when the subject of their meditation contains in it complex ideas. Which is a great evidence of the imperfection and uncertainty of our ideas of that kind, and may, if attentively made use of, serve for a mark to show us what are those things we have clear and perfect established ideas of, and what not. For if we will curiously observe the way our mind takes in thinking and reasoning, we shall find, I suppose, that when we make any propositions within our own thoughts about white or black, sweet or bitter, a triangle or a circle, we can and often do frame in our minds the ideas themselves, without reflecting on the names. But when we would consider, or make propositions about the more complex ideas, as of a man, vitriol, fortitude, glory, we usually put the name for the idea: because the ideas these names stand for, being for the most part imperfect, confused, and undetermined, we reflect on the names themselves, because they are more clear, certain, and distinct, and readier occur to our thoughts than the pure ideas: and so we make use of these words instead of the ideas themselves, even when we would meditate and reason within ourselves, and make tacit mental propositions. In substances, as has been already noticed, this is occasioned by the imperfections of our ideas: we making the name stand for the real essence, of which we have no idea at all. In modes, it is occasioned by the great number of simple ideas that go to the making them up. For many of them being compounded, the name occurs much easier than the complex idea itself, which requires time and attention to be recollected, and exactly represented to the mind, even in those men who have formerly been at the pains to do it; and is utterly impossible to be done by those who, though they have ready in their memory the greatest part of the common words of that language, yet perhaps never troubled themselves in all their lives to consider what precise ideas the most of them stood for. Some confused or obscure notions have served their turns; and many who talk very much of religion and conscience, of church and faith, of power and right, of obstructions and humours, melancholy and choler, would perhaps have little left in their thoughts and meditations if one should desire them to think only of the things themselves and lay by those words with which they so often confound others, and not seldom themselves also.

5. Mental and verbal propositions contrasted. But to return to the consideration of truth: we must, I say, observe two sorts of propositions that we are capable of making:—

First, mental, wherein the ideas in our understandings are without the use of words put together, or separated, by the mind perceiving or judging of their agreement or disagreement.

Secondly, Verbal propositions, which are words, the signs of our ideas, put together or separated in affirmative or negative sentences. By which way of affirming or denying, these signs, made by sounds, are, as it were, put together or separated one from another. So that proposition consists in joining or separating signs; and truth consists in the putting together or separating those signs, according as the things which they stand for agree or disagree.

6. When mental propositions contain real truth, and when verbal. Every one's experience will

satisfy him, that the mind, either by perceiving, or supposing, the agreement or disagreement of any of its ideas, does tacitly within itself put them into a kind of proposition affirmative or negative; which I have endeavoured to express by the terms putting together and separating. But this action of the mind, which is so familiar to every thinking and reasoning man, is easier to be conceived by reflecting on what passes in us when we affirm or deny, than to be explained by words. When a man has in his head the idea of two lines, viz. the side and diagonal of a square, whereof the diagonal is an inch long, he may have the idea also of the division of that line into a certain number of equal parts: v.g. into five, ten, a hundred, a thousand, or any other number, and may have the idea of that inch line being divisible, or not divisible, into such equal parts, as a certain number of them will be equal to the sideline. Now, whenever he perceives, believes, or supposes such a kind of divisibility to agree or disagree to his idea of that line, he, as it were, joins or separates those two ideas, viz. the idea of that line, and the idea of that kind of divisibility; and so makes a mental proposition, which is true or false, according as such a kind of divisibility; a divisibility into such aliquot parts, does really agree to that line or no. When ideas are so put together, or separated in the mind, as they or the things they stand for do agree or not, that is, as I may call it, mental truth. But truth of words is something more; and that is the affirming or denying of words one of another, as the ideas they stand for agree or disagree: and this again is two-fold; either purely verbal and trifling, which I shall speak of, (chap. viii.,) or real and instructive; which is the object of that real knowledge which we have spoken of already.

7. Objection against verbal truth, that "thus it may all be chimerical." But here again will be apt to occur the same doubt about truth, that did about knowledge: and it will be objected, that if truth be nothing but the joining and separating of words in propositions, as the ideas they stand for agree or disagree in men's minds, the knowledge of truth is not so valuable a thing as it is taken to be, nor worth the pains and time men employ in the search of it: since by this account it amounts to no more than the conformity of words to the chimeras of men's brains. Who knows not what odd notions many men's heads are filled with, and what strange ideas all men's brains are capable of? But if we rest here, we know the truth of nothing by this rule, but of the visionary words in our own imaginations; nor have other truth, but what as much concerns harpies and centaurs, as men and horses. For those, and the like, may be ideas in our heads, and have their agreement or disagreement there, as well as the ideas of real beings, and so have as true propositions made about them. And it will be altogether as true a proposition to say all centaurs are animals, as that all men are animals; and the certainty of one as great as the other. For in both the propositions, the words are put together according to the agreement of the ideas in our minds: and the agreement of the idea of animal with that of centaur is as clear and visible to the mind, as the agreement of the idea of animal with that of man; and so these two propositions are equally true, equally certain. But of what use is all such truth to us?

8. Answered, "Real truth is about ideas agreeing to things." Though what has been said in the foregoing chapter to distinguish real from imaginary knowledge might suffice here, in answer to this doubt, to distinguish real truth from chimerical, or (if you please) barely nominal, they depending both on the same foundation; yet it may not be amiss here again to consider, that though our words signify nothing but our ideas, yet being designed by them to signify things, the truth they contain when put into propositions will be only verbal, when they stand for ideas in the mind that have not an agreement with the reality of things. And therefore truth as well as knowledge may well come under the distinction of verbal and real; that being only verbal truth, wherein terms are joined according to the agreement or disagreement of the ideas they stand for; without regarding whether our ideas are such as really have, or are capable of having, an existence in nature. But then it is they contain real truth, when these signs are joined, as our ideas agree; and when our ideas are such as we know are capable of having an existence in nature: which in substances we cannot know, but by knowing that such have existed.

9. Truth and falsehood in general. Truth is the marking down in words the agreement or

disagreement of ideas as it is. Falsehood is the marking down in words the agreement or disagreement of ideas otherwise than it is. And so far as these ideas, thus marked by sounds, agree to their archetypes, so far only is the truth real. The knowledge of this truth consists in knowing what ideas the words stand for, and the perception of the agreement or disagreement of those ideas, according as it is marked by those words.

10. General propositions to be treated of more at large. But because words are looked on as the great conduits of truth and knowledge, and that in conveying and receiving of truth, and commonly in reasoning about it, we make use of words and propositions, I shall more at large inquire wherein the certainty of real truths contained in propositions consists, and where it is to be had; and endeavour to show in what sort of universal propositions we are capable of being certain of their real truth or falsehood.

I shall begin with general propositions, as those which most employ our thoughts, and exercise our contemplation. General truths are most looked after by the mind as those that most enlarge our knowledge; and by their comprehensiveness satisfying us at once of many particulars, enlarge our view, and shorten our way to knowledge.

11. Moral and metaphysical truth. Besides truth taken in the strict sense before mentioned, there are other sorts of truths: As, 1. Moral truth, which is speaking of things according to the persuasion of our own minds, though the proposition we speak agree not to the reality of things; 2. Metaphysical truth, which is nothing but the real existence of things, conformable to the ideas to which we have annexed their names. This, though it seems to consist in the very beings of things, yet, when considered a little nearly, will appear to include a tacit proposition, whereby the mind joins that particular thing to the idea it had before settled with the name to it. But these considerations of truth, either having been before taken notice of, or not being much to our present purpose, it may suffice here only to have mentioned them.

Chapter VI.Of Universal Propositions: their Truth and Certainty

1. Treating of words necessary to knowledge. Though the examining and judging of ideas by themselves, their names being quite laid aside, be the best and surest way to clear and distinct knowledge: yet, through the prevailing custom of using sounds for ideas, I think it is very seldom practised. Every one may observe how common it is for names to be made use of, instead of the ideas themselves, even when men think and reason within their own breasts; especially if the ideas be very complex, and made up of a great collection of simple ones. This makes the consideration of words and propositions so necessary a part of the Treatise of Knowledge, that it is very hard to speak intelligibly of the one, without explaining the other.

2. General truths hardly to be understood, but in verbal propositions. All the knowledge we have, being only of particular or general truths, it is evident that whatever may be done in the former of these, the latter, which is that which with reason is most sought after, can never be well made known, and is very seldom apprehended, but as conceived and expressed in words. It is not, therefore, out of our way, in the examination of our knowledge, to inquire into the truth and certainty of universal propositions.

3. Certainty twofold — of truth and of knowledge. But that we may not be misled in this case by that which is the danger everywhere, I mean by the doubtfulness of terms, it is fit to observe that certainty is twofold: certainty of truth and certainty of knowledge. Certainty of truth is, when words are so put together in propositions as exactly to express the agreement or disagreement of the ideas they stand for, as really it is. Certainty of knowledge is to perceive the agreement or disagreement of ideas, as expressed in any proposition. This we usually call knowing, or being certain of the truth of any proposition.

4. No proposition can be certainly known to be true, where the real essence of each species mentioned is not known. Now, because we cannot be certain of the truth of any general

proposition, unless we know the precise bounds and extent of the species its terms stand for, it is necessary we should know the essence of each species, which is that which constitutes and bounds it.

This, in all simple ideas and modes, is not hard to do. For in these the real and nominal essence being the same, or, which is all one, the abstract idea which the general term stands for being the sole essence and boundary that is or can be supposed of the species, there can be no doubt how far the species extends, or what things are comprehended under each term; which, it is evident, are all that have an exact conformity with the idea it stands for, and no other.

But in substances, wherein a real essence, distinct from the nominal, is supposed to constitute, determine, and bound the species, the extent of the general word is very uncertain; because, not knowing this real essence, we cannot know what is, or what is not of that species; and, consequently, what may or may not with certainty be affirmed of it. And thus, speaking of a man, or gold, or any other species of natural substances, as supposed constituted by a precise and real essence which nature regularly imparts to every individual of that kind, whereby it is made to be of that species, we cannot be certain of the truth of any affirmation or negation made of it. For man or gold, taken in this sense, and used for species of things constituted by real essences, different from the complex idea in the mind of the speaker, stand for we know not what; and the extent of these species, with such boundaries, are so unknown and undetermined, that it is impossible with any certainty to affirm, that all men are rational, or that all gold is yellow. But where the nominal essence is kept to, as the boundary of each species, and men extend the application of any general term no further than to the particular things in which the complex idea it stands for is to be found, there they are in no danger to mistake the bounds of each species, nor can be in doubt, on this account, whether any proposition be true or not. I have chosen to explain this uncertainty of propositions in this scholastic way, and have made use of the terms of essences, and species, on purpose to show the absurdity and inconvenience there is to think of them as of any other sort of realities, than barely abstract ideas with names to them. To suppose that the species of things are anything but the sorting of them under general names, according as they agree to several abstract ideas of which we make those names the signs, is to confound truth, and introduce uncertainty into all general propositions that can be made about them. Though therefore these things might, to people not possessed with scholastic learning, be treated of in a better and clearer way; yet those wrong notions of essences or species having got root in most people's minds who have received any tincture from the learning which has prevailed in this part of the world, are to be discovered and removed, to make way for that use of words which should convey certainty with it.

5. This more particularly concerns substances. The names of substances, then, whenever made to stand for species which are supposed to be constituted by real essences which we know not, are not capable to convey certainty to the understanding. Of the truth of general propositions made up of such terms we cannot be sure. The reason whereof is plain: for how can we be sure that this or that quality is in gold, when we know not what is or is not gold? Since in this way of speaking, nothing is gold but what partakes of an essence, which we, not knowing, cannot know where it is or is not, and so cannot be sure that any parcel of matter in the world is or is not in this sense gold; being incurably ignorant whether it has or has not that which makes anything to be called gold; i.e. that real essence of gold whereof we have no idea at all. This being as impossible for us to know as it is for a blind man to tell in what flower the colour of a pansy is or is not to be found, whilst he has no idea of the colour of a pansy at an. Or if we could (which is impossible) certainly know where a real essence, which we know not, is, v.g. in what parcels of matter the real essence of gold is, yet could we not be sure that this or that quality could with truth be affirmed of gold; since it is impossible for us to know that this or that quality or idea has a necessary connexion with a real essence of which we have no idea at all, whatever species that supposed real essence may be imagined to constitute.

6. The truth of few universal propositions concerning substances is to be known. On the other side, the names of substances, when made use of as they should be, for the ideas men have in their minds, though they carry a clear and determinate signification with them, will not yet serve us to make many universal propositions of whose truth we can be certain. Not because in this use of them we are uncertain what things are signified by them, but because the complex ideas they stand for are such combinations of simple ones as carry not with them any discoverable connexion or repugnancy, but with a very few other ideas.

7. Because necessary co-existence of simple ideas in substances can in few cases be known. The complex ideas that our names of the species of substances properly stand for, are collections of such qualities as have been observed to co-exist in an unknown substratum, which we call substance; but what other qualities necessarily co-exist with such combinations, we cannot certainly know, unless we can discover their natural dependence; which, in their primary qualities, we can go but a very little way in; and in all their secondary qualities we can discover no connexion at all: for the reasons mentioned, chap. iii. Viz. 1. Because we know not the real constitutions of substances, on which each secondary quality particularly depends. 2. Did we know that, it would serve us only for experimental (not universal) knowledge; and reach with certainty no further than that bare instance: because our understandings can discover no conceivable connexion between any secondary quality and any modification whatsoever of any of the primary ones. And therefore there are very few general propositions to be made concerning substances, which can carry with them undoubted certainty.

8. Instance in gold. "All gold is fixed," is a proposition whose truth we cannot be certain of, how universally soever it be believed. For if, according to the useless imagination of the Schools, any one supposes the term gold to stand for a species of things set out by nature, by a real essence belonging to it, it is evident he knows not what particular substances are of that species; and so cannot with certainty affirm anything universally of gold. But if he makes gold stand for a species determined by its nominal essence, let the nominal essence, for example, be the complex idea of a body of a certain yellow colour, malleable, fusible, and heavier than any other known;— in this proper use of the word gold, there is no difficulty to know what is or is not gold. But yet no other quality can with certainty be universally affirmed or denied of gold, but what hath a discoverable connexion or inconsistency with that nominal essence. Fixedness, for example, having no necessary connexion that we can discover, with the colour, weight, or any other simple idea of our complex one, or with the whole combination together; it is impossible that we should certainly know the truth of this proposition, that all gold is fixed.

9. No discoverable necessary connexion between nominal essence of gold and other simple ideas. As there is no discoverable connexion between fixedness and the colour, weight, and other simple ideas of that nominal essence of gold; so, if we make our complex idea of gold, a body yellow, fusible, ductile, weighty, and fixed, we shall be at the same uncertainty concerning solubility in aqua regia, and for the same reason. Since we can never, from consideration of the ideas themselves, with certainty affirm or deny of a body whose complex idea is made up of yellow, very weighty, ductile, fusible, and fixed, that it is soluble in aqua regia: and so on of the rest of its qualities. I would gladly meet with one general affirmation concerning any quality of gold, that any one can certainly know is true. It will, no doubt, be presently objected, Is not this an universal proposition, All gold is malleable? To which I answer, It is a very certain proposition, if malleableness be a part of the complex idea the word gold stands for. But then here is nothing affirmed of gold, but that that sound stands for an idea in which malleableness is contained: and such a sort of truth and certainty as this it is, to say a centaur is four-footed. But if malleableness make not a part of the specific essence the name of gold stands for, it is plain, all gold is malleable, is not a certain proposition. Because, let the complex idea of gold be made up of whichsoever of its other qualities you please, malleableness will not appear to depend on that complex idea, nor follow from any simple one contained in it: the connexion that malleableness has (if it has any) with those other qualities being only by the intervention of the real constitution of its insensible parts; which, since we

know not, it is impossible we should perceive that connexion, unless we could discover that which ties them together.

10. As far as any such co-existence can be known, so far universal propositions may be certain. But this will go but a little way. The more, indeed, of these coexisting qualities we unite into one complex idea, under one name, the more precise and determinate we make the signification of that word; but never yet make it thereby more capable of universal certainty, in respect of other qualities not contained in our complex idea: since we perceive not their connexion or dependence on one another; being ignorant both of that real constitution in which they are all founded, and also how they flow from it. For the chief part of our knowledge concerning substances is not, as in other things, barely of the relation of two ideas that may exist separately; but is of the necessary connexion and co-existence of several distinct ideas in the same subject, or of their repugnancy so to co-exist. Could we begin at the other end, and discover what it was wherein that colour consisted, what made a body lighter or heavier, what texture of parts made it malleable, fusible, and fixed, and fit to be dissolved in this sort of liquor, and not in another;— if, I say, we had such an idea as this of bodies, and could perceive wherein all sensible qualities originally consist, and how they are produced; we might frame such abstract ideas of them as would furnish us with matter of more general knowledge, and enable us to make universal propositions, that should carry general truth and certainty with them. But whilst our complex ideas of the sorts of substances are so remote from that internal real constitution on which their sensible qualities depend, and are made up of nothing but an imperfect collection of those apparent qualities our senses can discover, there can be few general propositions concerning substances of whose real truth we can be certainly assured; since there are but few simple ideas of whose connexion and necessary coexistence we can have certain and undoubted knowledge. I imagine, amongst all the secondary qualities of substances, and the powers relating to them, there cannot any two be named, whose necessary co-existence, or repugnance to coexist, can certainly be known; unless in those of the same sense, which necessarily exclude one another, as I have elsewhere shown. No one, I think, by the colour that is in any body, can certainly know what smell, taste, sound, or tangible qualities it has, nor what alterations it is capable to make or receive on or from other bodies. The same may be said of the sound or taste, &c. Our specific names of substances standing for any collections of such ideas, it is not to be wondered that we can with them make very few general propositions of undoubted real certainty. But yet so far as any complex idea of any sort of substances contains in it any simple idea, whose necessary existence with any other may be discovered, so far universal propositions may with certainty be made concerning it: v.g. could any one discover a necessary connexion between malleableness and the colour or weight of gold, or any other part of the complex idea signified by that name, he might make a certain universal proposition concerning gold in this respect; and the real truth of this proposition, that all gold is malleable, would be as certain as of this, the three angles of all right-lined triangles are all equal to two right ones.

11. The qualities which make our complex ideas of substances depend mostly on external, remote, and unperceived causes. Had we such ideas of substances as to know what real constitutions produce those sensible qualities we find in them, and how those qualities flowed from thence, we could, by the specific ideas of their real essences in our own minds, more certainly find out their properties, and discover what qualities they had or had not, than we can now by our senses: and to know the properties of gold, it would be no more necessary that gold should exist, and that we should make experiments upon it, than it is necessary for the knowing the properties of a triangle, that a triangle should exist in any matter, the idea in our minds would serve for the one as well as the other. But we are so far from being admitted into the secrets of nature, that we scarce so much as ever approach the first entrance towards them. For we are wont to consider the substances we meet with, each of them, as an entire thing by itself, having all its qualities in itself, and independent of other things; overlooking, for the most part, the operations of those invisible fluids they are encompassed with, and upon whose

motions and operations depend the greatest part of those qualities which are taken notice of in them, and are made by us the inherent marks of distinction whereby we know and denominate them. Put a piece of gold anywhere by itself, separate from the reach and influence of all other bodies, it will immediately lose all its colour and weight, and perhaps malleableness too; which, for aught I know, would be changed into a perfect friability. Water, in which to us fluidity is an essential quality, left to itself, would cease to be fluid. But if inanimate bodies owe so much of their present state to other bodies without them, that they would not be what they appear to us were those bodies that environ them removed; it is yet more so in vegetables, which are nourished, grow, and produce leaves, flowers, and seeds, in a constant succession. And if we look a little nearer into the state of animals, we shall find that their dependence, as to life, motion, and the most considerable qualities to be observed in them, is so wholly on extrinsical causes and qualities of other bodies that make no part of them, that they cannot subsist a moment without them: though yet those bodies on which they depend are little taken notice of, and make no part of the complex ideas we frame of those animals. Take the air but for a minute from the greatest part of living creatures, and they presently lose sense, life, and motion. This the necessity of breathing has forced into our knowledge. But how many other extrinsical and possibly very remote bodies do the springs of these admirable machines depend on, which are not vulgarly observed, or so much as thought on; and how many are there which the severest inquiry can never discover? The inhabitants of this spot of the universe, though removed so many millions of miles from the sun, yet depend so much on the duly tempered motion of particles coming from or agitated by it, that were this earth removed but a small part of the distance out of its present situation, and placed a little further or nearer that source of heat, it is more than probable that the greatest part of the animals in it would immediately perish: since we find them so often destroyed by an excess or defect of the sun's warmth, which an accidental position in some parts of this our little globe exposes them to. The qualities observed in a loadstone must needs have their source far beyond the confines of that body; and the ravage made often on several sorts of animals by invisible causes, the certain death (as we are told) of some of them, by barely passing the line, or, as it is certain of other, by being removed into a neighbouring country; evidently show that the concurrence and operations of several bodies, with which they are seldom thought to have anything to do, is absolutely necessary to make them be what they appear to us, and to preserve those qualities by which we know and distinguish them. We are then quite out of the way, when we think that things contain within themselves the qualities that appear to us in them; and we in vain search for that constitution within the body of a fly or an elephant, upon which depend those qualities and powers we observe in them. For which, perhaps, to understand them aright, we ought to look not only beyond this our earth and atmosphere, but even beyond the sun or remotest star our eyes have yet discovered. For how much the being and operation of particular substances in this our globe depends on causes utterly beyond our view, is impossible for us to determine. We see and perceive some of the motions and grosser operations of things here about us; but whence the streams come that keep all these curious machines in motion and repair, how conveyed and modified, is beyond our notice and apprehension: and the great parts and wheels, as I may say so, of this stupendous structure of the universe, may, for aught we know, have such a connexion and dependence in their influences and operations one upon another, that perhaps things in this our mansion would put on quite another face, and cease to be what they are, if some one of the stars or great bodies incomprehensibly remote from us, should cease to be or move as it does. This is certain: things, however absolute and entire they seem in themselves, are but retainers to other parts of nature, for that which they are most taken notice of by us. Their observable qualities, actions, and powers are owing to something without them; and there is not so complete and perfect a part that we know of nature, which does not owe the being it has, and the excellences of it, to its neighbours; and we must not confine our thoughts within the surface of any body, but look a great deal further, to comprehend perfectly those qualities that are in it.

12. Our nominal essences of substances furnish few universal propositions about them that are certain. If this be so, it is not to be wondered that we have very imperfect ideas of substances, and that the real essences, on which depend their properties and operations, are unknown to us. We cannot discover so much as that size, figure, and texture of their minute and active parts, which is really in them; much less the different motions and impulses made in and upon them by bodies from without, upon which depends, and by which is formed the greatest and most remarkable part of those qualities we observe in them, and of which our complex ideas of them are made up. This consideration alone is enough to put an end to all our hopes of ever having the ideas of their real essences; which whilst we want, the nominal essences we make use of instead of them will be able to furnish us but very sparingly with any general knowledge, or universal propositions capable of real certainty.

13. Judgment of probability concerning substances may reach further: but that is not knowledge. We are not therefore to wonder, if certainty be to be found in very few general propositions made concerning substances: our knowledge of their qualities and properties goes very seldom further than our senses reach and inform us. Possibly inquisitive and observing men may, by strength of judgment, penetrate further, and, on probabilities taken from wary observation, and hints well laid together, often guess right at what experience has not yet discovered to them. But this is but guessing still; it amounts only to opinion, and has not that certainty which is requisite to knowledge. For all general knowledge lies only in our own thoughts, and consists barely in the contemplation of our own abstract ideas. Wherever we perceive any agreement or disagreement amongst them, there we have general knowledge; and by putting the names of those ideas together accordingly in propositions, can with certainty pronounce general truths. But because the abstract ideas of substances, for which their specific names stand, whenever they have any distinct and determinate signification, have a discoverable connexion or inconsistency with but a very few other ideas, the certainty of universal propositions concerning substances is very narrow and scanty, in that part which is our principal inquiry concerning them; and there are scarce any of the names of substances, let the idea it is applied to be what it will, of which we can generally, and with certainty, pronounce, that it has or has not this or that other quality belonging to it, and constantly co-existing or inconsistent with that idea, wherever it is to be found.

14. What is requisite for our knowledge of substances. Before we can have any tolerable knowledge of this kind, we must First know what changes the primary qualities of one body do regularly produce in the primary qualities of another, and how. Secondly, We must know what primary qualities of any body produce certain sensations or ideas in us. This is in truth no less than to know all the effects of matter, under its divers modifications of bulk, figure, cohesion of parts, motion and rest. Which, I think every body will allow, is utterly impossible to be known by us without revelation. Nor if it were revealed to us what sort of figure, bulk, and motion of corpuscles would produce in us the sensation of a yellow colour, and what sort of figure, bulk, and texture of parts in the superficies of any body were fit to give such corpuscles their due motion to produce that colour; would that be enough to make universal propositions with certainty, concerning the several sorts of them; unless we had faculties acute enough to perceive the precise bulk, figure, texture, and motion of bodies, in those minute parts, by which they operate on our senses, so that we might by those frame our abstract ideas of them. I have mentioned here only corporeal substances, whose operations seem to lie more level to our understandings. For as to the operations of spirits, both their thinking and moving of bodies, we at first sight find ourselves at a loss; though perhaps, when we have applied our thoughts a little nearer to the consideration of bodies and their operations, and examined how far our notions, even in these, reach with any clearness beyond sensible matter of fact, we shall be bound to confess that, even in these too, our discoveries amount to very little beyond perfect ignorance and incapacity.

15. Whilst our complex ideas of substances contain not ideas of their real constitutions, we can make but few general certain propositions concerning them. This is evident, the abstract

complex ideas of substances, for which their general names stand, not comprehending their real constitutions, can afford us very little universal certainty. Because our ideas of them are not made up of that on which those qualities we observe in them, and would inform ourselves about, do depend, or with which they have any certain connexion: v.g. let the ideas to which we give the name man be, as it commonly is, a body of the ordinary shape, with sense, voluntary motion, and reason joined to it. This being the abstract idea, and consequently the essence of our species, man, we can make but very few general certain propositions concerning man, standing for such an idea. Because, not knowing the real constitution on which sensation, power of motion, and reasoning, with that peculiar shape, depend, and whereby they are united together in the same subject, there are very few other qualities with which we can perceive them to have a necessary connexion: and therefore we cannot with certainty affirm: That all men sleep by intervals; That no man can be nourished by wood or stones; That all men will be poisoned by hemlock: because these ideas have no connexion nor repugnancy with this our nominal essence of man, with this abstract idea that name stands for. We must, in these and the like, appeal to trial in particular subjects, which can reach but a little way. We must content ourselves with probability in the rest: but can have no general certainty, whilst our specific idea of man contains not that real constitution which is the root wherein all his inseparable qualities are united, and from whence they flow. Whilst our idea the word man stands for is only an imperfect collection of some sensible qualities and powers in him, there is no discernible connexion or repugnance between our specific idea, and the operation of either the parts of hemlock or stones upon his constitution. There are animals that safely eat hemlock, and others that are nourished by wood and stones: but as long as we want ideas of those real constitutions of different sorts of animals whereon these and the like qualities and powers depend, we must not hope to reach certainty in universal propositions concerning them. Those few ideas only which have a discernible connexion with our nominal essence, or any part of it, can afford us such propositions. But these are so few, and of so little moment, that we may justly look on our certain general knowledge of substances as almost none at all.
16. Wherein lies the general certainty of propositions. To conclude: general propositions, of what kind soever, are then only capable of certainty, when the terms used in them stand for such ideas, whose agreement or disagreement, as there expressed, is capable to be discovered by us. And we are then certain of their truth or falsehood, when we perceive the ideas the terms stand for to agree or not agree, according as they are affirmed or denied one of another. Whence we may take notice, that general certainty is never to be found but in our ideas. Whenever we go to seek it elsewhere, in experiment or observations without us, our knowledge goes not beyond particulars. It is the contemplation of our own abstract ideas that alone is able to afford us general knowledge.

Chapter VII.Of Maxims

1. Maxims or axioms are self-evident propositions. There are a sort of propositions, which, under the name of maxims and axioms, have passed for principles of science: and because they are self-evident, have been supposed innate, without that anybody (that I know) ever went about to show the reason and foundation of their clearness or cogency. It may, however, be worth while to inquire into the reason of their evidence, and see whether it be peculiar to them alone; and also to examine how far they influence and govern our other knowledge.
2. Wherein that self-evidence consists. Knowledge, as has been shown, consists in the perception of the agreement or disagreement of ideas. Now, where that agreement or disagreement is perceived immediately by itself, without the intervention or help of any other, there our knowledge is self-evident. This will appear to be so to any who will but consider any of those propositions which, without any proof, he assents to at first sight: for in all of them he will find that the reason of his assent is from that agreement or disagreement which the mind,

by an immediate comparing them, finds in those ideas answering the affirmation or negation in the proposition.

3. Self-evidence not peculiar to received axioms. This being so, in the next place, let us consider whether this self-evidence be peculiar only to those propositions which commonly pass under the name of maxims, and have the dignity of axioms allowed them. And here it is plain, that several other truths, not allowed to be axioms, partake equally with them in this self-evidence. This we shall see, if we go over these several sorts of agreement or disagreement of ideas which I have above mentioned, viz. identity, relation, coexistence, and real existence; which will discover to us, that not only those few propositions which have had the credit of maxims are self-evident, but a great many, even almost an infinite number of other propositions are such.

4. I. As to identity and diversity, all propositions are equally self-evident. For, First, The immediate perception of the agreement or disagreement of identity being founded in the mind's having distinct ideas, this affords us as many self-evident propositions as we have distinct ideas. Every one that has any knowledge at all, has, as the foundation of it, various and distinct ideas: and it is the first act of the mind (without which it can never be capable of any knowledge) to know every one of its ideas by itself, and distinguish it from others. Every one finds in himself, that he knows the ideas he has; that he knows also, when any one is in his understanding, and what it is; and that when more than one are there, he knows them distinctly and unconfusedly one from another; which always being so, (it being impossible but that he should perceive what he perceives,) he can never be in doubt when any idea is in his mind, that it is there, and is that idea it is; and that two distinct ideas, when they are in his mind, are there, and are not one and the same idea. So that all such affirmations and negations are made without any possibility of doubt, uncertainty, or hesitation, and must necessarily be assented to as soon as understood; that is, as soon as we have in our minds determined ideas, which the terms in the proposition stand for. And, therefore, whenever the mind with attention considers any proposition, so as to perceive the two ideas signified by the terms, and affirmed or denied one of the other to be the same or different; it is presently and infallibly certain of the truth of such a proposition; and this equally whether these propositions be in terms standing for more general ideas, or such as are less so: v.g. whether the general idea of Being be affirmed of itself, as in this proposition, "whatsoever is, is"; or a more particular idea be affirmed of itself, as "a man is a man"; or, "whatsoever is white is white"; or whether the idea of being in general be denied of not-Being, which is the only (if I may so call it) idea different from it, as in this other proposition, "it is impossible for the same thing to be and not to be": or any idea of any particular being be denied of another different from it, as "a man is not a horse"; "red is not blue." The difference of the ideas, as soon as the terms are understood, makes the truth of the proposition presently visible, and that with an equal certainty and easiness in the less as well as the more general propositions; and all for the same reason, viz. because the mind perceives, in any ideas that it has, the same idea to be the same with itself; and two different ideas to be different, and not the same; and this it is equally certain of, whether these ideas be more or less general, abstract, and comprehensive. It is not, therefore, alone to these two general propositions —"whatsoever is, is"; and "it is impossible for the same thing to be and not to be"— that this sort of self-evidence belongs by any peculiar right. The perception of being, or not being, belongs no more to these vague ideas, signified by the terms whatsoever, and thing, than it does to any other ideas. These two general maxims, amounting to no more, in short, but this, that the same is the same, and the same is not different, are truths known in more particular instances, as well as in those general maxims; and known also in particular instances, before these general maxims are ever thought on; and draw all their force from the discernment of the mind employed about particular ideas. There is nothing more visible than that the mind, without the help of any proof, or reflection on either of these general propositions, perceives so clearly, and knows so certainly, that the idea of white is the idea of white, and not the idea of blue; and that the idea of white, when it is in the mind, is there, and

is not absent; that the consideration of these axioms can add nothing to the evidence or certainty of its knowledge. Just so it is (as every one may experiment in himself) in all the ideas a man has in his mind: he knows each to be itself, and not to be another; and to be in his mind, and not away when it is there, with a certainty that cannot be greater; and, therefore, the truth of no general proposition can be known with a greater certainty, nor add anything to this. So that, in respect of identity, our intuitive knowledge reaches as far as our ideas. And we are capable of making as many self-evident propositions, as we have names for distinct ideas. And I appeal to every one's own mind, whether this proposition, "a circle is a circle," be not as self-evident a proposition as that consisting of more general terms, "whatsoever is, is"; and again, whether this proposition, "blue is not red," be not a proposition that the mind can no more doubt of, as soon as it understands the words, than it does of that axiom, "it is impossible for the same thing to be and not to be?" And so of all the like.

5. II. In co-existence we have few self-evident propositions. Secondly, as to co-existence, or such a necessary connexion between two ideas that, in the subject where one of them is supposed, there the other must necessarily be also: of such agreement or disagreement as this, the mind has an immediate perception but in very few of them. And therefore in this sort we have but very little intuitive knowledge: nor are there to be found very many propositions that are self-evident, though some there are: v.g. the idea of filling a place equal to the contents of its superficies, being annexed to our idea of body, I think it is a self-evident proposition, that two bodies cannot be in the same place.

6. III. In other relations we may have many. Thirdly, As to the relations of modes, mathematicians have framed many axioms concerning that one relation of equality. As, "equals taken from equals, the remainder will be equal"; which, with the rest of that kind, however they are received for maxims by the mathematicians, and are unquestionable truths, yet, I think, that any one who considers them will not find that they have a clearer self-evidence than these,— that "one and one are equal to two"; that "if you take from the five fingers of one hand two, and from the five fingers of the other hand two, the remaining numbers will be equal." These and a thousand other such propositions may be found in numbers, which, at the very first hearing, force the assent, and carry with them an equal, if not greater clearness, than those mathematical axioms.

7. IV. Concerning real existence, we have none. Fourthly, as to real existence, since that has no connexion with any other of our ideas, but that of ourselves, and of a First Being, we have in that, concerning the real existence of all other beings, not so much as demonstrative, much less a self-evident knowledge: and, therefore, concerning those there are no maxims.

8. These axioms do not much influence our other knowledge. In the next place let us consider, what influence these received maxims have upon the other parts of our knowledge. The rules established in the schools, that all reasonings are Ex praeognitis et praeconcessis, seem to lay the foundation of all other knowledge in these maxims, and to suppose them to be praecognita. Whereby, I think, are meant these two things: first, that these axioms are those truths that are first known to the mind; and, secondly, that upon them the other parts of our knowledge depend.

9. Because maxims or axioms are not the truths we first knew. First, That they are not the truths first known to the mind is evident to experience, as we have shown in another place. (Bk. I. chap. i.) Who perceives not that a child certainly knows that a stranger is not its mother; that its sucking-bottle is not the rod, long before he knows that "it is impossible for the same thing to be and not to be?" And how many truths are there about numbers, which it is obvious to observe that the mind is perfectly acquainted with, and fully convinced of, before it ever thought on these general maxims, to which mathematicians, in their arguings, do sometimes refer them? Whereof the reason is very plain: for that which makes the mind assent to such propositions, being nothing else but the perception it has of the agreement or disagreement of its ideas, according as it finds them affirmed or denied one of another in words it understands; and every idea being known to be what it is, and every two distinct ideas

being known not to be the same; it must necessarily follow, that such self-evident truths must be first known which consist of ideas that are first in the mind. And the ideas first in the mind, it is evident, are those of particular things, from whence, by slow degrees, the understanding proceeds to some few general ones; which being taken from the ordinary and familiar objects of sense, are settled in the mind, with general names to them. Thus particular ideas are first received and distinguished, and so knowledge got about them; and next to them, the less general or specific, which are next to particular. For abstract ideas are not so obvious or easy to children, or the yet unexercised mind, as particular ones. If they seem so to grown men, it is only because by constant and familiar use they are made so. For, when we nicely reflect upon them, we shall find that general ideas are fictions and contrivances of the mind, that carry difficulty with them, and do not so easily offer themselves as we are apt to imagine. For example, does it not require some pains and skill to form the general idea of a triangle, (which is yet none of the most abstract, comprehensive, and difficult,) for it must be neither oblique nor rectangle, neither equilateral, equicrural, nor scalenon; but all and none of these at once. In effect, it is something imperfect, that cannot exist; an idea wherein some parts of several different and inconsistent ideas are put together. It is true, the mind, in this imperfect state, has need of such ideas, and makes all the haste to them it can, for the conveniency of communication and enlargement of knowledge; to both which it is naturally very much inclined. But yet one has reason to suspect such ideas are marks of our imperfection; at least, this is enough to show that the most abstract and general ideas are not those that the mind is first and most easily acquainted with, nor such as its earliest knowledge is conversant about.

10. Because on perception of them the other parts of our knowledge do not depend. Secondly, from what has been said it plainly follows, that these magnified maxims are not the principles and foundations of all our other knowledge. For if there be a great many other truths, which have as much self-evidence as they, and a great many that we know before them, it is impossible they should be the principles from which we deduce all other truths. Is it impossible to know that one and two are equal to three, but by virtue of this, or some such axiom, viz. "the whole is equal to all its parts taken together?" Many a one knows that one and two are equal to three, without having heard, or thought on, that or any other axiom by which it might be proved; and knows it as certainly as any other man knows, that "the whole is equal to all its parts," or any other maxim; and all from the same reason of self-evidence: the equality of those ideas being as visible and certain to him without that or any other axiom as with it, it needing no proof to make it perceived. Nor after the knowledge, that the whole is equal to all its parts, does he know that one and two are equal to three, better or more certainly than he did before. For if there be any odds in those ideas, the whole and parts are more obscure, or at least more difficult to be settled in the mind than those of one, two, and three. And indeed, I think, I may ask these men, who will needs have all knowledge, besides those general principles themselves, to depend on general, innate, and self-evident principles. What principle is requisite to prove that one and one are two, that two and two are four, that three times two are six? Which being known without any proof, do evince, That either all knowledge does not depend on certain praecognita or general maxims, called principles; or else that these are principles: and if these are to be counted principles, a great part of numeration will be so. To which, if we add all the self-evident propositions which may be made about all our distinct ideas, principles will be almost infinite, at least innumerable, which men arrive to the knowledge of, at different ages; and a great many of these innate principles they never come to know all their lives. But whether they come in view of the mind earlier or later, this is true of them, that they are all known by their native evidence; are wholly independent; receive no light, nor are capable of any proof one from another; much less the more particular from the more general, or the more simple from the more compounded; the more simple and less abstract being the most familiar, and the easier and earlier apprehended. But whichever be the clearest ideas, the evidence and certainty of all such propositions is in this, That a man sees the same idea to be the same idea, and infallibly perceives two different

ideas to be different ideas. For when a man has in his understanding the ideas of one and of two, the idea of yellow, and the idea of blue, he cannot but certainly know that the idea of one is the idea of one, and not the idea of two; and that the idea of yellow is the idea of yellow, and not the idea of blue. For a man cannot confound the ideas in his mind, which he has distinct: that would be to have them confused and distinct at the same time, which is a contradiction: and to have none distinct, is to have no use of our faculties, to have no knowledge at all. And, therefore, what idea soever is affirmed of itself, or whatsoever two entire distinct ideas are denied one of another, the mind cannot but assent to such a proposition as infallibly true, as soon as it understands the terms, without hesitation or need of proof, or regarding those made in more general terms and called maxims.

11. What use these general maxims or axioms have. What shall we then say? Are these general maxims of no use? By no means; though perhaps their use is not that which it is commonly taken to be. But, since doubting in the least of what hath been by some men ascribed to these maxims may be apt to be cried out against, as overturning the foundations of all the sciences; it may be worth while to consider them with respect to other parts of our knowledge, and examine more particularly to what purposes they serve, and to what not.

(1) It is evident from what has been already said, that they are of no use to prove or confirm less general self-evident propositions.

(2) It is as plain that they are not, nor have been the foundations whereon any science hath been built. There is, I know, a great deal of talk, propagated from scholastic men, of sciences and the maxims on which they are built: but it has been my ill-luck never to meet with any such sciences; much less any one built upon these two maxims, what is, is; and it is impossible for the same thing to be and not to be. And I would be glad to be shown where any such science, erected upon these or any other general axioms is to be found: and should be obliged to any one who would lay before me the frame and system of any science so built on these or any such like maxims, that could not be shown to stand as firm without any consideration of them. I ask, Whether these general maxims have not the same use in the study of divinity, and in theological questions, that they have in other sciences? They serve here, too, to silence wranglers, and put an end to dispute. But I think that nobody will therefore say, that the Christian religion is built upon these maxims, or that the knowledge we have of it is derived from these principals. It is from revelation we have received it, and without revelation these maxims had never been able to help us to it. When we find out an idea by whose intervention we discover the connexion of two others, this is a revelation from God to us by the voice of reason: for we then come to know a truth that we did not know before. When God declares any truth to us, this is a revelation to us by the voice of his Spirit, and we are advanced in our knowledge. But in neither of these do we receive our light or knowledge from maxims. But in the one, the things themselves afford it: and we see the truth in them by perceiving their agreement or disagreement. In the other, God himself affords it immediately to us: and we see the truth of what he says in his unerring veracity.

(3) They are not of use to help men forward in the advancement of sciences, or new discoveries of yet unknown truths. Mr. Newton, in his never enough to be admired book, has demonstrated several propositions, which are so many new truths, before unknown to the world, and are further advances in mathematical knowledge: but, for the discovery of these, it was not the general maxims, "what is, is;" or, "the whole is bigger than a part," or the like, that helped him. These were not the clues that led him into the discovery of the truth and certainty of those propositions. Nor was it by them that he got the knowledge of those demonstrations, but by finding out intermediate ideas that showed the agreement or disagreement of the ideas, as expressed in the propositions he demonstrated. This is the greatest exercise and improvement of human understanding in the enlarging of knowledge, and advancing the sciences; wherein they are far enough from receiving any help from the contemplation of these or the like magnified maxims. Would those who have this traditional admiration of these propositions, that they think no step can be made in knowledge without the support of an

axiom, no stone laid in the building of the sciences without a general maxim, but distinguish between the method of acquiring knowledge, and of communicating it; between the method of raising any science, and that of teaching it to others, as far as it is advanced — they would see that those general maxims were not the foundations on which the first discoverers raised their admirable structures, not the keys that unlocked and opened those secrets of knowledge.

Though afterwards, when schools were erected, and sciences had their professors to teach what others had found out, they often made use of maxims, i.e. laid down certain propositions which were self-evident, or to be received for true; which being settled in the minds of their scholars as unquestionable verities they on occasion made use of, to convince them of truths in particular instances, that were not so familiar to their minds as those general axioms which had before been inculcated to them, and carefully settled in their minds. Though these particular instances, when well reflected on, are no less self-evident to the understanding than the general maxims brought to confirm them: and it was in those particular instances that the first discoverer found the truth, without the help of the general maxims: and so may any one else do, who with attention considers them.

Maxims of use in the exposition of what has been discovered, and in silencing obstinate wranglers. To come, therefore, to the use that is made of maxims.

(1) They are of use, as has been observed, in the ordinary methods of teaching sciences as far as they are advanced: but of little or none in advancing them further.

(2) They are of use in disputes, for the silencing of obstinate wranglers, and bringing those contests to some conclusion. Whether a need of them to that end came not in the manner following, I crave leave to inquire. The Schools having made disputation the touchstone of men's abilities, and the criterion of knowledge, adjudged victory to him that kept the field: and he that had the last word was concluded to have the better of the argument, if not of the cause. But because by this means there was like to be no decision between skilful combatants, whilst one never failed of a medius terminus to prove any proposition; and the other could as constantly, without or with a distinction, deny the major or minor; to prevent, as much as could be, running out of disputes into an endless train of syllogisms, certain general propositions — most of them, indeed, self-evident — were introduced into the Schools: which being such as all men allowed and agreed in, were looked on as general measures of truth, and served instead of principles (where the disputants had not lain down any other between them) beyond which there was no going, and which must not be receded from by either side. And thus these maxims, getting the name of principles, beyond which men in dispute could not retreat, were by mistake taken to be the originals and sources from whence all knowledge began, and the foundations whereon the sciences were built. Because when in their disputes they came to any of these, they stopped there, and went no further; the matter was determined. But how much this is a mistake, hath been already shown.

How maxims came to be so much in vogue. This method of the Schools, which have been thought the fountains of knowledge, introduced, as I suppose, the like use of these maxims into a great part of conversation out of the Schools, to stop the mouths of cavillers, whom any one is excused from arguing any longer with, when they deny these general self-evident principles received by all reasonable men who have once thought of them: but yet their use herein is but to put an end to wrangling. They in truth, when urged in such cases, teach nothing: that is already done by the intermediate ideas made use of in the debate, whose connexion may be seen without the help of those maxims, and so the truth known before the maxim is produced, and the argument brought to a first principle. Men would give off a wrong argument before it came to that, if in their disputes they proposed to themselves the finding and embracing of truth, and not a contest for victory. And thus maxims have their use to put a stop to their perverseness, whose ingenuity should have yielded sooner. But the method of the Schools having allowed and encouraged men to oppose and resist evident truth till they are baffled, i.e. till they are reduced to contradict themselves, or some established principles: it is no wonder that they should not in civil conversation be ashamed of that which in the Schools is counted a virtue and a glory, viz. obstinately to maintain that side of the question they have chosen, whether true or false, to the last extremity; even after conviction. A strange way to attain truth and knowledge: and that which I think the rational part of mankind, not corrupted by education, could scarce believe should ever be admitted amongst the lovers of truth, and students of religion or nature, or introduced into the seminaries of those who are to propagate the truths of religion or philosophy amongst the ignorant and unconvinced. How much such a way of learning is like to turn young men's minds from the sincere search and love of truth; nay, and to make them doubt whether there is any such thing, or, at least, worth the adhering to, I shall not now inquire. This I think, that, bating those places, which brought the Peripatetick Philosophy into their schools, where it continued many ages, without teaching the world anything but the art of wrangling, these maxims were nowhere thought the foundations on which the sciences were built, nor the great helps to the advancement of knowledge.

Of great use to stop wranglers in disputes, but of little use to the discovery of truths. As to these general maxims, therefore, they are, as I have said, of great use in disputes, to stop the mouths of wranglers; but not of much use to the discovery of unknown truths, or to help the mind forwards in its search after knowledge. For who ever began to build his knowledge on the general proposition, what is, is; or, it is impossible for the same thing to be and not to be: and from either of these, as from a principle of science, deduced a system of useful knowledge? Wrong opinions often involving contradictions, one of these maxims, as a touchstone, may serve well to show whither they lead. But yet, however fit to lay open the absurdity or mistake of a man's reasoning or opinion, they are of very little use for enlightening the understanding: and it will not be found that the mind receives much help from them in its progress in knowledge; which would be neither less, nor less certain, were these two general propositions never thought on. It is true, as I have said, they sometimes serve in argumentation to stop a wrangler's mouth, by showing the absurdity of what he saith, and by exposing him to the shame of contradicting what all the world knows, and he himself cannot but own to be true. But it is one thing to show a man that he is in an error, and another to put him in possession of truth; and I would fain know what truths these two propositions are able to teach, and by their influence make us know, which we did not know before, or could not know without them. Let us reason from them as well as we can, they are only about identical predications, and influence, if any at all, none but such. Each particular proposition concerning identity or diversity is as clearly and certainly known in itself, if attended to, as either of these general ones: only these general ones, as serving in all cases, are therefore more inculcated and insisted on. As to other less general maxims, many of them are no more than bare verbal propositions, and teach us nothing but the respect and import of names one to another. "The whole is equal to all its parts": what real truth, I beseech you, does it teach us? What more is contained in that maxim, than what the signification of the word totum, or the whole, does of itself import? And he that knows that the word whole stands for what is made up of all its parts, knows very little less than that the whole is equal to all its parts. And, upon the same ground, I think that this proposition, "A hill is higher than a valley," and several the like, may also pass for maxims. But yet masters of mathematics, when they would, as teachers of what they know, initiate others in that science, do not without reason place this and some other such maxims at the entrance of their systems; that their scholars, having in the beginning perfectly acquainted their thoughts with these propositions, made in such general terms, may be used to make such reflections, and have these more general propositions, as formed rules and sayings, ready to apply to all particular cases. Not that if they be equally weighed, they are more clear and evident than the particular instances they are brought to confirm; but that, being more familiar to the mind, the very naming them is enough to satisfy the understanding. But this, I say, is more from our custom of using them, and the establishment they have got in our minds by our often thinking of them, than from the different evidence of the things. But before custom has settled methods of thinking and reasoning in our minds, I am apt to imagine it is quite otherwise; and that the child, when a part of his apple is taken away, knows it better in that particular instance, than by this general proposition, "The whole is equal to all its parts"; and that, if one of these have need to be confirmed to him by the other, the general has more need to be let into his mind by the particular, than the particular by the general. For in particulars our knowledge begins, and so spreads itself, by degrees, to generals. Though afterwards the mind takes the quite contrary course, and having drawn its knowledge into as general propositions as it can, makes those familiar to its thoughts, and accustoms itself to have recourse to them, as to the standards of truth and falsehood. By which familiar use of them, as rules to measure the truth of other propositions, it comes in time to be thought, that more particular propositions have their truth and evidence from their conformity to these more general ones, which, in discourse and argumentation, are so frequently urged, and constantly admitted. And this I think to be the reason why, amongst so many self-evident propositions, the most general only have had the title of maxims.

12. Maxims, if care be not taken in the use of words, may prove contradictions. One thing further, I think, it may not be amiss to observe concerning these general maxims, That they are so far from improving or establishing our minds in true knowledge, that if our notions be wrong, loose, or unsteady, and we resign up our thoughts to the sound of words, rather than fix them on settled, determined ideas of things; I say these general maxims will serve to confirm us in mistakes; and in such a way of use of words, which is most common, will serve to prove contradictions: v.g. he that with Descartes shall frame in his mind an idea of what he calls body to be nothing but extension, may easily demonstrate that there is no vacuum, i.e. no space void of body, by this maxim, What is, is. For the idea to which he annexes the name body, being bare extension, his knowledge that space cannot be without body, is certain. For he knows his own idea of extension clearly and distinctly, and knows that it is what it is, and not another idea, though it be called by these three names,— extension, body, space. Which three words, standing for one and the same idea, may, no doubt, with the same evidence and certainty be affirmed one of another, as each of itself: and it is as certain, that, whilst I use them all to stand for one and the same idea, this predication is as true and identical in its signification, that "space is body," as this predication is true and identical, that "body is body," both in signification and sound.

13. Instance in vacuum. But if another should come and make to himself another idea, different from Descartes's, of the thing, which yet with Descartes he calls by the same name body, and make his idea, which he expresses by the word body, to be of a thing that hath both extension and solidity together; he will as easily demonstrate, that there may be a vacuum or space without a body, as Descartes demonstrated the contrary. Because the idea to which he gives the name space being barely the simple one of extension, and the idea to which he gives the name body being the complex idea of extension and resistibility or solidity, together in the same subject, these two ideas are not exactly one and the same, but in the understanding as distinct as the ideas of one and two, white and black, or as of corporeity and humanity, if I may use those barbarous terms: and therefore the predication of them in our minds, or in words standing for them, is not identical, but the negation of them one of another; viz. this proposition: "Extension or space is not body," is as true and evidently certain as this maxim, It is impossible for the same thing to be and not to be, can make any proposition.

14. But they prove not the existence of things without us. But yet, though both these propositions (as you see) may be equally demonstrated, viz. that there may be a vacuum, and that there cannot be a vacuum, by these two certain principles, viz. what is, is, and the same thing cannot be and not be: yet neither of these principles will serve to prove to us, that any, or what bodies do exist: for that we are left to our senses to discover to us as far as they can. Those universal and self-evident principles being only our constant, clear, and distinct knowledge of our own ideas, more general or comprehensive, can assure us of nothing that passes without the mind: their certainty is founded only upon the knowledge we have of each idea by itself, and of its distinction from others, about which we cannot be mistaken whilst they are in our minds; though we may be and often are mistaken when we retain the names

without the ideas; or use them confusedly, sometimes for one and sometimes for another idea. In which cases the force of these axioms, reaching only to the sound, and not the signification of the words, serves only to lead us into confusion, mistake, and error. It is to show men that these maxims, however cried up for the great guards of truth, will not secure them from error in a careless loose use of their words, that I have made this remark. In all that is here suggested concerning their little use for the improvement of knowledge, or dangerous use in undetermined ideas, I have been far enough from saying or intending they should be laid aside; as some have been too forward to charge me. I affirm them to be truths, self-evident truths; and so cannot be laid aside. As far as their influence will reach, it is in vain to endeavour, nor will I attempt, to abridge it. But yet, without any injury to truth or knowledge, I may have reason to think their use is not answerable to the great stress which seems to be laid on them; and I may warn men not to make an ill use of them, for the confirming themselves in errors.

15. They cannot add to our knowledge of substances, and their application to complex ideas is dangerous. But let them be of what use they will in verbal propositions, they cannot discover or prove to us the least knowledge of the nature of substances, as they are found and exist without us, any further than grounded on experience. And though the consequence of these two propositions, called principles, be very clear, and their use not dangerous or hurtful, in the probation of such things wherein there is no need at all of them for proof, but such as are clear by themselves without them, viz. where our ideas are [determined] and known by the names that stand for them: yet when these principles, viz. what is, is, and it is impossible for the same thing to be and not to be, are made use of in the probation of propositions wherein are words standing for complex ideas, v.g. man, horse, gold, virtue; there they are of infinite danger, and most commonly make men receive and retain falsehood for manifest truth, and uncertainty for demonstration: upon which follow error, obstinacy, and all the mischiefs that can happen from wrong reasoning. The reason whereof is not, that these principles are less true or of less force in proving propositions made of terms standing for complex ideas, than where the propositions are about simple ideas. But because men mistake generally,— thinking that where the same terms are preserved, the propositions are about the same things, though the ideas they stand for are in truth different, therefore these maxims are made use of to support those which in sound and appearance are contradictory propositions; and is clear in the demonstrations above mentioned about a vacuum. So that whilst men take words for things, as usually they do, these maxims may and do commonly serve to prove contradictory propositions; as shall yet be further made manifest.

16. Instance in demonstrations about man, which can only be verbal. For instance: let man be that concerning which you would by these first principles demonstrate anything, and we shall see, that so far as demonstration is by these principles, it is only verbal, and gives us no certain, universal, true proposition, or knowledge, of any being existing without us. First, a child having framed the idea of a man, it is probable that his idea is just like that picture which the painter makes of the visible appearances joined together; and such a complication of ideas together in his understanding makes up the single complex idea which he calls man, whereof white or flesh-colour in England being one, the child can demonstrate to you that a negro is not a man, because white colour was one of the constant simple ideas of the complex idea he calls man; and therefore he can demonstrate, by the principle, It is impossible for the same thing to be and not to be, that a negro is not a man; the foundation of his certainty being not that universal proposition, which perhaps he never heard nor thought of, but the clear, distinct perception he hath of his own simple ideas of black and white, which he cannot be persuaded to take, nor can ever mistake one for another, whether he knows that maxim or no. And to this child, or any one who hath such an idea, which he calls man, can you never demonstrate that a man hath a soul, because his idea of man includes no such notion or idea in it. And therefore, to him, the principle of What is, is, proves not this matter; but it depends upon collection and

observation, by which he is to make his complex idea called man.

17. Another instance. Secondly, Another that hath gone further in framing and collecting the idea he calls man, and to the outward shape adds laughter and rational discourse, may demonstrate that infants and changelings are no men, by this maxim, it is impossible for the same thing to he and not to be; and I have discoursed with very rational men, who have actually denied that they are men.

18. A third instance. Thirdly, Perhaps another makes up the complex idea which he calls man, only out of the ideas of body in general, and the powers of language and reason, and leaves out the shape wholly: this man is able to demonstrate that a man may have no hands, but be quadrupes, neither of those being included in his idea of man: and in whatever body or shape he found speech and reason joined, that was a man; because, having a clear knowledge of such a complex idea, it is certain that What is, is.

19. Little use of these maxims in proofs where we have clear and distinct ideas. So that, if rightly considered, I think we may say, That where our ideas are determined in our minds, and have annexed to them by us known and steady names under those settled determinations, there is little need, or no use at all of these maxims, to prove the agreement or disagreement of any of them. He that cannot discern the truth or falsehood of such propositions, without the help of these and the like maxims, will not be helped by these maxims to do it: since he cannot be supposed to know the truth of these maxims themselves without proof, if he cannot know the truth of others without proof, which are as self-evident as these. Upon this ground it is that intuitive knowledge neither requires nor admits any proof, one part of it more than another. He that will suppose it does, takes away the foundation of all knowledge and certainty; and he that needs any proof to make him certain, and give his assent to this proposition, that two are equal to two, will also have need of a proof to make him admit, that what is, is. He that needs a probation to convince him that two are not three, that white is not black, that a triangle is not a circle, &c., or any other two [determined] distinct ideas are not one and the same, will need also a demonstration to convince him that It is impossible for the same thing to be and not to be.

20. Their use dangerous, where our ideas are not determined. And as these maxims are of little use where we have determined ideas, so they are, as I have shown, of dangerous use where our ideas are not determined: and where we use words that are not annexed to determined ideas, but such as are of a loose and wandering signification, sometimes standing for one, and sometimes for another idea: from which follow mistake and error, which these maxims (brought as proofs to establish propositions, wherein the terms stand for undetermined ideas) do by their authority confirm and rivet.

Chapter VIII.Of Trifling Propositions

1. Some propositions bring no increase to our knowledge. Whether the maxims treated of in the foregoing chapter be of that use to real knowledge as is generally supposed, I leave to be considered. This, I think, may confidently be affirmed, That there are universal propositions, which, though they be certainly true, yet they add no light to our understanding; bring no increase to our knowledge. Such are —

2. I. As identical propositions. First, All purely identical propositions. These obviously and at first blush appear to contain no instruction in them; for when we affirm the said term of itself, whether it be barely verbal, or whether it contains any clear and real idea, it shows us nothing but what we must certainly know before, whether such a proposition be either made by, or proposed to us. Indeed, that most general one, what is, is, may serve sometimes to show a man the absurdity he is guilty of, when, by circumlocution or equivocal terms, he would in particular instances deny the same thing of itself; because nobody will so openly bid defiance to common sense, as to affirm visible and direct contradictions in plain words; or, if he does, a

man is excused if he breaks off any further discourse with him. But yet I think I may say, that neither that received maxim, nor any other identical proposition, teaches us anything; and though in such kind of propositions this great and magnified maxim, boasted to be the foundation of demonstration, may be and often is made use of to confirm them, yet all it proves amounts to no more than this, That the same word may with great certainty be affirmed of itself, without any doubt of the truth of any such proposition; and let me add, also, without any real knowledge.

3. Examples. For, at this rate, any very ignorant person, who can but make a proposition, and knows what he means when he says ay or no, may make a million of propositions of whose truth he may be infallibly certain, and yet not know one thing in the world thereby; v.g. "what is a soul, is a soul,"; or, "a soul is a soul"; "a spirit is a spirit"; "a fetiche is a fetiche," &c. These all being equivalent to this proposition, viz. what is, is; i.e. what hath existence, hath existence; or, who hath a soul, hath a soul. What is this more than trifling with words? It is but like a monkey shifting his oyster from one hand to the other: and had he but words, might no doubt have said, "Oyster in right hand is subject, and oyster in left hand is predicate": and so might have made a self-evident proposition of oyster, i.e. oyster is oyster; and yet, with all this, not have been one whit the wiser or more knowing: and that way of handling the matter would much at once have satisfied the monkey's hunger, or a man's understanding, and they would have improved in knowledge and bulk together.

How identical propositions are trifling. I know there are some who, because identical propositions are self-evident, show a great concern for them, and think they do great service to philosophy by crying them up; as if in them was contained all knowledge, and the understanding were led into all truth by them only. I grant as forwardly as any one, that they are all true and self-evident. I grant further, that the foundation of all our knowledge lies in the faculty we have of perceiving the same idea to be the same, and of discerning it from those that are different; as I have shown in the foregoing chapter. But how that vindicates the making use of identical propositions, for the improvement of knowledge, from the imputation of trifling, I do not see. Let any one repeat, as often as he pleases, that "the will is the will," or lay what stress on it he thinks fit; of what use is this, and an infinite the like propositions, for the enlarging our knowledge? Let a man abound, as much as the plenty of words which he has will permit, in such propositions as these: "a law is a law," and "obligation is obligation"; "right is right," and "wrong is wrong":— will these and the like ever help him to an acquaintance with ethics, or instruct him or others in the knowledge of morality? Those who know not, nor perhaps ever will know, what is right and what is wrong, nor the measures of them, can with as much assurance make, and infallibly know, the truth of these and all such propositions, as he that is best instructed in morality can do. But what advance do such propositions give in the knowledge of anything necessary or useful for their conduct?

He would be thought to do little less than trifle, who, for the enlightening the understanding in any part of knowledge, should be busy with identical propositions and insist on such maxims as these: "substance is substance," and "body is body"; "a vacuum is a vacuum," and "a vortex is a vortex"; "a centaur is a centaur," and "a chimera is a chimera," &c. For these and all such are equally true, equally certain, and equally self-evident. But yet they cannot but be counted trifling, when made use of as principles of instruction, and stress laid on them as helps to knowledge; since they teach nothing but what every one who is capable of discourse knows without being told, viz. that the same term is the same term, and the same idea the same idea. And upon this account it was that I formerly did, and do still think, the offering and inculcating such propositions, in order to give the understanding any new light, or inlet into the knowledge of things, no better than trifling.

Instruction lies in something very different; and he that would enlarge his own or another's mind to truths he does not yet know, must find out intermediate ideas, and then lay them in such order one by another, that the understanding may see the agreement or disagreement of those in question. Propositions that do this are instructive; but they are far from such as affirm the same term of itself; which is no way to advance one's self or others in any sort of knowledge. It no more helps to that than it would help any one in his learning to read, to have such propositions as these inculcated to him —"An A is an A," and "a B is a B"; which a man may know as well as any schoolmaster, and yet never be able to read a word as long as he lives. Nor do these, or any such identical propositions help him one jot forwards in the skill of reading, let him make what use of them he can.

If those who blame my calling them trifling propositions had but read and been at the pains to understand what I have above writ in very plain English, they could not but have seen that by identical propositions I mean only such wherein the same term, importing the same idea, is affirmed of itself: which I take to be the proper signification of identical propositions; and concerning all such, I think I may continue safely to say, that to propose them as instructive is no better than trifling. For no one who has the use of reason can miss them, where it is necessary they should be taken notice of; nor doubt of their truth when he does take notice of them.

But if men will call propositions identical, wherein the same term is not affirmed of itself, whether they speak more properly than I, others must judge; this is certain, all that they say of propositions that are not identical in my sense, concerns not me nor what I have said; all that I have said relating to those propositions wherein the same term is affirmed of itself. And I would fain see an instance wherein any such can be made use of, to the advantage and improvement of any one's knowledge. Instances of other kinds, whatever use may be made of them, concern not me, as not being such as I call identical.

4. II. Secondly, propositions in which a part of any complex idea is predicated of the whole. Another sort of trifling propositions is, when a part of the complex idea is predicated of the name of the whole; a part of the definition of the word defined. Such are all propositions wherein the genus is predicated of the species, or more comprehensive of less comprehensive terms. For what information, what knowledge, carries this proposition in it, viz. "Lead is a metal" to a man who knows the complex idea the name lead stands for? All the simple ideas that go to the complex one signified by the term metal, being nothing but what he before comprehended and signified by the name lead. Indeed, to a man that knows the signification of the word metal, and not of the word lead, it is a shorter way to explain the signification of the word lead, by saying it is a metal, which at once expresses several of its simple ideas, than to enumerate them one by one, telling him it is a body very heavy, fusible, and malleable.

5. As part of the definition of the term defined. Alike trifling it is to predicate any other part of the definition of the term defined, or to affirm any one of the simple ideas of a complex one of the name of the whole complex idea; as, "All gold is fusible." For fusibility being one of the simple ideas that goes to the making up the complex one the sound gold stands for, what can it be but playing with sounds, to affirm that of the name gold, which is comprehended in its received signification? It would be thought little better than ridiculous to affirm gravely, as a truth of moment, that gold is yellow; and I see not how it is any jot more material to say it is fusible, unless that quality be left out of the complex idea, of which the sound gold is the mark in ordinary speech. What instruction can it carry with it, to tell one that which he hath been told already, or he is supposed to know before? For I am supposed to know the signification of the word another uses to me, or else he is to tell me. And if I know that the name gold stands for this complex idea of body, yellow, heavy, fusible, malleable, it will not much instruct me to put it solemnly afterwards in a proposition, and gravely say, all gold is fusible. Such propositions can only serve to show the disingenuity of one who will go from the definition of his own terms, by reminding him sometimes of it; but carry no knowledge with them, but of the signification of words, however certain they be.

6. Instance, man and palfrey. "Every man is an animal, or living body," is as certain a proposition as can be; but no more conducing to the knowledge of things than to say, a palfrey is an ambling horse, or a neighing, ambling animal, both being only about the signification of words, and make me know but this — That body, sense, and motion, or power of sensation

and moving, are three of those ideas that I always comprehend and signify by the word man: and where they are not to be found together, the name man belongs not to that thing: and so of the other — That body, sense, and a certain way of going, with a certain kind of voice, are some of those ideas which I always comprehend and signify by the word palfrey; and when they are not to be found together, the name palfrey belongs not to that thing. It is just the same, and to the same purpose, when any term standing for any one or more of the simple ideas, that altogether make up that complex idea which is called man, is affirmed of the term man:— v.g. suppose a Roman signified by the word homo all these distinct ideas united in one subject, corporietas, sensibilitas, potentia se movendi rationalitas, risibilitas; he might, no doubt, with great certainty, universally affirm one, more, or all of these together of the word homo, but did no more than say that the word homo, in his country, comprehended in its signification all these ideas. Much like a romance knight, who by the word palfrey signified these ideas:— body of a certain figure, four-legged, with sense, motion, ambling, neighing, white, used to have a woman on his back — might with the same certainty universally affirm also any or all of these of the word palfrey: but did thereby teach no more, but that the word palfrey, in his or romance language, stood for all these, and was not to be applied to anything where any of these was wanting. But he that shall tell me, that in whatever thing sense, motion, reason, and laughter, were united, that thing had actually a notion of God, or would be cast into a sleep by opium, made indeed an instructive proposition: because neither having the notion of God, nor being cast into sleep by opium, being contained in the idea signified by the word man, we are by such propositions taught something more than barely what the word man stands for: and therefore the knowledge contained in it is more than verbal.

7. For this teaches but the signification of words. Before a man makes any proposition, he is supposed to understand the terms he uses in it, or else he talks like a parrot, only making a noise by imitation, and framing certain sounds, which he has learnt of others; but not as a rational creature, using them for signs of ideas which he has in his mind. The hearer also is supposed to understand the terms as the speaker uses them, or else he talks jargon, and makes an unintelligible noise. And therefore he trifles with words who makes such a proposition, which, when it is made, contains no more than one of the terms does, and which a man was supposed to know before: v.g. a triangle hath three sides, or saffron is yellow. And this is no further tolerable than where a man goes to explain his terms to one who is supposed or declares himself not to understand him; and then it teaches only the signification of that word, and the use of that sign.

8. But adds no real knowledge. We can know then the truth of two sorts of propositions with perfect certainty. The one is, of those trifling propositions which have a certainty in them, but it is only a verbal certainty, but not instructive. And, secondly, we can know the truth, and so may be certain in propositions, which affirm something of another, which is a necessary consequence of its precise complex idea, but not contained in it: as that the external angle of all triangles is bigger than either of the opposite internal angles. Which relation of the outward angle to either of the opposite internal angles, making no part of the complex idea signified by the name triangle, this is a real truth, and conveys with it instructive real knowledge.

9. General propositions concerning substances are often trifling. We having little or no knowledge of what combinations there be of simple ideas existing together in substances, but by our senses, we cannot make any universal certain propositions concerning them, any further than our nominal essences lead us. Which being to a very few and inconsiderable truths, in respect of those which depend on their real constitutions, the general propositions that are made about substances, if they are certain, are for the most part but trifling; and if they are instructive, are uncertain, and such as we can have no knowledge of their real truth, how much soever constant observation and analogy may assist our judgment in guessing. Hence it comes to pass, that one may often meet with very clear and coherent discourses, that amount yet to nothing. For it is plain that names of substantial beings, as well as others, as far as they have relative significations affixed to them, may, with great truth, be joined negatively and

affirmatively in propositions, as their relative definitions make them fit to be so joined; and propositions consisting of such terms, may, with the same clearness, be deduced one from another, as those that convey the most real truths: and all this without any knowledge of the nature or reality of things existing without us. By this method one may make demonstrations and undoubted propositions in words, and yet thereby advance not one jot in the knowledge of the truth of things: v.g. he that having learnt these following words, with their ordinary mutual relative acceptations annexed to them: v.g. substance, man, animal, form, soul, vegetative, sensitive, rational, may make several undoubted propositions about the soul, without knowing at all what the soul really is: and of this sort, a man may find an infinite number of propositions, reasonings, and conclusions, in books of metaphysics, school-divinity, and some sort of natural philosophy: and, after all, know as little of God, spirits, or bodies, as he did before he set out.

10. And why. He that hath liberty to define, i.e. to determine the signification of his names of substances (as certainly every one does in effect, who makes them stand for his own ideas), and makes their significations at a venture, taking them from his own or other men's fancies, and not from an examination or inquiry into the nature of things themselves; may with little trouble demonstrate them one of another, according to those several respects and mutual relations he has given them one to another; wherein, however things agree or disagree in their own nature, he needs mind nothing but his own notions, with the names he hath bestowed upon them: but thereby no more increases in his own knowledge than he does his riches, who, taking a bag of counters, calls one in a certain place a pound, another in another place a shilling, and a third in a third place a penny; and so proceeding, may undoubtedly reckon right, and cast up a great sum, according to his counters so placed, and standing for more or less as he pleases, without being one jot the richer, or without even knowing how much a pound, shilling, or penny is, but only that one is contained in the other twenty times, and contains the other twelve: which a man may also do in the signification of words, by making them, in respect of one another, more or less, or equally comprehensive.

11. Thirdly, using words variously is trifling with them. Though yet concerning most words used in discourses, equally argumentative and controversial, there is this more to be complained of, which is the worst sort of trifling, and which sets us yet further from the certainty of knowledge we hope to attain by them, or find in them; viz. that most writers are so far from instructing us in the nature and knowledge of things, that they use their words loosely and uncertainly, and do not, by using them constantly and steadily in the same significations, make plain and clear deductions of words one from another, and make their discourses coherent and clear, (how little soever they were instructive); which were not difficult to do, did they not find it convenient to shelter their ignorance or obstinacy under the obscurity and perplexedness of their terms: to which, perhaps, inadvertency and ill custom do in many men much contribute.

12. Marks of verbal propositions. To conclude. Barely verbal propositions may be known by these following marks:

Predication in abstract. First, All propositions wherein two abstract terms are affirmed one of another, are barely about the signification of sounds. For since no abstract idea can be the same with any other but itself, when its abstract name is affirmed of any other term, it can signify no more but this, that it may, or ought to be called by that name; or that these two names signify the same idea. Thus, should any one say that parsimony is frugality, that gratitude is justice, that this or that action is or is not temperate: however specious these and the like propositions may at first sight seem, yet when we come to press them, and examine nicely what they contain, we shall find that it all amounts to nothing but the signification of those terms.

13. A part of the definition predicated of any term. Secondly, All propositions wherein a part of the complex idea which any term stands for is predicated of that term, are only verbal: v.g. to say that gold is a metal, or heavy. And thus all propositions wherein more comprehensive

words, called genera, are affirmed of subordinate or less comprehensive, called species, or individuals, are barely verbal.

When by these two rules we have examined the propositions that make up the discourses we ordinarily meet with, both in and out of books, we shall perhaps find that a greater part of them than is usually suspected are purely about the signification of words, and contain nothing in them but the use and application of these signs.

This I think I may lay down for an infallible rule, That, wherever the distinct idea any word stands for is not known and considered, and something not contained in the idea is not affirmed or denied of it, there our thoughts stick wholly in sounds, and are able to attain no real truth or falsehood. This, perhaps, if well heeded, might save us a great deal of useless amusement and dispute; and very much shorten our trouble and wandering in the search of real and true knowledge.

Chapter IX.Of our Threefold Knowledge of Existence

1. General propositions that are certain concern not existence. Hitherto we have only considered the essences of things; which being only abstract ideas, and thereby removed in our thoughts from particular existence, (that being the proper operation of the mind, in abstraction, to consider an idea under no other existence but what it has in the understanding,) gives us no knowledge of real existence at all. Where, by the way, we may take notice, that universal propositions of whose truth or falsehood we can have certain knowledge concern not existence: and further, that all particular affirmations or negations that would not be certain if they were made general, are only concerning existence; they declaring only the accidental union or separation of ideas in things existing, which, in their abstract natures, have no known necessary union or repugnancy.

2. A threefold knowledge of existence. But, leaving the nature of propositions, and different ways of predication to be considered more at large in another place, let us proceed now to inquire concerning our knowledge of the existence of things, and how we come by it. I say, then, that we have the knowledge of our own existence by intuition; of the existence of God by demonstration; and of other things by sensation.

3. Our knowledge of our own existence is intuitive. As for our own existence, we perceive it so plainly and so certainly, that it neither needs nor is capable of any proof. For nothing can be more evident to us than our own existence. I think, I reason, I feel pleasure and pain: can any of these be more evident to me than my own existence? If I doubt of all other things, that very doubt makes me perceive my own existence, and will not suffer me to doubt of that. For if I know I feel pain, it is evident I have as certain perception of my own existence, as of the existence of the pain I feel: or if I know I doubt, I have as certain perception of the existence of the thing doubting, as of that thought which I call doubt. Experience then convinces us, that we have an intuitive knowledge of our own existence, and an internal infallible perception that we are. In every act of sensation, reasoning, or thinking, we are conscious to ourselves of our own being; and, in this matter, come not short of the highest degree of certainty.

Chapter X.Of our Knowledge of the Existence of a God

1. We are capable of knowing certainly that there is a God. Though God has given us no innate ideas of himself; though he has stamped no original characters on our minds, wherein we may read his being; yet having furnished us with those faculties our minds are endowed with, he hath not left himself without witness: since we have sense, perception, and reason, and cannot want a clear proof of him, as long as we carry ourselves about us. Nor can we justly complain of our ignorance in this great point; since he has so plentifully provided us

with the means to discover and know him; so far as is necessary to the end of our being, and the great concernment of our happiness. But, though this be the most obvious truth that reason discovers, and though its evidence be (if I mistake not) equal to mathematical certainty: yet it requires thought and attention; and the mind must apply itself to a regular deduction of it from some part of our intuitive knowledge, or else we shall be as uncertain and ignorant of this as of other propositions, which are in themselves capable of clear demonstration. To show, therefore, that we are capable of knowing, i.e. being certain that there is a God, and how we may come by this certainty, I think we need go no further than ourselves, and that undoubted knowledge we have of our own existence.

2. For man knows that he himself exists. I think it is beyond question, that man has a clear idea of his own being; he knows certainly he exists, and that he is something. He that can doubt whether he be anything or no, I speak not to; no more than I would argue with pure nothing, or endeavour to convince nonentity that it were something. If any one pretends to be so sceptical as to deny his own existence, (for really to doubt of it is manifestly impossible,) let him for me enjoy his beloved happiness of being nothing, until hunger or some other pain convince him of the contrary. This, then, I think I may take for a truth, which every one's certain knowledge assures him of, beyond the liberty of doubting, viz. that he is something that actually exists.

3 He knows also that nothing cannot produce a being; therefore something must have existed from eternity. In the next place, man knows, by an intuitive certainty, that bare nothing can no more produce any real being, than it can be equal to two right angles. If a man knows not that nonentity, or the absence of all being, cannot be equal to two right angles, it is impossible he should know any demonstration in Euclid. If, therefore, we know there is some real being, and that nonentity cannot produce any real being, it is an evident demonstration, that from eternity there has been something; since what was not from eternity had a beginning; and what had a beginning must be produced by something else.

4. And that eternal Being must be most powerful. Next, it is evident, that what had its being and beginning from another, must also have all that which is in and belongs to its being from another too. All the powers it has must be owing to and received from the same source. This eternal source, then, of all being must also be the source and original of all power; and so this eternal Being must be also the most powerful.

5. And most knowing. Again, a man finds in himself perception and knowledge. We have then got one step further; and we are certain now that there is not only some being, but some knowing, intelligent being in the world. There was a time, then, when there was no knowing being, and when knowledge began to be; or else there has been also a knowing being from eternity. If it be said, there was a time when no being had any knowledge, when that eternal being was void of all understanding; I reply, that then it was impossible there should ever have been any knowledge: it being as impossible that things wholly void of knowledge, and operating blindly, and without any perception, should produce a knowing being, as it is impossible that a triangle should make itself three angles bigger than two right ones. For it is as repugnant to the idea of senseless matter, that it should put into itself sense, perception, and knowledge, as it is repugnant to the idea of a triangle, that it should put into itself greater angles than two right ones.

6. And therefore God. Thus, from the consideration of ourselves, and what we infallibly find in our own constitutions, our reason leads us to the knowledge of this certain and evident truth,— That there is an eternal, most powerful, and most knowing Being; which whether any one will please to call God, it matters not. The thing is evident; and from this idea duly considered, will easily be deduced all those other attributes, which we ought to ascribe to this eternal Being. If, nevertheless, any one should be found so senselessly arrogant, as to suppose man alone knowing and wise, but yet the product of mere ignorance and chance; and that all the rest of the universe acted only by that blind haphazard; I shall leave with him that very rational and emphatical rebuke of Tully (I. ii. De Leg.), to be considered at his leisure: "What can be more sillily arrogant and misbecoming, than for a man to think that he has a mind and

understanding in him, but yet in all the universe beside there is no such thing? Or that those things, which with the utmost stretch of his reason he can scarce comprehend, should be moved and managed without any reason at all?" Quid est enim verius, quam neminem esse oportere tam stulte arrogantem, ut in se mentem et rationem putet inesse, in caelo mundoque non putet? Aut ea quae vix summa ingenii ratione comprehendat, nulla ratione moveri putet? From what has been said, it is plain to me we have a more certain knowledge of the existence of a God, than of anything our senses have not immediately discovered to us. Nay, I presume I may say, that we more certainly know that there is a God, than that there is anything else without us. When I say we know, I mean there is such a knowledge within our reach which we cannot miss, if we will but apply our minds to that, as we do to several other inquiries.

7. Our idea of a most perfect Being, not the sole proof of a God. How far the idea of a most perfect being, which a man may frame in his mind, does or does not prove the existence of a God, I will not here examine. For in the different make of men's tempers and application of their thoughts, some arguments prevail more on one, and some on another, for the confirmation of the same truth. But yet, I think, this I may say, that it is an ill way of establishing this truth, and silencing atheists, to lay the whole stress of so important a point as this upon that sole foundation: and take some men's having that idea of God in their minds, (for it is evident some men have none, and some worse than none, and the most very different,) for the only proof of a Deity; and out of an over fondness of that darling invention, cashier, or at least endeavour to invalidate all other arguments; and forbid us to hearken to those proofs, as being weak or fallacious, which our own existence, and the sensible parts of the universe offer so clearly and cogently to our thoughts, that I deem it impossible for a considering man to withstand them. For I judge it as certain and clear a truth as can anywhere be delivered, that "the invisible things of God are clearly seen from the creation of the world, being understood by the things that are made, even his eternal power and Godhead." Though our own being furnishes us, as I have shown, with an evident and incontestable proof of a Deity; and I believe nobody can avoid the cogency of it, who will but as carefully attend to it, as to any other demonstration of so many parts: yet this being so fundamental a truth, and of that consequence, that all religion and genuine morality depend thereon, I doubt not but I shall be forgiven by my reader if I go over some parts of this argument again, and enlarge a little more upon them.

8. Recapitulation — something from eternity. There is no truth more evident than that something must be from eternity. I never yet heard of any one so unreasonable, or that could suppose so manifest a contradiction, as a time wherein there was perfectly nothing. This being of all absurdities the greatest, to imagine that pure nothing, the perfect negation and absence of all beings, should ever produce any real existence.

It being, then, unavoidable for all rational creatures to conclude, that something has existed from eternity; let us next see what kind of thing that must be.

9. Two sorts of beings, cogitative and incogitative. There are but two sorts of beings in the world that man knows or conceives.

First, such as are purely material, without sense, perception, or thought, as the clippings of our beards, and parings of our nails.

Secondly, sensible, thinking, perceiving beings, such as we find ourselves to be. Which, if you please, we will hereafter call cogitative and incogitative beings; which to our present purpose, if for nothing else, are perhaps better terms than material and immaterial.

10. Incogitative being cannot produce a cogitative being. If, then, there must be something eternal, let us see what sort of being it must be. And to that it is very obvious to reason, that it must necessarily be a cogitative being. For it is as impossible to conceive that ever bare incogitative matter should produce a thinking intelligent being, as that nothing should of itself produce matter. Let us suppose any parcel of matter eternal, great or small, we shall find it, in itself, able to produce nothing. For example: let us suppose the matter of the next pebble we meet with eternal, closely united, and the parts firmly at rest together; if there were no other

being in the world, must it not eternally remain so, a dead inactive lump? Is it possible to conceive it can add motion to itself, being purely matter, or produce anything? Matter, then, by its own strength, cannot produce in itself so much as motion: the motion it has must also be from eternity, or else be produced, and added to matter by some other being more powerful than matter; matter, as is evident, having not power to produce motion in itself. But let us suppose motion eternal too: yet matter, incogitative matter and motion, whatever changes it might produce of figure and bulk, could never produce thought: knowledge will still be as far beyond the power of motion and matter to produce, as matter is beyond the power of nothing or nonentity to produce. And I appeal to every one's own thoughts, whether he cannot as easily conceive matter produced by nothing, as thought to be produced by pure matter, when, before, there was no such thing as thought or an intelligent being existing? Divide matter into as many parts as you will, (which we are apt to imagine a sort of spiritualizing, or making a thinking thing of it,) vary the figure and motion of it as much as you please — a globe, cube, cone, prism, cylinder, &c., whose diameters are but 100,000th part of a gry, will operate no otherwise upon other bodies of proportionable bulk, than those of an inch or foot diameter; and you may as rationally expect to produce sense, thought, and knowledge, by putting together, in a certain figure and motion, gross particles of matter, as by those that are the very minutest that do anywhere exist. They knock, impel, and resist one another, just as the greater do; and that is all they can do. So that, if we will suppose nothing first or eternal, matter can never begin to be: if we suppose bare matter without motion, eternal, motion can never begin to be: if we suppose only matter and motion first, or eternal, thought can never begin to be. For it is impossible to conceive that matter, either with or without motion, could have, originally, in and from itself, sense, perception, and knowledge; as is evident from hence, that then sense, perception, and knowledge, must be a property eternally inseparable from matter and every particle of it. Not to add, that, though our general or specific conception of matter makes us speak of it as one thing, yet really all matter is not one individual thing, neither is there any such thing existing as one material being, or one single body that we know or can conceive. And therefore, if matter were the eternal first cogitative being, there would not be one eternal, infinite, cogitative being, but an infinite number of eternal, finite, cogitative beings, independent one of another, of limited force, and distinct thoughts, which could never produce that order, harmony, and beauty which are to be found in nature. Since, therefore, whatsoever is the first eternal being must necessarily be cogitative; and whatsoever is first of all things must necessarily contain in it, and actually have, at least, all the perfections that can ever after exist; nor can it ever give to another any perfection that it hath not either actually in itself, or, at least, in a higher degree; it necessarily follows, that the first eternal being cannot be matter.

11. Therefore, there has been an eternal cogitative Being. If, therefore, it be evident, that something necessarily must exist from eternity, it is also as evident, that that something must necessarily be a cogitative being: for it is as impossible that incogitative matter should produce a cogitative being, as that nothing, or the negation of all being, should produce a positive being or matter.

12. The attributes of the eternal cogitative Being. Though this discovery of the necessary existence of an eternal Mind does sufficiently lead us into the knowledge of God; since it will hence follow, that all other knowing beings that have a beginning must depend on him, and have no other ways of knowledge or extent of power than what he gives them; and therefore, if he made those, he made also the less excellent pieces of this universe,— all inanimate beings, whereby his omniscience, power, and providence will be established, and all his other attributes necessarily follow: yet, to clear up this a little further, we will see what doubts can be raised against it.

13. Whether the eternal Mind may he also material or no. First, Perhaps it will be said, that, though it be as clear as demonstration can make it, that there must be an eternal Being, and that Being must also be knowing: yet it does not follow but that thinking Being may also be material. Let it be so, it equally still follows that there is a God. For if there be an eternal,

omniscient, omnipotent Being, it is certain that there is a God, whether you imagine that Being to be material or no. But herein, I suppose, lies the danger and deceit of that supposition:— there being no way to avoid the demonstration, that there is an eternal knowing Being, men, devoted to matter, would willingly have it granted, that this knowing Being is material; and then, letting slide out of their minds, or the discourse, the demonstration whereby an eternal knowing Being was proved necessarily to exist, would argue all to be matter, and so deny a God, that is, an eternal cogitative Being: whereby they are so far from establishing, that they destroy their own hypothesis. For, if there can be, in their opinion, eternal matter, without any eternal cogitative Being, they manifestly separate matter and thinking, and suppose no necessary connexion of the one with the other, and so establish the necessity of an eternal Spirit, but not of matter; since it has been proved already, that an eternal cogitative Being is unavoidably to be granted. Now, if thinking and matter may be separated, the eternal existence of matter will not follow from the eternal existence of a cogitative Being, and they suppose it to no purpose.

14. Not material: first, because each particle of matter is not cogitative. But now let us see how they can satisfy themselves, or others, that this eternal thinking Being is material.

I. I would ask them, whether they imagine that all matter, every particle of matter, thinks? This, I suppose, they will scarce say; since then there would be as many eternal thinking beings as there are particles of matter, and so an infinity of gods. And yet, if they will not allow matter as matter, that is, every particle of matter, to be as well cogitative as extended, they will have as hard a task to make out to their own reasons a cogitative being out of incogitative particles, as an extended being out of unextended parts, if I may so speak.

15. II. Secondly, because one particle alone of matter cannot be cogitative. If all matter does not think, I next ask, Whether it be only one atom that does so? This has as many absurdities as the other; for then this atom of matter must be alone eternal or not. If this alone be eternal, then this alone, by its powerful thought or will, made all the rest of matter. And so we have the creation of matter by a powerful thought, which is that the materialists stick at; for if they suppose one single thinking atom to have produced all the rest of matter, they cannot ascribe that pre-eminency to it upon any other account than that of its thinking, the only supposed difference. But allow it to be by some other way which is above our conception, it must still be creation; and these men must give up their great maxim, Ex nihilo nil fit. If it be said, that all the rest of matter is equally eternal as that thinking atom, it will be to say anything at pleasure, though ever so absurd. For to suppose all matter eternal, and yet one small particle in knowledge and power infinitely above all the rest, is without any the least appearance of reason to frame an hypothesis. Every particle of matter, as matter, is capable of all the same figures and motions of any other; and I challenge any one, in his thoughts, to add anything else to one above another.

16. III. Thirdly, because a system of incogitative matter cannot be cogitative. If then neither one peculiar atom alone can be this eternal thinking being; nor all matter, as matter, i.e. every particle of matter, can be it; it only remains, that it is some certain system of matter, duly put together, that is this thinking eternal Being. This is that which, I imagine, is that notion which men are aptest to have of God; who would have him a material being, as most readily suggested to them by the ordinary conceit they have of themselves and other men, which they take to be material thinking beings. But this imagination, however more natural, is no less absurd than the other: for to suppose the eternal thinking Being to be nothing else but a composition of particles of matter, each whereof is incogitative, is to ascribe all the wisdom and knowledge of that eternal Being only to the juxta-position of parts; than which nothing can be more absurd. For unthinking particles of matter, however put together, can have nothing thereby added to them, but a new relation of position, which it is impossible should give thought and knowledge to them.

17. And that whether this corporeal system is in motion or at rest. But further: this corporeal system either has all its parts at rest, or it is a certain motion of the parts wherein its thinking

consists. If it be perfectly at rest, it is but one lump, and so can have no privileges above one atom.

If it be the motion of its parts on which its thinking depends, all the thoughts there must be unavoidably accidental and limited; since all the particles that by motion cause thought, being each of them in itself without any thought, cannot regulate its own motions, much less be regulated by the thought of the whole; since that thought is not the cause of motion, (for then it must be antecedent to it, and so without it,) but the consequence of it; whereby freedom, power, choice, and all rational and wise thinking or acting, will be quite taken away: so that such a thinking being will be no better nor wiser than pure blind matter; since to resolve all into the accidental unguided motions of blind matter, or into thought depending on unguided motions of blind matter, is the same thing: not to mention the narrowness of such thoughts and knowledge that must depend on the motion of such parts. But there needs no enumeration of any more absurdities and impossibilities in this hypothesis (however full of them it be) than that before mentioned; since, let this thinking system be all or a part of the matter of the universe, it is impossible that any one particle should either know its own, or the motion of any other particle, or the whole know the motion of every particle; and so regulate its own thoughts or motions, or indeed have any thought resulting from such motion.

18. Matter not co-eternal with an eternal Mind. Secondly, Others would have Matter to be eternal, notwithstanding that they allow an eternal, cogitative, immaterial Being. This, though it take not away the being of a God, yet, since it denies one and the first great piece of his workmanship, the creation, let us consider it a little. Matter must be allowed eternal: Why? because you cannot conceive how it can be made out of nothing: why do you not also think yourself eternal? You will answer, perhaps, Because, about twenty or forty years since, you began to be. But if I ask you, what that you is, which began then to be, you can scarce tell me. The matter whereof you are made began not then to be: for if it did, then it is not eternal: but it began to be put together in such a fashion and frame as makes up your body; but yet that frame of particles is not you, it makes not that thinking thing you are; (for I have now to do with one who allows an eternal, immaterial, thinking Being, but would have unthinking Matter eternal too;) therefore, when did that thinking thing begin to be? If it did never begin to be, then have you always been a thinking thing from eternity; the absurdity whereof I need not confute, till I meet with one who is so void of understanding as to own it. If, therefore, you can allow a thinking thing to be made out of nothing, (as all things that are not eternal must be,) why also can you not allow it possible for a material being to be made out of nothing by an equal power, but that you have the experience of the one in view, and not of the other? Though, when well considered, creation of a spirit will be found to require no less power than the creation of matter. Nay, possibly, if we would emancipate ourselves from vulgar notions, and raise our thoughts, as far as they would reach, to a closer contemplation of things, we might be able to aim at some dim and seeming conception how matter might at first be made, and begin to exist, by the power of that eternal first Being: but to give beginning and being to a spirit would be found a more inconceivable effect of omnipotent power. But this being what would perhaps lead us too far from the notions on which the philosophy now in the world is built, it would not be pardonable to deviate so far from them; or to inquire, so far as grammar itself would authorize, if the common settled opinion opposes it: especially in this place, where the received doctrine serves well enough to our present purpose, and leaves this past doubt, that the creation or beginning of any one SUBSTANCE out of nothing being once admitted, the creation of all other but the CREATOR himself, may, with the same ease, be supposed.

19. Objection: "Creation out of nothing." But you will say, Is it not impossible to admit of the making anything out of nothing, since we cannot possibly conceive it? I answer, No. Because it is not reasonable to deny the power of an infinite being, because we cannot comprehend its operations. We do not deny other effects upon this ground, because we cannot possibly conceive the manner of their production. We cannot conceive how anything but impulse of body can move body; and yet that is not a reason sufficient to make us deny it possible, against

the constant experience we have of it in ourselves, in all our voluntary motions; which are produced in us only by the free action or thought of our own minds, and are not, nor can be, the effects of the impulse or determination of the motion of blind matter in or upon our own bodies; for then it could not be in our power or choice to alter it. For example: my right hand writes, whilst my left hand is still: What causes rest in one, and motion in the other? Nothing but my will,— a thought of my mind; my thought only changing, the right hand rests, and the left hand moves. This is matter of fact, which cannot be denied: explain this and make it intelligible, and then the next step will be to understand creation. For the giving a new determination to the motion of the animal spirits (which some make use of to explain voluntary motion) clears not the difficulty one jot. To alter the determination of motion, being in this case no easier nor less, than to give motion itself: since the new determination given to the animal spirits must be either immediately by thought, or by some other body put in their way by thought which was not in their way before, and so must owe its motion to thought: either of which leaves voluntary motion as unintelligible as it was before. In the meantime, it is an overvaluing ourselves to reduce all to the narrow measure of our capacities, and to conclude all things impossible to be done, whose manner of doing exceeds our comprehension. This is to make our comprehension infinite, or God finite, when what He can do is limited to what we can conceive of it. If you do not understand the operations of your own finite mind, that thinking thing within you, do not deem it strange that you cannot comprehend the operations of that eternal infinite Mind, who made and governs all things, and whom the heaven of heavens cannot contain.

Chapter XI.Of our Knowledge of the Existence of Other Things

1. Knowledge of the existence of other finite beings is to be had only by actual sensation. The knowledge of our own being we have by intuition. The existence of a God, reason clearly makes known to us, as has been shown.
The knowledge of the existence of any other thing we can have only by sensation: for there being no necessary connexion of real existence with any idea a man hath in his memory; nor of any other existence but that of God with the existence of any particular man: no particular man can know the existence of any other being, but only when, by actual operating upon him, it makes itself perceived by him. For, the having the idea of anything in our mind, no more proves the existence of that thing, than the picture of a man evidences his being in the world, or the visions of a dream make thereby a true history.
2. Instance: whiteness of this paper. It is therefore the actual receiving of ideas from without that gives us notice of the existence of other things, and makes us know, that something doth exist at that time without us, which causes that idea in us; though perhaps we neither know nor consider how it does it. For it takes not from the certainty of our senses, and the ideas we receive by them, that we know not the manner wherein they are produced: v.g. whilst I write this, I have, by the paper affecting my eyes, that idea produced in my mind, which, whatever object causes, I call white; by which I know that that quality or accident (i.e. whose appearance before my eyes always causes that idea) doth really exist, and hath a being without me. And of this, the greatest assurance I can possibly have, and to which my faculties can attain, is the testimony of my eyes, which are the proper and sole judges of this thing; whose testimony I have reason to rely on as so certain, that I can no more doubt, whilst I write this, that I see white and black, and that something really exists that causes that sensation in me, than that I write or move my hand; which is a certainty as great as human nature is capable of, concerning the existence of anything, but a man's self alone, and of God.
3. This notice by our senses, though not so certain as demonstration, yet may be called knowledge, and proves the existence of things without us. The notice we have by our senses of the existing of things without us, though it be not altogether so certain as our intuitive

knowledge, or the deductions of our reason employed about the clear abstract ideas of our own minds; yet it is an assurance that deserves the name of knowledge. If we persuade ourselves that our faculties act and inform us right concerning the existence of those objects that affect them, it cannot pass for an ill-grounded confidence: for I think nobody can, in earnest, be so sceptical as to be uncertain of the existence of those things which he sees and feels. At least, he that can doubt so far, (whatever he may have with his own thoughts,) will never have any controversy with me; since he can never be sure I say anything contrary to his own opinion. As to myself, I think God has given me assurance enough of the existence of things without me: since, by their different application, I can produce in myself both pleasure and pain, which is one great concernment of my present state. This is certain: the confidence that our faculties do not herein deceive us, is the greatest assurance we are capable of concerning the existence of material beings. For we cannot act anything but by our faculties; nor talk of knowledge itself, but by the help of those faculties which are fitted to apprehend even what knowledge is. But besides the assurance we have from our senses themselves, that they do not err in the information they give us of the existence of things without us, when they are affected by them, we are further confirmed in this assurance by other concurrent reasons:—

4. I. Confirmed by concurrent reasons:— First, because we cannot have ideas of sensation but by the inlet of the senses. It is plain those perceptions are produced in us by exterior causes affecting our senses: because those that want the organs of any sense, never can have the ideas belonging to that sense produced in their minds. This is too evident to be doubted: and therefore we cannot but be assured that they come in by the organs of that sense, and no other way. The organs themselves, it is plain, do not produce them: for then the eyes of a man in the dark would produce colours, and his nose smell roses in the winter: but we see nobody gets the relish of a pineapple, till he goes to the Indies, where it is, and tastes it.

5. II. Secondly, Because we find that an idea from actual sensation, and another from memory, are very distinct perceptions. Because sometimes I find that I cannot avoid the having those ideas produced in my mind. For though, when my eyes are shut, or windows fast, I can at pleasure recall to my mind the ideas of light, or the sun, which former sensations had lodged in my memory; so I can at pleasure lay by that idea, and take into my view that of the smell of a rose, or taste of sugar. But, if I turn my eyes at noon towards the sun, I cannot avoid the ideas which the light or sun then produces in me. So that there is a manifest difference between the ideas laid up in my memory, (over which, if they were there only, I should have constantly the same power to dispose of them, and lay them by at pleasure,) and those which force themselves upon me, and I cannot avoid having. And therefore it must needs be some exterior cause, and the brisk acting of some objects without me, whose efficacy I cannot resist, that produces those ideas in my mind, whether I will or no. Besides, there is nobody who doth not perceive the difference in himself between contemplating the sun, as he hath the idea of it in his memory, and actually looking upon it: of which two, his perception is so distinct, that few of his ideas are more distinguishable one from another. And therefore he hath certain knowledge that they are not both memory, or the actions of his mind, and fancies only within him; but that actual seeing hath a cause without.

6. III. Thirdly, because pleasure or pain, which accompanies actual sensation, accompanies not the returning of those ideas without the external objects. Add to this, that many of those ideas are produced in us with pain, which afterwards we remember without the least offence. Thus, the pain of heat or cold, when the idea of it is revived in our minds, gives us no disturbance; which, when felt, was very troublesome; and is again, when actually repeated: which is occasioned by the disorder the external object causes in our bodies when applied to them: and we remember the pains of hunger, thirst, or the headache, without any pain at all; which would either never disturb us, or else constantly do it, as often as we thought of it, were there nothing more but ideas floating in our minds, and appearances entertaining our fancies, without the real existence of things affecting us from abroad. The same may be said of pleasure,

accompanying several actual sensations. And though mathematical demonstration depends not upon sense, yet the examining them by diagrams gives great credit to the evidence of our sight, and seems to give it a certainty approaching to that of demonstration itself. For, it would be very strange, that a man should allow it for an undeniable truth, that two angles of a figure, which he measures by lines and angles of a diagram, should be bigger one than the other, and yet doubt of the existence of those lines and angles, which by looking on he makes use of to measure that by.

7. IV. Fourthly, because our senses assist one another's testimony of the existence of outward things, and enable us to predict. Our senses in many cases bear witness to the truth of each other's report, concerning the existence of sensible things without us. He that sees a fire, may, if he doubt whether it be anything more than a bare fancy, feel it too; and be convinced, by putting his hand in it. Which certainly could never be put into such exquisite pain by a bare idea or phantom, unless that the pain be a fancy too: which yet he cannot, when the burn is well, by raising the idea of it, bring upon himself again.

Thus I see, whilst I write this, I can change the appearance of the paper; and by designing the letters, tell beforehand what new idea it shall exhibit the very next moment, by barely drawing my pen over it: which will neither appear (let me fancy as much as I will) if my hands stand still; or though I move my pen, if my eyes be shut: nor, when those characters are once made on the paper, can I choose afterwards but see them as they are; that is, have the ideas of such letters as I have made. Whence it is manifest, that they are not barely the sport and play of my own imagination, when I find that the characters that were made at the pleasure of my own thoughts, do not obey them; nor yet cease to be, whenever I shall fancy it, but continue to affect my senses constantly and regularly, according to the figures I made them. To which if we will add, that the sight of those shall, from another man, draw such sounds as I beforehand design they shall stand for, there will be little reason left to doubt that those words I write do really exist without me, when they cause a long series of regular sounds to affect my ears, which could not be the effect of my imagination, nor could my memory retain them in that order.

8. This certainty is as great as our condition needs. But yet, if after all this any one will be so sceptical as to distrust his senses, and to affirm that all we see and hear, feel and taste, think and do, during our whole being, is but the series and deluding appearances of a long dream, whereof there is no reality; and therefore will question the existence of all things, or our knowledge of anything: I must desire him to consider, that, if all be a dream, then he doth but dream that he makes the question, and so it is not much matter that a waking man should answer him. But yet, if he pleases, he may dream that I make him this answer, That the certainty of things existing in rerum natura when we have the testimony of our senses for it is not only as great as our frame can attain to, but as our condition needs. For, our faculties being suited not to the full extent of being, nor to a perfect, clear, comprehensive knowledge of things free from all doubt and scruple; but to the preservation of us, in whom they are; and accommodated to the use of life: they serve to our purpose wen enough, if they will but give us certain notice of those things, which are convenient or inconvenient to us. For he that sees a candle burning, and hath experimented the force of its flame by putting his finger in it, will little doubt that this is something existing without him, which does him harm, and puts him to great pain; which is assurance enough, when no man requires greater certainty to govern his actions by than what is as certain as his actions themselves. And if our dreamer pleases to try whether the glowing heat of a glass furnace be barely a wandering imagination in a drowsy man's fancy, by putting his hand into it, he may perhaps be wakened into a certainty greater than he could wish, that it is something more than bare imagination. So that this evidence is as great as we can desire, being as certain to us as our pleasure or pain, i.e. happiness or misery; beyond which we have no concernment, either of knowing or being. Such an assurance of the existence of things without us is sufficient to direct us in the attaining the good and avoiding the evil which is caused by them, which is the important concernment we have of being made

acquainted with them.

9. But reaches no further than actual sensation. In fine, then, when our senses do actually convey into our understandings any idea, we cannot but be satisfied that there doth something at that time really exist without us, which doth affect our senses, and by them give notice of itself to our apprehensive faculties, and actually produce that idea which we then perceive: and we cannot so far distrust their testimony, as to doubt that such collections of simple ideas as we have observed by our senses to be united together, do really exist together. But this knowledge extends as far as the present testimony of our senses, employed about particular objects that do then affect them, and no further. For if I saw such a collection of simple ideas as is wont to be called man, existing together one minute since, and am now alone, I cannot be certain that the same man exists now, since there is no necessary connexion of his existence a minute since with his existence now: by a thousand ways he may cease to be, since I had the testimony of my senses for his existence. And if I cannot be certain that the man I saw last to-day is now in being, I can less be certain that he is so who hath been longer removed from my senses, and I have not seen since yesterday, or since the last year: and much less can I be certain of the existence of men that I never saw. And, therefore, though it be highly probable that millions of men do now exist, yet, whilst I am alone, writing this, I have not that certainty of it which we strictly call knowledge; though the great likelihood of it puts me past doubt, and it be reasonable for me to do several things upon the confidence that there are men (and men also of my acquaintance, with whom I have to do) now in the world: but this is but probability, not knowledge.

10. Folly to expect demonstration in everything. Whereby yet we may observe how foolish and vain a thing it is for a man of a narrow knowledge, who having reason given him to judge of the different evidence and probability of things, and to be swayed accordingly; how vain, I say, it is to expect demonstration and certainty in things not capable of it; and refuse assent to very rational propositions, and act contrary to very plain and clear truths, because they cannot be made out so evident, as to surmount every the least (I will not say reason, but) pretence of doubting. He that, in the ordinary affairs of life, would admit of nothing but direct plain demonstration, would be sure of nothing in this world, but of perishing quickly. The wholesomeness of his meat or drink would not give him reason to venture on it: and I would fain know what it is he could do upon such grounds as are capable of no doubt, no objection.

11. Past existence of other things is known by memory. As when our senses are actually employed about any object, we do know that it does exist; so by our memory we may be assured, that heretofore things that affected our senses have existed. And thus we have knowledge of the past existence of several things, whereof our senses having informed us, our memories still retain the ideas; and of this we are past all doubt, so long as we remember well. But this knowledge also reaches no further than our senses have formerly assured us. Thus, seeing water at this instant, it is an unquestionable truth to me that water doth exist: and remembering that I saw it yesterday, it will also be always true, and as long as my memory retains it always an undoubted proposition to me, that water did exist the 10th of July, 1688; as it will also be equally true that a certain number of very fine colours did exist, which at the same time I saw upon a bubble of that water: but, being now quite out of sight both of the water and bubbles too, it is no more certainly known to me that the water doth now exist, than that the bubbles or colours therein do so: it being no more necessary that water should exist to-day, because it existed yesterday, than that the colours or bubbles exist to-day, because they existed yesterday, though it be exceedingly much more probable; because water hath been observed to continue long in existence, but bubbles, and the colours on them, quickly cease to be.

12. The existence of other finite spirits not knowable, and rests on faith. What ideas we have of spirits, and how we come by them, I have already shown. But though we have those ideas in our minds, and know we have them there, the having the ideas of spirits does not make us know that any such things do exist without us, or that there are any finite spirits, or any other

spiritual beings, but the Eternal God. We have ground from revelation, and several other reasons, to believe with assurance that there are such creatures: but our senses not being able to discover them, we want the means of knowing their particular existences. For we can no more know that there are finite spirits really existing, by the idea we have of such beings in our minds, than by the ideas any one has of fairies or centaurs, he can come to know that things answering those ideas do really exist.

And therefore concerning the existence of finite spirits, as well as several other things, we must content ourselves with the evidence of faith; but universal, certain propositions concerning this matter are beyond our reach. For however true it may be, v.g., that all the intelligent spirits that God ever created do still exist, yet it can never make a part of our certain knowledge. These and the like propositions we may assent to, as highly probable, but are not, I fear, in this state capable of knowing. We are not, then, to put others upon demonstrating, nor ourselves upon search of universal certainty in all those matters; wherein we are not capable of any other knowledge, but what our senses give us in this or that particular.

13. Only particular propositions concerning concrete existences are knowable. By which it appears that there are two sorts of propositions:—(1) There is one sort of propositions concerning the existence of anything answerable to such an idea: as having the idea of an elephant, phoenix, motion, or an angel, in my mind, the first and natural inquiry is, Whether such a thing does anywhere exist? And this knowledge is only of particulars. No existence of anything without us, but only of God, can certainly be known further than our senses inform us. (2) There is another sort of propositions, wherein is expressed the agreement or disagreement of our abstract ideas, and their dependence on one another. Such propositions may be universal and certain. So, having the idea of God and myself, of fear and obedience, I cannot but be sure that God is to be feared and obeyed by me: and this proposition will be certain, concerning man in general, if I have made an abstract idea of such a species, whereof I am one particular. But yet this proposition, how certain soever, that "men ought to fear and obey God" proves not to me the existence of men in the world; but will be true of all such creatures, whenever they do exist: which certainty of such general propositions depends on the agreement or disagreement to be discovered in those abstract ideas.

14. And all general propositions that are known to be true concern abstract ideas. In the former case, our knowledge is the consequence of the existence of things, producing ideas in our minds by our senses: in the latter, knowledge is the consequence of the ideas (be they what they will) that are in our minds, producing there general certain propositions. Many of these are called aeternae veritates, and all of them indeed are so; not from being written, all or any of them, in the minds of all men; or that they were any of them propositions in any one's mind, till he, having got the abstract ideas, joined or separated them by affirmation or negation. But wheresoever we can suppose such a creature as man is, endowed with such faculties, and thereby furnished with such ideas as we have, we must conclude, he must needs, when he applies his thoughts to the consideration of his ideas, know the truth of certain propositions that will arise from the agreement or disagreement which he will perceive in his own ideas. Such propositions are therefore called eternal truths, not because they are eternal propositions actually formed, and antecedent to the understanding that at any time makes them; nor because they are imprinted on the mind from any patterns that are anywhere out of the mind, and existed before: but because, being once made about abstract ideas, so as to be true, they will, whenever they can be supposed to be made again at any time, past or to come, by a mind having those ideas, always actually be true. For names being supposed to stand perpetually for the same ideas, and the same ideas having immutably the same habitudes one to another, propositions concerning any abstract ideas that are once true must needs be eternal verities.

Chapter XII.Of the Improvement of our Knowledge

1. Knowledge is not got from maxims. It having been the common received opinion amongst men of letters, that maxims were the foundation of all knowledge; and that the sciences were each of them built upon certain praecognita from whence the understanding was to take its rise, and by which it was to conduct itself in its inquiries into the matters belonging to that science, the beaten road of the Schools has been, to lay down in the beginning one or more general propositions, as foundations whereon to build the knowledge that was to be had of that subject. These doctrines, thus laid down for foundations of any science, were called principles, as the beginnings from which we must set out, and look no further backwards in our inquiries, as we have already observed.

2. (The occasion of that opinion.) One thing which might probably give an occasion to this way of proceeding in other sciences, was (as I suppose) the good success it seemed to have in mathematics, wherein men, being observed to attain a great certainty of knowledge, these sciences came by pre-eminence to be called Mathemata, and Mathesis, learning, or things learned, thoroughly learned, as having of all others the greatest certainty, clearness, and evidence in them.

3. But from comparing clear and distinct ideas. But if any one will consider, he will (I guess) find, that the great advancement and certainty of real knowledge which men arrived to in these sciences, was not owing to the influence of these principles, nor derived from any peculiar advantage they received from two or three general maxims, laid down in the beginning; but from the clear, distinct, complete ideas their thoughts were employed about, and the relation of equality and excess so clear between some of them, that they had an intuitive knowledge, and by that a way to discover it in others; and this without the help of those maxims. For I ask, Is it not possible for a young lad to know that his whole body is bigger than his little finger, but by virtue of this axiom, that the whole is bigger than a part; nor be assured of it, till he has learned that maxim? Or cannot a country wench know that, having received a shilling from one that owes her three, and a shilling also from another that owes her three, the remaining debts in each of their hands are equal? Cannot she know this, I say, unless she fetch the certainty of it from this maxim, that if you take equals from equals, the remainder will be equals, a maxim which possibly she never heard or thought of? I desire any one to consider, from what has been elsewhere said, which is known first and clearest by most people, the particular instance, or the general rule; and which it is that gives life and birth to the other. These general rules are but the comparing our more general and abstract ideas, which are the workmanship of the mind, made, and names given to them for the easier dispatch in its reasonings, and drawing into comprehensive terms and short rules its various and multiplied observations. But knowledge began in the mind, and was founded on particulars; though afterwards, perhaps, no notice was taken thereof: it being natural for the mind (forward still to enlarge its knowledge) most attentively to lay up those general notions, and make the proper use of them, which is to disburden the memory of the cumbersome load of particulars. For I desire it may be considered, what more certainty there is to a child, or any one, that his body, little finger, and all, is bigger than his little finger alone, after you have given to his body the name whole, and to his little finger the name part, than he could have had before; or what new knowledge concerning his body can these two relative terms give him, which he could not have without them? Could he not know that his body was bigger than his little finger, if his language were yet so imperfect that he had no such relative terms as whole and part? I ask, further, when he has got these names, how is he more certain that his body is a whole, and his little finger a part, than he was or might be certain before he learnt those terms, that his body was bigger than his little finger? Any one may as reasonably doubt or deny that his little finger is a part of his body, as that it is less than his body. And he that can doubt whether it be less, will as certainly doubt whether it be a part. So that the maxim, the whole is bigger than a part, can never be made use of to prove the little finger less than the body, but when it is useless, by being brought to convince one of a truth which he knows already. For he that does not certainly know that any parcel of matter, with another parcel of matter joined to it, is bigger

than either of them alone, will never be able to know it by the help of these two relative terms, whole and part, make of them what maxim you please.

4. Dangerous to build upon precarious principles. But be it in the mathematics as it will, whether it be clearer, that, taking an inch from a black line of two inches, and an inch from a red line of two inches, the remaining parts of the two lines will be equal, or that if you take equals from equals, the remainder will be equals: which, I say, of these two is the clearer and first known, I leave to any one to determine, it not being material to my present occasion. That which I have here to do, is to inquire, whether, if it be the readiest way to knowledge to begin with general maxims, and build upon them, it be yet a safe way to take the principles which are laid down in any other science as unquestionable truths; and so receive them without examination, and adhere to them, without suffering them to be doubted of, because mathematicians have been so happy, or so fair, to use none but self-evident and undeniable. If this be so, I know not what may not pass for truth in morality, what may not be introduced and proved in natural philosophy.

Let that principle of some of the old philosophers, That all is Matter, and that there is nothing else, be received for certain and indubitable, and it will be easy to be seen by the writings of some that have revived it again in our days, what consequences it will lead us into. Let any one, with Polemo, take the world; or with the Stoics, the aether, or the sun; or with Anaximenes, the air, to be God; and what a divinity, religion, and worship must we needs have! Nothing can be so dangerous as principles thus taken up without questioning or examination; especially if they be such as concern morality, which influence men's lives, and give a bias to all their actions. Who might not justly expect another kind of life in Aristippus, who placed happiness in bodily pleasure; and in Antisthenes, who made virtue sufficient to felicity? And he who, with Plato, shall place beatitude in the knowledge of God, will have his thoughts raised to other contemplations than those who look not beyond this spot of earth, and those perishing things which are to be had in it. He that, with Archelaus, shall lay it down as a principle, that right and wrong, honest and dishonest, are defined only by laws, and not by nature, will have other measures of moral rectitude and pravity, than those who take it for granted that we are under obligations antecedent to all human constitutions.

5. To do so is no certain way to truth. If, therefore, those that pass for principles are not certain, (which we must have some way to know, that we may be able to distinguish them from those that are doubtful,) but are only made so to us by our blind assent, we are liable to be misled by them; and instead of being guided into truth, we shall, by principles, be only confirmed in mistake and error.

6. But to compare clear, complete ideas, under steady names. But since the knowledge of the certainty of principles, as well as of all other truths, depends only upon the perception we have of the agreement or disagreement of our ideas, the way to improve our knowledge is not, I am sure, blindly, and with an implicit faith, to receive and swallow principles; but is, I think, to get and fix in our minds clear, distinct, and complete ideas, as far as they are to be had, and annex to them proper and constant names. And thus, perhaps, without any other principles, but barely considering those perfect ideas, and by comparing them one with another, finding their agreement and disagreement, and their several relations and habitudes; we shall get more true and clear knowledge by the conduct of this one rule than by taking up principles, and thereby putting our minds into the disposal of others.

7. The true method of advancing knowledge is by considering our abstract ideas. We must, therefore, if we will proceed as reason advises, adapt our methods of inquiry to the nature of the ideas we examine, and the truth we search after. General and certain truths are only founded in the habitudes and relations of abstract ideas. A sagacious and methodical application of our thoughts. for the finding out these relations, is the only way to discover all that can be put with truth and certainty concerning them into general propositions. By what steps we are to proceed in these, is to be learned in the schools of the mathematicians, who, from very plain and easy beginnings, by gentle degrees, and a continued chain of reasonings,

proceed to the discovery and demonstration of truths that appear at first sight beyond human capacity. The art of finding proofs, and the admirable methods they have invented for the singling out and laying in order those intermediate ideas that demonstratively show the equality or inequality of unapplicable quantities, is that which has carried them so far, and produced such wonderful and unexpected discoveries: but whether something like this, in respect of other ideas, as well as those of magnitude, may not in time be found out, I will not determine. This, I think, I may say, that if other ideas that are the real as well as nominal essences of their species, were pursued in the way familiar to mathematicians, they would carry our thoughts further, and with greater evidence and clearness than possibly we are apt to imagine.

8. By which morality also may be made clearer. This gave me the confidence to advance that conjecture, which I suggest, (chap. iii.) viz. that morality is capable of demonstration as well as mathematics. For the ideas that ethics are conversant about, being all real essences, and such as I imagine have a discoverable connexion and agreement one with another; so far as we can find their habitudes and relations, so far we shall be possessed of certain, real, and general truths; and I doubt not but, if a right method were taken, a great part of morality might be made out with that clearness, that could leave, to a considering man, no more reason to doubt, than he could have to doubt of the truth of propositions in mathematics, which have been demonstrated to him.

9. Our knowledge of substances is to be improved, not by contemplation of abstract ideas, but only by experience. In our search after the knowledge of substances, our want of ideas that are suitable to such a way of proceeding obliges us to a quite different method. We advance not here, as in the other, (where our abstract ideas are real as well as nominal essences,) by contemplating our ideas, and considering their relations and correspondences; that helps us very little, for the reasons, that in another place we have at large set down. By which I think it is evident, that substances afford matter of very little general knowledge; and the bare contemplation of their abstract ideas will carry us but a very little way in the search of truth and certainty. What, then, are we to do for the improvement of our knowledge in substantial beings? Here we are to take a quite contrary course: the want of ideas of their real essences sends us from our own thoughts to the things themselves as they exist. Experience here must teach me what reason cannot: and it is by trying alone, that I can certainly know, what other qualities co-exist with those of my complex idea, v.g. whether that yellow, heavy, fusible body I call gold, be malleable, or no; which experience (which way ever it prove in that particular body I examine) makes me not certain, that it is so in all, or any other yellow, heavy, fusible bodies, but that which I have tried. Because it is no consequence one way or the other from my complex idea: the necessity or inconsistence of malleability hath no visible connexion with the combination of that colour, weight, and fusibility in any body. What I have said here of the nominal essence of gold, supposed to consist of a body of such a determinate colour, weight, and fusibility, will hold true, if malleableness, fixedness, and solubility in aqua regia be added to it. Our reasonings from these ideas will carry us but a little way in the certain discovery of the other properties in those masses of matter wherein all these are to be found. Because the other properties of such bodies, depending not on these, but on that unknown real essence on which these also depend, we cannot by them discover the rest; we can go no further than the simple ideas of our nominal essence will carry us, which is very little beyond themselves; and so afford us but very sparingly any certain, universal, and useful truths. For, upon trial, having found that particular piece (and all others of that colour, weight, and fusibility, that I ever tried) malleable, that also makes now, perhaps, a part of my complex idea, part of my nominal essence of gold: whereby though I make my complex idea to which I affix the name gold, to consist of more simple ideas than before; yet still, it not containing the real essence of any species of bodies, it helps me not certainly to know (I say to know, perhaps it may be to conjecture) the other remaining properties of that body, further than they have a visible connexion with some or all of the simple ideas that make up my nominal essence. For

example, I cannot be certain, from this complex idea, whether gold be fixed or no; because, as before, there is no necessary connexion or inconsistence to be discovered betwixt a complex idea of a body yellow, heavy, fusible, malleable; betwixt these, I say, and fixedness; so that I may certainly know, that in whatsoever body these are found, there fixedness is sure to be. Here, again, for assurance, I must apply myself to experience; as far as that reaches, I may have certain knowledge, but no further.

10. Experience may procure us convenience, not science. I deny not but a man, accustomed to rational and regular experiments, shall be able to see further into the nature of bodies and guess righter at their yet unknown properties than one that is a stranger to them: but yet, as I have said, this is but judgment and opinion, not knowledge and certainty. This way of getting and improving our knowledge in substances only by experience and history, which is all that the weakness of our faculties in this state of mediocrity which we are in in this world can attain to, makes me suspect that natural philosophy is not capable of being made a science. We are able, I imagine, to reach very little general knowledge concerning the species of bodies and their several properties. Experiments and historical observations we may have, from which we may draw advantages of ease and health, and thereby increase our stock of conveniences for this life; but beyond this I fear our talents reach not, nor are our faculties, as I guess, able to advance.

11. We are fitted for moral science, but only for probable interpretations of external nature. From whence it is obvious to conclude that, since our faculties are not fitted to penetrate into the internal fabric and real essences of bodies; but yet plainly discover to us the being of a God and the knowledge of ourselves, enough to lead us into a full and clear discovery of our duty and great concernment; it will become us, as rational creatures, to employ those faculties we have about what they are most adapted to, and follow the direction of nature, where it seems to point us out the way. For it is rational to conclude that our proper employment lies in those inquiries, and in that sort of knowledge which is most suited to our natural capacities, and carries in it our greatest interest, i.e. the condition of our eternal estate. Hence I think I may conclude that morality is the proper science and business of mankind in general, (who are both concerned and fitted to search out their summum bonum;) as several arts, conversant about several parts of nature, are the lot and private talent of particular men for the common use of human life and their own particular subsistence in this world. Of what consequence the discovery of one natural body and its properties may be to human life the whole great continent of America is a convincing instance: whose ignorance in useful arts, and want of the greatest part of the conveniences of life, in a country that abounded with all sorts of natural plenty, I think may be attributed to their ignorance of what was to be found in a very ordinary, despicable stone; I mean the mineral of iron. And whatever we think of our parts or improvements in this part of the world, where knowledge and plenty seem to vie with each other; yet to any one that will seriously reflect on it, I suppose it will appear past doubt, that, were the use of iron lost among us, we should in a few ages be unavoidably reduced to the wants and ignorance of the ancient savage Americans, whose natural endowments and provisions come no way short of those of the most flourishing and polite nations. So that he who first made known the use of that contemptible mineral, may be truly styled the father of arts, and author of plenty.

12. In the study of nature we must beware of hypotheses and wrong principles. I would not, therefore, be thought to disesteem or dissuade the study of nature. I readily agree the contemplation of his works gives us occasion to admire, revere, and glorify their Author: and, if rightly directed, may be of greater benefit to mankind than the monuments of exemplary charity that have at so great charge been raised by the founders of hospitals and almshouses. He that first invented printing, discovered the use of the compass, or made public the virture and right use of kin kina, did more for the propagation of knowledge, for the supply and increase of useful commodities, and saved more from the grave, than those who built colleges, workhouses, and hospitals. All that I would say is, that we should not be too forwardly

possessed with the opinion or expectation of knowledge, where it is not to be had, or by ways that will not attain to it: that we should not take doubtful systems for complete sciences; nor unintelligible notions for scientifical demonstrations. In the knowledge of bodies, we must be content to glean what we can from particular experiments: since we cannot, from a discovery of their real essences, grasp at a time whole sheaves, and in bundles comprehend the nature and properties of whole species together. Where our inquiry is concerning co-existence, or repugnancy to co-exist, which by contemplation of our ideas we cannot discover; there experience, observation, and natural history, must give us, by our senses and by retail, an insight into corporeal substances. The knowledge of bodies we must get by our senses, warily employed in taking notice of their qualities and operations on one another: and what we hope to know of separate spirits in this world, we must, I think, expect only from revelation. He that shall consider how little general maxims, precarious principles, and hypotheses laid down at pleasure, have promoted true knowledge, or helped to satisfy the inquiries of rational men after real improvements; how little, I say, the setting out at that end has, for many ages together, advanced men's progress, towards the knowledge of natural philosophy, will think we have reason to thank those who in this latter age have taken another course, and have trod out to us, though not an easier way to learned ignorance, yet a surer way to profitable knowledge.

13. The true use of hypotheses. Not that we may not, to explain any phenomena of nature, make use of any probable hypotheses whatsoever: hypotheses, if they are well made, are at least great helps to the memory, and often direct us to new discoveries. But my meaning is, that we should not take up any one too hastily (which the mind, that would always penetrate into the causes of things, and have principles to rest on, is very apt to do,) till we have very well examined particulars, and made several experiments, in that thing which we would explain by our hypothesis, and see whether it will agree to them all; whether our principles will carry us quite through, and not be as inconsistent with one phenomenon of nature, as they seem to accommodate and explain another. And at least that we take care that the name of principles deceive us not, nor impose on us, by making us receive that for an unquestionable truth, which is really at best but a very doubtful conjecture; such as are most (I had almost said all) of the hypotheses in natural philosophy.

14. Clear and distinct ideas with settled names, and the finding of those intermediate ideas which show their agreement or disagreement, are the ways to enlarge our knowledge. But whether natural philosophy be capable of certainty or no, the ways to enlarge our knowledge, as far as we are capable, seem to me, in short, to be these two:—

First, The first is to get and settle in our minds determined ideas of those things whereof we have general or specific names; at least, so many of them as we would consider and improve our knowledge in, or reason about. And if they be specific ideas of substances, we should endeavour also to make them as complete as we can, whereby I mean, that we should put together as many simple ideas as, being constantly observed to co-exist, may perfectly determine the species; and each of those simple ideas which are the ingredients of our complex ones, should be clear and distinct in our minds. For it being evident that our knowledge cannot exceed our ideas; as far as they are either imperfect, confused, or obscure, we cannot expect to have certain, perfect, or clear knowledge.

Secondly, The other is the art of finding out those intermediate ideas, which may show us the agreement or repugnancy of other ideas, which cannot be immediately compared.

15. Mathematics an instance of this. That these two (and not the relying on maxims, and drawing consequences from some general propositions) are the right methods of improving our knowledge in the ideas of other modes besides those of quantity, the consideration of mathematical knowledge will easily inform us. Where first we shall find that he that has not a perfect and clear idea of those angles or figures of which he desires to know anything, is utterly thereby incapable of any knowledge about them. Suppose but a man not to have a perfect exact idea of a right angle, a scalenum, or trapezium, and there is nothing more certain

than that he will in vain seek any demonstration about them. Further, it is evident that it was not the influence of those maxims which are taken for principles in mathematics that hath led the masters of that science into those wonderful discoveries they have made. Let a man of good parts know all the maxims generally made use of in mathematics ever so perfectly, and contemplate their extent and consequences as much as he pleases, he will, by their assistance, I suppose, scarce ever come to know that the square of the hypothenuse in a right-angled triangle is equal to the squares of the two other sides. The knowledge that "the whole is equal to all its parts," and "if you take equals from equals, the remainder will be equal," &c., helped him not, I presume, to this demonstration: and a man may, I think, pore long enough on those axioms without ever seeing one jot the more of mathematical truths. They have been discovered by the thoughts otherwise applied: the mind had other objects, other views before it, far different from those maxims, when it first got the knowledge of such truths in mathematics, which men, well enough acquainted with those received axioms, but ignorant of their method who first made these demonstrations, can never sufficiently admire. And who knows what methods to enlarge our knowledge in other parts of science may hereafter be invented, answering that of algebra in mathematics, which so readily finds out the ideas of quantities to measure others by; whose equality or proportion we could otherwise very hardly, or, perhaps, never come to know?

Chapter XIII.Some Further Considerations Concerning our Knowledge

1. Our knowledge partly necessary, partly voluntary. Our knowledge, as in other things, so in this, has so great a conformity with our sight, that it is neither wholly necessary, nor wholly voluntary. If our knowledge were altogether necessary, all men's knowledge would not only be alike, but every man would know all that is knowable; and if it were wholly voluntary, some men so little regard or value it that they would have extreme little, or none at all. Men that have senses cannot choose but receive some ideas by them; and if they have memory, they cannot but retain some of them; and if they have memory, they cannot but retain some of them; and if they have any distinguishing faculty, cannot but perceive the agreement or disagreement of some of them one with another; as he that has eyes, if he will open them by day, cannot but see some objects and perceive a difference in them. But though a man with his eyes open in the light, cannot but see, yet there be certain objects which he may choose whether he will turn his eyes to; there may be in his reach a book containing pictures and discourses, capable to delight or instruct him, which yet he may never have the will to open, never take the pains to look into.
2. The application of our faculties voluntary; but, they being employed, we know as things are, not as we please. There is also another thing in a man's power, and that is, though he turns his eyes sometimes towards an object, yet he may choose whether he will curiously survey it, and with an intent application endeavour to observe accurately all that is visible in it. But yet, what he does see, he cannot see otherwise than he does. It depends not on his will to see that black which appears yellow; nor to persuade himself that what actually scalds him, feels cold. The earth will not appear painted with flowers, nor the fields covered with verdure, whenever he has a mind to it: in the cold winter, he cannot help seeing it white and hoary, if he will look abroad. Just thus is it with our understanding: all that is voluntary in our knowledge is the employing or withholding any of our faculties from this or that sort of objects, and a more or less accurate survey of them: but, they being employed, our will hath no power to determine the knowledge of the mind one way or another; that is done only by the objects themselves, as far as they are clearly discovered. And therefore, as far as men's senses are conversant about external objects, the mind cannot but receive those ideas which are presented by them, and be informed of the existence of things without: and so far as men's thoughts converse with their

own determined ideas, they cannot but in some measure observe the agreement or disagreement that is to be found amongst some of them, which is so far knowledge: and if they have names for those ideas which they have thus considered, they must needs be assured of the truth of those propositions which express that agreement or disagreement they perceive in them, and be undoubtedly convinced of those truths. For what a man sees, he cannot but see; and what he perceives, he cannot but know that he perceives.

3. Instance in numbers. Thus he that has got the ideas of numbers, and hath taken the pains to compare one, two, and three, to six, cannot choose but know that they are equal: he that hath got the idea of a triangle, and found the ways to measure its angles and their magnitudes, is certain that its three angles are equal to two right ones; and can as little doubt of that, as of this truth, that it is impossible for the same thing to be, and not to be.

4. Instance in natural religion. He also that hath the idea of an intelligent, but frail and weak being, made by and depending on another, who is eternal, omnipotent, perfectly wise and good, will as certainly know that man is to honour, fear, and obey God, as that the sun shines when he sees it. For if he hath but the ideas of two such beings in his mind, and will turn his thoughts that way, and consider them, he will as certainly find that the inferior, finite, and dependent is under an obligation to obey the supreme and infinite, as he is certain to find that three, four, and seven are less than fifteen; if he will consider and compute those numbers: nor can he be surer in a clear morning that the sun is risen; if he will but open his eyes and turn them that way. But yet these truths, being ever so certain, ever so clear, he may be ignorant of either, or all of them, who will never take the pains to employ his faculties, as he should, to inform himself about them.

Chapter XIV. Of Judgment

1. Our knowledge being short, we want something else. The understanding faculties being given to man, not barely for speculation, but also for the conduct of his life, man would be at a great loss if he had nothing to direct him but what has the certainty of true knowledge. For that being very short and scanty, as we have seen, he would be often utterly in the dark, and in most of the actions of his life, perfectly at a stand, had he nothing to guide him in the absence of clear and certain knowledge. He that will not eat till he has demonstration that it will nourish him; he that will not stir till he infallibly knows the business he goes about will succeed, will have little else to do but to sit still and perish.

2. What use to be made of this twilight state. Therefore, as God has set some things in broad daylight; as he has given us some certain knowledge, though limited to a few things in comparison, probably as a taste of what intellectual creatures are capable of to excite in us a desire and endeavour after a better state: so, in the greatest part of our concernments, he has afforded us only the twilight, as I may so say, of probability; suitable, I presume, to that state of mediocrity and probationership he has been pleased to place us in here; wherein, to check our over-confidence and presumption, we might, by every day's experience, be made sensible of our short-sightedness and liableness to error; the sense whereof might be a constant admonition to us, to spend the days of this our pilgrimage with industry and care, in the search and following of that way which might lead us to a state of greater perfection. It being highly rational to think, even were revelation silent in the case, that, as men employ those talents God has given them here, they shall accordingly receive their rewards at the close of the day, when their sun shall set and night shall put an end to their labours.

3. Judgment, or assent to probability, supplies our want of knowledge. The faculty which God has given man to supply the want of clear and certain knowledge, in cases where that cannot be had, is judgment: whereby the mind takes its ideas to agree or disagree; or, which is the same, any proposition to be true or false, without perceiving a demonstrative evidence in the proofs. The mind sometimes exercises this judgment out of necessity, where demonstrative

proofs and certain knowledge are not to be had; and sometimes out of laziness, unskilfulness, or haste, even where demonstrative and certain proofs are to be had. Men often stay not warily to examine the agreement or disagreement of two ideas which they are desirous or concerned to know; but, either incapable of such attention as is requisite in a long train of gradations, or impatient of delay, lightly cast their eyes on, or wholly pass by the proofs; and so, without making out the demonstration, determine of the agreement or disagreement of two ideas, as it were by a view of them as they are at a distance, and take it to be the one or the other, as seems most likely to them upon such a loose survey. This faculty of the mind, when it is exercised immediately about things, is called judgment; when about truths delivered in words, is most commonly called assent or dissent: which being the most usual way, wherein the mind has occasion to employ this faculty, I shall, under these terms, treat of it, as least liable in our language to equivocation.

4. Judgement is the presuming things to be so, without perceiving it. Thus the mind has two faculties conversant about truth and falsehood:—

First, KNOWLEDGE, whereby it certainly perceives, and is undoubtedly satisfied of the agreement or disagreement of any ideas.

Secondly JUDGMENT, which is the putting ideas together, or separating them from one another in the mind, when their certain agreement or disagreement is not perceived, but presumed to be so; which is, as the word imports, taken to be so before it certainly appears. And if it so unites or separates them as in reality things are, it is right judgment.

Chapter XV.Of Probability

1. Probability is the appearance of agreement upon fallible proofs. As demonstration is the showing the agreement or disagreement of two ideas by the intervention of one or more proofs, which have a constant, immutable, and visible connexion one with another; so probability is nothing but the appearance of such an agreement or disagreement by the intervention of proofs, whose connexion is not constant and immutable, or at least is not perceived to be so, but is, or appears for the most part to be so, and is enough to induce the mind to judge the proposition to be true or false, rather than the contrary. For example: in the demonstration of it a man perceives the certain, immutable connexion there is of equality between the three angles of a triangle, and those intermediate ones which are made use of to show their equality to two right ones; and so, by an intuitive knowledge of the agreement or disagreement of the intermediate ideas in each step of the progress, the whole series is continued with an evidence, which clearly shows the agreement or disagreement of those three angles in equality to two right ones: and thus he has certain knowledge that it is so. But another man, who never took the pains to observe the demonstration, hearing a mathematician, a man of credit, affirm the three angles of a triangle to be equal to two right ones, assents to it, i.e. receives it for true: in which case the foundation of his assent is the probability of the thing; the proof being such as for the most part carries truth with it: the man on whose testimony he receives it, not being wont to affirm anything contrary to or besides his knowledge, especially in matters of this kind: so that that which causes his assent to this proposition, that the three angles of a triangle are equal to two right ones, that which makes him take these ideas to agree, without knowing them to do so, is the wonted veracity of the speaker in other cases, or his supposed veracity in this.

2. It is to supply our want of knowledge. Our knowledge, as has been shown, being very narrow, and we not happy enough to find certain truth in everything which we have occasion to consider; most of the propositions we think, reason, discourse — nay, act upon, are such as we cannot have undoubted knowledge of their truth: yet some of them border so near upon certainty, that we make no doubt at all about them; but assent to them as firmly, and act, according to that assent, as resolutely as if they were infallibly demonstrated, and that our

knowledge of them was perfect and certain. But there being degrees herein, from the very neighbourhood of certainty and demonstration, quite down to improbability and unlikeness, even to the confines of impossibility; and also degrees of assent from full assurance and confidence, quite down to conjecture, doubt, and distrust: I shall come now, (having, as I think, found out the bounds of human knowledge and certainty,) in the next place, to consider the several degrees and grounds of probability, and assent or faith.

3. Being that which makes us presume things to be true, before we know them to be so. Probability is likeliness to be true, the very notation of the word signifying such a proposition, for which there be arguments or proofs to make it pass, or be received for true. The entertainment the mind gives this sort of propositions is called belief, assent, or opinion, which is the admitting or receiving any proposition for true, upon arguments or proofs that are found to persuade us to receive it as true, without certain knowledge that it is so. And herein lies the difference between probability and certainty, faith, and knowledge, that in all the parts of knowledge there is intuition; each immediate idea, each step has its visible and certain connexion: in belief, not so. That which makes me believe, is something extraneous to the thing I believe; something not evidently joined on both sides to, and so not manifestly showing the agreement or disagreement of those ideas that are under consideration.

4. The grounds of probability are two: conformity with our own experience, or the testimony of others' experience. Probability then, being to supply the defect of our knowledge and to guide us where that fails, is always conversant about propositions whereof we have no certainty, but only some inducements to receive them for true. The grounds of it are, in short, these two following:—

First, The conformity of anything with our own knowledge, observation, and experience. Secondly, The testimony of others, vouching their observation and experience. In the testimony of others is to be considered: 1. The number. 2. The integrity. 3. The skill of the witnesses. 4. The design of the author, where it is a testimony out of a book cited. 5. The consistency of the parts, and circumstances of the relation. 6. Contrary testimonies.

5. In this, all the arguments pro and con ought to be examined, before we come to a judgment. Probability wanting that intuitive evidence which infallibly determines the understanding and produces certain knowledge, the mind, if it will proceed rationally, ought to examine all the grounds of probability, and see how they make more or less for or against any proposition, before it assents to or dissents from it; and, upon a due balancing the whole, reject or receive it, with a more or less firm assent, proportionably to the preponderancy of the greater grounds of probability on one side or the other. For example:—

If I myself see a man walk on the ice, it is past probability; it is knowledge. But if another tells me he saw a man in England, in the midst of a sharp winter, walk upon water hardened with cold, this has so great conformity with what is usually observed to happen that I am disposed by the nature of the thing itself to assent to it; unless some manifest suspicion attend the relation of that matter of fact. But if the same thing be told to one born between the tropics, who never saw nor heard of any such thing before, there the whole probability relies on testimony: and as the relators are more in number, and of more credit, and have no interest to speak contrary to the truth, so that matter of fact is like to find more or less belief. Though to a man whose experience has always been quite contrary, and who has never heard of anything like it, the most untainted credit of a witness will scarce be able to find belief.

The king of Siam. As it happened to a Dutch ambassador, who entertaining the king of Siam with the particularities of Holland, which he was inquisitive after, amongst other things told him that the water in his country would sometimes, in cold weather, be so hard that men walked upon it, and that it would bear an elephant, if he were there. To which the king replied, Hitherto I have believed the strange things you have told me, because I look upon you as a sober fair man, but now I am sure you lie.

6. Probable arguments capable of great variety. Upon these grounds depends the probability of any proposition: and as the conformity of our knowledge, as the certainty of observations, as

the frequency and constancy of experience and the number and credibility of testimonies do more or less agree or disagree with it, so is any proposition in itself more or less probable. There is another, I confess, which, though by itself it be no true ground of probability, yet is often made use of for one, by which men most commonly regulate their assent, and upon which they pin their faith more than anything else, and that is, the opinion of others; though there cannot be a more dangerous thing to rely on, nor more likely to mislead one; since there is much more falsehood and error among men than truth and knowledge. And if the opinions and persuasions of others, whom we know and think well of, be a ground of assent, men have reason to be Heathens in Japan, Mahometans in Turkey, Papists in Spain, Protestants in England, and Lutherans in Sweden. But of this wrong ground of assent I shall have occasion to speak more at large in another place.

Chapter XVI. Of the Degrees of Assent

1. Our assent ought to be regulated by the grounds of probability. The grounds of probability we have laid down in the foregoing chapter: as they are the foundations on which our assent is built, so are they also the measure whereby its several degrees are, or ought to be regulated: only we are to take notice that, whatever grounds of probability there may be, they yet operate no further on the mind which searches after truth, and endeavours to judge right, than they appear; at least, in the first judgment or search that the mind makes. I confess, in the opinions men have, and firmly stick to in the world, their assent is not always from an actual view of the reasons that at first prevailed with them: it being in many cases almost impossible, and in most, very hard, even for those who have very admirable memories, to retain all the proofs which, upon a due examination, made them embrace that side of the question. It suffices that they have once with care and fairness sifted the matter as far as they could; and that they have searched into all the particulars, that they could imagine to give any light to the question; and, with the best of their skill, cast up the account upon the whole evidence: and thus, having once found on which side the probability appeared to them, after as full and exact an inquiry as they can make, they lay up the conclusion in their memories as a truth they have discovered; and for the future they remain satisfied with the testimony of their memories that this is the opinion that, by the proofs they have once seen of it, deserves such a degree of their assent as they afford it.

2. These cannot always be actually in view; and then we must content ourselves with the remembrance that we once saw ground for such a degree of assent. This is all that the greatest part of men are capable of doing, in regulating their opinions and judgments; unless a man will exact of them, either to retain distinctly in their memories all the proofs concerning any probable truth, and that too, in the same order, and regular deduction of consequences in which they have formerly placed or seen them; which sometimes is enough to fill a large volume on one single question: or else they must require a man, for every opinion that he embraces, every day to examine the proofs: both which are impossible. It is unavoidable, therefore, that the memory be relied on in the case, and that men be persuaded of several opinions, whereof the proofs are not actually in their thoughts; nay, which perhaps they are not able actually to recall. Without this, the greatest part of men must be either very sceptic; or change every moment, and yield themselves up to whoever, having lately studied the question, offers them arguments, which, for want of memory, they are not able presently to answer.

3. The ill consequence of this, if our former judgments were not rightly made. I cannot but own, that men's sticking to their past judgment, and adhering firmly to conclusions formerly made, is often the cause of great obstinacy in error and mistake. But the fault is not that they rely on their memories for what they have before well judged, but because they judged before they had well examined. May we not find a great number (not to say the greatest part) of men that think they have formed right judgments of several matters; and that for no other reason,

but because they never thought otherwise? that imagine themselves to have judged right, only because they never questioned, never examined, their own opinions? Which is indeed to think they judged right, because they never judged at all. And yet these, of all men, hold their opinions with the greatest stiffness; those being generally the most fierce and firm in their tenets, who have least examined them. What we once know, we are certain is so: and we may be secure, that there are no latent proofs undiscovered, which may overturn our knowledge, or bring it in doubt. But, in matters of probability, it is not in every case we can be sure that we have all the particulars before us, that any way concern the question; and that there is no evidence behind, and yet unseen, which may cast the probability on the other side, and outweigh all that at present seems to preponderate with us. Who almost is there that hath the leisure, patience, and means to collect together all the proofs concerning most of the opinions he has, so as safely to conclude that he hath a clear and full view; and that there is no more to be alleged for his better information? And yet we are forced to determine ourselves on the one side or other. The conduct of our lives, and the management of our great concerns, will not bear delay: for those depend, for the most part, on the determination of our judgment in points wherein we are not capable of certain and demonstrative knowledge, and wherein it is necessary for us to embrace the one side or the other.

4. The right use of it, mutual charity and forbearance, in a necessary diversity of opinions. Since, therefore, it is unavoidable to the greatest part of men, if not all, to have several opinions, without certain and indubitable proofs of their truth; and it carries too great an imputation of ignorance, lightness, or folly for men to quit and renounce their former tenets presently upon the offer of an argument which they cannot immediately answer, and show the insufficiency of: it would, methinks, become all men to maintain peace, and the common offices of humanity, and friendship, in the diversity of opinions; since we cannot reasonably expect that any one should readily and obsequiously quit his own opinion, and embrace ours, with a blind resignation to an authority which the understanding of man acknowledges not. For however it may often mistake, it can own no other guide but reason, nor blindly submit to the will and dictates of another. If he you would bring over to your sentiments be one that examines before he assents, you must give him leave at his leisure to go over the account again, and, recalling what is out of his mind, examine all the particulars, to see on which side the advantage lies: and if he will not think our arguments of weight enough to engage him anew in so much pains, it is but what we often do ourselves in the like case; and we should take it amiss if others should prescribe to us what points we should study. And if he be one who takes his opinions upon trust, how can we imagine that he should renounce those tenets which time and custom have so settled in his mind, that he thinks them self-evident, and of an unquestionable certainty; or which he takes to be impressions he has received from God himself, or from men sent by him? How can we expect, I say, that opinions thus settled should be given up to the arguments or authority of a stranger or adversary, especially if there be any suspicion of interest or design, as there never fails to be, where men find themselves ill treated? We should do well to commiserate our mutual ignorance, and endeavour to remove it in all the gentle and fair ways of information; and not instantly treat others ill, as obstinate and perverse, because they will not renounce their own, and receive our opinions, or at least those we would force upon them, when it is more than probable that we are no less obstinate in not embracing some of theirs. For where is the man that has incontestable evidence of the truth of all that he holds, or of the falsehood of all he condemns; or can say that he has examined to the bottom all his own, or other men's opinions? The necessity of believing without knowledge, nay often upon very slight grounds, in this fleeting state of action and blindness we are in, should make us more busy and careful to inform ourselves than constrain others. At least, those who have not thoroughly examined to the bottom all their own tenets, must confess they are unfit to prescribe to others; and are unreasonable in imposing that as truth on other men's belief, which they themselves have not searched into, nor weighed the arguments of probability, on which they should receive or reject it. Those who have fairly and truly

examined, and are thereby got past doubt in all the doctrines they profess and govern themselves by, would have a juster pretence to require others to follow them: but these are so few in number, and find so little reason to be magisterial in their opinions, that nothing insolent and imperious is to be expected from them: and there is reason to think, that, if men were better instructed themselves, they would be less imposing on others.

5. Probability is either of sensible matter of fact, capable of human testimony, or of what is beyond the evidence of our senses. But to return to the grounds of assent, and the several degrees of it, we are to take notice, that the propositions we receive upon inducements of probability are of two sorts: either concerning some particular existence, or, as it is usually termed, matter of fact, which, falling under observation, is capable of human testimony; or else concerning things, which, being beyond the discovery of our senses, are not capable of any such testimony.

6. The concurrent experience of all other men with ours, produces assurance approaching to knowledge. Concerning the first of these, viz. Particular matter of fact.

I. Where any particular thing, consonant to the constant observation of ourselves and others in the like case, comes attested by the concurrent reports of all that mention it, we receive it as easily, and build as firmly upon it, as if it were certain knowledge; and we reason and act thereupon with as little doubt as if it were perfect demonstration. Thus, if all Englishmen, who have occasion to mention it, should affirm that it froze in England the last winter, or that there were swallows seen there in the summer, I think a man could almost as little doubt of it as that seven and four are eleven. The first, therefore, and highest degree of probability, is, when the general consent of all men, in all ages, as far as it can be known, concurs with a man's constant and never-failing experience in like cases, to confirm the truth of any particular matter of fact attested by fair witnesses: such are all the stated constitutions and properties of bodies, and the regular proceedings of causes and effects in the ordinary course of nature. This we call an argument from the nature of things themselves. For what our own and other men's constant observation has found always to be after the same manner, that we with reason conclude to be the effect of steady and regular causes; though they come not within the reach of our knowledge. Thus, That fire warmed a man, made lead fluid, and changes the colour or consistency in wood or charcoal; that iron sunk in water, and swam in quicksilver: these and the like propositions about particular facts, being agreeable to our constant experience, as often as we have to do with these matters; and being generally spoke of (when mentioned by others) as things found constantly to be so, and therefore not so much as controverted by anybody — we are put past doubt that a relation affirming any such thing to have been, or any prediction that it will happen again in the same manner, is very true. These probabilities rise so near to certainty, that they govern our thoughts as absolutely, and influence all our actions as fully, as the most evident demonstration; and in what concerns us we make little or no difference between them and certain knowledge. Our belief, thus grounded, rises to assurance.

7. II. Unquestionable testimony, and our own experience that a thing is for the most part so, produce confidence. The next degree of probability is, when I find by my own experience, and the agreement of all others that mention it, a thing to be for the most part so, and that the particular instance of it is attested by many and undoubted witnesses: v.g. history giving us such an account of men in all ages, and my own experience, as far as I had an opportunity to observe, confirming it, that most men prefer their private advantage to the public: if all historians that write of Tiberius, say that Tiberius did so, it is extremely probable. And in this case, our assent has a sufficient foundation to raise itself to a degree which we may call confidence.

8. III. Fair testimony, and the nature of the thing indifferent, produce unavoidable assent. In things that happen indifferently, as that a bird should fly this or that way; that it should thunder on a man's right or left hand, &c., when any particular matter of fact is vouched by the concurrent testimony of unsuspected witnesses, there our assent is also unavoidable. Thus: that there is such a city in Italy as Rome: that about one thousand seven hundred years ago, there

lived in it a man, called Julius Caesar; that he was a general, and that he won a battle against another, called Pompey. This, though in the nature of the thing there be nothing for nor against it, yet being related by historians of credit, and contradicted by no one writer, a man cannot avoid believing it, and can as little doubt of it as he does of the being and actions of his own acquaintance, whereof he himself is a witness.

9. Experience and testimonies clashing infinitely vary the degrees of probability. Thus far the matter goes easy enough. Probability upon such grounds carries so much evidence with it, that it naturally determines the judgment, and leaves us as little liberty to believe or disbelieve, as a demonstration does, whether we will know, or be ignorant. The difficulty is, when testimonies contradict common experience, and the reports of history and witnesses clash with the ordinary course of nature, or with one another; there it is, where diligence, attention, and exactness are required, to form a right judgment, and to proportion the assent to the different evidence and probability of the thing: which rises and falls, according as those two foundations of credibility, viz. common observation in like cases, and particular testimonies in that particular instance, favour or contradict it. These are liable to so great variety of contrary observations, circumstances, reports, different qualifications, tempers, designs, oversights, &c., of the reporters, that it is impossible to reduce to precise rules the various degrees wherein men give their assent. This only may be said in general, That as the arguments and proofs pro and con, upon due examination, nicely weighing every particular circumstance, shall to any one appear, upon the whole matter, in a greater or less degree to preponderate on either side; so they are fitted to produce in the mind such different entertainments, as we call belief, conjecture, guess, doubt, wavering, distrust, disbelief, &c.

10. Traditional testimonies, the further removed the less their proof becomes. This is what concerns assent in matters wherein testimony is made use of: concerning which, I think, it may not be amiss to take notice of a rule observed in the law of England; which is, That though the attested copy of a record be good proof, yet the copy of a copy, ever so well attested, and by ever so credible witnesses, will not be admitted as a proof in judicature. This is so generally approved as reasonable, and suited to the wisdom and caution to be used in our inquiry after material truths, that I never yet heard of any one that blamed it. This practice, if it be allowable in the decisions of right and wrong, carries this observation along with it, viz. That any testimony, the further off it is from the original truth, the less force and proof it has. The being and existence of the thing itself, is what I call the original truth. A credible man vouching his knowledge of it is a good proof; but if another equally credible do witness it from his report, the testimony is weaker: and a third that attests the hearsay of an hearsay is yet less considerable. So that in traditional truths, each remove weakens the force of the proof: and the more hands the tradition has successively passed through, the less strength and evidence does it receive from them. This I thought necessary to be taken notice of: because I find amongst some men the quite contrary commonly practised, who look on opinions to gain force by growing older; and what a thousand years since would not, to a rational man contemporary with the first voucher, have appeared at all probable, is now urged as certain beyond all question, only because several have since, from him, said it one after another. Upon this ground propositions, evidently false or doubtful enough in their first beginning, come, by an inverted rule of probability, to pass for authentic truths; and those which found or deserved little credit from the mouths of their first authors, are thought to grow venerable by age, are urged as undeniable.

11. Yet history is of great use. I would not be thought here to lessen the credit and use of history: it is all the light we have in many cases, and we have in many cases, and we receive from it a great part of the useful truths we have, with a convincing evidence. I think nothing more valuable than the records of antiquity: I wish we had more of them, and more uncorrupted. But this truth itself forces me to say, That no probability can rise higher than its first original. What has no other evidence than the single testimony of one only witness must stand or fall by his only testimony, whether good, bad, or indifferent; and though cited

afterwards by hundreds of others, one after another, is so far from receiving any strength thereby, that it is only the weaker. Passion, interest, inadvertency, mistake of his meaning, and a thousand odd reasons, or capricios, men's minds are acted by, (impossible to be discovered,) may make one man quote another man's words or meaning wrong. He that has but ever so little examined the citations of writers, cannot doubt how little credit the quotations deserve, where the originals are wanting; and consequently how much less quotations of quotations can be relied on. This is certain, that what in one age was affirmed upon slight grounds, can never after come to be more valid in future ages by being often repeated. But the further still it is from the original, the less valid it is, and has always less force in the mouth or writing of him that last made use of it than in his from whom he received it.

12. In things which sense cannot discover, analogy is the great rule of probability. [Secondly], The probabilities we have hitherto mentioned are only such as concern matter of fact, and such things as are capable of observation and testimony. There remains that other sort, concerning which men entertain opinions with variety of assent, though the things be such, that falling not under the reach of our senses, they are not capable of testimony. Such are, 1. The existence, nature and operations of finite immaterial beings without us; as spirits, angels, devils, &c. Or the existence of material beings which, either for their smallness in themselves or remoteness from us, our senses cannot take notice of — as, whether there be any plants, animals, and intelligent inhabitants in the planets, and other mansions of the vast universe. 2. Concerning the manner of operation in most parts of the works of nature: wherein, though we see the sensible effects, yet their causes are unknown, and we perceive not the ways and manner how they are produced. We see animals are generated, nourished, and move; the loadstone draws iron; and the parts of a candle, successively melting, turn into flame, and give us both light and heat. These and the like effects we see and know: but the causes that operate, and the manner they are produced in, we can only guess and probably conjecture. For these and the like, coming not within the scrutiny of human senses, cannot be examined by them, or be attested by anybody; and therefore can appear more or less probable, only as they more or less agree to truths that are established in our minds, and as they hold proportion to other parts of our knowledge and observation. Analogy in these matters is the only help we have, and it is from that alone we draw all our grounds of probability. Thus, observing that the bare rubbing of two bodies violently one upon another, produces heat, and very often fire itself, we have reason to think, that what we call heat and fire consists in a violent agitation of the imperceptible minute parts of the burning matter. Observing likewise that the different refractions of pellucid bodies produce in our eyes the different appearances of several colours; and also, that the different ranging and laying the superficial parts of several bodies, as of velvet, watered silk, &c., does the like, we think it probable that the colour and shining of bodies is in them nothing but the different arrangement and refraction of their minute and insensible parts. Thus, finding in all parts of the creation, that fall under human observation, that there is a gradual connexion of one with another, without any great or discernible gaps between, in all that great variety of things we see in the world, which are so closely linked together, that, in the several ranks of beings, it is not easy to discover the bounds betwixt them; we have reason to be persuaded that, by such gentle steps, things ascend upwards in degrees of perfection. It is a hard matter to say where sensible and rational begin, and where insensible and irrational end: and who is there quick-sighted enough to determine precisely which is the lowest species of living things, and which the first of those which have no life? Things, as far as we can observe, lessen and augment, as the quantity does in a regular cone; where, though there be a manifest odds betwixt the bigness of the diameter at a remote distance, yet the difference between the upper and under, where they touch one another, is hardly discernible. The difference is exceeding great between some men and some animals: but if we will compare the understanding and abilities of some men and some brutes, we shall find so little difference, that it will be hard to say, that that of the man is either clearer or larger. Observing, I say, such gradual and gentle descents downwards in those parts of the creation that are beneath man, the rule of analogy

may make it probable, that it is so also in things above us and our observation; and that there are several ranks of intelligent beings, excelling us in several degrees of perfection, ascending upwards towards the infinite perfection of the Creator, by gentle steps and differences, that are every one at no great distance from the next to it. This sort of probability, which is the best conduct of rational experiments, and the rise of hypothesis, has also its use and influence; and a wary reasoning from analogy leads us often into the discovery of truths and useful productions, which would otherwise lie concealed.

13. One case where contrary experience lessens not the testimony. Though the common experience and the ordinary course of things have justly a mighty influence on the minds of men, to make them give or refuse credit to anything proposed to their belief; yet there is one case, wherein the strangeness of the fact lessens not the assent to a fair testimony given of it. For where such supernatural events are suitable to ends aimed at by Him who has the power to change the course of nature, there, under such circumstances, that may be the fitter to procure belief, by how much the more they are beyond or contrary to ordinary observation. This is the proper case of miracles, which, well attested, do not only find credit themselves, but give it also to other truths, which need such confirmation.

14. The bare testimony of divine revelation is the highest certainty. Besides those we have hitherto mentioned, there is one sort of propositions that challenge the highest degree of our assent, upon bare testimony, whether the thing proposed agree or disagree with common experience, and the ordinary course of things, or no. The reason whereof is, because the testimony is of such an one as cannot deceive nor be deceived: and that is of God himself. This carries with it an assurance beyond doubt, evidence beyond exception. This is called by a peculiar name, revelation, and our assent to it, faith, which as absolutely determines our minds, and as perfectly excludes all wavering, as our knowledge itself; and we may as well doubt of our own being, as we can whether any revelation from God be true. So that faith is a settled and sure principle of assent and assurance, and leaves no manner of room for doubt or hesitation. Only we must be sure that it be a divine revelation, and that we understand it right: else we shall expose ourselves to all the extravagancy of enthusiasm, and all the error of wrong principles, if we have faith and assurance in what is not divine revelation. And therefore, in those cases, our assent can be rationally no higher than the evidence of its being a revelation, and that this is the meaning of the expressions it is delivered in. If the evidence of its being a revelation, or that this is its true sense, be only on probable proofs, our assent can reach no higher than an assurance or diffidence, arising from the more or less apparent probability of the proofs. But of faith, and the precedency it ought to have before other arguments of persuasion, I shall speak more hereafter; where I treat of it as it is ordinarily placed, in contradistinction to reason; though in truth it be nothing else but an assent founded on the highest reason.

Chapter XVII.Of Reason

1. Various significations of the word "reason". The word reason in the English language has different significations: sometimes it is taken for true and clear principles: sometimes for clear and fair deductions from those principles: and sometimes for the cause, and particularly the final cause. But the consideration I shall have of it here is in a signification different from all these; and that is, as it stands for a faculty in man, that faculty whereby man is supposed to be distinguished from beasts, and wherein it is evident he much surpasses them.

2. Wherein reasoning consists. If general knowledge, as has been shown, consists in a perception of the agreement or disagreement of our own ideas, and the knowledge of the existence of all things without us (except only of a God, whose existence every man may certainly know and demonstrate to himself from his own existence), be had only by our senses, what room is there for the exercise of any other faculty, but outward sense and inward

perception? What need it there of reason? Very much: both for the enlargement of our knowledge, and regulating our assent. For it hath to do both in knowledge and opinion, and is necessary and assisting to all our other intellectual faculties, and indeed contains two of them, viz. sagacity and illation. By the one, it finds out; and by the other, it so orders the intermediate ideas as to discover what connexion there is in each link of the chain, whereby the extremes are held together; and thereby, as it were, to draw into view the truth sought for, which is that which we call illation or inference, and consists in nothing but the perception of the connexion there is between the ideas, in each step of the deduction; whereby the mind comes to see, either the certain agreement or disagreement of any two ideas, as in demonstration, in which it arrives at knowledge; or their probable connexion, on which it gives or withholds its assent, as in opinion. Sense and intuition reach but a very little way. The greatest part of our knowledge depends upon deductions and intermediate ideas: and in those cases where we are fain to substitute assent instead of knowledge, and take propositions for true, without being certain they are so, we have need to find out, examine, and compare the grounds of their probability. In both these cases, the faculty which finds out the means, and rightly applies them, to discover certainty in the one, and probability in the other, is that which we call reason. For, as reason perceives the necessary and indubitable connexion of all the ideas or proofs one to another, in each step of any demonstration that produces knowledge; so it likewise perceives the probable connexion of all the ideas or proofs one to another, in every step of a discourse, to which it will think assent due. This is the lowest degree of that which can be truly called reason. For where the mind does not perceive this probable connexion, where it does not discern whether there be any such connexion or no; there men's opinions are not the product of judgment, or the consequence of reason, but the effects of chance and hazard, of a mind floating at all adventures, without choice and without direction.

3. Reason in its four degrees. So that we may in reason consider these degrees: four the first and highest is the discovering and finding out of truths; the second, the regular and methodical disposition of them, and laying them in a clear and fit order, to make their connexion and force be plainly and easily perceived; the third is the perceiving their connexion; and the fourth, a making a right conclusion. These several degrees may be observed in any mathematical demonstration; it being one thing to perceive the connexion of each part, as the demonstration is made by another; another to perceive the dependence of the conclusion on all the parts; a third, to make out a demonstration clearly and neatly one's self; and something different from all these, to have first found out these intermediate ideas or proofs by which it is made.

4. Whether syllogism is the great instrument of reason: first cause to doubt this. There is one thing more which I shall desire to be considered concerning reason; and that is, whether syllogism, as is generally thought, be the proper instrument of it, and the usefullest way of exercising this faculty. The causes I have to doubt are these:—

First, Because syllogism serves our reason but in one only of the forementioned parts of it; and that is, to show the connexion of the proofs in any one instance, and no more; but in this it is of no great use, since the mind can perceive such connexion, where it really is, as easily, nay, perhaps better, without it.

Men can reason well who cannot make a syllogism. If we will observe the actings of our own minds, we shall find that we reason best and clearest, when we only observe the connexion of the proof, without reducing our thoughts to any rule of syllogism. And therefore we may take notice, that there are many men that reason exceeding clear and rightly, who know not how to make a syllogism. He that will look into many parts of Asia and America, will find men reason there perhaps as acutely as himself, who yet never heard of a syllogism, nor can reduce any one argument to those forms: and I believe scarce any one makes syllogisms in reasoning within himself. Indeed syllogism is made use of, on occasion, to discover a fallacy hid in a rhetorical flourish, or cunningly wrapt up in a smooth period; and, stripping an absurdity of the cover of wit and good language, show it in its naked deformity. But the weakness or fallacy of such a loose discourse it shows, by the artificial form it is put into, only to those who have thoroughly studied mode and figure, and have so examined the many ways that three propositions may be put together, as to know which of them does certainly conclude right, and which not, and upon what grounds it is that they do so. All who have so far considered syllogism, as to see the reason why in three propositions laid together in one form, the conclusion will be certainly right, but in another not certainly so, I grant are certain of the conclusion they draw from the premises in the allowed modes and figures. But they who have not so far looked into those forms, are not sure by virtue of syllogism, that the conclusion certainly follows from the premises; they only take it to be so by an implicit faith in their teachers and a confidence in those forms of argumentation; but this is still but believing, not being certain. Now, if, of all mankind those who can make syllogisms are extremely few in comparison of those who cannot; and if, of those few who have been taught logic, there is but a very small number who do any more than believe that syllogisms, in the allowed modes and figures do conclude right, without knowing certainly that they do so: if syllogisms must be taken for the only proper instrument of reason and means of knowledge, it will follow, that, before Aristotle, there was not one man that did or could know anything by reason; and that, since the invention of syllogisms, there is not one of ten thousand that doth.

Aristotle. But God has not been so sparing to men to make them barely two-legged creatures, and left it to Aristotle to make them rational, i.e. those few of them that he could get so to examine the grounds of syllogisms, as to see that, in above three score ways that three propositions may be laid together, there are but about fourteen wherein one may be sure that the conclusion is right; and upon what grounds it is, that, in these few, the conclusion is certain, and in the other not. God has been more bountiful to mankind than so. He has given them a mind that can reason, without being instructed in methods of syllogizing: the understanding is not taught to reason by these rules; it has a native faculty to perceive the coherence or incoherence of its ideas, and can range them right, without any such perplexing repetitions. I say not this any way to lessen Aristotle, whom I look on as one of the greatest men amongst the ancients; whose large views, acuteness, and penetration of thought and strength of judgment, few have equalled; and who, in this very invention of forms of argumentation, wherein the conclusion may be shown to be rightly inferred, did great service against those who were not ashamed to deny anything. And I readily own, that all right reasoning may be reduced to his forms of syllogism. But yet I think, without any diminution to him, I may truly say, that they are not the only nor the best way of reasoning, for the leading of those into truth who are willing to find it, and desire to make the best use they may of their reason, for the attainment of knowledge. And he himself, it is plain, found out some forms to be conclusive, and others not, not by the forms themselves, but by the original way of knowledge, i.e. by the visible agreement of ideas. Tell a country gentlewoman that the wind is south-west, and the weather lowering, and like to rain, and she will easily understand it is not safe for her to go abroad thin clad in such a day, after a fever: she clearly sees the probable connexion of all these, viz. south-west wind, and clouds, rain, wetting, taking cold, relapse, and danger of death, without tying them together in those artificial and cumbersome fetters of several syllogisms, that clog and hinder the mind, which proceeds from one part to another quicker and clearer without them: and the probability which she easily perceives in things thus in their native state would be quite lost, if this argument were managed learnedly, and proposed in mode and figure. For it very often confounds the connexion; and, I think, every one will perceive in mathematical demonstrations, that the knowledge gained thereby comes shortest and clearest without syllogism.

Inference is looked on as the great act of the rational faculty, and so it is when it is rightly made: but the mind, either very desirous to enlarge its knowledge, or very apt to favour the sentiments it has once imbibed, is very forward to make inferences; and therefore often makes too much haste, before it perceives the connexion of the ideas that must hold the extremes together.

Syllogism does not discover ideas, or their connexions. To infer, is nothing but by virtue of

one proposition laid down as true, to draw in another as true, i.e. to see or suppose such a connexion of the two ideas of the inferred proposition. V.g. Let this be the proposition laid down, "Men shall be punished in another world," and from thence be inferred this other, "Then men can determine themselves." The question now is, to know whether the mind has made this inference right or no: if it has made it by finding out the intermediate ideas, and taking a view of the connexion of them, placed in a due order, it has proceeded rationally, and made a right inference: if it has done it without such a view, it has not so much made an inference that will hold, or an inference of right reason, as shown a willingness to have it be, or be taken for such. But in neither case is it syllogism that discovered those ideas, or showed the connexion of them; for they must be both found out, and the connexion everywhere perceived, before they can rationally be made use of in syllogism: unless it can be said, that any idea, without considering what connexion it hath with the two other, whose agreement should be shown by it, will do well enough in a syllogism, and may be taken at a venture for the medius terminus, to prove any conclusion. But this nobody will say; because it is by virtue of the perceived agreement of the intermediate idea with the extremes, that the extremes are concluded to agree; and therefore each intermediate idea must be such as in the whole chain hath a visible connexion with those two it has been placed between, or else thereby the conclusion cannot be inferred or drawn in: for wherever any link of the chain is loose and without connexion, there the whole strength of it is lost, and it hath no force to infer or draw in anything. In the instance above mentioned, what is it shows the force of the inference, and consequently the reasonableness of it, but a view of the connexion of all the intermediate ideas that draw in the conclusion, or proposition inferred? V.g. "Men shall be punished"; "God the punisher"; "Just punishment"; "The punished guilty"; "Could have done otherwise"; "Freedom"; "Self-determination"; by which chain of ideas thus visibly linked together in train, i.e. each intermediate idea agreeing on each side with those two it is immediately placed between, the ideas of men and self-determination appear to be connected, i.e. this proposition "men can determine themselves" is drawn in or inferred from this, "that they shall be punished in the other world." For here the mind, seeing the connexion there is between the idea of men's punishment in the other world and the idea of God punishing; between God punishing and the justice of the punishment; between justice of punishment and guilt; between guilt and a power to do otherwise; between a power to do otherwise and freedom; and between freedom and self-determination, sees the connexion between men and self-determination.
The connexion must be discovered before it can be put into syllogisms. Now I ask, whether the connexion of the extremes be not more clearly seen in this simple and natural disposition, than in the perplexed repetitions, and jumble of five or six syllogisms. I must beg pardon for calling it jumble, till somebody shall put these ideas into so many syllogisms, and then say that they are less jumbled, and their connexion more visible, when they are transposed and repeated, and spun out to a greater length in artificial forms, than in that short and natural plain order they are laid down in here, wherein everyone may see it, and wherein they must be seen before they can be put into a train of syllogisms. For the natural order of the connecting ideas must direct the order of the syllogisms, and a man must see the connexion of each intermediate idea with those that it connects, before he can with reason make use of it in a syllogism. And when all those syllogisms are made, neither those that are nor those that are not logicians will see the force of the argumentation, i.e., the connexion of the extremes, one jot the better. [For those that are not men of art, not knowing the true forms of syllogism, nor the reasons of them, cannot know whether they are made in right and conclusive modes and figures or no, and so are not at all helped by the forms they are put into; though by them the natural order, wherein the mind could judge of their respective connexion, being disturbed, renders the illation much more uncertain than without them.] And as for the logicians themselves, they see the connexion of each intermediate idea with those it stands between, (on which the force of the inference depends,) as well before as after the syllogism is made, or else they do not see it at all. For a syllogism neither shows nor strengthens the connexion of any two ideas immediately

put together, but only by the connexion seen in them shows what connexion the extremes have one with another. But what connexion the intermediate has with either of the extremes in the syllogism, that no syllogism does or can show. That the mind only doth or can perceive as they stand there in that juxta-position by its own view, to which the syllogistical form it happens to be in gives no help or light at all: it only shows that if the intermediate idea agrees with those it is on both sides immediately applied to; then those two remote ones, or, as they are called, extremes, do certainly agree; and therefore the immediate connexion of each idea to that which it is applied to on each side, on which the force of the reasoning depends, is as well seen before as after the syllogism is made, or else he that makes the syllogism could never see it at all. This, as has been already observed, is seen only by the eye, or the perceptive faculty, of the mind, taking a view of them laid together, in a juxta-position; which view of any two it has equally, whenever they are laid together in any proposition, whether that proposition be placed as a major or a minor, in a syllogism or no.

Use of syllogism. Of what use, then are syllogisms? I answer, their chief and main use is in the Schools, where men are allowed without shame to deny the agreement of ideas that do manifestly agree; or out of the Schools, to those who from thence have learned without shame to deny the connexion of ideas, which even to themselves is visible. But to an ingenuous searcher after truth, who has no other aim but to find it, there is no need of any such form to force the allowing of the inference: the truth and reasonableness of it is better seen in ranging of the ideas in a simple and plain order: and hence it is that men, in their own inquiries after truth, never use syllogisms to convince themselves or in teaching others to instruct willing learners. Because, before they can put them into a syllogism, they must see the connexion that is between the intermediate idea and the two other ideas it is set between and applied to, to show their agreement; and when they see that, they see whether the inference be good or no; and so syllogism comes too late to settle it. For to make use again of the former instance, I ask whether the mind, considering the idea of justice, placed as an intermediate idea between the punishment of men and the guilt of the punished, (and till it does so consider it, the mind cannot make use of it as a medius terminus,) does not as plainly see the force and strength of the inference as when it is formed into a syllogism. To show it in a very plain and easy example; let animal be the intermediate idea or medius terminus that the mind makes use of to show the connexion of homo and vivens; I ask whether the mind does not more readily and plainly see that connexion in the simple and proper position of the connecting idea in the middle thus: Homo — Animal — Vivens, than in this perplexed one, Animal — Vivens — Homo — Animal: which is the position these ideas have in a syllogism, to show the connexion between homo and vivens by the intervention of animal.

Not the only way to detect fallacies. Indeed syllogism is thought to be of necessary use, even to the lovers of truth, to show them the fallacies that are often concealed in florid, witty, or involved discourses. But that this is a mistake will appear, if we consider, that the reason why sometimes men who sincerely aim at truth are imposed upon by such loose, and, as they are called, rhetorical discourses, is, that their fancies being struck with some lively metaphorical representations, they neglect to observe, or do not easily perceive, what are the true ideas upon which the inference depends. Now, to show such men the weakness of such an argumentation, there needs no more but to strip if of the superfluous ideas, which, blended and confounded with those on which the inference depends, seem to show a connexion where there is none; or at least to hinder the discovery of the want of it; and then to lay the naked ideas on which the force of the argumentation depends in their due order; in which position the mind, taking a view of them, sees what connexion they have, and so is able to judge of the inference without any need of a syllogism at all.

I grant that mode and figure is commonly made use of in such cases, as if the detection of the incoherence of such loose discourses were wholly owing to the syllogistical form; and so I myself formerly thought, till, upon a stricter examination, I now find, that laying the intermediate ideas naked in their due order, shows the incoherence of the argumentation better than syllogism; not only as subjecting each link of the chain to the immediate view of the mind in its proper place, whereby its connexion is best observed; but also because syllogism shows the incoherence only to those (who are not one of ten thousand) who perfectly understand mode and figure, and the reason upon which those forms are established; whereas a due and orderly placing of the ideas upon which the inference is made, makes every one, whether logician or not logician, who understands the terms, and hath the faculty to perceive the agreement or disagreement of such ideas, (without which, in or out of syllogism, he cannot perceive the strength or weakness, coherence or incoherence of the discourse) see the want of connexion in the argumentation, and the absurdity of the inference.

And thus I have known a man unskilful in syllogism, who at first hearing could perceive the weakness and inconclusiveness of a long artificial and plausible discourse, wherewith others better skilled in syllogism have been misled: and I believe there are few of my readers who do not know such. And indeed, if it were not so, the debates of most princes' councils, and the business of assemblies, would be in danger to be mismanaged, since those who are relied upon, and have usually a great stroke in them, are not always such who have the good luck to be perfectly knowing in the forms of syllogism, or expert in mode and figure. And if syllogism were the only, or so much as the surest way to detect the fallacies of artificial discourses; I do not think that all mankind, even princes in matters that concern their crowns and dignities, are so much in love with falsehood and mistake, that they would everywhere have neglected to bring syllogism into the debates of moment; or thought it ridiculous so much as to offer them in affairs of consequence; a plain evidence to me, that men of parts and penetration, who were not idly to dispute at their ease, but were to act according to the result of their debates, and often pay for their mistakes with their heads or fortunes, found those scholastic forms were of little use to discover truth or fallacy, whilst both the one and the other might be shown, and better shown without them, to those who would not refuse to see what was visibly shown them.

Another cause to doubt whether syllogism be the only proper instrument of reason, in the discovery of truth. Secondly, Another reason that makes me doubt whether syllogism be the only proper instrument of reason, in the discovery of truth, is, that of whatever use mode and figure is pretended to be in the laying open of fallacy, (which has been above considered,) those scholastic forms of discourse are not less liable to fallacies than the plainer ways of argumentation; and for this I appeal to common observation, which has always found these artificial methods of reasoning more adapted to catch and entangle the mind, than to instruct and inform the understanding. And hence it is that men, even when they are baffled and silenced in this scholastic way, are seldom or never convinced, and so brought over to the conquering side: they perhaps acknowledge their adversary to be the more skilful disputant, but rest nevertheless persuaded of the truth on their side, and go away, worsted as they are, with the same opinion they brought with them: which they could not do if this way of argumentation carried light and conviction with it, and made men see where the truth lay; and therefore syllogism has been thought more proper for the attaining victory in dispute, than for the discovery or confirmation of truth in fair inquiries. And if it be certain, that fallacies can be couched in syllogism, as it cannot be denied; it must be something else, and not syllogism, that must discover them.

I have had experience how ready some men are, when all the use which they have been wont to ascribe to anything is not allowed, to cry out, that I am for laying it wholly aside. But to prevent such unjust and groundless imputations, I tell them, that I am not for taking away any helps to the understanding in the attainment of knowledge. And if men skilled in and used to syllogisms, find them assisting to their reason in the discovery of truth, I think they ought to make use of them. All that I aim at, is, that they should not ascribe more to these forms than belongs to them, and think that men have no use, or not so full an use, of their reasoning faculties without them. Some eyes want spectacles to see things clearly and distinctly; but let not those that use them therefore say nobody can see clearly without them: those who do so will be thought, in favour of art (which, perhaps, they are beholden to,) a little too much to depress and discredit nature. Reason, by its own penetration, where it is strong and exercised, usually sees quicker and clearer without syllogism. If use of those spectacles has so dimmed its sight, that it cannot without them see consequences or inconsequences in argumentation, I am not so unreasonable as to be against the using them. Every one knows what best fits his own sight; but let him not thence conclude all in the dark, who use not just the same helps that he finds a need of.

5. Syllogism helps little in demonstration, less in probability. But however it be in knowledge, I think I may truly say, it is of far less, or no use at all in probabilities. For the assent there being to be determined by the preponderancy, after due weighing of all the proofs, with all circumstances on both sides, nothing is so unfit to assist the mind in that as syllogism; which running away with one assumed probability, or one topical argument, pursues that till it has led the mind quite out of sight of the thing under consideration; and, forcing it upon some remote difficulty, holds it fast there; entangled perhaps, and, as it were, manacled, in the chain of syllogisms, without allowing it the liberty, much less affording it the helps, requisite to show on which side, all things considered, is the greater probability.

6. Serves not to increase our knowledge, but to fence with the knowledge we suppose we have. But let it help us (as perhaps may be said) in convincing men of their errors and mistakes: (and yet I would fain see the man that was forced out of his opinion by dint of syllogism,) yet still it fails our reason in that part, which, if not its highest perfection, is yet certainly its hardest task, and that which we most need its help in; and that is the finding out of proofs, and making new discoveries. The rules of syllogism serve not to furnish the mind with those intermediate ideas that may show the connexion of remote ones. This way of reasoning discovers no new proofs, but is the art of marshalling and ranging the old ones we have already. The forty-seventh proposition of the first book of Euclid is very true; but the discovery of it, I think, not owing to any rules of common logic. A man knows first, and then he is able to prove syllogistically. So that syllogism comes after knowledge, and then a man has little or no need of it. But it is chiefly by the finding out those ideas that show the connexion of distant ones, that our stock of knowledge is increased, and that useful arts and sciences are advanced. Syllogism, at best, is but the art of fencing with the little knowledge we have, without making any addition to it. And if a man should employ his reason all this way, he will not do much otherwise than he who, having got some iron out of the bowels of the earth, should have it beaten up all into swords, and put it into his servants' hands to fence with and bang one another. Had the King of Spain employed the hands of his people, and his Spanish iron so, he had brought to light but little of that treasure that lay so long hid in the dark entrails of America. And I am apt to think, that he who shall employ all the force of his reason only in brandishing of syllogisms, will discover very little of that mass of knowledge which lies yet concealed in the secret recesses of nature; and which, I am apt to think, native rustic reason (as it formerly has done) is likelier to open a way to, and add to the common stock of mankind, rather than any scholastic proceeding by the strict rules of mod, and figure.

7. Other helps to reason than syllogism should be sought. I doubt not, nevertheless, but there are ways to be found to assist our reason in this most useful part; and this the judicious Hooker encourages me to say, who in his Eccl. Pol. 1. i. SS 6, speaks thus: "If there might be added the right helps of true art and learning, (which helps, I must plainly confess, this age of the world, carrying the name of a learned age, doth neither much know nor generally regard,) there would undoubtedly be almost as much difference in maturity of judgment between men therewith inured, and that which men now are, as between men that are now, and innocents." I do not pretend to have found or discovered here any of those "right helps of art," this great man of deep thought mentions: but that is plain, that syllogism, and the logic now in use, which were as well known in his days, can be none of those he means. It is sufficient for me, if by a Discourse, perhaps something out of the way, I am sure, as to me, wholly new and unborrowed, I shall have given occasion to others to cast about for new discoveries, and to

seek in their own thoughts for those right helps of art, which will scarce be found, I fear, by those who servilely confine themselves to the rules and dictates of others. For beaten tracks lead this sort of cattle, (as an observing Roman calls them,) whose thoughts reach only to imitation, Non quo eundum est, sed quo itur. But I can be bold to say, that this age is adorned with some men of that strength of judgment and largeness of comprehension, that, if they would employ their thoughts on this subject, could open new and undiscovered ways to the advancement of knowledge.

8. We can reason about particulars; and the immediate object of all our reasonings is nothing but particular ideas. Having here had occasion to speak of syllogism in general, and the use of it in reasoning, and the improvement of our knowledge, it is fit, before I leave this subject, to take notice of one manifest mistake in the rules of syllogism: viz. that no syllogistical reasoning can be right and conclusive, but what has at least one general proposition in it. As if we could not reason, and have knowledge about particulars: whereas, in truth, the matter rightly considered, the immediate object of all our reasoning and knowledge, is nothing but particulars. Every man's reasoning and knowledge is only about the ideas existing in his own mind; which are truly, every one of them, particular existences: and our knowledge and reason about other things is only as they correspond with those particular ideas. So that the perception of the agreement or disagreement of our particular ideas is the whole and utmost of all our knowledge. Universality is but accidental to it, and consists only in this, that the particular ideas about which it is are such as more than one particular thing can correspond with and be represented by. But the perception of the agreement or disagreement of any two ideas, and consequently our knowledge, is equally clear and certain, whether either, or both, or neither of those ideas, be capable of representing more real beings than one, or no. One thing more I crave leave to offer about syllogism, before I leave it, viz. May one not upon just ground inquire whether the form syllogism now has, is that which in reason it ought to have? For the medius terminus being to join the extremes, i.e. the intermediate ideas, by its intervention, to show the agreement or disagreement of the two in question, would not the position of the medius terminus be more natural, and show the agreement or disagreement of the extremes clearer and better, if it were placed in the middle between them? Which might be easily done by transposing the propositions, and making the medius terminus the predicate of the first, and the subject of the second. As thus: Omnis homo est animal. Omne animal est vivens. Ergo, omnis homo est vivens. Omne corpus est extensum et solidum. Nullum extensum et solidum est pura extensio. Ergo, corpus non est pura extensio.

I need not trouble my reader with instances in syllogisms whose conclusions are particular. The same reason hold for the same form in them, as well as in the general.

9. Our reason often fails us. Reason, though it penetrates into the depths of the sea and earth, elevates our thoughts as high as the stars, and leads us through the vast spaces and large rooms of this mighty fabric, yet it comes far short of the real extent of even corporeal being. And there are many instances wherein it fails us: as,

I. In cases when we have no ideas. It perfectly fails us where our ideas fail. It neither does nor can extend itself further than they do. And therefore, wherever we have no ideas, our reasoning stops, and we are at an end of our reckoning: and if at any time we reason about words which do not stand for any ideas, it is only about those sounds, and nothing else.

10. II. Because our ideas are often obscure or imperfect. Our reason is often puzzled and at a loss because of the obscurity, confusion, or imperfection of the ideas it is employed about; and there we are involved in difficulties and contradictions. Thus, not having any perfect idea of the least extension of matter, nor of infinity, we are at a loss about the divisibility of matter; but having perfect, clear, and distinct ideas of number, our reason meets with none of those inextricable difficulties in numbers, nor finds itself involved in any contradictions about them. Thus, we having but imperfect ideas of the operations of out minds, and of the beginning of motion, or thought how the mind produces either of them in us, and much imperfecter yet of the operation of God, run into great difficulties about free created agents, which reason cannot

well extricate itself out of.

11. III. Because we perceive not intermediate ideas to show conclusions. Our reason is often at a stand because it perceives not those ideas, which could serve to show the certain or probable agreement or disagreement of any other two ideas: and in this some men's faculties far outgo others. Till algebra, that great instrument and instance of human sagacity, was discovered, men with amazement looked on several of the demonstrations of ancient mathematicians, and could scarce forbear to think the finding several of those proofs to be something more than human.

12. IV. Because we often proceed upon wrong principles. The mind, by proceeding upon false principles, is often engaged in absurdities and difficulties, brought into straits and contradictions, without knowing how to free itself: and in that case it is in vain to implore the help of reason, unless it be to discover the falsehood and reject the influence of those wrong principles. Reason is so far from clearing the difficulties which the building upon false foundations brings a man into, that if he will pursue it, it entangles him the more, and engages him deeper in perplexities.

13. V. Because we often employ doubtful terms. As obscure and imperfect ideas often involve our reason, so, upon the same ground, do dubious words and uncertain signs, often, in discourses and arguings, when not warily attended to, puzzle men's reason, and bring them to a nonplus. But these two latter are our fault, and not the fault of reason. But yet the consequences of them are nevertheless obvious; and the perplexities or errors they fill men's minds with are everywhere observable.

14. Our highest degree of knowledge is intuitive, without reasoning. Some of the ideas that are in the mind, are so there, that they can be by themselves immediately compared one with another: and in these the mind is able to perceive that they agree or disagree as clearly as that it has them. Thus the mind perceives, that an arch of a circle is less than the whole circle, as clearly as it does the idea of a circle: and this, therefore, as has been said, I call intuitive knowledge; which is certain, beyond all doubt, and needs no probation, nor can have any; this being the highest of all human certainty. In this consists the evidence of all those maxims which nobody has any doubt about, but every man (does not, as is said, only assent to, but) knows to be true, as soon as ever they are proposed to his understanding. In the discovery of and assent to these truths, there is no use of the discursive faculty, no need of reasoning, but they are known by a superior and higher degree of evidence. And such, if I may guess at things unknown, I am apt to think that angels have now, and the spirits of just men made perfect shall have, in a future state, of thousands of things which now either wholly escape our apprehensions, or which our short-sighted reason having got some faint glimpse of, we, in the dark, grope after.

15. The next is got by reasoning. But though we have, here and there, a little of this clear light, some sparks of bright knowledge, yet the greatest part of our ideas are such, that we cannot discern their agreement or disagreement by an immediate comparing them. And in all these we have need of reasoning, and must, by discourse and inference, make our discoveries. Now of these there are two sorts, which I shall take the liberty to mention here again:—

Through reasonings that are demonstrative. First, Those whose agreement or disagreement, though it cannot be seen by an immediate putting them together, yet may be examined by the intervention of other ideas which can be compared with them. In this case, when the agreement or disagreement of the intermediate idea, on both sides, with those which we would compare, is plainly discerned: there it amounts to demonstration whereby knowledge is produced, which, though it be certain, yet it is not so easy, nor altogether so clear as intuitive knowledge. Because in that there is barely one simple intuition, wherein there is no room for any the least mistake or doubt: the truth is seen all perfectly at once. In demonstration, it is true, there is intuition too, but not altogether at once; for there must be a remembrance of the intuition of the agreement of the medium, or intermediate idea, with that we compared it with before, when we compare it with the other: and where there be many mediums, there the danger of the mistake is the greater. For each agreement or disagreement of the ideas must be observed and seen in each step of the whole train, and retained in the memory, just as it is; and the mind must be sure that no part of what is necessary to make up the demonstration is omitted or overlooked. This makes some demonstrations long and perplexed, and too hard for those who have not strength of parts distinctly to perceive, and exactly carry so many particulars orderly in their heads. And even those who are able to master such intricate speculations, are fain sometimes to go over them again, and there is need of more than one review before they can arrive at certainty. But yet where the mind clearly retains the intuition it had of the agreement of any idea with another, and that with a third, and that with a fourth, &c., there the agreement of the first and the fourth is a demonstration, and produces certain knowledge; which may be called rational knowledge, as the other is intuitive.

16. To supply the narrowness of demonstrative and intuitive knowledge we have nothing but judgment upon probable reasoning. Secondly, There are other ideas, whose agreement or disagreement can no otherwise be judged of but by the intervention of others which have not a certain agreement with the extremes, but an usual or likely one: and in these it is that the judgment is properly exercised; which is the acquiescing of the mind, that any ideas do agree, by comparing them with such probable mediums. This, though it never amounts to knowledge, no, not to that which is the lowest degree of it; yet sometimes the intermediate ideas tie the extremes so firmly together, and the probability is so clear and strong, that assent as necessarily follows it, as knowledge does demonstration. The great excellency and use of the judgment is to observe right, and take a true estimate of the force and weight of each probability; and then casting them up all right together, choose that side which has the overbalance.

17. Intuitive knowledge is the perception of the certain agreement or disagreement of two ideas immediately compared together.

Rational knowledge is the perception of the certain agreement or disagreement of any two ideas, by the intervention of one or more other ideas.

Judgment is the thinking or taking two ideas to agree or disagree, by the intervention of one or more ideas, whose certain agreement or disagreement with them it does not perceive, but hath observed to be frequent and usual.

18. Consequences of words, and consequences of ideas. Though the deducing one proposition from another, or making inferences in words, be a great part of reason, and that which it is usually employed about; yet the principal act of ratiocination is the finding the agreement or disagreement of two ideas one with another, by the intervention of a third. As a man, by a yard, finds two houses to be of the same length, to measure their equality by juxta-position. Words have their consequences, as the signs of such ideas: and things agree or disagree, as really they are; but we observe it only by our ideas.

19. Four sorts of arguments. Before we quit this subject, it may be worth our while a little to reflect on four sorts of arguments, that men, in their reasonings with others, do ordinarily make use of to prevail on their assent; or at least to awe them as to silence their opposition.

I. Argumentum ad verecundiam. The first is, to allege the opinions of men, whose parts, learning, eminency, power, or some other cause has gained a name, and settled their reputation in the common esteem with some kind of authority. When men are established in any kind of dignity, it is thought a breach of modesty for others to derogate any way from it, and question the authority of men who are in possession of it. This is apt to be censured, as carrying with it too much pride, when a man does not readily yield to the determination of approved authors, which is wont to be received with respect and submission by others: and it is looked upon as insolence, for a man to set up and adhere to his own opinion against the current stream of antiquity; or to put it in the balance against that of some learned doctor, or otherwise approved writer. Whoever backs his tenets with such authorities, thinks he ought thereby to carry the cause, and is ready to style it impudence in any one who shall stand out against them. This I think may be called argumentum ad verecundiam.

20. II. Argumentum ad ignorantiam. Secondly, Another way that men ordinarily use to drive

others and force them to submit to their judgments, and receive their opinion in debate, is to require the adversary to admit what they allege as a proof, or to assign a better. And this I call argumentum ad ignorantiam.

21. III. Argumentum ad hominem. Thirdly, a third way is to press a man with consequences drawn from his own principles or concessions. This is already known under the name of argumentum ad hominem.

22. IV. Argumentum adjudicium. The fourth alone advances us in knowledge and judgment. The fourth is the using of proofs drawn from any of the foundations of knowledge or probability. This I call argumentum adjudicium. This alone, of all the four, brings true instruction with it, and advances us in our way to knowledge. For, 1. It argues not another man's opinion to be right, because I, out of respect, or any other consideration but that of conviction, will not contradict him. 2. It proves not another man to be in the right way, nor that I ought to take the same with him, because I know not a better. 3. Nor does it follow that another man is in the right way because he has shown me that I am in the wrong. I may be modest, and therefore not oppose another man's persuasion: I may be ignorant, and not be able to produce a better: I may be in an error, and another may show me that I am so. This may dispose me, perhaps, for the reception of truth, but helps me not to it: that must come from proofs and arguments, and light arising from the nature of things themselves, and not from my shamefacedness, ignorance, or error.

23. Above, contrary, and according to reason. By what has been before said of reason, we may be able to make some guess at the distinction of things into those that are according to, above, and contrary to reason. 1. According to reason are such propositions whose truth we can discover by examining and tracing those ideas we have from sensation and reflection; and by natural deduction find to be true or probable. 2. Above reason are such propositions whose truth or probability we cannot by reason derive from those principles. 3. Contrary to reason are such propositions as are inconsistent with or irreconcilable to our clear and distinct ideas. Thus the existence of one God is according to reason; the existence of more than one God, contrary to reason; the resurrection of the dead, above reason. Above reason also may be taken in a double sense, viz. either as signifying above probability, or above certainty: and in that large sense also, contrary to reason, is, I suppose, sometimes taken.

24. Reason and faith not opposite, for faith must be regulated by reason. There is another use of the word reason, wherein it is opposed to faith: which, though it be in itself a very improper way of speaking, yet common use has so authorized it, that it would be folly either to oppose or hope to remedy it. Only I think it may not be amiss to take notice that, however faith be opposed to reason, faith is nothing but a firm assent of the mind: which, if it be regulated, as is our duty, cannot be afforded to anything but upon good reason; and so cannot be opposite to it. He that believes without having any reason for believing, may be in love with his own fancies; but neither seeks truth as he ought, nor pays the obedience due to his Maker, who would have him use those discerning faculties he has given him, to keep him out of mistake and error. He that does not this to the best of his power, however he sometimes lights on truth, is in the right but by chance; and I know not whether the luckiness of the accident will excuse the irregularity of his proceeding. This at least is certain, that he must be accountable for whatever mistakes he runs into: whereas he that makes use of the light and faculties God has given him, and seeks sincerely to discover truth by those helps and abilities he has, may have this satisfaction in doing his duty as a rational creature, that, though he should miss truth, he will not miss the reward of it. For he governs his assent right, and places it as he should, who, in any case or matter whatsoever, believes or disbelieves according as reason directs him. He that doth otherwise, transgresses against his own light, and misuses those faculties which were given him to no other end, but to search and follow the clearer evidence and greater probability. But since reason and faith are by some men opposed, we will so consider them in the following chapter.

Chapter XVIII.Of Faith and Reason, and their Distinct Provinces

1. Necessary to know their boundaries. It has been above shown, 1. That we are of necessity ignorant, and want knowledge of all sorts, where we want ideas. 2. That we are ignorant, and want rational knowledge, where we want proofs. 3. That we want certain knowledge and certainty, as far as we want clear and determined specific ideas. 4. That we want probability to direct our assent in matters where we have neither knowledge of our own nor testimony of other men to bottom our reason upon.

From these things thus premised, I think we may come to lay down the measures and boundaries between faith and reason: the want whereof may possibly have been the cause, if not of great disorders, yet at least of great disputes, and perhaps mistakes in the world. For till it be resolved how far we are to be guided by reason, and how far by faith, we shall in vain dispute, and endeavour to convince one another in matters of religion.

2. Faith and reason, what, as contradistinguished. I find every sect, as far as reason will help them, make use of it gladly: and where it fails them, they cry out, It is matter of faith, and above reason. And I do not see how they can argue with any one, or ever convince a gainsayer who makes use of the same plea, without setting down strict boundaries between faith and reason; which ought to be the first point established in all questions where faith has anything to do.

Reason, therefore, here, as contradistinguished to faith, I take to be the discovery of the certainty or probability of such propositions or truths which the mind arrives at by deduction made from such ideas, which it has got by the use of its natural faculties; viz. by sensation or reflection.

Faith, on the other side, is the assent to any proposition, not thus made out by the deductions of reason, but upon the credit of the proposer, as coming from God, in some extraordinary way of communication. This way of discovering truths to men, we call revelation.

3. No new simple idea can be conveyed by traditional revelation. First, Then I say, that no man inspired by God can by any revelation communicate to others any new simple ideas which they had not before from sensation or reflection. For, whatsoever impressions he himself may have from the immediate hand of God, this revelation, if it be of new simple ideas, cannot be conveyed to another, either by words or any other signs. Because words, by their immediate operation on us, cause no other ideas but of their natural sounds: and it is by the custom of using them for signs, that they excite and revive in our minds latent ideas; but yet only such ideas as were there before. For words, seen or heard, recall to our thoughts those ideas only which to us they have been wont to be signs of, but cannot introduce any perfectly new and formerly unknown simple ideas. The same holds in all other signs; which cannot signify to us things of which we have before never had any idea at all.

Thus whatever things were discovered to St. Paul, when he was rapt up into the third heaven; whatever new ideas his mind there received, all the description he can make to others of that place, is only this, That there are such things, "as eye hath not seen, nor ear heard, nor hath it entered into the heart of man to conceive." And supposing God should discover to any one, supernaturally, a species of creatures inhabiting, for example, Jupiter or Saturn, (for that it is possible there may be such, nobody can deny,) which had six senses; and imprint on his mind the ideas conveyed to theirs by that sixth sense: he could no more, by words, produce in the minds of other men those ideas imprinted by that sixth sense, than one of us could convey the idea of any colour, by the sound of words, into a man who, having the other four senses perfect, had always totally wanted the fifth, of seeing. For our simple ideas, then, which are the foundation, and sole matter of all our notions and knowledge, we must depend wholly on our reason; I mean our natural faculties; and can by no means receive them, or any of them, from traditional revelation. I say, traditional revelation, in distinction to original revelation. By the one, I mean that first impression which is made immediately by God on the mind of any man, to which we cannot set any bounds; and by the other, those impressions delivered over to others in words, and the ordinary ways of conveying our conceptions one to another.

4. Traditional revelation may make us know propositions knowable also by reason, but not with the same certainty that reason doth. Secondly, I say that the same truths may be discovered, and conveyed down from revelation, which are discoverable to us by reason, and by those ideas we naturally may have. So God might, by revelation, discover the truth of any proposition in Euclid; as well as men, by the natural use of their faculties, come to make the discovery themselves. In all things of this kind there is little need or use of revelation, God having furnished us with natural and surer means to arrive at the knowledge of them. For whatsoever truth we come to the clear discovery of, from the knowledge and contemplation of our own ideas, will always be certainer to us than those which are conveyed to us by traditional revelation. For the knowledge we have that this revelation came at first from God can never be so sure as the knowledge we have from the clear and distinct perception of the agreement or disagreement of our own ideas: v.g. if it were revealed some ages since, that the three angles of a triangle were equal to two right ones, I might assent to the truth of that proposition, upon the credit of that tradition, that it was revealed: but that would never amount to so great a certainty as the knowledge of it, upon the comparing and measuring my own ideas of two right angles, and the three angles of a triangle. The like holds in matter of fact knowable by our senses; v.g. the history of the deluge is conveyed to us by writings which had their original from revelation: and yet nobody, I think, will say he has as certain and clear a knowledge of the flood as Noah, that saw it; or that he himself would have had, had he then been alive and seen it. For he has no greater an assurance than that of his senses, that it is writ in the book supposed writ by Moses inspired: but he has not so great an assurance that Moses wrote that book as if he had seen Moses write it. So that the assurance of its being a revelation is less still than the assurance of his senses.

5. Even original revelation cannot be admitted against the clear evidence of reason. In propositions, then, whose certainty is built upon the clear perception of the agreement or disagreement of our ideas, attained either by immediate intuition, as in self-evident propositions, or by evident deductions of reason in demonstrations we need not the assistance of revelation, as necessary to gain our assent, and introduce them into our minds. Because the natural ways of knowledge could settle them there, or had done it already; which is the greatest assurance we can possibly have of anything, unless where God immediately reveals it to us: and there too our assurance can be no greater than our knowledge is, that it is a revelation from God. But yet nothing, I think, can, under that title, shake or overrule plain knowledge; or rationally prevail with any man to admit it for true, in a direct contradiction to the clear evidence of his own understanding. For, since no evidence of our faculties, by which we receive such revelations, can exceed, if equal, the certainty of our intuitive knowledge, we can never receive for a truth anything that is directly contrary to our clear and distinct knowledge; v.g. the ideas of one body and one place do so clearly agree, and the mind has so evident a perception of their agreement, that we can never assent to a proposition that affirms the same body to be in two distant places at once, however it should pretend to the authority of a divine revelation: since the evidence, first, that we deceive not ourselves, in ascribing it to God; secondly, that we understand it right; can never be so great as the evidence of our own intuitive knowledge, whereby we discern it impossible for the same body to be in two places at once. And therefore no proposition can be received for divine revelation, or obtain the assent due to all such, if it be contradictory to our clear intuitive knowledge. Because this would be to subvert the principles and foundations of all knowledge, evidence, and assent whatsoever: and there would be left no difference between truth and falsehood, no measures of credible and incredible in the world, if doubtful propositions shall take place before self-evident; and what we certainly know give way to what we may possibly be mistaken in. In propositions therefore contrary to the clear perception of the agreement or disagreement of any of our ideas, it will be

in vain to urge them as matters of faith. They cannot move our assent under that or any other title whatsoever. For faith can never convince us of anything that contradicts our knowledge. Because, though faith be founded on the testimony of God (who cannot lie) revealing any proposition to us: yet we cannot have an assurance of the truth of its being a divine revelation greater than our own knowledge. Since the whole strength of the certainty depends upon our knowledge that God revealed it; which, in this case, where the proposition supposed revealed contradicts our knowledge or reason, will always have this objection hanging to it, viz. that we cannot tell how to conceive that to come from God, the bountiful Author of our being, which, if received for true, must overturn all the principles and foundations of knowledge he has given us; render all our faculties useless; wholly destroy the most excellent part of his workmanship, our understandings; and put a man in a condition wherein he will have less light, less conduct than the beast that perisheth. For if the mind of man can never have a clearer (and perhaps not so clear) evidence of anything to be a divine revelation, as it has of the principles of its own reason, it can never have a ground to quit the clear evidence of its reason, to give a place to a proposition, whose revelation has not a greater evidence than those principles have.

6. Traditional revelation much less. Thus far a man has use of reason, and ought to hearken to it, even in immediate and original revelation, where it is supposed to be made to himself. But to all those who pretend not to immediate revelation, but are required to pay obedience, and to receive the truths revealed to others, which, by the tradition of writings, or word of mouth, are conveyed down to them, reason has a great deal more to do, and is that only which can induce us to receive them. For matter of faith being only divine revelation, and nothing else, faith, as we use the word, (called commonly divine faith), has to do with no propositions, but those which are supposed to be divinely revealed. So that I do not see how those who make revelation alone the sole object of faith can say that it is a matter of faith, and not of reason, to believe that such or such a proposition, to be found in such or such a book, is of divine inspiration; unless it be revealed that that proposition, or all in that book, was communicated by divine inspiration. Without such a revelation, the believing, or not believing, that proposition, or book, to be of divine authority, can never be matter of faith, but matter of reason; and such as I must come to an assent to only by the use of my reason, which can never require or enable me to believe that which is contrary to itself: it being impossible for reason ever to procure any assent to that which to itself appears unreasonable.

In all things, therefore, where we have clear evidence from our ideas, and those principles of knowledge I have above mentioned, reason is the proper judge; and revelation, though it may, in consenting with it, confirm its dictates, yet cannot in such cases invalidate its decrees: nor can we be obliged, where we have the clear and evident sentience of reason, to quit it for the contrary opinion, under a pretence that it is matter of faith: which can have no authority against the plain and clear dictates of reason.

7. Things above reason are, when revealed, the proper matter of faith. But, Thirdly, There being many things wherein we have very imperfect notions, or none at all; and other things, of whose past, present, or future existence, by the natural use of our faculties, we can have no knowledge at all; these, as being beyond the discovery of our natural faculties, and above reason, are, when revealed, the proper matter of faith. Thus, that part of the angels rebelled against God, and thereby lost their first happy state: and that the dead shall rise, and live again: these and the like, being beyond the discovery of reason, are purely matters of faith, with which reason has directly nothing to do.

8. Or not contrary to reason, if revealed, are matter of faith; and must carry it against probable conjectures of reason. But since God, in giving us the light of reason, has not thereby tied up his own hands from affording us, when he thinks fit, the light of revelation in any of those matters wherein our natural faculties are able to give a probable determination; revelation, where God has been pleased to give it, must carry it against the probable conjectures of reason. Because the mind not being certain of the truth of that it does not evidently know, but

only yielding to the probability that appears in it, is bound to give up its assent to such a testimony which, it is satisfied, comes from one who cannot err, and will not deceive. But yet, it still belongs to reason to judge of the truth of its being a revelation, and of the signification of the words wherein it is delivered. Indeed, if anything shall be thought revelation which is contrary to the plain principles of reason, and the evident knowledge the mind has of its own clear and distinct ideas; there reason must be hearkened to, as to a matter within its province. Since a man can never have so certain a knowledge that a proposition which contradicts the clear principles and evidence of his own knowledge was divinely revealed, or that he understands the words rightly wherein it is delivered, as he has that the contrary is true, and so is bound to consider and judge of it as a matter of reason, and not swallow it, without examination, as a matter of faith.

9. Revelation in matters where reason cannot judge, or but probably, ought to be hearkened to. First, Whatever proposition is revealed, of whose truth our mind, by its natural faculties and notions, cannot judge, that is purely matter of faith, and above reason.

Secondly, All propositions whereof the mind, by the use of its natural faculties, can come to determine and judge, from naturally acquired ideas, are matter of reason; with this difference still, that, in those concerning which it has but an uncertain evidence, and so is persuaded of their truth only upon probable grounds, which still admit a possibility of the contrary to be true, without doing violence to the certain evidence of its own knowledge, and overturning the principles of all reason; in such probable propositions, I say, an evident revelation ought to determine our assent, even against probability. For where the principles of reason have not evidenced a proposition to be certainly true or false, there clear revelation, as another principle of truth and ground of assent, may determine; and so it may be matter of faith, and be also above reason. Because reason, in that particular matter, being able to reach no higher than probability, faith gave the determination where reason came short; and revelation discovered on which side the truth lay.

10. In matters where reason can afford certain knowledge, that is to be hearkened to. Thus far the dominion of faith reaches, and that without any violence or hindrance to reason; which is not injured or disturbed, but assisted and improved by new discoveries of truth, coming from the eternal fountain of all knowledge. Whatever God hath revealed is certainly true: no doubt can be made of it. This is the proper object of faith: but whether it be a divine revelation or no, reason must judge; which can never permit the mind to reject a greater evidence to embrace what is less evident, nor allow it to entertain probability in opposition to knowledge and certainty. There can be no evidence that any traditional revelation is of divine original, in the words we receive it, and in the sense we understand it, so clear and so certain as that of the principles of reason: and therefore Nothing that is contrary to, and inconsistent with, the clear and self-evident dictates of reason, has a right to he urged or assented to as a matter of faith, wherein reason hath nothing to do. Whatsoever is divine revelation, ought to overrule all our opinions, prejudices, and interest, and hath a right to be received with full assent. Such a submission as this, of our reason to faith, takes not away the landmarks of knowledge: this shakes not the foundations of reason, but leaves us that use of our faculties for which they were given us.

11. If the boundaries be not set between faith and reason, no enthusiasm or extravagancy in religion can be contradicted. If the provinces of faith and reason are not kept distinct by these boundaries, there will, in matters of religion, be no room for reason at all; and those extravagant opinions and ceremonies that are to be found in the several religions of the world will not deserve to be blamed. For, to this crying up of faith in opposition to reason, we may, I think, in good measure ascribe those absurdities that fill almost all the religions which possess and divide mankind. For men having been principled with an opinion that they must not consult reason in the things of religion, however apparently contradictory to common sense and the very principles of all their knowledge, have let loose their fancies and natural superstition; and have been by them led into so strange opinions, and extravagant practices in

religion, that a considerate man cannot but stand amazed at their follies, and judge them so far from being acceptable to the great and wise God, that he cannot avoid thinking them ridiculous and offensive to a sober good man. So that, in effect, religion, which should most distinguish us from beasts, and ought most peculiarly to elevate us, as rational creatures, above brutes, is that wherein men often appear most irrational, and more senseless than beasts themselves. Credo, quia impossibile est: I believe, because it is impossible, might, in a good man, pass for a sally of zeal; but would prove a very ill rule for men to choose their opinions or religion by.

Chapter XIX.Of Enthusiasm

1. Love of truth necessary. He that would seriously set upon the search of truth ought in the first place to prepare his mind with a love of it. For he that loves it not will not take much pains to get it; nor be much concerned when he misses it. There is nobody in the commonwealth of learning who does not profess himself a lover of truth: and there is not a rational creature that would not take it amiss to be thought otherwise of. And yet, for all this, one may truly say, that there are very few lovers of truth, for truth's sake, even amongst those who persuade themselves that they are so. How a man may know whether he be so in earnest, is worth inquiry: and I think there is one unerring mark of it, viz. The not entertaining any proposition with greater assurance than the proofs it is built upon will warrant. Whoever goes beyond this measure of assent, it is plain, receives not the truth in the love of it; loves not truth for truth's sake, but for some other bye-end. For the evidence that any proposition is true (except such as are self-evident) lying only in the proofs a man has of it, whatsoever degrees of assent he affords it beyond the degrees of that evidence, it is plain that all the surplusage of assurance is owing to some other affection, and not to the love of truth: it being as impossible that the love of truth should carry my assent above the evidence there is to me that it is true, as that the love of truth should make me assent to any proposition for the sake of that evidence which it has not, that it is true: which is in effect to love it as a truth, because it is possible or probable that it may not be true. In any truth that gets not possession of our minds by the irresistible light of self-evidence, or by the force of demonstration, the arguments that gain it assent are the vouchers and gage of its probability to us; and we can receive it for no other than such as they deliver it to our understandings. Whatsoever credit or authority we give to any proposition more than it receives from the principles and proofs it supports itself upon, is owing to our inclinations that way, and is so far a derogation from the love of truth as such: which, as it can receive no evidence from our passions or interests, so it should receive no tincture from them.

2. A forwardness to dictate another's beliefs, from whence. The assuming an authority of dictating to others, and a forwardness to prescribe to their opinions, is a constant concomitant of this bias and corruption of our judgments. For how almost can it be otherwise, but that he should be ready to impose on another's belief, who has already imposed on his own? Who can reasonably expect arguments and conviction from him in dealing with others, whose understanding is not accustomed to them in his dealing with himself? Who does violence to his own faculties, tyrannizes over his own mind, and usurps the prerogative that belongs to truth alone, which is to command assent by only its own authority, i.e. by and in proportion to that evidence which it carries with it.

3. Force of enthusiasm, in which reason is taken away. Upon this occasion I shall take the liberty to consider a third ground of assent, which with some men has the same authority, and is as confidently relied on as either faith or reason; I mean enthusiasm: which, laying by reason, would set up revelation without it. Whereby in effect it takes away both reason and revelation, and substitutes in the room of them the ungrounded fancies of a man's own brain, and assumes them for a foundation both of opinion and conduct.

4. Reason and revelation. Reason is natural revelation, whereby the eternal Father of light and fountain of all knowledge, communicates to mankind that portion of truth which he has laid within the reach of their natural faculties: revelation is natural reason enlarged by a new set of discoveries communicated by God immediately; which reason vouches the truth of, by the testimony and proofs it gives that they come from God. So that he that takes away reason to make way for revelation, puts out the light of both, and does much what the same as if he would persuade a man to put out his eyes, the better to receive the remote light of an invisible star by a telescope.

5. Rise of enthusiasm. Immediate revelation being a much easier way for men to establish their opinions and regulate their conduct than the tedious and not always successful labour of strict reasoning, it is no wonder that some have been very apt to pretend to revelation, and to persuade themselves that they are under the peculiar guidance of heaven in their actions and opinions, especially in those of them which they cannot account for by the ordinary methods of knowledge and principles of reason. Hence we see that, in all ages, men in whom melancholy has mixed with devotion, or whose conceit of themselves has raised them into an opinion of a greater familiarity with God, and a nearer admittance to his favour than is afforded to others, have often flattered themselves with a persuasion of an immediate intercourse with the Deity, and frequent communications from the Divine Spirit. God, I own, cannot be denied to be able to enlighten the understanding by a ray darted into the mind immediately from the fountain of light: this they understand he has promised to do, and who then has so good a title to expect it as those who are his peculiar people, chosen by him, and depending on him?

6. Enthusiastic impulse. Their minds being thus prepared, whatever groundless opinion comes to settle itself strongly upon their fancies is an illumination from the Spirit of God, and presently of divine authority: and whatsoever odd action they find in themselves a strong inclination to do, that impulse is concluded to be a call or direction from heaven, and must be obeyed: it is a commission from above, and they cannot err in executing it.

7. What is meant by enthusiasm. This I take to be properly enthusiasm, which, though founded neither on reason nor divine revelation, but rising from the conceits of a warmed or overweening brain, works yet, where it once gets footing, more powerfully on the persuasions and actions of men than either of those two, or both together: men being most forwardly obedient to the impulses they receive from themselves; and the whole man is sure to act more vigorously where the whole man is carried by a natural motion. For strong conceit, like a new principle, carries all easily with it, when got above common sense, and freed from all restraint of reason and check of reflection, it is heightened into a divine authority, in concurrence with our own temper and inclination.

8. Enthusiasm accepts its supposed illumination without search and proof. Though the odd opinions and extravagant actions enthusiasm has run men into were enough to warn them against this wrong principle, so apt to misguide them both in their belief and conduct: yet the love of something extraordinary, the ease and glory it is to be inspired, and be above the common and natural ways of knowledge, so flatters many men's laziness, ignorance, and vanity, that, when once they are got into this way of immediate revelation, of illumination without search, and of certainty without proof and without examination, it is a hard matter to get them out of it. Reason is lost upon them, they are above it: they see the light infused into their understandings, and cannot be mistaken; it is clear and visible there, like the light of bright sunshine; shows itself, and needs no other proof but its own evidence: they feel the hand of God moving them within, and the impulses of the Spirit, and cannot be mistaken in what they feel. Thus they support themselves, and are sure reasoning hath nothing to do with what they see and feel in themselves: what they have a sensible experience of admits no doubt, needs no probation. Would he not be ridiculous, who should require to have it proved to him that the light shines, and that he sees it? It is its own proof, and can have no other. When the Spirit brings light into our minds, it dispels darkness. We see it as we do that of the sun at

noon, and need not the twilight of reason to show it us. This light from heaven is strong, clear, and pure; carries its own demonstration with it: and we may as naturally take a glow-worm to assist us to discover the sun, as to examine the celestial ray by our dim candle, reason.

9. Enthusiasm how to be discovered. This is the way of talking of these men: they are sure, because they are sure: and their persuasions are right, because they are strong in them. For, when what they say is stripped of the metaphor of seeing and feeling, this is all it amounts to: and yet these similes so impose on them, that they serve them for certainty in themselves, and demonstration to others.

10. The supposed internal light examined. But to examine a little soberly this internal light, and this feeling on which they build so much. These men have, they say, clear light, and they see; they have awakened sense, and they feel: this cannot, they are sure, be disputed them. For when a man says he sees or feels, nobody can deny him that he does so. But here let me ask: This seeing, is it the perception of the truth of the proposition, or of this, that it is a revelation from God? This feeling, is it a perception of an inclination or fancy to do something, or of the Spirit of God moving that inclination? These are two very different perceptions, and must be carefully distinguished, if we would not impose upon ourselves. I may perceive the truth of a proposition, and yet not perceive that it is an immediate revelation from God. I may perceive the truth of a proposition in Euclid, without its being, or my perceiving it to be, a revelation: nay, I may perceive I came not by this knowledge in a natural way, and so may conclude it revealed, without perceiving that it is a revelation of God. Because there be spirits which, without being divinely commissioned, may excite those ideas in me, and lay them in such order before my mind, that I may perceive their connexion. So that the knowledge of any proposition coming into my mind, I know not how, is not a perception that it is from God. Much less is a strong persuasion that it is true, a perception that it is from God, or so much as true. But however it be called light and seeing, I suppose it is at most but belief and assurance: and the proposition taken for a revelation is not such as they know to be true, but take to be true. For where a proposition is known to be true, revelation is needless: and it is hard to conceive how there can be a revelation to any one of what he knows already. If therefore it be a proposition which they are persuaded, but do not know, to be true, whatever they may call it, it is not seeing, but believing. For these are two ways whereby truth comes into the mind, wholly distinct, so that one is not the other. What I see, I know to be so, by the evidence of the thing itself: what I believe, I take to be so upon the testimony of another. But this testimony I must know to be given, or else what ground have I of believing? I must see that it is God that reveals this to me, or else I see nothing. The question then here is: How do I know that God is the revealer of this to me; that this impression is made upon my mind by his Holy Spirit; and that therefore I ought to obey it? If I know not this, how great soever the assurance is that I am possessed with, it is groundless; whatever light I pretend to, it is but enthusiasm. For, whether the proposition supposed to be revealed be in itself evidently true, or visibly probable, or, by the natural ways of knowledge, uncertain, the proposition that must be well grounded and manifested to be true, is this, That God is the revealer of it, and that what I take to be a revelation is certainly put into my mind by Him, and is not an illusion dropped in by some other spirit, or raised by my own fancy. For, if I mistake not, these men receive it for true, because they presume God revealed it. Does it not, then, stand them upon to examine upon what grounds they presume it to be a revelation from God? or else all their confidence is mere presumption: and this light they are so dazzled with is nothing but an ignis fatuus, that leads them constantly round in this circle; It is a revelation, because they firmly believe it; and they believe it, because it is a revelation.

11. Enthusiasm fails of evidence, that the proposition is from God. In all that is of divine revelation, there is need of no other proof but that it is an inspiration from God: for he can neither deceive nor be deceived. But how shall it be known that any proposition in our minds is a truth infused by God; a truth that is revealed to us by him, which he declares to us, and therefore we ought to believe? Here it is that enthusiasm fails of the evidence it pretends to.

For men thus possessed, boast of a light whereby they say they are enlightened, and brought into the knowledge of this or that truth. But if they know it to be a truth, they must know it to be so, either by its own self-evidence to natural reason, or by the rational proofs that make it out to be so. If they see and know it to be a truth, either of these two ways, they in vain suppose it to be a revelation. For they know it to be true the same way that any other man naturally may know that it is so, without the help of revelation. For thus, all the truths, of what kind soever, that men uninspired are enlightened with, came into their minds, and are established there. If they say they know it to be true, because it is a revelation from God, the reason is good: but then it will be demanded how they know it to be a revelation from God. If they say, by the light it brings with it, which shines bright in their minds, and they cannot resist: I beseech them to consider whether this be any more than what we have taken notice of already, viz. that it is a revelation, because they strongly believe it to be true. For all the light they speak of is but a strong, though ungrounded persuasion of their own minds, that it is a truth. For rational grounds from proofs that it is a truth, they must acknowledge to have none; for then it is not received as a revelation, but upon the ordinary grounds that other truths are received: and if they believe it to be true because it is a revelation, and have no other reason for its being a revelation, but because they are fully persuaded, without any other reason, that it is true, then they believe it to be a revelation only because they strongly believe it to be a revelation; which is a very unsafe ground to proceed on, either in our tenets or actions. And what readier way can there be to run ourselves into the most extravagant errors and miscarriages, than thus to set up fancy for our supreme and sole guide, and to believe any proposition to be true, any action to be right, only because we believe it to be so? The strength of our persuasions is no evidence at all of their own rectitude: crooked things may be as stiff and inflexible as straight: and men may be as positive and peremptory in error as in truth. How come else the untractable zealots in different and opposite parties? For if the light, which every one thinks he has in his mind, which in this case is nothing but the strength of his own persuasion, be an evidence that it is from God, contrary opinions have the same title to be inspirations; and God will be not only the Father of lights, but of opposite and contradictory lights, leading men contrary ways; and contradictory propositions will be divine truths, if an ungrounded strength of assurance be an evidence that any proposition is a Divine Revelation.

12. Firmness of persuasion no Proof that any proposition is from God. This cannot be otherwise, whilst firmness of persuasion is made the cause of believing, and confidence of being in the right is made an argument of truth. St. Paul himself believed he did well, and that he had a call to it, when he persecuted the Christians, whom he confidently thought in the wrong: but yet it was he, and not they, who were mistaken. Good men are men still liable to mistakes, and are sometimes warmly engaged in errors, which they take for divine truths, shining in their minds with the clearest light.

13. Light in the mind, what. Light, true light, in the mind is, or can be, nothing else but the evidence of the truth of any proposition; and if it be not a self-evident proposition, all the light it has, or can have, is from the clearness and validity of those proofs upon which it is received. To talk of any other light in the understanding is to put ourselves in the dark, or in the power of the Prince of Darkness, and, by our own consent, to give ourselves up to delusion to believe a lie. For, if strength of persuasion be the light which must guide us; I ask how shall any one distinguish between the delusions of Satan, and the inspirations of the Holy Ghost? He can transform himself into an angel of light. And they who are led by this Son of the Morning are as fully satisfied of the illumination, i.e. are as strongly persuaded that they are enlightened by the Spirit of God as any one who is so: they acquiesce and rejoice in it, are actuated by it: and nobody can be more sure, nor more in the right (if their own belief may be judge) than they.

14. Revelation must be judged of by reason. He, therefore, that will not give himself up to all the extravagances of delusion and error must bring this guide of his light within to the trial. God when he makes the prophet does not unmake the man. He leaves all his faculties in the natural state, to enable him to judge of his inspirations, whether they be of divine original or

no. When he illuminates the mind with supernatural light, he does not extinguish that which is natural. If he would have us assent to the truth of any proposition, he either evidences that truth by the usual methods of natural reason, or else makes it known to be a truth which he would have us assent to by his authority, and convinces us that it is from him, by some marks which reason cannot be mistaken in. Reason must be our last judge and guide in everything. I do not mean that we must consult reason, and examine whether a proposition revealed from God can be made out by natural principles, and if it cannot, that then we may reject it: but consult it we must, and by it examine whether it be a revelation from God or no: and if reason finds it to be revealed from God, reason then declares for it as much as for any other truth, and makes it one of her dictates. Every conceit that thoroughly warms our fancies must pass for an inspiration, if there be nothing but the strength of our persuasions, whereby to judge of our persuasions: if reason must not examine their truth by something extrinsical to the persuasions themselves, inspirations and delusions, truth and falsehood, will have the same measure, and will not be possible to be distinguished.

15. Belief no proof of revelation. If this internal light, or any proposition which under that title we take for inspired, be conformable to the principles of reason, or to the word of God, which is attested revelation, reason warrants it, and we may safely receive it for true, and be guided by it in our belief and actions: if it receive no testimony nor evidence from either of these rules, we cannot take it for a revelation, or so much as for true, till we have some other mark that it is a revelation, besides our believing that it is so. Thus we see the holy men of old, who had revelations from God, had something else besides that internal light of assurance in their own minds, to testify to them that it was from God. They were not left to their own persuasions alone, that those persuasions were from God, but had outward signs to convince them of the Author of those revelations. And when they were to convince others, they had a power given them to justify the truth of their commission from heaven, and by visible signs to assert the divine authority of a message they were sent with. Moses saw the bush burn without being consumed, and heard a voice out of it: this was something besides finding an impulse upon his mind to go to Pharaoh, that he might bring his brethren out of Egypt: and yet he thought not this enough to authorize him to go with that message, till God, by another miracle of his rod turned into a serpent, had assured him of a power to testify his mission, by the same miracle repeated before them whom he was sent to. Gideon was sent by an angel to deliver Israel from the Midianites, and yet he desired a sign to convince him that this commission was from God. These, and several the like instances to be found among the prophets of old, are enough to show that they thought not an inward seeing or persuasion of their own minds, without any other proof, a sufficient evidence that it was from God; though the Scripture does not everywhere mention their demanding or having such proofs.

16. Criteria of a divine revelation. In what I have said I am far from denying, that God can, or doth sometimes enlighten men's minds in the apprehending of certain truths or excite them to good actions, by the immediate influence and assistance of the Holy Spirit, without any extraordinary signs accompanying it. But in such cases too we have reason and Scripture; unerring rules to know whether it be from God or no. Where the truth embraced is consonant to the revelation in the written word of God, or the action conformable to the dictates of right reason or holy writ, we may be assured that we run no risk in entertaining it as such: because, though perhaps it be not an immediate revelation from God, extraordinarily operating on our minds, yet we are sure it is warranted by that revelation which he has given us of truth. But it is not the strength of our private persuasion within ourselves, that can warrant it to be a light or motion from heaven: nothing can do that but the written Word of God without us, or that standard of reason which is common to us with all men. Where reason or Scripture is express for any opinion or action, we may receive it as of divine authority: but it is not the strength of our own persuasions which can by itself give it that stamp. The bent of our own minds may favour it as much as we please: that may show it to be a fondling of our own, but will by no means prove it to be an offspring of heaven, and of divine original.

Chapter XX.Of Wrong Assent, or Error

1. Causes of error, or how men come to give assent contrary to probability. Knowledge being to be had only of visible and certain truth, error is not a fault of our knowledge, but a mistake of our judgment giving assent to that which is not true.

But if assent be grounded on likelihood, if the proper object and motive of our assent be probability, and that probability consists in what is laid down in the foregoing chapters, it will be demanded how men come to give their assents contrary to probability. For there is nothing more common than contrariety of opinions; nothing more obvious than that one man wholly disbelieves what another only doubts of, and a third stedfastly believes and firmly adheres to. The reasons whereof, though they may be very various, yet, I suppose may all be reduced to these four: I. Want of proofs. II. Want of ability to use them. III. Want of will to see them. IV. Wrong measures of probability.

2. First cause of error, want of proofs. First, By want of proofs, I do not mean only the want of those proofs which are nowhere extant, and so are nowhere to be had; but the want even of those proofs which are in being, or might be procured. And thus men want proofs, who have not the convenience or opportunity to make experiments and observations themselves, tending to the proof of any proposition; nor likewise the convenience to inquire into and collect the testimonies of others: and in this state are the greatest part of mankind, who are given up to labour, and enslaved to the necessity of their mean condition, whose lives are worn out only in the provisions for living. These men's opportunities of knowledge and inquiry are commonly as narrow as their fortunes; and their understandings are but little instructed, when all their whole time and pains are laid out to still the croaking of their own bellies, or the cries of their children. It is not to be expected that a man who drudges on all his life in a laborious trade, should be more knowing in the variety of things done in the world than a packhorse, who is driven constantly forwards and backwards in a narrow lane and dirty road, only to market, should be skilled in the geography of the country. Nor is it at all more possible that he who wants leisure, books, and languages, and the opportunity of conversing with variety of men, should be in a condition to collect those testimonies and observations which are in being, and are necessary to make out many, nay most, of the propositions that, in the societies of men, are judged of the greatest moment; or to find out grounds of assurance so great as the belief of the points he would build on them is thought necessary. So that a great part of mankind are, by the natural and unalterable state of things in this world, and the constitution of human affairs, unavoidably given over to invincible ignorance of those proofs on which others build, and which are necessary to establish those opinions: the greatest part of men, having much to do to get the means of living, are not in a condition to look after those of learned and laborious inquiries.

3. Objection. "What shall become of those who want proofs?" Answered. What shall we say, then? Are the greatest part of mankind, by the necessity of their condition, subjected to unavoidable ignorance in those things which are of greatest importance to them? (for of those it is obvious to inquire). Have the bulk of mankind no other guide but accident and blind chance to conduct them to their happiness or misery? Are the current opinions, and licensed guides of every country sufficient evidence and security to every man to venture his great concernments on; nay, his everlasting happiness or misery? Or can those be the certain and infallible oracles and standards of truth, which teach one thing in Christendom and another in Turkey? Or shall a poor countryman be eternally happy, for having the chance to be born in Italy; or a day-labourer be unavoidably lost, because he had the ill-luck to be born in England? How ready some men may be to say some of these things, I will not here examine: but this I am sure, that men must allow one or other of these to be true, (let them choose which they

please,) or else grant that God has furnished men with faculties sufficient to direct them in the way they should take, if they will but seriously employ them that way, when their ordinary vocations allow them the leisure. No man is so wholly taken up with the attendance on the means of living, as to have no spare time at all to think of his soul, and inform himself in matters of religion. Were men as intent upon this as they are on things of lower concernment, there are none so enslaved to the necessities of life who might not find many vacancies that might be husbanded to this advantage of their knowledge.

4. People hindered from inquiry. Besides those whose improvements and informations are straitened by the narrowness of their fortunes, there are others whose largeness of fortune would plentifully enough supply books, and other requisites for clearing of doubts, and discovering of truth: but they are cooped in close, by the laws of their countries, and the strict guards of those whose interest it is to keep them ignorant, lest, knowing more, they should believe the less in them. These are as far, nay further, from the liberty and opportunities of a fair inquiry, than these poor and wretched labourers we before spoke of: and however they may seem high and great, are confined to narrowness of thought, and enslaved in that which should be the freest part of man, their understandings. This is generally the case of all those who live in places where care is taken to propagate truth without knowledge; where men are forced, at a venture, to be of the religion of the country; and must therefore swallow down opinions, as silly people do empiric's pills, without knowing what they are made of, or how they will work, and having nothing to do but believe that they will do the cure: but in this are much more miserable than they, in that they are not at liberty to refuse swallowing what perhaps they had rather let alone; or to choose the physician, to whose conduct they would trust themselves.

5. Second cause of error, want of skill to use proofs. Secondly, Those who want skill to use those evidences they have of probabilities; who cannot carry a train of consequences in their heads; nor weigh exactly the preponderancy of contrary proofs and testimonies, making every circumstance its due allowance; may be easily misled to assent to positions that are not probable. There are some men of one, some but of two syllogisms, and no more; and others that can but advance one step further. These cannot always discern that side on which the strongest proofs lie; cannot constantly follow that which in itself is the more probable opinion. Now that there is such a difference between men, in respect of their understandings, I think nobody, who has had any conversation with his neighbours, will question: though he never was at Westminster-Hall or the Exchange on the one hand, nor at Alms-houses or Bedlam on the other. Which great difference in men's intellectuals, whether it rises from any defect in the organs of the body particularly adapted to thinking; or in the dullness or untractableness of those faculties for want of use; or, as some think, in the natural differences of men's souls themselves; or some, or all of these together; it matters not here to examine: only this is evident, that there is a difference of degrees in men's understandings, apprehensions, and reasonings, to so great a latitude, that one may, without doing injury to mankind, affirm that there is a greater distance between some men and others in this respect than between some men and some beasts. But how this comes about is a speculation, though of great consequence, yet not necessary to our present purpose.

6. Third cause of error, want of will to use them. Thirdly, There are another sort of people that want proofs, not because they are out of their reach, but because they will not use them: who though they have riches and leisure enough and want neither parts nor other helps, are yet never the better for them. Their hot pursuit of pleasure, or constant drudgery in business, engages some men's thoughts elsewhere: laziness and oscitancy in general, or a particular aversion for books, study, and meditation, keep others from any serious thoughts at all; and some out of fear that an impartial inquiry would not favour those opinions which best suit their prejudices, lives, and designs, content themselves, without examination, to take upon trust what they find convenient and in fashion. Thus, most men, even of those that might do otherwise, pass their lives without an acquaintance with, much less a rational assent to,

probabilities they are concerned to know, though they lie so much within their view that, to be convinced of them, they need but turn their eyes that way. We know some men will not read a letter which is supposed to bring ill news; and many men forbear to cast up their accounts, or so much as think upon their estates, who have reason to fear their affairs are in no very good posture. How men, whose plentiful fortunes allow them leisure to improve their understandings, can satisfy themselves with a lazy ignorance, I cannot tell: but methinks they have a low opinion of their souls, who lay out all their incomes in provisions for the body, and employ none of it to procure the means and helps of knowledge; who take great care to appear always in a neat and splendid outside, and would think themselves miserable in coarse clothes, or a patched coat, and yet contentedly suffer their minds to appear abroad in a piebald livery of coarse patches and borrowed shreds, such as it has pleased chance, or their country tailor (I mean the common opinion of those they have conversed with) to clothe them in. I will not here mention how unreasonable this is for men that ever think of a future state, and their concernment in it, which no rational man can avoid to do sometimes: nor shall I take notice what a shame and confusion it is to the greatest contemners of knowledge, to be found ignorant in things they are concerned to know. But this at least is worth the consideration of those who call themselves gentlemen, That, however they may think credit, respect, power, and authority the concomitants of their birth and fortune, yet they will find all these still carried away from them by men of lower condition, who surpass them in knowledge. They who are blind will always be led by those that see, or else fall into the ditch: and he is certainly the most subjected, the most enslaved, who is so in his understanding.

In the foregoing instances some of the causes have been shown of wrong assent, and how it comes to pass that probable doctrines are not always received with an assent proportionable to the reasons which are to be had for their probability: but hitherto we have considered only such probabilities whose proofs do exist, but do not appear to him who embraces the error.

7. Fourth cause of error, wrong measures of Probability. Fourthly, There remains yet the last sort, who, even where the real probabilities appear, and are plainly laid before them, do not admit of the conviction, nor yield unto manifest reasons, but do either epechein, suspend their assent, or give it to the less probable opinion. And to this danger are those exposed who have taken up wrong measures of probability, which are: I. Propositions that are not in themselves certain and evident, but doubtful and false, taken up for principles. II. Received hypotheses. III. Predominant passions or inclinations. IV. Authority.

8. I. Doubtful propositions taken for principles. The first and firmest ground of probability is the conformity anything has to our own knowledge; especially that part of our knowledge which we have embraced, and continue to look on as principles. These have so great an influence upon our opinions, that it is usually by them we judge of truth, and measure probability; to that degree, that what is inconsistent with our principles, is so far from passing for probable with us, that it will not be allowed possible. The reverence borne to these principles is so great, and their authority so paramount to all other, that the testimony, not only of other men, but the evidence of our own senses are often rejected, when they offer to vouch anything contrary to these established rules. How much the doctrine of innate principles, and that principles are not to be proved or questioned, has contributed to this, I will not here examine. This I readily grant, that one truth cannot contradict another: but withal I take leave also to say, that every one ought very carefully to beware what he admits for a principle, to examine it strictly, and see whether he certainly knows it to be true of itself, by its own evidence, or whether he does only with assurance believe it to be so upon the authority of others. For he hath a strong bias put into his understanding, which will unavoidably misguide his assent, who hath imbibed wrong principles, and has blindly given himself up to the authority of any opinion in itself not evidently true.

9. Instilled in childhood. There is nothing more ordinary than children's receiving into their minds propositions (especially about matters of religion) from their parents, nurses, or those about them: which being insinuated into their unwary as well as unbiassed understandings, and

fastened by degrees, are at last (equally whether true or false) riveted there by long custom and education, beyond all possibility of being pulled out again. For men, when they are grown up, reflecting upon their opinions, and finding those of this sort to be as ancient in their minds as their very memories, not having observed their early insinuation, nor by what means they got them, they are apt to reverence them as sacred things, and not to suffer them to be profaned, touched, or questioned: they look on them as the Urim and Thummim set up in their minds immediately by God himself, to be the great and unerring deciders of truth and falsehood, and the judges to which they are to appeal in all manner of controversies.

10. Of irresistible efficacy. This opinion of his principles (let them be what they will) being once established in any one's mind, it is easy to be imagined what reception any proposition shall find, how clearly soever proved, that shall invalidate their authority, or at all thwart these internal oracles; whereas the grossest absurdities and improbabilities, being but agreeable to such principles, go down glibly, and are easily digested. The great obstinacy that is to be found in men firmly believing quite contrary opinions, though many times equally absurd, in the various religions of mankind, are as evident a proof as they are an unavoidable consequence of this way of reasoning from received traditional principles. So that men will disbelieve their own eyes, renounce the evidence of their senses, and give their own experience the lie, rather than admit of anything disagreeing with these sacred tenets. Take an intelligent Romanist that, from the first dawning of any notions in his understanding, hath had this principle constantly inculcated, viz. that he must believe as the church (i.e. those of his communion) believes, or that the pope is infallible, and this he never so much as heard questioned, till at forty or fifty years old he met with one of other principles: how is he prepared easily to swallow, not only against all probability, but even the clear evidence of his senses, the doctrine of transubstantiation? This principle has such an influence on his mind, that he will believe that to be flesh which he sees to be bread. And what way will you take to convince a man of any improbable opinion he holds, who, with some philosophers, hath laid down this as a foundation of reasoning, That he must believe his reason (for so men improperly call arguments drawn from their principles) against his senses? Let an enthusiast be principled that he or his teacher is inspired, and acted by an immediate communication of the Divine Spirit, and you in vain bring the evidence of clear reasons against his doctrine. Whoever, therefore, have imbibed wrong principles, are not, in things inconsistent with these principles, to be moved by the most apparent and convincing probabilities, till they are so candid and ingenuous to themselves, as to be persuaded to examine even those very principles, which many never suffer themselves to do.

11. II. Received hypotheses. Next to these are men whose understandings are cast into a mould, and fashioned just to the size of a received hypothesis. The difference between these and the former, is, that they will admit of matter of fact, and agree with dissenters in that; but differ only in assigning of reasons and explaining the manner of operation. These are not at that open defiance with their senses, with the former: they can endure to hearken to their information a little more patiently; but will by no means admit of their reports in the explanation of things; nor be prevailed on by probabilities, which would convince them that things are not brought about just after the same manner that they have decreed within themselves that they are. Would it not be an insufferable thing for a learned professor, and that which his scarlet would blush at, to have his authority of forty years, standing, wrought out of hard rock, Greek and Latin, with no small expense of time and candle, and confirmed by general tradition and a reverend beard, in an instant overturned by an upstart novelist? Can any one expect that he should be made to confess, that what he taught his scholars thirty years ago was all error and mistake; and that he sold them hard words and ignorance at a very dear rate. What probabilities, I say, are sufficient to prevail in such a case? And who ever, by the most cogent arguments, will be prevailed with to disrobe himself at once of all his old opinions, and pretences to knowledge and learning, which with hard study he hath all this time been labouring for; and turn himself out stark naked, in quest afresh of new notions? All the

arguments that can be used will be as little able to prevail, as the wind did with the traveller to part with his cloak, which he held only the faster. To this of wrong hypothesis may be reduced the errors that may be occasioned by a true hypothesis, or right principles, but not rightly understood. There is nothing more familiar than this. The instances of men contending for different opinions, which they all derive from the infallible truth of the Scripture, are an undeniable proof of it. All that call themselves Christians, allow the text that says, metanoeite, to carry in it the obligation to a very weighty duty. But yet how very erroneous will one of their practices be, who, understanding nothing but the French, take this rule with one translation to be, Repentez-vous, repent; or with the other, Fatiez penitence, do penance.

12. III. Predominant passions. Probabilities which cross men's appetites and prevailing passions run the same fate. Let ever so much probability hang on one side of a covetous man's reasoning, and money on the other; it is easy to foresee which will outweigh. Earthly minds, like mud walls, resist the strongest batteries: and though, perhaps, sometimes the force of a clear argument may make some impression, yet they nevertheless stand firm, and keep out the enemy, truth, that would captivate or disturb them. Tell a man passionately in love that he is jilted; bring a score of witnesses of the falsehood of his mistress, it is ten to one but three kind words of hers shall invalidate all their testimonies. Quod volumus, facile credimus; what suits our wishes, is forwardly believed, is, I suppose, what every one hath more than once experimented: and though men cannot always openly gainsay or resist the force of manifest probabilities that make against them, yet yield they not to the argument. Not but that it is the nature of the understanding constantly to close with the more probable side; but yet a man hath a power to suspend and restrain its inquiries, and not permit a full and satisfactory examination, as far as the matter in question is capable, and will bear it to be made. Until that be done, there will be always these two ways left of evading the most apparent probabilities:

13. Two means of evading probabilities: I. Supposed fallacy latent in the words employed. First, That the arguments being (as for the most part they are) brought in words, there may be a fallacy latent in them: and the consequences being, perhaps, many in train, they may be some of them incoherent. There are very few discourses so short, clear, and consistent, to which most men may not, with satisfaction enough to themselves, raise this doubt; and from whose conviction they may not, without reproach of disingenuity or unreasonableness, set themselves free with the old reply, Non persuadebis, etiamsi persuaseris; though I cannot answer, I will not yield.

14. Supposed unknown arguments for the contrary. Secondly, Manifest probabilities may be evaded, and the assent withheld, upon this suggestion, That I know not yet all that may he said on the contrary side. And therefore, though I be beaten, it is not necessary I should yield, not knowing what forces there are in reserve behind. This is a refuge against conviction so open and so wide, that it is hard to determine when a man is quite out of the verge of it. 15. What probabilities naturally determine the assent. But yet there is some end of it; and a man having carefully inquired into all the grounds of probability and unlikeliness; done his utmost to inform himself in all particulars fairly, and cast up the sum total on both sides; may, in most cases, come to acknowledge, upon the whole matter, on which side the probability rests: wherein some proofs in matter of reason, being suppositions upon universal experience, are so cogent and clear, and some testimonies in matter of fact so universal, that he cannot refuse his assent. So that I think we may conclude, that, in propositions, where though the proofs in view are of most moment, yet there are sufficient grounds to suspect that there is either fallacy in words, or certain proofs as considerable to be produced on the contrary side; there assent, suspense, or dissent, are often voluntary actions. But where the proofs are such as make it highly probable, and there is not sufficient ground to suspect that there is either fallacy of words (which sober and serious consideration may discover) nor equally valid proofs yet undiscovered, latent on the other side (which also the nature of the thing may, in some cases, make plain to a considerate man); there, I think, a man who has weighed them can scarce refuse his assent to the side on which the greater probability appears. Whether it be probable

that a promiscuous jumble of printing letters should often fall into a method and order, which should stamp on paper a coherent discourse; or that a blind fortuitous concourse of atoms, not guided by an understanding agent, should frequently constitute the bodies of any species of animals: in these and the like cases, I think, nobody that considers them can be one jot at a stand which side to take, nor at all waver in his assent. Lastly, when there can be no supposition (the thing in its own nature indifferent, and wholly depending upon the testimony of witnesses) that there is as fair testimony against, as for the matter of fact attested; which by inquiry is to be learned, v.g. whether there was one thousand seven hundred years ago such a man at Rome as Julius Caesar: in all such cases, I say, I think it is not in any rational man's power to refuse his assent; but that it necessarily follows, and closes with such probabilities. In other less clear cases, I think it is in man's power to suspend his assent; and perhaps content himself with the proofs he has, if they favour the opinion that suits with his inclination or interest, and so stop from further search. But that a man should afford his assent to that side on which the less probability appears to him, seems to me utterly impracticable, and as impossible as it is to believe the same thing probable and improbable at the same time.

16. Where it is in our power to suspend our judgment. As knowledge is no more arbitrary than perception; so, I think, assent is no more in our power than knowledge. When the agreement of any two ideas appears to our minds, whether immediately or by the assistance of reason, I can no more refuse to perceive, no more avoid knowing it, than I can avoid seeing those objects which I turn my eyes to, and look on in daylight; and what upon full examination I find the most probable, I cannot deny my assent to. But, though we cannot hinder our knowledge, where the agreement is once perceived; nor our assent, where the probability manifestly appears upon due consideration of all the measures of it: yet we can hinder both knowledge and assent, by stopping our inquiry, and not employing our faculties in the search of any truth. If it were not so, ignorance, error, or infidelity, could not in any case be a fault. Thus, in some cases we can prevent or suspend our assent: but can a man versed in modern or ancient history doubt whether there is such a place as Rome, or whether there was such a man as Julius Caesar? Indeed, there are millions of truths that a man is not, or may not think himself concerned to know; as whether our king Richard the Third was crooked or no; or whether Roger Bacon was a mathematician or a magician. In these and such like cases, where the assent one way or other is of no importance to the interest of any one; no action, no concernment of his following or depending thereon, there it is not strange that the mind should give itself up to the common opinion, or render itself to the first comer. These and the like opinions are of so little weight and moment, that, like motes in the sun, their tendencies are very rarely taken notice of. They are there, as it were, by chance, and the mind lets them float at liberty. But where the mind judges that the proposition has concernment in it: where the assent or not assenting is thought to draw consequences of moment after it, and good and evil to depend on choosing or refusing the right side, and the mind sets itself seriously to inquire and examine the probability: there I think it is not in our choice to take which side we please, if manifest odds appear on either. The greater probability, I think, in that case will determine the assent: and a man can no more avoid assenting, or taking it to be true, where he perceives the greater probability, than he can avoid knowing it to be true, where he perceives the agreement or disagreement of any two ideas.

If this be so, the foundation of error will lie in wrong measures of probability; as the foundation of vice in wrong measures of good.

17. IV. Authority. The fourth and last wrong measure of probability I shall take notice of, and which keeps in ignorance or error more people than all the other together, is that which I have mentioned in the foregoing chapter: I mean the giving up our assent to the common received opinions, either of our friends or party, neighbourhood or country. How many men have no other ground for their tenets, than the supposed honesty, or learning, or number of those of the same profession? As if honest or bookish men could not err; or truth were to be established by the vote of the multitude: yet this with most men serves the turn. The tenet has had the

attestation of reverend antiquity; it comes to me with the passport of former ages, and therefore I am secure in the reception I give it: other men have been and are of the same opinion, (for that is all is said,) and therefore it is reasonable for me to embrace it. A man may more justifiably throw up cross and pile for his opinions, than take them up by such measures. All men are liable to error, and most men are in many points, by passion or interest, under temptation to it. If we could but see the secret motives that influenced the men of name and learning in the world, and the leaders of parties, we should not always find that it was the embracing of truth for its own sake, that made them espouse the doctrines they owned and maintained. This at least is certain, there is not an opinion so absurd, which a man may not receive upon this ground. There is no error to be named, which has not had its professors: and a man shall never want crooked paths to walk in, if he thinks that he is in the right way, wherever he has the footsteps of others to follow.

18. Not so many men in errors as is commonly supposed. But, notwithstanding the great noise is made in the world about errors and opinions, I must do mankind that right as to say, There are not so many men in errors and wrong opinions as is commonly supposed. Not that I think they embrace the truth; but indeed, because concerning those doctrines they keep such a stir about, they have no thought, no opinion at all. For if any one should a little catechise the greatest part of the partizans of most of the sects in the world, he would not find, concerning those matters they are so zealous for, that they have any opinions of their own: much less would he have reason to think that they took them upon the examination of arguments and appearance of probability. They are resolved to stick to a party that education or interest has engaged them in; and there, like the common soldiers of an army, show their courage and warmth as their leaders direct, without ever examining, or so much as knowing, the cause they contend for. If a man's life shows that he has no serious regard for religion; for what reason should we think that he beats his head about the opinions of his church, and troubles himself to examine the grounds of this or that doctrine? It is enough for him to obey his leaders, to have his hand and his tongue ready for the support of the common cause, and thereby approve himself to those who can give him credit, preferment, or protection in that society. Thus men become professors of, and combatants for, those opinions they were never convinced of nor proselytes to; no, nor ever had so much as floating in their heads: and though one cannot say there are fewer improbable or erroneous opinions in the world than there are, yet this is certain; there are fewer that actually assent to them, and mistake them for truths, than is imagined.

Chapter XXI. Of the Division of the Sciences

1. Science may be divided into three sorts. All that can fall within the compass of human understanding, being either, First, the nature of things, as they are in themselves, their relations, and their manner of operation: or, Secondly, that which man himself ought to do, as a rational and voluntary agent, for the attainment of any end, especially happiness: or, Thirdly, the ways and means whereby the knowledge of both the one and the other of these is attained and communicated; I think science may be divided properly into these three sorts:—

2. Physica. First, The knowledge of things, as they are in their own proper beings, their constitution, properties, and operations; whereby I mean not only matter and body, but spirits also, which have their proper natures, constitutions, and operations, as well as bodies. This, in a little more enlarged sense of the word, I call Phusike, or natural philosophy. The end of this is bare speculative truth: and whatsoever can afford the mind of man any such, falls under this branch, whether it be God himself, angels, spirits, bodies; or any of their affections, as number, and figure, &c.

3. Practica. Secondly, Praktike, The skill of right applying our own powers and actions, for the attainment of things good and useful. The most considerable under this head is ethics, which is

the seeking out those rules and measures of human actions, which lead to happiness, and the means to practise them. The end of this is not bare speculation and the knowledge of truth; but right, and a conduct suitable to it.

4. Semeiotike. Thirdly, the third branch may be called Semeiotike, or the doctrine of signs; the most usual whereof being words, it is aptly enough termed also Logike, logic: the business whereof is to consider the nature of signs, the mind makes use of for the understanding of things, or conveying its knowledge to others. For, since the things the mind contemplates are none of them, besides itself, present to the understanding, it is necessary that something else, as a sign or representation of the thing it considers, should be present to it: and these are ideas. And because the scene of ideas that makes one man's thoughts cannot be laid open to the immediate view of another, nor laid up anywhere but in the memory, a no very sure repository: therefore to communicate our thoughts to one another, as well as record them for our own use, signs of our ideas are also necessary: those which men have found most convenient, and therefore generally make use of, are articulate sounds. The consideration, then, of ideas and words as the great instruments of knowledge, makes no despicable part of their contemplation who would take a view of human knowledge in the whole extent of it. And perhaps if they were distinctly weighed, and duly considered, they would afford us another sort of logic and critic, than what we have been hitherto acquainted with.

5. This is the first and most general division of the objects of our understanding. This seems to me the first and most general, as well as natural division of the objects of our understanding. For a man can employ his thoughts about nothing, but either, the contemplation of things themselves, for the discovery of truth; or about the things in his own power, which are his own actions, for the attainment of his own ends; or the signs the mind makes use of both in the one and the other, and the right ordering of them, for its clearer information. All which three, viz, things, as they are in themselves knowable; actions as they depend on us, in order to happiness; and the right use of signs in order to knowledge, being toto coelo different, they seemed to me to be the three great provinces of the intellectual world, wholly separate and distinct one from another.

Some Thoughts Concerning Education

Sections 1–10

§ 1. A SOUND mind in a sound body, is a short, but full description of a happy state in this world. He that has these two, has little more to wish for; and he that wants either of them, will be but little the better for any thing else. Men's happiness or misery is most part of their own making. He, whose mind directs not wisely, will never take the right way; and he, whose body is crazy and feeble, will never be able to advance in it. I confess, there are some men's constitutions of body and mind so vigorous, and well fram'd by nature, that they need not much assistance from others; but by the strength of their natural genius, they are from their cradles carried towards what is excellent; and by the privilege of their happy constitutions, are able to do wonders. But examples of this kind are but few; and I think I may say, that of all the men we meet with, nine parts of ten are what they are, good or evil, useful or not, by their education. 'Tis that which makes the great difference in mankind. The little, or almost insensible impressions on our tender infancies, have very important and lasting consequences: and there 'tis, as in the fountains of some rivers, where a gentle application of the hand turns the flexible waters in channels, that make them take quite contrary courses; and by this direction given them at first in the source, they receive different tendencies, and arrive at last at very remote and distant places.

§ 2. I imagine the minds of children as easily turn'd this or that way, as water it self: and though this be the principal part, and our main care should be about the inside, yet the clay-cottage is not to be neglected. I shall therefore begin with the case, and consider first the health of the body, as that which perhaps you may rather expect from that study I have been thought more peculiarly to have apply'd my self to; and that also which will be soonest dispatch'd, as lying, if I guess not amiss, in a very little compass.

§ 3. How necessary health is to our business and happiness; and how requisite a strong constitution, able to endure hardships and fatigue, is to one that will make any figure in the world, is too obvious to need any proof.

§ 4. The consideration I shall here have of health, shall be, not what a physician ought to do with a sick and crazy child; but what the parents, without the help of physick, should do for the preservation and improvement of an healthy, or at least not sickly constitution in their children. And this perhaps might be all dispatch'd in this one short rule, viz. That gentlemen should use their children, as the honest farmers and substantial yeomen do theirs. But because the mothers possibly may think this a little too hard, and the fathers too short, I shall explain my self more particularly; only laying down this as a general and certain observation for the women to consider, viz. That most children's constitutions are either spoil'd, or at least harm'd, by cockering and tenderness.

§ 5. The first thing to be taken care of, is, that children be not too warmly clad or cover'd, winter or summer. The face when we are born, is no less tender than any other part of the body. 'Tis use alone hardens it, and makes it more able to endure the cold. And therefore the Scythian philosopher gave a very significant answer to the Athenian, who wonder'd how he could go naked in frost and snow. How, said the Scythian, can you endure your face expos'd to the sharp winter air? My face is us'd to it, said the Athenian. Think me all face, reply'd the Scythian. Our bodies will endure any thing, that from the beginning they are accustom'd to.

An eminent instance of this, though in the contrary excess of heat, being to our present purpose, to shew what use can do, I shall set down in the author's words, as I meet with it in a late ingenious voyage. "The heats, says he, are more violent in Malta, than in any part of

Europe: they exceed those of Rome itself, and are perfectly stifling; and so much the more, because there are seldom any cooling breezes here. This makes the common people as black as gypsies: but yet the peasants defy the sun; they work on in the hottest part of the day, without intermission, or sheltering themselves from his scorching rays. This has convinc'd me, that nature can bring itself to many things, which seem impossible, provided we accustom ourselves from our infancy. The Malteses do so, who harden the bodies of their children, and reconcile them to the heat, by making them go stark naked, without shirt, drawers, or any thing on their heads, from their cradles till they are ten years old."

Give me leave therefore to advise you not to fence too carefully against the cold of this our climate. There are those in England, who wear the same clothes winter and summer, and that without any inconvenience, or more sense of cold than others find. But if the mother will needs have an allowance for frost and snow, for fear of harm, and the father, for fear of censure, be sure let not his winter clothing be too warm: And amongst other things, remember, that when nature has so well covered his head with hair, and strengthen'd it with a year or two's age, that he can run about by day without a cap, it is best that by night a child should also lie without one; there being nothing that more exposes to headaches, colds, catarrhs, coughs, and several other diseases, than keeping the head warm.

§ 6. I have said he here, because the principal aim of my discourse is, how a young gentleman should be brought up from his infancy, which in all things will not so perfectly suit the education of daughters; though where the difference of sex requires different treatment, 'twill be no hard matter to distinguish.

§ 7. I will also advise his feet to be wash'd every day in cold water, and to have his shoes so thin, that they might leak and let in water, whenever he comes near it. Here, I fear I shall have the mistress and maids too against me. One will think it too filthy, and the other perhaps too much pains, to make clean his stockings. But yet truth will have it, that his health is much more worth than all such considerations, and ten times as much more. And he that considers how mischievous and mortal a thing taking wet in the feet is, to those who have been bred nicely, will wish he had, with the poor people's children, gone bare-foot, who, by that means, come to be so reconcil'd by custom to wet in their feet, that they take no more cold or harm by it, than if they were wet in their hands. And what is it, I pray, that makes this great difference between the hands and the feet in others, but only custom? I doubt not, but if a man from his cradle had been always us'd to go bare-foot, whilst his hands were constantly wrapt up in warm mittins, and cover'd with hand-shoes, as the Dutch call gloves; I doubt not, I say, but such a custom would make taking wet in his hands as dangerous to him, as now taking wet in their feet is to great many others. The way to prevent this, is, to have his shoes made so as to leak water, and his feet wash'd constantly every day in cold water. It is recommendable for its cleanliness; but that which I aim at in it, is health; and therefore I limit it not precisely to any time of the day. I have known it us'd every night with very good success, and that all the winter, without the omitting it so much as one night in extreme cold weather; when thick ice cover'd the water, the child bathed his legs and feet in it, though he was of an age not big enough to rub and wipe them himself, and when he began this custom was puling and very tender. But the great end being to harden those parts by a frequent and familiar use of cold water, and thereby to prevent the mischiefs that usually attend accidental taking wet in the feet in those who are bred otherwise, I think it may be left to the prudence and convenience of the parents, to chuse either night or morning. The time I deem indifferent, so the thing be effectually done. The health and hardiness procured by it, would be a good purchase at a much dearer rate. To which if I add the preventing of corns, that to some men would be a very valuable consideration. But begin first in the spring with luke-warm, and so colder and colder every time, till in a few days you come to perfectly cold water, and then continue it so winter and summer. For it is to be observed in this, as in all other alterations from our ordinary way of living, the changes must be made by gentle and insensible degrees; and so we may bring our bodies to any thing, without pain, and without danger.

How fond mothers are like to receive this doctrine, is not hard to foresee. What can it be less, than to murder their tender babes, to use them thus? What! put their feet in cold water in frost and snow, when all one can do is little enough to keep them warm? A little to remove their fears by examples, without which the plainest reason is seldom hearken'd to: Seneca tells us of himself, Ep. 53, and 83, that he used to bathe himself in cold spring-water in the midst of winter. This, if he had not thought it not only tolerable, but healthy too, he would scarce have done, in an exorbitant fortune, that could well have borne the expence of a warm bath, and in an age (for he was then old) that would have excused greater indulgence. If we think his stoical principles led him to this severity, let it be so, that this sect reconciled cold water to his sufferance. What made it agreeable to his health? For that was not impair'd by this hard usage. But what shall we say to Horace, who warm'd not himself with the reputation of any sect, and least of all affected stoical austerities? yet he assures us, he was wont in the winter season to bathe himself in cold water. But, perhaps, Italy will be thought much warmer than England, and the chillness of their waters not to come near ours in winter. If the rivers of Italy are warmer, those of Germany and Poland are much colder, than any in this our country, and yet in these, the Jews, both men and women, bathe all over, at all seasons of the year, without any prejudice to their health. And every one is not apt to believe it is miracle, or any peculiar virtue of St. Winifred's Well, that makes the cold waters of that famous spring do no harm to the tender bodies that bathe in it. Every one is now full of the miracles done by cold baths on decay'd and weak constitutions, for the recovery of health and strength; and therefore they cannot be impracticable or intolerable for the improving and hardening the bodies of those tho are in better circumstances.

If these examples of grown men be not thought yet to reach the case of children, but that they may be judg'd still to be too tender, and unable to bear such usage, let them examine what the Germans of old, and the Irish now, do to them, and they will find, that infants too, as tender as they are thought, may, without any danger, endure bathing, not only of their feet, but of their whole bodies, in cold water. And there are, at this day, ladies in the Highlands of Scotland who use this discipline to their children in the midst of winter, and find that cold water does them no harm, even when there is ice in it.

§ 8. I shall not need here to mention swimming, when he is of an age able to learn, and has any one to teach him. 'Tis that saves many a man's life; and the Romans thought it so necessary, that they rank'd it with letters; and it was the common phrase to mark one ill-educated, and good for nothing, that he had neither learnt to read nor to swim: Nec literas didicit nec natare. But, besides the gaining a skill which may serve him at need, the advantages to health by often bathing in cold water during the heat of summer, are so many, that I think nothing need be said to encourage it; provided this one caution be us'd, that he never go into the water when exercise has at all warm'd him, or left any emotion in his blood or pulse.

§ 9. Another thing that is of great advantage to every one's health, but especially children's, is to be much in the open air, and as little as may be by the fire, even in winter. By this he will accustom himself also to heat and cold, shine and rain; all which if a man's body will not endure, it will serve him to very little purpose in this world; and when he is grown up, it is too late to begin to use him to it. It must be got early, and by degrees. Thus the body may be brought to bear almost any thing. If I should advise him to play in the wind and sun without a hat, I doubt whether it could be borne. There would a thousand objections be made against it, which at last would amount to no more, in truth, than being sun-burnt. And if my young master be to be kept always in the shade, and never expos'd to the sun and wind for fear of his complexion, it may be a good way to make him a beau, but not a man of business. And altho' greater regard be to be had to beauty in the daughters; yet I will take the liberty to say, that the more they are in the air, without prejudice to their faces, the stronger and healthier they will be; and the nearer they come to the hardships of their brothers in their education, the greater advantage will they receive from it all the remaining part of their lives.

§ 10. Playing in the open air has but this one danger in it, that I know; and that is, that when he is hot with running up and down, he should sit or lie down on the cold or moist earth. This I grant; and drinking cold drink, when they are hot with labour or exercise, brings more people to the grave, or to the brink of it, by fevers, and other diseases, than anything I know. These mischiefs are easily enough prevented whilst he is little, being then seldom out of sight. And if, during his childhood, he be constantly and rigorously kept form sitting on the ground, or drinking any cold liquor whilst he is hot, the custom of forbearing, grown into habit, will help much to preserve him, when he is no longer under his maid's or tutor's eye. This is all I think can be done in the case: for, as years increase, liberty must come with them; and in a great many things he must be trusted to his own conduct, since there cannot always be a guard upon him, except what you have put into his own mind by good principles, and establish'd habits, which is the best and surest, and therefore most to be taken care of. For, from repeated cautions and rules, never so often inculcated, you are not to expect any thing either in this, or any other case, farther than practice has establish'd them into habits.

Sections 11–20

§ 11. One thing the mention of the girls brings into my mind, which must not be forgot; and that is, that your son's clothes be never made strait, especially about the breast. Let nature have scope to fashion the body as she thinks best. She works of herself a great deal better and exacter than we can direct her. And if women were themselves to frame the bodies of their children in their wombs, as they often endeavour to mend their shapes when they are out, we should as certainly have no perfect children born, as we have few well-shap'd that are strait-lac'd, or much tamper'd with. This consideration should, methinks, keep busy people (I will not say ignorant nurses and bodice-makers) from meddling in a matter they understand not; and they should be afraid to put nature out of her way in fashioning the parts, when they know not how the least and meanest is made. And yet I have seen so many instances of children receiving great harm from strait-lacing, that I cannot but conclude there are other creatures as well as monkeys, who, little wiser than they, destroy their young ones by senseless fondness, and too much embracing.

§ 12. Narrow breasts, short and stinking breath, ill lungs, and crookedness, are natural and almost constant effects of hard bodice, and clothes that pinch. That way of making slender wastes, and fine shapes, serves but the more effectually to spoil them. Nor can there indeed but be disproportion in the parts, when the nourishment prepared in the several offices of the body cannot be distributed as nature designs. And therefore what wonder is it, if, it being laid where it can, on some part not so braced, it often makes a shoulder or hip higher or bigger than its just proportion? 'Tis generally known, that the women of China, (imagining I know not what kind of beauty in it) by bracing and binding them hard from their infancy, have very little feet. I saw lately a pair of China shoes, which I was told were for a grown woman: they were so exceedingly disproportion'd to the feet of one of the same age among us, that they would scarce have been big enough for one of our little girls. Besides this, 'tis observ'd, that their women are also very little, and short-liv'd; whereas the men are of the ordinary stature of other men, and live to a proportionable age. These defects in the female sex in that country, are by some imputed to the unreasonable binding of their feet, whereby the free circulation of the blood is hinder'd, and the growth and health of the whole body suffers. And how often do we see, that some small part of the foot being injur'd by a wrench or a blow, the whole leg or thigh thereby lose their strength and nourishment, and dwindle away? How much greater inconveniences may we expect, when the thorax, wherein is placed the heart and seat of life, is unnaturally compress'd, and hinder'd from its due expansion?

§ 13. As for his diet, it ought to be very plain and simple; and, if I might advise, flesh should be forborne as long as he is in coats, or at least till he is two or three years old. But whatever advantage this may be to his present and future health and strength, I fear it will hardly be consented to by parents, misled by the custom of eating too much flesh themselves, who will be apt to think their children, as they do themselves, in danger to be starv'd, if they have not flesh at least twice a-day. This I am sure, children would breed their teeth with much less danger, be freer from diseases whilst they were little, and lay the foundations of an healthy and strong constitution much surer, if they were not cramm'd so much as they are by fond mothers and foolish servants, and were kept wholly from flesh the first three or four years of their lives.

But if my young master must needs have flesh, let it be but once a day, and of one sort of a meal. Plain beef, mutton, veal, &c. without other sauce than hunger, is best; and great care should be used, that he eat bread plentifully, both alone and with every thing else; and whatever he eats that is solid, make him chew it well. We English are often negligent herein; from whence follow indigestion, and other great inconveniences.

§ 14. For breakfast and supper, milk, milk-pottage, water-gruel, flummery, and twenty other things, that we are wont to make in England, are very fit for children; only, in all these, let care be taken that they be plain, and without much mixture, and very sparingly season'd with sugar, or rather none at all; especially all spice, and other things that may heat the blood, are carefully to be avoided. Be sparing also of salt in the seasoning of all his victuals, and use him not to high-season'd meats. Our palates grow into a relish and liking of the seasoning and cookery which by custom they are set to; and an over-much use of salt, besides that it occasions thirst, and over-much drinking, has other ill effects upon the body. I should think that a good piece of well-made and well-bak'd brown bread, sometimes with, and sometimes without butter or cheese, would be often the best breakfast for my young master. I am sure 'tis as wholesome, and will make him as strong a man as greater delicacies; and if he be used to it, it will be as pleasant to him. If he at any time calls for victuals between meals, use him to nothing but dry bread. If he be hungry more than wanton, bread alone will down; and if he be not hungry, 'tis not fit he should eat. By this you will obtain two good effects: 1. That by custom he will come to be in love with bread; for, as I said, our palates and stomachs too are pleased with the things we are used to. 2. Another good you will gain hereby is, that you will not teach him to eat more nor oftener than nature requires. I do not think that all people's appetites are alike; some have naturally stronger, and some weaker stomachs. But this I think, that many are made gormands and gluttons by custom, that were not so by nature; and I see in some countries, men as lusty and strong, that eat but two meals a-day, as others that have set their stomachs by a constant usage, like larums, to call on them for four or five. The Romans usually fasted till supper, the only set meal even of those who eat more than once a-day; and those who us'd breakfast, as some did, at eight, some at ten, others at twelve of the clock, and some later, neither eat flesh, nor had any thing made ready for them. Augustus, when the greatest monarch on the earth, tells us, he took a bit of dry bread in his chariot. And Seneca, in his 83rd Epistle, giving an account how he managed himself, even when he was old, and his age permitted indulgence, says, that he used to eat a piece of dry bread for his dinner, without the formality of sitting to it, tho' his estate would as well have paid for a better meal (had health requir'd it) as any subject's in England, were it doubled. The masters of the world were bred up with this spare diet; and the young gentlemen of Rome felt no want of strength or spirit, because they eat but once a day. Or if it happen'd by chance, that any one could not fast so long as till supper, their only set meal, he took nothing but a bit of dry bread, or at most a few raisins, or some such slight thing with it, to stay his stomach. This part of temperance was found so necessary both for health and business, that the custom of only one meal a day held out against that prevailing luxury which their Eastern conquests and spoils had brought in amongst them; and those who had given up their old frugal eating, and made feasts, yet began them not till the evening. And more than one set meal a-day was thought so monstrous, that it was a reproach as low down as Cæsar's time, to make an entertainment, or sit down to a full table, till towards sun-set; and therefore, if it would not be thought too severe, I should judge it most convenient that my young master should have nothing but bread too for breakfast. You cannot imagine of what force custom is; and I impute a great part of our diseases in England, to our eating too much flesh, and too little bread.

§ 15. As to his meals, I should think it best, that as much as it can be conveniently avoided, they should not be kept constantly to an hour: for when custom has fix'd his eating to certain stated periods, his stomach will expect victuals at the usual hour, and grow peevish if he passes it; either fretting itself into a troublesome excess, or flagging into a downright want of appetite. Therefore I would have no time kept constantly to for his breakfast, dinner and supper, but rather vary'd almost every day. And if betwixt these, which I call meals, he will eat, let him have, as often as he calls for it, good dry bread. If any one think this too hard and sparing a diet for a child, let them know, that a child will never starve nor dwindle for want of nourishment, who, besides flesh at dinner, and spoon-meat, or some such other thing, at supper, may have good bread and beer as often as he has a stomach. For thus, upon second thoughts, I should judge it best for children to be order'd. The morning is generally design'd for study, to which a full stomach is but an ill preparation. Dry bread, though the best nourishment, has the least temptation; and no body would have a child cramm'd at breakfast, who has any regard to his mind or body, and would not have him dull and unhealthy. Nor let any one think this unsuitable to one of estate and condition. A gentleman in any age ought to be so bred, as to be fitted to bear arms, and be a soldier. But he that in this, breeds his son so, as if he design'd him to sleep over his life in the plenty and ease of a full fortune he intends to leave him, little considers the examples he has seen, or the age he lives in.

§ 16. His drink should be only small beer; and that too he should never be suffer'd to have between meals, but after he had eat a piece of bread. The reasons why I say this are these.

§ 17. I. More fevers and surfeits are got by people's drinking when they are hot, than by any one thing I know. Therefore, if by play he be hot and dry, bread will ill go down; and so if he cannot have drink but upon that condition, he will be forced to forbear; for, if he be very hot, he should by no means drink; at least a good piece of bread first to be eaten, will gain time to warm the beer blood-hot, which then he may drink safely. If he be very dry, it will go down so warm'd, and quench his thirst better; and if he will not drink it so warm'd, abstaining will not hurt him. Besides, this will teach him to forbear, which is an habit of greatest use for health of body and mind too.

§ 18. 2. Not being permitted to drink without eating, will prevent the custom of having the cup often at his nose; a dangerous beginning, and preparation to good-fellowship. Men often bring habitual hunger and thirst on themselves by custom. And if you please to try, you may, though he be wean'd from it, bring him by use to such a necessity again of drinking in the night, that he will not be able to sleep without it. It being the lullaby used by nurses to still crying children, I believe mothers generally find some difficulty to wean their children from drinking in the night, when they first take them home. Believe it, custom prevails as much by day as by night; and you may, if you please, bring any one to be thirsty every hour.

I once liv'd in a house, where, to appease a forward child, they gave him drink as often as he cry'd; so that he was constantly bibbing. And tho' he could not speak, yet he drank more in twenty-four hours than I did. Try it when you please, you may with small, as well as with strong beer, drink your self into a drought. The great thing to be minded in education is, what habits you settle; and therefore in this, as all other things, do not begin to make any thing customary, the practice whereof you would not have continue and increase. It is convenient for health and sobriety, to drink no more than natural thirst requires; and he that eats not salt meats, nor drinks strong drink, will seldom thirst between meals, unless he has been accustom'd to such unseasonable drinking.

§ 19. Above all, take great care that he seldom, if ever, taste any wine or strong drink. There is nothing so ordinarily given children in England, and nothing so destructive to them. They ought never to drink any strong liquor but when they need it as a cordial, and the doctor prescribes it. And in this case it is, that servants are most narrowly to be watch'd and most severely to be reprehended when they transgress. Those mean sort of people, placing a great part of their happiness in strong drink, are always forward to make court to my young master by offering him that which they love best themselves: and finding themselves made merry by it, they foolishly think 'twill do the child no harm. This you are carefully to have your eye upon, and restrain with all the skill and industry you can, there being nothing that lays a surer foundation of mischief, both to body and mind than children's being us'd to strong drink, especially to drink in private with the servants.

§ 20. Fruit makes one of the most difficult chapters in the government of health, especially that of children. Our first parents ventur'd Paradise for it; and 'tis no wonder our children cannot stand the temptation, tho' it cost them their health. The regulation of this cannot come under any one general rule; for I am by no means of their mind, who would keep children almost wholly from fruit, as a thing totally unwholesome for them; by which strict way, they make them but the more ravenous after it, and to eat good or bad, ripe or unripe, all that they can get, whenever they come at it. Melons, peaches, most sorts of plums, and all sorts of grapes in England, I think children should be wholly kept from, as having a very tempting taste, in a very unwholesome juice; so that if it were possible, they should never so much as see them, or know there were any such thing. But strawberries, cherries, gooseberries, or currants, when thorough ripe, I think may be very safely allow'd them, and that with a pretty liberal hand, if they be eaten with these cautions: 1. Not after meals, as we usually do, when the stomach is already full of other food: but I think they should be eaten rather before or between meals, and children should have them for their breakfast. 2. Bread eaten with them. 3. Perfectly ripe. If they are thus eaten, I imagine them rather conducing than hurtful to our health. Summer-fruits, being suited to the hot season of the year they come in, refresh our stomachs, languishing and fainting under it; and therefore I should not be altogether so strict in this point, as some are to their children; who being kept so very short, instead of a moderate quantity of well-chosen fruit, which being allow'd them would content them, whenever they can get loose, or bribe a servant to supply them, satisfy their longing with any trash they can get, and eat to a surfeit.

Apples and pears too, which are thorough ripe, and have been gather'd some time, I think may be safely eaten at any time, and in pretty large quantities, especially apples; which never did any body hurt, that I have heard, after October.

Fruits also dry'd without sugar, I think very wholesome. But sweet-meats of all kinds are to be avoided; which whether they do more harm to the maker or eater, is not easy to tell. This I am sure, it is one of the most inconvenient ways of expence that vanity hath yet found out; and so I leave them to the ladies.

Sections 21–30

§ 21. Of all that looks soft and effeminate, nothing is more to be indulg'd children, than sleep. In this alone they are to be permitted to have their full satisfaction; nothing contributing more to the growth and health of children, than sleep. All that is to be regulated in it, is, in what part of the twenty-four hours they should take it; which will easily be resolved, by only saying that it is of great use to accustom 'em to rise early in the morning. It is best so to do, for health; and he that, from his childhood, has, by a settled custom, made rising betimes easy and familiar to him, will not, when he is a man, waste the best and most useful part of his life in drowsiness, and lying a-bed. If children therefore are to be call'd up early in the morning, it will follow of course, that they must go to bed betimes; whereby they will be accustom'd to avoid the unhealthy and unsafe hours of debauchery, which are those of the evenings; and they who keep good hours, seldom are guilty of any great disorders. I do not say this, as if your son, when grown up, should never be in company past eight, nor ever chat over a glass of wine 'till midnight. You are now, by the accustoming of his tender years, to indispose him to those inconveniences as much as you can; and it will be no small advantage, that contrary practice having made sitting up uneasy to him, it will make him often avoid, and very seldom propose midnight-revels. But if it should not reach so far, but fashion and company should prevail, and make him live as others do above twenty, 'tis worth the while to accustom him to early rising and early going to bed, between this and that, for the present improvement of his health and other advantages.

Though I have said, a large allowance of sleep, even as much as they will take, should be made to children when they are little; yet I do not mean, that it should always be continued to them in so large a proportion, and they suffer'd to indulge a drowsy laziness in their bed, as they grow up bigger. But whether they should begin to be restrained at seven or ten years old, or any other time, is impossible to be precisely determined. Their tempers, strength, and constitutions, must be consider'd. But some time between seven and fourteen, if they are too great lovers of their beds, I think it may be seasonable to begin to reduce them by degrees to about eight hours, which is generally rest enough for healthy grown people. If you have accustom'd him, as you should do, to rise constantly very early in the morning, this fault of being too long in bed will easily be reform'd, and most children will be forward enough to shorten that time themselves, by coveting to sit up with the company at night; tho' if they be not look'd after, they will be apt to take it out in the morning, which should by no means be permitted. They should constantly be call'd up and made to rise at their early hour; but great care should be taken in waking them, that it be not done hastily, nor with a loud or shrill voice, or any other sudden violent noise. This often affrights children, and does them great harm; and sound sleep thus broke off, with sudden alarms, is apt enough to discompose any one. When children are to be waken'd out of their sleep, be sure to begin with a low call, and some gentle motion, and so draw them out of it by degrees, and give them none but kind words and usage, 'till they are come perfectly to themselves, and being quite dress'd you are sure they are thoroughly awake. The being forc'd from their sleep, how gently so ever you do it, is pain enough to them; and care should be taken not to add any other uneasiness to it, especially such that may terrify them.

§ 22. Let his bed be hard, and rather quilts than feathers. Hard lodging strengthens the parts; whereas being bury'd every night in feathers melts and dissolves the body, is often the cause of weakness, and forerunner of an early grave. And, besides the stone, which has often its rise from this warm wrapping of the reins, several other indispositions, and that which is the root of them all, a tender weakly constitution, is very much owing to down-beds. Besides, he that is used to hard lodging at home, will not miss his sleep (where he has most need of it) in his travels abroad, for want of his soft bed, and his pillows laid in order. And therefore, I think it would not be amiss, to make his bed after different fashions, sometimes lay his head higher, sometimes lower, that he may not feel every little change he must be sure to meet with, who is not design'd to lie always in my young master's bed at home, and to have his maid lay all things in print, and tuck him in warm. The great cordial of nature is sleep. He that misses that, will suffer by it; and he is very unfortunate, who can take his cordial only in his mother's fine gilt cup, and not in a wooden dish. He that can sleep soundly, takes the cordial; and it matters not whether it be on a soft bed or the hard boards. 'Tis sleep only that is the thing necessary.

§ 23. One thing more there is, which has a great influence upon the health, and that is, going to stool regularly; people that are very loose, have seldom strong thoughts, or strong bodies. But the cure of this, both by diet and medicine, being much more easy than the contrary evil, there needs not much to be said about it; for if it come to threaten, either by its violence or duration, it will soon enough, and sometimes too soon, make a physician be sent for; and if it be moderate or short, it is commonly best to leave it to nature. On the other side, costiveness has too its ill effects, and is much harder to be dealt with by physick; purging medicines, which seem to give relief, rather increasing them than removing the evil.

§ 24. It being an indisposition I had a particular reason to enquire into, and not finding the cure of it in books, I set my thoughts on work, believing that greater changes than that might be made in our bodies, if we took the right course, and proceeded by rational steps.

1. Then I consider'd, that going to stool, was the effect of certain motions of the body;especially of the peristaltick motion of the guts.

2. I consider'd that several motions, that were not perfectly voluntary, might yet, by use and constant application, be brought to be habitual, if by an unintermitted custom they were at certain seasons endeavour'd to be constantly produced.

3. I had observ'd some men, who by taking after supper a pipe of tobacco, never fail'd of a stool, and began to doubt with myself, whether it were not more custom, than the tobacco, that gave them the benefit of nature; or at least, if the tobacco did it, it was rather by exciting a vigorous motion in the guts, than by any purging quality; for then it would have had other effects.

Having thus once got the opinion that it was possible to make it habitual, the next thing was to consider what way and means was the likeliest to obtain it.

4. Then I guess'd, that if a man, after his first eating in the morning, would presently solicit nature, and try whether he could strain himself so as to obtain a stool, he might in time, by constant application, bring it to be habitual.

§ 25. The reasons that made me chuse this time, were,

1. Because the stomach being then empty, if it receiv'd any thing grateful to it (for I would never, but in case of necessity, have any one eat but what he likes, and when he has an appetite) it was apt to embrace it close by a strong constriction of its fibres; which constriction, I suppos'd, might probably be continu'd on in the guts, and so increase their peristaltick motion, as we see in the Ileus, that an inverted motion, being begun any where below, continues itself all the whole length, and makes even the stomach obey that irregular motion.

2. Because when men eat, they usually relax their thoughts, and the spirits then, free from other employments, are more vigorously distributed into the lower belly, which thereby contribute to the same effect.

3. Because, whenever men have leisure to eat, they have leisure enough also to make so much court to Madam Cloacina, as would be necessary to our present purpose; but else, in the variety of human affairs and accidents, it was impossible to affix it to any hour certain, whereby the custom would be interrupted. Whereas men in health seldom failing to eat once a day, tho' the hour chang'd, the custom might still be preserv'd.

§ 26. Upon these grounds the experiment began to be try'd, and I have known none who have been steady in the prosecution of it, and taken care to go constantly to the necessary-house, after their first eating, whenever that happen'd, whether they found themselves call'd on or no, and there endeavoured to put nature upon her duty, but in a few months they obtain'd the desired success, and brought themselves to so regular an habit, that they seldom ever fail'd of a stool after their first eating, unless it were by their own neglect: for, whether they have any motion or no, if they go to the place, and do their part, they are sure to have nature very obedient.

§ 27. I would therefore advise, that this course should be taken with a child every day presently after he has eaten his breakfast. Let him be set upon the stool, as if disburthening were as much in his power as filling his belly; and let not him or his maid know any thing to the contrary, but that it is so; and if he be forc'd to endeavour, by being hinder'd from his play or eating again 'till he has been effectually at stool, or at least done his utmost, I doubt not but in a little while it will become natural to him. For there is reason to suspect, that children being usually intent on their play, and very heedless of any thing else, often let pass those motions of nature, when she calls them but gently; and so they, neglecting the seasonable offers, do by degrees bring themselves into an habitual costiveness. That by this method costiveness may be prevented, I do more than guess; having known by the constant practice of it for some time, a child brought to have a stool regularly after his breakfast every morning.

§ 28. How far any grown people will think fit to make trial of it, must be left to them; tho' I cannot but say, that considering the many evils that come from that defect, of a requisite easing of nature, I scarce know any thing more conducing to the preservation of health, than this is. Once in four and twenty hours, I think is enough; and no body, I guess, will think it too much. And by this means it is to be obtain'd without physick, which commonly proves very ineffectual in the cure of a settled and habitual costiveness.

§ 29. This is all I have to trouble you with concerning his management in the ordinary course of his health. Perhaps it will be expected from me, that I should give some directions of physick, to prevent diseases; for which I have only this one, very sacredly to be observ'd, never to give children any physick for prevention. The observation of what I have already advis'd, will, I suppose, do that better than the ladies' diet-drinks or apothecaries' medicines. Have a great care of tampering that way, lest, instead of preventing, you draw on diseases. Nor even upon every little indisposition is physick to be given, or the physician to be call'd to children, especially if he be a busy man, that will presently fill their windows with gally-pots, and their stomachs with drugs. It is safer to leave them wholly to nature, than to put 'em into the hands of one forward to tamper, or that thinks children are to be cur'd, in ordinary distempers, by any thing but diet, or by a method very little distant from it: it seeming suitable both to my reason and experience, that the tender constitutions of children should have as little done to them as is possible, and as the absolute necessity of the case requires. A little cold-still'd red poppy-water, which is the true surfeit-water with ease, and abstinence from flesh, often puts an end to several distempers in the beginning, which, by too forward applications, might have been made lusty diseases. When such a gentle treatment will not stop the growing mischief, nor hinder it from turning into a form'd disease, it will be time to seek the advice of some sober and discreet physician. In this part, I hope, I shall find an easy belief; and no body can have a pretence to doubt the advice of one who has spent some time in the study of physick, when he counsels you not to be too forward in making use of physick and physicians.

§ 30. And thus I have done with what concerns the body and health, which reduces itself to these few and easy observable rules: plenty of open air, exercise, and sleep, plain diet, no wine or strong drink, and very little or no physick, not too warm and strait clothing, especially the head and feet kept cold, and the feet often us'd to cold water, and expos'd to wet.

Sections 31–40

§ 31. Due care being had to keep the body in strength and vigour, so that it may be able to obey and execute the orders of the mind; the next and principal business is, to set the mind right, that on all occasions it may be dispos'd to consent to nothing but what may be suitable to the dignity and excellency of a rational creature.

§ 32. If what I have said in the beginning of this discourse be true, as I do not doubt but it is, viz. That the difference to be found in the manners and abilities of men is owing more to their education than to any thing else, we have reason to conclude, that great care is to be had of the forming children's minds, and giving them that seasoning early, which shall influence their lives always after: For when they do well or ill, the praise and blame will be laid there; and when any thing is done awkwardly, the common saying will pass upon them, that it's suitable to their breeding.

§ 33. As the strength of the body lies chiefly in being able to endure hardships, so also does that of the mind. And the great principle and foundation of all virtue and worth is plac'd in this: that a man is able to deny himself his own desires, cross his own inclinations, and purely follow what reason directs as best, tho' the appetite lean the other way.

§ 34. The great mistake I have observ'd in people's breeding their children, has been, that this has not been taken care enough of in its due season: that the mind has not been made obedient to discipline, and pliant to reason, when at first it was most tender, most easy to be bow'd. Parents being wisely ordain'd by nature to love their children, are very apt, if reason watch not that natural affection very warily, are apt, I say, to let it run into fondness. They love their little ones and it is their duty; but they often, with them, cherish their faults too. They must not be cross'd, forsooth; they must be permitted to have their wills in all things; and they being in their infancies not capable of great vices, their parents think they may safe enough indulge their irregularities, and make themselves sport with that pretty perverseness which they think well enough becomes that innocent age. But to a fond parent, that would not have his child corrected for a perverse trick, but excus'd it, saying it was a small matter, Solon very well reply'd, aye, but custom is a great one.

§ 35. The fondling must be taught to strike and call names, must have what he cries for, and do what he pleases. Thus parents, by humouring and cockering them when little, corrupt the principles of nature in their children, and wonder afterwards to taste the bitter waters, when they themselves have poison'd the fountain. For when their children are grown up, and these ill habits with them; when they are now too big to be dandled, and their parents can no longer make use of them as play-things, then they complain that the brats are untoward and perverse; then they are offended to see them wilful, and are troubled with those ill humours which they themselves infus'd and fomented in them; and then, perhaps too late, would be glad to get out those weeds which their own hands have planted, and which now have taken too deep root to be easily extirpated. For he that hath been us'd to have his will in every thing, as long as he was in coats, why should we think it strange, that he should desire it, and contend for it still, when he is in breeches? Indeed, as he grows more towards a man, age shews his faults the more; so that there be few parents then so blind as not to see them, few so insensible as not to feel the ill effects of their own indulgence. He had the will of his maid before he could speak or go; he had the mastery of his parents ever since he could prattle; and why, now he is grown up, is stronger and wiser than he was then, why now of a sudden must he be restrain'd and curb'd? Why must he at seven, fourteen, or twenty years old, lose the privilege, which the parents' indulgence 'till then so largely allow'd him? Try it in a dog or an horse or any other creature, and see whether the ill and resty tricks they have learn'd when young, are easily to be mended when they are knit; and yet none of those creatures are half so wilful and proud, or half so desirous to be masters of themselves and others, as man.

§ 36. We are generally wise enough to begin with them when they are very young, and discipline betimes those other creatures we would make useful and good for somewhat. They are only our own offspring, that we neglect in this point; and having made them ill children, we foolishly expect they should be good men. For if the child must have grapes or sugar-plums when he has a mind to them, rather than make the poor baby cry or be out of humour; why, when, he is grown up, must he not be satisfy'd too, if his desires carry him to wine or women? They are objects as suitable to the longing of one of more years, as what he cry'd for, when little, was to the inclinations of a child. The having desires accommodated to the apprehensions and relish of those several ages, is not the fault; but the not having them subject to the rules and restraints of reason: the difference lies not in having or not having appetites, but in the power to govern, and deny ourselves in them. He that is not us'd to submit his will to the reason of others when he is young, will scarce hearken to submit to his own reason when he is of an age to make use of it. And what kind of a man such an one is like to prove, is easy to foresee.

§ 37. These are oversights usually committed by those who seem to take the greatest care of their children's education. But if we look into the common management of children, we shall have reason to wonder, in the great dissoluteness of manners which the world complains of, that there are any footsteps at all left of virtue. I desire to know what vice can be nam'd, which parents, and those about children, do not season them with, and drop into 'em the seeds of, as soon as they are capable to receive them? I do not mean by the examples they give, and the patterns they set before them, which is encouragement enough; but that which I would take notice of here is, the downright teaching them vice, and actual putting them out of the way of virtue. Before they can go, they principle 'em with violence, revenge, and cruelty. Give me a blow, that I may beat him, is a lesson which most children every day hear; and it is thought nothing, because their hands have not strength to do any mischief. But I ask, does not this corrupt their mind? Is not this the way of force and violence, that they are set in? And if they have been taught when little, to strike and hurt others by proxy, and encourag'd to rejoice in the harm they have brought upon them, and see them suffer, are they not prepar'd to do it when they are strong enough to be felt themselves, and can strike to some purpose?

The coverings of our bodies which are for modesty, warmth and defence, are by the folly or vice of parents recommended to their children for other uses. They are made matters of vanity and emulation. A child is set a-longing after a new suit, for the finery of it; and when the little girl is trick'd up in her new gown and commode, how can her mother do less than teach her to admire herself, by calling her, her little queen and her princess? Thus the little ones are taught to be proud of their clothes before they can put them on. And why should they not continue to value themselves for their outside fashionableness of the taylor or tirewoman's making, when their parents have so early instructed them to do so?

Lying and equivocations, and excuses little different from lying, are put into the mouths of young people, and commended in apprentices and children, whilst they are for their master's or parents' advantage. And can it be thought, that he that finds the straining of truth dispens'd with, and encourag'd, whilst it is for his godly master's turn, will not make use of that privilege for himself, when it may be for his own profit?

Those of the meaner sort are hinder'd, by the straitness of their fortunes, from encouraging intemperance in their children by the temptation of their diet, or invitations to eat or drink more than enough; but their own ill examples, whenever plenty comes in their way, shew, that 'tis not the dislike of drunkenness or gluttony, that keeps them from excess, but want of materials. But if we look into the houses of those who are a little warmer in their fortunes, their eating and drinking are made so much the great business and happiness of life, that children are thought neglected, if they have not their share of it. Sauces and ragoos, and food disguis'd by all the arts of cookery, must tempt their palates, when their bellies are full; and then, for fear the stomach should be overcharg'd, a pretence is found for t'other glass of wine to help digestion, tho' it only serves to increase the surfeit.

Is my young master a little out of order, the first question is, What will my dear eat? What shall I get for thee? Eating and drinking are instantly press'd; and every body's invention is set on work, to find out something luscious and delicate enough to prevail over that want of appetite, which nature has wisely order'd in the beginning of distempers, as a defence against their increase; that being freed from the ordinary labour of digesting any new load in the stomach, she may be at leisure to correct and master the peccant humours.

And where children are so happy in the care of their parents, as by their prudence to be kept from the excess of their tables, to the sobriety of a plain and simple diet, yet there too they are scarce to be preserv'd from the contagion that poisons the mind; though, by a discreet management whilst they are under tuition, their healths perhaps may be pretty well secure, yet their desires must needs yield to the lessons which every where will be read to them upon this part of epicurism. The commendation that eating well has every where, cannot fail to be a successful incentive to natural appetites, and bring them quickly to the liking and expence of a fashionable table. This shall have from every one, even the reprovers of vice, the title of living well. And what shall sullen reason dare to say against the publick testimony? Or can it hope to be heard, if it should call that luxury, which is so much own'd and universally practis'd by those of the best quality?

This is now so grown a vice, and has so great supports, that I know not whether it do not put in for the name of virtue; and whether it will not be thought folly, or want of knowledge of the world, to open one's mouth against it? And truly I should suspect, that what I have here said of it, might be censur'd as a little satire out of my way, did I not mention it with this view, that it might awaken the care and watchfulness of parents in the education of their children, when they see how they are beset on every side, not only with temptations, but instructors to vice, and that, perhaps, in those they thought places of security.

I shall not dwell any longer on this subject, much less run over all the particulars that would shew what pains are us'd to corrupt children, and instil principles of vice into them: but I desire parents soberly to consider, what irregularity or vice there is which children are not visibly taught, and whether it be not their duty and wisdom to provide them other instructions.

§ 38. It seems plain to me, that the principle of all virtue and excellency lies in a power of denying ourselves the satisfaction of our own desires, where reason does not authorize them. This power is to be got and improv'd by custom, made easy and familiar by an early practice. If therefore I might be heard, I would advise, that, contrary to the ordinary way, children should be us'd to submit their desires, and go without their longings, even from their very cradles. The first thing they should learn to know, should be, that they were not to have anything because it pleas'd them, but because it was thought fit for them. If things suitable to their wants were supply'd to them, so that they were never suffer'd to have what they once cry'd for, they would learn to be content without it, would never, with bawling and peevishness, contend for mastery, nor be half so uneasy to themselves and others as they are, because from the first beginning they are not thus handled. If they were never suffer'd to obtain their desire by the impatience they express'd for it, they would no more cry for another thing, than they do for the moon.

§ 39. I say not this, as if children were not to be indulg'd in anything, or that I expected they should in hanging-sleeves have the reason and conduct of counsellors. I consider them as children, who must be tenderly us'd, who must play, and have play-things. That which I mean, is, that whenever they crav'd what was not fit for them to have or do, they should not be permitted it because they were little, and desir'd it: nay, whatever they were importunate for, they should be sure, for that very reason, to be deny'd. I have seen children at a table, who, whatever was there, never ask'd for anything, but contentedly took what was given them; and at another place, I have seen others cry for everything they saw; must be serv'd out of every dish, and that first too. What made this vast difference but this? that one was accustom'd to have what they call'd or cry'd for, the other to go without it. The younger they are, the less I think are their unruly and disorderly appetites to be comply'd with; and the less reason they have of their own, the more are they to be under the absolute power and restraint of those in whose hands they are. From which I confess it will follow, that none but discreet people should be about them. If the world commonly does otherwise, I cannot help that. I am saying what I think should be; which if it were already in fashion, I should not need to trouble the world with a discourse on this subject. But yet I doubt not, but when it is consider'd, there will be others of opinion with me, that the sooner this way is begun with children, the easier it will be for them and their governors too; and that this ought to be observ'd as an inviolable maxim, that whatever once is deny'd them, they are certainly not to obtain by crying or importunity, unless one has a mind to teach them to be impatient and troublesome, by rewarding them for it when they are so.

§ 40. Those therefore that intend ever to govern their children, should begin it whilst they are very little, and look that they perfectly comply with the will of their parents. Would you have your son obedient to you when past a child; be sure then to establish the authority of a father as soon as he is capable of submission, and can understand in whose power he is. If you would have him stand in awe of you, imprint it in his infancy; and as he approaches more to a man, admit him nearer to your familiarity; so shall you have him your obedient subject (as is fit) whilst he is a child, and your affectionate friend when he is a man. For methinks they mightily misplace the treatment due to their children, who are indulgent and familiar when they are little, but severe to them, and keep them at a distance, when they are grown up: for liberty and indulgence can do no good to children; their want of judgment makes them stand in need of restraint and discipline; and on the contrary, imperiousness and severity is but an ill way of treating men, who have reason of their own to guide them; unless you have a mind to make your children, when grown up, weary of you, and secretly to say within themselves, When will you die, father?

Sections 41–50

§ 41. I imagine every one will judge it reasonable, that their children, when little, should look upon their parents as their lords, their absolute governors, and as such stand in awe of them; and that when they come to riper years, they should look on them as their best, as their only sure friends, and as such love and reverence them. The way I have mention'd, if I mistake not, is the only one to obtain this. We must look upon our children, when grown up, to be like ourselves, with the same passions, the same desires. We would be thought rational creatures, and have our freedom; we love not to be uneasy under constant rebukes and brow-beatings, nor can we bear severe humours and great distance in those we converse with. Whoever has such treatment when he is a man, will look out other company, other friends, other conversation, with whom he can be at ease. If therefore a strict hand be kept over children from the beginning, they will in that age be tractable, and quietly submit to it, as never having known any other: and if, as they grow up to the use of reason, the rigour of government be, as they deserve it, gently relax'd, the father's brow more smooth'd to them, and the distance by degrees abated, his former restraints will increase their love, when they find it was only a kindness to them, and a care to make them capable to deserve the favour of their parents, and the esteem of everybody else.

§ 42. Thus much for the settling your authority over your children in general. Fear and awe ought to give you the first power over their minds, and love and friendship in riper years to hold it: for the time must come, when they will be past the rod and correction; and then, if the love of you make them not obedient and dutiful, if the love of virtue and reputation keep them not in laudable courses, I ask, what hold will you have upon them to turn them to it? Indeed, fear of having a scanty portion if they displease you, may make them slaves to your estate, but they will be nevertheless ill and wicked in private; and that restraint will not last always. Every man must some time or other be trusted to himself and his own conduct; and he that is a good, a virtuous, and able man, must be made so within. And therefore what he is to receive from education, what is to sway and influence his life, must be something put into him betimes; habits woven into the very principles of his nature, and not a counterfeit carriage, and dissembled outside, put on by fear, only to avoid the present anger of a father who perhaps may disinherit him.

§ 43. This being laid down in general, as the course that ought to be taken, 'tis fit we now come to consider the parts of the discipline to be us'd, a little more particularly. I have spoken so much of carrying a strict hand over children, that perhaps I shall be suspected of not considering enough, what is due to their tender age and constitutions. But that opinion will vanish, when you have heard me a little farther: for I am very apt to think, that great severity of punishment does but very little good, nay, great harm in education; and I believe it will be found that, cæteris paribus, those children who have been most chastis'd, seldom make the best men. All that I have hitherto contended for, is, that whatsoever rigor is necessary, it is more to be us'd, the younger children are; and having by a due application wrought its effect, it is to be relax'd, and chang'd into a milder sort of government.

§ 44. A compliance and suppleness of their wills, being by a steady hand introduc'd by parents, before children have memories to retain the beginnings of it, will seem natural to them, and work afterwards in them as if it were so, preventing all occasions of struggling or repining. The only care is, that it be begun early, and inflexibly kept to 'till awe and respect be grown familiar, and there appears not the least reluctancy in the submission, and ready obedience of their minds. When this reverence is once thus established, (which it must be early, or else it will cost pains and blows to recover it, and the more the longer it is deferr'd) 'tis by it, still mix'd with as much indulgence as they make not an ill use of, and not by beating, chiding, or other servile punishments, they are for the future to be govern'd as they grow up to more understanding.

§ 45. That this is so, will be easily allow'd, when it is but consider'd, what is to be aim'd at in an ingenuous education; and upon what it turns.

1. He that has not a mastery over his inclinations, he that knows not how to resist the importunity of present pleasure or pain, for the sake of what reason tells him is fit to be done, wants the true principle of virtue and industry, and is in danger never to be good for anything. This temper therefore, so contrary to unguided nature, is to be got betimes; and this habit, as the true foundation of future ability and happiness, is to be wrought into the mind as early as may be, even from the first dawnings of knowledge or apprehension in children, and so to be confirm'd in them, by all the care and ways imaginable, by those who have the oversight of their education.

§ 46. 2. On the other side, if the mind be curb'd, and humbled too much in children; if their spirits be abas'd and broken much, by too strict an hand over them, they lose all their vigour and industry, and are in a worse state than the former. For extravagant young fellows, that have liveliness and spirit, come sometimes to be set right, and so make able and great men; but dejected minds, timorous and tame, and low spirits, are hardly ever to be rais'd, and very seldom attain to any thing. To avoid the danger that is on either hand, is the great art; and he that has found a way how to keep up a child's spirit easy, active, and free, and yet at the same time to restrain him from many things he has a mind to, and to draw him to things that are uneasy to him; he, I say, that knows how to reconcile these seeming contradictions, has, in my opinion, got the true secret of education.

§ 47. The usual lazy and short way by chastisement and the rod, which is the only instrument of government that tutors generally know, or ever think of, is the most unfit of any to be us'd in education, because it tends to both those mischiefs; which, as we have shewn, are the Scylla and Charybdis, which on the one hand or the other ruin all that miscarry.

§ 48. 1. This kind of punishment contributes not at all to the mastery of our natural propensity to indulge corporal and present pleasure, and to avoid pain at any rate, but rather encourages it, and thereby strengthens that in us, which is the root from whence spring all vicious actions, and the irregularities of life. For what other motive, but of sensual pleasure and pain, does a child act by, who drudges at his book against his inclination, or abstains from eating unwholesome fruit, that he takes pleasure in, only out of fear of whipping? He in this only prefers the greater corporal pleasure, or avoids the greater corporal pain. And what is it, to govern his actions, and direct his conduct by such motives as these? What is it, I say, but to cherish that principle in him, which it is our business to root out and destroy? And therefore I cannot think any correction useful to a child, where the shame of suffering for having done amiss, does not work more upon him than the pain.

§ 49. 2. This sort of correction naturally breeds an aversion to that which 'tis the tutor's business to create a liking to. How obvious is it to observe, that children come to hate things which were at first acceptable to them, when they find themselves whipp'd, and chid, and teas'd about them? And it is not to be wonder'd at in them, when grown men would not be able to be reconcil'd to any thing by such ways. Who is there that would not be disgusted with any innocent recreation, in itself indifferent to him, if he should with blows or ill language be haled to it, when he had no mind? Or be constantly so treated, for some circumstances in his application to it? This is natural to be so. Offensive circumstances ordinarily infect innocent things which they are join'd with; and the very sight of a cup wherein any one uses to take nauseous physick, turns his stomach, so that nothing will relish well out of it, tho' the cup be never so clean and well-shap'd, and of the richest materials.

§ 50. 3. Such a sort of slavish discipline makes a slavish temper. The child submits, and dissembles obedience, whilst the fear of the rod hangs over him; but when that is remov'd, and by being out of sight, he can promise himself impunity, he gives the greater scope to his natural inclination; which by this way is not at all alter'd, but, on the contrary, heighten'd and increas'd in him; and after such restraint, breaks out usually with the more violence; or,

Sections 51–60

§ 51. 4. If severity carry'd to the highest pitch does prevail, and works a cure upon the present unruly distemper, it often brings in the room of it a worse and more dangerous disease, by breaking the mind; and then, in the place of a disorderly young fellow, you have a low spirited moap'd creature, who, however with his unnatural sobriety he may please silly people, who commend tame unactive children, because they make no noise, nor give them any trouble; yet at last, will probably prove as uncomfortable a thing to his friends, as he will be all his life an useless thing to himself and others.

§ 52. Beating them, and all other sorts of slavish and corporal punishments, are not the discipline fit to be used in the education of those we would have wise, good, and ingenuous men; and therefore very rarely to be apply'd, and that only in great occasions, and cases of extremity. On the other side, to flatter children by rewards of things that are pleasant to them, is as carefully to be avoided. He that will give to his son apples or sugar-plumbs, or what else of this kind he is most delighted with, to make him learn his book, does but authorize his love of pleasure, and cocker up that dangerous propensity, which he ought by all means to subdue and stifle in him. You can never hope to teach him to master it, whilst you compound for the check you gave his inclination in one place, by the satisfaction you propose to it in another. To make a good, a wise, and a virtuous man, 'tis fit he should learn to cross his appetite, and deny his inclination to riches, finery, or pleasing his palate, &c. whenever his reason advises the contrary, and his duty requires it. But when you draw him to do any thing that is fit by the offer of money, or reward the pains of learning his book by the pleasure of a luscious morsel; when you promise him a lace-cravat or a fine new suit, upon performance of some of his little tasks; what do you by proposing these as rewards, but allow them to be the good things he should aim at, and thereby encourage his longing for 'em, and accustom him to place his happiness in them? Thus people, to prevail with children to be industrious about their grammar, dancing, or some other such matter, of no great moment to the happiness or usefulness of their lives, by misapply'd rewards and punishments, sacrifice their virtue, invert the order of their education, and teach them luxury, pride, or covetousness, &c. For in this way, flattering those wrong inclinations which they should restrain and suppress, they lay the foundations of those future vices, which cannot be avoided but by curbing our desires and accustoming them early to submit to reason.

§ 53. I say not this, that I would have children kept from the conveniences or pleasures of life, that are not injurious to their health or virtue. On the contrary, I would have their lives made as pleasant and as agreeable to them as may be, in a plentiful enjoyment of whatsoever might innocently delight them; provided it be with this caution, that they have those enjoyments, only as the consequences of the state of esteem and acceptation they are in with their parents and governors; but they should never be offer'd or bestow'd on them, as the rewards of this or that particular performance, that they shew an aversion to, or to which they would not have apply'd themselves without that temptation.

§ 54. But if you take away the rod on one hand, and these little encouragements which they are taken with, on the other, how then (will you say) shall children be govern'd? Remove hope and fear, and there is an end of all discipline. I grant that good and evil, reward and punishment, are the only motives to a rational creature: these are the spur and reins whereby all mankind are set on work, and guided, and therefore they are to be made use of to children too. For I advise their parents and governors always to carry this in their minds, that children are to be treated as rational creatures.

§ 55. Rewards, I grant, and punishments must be proposed to children, if we intend to work upon them. The mistake I imagine is, that those that are generally made use of, are ill chosen. The pains and pleasures of the body are, I think, of ill consequence, when made the rewards and punishments whereby men would prevail on their children; for, as I said before, they serve but to increase and strengthen those inclinations, which 'tis our business to subdue and master. What principle of virtue do you lay in a child, if you will redeem his desires of one pleasure, by the proposal of another? This is but to enlarge his appetite, and instruct it to wander. If a child cries for an unwholesome and dangerous fruit, you purchase his quiet by giving him a less hurtful sweet-meat. This perhaps may preserve his health, but spoils his mind, and sets that farther out of order. For here you only change the object, but flatter still his appetite, and allow that must be satisfy'd, wherein, as I have shew'd, lies the root of the mischief; and till you bring him to be able to bear a denial of that satisfaction, the child may at present be quiet and orderly, but the disease is not cured. By this way of proceeding, you foment and cherish in him that which is the spring from whence all the evil flows, which will be sure on the next occasion to break out again with more violence, give him stronger longings, and you more trouble.

§ 56. The rewards and punishments then, whereby we should keep children in order, are quite of another kind, and of that force, that when we can get them once to work, the business, I think, is done, and the difficulty is over. Esteem and disgrace are, of all others, the most powerful incentives to the mind, when once it is brought to relish them. If you can once get into children a love of credit, and an apprehension of shame and disgrace, you have put into 'em the true principle, which will constantly work and incline them to the right. But it will be ask'd, How shall this be done?

I confess it does not at first appearance want some difficulty; but yet I think it worth our while to seek the ways (and practise them when found) to attain this, which I look on as the great secret of education.

§ 57. First, children (earlier perhaps than we think) are very sensible of praise and commendation. They find a pleasure in being esteem'd and valu'd, especially by their parents and those whom they depend on. If therefore the father caress and commend them when they do well, shew a cold and neglectful countenance to them upon doing ill, and this accompany'd by a like carriage of the mother and all others that are about them, it will, in a little time, make them sensible of the difference; and this, if constantly observ'd, I doubt not but will of itself work more than threats or blows, which lose their force when once grown common, and are of no use when shame does not attend them; and therefore are to be forborne, and never to be us'd, but in the case hereafter-mention'd, when it is brought to extremity.

§ 58. But secondly, to make the sense of esteem or disgrace sink the deeper, and be of the more weight, other agreeable or disagreeable things should constantly accompany these different states; not as particular rewards and punishments of this or that particular action, but as necessarily belonging to, and constantly attending one, who by his carriage has brought himself into a state of disgrace or commendation. By which way of treating them, children may as much as possible be brought to conceive, that those that are commended, and in esteem for doing well, will necessarily be belov'd and cherish'd by every body, and have all other good things as a consequence of it; and on the other side, when any one by miscarriage falls into disesteem, and cares not to preserve his credit, he will unavoidably fall under neglect and contempt; and in that state, the want of whatever might satisfy or delight him will follow. In this way the objects of their desires are made assisting to virtue, when a settled experience from the beginning teaches children that the things they delight in, belong to, and are to be enjoy'd by those only who are in a state of reputation. If by these means you can come once to shame them out of their faults, (for besides that, I would willingly have no punishment) and make them in love with the pleasure of being well thought on, you may turn them as you please, and they will be in love with all the ways of virtue.

§ 59. The great difficulty here is, I imagine, from the folly and perverseness of servants, who are hardly to be hinder'd from crossing herein the design of the father and mother. Children discountenanc'd by their parents for any fault, find usually a refuge and relief in the caresses of those foolish flatterers, who thereby undo whatever the parents endeavour to establish. When the father or mother looks sowre on the child, everybody else should put on the same coldness to him, and nobody give him countenance, 'till forgiveness ask'd, and a reformation of his fault has set him right again, and restor'd him to his former credit. If this were constantly observ'd, I guess there would be little need of blows or chiding: their own ease and satisfaction would quickly teach children to court commendation, and avoid doing that which they found everybody condemn'd and they were sure to suffer for, without being chid or beaten. This would teach them modesty and shame; and they would quickly come to have a natural abhorrence for that which they found made them slighted and neglected by every body. But how this inconvenience from servants is to be remedy'd, I must leave to parents' care and consideration. Only I think it of great importance; and that they are very happy who can get discreet people about their children.

§ 60. Frequent beating or chiding is therefore carefully to be avoided: because this sort of correction never produces any good, farther than it serves to raise shame and abhorrence of the miscarriage that brought it on them. And if the greatest part of the trouble be not the sense that they have done amiss, and the apprehension that they have drawn on themselves the just displeasure of their best friends, the pain of whipping will work but an imperfect cure. It only patches up for the present, and skins it over, but reaches not to the bottom of the sore; ingenuous shame, and the apprehensions of displeasure, are the only true restraint. These alone ought to hold the reins, and keep the child in order. But corporal punishments must necessarily lose that effect, and wear out the sense of shame, where they frequently return. Shame in children has the same place that modesty has in women, which cannot be kept and often transgress'd against. And as to the apprehension of displeasure in the parents, that will come to be very insignificant, if the marks of that displeasure quickly cease, and a few blows fully expiate. Parents should well consider what faults in their children are weighty enough to deserve the declaration of their anger: but when their displeasure is once declar'd to a degree that carries any punishment with it, they ought not presently to lay by the severity of their brows, but to restore their children to their former grace with some difficulty, and delay a full reconciliation, 'till their conformity and more than ordinary merit, make good their amendment. If this be not so order'd, punishment will, by familiarity, become a mere thing of course, and lose all its influence; offending, being chastised, and then forgiven, will be thought as natural and necessary, as noon, night, and morning following one another.

Sections 61–70

§ 61. Concerning reputation, I shall only remark this one thing more of it, that though it be not the true principle and measure of virtue, (for that is the knowledge of a man's duty, and the satisfaction it is to obey his maker, in following the dictates of that light God has given him, with the hopes of acceptation and reward) yet it is that which comes nearest to it: and being the testimony and applause that other people's reason, as it were by a common consent, gives to virtuous and well-order'd actions, it is the proper guide and encouragement of children, 'till they grow able to judge for themselves, and to find what is right by their own reason.

§ 62. This consideration may direct parents how to manage themselves in reproving and commending their children. The rebukes and chiding, which their faults will sometimes make hardly to be avoided, should not only be in sober, grave, and unpassionate words, but also alone and in private: but the commendations children deserve, they should receive before others. This doubles the reward, by spreading their praise: but the backwardness parents shew in divulging their faults, will make them set a greater value on their credit themselves, and teach them to be the more careful to preserve the good opinion of others, whilst they think they have it: but when being expos'd to shame by publishing their miscarriages, they give it up for lost, that check upon them is taken off, and they will be the less careful to preserve others' good thoughts of them, the more they suspect that their reputation with them is already blemish'd.

§ 63. But if a right course be taken with children, there will not be so much need of the application of the common rewards and punishments as we imagine, and as the general practice has establish'd. For all their innocent folly, playing and childish actions, are to be left perfectly free and unrestrain'd, as far as they can consist with the respect due to those that are present; and that with the greatest allowance. If these faults of their age, rather than of the children themselves, were, as they should be, left only to time and imitation and riper years to cure, children would escape a great deal of misapply'd and useless correction, which either fails to overpower the natural disposition of their childhood, and so by an ineffectual familiarity, makes correction in other necessary cases of less use; or else if it be of force to restrain the natural gaiety of that age, it serves only to spoil the temper both of body and mind. If the noise and bustle of their play prove at any time inconvenient, or unsuitable to the place or company they are in, (which can only be where their parents are) a look or a word from the father or mother, if they have establish'd the authority they should, will be enough either to remove or quiet them for that time. But this gamesome humour, which is wisely adapted by nature to their age and temper, should rather be encourag'd to keep up their spirits, and improve their strength and health, than curb'd and restrain'd; and the chief art is to make all that they have to do, sport and play too.

§ 64. And here give me leave to take notice of one thing I think a fault in the ordinary method of education; and that is, the charging of children's memories, upon all occasions, with rules and precepts, which they often do not understand, and constantly as soon forget as given. It be some action you would have done, or done otherwise, whenever they forget, or do it awkwardly, make them do it over and over again, 'till they are perfect, whereby you will get these two advantages. First, to see whether it be an action they can do, or is fit to be expected of them: for sometimes children are bid to do things which upon trial they are found not able to do, and had need be taught and exercis'd in before they are requir'd to do them. But it is much easier for a tutor to command than to teach. Secondly, another thing got by it will be this, that by repeating the same action 'till it be grown habitual in them, the performance will not depend on memory or reflection, the concomitant of prudence and age, and not of childhood, but will be natural in them. Thus bowing to a gentleman, when he salutes him, and looking in his face, when he speaks to him, is by constant use as natural to a well-bred man, as breathing; it requires no thought, no reflection. Having this way cured in your child any fault, it is cured for ever: and thus one by one you may weed them out all, and plant what habits you please.

§ 65. I have seen parents so heap rules on their children, that it was impossible for the poor little ones to remember a tenth part of them, much less to observe them. However, they were either by words or blows corrected for the breach of those multiply'd and often very impertinent precepts. Whence it naturally follow'd that the children minded not what was said to them, when it was evident to them that no attention they were capable of was sufficient to preserve them from transgression, and the rebukes which follow'd it.

Let therefore your rules to your son be as few as possible, and rather fewer than more than seem absolutely necessary. For if you burden him with many rules, one of these two things must necessarily follow; that either he must be very often punish'd, which will be of ill consequence, by making punishment too frequent and familiar; or else you must let the transgressions of some of your rules go unpunish'd, whereby they will of course grow contemptible, and your authority become cheap to him. Make but few laws, but see they be well observ'd when once made. Few years require but few laws, and as his age increases, when one rule is by practice well establish'd, you may add another.

§ 66. But pray remember, children are not to be taught by rules which will be always slipping out of their memories. What you think necessary for them to do, settle in them by an indispensable practice, as often as the occasion returns; and if it be possible, make occasions. This will beget habits in them which being once establish'd, operate of themselves easily and naturally, without the assistance of the memory. But here let me give two cautions. 1. The one is, that you keep them to the practice of what you would have grow into a habit in them, by kind words, and gentle admonitions, rather as minding them of what they forget, than by harsh rebukes and chiding, as if they were wilfully guilty. 2. Another thing you are to take care of, is, not to endeavour to settle too many habits at once, lest by variety you confound them, and so perfect none. When constant custom has made any one thing easy and natural to 'em, and they practise it without reflection, you may then go on to another.

This method of teaching children by a repeated practice, and the same action done over and over again, under the eye and direction of the tutor, 'till they have got the habit of doing it well, and not by relying on rules trusted to their memories, has so many advantages, which way soever we consider it, that I cannot but wonder (if ill customs could be wondered at in any thing) how it could possibly be so much neglected. I shall name one more that comes now in my way. By this method we shall see whether what is requir'd of him be adapted to his capacity, and any way suited to the child's natural genius and constitution; for that too much be consider'd in a right education. We must not hope wholly to change their original tempers, nor make the gay pensive and grave, nor the melancholy sportive, without spoiling them. God has stamp'd certain characters upon men's minds, which like their shapes, may perhaps be a little mended, but can hardly be totally alter'd and transform'd into the contrary.

He therefore that is about children should well study their natures and aptitudes, and see by often trials what turn they easily take, and what becomes them; observe what their native stock is, how it may be improv'd, and what it is fit for: he should consider what they want, whether they be capable of having it wrought into them by industry, and incorporated there by practice; and whether it be worth while to endeavour it. For in many cases, all that we can do, or should aim at, is, to make the best of what nature has given, to prevent the vices and faults to which such a constitution is most inclin'd, and give it all the advantages it is capable of. Every one's natural genius should be carry'd as far as it could; but to attempt the putting another upon him, will be but labour in vain; and what is so plaister'd on, will at best sit but untowardly, and have always hanging to it the ungracefulness of constraint and affectation.

Affectation is not, I confess, an early fault of childhood, or the product of untaught nature. It is of that sort of weeds which grow not in the wild uncultivated waste, but in garden-plots, under the negligent hand or unskilful care of a gardener. Management and instruction, and some sense of the necessity of breeding, are requisite to make any one capable of affectation, which endeavours to correct natural defects, and has always the laudable aim of pleasing, though it always misses it; and the more it labours to put on gracefulness, the farther it is from it. For this reason, it is the more carefully to be watch'd, because it is the proper fault of education; a perverted education indeed, but such as young people often fall into, either by their own mistake, or the ill conduct of those about them.

He that will examine wherein that gracefulness lies, which always pleases, will find it arises from that natural coherence which appears between the thing done and such a temper of mind as cannot but be approv'd of as suitable to the occasion. We cannot but be pleas'd with an humane, friendly, civil temper wherever we meet with it. A mind free, and master of itself and all its actions, not low and narrow, not haughty and insolent, not blemish'd with any great defect, is what every one is taken with. The actions which naturally flow from such a well-form'd mind, please us also, as the genuine marks of it; and being as it were natural emanations from the spirit and disposition within, cannot but be easy and unconstrain'd. This seems to me to be that beauty which shines through some men's actions, sets off all that they do, and takes all they come near; when by a constant practice, they have fashion'd their carriage, and made all those little expressions of civility and respect, which nature or custom has establish'd in conversation, so easy to themselves, that they seem not artificial or studied, but naturally to follow from a sweetness of mind and a well-turn'd disposition.

On the other side, affectation is an awkward and forc'd imitation of what should be genuine and easy, wanting the beauty that accompanies what is natural; because there is always a disagreement between the outward action, and the mind within, one of these two ways: 1. Either when a man would outwardly put on a disposition of mind, which then he really has not, but endeavours by a forc'd carriage to make shew of; yet so, that the constraint he is under discovers itself: and thus men affect sometimes to appear sad, merry, or kind, when in truth they are not so.

The other is, when they do not endeavour to make shew of dispositions of mind, which they have not, but to express those they have by a carriage not suited to them. And such in conversation are all constrain'd motions, actions, words, or looks, which, though design'd to shew either their respect or civility to the company, or their satisfaction and easiness in it, are not yet natural nor genuine marks of the one or the other, but rather of some defect or mistake within. Imitation of others, without discerning what is graceful in them, or what is peculiar to their characters, often makes a great part of this. But affectation of all kinds, whencesoever it proceeds, is always offensive; because we naturally hate whatever is counterfeit, and condemn those who have nothing better to recommend themselves by.

Plain and rough nature, left to itself, is much better than an artificial ungracefulness, and such study'd ways of being illfashion'd. The want of an accomplishment, or some defect in our behaviour, coming short of the utmost gracefulness, often escapes observation and censure. But affectation in any part of our carriage is lighting up a candle to our defects, and never fails to make us be taken notice of, either as wanting sense, or wanting sincerity. This governors ought the more diligently to look after, because, as I above observ'd, 'tis an acquir'd ugliness, owing to mistaken education, few being guilty of it but those who pretend to breeding, and would not be thought ignorant of what is fashionable and becoming in conversation; and, if I mistake not, it has often its rise from the lazy admonitions of those who give rules, and propose examples, without joining practice with their instructions and making their pupils repeat the action in their sight, that they may correct what is indecent or constrain'd in it, till it be perfected into an habitual and becoming easiness.

§ 67. Manners, as they call it, about which children are so often perplex'd, and have so many goodly exhortations made them by their wise maids and governesses, I think, are rather to be learnt by example than rules; and then children, if kept out of ill company, will take a pride to behave themselves prettily, after the fashion of others, perceiving themselves esteem'd and commended for it. But if by a little negligence in this part, the boy should not pull off his hat, nor make legs very gracefully, a dancing-master will cure that defect, and wipe off all that plainness of nature, which the a-la-mode people call clownishness. And since nothing appears to me to give children so much becoming confidence and behaviour, and so to raise them to the conversation of those above their age, as dancing, I think they should be taught to dance as soon as they are capable of learning it. For tho' this consist only in outward gracefulness of motion, yet, I know not how, it gives children manly thoughts and carriage, more than any thing. But otherwise, I would not have little children much tormented about punctilio's or niceties of breeding.

Never trouble your self about those faults in them, which you know age will cure: and therefore want of well-fashion'd civility in the carriage, whilst civility is not wanting in the mind, (for there you must take care to plant it early) should be the parents' least care, whilst they are young. If his tender mind be fill'd with a veneration for his parents and teachers, which consists of love and esteem, and a fear to offend them: and with respect and good will to all people; that respect will of itself teach those ways of expressing it, which he observes most acceptable. Be sure to keep up in him the principles of good nature and kindness; make them as habitual as you can, by credit and commendation, and the good things accompanying that state: and when they have taken root in his mind, and are settled there by a continued practice, fear not, the ornaments of conversation, and the outside of fashionable manners, will come in their due time: if when they are remov'd out of their maid's care, they are put into the hands of a well-bred man to be their governor.

Whilst they are very young, any carelessness is to be borne with in children, that carries not with it the marks of pride or ill nature; but those, whenever they appear in any action, are to be corrected immediately by the ways above-mention'd. What I have said concerning manners, I would not have so understood, as if I meant that those who have the judgment to do it, should not gently fashion the motions and carriage of children, when they are very young. It would be of great advantage, if they had people about them from their being first able to go, that had the skill, and would take the right way to do it. That which I complain of, is the wrong course that is usually taken in this matter. Children, who were never taught any such thing as behaviour, are often (especially when strangers are present) chid for having some way or other fail'd in good manners, and have thereupon reproofs and precepts heap'd upon them, concerning putting off their hats, or making of legs, &c. Though in this, those concern'd pretend to correct the child, yet in truth, for the most part, it is but to cover their own shame; and they lay the blame on the poor little ones, sometimes passionately enough, to divert it from themselves, for fear the by-standers should impute to their want of care and skill the child's ill behaviour.

For, as for the children themselves, they are never one jot better'd by such occasional lectures. They at other times should be shewn what to do, and by reiterated actions be fashion'd beforehand into the practice of what is fit and becoming, and not told and talk'd to do upon the spot, of what they have never been accustom'd nor know how to do as they should. To hare and rate them thus at every turn, is not to teach them, but to vex and torment them to no purpose. They should be let alone, rather than chid for a fault which is none of theirs, nor is in their power to mend for speaking to. And it were much better their natural childish negligence or plainness should be left to the care of riper years, than that they should frequently have rebukes misplac'd upon them, which neither do nor can give them graceful motions. If their minds are well-dispos'd, and principled with inward civility, a great part of the roughness which sticks to the outside for want of better teaching, time and observation will rub off, as they grow up, if they are bred in good company; but if in ill, all the rules in the world, all the correction imaginable, will not be able to polish them. For you must take this for a certain truth, that let them have what instructions you will, and ever so learned lectures of breeding daily inculcated into them, that which will most influence their carriage will be the company they converse with, and the fashion of those about them. Children (nay, and men too) do most by example. We are all a sort of camelions, that still take a tincture from things near us; nor is it to be wonder'd at in children, who better understand what they see than what they hear.

§ 68. I mention'd above one great mischief that came by servants to children, when by their flatteries they take off the edge and force of the parents' rebukes, and so lessen their authority: and here is another great inconvenience which children receive from the ill examples which they meet with amongst the meaner servants.

They are wholly, if possible, to be kept from such conversation; for the contagion of these ill precedents, both in civility and virtue, horribly infects children, as often as they come within reach of it. They frequently learn from unbred or debauch'd servants such language, untowardly tricks and vices, as otherwise they possibly would be ignorant of all their lives.

§ 69. 'Tis a hard matter wholly to prevent this mischief. You will have very good luck, if you never have a clownish or vicious servant, and if from them your children never get any infection: but yet as much must be done towards it as can be, and the children kept as much as may be 1 in the company of their parents, and those to whose care they are committed. To this purpose, their being in their presence should be made easy to them; they should be allow'd the liberties and freedoms suitable to their ages, and not be held under unnecessary restraints, when in their parents' or governor's sight. If it be a prison to them, 'tis no wonder they should not like it. They must not be hinder'd from being children, or from playing, or doing as children, but from doing ill; all other liberty is to be allow'd them. Next, to make them in love with the company of their parents, they should receive all their good things there, and from their hands. The servants should be hinder'd from making court to them by giving them strong drink, wine, fruit, playthings, and other such matters, which may make them in love with their conversation.

§ 70. Having nam'd company, I am almost ready to throw away my pen, and trouble you no farther on this subject: for since that does more than all precepts, rules and instructions, methinks 'tis almost wholly in vain to make a long discourse of other things, and to talk of that almost to no purpose. For you will be ready to say, what shall I do with my son? If I keep him always at home, he will be in danger to be my young master; and if I send him abroad, how is it possible to keep him from the contagion of rudeness and vice, which is every where so in fashion? In my house he will perhaps be more innocent, but more ignorant too of the world; wanting there change of company, and being us'd constantly to the same faces, he will, when he comes abroad, be a sheepish or conceited creature.

I confess both sides have their inconveniences. Being abroad, 'tis true, will make him bolder, and better able to bustle and shift among boys of his own age; and the emulation of school-fellows often puts life and industry into young lads. But still you can find a school, wherein it is possible for the master to look after the manners of his scholars, and can shew as great effects of his care of forming their minds to virtue, and their carriage to good breeding, as of forming their tongues to the learned languages, you must confess, that you have a strange value for words, when preferring the languages of the antient Greeks and Romans to that which made 'em such brave men, you think it worth while to hazard your son's innocence and virtue for a little Greek and Latin. For, as for that boldness and spirit which lads get amongst their play-fellows at school, it has ordinarily such a mixture of rudeness and ill-turn'd confidence, that those misbecoming and disingenuous ways of shifting in the world must be unlearnt, and all the tincture wash'd out again, to make way for better principles, and such manners as make a truly worthy man. He that considers how diametrically opposite the skill of living well, and managing, as a man should do, his affairs in the world, is to that mal-pertness, tricking, or violence learnt amongst schoolboys, will think the faults of a privater education infinitely to be preferr'd to such improvements, and will take care to preserve his child's innocence and modesty at home, as being nearer of kin, and more in the way of those qualities which make an useful and able man. Nor does any one find, or so much as suspect, that that retirement and bashfulness which their daughters are brought up in, makes them less knowing, or less able women. Conversation, when they come into the world, soon gives them a becoming assurance; and whatsoever, beyond that, there is of rough and boisterous, may in men be very well spar'd too; for courage and steadiness, as I take it, lie not in roughness and ill breeding.

Virtue is harder to be got than a knowledge of the world; and if lost in a young man, is seldom recover'd. Sheepishness and ignorance of the world, the faults imputed to a private education, are neither the necessary consequences of being bred at home, nor if they were, are they incurable evils. Vice is the more stubborn, as well as the more dangerous evil of the two; and therefore in the first place to be fenced against. If that sheepish softness which often enervates those who are bred like fondlings at home, be carefully to be avoided, it is principally so for virtue's sake; for fear lest such a yielding temper should be too susceptible of vicious impressions, and expose the novice too easily to be corrupted. A young man before he leaves the shelter of his father's house, and the guard of a tutor, should be fortify'd with resolution, and made acquainted with men, to secure his virtues, lest he should be led into some ruinous course, or fatal precipice, before he is sufficiently acquainted with the dangers of conversation, and has steadiness enough not to yield to every temptation. Were it not for this, a young man's bashfulness and ignorance in the world, would not so much need an early care. Conversation would cure it in a great measure; or if that will not do it early enough, it is only a stronger reason for a good tutor at home. For if pains be to be taken to give him a manly air and assurance betimes, it is chiefly as a fence to his virtue when he goes into the world under his own conduct.

It is preposterous therefore to sacrifice his innocency to the attaining of confidence and some little skill of bustling for himself among others, by his conversation with ill-bred and vicious boys; when the chief use of that sturdiness, and standing upon his own legs, is only for the preservation of his virtue. For if confidence or cunning come once to mix with vice, and support his miscarriages, he is only the surer lost; and you must undo again, and strip him of that he has got from his companions, or give him up to ruin. Boys will unavoidably be taught assurance by conversation with men, when they are brought into it; and that is time enough. Modesty and submission, till then, better fits them for instruction; and therefore there needs not any great care to stock them with confidence beforehand. That which requires most time, pains, and assiduity, is, to work into them the principles and practice of virtue and good breeding. This is the seasoning they should be prepar'd with, so as not easily to be got out again. This they had need to be well provided with, for conversation, when they come into the world, will add to their knowledge and assurance, but be too apt to take from their virtue; which therefore they ought to be plentifully stor'd with, and have that tincture sunk deep into them.

How they should be fitted for conversation, and enter'd into the world, when they are ripe for it, we shall consider in another place. But how any one's being put into a mix'd herd of unruly boys, and there learning to wrangle at trap, or rook at span-farthing, fits him for civil conversation or business, I do not see. And what qualities are ordinarily to be got from such a troop of play-fellows as schools usually assemble together from parents of all kinds, that a father should so much covet, is hard to divine. I am sure, he who is able to be at the charge of a tutor at home, may there give his son a more genteel carriage, more manly thoughts, and a sense of what is worthy and becoming, with a greater proficiency in learning into the bargain, and ripen him up sooner into a man, than any at school can do. Not that I blame the schoolmaster in this, or think it to be laid to his charge. The difference is great between two or three pupils in the same house, and three or four score boys lodg'd up and down: for let the master's industry and skill be never so great, it is impossible he should have fifty or an hundred scholars under his eye, any longer than they are in the school together: Nor can it be expected, that he should instruct them successfully in any thing but their books; the forming of their minds and manners requiring a constant attention, and particular application to every single boy, which is impossible in a numerous flock, and would be wholly in vain (could he have time to study and correct every one's particular defects and wrong inclinations) when the lad was to be left to himself, or the prevailing infection of his fellows, the greatest part of the four and twenty hours.

But fathers, observing that fortune is often most successfully courted by bold and bustling men, are glad to see their sons pert and forward betimes; take it for an happy omen that they will be thriving men, and look on the tricks they play their school-fellows, or learn from them, as a proficiency in the art of living, and making their way through the world. But I must take the liberty to say, that he that lays the foundation of his son's fortune in virtue and good breeding, takes the only sure and warrantable way. And 'tis not the waggeries or cheats practis'd amongst school-boys, 'tis not their roughness one to another, nor the well-laid plots of robbing an orchard together, that make an able man; but the principles of justice, generosity, and sobriety, join'd with observation and industry, qualities which I judge school-boys do not learn much of one another. And if a young gentleman bred at home, be not taught more of them than he could learn at school, his father has made a very ill choice of a tutor. Take a boy from the top of a grammar-school, and one of the same age bred as he should be in his father's family, and bring them into good company together, and then see which of the two will have the more manly carriage, and address himself with the more becoming assurance to strangers. Here I imagine the school-boy's confidence will either fail or discredit him; and if it be such as fits him only for the conversation of boys, he were better to be without it.

Vice, if we may believe the general complaint, ripens so fast now-a-days, and runs up to seed to early in young people, that it is impossible to keep a lad from the spreading contagion, if you will venture him abroad in the herd, and trust to chance or his own inclination for the choice of his company at school. By what fate Vice has so thriven amongst us these years past, and by what hands it has been nurs'd up into so uncontroul'd a dominion, I shall leave to others to enquire. I wish that those who complain of the great decay of Christian piety and virtue every where, and of learning and acquir'd improvements in the gentry of this generation, would consider how to retrieve them in the next. This I am sure, that if the foundation of it be not laid in the education and principling of the youth, all other endeavours will be in vain. And if the innocence, sobriety, and industry of those who are coming up, be not taken care of and preserv'd, 'twill be ridiculous to expect, that those who are to succeed next on the stage, should abound in that virtue, ability, and learning, which has hitherto made England considerable in the world. I was going to add courage too, though it has been look'd on as the natural inheritance of Englishmen. What has been talk'd of some late actions at sea, of a kind unknown to our ancestors, gives me occasion to say, that debauchery sinks the courage of men; and when dissoluteness has eaten out the sense of true honour, bravery seldom stays long after it. And I think it impossible to find an instance of any nation, however renown'd for their valour, who ever kept their credit in arms, or made themselves redoubtable amongst their neighbours, after corruption had once broke through and dissolv'd the restraint of discipline, and vice was grown to such an head, that it durst shew itself barefac'd without being out of countenance.

'Tis virtue then, direct virtue, which is the hard and valuable part to be aim'd at in education, and not a forward pertness, or any little arts of shifting. All other considerations and accomplishments should give way and be postpon'd to this. This is the solid and substantial good which tutors should not only read lectures, and talk of, but the labour and art of education should furnish the mind with, and fasten there, and never cease till the young man had a true relish of it, and plac'd his strength, his glory, and his pleasure in it.

The more this advances, the easier way will be made for other accomplishments in their turns. For he that is brought to submit to virtue, will not be refractory, or resty, in any thing that becomes him; and therefore I cannot but prefer breeding of a young gentleman at home in his father's sight, under a good governour, as much the best and safest way to this great and main end of education, when it can be had, and is order'd as it should be. Gentlemen's houses are seldom without variety of company. They should use their sons to all the strange faces that come here, and engage them in conversation with men of parts and breeding, as soon as they are capable of it. And why those who live in the country should not take them with them, when they make visits of civility to their neighbours, I know not. This I am sure, a father that breeds his son at home, has the opportunity to have him more in his own company, and there give him what encouragement he thinks fit, and can keep him better from the taint of servants and the meaner sort of people, than is possible to be done abroad. But what shall be resolv'd in the case, must in great measure be left to the parents, to be determin'd by their circumstances and conveniences; only I think it the worst sort of good husbandry for a father not to strain himself a little for his son's breeding; which, let his condition be what it will, is the best portion he can leave him. But if, after all, it shall be thought by some, that the breeding at home has too little company, and that at ordinary schools, not such as it should be for a young gentleman, I think there might be ways found out to avoid the inconveniences on the one side and the other.

Note 1. How much the Romans thought the education of their children a business that properly belong'd to the parents themselves, see in Suetonius, August. § 64. Plutarch in vita Catonis Censoris, Diodorus Siculus, l. 2, cap. 3.

Sections 71–80

§ 71. Having under consideration how great the influence of company is, and how prone we are all, especially children, to imitation, I must here take the liberty to mind parents of this one thing, viz. That he that will have his son have a respect for him and his orders, must himself have a great reverence for his son. Maxima debetur pueris reverentia. You must do nothing before him, which you would not have him imitate. If any thing escape you, which you would have pass for a fault in him, he will be sure to shelter himself under your example, and shelter himself so as that it will not be easy to come at him, to correct it in him the right way. If you punish him for what he sees you practise yourself, he will not think that severity to proceed from kindness in you, careful to amend a fault in him; but will be apt to interpret it the peevishness and arbitrary imperiousness of a father, who, without any ground for it, would deny his son the liberty and pleasures he takes himself. Or if you assume to yourself the liberty you have taken, as a privilege belonging to riper years, to which a child must not aspire, you do but add new force to your example, and recommend the action the more powerfully to him. For you must always remember, that children affect to be men earlier than is thought; and they love breeches, not for their cut or ease, but because the having them is a mark or step towards manhood. What I say of the father's carriage before his children, must extend itself to all those who have any authority over them, or for whom he would have them have any respect.

§ 72. But to return to the business of rewards and punishments. All the actions of childishness, and unfashionable carriage, and whatever time and age will of itself be sure to reform, being (as I have said) exempt from the discipline of the rod, there will not be so much need of beating children as is generally made use of. To which if we add learning to read, write, dance, foreign language, &c. as under the same privilege, there will be but very rarely an occasion for blows or force in an ingenuous education. The right way to teach them those things, is, to give them a liking and inclination to what you suppose to them to be learn'd, and that will engage their industry and application. This I think no hard matter to do, if children be handled as they should be, and the rewards and punishments above-mention'd be carefully apply'd, and with them these few rules observ'd in the method of instructing them.

§ 73. 1. None of the things they are to learn, should ever be made a burthen to them, or impos'd on them as a task. Whatever is so propos'd, presently becomes irksome; the mind takes an aversion to it, though before it were a thing of delight or indifference. Let a child but be order'd to whip his top at a certain time every day, whether he has or has not a mind to it; let this be but requir'd of him as a duty, wherein he must spend so many hours morning and afternoon, and see whether he will not soon be weary of any play at this rate. Is it not so with grown men? What they do chearfully of themselves, do they not presently grow sick of, and can no more endure, as soon as they find it is expected of them as a duty? Children have as much a mind to shew that they are free, that their own good actions come from themselves, that they are absolute and independent, as any of the proudest of you grown men, think of them as you please.

§ 74. 2. As a consequence of this, they should seldom be put about doing even those things you have got an inclination in them to, but when they have a mind and disposition to it. He that loves reading, writing, musick, &c. finds yet in himself certain seasons wherein those things have no relish to him; and if at that time he forces himself to it, he only pothers and wearies himself to no purpose. So it is with children. This change of temper should be carefully observ'd in them, and the favourable seasons of aptitude and inclination be heedfully laid hold of: and if they are not often enough forward of themselves, a good disposition should be talk'd into them, before they be set upon any thing. This I think no hard matter for a discreet tutor to do, who has study'd his pupil's temper, and will be at a little pains to fill his head with suitable ideas, such as may make him in love with the present business. By this means a great deal of time and tiring would be sav'd: for a child will learn three times as much when he is in tune, as he will with double the time and pains when he goes awkwardly or is dragg'd unwillingly to it. If this were minded as it should, children might be permitted to weary themselves with play, and yet have time enough to learn what is suited to the capacity of each age. But no such thing is consider'd in the ordinary way of education, nor can it well be. That rough discipline of the rod is built upon other principles, has no attraction in it, regards not what humour children are in, nor looks after favourable seasons of inclination. And indeed it would be ridiculous, when compulsion and blows have rais'd an aversion in the child to his task, to expect he should freely of his own accord leave his play, and with pleasure court the occasions of learning; whereas, were matters order'd right, learning anything they should be taught might be made as much a recreation to their play, as their play is to their learning. The pains are equal on both sides. Nor is it that which troubles them; for they love to be busy, and the change and variety is that which naturally delights them. The only odds is, in that which we call play they act at liberty, and employ their pains (whereof you may observe them never sparing) freely; but what they are to learn is forc'd upon them, they are call'd, compell'd, and driven to it. This is that, that at first entrance balks and cools them; they want their liberty. Get them but to ask their tutor to teach them, as they do often their play-fellows, instead of his calling upon them to learn, and they being satisfy'd that they act as freely in this as they do in other things, they will go on with as much pleasure in it, and it will not differ from their other sports and play. By these ways, carefully pursu'd, a child may be brought to desire to be taught any thing you have a mind he should learn. The hardest part, I confess, is with the first or eldest; but when once he is set right, it is easy by him to lead the rest whither one will.

§ 75. Though it be past doubt, that the fittest time for children to learn any thing, is, when their minds are in tune, and well dispos'd to it; when neither flagging of spirit, nor intentness of thought upon something else, makes them awkward and averse; yet two things are to be taken care of: 1. That these seasons either not being warily observ'd, and laid hold on as often as they return, or else, not returning as often as they should, the improvement of the child be not thereby neglected, and so he be let grow into an habitual idleness, and confirm'd in this disposition: 2. That though other things are ill learn'd, when the mind is either indispos'd, or otherwise taken up; yet it is of great moment, and worth our endeavours, to teach the mind to get the mastery over itself, and to be able, upon choice, to take itself off from the hot pursuit of one thing, and set itself upon another with facility and delight, or at any time to shake off its sluggishness, and vigorously employ itself about what reason, or the advice of another shall direct. This is to be done in children, by trying them sometimes, when they are by laziness unbent, or by avocation bent another way, and endeavouring to make them buckle to the thing propos'd. If by this means the mind can get an habitual dominion over itself, lay by ideas or business as occasion requires, and betake itself to new and less acceptable employments without reluctancy or discomposure, it will be an advantage of more consequence than Latin or logick or most of those things children are usually requir'd to learn.

§ 76. Children being more active and busy in that age, than in any other part of their life, and being indifferent to any thing they can do, so they may be but doing, dancing and Scotch-hoppers would be the same thing to them, were the encouragements and discouragements equal. But to things we would have them learn, the great and only discouragement I can observe, is, that they are call'd to it, 'tis made their business, they are teaz'd and chid about it, and do it with trembling and apprehension; or, when they come willingly to it, are kept too long at it, till they are quite tir'd: all which intrenches too much on that natural freedom they extremely affect. And it is that liberty alone which gives the true relish and delight to their ordinary play-games. Turn the tables, and you will find they will soon change their application; especially if they see the examples of others whom they esteem and think above themselves. And if the things which they observe others to do, be order'd so, that they insinuate themselves into them as the privilege of an age or condition above theirs; then ambition, and the desire still to get forward and higher, and to be like those above them, will set them on work, and make them go on with vigour and pleasure; pleasure in what they have begun by their own desire, in which way the enjoyment of their dearly beloved freedom will be no small encouragement to them. To all which, if there be added the satisfaction of credit and reputation, I am apt to think there will need no other spur to excite their application and assiduity, as much as is necessary. I confess, there needs patience and skill, gentleness and attention, and a prudent conduct to attain this at first. But why have you a tutor, if there needed no pains? But when this is once establish'd, all the rest will follow, more easily than in any more severe and imperious discipline. And I think it no hard matter to gain this point; I am sure it will not be, where children have no ill examples set before them. The great danger therefore, I apprehend, is only from servants, and other ill-order'd children, or such other vicious or foolish people, who spoil children both by the ill pattern they set before them in their own ill manners, and by giving them together the two things they should never have at once; I mean vicious pleasures and commendation.

§ 77. As children should very seldom be corrected by blows, so I think frequent, and especially passionate chiding of almost as ill consequence. It lessens the authority of the parents, and the respect of the child; for I bid you still remember, they distinguish early betwixt passion and reason: and as they cannot but have a reverence for what comes from the latter, so they quickly grow into a contempt of the former; or if it causes a present terror, yet it soon wears off, and natural inclination will easily learn to slight such scare-crows which make a noise, but are not animated by reason. Children being to be restrain'd by the parents only in vicious (which, in their tender years, are only a few) things, a look or nod only ought to correct them when they do amiss; or, if words are sometimes to be us'd, they ought to be grave, kind, and sober, representing the ill or unbecomingness of the faults, rather than a hasty rating of the child for it; which makes him not sufficiently distinguish, whether your dislike be not more directed to him than his fault. Passionate chiding usually carries rough and ill language with it, which has this fartser ill effect, that it teaches and justifies it in children: and the names that their parents or præceptors give them, they will not be asham'd or backward to bestow on others, having so good authority for the use of them.

§ 78. I foresee here it will be objected to me, what then, will you have children never beaten nor chid for any fault? This will be to let loose the reins to all kind of disorder. Not so much, as is imagin'd, if a right course has been taken in the first seasoning of their minds, and implanting that awe of their parents above mentioned. For beating, by constant observation, is found to do little good, where the smart of it is all the punishment is fear'd or felt in it; for the influence of that quickly wears out, with the memory of it. But yet there is one, and but one fault, for which, I think, children should be beaten, and that is, obstinacy or rebellion. And in this too, I would have it order'd so, if it can be, that the shame of the whipping, and not the pain, should be the greatest part of the punishment. Shame of doing amiss, and deserving chastisement, is the only true restraint belonging to virtue. The smart of the rod, if shame accompanies it not, soon ceases, and is forgotten, and will quickly by use lose its terror. I have known the children of a person of quality kept in awe by the fear of having their shoes pull'd off, as much as others by apprehensions of a rod hanging over them. Some such punishment I think better than beating; for 'tis shame of the fault, and the disgrace that attends it, that they should stand in fear of, rather than pain, if you would have them have a temper truly ingenuous. But stubbornness, and an obstinate disobedience, must be master'd with force and blows; for this there is no other remedy. Whatever particular action you bid him do, or forbear, you must be sure to see your self obey'd; no quarter in this case, no resistance: for when once it comes to be a trial of skill, a contest for mastery betwixt you, as it is if you command and he refuses, you must be sure to carry it, whatever blows it costs, if a nod or words will not prevail; unless, for ever after you intend to live in obedience to your son. A prudent and kind mother of my acquaintance, was, on such an occasion, forc'd to whip her little daughter, at her first coming home from nurse, eight times successively the same morning, before she could master her stubbornness, and obtain a compliance in a very easy and indifferent matter. If she had left off sooner, and stopp'd at the seventh whipping, she had spoil'd the child for ever, and, by her unprevailing blows, only confirm'd her refractoriness, very hardly afterwards to be cur'd: but wisely persisting till she had bent her mind, and suppled her will, the only end of correction and chastisement, she establish'd her authority thoroughly in the very first occasions, and had ever after a very ready compliance and obedience in all things from her daughter; for as this was the first time, so I think it was the last too she ever struck her.

The pain of the rod, the first occasion that requires it, continu'd and increas'd, without leaving off till it has throughly prevail'd, should first bend the mind, and settle the parent's authority; and then gravity, mix'd with kindness, should for ever after keep it.

This, if well reflected on, would make people more wary in the use of the rod and the cudgel, and keep them from being so apt to think beating the safe and universal remedy to be apply'd at random on all occasions. This is certain, however, if it does no good, it does great harm; if it reaches not the mind, and makes not the will supple, it hardens the offender; and whatever pain he has suffer'd for it, does but endear him to his beloved stubbornness, which has got him this time the victory, and prepares him to contest, and hope for it for the future. This I doubt not but by ill-order'd correction many have been taught to be obstinate and refractory who otherwise would have been very pliant and tractable. For if you punish a child so, as if it were only to revenge the past fault, which has rais'd your choler, what operation can this have upon his mind, which is the part to be amended? If there were no sturdy humor or wilfulness mix'd with his fault, there was nothing in it that requir'd the severity of blows. A kind or grave admonition is enough to remedy the slips of frailty, forgetfulness, or inadvertency, and is as much as they will stand in need of. But if there were a perverseness in the will, if it were a design'd, resolv'd disobedience, the punishment is not to be measur'd by the greatness or smallness of the matter wherein it appear'd, but by the opposition it carries, and stands in, to that respect and submission is due to the father's orders; which must always be rigorously exacted, and the blows by pauses laid on, till they reach the mind, and you perceive the signs of a true sorrow, shame, and purpose of obedience.

This, I confess, requires something more than setting children a task, and whipping them without any more a-do if it be not done, and done to our fancy. This requires care, attention, observation, and a nice study of children's tempers, and weighing their faults well, before we come to this sort of punishment. But is not that better than always to have the rod in hand as the only instrument of government? And by frequent use of it on all occasions, misapply and render inefficacious this last and useful remedy, where there is need of it? For what else can be expected, when it is promiscuously us'd upon every little slip? When a mistake in concordance, or a wrong position in verse, shall have the severity of the lash, in a well-temper'd and industrious lad, as surely as a wilful crime in an obstinate and perverse offender; how can such a way of correction be expected to do good on the mind, and set that right? Which is the only thing to be look'd after; and when set right, brings all the rest that you can desire along with it.

§ 79. Where a wrong bent of the will wants not amendment, there can be no need of blows. All other faults, where the mind is rightly dispos'd, and refuses not the government and authority of the father or tutor, are but mistakes, and may often be overlook'd; or when they are taken notice of, need no other but the gentle remedies of advice, direction, and reproof, till the repeated and wilful neglect of those, shews the fault to be in the mind, and that a manifest perverseness of the will lies at the root of their disobedience. But whenever obstinacy, which is an open defiance, appears, that cannot be wink'd at or neglected, but must, in the first instance, be subdu'd and master'd; only care must be had, that we mistake not and we must be sure it is obstinacy and nothing else.

§ 80. But since the occasions of punishment, especially beating, are as much to be avoided as may be, I think it should not be often brought to this point. If the awe I spoke of be once got, a look will be sufficient in most cases. Nor indeed should the same carriage, seriousness, or application be expected from young children as from those of riper growth. They must be permitted, as I said, the foolish and childish actions suitable to their years, without taking notice of them. Inadvertency, carelessness, and gayety, is the character of that age. I think the severity I spoke of is not to extend itself to such unseasonable restraints. Nor is that hastily to be interpreted obstinacy or wilfulness, which is the natural product of their age or temper. In such miscarriages they are to be assisted, and help'd towards an amendment, as weak people under a natural infirmity; which, though they are warn'd of, yet every relapse must not be counted a perfect neglect, and they presently treated as obstinate. Faults of frailty, as they should never be neglected, or let pass without minding, so, unless the will mix with them, they should never be exaggerated, or very sharply reprov'd; but with a gentle hand set right, as time and age permit. By this means, children will come to see what 'tis in any miscarriage that is chiefly offensive, and so learn to avoid it. This will encourage them to keep their wills right; which is the great business, when they find that it preserves them from any great displeasure, and that in all their other failings they meet with the kind concern and help, rather than the anger and passionate reproaches of their tutor and parents. Keep them from vice and vicious dispositions, and such a kind of behaviour in general will come with every degree of their age, as is suitable to that age and the company they ordinarily converse with; and as they grow in years, they will grow in attention and application. But that your words may always carry weight and authority with them, if it shall happen, upon any occasion, that you bid him leave off the doing of any even childish things, you must be sure to carry the point, and not let him have the mastery. But yet, I say, I would have the father seldom interpose his authority and command in these cases, or in any other, but such as have a tendency to vicious habits. I think there are better ways of prevailing with them: and a gentle persuasion in reasoning, (when the first point of submission to your will is got) will most times do much better.

Sections 81–90

§ 81. It will perhaps be wonder'd, that I mention reasoning with children; and yet I cannot but think that the true way of dealing with them. They understand it as early as they do language; and, if I misobserve not, they love to be treated as rational creatures, sooner than is imagin'd. 'Tis a pride should be cherish'd in them, and, as much as can be, made the greatest instrument to turn them by.

But when I talk of reasoning, I do not intend any other but such as is suited to the child's capacity and apprehension. No body can think a boy or three of seven years old should be argu'd with as a grown man. Long discourses, and philosophical reasonings, at best, amaze and confound, but do not instruct children. When I say, therefore, that they must be treated as rational creatures, I mean that you should make them sensible, by the mildness of your carriage, and the composure even in your correction of them, that what you do is reasonable in you, and useful and necessary for them; and that it is not out of caprichio, passion or fancy, that you command or forbid them any thing. This they are capable of understanding; and there is no virtue they should be excited to, nor fault they should be kept from, which I do not think they may be convinced of; but it must be by such reasons as their age and understandings are capable of, and those propos'd always in very few and plain words. The foundations on which several duties are built, and the fountains of right and wrong from which they spring, are not perhaps easily to be let into the minds of grown men, not us'd to abstract their thoughts from common receiv'd opinions. Much less are children capable of reasonings from remote principles. They cannot conceive the force of long deductions. The reasons that move them must be obvious, and level to their thoughts, and such as may (if I may so say) be felt and touch'd. But yet, if their age, temper, and inclination be consider'd, there will never want such motives as may be sufficient to convince them. If there be no other more particular, yet these will always be intelligible, and of force, to deter them from any fault fit to be taken notice of in them, (viz.) That it will be a discredit and disgrace to them, and displease you.

§ 82. But of all the ways whereby children are to be instructed, and their manners formed, the plainest, easiest, and most efficacious, is, to set before their eyes the examples of those things you would have them do, or avoid; which, when they are pointed out to them, in the practice of persons within their knowledge, with some reflections on their beauty and unbecomingness, are of more force to draw or deter their imitation, than any discourses which can be made to them. Virtues and vices can by no words be so plainly set before their understandings as the actions of other men will shew them, when you direct their observation, and bid them view this or that good or bad quality in their practice. And the beauty or uncomeliness of many things, in good and ill breeding, will be better learnt, and make deeper impressions on them, in the examples of others, than from any rules or instructions can be given about them.

This is a method to be us'd, not only whilst they are young, but to be continu'd even as long as they shall be under another's tuition or conduct; nay, I know not whether it be not the best way to be us'd by a father, as long as he shall think fit, on any occasion, to reform any thing he wishes mended in his son; nothing sinking so gently, and so deep, into men's minds, as example. And what ill they either overlook or indulge in themselves, they cannot but dislike and be asham'd of, when it is set before them in another.

§ 83. It may be doubted, concerning whipping, when as the last remedy, it comes to be necessary, at what times, and by whom it should be done; whether presently upon the committing the fault, whilst it is yet fresh and hot; and whether parents themselves should beat their children. As to the first, I think it should not be done presently, lest passion mingle with it; and so, though it exceed the just proportion, yet it lose of its due weight: for even children discern when we do things in passion. But, as I said before, that has most weight with them, that appears sedately to come from their parents' reason; and they are not without this distinction. Next, if you have any discreet servant capable of it, and has the place of governing your child (for if you have a tutor, there is no doubt) I think it is best the smart should come immediately from another's hand, though by the parent's order, who should see it done; whereby the parent's authority will be preserv'd, and the child's aversion, for the pain it suffers, rather to be turn'd on the person that immediately inflicts. For I would have a father seldom strike his child, but upon very urgent necessity, and as the last remedy; and then perhaps it will be fit to do it so that the child should not quickly forget it.

§ 84. But, as I said before, beating is the worst, and therefore the last means to be us'd in the correction of children, and that only in cases of extremity, after all gentle ways have been try'd, and prov'd unsuccessful; which, if well observ'd, there will be very seldom any need of blows. For, it not being to be imagin'd that a child will often, if ever, dispute his father's present command in any particular instance, and the father not interposing his absolute authority, in peremptory rules, concerning either childish or indifferent actions, wherein his son is to have his liberty, or concerning his learning or improvement, wherein there is no compulsion to be us'd: there remains only the prohibition of some vicious actions, wherein a child is capable of obstinacy, and consequently can deserve beating; and so there will be but very few occasions of that discipline to be us'd by any one who considers well and orders his child's education as it should be. For the first seven years, what vices can a child be guilty of, but lying or some ill-natur'd tricks; the repeated commission whereof, after his father's direct command against it, shall bring him into the condemnation of obstinacy, and the chastisement of the rod? If any vicious inclination in him be, in the first appearance and instances of it, treated as it should be, first with your wonder, and then, if returning again, a second time discountenanc'd with the severe brow of a father, tutor, and all about him, and a treatment suitable to the state of discredit before-mention'd; and this continu'd till he be made sensible and asham'd of his fault, I imagine there will be no need of any other correction, nor ever any occasion to come to blows. The necessity of such chastisement is usually the consequence only of former indulgences or neglects: If vicious inclinations were watch'd from the beginning, and the first irregularities which they cause, corrected by those gentler ways, we should seldom have to do with more than one disorder at once; which would be easily set right without any stir or noise, and not require so harsh a discipline as beating. Thus one by one as they appear'd, they might all be weeded out, without any signs or memory that ever they had been there. But we letting their faults (by indulging and humouring our little ones) grow up, till they are sturdy and numerous, and the deformity of them makes us asham'd and uneasy, we are fain to come to the plough and the harrow; the spade and the pick-ax must go deep to come at the roots; and all the force, skill, and diligence we can use, is scarce enough to cleanse the vitiated seed-plat, overgrown with weeds, and restore us the hopes of fruits, to reward our pains in its season.

§ 85. This course, if observ'd, will spare both father and child the trouble of repeated injunctions, and multiply'd rules of doing and forbearing. For I am of opinion, that of those actions which tend to vicious habits, (which are those alone that a father should interpose his authority and commands in) none should be forbidden children till they are found guilty of them. For such untimely prohibitions, if they do nothing worse, do at least so much towards teaching and allowing 'em, that they suppose that children may be guilty of them, who would possibly be safer in the ignorance of any such faults. And the best remedy to stop them, is, as I have said, to shew wonder and amazement at any such action as hath a vicious tendency, when it is first taken notice of in a child. For example, when he is first found in a lie, or any ill-natur'd trick, the first remedy should be, to talk to him of it as a strange monstrous matter, that it could not be imagin'd he would have done, and so shame him out of it.

§ 86. It will be ('tis like) objected, that whatsoever I fancy of the tractableness of children, and the prevalency of those softer ways of shame and commendation; yet there are many who will never apply themselves to their books, and to what they ought to learn, unless they are scourg'd to it. This, I fear, is nothing but the language of ordinary schools and fashion, which have never suffer'd the other to be try'd as it should be, in places where it could be taken notice of. Why, else, does the learning of Latin and Greek need the rod, when French and Italian need it not? Children learn to dance and fence without whipping; nay, Arithmetick, drawing, &c. they apply themselves well enough to without beating: which would make one suspect, that there is something strange, unnatural, and disagreeable to that Age, in the things required in grammar-schools, or in the methods us'd there, that children cannot be brought to, without the severity of the lash, and hardly with that too; or else, that it is a mistake, that those tongues could not be taught them without beating.

§ 87. But let us suppose some so negligent or idle, that they will not be brought to learn by the gentle ways propos'd, (for we must grant, that there will be children found of all tempers,) yet it does not thence follow, that the rough discipline of the cudgel is to be us'd to all. Nor can any one be concluded unmanageable by the milder methods of government, till they have been thoroughly try'd upon him; and if they will not prevail with him to use his endeavours, and do what is in his power to do, we make no excuses for the obstinate. Blows are the proper remedies for those; but blows laid on in a way different from the ordinary. He that wilfully neglects his book, and stubbornly refuses any thing he can do, requir'd of him by his father, expressing himself in a positive serious command, should not be corrected with two or three angry lashes, for not performing his task, and the same punishment repeated again and again upon every the like default; but when it is brought to that pass, that wilfulness evidently shews itself, and makes blows necessary, I think the chastisement should be a little more sedate, and a little more severe, and the whipping (mingled with admonition between) so continu'd, till the impressions of it on the mind were found legible in the face, voice, and submission of the child, not so sensible of the smart as of the fault he has been guilty of, and melting in true sorrow under it. If such a correction as this, try'd some few times at fit distances, and carry'd to the utmost severity, with the visible displeasure of the father all the while, will not work the effect, turn the mind, and produce a future compliance, what can be hop'd from blows, and to what purpose should they be any more us'd? Beating, when you can expect no good from it, will look more like the fury of an enrag'd enemy, than the good-will of a compassionate friend; and such chastisement carries with it only provocation, without any prospect of amendment. If it be any father's misfortune to have a son thus perverse and untractable, I know not what more he can do but pray for him. But, I imagine, if a right course be taken with children from the beginning, very few will be found to be such; and when there are any such instances, they are not to be the rule for the education of those who are better natur'd, and may be manag'd with better usage.

§ 88. If a tutor can be got, that, thinking himself in the father's place, charg'd with his care, and relishing these things, will at the beginning apply himself to put them in practice, he will afterwards find his work very easy; and you will, I guess, have your son in a little time a greater proficient in both learning and breeding than perhaps you imagine. But let him by no means beat him at any time without your consent and direction; at least till you have experience of his discretion and temper. But yet, to keep up his authority with his pupil, besides concealing that he has not the power of the rod, you must be sure to use him with great respect yourself, and cause all your family to do so too: for you cannot expect your son should have any regard for one whom he sees you, or his mother, or others slight. If you think him worthy of contempt, you have chosen amiss; and if you shew any contempt of him, he will hardly escape it from your son: and whenever that happens, whatever worth he may have in himself, and abilities for this employment, they are all lost to your child, and can afterwards never be made useful to him.

§ 89. As the father's example must teach the child respect for his tutor, so the tutor's example must lead the child into those actions he would have him do. His practice must by no means cross his precepts, unless he intend to set him wrong. It will be to no purpose for the tutor to talk of the restraint of the passions whilst any of his own are let loose; and he will in vain endeavour to reform any vice or indecency in his pupil, which he allows in himself. Ill patterns are sure to be follow'd more than good rules; and therefore he must always carefully preserve him from the influence of ill precedents, especially the most dangerous of all, the examples of the servants; from whose company he is to be kept, not by prohibitions, for that will but give him an itch after it, but by other ways I have mention'd.

§ 90. In all the whole business of education, there is nothing like to be less hearken'd to, or harder to be well observ'd, than what I am now going to say; and that is, that children should, from their first beginning to talk, have some discreet, sober, nay, wise person about them, whose care it should be to fashion them aright, and keep them from all ill, especially the infection of bad company. I think this province requires great sobriety, temperance, tenderness, diligence, and discretion; qualities hardly to be found united in persons that are to be had for ordinary salaries, nor easily to be found any where. As to the charge of it, I think it will be the money best laid out that can be, about our children; and therefore, though it may be expensive more than is ordinary, yet it cannot be thought dear. He that at any rate procures his child a good mind, well-principled, temper'd to virtue and usefulness, and adorn'd with civility and good breeding, makes a better purchase for him that if he laid out the money for an addition of more earth to his former acres. Spare it in toys and play-games, in silk and ribbons, laces, and other useless expenses, as much as you please; but be not sparing in so necessary a part as this. 'Tis not good husbandry to make his fortune rich, and his mind poor. I have often with great admiration seen people lavish it profusely in tricking up their children in fine clothes, lodging and feeding them sumptuously, allowing them more than enough of useless servants, and yet at the same time starve their minds, and not take sufficient care to cover that which is the most shameful nakedness, viz. their natural wrong inclinations and ignorance. This I can look on as no other than a sacrificing to their own vanity, it shewing more their pride than true care of the good of their children; whatsoever you employ to the advantage of your son's mind, will shew your true kindness, tho' it be to the lessening of his estate. A wise and good man can hardly want either the opinion or reality of being great and happy; but he that is foolish or vicious, can be neither great nor happy, what estate soever you leave him: and I ask you whether there be not men in the world, whom you had rather have your son be with five hundred pounds per annum, than some other you know with five thousand pounds.

Sections 91–100

§ 91. The consideration of charge ought not therefore to deter those who are able. The great difficulty will be where to find a proper person: for those of small age, parts, and virtue, are unfit for this employment, and those that have greater, will hardly be got to undertake such a charge. You must therefore look out early, and enquire every where; for the world has people of all sorts. And I remember, Montaigne says in one of his essays, that the learned Castalio was fain to make trenchers at Basle, to keep himself from starving, when his father would have given any money for such a tutor for his son, and Castalio have willingly embrac'd such an employment upon very reasonable terms; but this was for want of intelligence.

§ 92. If you find it difficult to meet with such a tutor as we desire, you are not to wonder. I only can say, spare no care nor cost to get such an one. All things are to be had that way: and I dare assure you, that if you can get a good one, you will never repent the charge; but will always have the satisfaction to think it the money of all other the best laid out. But be sure take no body upon friends, or charity, no, nor upon great commendations. Nay, if you will do as you ought, the reputation of a sober man, with a good stock of learning, (which is all usually requir'd in a tutor) will not be enough to serve your turn. In this choice be as curious as you would be in that of a wife for him; for you must not think of trial or changing afterwards: This will cause great inconvenience to you, and greater to your son. When I consider the scruples and cautions I here lay in your way, methinks it looks as if I advis'd you to something which I would have offer'd at, but in effect not done. But he that shall consider how much the business of a tutor, rightly employ'd, lies out of the road, and how remote it is from the thoughts of many, even of those who propose to themselves this employment, will perhaps be of my mind, that one fit to educate and form the mind of a young gentleman is not everywhere to be found, and that more than ordinary care is to be taken in the choice of him, or else you may fail of your end.

§ 93. The character of a sober man and a scholar is, as I have above observ'd, what every one expects in a tutor. This generally is thought enough, and is all that parents commonly look for: But when such an one has empty'd out into his pupil all the Latin and logick he has brought from the university, will that furniture make him a fine gentleman? Or can it be expected, that he should be better bred, better skill'd in the world, better principled in the grounds and foundations of true virtue and generosity, than his young tutor is?

To form a young gentleman as he should be, 'tis fit his governor should himself be well-bred, understanding the ways of carriage and measures of civility in all the variety of persons, times, and places; and keep his pupil, as much as his age requires, constantly to the observation of them. This is an art not to be learnt nor taught by books. Nothing can give it but good company and observation join'd together. The taylor may make his clothes modish, and the dancing-master give fashion to his motions; yet neither of these, tho' they set off well, make a well-bred gentleman: no, tho' he have learning to boot, which, if not well manag'd, makes him more impertinent and intolerable in conversation. Breeding is that which sets a gloss upon all his other good qualities, and renders them useful to him, in procuring him the esteem and good-will of all that he comes near. Without good breeding his other accomplishments make him pass but for proud, conceited, vain, or foolish.

Courage in an ill-bred man has the air and escapes not the opinion of brutality: Learning becomes pedantry; wit, buffoonery; plainness, rusticity; good nature, fawning. And there cannot be a good quality in him, which want of breeding will not warp and disfigure to his disadvantage. Nay, virtue and parts, though they are allow'd their due commendation, yet are not enough to procure a man a good reception, and make him welcome wherever he comes. No body contents himself with rough diamonds, and wears them so, who would appear with advantage. When they are polish'd and set, then they give a lustre. Good qualities are the substantial riches of the mind, but 'tis good breeding sets them off: and he that will be acceptable, must give beauty, as well as strength, to his actions. Solidity, or even usefulness, is not enough: a graceful way and fashion in every thing, is that which gives the ornament and liking. And in most cases, the manner of doing is of more consequence than the thing done; and upon that depends the satisfaction or disgust wherewith it is receiv'd. This therefore, which lies not in the putting off the hat, nor making of compliments, but in a due and free composure of language, looks, motion, posture, place, &c. suited to persons and occasions, and can be learn'd only by habit and use, though it be above the capacity of children, and little ones should not be perplex'd about it, yet it ought to be begun and in a good measure learn'd by a young gentleman whilst he is under a tutor, before he comes into the world upon his own legs: for then usually it is too late to hope to reform several habitual indecencies, which lie in little things. For the carriage is not as it should be, till it is become natural in every part, falling, as skilful musicians' fingers do, into harmonious order without care and without thought. If in conversation a man's mind be taken up with a solicitous watchfulness about any part of his behaviour; instead of being mended by it, it will be constrain'd, uneasy, and ungraceful.

Besides, this part is most necessary to be form'd by the hand and care of a governor, because, though the errors committed in breeding are the first that are taken notice of by others, yet they are the last that any one is told of; not but that the malice of the world is forward enough to tattle of them; but it is always out of his hearing, who should make profit of their judgment and reform himself by their censure. And indeed, this is so nice a point to be meddled with, that even those who are friends, and wish it were mended, scarce ever dare mention it, and tell those they love that they are guilty in such or such cases of ill breeding. Errors in other things may often with civility be shewn another; and 'tis no breach of good manners or friendship to set him right in other mistakes; but good breeding itself allows not a man to touch upon this, or to insinuate to another that he is guilty of want of breeding. Such information can come only from those who have authority over them; and from them too it comes very hardly and harshly to a grown man; and however soften'd, goes but ill down with any one who has liv'd ever so little in the world. Wherefore it is necessary that this part should be the governor's principal care, that an habitual gracefulness, and politeness in all his carriage, may be settled in his charge, as much as may be, before he goes out of his hands; and that he may not need advice in this point when he has neither time nor disposition to receive it, nor has any body left to give it him. The tutor therefore ought in the first place to be well-bred: and a young gentleman, who gets this one qualification from his governor, sets out with great advantage, and will find that this one accomplishment will more open his way to him, get him more friends, and carry him farther in the world, than all the hard words or real knowledge he has got from the liberal arts, or his tutor's learned encyclopaedia: not that those should be neglected, but by no means preferr'd, or suffer'd to thrust out the other.

§ 94. Besides being well-bred, the tutor should know the world well; the ways, the humours, the follies, the cheats, the faults of the age he is fallen into, and particularly of the country he lives in. These he should be able to shew to his pupil, as he finds him capable; teach him skill in men, and their manners; pull off the mask which their several callings and pretences cover them with, and make his pupil discern what lies at the bottom under such appearances, that he may not, as unexperienc'd young men are apt to do if they are unwarn'd, take one thing for another, judge by the outside, and give himself up to shew, and the insinuation of a fair carriage, or an obliging application. A governor should teach his scholar to guess at and beware of the designs of men he hath to do with, neither with too much suspicion, nor too much confidence; but as the young man is by nature most inclin'd to either side, rectify him, and bend him the other way. He should accustom him to make, as much as is possible, a true judgment of men by those marks which serve best to shew what they are, and give a prospect into their inside, which often shows itself in little things, especially when they are not in parade, and upon their guard. He should acquaint him with the true state of the world, and dispose him to think no man better or worse, wiser or foolisher, than he really is. Thus, by safe and insensible degrees, he will pass from a boy to a man; which is the most hazardous step in all the whole course of life. This therefore should be carefully watch'd, and a young man with great diligence handed over it; and not as now usually is done, be taken from a governor's conduct, and all at once thrown into the world under his own, not without manifest dangers of immediate spoiling; there being nothing more frequent than instances of the great looseness, extravagancy, and debauchery, which young men have run into as soon as they have been let loose from a severe and strict education: Which I think may be chiefly imputed to their wrong way of breeding, especially in this part; for having been bred up in a great ignorance of what the world truly is, and finding it a quite other thing, when they come into it, than what they were taught it should be, and so imagin'd it was, are easily persuaded, by other kind of tutors, which they are sure to meet with, that the discipline they were kept under, and the lectures read to them, were but the formalities of education and the restraints of childhood; that the freedom belonging to men is to take their swing in a full enjoyment of what was before forbidden them. They shew the young novice the world full of fashionable and glittering examples of this every where, and he is presently dazzled with them. My young master failing not to be willing to shew himself a man, as much as any of the sparks of his years, lets himself loose to all the irregularities he finds in the most debauch'd; and thus courts credit and manliness in the casting off the modesty and sobriety he has till then been kept in; and thinks it brave, at his first setting out, to signalize himself in running counter to all the rules of virtue which have been preach'd to him by his tutor.

The shewing him the world as really it is, before he comes wholly into it, is one of the best means, I think, to prevent this mischief. He should by degrees be informed of the vices in fashion, and warned of the applications and designs of those who will make it their business to corrupt him. He should be told the arts they use, and the trains they lay; and now and then have set before him the tragical or ridiculous examples of those who are ruining or ruin'd this way. The age is not like to want instances of this kind, which should be made land-marks to him, that by the disgraces, diseases, beggary, and shame of hopeful young men thus brought to ruin, he may be precaution'd, and be made see, how those join in the contempt and neglect of them that are undone, who, by pretences of friendship and respect, lead them to it, and help to prey upon them whilst they were undoing; that he may see, before he buys it by a too dear experience, that those who persuade him not to follow the sober advices he has receiv'd from his governors, and the counsel of his own reason, which they call being govern'd by others, do it only that they may have the government of him themselves; and make him believe, he goes like a man of himself, by his own conduct, and for his own pleasure, when in truth he is wholly as a child led by them into those vices which best serve their purposes. This is a knowledge which, upon all occasions, a tutor should endeavour to instil, and by all methods try to make him comprehend, and thoroughly relish.

I know it is often said, that to discover to a young man the vices of the age is to teach them him. That, I confess, is a good deal so, according as it is done; and therefore requires a discreet man of parts, who knows the world, and can judge of the temper, inclination, and weak side of his pupil. This farther is to be remember'd, that it is not possible now (as perhaps formerly it was) to keep a young gentleman from vice by a total ignorance of it, unless you will all his life mew him up in a closet, and never let him go into company. The longer he is kept thus hoodwink'd, the less he will see when he comes abroad into open daylight, and be the more expos'd to be a prey to himself and others. And an old boy, at his first appearance, with all the gravity of his ivy-bush about him, is sure to draw on him the eyes and chirping of the whole town volery; amongst which there will not be wanting some birds of prey, that will presently be on the wing for him.

The only fence against the world, is, a thorough knowledge of it, into which a young gentleman should be enter'd by degrees, as he can bear it; and the earlier the better, so he be in safe and skilful hands to guide him. The scene should be gently open'd, and his entrance made step by step, and the dangers pointed out that attend him from the several degrees, tempers, designs, and clubs of men. He should be prepar'd to be shock'd by some, and caress'd by others; warn'd who are like to oppose, who to mislead, who to undermine him, and who to serve him. He should be instructed how to know and distinguish them; where he should let them see, and when dissemble the knowledge of them and their aims and workings. And if he be too forward to venture upon his own strength and skill, the perplexity and trouble of a misadventure now and then, that reaches not his innocence, his health, or reputation, may not be an ill way to teach him more caution.

This, I confess, containing one great part of wisdom, is not the product of some superficial thoughts, or much reading; but the effect of experience and observation in a man who has liv'd in the world with his eyes open, and convers'd with men of all sorts. And therefore I think it of most value to be instill'd into a young man upon all occasions which offer themselves, that when he comes to launch into the deep himself, he may not be like one at sea without a line, compass or sea-chart; but may have some notice before-hand of the rocks and shoals, the currents and quick-sands, and know a little how to steer, that he sink not before he get experience. He that thinks not this of more moment to his son, and for which he more needs a governor, than the languages and learned sciences, forgets of how much more use it is to judge right of men, and manage his affairs wisely with them, than to speak Greek and Latin, or argue in mood and figure; or to have his head fill'd with the abstruse speculations of natural philosophy and metaphysicks; nay, than to be well vers'd in Greek and Roman writers, though that be much better for a gentleman than to be a good Peripatetick or Cartesian, because those antient authors observ'd and painted mankind well, and give the best light into that kind of knowledge. He that goes into the eastern parts of Asia, will find able and acceptable men without any of these; but without virtue, knowledge of the world, and civility, an accomplish'd and valuable man can be found no where.

A great part of the learning now in fashion in the schools of Europe, and that goes ordinarily into the round of education, a gentleman may in a good measure be unfurnish'd with, without any great disparagement to himself or prejudice to his affairs. But prudence and good breeding are in all the stations and occurrences of life necessary; and most young men suffer in the want of them, and come rawer and more awkward into the world than they should, for this very reason, because these qualities, which are of all other the most necessary to be taught, and stand most in need of the assistance and help of a teacher, are generally neglected and thought but a slight or no part of a tutor's business. Latin and learning make all the noise; and the main stress is laid upon his proficiency in things a great part whereof belong not to a gentleman's calling; which is to have the knowledge of a man of business, a carriage suitable to his rank, and to be eminent and useful in his country, according to his station. Whenever either spare hours from that, or an inclination to perfect himself in some parts of knowledge, which his tutor did but just enter him in, set him upon any study, the first rudiments of it, which he learn'd before, will open the way enough for his own industry to carry him as far as his fancy will prompt, or his parts enable him to go. Or, if he thinks it may save his time and pains to be help'd over some difficulties by the hand of a master, he may then take a man that is perfectly well skilled in it, or chuse such an one as he thinks fittest for his purpose. But to initiate his pupil in any part of learning, as far as is necessary for a young man in the ordinary course of his studies, an ordinary skill in the governor is enough. Nor is it requisite that he should be a thorough scholar, or possess in perfection all those sciences which 'tis convenient a young gentleman should have a taste of in some general view, or short system. A gentleman that would penetrate deeper must do it by his own genius and industry afterwards: For no body ever went far in knowledge, or became eminent in any of the sciences, by the discipline and constraint of a master.

The great work of a governor, is to fashion the carriage, and form the mind; to settle in his pupil good habits and the principles of virtue and wisdom; to give him by little and little a view of mankind, and work him into a love and imitation of what is excellent and praise-worthy; and, in the prosecution of it, to give him vigour, activity, and industry. The studies which he sets him upon, are but as it were the exercises of his faculties, and employment of his time, to keep him from sauntering and idleness, to teach him application, and accustom him to take pains, and to give him some little taste of what his own industry must perfect. For who expects, that under a tutor a young gentleman should be an accomplish'd critick, orator, or logician? go to the bottom of metaphysicks, natural philosophy, or mathematicks? or be a master in history or chronology? though something of each of these is to be taught him: But it is only to open the door, that he may look in, and as it were begin an acquaintance, but not to dwell there: And a governor would be much blam'd that should keep his pupil too long, and lead him too far in most of them. But of good breeding, knowledge of the world, virtue industry, and a love of reputation, he cannot have too much: And if he have these, he will not long want what he needs or desires of the other.

And since it cannot be hop'd he should have time and strength to learn all things, most pains should be taken about that which is most necessary; and that principally look'd after which will be of most and frequentest use to him in the world.

Seneca complains of the contrary practice in his time; and yet the Burgursdicius's and the Scheiblers did not swarm in those days as they do now in these. What would he have thought if he had liv'd now, when the tutors think it their great business to fill the studies and heads of their pupils with such authors as these? He would have had much more reason to say, as he does, non vitæ sed scholæ discimus, we learn not to live, but to dispute; and our education fits us rather for the university than the world. But 'tis no wonder if those who make the fashion suit it to what they have, and not to what their pupils want. The fashion being once establish'd, who can think it strange, that in this, as well as in all other things, it should prevail? And that the greatest part of those, who find their account in an easy submission to it, should be ready to cry out, Heresy, when any one departs from it? 'Tis nevertheless matter of astonishment that men of quality and parts should suffer themselves to be so far misled by custom and implicit faith. Reason, if consulted with, would advise, that their children's time should be spent in acquiring what might be useful to them when they come to be men, rather than to have their heads stuff'd with a deal of trash, a great part whereof they usually never do ('tis certain they never need to) think on again as long as they live: and so much of it as does stick by them they are only the worse for. This is so well known, that I appeal to parents themselves, who have been at cost to have their young heirs taught it, whether it be not ridiculous for their sons to have any tincture of that sort of learning, when they come abroad into the world? whether any appearance of it would not lessen and disgrace them in company? And that certainly must be an admirable acquisition, and deserves well to make a part in education, which men are asham'd of where they are most concern'd to shew their parts and breeding.

There is yet another reason why politeness of manners, and knowledge of the world should principally be look'd after in a tutor; and that is, because a man of parts and years may enter a lad far enough in any of those sciences, which he has no deep insight into himself. Books in these will be able to furnish him, and give him light and precedency enough to go before a young follower: but he will never be able to set another right in the knowledge of the world, and above all in breeding, who is a novice in them himself.

This is a knowledge he must have about him, worn into him by use and conversation and a long forming himself by what he has observ'd to be practis'd and allow'd in the best company. This, if he has it not of his own, is no where to be borrowed for the use of his pupil; or if he could find pertinent treatises of it in books that would reach all the particulars of an English gentleman's behaviour, his own ill-fashion'd example, if he be not well-bred himself, would spoil all his lectures; it being impossible, that any one should come forth well-fashion'd out of unpolish'd, ill-bred company.

I say this, not that I think such a tutor is every day to be met with, or to be had at the ordinary rates; but that those who are able, may not be sparing of enquiry or cost in what is of so great moment; and that other parents, whose estates will not reach to greater salaries, may yet remember what they should principally have an eye to in the choice of one to whom they would commit the education of their children; and what part they should chiefly look after themselves, whilst they are under their care, and as often as they come within their observation; and not think that all lies in Latin and French or some dry systems of logick and philosophy.

§ 95. But to return to our method again. Though I have mention'd the severity of the father's brow, and the awe settled thereby in the mind of children when young, as one main instrument whereby their education is to be manag'd; yet I am far from being of an opinion that it should be continu'd all along to them, whilst they are under the discipline and government of pupilage; I think it should be relax'd, as fast as their age, discretion and good behaviour could allow it; even to that degree, that a father will do well, as his son grows up, and is capable of it, to talk familiarly with him; nay, ask his advice, and consult with him about those things wherein he has any knowledge or understanding. By this, the father will gain two things, both of great moment. The one is, that it will put serious considerations into his son's thoughts, better than any rules or advices he can give him. The sooner you treat him as a man, the sooner he will begin to be one: and if you admit him into serious discourses sometimes with you, you will insensibly raise his mind above the usual amusements of youth, and those trifling occupations which it is commonly wasted in. For it is easy to observe, that many young men continue longer in the thought and conversation of school-boys than otherwise they would, because their parents keep them at that distance, and in that low rank, by all their carriage to them.

§ 96. Another thing of greater consequence, which you will obtain by such a way of treating him, will be his friendship. Many fathers, though they proportion to their sons liberal allowances, according to their age and condition, yet they keep the knowledge of their estates and concerns from them with as much reservedness as if they were guarding a secret of state from a spy or an enemy. This, if it looks not like jealousy, yet it wants those marks of kindness and intimacy which a father should shew to his son, and no doubt often hinders or abates that chearfulness and satisfaction wherewith a son should address himself to and rely upon his father. And I cannot but often wonder to see fathers who love their sons very well, yet so order the matter by a constant stiffness and a mien of authority and distance to them all their lives, as if they were never to enjoy, or have any comfort from those they love best in the world, till they had lost them by being remov'd into another. Nothing cements and establishes friendship and good-will so much as confident communication of concernments and affairs. Other kindnesses, without this, leave still some doubts: but when your son sees you open your mind to him, when he finds that you interest him in your affairs, as things you are willing should in their turn come into his hands, he will be concern'd for them as for his own, wait his season with patience, and love you in the mean time, who keep him not at the distance of a stranger. This will also make him see, that the enjoyment you have, is not without care; which the more he is sensible of, the less will he envy you the possession, and the more think himself happy under the management of so favourable a friend and so careful a father. There is scarce any young man of so little thought, or so void of sense, that would not be glad of a sure friend, that he might have recourse to, and freely consult on occasion. The reservedness and distance that fathers keep, often deprive their sons of that refuge which would be of more advantage to them than an hundred rebukes and chidings. Would your son engage in some frolick, or take a vagary, were it not much better he should do it with, than without your knowledge? For since allowances for such things must be made to young men, the more you know of his intrigues and designs, the better will you be able to prevent great mischiefs; and by letting him see what is like to follow, take the right way of prevailing with him to avoid less inconveniences. Would you have him open his heart to you, and ask your advice? you must begin to do so with him first, and by your carriage beget that confidence.

§ 97. But whatever he consults you about, unless it lead to some fatal and irremediable mischief, be sure you advise only as a friend of more experience; but with your advice mingle nothing of command or authority, nor more than you would to your equal or a stranger. That would be to drive him for ever from any farther demanding, or receiving advantage from your counsel. You must consider that he is a young man, and has pleasures and fancies which you are pass'd. You must not expect his inclination should be just as yours, nor that at twenty he should have the same thoughts you have at fifty. All that you can wish, is, that since youth must have some liberty, some outleaps, they might be with the ingenuity of a son, and under the eye of a father, and then no very great harm can come of it. The way to obtain this, as I said before, is (according as you find him capable) to talk with him about your affairs, propose matters to him familiarly, and ask his advice; and when he ever lights on the right, follow it as his; and if it succeed well, let him have the commendation. This will not at all lessen your authority, but increase his love and esteem of you. Whilst you keep your estate, the staff will be in your own hands; and your authority the surer, the more it is strengthen'd with confidence and kindness. For you have not that power you ought to have over him, till he comes to be more afraid of offending so good a friend than of losing some part of his future expectation.

§ 98. Familiarity of discourse, if it can become a father to his son, may much more be condescended to by a tutor to his pupil. All their time together should not be spent in reading of lectures, and magisterially dictating to him what he is to observe and follow. Hearing him in his turn, and using him to reason about what is propos'd, will make the rules go down the easier and sink the deeper, and will give him a liking to study and instruction: And he will then begin to value knowledge, when he sees that it enables him to discourse, and he finds the pleasure and credit of bearing a part in the conversation, and of having his reasons sometimes approv'd and hearken'd to; particularly in morality, prudence, and breeding, cases should be put to him, and his judgment ask'd. This opens the understanding better than maxims, how well soever explain'd, and settles the rules better in the memory for practice. This way lets things into the mind which stick there, and retain their evidence with them; whereas words at best are faint representations, being not so much as the true shadows of things, and are much sooner forgotten. He will better comprehend the foundations and measures of decency and justice, and have livelier, and more lasting impressions of what he ought to do, by giving his opinion on cases propos'd, and reasoning with his tutor on fit instances, than by giving a silent, negligent, sleepy audience to his tutor's lectures; and much more than by captious logical disputes, or set declamations of his own, upon any question. The one sets the thoughts upon wit and false colours, and not upon truth; the other teaches fallacy, wrangling, and opiniatry; and they are both of them things that spoil the judgment, and put a man out of the way of right and fair reasoning; and therefore carefully to be avoided by one who would improve himself, and be acceptable to others.

§ 99. When by making your son sensible that he depends on you, and is in your power, you have established your authority; and by being inflexibly severe in your carriage to him when obstinately persisting in any ill-natur'd trick which you have forbidden, especially lying, you have imprinted on his mind that awe which is necessary; and, on the other side, when (by permitting him the full liberty due to his age, and laying no restraint in your presence to those childish actions and gaiety of carriage, which, whilst he is very young, is as necessary to him as meat or sleep) you have reconcil'd him to your company, and made him sensible of your care and love of him, by indulgence and tenderness, especially caressing him on all occasions wherein he does any thing well, and being kind to him after a thousand fashions suitable to his age, which nature teaches parents better than I can: When, I say, by these ways of tenderness and affection, which parents never want for their children, you have also planted in him a particular affection for you; he is then in the state you could desire, and you have form'd in his mind that true reverence which is always afterwards carefully to be continu'd, and maintain'd in both parts of it, love, and fear, as the great principles whereby you will always have hold upon him, to turn his mind to the ways of virtue and honour.

§ 100. When this foundation is once well lay'd, and you find this reverence begin to work in him, the next thing to be done, is carefully to consider his temper, and the particular constitution of his mind. Stubbornness, lying, and ill-natur'd actions, are not (as has been said) to be permitted in him from the beginning, whatever his temper be. Those seeds of vices are not to be suffer'd to take any root, but must be carefully weeded out, as soon as ever they begin to shew themselves in him; and your authority is to take place and influence his mind, from the very dawning of any knowledge in him, that it may operate as a natural principle, whereof he never perceiv'd the beginning, never knew that it was, or could be otherwise. By this, if the reverence he owes you be establish'd early, it will always be sacred to him, and it will be as hard for him to resist as the principles of his nature.

Sections 101–110

§ 101. Having thus very early set up your authority, and by the gentler applications of it sham'd him out of what leads towards an immoral habit, as soon as you have observ'd it in him, (for I would by no means have chiding us'd, much less blows, till obstinacy and incorrigibleness make it absolutely necessary) it will be fit to consider which way the natural make of his mind inclines him. Some men by the unalterable frame of their constitutions, are stout, others timorous, some confident, others modest, tractable, or obstinate, curious or careless, quick or slow. There are not more differences in men's faces, and the outward lineaments of their bodies, than there are in the makes and tempers of their minds; only there is this difference, that the distinguishing characters of the face, and the lineaments of the body, grow more plain and visible with time and age; but the peculiar physiognomy of the mind is most discernible in children, before art and cunning have taught them to hide their deformities, and conceal their ill inclinations under a dissembled outside.

§ 102. Begin therefore betimes nicely to observe your son's temper; and that, when he is under least restraint, in his play, and as he thinks out of your sight. See what are his predominate passions and prevailing inclinations; whether he be fierce or mild, bold or bashful, compassionate or cruel, open or reserv'd, &c. For as these are different in him, so are your methods to be different, and your authority must hence take measures to apply itself different ways to him. These native propensities, these prevalencies of constitution, are not to be cur'd by rules, or a direct contest, especially those of them that are the humbler and meaner sort, which proceed from fear, and lowness of spirit; though with art they may be much mended, and turn'd to good purposes. But this, be sure, after all is done, the byass will always hang on that side that nature first plac'd it: And if you carefully observe the characters of his mind, now in the first scenes of his life, you will ever after be able to judge which way his thoughts lean, and what he aims at even hereafter, when, as he grows up, the plot thickens, and he puts on several shapes to act it.

§ 103. I told you before, that children love liberty; and therefore they should be brought to do the things are fit for them, without feeling any restraint laid upon them. I now tell you, they love something more; and that is dominion: And this is the first original of most vicious habits, that are ordinary and natural. This love of power and dominion shews itself very early, and that in these two things.

§ 104. 1. We see children, as soon almost as they are born (I am sure long before they can speak) cry, grow peevish, sullen, and out of humour, for nothing but to have their wills. They would have their desires submitted to by others; they contend for a ready compliance from all about them, especially from those that stand near or beneath them in age or degree, as soon as they come to consider others with those distinctions.

§ 105. 2. Another thing wherein they shew their love of dominion, is, their desire to have things to be theirs: They would have propriety and possession, pleasing themselves with the power which that seems to give, and the right they thereby have, to dispose of them as they please. He that has not observ'd these two humours working very betimes in children, has taken little notice of their actions: And he who thinks that these two roots of almost all the injustice and contention that so disturb human life, are not early to be weeded out, and contrary habits introduc'd, neglects the proper season to lay the foundations of a good and worthy man. To do this, I imagine these following things may somewhat conduce.

§ 106. 1. That a child should never be suffer'd to have what he craves, much less what he cries for, I had said, or so much as speaks for: But that being apt to the misunderstood, and interpreted as if I meant a child should never speak to his parents for any thing, which will perhaps be thought to lay too great a curb on the minds of children, to the prejudice of that love and affection which should be between them and their parents; I shall explain my self a little more particularly. It is fit that they should have liberty to declare their wants to their parents, and that with all tenderness they should be hearken'd to, and supply'd, at least whilst they are very little. But 'tis one thing to say, I am hungry, another to say, I would have roastmeat. Having declar'd their wants, their natural wants, the pain they feel from hunger, thirst, cold, or any other necessity of nature, 'tis the duty of their parents and those about them to relieve them: But children must leave it to the choice and ordering of their parents, what they think properest for them, and how much; and must not be permitted to chuse for themselves, and say, I would have wine, or white-bread; the very naming of it should make them lose it.

§ 107. That which parents should take care of here, is to distinguish between the wants of fancy, and those of nature; which Horace has well taught them to do in this verse:Queis humana sibi doleat natura negatis.

Those are truly natural wants, which reason alone, without some other help, is not able to fence against, nor keep from disturbing us. The pains of sickness and hurts, hunger, thirst, and cold, want of sleep and rest or relaxation of the part weary'd with labour, are what all men feel and the best dispos'd minds cannot but be sensible of their uneasiness; and therefore ought, by fit applications, to seek their removal, though not with impatience, or over great haste, upon the first approaches of them, where delay does not threaten some irreparable harm. The pains that come from the necessities of nature, are monitors to us to beware of greater mischiefs, which they are the forerunners of; and therefore they must not be wholly neglected, nor strain'd too far. But yet the more children can be inur'd to hardships of this kind, by a wise care to make them stronger in body and mind, the better it will be for them. I need not here give any caution to keep within the bounds of doing them good, and to take care, that what children are made to suffer, should neither break their spirits, nor injure their health, parents being but too apt of themselves to incline more than they should to the softer side.

But whatever compliance the necessities of nature may require, the wants of fancy children should never be gratify'd in, nor suffered to mention. The very speaking for any such thing should make them lose it. Clothes, when they need, they must have; but if they speak for this stuff or that colour, they should be sure to go without it. Not that I would have parents purposely cross the desires of their children in matters of indifference,; on the contrary, where their carriage deserves it, and one is sure it will not corrupt or effeminate their minds, and make them fond of trifles, I think all things should be contriv'd, as much as could be, to their satisfaction, that they may find the ease and pleasure of doing well. The best for children is that they should not place any pleasure in such things at all, nor regulate their delight by their fancies, but be indifferent to all that nature has made so. This is what their parents and teachers should chiefly aim at; but till this be obtain'd, all that I oppose here, is the liberty of asking, which in these things of conceit ought to be restrain'd by a constant forfeiture annex'd to it.

This may perhaps be thought a little too severe by the natural indulgence of tender parents; but yet it is no more than necessary: For since the method I propose is to banish the rod, this restraint of their tongues will be of great use to settle that awe we have elsewhere spoken of, and to keep up in them the respect and reverence due to their parents. Next, it will teach to keep in, and so master their inclinations. By this means they will be brought to learn the art of stifling their desires, as soon as they rise up in them, when they are easiest to be subdu'd. For giving vent, gives life and strength to our appetites; and he that has the confidence to turn his wishes into demands, will be but a little way from thinking he ought to obtain them. This, I am sure, every one can more easily bear a denial from himself, than from any body else. They should therefore be accustom'd betimes to consult, and make use of their reason, before they give allowance to their inclinations. 'Tis a great step towards the mastery of our desires, to give this stop to them, and shut them up in silence. This habit got by children, of staying the forwardness of their fancies, and deliberating whether it be fit or no, before they speak, will be of no small advantage to them in matters of greater consequence, in the future course of their lives. For that which I cannot too often inculcate, is, that whatever the matter be about which it is conversant, whether great or small, the main (I had almost said only) thing to be consider'd in every action of a child, is, what influence it will have upon his mind; what habit it tends to, and is like to settle in him; how it will become him when he is bigger; and if it be encourag'd, whither it will lead him when he is grown up.

My meaning therefore is not, that children should purposely be made uneasy. This would relish too much of inhumanity and ill-nature, and be apt to infect them with it. They should be brought to deny their appetites; and their minds, as well as bodies, be made vigorous, easy, and strong, by the custom of having their inclinations in subjection, and their bodies exercis'd with hardships: But all this, without giving them any mark or apprehension of ill-will towards them. The constant loss of what they crav'd or carv'd to themselves, should teach them modesty, submission, and a power to forbear: But the rewarding their modesty, and silence, by giving them what they lik'd, should also assure them of the love of those who rigorously exacted this obedience. The contenting themselves now in the want of what they wish'd for, is a virtue that another time should be rewarded with what is suited and acceptable to them; which should be bestow'd on them as if it were a natural consequence of their good behaviour, and not a bargain about it. But you will lose your labour, and what is more, their love and reverence too, if they can receive from others what you deny them. This is to be kept very staunch, and carefully to be watch'd. And here the servants come again my way.

§ 108. If this be begun betimes, and they accustom themselves early to silence their desires, this useful habit will settle them; and as they come to grow up in age and discretion, they may be allow'd greater liberty, when reason comes to speak in 'em, and not passion: For whenever reason would speak, it should be hearken'd to. But as they should never be heard, when they speak for any particular thing they would have, unless it be first propos'd to them; so they should always be heard, and fairly and kindly answer'd, when they ask after any thing they would know, and desire to be inform'd about. Curiosity should be as carefully cherish'd in children, as other appetites suppress'd.

However strict an hand is to be kept upon all desires of fancy, yet there is one case wherein fancy must be permitted to speak, and be hearken'd to also. Recreation is as necessary as labour or food. But because there can be no recreation without delight, which depends not always on reason, but oftner fancy, it must be permitted children not only to divert themselves, but to do it after their own fashion, provided it be innocently, and without prejudice to their health; and therefore in this case they should not be deny'd, if they proposed any particular kind of recreation. Tho' I think in a well-order'd education, they will seldom be brought to the necessity of asking any such liberty. Care should be taken, that what is of advantage to them, they should always do with delight; and before they are weary'd with one, they should be timely diverted to some other useful employment. But if they are not yet brought to that degree of perfection, that one way of improvement can be made a recreation to them, they must be let loose to the childish play they fancy; which they should be wean'd from by being made to surfeit of it: But from things of use, that they are employ'd in, they should always be sent away with an appetite; at least be dismiss'd before they are tir'd, and grow quite sick of it, that so they may return to it again, as to a pleasure that diverts them. For you must never think them set right, till they can find delight in the practice of laudable things; and the useful exercises of the body and mind, taking their turns, make their lives and improvement pleasant in a continu'd train of recreations, wherein the weary'd part is constantly reliev'd and refresh'd. Whether this can be done in every temper, or whether tutors and parents will be at the pains, and have the discretion and patience to bring them to this, I know not; but that it may be done in most children, if a right course be taken to raise in them the desire of credit, esteem, and reputation, I do not at all doubt. And when they have so much true life put into them, they may freely be talk'd with about what most delights them, and be directed or let loose to it; so that they may perceive that they are belov'd and cherish'd, and that those under whose tuition they are, are not enemies to their satisfaction. Such a management will make them in love with the hand that directs them, and the virtue they are directed to.

This farther advantage may be made by a free liberty permitted them in their recreations, that it will discover their natural tempers, shew their inclinations and aptitudes, and thereby direct wise parents in the choice both of the course of life and employment they shall design them for, and of fit remedies, in the mean time, to be apply'd to whatever bent of nature they may observe most likely to mislead any of their children.

§ 109. 2. Children who live together, often strive for mastery, whose wills shall carry it over the rest: whoever begins the contest, should be sure to be cross'd in it. But not only that, but they should be taught to have all the deference, complaisance, and civility one for the other imaginable. This, when they see it procures them respect, love and esteem, and that they lose no superiority by it, they will take more pleasure in, than in insolent domineering; for so plainly is the other.

The accusations of children one against another, which usually are but the clamours of anger and revenge desiring aid, should not be favourably received, nor hearken'd to. It weakens and effeminates their minds to suffer them to complain; and if they endure sometimes crossing or pain from others without being permitted to think it strange or intolerable, it will do them no harm to learn sufferance, and harden them early. But though you give no countenance to the complaints of the querulous, yet take care to curb the insolence and ill nature of the injurious. When you observe it yourself, reprove it before the injur'd party: but if the complaint be of something really worth your notice, and prevention another time, then reprove the offender by himself alone, out of sight of him that complain'd and make him go and ask pardon, and make reparation: which coming thus, as it were from himself, will be the more chearfully performed, and more kindly receiv'd, the love strengthen'd between them, and a custom of civility grow familiar amongst your children.

§ 110. 3. As to the having and possessing of things, teach them to part with what they have, easily and freely to their friends, and let them find by experience that the most liberal has always the most plenty, with esteem and commendation to boot, and they will quickly learn to practise it. This I imagine, will make brothers and sisters kinder and civiller to one another, and consequently to others, than twenty rules about good manners, with which children are ordinarily perplex'd and cumber'd. Covetousness, and the desire of having in our possession, and under our dominion, more than we have need of, being the root of all evil, should be early and carefully weeded out, and the contrary quality of a readiness to impart to others, implanted. This should be encourag'd by great commendation and credit, and constantly taking care that he loses nothing by his liberality. Let all the instances he gives of such freeness be always repay'd, and with interest; and let him sensibly perceive, that the kindness he shews to others, is no ill husbandry for himself; but that it brings a return of kindness both from those that receive it, and those who look on. Make this a contest among children, who shall out-do one another this way: and by this means, by a constant practice, children having made it easy to themselves to part with what they have, good nature may be settled in them into an habit, and they may take pleasure, and pique themselves in being kind, liberal and civil, to others.

If liberality ought to be encourag'd certainly great care is to be taken that children transgress not the rules of Justice: and whenever they do, they should be set right, and if there be occasion for it, severely rebuk'd.

Our first actions being guided more by self-love than reason or reflection, 'tis no wonder that in children they should be very apt to deviate from the just measures of right and wrong; which are in the mind the result of improv'd reason and serious meditation. This the more they are apt to mistake, the more careful guard ought to be kept over them; and every the least slip in this great social virtue taken notice of, and rectify'd; and that in things of the least weight and moment, both to instruct their ignorance, and prevent ill habits; which from small beginnings in pins and cherry-stones, will, if let alone, grow up to higher frauds, and be in danger to end at last in downright harden'd dishonesty. The first tendency to any injustice that appears, must be suppress'd with a shew of wonder and abhorrence in the parents and governors. But because children cannot well comprehend what injustice is, till they understand property, and how particular persons come by it, the safest way to secure honesty, is to lay the foundations of it early in liberality, and an easiness to part with to others whatever they have or like themselves. This may be taught them early, before they have language and understanding enough to form distinct notions of property, and to know what is theirs by a peculiar right exclusive of others. And since children seldom have any thing but by gift, and that for the most part from their parents, they may be at first taught not to take or keep any thing but what is given them by those, whom they take to have power over it. And as their capacities enlarge, other rules and cases of justice, and rights concerning Meum and Tuum, may be propos'd and inculcated. If any act of injustice in them appears to proceed, not from mistake, but a perverseness in their wills, when a gentle rebuke and shame will not reform this irregular and covetous inclination, rougher remedies must be apply'd: And 'tis but for the father and tutor to take and keep from them something that they value and think their own, or order somebody else to do it; and by such instances, make them sensible what little advantage they are like to make by possessing themselves unjustly of what is another's, whilst there are in the world stronger and more men than they. But if an ingenuous detestation of this shameful vice be but carefully and early instill'd into 'em, as I think it may, that is the true and genuine method to obviate this crime, and will be a better guard against dishonesty than any considerations drawn from interest; habits working more constantly, and with greater facility, than reason, which, when we have most need of it, is seldom fairly consulted, and more rarely obey'd.

Sections 111–120

§ 111. Crying is a fault that should not be tolerated in children; not only for the unpleasant and unbecoming noise it fills the house with, but for more considerable reasons, in reference to the children themselves; which is to be our aim in education.

Their crying is of two sorts; either stubborn and domineering, or querulous and whining.

1. Their crying is very often a striving for mastery, and an open declaration of their insolence or obstinacy; when they have not the power to obtain their desire, they will, by their clamour and sobbing, maintain their title and right to it. This is an avow'd continuing their claim, and a sort of remonstrance against the oppression and injustice of those who deny them what they have a mind to.

§ 112. 2. Sometimes their crying is the effect of pain, or true sorrow, and a bemoaning themselves under it.

These two, if carefully observ'd, may, by the mien, looks, actions, and particularly by the tone of their crying be easily distinguished; but neither of them must be suffer'd, much less encourag'd.

1. The obstinate or stomachful crying should by no means be permitted, because it is but another way of flattering their desires, and encouraging those passions which 'tis our main business to subdue: and if it be, as often it is, upon the receiving any correction, it quite defeats all the good effects of it; for any chastisement which leaves them in this declar'd opposition, only serves to make them worse. The restraints and punishments laid on children are all misapply'd and lost, as far as they do not prevail over their wills, teach them to submit their passions, and make their minds supple and pliant to what their parents' reason advises them now, and so prepare them to obey what their own reason shall advise hereafter. But if in any thing wherein they are cross'd, they may be suffer'd to go away crying, they confirm themselves in their desires, and cherish the ill humour, with a declaration of their right, and a resolution to satisfy their inclination the first opportunity. This therefore is another argument against the frequent use of blows: for, whenever you come to that extremity, 'tis not enough to whip or beat them, you must do it, till you find you have subdu'd their minds, till with submission and patience they yield to the correction; which you shall best discover by their crying, and their ceasing from it upon your bidding. Without this, the beating of children is but a passionate tyranny over them; and it is mere cruelty, and not correction, to put their bodies in pain, without doing their minds any good. As this gives us a reason why children should seldom be corrected, so it also prevents their being so. For if, whenever they are chastis'd, it were done thus without passion, soberly, and yet effectually too, laying on the blows and smart not furiously, and all at once, but slowly, with reasoning between, and with observation how it wrought, stopping when it had made them pliant, penitent and yielding; they would seldom need the like punishment again, being made careful to avoid the fault that deserv'd it. Besides, by this means, as the punishment would not be lost for being too little, and not effectual, so it would be kept from being too much, if we gave off as soon as we perceiv'd that it reach'd the mind, and that was better'd. For since the chiding or beating of children should be always the least that possibly may be, that which is laid on in the heat of anger, seldom observes that measure, but is commonly more than it should be, though it prove less than enough.

§ 113. 2. Many children are apt to cry, upon any little pain they suffer, and the least harm that befalls them puts them into complaints and bawling. This few children avoid: for it being the first and natural way to declare their sufferings or wants, before they can speak, the compassion that is thought due to that tender age foolishly encourages, and continues it in them long after they can speak. 'Tis the duty, I confess, of those about children, to compassionate them, whenever they suffer any hurt; but not to shew it in pitying them. Help and ease them the best you can, but by no means bemoan them. This softens their minds, and makes them yield to the little harms that happen to them; whereby they sink deeper into that part which alone feels, and makes larger wounds there, than otherwise they would. They should be harden'd against all sufferings, especially of the body, and have no tenderness but what rises from an ingenuous shame, and a quick sense of reputation. The many inconveniences this life is expos'd to, require we should not be too sensible of every little hurt. What our minds yield not to, makes but a slight impression, and does us but very little harm.

'Tis the suffering of our spirits that gives and continues the pain. This brawniness and insensibility of mind, is the best armour we can have against the common evils and accidents of life; and being a temper that is to be got by exercise and custom, more than any other way, the practice of it should be begun betimes; and happy is he that is taught it early. That effeminacy of spirit, which is to be prevented or cured, as nothing that I know so much increases in children as crying; so nothing, on the other side, so much checks and restrains, as their being hinder'd from that sort of complaining. In the little harms they suffer from knocks and falls, they should not be pitied for falling, but bid do so again; which besides that it stops their crying, is a better way to cure their heedlessness, and prevent their tumbling another time, than either chiding or bemoaning them. But, let the hurts they receive be what they will, stop their crying, and that will give them more quiet and ease at present, and harden them for the future.

§ 114. The former sort of crying requires severity to silence it; and where a look, or a positive command will not do it, blows must: for it proceeding from pride, obstinacy, and stomach, the will, where the fault lies, must be bent, and made to comply, by a rigour sufficient to master it. But this latter being ordinarily from softness of mind, a quite contrary cause, ought to be treated with a gentler hand. Persuasion, or diverting the thoughts another way, or laughing at their whining, may perhaps be at first the proper method: but for this, the circumstances of the thing, and the particular temper of the child, must be considered. No certain unvariable rules can be given about it; but it must be left to the prudence of the parents or tutor. But this, I think, I may say in general, that there should be a constant discountenancing of this sort of crying also; and that the father, by his authority, should always stop it, mixing a greater degree of roughness in his looks or words, proportionately as the child is of a greater age, or a sturdier temper: But always let it be enough to silence their whimpering, and put an end to the disorder.

§ 115. Cowardice and courage are so nearly related to the foremention'd tempers, that it may not be amiss here to take notice of them. Fear is a passion that, if rightly governed, has its use. And though self-love seldom fails to keep it watchful and high enough in us, yet there may be an excess on the daring side; fool-hardiness and insensibility of danger being as little reasonable, as trembling and shrinking at the approach of every little evil. Fear was given us as a monitor to quicken our industry, and keep us upon our guard against the approaches of evil; and therefore to have no apprehension of mischief at hand, not to make a just estimate of the danger, but heedlessly to run into it, be the hazard what it will, without considering of what use or consequence it may be, is not the resolution of a rational creature, but brutish fury. Those who have children of this temper, have nothing to do, but a little to awaken their reason, which self-preservation will quickly dispose them to hearken to, unless (which is usually the case) some other passion hurries them on head-long, without sense and without consideration. A dislike of evil is so natural to mankind, that nobody, I think, can be without fear of it: fear being nothing but an uneasiness under the apprehension of that coming upon us, which we dislike. And therefore, whenever any one runs into danger, we may say, 'tis under the conduct of ignorance, or the command of some more imperious passion, nobody being so much an enemy to himself, as to come within the reach of evil, out of free choice, and court danger for danger's sake. If it be therefore pride, vain-glory, or rage, that silences a child's fear, or makes him not hearken to its advice, those are by fit means to be abated, that a little consideration may allay his heat, and make him bethink himself, whether this attempt be worth the venture. But this being a fault that children are not so often guilty of, I shall not be more particular in its cure. Weakness of spirit is the more common defect, and therefore will require the greater care.

Fortitude is the guard and support of the other virtues; and without courage a man will scarce keep steady to his duty, and fill up the character of a truly worthy man.

Courage, that makes us bear up against dangers that we fear and evils that we feel, is of great use in an estate, as ours is in this life, expos'd to assaults on all hands: and therefore it is very advisable to get children into this armour as early as we can. Natural temper, I confess, does here a great deal: but even where that is defective, and the heart is in itself weak and timorous, it may, by a right management, be brought to a better resolution. What is to be done to prevent breaking children's spirits by frightful apprehensions instill'd into them when young, or bemoaning themselves under every little suffering, I have already taken notice; how to harden their tempers, and raise their courage, if we find them too much subject to fear, is farther to be consider'd.

True fortitude, I take to be the quiet possession of a man's self, and an undisturb'd doing his duty, whatever evil besets, or danger lies in his way. This there are so few men attain to, that we are not to expect it from children. But yet something may be done: and a wise conduct by insensible degrees may carry them farther than one expects.

The neglect of this great care of them, whilst they are young, is the reason, perhaps, why there are so few that have this virtue in its full latitude when they are men. I should not say this in a nation so naturally brave, as ours is, did I think that true fortitude required nothing but courage in the field, and a contempt of life in the face of an enemy. This, I confess, is not the least part of it, nor can be denied the laurels and honours always justly due to the valour of those who venture their lives for their country. But yet this is not all. Dangers attack us in other places besides the field of battle; and though death be the king of terrors, yet pain, disgrace and poverty, have frightful looks, able to discompose most men whom they seem ready to seize on: and there are those who contemn some of these, and yet are heartily frighted with the other. True fortitude is prepar'd for dangers of all kinds, and unmoved, whatsoever evil it be that threatens. I do not mean unmoved with any fear at all. Where danger shews it self, apprehension cannot, without stupidity, be wanting; where danger is, sense of danger should be; and so much fear as should keep us awake, and excite our attention, industry, and vigour; but not disturb the calm use of our reason, nor hinder the execution of what that dictates.

The first step to get this noble and manly steadiness, is, what I have above mentioned, carefully to keep children from frights of all kinds, when they are young. Let not any fearful apprehensions be talk'd into them, nor terrible objects surprise them. This often so shatters and discomposes the spirits, that they never recover it again; but during their whole life, upon the first suggestion or appearance of any terrifying idea, are scatter'd and confounded; the body is enervated, and the mind disturb'd, and the man scarce himself, or capable of any composed or rational action. Whether this be from an habitual motion of the animal spirits, introduc'd by the first strong impression, or from the alteration of the constitution by some more unaccountable way, this is certain, that so it is. Instances of such who in a weak timorous mind, have borne, all their whole lives through, the effects of a fright when they were young, are every where to be seen, and therefore as much as may be to be prevented.

The next thing is by gentle degrees to accustom children to those things they are too much afraid of. But here great caution is to be used, that you do not make too much haste, nor attempt this cure too early, for fear lest you increase the mischief instead of remedying it. Little ones in arms may be easily kept out of the way of terrifying objects, and till they can talk and understand what is said to them, are scarce capable of that reasoning and discourse which should be used to let them know there is no harm in those frightful objects, which we would make them familiar with, and do, to that purpose by gentle degrees bring nearer and nearer to them. And therefore 'tis seldom there is need of any application to them of this kind, till after they can run about and talk. But yet, if it should happen that infants should have taken offence at any thing which cannot be easily kept out of their way, and that they shew marks of terror as often as it comes in sight; all the allays of fright, by diverting their thoughts, or mixing pleasant and agreeable appearances with it, must be used, till it be grown familiar and inoffensive to them.

I think we may observe, that, when children are first born, all objects of sight that do not hurt the eyes, are indifferent to them; and they are no more afraid of a blackamoor or a lion, than of their nurse or a cat. What is it then, that afterwards, in certain mixtures of shape and colour, comes to affright them? Nothing but the apprehensions of harm that accompanies those things. Did a child suck every day a new nurse, I make account it would be no more affrighted with the change of faces at six months old, than at sixty. The reason then why it will not come to a stranger, is, because having been accustomed to receive its food and kind usage only from one or two that are about it, the child apprehends, by coming into the arms of a stranger, the being taken from what delights and feeds it and every moment supplies its wants, which it often feels, and therefore fears when the nurse is away.

The only thing we naturally are afraid of is pain, or loss of pleasure. And because these are not annexed to any shape, colour, or size of visible objects, we are frighted with none of them, till either we have felt pain from them, or have notions put into us that they will do us harm. The pleasant brightness and lustre of flame and fire so delights children, that at first they always desire to be handling of it: but when constant experience has convinced them, by the exquisite pain it has put them to, how cruel and unmerciful it is, they are afraid to touch it, and carefully avoid it. This being the ground of fear, 'tis not hard to find whence it arises, and how it is to be cured in all mistaken objects of terror. And when the mind is confirm'd against them, and has got a mastery over it self and its usual fears in lighter occasions, it is in good preparation to meet more real dangers. Your child shrieks, and runs away at the sight of a frog; let another catch it, and lay it down at a good distance from him: at first accustom him to look upon it; when he can do that, then to come nearer to it, and see it leap without emotion; then to touch it lightly, when it is held fast in another's hand; and so on, till he can come to handle it as confidently as a butterfly or a sparrow. By the same way any other vain terrors may be remov'd; if care be taken, that you go not too fast, and push not the child on to a new degree of assurance, till he be thoroughly confirm'd in the former. And thus the young soldier is to be train'd on to the warfare of life; wherein care is to be taken, that more things be not represented as dangerous than really are so; and then, that whatever you observe him to be more frighted at than he should, you be sure to tole him on to by insensible degrees, till he at last, quitting his fears, masters the difficulty, and comes off with applause. Successes of this kind, often repeated, will make him find, that evils are not always so certain or so great as our fears represent them; and that the way to avoid them, is not to run away, or be discompos'd, dejected, and deterr'd by fear, where either our credit or duty requires us to go on.

But since the great foundation of fear in children is pain, the way to harden and fortify children against fear and danger is to accustom them to suffer pain. This 'tis possible will be thought, by kind parents, a very unnatural thing towards their children; and by most, unreasonable, to endeavour to reconcile any one to the sense of pain, by bringing it upon him. 'Twill be said: 'It may perhaps give the child an aversion for him that makes him suffer; but can never recommend to him suffering itself. This is a strange method. You will not have children whipp'd and punish'd for their faults, but you would have them tormented for doing well, or for tormenting sake.' I doubt not but such objections as these will be made, and I shall be thought inconsistent with my self, or fantastical, in proposing it. I confess, it is a thing to be managed with great discretion, and therefore it falls not out amiss, that it will not be receiv'd or relish'd, but by those who consider well, and look into the reason of things. I would not have children much beaten for their faults, because I would not have them think bodily pain the greatest punishment: and I would have them, when they do well, be sometimes put in pain, for the same reason, that they might be accustom'd to bear it, without looking on it as the greatest evil. How much education may reconcile young people to pain and sufference, the examples of Sparta do sufficiently shew: and they who have once brought themselves not to think bodily pain the greatest of evils, or that which they ought to stand most in fear of, have made no small advance towards virtue. But I am not so foolish to propose the Lacedæmonian discipline in our age or constitution. But yet I do say, that inuring children gently to suffer some degrees of pain without shrinking, is a way to gain firmness to their minds, and lay a foundation for courage and resolution in the future part of their lives.

Not to bemoan them, or permit them to bemoan themselves, on every little pain they suffer, is the first step to be made. But of this I have spoken elsewhere.

The next thing is, sometimes designedly to put them in pain: but care must be taken that this be done when the child is in good humour, and satisfied of the good-will and kindness of him that hurts him, at the time that he does it. There must no marks of anger or displeasure on the one side, nor compassion or repenting on the other, go along with it: and it must be sure to be no more than the child can bear without repining or taking it amiss, or for a punishment. Managed by these degrees, and with such circumstances, I have seen a child run away laughing with good smart blows of a wand on his back, who would have cried for an unkind word, and have been very sensible of the chastisement of a cold look, from the same person. Satisfy a child by a constant course of your care and kindness, that you perfectly love him, and he may by degrees be accustom'd to bear very painful and rough usage from you, without flinching or complaining: and this we see children do every day in play one with another. The softer you find your child is, the more you are to seek occasions, at fit times, thus to harden him. The great art in this is, to begin with what is but very little painful, and to proceed by insensible degrees, when you are playing, and in good humour with him, and speaking well of him: and when you have once got him to think himself made amends for his suffering by the praise is given him for his courage; when he can take a pride in giving such marks of his manliness, and can prefer the reputation of being brave and stout, to the avoiding a little pain, or the shrinking under it; you need not despair in time and by the assistance of his growing reason, to master his timorousness, and mend the weakness of his constitution. As he grows bigger, he is to be set upon bolder attempts than his natural temper carries him to; and whenever he is observ'd to flinch from what one has reason to think he would come off well in, if he had but courage to undertake, that he should be assisted in at first, and by degrees sham'd to, till at last practice has given more assurance, and with it a mastery; which must be rewarded with great praise, and the good opinion of others, for his performance. When by these steps he has got resolution enough not to be deterr'd from what he ought to do, by the apprehension of danger; when fear does not, in sudden or hazardous occurrences, discompose his mind, set his body a-trembling, and make him unfit for action, or run away from it, he has then the courage of a rational creature: and such an hardiness we should endeavour by custom and use to bring children to, as proper occasions come in our way.

§ 116. One thing I have frequently observ'd in children, that when they have got possession of any poor creature, they are apt to use it ill: they often torment, and treat very roughly, young birds, butterflies, and such other poor animals which fall into their hands, and that with a seeming kind of pleasure. This I think should be watched in them, and if they incline to any such cruelty, they should be taught to contrary usage. For the custom of tormenting and killing of beasts, will, by degrees, harden their minds even towards men; and they who delight in the suffering and destruction of inferior creatures, will not be apt to be very compassionate or benign to those of their own kind. Our practice takes notice of this in the exclusion of butchers from juries of life and death. Children should from the beginning be bred up in an abhorrence of killing or tormenting any living creature; and be taught not to spoil or destroy any thing, unless it be for the preservation or advantage of some other that is nobler. And truly, if the preservation of all mankind, as much as in him lies, were every one's persuasion, as indeed it is every one's duty, and the true principle to regulate our religion, politics and morality by, the world would be much quieter, and better natur'd than it is. But to return to our present business; I cannot but commend both the kindness and prudence of a mother I knew, who was wont always to indulge her daughters, when any of them desired dogs, squirrels, birds, or any such things as young girls use to be delighted with: but then, when they had them, they must be sure to keep them well, and look diligently after them, that they wanted nothing, or were not ill used. For if they were negligent in their care of them, it was counted a great fault, which often forfeited their possession, or at least they fail'd not to be rebuked for it; whereby they were early taught diligence and good nature. And indeed, I think people should be accustomed, from their cradles, to be tender to all sensible creatures, and to spoil or waste nothing at all.

This delight they take in doing of mischief, whereby I mean spoiling of any thing to no purpose, but more especially the pleasure they take to put any thing in pain, that is capable of it; I cannot persuade my self to be any other than a foreign and introduced disposition, an habit borrowed from custom and conversation. People teach children to strike, and laugh when they hurt or see harm come to others: and they have the examples of most about them, to confirm them in it. All the entertainment and talk of history is nothing almost but fighting and killing: and the honour and renown that is bestowed on conquerors (who for the most part are but the great butchers of mankind) farther mislead growing youth, who by this means come to think slaughter the laudable business of mankind, and the most heroic of virtues. By these steps unnatural cruelty is planted in us; and what humanity abhors, custom reconciles and recommends to us, by laying it in the way to honour. Thus, by fashion and opinion, that comes to be a pleasure, which in itself neither is, nor can be any. This ought carefully to be watched, and early remedied; so as to settle and cherish the contrary and more natural temper of benignity and compassion in the room of it; but still by the same gentle methods which are to be applied to the other two faults before mention'd. It may not perhaps be unreasonable here to add this farther caution, viz., That the mischiefs or harms that come by play, inadvertency, or ignorance, and were not known to be harms, or design'd for mischief's sake, though they may perhaps be sometimes of considerable damage, yet are not at all, or but very gently, to be taken notice of. For this, I think, I cannot too often inculcate, that whatever miscarriage a child is guilty of, and whatever be the consequence of it, the thing to be regarded in taking notice of it, is only what root it springs from, and what habit it is like to establish: and to that the correction ought to be directed, and the child not to suffer any punishment for any harm which may have come by his play or inadvertency. The faults to be amended lie in the mind; and if they are such as either age will cure, or no ill habits will follow from, the present action, whatever displeasing circumstances it may have, is to be passed by without any animadversion.

§ 117. Another way to instill sentiments of humanity, and to keep them lively in young folks, will be, to accustom them to civility in their language and deportment towards their inferiors and the meaner sort of people, particularly servants. It is not unusual to observe the children in gentlemen's families treat the servants of the house with domineering words, names of contempt, and an imperious carriage; as if they were of another race and species beneath them. Whether ill example, the advantage of fortune, or their natural vanity, inspire this haughtiness, it should be prevented, or weeded out; and a gentle, courteous, affable carriage towards the lower ranks of men, placed in the room of it. No part of their superiority will be hereby lost; but the distinction increased, and their authority strengthen'd; when love in inferiors is join'd to outward respect, and an esteem of the person has a share in their submission: and domestics will pay a more ready and chearful service, when they find themselves not spurn'd because fortune has laid them below the level of others at their master's feet. Children should not be suffer'd to lose the consideration of human nature in the shufflings of outward conditions. The more they have, the better humor'd they should be taught to be, and the more compassionate and gentle to those of their brethren who are placed lower, and have scantier portions. If they are suffer'd from their cradles to treat men ill and rudely, because, by their father's title, they think they have a little power over them, at best it is ill-bred; and if care be not taken, will by degrees nurse up their natural pride into an habitual contempt of those beneath them. And where will that probably end but in oppression and cruelty?

§ 118. Curiosity in children (which I had occasion just to mention § 108) is but an appetite after knowledge; and therefore ought to be encouraged in them, not only as a good sign, but as the great instrument nature has provided to remove that ignorance they were born with; and which, without this busy inquisitiveness, will make them dull and useless creatures. The ways to encourage it, and keep it active and busy, are, I suppose, these following:

1. Not to check or discountenance any enquiries he shall make, nor suffer them to be laugh'd at; but to answer all his questions, and explain the matter he desires to know, so as to make them as much intelligible to him as suits the capacity of his age and knowledge. But confound not his understanding with explications or notions that are above it; or with the variety or number of things that are not to his present purpose. Mark what 'tis his mind aims at in the question, and not what words he expresses it in: and when you have informed and satisfied him in that, you shall see how his thoughts will enlarge themselves, and how by fit answers he may be led on farther than perhaps you could imagine. For knowledge is grateful to the understanding, as light to the eyes: children are pleased and delighted with it exceedingly, especially if they see that their enquiries are regarded, and that their desire of knowing is encouraged and commended. And I doubt not but one great reason why many children abandon themselves wholly to silly sports, and trifle away all their time insipidly, is, because they have found their curiosity baulk'd, and their enquiries neglected. But had they been treated with more kindness and respect, and their questions answered, as they should, to their satisfaction; I doubt not but they would have taken more pleasure in learning, and improving their knowledge, wherein there would be still newness and variety, which is what they are delighted with, than in returning over and over to the same play and play-things.

§ 119. 2. To this serious answering their questions, and informing their understandings, in what they desire, as if it were a matter that needed it, should be added some peculiar ways of commendation. Let others whom they esteem, be told before their faces of the knowledge they have in such and such things; and since we are all, even from our cradles, vain and proud creatures, let their vanity be flatter'd with things that will do them good; and let their pride set them on work on something which may turn to their advantage. Upon this ground you shall find, that there cannot be a greater spur to the attaining what you would have the eldest learn, and know himself, than to set him upon teaching it his younger brothers and sisters.

§ 120. 3. As children's enquiries are not to be slighted; so also great care is to be taken, that they never receive deceitful and eluding answers. They easily perceive when they are slighted or deceived; and quickly learn the trick of neglect, dissimulation and falsehood, which they observe others to make use of. We are not to intrench upon truth in any conversation, but least of all with children; since if we play false with them, we not only deceive their expectation, and hinder their knowledge, but corrupt their innocence, and teach them the worst of vices. They are travellers newly arrived in a strange country, of which they know nothing; we should therefore make conscience not to mislead them. And though their questions seem sometimes not very material, yet they should be seriously answer'd; for however they may appear to us (to whom they are long since known) enquiries not worth the making; they are of moment to those who are wholly ignorant. Children are strangers to all we are acquainted with; and all the things they meet with, are at first unknown to them, as they once were to us: and happy are they who meet with civil people, that will comply with their ignorance, and help them to get out of it.

If you or I now should be set down in Japan, with all our prudence and knowledge about us, a conceit whereof makes us, perhaps, so apt to slight the thoughts and enquiries of children; should we, I say, be set down in Japan, we should, no doubt (if we would inform our selves of what is there to be known) ask a thousand questions, which, to a supercilious or inconsiderate Japaner, would seem very idle and impertinent; though to us they would be very material and of importance to be resolved; and we should be glad to find a man so complaisant and courteous, as to satisfy our demands, and instruct our ignorance.

When any new thing comes in their way, children usually ask the common question of a stranger: What is it? Whereby they ordinarily mean nothing but the name; and therefore to tell them how it is call'd, is usually the proper answer to that demand. And the next question usually is, What is it for? And to this it should be answered truly and directly. The use of the thing should be told, and the way explained, how it serves to such a purpose, as far as their capacities can comprehend it. And so of any other circumstances they shall ask about it; not turning them going, till you have given them all the satisfaction they are capable of; and so leading them by your answers into farther questions. And perhaps to a grown man, such conversation will not be altogether so idle and insignificant as we are apt to imagine. The native and untaught suggestions of inquisitive children do often offer things, that may set a considering man's thoughts on work. And I think there is frequently more to be learn'd from the unexpected questions of a child, than the discourses of men, who talk in a road, according to the notions they have borrowed, and the prejudices of their education.

Sections 121–130

§ 121. 4. Perhaps it may not sometimes be amiss to excite their curiosity by bringing strange and new things in their way, on purpose to engage their enquiry, and give them occasion to inform themselves about them and if by chance their curiosity leads them to ask what they should not know, it is a great deal better to tell them plainly, that it is a thing that belongs not to them to know, than to pop them off with a falsehood of a frivolous answer.

§ 122. Pertness, that appears sometimes so early, proceeds from a principle that seldom accompanies a strong constitution of body, or ripens into a strong judgment of mind. If it were desirable to have a child a more brisk talker, I believe there might be ways found to make him so: But I suppose a wise father had rather that his son should be able and useful, when a man, than pretty company, and a diversion to others, whilst a child: though if that too were to be consider'd, I think I may say, there is not so much pleasure to have a child prattle agreeably, as to reason well. Encourage therefore his inquisitiveness all you can, by satisfying his demands, and informing his judgment, as far as it is capable. When his reasons are any way tolerable, let him find the credit and commendation of it: and when they are quite out of the way, let him, without being laugh'd at for his mistake be gently put into the right; and if he shew a forwardness to be reasoning about things that come in his way, take care, as much as you can, that no body check this inclination in him, or mislead it by captious or fallacious ways of talking with him. For when all is done, this, as the highest and most important faculty of our minds, deserves the greatest care and attention in cultivating it: the right improvement, and exercise of our reason being the highest perfection that a man can attain to in this life.

§ 123. Contrary to this busy inquisitive temper, there is sometimes observable in children, a listless carelessness, a want of regard to any thing, and a sort of trifling even at their business. This sauntring humour I look on as one of the worst qualities can appear in a child, as well as one of the hardest to be cured, where it is natural. But it being liable to be mistaken in some cases, care must be taken to make a right judgment concerning than trifling at their books or business, which may sometimes be complained of in a child. Upon the first suspicion a father has, that his son is of a sauntring temper, he must carefully observe him, whether he be listless and indifferent in all in his actions, or whether in some things alone he be slow and sluggish, but in others vigorous and eager. For tho' we find that he does loiter at his book, and let a good deal of the time he spends in his chamber or study, run idly away; he must not presently conclude, that this is from a sauntring humour in his temper. It may be childishness, and a preferring something to his study, which his thoughts run on; and he dislikes his book, as is natural, because it is forced upon him as a task. To know this perfectly, you must watch him at play, when he is out of his place and time of study, following his own inclination; and see there whether he be stirring and active; whether he designs any thing, and with labour and eagerness pursues it, till he has accomplished what he aimed at, or whether he lazily and listlessly dreams away his time. If this sloth be only when he is about his book, I think it may be easily cured. If it be in his temper, it will require a little more pains and attention to remedy it.

§ 124. If you are satisfied by his earnestness at play, or any thing else he sets his mind on, in the intervals between his hours of business, that he is not of himself inclined to laziness, but that only want of relish of his book makes him negligent and sluggish in his application to it; the first step is to try by talking to him kindly of the folly and inconvenience of it, whereby he loses a good part of his time, which he might have for his diversion: but be sure to talk calmly and kindly, and not much at first, but only these plain reasons in short. If this prevails, you have gain'd the point in the most desirable way, which is that of reason and kindness. If this softer application prevails not, try to shame him out of it, by laughing at him for it, asking every day, when he comes to table, if there be no strangers there, how long he was that day about his business: And if he has not done it in the time he might be well supposed to have dispatched it, expose and turn him into ridicule for it; but mix no chiding, only put on a pretty cold brow towards him, and keep it till he reform; and let his mother, tutor, and all about him do so too. If this work not the effect you desire, then tell him he shall be no longer troubled with a tutor to take care of his education, you will not be at the charge to have him spend his time idly with him; but since he prefers this or that [whatever play he delights in] to his book, that only he shall do; and so in earnest set him to work on his beloved play, and keep him steadily, and in earnest, to it morning and afternoon, till he be fully surfeited, and would, at any rate, change it for some hours at his book again. But when you thus set him his task of play, you must be sure to look after him your self, or set somebody else to do it, that may constantly see him employed in it, and that he be not permitted to be idle at that too. I say, your self look after him; for it is worth a father's while, whatever business he has, to bestow two or three days upon his son, to cure so great a mischief as his sauntring at his business.

§ 125. This is what I propose, if it be idleness, not from his general temper, but a peculiar or acquir'd aversion to learning, which you must be careful to examine and distinguish. But though you have your eyes upon him, to watch what he does with the time which he has at his own disposal, yet you must not let him perceive that you or any body else do so; for that may hinder him from following his own inclination, which he being full of, and not daring, for fear of you, to prosecute what his head and heart are set upon, he may neglect all other things, which then he relishes not, and so may seem to be idle and listless, when in truth it is nothing but being intent on that, which the fear of your eye or knowledge keeps him from executing. To be clear in this point, the observation must be made when you are out of the way, and he not so much as under the restraint of a suspicion that any body has an eye upon him. In those seasons of perfect freedom, let some body you can trust mark how he spends his time, whether he unactively loiters it away, when without any check he is left to his own inclination. Thus, by his employing of such times of liberty, you will easily discern, whether it be listlessness in his temper, or aversion to his book, that makes him saunter away his time of study.

§ 126. If some defect in his constitution has cast a damp on his mind, and he be naturally listless and dreaming, this unpromising disposition is none of the easiest to be dealt with, because, generally carrying with it an unconcernedness for the future, it wants the two great springs of action, foresight and desire; which how to plant and increase, where nature has given a cold and contrary temper, will be the question. As soon as you are satisfied that this is the case, you must carefully enquire whether there be nothing he delights in; Inform your self what it is he is most pleased with; and if you can find any particular tendency his mind hath, increase it all you can, and make use of that to set him on work, and to excite his industry. If he loves praise, or play, or fine clothes, &c. or, on the other side, dreads pain, disgrace, or your displeasure, &c., whatever it be that he loves most, except it be sloth (for that will never set him on work) let that be made use of to quicken him, and make him bestir himself. For in this listless temper, you are not to fear an excess of appetite (as in all other cases) by cherishing it. 'Tis that which you want, and therefore must labour to raise and increase; for where there is no desire, there will be no industry.

§ 127. If you have not hold enough upon him this way, to stir up vigour and activity in him, you must employ him in some constant bodily labour, whereby he may get an habit of doing something. The keeping him hard to some study were the better way to get him an habit of exercising and applying his mind. But because this is an invisible attention, and no body can tell when he is or is not idle at it, you must find bodily employments for him, which he must be constantly busied in, and kept to; and if they have some little hardship and shame in them, it may not be the worse, that they may the sooner weary him, and make him desire to return to his book. But be sure, when you exchange his book for his other labour, set him such a task, to be done in such a time as may allow him no opportunity to be idle. Only after you have by this way brought him to be attentive and industrious at his book, you may, upon his dispatching his study within the time set him, give him as a reward some respite from his other labour; which you may diminish as you find him grow more and more steady in his application, and at last wholly take off when his sauntring at his book is cured.

§ 128. We formerly observed, that variety and freedom was that that delighted children, and recommended their plays to them; and that therefore their book or any thing we would have them learn, should not be enjoined them as business. This their parents, tutors, and teachers are apt to forget; and their impatience to have them busied in what is fit for them to do, suffers them not to deceive them into it: but by the repeated injunctions they meet with, children quickly distinguish between what is required of them, and what not. When this mistake has once made his book uneasy to him, the cure is to be applied at the other end. And since it will be then too late to endeavour to make it a play to him, you must take the contrary course: observe what play he is most delighted with; enjoin that, and make him play so many hours every day, not as a punishment for playing, but as if it were the business required of him. This, if I mistake not, will in a few days make him so weary of his most beloved sport, that he will prefer his book, or any thing to it, especially if it may redeem him from any part of the task of play is set him, and he may be suffered to employ some part of the time destined to his task of play in his book, or such other exercise as is really useful to him. This I at least think a better cure than that forbidding, (which usually increases the desire) or any other punishment should be made use of to remedy it: for when you have once glutted his appetite (which may safely be done in all things but eating and drinking) and made him surfeit of what you would have him avoid, you have put into him a principle of aversion, and you need not so much fear afterwards his longing for the same thing again.

§ 129. This I think is sufficiently evident, that children generally hate to be idle. All the care then is, that their busy humour should be constantly employ'd in something of use to them; which, if you will attain, you must make what you would have them do a recreation to them, and not a business. The way to do this, so that they may not perceive you have any hand in it, is this proposed here; viz. To make them weary of that which you would not have them do, by enjoining and making them under some pretence or other do it, till they are surfeited. For example: Does your son play at top and scourge too much? Enjoin him to play so many hours every day, and look that he do it; and you shall see he will quickly be sick of it, and willing to leave it. By this means making the recreations you dislike a business to him, he will of himself with delight betake himself to those things you would have him do, especially if they be proposed as rewards for having performed his task in that play which is commanded him. For if he be ordered every day to whip his top so long as to make him sufficiently weary, do you not think he will apply himself with eagerness to his book, and wish for it, if you promise it him as a reward of having whipped his top lustily, quite out all the time that is set him? Children, in the things they do, if they comport with their age, find little difference so they may be doing: the esteem they have for one thing above another they borrow from others; so that what those about them make to be a reward to them, will really be so. By this art it is in their governor's choice, whether scotchhoppers shall reward their dancing, or dancing their scotchhoppers; whether peg-top, or reading; playing at trap, or studying the globes, shall be more acceptable and pleasing to them; all that they desire being to be busy, and busy, as they imagine, in things of their own choice, and which they receive as favours from their parents or others for whom they have respect and with whom they would be in credit. A set of children thus ordered and kept from the ill example of others, would all of them, I suppose, with as much earnestness and delight, learn to read, write, and what else one would have them, as others do their ordinary plays: and the eldest being thus entered, and this made the fashion of the place, it would be as impossible to hinder them from learning the one, as it is ordinarily to keep them from the other.

§ 130. Play-things, I think, children should have, and of divers sorts; but still to be in the custody of their tutors or some body else, whereof the child should have in his power but one at once, and should not be suffered to have another but when he restored that. This teaches them betimes to be careful of not losing or spoiling the things they have; whereas plenty and variety in their own keeping, makes them wanton and careless, and teaches them from the beginning to be squanderers and wasters. These, I confess, are little things, and such as will seem beneath the care of a governor; but nothing that may form children's minds is to be overlooked and neglected, and whatsoever introduces habits, and settles customs in them, deserves the care and attention of their governors, and is not a small thing in its consequences.

One thing more about children's play-things may be worth their parents' care. Though it be agreed they should have of several sorts, yet, I think, they should have none bought for them. This will hinder that great variety they are often overcharged with, which serves only to teach the mind to wander after change and superfluity, to be unquiet, and perpetually stretching itself after something more still, though it knows not what, and never to be satisfied with what it hath. The court that is made to people of condition in such kind of presents to their children, does the little ones great harm. By it they are taught pride, vanity and covetousness, almost before they can speak: and I have known a young child so distracted with the number and variety of his play-games, that he tired his maid every day to look them over; and was so accustomed to abundance, that he never thought he had enough, but was always asking, What more? What more? What new thing shall I have? A good introduction to moderate desires, and the ready way to make a contented happy man!

"How then shall they have the play-games you allow them, if none must be bought for them?" I answer, they should make them themselves, or at least endeavour it, and set themselves about it; till then they should have none, and till then they will want none of any great artifice. A smooth pebble, a piece of paper, the mother's bunch of keys, or any thing they cannot hurt themselves with, serves as much to divert little children as those more chargeable and curious toys from the shops, which are presently put out of order and broken. Children are never dull, or out of humour, for want of such playthings, unless they have been used to them; when they are little, whatever occurs serves the turn; and as they grow bigger, if they are not stored by the expensive folly of others, they will make them themselves. Indeed, when they once begin to set themselves to work about any of their inventions, they should be taught and assisted; but should have nothing whilst they lazily sit still, expecting to be furnish'd from other hands, without employing their own. And if you help them where they are at a stand, it will more endear you to them than any chargeable toys you shall buy for them. Play-things which are above their skill to make, as tops, gigs, battledores, and the like, which are to be used with labour, should indeed be procured them. These 'tis convenient they should have, not for variety but exercise; but these too should be given them as bare as might be. If they had a top, the scourge-stick and leather-strap should be left to their own making and fitting. If they sit gaping to have such things drop into their mouths, they should go without them. This will accustom them to seek for what they want, in themselves and in their own endeavours; whereby they will be taught moderation in their desires, application, industry, thought, contrivance, and good husbandry; qualities that will be useful to them when they are men, and therefore cannot be learned too soon, nor fixed too deep. All the plays and diversions of children should be directed towards good and useful habits, or else they will introduce ill ones. Whatever they do, leaves some impression on that tender age, and from thence they receive a tendency to good or evil: and whatever hath such an influence, ought not to be neglected.

Sections 131–140

§ 131. Lying is so ready and cheap a cover for any miscarriage, and so much in fashion among all sorts of people, that a child can hardly avoid observing the use is made of it on all occasions, and so can scarce be kept without great care from getting into it. But it is so ill a quality, and the mother of so many ill ones that spawn from it, and take shelter under it, that a child should be brought up in the greatest abhorrence of it imaginable. It should be always (when occasionally it comes to be mention'd) spoke of before him with the utmost detestation, as a quality so wholly inconsistent with the name and character of a gentleman, that no body of any credit can bear the imputation of a lie; a mark that is judg'd the utmost disgrace, which debases a man to the lowest degree of a shameful meanness, and ranks him with the most contemptible part of mankind and the abhorred rascality; and is not to be endured in any one who would converse with people of condition, or have any esteem or reputation in the world. The first time he is found in a lie, it should rather be wondered at as a monstrous thing in him, than reproved as an ordinary fault. If that keeps him not from relapsing, the next time he must be sharply rebuked, and fall into the state of great displeasure of his father and mother and all about him who take notice of it. And if this way work not the cure, you must come to blows; for after he has been thus warned, a premeditated lie must always be looked upon as obstinacy, and never be permitted to escape unpunished.

§ 132. Children, afraid to have their faults seen in their naked colours, will, like the rest of the sons of Adam, be apt to make excuses. This is a fault usually bordering upon, and leading to untruth, and is not to be indulged in them; but yet it ought to be cured rather with shame than roughness. If therefore, when a child is questioned for any thing, his first answer be an excuse, warn him soberly to tell the truth; and then if he persists to shuffle it off with a falsehood, he must be chastised; but if he directly confess, you must commend his ingenuity, and pardon the fault, be it what it will; and pardon it so, that you never so much as reproach him with it, or mention it to him again: for if you would have him in love with ingenuity, and by a constant practice make it habitual to him, you must take care that it never procure him the least inconvenience; but on the contrary, his own confession bringing always with it perfect impunity, should be besides encouraged by some marks of approbation. If his excuse be such at any time that you cannot prove it to have any falsehood in it, let it pass for true, and be sure not to shew any suspicion of it. Let him keep up his reputation with you as high as is possible; for when once he finds he has lost that, you have lost a great, and your best hold upon him. Therefore let him not think he has the character of a liar with you, as long as you can avoid it without flattering him in it. Thus some slips in truth may be overlooked. But after he has once been corrected for a lie, you must be sure never after to pardon it in him, whenever you find and take notice to him that he is guilty of it: for it being a fault which he has been forbid, and may, unless he be wilful, avoid, the repeating of it is perfect perverseness, and must have the chastisement due to that offence.

§ 133. This is what I have thought concerning the general method of educating a young gentleman; which, though I am apt to suppose may have some influence on the whole course of his education, yet I am far from imagining it contains all those particulars which his growing years or peculiar temper may require. But this being premised in general, we shall in the next place, descend to a more particular consideration of the several parts of his education.

§ 134. That which every gentleman (that takes any care of his education) desires for his son, besides the estate he leaves him, is contain'd (I suppose) in these four things, virtue, wisdom, breeding and learning. I will not trouble my self whether these names do not some of them sometimes stand for the same thing, or really include one another. It serves my turn here to follow the popular use of these words, which, I presume, is clear enough to make me be understood, and I hope there will be no difficulty to comprehend my meaning.

§ 135. I place virtue as the first and most necessary of those endowments that belong to a man or a gentleman; as absolutely requisite to make him valued and beloved by others, acceptable or tolerable to himself. Without that, I think, he will be happy neither in this nor the other world.

§ 136. As the foundation of this, there ought very early to be imprinted on his mind a true notion of God, as of the independent Supreme Being, Author and Maker of all things, from Whom we receive all our good, Who loves us, and gives us all things. And consequent to this, instil into him a love and reverence of this Supreme Being. This is enough to begin with, without going to explain this matter any farther; for fear lest by talking too early to him of spirits, and being unseasonably forward to make him understand the incomprehensible nature of that Infinite Being, his head be either fill'd with false, or perplex'd with unintelligible notions of Him. Let him only be told upon occasion, that God made and governs all things, hears and sees every thing, and does all manner of good to those that love and obey Him; you will find, that being told of such a God, other thoughts will be apt to rise up fast enough in his mind about Him; which, as you observe them to have any mistakes, you must set right. And I think it would be better if men generally rested in such an idea of God, without being too curious in their notions about a Being which all must acknowledge incomprehensible; whereby many, who have not strength and clearness of thought to distinguish between what they can, and what they cannot know, run themselves in superstitions or atheism, making God like themselves, or (because they cannot comprehend any thing else) none at all. And I am apt to think, the keeping children constantly morning and evening to acts of devotion to God, as to their Maker, Preserver and Benefactor, in some plain and short form of prayer, suitable to their age and capacity, will be of much more use to them in religion, knowledge, and virtue, than to distract their thoughts with curious enquiries into His inscrutable essence and being.

§ 137. Having by gentle degrees, as you find him capable of it, settled such an idea of God in his mind, and taught him to pray to Him, and praise Him as the Author of his being, and of all the good he does or can enjoy; forbear any discourse of other spirits, till the mention of them coming in his way, upon occasion hereafter to be set down, and his reading the scripture-history, put him upon that enquiry.

§ 138. But even then, and always whilst he is young, be sure to preserve his tender mind from all impressions and notions of spirits and goblins, or any fearful apprehensions in the dark. This he will be in danger of from the indiscretion of servants, whose usual method is to awe children, and keep them in subjection, by telling them of raw-head and bloody-bones, and such other names as carry with them the ideas of something terrible and hurtful, which they have reason to be afraid of when alone, especially in the dark. This must be carefully prevented: for though by this foolish way, they may keep them from little faults, yet the remedy is much worse than the disease; and there are stamped upon their imaginations ideas that follow them with terror and affrightment. Such bug-bear thoughts once got into the tender minds of children, and being set on with a strong impression from the dread that accompanies such apprehensions, sink deep, and fasten themselves so as not easily, if ever, to be got out again; and whilst they are there, frequently haunt them with strange visions, making children dastards when alone, and afraid of their shadows and darkness all their lives after. I have had those complain to me, when men, who had been thus used when young; that though their reason corrected the wrong ideas they had taken in, and they were satisfied that there was no cause to fear invisible beings more in the dark than in the light, yet that these notions were apt still upon any occasion to start up first in their prepossessed fancies, and not to be removed without some pains. And to let you see how lasting and frightful images are, that take place in the mind early, I shall here tell you a pretty remarkable but true story. There was in a town in the west a man of a disturbed brain, whom the boys used to teaze when he came in their way: this fellow one day seeing in the street one of those lads, that used to vex him, stepped into a cutler's shop he was near, and there seizing on a naked sword, made after the boy; who seeing him coming so armed, betook himself to his feet, and ran for his life, and by good luck had strength and heels enough to reach his father's house before the mad-man could get up to him. The door was only latch'd; and when he had the latch in his hand, he turn'd about his head, to see how near his pursuer was, who was at the entrance of the porch, with his sword up ready to strike; and he had just time to get in, and clap to the door to avoid the blow, which, though his body escaped, his mind did not. This frightening idea made so deep an impression there, that it lasted many years, if not all his life after. For, telling this story when he was a man, he said, that after that time till then, he never went in at that door (that he could remember) at any time without looking back, whatever business he had in his head, or how little soever before he came thither he thought of this mad-man.

If children were let alone, they would be no more afraid in the dark, than in broad sun-shine; they would in their turns as much welcome the one for sleep as the other to play in. There should be no distinction made to them by any discourse of more danger or terrible things in the one than the other: but if the folly of any one about them should do them this harm, and make them think there is any difference between being in the dark and winking, you must get it out of their minds as soon as you can; and let them know, that God, who made all things good for them, made the night that they might sleep the better and the quieter; and that they being under his protection, there is nothing in the dark to hurt them. What is to be known more of God and good spirits, is to be deferr'd till the time we shall hereafter mention; and of evil spirits, 'twill be well if you can keep him from wrong fancies about them till he is ripe for that sort of knowledge.

§ 139. Having laid the foundations of virtue in a true notion of a God, such as the creed wisely teaches, as far as his age is capable, and by accustoming him to pray to Him; the next thing to be taken care of is to keep him exactly to speaking of truth, and by all the ways imaginable inclining him to be good-natur'd. Let him know that twenty faults are sooner to be forgiven than the straining of truth to cover any one by an excuse. And to teach him betimes to love and be good-natur'd to others, is to lay early the true foundation of an honest man; all injustice generally springing from too great love of ourselves and too little of others.

This is all I shall say of this matter in general, and is enough for laying the first foundations of virtue in a child: as he grows up, the tendency of his natural inclination must be observed; which, as it inclines him more than is convenient on one or t'other side from the right path of virtue, ought to have proper remedies applied. For few of Adam's children are so happy, as not to be born with some byass in their natural temper, which it is the business of education either to take off, or counterbalance. But to enter into particulars of this, would be beyond the design of this short treatise of education. I intend not a discourse of all the virtues and vices, how each virtue is to be attained, and every particular vice by its peculiar remedies cured: though I have mentioned some of the most ordinary faults, and the ways to be used in correcting them.

§ 140. Wisdom I take in the popular acceptation, for a man's managing his business ably and with foresight in this world. This is the product of a good natural temper, application of mind, and experience together, and so above the reach of children. The greatest thing that in them can be done towards it, is to hinder them, as much as may be, from being cunning; which, being the ape of wisdom, is the most distant from it that can be: and as an ape for the likeness it has to a man, wanting what really should make him so, is by so much the uglier; cunning is only the want of understanding, which because it cannot compass its ends by direct ways, would do it by a trick and circumvention; and the mischief of it is, a cunning trick helps but once, but hinders ever after. No cover was ever made so big or so fine as to hide it self: no body was ever so cunning as to conceal their being so: and when they are once discovered, every body is shy, every body distrustful of crafty men; and all the world forwardly join to oppose and defeat them; whilst the open, fair, wise man has every body to make way for him, and goes directly to his business. To accustom a child to have true notions of things, and not to be satisfied till he has them; to raise his mind to great and worthy thoughts, and to keep him at a distance from falsehood and cunning, which has always a broad mixture of falsehood in it; is the fittest preparation of a child for wisdom. The rest, which is to be learn'd from time, experience, and observation, and an acquaintance with men, their tempers and designs, is not to be expected in the ignorance and inadvertency of childhood, or the inconsiderate heat and unweariness of youth: all that can be done towards it, during this unripe age, is, as I have said, to accustom them to truth and sincerity; to a submission to reason; and as much as may be, to reflection on their own actions.

Sections 141–150

§ 141. The next good quality belonging to a gentleman, is good breeding. There are two sorts of ill-breeding: the one a sheepish bashfulness, and the other a mis-becoming negligence and disrespect in our carriage; both which are avoided by duly observing this one rule, not to think meanly of ourselves, and not to think meanly of others.

§ 142. The first part of this rule must not be understood in opposition to humility, but to assurance. We ought not to think so well of our selves, as to stand upon our own value; and assume to our selves a preference before others, because of any advantage we may imagine we have over them; but modestly to take what is offered, when it is our due. But yet we ought to think so well of our selves, as to perform those actions which are incumbent on, and expected of us, without discomposure or disorder, in whose presence soever we are; keeping that respect and distance which is due to every one's rank and quality. There is often in people, especially children, a clownish shamefacedness before strangers or those above them: they are confounded in their thoughts, words, and looks; and so lose themselves in that confusion as not to be able to do any thing, or at least not to do it with that freedom and gracefulness which pleases, and makes them be acceptable. The only cure for this, as for any other miscarriage, is by use to introduce the contrary habit. But since we cannot accustom ourselves to converse with strangers and persons of quality without being in their company, nothing can cure this part of ill-breeding but change and variety of company, and that of persons above us.

§ 143. As the before-mentioned consists in too great a concern how to behave ourselves towards others; so the other part of ill-breeding lies in the appearance of too little care of pleasing or shewing respect to those we have to do with. To avoid this these two things are requisite: first, a disposition of the mind not to offend others; and secondly, the most acceptable and agreeable way of expressing that disposition. From the one men are called civil; from the other well-fashion'd. The latter of these is that decency and gracefulness of looks, voice, words, motions, gestures, and of all the whole outward demeanour, which takes in company, and makes those with whom we may converse, easy and well pleased. This is, as it were, the language whereby that internal civility of the mind is expressed; which, as other languages are, being very much governed by the fashion and custom of every country, must, in the rules and practice of it, be learn'd chiefly from observation, and the carriage of those who are allow'd to be exactly well-bred. The other part, which lies deeper than the outside, is that general good-will and regard for all people, which makes any one have a care not to shew in his carriage any contempt, disrespect, or neglect of them; but to express, according to the fashion and way of that country, a respect and value for them according to their rank and condition. It is a disposition of the mind that shews it self in the carriage, whereby a man avoids making any one uneasy in conversation.

I shall take notice of four qualities, that are most directly opposite to this first and most taking of all the social virtues. And from some one of these four it is, that incivility commonly has its rise. I shall set them down, that children may be preserv'd or recover'd from their ill influence.

1. The first is, a natural roughness, which makes a man uncomplaisant to others, so that he has no deference for their inclinations, tempers, or conditions. 'Tis the sure badge of a clown,

not to mind what pleases or displeases those he is with; and yet one may often find a man in fashionable clothes give an unbounded swing to his own humour, and suffer it to justle or over-run any one that stands in its way, with a perfect indifference how they take it. This is a brutality that every one sees and abhors, and nobody can be easy with: and therefore this finds no place in any one who would be thought to have the least tincture of good-breeding. For the very end and business of good-breeding is to supple the natural stiffness, and so soften men's tempers, that they may bend to a compliance, and accommodate themselves to those they have to do with.

2. Contempt, or want of due respect, discovered either in looks, words, or gesture: this, from whomsoever it comes, brings always uneasiness with it. For nobody can contentedly bear being slighted.

3. Censoriousness, and finding fault with others, has a direct opposition to civility. Men, whatever they are or are not guilty of, would not have their faults display'd and set in open view and broad day-light, before their own or other people's eyes. Blemishes affixed to any one always carry shame with them: and the discovery, or even bare imputation of any defect is not borne without some uneasiness. Raillery is the most refined way of exposing the faults of others: but, because it is usually done with wit and good language, and gives entertainment to the company, people are led into a mistake, that where it keeps within fair bounds there is no incivility in it. And so the pleasantry of this sort of conversation often introduces it amongst people of the better rank; and such talkers are favourably heard and generally applauded by the laughter of the bystanders on their side. But they ought to consider, that the entertainment of the rest of the company is at the cost of that one who is set out in their burlesque colours, who therefore is not without uneasiness, unless the subject for which he is rallied be really in itself matter of commendation. For then the pleasant images and representations which make the raillery carrying praise as well as sport with them, the rallied person also finds his account, and takes part in the diversion. But because the right management of so nice and ticklish a business, wherein a little slip may spoil all, is not every body's talent, I think those who would secure themselves from provoking others, especially all young people, should carefully abstain from raillery, which by a small mistake or any wrong turn, may leave upon the mind of those who are made uneasy by it, the lasting memory of having been piquantly, tho' wittily, taunted for some thing censurable in them.

Besides raillery, contradiction is a sort of censoriousness wherein ill-breeding often shews it self. Complaisance does not require that we should always admit all the reasonings or relations that the company is entertain'd with, no, nor silently to let pass all that is vented in our hearing. The opposing the opinions, and rectifying the mistakes of others, is what truth and charity sometimes require of us, and civility does not oppose, if it be done with due caution and care of circumstances. But there are some people, that one may observe, possessed as it were with the spirit of contradiction, that steadily, and without regard to right or wrong, oppose some one, or, perhaps, every one of the company, whatever they say. This is so visible and outrageous a way of censuring, that nobody can avoid thinking himself injur'd by it. All opposition to what another man has said, is so apt to be suspected of censoriousness, and is so seldom received without some sort of humiliation, that it ought to be made in the gentlest manner, and softest words can be found, and such as with the whole deportment may express no forwardness to contradict. All marks of respect and good will ought to accompany it, that whilst we gain the argument, we may not lose the esteem of those that hear us.

4. Captiousness is another fault opposite to civility; not only because it often produces misbecoming and provoking expressions and carriage; but because it is a tacit accusation and reproach of some incivility taken notice of in those whom we are angry with. Such a suspicion or intimation cannot be borne by any one without uneasiness. Besides, one angry body discomposes the whole company, and the harmony ceases upon any such jarring.

The happiness that all men so steadily pursue consisting in pleasure, it is easy to see why the civil are more acceptable than the useful. The ability, sincerity, and good intention of a man of weight and worth, or a real friend, seldom atones for the uneasiness that is produced by his grave and solid representations. Power and riches, nay virtue itself, are valued only as conducing to our happiness. And therefore he recommends himself ill to another as aiming at his happiness, who, in the services he does him, makes him uneasy in the manner of doing them. He that knows how to make those he converses with easy, without debasing himself to low and servile flattery, has found the true art of living in the world, and being both welcome and valued every where. Civility therefore is what in the first place should with great care be made habitual to children and young people.

§ 144. There is another fault in good manners, and that is excess of ceremony, and an obstinate persisting to force upon another what is not his due, and what he cannot take without folly or shame. This seems rather a design to expose than oblige: or at least looks like a contest for mastery, and at best is but troublesome, and so can be no part of good-breeding, which has no other use or end but to make people easy and satisfied in their conversation with us. This is a fault few young people are apt to fall into; but yet if they are ever guilty of it, or are suspected to incline that way, they should be told of it, and warned of this mistaken civility. The thing they should endeavour and aim at in conversation, should be to shew respect, esteem, and good-will, by paying to every one that common ceremony and regard which is in civility due to them. To do this without a suspicion of flattery, dissimulation, or meanness, is a great skill, which good sense, reason, and good company can only teach; but is of so much use in civil life that it is well worth the studying.

§ 145. Though the managing ourselves well in this part of our behaviour has the name of good-breeding, as if peculiarly the effect of education; yet, as I have said, young children should not be much perplexed about it; I mean, about putting off their hats, and making legs modishly. Teach them humility, and to be good-natur'd, if you can, and this sort of manners will not be wanting; civility being in truth nothing but a care not to shew any slighting or contempt of any one in conversation. What are the most allow'd and esteem'd ways of expressing this, we have above observ'd. It is as peculiar and different, in several countries of the world, as their languages; and therefore, if it be rightly considered, rules and discourses made to children about it, are as useless and impertinent, as it would be now and then to give a rule or two of the Spanish tongue to one that converses only with Englishmen. Be as busy as you please with discourses of civility to your son, such as is his company, such will be his manners. A plough-man of your neighbourhood that has never been out of his parish, read what lectures you please to him, will be as soon in his language as his carriage a courtier; that is, in neither will be more polite than those he uses to converse with: and therefore, of this no other care can be taken till he be of an age to have a tutor put to him, who must not fail to be a well-bred man. And, in good earnest, if I were to speak my mind freely, so children do nothing out of obstinacy, pride, and ill-nature, 'tis no great matter how they put off their hats or make legs. If you can teach them to love and respect other people, they will, as their age requires it, find ways to express it acceptably to every one, according to the fashions they have been used to: and as to their motions and carriage of their bodies, a dancing-master, as has been said, when it is fit, will teach them what is most becoming. In the mean time, when they are young, people expect not that children should be over-mindful of these ceremonies; carelessness is allow'd to that age, and becomes them as well as compliments do grown people: or, at least, if some very nice people will think it a fault, I am sure it is a fault that should be over-look'd, and left to time, a tutor and conversation to cure. And therefore I think it not worth your while to have your son (as I often see children are) molested or chid about it: but where there is pride or ill-nature appearing in his carriage, there he must be persuaded or shamed out of it.

Though children, when little, should not be much perplexed with rules and ceremonious parts of breeding, yet there is a sort of unmannerliness very apt to grow up with young people, if not early restrained, and that is, a forwardness to interrupt others that are speaking; and to stop them with some contradiction. Whether the custom of disputing, and the reputation of parts and learning usually given to it as if it were the only standard and evidence of knowledge, make young men so forward to watch occasions to correct others in their discourse, and not to slip any opportunity of shewing their talents: so it is, that I have found scholars most blamed in this point. There cannot be a greater rudeness, than to interrupt another in the current of his discourse; for if there be not impertinent folly in answering a man before we know what he will say, yet it is a plain declaration, that we are weary to hear him talk any longer, and have a dis-esteem of what he says; which we judging not fit to entertain the company, desire them to give audience to us, who have something to produce worth their attention. This shews a very great disrespect, and cannot but be offensive: and yet this is what almost all interruption constantly carries with it. To which, if there be added, as is usual, a correcting of any mistake, or a contradiction of what has been said, it is a mark of yet greater pride and self-conceitedness, when we thus intrude our selves for teachers, and take upon us either to set another right in his story, or shew the mistakes of his judgment.

I do not say this, that I think there should be no difference of opinions in conversation, nor opposition in men's discourses: this would be to take away the greatest advantage of society, and the improvements are to be made by ingenious company; where the light is to be got from the opposite arguings of men of parts, shewing the different sides of things and their various aspects and probabilities, would be quite lost, if every one were obliged to assent to, and say after the first speaker. 'Tis not the owning one's dissent from another, that I speak against, but the manner of doing it. Young men should be taught not to be forward to interpose their opinions, unless asked, or when others have done, and are silent; and then only by way of enquiry, not instruction. The positive asserting, and the magisterial air should be avoided; and when a general pause of the whole company affords an opportunity, they may modestly put in their question as learners.

This becoming decency will not cloud their parts, nor weaken the strength of their reason; but bespeak the more favourable attention, and give what they say the greater advantage. An ill argument, or ordinary observation, thus introduc'd, with some civil preface of deference and respect to the opinions of others, will procure them more credit and esteem than the sharpest wit, or profoundest science, with a rough, insolent, or noisy management, which always shocks the hearers, leaves an ill opinion of the man, though he get the better of it in the argument.

This therefore should be carefully watched in young people, stopp'd in the beginning, and the contrary habit introduced in all their conversation. And the rather, because forwardness to talk, frequent interruptions in arguing, and loud wrangling, are too often observable amongst grown people, even of rank, amongst us. The Indians, whom we call barbarous, observe much more decency and civility in their discourses and conversation, giving one another a fair silent hearing till they have quite done; and then answering them calmly, and without noise or passion. And if it be not so in this civiliz'd part of the world, we must impute it to a neglect in education, which has not yet reform'd this antient piece of barbarity amongst us. Was it not, think you, an entertaining spectacle, to see two ladies of quality accidentally seated on the opposite sides of a room, set round with company, fall into a dispute, and grow so eager in it, that in the heat of the controversy, edging by degrees their chairs forwards, they were in a little time got up close to one another in the middle of the room; where they for a good while managed the dispute as fiercely as two game-cocks in the pit, without minding or taking any notice of the circle, which could not all the while forbear smiling? This I was told by a person of quality, who was present at the combat, and did not omit to reflect upon the indecencies that warmth in dispute often runs people into; which, since custom makes too frequent, education should take the more care of. There is no body but condemns this in others, though they overlook it in themselves; and many who are sensible of it in themselves, and resolve against it, cannot yet get rid of an ill custom, which neglect in their education has suffer'd to settle into an habit.

§ 146. What has been above said concerning company, would perhaps, if it were well reflected on, give us a larger prospect, and let us see how much farther its influence reaches.

'Tis not the modes of civility alone, that are imprinted by conversation: the tincture of company sinks deeper than the out-side; and possibly, if a true estimate were made of the morality and religions of the world, we should find that the far greater part of mankind received even those opinions, and ceremonies they would die for, rather from the fashions of their countries, and the constant practice of those about them, than from any conviction of their reasons. I mention this only to let you see of what moment I think company is to your son in all the parts of his life, and therefore how much that one part is to be weighed and provided for; it being of greater force to work upon him, than all you can do besides.

§ 147. You will wonder, perhaps, that I put learning last, especially if I tell you I think it the least part. This may seem strange in the mouth of a bookish man; and this making usually the chief, if not only bustle and stir about children, this being almost that alone which is thought on, when people talk of education, makes it the greater paradox. When I consider, what ado is made about a little Latin and Greek, how many years are spent in it, and what a noise and business it makes to no purpose, I can hardly forbear thinking that the parents of children still live in fear of the school-master's rod, which they look on as the only instrument of education; as a language or two to be its whole business. How else is it possible that a child should be chain'd to the oar seven, eight, or ten of the best years of his life, to get a language or two, which, I think, might be had at a great deal cheaper rate of pains and time, and be learn'd almost in playing?

Forgive me therefore if I say, I cannot with patience think, that a young gentleman should be put into the herd, and be driven with a whip and scourge, as if he were to run the gantlet through the several classes, ad capiendum ingenii cultum. What then? say you, would you not have him write and read? Shall he be more ignorant than the clerk of our parish, who takes Hopkins and Sternhold for the best poets in the world, whom yet he makes worse than they are by his ill reading? Not so, not so fast, I beseech you. Reading and writing and learning I allow to be necessary, but yet not the chief business. I imagine you would think him a very foolish fellow, that should not value a virtuous or a wise man infinitely before a great scholar. Not but that I think learning a great help to both in well-dispos'd minds; but yet it must be confess'd also, that in others not so dispos'd, it helps them only to be the more foolish, or worse men. I say this, that when you consider the breeding of your son, and are looking out for a school-master or a tutor, you would not have (as is usual) Latin and logick only in your thoughts. Learning must be had, but in the second place, as subservient only to greater qualities. Seek out somebody that may know how discreetly to frame his manners: place him in hands where you may, as much as possible, secure his innocence, cherish and nurse up the good, and gently correct and weed out any bad inclinations, and settle in him good habits. This is the main point, and this being provided for, learning may be had into the bargain, and that, as I think, at a very easy rate, by methods that may be thought on.

§ 148. When he can talk, 'tis time he should begin to learn to read. But as to this, give me leave here to inculcate again, what is very apt to be forgotten, viz. That great care is to be taken, that it be never made as a business to him, nor he look on it as a task. We naturally, as I said, even from our cradles, love liberty, and have therefore an aversion to many things for no other reason but because they are enjoin'd us. I have always had a fancy that learning might be made a play and recreation to children: and that they might be brought to desire to be taught, if it were proposed to them as a thing of honour, credit, delight, and recreation, or as a reward for doing something else; and if they were never chid or corrected for the neglect of it. That which confirms me in this opinion is, that amongst the Portuguese, 'tis so much a fashion and emulation amongst their children, to learn to read and write, that they cannot hinder them from it: they will learn it one from another, and are as intent on it, as if it were forbidden them. I remember that being at a friend's house, whose younger son, a child in coats, was not easily brought to his book (being taught to read at home by his mother) I advised to try another way, than requiring it of him as his duty; we therefore, in a discourse on purpose amongst our selves, in his hearing, but without taking any notice of him, declared, that it was the privilege and advantage of heirs and elder brothers, to be scholars; that this made them fine gentlemen, and beloved by every body: and that for younger brothers, 'twas a favour to admit them to breeding; to be taught to read and write, was more than came to their share; they might be ignorant bumpkins and clowns, if they pleased. This so wrought upon the child, that afterwards he desired to be taught; would come himself to his mother to learn, and would not let his maid be quiet till she heard him his lesson. I doubt not but some way like this might be taken with other children; and when their tempers are found, some thoughts be instill'd into them, that might set them upon desiring of learning, themselves, and make them seek it as another sort of play or recreation. But then, as I said before, it must never be imposed as a task, nor made a trouble to them. There may be dice and play-things, with the letters on them to teach children the alphabet by playing; and twenty other ways may be found, suitable to their particular tempers, to make this kind of learning a sport to them.

§ 149. Thus children may be cozen'd into a knowledge of the letters; be taught to read, without perceiving it to be any thing but a sport, and play themselves into that which others are whipp'd for. Children should not have any thing like work, or serious, laid on them; neither their minds, nor bodies will bear it. It injures their healths; and their being forced and tied down to their books in an age at enmity with all such restraint, has, I doubt not, been the reason, why a great many have hated books and learning all their lives after. 'Tis like a surfeit, that leaves an aversion behind not to be removed.

§ 150. I have therefore thought, that if play-things were fitted to this purpose, as they are usually to none, contrivances might be made to teach children to read, whilst they thought they were only playing. For example, what if an ivory-ball were made like that of the royal-oak lottery, with thirty two sides, or one rather of twenty four or twenty five sides; and upon several of those sides pasted on an A, upon several others B, on others C, and on others D? I would have you begin with but these four letters, or perhaps only two at first; and when he is perfect in them, then add another; and so on till each side having one letter, there be on it the whole alphabet. This I would have others play with before him, it being as good a sort of play to lay a stake who shall first throw an A or B, as who upon dice shall throw six or seven. This being a play amongst you, tempt him not to it, lest you make it business; for I would not have him understand 'tis any thing but a play of older people, and I doubt not but he will take to it of himself. And that he may have the more reason to think it is a play, that he is sometimes in favour admitted to, when the play is done the ball should be laid up safe out of his reach, that so it may not, by his having it in his keeping at any time, grow stale to him.

Sections 151–160

§ 151. To keep up his eagerness to it, let him think it a game belonging to those above him: and when, by this means, he knows the letters, by changing them into syllables, he may learn to read, without knowing how he did so, and never have any chiding or trouble about it, nor fall out with books because of the hard usage and vexation they have caus'd him. Children, if you observe them, take abundance of pains to learn several games, which, if they should be enjoined them, they would abhor as a task and business. I know a person of great quality (more yet to be honoured for his learning and virtue than for his rank and high place) who by pasting on the six vowels (for in our language Y is one) on the six sides of a die, and the remaining eighteen consonants on the sides of three other dice, has made this a play for his children, that he shall win who, at one cast, throws most words on these four dice; whereby his eldest son, yet in coats, has play'd himself into spelling, with great eagerness, and without once having been chid for it or forced to it.

§ 152. I have seen little girls exercise whole hours together and take abundance of pains to be expert at dibstones as they call it. Whilst I have been looking on, I have thought it wanted only some good contrivance to make them employ all that industry about something that might be more useful to them; and methinks 'tis only the fault and negligence of elder people that it is not so. Children are much less apt to be idle than men; and men are to be blamed if some part of that busy humour be not turned to useful things; which might be made usually as delightful to them as those they are employed in, if men would be but half so forward to lead the way, as these little apes would be to follow. I imagine some wise Portuguese heretofore began this fashion amongst the children of his country, where I have been told, as I said, it is impossible to hinder the children from learning to read and write: and in some parts of France they teach one another to sing and dance from the cradle.

§ 153. The letters pasted upon the sides of the dice, or polygon, were best to be of the size of those of the folio Bible, to begin with, and none of them capital letters; when once he can read what is printed in such letters, he will not long be ignorant of the great ones: and in the beginning he should not be perplexed with variety. With this die also, you might have a play just like the royal oak, which would be another variety, and play for cherries or apples, &c.

§ 154. Besides these, twenty other plays might be invented depending on letters, which those who like this way, may easily contrive and get made to this use if they will. But the four dice above-mention'd I think so easy and useful, that it will be hard to find any better, and there will be scarce need of any other.

§ 155. Thus much for learning to read, which let him never be driven to, nor chid for; cheat him into it if you can, but make it not a business for him. 'Tis better it be a year later before he can read, than that he should this way get an aversion to learning. If you have any contest with him, let it be in matters of moment, of truth, and good nature; but lay no task on him about A B C. Use your skill to make his will supple and pliant to reason: teach him to love credit and commendation; to abhor being thought ill or meanly of, especially by you and his mother, and then the rest will come all easily. But I think if you will do that, you must not shackle and tie him up with rules about indifferent matters, nor rebuke him for every little fault, or perhaps some that to others would seem great ones; but of this I have said enough already.

§ 156. When by these gentle ways he begins to read, some easy pleasant book, suited to his capacity, should be put into his hands, wherein the entertainment that he finds might draw him on, and reward his pains in reading, and yet not such as should fill his head with perfectly useless trumpery, or lay the principles of vice and folly. To this purpose, I think Æsop's Fables the best, which being stories apt to delight and entertain a child, may yet afford useful reflections to a grown man; and if his memory retain them all his life after, he will not repent to find them there, amongst his manly thoughts and serious business. If his Æsop has pictures in it, it will entertain him much the better, and encourage him to read, when it carries the increase of knowledge with it: for such visible objects children hear talked of in vain and without any satisfaction whilst they have no ideas of them; those ideas being not to be had from sounds, but from the things themselves or their pictures. And therefore I think as soon as he begins to spell, as many pictures of animals should be got him as can be found, with the printed names to them, which at the same time will invite him to read, and afford him matter of enquiry and knowledge. Reynard the Fox is another book I think may be made use of to the same purpose. And if those about him will talk to him often about the stories he has read, and hear him tell them, it will, besides other advantages, add encouragement and delight to his reading, when he finds there is some use and pleasure in it. These baits seem wholly neglected in the ordinary method; and 'tis usually long before learners find any use or pleasure in reading, which may tempt them to it, and so take books only for fashionable amusements, or impertinent troubles, good for nothing.

§ 157. The Lord's Prayer, the Creeds, and Ten Commandments, 'tis necessary he should learn perfectly by heart; but, I think, not by reading them himself in his primer, but by somebody's repeating them to him, even before he can read. But learning by heart, and learning to read, should not I think be mix'd, and so one made to clog the other. But his learning to read should be made as little trouble or business to him as might be.

What other books there are in English of the kind of those above-mentioned, fit to engage the liking of children, and tempt them to read, I do not know: but am apt to think, that children being generally delivered over to the method of schools, where the fear of the rod is to inforce, and not any pleasure of the employment to invite them to learn, this sort of useful books, amongst the number of silly ones that are of all sorts, have yet had the fate to be neglected; and nothing that I know has been considered of this kind out of the ordinary road of the hornbook, primer, psalter, Testament, and Bible.

§ 158. As for the Bible, which children are usually employ'd in to exercise and improve their talent in reading, I think the promiscuous reading of it through by chapters as they lie in order, is so far from being of any advantage to children, either for the perfecting their reading, or principling their religion, that perhaps a worse could not be found. For what pleasure or encouragement can it be to a child to exercise himself in reading those parts of a book where he understands nothing? And how little are the law of Moses, the song of Solomon, the prophecies in the Old, and the Epistles and Apocalypse in the New Testament, suited to a child's capacity? And though the history of the Evangelists and the Acts have something easier, yet, taken altogether, it is very disproportional to the understanding of childhood. I grant that the principles of religion are to be drawn from thence, and in the words of the scripture; yet none should be propos'd to a child, but such as are suited to a child's capacity and notions. But 'tis far from this to read through the whole Bible, and that for reading's sake. And what an odd jumble of thoughts must a child have in his head, if he have any at all, such as he should have concerning religion, who in his tender age reads all the parts of the Bible indifferently as the word of God without any other distinction! I am apt to think, that this in some men has been the very reason why they never had clear and distinct thoughts of it all their lifetime.

§ 159. And now I am by chance fallen on this subject, give me leave to say, that there are some parts of the Scripture which may be proper to be put into the hands of a child to engage him to read; such as are the story of Joseph and his brethren, of David and Goliath, of David and Jonathan, &c. and others that he should be made to read for his instruction, as that, What you would have others do unto you, do you the same unto them; and such other easy and plain moral rules, which being fitly chosen, might often be made use of, both for reading and instruction together; and so often read till they are throughly fixed in the memory; and then afterwards, as he grows ripe for them, may in their turns on fit occasions be inculcated as the standing and sacred rules of his life and actions. But the reading of the whole Scripture indifferently, is what I think very inconvenient for children, till after having been made acquainted with the plainest fundamental parts of it, they have got some kind of general view of what they ought principally to believe and practise; which yet, I think, they ought to receive in the very words of the scripture, and not in such as men prepossess'd by systems and analogies are apt in this case to make use of and force upon them. Dr. Worthington, to avoid this, has made a catechism, which has all its answers in the precise words of the Scripture; a thing of good example, and such a sound form of words as no Christian can except against as not fit for his child to learn. Of this, as soon as he can say the Lord's Prayer, Creed, the Ten Commandments, by heart, it may be fit for him to learn a question every day, or every week, as his understanding is able to receive and his memory to retain them. And when he has this catechism perfectly by heart, so as readily and roundly to answer to any question in the whole book, it may be convenient to lodge in his mind the remaining moral rules scatter'd up and down in the Bible, as the best exercise of his memory, and that which may be always a rule to him, ready at hand, in the whole conduct of his life.

§ 160. When he can read English well, it will be seasonable to enter him in writing: and here the first thing should be taught him is to hold his pen right; and this he should be perfect in before he should be suffered to put it to paper: For not only children but any body else that would do any thing well, should never be put upon too much of it at once, or be set to perfect themselves in two parts of an action at the same time, if they can possibly be separated. I think the Italian way of holding the pen between the thumb and the forefinger alone, may be best; but in this you may consult some good writing-master, or any other person who writes well and quick. When he has learn'd to hold his pen right, in the next place he should learn how to lay his paper, and place his arm and body to it. These practices being got over, the way to teach him to write without much trouble, is to get a plate graved with the characters of such a hand as you like best: but you must remember to have them a pretty deal bigger than he should ordinarily write; for every one naturally comes by degrees to write a less hand than he at first was taught, but never a bigger. Such a plate being graved, let several sheets of good writing-paper be printed off with red ink, which he has nothing to do but go over with a good pen fill'd with black ink, which will quickly bring his hand to the formation of those characters, being at first shewed where to begin, and how to form every letter. And when he can do that well, he must then exercise on fair paper; and so may easily be brought to write the hand you desire.

Sections 161–170

§ 161. When he can write well and quick, I think it may be convenient not only to continue the exercise of his hand in writing, but also to improve the use of it farther in drawing; a thing very useful to a gentleman in several occasions; but especially if he travel, as that which helps a man often to express, in a few lines well put together, what a whole sheet of paper in writing would not be able to represent and make intelligible. How many buildings may a man see, how many machines and habits meet with, the ideas whereof would be easily retain'd and communicated by a little skill in drawing; which being committed to words, are in danger to be lost, or at best but ill retained in the most exact descriptions? I do not mean that I would have your son a perfect painter; to be that to any tolerable degree, will require more time than a young gentleman can spare from his other improvements of greater moment. But so much insight into perspective and skill in drawing, as will enable him to represent tolerably on paper any thing he sees, except faces, may, I think, be got in a little time, especially if he have a genius to it; but where that is wanting, unless it be in the things absolutely necessary, it is better to let him pass them by quietly, than to vex him about them to no purpose: and therefore in this, as in all other things not absolutely necessary, the rule holds, nil invita Minerva.

¶ 1. Short-hand, an art, as I have been told, known only in England, may perhaps be thought worth the learning, both for dispatch in what men write for their own memory, and concealment of what they would not have lie open to every eye. For he that has once learn'd any sort of character, may easily vary it to his own private use or fancy, and with more contraction suit it to the business he would employ in. Mr. Rich's, the best contriv'd of any I have seen, may, as I think, by one who knows and considers grammar well, be made much easier and shorter. But for the learning this compendious way of writing, there will be no need hastily to look out a master; it will be early enough when any convenient opportunity offers itself at any time, after his hand is well settled in fair and quick writing. For boys have but little use of short hand, and should by no means practise it till they write perfectly well, and have throughly fixed the habit of doing so.

§ 162. As soon as he can speak English, 'tis time for him to learn some other language. This no body doubts of, when French is propos'd. And the reason is, because people are accustomed to the right way of teaching that language, which is by talking it into children in constant conversation, and not by grammatical rules. The Latin tongue would easily be taught the same way, if his tutor, being constantly with him, would talk nothing else to him, and make him answer still in the same language. But because French is a living language, and to be used more in speaking, that should be first learned, that the yet pliant organs of speech might be accustomed to a due formation of those sounds, and he get the habit of pronouncing

French well, which is the harder to be done the longer it is delay'd.

§ 163. When he can speak and read French well, which in this method is usually in a year or two, he should proceed to Latin, which 'tis a wonder parents, when they have had the experiment in French, should not think ought to be learned the same way, by talking and reading. Only care is to be taken whilst he is learning these foreign languages, by speaking and reading nothing else with his tutor, that he do not forget to read English, which may be preserved by his mother or some body else hearing him read some chosen parts of the scripture or other English book every day.

§ 164. Latin I look upon as absolutely necessary to a gentleman; and indeed custom, which prevails over every thing, has made it so much a part of education, that even those children are whipp'd to it, and made spend many hours of their precious time uneasily in Latin, who after they are once gone from school, are never to have more to do with it as long as they live. Can there be any thing more ridiculous, than that a father should waste his own money and his son's time in setting him to learn the Roman language, when at the same time he designs him for a trade, wherein he having no use of Latin, fails not to forget that little which he brought from school, and which 'tis ten to one he abhors for the ill usage it procured him? Could it be believed, unless we had every where amongst us examples of it, that a child should be forced to learn the rudiments of a language which he is never to use in the course of life that he is designed to, and neglect all the while the writing a good hand and casting accounts, which are of great advantage in all conditions of life, and to most trades indispensably necessary? But though these qualifications, requisite to trade and commerce and the business of the world, are seldom or never to be had at grammar-schools, yet thither not only gentlemen send their younger sons, intended for trades, but even tradesmen and farmers fail not to send their children, though they have neither intention nor ability to make them scholars. If you ask them why they do this, they think it as strange a question as if you should ask them, why they go to church. Custom serves for reason, and has, to those who take it for reason, so consecrated this method, that it is almost religiously observed by them, and they stick to it, as if their children had scarce an orthodox education unless they learned Lilly's grammar.

§ 165. But how necessary soever Latin be to some, and is thought to be to others to whom it is of no manner of use and service; yet the ordinary way of learning it in a grammar-school is that which having had thoughts about I cannot be forward to encourage. The reasons against it are so evident and cogent, that they have prevailed with some intelligent persons to quit the ordinary road, not without success, though the method made use of was not exactly what I imagine the easiest, and in short is this. To trouble the child with no grammar at all, but to have Latin, as English has been, without the perplexity of rules, talked into him; for if you will consider it, Latin is no more unknown to a child, when he comes into the world, than English: and yet he learns English without master, rule, or grammar; and so might he Latin too, as Tully did, if he had some body always to talk to him in this language. And when we so often see a French woman teach an English girl to speak and read French perfectly in a year or two, without any rule of grammar, or any thing else but prattling to her, I cannot but wonder how gentlemen have overseen this way for their sons, and thought them more dull or incapable than their daughters.

§ 166. If therefore a man could be got, who himself speaking good Latin, would always be about your son, talk constantly to him, and suffer him to speak or read nothing else, this would be the true and genuine way, and that which I would propose, not only as the easiest and best, wherein a child might, without pains or chiding, get a language, which others are wont to be whipt for at school six or seven years together: but also as that, wherein at the same time he might have his mind and manners formed, and he be instructed to boot in several sciences, such as are a good part of geography, astronomy, chronology, anatomy, besides some parts of history, and all other parts of knowledge of things that fall under the senses and require little more than memory. For there, if we would take the true way, our knowledge should begin, and in those things be laid the foundation; and not in the abstract notions of logick and metaphysicks, which are fitter to amuse than inform the understanding in its first setting out towards knowledge. When young men have had their heads employ'd a while in those abstract speculations without finding the success and improvement, or that use of them, which they expected, they are apt to have mean thoughts either of learning or themselves; they are tempted to quit their studies, and throw away their books as containing nothing but hard words and empty sounds; or else, to conclude, that if there be any real knowledge in them, they themselves have not understandings capable of it. That this is so, perhaps I could assure you upon my own experience. Amongst other things to be learned by a young gentleman in this method, whilst others of his age are wholly taken up with Latin and languages, I may also set down geometry for one; having known a young gentleman, bred something after this way, able to demonstrate several propositions in Euclid before he was thirteen.

§ 167. But if such a man cannot be got, who speaks good Latin, and being able to instruct your son in all these parts of knowledge, will undertake it by this method; the next best is to have him taught as near this way as may be, which is by taking some easy and pleasant book, such as Æsop's Fables, and writing the English translation (made as literal as it can be) in one line, and the Latin words which answer each of them, just over it in another. These let him read every day over and over again, till he perfectly understands the Latin; and then go on to another fable, till he be also perfect in that, not omitting what he is already perfect in, but sometimes reviewing that, to keep it in his memory. And when he comes to write, let these be set him for copies, which with the exercise of his hand will also advance him to Latin. This being a more imperfect way than by talking Latin unto him; the formation of the verbs first, and afterwards the declensions of the nouns and pronouns perfectly learned by heart, may facilitate his acquaintance with the genius and manner of the Latin tongue, which varies the signification of verbs and nouns, not as the modern languages do by particles prefix'd, but by changing the last syllables. More than this of grammar, It think he need not have, till he can read himself Sanctii Minerva, with Scioppius and Perizonius's notes.

In teaching of children, this too, I think, is to be observed, that in most cases where they stick, they are not to be farther puzzled by putting them upon finding it out themselves; as by asking such questions as these, (viz.) which is the nominative case, in the sentence they are to construe; or demanding what aufero signifies, to lead them to the knowledge what abstlere signifies, &c., when they cannot readily tell. This wastes time only in disturbing them; for whilst they are learning, and apply themselves with attention, they are to be kept in good humour, and every thing made easy to them, and as pleasant as possible. Therefore, wherever they are at a stand, and are willing to go forwards, help them presently over the difficulty, without any rebuke or chiding, remembering, that where harsher ways are taken, they are the effect only of pride and peevishness in the teacher, who expects children should instantly be masters of as much as he knows; whereas he should rather consider, that his business is to settle in them habits, not angrily to inculcate rules, which serve for little in the conduct of our lives; at least are of no use to children, who forget them as soon as given. In sciences where their reason is to be exercised, I will not deny but this method may sometimes be varied, and difficulties proposed on purpose to excite industry, and accustom the mind to employ its own strength and sagacity in reasoning. But yet, I guess, this is not to be done to children, whilst very young, nor at their entrance upon any sort of knowledge: then every thing of itself is difficult, and the great use and skill of a teacher is to make all as easy as he can: but particularly in learning of languages there is least occasion for posing of children. For languages being to be learned by rote, custom and memory, are then spoken in greatest perfection, when all rules of grammar are utterly forgotten. I grant the grammar of a language is sometimes very carefully to be studied, but it is not to be studied but by a grown man, when he applies himself to the understanding of any language critically, which is seldom the business of any but professed scholars. This I think will be agreed to, that if a gentleman be to study any language, it ought to be that of his own country, that he may understand the language which he has constant use of, with the utmost accuracy.

There is yet a further reason, why masters and teachers should raise no difficulties to their scholars; but on the contrary should smooth their way, and readily help them forwards, where they find them stop. Children's minds are narrow and weak, and usually susceptible but of one thought at once. Whatever is in a child's head, fills it for the time, especially if set on with any passion. It should therefore be the skill and art of the teacher to clear their heads of all other thoughts whilst they are learning of any thing, the better to make room for what he would instil into them, that it may be received with attention and application, without which it leaves no impression. The natural temper of children disposes their minds to wander. Novelty alone takes them; whatever that presents, they are presently eager to have a taste of, and are as soon satiated with it. They quickly grow weary of the same thing, and so have almost their whole delight in change and variety. It is a contradiction to the natural state of childhood for them to fix their fleeting thoughts. Whether this be owing to the temper of their brains, or the quickness or instability of their animal spirits, over which the mind has not yet got a full command; this is visible, that it is a pain to children to keep their thoughts steady to any thing. A lasting continued attention is one of the hardest tasks can be imposed on them; and therefore, he that requires their application, should endeavour to make what he proposes as grateful and agreeable as possible; at least he ought to take care not to join any displeasing or frightful idea with it. If they come not to their books with some kind of liking and relish, 'tis no wonder their thoughts should be perpetually shifting from what disgusts them; and seek better entertainment in more pleasing objects, after which they will unavoidably be gadding.

'Tis, I know, the usual method of tutors, to endeavour to procure attention in their scholars, and to fix their minds to the business in hand, by rebukes and corrections, if they find them ever so little wandering. But such treatment is sure to produce the quite contrary effect. Passionate words or blows from the tutor fill the child's mind with terror and affrightment, which immediately takes it wholly up, and leaves no room for other impressions. I believe there is nobody that reads this, but may recollect what disorder hasty or imperious words from his parents or teachers have caused in his thoughts; how for the time it has turned his brains, so that he scarce knew what was said by or to him. He presently lost the sight of what he was upon, his mind was filled with disorder and confusion, and in that state was no longer capable of attention to any thing else.

'Tis true, parents and governors ought to settle and establish their authority by an awe over the minds of those under their tuition; and to rule them by that: but when they have got an ascendant over them, they should use it with great moderation, and not make themselves such scare-crows that their scholars should always tremble in their sight. Such an austerity may make their government easy to themselves, but of very little use to their pupils. 'Tis impossible children should learn any thing whilst their thoughts are possessed and disturbed with any passion, especially fear, which makes the strongest impression on their yet tender and weak spirits. Keep the mind in an easy calm temper, when you would have it receive your instructions or any increase of knowledge. 'Tis as impossible to draw fair and regular characters on a trembling mind as on a shaking paper.

The great skill of a teacher is to get and keep the attention of his scholar; whilst he has that, he is sure to advance as fast as the learner's abilities will carry him; and without that, all his bustle and pother will be to little or no purpose. To attain this, he should make the child comprehend (as much as may be) the usefulness of what he teaches him, and let him see, by what he has learnt, that he can do something which he could not do before; something, which gives him some power and real advantage above others who are ignorant of it. To this he should add sweetness in all his instructions, and by a certain tenderness in his whole carriage, make the child sensible that he loves him and designs nothing but his good, the only way to beget love in the child, which will make him hearken to his lessons, and relish what he teaches him.

Nothing but obstinacy should meet with any imperiousness or rough usage. All other faults should be corrected with a gentle hand; and kind engaging words will work better and more effectually upon a willing mind, and even prevent a good deal of that perverseness which rough and imperious usage often produces in well disposed and generous minds. 'Tis true, obstinacy and wilful neglects must be mastered, even though it cost blows to do it: but I am apt to think perverseness in the pupils is often the effect of frowardness in the tutor; and that most children would seldom have deserved blows, if needless and misapplied roughness had not taught them ill-nature, and given them an aversion for their teacher and all that comes from him.

Inadvertency, forgetfulness, unsteadiness, and wandering of thought, are the natural faults of childhood; and therefore, where they are not observed to be wilful, are to be mention'd softly, and gain'd upon by time. If every slip of this kind produces anger and rating, the occasions of rebuke and corrections will return so often, that the tutor will be a constant terror and uneasiness to his pupils. Which one thing is enough to hinder their profiting by his lessons, and to defeat all his methods of instruction.

Let the awe he has got upon their minds be so tempered with the constant marks of tenderness and good will, that affection may spur them to their duty, and make them find a pleasure in complying with his dictates. This will bring them with satisfaction to their tutor; make them hearken to him, as to one who is their friend, that cherishes them, and takes pains for their good: this will keep their thoughts easy and free whilst they are with him, the only temper wherein the mind is capable of receiving new informations, and of admitting into itself those impressions, which, if not taken and retain'd, all that they and their teachers do together is lost labour; there is much uneasiness and little learning.

§ 168. When by this way of interlining Latin and English one with another, he has got a moderate knowledge of the Latin tongue, he may then be advanced a little farther to the reading of some other easy Latin-book, such as Justin or Eutropius; and to make the reading and understanding of it the less tedious and difficult to him, let him help himself if he pleases with the English translation. Nor let the objection that he will then know it only by rote, fright any one. This, when well consider'd, is not of any moment against, but plainly for this way of learning a language. For languages are only to be learned by rote; and a man who does not speak English or Latin perfectly by rote, so that having thought of the thing he would speak of, his tongue of course, without thought of rule or grammar, falls into the proper expression and idiom of that language, does not speak it well, nor is master of it. And I would fain have any one name to me that tongue, that any one can learn, or speak as he should do, by the rules of grammar. Languages were made not by rules or art, but by accident, and the common use of the people. And he that will speak them well, has no other rule but that; nor any thing to trust to, but his memory, and the habit of speaking after the fashion learned from those, that are allowed to speak properly, which in other words is only to speak by rote.

It will possibly be asked here, is grammar then of no use? and have those who have taken so much pains in reducing several languages to rules and observations; who have writ so much about declensions and conjugations, about concords and syntaxis, lost their labour, and been learned to no purpose? I say not so; grammar has its place too. But this I think I may say, there is more stir a great deal made with it than there needs, and those are tormented about it, to whom it does not at all belong; I mean children, at the age wherein they are usually perplexed with it in grammar-schools.

There is nothing more evident, than that languages learnt by rote serve well enough for the common affairs of life and ordinary commerce. Nay, persons of quality of the softer sex, and such of them as have spent their time in well-bred company, shew us, that this plain natural way, without the least study or knowledge of grammar, can carry them to a great degree of elegancy and politeness in their language: and there are ladies who, without knowing what tenses and participles, adverbs and prepositions are, speak as properly and as correctly (they might take it for an ill compliment if I said as any country school-master) as most gentlemen who have been bred up in the ordinary methods of grammar-schools. Grammar therefore we see may be spared in some cases. The question then will be, to whom should it be taught, and when? To this I answer:

1. Men learn languages for the ordinary intercourse of society and communication of thoughts in common life, without any farther design in the use of them. And for this purpose, the original way of learning a language by conversation not only serves well enough, but is to be preferred as the most expedite, proper and natural. Therefore, to this use of language one may answer, that grammar is not necessary. This so many of my readers must be forced to allow, as understand what I here say, and who conversing with others, understand them without having ever been taught the grammar of the English tongue. Which I suppose is the case of incomparably the greatest part of English men, of whom I have never yet known any one who learned his mother-tongue by rules.

2. Others there are, the greatest part of whose business in this world is to be done with their tongues and with their pens; and to these it is convenient, if not necessary, that they should speak properly and correctly, whereby they may let their thoughts into other men's minds the more easily, and with the greater impression. Upon this account it is, that any sort of speaking, so as will make him be understood, is not thought enough for a gentleman. He ought to study grammar amongst the other helps of speaking well, but it must be the grammar of his own tongue, of the language he uses, that he may understand his own country speech nicely, and speak it properly, without shocking the ears of those it is addressed to, with solecisms and offensive irregularities. And to this purpose grammar is necessary; but it is the grammar only of their own proper tongues, and to those only who would take pains in cultivating their language, and in perfecting their stiles. Whether all gentlemen should not do this, I leave to be considered, since the want of propriety and grammatical exactness is thought very misbecoming one of that rank, and usually draws on one guilty of such faults the censure of having had a lower breeding and worse company than suits with his quality. If this be so, (as I suppose it is) it will be matter of wonder why young gentlemen are forced to learn the grammars of foreign and dead languages, and are never once told of the grammar of their own tongues, they do not so much as know there is any such thing, much less is it made their business to be instructed in it. Nor is their own language ever proposed to them as worthy their care and cultivating, though they have daily use of it, and are not seldom, in the future course of their lives, judg'd of by their handsome or awkward way of expressing themselves in it. Whereas the languages whose grammars they have been so much employed in, are such as probably they shall scarce ever speak or write; or if, upon occasion, this should happen, they should be excused for the mistakes and faults they make in it. Would not a Chinese who took notice of this way of breeding, be apt to imagine that all our young gentlemen were designed to be teachers and professors of the dead languages of foreign countries, and not to be men of business in their own?

3. There is a third sort of men, who apply themselves to two or three foreign, dead, and (which amongst us are called the) learned languages, make them their study, and pique themselves upon their skill in them. No doubt, those who propose to themselves the learning of any language with this view, and would be critically exact in it, ought carefully to study the grammar of it. I would not be mistaken here, as if this were to undervalue Greek and Latin. I grant these are languages of great use and excellency, and a man can have no place among the learned in this part of the world, who is a stranger to them. But the knowledge a gentleman would ordinarily draw for his use out of the Roman and Greek writers, I think he may attain without studying the grammars of those tongues, and by bare reading, may come to understand them sufficiently for all his purposes. How much farther he shall at any time be concerned to look into the grammar and critical niceties of either of these tongues, he himself will be able to determine when he comes to propose to himself the study of any thing that shall require it. Which brings me to the other part of the enquiry, viz.

When Grammar should be taught?

To which, upon the premised grounds, the answer is obvious, viz.

That if grammar ought to be taught at any time, it must be to one that can speak the language already; how else can he be taught the grammar of it? This at least is evident from the practice of the wise and learned nations amongst the antients. They made it a part of education to cultivate their own, not foreign tongues. The Greeks counted all other nations barbarous, and had a contempt for their languages. And tho' the Greek learning grew in credit amongst the Romans, towards the end of their commonwealth, yet it was the Roman tongue that was made the study of their youth: their own language they were to make use of, and therefore it was their own language they were instructed and exercised in.

But, more particularly to determine the proper season for grammar, I do not see how it can reasonably be made any one's study, but as an introduction to rhetorick; when it is thought time to put any one upon the care of polishing his tongue, and of speaking better than the illiterate, then is the time for him to be instructed in the rules of grammar, and not before. For grammar being to teach men not to speak, but to speak correctly and according to the exact rules of the tongue, which is one part of elegancy, there is little use of the one to him that has no need of the other; where rhetorick is not necessary, grammar may be spared. I know not why any one should waste his time, and beat his head about the Latin grammar, who does not intend to be a critick, or make speeches and write dispatches in it. When any one finds in himself a necessity or disposition to study any foreign language to the bottom, and to be nicely exact in the knowledge of it, it will be time enough to take a grammatical survey of it. If his use of it be only to understand some books writ in it, without a critical knowledge of the tongue itself, reading alone, as I have said, will attain this end, without charging the mind with the multiplied rules and intricacies of grammar.

§ 169. For the exercise of his writing, let him sometimes translate Latin into English: but the learning of Latin being nothing but the learning of words, a very unpleasant business both to young and old, join as much other real knowledge with it as you can, beginning still with that which lies most obvious to the senses; such as is the knowledge of minerals, plants and animals, and particularly timber and fruit-trees, their parts, and ways of propagation, wherein a great deal may be taught a child which will not be useless to the man: but more especially geography, astronomy, and anatomy. But whatever you are teaching him, have a care still that you do not clog him with too much at once; or make anything his business but downright virtue, or reprove him for any thing but vice, or some apparent tendency to it.

§ 170. But if after all his fate be to go to school to get the Latin tongue, 'twill be in vain to talk to you concerning the method I think best to be observ'd in schools; you must submit to that you find there, not expect to have it changed for your son; but yet by all means obtain, if you can, that he be not employed in making Latin themes and declamations, and least of all, verses of any kind. You may insist on it, if it will do any good, that you have no design to make him either a Latin orator or poet, but barely would have him understand perfectly a Latin author; and that you observe, those who teach any of the modern languages, and that with success, never amuse their scholars to make speeches or verses either in French or Italian, their business being language barely, and not invention.

Sections 171–180

§ 171. But to tell you a little more fully why I would not have him exercised in making of themes and verses. 1. As to themes, they have, I confess, the pretence of something useful, which is to teach people to speak handsomely and well on any subject; which, if it could be attained this way, I own would be a great advantage, there being nothing more becoming a gentleman, nor more useful in all the occurrences of life, than to be able, on any occasion, to speak well and to the purpose. But this I say, that the making of themes, as is usual at schools, helps not one jot towards it: for do but consider what it is, in making a theme, that a young lad is employed about; it is to make a speech on some Latin saying; as Omnia vincit amor; or Non licet in Bello bis peccare, &c. And here the poor lad, who wants knowledge of those things he is to speak of, which is to be had only from time and observation, must set his invention on the rack, to say something where he knows nothing; which is a sort of Egyptian tyranny, to bid them make bricks who have not yet any of the materials. And therefore it is usual in such cases for the poor children to go to those of higher forms with this petition, Pray give me a little sense; which, whether it be more reasonable or more ridiculous, it is not easy to determine. Before a man can be in any capacity to speak on any subject, 'tis necessary he be acquainted with it; or else it is as foolish to set him to discourse of it, as to set a blind man to talk of colours, or a deaf man of musick. And would you not think him a little crack'd, who would require another to make an argument on a moot point, who understands nothing of our laws? And what, I pray, do school-boys understand concerning those matters which are used to be proposed to them in their themes as subjects to discourse on, to whet and exercise their fancies?

§ 172. In the next place, consider the language that their themes are made in: 'tis Latin, a language foreign in their country, and long since dead every where: a language which your son, 'tis a thousand to one, shall never have an occasion once to make a speech in as long as he lives after he comes to be a man; and a language wherein the manner of expressing one's self is so far different from ours, that to be perfect in that would very little improve the purity and facility of his English stile. Besides that, there is now so little room or use for set speeches in our own language in any part of our English business, that I can see no pretence for this sort of exercise in our schools, unless it can be supposed, that the making of set Latin speeches should be the way to teach men to speak well in English extempore. The way to that, I should think rather to be this: that there should be propos'd to young gentlemen rational and useful questions, suited to their age and capacities, and on subjects not wholly unknown to them nor out of their way: such as these, when they are ripe for exercises of this nature, they should extempore, or after a little meditation upon the spot, speak to, without penning of any thing: for I ask, if we will examine the effects of this way of learning to speak well, who speak best in any business, when occasion calls them to it upon any debate, either those who have accustomed themselves to compose and write down beforehand what they would say; or those, who thinking only of the matter, to understand that as well as they can, use themselves only to speak extempore? And he that shall judge by this, will be little apt to think, that the accustoming him to studied speeches and set compositions, is the way to fit a young gentleman for business.

§ 173. But perhaps we shall be told, 'tis to improve and perfect them in the Latin tongue. 'Tis true, that is their proper business at school; but the making of themes is not the way to it: that perplexes their brains about invention of things to be said, not about the signification of words to be learn'd; and when they are making a theme, 'tis thoughts they search and sweat for, and not language. But the learning and mastery of a tongue being uneasy and unpleasant enough in itself, should not be cumbred with any other difficulties, as is done in this way of proceeding. In fine, if boys' invention be to be quicken'd by such exercise, let them make themes in English, where they have facility and a command of words, and will better see what kind of thoughts they have, when put into their own language. And if the Latin tongue be to be learned, let it be done the easiest way, without toiling and disgusting the mind by so uneasy an employment as that of making speeches joined to it.

§ 174. If these may be any reasons against children's making Latin themes at school, I have much more to say, and of more weight, against their making verses; verses of any sort: for if he has no genius to poetry, 'tis the most unreasonable thing in the world to torment a child and waste his time about that which can never succeed; and if he have a poetick vein, 'tis to me the strangest thing in the world that the father should desire or suffer it to be cherished or improved. Methinks the parents should labour to have it stifled and suppressed as much as may be; and I know not what reason a father can have to wish his son a poet, who does not desire to have him bid defiance to all other callings and business; which is not yet the worst of the case; for if he proves a successful rhymer, and gets once the reputation of a wit, I desire it may be considered what company and places he is like to spend his time in, nay, and estate too: for it is very seldom seen, that any one discovers mines of gold or silver in Parnassus. 'Tis a pleasant air, but a barren soil; and there are very few instances of those who have added to their patrimony by any thing they have reaped from thence. Poetry and gaming, which usually go together, are alike in this too, that they seldom bring any advantage but to those who have nothing else to live on. Men of estates almost constantly go away losers; and 'tis well if they escape at a cheaper rate than their whole estates, or the greatest part of them. If therefore you would not have your son the fiddle to every jovial company, without whom the sparks could not relish their wine nor know how to pass an afternoon idly; if you would not have him to waste his time and estate to divert others, and contemn the dirty acres left him by his ancestors, I do not think you will much care he should be a poet, or that his school-master should enter him in versifying. But yet, if any one will think poetry a desirable quality in his son, and that the study of it would raise his fancy and parts, he must needs yet confess, that to that end reading the excellent Greek and Roman poets is of more use than making bad verses of his own, in a language that is not his own. And he whose design it is to excel in English poetry, would not, I guess, think the way to it were to make his first essays in Latin verses.

§ 175. Another thing very ordinary in the vulgar method of grammar-schools there is, of which I see no use at all, unless it be to baulk young lads in the way to learning languages, which, in my opinion, should be made as easy and pleasant as may be; and that which was painful in it, as much as possible quite removed. That which I mean, and here complain of, is, their being to learn by heart, great parcels of the authors which are taught them; wherein I can discover no advantage at all, especially to the business they are upon. Languages are to be learned only by reading and talking, and not by scraps of authors got by heart; which when a man's head is stuffed with, he has got the just furniture of a pedant, and 'tis the ready way to make him one; than which there is nothing less becoming a gentleman. For what can be more ridiculous, than to mix the rich and handsome thoughts and sayings of others with a deal of poor stuff of his own; which is thereby the more exposed, and has no other grace in it, nor will otherwise recommend the speaker, than a thread-bare russet coat would, that was set off with large patches of scarlet and glittering brocade. Indeed, where a passage comes in the way, whose matter is worth remembrance, and the expression of it very close and excellent, (as there are many such in the antient authors) it may not be amiss to lodge it in the mind of young scholars, and with such admirable strokes of those great masters sometimes exercise the memories of school-boys. But their learning of their lessons by heart, as they happen to fall out in their books, without choice or distinction, I know not what it serves for, but no misspend their time and pains, and give them a disgust and aversion to their books, wherein they find nothing but useless trouble.

§ 176. I hear it is said, that children should be employ'd in getting things by heart, to exercise and improve their memories. I could wish this were said with as much authority of reason, as it is with forwardness of assurance, and that this practice were established upon good observation more than old custom; for it is evident, that strength of memory is owing to an happy constitution, and not to any habitual improvement got by exercise. 'Tis true, what the mind is intent upon, and, for fear of letting it slip, often imprints afresh on itself by frequent reflection, that it is apt to retain, but still according to its own natural strength of retention. An impression made on bees-wax or lead, will not last so long as on brass or steel. Indeed, if it be renew'd often, it may last the longer; but every new reflecting on it is a new impression; and 'tis from thence one is to reckon, if one would know how long the mind retains it. But the learning pages of Latin by heart, no more fits the memory for retention of any thing else, than the graving of one sentence in lead makes it the more capable of retaining firmly any other characters. If such a sort of exercise of the memory were able to give it strength, and improve our parts, players of all other people must needs have the best memories and be the best company. But whether the scraps they have got into their heads this way, make them remember other things the better; and whether their parts be improved proportionably to the pains they have taken in getting by heart others' sayings, experience will shew. Memory is so necessary to all parts and conditions of life, and so little is to be done without it, that we are not to fear it should grow dull and useless for want of exercise, if exercise would make it grow stronger. But I fear this faculty of the mind is not capable of much help and amendment in general by any exercise or endeavour of ours, at least not by that used upon this pretence in grammar-schools. And if Xerxes was able to call every common soldier by name in his army that consisted of no less than an hundred thousand men, I think it may be guessed, he got not this wonderful ability by learning his lessons by heart when he was a boy. This method of exercising and improving the memory by toilsome repetitions without book of what they read, is, I think, little used in the education of princes, which if it had that advantage is talked of, should be as little neglected in them as in the meanest school-boys: princes having as much need of good memories as any men living, and have generally an equal share in this faculty with other men; though it has never been taken care of this way. What the mind is intent upon and careful of, that it remembers best, and for the reason above-mentioned: to which, if method and order be joined, all is done, I think, that can be, for the help of a weak memory; and he that will take any other way to do it, especially that of charging it with a train of other peoples' words, which he that learns cares not for, will, I guess, scarce find the profit answer half the time and pains employ'd in it.

I do not mean hereby, that there should be no exercise given to children's memories. I think their memories should be employ'd, but not in learning by rote whole pages out of books, which, the lesson being once said, and that task over, are delivered up again to oblivion and neglected for ever. This mends neither the memory nor the mind. What they should learn by heart out of authors, I have above mentioned: and such wise and useful sentences being once being once given in charge to their memories, they should never be suffer'd to forget again, but be often called to account for them: whereby, besides the use those sayings may be to them in their future life, as so many good rules and observations, they will be taught to reflect often, and bethink themselves what they have to remember, which is the only way to make the memory quick and useful. The custom of frequent reflection will keep their minds from running adrift, and call their thoughts home from useless unattentive roving: and therefore I think it may do well, to give them something every day to remember, but something still, that is in itself worth the remembering, and what you would never have out of mind, whenever you call, or they themselves search for it. This will oblige them often to turn their thoughts inwards, than which you cannot wish them a better intellectual habit.

§ 177. But under whose care soever a child is put to be taught during the tender and flexible years of his life, this is certain, it should be one who thinks Latin and language the least part of education; one who knowing how much virtue and a well-temper'd soul is to be preferred to any sort of learning or language, makes it his chief business to form the mind of his scholars, and give that a right disposition; which if once got, though all the rest should be neglected, would in due time produce all the rest; and which, if it be not got and settled so as to keep out ill and vicious habits, languages and sciences and all the other accomplishments of education, will be to no purpose but to make the worse or more dangerous man. And indeed whatever stir there is made about getting of Latin as the great and difficult business, his mother may teach it him herself, if she will but spend two or three hours in a day with him, and make him read the Evangelists in Latin to her: for she need but buy a Latin Testament, and having got some body to mark the last syllable but one where it is long in words above two syllables, (which is enough to regulate her pronunciation, and accenting the words) read daily in the Gospels, and then let her avoid understanding them in Latin if she can. And when she understands the Evangelists in Latin, let her, in the same manner, read Æsop's Fables, and so proceed on to Eutropius, Justin, and other such books. I do not mention this, as an imagination of what I fancy may do, but as of a thing I have known done, and the Latin tongue with ease got this way.

But, to return to what I was saying: he that takes on him the charge of bringing up young men, especially young gentlemen, should have something more in him than Latin, more than even a knowledge in the liberal sciences: he should be a person of eminent virtue and prudence, and with good sense, have good humour, and the skill to carry himself with gravity, ease and kindness, in a constant conversation with his pupils. But of this I have spoken at large in another place.

§ 178. At the same time that he is learning French and Latin, a child, as has been said, may also be enter'd in Arithmetick, Geography, Chronology, History and Geometry too. For if these be taught him in French or Latin, when he begins once to understand either of these tongues, he will get a knowledge in these sciences, and the language to boot.

Geography I think should be begun with: for the learning of the figure of the globe, the situation and boundaries of the four parts of the world, and that of particular kingdoms and countries, being only an exercise of the eyes and memory, a child with pleasure will learn and retain them. And this is so certain, that I now live in the house with a child whom his mother has so well instructed this way in geography, that he knew the limits of the four parts of the world, could readily point, being ask'd, to any country upon the globe, or any county in the map of England; knew all the great rivers, promontories, straits and bays in the world, and could find the longitude and latitude of any place, before he was six years old. These things, that he will thus learn by sight, and have by rote in his memory, are not all, I confess, that he is to learn upon the globes. But yet it is a good step and preparation to it, and will make the remainder much easier, when his judgment is grown ripe enough for it: besides that, it gets so much time now; and by the pleasure of knowing things, leads him on insensibly to the gaining of languages.

§ 179. When he has the natural parts of the globe well fix'd in his memory, it may then be time to begin arithmetick. By the natural parts of the globe, I mean the several positions of the parts of the earth and sea, under different names and distinctions of countries, not coming yet to those artificial and imaginary lines which have been invented, and are only suppos'd for the better improvement of that science.

§ 180. Arithmetick is the easiest, and consequently the first sort of abstract reasoning, which the mind commonly bears or accustoms itself to: and is of so general use in all parts of life and business, that scarce any thing is to be done without it. This is certain, a man cannot have too much of it, nor too perfectly: he should therefore begin to be exercis'd in counting, as soon, and as far, as he is capable of it; and do something in it every day, till he is master of the art of numbers. When he understands addition and subtraction, he then may be advanced farther in geography, after he is acquainted with the poles, zones, parallel circles, and meridians, be taught longitude and latitude, and by them be made to understand the use of maps, and by the numbers placed on their sides, to know the respective situation of countries, and how to find them out on the terrestrial globe. Which when he can readily do, he may then be entered in the celestial; and there going over all the circles again, with a more particular observation of the Ecliptick, or Zodiack, to fix them all very clearly and distinctly in his mind, he may be taught the figure and position of the several constellations, which may be shewed him first upon the globe, and then in the heavens.

When that is done, and he knows pretty well the constellations of this our hemisphere, it may be time to give him some notions of this our planetary world; and to that purpose, it may not be amiss to make him a draught of the Copernican system, and therein explain to him the situation of the planets, their respective distances from the sun, the centre of their revolutions. This will prepare him to understand the motion and theory of the planets, the most easy and natural way. For since astronomers no longer doubt of the motion of the planets about the sun, it is fit he should proceed upon that hypothesis, which is not only the simplest and least perplexed for a learner, but also the likeliest to be true in itself. But in this, as in all other parts of instruction, great care must be taken with children, to begin with that which is plain and simple, and to teach them as little as can be at once, and settle that well in their heads before you proceed to the next, or any thing new in that science. Give them first one simple idea, and see that they take it right, and perfectly comprehend it before you go any farther, and then add some other simple idea which lies next in your way to what you aim at; and so proceeding by gentle and insensible steps, children without confusion and amazement will have their understandings opened and their thoughts extended farther than could have been expected. And when any one has learn'd any thing himself, there is no such way to fix it in his memory, and to encourage him to go on, as to set him to teach it others.

Sections 181–190

§ 181. When he has once got such an acquaintance with the globes, as is above mentioned, he may be fit to be tried in a little geometry; wherein I think the first six books of Euclid enough for him to be taught. For I am in some doubt, whether more to a man of business be necessary or useful. At least, if he have a genius and inclination to it, being enter'd so far by his tutor, he will be able to go on of himself without a teacher.

The globes therefore must be studied, and that diligently; and I think may be begun betimes, if the tutor will be but careful to distinguish what the child is capable of knowing, and what not; for which this may be a rule that perhaps will go a pretty way, viz. that children may be taught anything that falls under their senses, especially their sight, as far as their memories only are exercised: and thus a child very young may learn, which is the Æquator, which the Meridian, &c. which Europe, and which England, upon the globes, as soon almost as he knows the rooms of the house he lives in, if care be taken not to teach him too much at once, nor to set him upon a new part, till that which he is upon be perfectly learned and fixed in his memory.

§ 182. With geography, chronology ought to go hand in hand. I mean the general part of it, so that he may have in his mind a view of the whole current of time, and the several considerable epochs that are made use of in history. Without these two, history, which is the great mistress of prudence and civil knowledge, and ought to be the proper study of a gentleman, or man of business in the world; without geography and chronology, I say, history will be very ill retain'd, and very little useful; but be only a jumble of matters of fact, confusedly heaped together without order or instruction. 'Tis by these two that the actions of mankind are ranked into their proper places of time and countries, under which circumstances they are not only much easier kept in the memory, but in that natural order, are only capable to afford those observations which make a man the better and the abler for reading them.

§ 183. When I speak of chronology as a science he should be perfect in, I do not mean the little controversies that are in it. These are endless, and most of them of so little importance to a gentleman, as not to deserve to be enquir'd into, were they capable of an easy decision. And therefore all that learned noise and dust of the chronologist is wholly to be avoided. The most useful book I have seen in that part of learning, is a small treatise of Strauchius, which is printed in twelves, under the title of Breviarium Chronologicum, out of which may be selected all that is necessary to be taught a young gentleman concerning chronology; for all that is in that treatise a learner need not be cumbred with. He has in him the most remarkable or useful epochs reduced all to that of the Julian Period, which is the easiest and plainest and surest method that can be made use of in chronology. To this treatise of Strauchius, Helvicus's tables may be added, as a book to be turned to on all occasions.

§ 184. As nothing teaches, so nothing delights more than history. The first of these recommends it to the study of grown men, the latter makes me think it the fittest for a young lad, who as soon as he is instructed in chronology, and acquainted with the several epochs in use in this part of the world, and can reduce them to the Julian Period, should then have some Latin history put into his hand. The choice should be directed by the easiness of the stile; for wherever he begins, chronology will keep it from confusion; and the pleasantness of the subject inviting him to read, the language will insensibly be got without that terrible vexation and uneasiness which children suffer where they are put into books beyond their capacity; such as are the Roman orators and poets, only to learn the Roman language. When he has by reading master'd the easier, such perhaps as Justin, Eutropius, Quintius Curtius, &c. the next degree to these will give him no great trouble: and thus by a gradual progress from the plaintest and easiest historians, he may at last come to read the most difficult and sublime of the Latin authors, such as are Tully, Virgil, and Horace.

§ 185. The knowledge of virtue, all along from the beginning, in all the instances he is capable of, being taught him more by practice than rules; and the love of reputation, instead of satisfying his appetite, being made habitual in him, I know not whether he should read any other discourses of morality but what he finds in the Bible; or have any system of ethicks put into his hand till he can read Tully's Offices not as a school-boy to learn Latin, but as one that would be informed in the principles and precepts of virtue for the conduct of his life.

§ 186. When he has pretty well digested Tully's Offices, and added to it, Puffendorf de Officio Hominis & Civis, it may be seasonable to set him upon Grotius de Jure Belli & Pacis, or, which perhaps is the better of the two, Puffendorf de Jure naturali & Gentium; wherein he will be instructed in the natural rights of men, and the original and foundations of society, and the duties resulting from thence. This general part of civil-law and history, are studies which a gentleman should not barely touch at, but constantly dwell upon, and never have done with. A virtuous and well-behaved young man, that is well-versed in the general part of the civil-law (which concerns not the chicane of private cases, but the affairs and intercourse of civilized nations in general, grounded upon principles of reason) understands Latin well, and can write a good hand, one may turn loose into the world with great assurance that he will find employment and esteem every where.

§ 187. It would be strange to suppose an English gentleman should be ignorant of the law of his country. This, whatever station he is in, is so requisite, that from a Justice of the Peace to a Minister of State I know no place he can well fill without it. I do not mean the chicane or wrangling and captious part of the law: a gentleman, whose business is to seek the true measures of right and wrong, and not the arts how to avoid doing the one, and secure himself in doing the other, ought to be as far from such a study of the law, as he is concerned diligently to apply himself to that wherein he may be serviceable to his country. And to that purpose, I think the right way for a gentleman to study our law, which he does not design for his calling, is to take a view of our English constitution and government in the antient books of the common-law, and some more modern writers, who out of them have given an account of this government. And having got a true idea of that, then to read our history, and with it join in every king's reign the laws then made. This will give an insight into the reason of our statutes, and shew the true ground upon which they came to be made, and what weight they ought to have.

§ 188. Rhetorick and logick being the arts that in the ordinary method usually follow immediately after grammar, it may perhaps be wondered that I have said to little of them. The reason is, because of the little advantage young people receive by them: for I have seldom or never observed any one to get the skill of reasoning well, or speaking handsomely, by studying those rules which pretend to reach it: and therefore I would have a young gentleman take a view of them in the shortest systems could be found, without dwelling long on the contemplation and study of those formalities. Right reasoning is founded on something else than the predicaments and predicables, and does not consist in talking in mode and figure it self. But 'tis beside my present business to enlarge upon this speculation. To come therefore to what we have in hand; if you would have your son reason well, let him read Chillingworth; and if you would have him speak well, let him be conversant in Tully, to give him the true idea of eloquence; and let him read those things that are well writ in English, to perfect his style in the purity of our language.

§ 189. If the use and end of right reasoning be to have right notions and a right judgment of things, to distinguish betwixt truth and falsehood, right and wrong, and to act accordingly; be sure not to let your son be bred up in the art and formality of disputing, either practising it himself, or admiring it in others; unless instead of an able man, you desire to have him an insignificant wrangler, opiniator in discourse, and priding himself in contradicting others; or, which is worse, questioning every thing, and thinking there is no such thing as truth to be sought, but only victory, in disputing. There cannot be any thing so disingenuous, so misbecoming a gentleman or any one who pretends to be a rational creature, as not to yield to plain reason and the conviction of clear arguments. Is there any thing more consistent with civil conversation, and the end of all debate, than not to take an answer, though never so full and satisfactory, but still to go on with the dispute as long as equivocal sounds can furnish (a medius terminus) a term to wrangle with on the one side, or a distinction on the other; whether pertinent or impertinent, sense or nonsense, agreeing with or contrary to what he had said before, it matters not. For this, in short, is the way and perfection of logical disputes, that the opponent never takes any answer, nor the respondent ever yields to any argument. This neither of them must do, whatever becomes of truth or knowledge, unless he will pass for a poor baffled wretch, and lie under the disgrace of not being able to maintain whatever he has once affirm'd, which is the great aim and glory in disputing. Truth is to be found and supported by a mature and due consideration of things themselves, and not by artificial terms and ways of arguing: these lead not men so much into the discovery of truth, as into a captious and fallacious use of doubtful words, which is the most useless and most offensive way of talking, and such as least suits a gentleman or a lover of truth of any thing in the world.

There can scarce be a greater defect in a gentleman than not to express himself well either in writing or speaking. But yet I think I may ask my reader, whether he doth not know a great many, who live upon their estates, and so with the name should have the qualities of gentlemen, who cannot so much as tell a story as they should, much less speak clearly and persuasively in any business. This I think not to be so much their fault, as the fault of their education; for I must, without partiality, do my countrymen this right, that where they apply themselves, I see none of their neighbours outgo them. They have been taught rhetorick, but yet never taught how to express themselves handsomely with their tongues or pens in the language they are always to use; as if the names of the figures that embellish'd the discourses of those who understood the art of speaking, were the very art and skill of speaking well. This, as all other things of practice, is to be learn'd not by a few or a great many rules given, but by exercise and application according to good rules, or rather patterns, till habits are got, and a facility of doing it well.

Agreeable hereunto, perhaps it might not be amiss to make children, as soon as they are capable of it, often to tell a story of any thing they know; and to correct at first the most remarkable fault they are guilty of in their way putting it together. When that fault is cured, then to shew them the next, and so on, till one after another, all, at least the gross ones, are mended. When they can tell tales pretty well, then it may be the time to make them write them. The Fables of Æsop, the only book almost that I know fit for children, may afford them matter for this exercise of writing English, as well as for reading and translating, to enter them in the Latin tongue. When they have got past the faults of grammar, and can join in a continued coherent discourse the several parts of a story, without bald and unhandsome forms of transition (as is usual) often repeated, he that desires to perfect them yet farther in this, which is the first step to speaking well and needs no invention, may have recourse to Tully, and by putting in practice those rules which that master of eloquence gives in his first book de inventione, § 20, make them know wherein the skill and graces of an handsome narrative, according to the several subjects and designs of it, lie. Of each of which rules fit examples may be found out, and therein they may be shewn how others have practised them. The antient classick authors afford plenty of such examples, which they should be made not only to translate, but have set before them as patterns for their daily imitation.

When they understand how to write English with due connexion, propriety and order, and are pretty well masters of a tolerable narrative style, they may be advanced to writing of letters; wherein they should not be put upon any strains of wit or compliment, but taught to express their own plain easy sense, without any incoherence, confusion or roughness. And when they are perfect in this, they may, to raise their thoughts, have set before them the examples of Voitures, for the entertainment of their friends at a distance, with letters of compliment, mirth, raillery or diversion; and Tully's Epistles, as the best pattern whether for business or conversation. The writing of letters has so much to do in all the occurrences of human life, that no gentleman can avoid shewing himself in this kind of writing. Occasions will daily force him to make this use of his pen, which, besides the consequences that, in his affairs, his well or ill managing of it often draws after it, always lays him open to a severer examination of his breeding, sense, and abilities, than oral discourses; whose transient faults dying for the most part with the sound that gives them life, and so not subject to a strict review, more easily escape observation and censure.

Had the methods of education been directed to their right end, one would have thought this so necessary a part could not have been neglected whilst themes and verses in Latin, of no use at all, were so constantly every where pressed, to the racking of children's inventions beyond their strength and hindering their chearful progress in learning the tongues by unnatural difficulties. But custom has so ordain'd it, and who dares disobey? And would it not be very unreasonable to require of a learned country school-master (who has all the tropes and figures in Farnaby's Rhetorick at his fingers' ends) to teach his scholar to express himself handsomely in English, when it appears to be so little his business or thought, that the boy's mother (despised, 'tis like, as illiterate for not having read a system of logick and rhetorick) outdoes him in it?

To write and speak correctly gives a grace and gains a favourable attention to what one has to say: and since 'tis English that an English gentleman will have constant use of, that is the language he should chiefly cultivate, and wherein most care should be taken to polish and perfect his style. To speak or write better Latin than English, may make a man be talk'd of, but he would find it more to his purpose to express himself well in his own tongue, that he uses every moment, than to have the vain commendation of others for a very insignificant quality. This I find universally neglected, and no care taken any where to improve young men in their own language, that they may thoroughly understand and be masters of it. If any one among us have a facility or purity more than ordinary in his mother tongue, it is owing to chance, or his genius, or any thing rather than to his education or any care of his teacher. To mind what English his pupil speaks or writes, is below the dignity of one bred up amongst Greek and Latin, though he have but little of them himself. These are the learned languages fit only for learned men to meddle with and teach; English is the language of the illiterate vulgar: tho' yet we see the polity of some of our neighbours hath not thought it beneath the publick care to promote and reward the improvement of their own language. Polishing and enriching their tongue is no small business amongst them; it hath colleges and stipends appointed it, and there is raised amongst them a great ambition and emulation of writing correctly: and we see what they are come to by it, and how far they have spread one of the worst languages possibly in this part of the world, if we look upon it as it was in some few reigns backwards, whatever it be now. The great men among the Romans were daily exercising themselves in their own language; and we find yet upon record the names of orators, who taught some of their emperors Latin, though it were their mother tongue.

'Tis plain the Greeks were yet more nice in theirs. All other speech was barbarous to them but their own, and no foreign language appears to have been studied or valued amongst that learned and acute people; tho' it be past doubt that they borrowed their learning and philosophy from abroad.

I am not here speaking against Greek and Latin; I think they ought to be studied, and the Latin at least understood well by every gentleman. But whatever foreign languages a young man meddles with (and the more he knows the better) that which he should critically study, and labour to get a facility, clearness and elegancy to express himself in, should be his own; and to this purpose he should daily be exercised in it.

§ 190. Natural philosophy, as a speculative science, I imagine we have none, and perhaps I may think I have reason to say we never shall be able to make a science of it. The works of nature are contrived by a wisdom, and operate by ways too far surpassing our faculties to discover or capacities to conceive, for us ever to be able to reduce them into a science. Natural philosophy being the knowledge of the principles, properties and operations of things as they are in themselves, I imagine there are two parts of it, one comprehending spirits, with their nature and qualities, and the other bodies. The first of these is usually referred to metaphysicks: but under what title soever the consideration of spirits comes, I think it ought to go before the study of matter and body, not as a science that can be methodized into a system, and treated of upon principles of knowledge; but as an enlargement of our minds towards a truer and fuller comprehension of the intellectual world to which we are led both by reason and revelation. And since the clearest and largest discoveries we have of other spirits, besides God and our own souls, is imparted to us from heaven by revelation, I think the information that at least young people should have of them, should be taken from that revelation. To this purpose, I conclude, it would be well, if there were made a good history of the Bible, for young people to read; wherein if every thing that is fit to be put into it, were laid down in its due order of time, and several things omitted which are suited only to riper age, that confusion which is usually produced by promiscuous reading of the Scripture, as it lies now bound up in our Bibles, would be avoided. And also this other good obtained, that by reading of it constantly, there would be instilled into the minds of children a notion and belief of spirits, they having so much to do in all the transactions of that history, which will be a good preparation to the study of bodies. For without the notion and allowance of spirit, our philosophy will be lame and defective in one main part of it, when it leaves out the contemplation of the most excellent and powerful part of the creation.

Sections 191–200

§ 191. Of this History of the Bible, I think too it would be well if there were a short and plain epitome made, containing the chief and most material heads, for children to be conversant in as soon as they can read. This, though it will lead them early into some notion of spirits, yet it is not contrary to what I said above, that I would not have children troubled, whilst young, with notions of spirits; whereby my meaning was, that I think it inconvenient that their yet tender minds should receive early impressions of goblins, spectres, and apparitions, wherewith their maids and those about them are apt to fright them into a compliance with their orders, which often proves a great inconvenience to them all their lives after, by subjecting their minds to frights, fearful apprehensions, weakness and superstition; which when coming abroad into the world and conversation they grow weary and ashamed of, it not seldom happens, that to make, as they think, a thorough cure, and ease themselves of a load which has sat so heavy on them, they throw away the thoughts of all spirits together, and so run into the other, but worse, extream.

§ 192. The reason why I would have this premised to the study of bodies, and the Doctrine of the Scriptures well imbibed before young men be entered in natural philosophy, is, because matter, being a thing that all our senses are constantly conversant with, it is so apt to possess the mind, and exclude all other beings but matter, that prejudice, grounded on such principles, often leaves no room for the admittance of spirits, or the allowing any such things as immaterial beings in rerum natura; when yet it is evident that by mere matter and motion none of the great phaenomena of nature can be resolved, to instance but in that common one of gravity, which I think impossible to be explained by any natural operation of matter, or any other law of motion, but the positive will of a superior being so ordering it. And therefore since the deluge cannot be well explained without admitting something out of the ordinary course of nature, I propose it to be considered whether God's altering the centre of gravity in the earth for a time (a thing as intelligible as gravity it self, which perhaps a little variation of causes unknown to us would produce) will not more easily account for Noah's flood than any hypothesis yet made use of to solve it. I hear the great objection to this, is, that it would produce but a partial deluge. But the alteration of the centre of gravity once allowed, 'tis no hard matter to conceive that the divine power might make the centre of gravity, plac'd at a due distance from the centre of the earth, move round it in a convenient space of time, whereby the flood would become universal, and, as I think, answer all the phaenomena of the deluge as delivered by Moses, at an easier rate than those many hard suppositions that are made use of to explain it. But this is not a place for that argument, which is here only mentioned by the bye, to shew the necessity of having recourse to something beyond bare matter and its motion in the explication of nature; to which the notions of spirits and their power, as delivered in the Bible, where so much is attributed to their operation, may be a fit preparative, reserving to a fitter opportunity a fuller explication of this hypothesis, and the application of it to all the parts of the deluge, and any difficulties can be supposed in the history of the flood, as recorded in the scripture.

§ 193. But to return to the study of natural philosophy. Tho' the world be full of systems of it, yet I cannot say, I know any one which can be taught a young man as a science wherein he may be sure to find truth and certainty, which is what all sciences give an expectation of. I do not hence conclude, that none of them are to be read. It is necessary for a gentleman in this learned age to look into some of them to fit himself for conversation: but whether that of Des Cartes be put into his hands, as that which is most in fashion, or it be thought fit to give him a short view of that and several others also, I think the systems of natural philosophy that have obtained in this part of the world, are to be read more to know the hypotheses, and to understand the terms and ways of talking of the several sects, than with hopes to gain thereby a comprehensive, scientifical and satisfactory knowledge of the works of nature. Only this may be said, that the modern Corpuscularians talk in most things more intelligibly than the Peripateticks, who possessed the schools immediately before them. He that would look further back, and acquaint himself with the several opinions of the antients, may consult Dr. Cudworth's Intellectual System, wherein that very learned author hath with such accurateness and judgment collected and explained the opinions of the Greek philosophers, that what principles they built on, and what were the chief hypotheses that divided them, is better to be seen in him than any where else that I know. But I would not deter any one from the study of nature because all the knowledge we have or possibly can have of it cannot be brought into a science. There are very many things in it that are convenient and necessary to be known to a gentleman; and a great many other that will abundantly reward the pains of the curious with delight and advantage. But these, I think, are rather to be found amongst such writers as have employed themselves in making rational experiments and observations than in starting barely speculative systems. Such writings therefore, as many of Mr. Boyle's are, with others that have writ of husbandry, planting, gardening, and the like, may be fit for a gentleman, when he has a little acquainted himself with some of the systems of the natural philosophy in fashion.

§ 194. Though the systems of physicks that I have met with, afford little encouragement to look for certainty or science in any treatise which shall pretend to give us a body of natural philosophy from the first principles of bodies in general, yet the incomparable Mr. Newton has shewn, how far mathematicks applied to some parts of nature may, upon principles that matter of fact justify, carry us in the knowledge of some, as I may so call them, particular provinces of the incomprehensible universe. And if others could give us so good and clear an account of other parts of nature, as he has of this our planetary world, and the most considerable phænomena observable in it, in his admirable book, Philosophiæ naturalis Principia Mathematica, we might in time hope to be furnished with more true and certain knowledge in several parts of this stupendous machine, than hitherto we could have expected. And though there are very few that have mathematicks enough to understand his demonstrations, yet the most accurate mathematicians who have examin'd them allowing them to be such, his book will deserve to be read, and give no small light and pleasure to those, who, willing to understand the motions, properties, and operations of the great masses of matter, in this our solar system, will but carefully mind his conclusions, which may be depended on as propositions well proved.

§ 195. This is, in short, what I have thought concerning a young gentleman's studies; wherein it will possibly be wonder'd that I should omit Greek, since amongst the Grecians is to be found the original as it were, and foundation of all that learning which we have in this part of the world. I grant it so; and will add, that no man can pass for a scholar that is ignorant of the Greek tongue. But I am not here considering the education of a profess'd scholar, but of a gentleman, to whom Latin and French, as the world now goes, is by every one acknowledg'd to be necessary. When he comes to be a man, if he has a mind to carry his studies farther, and look into the Greek learning, he will then easily get that tongue himself: and if he has not that inclination, his learning of it under a tutor will be but lost labour, and much of his time and pains spent in that which will be neglected and thrown away as soon as he is at liberty. For how many are there of an hundred, ever amongst scholars themselves, who retain the Greek they carried from school; or ever improve it to a familiar reading and perfect understanding of Greek authors?

To conclude this part, which concerns a young gentleman's studies, his tutor should remember, that his business is not so much to teach him all that is knowable, as to raise in him a love and esteem of knowledge; and to put him in the right way of knowing and improving himself when he has a mind to it.

The thoughts of a judicious author on the subject of languages, I shall here give the reader, as near as I can, in his own way of expressing them: he says, "One can scarce burden children too much with the knowledge of languages. They are useful to men of all conditions, and they equally open them the entrance, either to the most profound, or the more easy and entertaining parts of learning. If this irksome study be put off to a little more advanced age, young men either have not resolution enough to apply it out of choice or steadiness to carry it on. And if any one has the gift of perseverance, it is not without the inconvenience of spending that time upon languages, which is destined to other uses: and he confines to the study of words that age of his life that is above it, and requires things; at least it is the losing the best and beautifullest season of one's life. This large foundation of languages cannot be well laid but when every thing makes an easy and deep impression on the mind; when the memory is fresh, ready, and tenacious; when the head and heart are as yet free from cares, passions, and designs; and those on whom the child depends have authority enough to keep him close to a long continued application. I am persuaded that the small number of truly learned, and the multitude of superficial pretenders, is owing to the neglect of this."

I think every body will agree with this observing gentleman, that languages are the proper study of our first years. But 'tis to be consider'd by the parents and tutors, what tongues 'tis fit the child should learn. For it must be confessed, that it is fruitless pains and loss of time, to learn a language which in the course of life that he is designed to, he is never like to make use of, or which one may guess by his temper he will wholly neglect and lose again, as soon as an approach to manhood, setting him free from a governor, shall put him into the hands of his own inclination, which is not likely to allot any of his time to the cultivating the learned tongues, or dispose him to mind any other language but what daily use or some particular necessity shall force upon him.

But yet for the sake of those who are designed to be scholars, I will add what the same author subjoins to make good his foregoing remark. It will deserve to be considered by all who desire to be truly learned, and therefore may be a fit rule for tutors to inculcate and leave with their pupils to guide their future studies.

"The study, says he, of the original text can never be sufficiently recommended. 'Tis the shortest, surest, and most agreeable way to all sorts of learning. Draw from the spring-head, and take not things at second hand. Let the writings of the great masters be never laid aside, dwell upon them, settle them in your mind, and cite them upon occasion; make it your business throughly to understand them in their full extent and all their circumstances: acquaint yourself fully with the principles of original authors; bring them to a consistency, and then do you yourself make your deductions. In this state were the first commentators, and do not you rest till you bring yourself to the same. Content not yourself with those borrowed lights, nor guide yourself by their views but where your own fails you and leaves you in the dark. Their explications are not yours, and will give you the slip. On the contrary, your own observations are the product of your own mind, where they will abide and be ready at hand upon all occasions in converse, consultation, and dispute. Lose not the pleasure it is to see that you are not stopp'd in your reading but by difficulties that are invincible; where the commentators and scholiasts themselves are at a stand and have nothing to say. Those copious expositors of other places, who with a vain and pompous overflow of learning poured out on passages plain and easy in themselves, are very free of their words and pains, where there is no need. Convince yourself full by this ordering your studies, that 'tis nothing but men's laziness which hath encouraged pedantry to cram rather than enrich libraries, and to bury good authors under heaps of notes and commentaries, and you will perceive that sloth herein hath acted against itself and its own interest by multiplying reading and enquiries, and encreasing the pains it endeavoured to avoid."

This, tho' it may seem to concern none but direct scholars, is of so great moment for the right ordering of their education and studies, that I hope I shall not be blamed for inserting of it here; especially if it be considered, that it may be of use to gentlemen too, when at any time they have a mind to go deeper than the surface, and get to themselves a solid, satisfactory, and masterly insight in any part of learning.

Order and constancy are said to make the great difference between one man and another: this I am sure, nothing so much clears a learner's way, helps him so much on in it, and makes him go so easy and so far in any enquiry, as a good method. His governor should take pains to make him sensible of this, accustom him to order, and teach him method in all the applications of his thoughts; shew him wherein it lies, and the advantages of it; acquaint him with the several sorts of it, either from general to particulars, or from particulars to what is more general; exercise him in both of them, and make him see in what cases each different method is most proper, and to what ends it best serves.

In history the order of time should govern, in philosophical enquiries that of nature, which in all progression is to go from the place one is then in, to that which joins and lies next to it; and so it is in the mind, from the knowledge it stands possessed of already, to that which lies next, and is coherent to it, and so on to what it aims at, by the simplest and most uncompounded parts it can divide the matter into. To this purpose, it will be of great use to his pupil to accustom him to distinguish well, that is, to have distinct notions, whereever the mind can find any real difference; but as carefully to avoid distinctions in terms, where he has not distinct and different clear ideas.

§ 196. Besides what is to be had from study and books, there are other accomplishments necessary for a gentleman, to be got by exercise, and to which time is to be allowed, and for which masters must be had.

Dancing being that which gives graceful motions all the life, and above all things manliness, and a becoming confidence to young children, I think it cannot be learned too early, after they are once of an age and strength capable of it. But you must be sure to have a good master, that knows, and can teach, what is graceful and becoming, and what gives a freedom and easiness to all the motions of the body. One that teaches not this, is worse than none at all: natural unfashionableness being much better than apish affected postures; and I think it much more passable, to put off the hat and make a leg like an honest country gentleman than like an ill-fashioned dancing-master. For as for the jigging part, and the figures of dances, I count that little or nothing, farther than as it tends to perfect graceful carriage.

§ 197. Musick is thought to have some affinity with dancing, and a good hand upon some instruments is by many people mightily valued. But it wastes so much of a young man's time to gain but a moderate skill in it; and engages often in such odd company, that many think it much better spared: and I have amongst men of parts and business so seldom heard any one commended or esteemed for having an excellency in musick, that amongst all those things that ever came into the list of accomplishments, I think I may give it the last place. Our short lives will not serve us for the attainment of all things; nor can our minds be always intent on something to be learned. The weakness of our constitutions both of mind and body, requires that we should be often unbent: and he that will make a good use of any part of his life, must allow a large portion of it to recreation. At least, this must not be denied to young people; unless whilst you with too much haste make them old, you have the displeasure to set them in their graves or a second childhood sooner than you could wish. And therefore, I think, that the time and pains allotted to serious improvements, should be employed about things of most use and consequence, and that too in the methods the most easy and short that could be at any rate obtained: and perhaps, as I have above said, it would be none of the least secrets of education, to make the exercises of the body and the mind the recreation one to another. I doubt not but that something might be done in it, by a prudent man, that would well consider the temper and inclination of his pupil. For he that is wearied either with study or dancing does not desire presently to go to sleep, but to do something else which may divert and delight him. But this must be always remembered, that nothing can come into the account of recreation, that is not done with delight.

§ 198. Fencing and riding the great horse, are looked upon so necessary parts of breeding, that it would be thought a great omission to neglect them; the latter of the two being for the most part to be learned only in great towns, is one of the best exercises for health, which is to be had in those places of ease and luxury: and upon that account makes a fit part of a young gentleman's employment during his abode there. And as far as it conduces to give a man a firm and graceful seat on horseback, and to make him able to teach his horse to stop and turn quick, and to rest on his hanches, is of use to a gentleman both in peace and war. But whether it be of moment enough to be made a business of, and deserve to take up more of his time than should barely for his health be employed at due intervals in some such vigorous exercise, I shall leave to the discretion of parents and tutors; who will do well to remember, in all the parts of education, that most time and application is to be bestowed on that which is like to be of greatest consequence and frequentest use in the ordinary course and occurrences of that life the young man is designed for.

§ 199. As for fencing, it seems to me a good exercise for health, but dangerous to the life; the confidence of their skill being apt to engage in quarrels those that think they have learned to use their swords. This presumption makes them often more touchy than needs on point of honour and slight or no provocations. Young men, in their warm blood, are forward to think they have in vain learned to fence, if they never shew their skill and courage in a duel; and they seem to have reason. But how many sad tragedies that reason has been the occasion of, the tears of many a mother can witness. A man that cannot fence, will be more careful to keep out of bullies' and gamesters' company, and will not be half so apt to stand upon punctilios, nor to give affronts, or fiercely justify them when given, which is that which usually makes the quarrel. And when a man is in the field, a moderate skill in fencing rather exposes him to the sword of his enemy than secures him from it. And certainly a man of courage who cannot fence at all and therefore will put all upon one thrust and not stand parrying, has the odds against a moderate fencer, especially if he has skill in wrestling. And therefore, if any provision be to be made against such accidents, and a man be to prepare his son for duels, I had much rather mine should be a good wrestler than an ordinary fencer, which is the most a gentleman can attain to in it, unless he will be constantly in the fencing-school and every day exercising. But since fencing and riding the great horse are so generally looked upon as necessary qualifications in the breeding of a gentleman, it will be hard wholly to deny any one of that rank these marks of distinction. I shall leave it therefore to the father to consider, how far the temper of his son and the station he is like to be in, will allow or encourage him to comply with fashions which, having very little to do with civil life, were yet formerly unknown to the most warlike nations, and seem to have added little of force or courage to those who have received them; unless we will think martial skill or prowess have been improved by duelling, with which fencing came into, and with which I presume it will go out of the world.

§ 200. These are my present thoughts concerning learning and accomplishments. The great business of all is virtue and wisdom:

Nullum numen abest si sit Prudentia.

Teach him to get a mastery over his inclinations, and submit his appetite to reason. This being obtained, and by constant practice settled into habit, the hardest part of the task is over. To bring a young man to this, I know nothing which so much contributes as the love of praise and commendation, which should therefore be instilled into him by all arts imaginable. Make his mind as sensible of credit and shame as may be; and when you have done that, you have put a principle into him, which will influence his actions when you are not by, to which the fear of a little smart of a rod is not comparable, and which will be the proper stock whereon afterwards to graff the true principles of morality and religion.

Sections 201–210

§ 201. I have one thing more to add, which as soon as I mention I shall run the danger of being suspected to have forgot what I am about, and what I have above written concerning education all tending towards a gentleman's calling, with which a trade seems wholly inconsistent. And yet I cannot forbear to say, I would have him learn a trade, a manual trade; nay two or three, but one more particularly.

§ 202. The busy inclination of children being always to be directed to something that may be useful to them, the advantages proposed from what they are set about may be considered of two kinds: 1. Where the skill itself that is got by exercise is worth the having. Thus skill not only in languages and learned sciences, but in painting, turning, gardening, tempering and working in iron, and all other useful arts is worth the having. 2. Where the exercise itself, without any consideration, is necessary or useful for health. Knowledge in some things is so necessary to be got by children whilst they are young, that some part of their time is to be allotted to their improvement in them, though those employments contribute nothing at all to their health. Such are reading and writing and all other sedentary studies for the cultivating of the mind, which unavoidably take up a great part of a gentleman's time, quite from their cradles. Other manual arts, which are both got and exercised by labour, do many of them by that exercise not only increase our dexterity and skill, but contribute to our health too, especially such as employ us in the open air. In these, then, health and improvement may be join'd together; and of these should some fit ones be chosen, to be made the recreations of one whose chief business is with books and study. In this choice the age and inclination of the person is to be considered, and constraint always to be avoided in bringing him to it. For command and force may often create, but can never cure, an aversion: and whatever any one is brought to by compulsion, he will leave as soon as he can, and be little profited and less recreated by, whilst he is at it.

§ 203. That which of all others would please me best, would be a painter, were there not an argument or two against it not easy to be answered. First, ill painting is one of the worst things in the world; and to attain a tolerable degree of skill in it, requires too much of a man's time. If he has a natural inclination to it, it will endanger the neglect of all other more useful studies to give way to that; and if he have no inclination to it, all the time, pains and money shall be employed in it, will be thrown away to no purpose. Another reason why I am not for painting in a gentleman, is, because it is a sedentary recreation, which more employs the mind than the body. A gentleman's more serious employment I look on to be study; and when that demands relaxation and refreshment, it should be in some exercise of the body, which unbends the thought, and confirms the health and strength. For these two reasons I am not for painting.

§ 204. In the next place, for a country gentleman I should propose one, or rather both these, viz. Gardening or husbandry in general, and working in wood, as a carpenter, joiner, or turner, these being fit and healthy recreations for a man of study or business. For since the mind endures not to be constantly employed in the same thing or way, and sedentary or studious men should have some exercise, that at the same time might divert their minds and employ their bodies, I know none that could do it better for a country gentleman than these two; the one of them affording him exercise when the weather or season keeps him from the other. Besides that, by being skill'd in the one of them, he will be able to govern and teach his gardener; by the other, contrive and make a great many things both of delight and use: though these I propose not as the chief end of his labour, but as temptations to it; diversion from his other more serious thoughts and employments by useful and healthy manual exercise being what I chiefly aim at in it.

§ 205. The great men among the antients understood very well how to reconcile manual labour with affairs of state, and thought it no lessening to their dignity to make the one the recreation to the other. That indeed which seems most generally to have employed and diverted their spare hours, was agriculture. Gideon among the Jews was taken from threshing, as well as Cincinnatus amongst the Romans from the plough, to command the armies of their countries against their enemies; and 'tis plain their dexterous handling of the flayl or the plough, and being good workmen with these tools, did not hinder their skill in arms, nor make them less able in the arts of war or government. They were great captains and statesmen as well as husbandmen. Cato Major, who had with great reputation born all the great offices of the commonwealth, has left us an evidence under his own hand, how much he was versed in country affairs; and, as I remember, Cyrus thought gardening so little beneath the dignity and grandeur of a throne, that he shew'd Xenophon a large field of fruit-trees all of his own planting. The records of antiquity, both among Jews and Gentiles, are full of instances of this kind, if it were necessary to recommend useful recreations by examples.

§ 206. Nor let it be thought that I mistake, when I call these or the like exercises of manual arts, diversions or recreations: for recreation is not being idle (as every one may observe) but easing the wearied part by change of business: and he that thinks diversion may not lie in hard and painful labour, forgets the early rising, hard riding, heat, cold and hunger of huntsmen, which is yet known to be the constant recreation of men of the greatest condition. Delving, planting, inoculating, or any the like profitable employments, would be no less a diversion than any of the idle sports in fashion, if men could but be brought to delight in them, which custom and skill in a trade will quickly bring any one to do. And I doubt not but there are to be found those, who being frequently called to cards or any other play by those they could not refuse, have been more tired with these recreations than with any the most serious employment of life, though the play has been such as they have naturally had no aversion to, and with which they could willingly sometimes divert themselves.

§ 207. Play, wherein persons of condition, especially ladies, waste so much of their time, is a plain instance to me that men cannot be perfectly idle; they must be doing something; for how else could they sit so many hours toiling at that which generally gives more vexation than delight to people whilst they are actually engag'd in it? 'Tis certain, gaming leaves no satisfaction behind it to those who reflect when it is over, and it no way profits either body or mind: as to their estates, if it strike so deep as to concern them, it is a trade then, and not a recreation, wherein few that have any thing else to live on thrive: and at best, a thriving gamester has but a poor trade on't, who fills his pockets at the price of his reputation.

Recreation belongs not to people who are strangers to business, and are not wasted and wearied with the employment of their calling. The skill should be, so to order their time of recreation, that it may relax and refresh the part that has been exercised and is tired, and yet do something which besides the present delight and ease, may produce what will afterwards be profitable. It has been nothing but the vanity and pride of greatness and riches, that has brought unprofitable and dangerous pastimes (as they are called) into fashion, and persuaded people into a belief, that the learning or putting their hands to any thing that was useful, could not be a diversion fit for a gentleman. This has been that which has given cards, dice and drinking so much credit in the world: and a great many throw away their spare hours in them, through the prevalency of custom, and want of some better employment to fill up the vacancy of leisure, more than from any real delight is to be found in them. They cannot bear the dead weight of unemployed time lying upon their hands, nor the uneasiness it is to do nothing at all: and having never learned any laudable manual art wherewith to divert themselves, they have recourse to those foolish or ill ways in use, to help off their time, which a rational man, till corrupted by custom, could find very little pleasure in.

§ 208. I say not this, that I would never have a young gentleman accommodate himself to the innocent diversions in fashion amongst those of his age and condition. I am so far from having him austere and morose to that degree, that I would persuade him to more than ordinary complaisance for all the gaieties and diversions of those he converses with, and be averse or testy in nothing they should desire of him, that might become a gentleman and an honest man. Though as to cards and dice, I think the safest and best way is never to learn any play upon them, and so to be incapacitated for those dangerous temptations and incroaching wasters of useful time. But allowance being made for idle and jovial conversation and all fashionable becoming recreations; I say, a young man will have time enough from his serious and main business, to learn almost any trade. 'Tis want of application, and not of leisure, that men are not skilful in more arts than one; and an hour in a day, constantly employed in such a way of diversion, will carry a man in a short time a great deal farther than he can imagine: which, if it were of no other use but to drive the common, vicious, useless, and dangerous pastimes out of fashion, and to shew there was no need of them, would deserve to be encouraged. If men from their youth were weaned from that sauntring humour wherein some out of custom let a good part of their lives run uselessly away, without either business or recreation, they would find time enough to acquire dexterity and skill in hundreds of things, which, though remote from their proper callings, would not at all interfere with them. And therefore, I think, for this, as well as other reasons before-mentioned, a lazy, listless humour that idly dreams away the days, is of all others the least to be indulged or permitted in young people. It is the proper state of one sick and out of order in his health, and is tolerable in nobody else of what age or condition soever.

§ 209. To the arts above-mentioned may be added perfuming, varnishing, graving, and several sorts of working in iron, brass, and silver; and if, as it happens to most young gentlemen, that a considerable part of his time be spent in a great town, he may learn to cut, polish, and set precious stones, or employ himself in grinding and polishing optical glasses. Amongst the great variety there is of ingenious manual arts, 'twill be impossible that no one should be found to please and delight him, unless he be either idle or debauched, which is not to be supposed in a right way of education. And since he cannot be always employ'd in study, reading, and conversation, there will be many an hour, besides what his exercises will take up, which, if not spent this way, will be spent worse. For I conclude, a young man will seldom desire to sit perfectly still and idle; or, if he does, 'tis a fault that ought to be mended.

§ 210. But if his mistaken parents, frighted with the disgraceful names of mechanick and trade, shall have an aversion to any thing of this kind in their children; yet there is one thing relating to trade, which, when they consider, they will think absolutely necessary for their sons to learn.

Merchants' accompts, tho' a science not likely to help a gentleman to get an estate, yet possibly there is not any thing of more use and efficacy, to make him preserve the estate he has. 'Tis seldom observed, that he keeps an accompt of his income and expenses, and thereby has constantly under view the course of his domestick affairs, lets them run to ruin: and I doubt not but many a man gets behind-hand before he is aware, or runs farther on when he is once in, for want of this care, or the skill to do it. I would therefore advise all gentlemen to learn perfectly merchants' accompts, and not to think it is a skill that belongs not to them, because it has received its name from, and has been chiefly practised by men of traffick.

Sections 211–217

§ 211. When my young master has once got the skill of keeping accounts (which is a business of reason more than arithmetick) perhaps it will not be amiss that his father from thenceforth require him to do it in all his concernments. Not that I would have him set down every pint of wine or play that costs him money; the general name of expenses will serve for such things well enough: nor would I have his father look so narrowly into these accompts, as to take occasion from thence to criticise on his expences; he must remember that he himself was once a young man, and not forget the thoughts he had then, nor the right his son has to have the same, and to have allowance made for them. If therefore I would have the young gentleman oblig'd to keep an account, it is not at all to have that way a check upon his expenses (for what the father allows him, he ought to let him be fully master of) but only, that he might be brought early into the custom of doing it, and that it might be made familiar and habitual to him betimes, which will be so useful and necessary to be constantly practised the whole course of his life. A noble Venetian, whose son wallowed in the plenty of his father's riches, finding his son's expenses grow very high and extravagant, ordered his cashier to let him have for the future no more money than what he should count when he received it. This one would think no great restraint to a young gentleman's expenses; who could freely have as much money as he would tell. But yet this, to one that was used to nothing but the pursuit of his pleasures, prov'd a very great trouble, which at last ended in this sober and advantageous reflection: if it be so much pains to me barely to count the money I would spend, what labour and pains did it cost my ancestors, not only to count, but get it? This rational thought, suggested by this little pains impos'd upon him, wrought so effectually upon his mind, that it made him take up, and from that time forwards prove a good husband. This, at least, every body must allow, that nothing is likelier to keep a man within compass than the having constantly before his eyes the state of his affairs in a regular course of accompt.

§ 212. The last part usually in education is travel, which is commonly thought to finish the work, and complete the gentleman. I confess travel into foreign countries has great advantages, but the time usually chosen to send young men abroad, is, I think, of all other, that which renders their least capable of reaping those advantages. Those which are propos'd, as to the main of them, may be reduced to these two: first, language, secondly, an improvement in wisdom and prudence, by seeing men, and conversing with people of tempers, customs and ways of living, different from one another, and especially from those of his parish and neighbourhood. But from sixteen to one and twenty, which is the ordinary time of travel, men are, of all their lives, the least suited to these improvements. The first season to get foreign languages, and form the tongue to their true accents, I should think, should be from seven to fourteen or sixteen, and then too a tutor with them is useful and necessary, who may with those languages teach them other things. But to put them out of their parents' view at a great distance under a governor, when they think themselves to be too much men to be governed by others, and yet have not prudence and experience enough to govern themselves, what is it, but to expose them to all the greatest dangers of their whole life, when they have the least fence and guard against them? 'Till that boiling boisterous part of life comes in, it may be hoped the tutor may have some authority: neither the stubbornness of age, nor the temptation or examples of others, can take him from his tutor's conduct till fifteen or sixteen; but then, when he begins to comfort himself with men, and thinks himself one; when he comes to relish and pride himself in manly vices, and thinks it a shame to be any longer under the controul and conduct of another, what can be hoped from even the most careful and discreet governor, when neither he has power to compel, nor his pupil a disposition to be persuaded; but on the contrary, has the advice of warm blood and prevailing fashion, to hearken to the temptations of his companions, just as wise as himself, rather than to the persuasions of his tutor, who is now looked on as an enemy to his freedom? And when is a man so like to miscarry, as when at the same time he is both raw and unruly? This is the season of all his life that most requires the eye and authority of his parents and friends to govern it. The flexibleness of the former part of a man's age, not yet grown up to be headstrong, makes it more governable and safe; and in the afterpart, reason and foresight begin a little to take place, and mind a man of his safety and improvement. The time therefore I should think the fittest for a young gentleman to be sent abroad, would be, either when he is younger, under a tutor, whom he might be the better for; or when he is some years older, without a governor; when he is of age to govern himself, and make observations of what he finds in other countries worthy his notice, and that might be of use to him after his return; and when too, being throughly acquainted with the laws and fashions, the natural and moral advantages and defects of his own country, he has something to exchange with those abroad, from whose conversation he hoped to reap any knowledge.

§ 213. [Wanting].

§ 214. The ordering of travel otherwise, is that, I imagine, which makes so many young gentlemen come back so little improved by it. And if they do bring home with them any knowledge of the places and people they have seen, it is often an admiration of the worst and vainest practices they met with abroad; retaining a relish and memory of those things wherein their liberty took its first swing, rather than of what should make them better and wiser after their return. And indeed how can it be otherwise, going abroad at the age they do under the care of another, who is to provide their necessaries, and make their observations for them? Thus under the shelter and pretence of a governor, thinking themselves excused from standing upon their own legs or being accountable for their own conduct, they very seldom trouble themselves with enquiries or making useful observations of their own. Their thoughts run after play and pleasure, wherein they take it as a lessening to be controll'd; but seldom trouble themselves to examine the designs, observe the address, and consider the arts, tempers, and inclinations of men they meet with; that so they may know how to comport themselves towards them. Here he that travels with them is to screen them; get them out when they have run themselves into the briars; and in all their miscarriages be answerable for them.

§ 215. I confess, the knowledge of men is so great a skill, that it is not to be expected a young man should presently be perfect in it. But yet his going abroad is to little purpose, if travel does not sometimes open his eyes, make him cautious and wary, and accustom him to look beyond the outside, and, under the inoffensive guard of a civil and obliging carriage, keep himself free and safe in his conversation with strangers and all sorts of people without forfeiting their good opinion. He that is sent out to travel at the age, and with the thoughts of a man designing to improve himself, may get into the conversation and acquaintance of persons of condition where he comes; which, tho' a thing of most advantage to a gentleman that travels, yet I ask, amongst our young men that go abroad under tutors, what one is there of an hundred, that ever visits any person of quality? Much less makes an acquaintance with such, from whose conversation he may learn what is good breeding in that country, and what is worth observation in it; tho' from such persons it is, one may learn more in one day, than in a year's rambling from one inn to another. Nor indeed, is it to be wondered; for men of worth and parts will not easily admit the familiarity of boys who yet need the care of a tutor; tho' a young gentleman and stranger, appearing like a man, and shewing a desire to inform himself in the customs, manners, laws, and government of the country he is in, will find welcome assistance and entertainment amongst the best and most knowing persons every where, who will be ready to receive, encourage and countenance, an ingenuous and inquisitive foreigner.

§ 216. This, how true soever it be, will not I fear alter the custom, which has cast the time of travel upon the worst part of a man's life; but for reasons not taken from their improvement. The young lad must not be ventured abroad at eight or ten, for fear of what may happen to the tender child, tho' he then runs ten times less risque than at sixteen or eighteen. Nor must he stay at home till that dangerous, heady age be over, because he must be back again by one and twenty, to marry and propagate. The father cannot stay any longer for the portion, nor the mother for a new set of babies to play with; and so my young master, whatever comes on it, must have a wife look'd out for him by that time he is of age; tho' it would be no prejudice to his strength, his parts, or his issue, if it were respited for some time, and he had leave to get, in years and knowledge, the start a little of his children, who are often found to tread too near upon the heels of their fathers, to the no great satisfaction either of son or father. But the young gentleman being got within view of matrimony, 'tis time to leave him to his mistress.

§ 217. Tho' I am now come to a conclusion of what obvious remarks have suggested to me concerning education, I would not have it thought that I look on it as a just treatise on this subject. There are a thousand other things that may need consideration; especially if one should take in the various tempers, different inclinations, and particular defaults, that are to be found in children, and prescribe proper remedies. The variety is so great that it would require a volume; nor would that reach it. Each man's mind has some peculiarity, as well as his face, that distinguishes him from all others; and there are possibly scarce two children who can be conducted by exactly the same method. Besides that, I think a prince, a nobleman, and an ordinary gentleman's son, should have different ways of breeding. But having had here only some general views in reference to the main end and aims in education, and those designed for a gentleman's son, whom, being then very little, I considered only as white paper, or wax, to be moulded and fashioned as one pleases; I have touched little more than those heads which I judged necessary for the breeding of a young gentleman of his condition in general; and have now published these my occasional thoughts with this hope, that tho' this be far from being a complete treatise on this subject, or such as that every one may find what will just fit his child in it, yet it may give some small light to those, whose concern for their dear little ones makes them so irregularly bold, that they dare venture to consult their own reason in the education of their children, rather than wholly to rely upon old custom.

Made in the USA
San Bernardino, CA
21 January 2016